Sentencing Law and Policy

ASPEN PUBLISHERS

Sentencing Law and Policy

Cases, Statutes, and Guidelines

Second Edition

Nora V. Demleitner

Interim Dean
Professor of Law
Hofstra University School of Law

Douglas A. Berman

William B. Saxbe Designated Professor of Law
The Ohio State University
Moritz College of Law

Marc L. Miller

Ralph W. Bilby Professor of Law
University of Arizona Jame E. Rogers College of Law

Ronald F. Wright

Professor of Law
Wake Forest University School of Law

 Wolters Kluwer

Law & Business

AUSTIN   BOSTON   CHICAGO   NEW YORK   THE NETHERLANDS

Aspen Publishers
Attn: Permissions Department
76 Ninth Avenue, 7th Floor
New York, NY 10011-5201

To contact Customer Care, e-mail customer.care@aspenpublishers.com,
call 1-800-234-1660, fax 1-800-901-9075, or mail correspondence to:

Aspen Publishers
Attn: Order Department
PO Box 990
Frederick, MD 21705

Printed in the United States of America.

1 2 3 4 5 6 7 8 9 0

ISBN 978-0-7355-6361-2

Library of Congress Cataloging-in-Publication Data

Sentencing law and policy: cases, statutes, and guidelines/Nora V. Demleitner ...
[et al.]. — [2nd ed.].
    p. cm.
  ISBN 978-0-7355-6361-2 (perfectbound : alk. paper)
   1. Sentences (Criminal procedure) — United States — Cases. I. Demleitner, Nora V., 1966-
KF9685.A7S46 2007
345.73'07720264 — dc22
                                                  2007031943

About Wolters Kluwer Law & Business

Wolters Kluwer Law & Business is a leading provider of research information and workflow solutions in key specialty areas. The strengths of the individual brands of Aspen Publishers, CCH, Kluwer Law International and Loislaw are aligned within Wolters Kluwer Law & Business to provide comprehensive, in-depth solutions and expert-authored content for the legal, professional and education markets.

CCH was founded in 1913 and has served more than four generations of business professionals and their clients. The CCH products in the Wolters Kluwer Law & Business group are highly regarded electronic and print resources for legal, securities, antitrust and trade regulation, government contracting, banking, pension, payroll, employment and labor, and healthcare reimbursement and compliance professionals.

Aspen Publishers is a leading information provider for attorneys, business professionals and law students. Written by preeminent authorities, Aspen products offer analytical and practical information in a range of specialty practice areas from securities law and intellectual property to mergers and acquisitions and pension/benefits. Aspen's trusted legal education resources provide professors and students with high-quality, up-to-date and effective resources for successful instruction and study in all areas of the law.

Kluwer Law International supplies the global business community with comprehensive English-language international legal information. Legal practitioners, corporate counsel and business executives around the world rely on the Kluwer Law International journals, loose-leafs, books and electronic products for authoritative information in many areas of international legal practice.

Loislaw is a premier provider of digitized legal content to small law firm practitioners of various specializations. Loislaw provides attorneys with the ability to quickly and efficiently find the necessary legal information they need, when and where they need it, by facilitating access to primary law as well as state-specific law, records, forms and treatises.

Wolters Kluwer Law & Business, a unit of Wolters Kluwer, is headquartered in New York and Riverwoods, Illinois. Wolters Kluwer is a leading multinational publisher and information services company.

To my parents, Alfred and
Walburga Demleitner.

NVD

To my grandfather and mother,
Seymour Kleinman and Dale Berman.

DAB

To Daniel J. Freed.

MLM

To my mother, Marian Stallings Wright.

RFW

Summary of Contents

Contents

— 1 —
The Purposes of Punishment and Sentencing   1

— 2 —

Who Sentences?   *85*

— 3 —

‖ *Regulating Discretion* ‖

— **4** —

|| *Sentencing Inputs: The Crime and Its Effects* || *273*

— 5 —

‖ *Sentencing Inputs: The Offender's Record and Background* ‖   *339*

— 6 —

‖ *Procedure and Proof at Sentencing* ‖   *433*

— 7 —

Sentencing Outcomes: The Scale of Imprisonment   *517*

— 8 —

|| *Sentencing Outcomes: Nonprison Punishments* || 587

— 9 —

Race, Class, and Gender

—10—

Alternatives to Criminal Sentences   *733*

—11—
Sentences Reconsidered   779

Preface

What claim does sentencing have in the modern law school curriculum, which already seems filled to capacity? We believe that the law of sentencing has plenty to offer all law students, even those not inclined toward a career in criminal law. This field provides an insightful case study in the dynamics of law reform; requires synthesis of theoretical and practical issues of doctrine, procedure, and policy; and touches deep and abiding issues about the nature and structure of law in society. Sentencing, in our view, illustrates superbly what advanced courses should offer, with its virtues extending to all law students by building effectively on the themes and goals pursued in an introductory criminal law and procedure class.

Of course, for students interested in a career in criminal law, the law of sentencing will serve as the central legal framework defining their day-to-day practice. Sentencing outcomes are the true bottom line of criminal law practice, and thoughtful defense attorneys and candid prosecutors regularly state that sentencing rules should be a lawyer's very first consideration in a criminal case. Moreover, because sentencing issues are frequently the focal point of criminal justice policy debates, many lawyers working for the government or for public interest groups are regularly engaged with sentencing controversies and concerns. Since criminal cases occupy such a large part of the courts' dockets, all judges (and their law clerks) spend a considerable portion of their working days on issues of sentencing law and policy.

A Law Reform Experiment

Criminal sentences involve some of the most severe actions that governments take against their own citizens and residents. Because every criminal conviction results in some kind of sentence, sentencing occurs all the time and involves a huge number of people. In an average year, federal, state, and local governments make more than 15 million arrests and obtain around 1 million felony convictions and several million additional misdemeanor convictions. Right now, more than 1.5 million people are serving time in U.S. prisons. Another 750,000 are held in jail, and an additional 5 million are on probation or parole.

Sentences are essential (though often hidden) elements of every substantive crime and every criminal process. Teachers in the first-year criminal law course point again and again to issues that will be resolved at sentencing; they explain that finer gradations or more subtle principles are possible at sentencing than in the rough-cut efforts to define crimes. Teachers of criminal procedure often note that defendants and their lawyers, as well as prosecutors, care most about the sentence because it represents the bottom line of all their procedural transactions.

Given the elemental role of sentencing in criminal law and procedure and the large social costs and benefits of criminal sentences, one might expect the law in this area to be highly evolved. In fact, for much of our history there has been very little law of sentencing. While some sentencing principles and punishments are ancient, the body of law that regulates sentences has remained undeveloped and unexamined until recently.

Rules prescribing the punishment for wrongdoers are found in the Bible and in the Koran. The earliest recorded legal codes, such as the Babylonian Code of Hammurabi (c. 1780 B.C.E.), spell out sanctions for various harms. Yet by the late twentieth century, 4,000 years of world civilization had resulted in sentencing systems in the United States (and in many other countries) that reflected only the most rudimentary qualities of law—for most offenses, only broad legislative specification of sentencing ranges, an absence of rules to guide judges in sentencing within those ranges, and actual determinations of sentences made not by judges but by executive release authorities.

Social and legal evolution can occur in the blink of an eye, and that has been the case for the law of sentencing. Since the 1970s, sentencing has undergone a political and legal revolution; it has become an area replete with law. Various kinds of "structured" or "guideline" systems now govern felony sentencing in many states and in the federal system; another intricate body of law now applies to capital sentencing, driven by an ongoing constitutional and policy dialogue between courts and legislatures. The emergence of sentencing law is one of the most dramatic and interesting law reform experiments in American legal history.

Sentencing, Law School, and the Nature of Law

Though young in its details, the law of sentencing wrestles with profound and ancient themes of justice and the nature of law. These themes echo throughout the law: what makes rules and procedures wise, which institutions should design and implement these rules, how much discretion should (or must) be allowed in each case, and what impact the law will have on human lives. This combination of new laws and long-standing problems, of the familiar and the unfamiliar, gives students an opportunity to synthesize many aspects of the lawyer's art.

Some law students end their first year of studies (or their second) and yearn for more opportunities to confront questions of justice, fairness, politics, and efficiency. Even the most cursory reading of daily newspapers will confirm that sentencing is an area in which all these concepts remain openly in play.

Indeed, media coverage of current sentencing debates enriches students' appreciation of the importance of this field and enables teachers to place current controversies within the enduring theoretical and doctrinal issues of sentencing law and policy.

Advanced courses should move beyond the mastery of doctrines and the already honed skill of reading appellate decisions. Sentencing integrates substantive criminal law with criminal procedure, and it often does so through institutions other than appellate courts. Sentencing law adds a strong dose of a subject not taught in most law schools — criminal justice policy (or criminology). The emergence of a language and grammar for sentencing has made it possible to explore the substantive, procedural, and policy aspects of criminal justice together in one place in the law school curriculum.

The Approach of This Book

Two particular areas of sentencing law have received the most attention in law schools. The promulgation of the federal sentencing guidelines has interested many scholars, and courses and seminars on federal sentencing have been developed at a number of schools. The persistence of capital sentencing in the American agenda has also sparked substantial scholarly and classroom interest in the death penalty.

But these dramatic areas of sentencing turn out to be only two slices of a much larger pie. The rapid emergence of sentencing as an area of law has created legal flux and remarkable variety. Drawing from a rich background, the book presents the common themes and trends in this emerging field of law, looking to its practical, political, social, and historical roots. We do not focus on a single system or jurisdiction, but rather try to capture the central issues and elements for all systems in all places.

This book has no separate sections for guideline versus indeterminate sentencing, state versus federal systems, or domestic versus foreign systems. Nor are constitutional issues segregated into a separate unit. This is because lawyers do not think about all of the constitutional doctrine together. Instead, they think about stages of the process, and how various sources of law — constitutional and otherwise — have some bearing on a particular stage.

Throughout the book, we draw on the most relevant examples from three distinct sentencing worlds: guideline/determinate, indeterminate, and capital. The examples from structured guideline jurisdictions — the dominant modern sentencing reform — occupy the center of attention. There is simply more "law" in a determinate system than in an indeterminate one, and more explicit discussion of what remains implicit in the older, discretionary systems. Because the federal system is so well funded and closely critiqued, the book devotes thorough attention to that system, but it features several key state systems as well.

We also examine capital punishment materials from time to time. Although detailed coverage of capital sentencing merits a full course and a full book in its own right, we focus here on the revealing comparisons between capital and noncapital sentencing practices.

Organization and Selection of Materials

An introductory unit surveys the social purposes (Chapter 1) and social institutions at work (Chapter 2) in the sentencing area, and then presents two case studies — involving guideline and capital regimes — showing how the legal system regulates the exercise of sentencing discretion (Chapter 3).

After this introduction, the volume follows an intuitive organization that tracks the basic sequence of decisions made in criminal sentencing. The book first reviews the basic "inputs" to the sentencing decision: Chapter 4 weighs the importance of the crime and its effects, and Chapter 5 considers the background of the offender. Chapter 6 reviews the distinctive procedures that shape how judges and others evaluate these sentencing inputs, both before and during the sentencing hearing.

The next three chapters explore the "outputs" of sentencing: prison (Chapter 7), nonprison punishments (Chapter 8), and the patterns of race, gender, and class that emerge in sentencing outcomes (Chapter 9).

The book closes by discussing punishment choices that arise in institutional settings other than the criminal trial court. Chapter 10 looks at alternatives to criminal sentences, and Chapter 11 highlights the important judicial and executive review that can occur after sentences are imposed.

Our principal materials come from many sources, reflecting the many institutions that shape and apply sentencing law. The U.S. Supreme Court makes occasional forays into the noncapital sentencing realm, but it leaves the great majority of the legal questions for others to address. We blend decisions from the U.S. Supreme Court, state high courts, and the federal appellate courts, along with a sprinkling of cases from foreign jurisdictions and supranational tribunals.

State cases carry substantial weight in this book, since well over 95% of criminal defendants are sentenced in state court and many of the most interesting modern sentencing reforms have occurred in the states. The amazing variety among state systems also allows instructive class discussions about the sentencing choices available.

We do not reprint only appellate judicial opinions as principal materials. We often use statutes or guideline provisions to lay out the common choices made by those who try to change sentencing practices. Reports and data from sentencing commissions and other agencies also help set the scene.

To keep track of the options and to prevent our celebration of variety from obscuring core concepts, we strive in the notes to tell readers directly what the most common practices are in various U.S. jurisdictions. The principal materials usually explain (and often embody) this majority position, but we also underscore it in the notes. To the extent possible in an emerging field of law such as sentencing, we estimate in the notes how often a lawyer is likely to encounter a given practice in American jurisdictions.

Central Themes in This Book

A small number of themes are central to the study of sentencing; these themes are present throughout the study of the law, even in areas completely unrelated to the criminal process. The book returns regularly to five major themes:

1. *Variety and change.* There is no single law of sentencing but rather many laws of sentencing, providing varied answers to a range of similar problems. This variation is apparent both across jurisdictions and within jurisdictions over time. Why are there different answers to similar questions?

2. *Multiple institutions.* One of the most striking aspects of sentencing is the variety of participants, both in lawmaking and in application. These participants include not only the top officials within the legislative, executive, and judicial branches but also various lower-level actors and institutions. Thus, we highlight distinctions between the roles of sentencing judges and appellate judges, spotlight the role of prosecutors, and consider the special role of sentencing commissions, parole boards, and probation officers. We continually ask students to compare decision makers both descriptively and normatively: when does it (and when should it) matter whether judges or legislators make a certain type of decision?

3. *Purposes and politics.* Sentencing and punishment serve many different purposes — some explicit and others implicit, some philosophical and others practical and perhaps base. We repeatedly ask students to consider the connections between specific sentencing rules and the purposes, politics, and practicalities of criminal justice.

4. *Impact and knowledge.* Modern sentencing law sometimes invokes the optimistic belief that knowledge and research can form a sound basis for creating and improving legal systems. Most research considers the visible impact of different sentencing rules on crime and on actual sentencing patterns. Experience, however, tempers the perhaps naïve hope for empirically grounded reform. Still, the materials in this book aim to identify the effects of sentencing practices on the work of judges and attorneys and on defendants of different social groups.

5. *Discretion and equality.* A major theme of sentencing across systems has been the need to individualize sentences to account for relevant variations among convicted offenders. At the same time, one of the major goals of modern sentencing reform has been to regulate the discretion of those who sentence and punish individuals, with the aim of reducing or eliminating unjust disparity. Of particular concern here are sentencing disparities based on race, class, or gender. We believe it is impossible to assess properly any aspect of criminal justice in the United States, including sentencing, without explicit and steady attention to issues of race. One chapter in the book specifically addresses issues of race, class, and gender, but these themes are raised throughout the volume.

Each of these larger lessons attends to the nature of law. The dramatic construction of a new field over a relatively short time — although a field replete with links to ancient puzzles and problems—provides a special kind of clarity into these deeper themes.

The Second Edition

Sentencing remains an active—and at times a hyperactive—field. This activity reflects the relative youth of sentencing as a discrete area of law and the focus of politicians, system participants, and the public on issues of crime and punishment.

This new edition reflects widely noted and dramatic shifts in constitutional sentencing law along with a host of significant changes in law and policy at the federal and state levels. This edition also reflects our education as teachers and editors as we have taught sentencing courses and heard from teachers around the country about which cases and materials have proved most effective in the classroom and which less so.

The pressures for change in sentencing policy and practice come from many directions. The United States Supreme Court has taken a dramatic turn in constitutionalizing aspects of charging, crime definition, and punishment through the *Apprendi-Blakely* line of cases. These cases have had widely varying impacts in different jurisdictions, but even if most systems find ways to accommodate these decisions, or if in the end the federal constitutional mandates of *Apprendi* and *Blakely* are watered down, these cases have become a pervasive part of sentencing discussions. This constitutional sentencing revolution demands explicit attention—at times in passing, at times as a focal point—throughout this volume and prompted the production of a second edition of this casebook.

The world-leading level and rate of imprisonment in the United States have drawn increasing attention in states confronting the "bill due" for so much punishment. A quieter but emerging theme in both national and state discourse is the idea of shifting from the maximum punishment to "smart" punishment. The "smart" punishment (and parallel "smart policing" and nascent "smart prosecution") movements are, among other things, a more policy-centered way of rejuvenating debates over the purposes and value of punishment.

Commentators have raised questions not only about the efficiency of modern punishment regimes, but also about the fairness of modern sentencing systems and the criminal justice systems that generate convictions and sentencing in the first place. The gentle but continuing stream of DNA-related and other innocence cases, often nullifying convictions and long punishments (or the threat of the death penalty), have been one motivation for this renewed attention to fairness. Also burbling at the margins of social and legal policy are voices concerned with race and class bias in United States criminal justice and punishment systems.

Most sentencing commissions have established a role as a steady voice for punishment moderation and sound policy. In particular, the commissions have reminded legislatures and executive branch agencies of the prospects for rational and cost-effective punishment. They seem to have blunted some of the more extreme policies that tend to result from public and political debate uninformed by bureaucratic expertise.

All of these pressures for change combine to produce a dramatic field of study. We have developed this second edition with the continuing sense of intellectual challenge, real-world demands, and drama that led us to produce the first one.

Our Hopes

We continue to believe that sentencing has blossomed into one of the most provocative and revealing areas of the law. It has become a powerful entry point into the workings of the law itself and into the nature of our social order. We wrote this book in the belief that the study of sentencing will be valuable to all lawyers and law students, not only to those with a commitment to criminal justice practice and policy.

Sentencing law itself is still a legal toddler. For sentencing law to become not only an illustration of the striking change taking place in the law but a model of legal reform and justice as well, the sentencing arena is in desperate need of excellent lawyers, well-informed legislators, and knowledgeable commissioners. We hope that some of those who study sentencing will be ready and willing to join the fray and work to produce better systems and greater justice.

Nora V. Demleitner
Douglas A. Berman
Marc L. Miller
Ronald F. Wright

July 2007

Acknowledgments

Modern sentencing law, with structured sentencing at its core, has emerged over the past 30 years, and a community of sentencing scholars, judges, and practitioners has emerged along with it. We have all spent part of our scholarly careers nurturing and critiquing the work that takes place in this field; it is terrifically gratifying for us to see criminal sentencing treated, at long last, as a "field" for study.

Course books reflect not only the immediate work of the editors but also the influence of colleagues and friends. Some of the most important influences on this book came from our close collaborators on other sentencing projects, most notably our fellow editors of the *Federal Sentencing Reporter* over the years: Dan Freed, Frank Bowman, Steve Chanenson, Michael O'Hear, Mark Harris, and Aaron Rappaport.

A special word is in order about Dan Freed: there is a part of Dan in everything we see or do in the area of sentencing. His farsighted and impassioned work for sentencing justice draws others, including us, to this corner of the world. We hope this book reflects Dan's joyful engagement with the ideas and realities of criminal sentencing.

Colleagues in this field around the country have been generous with their observations and encouragement during this project. Steve Chanenson and Michael E. Smith gave us crucial feedback on this book by teaching from the manuscripts and offering us wise suggestions along the way. There are a number of scholars and teachers whose work in sentencing and related areas have influenced this volume. On this score, we thank Albert Alschuler, Rachel Barkow, Sara Sun Beale, Stephanos Bibas, David Boerner, Dennis Curtis, Kara Dansky, George Fisher, George Fletcher, Richard Frase, Jim Jacobs, Eric Janus, Pam Karlan, Joe Kennedy, Nancy King, Susan Klein, Dan Markel, Tracy Meares, Michael O'Hear, Kevin Reitz, Alice Ristroph, Max Schanzenbach, Michael Simons, Kate Stith, Kimberly Thomas, Sandra Guerra Thompson, Michael Tonry, Robert Weisberg, Bert Westbrook, James Q. Whitman, and Deborah Young.

Advice and support also came from our home institutions, and we want to thank Jack Chin, Jennifer Collins, Sharon Davies, Terry Gordon, Kay Levine,

Alan Michaels, Nancy Rogers, Charley Rose, Robert Schapiro, Charlie Shanor, Kami Simmons, and David Yellen. Assistance with this volume also came from Kristie Gallardo, Melissa Haun, Barbara Lopez, and Marissa White. We received timely and thorough research assistance from several students, including Kris Armstrong, Leslie Cory, Jon Cowley, Jeffrey Davis, Amy DeWitt, Rudolph Fusco, Andrew Harris, Christine Robek, Daniel Smith, Jennifer Wiggins, and Robert Zayac. And, of course, the long-suffering students in our courses and seminars tolerated many drafts and many false starts to help us bring the book to its present form.

It is encouraging to meet so many judges around the country who offer important insights about the work of sentencing, which commands so much of their time and energy. We particularly want to thank Justice Samuel Alito Jr., Myron Bright, Guido Calabresi, Paul Cassell, Avern Cohen, Nancy Gertner, John Godbold, Frank Johnson, Gerard Lynch, John Martin, Michael Mihm, Jon O. Newman, Jim Rosenbaum, and Jack Weinstein. Prosecutors and defense attorneys, such as Stephen Bright, Judy Clarke, Roger Haines, Tom Hillier, Margy Love, Jon Sands, and Benson Weintraub, prevented us from losing sight of the realities on the ground as we observe events from our academic vantage points. In addition, probation officers, including Maggie Jensen and Matt Rowland, have provided us with useful glimpses into the difficulties of their work. Finally, our gratitude extends to scholars and researchers outside the United States. Their contributions to sentencing have informed our thinking about reforms and other changes. Among them are Hans-Jörg Albrecht, Andrew Ashworth, Albin Eser, Andrew von Hirsch, Geraldine Mackenzie, Stephan Terblanche, Dirk van Zyl Smit, Andrew Vincent, Susanne Walther, John Zeleznikow, and Emily Zimmerman.

Sentencing law and policy benefit from the vision and tireless work of reformers, based at institutions such as the Vera Institute, the Sentencing Project, the Urban Institute, the U.S. Sentencing Commission, and many state sentencing commissions. We are grateful for insights from Mark Bergstrom, Adam Gelb, Paul Hofer, Kim Hunt, Susan Katzenelson, Cynthia Kempenin, Rick Kearn, Robin Lubitz, Marc Mauer, Linda Drazga Maxfield, John O'Connell, Tom Ross, Julie Stewart, Chris Stone, Barbara Toombs, Jeremy Travis, Nick Turner, Ronald Weich, and Dan Wilhelm.

All writers of texts for students come to appreciate their own teachers even more. We are grateful, more than ever, to Steven Duke, Dan Freed, Owen Fiss, Edward Levi, Norval Morris, and Frank Zimring.

The editors at Aspen Publishers remained supportive throughout. Richard Mixter got the ball rolling and shared with us his wisdom about the nature of learning and the direction of legal education. We deeply value the encouragement and advice we received from Carol McGeehan, whose work with us—including discussions about when it would be appropriate to produce a volume on sentencing law—now stretches back over a decade. The book also profited from the great talents of Curt Berkowitz, Melody Davies, John Devins, Michael Gregory, Katy Guimon, Leslie Keros, and Barbara Roth.

Books do not take shape only in professional surroundings; this book followed us home and lived among our families. We are grateful to our families for playing host to this book in their lives, even though the guest may have overstayed its welcome. Our thanks and our love go to Michael D. Smith, Cordell

Demleitner Smith, Walburga Demleitner, Christine Anne Berman, Charlotte Lindsay Berman, Rebecca Elise Berman, Chris Cutshaw, Owen Miller, Evelyn Miller, Amy Wright, Andrew Wright, and Joanna Wright. Without them, the creation of this book, like everything else we do, would be unthinkable.

The authors acknowledge the following authors and copyright holders for permission to use material reprinted in this book.

American Bar Association, Standards for Criminal Justice Sentencing (3d ed. 1994). Copyright © 1994 by the American Bar Association. Reprinted with permission.

Americans for Gun Safety Foundation, The Enforcement Gap: Federal Gun Laws Ignored (2003). Copyright © 2003 by the Americans for Gun Safety Foundation. Reprinted by permission.

Hugo Adam Bedau, The Death Penalty in America (3d ed. 1982). Copyright © 1982 by Oxford University Press, Inc. Used by permission of Oxford University Press, Inc.

Walter Berns, For Capital Punishment: The Morality of Anger, Harper's (April 1979) at 15-20. Copyright © 1979 by Harper's. Reprinted with permission.

Alfred Blumstein, Jacqueline Cohen, Susan E. Martin, and Michael H. Tonry, Research on Sentencing: The Search for Reform (1983). Copyright © 1983 by National Academy Press. Reprinted with permission.

William J. Bowers, The Capital Jury Project: Rationale, Design, and Preview of Early Findings, 70 Ind. L.J. 1043 (1995). Copyright © 1995 by the Indiana Law Journal. Reprinted with permission.

Francesca D. Bowman, The Greening of Probation Officers in Their New Role, 4 Fed. Sent'g Rep. 99 (1991). Copyright © 1991 The Vera Institute of Justice. Reprinted with permission from the author and the Federal Sentencing Reporter.

Stephen Breyer, Speech to the University of Nebraska College of Law (Nov. 18, 1998), in 11 Fed. Sent'g Rep. 180 (1999). Copyright © 1999 The Vera Institute of Justice. Reprinted with permission.

Teresa Carns, Michael Hotchkin, and Elaine Andrews, Therapeutic Justice in Alaska's Courts, 19 Alaska L. Rev. 1 (2002). Copyright © 2002 by the Alaska Law Review. Reprinted with permission.

Leslie A. Cory, Looking at the Federal Sentencing Process One Judge at a Time, One Probation Officer at a Time, 51 Emory L.J. 379 (2002). Copyright © 2002 Emory Law Journal. Reprinted with permission.

Anthony N. Doob & Cheryl Marie Webster, Countering Punitiveness: Understanding Stability in Canada's Imprisonment Rate, 40 Law & Soc'y Rev. 325 (2006). Copyright 2006. Basil Blackwell, Publishing. Reprinted with permission.

Michel Foucault, Discipline and Punish: The Birth of the Prison (1977). Copyright © 1977 by Pantheon Books. Reprinted with permission.

Marvin E. Frankel, Criminal Sentencing: Law Without Order (1973). Copyright © 1973 by Hill and Wang Publishers. Reprinted with permission.

Sentencing Law and Policy

=1=

The Purposes of Punishment and Sentencing

The simplest question about sentencing is also one of the hardest to answer: what purposes does society achieve, or hope to achieve, when it sentences people convicted of crimes? One dominant and long-standing view is that society wishes to punish individuals who violate social norms and that sentencing systems are the means to impose such punishment. But this basic observation raises myriad problems: governments sometimes punish individuals outside of the criminal justice system; and if criminal sentencing is about imposing punishment, what is the purpose for the imposition of punishment?

Such fundamental issues concerning the purpose of punishment confront all organized societies, but they are especially important in the United States, which is now a world leader in punishing its citizens. As of 2007, more than 2 million persons are incarcerated in prisons and jails in the United States, and more than 5 million others are subject to criminal justice supervision through probation or parole. Altogether, more than 7 million people in the United States are under the control of the criminal justice system. (For point of reference, this is a group larger than the combined populations of all but the 11 largest states, and larger than the entire population of Indiana, Massachusetts, or Virginia — or roughly equal to the population of Switzerland, Honduras, or Bulgaria.) These basic numbers, however, mask enormous variation across the United States in how offenders are sentenced and punished.

Although sentencing is an important and dynamic field, discussions and decision making regarding sentencing often take place without any explicit reference to its underlying purposes. It is possible to study the law of sentencing without considering its fundamental purposes, but doing so would produce at best expertise in technical rules and procedures without a deep understanding of the reasons (or lack of reasons) for those rules and procedures. Although such crabbed discussions are found in many legal, political, and administrative settings, it is important to recognize that sentencing decisions reflect implicit or unconscious choices about the purposes of sentencing even when such purposes

1

are not considered explicitly. Consequently, to acquire knowledge and make sound policy about sentencing, and more generally about law and society, we must address the purposes of sentencing up front and maintain an awareness of the theoretical underpinning of different rules and procedures.

The first part of this chapter considers the various stated or implicit purposes that society tries to achieve through the sentencing process. This analysis reveals that none of the "traditional" justifications for punishment— retribution, deterrence, incapacitation, and rehabilitation—is self-defining, and that each is contested, both conceptually and practically. This discussion also examines other social purposes that have been suggested formally by philosophers and informally by observers of actual punishment and sentencing systems.

The second part of this chapter illuminates three fundamental points that demonstrate why it is unrealistic and probably inappropriate to posit a single purpose for sentencing and punishment. First, several different purposes may operate together to justify or limit punishment structures or sentencing systems in various ways. Second, the purposes that may justify certain systemwide sentencing rules or procedures may differ from those that justify case-specific sentencing outcomes. Third, purposes are constantly contested in both political and legal realms, and the focal points for debate and policy change over time.

A. SOCIAL PURPOSES OF SENTENCING

Organized societies devise many ways to sanction individuals who violate social norms. But formal and substantial punishments are delivered through the criminal justice system, where governments consciously and intentionally seek to condemn individuals. All aspects of criminal law— substantive, procedural, and political—must grapple with the core question of purpose and justification: Why should governments condemn and harm their own citizens?

In answering this question, philosophers have traditionally fallen into two camps. *Consequentialist philosophers,* who judge actions based on their consequences, justify state punishment as a means of reducing the overall harms created by criminal behavior. *Deontological philosophers,* who judge actions based on notions of moral duty, justify state punishment as a means of righting the moral wrongs of criminal behavior. Consequentialist philosophers generally endorse forward-looking, utilitarian theories of punishment, believing that punishment can benefit society through *deterrence* of potential offenders from committing future crimes, through *incapacitation* to render the current offender unable to commit future crimes, or through *rehabilitation* of the offender to prevent any further wrongdoing. Deontological philosophers generally endorse backward-looking theories of punishment, described in terms of *retribution* or *just deserts* and based on the notion that punishment is just when it restores the moral balance that criminal behavior upsets.

The materials in this section raise a number of questions: What purposes should a sentencing system seek? Is it possible or helpful to state those purposes explicitly? Can any unstated purposes be discovered? Can a system pursue multiple purposes, and if so, can it produce reasonably coherent and consistent outcomes across cases? We also consider whether the philosophical justifications for punishment are necessary for a principled system, and whether it is possible to describe and implement a decent system without any guiding purpose or purposes.

It is useful to stop at this point and articulate an initial reason or set of reasons why a government is justified in condemning and harming its own citizens through criminal punishment. You should attempt to rank the importance of these reasons if you list more than one. The coherence and relevance of various purposes will become clearer if you compare the purposes as described in this chapter with your own initial beliefs.

1. Stated Purposes

How can we tell what purposes a system serves? Actors in a variety of settings often make explicit claims to serve particular purposes. This section explores illustrations of explicit claims.

a. Purposes Statutes

Some systems in statutes, and some sentencers in opinions, articulate one or more purposes to justify a sentence. What is the impact and relevance of expressed and intentional assertions of purposes by the legislator or sentencer?

When legislators consider the purposes of criminal sentences and punishment, they often articulate goals that do not fit neatly into the traditional philosophical categories. They also likely do not think about individual offenders, but rather imagine more broadly the values and interests that they hope their jurisdiction's entire criminal justice system will pursue. An ever-present challenge in modern sentencing systems is to connect legislative statements of purpose with the traditional purposes discussed by philosophers and with actual offenders who confront judges. Consider first in the abstract the various kinds of purposes and goals identified in the following state statutes, and then try to effectuate those purposes and goals in the context of the case study presented in Problem 1-2. Ask yourself whether legislators provide useful guidance to prosecutors or sentencing judges, and why legislators may highlight purposes different in some important ways from the classic philosophical justifications.

This section begins with an effort by model law reformers (in this case the American Bar Association (ABA)) to state explicitly which purposes legislatures should consider when designing a sentencing system. Is this statement of purposes complete? If not, what is missing? Is it too sweeping? Is it helpful?

In this section we see how Congress, the Tennessee legislature and the Montana legislature have specified sentencing purposes. The second part illustrates more overtly political assertions about the purposes of punishment. The third part offers a radically different approach to sentencing dynamics than those presented by traditional court systems. It highlights a different perspective on the purposes that punishment and sentencing systems can (and should?) serve.

|| *ABA Standards for Criminal Justice,* ||
Sentencing 18-2.1
(3d ed. 1994)

MULTIPLE PURPOSES; CONSEQUENTIAL AND
RETRIBUTIVE APPROACHES

(a) The legislature should consider at least five different societal purposes in designing a sentencing system:
(i) To foster respect for the law and to deter criminal conduct.
(ii) To incapacitate offenders.
(iii) To punish offenders.
(iv) To provide restitution or reparation to victims of crimes.
(v) To rehabilitate offenders.
(b) Determination of the societal purposes for sentencing is a primary element of the legislative function. . . .

COMMENTARY

Every aspect of a criminal justice system, including sentencing, derives legitimacy from the advancement of social ends.[2] Current criminal codes are generally lacking in useful articulation of the policy objectives sought in the sentencing of offenders. This Standard calls attention to the vital need for a policy foundation upon which the sentencing system can be built. Without reasonably clear identification of goals and purposes, the administration of criminal justice will be inconsistent, incoherent, and ineffectual.

THE CHOICE OF SOCIETAL PURPOSES

The Standards' drafters recognized that there is no national consensus regarding the operative purposes of criminal sentencing. Indeed, even among philosophers there has been unceasing disagreement over the goals of sanctions. Some current systems have been characterized as predominantly retributive in nature. Other observers have claimed that the prevailing penology of the 1980s and early 1990s has been that of incapacitation. One need not go far back in time to find periods in which theories of rehabilitation and deterrence were of high prominence. Indeed, the resurgence of interest in community-based sanctions signals that, at least for the sentencing of some offenders, rehabilitative theory is alive and flourishing.

Paragraph (a) catalogs five different societal purposes a legislature should consider when designing a sentencing system. No hierarchy of importance is intended in the ordering of the five subsections, nor is it contemplated that

---

2. This statement is meant to encompass both consequentialist and retributive views of criminal justice policy. Consequentialists seek to promote the prospective social good of reducing future crime. Retributivists find a different social end in the punishment of past criminal acts, even where no forward-looking benefits result.

every jurisdiction must implement all five purposes. Rather, the Standard is drafted in recognition of the wide diversity of viewpoints that exist concerning ultimate goals, and is meant to express a conclusion that different schemas can be imagined consistent with rational and desirable public policy.

Subparagraph (a)(i) recognizes that criminal sanctions may be used in an attempt to foster respect for the law and deter criminal conduct. This goal might be understood as "general deterrence," which operates through the exemplary and educative force of criminal law.[7] If the public is made to believe that criminal behavior will be answered by painful consequences, it is hoped that some individuals will be discouraged from risking such consequences. On a more abstract plane, the imposition of punishment may disseminate a generalized message that criminal transgressions are treated seriously by society. Thus, information about criminal sentences may encourage people to respect the law as a whole and increase the numbers of law-abiding citizens.

Subparagraph (a)(ii) states that a jurisdiction may legitimately consider the goal of incapacitating offenders in designing a sentencing system. There is no question that some degree of disablement occurs whenever groups of offenders are incarcerated or are subjected to the restraint and surveillance of nonprison sanctions. To this extent, all sentencing systems are incapacitative, intentionally or not. A jurisdiction may further choose to pursue incapacitation in deliberate and targeted ways, however, and such choices are matters of fair policy debate.

Subparagraph (a)(iii) acknowledges that the punishment of offenders is a reasonable objective that legislatures may incorporate into a sentencing system. While retributivism had fallen from favor in the middle of this century, at least in the academic community, the theory has enjoyed both a scholarly and political rejuvenation since the 1970s. Today, a number of states have identified punishment or the meting out of "just deserts" as the central objective of their sentencing laws.

Subparagraph (a)(iv) identifies victim restitution and reparation as an eligible goal of sentencing. This consequentialist purpose aims toward the restoration of losses suffered by crime victims, when possible. Obviously, restitution cannot adequately be achieved in all criminal cases. Some injuries defy compensation and most offenders lack the resources to make adequate payments. Where restitution can be made, however, it is hard to posit a reason not to provide for it in the criminal justice system. Accordingly, the Standards elsewhere take the position that victim restitution should be given priority over the assessment and collection of other economic sanctions.

Last, subparagraph (a)(v) states that the legislature should consider the goal of rehabilitation of offenders when designing a sentencing system. As recently as the 1960s and early 1970s, rehabilitation was the prevailing theory of sentencing and corrections, and was the principal justification for the traditional structure of indeterminate sentences and parole. In the intervening years rehabilitation has lost its position of preeminence almost everywhere, but has hardly disappeared from view. Many incarcerative and nonincarcerative programs continue to attempt to reform offenders while at the same time serving

---

7. Some theorists have spoken in terms of "general deterrence" and "specific deterrence." The latter term refers to the tendency of painful punishments to deter the offender, who experiences them directly, from future criminal conduct. Under this Standard, such offender-specific effects are classified as "rehabilitation."

other goals, such as punishment, deterrence, and incapacitation. The Standards endorse this as a worthy aim. It should be noted, in this regard, that the Standards take the view that rehabilitation, standing alone, is never an adequate basis for criminal punishment. In effect, reform should be attempted only in connection with sentences that are independently justified on some other ground.

The preceding description of eligible purposes is only a starting point in the development of a meaningful statement of societal goals for a working sentencing system. To be useful, such a statement must identify which purpose or purposes the legislature wishes to pursue. If multiple goals are selected, a system of priorities is needed so that when two purposes conflict, decision makers have a guidepost for choosing between competing objectives. [T]he legislature may even wish the hierarchy of relevant goals to change for crimes of lesser and greater severity.

‖ 18 United States Code §3553 ‖

IMPOSITION OF A SENTENCE

(a) Factors to be considered in imposing a sentence. — The court shall impose a sentence sufficient, but not greater than necessary, to comply with the purposes set forth in paragraph (2) of this subsection. The court, in determining the particular sentence to be imposed, shall consider —

(1) the nature and circumstances of the offense and the history and characteristics of the defendant;

(2) the need for the sentence imposed —

(A) to reflect the seriousness of the offense, to promote respect for the law, and to provide just punishment for the offense;

(B) to afford adequate deterrence to criminal conduct;

(C) to protect the public from further crimes of the defendant; and

(D) to provide the defendant with needed educational or vocational training, medical care, or other correctional treatment in the most effective manner;

(3) the kinds of sentences available;

(4) the kinds of sentence and the sentencing range established [in the federal sentencing guidelines]; . . .

(6) the need to avoid unwarranted sentence disparities among defendants with similar records who have been found guilty of similar conduct; and

(7) the need to provide restitution to any victims of the offense.

‖ Tennessee Code §40-35-102 ‖

PURPOSE AND INTENT

The foremost purpose of this chapter [on criminal sentencing] is to promote justice [and] in so doing, the following principles are hereby adopted:

(1) Every defendant shall be punished by the imposition of a sentence justly deserved in relation to the seriousness of the offense;

(2) This chapter is to assure fair and consistent treatment of all defendants by eliminating unjustified disparity in sentencing and providing a fair sense of predictability of the criminal law and its sanctions;

(3) Punishment shall be imposed to prevent crime and promote respect for the law by:

(A) Providing an effective general deterrent to those likely to violate the criminal laws of this state;

(B) Restraining defendants with a lengthy history of criminal conduct;

(C) Encouraging effective rehabilitation of those defendants, where reasonably feasible, by promoting the use of alternative sentencing and correctional programs that elicit voluntary cooperation of defendants; and

(D) Encouraging restitution to victims where appropriate;

(4) Sentencing should exclude all considerations respecting race, gender, creed, religion, national origin and social status of the individual;

(5) In recognition that state prison capacities and the funds to build and maintain them are limited, convicted felons committing the most severe offenses, possessing criminal histories evincing a clear disregard for the laws and morals of society, and evincing failure of past efforts at rehabilitation shall be given first priority regarding sentencing involving incarceration; and

(6) A defendant who does not fall within the parameters of subdivision (5) and who is an especially mitigated or standard offender convicted of a Class C, D or E felony is presumed to be a favorable candidate for alternative sentencing options in the absence of evidence to the contrary.

NOTES

1. *Structure, content, and meaning.* The structure and language of the "purposes" statutes reprinted above vary considerably. Do the content and meaning of these statutes vary along with their structure? Which theory or theories of punishment are adopted in the federal system? In Tennessee? Which theory or theories of punishment do these jurisdictions reject? Note that the opening line in the federal statute provides what has been called a "parsimony" requirement by stating that the court "shall impose a sentence sufficient, but not greater than necessary, to comply with the purposes" of punishment. Why do you think Congress included this provision, and what do you think it means? Does it reflect one of the traditional theories of punishment or a different set of values? Do subdivisions (5) and (6) of Tennessee's statute to pursue related interests? In the federal system, the parsimony provision has been ignored by the courts and by commentators. How could such strong language have so little impact?

2. *Historical trends in punishment theory.* Adoption of particular theories of sentencing and punishment has varied greatly by jurisdiction and especially by era. Retribution is perhaps the oldest theory of punishment, with clear biblical roots and a beautiful illustration in the Code of Hammurabi, a set of laws created by a ruler of Babylon in the eighteenth century B.C. (excerpts reprinted in Chapter 2). More modern history marks a turn in punishment theory in the late 1700s and early 1800s due to the influential writings of Jeremy Bentham, an English philosopher and social scientist who argued against natural law theories

and urged an approach to law and punishment grounded in principles of utility. Writing around this same period, the equally influential German philosopher Immanuel Kant provided a more contemporary argument that retribution is the proper moral justification for punishment.

As a result of a variety of social forces, including the development of prison systems and modern American optimism concerning the ability of humans to improve other humans, during the nineteenth and early twentieth centuries rehabilitation took center stage as the dominant (though not the only) theory justifying punishment. See Williams v. New York, 337 U.S. 241 (1949). But rehabilitation as a general justifying theory came under a sustained attack in the 1960s and 1970s, as illustrated by Professor Francis Allen's famous book *The Decline of the Rehabilitative Ideal: Penal Policy and Social Purpose* (1981). These attacks were capped by Robert Martinson's widely discussed short paper What Works? — Questions and Answers About Prison Reform, 25 The Public Interest 25 (1974), which reviewed numerous studies evaluating efforts at penal rehabilitation. Martinson's conclusions, which were generally discouraging, quickly became oversimplified into the assertion that "nothing works." Commentators and others have tended to overstate the prior dominance of rehabilitation, as well as the modern failings of rehabilitative efforts and the general decline of the role of rehabilitation in sentencing. Indeed, though different theories of punishment have been expressly favored or disfavored in different eras, a thoughtful observer can probably identify the impact of each classic theory in nearly every punishment or sentencing system throughout history.

3. *Modern views of punishment theory.*   As the ABA excerpt highlights, the academic debates and practical realities surrounding punishment theories remain dynamic and contested today. It is probably fair to say that most systems now recognize, either expressly or implicitly, some combination of retribution, deterrence, and incapacitation, along with a sprinkling of other rationales. One of the most interesting developments in modern thinking about punishment is the decline of the once-dominant theory of rehabilitation: note that the ABA states expressly that "rehabilitation, standing alone, is never an adequate basis for criminal punishment [and] reform should be attempted only in connection with sentences that are independently justified on some other ground." Why do you think the ABA declared rehabilitation to be the one traditional theory that cannot alone provide an adequate justification for punishment?

Some scholars assert that a dominant modern rationale has emerged through the idea of "limiting retributivism," an idea often attributed to Professors H. L. A. Hart and Norval Morris (writing separately). This theory suggests that retribution sets the upper and lower boundaries of just punishment, within which other purposes can hold sway, including utilitarian theories of deterrence, incapacitation, and rehabilitation. See Richard Frase, Limiting Retributivism: The Consensus Model of Criminal Punishment, in Michael Tonry, ed., The Future of Imprisonment (2004). This theory has recently been endorsed by the American Law Institute during its ongoing effort to revise the Model Penal Code's sentencing provisions, although the exact meaning and the appropriateness of this decision is already being debated in academic circles. See Paul Robinson, The A.L.I.'s Proposed Distributive Principle of "Limiting

Retributivism": Does It Mean in Practice Pure Desert?, 7 Buff. Crim. L. Rev. 3 (2004); Edward Rubin, Just Say No to Retribution, 7 Buff. Crim. L. Rev. 17 (2003).

4. *Single or multiple theories?* Some philosophers have contended that utilitarian and retributive theories of punishment are incommensurable and that an initial choice must be made between them to develop a truly principled sentencing system. Others, however, perhaps because of the strong intuitive appeal of both approaches, have endeavored to develop hybrid theories of punishment that are compatible with both theoretical perspectives. The theory of limiting retributivism may be popular in large part because it seems to be one of the more satisfying hybrid theories. The ABA sentencing standards suggest that a legislature may legitimately select multiple purposes for its sentencing system, but "[i]f multiple goals are selected, a system of priorities is needed so that when two purposes conflict, decision makers have a guidepost for choosing between competing objectives."

Punishment and sentencing choices frequently reflect a variety of purposes, as Professor Norval Morris astutely observed more than 50 years ago:

> No one theory explains the different punitive measures to be found in our criminal law. . . . *All too often the purposes of punishment are discussed as if they could be treated as a single problem. . . . Surely the truth is that we have a series of related problems rather than a single problem.* . . . Surely, at the present level of our knowledge, we aim at a whole congeries of various purposes in respect not only of various types of crime but various types of criminals. . . . [B]ecause we do not seek any single purpose or set of purposes through our penal sanctions, we must not suppose we are facing an academic and impractical problem. . . . Prevention, reformation, deterrence, retribution, expiation, vindication of the law, and the Kantian argument that punishment is an end in itself all mingle in the wild dialectic confusion which constitutes most discussions of the purposes of punishment. . . .

Norval Morris, Sentencing Convicted Criminals, 27 Austl. L.J. 186, 188-189 (1953) (emphasis added).

5. *Inherent conundrums in applying punishment theory.* Though selection of multiple purposes creates the added challenge of establishing priorities, even a jurisdiction's decision to pursue only one theory of punishment does not magically simplify the conundrums inherent in developing a sound sentencing system. For one thing, each theory of punishment has conceptual variations. Retributive principles of just deserts can focus on the subjective culpability of an offender or the objective harms created by the offense; rehabilitation can be understood simply in terms of offenders no longer committing crimes or more dynamically in terms of offenders becoming productive contributors to the community. In addition, each goal raises challenging (and perhaps unanswerable) empirical and factual questions. Rarely do we have unassailable evidence about what punishments will deter (or rehabilitate) which offenders, and rarely can we establish indisputably what an offender thought (or did) to assess just deserts. Further, punishment goals must be reconciled with a jurisdiction's various other commitments and limitations; a commitment to the right of due process, for example, may make a particular theory of punishment more difficult to pursue, as can limitations on the resources that a jurisdiction is able to devote to these matters.

PROBLEM 1-1.   RICHARD GRAVES

One summer evening, Betsy Baker and her boyfriend ate dinner and had several beers at a local bar. As they drove home, Betsy's boyfriend was arrested for driving while under the influence (DUI). Richard Graves, a stranger, approached Betsy and offered to drive her truck home. Betsy agreed. After Richard returned with Betsy to her trailer, he followed Betsy inside. Betsy allowed Richard to stay, but told him he could sleep either on the bed or on the couch and she would stay on the other because they were not sleeping together.

Betsy awakened when she felt someone penetrating her vagina from behind her. She dove off of the bed and yelled at Richard to leave. Richard told Betsy to "hold on" and calm down, but she kept yelling for him to get out. Before he left, Betsy asked Richard, "Did we make love?" Richard replied, "I didn't mean to hurt you," then ran out the door. Betsy's loud crying brought a neighbor to her door, and she asked the neighbor to call the police. An officer arrived, who recognized Betsy from the earlier DUI stop and arrest. After Betsy calmed down, she told the officer that a man offered to drive her home after the arrest and that she had been raped.

The officer located Richard Graves based on Betsy's description. When the officer asked what had happened that night, Richard said, "What, nothing happened." When the officer said he knew something happened, Richard told him that Betsy offered to let him sleep in the bed, but that he declined, telling Betsy, "No, that's your bed. I'll sleep on the couch." Richard then said Betsy was with him on the bed and began touching him, but then they fell asleep and that "nothing really happened after that." After Richard became evasive answering follow-up questions, the officer advised him of his rights.

After Richard was booked, he and Betsy were both taken for a rape examination, which revealed sperm, biologically consistent with Richard, in Betsy. Richard was charged with the offense of sexual intercourse without consent. He was tried before a jury and testified on his own behalf. Richard claimed that, as he drove Betsy home, she flirted with him and gave him a hug and kissed him affectionately. Richard also testified that after he had fallen asleep in her trailer, he awoke to find Betsy fondling his groin area. He testified that after brief foreplay, intercourse took place.

Based on Betsy's testimony and other corroborating evidence, the jury found Richard Graves guilty of sexual intercourse without consent. Montana law provides that "[a] person convicted of sexual intercourse without consent shall be punished by life imprisonment or by imprisonment in the state prison for a term of not less than 2 years or more than 100 years and may be fined not more than $50,000."

At a hearing before the judge at sentencing, Richard again admitted to having sexual intercourse with Betsy, and he suggested that any mistake as to consent might have resulted from the fact that he had a lot to drink that night. Richard said he was sorry for any harm he caused, and also indicated that he had enrolled in a treatment program to deal with his alcohol problems. Richard also noted that despite a disadvantaged upbringing, which included a brief stint in a juvenile corrections facility following an assault conviction, he had had only minor contacts with the criminal justice system since becoming an adult. The Montana Codes provides the following guidance about purposes at sentencing.

‖ *Montana Code Annotated §46-18-101* ‖

CORRECTIONAL AND SENTENCING POLICY

(1) It is the purpose of this section to establish the correctional and sentencing policy of the state of Montana. Laws for the punishment of crime are drawn to implement the policy established by this section.

(2) The correctional and sentencing policy of the state of Montana is to:

(a) punish each offender commensurate with the nature and degree of harm caused by the offense and to hold an offender accountable;

(b) protect the public, reduce crime, and increase the public sense of safety by incarcerating violent offenders and serious repeat offenders;

(c) provide restitution, reparation, and restoration to the victim of the offense; and

(d) encourage and provide opportunities for the offender's self-improvement to provide rehabilitation and reintegration of offenders back into the community.

(3) To achieve the policy outlined in subsection (2), the state of Montana adopts the following principles:

(a) Sentencing and punishment must be certain, timely, consistent, and understandable.

(b) Sentences should be commensurate with the punishment imposed on other persons committing the same offenses.

(c) Sentencing practices must be neutral with respect to the offender's race, gender, religion, national origin, or social or economic status.

(d) Sentencing practices must permit judicial discretion to consider aggravating and mitigating circumstances.

(e) Sentencing practices must include punishing violent and serious repeat felony offenders with incarceration.

(f) Sentencing practices must provide alternatives to imprisonment for the punishment of those nonviolent felony offenders who do not have serious criminal records.

(g) Sentencing and correctional practices must emphasize that the offender is responsible for obeying the law and must hold the offender accountable for the offender's actions. . . .

(h) Sentencing practices must emphasize restitution to the victim by the offender. . . .

(i) Sentencing practices should promote and support practices, policies, and programs that focus on restorative justice principles.

If you were the prosecutor in Richard Graves's case, what sentence would you recommend? If you were a defense attorney assigned to represent Richard Graves, what sentence would you recommend? How would the provisions of Mont. Code Ann. §46-18-101 influence your recommendation? Would you seek additional information before making a specific recommendation to the judge? Would you emphasize a particular theory or theories of punishment in your recommendation?

If you were the sentencing judge in Richard Graves's case, what sentence would you impose? How would the provisions of Mont. Code Ann. §46-18-101 influence your decision? Would you want additional information before making your decision? Would you emphasize a particular theory or theories of punishment in your decision?

Cf. State v. Graves, 901 P.2d 549 (Mont. 1995).

NOTES

1. *Deterrence.*   Deterrence is not only a plausible concept but one that most people rely on in their everyday activities. Indeed, no one seriously disputes that creating a criminal justice system that punishes wrongdoing has some deterrent impact. But far more debatable — indeed, hotly debated — is the concept of marginal deterrence, which postulates that an additional quantum of punishment can lead to a measurable decrease in a particular crime (or all crimes). Complicating this issue is the likelihood, according to many researchers, that extralegal factors such as moral views, family, and community structures and other social dynamics have more of a deterrent impact than specific legal sanctions.

Defenders of deterrence as a justification for punishment must confront the argument that it is immoral to punish one person to deter others. Because of his eloquence, philosopher Immanuel Kant's arguments classically set out the terms of this debate:

> [P]unishment [by government for crime] can never be administered merely as a means for promoting another good either with regard to the criminal himself or to civil society, but must in all cases be imposed only because the individual on whom it is inflicted has committed a crime. For one man ought never to be dealt with merely as a means subservient to the purpose of another, nor be mixed up with the subjects of real right. . . . He must first be found guilty and punishable, before there can be any thought of drawing from his punishment any benefit for himself or his fellow-citizens. The penal law is a categorical imperative; and woe to him who creeps through the serpent-windings of utilitarianism to discover some advantage that may discharge him from the justice of punishment, or even from the due measure of it. . . .

Immanuel Kant, The Science of Right 195 (W. Hastie trans., 1790). This statement is often read solely as a justification for retribution or just deserts. But notice that Kant argues that it is immoral to punish an individual "merely" to promote another good. Kant recognizes that if a person is guilty of crime, then utilitarian reasons might come into play.

A growing body of social science research suggests that we should not expect to decrease crime rates significantly through changes in criminal law rules or through the specific distribution of criminal punishments. See Paul H. Robinson and John M. Darley, Does Criminal Law Deter? A Behavioral Science Investigation, 24 Oxford J. Legal Stud. 173 (2004). Professor Michael Tonry summarizes the state of empirical knowledge about deterrence:

> Current knowledge concerning deterrence is little different than eighteenth-century theorists such as Beccaria ([1764] 1995) supposed it to be: certainty and promptness of punishment are more powerful deterrents than severity. This does not mean that punishments do not deter. No one doubts that having a

system of punishment has crime-preventive effects. The important question is whether changes in punishments have marginal deterrent effects, that is, whether a new policy causes crime rates to fall from whatever level they would otherwise have been at. Modern deterrent strategies, through sentencing law changes, take two forms: increases in punishments for particular offenses and mandatory minimum sentence (including "three-strikes") laws.

Imaginable increases in severity of punishments do not yield significant (if any) marginal deterrent effects. Three National Academy of Sciences panels, all appointed by Republican presidents, reached that conclusion, as has every major survey of the evidence. There are a number of good practical reasons why this widely reached conclusion makes sense. First, serious sexual and violent crimes are generally committed under circumstances of extreme emotion, often exacerbated by the influence of alcohol or drugs. Detached reflection on possible penalties or recent changes in penalties seldom if ever occurs in such circumstances. Second, most minor and middling and many serious crimes do not result in arrests or prosecutions; most offenders committing them, naively but realistically, do not expect to be caught. Third, those who are caught and prosecuted almost always are offered plea bargains that break the link between the crime and the prescribed punishment. Fourth, when penalties are especially severe, they are often, albeit inconsistently, circumvented by prosecutors and judges. Fifth, for many crimes including drug trafficking, prostitution, and much gang-related activity, removing individual offenders does not alter the structural circumstances conducing to the crime. Sixth, even when one ignores all those considerations, the idea that increased penalties have sizable marginal deterrent effects requires heroic and unrealistic assumptions about "threat communication," the process by which would-be offenders learn that penalty increases have been legislated or are being implemented.

Michael Tonry, Purposes and Foundations of Sentencing, 34 Crime & Just. 28-29 (2006).

2. *Incapacitation.*   Because of the indisputable efficacy of some punishments to incapacitate offenders, one could reasonably view incapacitation as the most tangible and certain goal for punishment. (In addition, one could, after examining the history of punishment laws and the realities of punishment practices, reasonably conclude that incapacitation has been the goal most regularly and consistently pursued.) But because of the almost limitless reach of a theory of incapacitation and the obvious costs of its blind pursuit — to achieve "perfect" incapacitation, every offender would be executed — deciding how to pursue the theory poses a very serious challenge.

In the mid-twentieth century, a somewhat refined approach to incapacitation — operating under the label "selective incapacitation" — gained adherents based on the contention that judges and parole officials could accurately determine which offenders were especially dangerous to society and thus should serve longer prison terms than typical offenders. But much research conducted over the past four decades has shown that it is exceedingly difficult to predict future serious criminal behavior. Researchers generally concluded that even with the best information, predictions of future dangerousness would be wrong more often than right, and the challenge of obtaining all needed information for these assessments only increased the risk of "false positives." See Norval Morris and Marc Miller, Predictions of Dangerousness, 6 Crime & Just. 1 (1985).

Micheal Tonry summarizes the empirical research on incapacitation:

Incapacitative crime control strategies have some potential if used discriminatingly for people who commit very serious crimes at high rates. Offenders in confinement necessarily are disabled from committing offenses in the free community. We know a good bit more about incapacitation than we did thirty years ago. For a time, policies referred to as "collective incapacitation" were in vogue, influenced or at least evidenced by proposals in James Q. Wilson's Thinking about Crime (1976): extend all sentences of people convicted of violent crimes such as robbery by several years. This was soon shown to be impracticable. Large numbers of people are convicted of such crimes, but the average likelihood of recidivism is too low for the resulting huge increases in imprisonment to be justified.

This was followed by proposals for "selective incapacitation," catalyzed by a RAND Corporation report purporting to show the feasibility of such policies. This was soon discredited by a National Academy of Sciences report that showed that RAND's proposals worked with hindsight — it was based on self-reported past crimes of imprisoned violent offenders and in retrospect seemed to characterize those prisoners — but not prospectively. The prediction methods proposed were so over-inclusive, producing so many "false positives," that selective incapacitation was dismissed as impracticable.

After that, the theoretical writing and related empirical research on incapacitation pretty much came to a halt, but policy makers kept increasing lengths of sentences and accepted the imprisonment numbers that in the 1970s and early 1980s appeared unimaginable. Collective incapacitation, in effect, became national policy, though not under that name. Studies in the late 1990s and early in [the twenty-first] century concluded that mass imprisonment had reduced crime rates by 10-25 percent.

That last conclusion needs to be taken with a grain of salt for two reasons. First, comparable declines in crime rates occurred throughout the Western world, and no country other than the United States quintupled its imprisonment rate and experimented with mass imprisonment. There is a reasonably good chance that American crime rates would have fallen like every other Western country's. The contrast with Canada — a flat imprisonment rate of 100 per 100,000 population for forty years but crime rate trends closely paralleling those in the United States — is especially cautionary. Second, and no less important, the studies concluding that incapacitation caused significant declines in crime rates are based on exceedingly complex modeling, which like all such modeling is highly vulnerable to the assumptions on which it is based and the modeling technique used; even highly sophisticated modelers seldom agree about either.

Michael Tonry, Purposes and Foundations of Sentencing, 34 Crime & Just. 30-31 (2006).

3. *Retribution.*   Though having intuitive appeal, the seemingly simple retributivist notion that offenders deserve to be, and thus should be, punished proves to be a difficult concept to pin down. As Professor Richard Frase explains, the theory of retribution can have many facets:

The theory of retribution (or "just deserts") views punishment as being proper for its own sake, or for the sake of fairness to the victims of crime; to law-abiding offenders; to other offenders who have been punished for the same offense; and to this offender (who deserves to be punished no more severely than other, similar offenders were punished). There are several versions of retributive theory. What some have called "defining" retributivism seeks to impose penalties which are directly proportional to the seriousness of the offense and the offender's blameworthiness. A more modest version of desert theory, "limiting" retributivism, merely sets upper and lower bounds — sentences must not be excessively severe or unduly lenient; within these outer limits, punishment is scaled according to what is needed to achieve other purposes . . . and should be the least severe sanction necessary to achieve all of these other punishment goals (a concept sometimes referred to as sentencing parsimony).

Richard S. Frase, Criminal Punishment, in Encyclopedia of Crime and Justice 197 (2003). Though the concept of just deserts has broad appeal in the abstract, the difficulty of deciding exactly what punishment and how much punishment is "deserved" has proven to be the greatest enduring challenge in turning retributive theory into sentencing practice. Indeed, the hybrid theory of limiting retributivism may garner many adherents because it does not actually try to ascribe specific punishments based on notions of desert.

4. *Rehabilitation.* As a theory of punishment, rehabilitation is at once inevitable and oxymoronic. Interest in rehabilitation is inevitable because, unless every offender is to be executed or locked away for life, jurisdictions will want their punishment systems to reduce the likelihood that past offenders will re-offend when returned to the community. Yet a commitment to rehabilitation is oxymoronic because efforts by the state to improve the life and behavior of criminal offenders — through counseling, treatment, education, or training — do not seem like a form of punishment at all. These practical tensions have persistently burdened the concept of rehabilitation as a theory of punishment: jurisdictions have always recognized the importance of rehabilitating criminals, but they have rarely devoted sufficient money and energy to the programs most likely to succeed.

The conclusion drawn from Robert Martinson's famous article that "nothing works" to rehabilitate criminals is now well known to be a gross overstatement. Martinson himself came to recognize this, and within several years he published partial retractions of his position, noting that many rehabilitation programs had some modest impacts on individual behavior. See Robert Martinson, New Findings, New Views: A Note of Caution Regarding Sentencing Reform, 7 Hofstra L. Rev. 243 (1979). But continued research on rehabilitative efforts has tended to support a pessimistic view of the criminal justice system's ability to effectively reform offenders, although a few programs do have a track record of success. See Gerald G. Gaes et al., Adult Correction Treatment, 26 Crime & Just. 361 (1999); see also Rick Sarre, Beyond "What Works?" A 25-Year Jubilee Retrospective of Robert Martinson's Famous Article, 34 Austl. & N.Z. J. Criminology 1 (April 2001).

Michael Tonry summarizes empirical work on rehabilitation:

Prevention through rehabilitation looks to be a considerably more viable strategy in the early twenty-first century than it did during the closing decades of the twentieth. The view that "nothing works" was an important backdrop to the shift toward determinate sentencing, the abolition of parole, and adoption of incapacitative and deterrent crime control strategies. If we do not know how to reduce offenders' prospects for later offending, it is hard to justify giving judges and parole boards broad discretion to individualize sentencing.

The prospects for rehabilitation, however, have changed radically. Evidence is accumulating from many sources — individual evaluations, meta-analyses, literature reviews, and practical experience — that well-managed, well-targeted programs can reduce participants' probability of reoffending. A wide range of programs, including drug treatment, anger management, cognitive-skills programs, sex offender treatment, and various educational- and vocational-skills programs, have been shown to reduce reoffending. A report from the English Home Office, which underpinned a massive reorganization of the English criminal justice system mandated by the Criminal Justice Act of 2003, concluded that "a reasonable estimate at this stage is that, if the [treatment] programmes are developed and applied as intended, to the maximum extent possible, reconviction rates might be reduced by 5-25 percentage points (i.e., from the present level of 56 percent within two years to (perhaps) 40 percent)." The most recent meta-analysis of the effects of cognitive-behavioral programs concluded that, on average, they reduced reoffending by 27 percent. The proliferation of drug courts and prisoner reentry programs in the United States bears witness to the widely shared perception that some things work.

That litany of positive findings does not mean that reducing reoffending rates is easy. The results obtained from a well-funded pilot project, led by motivated people, cannot automatically be obtained by institutionalizing a new program model throughout a jurisdiction. A recent survey of violence prevention programs by the U.S. Surgeon General (2001) concluded that many programs can reduce violent offending but that the challenge is broad-based implementation. This is nonetheless much better news than the state of the evidence twenty-five years ago. We now know what we do; we need to figure out how to do it on a large scale.

An important implication is that rigid sentencing policies obstruct efforts to prevent crime through rehabilitation of offenders. For drug and other treatment programs to work, they must be targeted to the characteristics and needs of particular offenders, and this requires sentences to be individualized. With the fall of the nothing works psychology goes much of the case for rigid sentencing standards.

Michael Tonry, Purposes and Foundations of Sentencing, 34 Crime & Just. 32-33 (2006).

b. Politicians' Purposes

Politicians often make statements about crime policy that hint at or assume a role and justifications for punishment. Consider the following official Democratic and Republican North Carolina party platforms on crime. Do the political parties take an explicit position on the role and justifications for punishment? Should they? Should individual politicians have a substantial answer to the question "what is the purpose of punishment?" or, more broadly, "what is the purpose of the criminal justice system?" The question may be more important than the answer: would the answer change (for a party or an individual) if the question were "what is your policy on public safety?"

> ### *North Carolina Republican Party Platform* *(2004),* *Article VIII: Justice*

1. One of the first duties of government is maintaining law and order, thereby allowing citizens freedom to pursue the blessings of life and liberty.

2. Law-abiding citizens often live in fear of crime in their neighborhoods and schools. By better allocation of resources and tax dollars, the crime rate can be reduced and the state can ensure the rights of innocent people and victims, as well as the legitimate rights of the accused. We support the principle of victim's rights, including restitution and notification.

3. We believe the death penalty deters some murders. But we also believe crime calls for punishment directly proportional to the wrong perpetrated against its victims and against the moral order. Therefore, we believe the death penalty, whether or not it serves to deter other criminal acts, is the right punishment for premeditated murder. We call for legislation to drastically reduce the time between death sentence and executions that lasts for years and years making a mockery of the law.

4. Drug and alcohol abuse are major problems in North Carolina. We support effective educational and treatment programs to address these problems. We call for stiffer punishment for drivers who drive while impaired by drugs or alcohol. We oppose decriminalizing or legalizing drugs that are currently illegal. Drug users must face stiffer penalties for contributing to the supply of these poisonous products. We applaud new laws that have lengthened prison terms for persons convicted of selling illegal drugs. . . .

6. We endorse new laws that stiffen penalties for abducting, exploiting or abusing children. We oppose domestic violence and spousal abuse. We support community organizations that work with the justice system to provide efficient and effective solutions for family members facing domestic violence and abuse.

7. We support military-style boot camps and prisons with less attention to inmate comfort and more direction toward security, labor, and education. Prison labor should be used for construction of the facilities when possible. All inmates should be required to work and pay for their incarceration, including reasonable payment for health and dental care. . . .

|| *North Carolina Democratic Party Platform*
(2006) ||

CRIMINAL JUSTICE

The North Carolina Democratic Party believes that every person should be safe from crime. We also believe that crime is prevented not only through swift punishment for lawbreakers, but also by rearing children in loving, stable families that teach moral values and by having social, educational, and economic systems that give our people a sense of hope and community.

Capital punishment: In granting to our government the ultimate power to take the lives of individuals convicted of capital offenses, we have given it the most far-reaching power that can be bestowed upon any government. For this reason, we support both stronger due process safeguards and a moratorium in the application of this power until such safeguards are in place. With the advent of enhanced technology we believe it is incumbent for the State to use it so that no innocent person is mistakenly put to death by the State or wrongfully imprisoned. Neither a victim's nor a perpetrator's race, sex, or economic status should be a factor in sentencing or execution in North Carolina.

Gun safety: We support efforts to increase safety and education in the handling and ownership of firearms. Furthermore, we avidly support strict enforcement of existing firearms laws.

Hate crimes: We support increased penalties for violent crimes motivated solely by hatred towards the victim's race, gender, ethnicity, religion, disability, political beliefs, or sexual orientation.

Prisons/prisoners: We support efforts to relieve prison overcrowding, including efforts to fund additional facilities and to find effective alternatives to incarceration. We oppose the privatization of prisons. Inmates should work hard to earn their keep and learn the values of hard work, respect, discipline, and teamwork. We support efforts to achieve that goal, including making sure every able-bodied prisoner is participating in work or education programs, receiving appropriate mental health and substance abuse treatment and parental training, learning a trade or getting a diploma, and to making sure prisoners do not return to a life of crime when they are released.

Victims' rights: We believe that the effect of crime on victims should be considered in imposing punishment, that restitution should be required where possible, and that appropriate services to victims should be available.

Youhtful offenders: The rise in juvenile crime, including gang violence, is an alarming trend that must be reversed. We support the implementation of appropriate alternative sentencing programs designed to turn around troubled youths.

DRUGS AND ALCOHOL ABUSE

The abuse of drugs — including prescription drugs and alcohol — drains our State of the creativity, energy, and vitality we need for continued progress. We believe that efforts to reduce the demand for drugs and alcohol should be a major focus of our State's anti-drug strategy. We believe that law enforcement plays a crucial role in stemming the use of illegal drugs, and that both courts and police agencies should be given the support and resources they need to fight this battle. To that end, we enthusiastically support family, neighborhood, and school-based programs aimed at turning young people away from the use of illegal drugs and alcohol. We support the efforts of State and local law-enforcement agencies to deal severely with drug trafficking and alcohol-impaired driving, and we call for effective sentences for repeat drug and alcohol offenders. We also call for strong State support of treatment facilities, halfway houses, and drug courts for drug and alcohol abusers to help break the cycle of addiction. We also believe firmly in the concept of rehabilitation.

NOTES

What is the relationship between the purposes of punishment identified by political parties and politicians, and the purposes identified by legislators in statutes? How often do politicians and political parties focus on particular sanctions and their justifications? What is the framework for political claims about crime, justice, and punishment?

c.   Community Purposes

Although debate over the traditional theories of punishment has raged for centuries and continues to be quite lively, a number of philosophers and policymakers who have found the traditional debate unsatisfying or unhelpful have explored other approaches to punishment and sentencing. Notice that the ABA sentencing standards, for example, endorse sentencing systems that "foster respect for the law" and "provide restitution or reparation to victims of crimes." Michael Tonry notes:

> Deterrence, incapacitation, and rehabilitation are not needed to restrain most adults from selling drugs, burglarizing houses, holding up convenience stores, or mugging passersby. Most people's personal norms and values make predatory crime almost unthinkable. European scholars and theorists have long observed that the criminal law's main function is "general prevention": reinforcement of basic social norms that are learned in the home, the church, the school, and the neighborhood (Lappi-Seppala, T. (2001) Sentencing and Punishment in Finland. In Tonry, M. and Frase, R.S. (Eds.) — Sentencing and Sanctions in Western Countries. Oxford University Press (2001)). These primary socializing institutions must do the heavy lifting — what the criminal courts can do is too little and too late for the criminal justice system to serve as a primary socializing institution — but it is important that law and the legal system reinforce those norms and not undermine them.

Michael Tonry, Purposes and Fundations of Sentencing, 34 Crime & Just. 34 (2006).

Taking account of the limits of the criminal sanction, or the comparative benefits of noncriminal responses to various social problems, does not provide much affirmative guidance in setting punishments. Stressing the role and importance of the criminal law in establishing norms of behavior in society, modern philosophers have often spoken of the "educative" or "expressive" value of punishment and have stressed the ways in which criminal justice systems can and should communicate societal condemnation of crime and criminals. See Joel Feinberg, The Expressive Function of Punishment, in Doing and Deserving 98 (1970); Dan M. Kahan, What Do Alternative Sanctions Mean?, 63 U. Chi. L. Rev. 591 (1996). Though some suggest that the educative and expressive approaches to punishment are simply intriguing hybrid theories

melding aspects of retributivist and utilitarian philosophy, they define sufficiently distinct perspectives that their proponents often argue for different
sorts of punishment schemes.

Highlighting harms suffered by both offenders and their victims in traditional sentencing and punishment schemes, many modern advocates of reform
have urged the application of "restorative justice" principles throughout the
criminal justice system. In its broadest terms, restorative justice is fundamentally
concerned with restoring social relationships; in the context of crime and punishment, restorative justice has been described as a process through which all the
parties with a stake in a particular offense come together to resolve collectively
how to deal with the aftermath of the offense and its implications for the future.
The growing interest in restorative justice ideas can be seen in Montana's 2001
amendment to the statute reprinted in Problem 1-1, which added subsection (i),
stating that "[s]entencing practices should promote and support practices,
policies, and programs that focus on restorative justice principles."

One of the most tangible expressions of restorative justice concepts is the
use of sentencing circles in some criminal justice systems. Sentencing circles are
based on sentencing practices typical of Native communities in Canada, the
United States, and Australia. Their value is being increasingly emphasized by
those interested in broadening the applicability and usefulness of restorative
justice ideas to all members of society.

A sentencing circle is typically a community-directed process, conducted in
partnership with the criminal justice system, to develop consensus on an appropriate sentencing plan that addresses the concerns of all interested parties.
Sentencing circles are traditional peacemaking rituals and are structured to
involve the victim, victim supporters, the offender, offender supporters, traditional criminal justice personnel, and other community members. Within the
circle, people are asked to speak from the heart in a shared search for
understanding of the event, and together try to identify the steps necessary to
assist in healing all affected parties and prevent future crimes.

Modern sentencing circles have been developed most extensively in
Saskatchewan, Manitoba, and the Yukon and have been used occasionally in
several other communities. Their use spread to the United States in 1996, when
a pilot project was initiated in Minnesota. As you review the following discussion
of one sentencing circle experience, consider what values and goals find expression in this sort of response to criminal wrongdoing. Also consider whether
sentencing circles, and the ideas of restorative justice more generally, have
the potential to transform traditional perspectives on theories of punishment.

A Healing Circle in the Innu Community
of Sheshashit
Justice as Healing (Native Law Centre of Canada),
Summer 1997

[During the fall of 1994 Gavin Sellon, while attending a clinic for alcohol
and substance abuse, disclosed to counsellors that he had committed a sexual
assault the year before. On his return to Sheshashit, Labrador, Mr. Sellon went
to the Royal Canadian Mounted Police detachment and gave a cautioned

statement admitting to having intercourse with L. without her consent. The police then began to investigate the incident.

The accused first appeared in provincial court on June 12, 1995, where he elected to be tried in the Newfoundland Supreme Court, Trial Division, waiving the preliminary inquiry. On August 9, 1995, in the supreme court, the accused indicated that he wished to plead guilty and to make an application for a sentencing circle. The Crown opposed the motion and the matter was set over to December 18, 1995, for argument, at which time the application for a sentencing circle was withdrawn. Counsel for the accused indicated that he intended to pursue an informal healing circle outside the courtroom setting and in the community of Sheshashit, and asked Judge O'Regan to give strong consideration to viewing the sentencing of Sellon with a restorative approach rather than a punitive approach. Counsel for the Crown argued that the accused, being a non-native, should be treated using the traditional methods of sentencing. Judge O'Regan indicated to both counsel that if they wished to attend the healing circle they could do so and he would place what he deemed to be appropriate weight on the results of the healing circle.]

On Sunday January 21, 1996 a circle was held in the Alcohol Centre in Sheshashit. This circle was unique because unlike previous circles that have been held, the participants of this circle were aware in advance of the circle that a written report about the circle would be completed to share with the court. The following is a report of that circle.

Much thought and discussion went into the planning and preparation for this circle. Initially Innu Nation workers in health and justice were involved in this planning. Workers all began by referring to this circle as a "sentencing" circle. Workers discussed what needs and whose needs were to be met with this circle and how best to try and meet these varied needs. There was a great deal of concern expressed that the circle needed to be witnessed by members of the justice system so that Innu would not be open to seemingly inevitable criticism that we had something to hide or fear in the circle process. The same concern was raised should we not have witnesses from the Innu public.

Those involved in planning the circle were all able to agree that as the service provider, Innu Nation has a real need to demonstrate, both to Innu and the non Innu public and justice system, that Innu can develop and deliver services best suited to meet the needs of Innu. . . . We knew that this particular circle, with its direct connection to the court, would have a bearing on any future circles, court related or not. . . .

Therefore a conscious decision was made to be clear and specific about what needs and whose needs we were trying to meet through this process. We could then evaluate the effectiveness of the circle based clearly on what we set out to do. It was decided to tailor the circle to meet L.'s need for an opportunity to be heard within a supportive circle of those most directly affected by and involved with what happened between Gavin and her.

We also made a deliberate decision that it was not suitable or accurate to call this planned circle a "sentencing" circle. Sentencing is a justice system process to be done in court by court participants and the Judge. This circle would be held as a circle of concern and support for L. and Gavin. Included in the circle as part of the process would be recommendations made by the participants which would be shared with the court to be used by the Judge as he saw fit. . . .

We are able to determine the purpose of this circle as twofold:

1. to provide Gavin an opportunity to acknowledge responsibility for his actions and
2. to provide L. an opportunity to say what needed to happen for her to feel that the situation was being made more right.

Several weeks prior to the circle Jack Penashue met with L. to ask if she would be willing and able to participate in a circle with Gavin and others to deal with the incident which had resulted in a charge of sexual assault against Gavin. L. said she was willing and able to participate. After this, separate meetings were held with her father and then her mother to determine their support for their daughter's decision to participate as well as their own willingness to participate. They said they supported their daughter in her decision and were themselves willing to participate if asked by L.

Another meeting was then held with L. and Lyla Andrew [the facilitator]. Again she was asked if she felt comfortable about participating and was asked who she wanted to have participate in the circle. She said she wanted to have her sisters and parents be present. The names of other possible participants, Innu and non Innu . . . were given to L. and she indicated that "it was fine" if they wanted to attend. More information was shared with L. about the purpose of the circle and about the way it was thought the circle would happen. L. again indicated her willingness to participate. Her only request was that the circle take place soon. When she was told that her Dad would be working in Davis Inlet and not able to attend anytime soon, L. asked that the circle go ahead anyway and so the January 21 date was set.

Once this date was set Lyla met with Gavin Sellon to invite his participation in the circle. He was told who L. had invited and was asked if there were people he wanted to invite. He requested his mother, stepfather and his spouse. L. had already agreed to their participation and Gavin was told this. He also asked if Jack Penashue could attend and was informed that Jack would be a facilitator of the circle. . . .

Sunday there were 10 participants: L., G. (L.'s mom), R.N. (L.'s sister), Gavin Sellon, Patricia Nuna (Gavin's spouse), Lynne Gregory (Gavin's mom), Apenam Pone (Gavin's stepfather), Germaine Benuen [Labrador Legal Services court liaison in Sheshashit], Jack Penashue (facilitator) and Lyla Andrew (facilitator).

The participants had coffee and tea prior to the circle starting. Then all participants moved into the large meeting room and sat in a circle on the floor. With joined hands a prayer was shared. Jack then explained to the participants the symbolism of burning sweetgrass and smudging. If participants found it meaningful, they were invited to smudge and Jack went around the circle. He spoke Innuaimum first and then in English. When this was completed, Jack asked Lyla to explain the process.

It was explained to participants that what happened in the circle should be guided by the participants' acceptance and use of four principles: honesty, kindness, sharing and respect. Each person in turn would have the chance to speak uninterrupted. If they chose not to speak, they would pass the small "talking stone" on to the next person because no one would be forced to speak. There were four rounds of the circle so there were four opportunities for speaking.

The first round of the circle was for each participant to explain why they were present in the circle. The second round was a chance for each participant to speak directly to L., to share concern, support and encouragement. The third round was for each participant to speak directly to Gavin, to share with him directly feelings about him. The fourth round was the chance for each participant to make recommendations to those in the circle, and especially to Gavin, about what could or should be done at this point in time to help bring about resolution to this situation.

Before the facilitators began the rounds, the possible need for interpretation between Innuaimum and English was discussed. It was agreed that participants would speak the language of their choice and anyone could request interpretation. Jack Penashue agreed to provide the interpretation. . . .

When the fourth and final round was completed . . . participants joined hands and closed the circle with a shared prayer.

It is very difficult to put into words an assessment of the effectiveness and power of this circle. Participants in circles learn the power of the circle through their active participation and learn that equally important to what is said by the participants is the atmosphere or feeling created within the circle by the participants. The comments which follow are those of the facilitators and Germaine Benuen in relation to their impressions about the intangibles of the circle process, about why it was effective and powerful.

As the participants began arriving at the building there was a noticeable tension among some. L. arrived with her mom and was quiet, almost sad, speaking little, standing off to the side while others chatted in twos or threes. All the participants seemed to be nervous. The facilitators had to be very direct to get participants into the room to start the circle. L.'s mother (G.) was the third participant to speak and she said directly that she was scared. The tension noticeably lessened and participants explained why they were present. It seemed to help that all participants had equal opportunity to say something. Even when L. did not speak in the first round, she began to appear less tense and less pressured, perhaps because she was not put on the spot to speak. We felt that in a way the process, and the participants in the process, showed respect to L. by not forcing her to speak. . . . When the circle started L. was seated in between her mom and Gavin's mom. She sat herself in such a way that she could look at her mom and at her cousin, but she had her back to almost everyone else in the circle. By the fourth round she had shifted around so that she could see and be seen by all the participants. She was smiling sometimes and by the end of the circle was laughing when appropriate with the other participants.

Another important aspect of the circle process was the expression of emotion by participants. Facilitators had no way to know what emotions, whether anger, sadness or frustration, might be voiced and/or displayed by the participants. Facilitators knew from previous experiences that the process of the circle was powerful because honesty and emotion are an integral part of the process.

How people spoke would in many ways be just as important to the impact of the circle as what people had to say.

There were two occasions when participants broke down weeping. Both L. and Gavin's mom wept. The other circle participants remained seated without speaking and waited for the person to compose themselves and then proceed when they were able. . . . G. commented that if she had been crying and some-one had asked that there be a break to give her time to stop crying that it would feel like a rejection of her and her genuine feelings. She felt it was respectful of people to let them show emotion in a setting that was safe. If participants had taken a break, it would have been more because of participants' discomfort than anything else. Participants had been asked to try and be honest and respectful, and accepting the expression of emotion seemed very much a part of that honesty and respect. . . .

An assumption is made that the recommendations of the circle partici-pants in the final round are of most importance to the court. Prior to the circle meeting, participants had been asked in preparation for the circle to think about recommendations they would want to make to be shared with the court. However, it is important to stress that what was said in the earlier three rounds and how that was expressed, had great influence on, indeed shaped the recommendations which eventually were made.

Probably the single most important comments made by any participant affecting the recommendations finally offered, were the comments made by Gavin. In the first round Gavin spoke in a clear voice, in a direct way that he had come to the circle to apologize to everyone that he had hurt for what he had done. He said that he wanted to find out what people wanted from him, what they expected from him and he repeated that he had come to apologize and to say that he was sorry for his behaviour. In the round when everyone was invited to speak to L. Gavin spoke emphasizing that L. was in no way to blame for what had happened, that he took full responsibility for his actions. He explained that when he had gone to the Brentwood Treatment Centre that he had shared a lot of things that had happened in his life and that one of those things was what had happened between him and L. He said the reason he shared that at treat-ment was because of his shame. He told us that he knew that what he had done was wrong and he thought that if he shared how he felt about what he had done that it might help him to get better. He also thanked people for coming to the circle.

Because of the seating, L. had the opportunity in each round to speak before Gavin. She didn't speak in the first or second rounds but she spoke in the third round to Gavin and said that she was happy that he had opened up about what had happened between them. She said she would not have been strong enough to open up to others about what happened but she was glad he had. She also told participants she was happy to be a part of the circle. After this when Gavin spoke he said he wanted L. to know that what had happened was his fault. He also wanted his family to know that he was not blaming them in any way, that his actions were his own and he was responsible for his behaviour. . . .

Jack began the final round by saying that he felt what needed to be said had been said. He said he saw what had happened in the circle . . . and he felt honoured to have been a part of the process where participants who cared about each other were able to say the things they needed to say. Jack spoke about his hesitation to say anything more but on a very personal note he said that he wanted to say what he felt should now happen, what could now happen. He said he thought that L. and Gavin should start talking to one another if they were not already doing so, that they both needed to accept what had happened because it was his experience that people sometimes "over say things and over think things." He said maybe it wouldn't happen right now but what needed to happen was for L. and Gavin to start having contact again maybe to try and hug each other. . . .

Lyla then began speaking and said she too found the last round the most difficult even though she knew that the earlier rounds had been difficult because what was said and expressed was more painful. The difficulty with making recommendations came with a sense of having to satisfy someone or [some] group outside the circle, someone who hadn't experienced what had happened in the circle.

She then shared the same concern as Jack that where there had been friendships and family ties connecting Gavin and L. and Gavin's spouse and children, and where those connections had been broken or damaged, that through Gavin's actions, with the permission and agreement of others, that he needed to try and mend those connections. . . .

One recommendation was shared with L. This was that she accept and use . . . the caring that her family clearly has for her . . . to grow into being her own person. . . .

Another specific recommendation was made about Gavin. If he were to be placed on probation, and obviously we couldn't know this, but if he was, it was recommended that rather than being supervised directly by the adult probation office, that he be made accountable through a period of probation to people in the community to whom he is connected and who know why he would be on probation and who would have real concern about how he was going to do while on probation. . . .

Through interpretation L.'s mom G. said that she was really happy that Gavin had come to the circle and shared what he had with the participants. It was her opinion that Gavin was a strong young man because he had shared so much and taken responsibility. . . .

Apenam [Gavin's stepfather] recommended to Gavin that he continue to work at what Apenam knew Gavin had learned from going to the Brentwood treatment program. Apenam recommended this because he himself had gone to Brentwood many years before Gavin to change his own behaviour. . . .

Apenam said he wanted to say openly that he loves Gavin. Apenam said he doesn't always know how to show his love and that this is one of the biggest problems in his own life. He said he knows Gavin has a birth father but that he still wants to continue to be a father to Gavin as he has tried to be for many years, and if Gavin needs his help, Apenam offers it to him. . . .

In Innuaimum, L. was asked by Jack if she understood and she made a reply right away. . . . Everyone agreed to close the circle and stood up with hands joined and together repeated the "serenity prayer."

At this point the tape was turned off and participants embraced one another at their own choosing. It is noted that L.'s mom went over to Gavin and embraced him and most significantly that L. and Gavin embraced one another. . . .

[A report of the circle was prepared and attached . . . to the decision of Judge O'Regan of the Newfoundland Supreme Court, Trial Division. In considering sentencing, Judge O'Regan found that "the concern of the Crown" that Gavin was non Inuit was "a non-issue," especially since Gavin "did grow up in the community of Sheshashit and was exposed to the Innu Culture and thus can benefit from the community's involvement in such things as a 'healing circle' which he attended." Judge O'Regan accepted the recommendations of the healing circle and imposed a noncustodial sentence.]

NOTES

1. *Sentencing circles, restorative justice, and traditional purposes.*   Do sentencing circles serve all, or even any, of the traditional purposes of punishment? Which traditional purposes were served or not served by the healing circle involving Gavin, L., and their families? See Julian V. Roberts & Carol LaPrairie, Sentencing Circles: Some Unanswered Questions, 39 Crim. L.Q. 69 (1997) (exploring the relationship of sentencing circles to traditional purposes of punishment).

What nontraditional purposes were served in the sentencing of Gavin? Proponents of sentencing circles say the goals of the process are to promote healing for all affected parties; provide an opportunity for the offender to make amends; empower victims, community members, families, and offenders by giving them a voice and a shared responsibility in finding constructive resolutions; address the underlying causes of criminal behavior; build a sense of community and enhance its capacity for resolving conflict; and promote and share community values. Do you think sentencing circles represent a radically different substantive approach to crime and punishment? Or do they simply represent a more meaningful and effective means to achieve traditional goals?

Proponents of sentencing circles readily concede that the process is not appropriate for all offenders. They stress the importance of several factors in determining whether a case is appropriate for a sentencing circle, including the strength of the offender's connection to the community, the sincerity and nature of the offender's efforts to be healed, the input of victims, and the dedication of the offender's support group. What about the nature of the offense itself? Would a sentencing circle be useful for an offender convicted of murder? For an offender convicted of stock fraud? For an offender convicted of trafficking in cocaine? For an offender convicted of domestic violence? Cf. Rashmi Goel, No Women at the Center: The Use of the Canadian Sentencing Circle in Domestic Violence Cases, 15 Wis. Women's L.J. 293 (2000).

2. *Assessing the efficacy of sentencing circles.*   Very little research has been conducted to date on the effectiveness of sentencing circles, in part because most punishment systems are judged in terms of crime rates whereas sentencing circles are clearly concerned with a range of other interests. There have been a number of positive anecdotal reports about sentencing circles, but they have not been seriously examined empirically. See Roberts & LaPrairie, Sentencing Circles at 82-83 (arguing that before sentencing circles are used broadly, "it is

incumbent upon advocates to produce the kind of rigorous scientific evidence that sentencing circles are more effective than the current system").

_____

Should sentencing circles be an option in all criminal justice settings — that is, should jurisdictions explore the possibility of using sentencing circles for all sorts of crimes and all sorts of offenders? Consider the following sentencing and justice experiment.

PROBLEM 1-2.   RED HOOK COMMUNITY COURT

Red Hook, a Brooklyn neighborhood notorious for drugs and crime, is home to one of New York's oldest and largest public housing developments. It is also home to a multi-jurisdictional community court, the Red Hook Community Justice Center (RHCJC). In the court, one judge hears cases that would otherwise be divided among civil, family, and criminal courts. Typical cases involve common neighborhood problems: drugs, domestic violence, and landlord-tenant disputes. The judge has a variety of sanctions and services available, and the judge, prosecutor, and public defender work together to achieve the best plan for the particular individual. For example, the court can require drug treatment or counseling for mental health or domestic violence. Offenders can also be required to participate in community restitution projects. There are on-site educational workshops as well, including job training and GED classes. These programs are available to all community members, regardless of court involvement.

You work for the District Attorney's office of a community similarly plagued by chronic street crime, drugs, and unemployment. Your boss has heard of Red Hook and other community courts, as well as funding sources in the Department of Justice to underwrite experimental community courts. You are tasked with proposing the jurisdiction for the court, and presenting the idea to city officials, community leaders, and members of the public. How would you explain the benefits of a community court? Would you focus on the success of other courts by highlighting the decline in recidivism rates or would you emphasize the long-term benefits of increased community involvement? What are the similarities between a community court and a traditional court? What would you say to those concerned that the lack of an adversarial process is damaging the rights of the individuals sentenced by community courts?

For a firsthand account of the RHCJC, see Greg Berman & Aubrey Fox, Justice in Red Hook, 26 Just. Sys. J. 77 (2005).

NOTES

1. *Other approaches to restorative justice.* The movement toward restorative justice finds many manifestations besides sentencing circles. Especially for less serious offenses, a number of jurisdictions have developed various novel criminal justice forums and procedures that emphasize repairing harm, healing,

and rebuilding relations among victims, offenders, and communities. In addition to sentencing circles, popular restorative justice practices include victim-offender mediation, family group conferencing, citizen panels, and various restitution initiatives. See generally Leena Kurki, Restorative and Community Justice in the United States, 27 Crime & Just. 235 (2000); Frederick W. Gay, Restorative Justice and the Prosecutor, 27 Fordham Urb. L.J. 1651 (2000). A parallel development is the recognition by both traditional and specialty courts of "therapeutic jurisprudence," which treats the law and its institutions and agents as potentially organized around problem solving and individualized justice. David Wexler, Dennis Stolle & Bruce Winick, eds., Practicing Therapeutic Jurisprudence: Law as a Helping Profession (2000); David Wexler, Therapeutic Jurisprudence: It's Not Just for Problem-Solving Courts and Calendars Anymore, in National Center for State Courts, Future Trends in State Courts 2004 87 (2004).

2.   *Implicit Purposes*

The American Bar Association states in its model sentencing standards that "[w]ithout reasonably clear identification of goals and purposes, the administration of criminal justice will be inconsistent, incoherent, and ineffectual." Yet most criminal justice systems operate without reasonably clear identification of goals and purposes. But just because goals and purposes have not been articulated does not mean that they do not operate. And even in systems with explicit purposes, truer, deeper purposes (acknowledged or unacknowledged) may operate. Consider the implicit purpose or purposes of punishment suggested in the following materials.

The traditional justifications for punishment are profoundly unsatisfying to many scholars and system actors for their inability to justify or explain the actual behavior of legislators, prosecutors, and judges. Consider the following critique by Professor Michael Tonry, which suggests a much wider range of purposes to justify punishment and sentencing policy. Does Tonry add a touch of hard-nosed realism to unduly arid philosophical discussions? If his critical perspective is more satisfying than the traditional and abstract list (deterrence, just deserts, incapacitation, rehabilitation), does it also help to solve the practical challenges of the design and application of sentencing systems?

	Purposes and Functions of Sentencing,	
	Michael Tonry	
	34 Crime & Just. 10-12, 42-43 (2006)	

The fundamental purposes and primary functions of sentencing are clear, and are the same: to punish criminals and prevent crimes. There are, however, other functions that concern officials and policy makers. They range from encouraging most defendants to plead guilty and managing criminal justice budgets to reassuring the public and getting reelected.

People concerned primarily with the word "justice" in "criminal justice" would say that the overriding purpose of sentencing is the imposition of punishments that are just relative to prevailing normative criteria; the overriding functional goal would be to ensure, or at least maximize the likelihood of, imposition of just punishments according to those criteria. People concerned primarily with the word "criminal" would say that the overriding purpose of sentencing is the prevention of crime and accordingly that the overriding functional goal is to minimize the incidence of crime and its consequences. To distinguish the question of what purposes should be pursued from the question of whether laws have been fairly and effectively applied relative to those purposes, I refer to the first as purposes and the second as distributive functions. . . .

All mainstream contemporary theories include crime prevention among the purposes of punishment, though they vary widely in what ways, with what weight, and subject to what constraints prevention may be taken into account. Most people, however, believe that prevention and diminution of crime, fear of crime, and their consequences are important and legitimate functions of sentencing. These are the preventive functions.

Many practitioners would also include efficiency, cost-effectiveness, and resource management among the functional goals of an acceptable sentencing system. Managers need to set and pursue substantive priorities, allocate personnel and resources, meet performance goals, and operate within their budgets. They also need to maintain good working relations with other agencies and officials who can make their work easier or harder, and thereby make achievement of other goals easier or harder. These are management functions.

Some policy makers and analysts urge that it is important that governments reassure the public, maintain confidence in the legal system, denounce wrongful behavior, and reinforce basic social norms. Contemporary analyses of "expressive" policies emphasize government officials' wishes and needs to assure the public that things are being done to address subjects that trouble them [David Garland, The Culture of Control: Crime and Social Order in Contemporary Society (Univ. of Chicago Press 2001)]. Recent work on legitimacy and procedural justice emphasizes that justice needs to be seen to be done [Tom R. Tyler, Procedural Justice, Legitimacy, and the Effective Rule of Law, 30 Crime & Just. 431 (2003)]. Durkheimian analyses portray criminal law as a primary contributor to maintenance and refinement of basic social norms and its dramaturgical features as key sources of social cohesion [Emile Durkheim, Division of Labor in Society (1893/1933)]. These are communicative functions.

The first two of these, distribution and prevention, concern primary goals (what sentencing "is supposed to do"). The third, management, is an ancillary goal (how institutional imperatives can be acknowledged while pursuing primary goals).

The fourth, communication, is the most complex and multifaceted and operates at all three functional levels. Communication of legal threats and acknowledgment in court processes and outcomes of basic social norms are necessary to achieve the primary goals of distribution and prevention. Communication about court processes and procedures and likely punishments is key to achievement of a variety of management goals. These might, however, be thought of as incidental components of primary and ancillary functions. . . .

The more controversial forms of communication relate to latent functions. Practitioners and policy makers are sometimes moved by personal, ideological, and partisan objectives. People sometimes make decisions or support policies because it is in their personal self-interest, because they want to bear witness to their ideological beliefs, or because they want to pursue partisan political advantage. . . . [To summarize:]

A. Purposes (. . . these could be called normative functions)
B. Primary functions
   1. Distribution (consistency, evenhandedness, fairness)
   2. Prevention (crime, fear of crime, costs and consequences of both)
   3. Communication (threat communication, denunciation of wrongful behavior, reinforcement of basic social norms)
C. Ancillary functions
   1. Management (efficiency, cost-effectiveness, resource management)
   2. Communication (procedural justice, legitimacy, public confidence)
D. Latent functions
   1. Self-interest
   2. Ideology
   3. Partisanship
   4. Communication. . . .

Purely personal ambitions and self-serving motives are illegitimate considerations in decision making by prosecutors and judges about individual cases. Performance of the distributive, preventive, and communicative functions is undermined when cases are dealt with in a particular way because a practitioner believes she is likelier to gain a nomination, win an election, or obtain a new job. . . . When a prosecutor or judge treats an offender in a particular way to realize a purely personal goal, there is no arguable public benefit that can be said to outweigh or counterbalance the harm done the offender. When an entirely self-motivated legislator votes to support a particular policy for which there is little substantive justification, but claims in good faith to be trying to reassure the public or, more complicatedly, claims a need to vote in a particular way on this subject in order to win others' support for a vote on a more important subject, it is almost impossible to assess what the real motives are. The governing ethical premise, however, should be the same as for a prosecutor or a judge: only disinterested motives are legitimate. . . .

Sometimes penal policies are proposed for reasons having nothing to do with the goals of punishment per se. The prison guards union in California, for example, is often said to promote harsher policies as means to the ends of job creation and maintenance. Many communities have sought placement of prisons within their boundaries and, implicitly, increased use of imprisonment, as a form of economic development. On the face of it these considerations are entirely unrelated to punishment and prevention. . . .

Crime control policy in our time has become entangled in ideological conflict. Recent conflicts over medical use of marijuana and Oregon's assisted-suicide law offer front-page examples. . . .

Ideology is at least as powerful an influence on sentencing policy. Drug policy offers stark examples. The federal 100-to-one law punishes people, mostly black, convicted of crack cocaine offenses as severely as people, many white, convicted of powder cocaine offenses involving amounts that are 100 times larger. The law was enacted in 1986, after the much-publicized death, generally attributed to a crack overdose, of Len Bias, a University of Maryland basketball player forecast to become a National Basketball Association superstar. The law's role in exacerbating racial disparities in federal prisons soon became clear, and the U.S. Sentencing Commission proposed that the differential be eliminated. Both the Clinton White House and the Congress opposed any change, and none was made. In later years Attorney General Janet Reno, Drug Czar Barry McCaffrey, and the U.S. Sentencing Commission proposed that the differential be reduced. The Clinton and Bush II White Houses opposed all changes, and the differential remains. No one presumably wants federal sentencing laws to worsen racial disparities, but neither successive administration nor congressional leaders have been willing to risk being accused of condoning drug use or trafficking.

Mandatory minimum and three-strikes laws, for other examples, often are primarily based on ideology. Research findings discussed in earlier sections make it clear, and for at least a century have made it clear, that such laws seldom achieve their putative goals and always produce undesirable and unwanted consequences. Ideological posturing is no better an explanation for why an offender is punished unjustly than is a judge's hope for reelection.

Pursuit of partisan advantage is the most cynical of the latent functions. Ideological influences grow out of deeply held beliefs; those beliefs may sometimes be blinding. . . . Decisions made for partisan reasons, by contrast, are made in cold calculation. Partisan influences often result in the passage of laws that cannot be justified on the substantive merits and foreseeably produce unjust results. Republican Senator Orrin Hatch, according to a member of his staff, for example, long believed reducing sentences for drug offenders "was the right thing to do, but he couldn't do it for political reasons."

California's three-strikes law, according to Frank Zimring's account, resulted from politicians' competing attempts to use punishment policies to pursue partisan advantage. It was enacted not because thoughtful policy makers really believed that people who stole pizza slices in schoolyards or handfuls of compact discs from Wal-Mart deserved decades-long prison sentences, but because Republican Governor Pete Wilson and California Assembly leader Willie Brown played a game of chicken in which, in the end, neither backed down. Democratic legislators agreed among themselves to pass any proposal Governor Wilson offered, in hopes "that he would back down from an unqualified 'get tough' stand or be politically neutralized if he persisted." . . . Neither Wilson nor Brown was willing to propose refinements to Wilson's extreme initial proposal and thereby expose himself and his party to the other's accusation of softness. As a result California adopted the most far-reaching, rigid, and unjust three-strikes law in the country. . . .

	Discipline and Punish: The Birth of the Prison,	
	Michel Foucault	
	Pages 3-8, 16-30, 200-221 (1977)	

On 1 March 1757 Damiens the regicide was condemned "to make the *amende honorable* before the main door of the Church of Paris," where he was to be "taken and conveyed in a cart, wearing nothing but a shirt, holding a torch of burning wax weighing two pounds"; then, "in the said cart, to the Place de Grève, where, on a scaffold that will be erected there, the flesh will be torn from his breasts, arms, thighs and calves with red-hot pincers, his right hand, holding the knife with which he committed the said parricide, burnt with sulphur, and, on those places where the flesh will be torn away, poured molten lead, boiling oil, burning resin, wax and sulphur melted together and then his body drawn and quartered by four horses and his limbs and body consumed by fire, reduced to ashes and his ashes thrown to the winds" (*Pièces originales*, 372-4).

"Finally, he was quartered," recounts the *Gazette d'Amsterdam* of 1 April 1757. "This last operation was very long, because the horses used were not accustomed to drawing; consequently, instead of four, six were needed; and when that did not suffice, they were forced, in order to cut off the wretch's thighs, to sever the sinews and hack at the joints. . . . It is said that, though he was always a great swearer, no blashemy escaped his lips; but the excessive pain made him utter horrible cries, and he often repeated: 'My God, have pity on me! Jesus, help me!' The spectators were all edified by the solicitude of the parish priest of St Paul's who despite his great age did not spare himself in offering consolation to the patient." . . .

Eighty years later, Léon Faucher drew up his rules "for the House of young prisoners in Paris":

> Art. 17. The prisoners' day will begin at six in the morning in winter and at five in summer. They will work for nine hours a day throughout the year. Two hours a day will be devoted to instruction. Work and the day will end at nine o'clock in winter and at eight in summer.
>
> Art. 18. *Rising.* At the first drum-roll, the prisoners must rise and dress in silence, as the supervisor opens the cell doors. At the second drum-roll, they must be dressed and make their beds. At the third, they must line up and proceed to the chapel for morning prayer. There is a five-minute interval between each drum-roll.
>
> Art. 19. The prayers are conducted by the chaplain and followed by a moral or religious reading. This exercise must not last more than half an hour.
>
> Art. 20. *Work.* At a quarter to six in the summer, a quarter to seven in winter, the prisoners go down into the courtyard where they must wash their hands and faces, and receive their first ration of bread. Immediately afterwards, they form into work-teams and go off to work, which must begin at six in summer and seven in winter.
>
> Art. 21. *Meal.* At ten o'clock the prisoners leave their work and go to the refectory; they wash their hands in their courtyards and assemble in

divisions. After the dinner, there is recreation until twenty minutes to eleven.

Art. 22. *School.* At twenty minutes to eleven, at the drum-roll, the prisoners form into ranks, and proceed in divisions to the school. The class lasts two hours and consists alternately of reading, writing, drawing and arithmetic.

Art. 23. At twenty minutes to one, the prisoners leave the school, in divisions, and return to their courtyards for recreation. At five minutes to one, at the drum-roll, they form into workteams.

Art. 24. At one o'clock they must be back in the workshops: they work until four o'clock.

Art. 25. At four o'clock the prisoners leave their workshops and go into the courtyards where they wash their hands and form into divisions for the refectory.

Art. 26. Supper and the recreation that follows it last until five o'clock: the prisoners then return to the workshops.

Art. 27. At seven o'clock in the summer, at eight in winter, work stops; bread is distributed for the last time in the workshops. For a quarter of an hour one of the prisoners or supervisors reads a passage from some instructive or uplifting work. This is followed by evening prayer.

Art. 28. At half-past seven in summer, half-past eight in winter, the prisoners must be back in their cells after the washing of hands and the inspection of clothes in the courtyard; at the first drum-roll, they must undress, and at the second get into bed. The cell doors are closed and the supervisors go the rounds in the corridors, to ensure order and silence" (Faucher, 274, 82).

We have, then, [from the two distinct examples] a public execution and a timetable. They do not punish the same crimes or the same type of delinquent. But they each define a certain penal style. Less than a century separates them. [Between 1760 and 1840] in Europe and in the United States, the entire economy of punishment was redistributed. It was a time of great "scandals" for traditional justice, a time of innumerable projects for reform. It saw a new theory of law and crime, a new moral or political justification of the right to punish; old laws were abolished, old customs died out. "Modern" codes were planned or drawn up: Russia, 1769; Prussia, 1780; Pennsylvania and Tuscany, 1786; Austria, 1788; France, 1791, Year IV, 1808 and 1810. It was a new age for penal justice.

Among so many changes, I shall consider one: the disappearance of torture as a public spectacle. Today we are rather inclined to ignore it; perhaps, in its time, it gave rise to too much inflated rhetoric; perhaps it has been attributed too readily and too emphatically to a process of "humanization," thus dispensing with the need for further analysis. And, in any case, how important is such a change, when compared with the great institutional transformations, the formulation of explicit, general codes and unified rules of procedure; with the almost universal adoption of the jury system, the definition of the essentially corrective character of the penalty and the tendency, which has become increasingly marked since the nineteenth century, to adapt punishment to the individual offender? Punishment of a less immediately physical kind, a certain discretion in the art of inflicting pain, a combination of more subtle, more subdued sufferings, deprived of their visible display, should not all this be treated as a special case, an incidental effect of deeper changes? And yet the fact remains that a few decades saw the disappearance of the tortured, dismembered, amputated body, symbolically branded on face or shoulder, exposed alive or dead to public view. The body as the major target of penal repression disappeared.

If the penalty in its most severe forms no longer addresses itself to the body, on what does it lay hold? The answer of the theoreticians — those who, about 1760, opened up a new period that is not yet at an end — is simple, almost obvious. It seems to be contained in the question itself: since it is no longer the body, it must be the soul. The expiation that once rained down upon the body must be replaced by a punishment that acts in depth on the heart, the thoughts, the will, the inclinations. Mably formulated the principle once and for all: "Punishment, if I may so put it, should strike the soul rather than the body." . . .

Bentham's Panopticon is the architectural figure of this composition. We know the principle on which it was based: at the periphery, an annular building; at the centre, a tower; this tower is pierced with wide windows that open onto the inner side of the ring; the peripheric building is divided into cells, each of which extends the whole width of the building; they have two windows, one on the inside, corresponding to the windows of the tower; the other, on the outside, allows the light to cross the cell from one end to the other. All that is needed, then, is to place a supervisor in a central tower and to shut up in each cell a madman, a patient, a condemned man, a worker or a schoolboy. By the effect of backlighting, one can observe from the tower, standing out precisely against the light, the small captive shadows in the cells of the periphery. They are like so many cages, so many small theaters, in which each actor is alone, perfectly individualized and constantly visible.

. . . Each individual, in his place, is securely confined to a cell from which he is seen from the front by the supervisor; but the side walls prevent him from coming into contact with his companions. He is seen, but he does not see; he is the object of information, never a subject in communication. The arrangement of his room, opposite the central tower, imposes on him an axial visibility. And this invisibility is a guarantee of order. If the inmates are convicts, there is no danger of a plot, an attempt at collective escape, the planning of new crimes for the future, bad reciprocal influences; if they are patients, there is no danger of contagion; if they are madmen there is no risk of their committing violence upon one another; if they are schoolchildren, there is no copying, no noise, no chatter, no waste of time; if they are workers, there are no disorders, no theft, no coalitions, none of those distractions that slow down the rate of work, make it less perfect or cause accidents. The crowd, a compact mass, a locus of multiple exchanges, individualities merging together, a collective effect, is abolished and replaced by a collection of separated individualities. . . . (Bentham, 60-64).

Hence the major effect of the Panopticon: to induce in the inmate a state of conscious and permanent visibility that assures the automatic functioning of power. So to arrange things that the surveillance is permanent in its effects, even if it is discontinuous in its action; that the perfection of power should tend to render its actual exercise unnecessary; that this architectural apparatus should be a machine for creating and sustaining a power relation independent of the person who exercises it; in short, that the inmates should be caught up in a power situation of which they are themselves the bearers. . . .

So much for the question of observation. But the Panopticon was also a laboratory; it could be used as a machine to carry out experiments, to alter behaviour, to train or correct individuals. To experiment with medicines and monitor their effects. To try out different punishments on prisoners, according to their crimes and character, and to seek the most effective ones. To teach different techniques simultaneously to the workers, to decide which is the best. To try out pedagogical experiments. . . . The Panopticon is a privileged place for experiment on men, and for analysing with complete certainty the transformations that may be obtained from them. The Panopticon may even provide an apparatus for supervising its own mechanisms. In this central tower, the director may spy on all the employees that he has under his orders: nurses, doctors, foremen, teachers, warders; he will be able to judge them continuously, alter their behaviour, impose upon them the methods he thinks best; and it will even be possible to observe the director himself. . . .

. . . The Panopticon . . . is polyvalent in its applications; it serves to reform prisoners, but also to treat patients, to instruct schoolchildren, to confine the insane, to supervise workers, to put beggars and idlers to work. It is a type of location of bodies in space, of distribution of individuals in relation to one another, of hierarchical organization, of disposition of centres and channels of power, of definition of the instruments and modes of intervention of power, which can be implemented in hospitals, workshops, schools, prisons. . . .

[I]t is not that the beautiful totality of the individual is amputate, repressed, altered by our social order, it is rather that the individual is carefully fabricated in it, according to a whole technique of forces and bodies. . . . The panoptic modality of power . . . is not under the immediate dependence or a direct extension of the great juridical-political structures of a society; it is nonetheless not absolutely independent. Historically, the process by which the bourgeoisie became in the course of the eighteenth century the politically dominant class was masked by the establishment of an explicit, coded and formally egalitarian juridical framework, made possible by the organization of a parliamentary, representative regime. But the development and generalization of disciplinary mechanisms constituted the other, dark side of these processes. The general juridical form that guaranteed a system of rights that were egalitarian in principle was supported by these tiny, everyday, physical mechanisms, by all those systems of micro-power that are essentially non-egalitarian and asymmetrical that we call the disciplines. And although, in a formal way, the representative regime makes it possible . . . for the will of all to form the fundamental authority of sovereignty, the disciplines provide, at the base, a guarantee of the submission of forces and bodies. The real, corporal disciplines constituted the foundation of the formal, juridical liberties. The contract may have been regarded as the ideal foundation of law and political power; panopticism constituted the technique, universally widespread, of coercion. It continued to work in depth on the juridical structures of society, in order to make the effective mechanisms of power function in opposition to the formal framework that it had acquired. The "Enlightenment," which discovered the liberties, also invented the disciplines.

How can we determine any implicit purposes of sentencing in the United States at the start of the twenty-first century? Perhaps one way is to offer a snapshot of current punishment — what sanctions are used, for how many, and for whom.[*] Imagine this is not a country you know, but a foreign country. If you look only at the picture of punishment described below, what possible theories of implicit purpose can you discern (despite whatever explicit claims might be made)?

- At midyear 2005 the nation's prisons and jails incarcerated 2,186,230 persons. Prisoners in the custody of the 50 states and the federal system accounted for two-thirds of the incarcerated population (1,438,701 inmates). The other third were held in local jails (747,529), not including persons in community-based programs.
- The rate of incarceration in prison and jail was 738 inmates per 100,000 residents in midyear 2005, up from 601 in 1995. At midyear 2005, 1 of every 136 U.S. residents was incarcerated in state or federal prison or a local jail.
- The five states with the highest incarceration rates at midyear 2005 were all in the South. Louisiana had the highest prison incarceration rate (1,138 sentenced inmates per 100,000 residents), followed by Georgia (1,021), Texas (976), Mississippi (955), and Oklahoma (919). The five states with the lowest incarceration rates at midyear 2005 were all in the North: Maine (273), Minnesota (300), Rhode Island (313), Vermont (317), and New Hampshire (319).
- Among the nearly 2.2 million offenders incarcerated as of June 30, 2005, an estimated 548,300 were black males between the ages of 20 and 39. Of black non-Hispanic males age 25 to 29, 11.9% were in prison or jail, compared with 3.9% of Hispanic males and about 1.7% of white males in the same age group. In general, the incarceration rates for black males of all ages were five to seven times greater than those for white males in the same age groups.
- An estimated 12% of black males, 3.7% of Hispanic males, and 1.7% of white males in their late 20s were in prison or jail.
- In 2005 a total of 60 persons were executed in 16 states: 19 in Texas; 5 each in Indiana, Missouri, and North Carolina; 4 each in Ohio, Alabama, and Oklahoma; 3 each in Georgia and South Carolina; 2 in California; and 1 each in Connecticut, Arkansas, Delaware, Florida, Maryland, and Mississippi. Those executed during 2005 had been under sentence of death an average of 12 years and 3 months. In 2005 a total of 59 men and 1 woman were executed. The racial/ethnic distribution of those executed included 38 whites, 19 blacks, and 3 Hispanics (all white). Thirty-eight states and the federal government had capital statutes as of 2005.
- At the end of 2005 there were 3,254 prisoners under sentence of death. California held the largest number on death row (646), followed by Texas (411), Florida (372), and Pennsylvania (218). Thirty-seven people were under a federal death sentence. Men made up 98% (3,202) of all prisoners under sentence of death. Whites accounted for 56%, blacks 42%, and other races 2%. Those of

---

[*] Bureau of Justice Statistics, Prison and Jail Inmates, Mid-Year 2005 (May 2006); Bureau of Justice Statitistics, Capital Punishement — 2005 (Dec. 2006).

Adult Correctional Populations 1980-2005

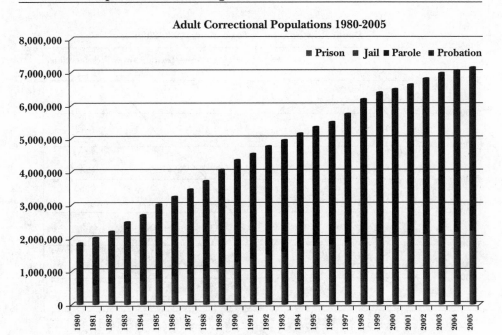

Source: From http://www.ojp.usdoj.gov/bjs/glance/corr2.htm.

Prisoners—Rate/100,000

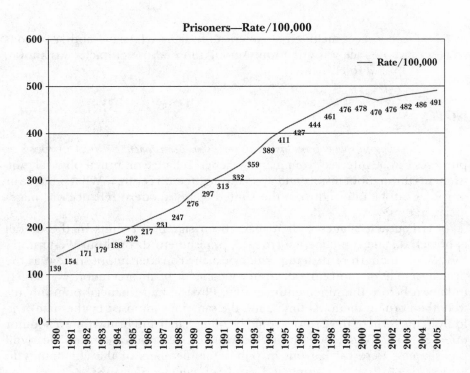

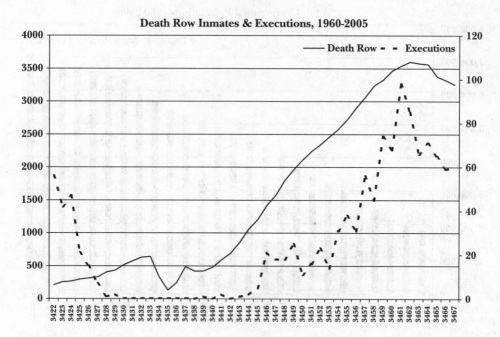

Source: From http://www.ojp.usdoj.gov/bjs/glance/dr.htm.

other races included 31 American Indians, 34 Asians, and 12 persons whose race was unknown. Among those whose ethnicity was known, 13% were Hispanic.

NOTES

1. *Inferring purposes from historical trends in punishment.* What purpose or purposes can be inferred from many societies' reliance on brutal physical punishments throughout history and up to the eighteenth century? What purpose or purposes can be inferred from the United States' modern reliance on (mass) incarceration?

As Foucault suggests, there have been significant shifts in the overall approach to, and fundamental types of, punishment throughout Western history. While modern sentencing systems usually consider imprisonment as the primary mode of punishment, the very concept of incarceration was largely unknown before the nineteenth century. Physical and financial punishments were the norm in medieval times, and the sanctions imposed by the state (typically in the form of the Crown) could be quite harsh and brutal for even minor offenses. Serious crimes were punished with death or banishment, and nearly all punishments were carried out in public for members of the community to witness. See Arthur W. Campbell, Law of Sentencing, §1 (1978).

Influenced in part by the development and ascendancy of imprisonment as a principal mode of punishment, nearly all Western societies have abandoned the official use of brutal physical punishments, and rarely are punishments carried out in public settings. Though these "modernizing" trends seem to make our systems of punishment more "civilized," the Foucault reading should lead you to consider whether torturing the human soul may in fact be worse than torturing the human body. Another question to consider is whether the "civilization" of our methods of punishment may make them less effective when judged against our theories of punishment. Might certain theories of punishment be better served by forms of physical torture imposed in public than by terms of imprisonment served in private?

2. *Modern variations in types of punishment.*   The cumulative statistics presented above do not reveal the significant variations in how individuals are incarcerated and how terms of probation and parole are structured and controlled. The experience of incarceration for offenders can and does vary greatly depending in part on whether the time is served in halfway houses, local jails, minimum-security prisons, general state or federal prisons, or high-security (supermax) prisons. See generally Norval Morris, The Contemporary Prison: 1965-Present, in The Oxford History of the Prison 227 (1995). The experience of probation or parole likewise can and does vary considerably depending on the nature and type of conditions placed on probationers or parolees and on other forms of sanctions (both official and unofficial) that can accompany community supervision. See generally Andrew Horwitz, Coercion, Pop-Psychology, and Judicial Moralizing: Some Proposals for Curbing Judicial Abuse of Probation Conditions, 57 Wash. & Lee L. Rev. 75 (2000); Nora V. Demleitner, Preventing Internal Exile: The Need for Restrictions on Collateral Sentencing Consequences, 11 Stan. L. & Pol'y Rev. 153 (1999).

3. *Questions about U.S. punishment practices.*   Which of the statistics reflecting modern sentencing and punishment dynamics in the United States surprises you the most? Which of the statistics disturbs you the most?

B. PURPOSES IN PRACTICAL CONTEXT

For several millennia philosophers have discussed the ins and outs, the pros and cons, of different theories of punishment. English philosopher H. L. A. Hart advanced the theoretical debate when he observed that these discussions involve three conceptually distinct issues:

(1) The "general justifying aim" — the general goal of the social institution of punishment
(2) The question of liability — who specifically should be punished for certain behavior
(3) The question of amount — exactly how much punishment should be administered

See H. L. A. Hart, Prolegomenon to the Principles of Punishment, in Punishment and Responsibility 1-28 (1968). Hart's insight reinforces the fact that while philosophers have the luxury of discussing theoretical issues in the abstract, societies must confront the complicated practical realities of constructing and operating a workable criminal justice system and then distributing specific punishments to offenders. The materials in this section demonstrate that the actual practice of administering and enforcing punishments through a sentencing and corrections system implicates many levels of complexity beyond the basic questions of punishment theory. Rather than working through these issues by starting with general questions and then moving to specific cases, we will begin with a specific case and then telescope out to broader, systemwide questions.

1.   Use of Purposes in Sentencing an Individual Offender

Though the purposes of punishment are often debated at a high level of abstraction, individual decision makers (usually judges) necessarily confront them when deciding what sentence to impose in a particular case. Norval Morris, writing in 1953, noted not only the inevitability of considering purposes in sentencing individual offenders but also the importance of blending purposes on a case-by-case basis:

> When a court decides what sentence to impose on a criminal . . . , it must do so with reference to some purpose or purposes, conscious or unconscious, articulate or inarticulate. [A] compass is desirable . . . , even if only for a short distance and over a particular part of the journey. [F]or certain types of criminals reformation is one important aim. None will dispute that our hope of deterring the criminal from repeating his crime by the punishment we inflict and by that same punishment deterring others who are like-minded also plays a considerable part. Few will deny that there is in the community a deep-rooted hatred of the criminal . . . and that in our penal sanctions we must take into account these emotional demands of the community. The extent to which these aims of reformation, deterrence and community satisfaction blend in relation to any particular offender will vary considerably.

Norval Morris, Sentencing Convicted Criminals, 27 Austl. L.J. 186, 192-198 (1953).

Many modern sentencing systems that structure how judges can exercise their sentencing power often prescribe certain sentencing ranges for particular offenders committing particular offenses, but then allow the judge to move outside these ranges in "extraordinary" circumstances or for "substantial and compelling" reasons. Judges in these systems thus have an opportunity to consider the purposes of sentencing in the selection of specific sentences both within and outside of the prescribed ranges.

For example, the Washington State Sentencing Reform Act of 1981 provides that the purposes of sentencing are to: (1) ensure that the punishment for a criminal offense is proportionate to the seriousness of the offense and the offender's criminal history; (2) promote respect for the law by providing punishment that is just; (3) impose punishment that is commensurate with the punishment imposed on others committing similar offenses; (4) protect the public; (5) offer offenders an opportunity to improve themselves; and (6) make frugal use of the state's resources. See Wash. Rev. Code §9.94A.010. The following case comes not from the Northwest but from the Southeast—and to make matters even more interesting, it is from the southeastern Australian territory of Victoria! There are untold riches in the sentencing practices, procedures, and decisions of several Australian jurisdictions, nicely illustrated by this decision. In the following sentencing decision, consider the role of purposes and the kinds of purposes the court uses to decide whether an exceptional sentence was appropriate.

The Queen v. Robert James Arnautovic
[2007] VCC 597 (9 June 2005),
County Court of Victoria,
Melbourne Criminal Division

Her Honour, Judge Gaynor:

1. Robert James Arnautovic, you have pleaded guilty before me to seven counts of burglary, seven counts of theft and one count of armed robbery and have admitted prior convictions. The facts underlying the offending which took place between November 1998 and March 2002 are as follows.

2. Counts 1 and 2 relate to an incident which occurred on the afternoon of 13 November 1998 when you entered the rear yard of a house at 56 Stafford Street, Abbotsford, smashing two windows to gain entry. You stole from that house property to the value of approximately $18,300 consisting of electronic equipment, computer equipment, a mobile phone, a watch, cameras, camera equipment, VCRs, CD players, disk players and CDs. . . .

3. [Counts 3-10 relate to similar criminal incidents during 1999 and 2000.]

7. Count 11 refers to an incident on the morning of 4 December 2001 when you forced a side window of a house at 5 York Street, Albion through which you gained entry and then stole a bag which you filled with items of property. While you were in the house the occupier, one Xavier Haveraux and his three year old daughter Kemely returned home entering through the front door. You rushed at Mr. Haveraux striking him to the head three times with a flat instrument similar to a small jemmy bar causing Mr. Haveraux to fall on the floor. Whilst he was on the floor you searched him taking his watch which was valued at $65 and demanding money from him, you ultimately being given $10. Whilst this was occurring you kept accusing Mr. Haveraux of "ripping you off" to the tune of $50 a couple of weeks earlier and claimed you had followed him home.

8. You then asked Mr. Haveraux to drive you in his car to get more money but Mr. Haveraux talked you out of this and got you to leave. You then left the premises and walked down the street before which you apologised to Mr. Haveraux's three year old daughter who was present during the entire incident. Once you had left Mr. Haveraux grabbed an old cricket bat and followed you to see where you were going and as he followed you down the street you turned back towards him and approached him saying, "Come on."

9. You and Mr. Haveraux then struggled, wrestling to the ground during the course of which Mr. Haveraux managed to hit you over the head with the cricket bat causing you to bleed. Eventually you both stood up and you walked off, Mr. Haveraux going back to his house and calling police. A sample of your bloodstains obtained from the footpath in York Street was subsequently obtained and examined.

10. Counts 12 and 13 relate to an incident which occurred on 8 December 2001 when you entered the back yard of a house at 1 Cowper Street, Footscray, smashing the window with a pitchfork you obtained from a garden shed, thereby gaining entry to the house from which you stole an IBM laptop computer, a Packlite backpack, a Kathmandu backpack, gold jewellery, a camera, a watch and a Sharp remote control valued at approximately $10,190.

11. Counts 14 and 15 relate to an incident 14 March 2002 when you entered the back yard of a house at 36 Princess Street, Kew, smashing and removing slats from a louvre window to gain access to the house from which you stole UK Sterling cash, a video game unit, confectionary, a Samsung mobile telephone, sunglasses, a video game, a Walkman and a backpack to the value of approximately $600.

12. This offending was ultimately linked to you because in each case police obtained blood samples from the scenes of the crimes left by you on entering premises via broken windows or in the case of Count 11 from the pavement of York Street, Albion, following the contretemps with Mr. Haveraux. You were arrested on 4 March 2004. . . .

13. You have admitted extensive prior convictions, they being 39 prior convictions for burglary, 57 prior convictions for theft, and you have in the course of your offending previously received eight gaol terms and in that course breaching three suspended sentences imposed upon you.

14. You are now 30 years of age, the youngest of three children born to your parents who separated when you were still a baby. Your mother was a heroin addict who now resides in a nursing home after suffering a stroke as a result of a heroin overdose about five years ago. You have had virtually no contact with your father who remarried, had further children and was himself gaoled for subsequent criminal behaviour.

15. At the age of one you were placed in foster care and remained in departmental care for the next 15 years. Your placements were changed every two to three years. You were rarely visited by your mother who continued with drug problems and was apparently regularly in and out of gaol.

16. You have one sister who remained in your father's care but you and your brother went into the foster care system. You had difficulty with learning due to a hearing problem and needed to attend speech therapy and physiotherapy. Despite the disruption to your early years, it appears your offending behaviour did not begin until your adolescence which began promisingly when you were initially attending St Bernard's College in Essendon where you were an excellent sportsman being a Victorian champion in running. However your behaviour deteriorated, you were expelled from that school in Year 9, then attended St Albans High School, then Kensington Community School.

17. At the age of 15 you were placed to live with your mother for six months, she then just having come out of gaol. She introduced you to heroin. You quickly became addicted and this has been the drug that has bedevilled you ever since although there is also some history of earlier amphetamine use.

18. You have a limited employment history, in 1997 working as a furniture removalist for about eight months, then briefly as a truck jockey and then with a garden program. The dominating theme of your life however from the age of 15 until two years ago was your heroin addiction and associated offending in support of that habit. [That offending saw you] in July 1999 placed on a

combined custody and treatment order and in August 2000 you were sentenced to a total effective sentence of 14 months. . . .

19. You were released in October 2001 and it is clear that both your heroin addiction and associated offending continued as shown in Counts 11 to 15 on the presentment in this matter, being the armed robbery, burglaries and theft committed between 4 December 2001 and 14 March 2002.

20. On your release from prison in October 2001, you admitted yourself to a rehabilitation centre to detoxify but stayed only eight weeks before moving to various boarding houses in Footscray. In that time you met Rebecca Gibbons, also a heroin user with whom you commenced a relationship. On 15 October 2002 your daughter Shakira was born. Her birth saw a remarkable transformation by you in terms of your drug addiction and lifestyle.

21. Before turning to this aspect of your life however, the observations and psychological testing upon you by forensic psychologist Dr. Carla Lechner as contained in her report of 27 May 2005 are important. . . .

22. It is Dr. Lechner's view that you demonstrate symptoms [consistent] with a diagnosis of clinical depression and states that you told her you had been depressed for as long as you can remember, your mood at present being further lowered by an intense anxiety over the outcome of this proceeding and your fear of prison and of course the effect of that upon your daughter, Shakira.

23. Dr. Lechner says you impressed as cognitively and emotionally immature, which she attributed to a retardation of your emotional development in the years of your heavy drug use. Formal psychological testing to determine your level of comprehension, reason and judgment skills rated you in the low average borderline range of verbal intelligence with approximately 91 per cent of the adult population performing better than you.

24. I now return to the issue of your daughter. Shakira, as I have stated, was born on 15 October 2002. According to the report of Dr. Juliana Antolovic, a paediatrician in child development and rehabilitation at the Royal Children's Hospital, whose report, dated 20 March 2005, was tendered on your behalf, Shakira was born with a significant medical condition, Pierre Robin Syndrome, which is associated with abnormal development of the jaw, tongue and mouth, and children with this condition often have a cleft palate and can have significant problems with breathing and feeding.

25. Indeed, according to Dr. Antolovic, who appears to have been Shakira's paediatrician since her birth, Shakira had a number of complications related to this condition and since her birth has had multiple admissions to hospital, a number of investigations and surgery to repair her very large cleft palate. For the first 18 months of her life she was dependent upon tube feeding for her growth and nutrition. Dr. Antolovic states: "Shakira's care needs have been extremely high. In addition to two weekly visits to the Child Development and Rehabilitation Centre, Shakira and her family have also regularly attended the Royal Children's Hospital for routine follow up with a dietician and in a cleft palate splint. During the time Shakira was fed by a nasogastric tube (the first 18 months of her life) there were multiple visits to the emergency department for replacement of her neo-gastric tube. These visits sometimes occurred up to three times a week, which is not uncommon in the circumstances."

26. At the age of 17 a daughter was born to you and your then partner, a lady named Narelle. That daughter and her mother were taken in by the

maternal grandmother with whom they still live and with whom you continue to have contact. However, you did not play a significant parenting role in that daughter's life, you remaining in the grip of your heroin addiction and continuing to offend in support of it and to be gaoled regularly by the court.

27. However, it is clear that the birth of this second gravely physically compromised daughter has wrought the transformation in you and you have entirely devoted yourself to her care since her birth. You have been her primary caregiver since her birth. Concomitant with this dedication to your daughter and her various needs, you have entirely ceased heroin use and criminal offending.

28. In December 2004 the Department of Human Services became involved because of concerns over verbal domestic violence taking place between yourself and Rebecca, who had remained a drug user, you perceiving that she was failing to fulfil her role as Shakira's mother.

29. Shakira was removed from your care for one night then returned to you as her sole carer and you remain in that position to this day. You and the child's mother, Rebecca, remained in a relationship until December 2004. . . .

30. You and Shakira were initially placed by DHS for a six week period in a caravan park by way of emergency housing whilst arrangements were made for more appropriate accommodation which was ultimately provided through Hanover Family Services. . . .

40. Howard Draper, a solicitor who represented you in the Children's Court proceedings relating to Shakira [notes that in] February 2005 the Children's Court made an interim protection order placing the child in your care on certain conditions and that by the return of that order on 16 May 2005 DHS was recommending that there was no need for any further involvement by that department due to the progress made by you. He states: "According to the latest DHS report, 16 May 2005, my client is currently on methadone and is no longer required to provide drug screens to DHS. It appears that DHS is satisfied that my client is not abusing substances." . . .

42. Mr. Draper concludes, "As a legal practitioner I have been practising in the Children's Court for about 21 years and for the past seven to eight years most of my practice has involved Children's Court matters. I have no hesitation in noting that the efforts of Mr. Arnautovic in addressing the protective concerns and providing a safe and secure environment for his daughter, have been exceptional."

43. . . . During the plea evidence was given by Daheyamima Matthew, a senior Child Protection worker, who is the case manager for Shakira from the Child Protection Unit. Ms. Matthew has been employed with DHS for ten years.

44. She stated that since December you have been the sole carer for Shakira. She said that Rebecca, Shakira's mother, continues to have access to her daughter, which was initially supervised and which is supposed to occur for about two and a half hours a week. This, she said, is either usually cancelled or shortened by Rebecca, who generally wants the child for an hour only. She stated that Rebecca had no capacity to care for Shakira and in the department's view she was not an option as a carer for her daughter. She said Shakira's best interests were the first priority in your life and that, unusually in her experience, you had welcomed DHS's involvement.

45. Ms. Matthew said she had no concerns regarding your heroin use and noted that you were keen to ultimately get off methadone. She said she had never seen you under the influence of any drug. Ms. Matthew said DHS had linked you in with a number of anger management programs which you had undertaken and describes you as honest and open in your dealings with various services. Ms. Matthew said Shakira had a severe deformity and consequent hearing and speech problems requiring regular attendance upon a paediatrician and other services, which was carried out by you. She said there was a strong attachment and bond between yourself and your daughter, and she said that when Shakira was taken to access with her mother you made sure she was well clothed and that appropriate food and nappies went with her. Shakira currently attends crèche two days a week and staff there have requested the attendance of a speech therapist at that crèche to address Shakira's apprehended delay in those areas of her development. . . .

47. Ms. Matthew said it was imperative that Shakira have a constant carer to reach her potentials in life. She said that the only extended family with whom you have contact is your sister who, however, lives in Ballarat, but this was not a close relationship either between your sister and yourself, and Shakira and that sister, and further, given Shakira's medical needs, she must be able to continue with those services in Melbourne. She said there could be some difficulties initially in placing Shakira in foster care given her special needs. . . .

52. I am satisfied that since the birth of Shakira you have ceased to use heroin. You did admit, when giving evidence in the pre-sentence before me, to occasionally smoking marijuana at night after Shakira was in bed. I am satisfied that you have ceased offending and have carried out to the fullest extent to which you are capable, care which has proved difficult and demanding, of your disabled child.

53. This is, however, not the only aspect to which the court must have regard. A medical report dated 8 October 2003 from Dr. Denis Yeung of the Sunshine Brimbank Clinic, notes that the victim of the armed robbery, Mr. Haveraux, sustained the following injuries as a result upon your assault upon him—bruising on the left side of his skull, sore fingers on the left hand, abrasions on the right little finger, bruises on the back of the right hand and wrist, and whilst X-ray did not show any fracture, a diagnosis of ligamentous strain was made.

54. In his victim impact statement dated 27 May 2005 Mr. Haveraux stated: "For the next week after the attack I found it difficult to enter the empty house. This was the reason for installing the alarm as it would give me prior warning. I do feel that I have been affected psychologically as I now tend to enter empty rooms as if somebody may be waiting around the corner for me."

55. He further states: "I feel that no mercy should be shown because of the fact that the attack took place in front of my three year old daughter and that he wanted to take a hostage to the bank so we could give him all we had. If this attack had involved a weaker person (that is somebody that hadn't played soccer for 20 years) what damage could he have caused? Put him away before he really hurts somebody."

56. Your counsel informed me that regularly throughout the years of your drug addiction you would turn to the use of prescription drugs when your heroin supply failed and at the time of the armed robbery you had taken

Rohypnol to this end. . . . These courts are sadly familiar with the elevation in violent offending that can occur when the offender is under the influence of this prescription drug. This appears to have been the case at the time of the armed robbery, the violence involved not being characteristic of your previous offending. . . .

58. Appallingly, this violent offending, however, took place before the undoubtedly terrified gaze of a three year old child. This offending in particular was abhorrent in the extreme. In the absence of mitigatory material, indeed in the absence of any but the most compelling mitigatory material, the court would, in a case such as this involving the intrusion into a home, a violent attack upon the occupier of the house, the terrifying of a little girl in her own home, watching her father being assaulted, would undoubtedly result in a sentence of imprisonment to be served immediately. Such offending cannot and should not be tolerated. I make it clear to you, Mr. Arnautovic, that I condemn your behaviour and I do so in the strongest possible terms. The fact of your difficult personal history, the fact of your heroin addiction, the fact of your Rohypnol use at the time, are of no moment. This was an appalling and dangerous attack and one cannot wonder at the sentiments expressed by Mr. Haveraux in the victim impact statement. . . .

60. The question is whether your undoubted reformation, together with the needs of your highly dependent little daughter, are such that a sentence of imprisonment to be immediately served should be averted. This is the course that I am urged to take by your counsel on the basis of your reformation and the needs of your daughter. This course is resisted by the prosecution, which contends that a sentence of imprisonment to be immediately served should indeed be visited upon you. It is their contention firstly that the hardship to your daughter, should you be incarcerated, would not be such as to answer the "test" contained in the judgment of Wells, J. in *Worth* (1976) 14 S.A.S.R. 291 where . . . His Honour stated: "the hardship caused directly or indirectly by a proposed sentence of imprisonment to the family of or to others closely associated with the offender [should] be taken into account by the court in mitigation of that sentence . . . where the circumstances are highly exceptional where it would be, in effect, inhuman to refuse to do so."

61. Insofar as your rehabilitation is concerned the prosecution referred to the case of *DPP v. Jovasici*, a decision of the Court of Appeal of the Supreme Court of Victoria delivered on March 22, 2001. There, in essence, it was held that notwithstanding the demonstrated rehabilitation of two professional burglars, including drug rehabilitation, the requirement for general and specific deterrence, denunciation and punishment, were such that gaol sentences to be immediately served, which had been received in the first instance, were in fact manifestly inadequate and were, accordingly, increased by the Court of Appeal. There are, however, in my view, important distinguishing factors between those authorities and this case. Dealing first with the case of *Jovasici*, this involves the participation of perpetrators in a highly organised professional ring of burglars which targeted goods of particular value centring around a particular receiver of stolen goods and the activities of which clearly resulted in the theft and on selling of a vast array of valuable items stolen from a myriad of residences. It involved organised and sophisticated offending. Further, it was not accepted by the sentencing judge in that case that either of the perpetrators,

neither of whom gave evidence in their hearings, were remorseful, nor was it accepted that the offending occurred solely to support the drug addiction suffered by both men.

62. During the plea before me you did give evidence on oath, saying there were no apologies you could make to Mr. Haveraux that he could accept. You said you did not blame him for his comments relating to you and described what you had done to him as the "lowest act" you had committed in your life. You said you were still dealing with what you had done in that it continued to play on your conscience. You were concerned that you could have "devastated that little girl" and said that you thought about what you have done all the time. . . .

64. In relation to your daughter reference is also made by the prosecution to the decision of *R v. Holland*, a decision of the Court of Appeal of the Supreme Court of Victoria delivered on 12 August 2002. There the sole ground of appeal by the appellant, who had been incarcerated for cultivating a commercial quantity of narcotic plants, was the effect of her imprisonment on her seven year old daughter who was in the care of her grandparents who did not believe they could continue to care for her. This case was tendered in support of the prosecution's contention that Shakira's plight, should you be incarcerated, would not amount to the exceptional circumstances I have previously referred to as outlined by Wells, J.

65. Importantly, in . . . the case of *Holland*, in disallowing the appeal, the court expressed a doubt that the grandparents would not in fact continue to be able to care for their grandchild in the months remaining of her mother's sentence, and in the words of Batt, J., . . . "In the circumstances of this case the incarceration of both parents of one healthy child of seven is not sufficient to constitute exceptional circumstances."

66. I am satisfied, however, that the hardship which would be faced by Shakira if you were incarcerated would amount to be extreme and exceptional circumstances as demanded by the authority. Shakira is only two and a half years old, a far more vulnerable age than the child in the case of *Holland*. She has disabilities that require particular care and according to the evidence of Ms. Matthew, this will be ongoing for some four years.

67. Further, and unusually, she has no meaningful relationships with any adult other than yourself, thus she is in familial terms, apart from yourself, an isolated, disabled toddler, and your removal from her life would see her placed either in foster care with strangers or, if the department was willing to consider the few persons named by you when pressed in cross-examination as possibly suitable, with adults who are neither related to her or whom it appears she knows particularly well. Mention has been made in more than one report and by myself earlier in this judgment of your social isolation as a result of your change of lifestyle. . . .

69. [It] is my view that Shakira's case is one in which mercy should be exercised. If I be wrong in that it is my view that Shakira's dependence upon you, coupled with your personal transformation and general remorse, are sufficient that I should sentence you in a way which does not require your immediate incarceration. I should add, Mr. Arnautovic, however, that I have made this decision only after anxiously considering all the competing sentencing demands and emphasise that I am fully alive to the appalling and noxious nature of your offending. It is my view, however, that the long term interests of the community and Shakira are best served by your continuing on your path of reformation and

your care of your daughter. It is my view that were you to be incarcerated and separated from Shakira the effects upon her would be grievous, long lasting and possibly irretrievable. The effect upon yourself would likely ignite such anxiety in view of your daughter's position that you could well collapse, and even did you not, the additional problems faced by you on your release insofar as the trauma-tising effects upon Shakira as a result of your separation, could interfere substan-tially with, if not destroy, your capacity to continue to care for her and her to respond and thus the exceptional work of the past two years be totally undone.

70. I therefore propose to deal with you by way of a non-custodial dispo-sition which will involve not only suspended sentences but the imposition of a community based order for which you have been assessed as suitable. . . .

71. I am including a community based order in the disposition, both because I think the gravity of your offending requires it and because, in my view, you have ongoing personal difficulties and frailties which require attention and you have indicated through your work with DHS that you are capable of taking advantage of assistance offered to you and, indeed, have been reliant upon it to such an extent that it appears your main social interaction in life is with DHS workers. That support is to be withdrawn in June of this year and it is my view that replacement of it with the supports that can be obtained by a Community Based Order is important in terms of your ongoing reform which is, of course, inextricably linked with Shakira's welfare. . . .

73. I therefore sentence you as follows, and can you stand up, please? On counts 1, 3, 5, 7, 9, 12 and 14 you are sentenced to 12 months' imprisonment. On Count 4 you are sentenced to six months' imprisonment. On counts 6, 8, 10, 13 and 15 you are sentenced to nine months' imprisonment. On Count 11 you are sentenced to two years and nine months' imprisonment. I order that 12 days of each of the sentences imposed on counts 1, 3, 5, 7, 9, 12 and 14 be served cumulatively to the sentence imposed on Count 11 and to each other, giving a total effective sentence of three years. This sentence is to be wholly suspended for a period of three years. On Count 2 you are placed on a community based order for two years. . . .

75. The order will last for two years. You must attend at the Sunshine Community Corrections Centre at 10 Foundry Road, Sunshine within two clear working days, all right? . . . You must report to and receive visits from a Community Corrections officer. You must notify an officer at the specified Community Corrections Centre of any change of address or employment within two clear working days of that change. You may not leave Victoria without the consent of the specified Community Corrections officer and you must obey all lawful instructions and directions of the Community Corrections officer.

76. I order that you perform 150 hours of unpaid community work over a 24 month period as directed. I order that you be under the supervision of a Community Corrections officer. [The comment of Ms. Evans was that an oner-ous level of unpaid community work may place you under a detrimental amount of pressure and may affect your ability to successfully negotiate both your par-enting and order commitments.] I order that you undergo assessment and treatment for alcohol or drug addiction or submit to medical, psychological or psychiatric assessment and treatment as directed by the regional manager. I order that you submit to testing for alcohol or drug use as directed by the regional manager and I further order, as a special condition, that you undergo

programs to reduce the risk of re-offending and participate in such programs as directed by the Community Corrections officer. . . .

100. . . . Can you stand up Mr. Arnautovic? Because before you leave I have to explain to you the consequences of breaching the suspended sentence. You need to understand that any offending which can result in a sentence of imprisonment, it does not have to, so, for example, if you commit a very small shoplifting offence you might not get a sentence of imprisonment but because that is an offence that you can be sentenced to gaol for, you would have breached the suspended sentence.

101. The legislation makes it very clear that unless there are exceptional circumstances, if a person breaches a suspended sentence the court must make that person serve the whole of the sentence that was suspended. So if you commit an offence — you need to have a look at your marijuana smoking in that respect as well, OK?

102. PRISONER: Yes.

103. HER HONOUR: If you commit an offence you will be looking at three years' imprisonment. I imagine that would ruin your life and it would certainly ruin Shakira's life. Do you understand? All right. I am confident enough in your progress to place you on a disposition which can be very dangerous for persons who have got long offending histories and drug addictions, all right? You just keep going the way you are going and all will be well, but you need to understand that for the next three years you have got to be incredibly careful. All right?

104. PRISONER: Yes.

105. HER HONOUR: Thank you. You can have a seat.

NOTES

1. *Applying purposes in individual cases.* Is the application of punishment purposes in individual sentencing decisions a factual issue or a legal issue? Is it a decision best made by legislatures, trial courts, appellate courts, or some other decision maker? Was the Australian court in *Arnautovic* making judgments that are better left to the legislature? Does the legislature make its own attempt to accommodate the purposes of punishment through the establishment of the standard sentencing terms? Compare State v. Gaines, 859 P.2d 36 (Wash. 1993).

2. *"Consistency" affecting the application of purposes.* If courts make case-specific judgments as we saw in *Arautovic*, what techniques might be available to ensure reasonable consistency from case to case? Perhaps appellate review of sentencing decisions could exert some unifying force on the choices of sentencing judges. What purpose does consistency serve? Is furthering consistency across cases more important than furthering the purposes of punishment in individual cases?

PROBLEM 1-3. BROMLEY HEATH

A federal grand jury indicted John Thompson, a 24-year-old African American man, on narcotics violations stemming from an investigation of crack cocaine trafficking at the Bromley Heath Housing Development in Jamaica Plain, Massachusetts. The charges grew out of a joint federal-state investigation of crack cocaine trafficking at Bromley Heath. Pursuant to a plea agreement, the defendant pled guilty to one count of distributing cocaine base in violation of 21 U.S.C. §841(a)(1).

Thompson has one prior conviction but has never been incarcerated. His criminal record includes possession of a controlled substance at age 17, a charge that was dismissed; assault and battery at age 19, which resulted in a guilty finding and a six-month probation term; drinking alcohol in public at age 20, a charge that was dismissed; and another, recent charge of possession with intent to distribute a controlled substance (a charge brought shortly after the events that form the basis of the current charge, to which he pled guilty).

Thompson lived his entire life in Bromley Heath. He describes his child-hood as rough; the majority of it was spent without his father, who was incar-cerated much of the time. Thompson dropped out of high school in the eleventh grade when he learned that his girlfriend, Breii Murray, was pregnant with their first child. Thompson was determined to provide for her and their daughter, Jabria, despite his youth and lack of education.

Thompson became a member of Union Local 223 and maintained steady employment until his arrest on these charges. At the time of his arrest, he was employed by M. Solberg Enterprises Corp. and earned about $2,000 per month setting planks, drilling cords, and cutting concrete. His employer has provided a letter saying that Thompson was wanted back at his job.

Murray and Thompson have been in a steady relationship for seven years and are engaged to be married. They now have two daughters together. Thompson is a good father who spends a lot of time with his daughters and enjoys a solid relationship with both of them, particularly Jabria, the elder daughter. He supports his fiancée, their children, and his fiancée's family both economically and emotionally. Murray, along with Murray's mother, aunt, and grandmother, are all supportive of Thompson. They describe him as a wonderful person who has substantially assisted in the upkeep of their home by running errands, doing chores, and contributing $100 per week. All of the women stressed that Thompson's incarceration would make a detrimental impact on their lives, and particularly on the lives of his daughters.

What should Thompson's sentence be? What purposes should guide that sentence? See United States v. Thompson, 190 F. Supp. 2d 138 (D. Mass. 2002).

2. Use of Purposes in System Components

Not only do judges and other decision makers face challenges in trying to inte-grate purposes into case-specific sentencing judgments, but legislators and other rule makers also confront challenges when integrating purposes into structural aspects of a sentencing system. Institutions responsible for creating sentencing rules that apply to a range of cases must consider whether and to what extent particular purposes should be considered for certain types of crimes, certain types of offenders, and certain types of punishment.

As you review the materials in the following sections, consider how your initial beliefs about the purposes of punishment bear on issues such as the appropriate sentencing rules for repeat offenders or the appropriateness of the death penalty.

a. The Relevance of Prior Crimes to Current Punishment

The justifications for punishment may help to explain specific sentencing rules. Consider some of the most basic sentencing questions: Should an offender be punished more severely if she has a prior conviction? Multiple convictions? Does it matter if the prior offense is the same as the current offense? How old the prior offense is? How the offender was punished for the prior offense?

First write down your answers to these questions. Then, informed by your own instincts and insights, consider the following materials, where the U.S. Sentencing Commission explores the ways and means of developing concrete and comprehensive criminal history rules for the federal guideline sentencing system.

‖ *Simplification Paper: Criminal History* ‖
U.S. Sentencing Commission, reprinted in
9 Fed. Sent'g Rep. 216 (1997)

Criminal history [is incorporated in the federal sentencing guidelines through a series of rules that], in conjunction with [rules for defining the seriousness of the current offense], determines the guideline range. This paper discusses Chapter Four [which establishes the rules for sentencing consideration of criminal history].

There are both philosophical and practical reasons for including criminal history as a major component of the federal sentencing guidelines. Criminal history can serve several important functions in setting sentencing recommendations. It can be used to measure increased culpability, predict future criminality, and selectively target dangerous offenders. . . .

There have been various debates as to propriety and purpose of using criminal history to determine a defendant's sentence. Retributionists or those who believe in the "just deserts" philosophy argue that punishment should be proportionate to the defendant's culpability for his/her current offense of conviction. Those who argue that retribution is a key principle in sentencing argue for a significantly reduced role for criminal history. For example, Richard Singer (1978) argues that criminal history is inappropriate to consider at sentencing because the defendant has already been punished for the previous offense. He contends that a defendant has no greater culpability (blameworthiness) because of having committed the prior offense; nor is victimization greater in the current offense as a result of the prior offense.

Andrew Von Hirsch, a noted retributionist, argues that criminal history should play only a minor role at sentencing, impacting sentence only to the extent that the defendant's culpability is enhanced due to his/her prior offenses. Von Hirsch argues that offenders who are being sentenced for their first offense have less culpability due to their not having been punished previously. According to Von Hirsch, the first sentence communicates that the behavior is wrong and will not be tolerated. A sentence for a second violation can reflect the "full" weight of the law because the offender has been alerted previously to the unacceptability of the behavior.[2]

A contrary theory of the role of criminal justice is incapacitation. This approach advocates the expanded use of imprisonment to incapacitate offenders. Incapacitation takes two forms: collective and selective. Both forms assume that while offenders are incarcerated they will not be able to engage in additional criminal behavior. Collective incapacitation seeks to prevent crime by increasing the rate and duration of imprisonment for a broad range of offenders, without specific prediction of future criminality. In contrast, selective incapacitation seeks to prevent crime by using certain criteria to identify for restraint a smaller number of offenders who are predicted to commit more crime and/or serious crime. Selective incapacitation also can reduce punishment for persons who are predicted to be less likely to commit additional crimes or to commit serious crimes.

Society and its elected representatives have reached a level of frustration with crime so that current policies more frequently tend to reflect the selective incapacitation philosophy in sentencing practices in general and criminal history in particular. Advocates of selective incapacitation argue that some offenders have shown themselves to be too dangerous (given the frequency or severity of their criminal conduct) to be permitted to remain in society. These advocates have successfully swayed Congress and state legislators that, for the safety of society, presence of an extensive or violent prior record warrants severe sanction for the current offense (e.g., habitual offender provisions in the states and career offender provision in the federal system).[3] Consequently, in many criminal justice systems, criminal history is seen as a crucial component of the determination of an offender's sentence because of its use as a predictor of future criminality.

The Commission determined that criminal history was a major factor in past sentencing practices and should be a major component in the sentencing guidelines. In addition, the Commission believed that with its congressional mandate to consider the breadth of sentencing purposes (rehabilitation, deterrence, incapacitation, and just punishment), it had to consider criminal history as a major component of the guideline sentence. In designing Chapter Four, the Commission considered various philosophical arguments regarding the appropriate use of prior record in determining a defendant's sentence, including arguments regarding "just deserts" and selective incapacitation.

---

2. Currently, no guideline system completely disregards the defendant's prior record in the determination of sentence. However, some states do consider aspects of retributionist theory. Minnesota, for example, used this theory in a modified format by adjusting the slope of its imprisonment/non-imprisonment line to focus more on the current offense.

3. States vary in their use of selective incapacitation. For example, in the Pennsylvania guidelines, all prior convictions are included in the computation of the criminal history score, although some offenses are weighed more heavily than others. Because the focus is on the number of prior offenses, little distinction is made between types of offender. In contrast, Oregon uses a typography classification of offenders that focuses not on the number of prior convictions, but, instead, the type of prior offenses committed with violent offenders and repeat non-violent felony offenders targeted for longer sentences. Each prior conviction does not necessarily contribute to the criminal history score.

The Commission hoped to diminish the conflict between the two ideologies by incorporating elements from both in assessing criminal history.

A defendant with a record of prior criminal behavior is more culpable than a first offender and thus deserving of a greater punishment. General deterrence of criminal conduct dictates that a clear message be sent to society that repeated criminal behavior will aggravate the need for punishment with each recurrence. To protect the public from further crimes of the particular defendant, the likelihood of recidivism and future criminal behavior must be considered. Repeated criminal behavior is an indicator of a limited likelihood of successful rehabilitation.

In the end, Chapter Four was designed to address the frequency, seriousness, and recency of the defendant's prior record. The Commission believed these items were reliable predictors of future criminal conduct. . . .

[T]he federal sentencing guidelines are unique in their approach to criminal history. It is the only system that measures the severity of the prior offense by the length of the sentence imposed for the previous conviction. Specifically, the guidelines give three points for each sentence greater than one year and one month, two points for each sentence of 60 days but not more than one year and one month, and one point for any other sentence. Up to three points also can be assigned if the defendant was under a criminal justice sentence at the time the instant offense was committed, and he/she had been released from a sentence of imprisonment within two years of the commencement of the instant offense. This criminal history score is translated into one of six criminal history categories in the Sentencing Table. The higher the category, the higher the guideline sentence for any given offense level. . . .

While there is some variation in approach, almost every sentencing guideline system considers a defendant's prior record in the determination of the sentence. Most states measure both the number and seriousness of prior convictions. Some states weigh prior convictions depending on their severity. Minnesota, for example, assigns prior felony offenses from one-half to two points depending upon the offense's "severity level." [I]n the Pennsylvania Sentencing Guidelines, the most serious category of prior convictions includes murder, voluntary manslaughter, kidnapping, rape, involuntary deviate intercourse, arson, and robbery. Convictions for these offenses receive four points, the maximum amount assessable for a prior conviction. Similarly, in Oregon, criminal history is categorized by prior offense type specifically violent versus nonviolent offenses. . . .

[One] criticism of the federal guidelines' present scheme is its lack of precision in measuring the severity of prior record. For example, because three points are given for each sentence of more than one year and one month, the guidelines make no distinction between a 14-month sentence and a 15-year sentence. Arguably, these two sentences may reflect the seriousness of substantially different prior offenses. Under the current system, there is no differentiation between a fraud and a rape if they both receive sentences of imprisonment of more than one year and one month.

Another area in which the current criminal history score treats seemingly different offenders the same is in Criminal History Category I. . . . Currently, Criminal History Category I treats a wide range of defendants similarly despite the fact that they have dissimilar levels of previous contact with the criminal justice system. For example, defendants who have no prior record (no prior arrests, no pending charges, no dismissed charges, no prior convictions) are in Category I along with defendants who have at least one prior conviction that received a sentence of imprisonment of at least 60 days.[13] Title 28, section 994(j) requires the Commission to "insure that the guidelines reflect the general appropriateness of imposing a sentence other than imprisonment in cases in which the defendant is a first offender who has not been convicted of a crime of violence or an otherwise serious offense. . . ." By not incorporating a "first offender category" in the guidelines, critics argue that the Commission did not adequately address the statutory directive at Title 28, section 994(j) related to first offenders. However, the Commission's compliance with this directive has been challenged in a number of cases and uniformly rejected. . . .

There is general agreement among sentencing theorists that the importance of a previous conviction diminishes over time. In keeping with this theory, the Commission chose to limit the impact of "decaying" prior convictions by requiring that they fall within various time periods. It is not the limitation of old prior convictions that adds complexity. The complexity results because the guidelines have five different applicable time periods for the assessment of criminal history points. These time periods depend upon both the length of the sentence imposed and the age of the defendant when the prior offense was committed, and in one instance, whether the prior was imposed as an adult or juvenile sentence.

State guideline systems vary in their use of applicable time periods. States that limit consideration of offenses generally use one applicable time period for all offenses. . . . Some states that do not restrict the time period in which prior offenses can be counted instead have "crime-free" periods from which the defendant benefits. In these states, if the defendant remains "conviction free" for a period of time (usually 10 or 15 years not including periods of imprisonment or release on probation or parole) prior to the instant offense, any convictions prior to that period are not counted. Others leave this item as a departure consideration.

One of the frequently debated issues regarding the prior record measurement is whether to include juvenile adjudications, and if so, to what extent. Currently, the federal guidelines consider offenses that occurred prior to the defendant's eighteenth birthday, except under certain circumstances. Some would argue that juvenile adjudications should not contribute to the criminal history score because juvenile courts typically focus on the juvenile's welfare and treatment, and generally have a more informal process. Moreover, the juvenile courts' standard of proof may be somewhat lower than adult courts. More importantly, juvenile records are less reliable than adult records because of different jurisdictional policies on recording and disclosing juvenile offenses. This inconsistency can result in great disparity in the criminal history score computation.

---

13. This category includes the following defendants: (1) a person with no contact with any criminal justice system of any kind, (2) a person who may have had contact with the criminal justice system, such as arrests or dismissed charges, and (3) a person with convictions not countable under the guidelines for a variety of reasons, such as the "age" of the conviction, the locality where the conviction occurred, and the minor nature of the offense.

Nonetheless, most states include juvenile adjudications in the computation of criminal history score because many argue that juvenile record, in particular violent behavior, is a strong predictor of future criminal conduct. In fact, some restrict the use of juvenile offenses to include only convictions for violent offenses. Others restrict the use of juvenile offenses if the defendant is an older offender. For example, in Maryland, juvenile convictions are not included in the sentence determination if the defendant is 26 years of age or older at the time of commission of the instant offense; the argument being that as the offender gets older, the use of a juvenile record as predictor of criminality diminishes. . . .

NOTES

1. *Recidivism and punishment theory in practice.*   The above discussion of criminal history rules in the federal sentencing guidelines begins by highlighting the linkage between considerations of prior criminal history and sentencing theories, as well as the robust debate among theorists about these matters. But note the conclusion of this theoretical discussion:

In designing Chapter Four, the Commission considered various philosophical arguments regarding the appropriate use of prior record in determining a defendant's sentence, including arguments regarding "just deserts" and selective incapacitation. The Commission hoped to diminish the conflict between the two ideologies by incorporating elements from both in assessing criminal history.

Is it possible to design sentencing rules to "diminish the conflict" between the just-deserts and incapacitation theories? Do the rules for considering criminal history under the federal sentencing guidelines as described in this excerpt succeed in diminishing the conflict? Consider the following assessment of the actual rules developed for the federal sentencing guidelines:

[T]he arguments for viewing the criminal history guidelines as utilitarian in orientation are powerful. Utilitarianism offers a coherent justification for taking prior criminal records into account generally. It helps to explain specific structural features of the Commission's rules. It is consistent with the considerations the Commission actually took into account when developing these guidelines. In its Supplementary Report on the original guidelines, the Commission virtually acknowledged that utilitarianism was the dominant justification for the criminal history rules [by stating the rules were] "included primarily for crime-control considerations."

Aaron J. Rappaport, Rationalizing the Commission: The Philosophical Premises of the U.S. Sentencing Guidelines, 52 Emory L.J. 558, 594-595 (2003).

2. *Detailed sentencing rules and punishment theory in practice.*   As the excerpt above highlights, numerous complications and many intricate details arise in the development of structured sentencing rules; this is true not only for criminal history issues but for all areas of sentencing decision making, as we shall see throughout the book. Can the resolution of these complications and details turn on matters of punishment theory? Should they?

b.   Justifying Particular Forms of Punishment Such as the Death Penalty

Should the consideration and application of theories of punishment change when particular forms of punishment are being considered? Historically, there has often been a direct connection between the forms of punishment employed and the theories of punishment being pursued. Theories of punishment may also shift for different crimes and different classes of offenders—with crimes and offenders being correlated with different kinds of punishments.

For example, one of the most important (and ironic) modern sentencing developments concerns the evolution of imprisonment as a form of punishment and of prisons as an institution for punishment. The penitentiary was developed and structured as a form of punishment with the express goal of "curing" offenders of their criminal tendencies. The belief in the nineteenth century was that imprisonment, by removing an offender from certain corrupting influences in his community while also providing an offender with the time and opportunity to reflect on his misdeeds, would reform and rehabilitate criminals in ways that physical punishment could not. See generally David J. Rothman, Perfecting the Prison: United States, 1789-1865, in The Oxford History of the Prison 111 (1995). For more than a century, many proponents of imprisonment continued to argue that rehabilitation could be furthered through incarceration.

But by the mid-1980s, many observers had come to recognize that most prison environments, in which prisoners were more often warehoused than treated, were more likely to provide criminal training than to rehabilitate effectively. Consequently, in the Sentencing Reform Act of 1984, Congress expressly instructed the U.S. Sentencing Commission that its development of federal sentencing rules should "reflect the inappropriateness of imposing a sentence to a term of imprisonment for the purpose of rehabilitating the defendant or providing the defendant with needed educational or vocational training, medical care, or other correctional treatment." 28 U.S.C. §994(k). But even today, despite the widespread belief that prison is not an effective environment for rehabilitation, many state sentencing systems (and even aspects of the federal system) continue to pursue rehabilitative goals through incarceration. Indeed, at least one scholar has recently asserted that the "only rationale for the design of prison programs that is possible and acceptable in this society is rehabilitation." Edward Rubin, The Inevitability of Rehabilitation, 19 Law & Ineq. 343 (2001).

Perhaps even more than imprisonment, the use of the death penalty has generated considerable debate and commentary about the connection between certain forms of punishment and the purposes of punishment. In fact, though most public debates over sentencing issues are rarely cast in theoretical terms, modern public debates over the death penalty frequently explore whether it is an effective deterrent to murder, whether a life sentence without the possibility of parole can incapacitate as well as an execution, whether concepts of retribution justify use of this ultimate punishment for the most heinous of crimes, and whether the death penalty can be administered fairly or efficiently. The unique severity and finality of the death penalty always brings added attention and a heightened dynamic to traditional debates over the theories of punishment.

Many insights can be drawn from a close examination of the classic theoretical debates surrounding the death penalty. Perhaps an even deeper insight might be drawn from the fact that capital punishment's severity prompts us to explore these theoretical issues more frequently and explicitly. Part of what makes the death penalty so worthy of study is that the unique mental impact of life-and-death decision making helps ensure that we do not become complacent in our consideration of the issues that surround sentencing and punishment choices. To seize on a well-worn phrase in these debates, "death is different," and that difference informs our thinking about sentencing theory in ways that few other punishments can.

Among the scholarly and policy developments in recent years that have led to editorial page (public) debate and even proposed state legislation to abolish the death penalty in some states are the large and increasing number of convicts being later found to be innocent, often through the use of DNA evidence and the diligence of lawyers and students; attention to the high cost of death penalty prosecutions and the massive cost of high-profile death cases; renewed attention to the manner of execution and recognition of the small number of executions compared with the larger numbers on death row; and continuing concern for racial and new concern for geographic inequalities.

Pointing in the other direction, recent studies by economists have renewed interest in the deterrent effect of the death penalty. A number of studies since 2001, mostly by economists, have purported to establish that the death penalty has a deterrent impact in modern times. As with prior studies making such claims, the data and conclusions in these papers are hotly disputed, and it still is (and likely will always be) difficult to make conclusive statements about the deterrent effect of capital punishment. Though strong proof of deterrence may always be elusive, would a truly conclusive and indisputable study resolve the debate over the death penalty? Suppose we could be absolutely positive that each execution of a convicted murderer would deter ten murders and thus save ten innocent lives. In light of such data, could there be any conclusive argument against the death penalty? Imagine the empirical evidence running the other way. Suppose we could be absolutely positive that each execution of a convicted murderer would cause ten additional murders (because of the brutalization impact of having society in the business of state killing) and thus cost ten innocent lives. In light of such data, could there be any conclusive argument for the death penalty?

The next set of readings turn on the moral questions sitting before, under, around, and after the deterrence debates. The first is a short statement about the moral justifications for the death penalty. The second reading responds to two prominent legal scholars, Cass Sunstein and Adrian Vermeule, who have taken the position that, in light of the new deterrence data, society (including those with a liberal bent) should as a moral matter support the imposition of the death penalty. See Cass R. Sunstein & Adrian Vermeule, Is Capital Punishment Morally Required? Acts, Omissions, and Life-Life Tradeoffs, 58 Stan. L. Rev. 703 (2005).

For Capital Punishment: The Morality of Anger,
Walter Berns
Harper's, Apr. 1979, at 15-20

Anger is expressed or manifested on those occasions when someone has acted in a manner that is thought to be unjust, and one of its origins is the opinion that men are responsible, and should be held responsible, for what they do. Thus, as Aristotle teaches us, anger is accompanied not only by the pain caused by the one who is the object of anger, but by the pleasure arising from the expectation of inflicting revenge on someone who is thought to deserve it. We can become angry with an inanimate object (the door we run into and then kick in return) only by foolishly attributing responsibility to it, and we cannot do that for long, which is why we do not think of returning later to revenge ourselves on the door. For the same reason, we cannot be more than momentarily angry with any one creature other than man; only a fool and worse would dream of taking revenge on a dog. And, finally, we tend to pity rather than to be angry with men who — because they are insane, for example — are not responsible for their acts. Anger, then, is a very human passion not only because only a human being can be angry, but also because anger acknowledges the humanity of its objects: it holds them accountable for what they do. And in holding particular men responsible, it pays them the respect that is due them as men. Anger recognizes that only men have the capacity to be moral beings and, in so doing, acknowledges the dignity of human beings. Anger is somehow connected with justice, and it is this that modern penology has not understood; it tends, on the whole, to regard anger as a selfish indulgence. . . .

Criminals are properly the objects of anger, and the perpetrators of terrible crimes — for example, Lee Harvey Oswald and James Earl Ray — are properly the objects of great anger. They have done more than inflict an injury on an isolated individual; they have violated the foundations of trust and friendship, the necessary elements of a moral community, the only community worth living in. A moral community, unlike a hive of bees or a hill of ants, is one whose members are expected freely to obey the laws, and unlike those in a tyranny, are trusted to obey the laws. The criminal has violated that trust, and in so doing has injured not merely his immediate victim but the community as such. He has called into question the very possibility of that community by suggesting that men cannot be trusted to respect freely the property, the person, and the dignity of those with whom they are associated. If, then, men are not angry when someone else is robbed, raped, or murdered, the implication is that no moral community exists, because those men do not care for anyone other than themselves. Anger is an expression of that caring, and society needs men who care for one another, who share their pleasures and their pains, and do so for the sake of the others. It is the passion that can cause us to act for reasons having nothing to do with selfish or mean calculation; indeed, when educated, it can become a generous passion, the passion that protects the community or country by demanding punishment for its enemies. It is the stuff from which heroes are made. . . .

. . . The law must not be understood to be merely a statute that we enact or repeal at our will, and obey or disobey at our convenience — especially not the criminal law. Wherever law is regarded as merely statutory, men will soon enough disobey it, and will learn how to do so without any inconvenience to themselves. The criminal law must possess a dignity far beyond that possessed by mere statutory enactment or utilitarian and self-interested calculations. The most powerful means we have to give it that dignity is to authorize it to impose the ultimate penalty. The criminal law must be made awful, by which I mean inspiring, or commanding "profound respect or reverential fear." It must remind us of the moral order by which alone we can live as *human* beings, and in America, now that the Supreme Court has outlawed banishment, the only punishment that can do this is capital punishment.

The founder of modern criminology, the eighteenth-century Italian Cesare Beccaria, opposed both banishment and capital punishment because he understood that both were inconsistent with the principle of self-interest, and self-interest was the basis of the political order he favored. If a man's first and only duty is to himself, of course he will prefer his money to his country; he will also prefer his money to his brother. In fact, he will prefer his brother's money to his brother, and a people of this description, or a country that understands itself in this Beccarian manner, can put the mark of Cain on no one. For the same reason, such a country can have no legitimate reason to execute its criminals, or, indeed, to punish them in any manner. What would be accomplished by punishment in such a place? Punishment arises out of the demand for justice, and justice is demanded by angry, morally indignant men; its purpose is to satisfy that moral indignation and thereby promote the law-abidingness that, it is assumed, accompanies it. But the principle of self-interest denies the moral basis of that indignation.

Not only will a country based solely on self-interest have no legitimate reason to punish; it may have no need to punish. It may be able to solve what we call the crime problem by substituting a law of contracts for a law of crimes. According to Beccaria's social contract, men agree to yield their natural freedom to the "sovereign" in exchange for his promise to keep the peace. As it becomes more difficult for the sovereign to fulfill his part of the contract, there is a demand that he be made to pay for his nonperformance. From this comes compensation or insurance schemes embodied in statutes whereby the sovereign (or state), being unable to keep the peace by punishing criminals, agrees to compensate its contractual partners for injuries suffered at the hands of criminals, injuries the police are unable to prevent. The insurance policy takes the place of law enforcement and the *posse comitatus,* and John Wayne and Gary Cooper give way to Mutual of Omaha. There is no anger in this kind of law, and none (or no reason for any) in the society. . . .

No, Capital Punishment Is Not Morally Required: Deterrence, Deontology, and the Death Penalty,
Carol S. Steiker
58 Stan. L. Rev. 751-756, 765-770, 773-774 (2005)

As an opponent of capital punishment, I have participated in many (and witnessed many more) debates about the morality and wisdom of the death penalty. The debate usually begins with one of two dramatic gambits by the proponent of capital punishment, both of which derive their power from the grievous harms suffered by murder victims and their loved ones. The first gambit is to consider in detail the facts of one or more capital murders and to propose that only the punishment of death is an adequate and proportional response to the terrible suffering of the victim intentionally inflicted by the perpetrator — a predominantly retributive argument. The second gambit — a modified version of which Cass Sunstein and Adrian Vermeule use to begin their provocative article[1] — is predominantly consequentialist. This gambit is to suggest that if the death penalty can prevent — through incapacitation of the offender or general deterrence — the loss to murder of even one innocent life, then it is a morally justified or perhaps even morally required penal response. A common response to both of these gambits is to ask why it is we do not rape rapists, torture torturers, or rape and then murder those who rape and murder in order to provide a proportional response to the suffering they have inflicted or to adequately deter future rapists, torturers, and rapist/murderers. This response suggests that our rejection of such extreme punishments points the way to a categorical, deontological limitation on the kinds of punishments we are justified in imposing, on either retributive or consequentialist grounds. The usual counter to this response is to acknowledge that we do not and should not impose such extreme punishments — that there is some moral limit to what we can justify as punishment — but to deny that the use of the death penalty crosses that line.

The debate — like a stylized form of dance — then tends to move from consideration of capital punishment in the abstract to its application in contemporary society. Here the opponent of the death penalty goes on the offensive, arguing that regardless of whether capital punishment is justified in the abstract, the fact that it is too often imposed arbitrarily, invidiously, or in error in our imperfect legal system renders it a morally unacceptable practice in contemporary society. The usual counter here is some combination of denying that the problems are as big as the opponent claims (citing the opponent's abolitionist bias), denying that problems of arbitrariness and discrimination affect the justice of imposing the death penalty if the defendant is guilty, and acknowledging that the erroneous conviction and execution of innocents is unjust but maintaining that the problem is either small enough to be acceptable (in light of the greater number of innocent lives saved) or fixable.

Sunstein and Vermeule want to dance to a very different tune. They start with some recent statistical studies of the impact of capital punishment on homicide rates — studies that claim to find strong deterrent effects after controlling for potentially confounding variables with multiple regression analysis.[2] Sunstein and Vermeule do not purport to vouch for the validity of this recent spate of studies, acknowledging that "it remains possible that the recent findings

---

1. Cass R. Sunstein & Adrian Vermeule, Is Capital Punishment Morally Required? Acts, Omissions, and Life-Life Tradeoffs, 58 Stan. L. Rev. 703, 705 (2005) (suggesting that "on certain empirical assumptions, capital punishment may be morally required, not for retributive reasons, but rather to prevent the taking of innocent lives").

2. Id. at 706 & n.9 (citing Hashem Dezhbakhsh et al., Does Capital Punishment Have a Deterrent Effect? New Evidence from Postmoratorium Panel Data, 5 Am. L. & Econ. Rev. 344 (2003) (suggesting that each execution on average prevents eighteen murders)).

will be exposed as statistical artifacts or found to rest on flawed econometric methods." This is a prudent concession, given the powerful reasons that are offered by John Donohue and Justin Wolfers,[4] along with many other experts,[5] to reject this body of work as the basis for any public policy initiative. Rather, Sunstein and Vermeule argue that if such deterrent effects could ever be reliably proven or even if the evidence demonstrated a "significant possibility" that the use of capital punishment saves a substantial number of lives by preventing future murders, then consequentialists and deontologists alike should join in supporting the retention and vigorous use of the death penalty. Indeed, they contend that under such conditions, capital punishment should be considered not merely morally permissible (as any consequentialist would hold) but actually "morally obligatory." What Sunstein and Vermeule add to prior debates between consequentialists and deontologists regarding the death penalty is their insistence that recognition of the inapplicability of the act/omission distinction to the government as a distinctive kind of moral agent should strengthen the consequentialist argument in favor of capital punishment and undermine deontological objections to capital punishment, under the stipulated conditions of deterrence from which the argument proceeds.

This argument neatly sidesteps some of the central wrangles in the typical death penalty debate described above. First, under the terms of Sunstein and Vermeule's argument, there is no need to "draw the line" excluding some extreme punishments (like torture), because the argument denies the existence of any such categorical line prohibiting extreme punishments as a moral matter; the only question is whether the government can prevent more suffering inflicted by future offenders than it metes out as punishment on current offenders. Second, there is no need to address the vexing issue of how to weigh innocent lives of murder victims against (usually, but not always) guilty lives of convicted capital defendants because the argument holds that the government is equally responsible for the harms that flow from its failure to impose the death penalty and for those that flow from its imposition. Thus, all lives (innocent or guilty) are counted equally, and all that remains to do is count:

---

4. See John J. Donohue & Justin Wolfers, Uses and Abuses of Empirical Evidence in the Death Penalty Debate, 58 Stan. L. Rev. 791, 794 (2005) (reviewing the studies relied upon by Sunstein and Vermeule and finding "that the existing evidence for deterrence is surprisingly fragile").

5. See Richard Berk, New Claims About Executions and General Deterrence: Déjà Vu All Over Again?, 2 J. Empirical Legal Stud. 303, 328 (2005) (noting that "it would be bad statistics and bad social policy" to generalize from one percent of the data to the remaining ninety-nine percent, and concluding that "for the vast majority of states for the vast majority of years there is no evidence for deterrence" and that even for the remaining one percent, "credible evidence for deterrence is lacking"); see also Deterrence and the Death Penalty: A Critical Review of New Evidence: Hearings on the Future of Capital Punishment in the State of New York Before the New York State Assemb. Standing Comm. on Codes, Assemb. Standing Comm. on Judiciary, and Assemb. Standing Comm. on Correction, 2005 Leg., 228th Sess. 1-12 (N.Y. 2005) (statement of Jeffrey Fagan, Professor of Law and Pub. Health, Columbia Univ.), available at www.deathpenaltyinfo.org/FaganTestimony.pdf; Jeffrey Fagan, Death and Deterrence Redux: Science, Law, and Causal Reasoning on Capital Punishment, 4 Ohio St. J. Crim. L. 255 (2006); Ted Goertzel, Capital Punishment and Homicide: Sociological Realities and Econometric Illusions, Skeptical Inquirer, July-Aug. 2004, available at http://www.findarticles.com/p/articles/mi_m2843/is_4_28/ai_n6145278.

if more private murders would be prevented than executions imposed, the balance favors executions. Third, the argument insists that the distributional problems of arbitrary or invidious infliction of the death penalty disappear as moral problems, at least when there is reason to believe that private murders are at least equally arbitrary or invidious in their distribution. Sunstein and Vermeule contend that the belief that there is a categorical prohibition of extreme punishments or the belief that arbitrariness, discrimination, or error in the distribution of capital punishment count as distinctive moral failures are examples of the operation of a "moral heuristic" — by which they mean a form of moral shorthand that leads to error. Specifically, they refer to error arising from the failure to fully appreciate the distinctiveness of the government as a moral agent that must treat the death penalty as an example of a "life-life tradeoff."

The problem with Sunstein and Vermeule's argument is not their general premise regarding the government's distinctive moral agency, which, as they acknowledge, is likely to be far more congenial to the political opponents of capital punishment than to its supporters. Rather, Sunstein and Vermeule's argument runs into serious problems when they attempt to transplant their insight about government agency from the arena of civil regulation to the arena of criminal justice. Sunstein and Vermeule's assertion that the state's execution of murderers is equivalent to its failure to adequately deter murders by private actors ignores the ways in which the construction of a governmental choice as a "life-life tradeoff" in the regulatory context does not map congruently onto the criminal justice context, either as a matter of morality or as a matter of justice.

As a matter of morality, Sunstein and Vermeule fail to grapple adequately with the fact that for their argument to succeed in the criminal context, they must jettison not only the act/omission distinction in the context of government action but also — and less convincingly — the distinction between purposeful wrongdoing on the one hand and merely reckless or even knowing wrongdoing on the other. Even more problematic is Sunstein and Vermeule's failure to acknowledge the social and political fact that executions are not mere fungible "killings" but rather are part of a practice of state punishment that can be unjust in ways quite distinct from the general wrongness of killing. Sunstein and Vermeule's reduction of the deontological objections to capital punishment to some version of the moral intuition that "killing is wrong" thus evades and fails even to acknowledge long-standing and widely discussed deontological objections to capital punishment qua punishment.

Moreover, despite their protestations to the contrary, Sunstein and Vermeule's argument in favor of capital punishment presents some conceptual slippery slopes upon which only the deontological arguments that they evade can offer some purchase. Their argument is unable to explain why we might not, under conceivable circumstances, be morally obligated to adopt punishments far more brutal and extreme even than execution, or to inflict similarly brutal and extreme harms on innocent members of an offender's family (as punishment of the offender, not of the innocent), or to extend the use of capital punishment to contexts in which many deaths result from behavior far less culpable than murder, such as highway fatalities due to drunkenness or negligence. From their moral position, the only arguments available to Sunstein and Vermeule against any of these practices are unsatisfactorily contingent on prudential considerations, which will not always provide plausible reasons to avoid such practices.

Sunstein and Vermeule wish to avoid making an exclusively consequentialist argument that appeals only to precommitted consequentialists. Thus, they insist that their argument not only puts consequentialist justifications for capital punishment on a surer footing but also should be persuasive to some deontologists (at least if the number of lives saved by capital punishment reaches a certain level). Here, too, they fail to see that the context of criminal punishment changes arguments about "threshold" deontology — the acknowledgement by some deontologists that at some "threshold" of catastrophic consequences, categorical moral prohibitions should give way to consequentialist concerns.

Perhaps most surprising, it is not only deontologists who will fail to be moved by Sunstein and Vermeule's arguments. If one applies to the question of how deterrence works (when it does) some of the same nuanced consideration of the operation of human cognition upon which Sunstein and Vermeule seek to draw to make their argument in favor of capital punishment, one sees that even committed consequentialists should not be convinced by Sunstein and Vermeule's argument for the retention and use of capital punishment, even under the hypothetical conditions of deterrence that they assume. . . .

A venerable deontological tradition with roots in Kantian retributivism holds that punishment is justified only as a response to wrongdoing by the offender and not by its consequential effects.[43] In its strongest form, retributivism imposes a duty to punish offenders according to their desert. In its weakest and perhaps most widely accepted form — as a side constraint on the useful deterrent, incapacitative, or rehabilitative functions that punishment can serve in a society — retributivism requires, at a bare minimum, that the uses of punishment be limited to situations in which the punishment is deserved by the offender and is proportional to the offender's wrongdoing. Under this theory, if the suffering caused by punishment is not deserved and is not proportional to the wrongdoing of those upon whom it is inflicted, then the infliction of such suffering constitutes a wrong — the imposition of unjust punishment — distinct from and worse than merely the suffering itself.

At first glance, a retributive argument might seem an odd one to make against capital punishment, as it is retributivism that offers some of the strongest arguments in favor of the death penalty. (Reconsider the depiction of a generic death penalty debate with which I began, in which retributive arguments are deployed by the proponent of capital punishment.) Kant's famous injunction — that a desert-island society about to disperse would still have an obligation to kill its last murderer — stands for the strong form of retributivism. This form of retributivism holds that the duty to impose deserved punishment exists regardless of any beneficial consequences that might be thought to flow from it. Kant's use of the death penalty as the quintessential example of deserved punishment for the crime of murder seems, at first blush, natural and unobjectionable.

---

43. See Immanuel Kant, The Philosophy of Law: An Exposition of the Fundamental Principles of Jurisprudence as the Science of Right 198 (W. Hastrie trans. 1887) (1797).

But there is good reason to think that capital punishment—at least as imposed in our contemporary society—routinely and inevitably runs afoul of retributivism's bedrock proportionality constraint. It is rarely the case that execution as a form of suffering can confidently be viewed as disproportionate to the harms inflicted on the victims of capital murders.[47] Rather, the strongest argument for such disproportionality lies in the reduced culpability of most convicted capital offenders; this is an argument that remains powerful even today, after the Supreme Court has recently declared that mentally retarded and juvenile offenders may no longer be executed for their crimes. Though capital defendants have usually committed (or participated in) heinous murders, they very frequently are extremely intellectually limited, are suffering from some form of mental illness, are in the powerful grip of a drug or alcohol addiction, are survivors of childhood abuse, or are the victims of some sort of societal deprivation (be it poverty, racism, poor education, inadequate health care, or some noxious combination of the above). In such circumstances, it is difficult to say that these defendants deserve all of the blame for their terrible acts; if their families or societies share responsibility—even in some small measure—for the tragic results, then the extreme punishment of death should be considered undeserved. Indeed, this point follows directly from Sunstein and Vermeule's own logic. If the government is responsible for private murders that it fails to prevent by providing adequate deterrence, is it not also responsible for private murders that it fails to prevent by providing adequate poverty relief, support for families, education, health care, and initiatives to promote racial equality? This recognition of the conflict between collective responsibility for crimogenic conditions and the imposition of individual criminal responsibility for crime is best captured by a New Yorker cartoon in which a jury foreperson delivers the following verdict: "We find that all of us, as a society, are to blame, but only the defendant is guilty."

For this point to hold, it is not necessary to say that there are no capital defendants in our society who could be deemed sufficiently blameworthy so as to deserve the death penalty, or that all capital defendants not sufficiently blameworthy for capital punishment are blameless for their actions and deserve no punishment at all, or that criminal defendants in general are blameless and undeserving of any criminal punishment. Rather, the more modest point is simply the uncontroversial empirical fact that in our contemporary society, those most likely to commit the worst crimes (capital murders) are, as a group, also most likely to have had their volitional capacities affected or impaired by societal conditions for which we collectively bear some responsibility. Thus, it cannot fairly be said that this group is deserving of our worst punishment,

---

47. The lengthy waits on death row in anticipation of execution are the strongest current argument for this sort of disproportionality. See, e.g., Soering v. United Kingdom, 11 Eur. Ct. H.R. 439 (1989) (holding that a person sought for extradition from the United Kingdom to the United States could not be extradited because of the likelihood that he would suffer "death row phenomenon" in the prolonged and uncertain wait for his execution, which would violate the European Convention on Human Rights). Some also argue that electrocution is excessively painful, but this argument is less compelling now that lethal injection has replaced electrocution as the predominant means of execution. See generally Deborah W. Denno, Is Electrocution an Unconstitutional Method of Execution? The Engineering of Death over the Century, 35 Wm. & Mary L. Rev. 551 (1994).

or, more affirmatively, it must be acknowledged that there is a retributive gap between the culpability of such offenders and the punishment inflicted upon them.

Moreover, from the standpoint of retributive justice, the strong evidence of discrimination (on the basis of race) or mere arbitrariness (on the basis of geography, among other things) in the imposition of capital punishment takes on a new and different significance from the disparate impact of the private murders that the government might fail to deter. The fact that the race of the defendant and/or the race of the victim frequently have been found to have salience in predicting whether a defendant will be sentenced to death shows not only that there is some racial skewing in the distribution of capital sentences, but also that there is reason to question the underlying moral and legal judgment that any particular murder is one for which capital punishment is a proportional response. Similarly, the fact that defendants from otherwise similar counties in the same state face radically different prospects of receiving capital punishment calls into question not only the procedures by which those deserving of capital punishment are chosen but also the reliability of the underlying judgment that any particular defendant so chosen deserves the death penalty. Unless one takes the position that capital punishment is a deserved and proportional response to every intentional killing no matter what the circumstances (a position neither required by retributivism nor permitted by American law), one can take no recourse in the argument that discrimination and arbitrariness merely exclude some deserving defendants from execution. Rather, discrimination and arbitrariness undermine our confidence in the very attribution of desert to the defendants chosen for execution.

The strongest case for a retributive gap, of course, lies in the conviction and execution of the innocent — a moral wrong that we have new reason to believe is disturbingly prevalent in our capital punishment system. . . .

There is a second and distinct flaw in the equivalence that Sunstein and Vermeule seek to maintain between racial inequality in the administration of capital punishment and racial inequality in the distribution of private murders. The racial inequalities in the administration of capital punishment — both the failure to give equal weight to the deaths of black victims as compared to white victims in similar cases and the greater willingness to take the lives of black defendants as compared to white defendants in similar cases — give rise to an inference of racial animus on the part of state actors (prosecutors and jurors). That is, these disparities reveal the unwillingness or inability, whether conscious or unconscious, of governmental actors to treat black citizens with equal concern and respect. But the racial inequality in the distribution of private murders does not plausibly reflect such pervasive animus on the part either of the murderers or the government. . . .

A third major wellspring of deontological objection to the justice of capital punishment is the claim that, unlike many ordinary punishments, it violates human dignity. This view has been given its most prominent exposition in Justice Brennan's concurring opinion on the unconstitutionality of the death penalty as "cruel and unusual punishment" under the Eighth Amendment in Furman v. Georgia. This claim has an abstract, slippery quality to it that makes it difficult to assess whether the violence done to human dignity through the imposition of death as punishment is different in any meaningful way from the violence done to human dignity through the crime of murder. . . .

The imposition of extreme punishments such as execution (or rape or torture), even in cases involving the most deserving of murderers (or rapists or torturers), violates human dignity—not because of what it does to the punished, but rather because of what it does to all of us. Death, from either execution or murder, by definition destroys the human capacities of the person killed, but inflicting death (or rape or torture) as punishment can, in addition, damage or destroy the human capacities of those of us in whose name the punishment is publicly inflicted.

This threat to dignity stems from certain sociological facts about the way punishment works as a social practice. Punishment is a public act; it is generally presented by the government as deserved by the recipient, and that imputation of desert is generally accepted by the public; the imposition of punishment tends to elicit gratifying emotions of satisfaction because the public condemnation and suffering of an offender assuage to some degree the anger and hatred provoked by the offense. Nothing in this characterization is meant as a normative justification of punishment practices. I mean to take no position here on whether the "retributive hatred" that wrongdoing inspires is a moral good,[72] or whether the public satisfaction of vengeful urges offers a satisfactory consequentialist defense of punishment. Rather, I mean simply to suggest that when the purposeful infliction of extreme suffering is yoked with emotions of righteousness and satisfaction, it will inevitably suppress our ordinary human capacities for compassion and empathy. To be sure, the desire to punish may itself spring, at least in part, from compassion and empathy for crime victims. And not every kind of punishment necessarily suppresses to any great extent our capacities for compassion and empathy. But the inherent moral satisfaction that attends the practice of punishment when it includes the infliction of death or other very extreme forms of suffering does seem to permit, or even require, the weakening of important psychological constraints against brutality. In this way, brutal punishment poses threats to our human capacities distinct from and more insidious than other forms of brutality that might be authorized or tolerated by the government because punishment has a distinctive connection to powerful human emotions. . . .

NOTES

1. *Arguments for and against the death penalty.*   For many observers, the fundamental question about the legitimacy of the death penalty turns on moral arguments. Walter Berns has developed the argument presented above in more detail in his book For Capital Punishment (1979). Sunstein and Vermeule are the latest prominent intellectuals to make a sustained moral argument in favor of the death penalty. In response critics argue that the taking of life is immoral, even when done by the state. Other critics attack the barbarity of

---

72. See, e.g., Jeffrie G. Murphy, Hatred: A Qualified Defense, in Forgiveness and Mercy 88, 91-92 (Jeffrie G. Murphy & Jean Hampton eds., 1988) (defending "retributive hatred" as an appropriate moral response to certain types of wrongdoing).

the sanction itself. Yet others question whether any government can be trusted with such an awesome power, even if the morality of retribution itself is recognized. The literature is vast and impassioned, and includes striking historical, geographical, social, and comparative arguments. See, e.g., Encyclopedia of Capital Punishment (1998); Franklin Zimring, The Contradictions of American Capital Punishment (2003).

2. *New deterrence literature.*   The question whether the death penalty deters has a long history. Professor Bernard Harcourt observes:

> Beccaria, the first true rational choice theorist, did not believe that capital punishment fell within the domain of the sovereign's right to punish, but instead within the domain of war, which, he argued, was ruled by necessity and utility. But the death penalty, according to Beccaria, served neither interest. It was not necessary because long-draw-out punishments, such as penal servitude or slavery for life, were more effective and fear-inducing than the fleeting shock of death. It was also not useful because capital punishment had a brutalizing effect on society. Jeremy Bentham — the very spokesman for the theory of marginal deterrence in the modern era — agreed entirely: "the more attention one gives to the punishment of death the more he will be inclined to adopt the opinion of Beccaria — that it ought to be disused. This subject is so ably discussed in his book that to treat it after him is a work that may well be dispensed with."

See Bernard Harcourt, Randomization and Social Physics: Post-Modern Meditations on Punishment, A Polemic and Manifesto for the 21st Century (working draft, February 2007).

Neither scholars nor politicians in the United States have treated Beccaria and Bentham as having the last word on the subject. In 1975 Professor Isaac Ehrlich influenced the course of this debate when he concluded, based on a sophisticated study on data from 1933 to 1969 in the United States, that "an additional execution per year . . . may have resulted (on the average) in 7 or 8 fewer murders." Isaac Ehrlich, The Deterrent Effect of Capital Punishment: A Question of Life and Death, 65 Am. Econ. Rev. 414 (June 1975). Though Ehrlich's data analysis and conclusions have been widely and powerfully assailed, his work succeeded at the time in convincing at least some persons of the potential deterrent impact of capital punishment. See Ernest Van Den Haag, In Defense of the Death Penalty: A Practical and Moral Analysis, 14 Crim. L. Bull. 51 (1978). Sharply critical reviews of Ehrlich's studies led most observers in the 1980s and 1990s to treat the deterrent impact of the death penalty as an open question. Ehrlich's work was conducted before the modern reconstruction of the death penalty in America, a story told in brief in Chapter 3 of this volume. A number of new studies, however, have purported to establish that the death penalty has a deterrent impact in modern times. See Dale O. Cloninger & Roberto Marchesini, Execution and Deterrence: A Quasi-Controlled Group Experiment, 33 Applied Econ. 569 (2001); Hashem Dezhbakhsh, Paul H. Rubin & Joanna M. Shepherd, Does Capital Punishment Have a Deterrent Effect? New Evidence from Postmoratorium Panel Data, 5 Am. L. & Econ. Rev. 344 (2003); H. Naci Mocan & R. Kaj Gittings, Pardons, Executions, and Homicide, NBER Working Paper 8639 (Dec. 2001).

3. *At what price?*   One fairly isolated argument concerning the death penalty involves the financial cost of operating a functional capital punishment system. Death penalty cases are enormously expensive. See The Costs of the

Death Penalty, testimony of Richard C. Deiter, executive director of the Death Penalty Information Center, before the Massachusetts Legislature, Joint Committee on Criminal Justice (available at http://www.deathpenaltyinfo.org/MassCostTestimony.pdf) (reporting various calculations and estimates of the cost of capital cases in different jurisdictions). Indeed, many prosecutors with capital charging authority use it rarely or not at all, in part to shepherd resources for the full range of cases, apart from moral, philosophical, or political concerns. See E. Michael McCann, Opposing Capital Punishment: A Prosecutor's Perspective, 79 Marq. L. Rev. 649 (1996) (noting prosecutors' concerns about the costs of the death penalty). Death penalty proponents respond that the costs are high in part because of excessive relitigation of capital claims, and that even at a high cost, a capital sentence may be justified. Other observers find the entire conversation about the cost of the capital system distasteful, holding that moral arguments should be determinative. Some people consider the idea of assessing economic costs in the absence of measures of human cost stilted.

4. *Death as the appropriate penalty for what types of crimes?*   Walter Berns points to the atrocities of the Nazi regime, including genocide and crimes against humanity, as offenses meriting death. Compared with the magnitude of those crimes, what other crimes, if any, deserve the death penalty? Does it not denigrate the enormity and brutality of those offenses if death becomes the punishment for any murder? Consider also that the judges of the recently instituted International Criminal Court cannot impose death sentences even though they try cases of genocide, crimes against humanity, war crimes, and the crime of aggression.

3.   Politics, Philosophy, and Economics ("PP&E")

Criminal punishments are the product of a series of public acts. It is striking to look at the justifications offered by politicians both for expanding and for restricting or regulating the use of punishment. Often the justifications for particular crimes, sanctions, or policies are unarticulated or poorly articulated. But compared with philosophical claims, public officials in the legislative and executive branch (but typically not judges) more often resort to claims based on concerns of equal treatment (either for its own sake, or to achieve equal severity or leniency for classes of offense or offender) or concerns for the public fisc, given the massive role of public safety, criminal justice and punishment, especially in state and local budgets, and to assertions that political actors are serving in a representative capacity and responding to public demands. This part of the chapter introduces these functional and political claims, which sometimes are visible and often are found to underlie policy initiatives.

a.   Equality/Disparity Concerns

Ohio Rev. Code §2929.11(C) provides that a court "shall not base the sentence upon the race, ethnic background, gender, or religion of the offender." Tennessee similarly provides that sentencing "should exclude all considerations respecting race, gender, creed, religion, national origin and social status of the individual," and Montana states that sentencing practices "must be neutral with respect to the offender's race, gender, religion, national origin, or social or economic status." Federal law has a similar provision, 28 U.S.C. §994(d), which instructs the U.S. Sentencing Commission to "assure that the [sentencing] guidelines and policy statements are entirely neutral as to the race, sex, national origin, creed, and socioeconomic status of offenders."

Do you think these requirements of equality are readily integrated with traditional purposes of punishment, or can you envision some tensions between traditional notions of equality and traditional theories of punishment? Consider the following recommendation from the ABA, which focuses on the importance of ensuring that principles of equality are safeguarded in sentencing systems.

ABA Standards for Criminal Justice, Sentencing 18-2.5
(3d ed. 1994)

(a) The legislature should create a sentencing structure that enables the agency performing the intermediate function to make reasonably accurate forecasts of the aggregate of sentencing decisions, including forecasts of the types of sanctions and severity of sentences imposed, so that the legislature can make informed changes in sentence patterns through amendment of the criminal code, or the agency can do so through revised guidance to sentencing courts.

(b) The legislature should create a sentencing structure that sufficiently guides the exercise of sentencing courts' discretion to the end that unwarranted and inequitable disparities in sentences are avoided. . . .

COMMENTARY

Systems of "indeterminate" sentencing, which invest sentencing judges and parole boards with broad discretion in making sentencing decisions, have resulted in unwarranted disparity in individual sentences. . . . [1] Prior editions of these Standards have noted the prevalence of unwarranted sentencing disparities in specific cases, demonstrated in analyses of sentence patterns for similar offenses and in studies of sentence choices by different judges considering identical cases. Some observers have condemned the arbitrary and random nature of indeterminate sentences; others have claimed that such a sentencing structure allows racial and class biases to infect sentencing decisions.

At every level of the drafting process (in the Task Force, the Standards Committee, and the Criminal Justice Section Council), the ABA consistently decided that the traditional practices of indeterminate sentencing, still followed in most states, should be rejected. It is a telling point that through four years of ABA debate, no defense was raised of the old practices of indeterminacy. . . .

---

1. As to the injustices of individualized disparities, the classic work is Marvin E. Frankel, Criminal Sentences: Law Without Order (1973). A valuable study of the unplanned expansion of American prison systems since the 1970s is Franklin E. Zimring & Gordon Hawkins, The Scale of Imprisonment (1991).

The third edition adds an important new component of the requirement of determinacy: Standard 18-2.5(a) states that the sentencing structure should be sufficiently determinate to allow for reasonably accurate forecasts of aggregate sentencing decisions so that the legislature can make informed changes in sentence patterns through amendment of the criminal code, or the agency can do so through revised guidance to sentencing courts. Thus, the Standard contemplates a system in which policy decisions can be made to have predictable impacts on the system as a whole. Also, with adequate determinacy the legislature and agency can address discrete problems in targeted ways. For example, a jurisdiction that wants to heighten the severity of sentences for violent crimes can do so with some precision. If the resulting changes will overload the prison system, the agency can propose offsetting amendments, such as fractional reductions in sentences for nonviolent crimes. Substantial state experience through the 1980s has shown that the related goals of predictability and manageability can be realized in determinate sentencing structures.

This Standard must be read in conjunction with Standard 18-2.6 regarding the "individualization of sentences." Determinacy, as a systemic and case-specific value, is not an absolute good that must be pursued to the exclusion of other concerns. As argued by Kenneth Culp Davis, predictable and uniform rules must always coexist with a degree of flexibility and discretion. The problem is finding the optimum balance between rule and discretion. In the realm of sentencing, this tension is vividly pronounced. . . .

NOTES

1. *The goal of reducing sentencing disparity.* As discussed more fully in Chapter 3, one of the most prominent goals of modern sentencing reform has been to reduce unwarranted sentencing disparity. The problems of defining, measuring, and finding solutions to disparity arise throughout sentencing systems. Some of these problems are endemic to discussions of equality and disparity in all contexts. When, for example, are two individuals similar and when are they different? Other problems are especially acute in sentencing; these include the difficulty of describing each offense and offender (for example, is similarity based on offenders' "actual" behavior or the charges for which offenders are convicted?) and the difficulty of measuring and assessing actual sentences (are we concerned with sentences imposed or sentences served? Should fines of fixed dollar amounts be the same if offenders have vastly different resources?).

In practice, among the greatest areas of concern in modern reforms for both apparent and actual inequalities are disparities in treatment by race and, to a lesser extent, gender. Yet there have also been, both historically and throughout modern systems, wide sentencing disparities based on socioeconomic class, geography, and other "status" characteristics. Given the wide range of potential sentencing disparities (and the challenges in defining, measuring, and remedying such disparities), are there certain types of disparity that call for extra attention? In considering this question, examine again the somewhat different groups and commands articulated in the equality provisions of the state statutes reprinted above.

2. *Surface equality and a deep understanding of disparity.*   Concepts of disparity and equality in sentencing can be baffling in part because of three additional
puzzles that are worth noting as an introduction to this topic. First, what might
be seen as apparent equality—such as giving every offender a five-year
sentence—can in fact represent great inequality if offenders or their offenses
or both are different in pertinent ways. Because equality means not only treating
like cases alike, but also treating different cases differently, an example of two
cases sentenced in the same way could actually be evidence of *inequality* if these
cases were different in ways that should have led to different sentences. Second,
even when two convicted offenders who are similar are sentenced in the same
way, inequality can exist if a third, similar offender either escapes without being
charged or is prosecuted in a different jurisdiction or is charged with a different
offense. The different treatment of the third, similar offender who "escapes"
the standard punishment creates a form of disparity that, although very difficult
to measure, undermines efforts to achieve true sentencing equality. Finally, the
very ability to assess what factors can and should matter in judging equality and
disparity depends in large part on initially selecting an underlying theory of
punishment. Two offenders committing similar crimes might deserve similar
punishments if sentenced according to retributivist theory, but their personal
backgrounds might call for quite different punishments if sentencing is based
on the goal of rehabilitation. If we cannot or do not adopt defined theories of
punishment, it becomes very hard to distinguish *warranted* from *unwarranted*
sentencing disparity. See Marc Miller, Sentencing Equality Pathology, 53
Emory L.J. 271 (2005); Kevin Cole, The Empty Idea of Sentencing Disparity,
91 Nw. U. L. Rev. 1336 (1997).

b. Cents and Sentencing Ability

A central aspect of most legislative sentencing discussions does not
concern traditional justifications for punishment at all. Consider the following
document developed by criminal justice policy experts in Ohio to explain to
the public what factors influence criminal punishments and sentencing outcomes in that state. What non-philosophical justifications are offered to define,
justify, or limit sentences? How might you characterize these additional kinds of
justifications?

|| *The State of Crime and Criminal Justice in Ohio* ||
|| **The Office of Criminal Justice Services (Jan. 1995)** ||

REASONS FOR CRIMINAL SANCTIONS IN OHIO

HOW SHOULD CRIME BE PUNISHED?

The question, itself, testifies to the complexity of the issue in that it wrongly
assumes that punishment (e.g., imprisonment, death) is the only legitimate
function of justice at the sentencing level. Incapacitation, deterrence,

rehabilitation, restitution and, more recently, forfeiture, are other goals which can and do drive the decisions of legislators, judges, parole officials, corrections authorities, and others who administer criminal sanctions—the carrying out of court sentences—in this State.

For these reasons and others (e.g., legal issues, humane and equitable treatment of offenders) prisons and jails are not necessarily the best sanctions for all felony offenders, as is often assumed. "Alternatives to incarceration," rather than suggesting a second or third preferred choice in the sanctioning process, may in fact provide the best means at a government's disposal for dealing with certain kinds of offenders. . . .

Resources can also dictate choice of sanctions, where judges are given such sentencing discretion. Sometimes judges, faced with severely crowded local jails and little in the way of intermediate options, must choose between the polar extremes of prison and probation in felony sentencing. The problem has grown more extreme in recent years in the face of a dramatic increase in drug-related prison sentences which could be diminished, in number and perhaps severity, by sufficient resources devoted to treatment programs.

Ohioans' attitudes and opinions about sanctions reflect uncertainty about appropriate responses to criminal offenders. There appears to be a general presumption that citizens are frustrated by the leniency and inefficiency of the Criminal Justice System, that they are continually seeking harsher felony punishments than those being handed down in Ohio's criminal courts. Research in Ohio and at the national level suggests that key decision makers, such as legislators, rather consistently assume that the public will not support sanctions which propose something in lieu of prison/jail sentences. However, citizen attitude surveys in Ohio and elsewhere have found that these assumptions overestimate public inflexibility, and that given sufficient information regarding the circumstances of the criminal behavior citizens will support a wide range of other sanction options.

Less than one-third of the citizen respondents in a statewide Office of Criminal Justice Services (OCJS) survey readied for release in 1993 stated a preference for building our way out of the prison/jail crowding crisis in Ohio, while more than half opted for community treatment centers (35%), emergency releases (18%), and more use of probation (7%).

When presented a list of six specific options which could be used to replace or ease incarceration for non-violent offenders the same respondents found five of the six options agreeable by margins ranging from 68% to 76%. Only "fines" fell below the level of public acceptability (48%). "Victim compensation" (68%), "community supervision" (69%), "work release" (73%), "education release" (76%), and "early release" (78%) all found solid support. These results were virtually unchanged from those obtained in a 1984 survey which examined the same question.

Five critical issues largely determine Ohio's capacity to administer effective criminal justice sanctions.

Institutional crowding: Both the Departments of Youth Services (DYS) and Rehabilitation and Correction (DRC) have experienced unprecedented increases in institutional populations during the past decade. DYS populations have risen by half, while DRC's numbers have doubled. Virtually all of the 24 DRC institutions are operating above capacity—180% statewide. The tremendous growth in numbers appears largely unrelated to broader crime trends, instead being driven by decision choices within the criminal justice system (i.e., legislative, prosecutorial/judicial, parole). Every aspect of Ohio's sanctioning procedures is negatively affected by the institutional crowding crisis.

Impact of substance abuse: This nationwide problem has created special stress for the sanctioning function in criminal justice. Tougher laws and sentencing relative to drunk driving and drug abuse, combined with the usage explosion of crack-cocaine in the latter 1980s have proven especially burdensome for already crowded prisons, jails, youth detention facilities, and treatment programs.

Escalating costs: Funding for new institutional construction is not the major economic cost concern relative to sanctions; the cost of running those institutions is. The average per-year, per-prisoner operational cost to DRC exceeds $12,000, ballooning that agency's annual budget to the three-quarters of a billion dollar range. Meeting the basic needs of county jail inmates and juvenile offenders adds more hundreds of millions of dollars each year. In the aftermath of the Lucasville uprising it appears that security costs will dramatically increase in at least some state facilities. While technology promises hope for minimizing the costs of some sanctions (e.g., ankle bracelets for electronic monitoring of house arrestees, hair testing for drug usage supervision of parolees, etc.), the fact remains that Ohio's expenditures on criminal sanctions are increasing dramatically at a time when most items in government budgets are holding level or being reduced.

Effectiveness of treatment: Sentenced criminal offenders bring a wide range of social disorders relating to sexual problems, gambling, child abuse, substance addiction, learning disabilities, and others. Frequently, criminal sanctions include treatment provisions for these disorders, but it is difficult to determine how effective these treatment programs are, especially in light of very limited treatment resources. Much of the future of criminal sanctions may ride on treatment programs with a proven capacity to interrupt criminal careers.

Availability of sanctioning options: Ohio's institutional crowding crisis alone, with its enormous implications for state and local budgets, strongly suggests the development of non-incarceration options for at least some types of offenders. Other issues of justice are also linked to this development, such as sentencing equity, long-term crime costs to society, and the potential tapping of resources outside of the traditional criminal justice arena (e.g., public health).

NOTES

1. *Functional purposes: politics.* Why does this excerpt discuss at some length the results of a survey of Ohio citizens about their attitudes concerning punishment and sentencing? Why should decision makers, who presumably have more knowledge about and time to consider the reasons for and consequences of particular punishment and sentencing issues, be concerned with the opinions of average citizens? Do any of the traditional purposes of punishment depend on or incorporate the perspectives of a majority of average citizens?

Although one can debate whether the views of the general public should matter in sentencing and punishment decision making, there is little question that they do have a profound influence on sentencing systems in the United

States. Every legislature making sentencing rules in the United States is elected by popular vote, and most judges and prosecutors in state systems are also elected officials. Even sentencing decision makers who are appointed, including some judges and prosecutors and most members of sentencing commissions, typically can attribute their position to being well regarded by an elected official who is in turn well regarded by a majority of the electorate. A profound and enduring issue in modern sentencing systems, and in many specific sentencing decisions, is the role of politics in the development of sentencing rules. See generally Carol A. Bergman, The Politics of Federal Sentencing on Cocaine, 10 Fed. Sent'g Rep. 196 (1998); Peter J. Benekos & Alida V. Merlo, Three Strikes and You're Out! The Political Sentencing Game, 59 Fed. Probation, Mar. 1995, at 3; Stephen B. Bright & Patrick J. Keenen, Judges and the Politics of Death: Deciding Between the Bill of Rights and the Next Election in Capital Cases, 75 B.U. L. Rev. 760 (1995).

2. *Functional purposes: costs.*   An obvious theme running through the "five critical issues" influencing Ohio's capacity to administer effective criminal justice sanctions is money (or the lack thereof). In other words, limited resources are another powerful purpose guiding sentencing decision making, especially in states where punishment resources (prisons, jails, probation officers) and prosecutorial and judicial resources are always scarce. Sometimes resource constraints provide the superstructure within which policymakers must allocate sentences. An illustration of this approach is the "capacity constraint" provision in some states, which directs sentencing commissions to design sentencing rules that take into account limitations in available prison space. Some states explain punishment priorities in light of limited resources. For example, Florida's legislature has decided that punishment is the primary purpose of sentencing. Along with other limitations, the Florida legislature prioritizes the incarceration of serious offenders and recidivists "in order to maximize the finite capacities of state and local correctional facilities." Fla. Stat. §921.002.

Resources can constrain sentencing and punishment systems driven initially by philosophical, political, or more random considerations. Consider the developments in state sentencing described by Daniel Wilhelm and Nicholas Turner in late 2002:

> Corrections budgets have been especially hard hit by the current [fiscal] crisis. In FY 2002, 25 states were forced to reduce their corrections budgets. Higher education was the only government sector affected more often, in 29 states. As budget cuts have been imposed or threatened, corrections departments have responded in three predominant ways: closing prisons, reducing staff, and curtailing programs. . . .
>
> Concern about the spiraling cost of incarcerating offenders has created pressure on corrections administrators to do more than cut costs quickly. In a number of states, lawmakers have used the moment to re-examine sentencing schemes and to engage in targeted mitigation of certain punishments. In some cases, this has resulted in the repeal of mandatory minimum sentences now perceived as too harsh and too financially onerous. In others, it has led to the reclassification of certain offenses so that they no longer automatically result in prison sentences.
>
> In 2001 and 2002, 13 states took legislative action to ameliorate the effects of stringent sentencing laws. Of these, Connecticut, Indiana, and North Dakota repealed mandatory minimum sentences relating to some nonviolent offenses.

(Legislation has also been introduced in three other jurisdictions — Colorado, Delaware, and Michigan — tempering mandatory minimum sentences.) Mississippi pared back truth-in-sentencing requirements. Louisiana, Virginia, and Texas expanded the number of inmates eligible for early release. Iowa granted judges greater discretion in sentencing certain felony offenders. Alabama and New Mexico eased habitual offender laws. And Idaho, Oregon, and Washington enhanced treatment options for nonviolent drug offenders. In many of these states, rising prison populations and incarceration costs were factors for winning passage of legislation.

Daniel Wilhelm & Nicholas Turner, Is the Budget Crisis Changing the Way We Look at Sentencing and Incarceration?, 15 Fed. Sent'g Rep. 41, 41-44 (2002).

PROBLEM 1-4. SENTENCING WITHOUT PRISON OR DEATH

If prisons and the death penalty were declared unconstitutional or became wildly unpopular politically (perhaps on moral or economic grounds), would the only option be anarchy? How might policymakers respond to a world with crime but without prisons or capital punishment as sentencing options?

PROBLEM 1-5. SENTENCING BUDGETS

Given the profound difficulty of specifying, finding political agreement on, and applying purposes of punishment, do functional justifications or other practical resource limits offer the best hope for "forcing" relatively principled sentencing and use of punishment?

Should a legislature decide how many prison beds it wants, and then tell an executive agency to allocate those beds to best achieve one or more stated purposes as opposed to serving whatever mix of purposes the executive agency decides? Are there more profound kinds of budgets that might produce a fairer or more decent society? What if legislatures specified a particular number of prosecutions, convictions, or prison cells for a specific crime — say, 300 person-years for persons convicted of possession of narcotics with intent to sell?

c. Public Sentiment

In democratic systems there is a strong belief that fundamental normative choices ought to be made by the people. Few political systems function in such a purely democratic form, and the relationship between legislative and executive representatives and citizens is a relationship reflecting both the puzzles of agency and the puzzles of politics. Any conception of political accountability must also reflect a theory or conception of public preference and value. The next reading explores the difference between uninformed (background) and informed public preference about punishment. Consider the relevance of these materials for politicians, prosecutors, policy advocates — and for theories of just punishment.

Myths and Misconceptions: Public Opinion versus
Public Judgment about Sentencing, Karen Gelb
Sentencing Advisory Council (July 2006),
pp. 4, 11-14, 17, 24-25

[The Sentencing Advisory Council (SAC) was established in Victoria in 2004 as an "independent statutory body." The SAC funnels informed public opinion about the sentencing process to advise the necessary lawmakers, including Victoria's Court of Appeal and Attorney General. The following report examines national and international public opinions on sentencing. The report was the product of a year-long study where the SAC wanted to ascertain current public opinions on sentencing, to analyze the methodologies used to obtain the information and whether certain methodologies influenced the results, and to develop a toolkit of methodologies that can provide the most accurate public opinion to aid review of the sentencing process.]

Most Western governments now routinely conduct public opinion polls about attitudes to important issues in criminal justice. Recent surveys measuring levels of public confidence in the criminal justice system have found that public trust and confidence are at critically low levels around the world. Such findings have led to attempts to promote public confidence and to ensure that the system — in particular the court component — does not lose touch with the community that it serves. In Australia one manifestation of this concern has been a focus for court administrators on ways to improve the relationship between the courts and their various publics.

To some degree, this heightened sensitivity to the views of the public reflects an element of penal populism. Anthony Bottoms recently coined the phrase 'populist punitiveness' to describe 'the notion of politicians tapping into, and using for their own purposes, what they believe to be the public's generally punitive stance'. Policies are populist if they are used for winning votes without regard for their effectiveness in reducing crime or promoting justice — allowing the electoral advantage of a policy to take precedence over its penal effectiveness.

The central tool of penal populism is imprisonment. Penal populism provides a framework within which to understand increasing imprisonment rates around the world as well as the proliferation of punitive sentencing policies. Justification for policies such as three-strikes legislation, mandatory minimum sentences and sex offender notification laws is found in this framework of penal populism, which describes a punitive public fed up with crime and with the perceived leniency of the criminal justice system. . . .

When representative surveys first came into widespread use, the most common way of measuring public opinion on sentencing was to use the general question of whether sentences are 'too harsh, about right or too lenient'. This question, in some variant or another, has been used in opinion polls across the world for the last forty years. Responses to this question have been remarkably consistent both over time (from the 1970s to current research) and across countries (from North America and Australia to the United Kingdom and Europe): over the past three decades about 70%-80% of respondents in these countries reported that sentences are too lenient, with slightly lower rates in Canada in recent years (60%-70%) and slightly higher rates in the United States (up to 85%). When asked about juvenile offenders, slightly higher proportions of respondents felt that sentences are too lenient: ranging from 71% in a 2003 Office of National Statistics Omnibus Survey in the United Kingdom to 88% of respondents in a 1997 Canadian survey. . . .

In more recent years, however, this conclusion has been called into question. In particular, researchers have hypothesized that the finding of a highly punitive public is merely a methodological artifact—a result of the way in which public opinion has been measured. Since the 1980s researchers have attempted to go beyond the single question poll to include further questions in representative surveys that can clarify and further explain the apparent harshness of public attitudes. In this way the research has attempted to address the methodological limitations of using a single abstract question to measure complex and nuanced public attitudes.

In the abstract, people tend to think about violent and repeat offenders when reporting that sentencing is too lenient.

A simple yet highly effective way of explaining public punitiveness has been the inclusion of a second question in representative surveys that asks people about the kind of offender they were thinking about when answering the question about perceived leniency of sentencing. Doob and Roberts [An Analysis of the Public's View of Sentencing: A Report to the Department of Justice, Canada (1983)] developed this approach, which has provided valuable insight into the stereotypical offender: most people (57%) report that they had been thinking about a violent or repeat offender when stating that sentences are too lenient. These same results have been found when asking respondents about juvenile offenders. Violent crimes account for only a very small proportion (no more than about 10% in the United States, the United Kingdom, Canada and Australia) of all crimes recorded by police. Repeat offenders also only account for a small proportion of all offenders. Despite these facts, the public thinks of violent recidivists when claiming that sentences are too lenient.

Doob and Roberts conducted a series of studies examining public opinion on crime and justice. One of these involved a representative nationwide survey in Canada and found that 80% of respondents felt that sentences were not severe enough. [Seventy-four percent] of respondents greatly overestimated the proportion of crimes involving violence; 34% greatly overestimated the proportion of property offenders who would be reconvicted in 5 years; and 45% greatly overestimated the proportion of violent offenders who would be reconvicted in 5 years.

After giving their views on sentences as a whole, respondents were asked what kind of offender they were thinking of when they answered the question. Responses showed that 38% thought of violent offenders and 16% of repeat offenders. Only 4% were thinking of first offenders and 3% of property offenders. This is vastly different from the kinds of offenders that typically come before the courts. . . .

People have very little accurate knowledge of crime and the criminal justice system.

Misunderstanding of the facts is not restricted to the prevalence of violent offenders in the criminal justice system. Indeed, research has shown that public misperceptions are rife in relation to every stage of the criminal justice system.

Looking at large-scale surveys of public opinion about crime and punishment in the United States, United Kingdom, Canada, Australia and New Zealand, Roberts et al. [Penal Populism and Public Opinion: Lessons from Five Countries (2003)] conclude that the public has very little accurate knowledge about the criminal justice system. Of particular relevance to attitudes to sentencing are findings that show that people have extensive misperceptions about the nature and extent of crime, about court outcomes and about the use of imprisonment and parole. Consistent results from many of the studies in this field show that people tend to:

- perceive crime to be constantly increasing, particularly crimes of violence;
- over-estimate the proportion of recorded crime that involves violence;
- over-estimate the proportion of juvenile crime that involves violence;
- over-estimate the proportion of crime for which juveniles are responsible;
- over-estimate the number of homicides committed;
- over-estimate the percentage of offenders who re-offend;
- under-estimate the severity of maximum penalties;
- under-estimate the severity of sentencing practices (e.g., the incarceration rate);
- have little accurate knowledge of statutory sentencing;
- have little accurate knowledge of the juvenile justice system;
- know little about sentencing alternatives and focus instead on imprisonment;
- under-estimate the severity of sentencing practices for specific offences;
- under-estimate the severity of prison life;
- over-estimate the percentage of offenders released on parole;
- over-estimate the proportion of prison terms served in the community on parole;
- over-estimate the percentage of parolees who will re-offend while on parole; and
- over-estimate the proportion of young offenders who will be reconvicted of a criminal offence.

It is clear that the public lacks accurate information about crime and criminal justice system practices. Despite this lack of knowledge, people nonetheless have strongly held and confident opinions about crime and justice issues. In fact, representative surveys have shown that it is those who have the lowest levels of knowledge who also hold the most punitive views. For example, Doob and Roberts (1983) found that those who think that sentences are too lenient are more likely to think that crime overall is violent and to underestimate the proportion of offenders convicted of robbery and assault who are sent to prison. . . .

When people are given more information, their levels of putitiveness drop dramatically.

There is substantial evidence that the public's lack of knowledge about crime and justice is related to the high levels of punitiveness reported as a response to a general, abstract question about sentencing. Based upon the conclusion that increasing the provision of information will decrease levels of punitiveness, many researchers have moved from traditional survey questions to those which provide much more information to people before asking for a response. The crime vignette approach in a representative survey is a way in which to provide more information about the offence, the offender and the impact on the victim. This approach uses brief case studies to achieve two goals:

- to provide a more accurate picture of public opinion based on an *informed* public; and
- to determine the effect of information provision on respondents' perceptions of sentencing.

By providing the opportunity to ascertain a more informed public opinion, crime vignettes address one of the disadvantages of the traditional survey question — that such questions cannot adequately uncover the nuances of public opinion on the complex issues of crime and justice. . . .

In [a] groundbreaking [study, two researchers] conducted a series of 13 studies for the Canadian Department of Justice. In a small study of 116 randomly selected respondents, [the researchers] contrasted the response given to brief descriptions of unusual sentences (only offence and sentence information) to those given to more complete descriptions of the same cases (including a case summary). Respondents were initially asked a general question about their perceptions of court sentencing practice. In the abstract, over 90% of the total group reported that in general the courts are too lenient.

Respondents were then randomly assigned to one of two groups, one to receive a brief description of a manslaughter case (similar to a media report) and one to receive a more detailed description with information on incident and offender characteristics.

Most of the respondents provided with a short description of the case felt that the sentence was too lenient (80%), while only 7% felt the sentence was about right. For those given a longer description of the case, 15% felt that the sentence was too lenient and 30% felt that the sentence was about right. It is interesting to note that fully 45% of this group described the sentence as too harsh (citation omitted).

[T]hese studies show that sentences described in the media are perceived by most people as being too lenient, while those described in detail in court transcripts are mostly seen as appropriate. [The researchers] conclude that, were the public to form opinions from court-based information instead of through the lens of the mass media, there would be fewer instances of calls for harsher sentences. Caution should thus be exercised in responding to calls for harsher penalties as a fully informed public could well be quite content with the current level of severity of penalties.

. . . Rethinking Crime & Punishment (RCP) was set up in 2001 in response to widespread concern about the United Kingdom's growing reliance on imprisonment. A key reason for this has been the perceived pressure of public opinion, as politicians, judges and magistrates have responded to a supposed climate of opinion that demands an increasingly harsh response to crime. The specific aims of RCP have been to increase public knowledge and improve public debate about prison and alternatives. It has been suggested that studies on attitudes to

imprisonment might be tapping top-of-the-head reactions, rather than enduring and well-considered beliefs.

In [a] 1996 British Crime Survey, respondents were given a description of a
real case and were asked to impose one or more sentences for a 23 year-old male
repeat offender convicted of the burglary of an elderly man's house. Half the
sample was given a menu of options from which to choose, while the other half
was asked to give unprompted responses. This allowed testing of the hypothesis
that there would be less support for imprisonment when respondents were
made aware of alternative options.

While a majority of respondents in both groups [favored] imprisonment,
the figure was significantly higher for those without the menu of options (67%)
than for those given information on other sentencing options available (54%).
Respondents with the sentencing menu were more likely to favour non-custodial
options such as suspended sentences, community service, compensation and
probation (citation omitted).

[When exposed to additional, accurate information about current sentencing tools, such as mandatory sentencing, the public also shows a lack of a punitive bent.] The main justification for [mandatory sentencing] has been
supposed public demand for more severe sentencing.

People have little knowledge about mandatory sentencing, the offences
that attract this response and the actual minimum and maximum penalties that
apply. They are also unaware of the extent to which mandatory sentencing laws
affect large numbers of offenders convicted of non-violent offences, particularly
drug crimes. . . .

In a study that specifically examined public attitudes to 'three-strikes' laws,
a random sample of Ohio residents [were asked] whether they supported or
opposed implementing such a law in their state. In response to a single question
with no context provided, 88% expressed support for the proposal. But when
asked to impose sentences for a number of case studies, the percentage endors-
ing the 'three-strikes' sentence dropped to only 17%.

A more recent national survey of 2,000 adults in the United States found
even lower levels of support for mandatory sentencing. Respondents were first
asked a general question: 'In recent years, some states have required that certain
crimes, including non-violent crimes, carry a mandatory minimum prison
sentence regardless of the circumstances of the crime. Do you support or oppose
the idea of mandatory prison sentences for non-violent crime?' In response to
this question, 61% were opposed to mandatory prison terms while 35% supported them. . . . Clearly there is less support for mandatory prison terms in the
United States than is suggested by the proliferation of such laws. . . .

Evidence of the often contradictory nature of public opinion on sentencing can be found when people are asked how to "fix" the criminal justice system.
The responses vary based on the nature of the question (whether the question is
the open-ended "what is the most effective way to reduce crime" or the binary
"which would you choose to reduce prison over-crowding: build more prisons or
increase the use of alternative prisons").

Despite a lack of knowledge about the criminal justice system, public sentencing preferences are actually very similar to those expressed by the judiciary
or actually used by the courts. To test the hypothesis that the public is more
punitive than judges, [researchers] looked at a 1986 representative survey

conducted by Gallup for the Canadian Sentencing Commission. The survey asked respondents what proportion of offenders should be incarcerated for various crimes. These preferences were then compared to the proportion of convictions for this offence that actually resulted in custody in the Canadian courts. No significant difference was found between the two groups — average incarceration rates across ten offences (both violent and property offences) were 66% for the public and 67% for the courts.

A similar approach was adopted . . . in [a] 1989 comparison of lay and judicial responses to case study vignettes in Illinois, in which respondents were asked to impose sentences on the same four moderately severe cases in which prison was a possible, but not inevitable sentencing outcome. A total of 325 respondents participated in the research: [including] state judges who participated as part of seminars on sentencing; . . . jurors who reported for jury duty but who were not needed by the court that day; and . . . university students who participated for course credit.

Respondents were presented with detailed information about each of the four cases, including a presentence report (including information on the nature of the offence and on the offender's background) and a video of the sentencing hearing. Respondents were told the range of possible sentencing options legally available for that case and then completed a questionnaire indicating sentencing preferences. The non-judicial respondents were also told that offenders sentenced to prison would typically serve about half of their prison terms.

[The results] found that there was no evidence in any of the four cases that judicial sentences were more lenient than the sentences of the lay respondents. Judges' sentences in this study were as severe or more severe than those of lay respondents. They conclude that the perception that judges are more lenient than the public is simply a myth. . . .

Evidence of the often contradictory nature of public opinion on sentencing can be found in the literature showing that people favour non-imprisonment mechanisms, even when they have reported that they perceive sentences to be overly lenient. This result has been found in surveys asking two types of questions: those that ask respondents about the most effective way to reduce crime and those that offer respondents a choice between building more prisons and increasing the use of alternatives to prison as possible options for reducing prison over-crowding.

WHAT DO WE KNOW ABOUT PUBLIC OPINION INTERNATIONALLY?

The Canadian Sentencing Commission commissioned a survey in 1986 that asked respondents about the most effective way of controlling crime. While 28% of respondents felt that sentences should be made harsher, fully 43% suggested that reducing unemployment would be most effective. A further 14% favoured increasing the use of alternatives to incarceration and 11% suggested increasing the number of social programs. Respondents were then asked a follow-up question asking them to choose between spending money on building more prisons or on developing alternatives to incarceration. While 23% favoured the prison approach, fully 70% chose alternatives to imprisonment.

A more recent Canadian survey examined people's attitudes to sentencing for adults and juveniles separately. Respondents were asked about the most effective way to control crime. Half were asked about controlling youth crime, while the others were asked about controlling adult crime. Fewer than a third of respondents thought that making sentences harsher was the best way to control adult crime, and fewer than a quarter of respondents thought that this was the best way to reduce youth crime. Incapacitation is seen as being more important for adult offenders than for youth, for whom expressions of community disapproval and rehabilitation are seen as being more important.

A 2001 survey of 1,056 adults in the United States found that Americans clearly preferred prevention as the best strategy for dealing with crime. More respondents felt that prevention in the form of education and youth programs was the most effective way to control crime (37%), while 20% preferred punishment in the form of longer sentences and more prisons. Enforcement (more police officers) was considered the best approach by 19% of respondents, while prison rehabilitation and education programs were favoured by 17% of respondents. This same study also found that 65% of adults surveyed favoured dealing with the root causes of crime while only 32% preferred the punitive approach in the form of strict sentencing. Respondents reported that they strongly favoured rehabilitation and re-entry programs over incapacitation as the best method of ensuring public safety: 66% felt that the best way to reduce crime was to rehabilitate offenders while only 28% felt that keeping criminals off the street through long prison sentences would be more effective. The authors of this report concluded that conventional wisdom about public punitiveness misjudges the mood of the voters, who now see the 'lock-'em-up' strategy as having failed.

The most recent study to examine public opinion about crime control strategies asked victims of crime about the effectiveness of various methods for reducing re-offending. The survey of 982 victims in the United Kingdom, conducted on behalf of the Smart Justice and Victim Support agencies, found that 61% of respondents believed that prison does not reduce re-offending. Rather, 80% of respondents believed that better supervision of young people by parents is effective in reducing crime in the long run while 83% felt that more constructive activities for young people would be effective in reducing crime.

Representatives of the sponsoring agencies concluded from this research that victims do not want retribution and vengeance but instead want constructive and effective methods to tackle the root causes of offending and thus prevent further offending. . . .

NOTE

Public opinion and sentencing. Politicians, criminal justice scholars in general, and desert theorists in particular often refer to public opinion to justify particular sanctions or policy recommendations. Typically the unstated assumption in such assertions is that the public belief is innate or static. Why should anyone assume that uninformed rather than informed opinion is the proper basis for any policy or decision? Are juries — one model of citizen involvement in the criminal justice process — more fairly described as "informed" or "uninformed" actors?

PROBLEM 1-6.   CRIME IN AMERICA

Imagine that you are a member of the state legislature who has been elected on a "public safety" platform. You now wish to join committees and to introduce and support legislation and funding consistent with your public commitments. You meet with your staff and several invited "public safety" experts for a nonpublic discussion. You ask the following question: what are the top ten policies that will reduce crime in America, or that will reduce the particular kinds of crime that are most in the news, or that are the most socially costly? You encourage each person at the meeting to think silently for ten minutes and then to write down those ten policies, with a short explanation of the assumptions underlying the recommendations. Now you go around the room and ask: how many of the top ten policies involve changes in sentencing or punishment? Indeed, how many of the policies involve the criminal justice system at all?

Now, in your role as one of the sentencing experts in the room and based on the results of this exercise, does this discussion make you rethink your response to the question of the justifications for sentencing and punishment?

NOTE

Crime in America.   In discussing the purposes of sentencing, it is critical to "frame" the question properly. In this chapter we have emphasized the different jurisprudential roles that the purposes of punishment play at the case, rule, and systemic levels. We have noted the variety of functional and political goals (both legitimate and illegitimate, express and implied, conscious and unintentional) that may be served by criminal sanctions. But perhaps the proper question is not how punishment is justified, but what role punishment (or the criminal justice system as a whole) serves relative to other forms of social control, including education, labor, housing, health and welfare policies, systems for responding to mental health issues and drug and alcohol dependency, and other private or public tools and initiatives.

= 2 =
‖ *Who Sentences?* ‖

In most criminal justice systems, several institutions share the decision about the proper sentence to impose: Legislatures and judges always have a say in the sentence, and juries, parole boards, and sentencing commissions may participate. But the precise division of labor in setting general sentencing policy and sentences in particular cases varies a great deal from place to place. We begin with a survey of the actors, and then we take a closer look at the distinctive capabilities of each.

‖ ***Research on Sentencing: The Search for Reform,***
Alfred Blumstein, Jacqueline Cohen,
Susan Martin, and Michael Tonry
Vol. 1, pp. 41-47 (1983) ‖

Any effort . . . to understand sentencing must take into account the existence of the many participants and decisions that together constitute "sentencing" and the conflicting values, perspectives, and interests among them. This very complexity, however, frustrates efforts to change the criminal justice process in America.

Victims and Witnesses. Victims initiate criminal justice action when they decide to complain to the police. They also, subsequently, affect the likelihood of conviction and punishment through their ability and willingness to cooperate with the prosecution. Victim and witness noncooperation is a major cause of charge dismissal in the United States. According to the National Crime Survey, 56 percent of violent crimes went unreported in 1978 (including 35 percent of robberies with injury), as did 75 percent of personal crimes of theft and 64 percent of household crimes. . . .

Police. Police decide whom to notice, to stop, to arrest, to book, and (in some jurisdictions) to charge. Police officers have the primary authority to decide who will *not* be pursued by the criminal justice system. . . . The exercise of discretion in the police decision to arrest largely dictates the outcome in [misdemeanor cases involving public disorder, family violence, and small-scale drug trafficking]. The police also possess substantial autonomy in handling serious crimes of violence and investigating organized illegal activities and large property loss or damage. Police are relatively free to decide which complaints to follow up, with what diligence and resources, and to select their means of investigation. . . .

    Prosecutors.   Prosecutors establish priorities and determine the vigor with which various kinds of cases will be pursued. In the 1970s, for example, many prosecutors ceased prosecuting marijuana possession cases; in effect, those prosecutors decriminalized marijuana use in their jurisdictions.

    Prosecutors also exercise substantial discretion over individual cases. Prosecutors decide what charges to file or, if the police file charges, what to dismiss. Like the decisions of police officers, prosecutors' decisions to [dismiss or reduce charges] are not subject to independent review. . . .

    Plea bargaining takes diverse forms. In *horizontal charge bargains,* a prosecutor agrees to drop several charges for an offense type if the defendant pleads guilty to the remaining charges (e.g., three burglary charges are dropped when the defendant pleads guilty to a fourth). In *vertical charge bargains,* a prosecutor agrees to drop the highest charge if the defendant pleads guilty to a less serious charge (e.g., a narcotics trafficking charge is dropped if the defendant pleads guilty to a narcotics possession charge, or a charge of armed robbery is dropped if the defendant pleads guilty to a charge of robbery). In sentence bargains, a prosecutor agrees that the defendant will receive a specific sentence in return for a guilty plea. In fact bargains, a prosecutor agrees not to introduce evidence of specific aggravating circumstances. Other plea bargaining variants involve prosecutorial agreements to recommend or not to oppose particular sentences or to dismiss charges in consideration of the defendant's cooperation in other prosecutions or investigations. Whatever form plea bargaining takes, the prosecutor and to a lesser extent the defense counsel often stand supreme. The judge sometimes has little choice but to ratify their decisions. . . .

    Judges.   Judges impose sentences. They decide who goes to prison and who does not; they set the terms of nonincarcerative sentences; and (depending on whether there is a parole board and on the rules governing parole eligibility) they set minimum, maximum, or actual lengths of jail and prison terms. . . .

    Judges' powers [are also] informally but importantly affected by the work of other court personnel. First, in jurisdictions in which sentence bargaining is common, often a judge's choice is whether to ratify the negotiated sentence. Second, where charge bargaining is prevalent, a judge usually accedes to proposed charge dismissals and may impose a sentence only within the constraints set by any statutory sentence provisions. Third, probation officers devote more time to investigation of the offender's circumstances and to consideration of the case than judges possibly can, and so they control the flow of information to judges. Probation officers are attached to most modern felony courts; presentence reports containing their recommendations are commonly provided to judges, and these recommendations are usually followed.

Parole Boards.   Although parole boards have been abolished in some jurisdictions — and in others they have lost their authority to determine release dates — in the majority of states they retain control over parole release. Judges often set maximum sentences (and in some states minimums as well), but the maximum is often very long; parole boards decide who and when to release prior to sentence expiration; the conditions to which a parolee will be subject while on parole; when and why parole can be revoked; and when after revocation, if at all, an offender can be re-released prior to the end of the maximum sentence. . . .

Parole boards traditionally make individualized release decisions, taking account of a wide variety of offender characteristics. In establishing uniform criteria for releasing offenders, they, too, face the basic dilemma in criminal justice: How much emphasis should be placed on the seriousness of the conviction offense in attempting to follow the injunction to "treat like cases alike" and how much on the characteristics of the defendant, including prior record and employment status, in predicting whether the release constitutes a danger to the community?

Corrections Administrators.   Corrections administrators affect the duration of imprisonment by the award, withdrawal, or denial of time off for good behavior and by their recommendations and reports to parole boards when a prisoner is being considered for early release. Corrections administrators also influence the quality of a prisoner's confinement through decisions about institutional assignments and participation in various kinds of furlough programs. Whether an inmate spends time in a maximum security prison, in a less restrictive minimum security facility, or in a group home in his or her hometown is almost entirely in the hands of corrections authorities. . . .

Executive Clemency: Commutations and Pardons.   Although pardons and similar executive release mechanisms once played a major part in prison releases, these ad hoc powers are no longer extensively used in most states.

Legislatures.   Legislative influence in sentencing is first and last: it is first because a legislature constructs and can always alter the basic statutory framework that other officials are charged to carry out; it is last because most punishments prescribed by law are not self-executing but can be realized only through other officials. If those officials behave inconsistently with the law, there is little a legislature can do. Even such seemingly authoritative laws as those calling for mandatory minimum sentences can be effected only through others; if prosecutors and judges choose to circumvent the law, mandatory terms will not be imposed. . . . Sometimes statutes are drafted so broadly that they provide little guidance in individual cases. For example, the maximum prison terms authorized for most offenses — 5 or 10 or 25 years — are so much longer than the sentences typically imposed or served that the legislative decision has little significance for the operation of the system.

The System as a Whole.   The operations of this complex system of criminal justice, with its network of multiple, overlapping, and interconnecting discretions and conflicting goals, are not easily altered; like the operation of any complex system, they are influenced by powerful forces of tradition, institutional convenience, scarcity of resources, and self-interest. Officials who wish to circumvent or undermine a new law can usually find ways to do so; legislative changes are impositions from outside and are often resisted. . . .

Such reactions are foreseeable. The staffs of prosecutors' offices and the courts have institutional goals and personal interests to serve and limited resources to expend. Sometimes their personal views of justice and injustice may not easily accept legislative solutions to the crime problem. Since new laws are seldom accompanied by appropriation of funds sufficient to permit literal and wholehearted compliance with them, something must give, and that something is often compliance. The complexity of the system also often confounds reform initiatives by merely shifting the locus of decision-making power from one agency to another. . . .

NOTES

1. *Victim participation in sentencing.*   Victim participation in criminal justice has grown more important since the original publication of the passage reprinted above. Legislation in all 50 states now formalizes victim participation at various stages in the criminal process. For instance, laws in many states require the prosecutor to notify the victim before dismissing any serious charges, and the law often gives the victim the opportunity to speak at the offender's sentencing hearing and sometimes to recommend a sentence. Victims also figure prominently in some parole hearings. Do these contacts between the victim and various government officials amount to a grant of "sentencing" power to the victim?

In 2004 Congress passed the Crime Victims' Rights Act (CVRA), Pub. L. No. 108-405, §§101-104, 118 Stat. 2260, 2261-2265 (2004) (codified at 18 U.S.C. §3771). The CVRA guarantees crime victims eight different rights, and unlike the prior crime victims' rights statute, allows both the government and the victims to enforce them. One of the rights guaranteed by the CVRA is the "right to be reasonably heard at any public proceeding in the district court involving release, plea, sentencing, or any parole proceeding." 18 U.S.C. §3771(a)(4). As discussed more fully in Chapter 4, the Ninth Circuit has held that the CVRA "gives victims the right to allocute at sentencing." Kenna v. District Court, 435 F.3d 1011 (9th Cir. 2006).

2. *Pardon and clemency boards.*   The passage above mentions that executive clemency is "no longer extensively used in most states," and it is true that governors today grant pardons and commute sentences far less often than they once did. Governors do still grant pardons, however, and there are now active and elaborate bureaucracies at work in many states to assist the governor in deciding when to grant pardons and when to commute sentences. About two-thirds of the states leave the pardon decision entirely to the discretion of the governor. In about ten states, the governor can consider only clemency recommendations issued by a clemency board. We discuss the pardon and clemency power in Chapter 11.

3. *Involvement of unexpected actors.*   In various settings and in various ways, additional actors can play a direct or indirect role in the development of sentencing policies and punishment practices. For example, concerns about the

post-release activities of sex offenders has led numerous localities to enact regional residency restrictions on persons previously convicted of certain crimes. And in recent debates and litigation over execution methods, doctors and other medical professionals have sometimes been requested — and have sometimes refused — to assess and participate in lethal injection protocols. Can you identify any other types of unexpected actors who may, either systematically or sporadically, have a role in sentencing decision making?

A. SENTENCING IN THE COURTROOM

The immediate answer to the question of "who sentences" may be the judge who announces a sentence in the courtroom. But the legal framework for sentencing is always more complex. In the United States, the closest approximation to the pure, unadulterated image of the judge as law giver and law applier is found in "indeterminate" sentencing systems, which traditionally vest enormous discretion in the sentencing judge and provide little review of the sentences imposed. But even in indeterminate systems, the seemingly vast power of the judge is circumscribed by modest guidance from legislatures and, more important, by post-sentence executive branch review by parole boards.

The materials that follow illuminate the nature of sentencing by judges and parole boards in indeterminate systems. If one of the purposes of criminal sentences is to reflect the community's response to the violation of social norms, should a group of representative community members, in the familiar form of a jury, decide the sentence? While conceptually intriguing, jury sentencing has played a major role in the United States only in capital cases. The second section below examines one special noncapital setting and the handful of states that grant juries the authority to sentence.

1. Judges and Parole Boards in Indeterminate Sentencing

Until recently, sentencing in the United States was characterized more by discretion than by law. In 1950 every state and the federal system used indeterminate sentencing. Under this type of system, the legislature prescribes broad potential sentencing ranges and the trial judge sentences without meaningful legal guidance and typically without offering a detailed explanation for the sentence. An executive branch agency (usually a parole board) ultimately determines the actual sentence each defendant serves. There are virtually no judicial opinions explaining or reviewing a sentence, and legal counsel ordinarily makes oral arguments at sentencing hearings without any written submissions to the court. The unwritten nature of the arguments and the decisions make it difficult for anyone to get a handle on sentencing law and practice. Perhaps that reality demonstrates the most important point about such a system: sentencing occurs without much law.

The following materials offer a glimpse of indeterminate sentencing systems at work. The U.S. Supreme Court's 1949 decision in Williams v. New York, which came at the high-water mark of indeterminate sentencing, reveals not only the extensive discretion given to trial judges but also some of the principles underlying that discretion.

Samuel Williams v. New York
337 U.S. 241 (1949)

BLACK, J.

A jury in a New York state court found appellant guilty of murder in the first degree. The jury recommended life imprisonment, but the trial judge imposed a sentence of death. In giving his reasons for imposing the death sentence the judge discussed in open court the evidence upon which the jury had convicted stating that this evidence had been considered in the light of additional information obtained through the court's "Probation Department, and through other sources." [A New York statute authorized the court to consider "any information that will aid the court in determining the proper treatment of such defendant." Williams claimed that the sentence, which was based on information supplied by witnesses, violated his due process rights because he had no chance to confront or cross-examine the witnesses or to rebut the evidence.]

The record shows a carefully conducted trial lasting more than two weeks in which appellant was represented by three appointed lawyers who conducted his defense with fidelity and zeal. The evidence proved a wholly indefensible murder committed by a person engaged in a burglary. . . .

About five weeks after the verdict of guilty with recommendation of life imprisonment, and after a statutory pre-sentence investigation report to the judge, the defendant was brought to court to be sentenced. [T]he judge gave reasons why he felt that the death sentence should be imposed. . . . He stated that the pre-sentence investigation revealed many material facts concerning appellant's background which though relevant to the question of punishment could not properly have been brought to the attention of the jury in its consideration of the question of guilt. He referred to the experience appellant "had had on 30 other burglaries in and about the same vicinity" where the murder had been committed. The appellant had not been convicted of these burglaries although the judge had information that he had confessed to some and had been identified as the perpetrator of some of the others. The judge also referred to certain activities of appellant as shown by the probation report that indicated appellant possessed "a morbid sexuality" and classified him as a "menace to society." The accuracy of the statements made by the judge as to appellant's background and past practices [was] not challenged by appellant or his counsel, nor was the judge asked to disregard any of them or to afford appellant a chance to refute or discredit any of them by cross-examination or otherwise.

The case presents a serious and difficult question. The question relates to the rules of evidence applicable to the manner in which a judge may obtain information to guide him in the imposition of sentence upon an already convicted defendant. . . . To aid a judge in exercising this discretion intelligently the New York procedural policy encourages him to consider information about the convicted person's past life, health, habits, conduct, and mental and moral propensities. The sentencing judge may consider such information even though obtained outside the courtroom from persons whom a defendant has not been permitted to confront or cross-examine. . . .

Tribunals passing on the guilt of a defendant always have been hedged in by strict evidentiary procedural limitations. But both before and since the American colonies became a nation, courts in this country and in England practiced a policy under which a sentencing judge could exercise a wide discretion in the sources and types of evidence used to assist him in determining the kind and the extent of punishment to be imposed within limits fixed by law. Out-of-court affidavits have been used frequently, and of course in the smaller communities sentencing judges naturally have in mind their knowledge of the personalities and backgrounds of convicted offenders. . . .

In addition to the historical basis for different evidentiary rules governing trial and sentencing procedures there are sound practical reasons for the distinction. In a trial before verdict the issue is whether a defendant is guilty of having engaged in certain criminal conduct of which he has been specifically accused. Rules of evidence have been fashioned for criminal trials which narrowly confine the trial contest to evidence that is strictly relevant to the particular offense charged. These rules rest in part on a necessity to prevent a time-consuming and confusing trial of collateral issues. They were also designed to prevent tribunals concerned solely with the issue of guilt of a particular offense from being influenced to convict for that offense by evidence that the defendant had habitually engaged in other misconduct. A sentencing judge, however, is not confined to the narrow issue of guilt. His task within fixed statutory or constitutional limits is to determine the type and extent of punishment after the issue of guilt has been determined. Highly relevant — if not essential — to his selection of an appropriate sentence is the possession of the fullest information possible concerning the defendant's life and characteristics. And modern concepts individualizing punishment have made it all the more necessary that a sentencing judge not be denied an opportunity to obtain pertinent information by a requirement of rigid adherence to restrictive rules of evidence properly applicable to the trial.

Undoubtedly the New York statutes emphasize a prevalent modern philosophy of penology that the punishment should fit the offender and not merely the crime. The belief no longer prevails that every offense in a like legal category calls for an identical punishment without regard to the past life and habits of a particular offender. This whole country has traveled far from the period in which the death sentence was an automatic and commonplace result of convictions — even for offenses today deemed trivial. . . . Indeterminate sentences, the ultimate termination of which are sometimes decided by nonjudicial agencies, have to a large extent taken the place of the old rigidly fixed punishments. . . . Retribution is no longer the dominant objective of the criminal law. Reformation and rehabilitation of offenders have become important goals of criminal jurisprudence. . . .

Under the practice of individualizing punishments, investigation techniques have been given an important role. Probation workers making reports of their investigations have not been trained to prosecute but to aid offenders. Their reports have been given a high value by conscientious judges who want to sentence persons on the best available information rather than on guesswork and inadequate information. To deprive sentencing judges of this kind of information would undermine modern penological procedural policies that have been cautiously adopted throughout the nation after careful consideration and experimentation. We must recognize that most of the information now relied upon by judges to guide them in the intelligent imposition of sentences would be unavailable if information were restricted to that given in open court by witnesses subject to cross-examination. And the modern probation report draws on information concerning every aspect of a defendant's life. The type and extent of this information make totally impractical if not impossible open court testimony with cross-examination. Such a procedure could endlessly delay criminal administration in a retrial of collateral issues. The considerations we have set out admonish us against treating the due-process clause as a uniform command that courts throughout the nation abandon their age-old practice of seeking information from out-of-court sources to guide their judgment toward a more enlightened and just sentence.... So to treat the due-process clause would hinder if not preclude all courts — state and federal — from making progressive efforts to improve the administration of criminal justice. We hold that appellant was not denied due process of law....

NOTES

1. *Informal procedure at sentencing: majority position.*   The New York statute discussed in *Williams,* allowing the sentencing judge to consider evidence inadmissible at trial under the rules of evidence, typifies sentencing practices in most states. See Tex. Crim. Proc. Code Ann. §37.07(3). The informal presentation of evidence supposedly supports an effort to obtain the most information possible about the offender and the offense and to make an individualized (perhaps even clinical) decision. Over time, many different actors participate in the decision about how best to respond to an individual offender. Thus, the indeterminate sentencing system is one of "multiple discretions." More than half the states use this system for large groups of cases, although many of these states use more narrowly circumscribed sentencing rules for some crimes.

As discussed more fully in Chapter 6, recent Supreme Court decisions that are primarily concerned with the Sixth Amendment right to a jury trial have arguably undercut some of the principles of *Williams,* although *Williams* remains good law. See generally Douglas A. Berman, Beyond *Blakely* and *Booker:* Pondering Modern Sentencing Process, 95 J. Crim. L. & Criminology 654 (2005)

2. Williams *revisited.*   Samuel Titto Williams, a black man, was 18 years old at the time he killed 15-year-old Selma Graff, who surprised him during a burglary. Williams had no record of prior convictions, but he had been accused of burglary at age 11. The judgment in juvenile court was suspended. The probation report — a report prepared by probation officers prior to sentencing, also called a presentence investigation report — informed the judge that Williams was suspected of (but not charged with) committing 30 burglaries during the two months before the murder. A 7-year-old girl who was present during one of those burglaries told the probation officer that Williams had sexually molested her. She identified Williams as the perpetrator two weeks after the incident. The

probation report also stated that Williams was living with two women, and brought different men into the apartment for the purpose of having sexual relations with the women. It alleged that Williams had once gone to a local school to photograph "private parts of young children." Finally, the sentencing judge relied on injuries inflicted on the murder victim's brother during the burglary. The prosecutor did not bring any charges based on the assault. See Kevin Reitz, Sentencing Facts: Travesties of Real-Offense Sentencing, 45 Stan. L. Rev. 523 (1993). Is the problem in *Williams* the presentation of new offender information at sentencing or the fact that Williams did not know the judge would hear these allegations?

3. *Capital punishment and informal procedure.*   Although the *Williams* Court emphasized that rehabilitative purposes of sentencing required far-reaching information about an offender, the proposed "treatment" for Williams was execution. It brings to mind the statement attributed to the comedian W. C. Fields, who quoted a condemned prisoner on his way to the electric chair, saying, "This will certainly be a lesson to me." *Williams* is still cited with approval in support of informal sentencing procedures generally, but it has been partially overruled in the context of capital sentencing. In Gardner v. Florida, 430 U.S. 349 (1977), the trial judge sentenced a defendant to death after consulting confidential and unrebutted information in the presentence investigation report. A plurality of the Supreme Court found that due process required, at least in capital cases, that the defendant have access to information that will influence the sentencing judge and have an opportunity to test its reliability.

4. *Styles of argument in indeterminate sentencing.*   When judges describe the factors they consider in sentencing under an indeterminate system, they often discuss the traditional purposes of sentencing examined in Chapter 1 and try to operationalize those purposes in light of the specific facts of the offense and the background of the offender. One study of sentences in federal white-collar crime cases concluded that judges considered three common principles during sentencing: (1) the harm the offense produced; (2) the blameworthiness of the defendant, judged from the defendant's criminal intent, from other details of the crime, and from the defendant's earlier life; and (3) the consequences of the punishment, both for deterring future wrongdoing and for the well-being of the defendant's family and community. Despite the presence of these common principles for sentencing, judges selected very different sentences because they did not agree on how to measure each of the principles or the relative weight to place on each. See Stanton Wheeler, Kenneth Mann & Austin Sarat, Sitting in Judgment: The Sentencing of White-Collar Criminals (1988).

Observers in higher-volume courts, such as state misdemeanor courts, describe a very different reality. During plea bargaining the parties settle quickly on a proper sentence, which hinges largely on the charges filed and the parties' interpretation of the facts as reflected in the police reports. These negotiations do not often involve individualized haggling; rather, they are "more akin to modern supermarkets in which prices for various commodities have been clearly established and labeled." Malcolm Feeley, The Process Is the Punishment: Handling Cases in a Lower Criminal Court 187 (1979). What determines whether a given case will receive the "supermarket" form of sentencing or a more individualized assessment?

5. *Probation officers.*   Judges who sentence a defendant after a guilty plea have not heard an extensive presentation of the evidence at trial and thus depend heavily on the presentence investigation that probation officers perform to provide information about the offender and the offense. How might a prosecutor or a defense attorney influence the recommendations of the probation officer? What institutional or individual biases might the probation officer bring to her assessment (and recommendation) of proper sentences? We consider further the work of probation officers and their interaction with attorneys and judges in Chapter 6.

PROBLEM 2-1.   DETERMINING THE INDETERMINABLE

On February 20, 2003, at The Station nightclub in West Warwick, Rhode Island, the metal band Great White took the stage around 11 p.m. and broke into their first song. Daniel Biechele, the tour manager for Great White, then ignited the pyrotechnics he set up to accompany the band's performance. Almost instantly, the combustible soundproofing material that surrounded the stage caught on fire, and the fire quickly spread throughout the wood-paneled club.

Exactly 100 persons died in the resulting blaze: rescue teams pulled 96 bodies from the nightclub after the fire was contained, and 4 more people died in the hospital. Almost 200 other people were treated for their injuries. The victims included teens, married couples, and roadies.

As part of a plea agreement, Biechele ultimately pleaded guilty to 100 counts of involuntary manslaughter for his role in this tragedy. In exchange for a recommended sentence from the prosecution of 10 years in prison and 5 years on probation, Biechele admitted that he set off the pyrotechnics without a permit or license. The plea agreement clarifies that the Rhode Island sentencing judge will have complete discretion to adjust the balance of the prison time against probation as long as the total term does not exceed 15 years.

Representatives from many victims' families have expressed outrage at the plea deal. The sentencing judge has scheduled a set of hearings in which he will permit any and every victim and family member to address the court before the judge determines Biechele's sentence.

If you were the lawyer representing Biechele, what sentence would you request and what sorts of evidence and arguments would you marshal in support of that request?

PROBLEM 2-2.   DUE NORTH

Oliver North was a marine lieutenant colonel assigned in 1981 to the National Security Council (NSC) staff. By 1984 North was responsible for two principal areas: counterterrorism and Central America. North was prosecuted by an independent counsel and was convicted of aiding and abetting an obstruction of Congress, for his removal and destruction of the permanent historical records of the NSC and for receiving an illegal gratuity. North was a very controversial public figure. The battle between the independent counsel and

North's defense lawyers — and between critics and supporters of the Reagan administration policies with respect to Central America — turned on whether North would receive any time in prison. The high-profile nature of the case provides a better picture than do most (unreported) cases of the nature of sentencing arguments in the indeterminate sentencing era, at least in widely publicized cases.

The independent counsel wrote in its sentencing memorandum:

> The most striking thing about North's posture on the eve of sentencing is his insistence that he has done nothing wrong. Instead, on the day of the verdict, he declared that his "vindication" was not "complete," and promised to "continue the fight" until it is. . . .
>
> [North] apparently sees nothing wrong with alteration and destruction of official national security records. His participation in the preparation of a false and misleading chronology [to present during a congressional hearing on the Iran-Contra affair] has not led to any acknowledgment of wrongdoing. Certainly, he sees nothing wrong with lying to Congress, when in the view of himself and his superiors lying is necessary. . . .
>
> In fashioning a just sentence in this case, we urge the Court to consider the seriousness of North's abuse of the public trust, the need for deterrence, North's failure to accept personal responsibility for his actions, his lack of remorse and his perjury on the witness stand. Taking all of these factors into account . . . the Government submits that a term of incarceration is appropriate and necessary.
>
> [The] Court, in its sentence, should [demonstrate] that if officials engaging in such conduct are caught and convicted, the punishment will be severe. Further, the private citizens of this country, who continue to follow this case closely, are entitled to the reassurance only this Court can give that these are serious crimes and that powerful government officials are not accorded special treatment. . . .
>
> A sentence in this case that included no period of incarceration would send exactly the wrong message to government officials and to the public. It would be a statement that 15 years after Watergate, government officials can participate in a brazen cover-up, lie to Congress and collect a substantial gratuity and still receive only a slap on the wrist. . . .
>
> Oliver North's sentence will be known to, and closely evaluated by, all who view the perversion of government as a permissible means to the attainment of their goals. The sentence will also be carefully considered by those officials who may now be weighing the advantages of deception, obstruction and personal greed against the risks of punishment. It will also be noted by those serving substantial prison sentences for more personal crimes far less damaging to the nation. Most importantly, the sentence will be closely scrutinized by a citizenry whose confidence in government and the political system has been seriously undermined by the activities of this defendant. . . . Under all these circumstances, we respectfully submit that a term of incarceration is appropriate and necessary.

North's lawyers responded as follows:

> Lt. Col. Oliver L. North is before the court for sentencing upon being found guilty of 3 of the 16 charges brought against him by the IC. . . . The IC's memorandum demonstrates that it will stop at nothing in its effort to crush Oliver North. . . .
>
> We submit that Lt. Col. North has already been punished sufficiently for the three offenses of which he was found guilty. He was fired from his job at the NSC. He has lost his career as a Marine Corps officer. He may lose his Marine Corps pension after 20 years of service. He remains under threat of assassination

by a dangerous terrorist organization as a direct result of his service to this country. He has been subjected to unrelenting and often hostile press scrutiny for the past two-and-a-half years. Every detail of his life has been probed, first in nationally televised hearings conducted by the joint Iran/Contra committee and then by the IC. He has heard himself likened to Hitler by a prosecutor who appears to lack any sense of fairness and [has heard] rumors in the press, before Congress, in court, in a nationally televised "docudrama," and now in the IC's memorandum. His children have been tormented. By any standard, the toll that this ordeal has already taken on Lt. Col. North and his family fulfills every legitimate purpose of punishment. If the Court accepts the IC's view that this punishment is not enough — that Oliver North must be punished further for the three offenses of which he was found guilty — then that punishment should take the form of probation conditioned on community service. . . .

In determining the proper sentence for Oliver North, the Court should consider the man as an individual, not — as the IC would have it — merely as a vehicle through which to send a "public message." The Court should weigh carefully Lt. Col. North's service to this country and to society, the devastating impact that imprisonment would have on his family, and the unique confluence of circumstances that gave rise to his conduct. This careful, individualized sentencing is essential to ensure that "the punishment should fit the offender and not merely the crime." Williams v. New York, 337 U.S. 241 (1949).

Oliver North devoted 20 years to the service of this country, from Vietnam to Tehran to Beirut. He has risked his own life and saved the lives of others. We submit that the Court should weigh this service in Lt. Col. North's favor at sentencing. . . .

Oliver North . . . has worked to improve society in other ways as well. Since the Congressional hearings of 1987, he has put his unsought and unwanted notoriety to use in service of his fellow citizens, particularly America's youth. Two examples illustrate Lt. Col. North's compassion and concern — and put the lie to the IC's claim that Lt. Col. North displays "contempt for the public."

First, shortly after his Congressional testimony, Lt. Col. North learned that it was the dream of a terminally ill boy to see him before the boy died. Lt. Col. North agreed to meet the boy to give him courage in his final days. The woman who arranged the meeting describes what happened in her letter to the Court:

> [The boy] told me he wanted to meet Lt. Col. North because this was the strongest person that he could ever know. [The boy] said that he needed this man to teach him how to become stronger mentally so that he could deal with his fast-approaching death. . . .
>
> To my amazement and delight, Lt. Col. North brought with him a large Bible with certain scriptures marked throughout the Bible that he said he lives by, that his strength comes from his faith in God. He sat down and read with the child from the Bible and they prayed together that [the boy] would find his answers. Lt. Col. North spent one and a half hours alone with [the boy] helping him to find the strength that the child was very much in need of. . . .
>
> Lt. Col. North placed the following inscription on a photograph for the dying boy: "Courageous Hero, Inspiration, Fighter — Semper Fidelis. 18 September '87, Oliver L. North."

Second, Lt. Col. North has spoken out throughout America against drug use and in favor of improved drug prevention and rehabilitation. As but one example, he delivered a speech on behalf of the drug-prevention organization Reach Out America. . . .

Criminal punishment serves four legitimate purposes: it incapacitates the offender, to prevent him from harming society; it rehabilitates him; it deters him and others from committing further offenses; and it reflects the seriousness of the offenses. The punishment that Oliver North and his family have suffered to date more than adequately fulfills each of these purposes.

1. *Incapacitation.* There is no need to incapacitate Oliver North. Far from representing a threat to society, Lt. Col. North devoted his professional life to ensuring the safety of Americans at home and abroad. . . .
2. *Rehabilitation.* No one can seriously contend that Oliver North needs rehabilitation, and it would be preposterous to suggest that, if rehabilitation *were* necessary, it would occur in prison. . . .
3. *Deterrence.* The punishment that Oliver North has suffered to date fully satisfied any need for deterrence; no additional sentence is necessary. First, there is no need for a harsh punishment to achieve *specific* deterrence — deterrence of Lt. Col. North from future unlawful acts. In light of his record of service to this country and the excruciating ordeal that he and his family have endured, there is no chance that he will commit offenses in the future. Second, *general* deterrence — deterrence of those other than Lt. Col. North — provides no basis for harsh punishment. The punishment that Lt. Col. North has suffered to date — including the loss of his position at the NSC, the loss of his career in the Marine Corps, and the minute and public scrutiny of his most private affairs by Congress, the IC, and frequently the media — should amply deter others. . . .
4. *The Seriousness of the Offense.* The punishment that Lt. Col. North has suffered to date more than adequately reflects the gravity of the offenses of which he was found guilty. The three offenses — aiding and abetting an obstruction of Congress, destroying, altering, and/or removing official NSC documents, and accepting an unlawful gratuity — are serious. Each is a felony; each has a maximum prison term of between two and five years; and each carries a maximum fine of $250,000. But the seriousness of these offenses is significantly reduced by the unique circumstances of this case. . . .

Can both of these pictures be true? Is purpose-driven picture painting a useful way to help courts decide on a proper sentence? If not, are there any virtues or lessons to be learned from such advocacy?

NOTE

In United States v. Oliver North, Judge Gerhard Gesell of the United States District Court for the District of Columbia acknowledged North's service, but pointed out that the "case has little to do with your military behavior, commitment or expertise" (Transcript, D.D.C., July 5, 1989). At the same time, Judge Gesell observed that North was "really a low ranking subordinate working to carry out initiatives of a few cynical superiors." Judge Gesell sentenced North as follows:

I fashioned a sentence that punishes you. It is my duty to do that. But it leaves the future up to you. . . . On count six where you are found guilty of aiding and abetting [an] obstruction of Congress, I'm going to impose a sentence of three years and suspend the execution of the sentence, place you on probation for two years, fine you $100,000 and I have to impose a special assessment of $50. Under count nine, altering, removing and destroying the permanent historical records of the National Security Council, I impose a sentence of two years, suspend the execution of sentence, place you on probation for two years, fine you $35,000 and impose a special assessment of $50 and I am required by the statute to impose another mandatory penalty. You are hereby disqualified from holding any office under the United States. Under count ten, receiving an illegal gratuity, I'll impose a sentence of one year, suspend the execution of that sentence, place you on probation for two years, fine you $15,000 and impose a special assessment again of $50. These sentences and the probation are to run concurrently. The fines are to run consecutively. Your probation shall consist . . . of community service in a total amount of 1200, 800 the first year, and 400 the second year. . . .

North's conviction was later reversed on the ground that witnesses in his trial had been exposed to North's immunized congressional testimony. United States v. North, 920 F.2d 940 (D.C. Cir. 1990).

Parole Consideration and Eligibility, Georgia Board of Pardons and Paroles

http://www.pap.state.ga.us/parole_consideration. htm (2003)

. . . Before the Board considers an inmate for parole, it conducts investigations, detailed reports of which become a part of the Board's case file. . . . First, a parole officer studies arrest and court records and may talk with arresting officers, court officials, victims, and witnesses in order to write a Legal Investigation report on the details of the inmate's current offense and a summary of any prior offenses in the same county. Next, a parole officer interviews the inmate and completes a Personal History Statement questionnaire. The inmate is asked, among other things, where he has resided and worked; who his family members are and where they live; where he plans to live and work; and what his own account is of his crime. Finally, a parole officer conducts a Social Investigation, which includes interviews with persons mentioned in the Personal History Statement as well as others. The written report presents a revealing picture of the inmate's life from birth to current imprisonment and may also indicate the degree of his truthfulness.

Before the inmate is paroled, the Board receives a Parole Review Summary from the Department of Corrections. This discusses the inmate's behavior, attitude, physical status, mental and emotional condition, participation in activities, and performance in work and training. The Board may, at its discretion, request detailed psychological or psychiatric opinions. Other documents in the case file usually include a Federal Bureau of Investigation or Georgia Crime Information Center record of arrests and convictions. . . .

For inmates serving non-life sentences, the Board generally establishes a Tentative Parole Month within eight to ten months after the inmate enters state prison. . . . The Parole Board requires all violent offenders as well as residential burglars to serve a minimum of 90 percent of their court-imposed terms of incarceration. The policy affects offenders convicted . . . for twenty crimes not covered under two strikes legislation. That legislation, passed in 1994, already requires offenders convicted of murder, rape, aggravated sodomy, armed robbery, kidnapping, aggravated child molestation, and aggravated sexual battery to serve 100 percent of their prison sentence.

Crimes covered under the Board's 90-percent policy are: attempted rape, voluntary manslaughter, aggravated battery on a police officer, aggravated battery, child molestation, hijacking a motor vehicle, robbery, aggravated assault on a police officer, aggravated assault (with injury or weapon), enticing a child for indecent purposes, cruelty to children, feticide, incest, statutory rape, criminal attempt to murder, bus hijacking, vehicular homicide (while DUI or habitual violator), involuntary manslaughter, aggravated stalking, and residential burglary.

Offenders released under the 90-percent policy will serve the remainder of their sentence under parole supervision so they can be reintegrated into the community with structure and surveillance. . . .

Parole Decision Guidelines assist the State Board of Pardons and Paroles in making consistent, soundly based, and understandable parole decisions on inmates serving non-life sentences. Guidelines help the Board decide on a Tentative Parole Month (TPM) for the inmate or that he will complete his sentence without parole.

A Board hearing examiner identifies an inmate's Crime Severity Level from a table of offenses ranked in seven levels. The higher the severity, the longer the inmate is recommended to serve. Then the hearing examiner calculates the inmate's Parole Success Likelihood Score by adding weighted factors with proven predictive value from the inmate's criminal and social history, . . . such as a juvenile record, prior imprisonment, parole or probation failure, heroin or cocaine use or possession, and joblessness. . . . The hearing examiner cross-refers the inmate's Crime Severity Level and Parole Success Likelihood Factor Score on the Guidelines Grid [to obtain] a months-to-serve recommendation for the Board's discretionary consideration.

The Board votes to accept or reject the months-to-serve recommendation. If the Board votes to reject the recommendation, the Board then makes a fully discretionary clemency determination which may or may not permit parole for the inmate. [Any] TPM is conditioned on good conduct in prison and sometimes also on successful completion of a drug, alcohol, sex-offender counseling program, or other pre-condition. . . . Parole Guidelines help keep the Board on track toward its goal of seeing that inmates serving for similar offenses with similar histories are treated the same. . . .

Board members select the lowest-risk offenders for parole, acknowledging that a certain number of inmates must be paroled to allow room for newly sentenced, incoming prisoners. The "least risky" offender is therefore correlated to the characteristics of an ever-changing prison population, with its steady influx of both violent and non-violent, first-time and serial felons. One of Georgia Parole's strengths, in addition to its careful parole-selection process, is its ability to tailor parole community supervision strategies to the risk and needs presented by each offender.[*]

Georgia's Correctional Population — FY 2001

Crime Type	Probation		Inmate		Parole		Total
Violent personal	17,960	44%	19,813	48%	3,321	8%	41,094
Sex offense	5,189	47%	5,730	52%	207	2%	11,126
Property	46,587	74%	10,058	16%	6,694	11%	63,330
Drug sales	8,525	50%	4,198	25%	4,260	25%	16,983
Drug possession	34,448	82%	3,454	8%	4,084	10%	41,986
Habitual violator, DUI	5,684	81%	588	8%	787	11%	7,059
Other	8,556	76%	1,662	15%	972	9%	11,190
TOTAL	126,940	66%	45,503	24%	20,325	10%	192,768

* This paragraph, along with the chart for 2001, derive from the board's 2001 Annual Report. — EDS.

PROBLEM 2-3.   SAVINGS PLAN

The state of Georgia is experiencing a budget crisis, and the governor's office has instructed various state agencies to trim their budgets. The Department of Corrections and the Board of Pardons and Paroles have been told that the state needs to reduce the number of corrections officers on staff and therefore needs to reduce the prison population by a significant amount.

You are a staff member working for the Board of Pardons and Paroles. What strategies would you recommend for increasing the number of prison inmates released on parole? Would you ask the board to restrict its "90 percent policy" to a shorter list of crimes? Perhaps you would recommend abandoning the policy altogether. Alternatively, you might concentrate on the method used to select prisoners to parole from among the groups that are currently eligible. Should the board amend its Parole Decision Guidelines or abandon those guidelines in favor of a case-by-case approach? Should the board lobby the legislature to change the two-strikes law, which makes offenders convicted of specified crimes ineligible for parole? Cf. Daniel F. Wilhelm & Nicholas R. Turner, Is the Budget Crisis Changing the Way We Look at Sentencing and Incarceration?, 15 Fed. Sent'g Rep. 41 (2002).

NOTES

1. *Parole and sentencing purposes.* When parole first appeared in this country, it embodied the rehabilitative ideal. Prisoners received longer prison terms to allow the criminal sanctions plenty of time to do their rehabilitative work, and parole marked the successful completion of the process. Parole also served an incapacitative purpose, because it was unfair to society to release prisoners before they were rehabilitated. In theory, the parole board assessed whether rehabilitation had taken place, but in practice this determination was far from precise. A staff member for Pennsylvania's parole commission described in 1927 the process for selecting prisoners for parole release:

> [Parole boards] must attempt to separate the sheep from the goats; to liberate certain prisoners and hold others. There are certain factors which generally influence this decision. Of these, prison conduct is usually given the greatest weight. . . . Another factor generally considered is the nature of the crime for which the prisoner was committed. . . . A third item which generally has weight with paroling authorities is the prior criminal record of the applicant for parole. . . . The only other factor generally entering into parole decisions is the appearance, personality, or general demeanor of the applicant. Truthfulness, square shoulders, a good voice, or a steady eye may go far toward winning a scoundrel his freedom in more than one State. Members of parole boards are human, like the rest of us, and are often inclined to congratulate themselves on their ability to read character at a glance. And so, shrewd but experimental guesswork, prejudices, and hunches many times decide whether a boy is to spend another two or three years behind prison walls or to be allowed to circulate among us.

National Commission on Law Observance and Enforcement (Wickersham Commission), Report on Penal Institutions, Probation and Parole (Report

No. 9) at 133 (1931). Does the Georgia Board of Pardons and Paroles still purport to serve both rehabilitation and incapacitation purposes?

2. *Parole and parole guidelines.*   Even with rehabilitation becoming less important and convincing as a purpose of criminal sentencing, states find it necessary to give parole or corrections authorities the power to review sentences. This later review imposes a centralized perspective on the decisions of judges or juries from all over the state, and it coordinates the sentences with the amount of correctional resources available. Parole boards decide on the actual time an offender will serve *after* the judge has announced a sentence. Some parole boards decide cases according to formal parole guidelines, while others make more ad hoc decisions, considering prison capacity and other factors. What are the advantages and disadvantages of setting the release date later in the process through a parole board as opposed to a judge applying up-front sentencing rules? We examine parole boards and parole guidelines in more detail in Chapter 11.

Parole today is less instrumental to sentencing in the United States than it was in the middle of the twentieth century. More than a dozen states have abolished parole, and the law in other states restricts parole to certain classes of cases or gives judges more power to set the minimum prison term to be served, leaving the parole authority with less to decide. The movement to restrict parole authority is part of the broader shift to more determinate sentencing laws, a topic we consider more fully in Chapter 3.

3. *Parole and the Constitution.*   Several procedural due process rulings affect the way parole boards decide whether to grant parole to inmates and whether to revoke the parole granted at some earlier time. In Morrissey v. Brewer, 408 U.S. 471 (1972), the Supreme Court held that due process requires that an informal hearing be held before a parole board can revoke an earlier grant of parole. The hearing must be conducted by an impartial hearing officer, and the parolee must receive written notice of the claimed violations and be given an opportunity to respond to the evidence. A discretionary decision to *grant or deny* parole requires a less formal hearing. Under Greenholtz v. Inmates of Nebraska Penal and Correctional Complex, 442 U.S. 1 (1979), the parole authority must simply review the prisoner's file, give the prisoner an opportunity to be heard, and inform the inmate who is denied parole the reasons that he or she falls short.

4. *Good-time reductions to prison terms.*   Prison officials also have some influence over the length of a prison sentence served. In most states, corrections officials have the power to reduce the sentence by up to one-third the maximum set by the judge or the parole authority. Prison authorities use this discretion to reward good behavior by inmates: the reductions are known as "good time." In the federal system, the maximum such reduction is 15%. The federal government encourages states to keep their good-time discounts below 15% by offering prison funding to states that comply with federal "truth in sentencing" guidelines. Jim Jacobs has pointed out the anomaly of placing legal controls on other sentencing decisions while leaving good-time decisions unregulated. Jacobs, Sentencing by Prison Personnel: Good Time, 30 UCLA L. Rev. 217 (1982). Which institutions would be best suited to create legal constraints on good-time decisions?

2.   *Sentencing Juries*

Juries play a central role in most capital sentencing systems. In a half-dozen states — Arkansas, Kentucky, Missouri, Oklahoma, Texas, and Virginia — juries in some noncapital cases not only rule on guilt or innocence but also decide the sentence to impose. If sentencing is a community judgment, should the community's representatives decide the sentence? Is a judge or legislature or sentencing commission as representative as a sentencing jury? Consider these questions in light of the following Arkansas statutes and the special and intriguing jury sentencing provisions for courts-martial under the Code of Military Justice.

|| *Arkansas Code §16-97-101* ||
Bifurcated Sentencing Procedures

The following procedure shall govern jury trials which include any felony charges:

(1) The jury shall first hear all evidence relevant to every charge on which a defendant is being tried and shall retire to reach a verdict on each charge.

(2) If the defendant is found guilty of one (1) or more charges, the jury shall then hear additional evidence relevant to sentencing on those charges. Evidence introduced in the guilt phase may be considered, but need not be reintroduced at the sentencing phase.

(3) Following the introduction of additional evidence relevant to sentencing, if any, instruction on the law, and argument, the jury shall again retire and determine a sentence within the statutory range.

(4) The court, in its discretion, may also instruct the jury that counsel may argue as to alternative sentences for which the defendant may qualify. The jury, in its discretion, may make a recommendation as to an alternative sentence. However, this recommendation shall not be binding on the court.

(5) After a jury finds guilt, the defendant, with the agreement of the prosecution and the consent of the court, may waive jury sentencing, in which case the court shall impose sentence.

(6) After a plea of guilty, the defendant, with the agreement of the prosecution and the consent of the court, may be sentenced by a jury impaneled for purposes of sentencing only.

|| *Arkansas Code §16-97-103* ||
Evidence

Evidence relevant to sentencing by either the court or a jury may include, but is not limited to, the following, provided no evidence shall be construed under this section as overriding the rape shield statute . . . :

(1) The law applicable to parole, meritorious good time, or transfer;

(2) Prior convictions of the defendant, both felony and misdemeanor. The jury may be advised as to the nature of the previous convictions, the date

and place thereof, the sentence received, and the date of release from confinement or supervision from all prior offenses;

(3) Prior judicial determinations of delinquency in juvenile court, subject to the following limitations:

(i) That prior delinquency adjudications be subject to a judicial determination that the relevant value of the prior juvenile adjudication outweigh its prejudicial value;

(ii) That consideration only be given to juvenile delinquency adjudications for crimes for which the juvenile could have been tried as an adult; and

(iii) That in no event shall delinquency adjudications for acts occurring more than ten (10) years prior to the commission of the offense charged be considered;

(4) Victim impact evidence or statements;

(5) Relevant character evidence;

(6) Evidence of aggravating and mitigating circumstances. The criteria for departure from the sentencing standards may serve as examples of this type of evidence;

(7) Evidence relevant to guilt presented in the first stage;

(8) Evidence held inadmissible in the first stage may be resubmitted for consideration in the second stage if the basis for exclusion did not apply to sentencing; and

(9) Rebuttal evidence.

‖ *Arkansas Code §16-90-107* ‖
Fixing of Punishment Generally

(a) When a jury finds a verdict of guilty and fails to agree on the punishment to be inflicted, or does not declare the punishment in its verdict, or if it assesses a punishment not authorized by law, and in all cases of a judgment on confession, the court shall assess and declare the punishment and render judgment accordingly.

(b) (1) Juries and courts shall have the power to assess the punishment of one convicted of a felony at a general sentence to the penitentiary. The sentence shall not be less than the minimum nor greater than the maximum time provided by law.

(2) At any time after the expiration of the minimum time, upon the recommendation of the superintendent and it appearing that a prisoner has a good record as a convict, his sentence may be terminated by the [parole] board.

(c) If the jury in any case assesses a greater punishment, whether of fine or imprisonment, than the highest limit declared by law for the offense for which they convict the defendant, the court shall disregard the excess and enter judgment and pronounce sentence according to the highest limit prescribed by law in the particular case.

(d) If the jury in any case assesses a punishment, whether of fine or imprisonment, below the limit prescribed by law for offenses of which the defendant is convicted, the court shall render judgment and pronounce sentence according to the lowest limit prescribed by law in such cases.

(e) The court shall have power, in all cases of conviction, to reduce the extent or duration of the punishment assessed by a jury if, in the opinion of the court, the conviction is proper and the punishment assessed is greater than, under the circumstances of the case, ought to be inflicted, so that the punishment is not, in any case, reduced below the limit prescribed by law in such cases.

Manual for Courts-Martial, United States
Exec. Order No. 12,473, 49 Fed. Reg. 17,152
(Apr. 13, 1984)

RULE 1002.   SENTENCE DETERMINATION

Subject to limitations in this Manual, the sentence to be adjudged is a matter within the discretion of the court-martial; except when a mandatory minimum sentence is prescribed by the code, a court-martial may adjudge any punishment authorized in this Manual, including the maximum punishment or any lesser punishment, or may adjudge a sentence of no punishment. . . .

RULE 1006.   DELIBERATIONS AND VOTING ON SENTENCE

(a) In general. The members shall deliberate and vote after the military judge instructs the members on sentence. Only the members shall be present during deliberations and voting. Superiority in rank shall not be used in any manner to control the independence of members in the exercise of their judgment.

(b) Deliberations. Deliberations may properly include full and free discussion of the sentence to be imposed in the case. Unless otherwise directed by the military judge, members may take with them in deliberations their notes, if any, any exhibits admitted in evidence, and any written instructions. Members may request that the court-martial be reopened and that portions of the record be read to them or additional evidence introduced. The military judge may, in the exercise of discretion, grant such requests.

(c) Proposal of sentences. Any member may propose a sentence. Each proposal shall be in writing and shall contain the complete sentence proposed. The junior member shall collect the proposed sentences and submit them to the president.

(d) Voting.

(1) Duty of members. Each member has the duty to vote for a proper sentence for the offenses of which the court-martial found the accused guilty, regardless of the member's vote or opinion as to the guilt of the accused.

(2) Secret ballot. Proposed sentences shall be voted on by secret written ballot.

(3) Procedure.

(A) Order. All members shall vote on each proposed sentence in its entirety beginning with the least severe and continuing, as necessary, with the next least severe, until a sentence is adopted by the concurrence of the number of members required under subsection (d)(4) of this rule. The process of proposing sentences and voting on them may be repeated as necessary until a sentence is adopted.

(B) Counting votes. The junior member shall collect the ballots and count the votes. The president shall check the count and inform the other members of the result.

(4) Number of votes required.

(A) Death. A sentence which includes death may be adjudged only if all members present vote for that sentence.

(B) Confinement for life or more than 10 years. A sentence which includes confinement for life or more than 10 years may be adjudged only if at least three-fourths of the members present vote for that sentence.

(C) Other. A sentence other than those described in subsection (d)(4)(A) or (B) of this rule may be adjudged only if at least two-thirds of the members present vote for that sentence.

(5) Mandatory sentence. When a mandatory minimum is prescribed under Article 118 the members shall vote on a sentence in accordance with this rule.

(6) Effect of failure to agree. If the required number of members do not agree on a sentence after a reasonable effort to do so, a mistrial may be declared as to the sentence and the case shall be returned to the convening authority, who may order a rehearing on sentence only or order that a sentence of no punishment be imposed. . . .

NOTES

1. *Sentencing juries.* As mentioned above, in a half-dozen states juries not only rule on guilt or innocence but can also decide the sentence to impose, even in noncapital cases. In some of these states, the jury's choice is binding. Va. Code Ann. §29.2-295.1 (jury sentences unless "jury cannot agree on a punishment" and defendant, prosecutor, and court agree that the court should determine punishment). In other states, such as Kentucky, "the judge can modify a jury sentence if the jury penalty is unduly harsh." Ky. Rev. Stat. §532.070. In Missouri, the sentencing jury recommends a range for sentencing. Mo. Rev. Stat. §557.036. See also Tex. Crim. Proc. Code Ann. §37.07 (judge can assess punishment if defendant does not request probation or jury sentence; jury must be instructed about parole and other devices for reducing actual amount of prison time offender must serve).

The ABA Standards for Criminal Justice, Sentencing 18-1.4 (3d ed. 1994), calls for the abolition of jury sentencing in noncapital cases. Earlier versions of the ABA standards took the same position, leading to the abolition of jury sentencing in Alabama (in 1977), Indiana (1976), and Montana (1967). Why do the ABA standards, along with the strong majority of the states, give sentencing responsibilities to the judge and not the jury, the representatives of the community? For a proposal to expand the use of jury sentencing, see Jenia Iontcheva, Jury Sentencing as Democratic Practice, 88 Va. L. Rev. 311 (2003).

Even in a system that gives no formal sentencing power to juries, the jury might consider likely punishments as it deliberates on the verdict in the case, and jurors might acquit if they believe the sanction is too severe. See Paul Butler, Racially Based Jury Nullification: Black Power in the Criminal Justice System, 105 Yale L.J. 677 (1995). As defense counsel, would you recommend that your client choose jury sentencing? If so, for what types of cases?

Interestingly, although sentencing juries are the exception in noncapital cases, they are the norm in death penalty cases. Is there a principled reason for juries to have a central role in capital sentencing systems but little or no role in noncapital sentencing systems? The role of the jury in sentencing systems is explored more fully in Chapters 3 and 6.

2. *Jury sentencing and disparity.*   One of the most significant concerns about jury sentencing in noncapital cases (and in capital cases as well) is that different juries might impose significantly different sentences in similar cases. Another source of potential disparity is the difference between judge and jury sentencing choices in states that give the defendant the option of jury or judge sentencing, such as Arkansas (see above) or Missouri (defendant must request in writing before voir dire that the judge assess the punishment in the case of a finding of guilt). Very little is known about whether jury sentencing in fact produces greater disparity. See Adriaan Lanni, Jury Sentencing in Non-Capital Cases: An Idea Whose Time Has Come (Again)?, 108 Yale L.J. 1775 (1999). Effectively allocating scarce punishment resources, another systematic concern of modern reformers, may also be difficult for juries to assess. Perhaps the several states that allow judges to reduce (but not increase) jury sentences, or that allow juries to recommend sentencing ranges, accommodate both the virtues of a jury's sentencing judgment and more systematic concerns.

Is sentencing an "expert" function? Is the expertise the product of sentencing experience, or life experience, or something else? If sentencing is appropriately a judicial function, does that function have constitutional foundations? See Mistretta v. United States, 488 U.S. 361 (1989). Can—and should—legislatures (or commissions) remove most, or all, sentencing discretion? See Nancy J. King & Rosevelt L. Noble, Felony Jury Sentencing in Practice: A Three-State Study, 57 Vand. L. Rev. 885 (2004) (arguing that juries cannot properly reflect community sentiment about the severity of sentences because juries do not have the range of information and sentencing options available to sentencing judges).

3. *Code of Military Justice and non-unanimous sentences.*   Should the sentencing jury be required to vote unanimously for a particular sentence? Should its voting rules be the same as the rules for its vote on guilt versus innocence? Recall that in the Manual for Courts-Martial, Rule 1006(c) and (d), members of the court-martial panel propose sentences, and the panel must consider each proposed sentence from least severe to most severe, with the necessary voting requirements turning on the nature of the sentence. How much less protection is provided to defendants by allowing for confinement for more than ten years subject to approval by three-fourths of the jury members? What aspects of the

military, if any, might justify the use of sentencing juries in courts-martial as distinguished from regular state felony juries?

B. LEGISLATURES AND COMMISSIONS

Although indeterminate sentencing was the norm in this country for most of the twentieth century, new arrangements have emerged over the past generation. Some of those alternative approaches put the legislature more firmly in control of sentencing. Legislators have decided for themselves the precise sentences that will attach to various types of offenses; other sentencing institutions such as courts are supposed to carry out the instructions of the legislature without adding any meaningful input of their own. For instance, under 18 U.S.C. §924(c), any person who "uses or carries" a firearm during any federal drug trafficking crime "shall, in addition to the punishment provided for [the] drug trafficking crime . . . be sentenced to a term of imprisonment of not less than 5 years [and] if the firearm is brandished, be sentenced to a term of imprisonment of not less than 7 years; and . . . if the firearm is discharged, be sentenced to a term of imprisonment of not less than 10 years."

Sentences dominated by legislative choices go back to some of the earliest recorded sources of law, including the Code of Hammurabi, excerpted below. This code reflects a society very different from our own; would a review of our current statutes on criminal punishments create a fairly accurate portrait of our own times?

‖ *Code of Hammurabi* ‖
(C. H. W. Johns trans., 1911)

§1: If a man weave a spell and put a ban upon a man, and has not justified himself, he that wove the spell upon him shall be put to death.

§8: If a man has stolen ox or sheep or ass, or pig, or ship, whether from the temple or the palace, he shall pay thirtyfold. If he be a poor man, he shall render tenfold. If the thief has naught to pay, he shall be put to death.

§195: If a man has struck his father, his hands one shall cut off.

§196: If a man has caused the loss of a gentleman's eye, his eye one shall cause to be lost.

§197: If he has shattered a gentleman's limb, one shall shatter his limb.

§198: If he has caused a poor man to lose his eye or shattered a poor man's limb, he shall pay one mina of silver.

§209: If a man has struck a gentleman's daughter and caused her to drop what is in her womb, he shall pay ten shekels of silver for what was in her womb.

§210: If that woman has died, one shall put to death his daughter.

§211: If the daughter of a poor man through his blows he has caused to drop that which is in her womb, he shall pay five shekels of silver.

§212: If that woman has died, he shall pay half a mina of silver.

	Mandatory Minimum Penalties in the	
	Federal Criminal Justice System	
	U.S. Sentencing Commission, pp. 5-15, 27-32 (1991)	

Mandatory minimum sentences are not new to the federal criminal justice system. As early as 1790, mandatory penalties had been established for capital offenses. In addition, at subsequent intervals throughout the 19th Century, Congress enacted provisions that required definite prison terms, typically quite short, for a variety of other crimes. Until recently, however, the enactment of mandatory minimum provisions was generally an occasional phenomenon that was not comprehensively aimed at whole classes of offenses.

A change in practice occurred with the passage of the Narcotic Control Act of 1956, which mandated minimum sentences of considerable length for most drug importation and distribution offenses. . . . In 1970, Congress drew back from the comprehensive application of mandatory minimum provisions to drug crimes enacted 14 years earlier. Finding that increases in sentence length "had not shown the expected overall reduction in drug law violations," Congress passed [legislation] that repealed virtually all mandatory penalties for drug violations.

[Growing criticism of efforts to rehabilitate inmates led lawmakers] to renew support for mandatory minimum penalties. On the state level this trend began in New York in 1973, with California and Massachusetts following soon thereafter. While the trend toward mandatory minimums in the states was gradual, by 1983, 49 of the 50 states had passed such provisions. . . . On the federal level, a comparable but more comprehensive trend was underway. Beginning in 1984, and every two years thereafter, Congress enacted an array of mandatory minimum penalties specifically targeted at drugs and violent crime. . . . Today there are approximately 100 separate federal mandatory minimum penalty provisions located in 60 different criminal statutes. . . . Of the 59,780 cases sentenced under mandatory minimum statutes [between 1984 and 1990], four statutes account for approximately 94 percent of the cases. These four statutes . . . all involve drugs and weapons violations. . . .

REASONS CITED IN SUPPORT OF MANDATORY MINIMUMS

[Field interviews with] judges, assistant United States attorneys, defense attorneys, and probation officers . . . identified six commonly-offered rationales for mandatory minimum sentencing provisions.

Retribution or "Just Deserts."   Perhaps the most commonly-voiced goal of mandatory minimum penalties is the "justness" of long prison terms for particularly serious offenses. Proponents generally agree that longer sentences are deserved and that, absent mandatory penalties, judges would impose sentences more lenient than would be appropriate.

Deterrence.   . . . Those supporting mandatory minimums on deterrence grounds point not only to the strong deterrent value of the *certainty* of substantial punishment these penalties are intended to provide, but also to the deterrent value of sentence *severity* that these penalties are intended to ensure in the war against crime.

Incapacitation, Especially of the Serious Offender. Mandating increased sentence severity aims to protect the public by incapacitating offenders convicted of serious crimes for definite, and generally substantial, periods of time. Proponents argue that one way to increase public safety, particularly with respect to guns and drugs, is to remove drug dealers and violent offenders from the streets for extended periods of time.

Disparity. Indeterminate sentencing systems permit substantial latitude in setting the sentence, which in turn can mean that defendants convicted of the same offense are sentenced to widely disparate sentences. Supporters of mandatory minimum penalties contend that they greatly reduce judicial discretion and are therefore more fair. Mandatory minimums are meant to ensure that defendants convicted of similar offenses receive penalties that at least begin at the same minimal point.

Inducement of Cooperation. Because they provide specific lengthy sentences, mandatory minimums encourage offenders to assist in the investigation of criminal conduct by others. This is because cooperation — that is, supplying information concerning the activities of other criminally involved individuals — is the only statutorily-recognized way to permit the court to impose a sentence below the length of imprisonment required by the mandatory minimum sentence.

Inducement of Pleas. Although infrequently cited by policymakers, prosecutors express the view that mandatory minimum sentences can be valuable tools in obtaining guilty pleas, saving scarce enforcement resources and increasing the certainty of at least some measure of punishment. In this context, the value of a mandatory minimum sentence lies not in its imposition, but in its value as a bargaining chip to be given away in return for the resource-saving plea from the defendant to a more leniently sanctioned charge.

[Now we turn to some of the criticisms of mandatory minimum sentences.]

THE "TARIFF" EFFECT OF MANDATORY MINIMUMS

Years ago, Congress used tariff sentences in sanctioning broad categories of offenses, ranging from quite serious crimes (e.g., homicide) to fairly minor property theft. This tariff approach has been rejected historically primarily because there were too many defendants whose important distinctions were obscured by this single, flat approach to sentencing. A more sophisticated, calibrated approach that takes into account gradations of offense seriousness, criminal record, and level of culpability has long since been recognized as a more appropriate and equitable method of sentencing. . . .

The mandatory minimums set forth in 21 U.S.C. §841(b), applicable to defendants convicted of trafficking in the more common street drugs, are illustrative. For those convicted of drug trafficking under this section, one offense-related factor, and only one, is determinative of whether the mandatory minimum applies: the weight of the drug or drug mixture. Any other sentence-individualizing factors that might pertain in a case are irrelevant as far as the statute is concerned. Thus, for example, whether the defendant was a peripheral participant or the drug ring's kingpin, whether the defendant used a weapon, whether the defendant accepted responsibility or, on the other hand, obstructed justice, have no bearing on the mandatory minimum to which each defendant is exposed. . . .

THE "CLIFF" EFFECT OF MANDATORY MINIMUMS

Related to the proportionality problems posed in mandatory minimums already described are the sharp differences in sentence between defendants who fall just below the threshold of a mandatory minimum compared with those whose criminal conduct just meets the criteria of the mandatory minimum penalty. Just as mandatory minimums fail to distinguish among defendants whose conduct and prior records in fact differ markedly, they distinguish far too greatly among defendants who have committed offense conduct of highly comparable seriousness.

[A] lack of coordination between statutory maximum and mandatory minimum penalties for the same or similar offenses can create dramatic sentencing cliffs among similarly-situated defendants. For example, 21 U.S.C. §884 mandates a minimum five-year term of imprisonment for a defendant convicted of first-offense, simple possession of 5.01 or more grams of "crack." . . . However, a first-offender convicted of simple possession of 5.0 grams of crack is subjected to a *maximum* statutory penalty of one year imprisonment. . . .

THE "CHARGE-SPECIFIC" NATURE OF MANDATORY MINIMUMS

. . . In general, a mandatory minimum becomes applicable only when the prosecutor elects to *charge* and the defendant is *convicted* of the specific offense carrying the mandatory sentence. . . . Mandatory minimums employ a structure that allows a shifting of discretion and control over the implementation of sentencing policies from courts to prosecutors. [There] is substantial reason to believe that mandatory minimums are not in fact pursued by prosecutors in all instances that the underlying statutes otherwise would require. . . .

PROBLEM 2-4.   LETTER FROM A CONGRESSMAN

A panel of the U.S. Court of Appeals for the Seventh Circuit issued an opinion stating that a 97-month sentence imposed on a drug dealer was contrary to statute, because the defendant was convicted under a statute calling for a 120-month mandatory minimum sentence. Nevertheless, the panel allowed the sentence to stand because the government did not appeal this aspect of the sentence.

News of this judicial opinion reached Rep. James Sensenbrenner, the chair of the House Judiciary Committee. Sensenbrenner immediately wrote letters about the case to the chief judge of the Seventh Circuit and to the attorney general. In his letter to attorney general, Sensenbrenner demanded that the Department of Justice file any available appeals in the case. In the letter to the chief judge, Sensenbrenner demanded "a prompt response" about what steps the judge would take "to rectify the panel's actions" in the case. He believed that the government's failure to appeal was not a sufficient reason to allow the reduced sentence to stand, and asked "that all necessary and appropriate measures be taken, whether by members of the panel and/or by the other judges of the court" to ensure that the higher sentence would be imposed in this case. See Maurice Possley, Lawmaker Prods Court, Raises Brows, Chi. Trib., July 10, 2005.

Does this letter qualify as legitimate "oversight" of the judiciary by a committee of Congress? Does it violate separation of powers principles? If there is a problem with sending a letter of this sort to judges, what can a member of Congress do about cases that appear to misapply a mandatory minimum sentencing law?

NOTES

1. *Judicial discretion and mandatory penalties.*   Many criticisms of mandatory minimum statutes focus on the loss of judicial discretion in sentencing. Consider, for example, the 1970 statement of then Representative George H.W. Bush:

> Federal judges are almost unanimously opposed to mandatory minimums, because they remove a great deal of the court's discretion. In the vast majority of cases which reach the sanctioning stage today, the bare minimum sentence is levied — and in some cases, less than the minimum mandatory is given. . . . - Probations and outright dismissals often result. Philosophical differences aside, practicality requires a sentence structure which is generally acceptable to the courts, to prosecutors, and to the general public.

116 Cong. Rec. H33314, Sept. 23, 1970. Many state and federal judges share these views and believe that mandatory minimum statutes too often force them to impose a fundamentally unjust sentence. In a 2003 survey of federal judges, most of the judges believed that mandatory minimum punishments had a negative effect on their ability to "impose sentences that reflect the statutory purposes of sentencing." See Survey of Article III Judges on the Federal Sentencing Guidelines, http://www.ussc.gov/judsurv/judsurv.htm. Are all mandatory minimums subject to the criticisms about uneven enforcement and loss of judicial discretion? Could a legislature address these problems by narrowly defining the offenses and offenders eligible for a mandatory sentence?

Can any decision maker other than a judge — who decides many individual cases — appreciate the facts about an offender's past that should lead to a lighter sentence? Why might judges impose sentences lighter than those set by the

legislature? Do judges generally share a different political view on crime control?
Do they see too many individual cases?

2. *Mandatory mandatories.*   Most mandatory minimum statutes instruct the
judge to impose a particular sentence for a particular charge, but they do not
require the prosecutor to file a given charge when adequate facts are present.
Thus, typical mandatory sentencing statutes give prosecutors considerable bargaining power during plea negotiations; they also offer prosecutors opportunities to avoid mandatory minimum sentences when they believe that such
sentences would be unjust or a poor use of resources. Stephen Schulhofer
and Ilene Nagel surveyed charging practices and concluded that prosecutors'
concerns about mandatory minimum sentences led them in a substantial
number of cases to charge some lesser crime even though the evidence was
available to charge for the mandatory minimum crime. Schulhofer & Nagel,
A Tale of Three Cities: An Empirical Study of Charging and Bargaining Practices
Under the Federal Sentencing Guidelines, 66 S. Cal. L. Rev. 501 (1992).

Legislatures sometimes constrain this prosecutorial power by passing statutes that prevent plea bargaining and require the prosecutor to file charges
whenever adequate evidence is available. For instance, in 1973 New York passed
a "Rockefeller drug law" imposing severe mandatory minimums and restricting
plea bargaining. After passage of this law, there were fewer arrests, indictments,
and convictions for drug offenses, but those convicted served longer terms.
Jacqueline Cohen & Michael Tonry, Sentencing Reforms and the Impacts, in
Research on Sentencing: The Search for Reform 348-349 (Alfred Blumstein et
al. eds., 1983). This sort of "mandatory mandatory" statute is rare. Why do
legislators hesitate to pass statutes that remove the prosecutor's discretion to
decline charges or to select a charge not subject to the minimum penalty?

3. *Net effects of mandatory minimum penalties on sentencing patterns.*   Studies of
mandatory minimum penalties have reached different conclusions about the
effect of these laws on the crime rates for the targeted offenses. Some studies
have found a deterrent effect for gun crimes and homicides, but other studies
have found no effect on the commission of drug crimes or violent crimes generally. The effects of mandatory minimum penalties on the criminal justice
system are clearer. These laws consistently lead to fewer arrests for the designated crimes, fewer charges filed, more dismissals of charges, more trials rather
than guilty pleas, and longer sentences imposed and served. See Dale Parent,
Terence Dunworth, Douglas McDonald & William Rhodes, Key Legislative
Issues in Criminal Justice: Mandatory Sentencing (National Institute of Justice,
Research in Action, NCJ 161839, Jan. 1997).

4. *Self-correcting democratic process.*   If mandatory minimum sentences truly
produced the ill effects described by critics, wouldn't the democratically elected
legislature recognize these flaws after a time and abandon the experiment? This
has happened in a few states. In 2001 the Connecticut legislature granted judges
authority to depart from mandatory minimum sentences for certain drug
crimes, such as first-time sales or possession within 1,500 feet of a school. Also
that year, Indiana eliminated mandatory 20-year sentences for cocaine dealers
(anyone caught with more than three grams of powder cocaine), and Louisiana
repealed mandatory sentences for some simple possession and other nonviolent

drug offenses. Meanwhile, other jurisdictions, such as New York, have debated for years about changing mandatory minimum drug sentences, without ever taking significant action. See Ronald F. Wright, Are the Drug Wars De-escalating? Where to Look for Evidence, 14 Fed. Sent'g Rep. 141 (2002). What might prevent the legislature from rethinking self-destructive legislation? Who brings information to the legislators' attention as they debate proposals or create an agenda? Is the problem a lack of information, a lack of time, or something else?

Legislatures in just under half of the states have empowered permanent "sentencing commissions" to create rules to guide judges as they select sentences within the statutory range. These guidelines (some embodied in statutes and others in administrative rules) are different from statutory maximum and minimum punishments because they allow judges, under some circumstances, to go above or below the recommended range so long as the final sentence remains within the statutorily authorized range.

Legislatures typically create sentencing commissions after other institutions fail. Judges, executive branch officials, and legislators have failed in predictable patterns over the years when they have tried to change or administer sentencing policy. You might think of these patterns of institutional failure as "pathologies," or deviations from the more ordinary and effective functions of these governmental institutions.

Judicial Pathologies.   Judges create two sorts of difficulties in the sentencing system, both arising because judges sentence individually rather than as a coordinated group. First, different judges sometimes give disparate sentences to offenders who, in every relevant way, seem to be alike. Second, sentencing judges do not conserve corrections resources. There are a fixed number of prison beds and slots in corrections programs, yet a judge has little incentive to use only her proportional share of this "public good."

A sentencing commission is one potential solution to both problems. A commission could reduce disparity by designating, within narrow boundaries, the "ordinary" sentences for particular types of offenses and offenders. A commission could also designate ordinary sentences at a level not likely to overburden the corrections system.

Executive Pathologies.   Some executive branch pathologies in sentencing are made possible because parole release decisions are not easily visible to the public. The parole decision receives less attention than the sentence itself, and it is made by an executive official who, unlike many state court judges, is not directly accountable to the voters.

The difficulties with low-visibility release decisions correspond to the classic objections to all low-visibility discretionary decisions: they may not be based on consistent or proper reasons. The release date may depend on no articulable principles at all, or it may depend on the personal views of the executive officer involved rather than on principles endorsed by the public. Sentencing commissions offer one way to make release decisions more visible and consistent. Under a guideline system, the release date turns on principles adopted through a public process, as applied and announced by a publicly accountable government official, the judge.

Legislative Pathologies.   Legislators make their own pathological contributions to sentencing policy. But the accounts of exactly how the legislature does so are not altogether consistent. According to some accounts, legislatures need to delegate sentencing authority to a permanent commission because they do not have enough time or expertise to make proper changes in sentencing laws. The complexity of sentencing issues makes it difficult, during the limited time available, for the legislators and their staffs to acquire the necessary information to make wise choices.

Other critics of the legislative role in sentencing argue that the legislature spends far too *much* time dealing with sentencing. Legislators, according to this view, pander to the perceived passions and frustrations of their constituents about crime; they pass laws that prove later to be expensive, ineffectual, and cruel. Periodic tinkering by the legislature creates an inconsistent sentencing scheme, riddled with exceptions. According to these critics, the legislature has more difficulty dealing rationally with crime than with most other subjects.

Just as the descriptions of legislative pathologies are not entirely consistent, the prescriptions for a commission's proper response to the legislative pathologies are in some tension with each other. Under one model, the ideal commission strategy is to minimize legislative involvement in criminal punishment issues. A successful system, in this view, will reduce the legislators' opportunities to interfere with the judgment of the expert members and staff of the commission. The commission will anticipate and deal with any criminal justice crises that could provoke the legislature to take action. Under a second model, the sentencing commission merely attempts to improve legislative deliberation about criminal legislation. The commission can inform the legislators about the consequences (especially the fiscal consequences) of different bills, and it can advocate consistency and rationality in sentencing.

The following materials highlight the different roles that sentencing commissions and sentencing guidelines play in a jurisdiction. They also point out how commissions, when they arrive on the scene, can change the established roles among the existing sentencing institutions in the jurisdiction.

ABA Standards for Criminal Justice, Sentencing 18-4.1
(3d ed. 1994)

(a) Implementation of legislative policy determinations within the statutory framework of the criminal code requires a state-wide agency to develop a more specific set of provisions that guide sentencing courts to presumptive sentences and in the appropriate use of aggravating and mitigating factors, offenders' criminal history, and offenders' personal characteristics. . . .

(b) The agency performing the intermediate function should be the information center for all elements of the criminal justice system. The agency should collect, analyze and disseminate information on the nature and effects of sentences imposed and carried out. The agency should develop means to monitor, evaluate, and predict patterns of sentencing, including levels of severity of sentences imposed and relative use of each type of sanction. . . .

Commentary. This standard gives definition to the concept of the "intermediate function" in sentencing systems. This term [describes] the work done "in between" the legislature's statutory commands and the case-by-case decisions of sentencing judges. Every jurisdiction should create a permanently chartered agency to perform the intermediate function, either in the form of a sentencing commission or an equivalent body in the legislative or judicial branch. . . .

Typically, statutory maxima are set at high levels so that the range of statutorily authorized penalties is wide indeed. One critical function of the sentencing agency, as intermediary between legislature and the courts, is to give structure to the decision-making process for selecting particular sentences within the expansive range allowed by the code.

The agency performs this role through the creation of presumptive sentences and other provisions for the guidance of sentencing judges, including provisions relating to aggravating and mitigating circumstances, and the effect of offenders' prior criminal histories and personal characteristics. Through such measures, courts across the jurisdiction can approach sentencing decisions from a common baseline and can employ similar steps of logic and analysis in adjusting sentences away from the presumptive baseline when required. . . .

Modeling Discretion in American Sentencing Systems, Kevin Reitz
20 Law & Pol'y 389 (1998)

. . . I have found it helpful to think in pictorial terms about an array of actors in sentencing systems who potentially have sentencing discretion. A generic "discretion diagram," such as that reproduced in Figure 1, can be used to visualize many of the important relationships in existing punishment systems.

[One] function of Figure 1 is to recognize that some discretionary actors operate primarily on the "systemic level" while others discharge their authorities primarily on the "case-specific level." . . . Systemic actors make discretionary decisions intended to influence whole categories of cases; case-specific actors make discretionary judgments that, for the most part, operate on the individual cases before them. . . .

Indeterminate Sentencing Systems

. . . Indeterminate schemes, still in effect in roughly half of the American states, are represented . . . in Figure 3. . . .

A number of the distinctive features of indeterminacy jump out from Figure 3. . . . First, the shrunken compartment for the legislature in Figure 3 indicates the very loose statutory boundaries upon punishment outcomes that

FIGURE 1
A Discretion Diagram for Sentencing Systems

Systemic Level

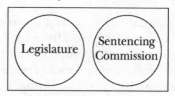

Case-Specific Level

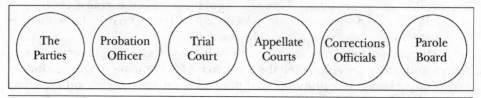

generally exist in the traditional systems. It would not be unusual in an indeterminate jurisdiction, for example, to find that the legislatively authorized sanction for a crime such as aggravated assault reaches as low as a suspended sentence without conditions, up to a term of incarceration in the ballpark of thirty-two years. . . .

FIGURE 3
A Discretion Diagram of Indeterminate Sentencing

Systemic Level

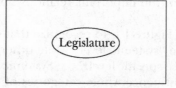

Case-Specific Level

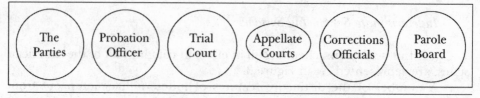

The second defining characteristic of indeterminate structures is their diffusion of meaningful sentencing discretion across numerous actors at the case-specific level. Prosecutors most of the time enjoy unregulated charging discretion; plea bargains between the parties (sometimes including sentence bargains) can have sizable impact on punishment; probation officers, at least in some jurisdictions, make sentence recommendations that are highly influential with judges; the judges themselves usually have a boggling array of choices remaining open to them on the day of sentencing; and following a judicially pronounced prison sentence, correctional officials and parole boards hold impressive powers to fix actual release dates — which can sometimes be set after only a small fraction of the court's sentence has been served.

The only case-specific actor without meaningful sentencing discretion in traditional indeterminate systems, as it turns out, is the appellate judiciary. For reasons of historical practice, deference to trial courts, and caseload pressures, appellate courts almost universally have resisted responsibility to participate in sentencing outcomes. . . .

THE FEDERAL SYSTEM

The most salient discretionary feature of the U.S. sentencing system, especially in comparison with its state counterparts, is the federal system's attempt to concentrate discretionary authority at the systemic level and to constrain such authority at the case-specific level. . . . In comparison with the weak legislative presence in indeterminate sentencing structures, Congress made itself an important discretionary actor in the new federal scheme. Through its many mandatory sentencing laws, and through oversight of the U.S. Sentencing Commission, Congress has assumed and held a major role in the ongoing determination of sentencing outcomes.

More distinctive than the enlargement of the legislative role, however, has been the great measure of authority granted to or assumed by the U.S. Sentencing Commission vis-à-vis downstream players in the sentencing system. [The] federal commission was introduced as a new and authoritative actor, absorbing important discretions that formerly were exercised by other decision makers. . . .

The systemic power wielded by the U.S. commission was compounded by the fact that, when creating the federal guidelines system, Congress abolished parole release and imposed sharp limits on the amount of good-time credit that may be awarded federal prisoners. . . . Thus, the commission's discretion to say what a sentence should be in a particular case could be overruled infrequently by a trial judge, and was subject only to minor adjustment at the "back door" of the incarceration process. . . .

PENNSYLVANIA

While the federal sentencing system may be seen primarily as an attempt to concentrate authority at the systemic level, the Pennsylvania guidelines structure is distinguished by its very weak exertions of systemwide control over punishment decisions. . . . In comparison with the detailed legislative mandate enacted

FIGURE 5
A Discretionary Diagram of the Pennsylvania System

Systemic Level

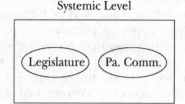

Case-Specific Level

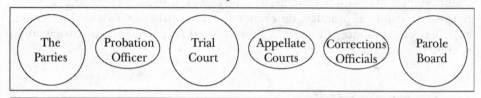

by Congress for the new federal structure, the Pennsylvania legislature authored a cryptic and open-ended scheme. Notably, the state legislature described the guidelines to be created by the commission as one factor among many, or as merely "considerations," for trial courts to weigh when imposing sentences. . . .

In Pennsylvania, as it turned out, the most important structural decisions about the apportionment of sentencing discretion were made by the state's appellate courts. . . . By the late 1980s, the state supreme court ruled that the new guidelines were only "advisory," that the legislature had required no more than that trial courts "take notice of" the commission's work before choosing a sentence, and that reviewing courts had no power to hear appeals based on the claim that the guidelines had not been followed, except in "exceptional cases." The discretionary implications of these decisions are pictured in Figure 5. . . .

The result, in Pennsylvania, has been to privilege trial court discretion while leaving the parties' plea negotiation powers unregulated. In these terms, Figure 5 still resembles the traditional indeterminate sentencing structure that preceded the Pennsylvania guidelines. No one is in charge at the systemic level; nearly all meaningful sentencing authority has settled down to the case-specific level. [The] discretionary patterns of the Pennsylvania system [reminds us that] not all guideline structures are created equal. With respect to one critical variable — the degree of systemwide control attempted in each structure — the [federal and Pennsylvania guidelines] could hardly be more different. . . .

NOTES

1. *Where's the jury?* One of the notable aspects of Professor Reitz's sentencing diagrams is the absence of any "bubbles" for juries. Professor Reitz's article was authored in the late 1990s, before the Supreme Court started to give

attention to the jury's role in sentencing determinations through the *Apprendi-Blakely* line of cases (which is discussed fully in Chapter 6).

2. *Reasons to create sentencing commissions and guidelines.* Almost half the states use sentencing guidelines created by sentencing commissions. The federal system also operates under sentencing guidelines, created in 1987 by the U.S. Sentencing Commission. A state sentencing commission typically drafts the initial set of guidelines on behalf of the legislature, which then enacts an integrated package of sentencing reforms. In states without a commission, the state judiciary adopts a package of guidelines as procedural rules or as informal guidance to judges.

Why would a legislature ask a commission to create a set of sentencing guidelines? Does a commission have any advantages over a legislature in setting specific sentencing ranges for particular types of offenses and offenders? Legislatures turn to commissions when the legislators recognize that they do not have enough time or expertise themselves to do the job well. Political theory also suggests some less noble motives that might lead legislators to deal with criminal sentencing through a commission. When it comes to statutes involving criminal punishments, legislators often have political incentives to advocate severe punishment so that they can be seen as tough on crime. Stiff penalties may be appropriate for the extreme cases that dominate legislative debates; a wide definition of the crime will include both the imagined and the as-yet-unimagined evils.

At the same time, legislators want to avoid blame for the costs of criminal punishments. They would rather leave it to prosecutors to weigh the human costs of unnecessarily strong punishments, since prosecutors can decline prosecution when justice requires it. And they might prefer some other institution, such as a sentencing commission, to make the hard decisions about how to economize on the limited prison and corrections resources available.

Very few jurisdictions outside the United States have created bodies such as sentencing commissions to serve an intermediate function between the legislature and the judges. If sentencing commissions are a good idea, why do we not see them in other places in the world?

3. *Research instead of rules.* Most guidelines created by commissions are, to some degree or another, presumptive. That is, a judge who sentences outside the presumed range for sentences risks reversal. Are presumptive sentencing rules, created by commissions and approved by legislatures, subject to the same criticisms leveled against legislatively determined sentences? Would sentencing commissions be more valuable if they limited their recommendations to the most commonly encountered "paradigm" cases for sentencing and conducted research into the effects of various types of sanctions? Is lack of knowledge a more pressing concern than lack of uniformity among sentencing judges? See Albert Alschuler, The Failure of Sentencing Guidelines: A Plea for Less Aggregation, 58 U. Chi. L. Rev. 901 (1991).

4. *Sentencing commissions coming and going.* Sentencing commissions (along with parole boards) are one of the few sentencing actors that can come and go. A number of states have never established sentencing commissions, and a few states eliminated or restructured their sentencing commissions after they were in operation only a short period of time. Interestingly, in 2004

the New Jersey legislature created the New Jersey Commission to Review Criminal Sentencing, but only on a temporary basis. As its term was coming to a close in summer 2006, this commission issued a report discussing the need for and importance of a permanent sentencing commission in the state. Here is part of its pitch:

> To continue its work and replicate the more ambitious initiatives now undertaken by more established sentencing commissions elsewhere, the Commission requires only a modest increase in funding. Moreover, a permanent sentencing commission, with clear, statutory authorization, is much better positioned to acquire assistance from federal and philanthropic organizations concerned with promoting rational sentencing policy. Simply stated, the prospect of securing such funding is contingent upon a showing of clear and unambiguous support for the Commission by both the Governor and the Legislature expressed through enactment of pending legislation to establish a permanent sentencing commission.

New Jersey Commission to Review Criminal Sentencing, Sentencing in the 21st Century and the Necessity of a Permanent Sentencing Commission in New Jersey (June 2006). Is it unseemly, or entirely appropriate, for a sentencing commission to be writing reports to justify its continued existence?

   5. *Sentencing information systems.*   Are there ways of achieving the goal of reasonable uniformity other than the issuance of detailed rules, whether by courts or sentencing commissions? One idea that has been explored in Scotland and South Australia—but has yet to be applied in the United States—is the creation of "information systems" that will let judges and lawyers know what sentences were imposed in "similar" cases (with great attention to what makes a case "similar"). See Marc Miller & Ronald Wright, The Wisdom We Have Lost: Sentencing Information and Its Uses, 58 Stan. L. Rev. 361 (2005); Marc Miller, A Map of Sentencing and a Compass for Judges: Sentencing Information Systems, Transparency, and the Next Generation of Reform, 105 Colum. L. Rev. 1351 (2005); Marc Miller, Sentencing "Reform Reform" Through Sentencing Information Systems, in The Future of Imprisonment 121-153(Michael Tonry ed., Oxford University Press 2004) (essays in honor of Norval Morris).

C.   PROSECUTORS

   Just as they are central to most other aspects of criminal justice, prosecutors are central to sentencing. Prosecutors select the charges that define the outer statutory boundaries for the sentence. Because criminal codes in the United States are typically stuffed with different crimes covering similar conduct, and specific crimes are often defined with broad terms that could cover a wide range of behavior, the prosecutor normally has a number of legal options that could plausibly fit the facts as alleged. Some crimes include mandatory sentences, and in some systems prosecutors can specify particular aggravating factors with dramatic sentencing implications.

   The prosecutor also can negotiate a plea agreement with the defendant. Defendants pleading guilty tend to receive substantially lower sentences than defendants who go to trial (in some studies the "plea discount" has been one-third or more off post-trial sentences), but judges tend to sentence based on the original charges filed rather than the charges forming the basis of the guilty plea. And the prosecutor often recommends a particular sentence to the judge—a recommendation that carries great weight, especially in high-volume courtrooms, where the judges and probation officers must depend heavily on the parties to inform them about each case.

Under these conditions, prosecutors have substantial and often determinative sentencing power. Do effective controls exist to prevent an individual prosecutor from misusing this power? As the materials below indicate, such controls are not likely to come from the judiciary, because judges are extremely reluctant to review the merits of prosecutorial charging decisions. The study of the prosecutor's office in New Orleans excerpted below raises the possibility of effective controls over individual prosecutors originating internally, from the prosecutor's office itself.

|| *People v. Wayne Robert Stewart* ||
|| 55 P.3d 107 (Colo. 2002) ||

MULLARKEY, C.J.

. . . The crimes occurred on a Sunday evening in March 1997 when Wayne Stewart left the bar of a restaurant located in a suburban shopping center. As Stewart began to drive his sports utility vehicle out of the shopping center parking lot, he encountered three pedestrians—Richard Ehrmann, Christine Castro, and Jeffrey Pippenger, in that order—walking abreast in the middle of the driving lane. The pedestrians had just left a video rental store and, as they walked to their vehicle, they were looking up at the Hale Bopp comet streaking across the sky. The testimony of disinterested bystanders established that Stewart veered toward the pedestrians at an angle; Ehrmann, who was closest to the traffic lane, was brushed by Stewart's vehicle. A verbal altercation ensued, after which Stewart began driving back and forth at an angle and in an aggressive manner. [Stewart's car hit Ehrmann, and when the car abruptly stopped, Ehrmann rolled off the hood and landed hard on the ground next to the driver's side. The SUV continued to roll forward, and the rear wheel on the driver's side ran over Ehrmann's head.] Stewart left the scene without stopping. As a result of the incident, Ehrmann suffered massive brain injury and lay comatose for approximately two and one-half years. Ultimately, the victim died.

The state charged Stewart with one count of first degree assault against Ehrmann, a class 3 felony in violation of section 18-3-202(1)(a); one count of reckless second degree assault against Ehrmann, a class 4 felony, in violation of §18-3-203(1)(d); four counts of violent crime, pursuant to §16-11-309; one count of vehicular assault against Ehrmann, a class 5 felony, in violation of §18-3-205(1)(a); and four counts of reckless endangerment against the other two pedestrians and two bystanders, a class 3 misdemeanor, in violation of §18-3-208. Stewart pleaded not guilty to the charges.

At trial, the People contended that Stewart intentionally hit Ehrmann or, in the alternative, that Stewart used his vehicle to scare and intimidate Ehrmann. Stewart took the position . . . that Ehrmann jumped onto [the hood of] Stewart's vehicle and that he was unaware that he ran over Ehrmann. . . .

A jury convicted Stewart of reckless second degree assault of Ehrmann and two counts of reckless endangerment against the other two pedestrians. At the sentencing hearing, the trial court found that Stewart "did drive his car at Mr. Ehrmann in an act of anger," and sentenced Stewart to five years in the Department of Corrections for the second degree assault conviction. . . .

Stewart argues that his conviction for reckless second degree assault with a deadly weapon violates his right to equal protection because the statutes governing vehicular assault and reckless second degree assault with a deadly weapon proscribe the same conduct but mete out disparate punishments. He asserts that there is no rational distinction between second degree reckless assault, a class 4 felony requiring mandatory sentencing for a term of five to sixteen years, and vehicular assault, a class 5 felony that is punishable by one to three years of imprisonment in the presumptive range and two to six years in the aggravated range, and which neither requires a mandatory sentence nor precludes probation. The lack of any rational basis for distinguishing the two offenses, he maintains, coupled with the significant difference in penalty, renders his conviction of second degree assault violative of equal protection by penalizing him more severely for the identical criminal conduct proscribed by the lesser offense of vehicular assault. We disagree.

The Fourteenth Amendment to the United States Constitution provides in part that no state "shall deny to any person within its jurisdiction the equal protection of the laws." A similar guarantee is implicit in the due process clause of the Colorado Constitution. Colo. Const., art. II, §25. Colorado, however, has taken a stricter view of the protections afforded by our equal protection guarantee than has the United States Supreme Court in interpreting the federal Constitution. The Supreme Court has held that equal protection is not offended when statutes proscribe identical conduct but authorize different penalties. United States v. Batchelder, 442 U.S. 114 (1979).

By contrast, we have consistently held that if a criminal statute proscribes different penalties for identical conduct, a person convicted under the harsher penalty is denied equal protection unless there are reasonable differences or distinctions between the proscribed behavior. The statutory classification of crimes must be based on differences that are both real in fact and also reasonably related to the general purposes of the criminal legislation.

Equally well established is the principle that a single act may violate more than one criminal statute. We have emphasized that equal protection is offended only when two statutes forbid *identical* conduct. . . . To determine whether two statutes proscribe identical conduct, we analyze the elements of each. We emphasize that this task requires a facial examination of the elements comprising each crime. . . . The crime of reckless second degree assault with a deadly weapon is defined in §18-3-203(1)(d), as follows: "(1) A person commits the crime of assault in the second degree if . . . (d) He recklessly causes serious bodily injury to another person by means of a deadly weapon." . . . Vehicular assault is defined in §18-3-205(1)(a), as follows: "If a person operates or drives a motor vehicle in a reckless manner, and this conduct is the proximate cause of serious bodily injury to another, such person commits vehicular assault." . . .

The language of the statutes differs in [several] ways. First, second degree assault applies to a range of unspecified conduct; the defendant can "recklessly cause" injury in a multitude of ways. The conduct specified in the vehicular assault statute, on the other hand, is strictly limited to "driving or operating" a motor vehicle. . . . An elemental comparison thus illustrates that the two statutes, by their terms, target different conduct. To achieve a conviction under the vehicular assault statute, the prosecution must demonstrate that the defendant drove or operated a motor vehicle. Accordingly, one who causes serious bodily injury by dint of a motor vehicle that is used as a weapon, but that is not driven or operated, could be convicted of reckless second degree assault with a deadly weapon but not vehicular assault. For example, if an adult locks a child in a car on a sweltering summer day to punish or intimidate the child, the adult obviously is not driving or operating the car. Assuming that the other elements of the crime are met, however, the adult could be charged with reckless second degree assault but not vehicular assault. . . .

[Another] difference between second degree assault and vehicular assault lies in the means by which the defendant allegedly caused serious bodily injury. The vehicular assault statute provides that, to be convicted, the defendant's reckless driving or operation of a "motor vehicle" must have proximately caused serious bodily injury. The second degree assault statute requires that the defendant use a "deadly weapon." . . . Section 18-1-901(3)(e), provides the statutory definition of deadly weapon:

> "Deadly weapon" means any of the following which in the manner it is used or intended to be used is capable of producing death or serious bodily injury: (I) A firearm, whether loaded or unloaded; (II) A knife; (III) A bludgeon; or (IV) Any other weapon, device, instrument, material, or substance, whether animate or inanimate. . . .

We have consistently held that whether an object is a deadly weapon for the purposes of section 18-1-903(e)(IV) depends on the manner in which the object is used. People v. Ross, 831 P.2d 1310 (Colo. 1992) (holding that a fist can be a deadly weapon). . . . Any object can be a deadly weapon if it is used in a manner capable of producing death or serious bodily injury. . . . The same is true of a motor vehicle. It is not always a deadly weapon under the statutory definition. A motor vehicle may be a deadly weapon, however, depending on how it is used in a particular situation.

The difference between the "deadly weapon" requirement of the second degree assault statute and the "motor vehicle" element of vehicular assault justifies the disparate penalties established by the General Assembly. The legislature could rationally decide that "road rage" or the use of a car as a deadly weapon justifies an increased penalty. At the same time, it could rationally determine that it is less reprehensible for one to cause serious bodily injury by mere reckless driving of a vehicle as a vehicle. This court cannot hold that the General Assembly has constitutionally erred in providing a more severe penalty for an act which it believes to be of greater social consequence. . . .

Stewart argues that even if the statutes are not identical, he can be convicted only of the more specific crime, motor vehicle assault, and not of the more general crime, second degree assault. Generally, the prosecution has discretion to determine what charges to file when a defendant's conduct violates more than one statute. See §18-1-408(7) ["If the same conduct is defined as criminal in different enactments or in different sections of this code, the offender may be prosecuted under any one or all of the sections or enactments"]. There are certain circumstances in which this general rule does not apply. See, e.g., People v. Smith, 938 P.2d 111, 115-116 (Colo. 1997) [General Assembly can supplant the more general offense by creating a specific offense supported by clear legislative intent to limit prosecution to that statute; in adopting the comprehensive Liquor Code, the General Assembly intended to require the offense of falsely filling out a liquor application to be prosecuted under the Liquor Code and not under the general felony offense of offering a false instrument for recording].

Stewart has failed to show that his crimes fall into this category. He simply asserts that the General Assembly intended to punish motor vehicle offenses pursuant to the motor vehicle statutes. He cites no authority such as statutory language or legislative history to support his theory and we reject it. The prosecution had discretion to charge second degree assault in this case and the jury verdict convicting Stewart on that charge stands. . . .

The Screening/Bargaining Tradeoff,
Ronald Wright and Marc Miller
55 Stan. L. Rev. 29 (2002)

[All] prosecutors "screen" when they make any charging decision. By prosecutorial screening we mean a far more structured and reasoned charge selection process than is typical in most prosecutors' offices in this country. The prosecutorial screening system we describe has four interrelated features, all internal to the prosecutor's office: early assessment, reasoned selection, barriers to bargains, and enforcement.

First, the prosecutor's office must make an early and careful assessment of each case, and demand that police and investigators provide sufficient information before the initial charge is filed. Second, the prosecutor's office must file only appropriate charges. Which charges are "appropriate" is determined by several factors. A prosecutor should only file charges that the office would generally want to result in a criminal conviction and sanction. In addition, appropriate charges must reflect reasonably accurately what actually occurred. They are charges that the prosecutor can very likely prove in court. Third, and critically, the office must severely restrict all plea bargaining, and most especially charge bargains. Prosecutors should also recognize explicitly that the screening process is the mechanism that makes such restrictions possible. Fourth, the kind of prosecutorial screening we advocate must include sufficient training, oversight, and other internal enforcement mechanisms to ensure reasonable uniformity in charging and relatively few changes to charges after they have been filed. If prosecutors treat hard screening decisions as the primary alternative to plea bargaining, they can produce changes in current criminal practice that would be fundamental, attractive, and viable. . . .

THE SCREENING/BARGAINING TRADEOFF IN PRACTICE: NODA DATA

. . . Harry Connick was elected as the District Attorney for Orleans Parish in 1974. He has remained in that office for the past twenty-eight years. Connick first ran for office in 1969 against incumbent Jim Garrison, the flamboyant District Attorney made famous in the film *JFK*. His first unsuccessful campaign did not focus on plea bargaining. He promised faster prosecution and better tracking of defendants who failed to appear for trial. His 1973 campaign began with a similar emphasis on swift prosecution. As the campaign wore on, however, Connick's speeches began to feature attacks on plea bargaining. . . .

Connick told voters that widespread plea bargaining was wrong; years later, he explained that victims were right to resent it when cases were bargained away simply because of a "lazy" prosecutor. He promised to eliminate "baseless" plea bargaining and to hire full-time prosecutors who would not use plea bargains just to move cases from the docket.

As in other American cities, the criminal courts in New Orleans deal with enormous volume. In the face of this large urban caseload, Connick needed a strategy to carry out his campaign statements about plea bargaining. During the weeks between his election victory and taking office, he started speaking publicly about a plan with two central components. First, Connick planned to devote expertise and resources to screening. He proposed a screening procedure that "would weed out those cases really not worthy of being on the criminal docket, so more courtroom emphasis can be devoted to the violent offender." Second, he instructed his prosecutors not to engage in plea bargaining — particularly charge bargaining — except under very limited circumstances. . . .

The distinctiveness of the screening process in the NODA office is apparent from a closer examination of the path each new case takes through the system. Police officers develop a case folder after they complete an investigation and file charges with the magistrate. The first stop for the case folder in the NODA office is the Magistrate Section, where the least experienced assistants work. They typically have logged six months or fewer on the job. The ADA from the Magistrate Section appears for the state at the first appearance and bail hearing before the magistrate. A public defender is also present for the first appearance, but the case is reassigned immediately after the hearing and there is typically no further defense presence or participation in the case until after the DA files an information or obtains an indictment.

After any proceedings in the Magistrate Division, the folder moves to the Screening Section of the NODA office. Connick devotes extraordinary resources to this operation. For instance, in the late 1990s, about fifteen of the eighty-five attorneys in the office worked in Screening. . . . All attorneys in the Screening Section served previously (usually a couple of years) in the Trial Section. This level of experience comes at a premium in New Orleans, where the turnover among prosecuting attorneys is quite high. The average tenure of an ADA in the NODA office is around two years. . . .

The screener reviews the investigation file, speaks to all the key witnesses and the victims (often by telephone, but sometimes in person), and generally gauges the strength of the case. If the police report neglects to mention a factual issue that is likely to arise at trial, the screening attorney will speak directly with the police officer to resolve it. There is a powerful office expectation that the Screening Attorney will make a decision within ten days of receiving the folder.

NODA instituted a variety of measures to ensure reasonable uniformity in screening decisions. Connick committed his screening principles to writing in an office policy manual. The general office policy is to charge the most serious

crime the facts will support at trial. The policy does not, on its face, allow
individual prosecutors to consider for themselves the equities in the case
when selecting the charge. By the same token, however, Connick insists that
overcharging is unacceptable, because the charges chosen for the information
will stay in place through the trial. If screening prosecutors overcharge cases too
often, the Chief of the Trial Section might send the screening attorney back into
the courtroom on at least one of those overcharged matters to "get his teeth
kicked in." Supervisors review all refusals to charge. . . .

Neither Connick nor any attorneys in his office claim to have abolished
plea bargaining entirely from the New Orleans system. Prosecutors in the office
acknowledge that sometimes new information appears and changes the value of
a case. Witnesses leave town, victims decide not to testify, new witnesses appear,
and investigators find new evidence. On occasion, the screening attorney makes
a bad judgment and overcharges, and a plea could save the case.

Nevertheless, office policy tries to keep these changes in charges to a
minimum. A supervisor must approve any decision to drop or change charges
after the information is filed. The attorney requesting the change must
complete a special form naming the screening and trial attorneys, and explaining the reason for the decision, drawing from a list of acceptable reasons. The
ADAs believe there is a "stigma" involved in reducing charges, however strong
the reasons for a reduction might be.

Attorneys from the NODA office believe that they decline to prosecute an
exceptional number of cases. They view this as a necessary part of training police
officers to investigate more thoroughly. The relatively high rate of declination
also created a political challenge for Connick over the years. During each of his
reelection campaigns — in 1978, 1984, 1990, and 1996 — Connick's challengers
criticized the number of cases that the NODA office declined to prosecute. As
his opponent Morris Reed put it in many public debates, "the PD arrests them
and the DA turns them loose." Connick had several replies. Poor police work
made declinations necessary. Further, he pointed to specific examples of how
his office dealt severely with defendants once they were charged. Connick also
explicitly linked his screening policies to his plea bargaining policies: Tough
screening, he said, made it possible to keep plea bargaining at low levels.

Connick drew on case data to make specific claims about low rates of plea
bargaining in the office: He asserted that plea bargaining in Jim Garrison's day
reached 60 to 70%, but fell to 7 or 8% of all cases filed under his office policy. He
also routinely mentioned the high number of trials in New Orleans compared to
other Louisiana jurisdictions. In addition, Connick pointed to his routine use of
the habitual felon law to enhance sentences. By the end of each of the four
reelection campaigns, Connick convinced the voters that it was possible both to
decline many cases and to run a tough prosecutor's office at the same time. . . .

NOTES

1. *Prosecutorial "sentencing" through selection of charges.* Prosecutorial selection of charges can have an immense impact on sentencing decisions. Scholars
concerned about the exercise of prosecutorial discretion often call for judicial
regulation of prosecutors, but as the decision in People v. Stewart illustrates,

courts have yet to hear their call, refusing to review prosecutorial decisions except in extraordinarily limited circumstances. See, e.g., James Vorenberg, Decent Restraint of Prosecutorial Power, 94 Harv. L. Rev. 1521 (1981). The experience described above in the New Orleans District Attorney's office under Harry Connick raises the question whether "decent restraint" might come from within prosecutor's offices rather than from external sources. See Michael Simons, Prosecutorial Discretion and Prosecution Guidelines: A Case Study in Controlling Federalization, 75 N.Y.U. L. Rev. 893 (2000). Prosecutorial control of sentences raises particular issues for guideline sentencing systems that claim to provide legislative or administrative guidance to sentencing judges but not to prosecutors. See David Boerner, Sentencing Guidelines and Prosecutorial Discretion, 78 Judicature 196 (1995). Guidelines or highly structured criminal codes may provide prosecutors with even greater authority to "specify" the effect at sentencing of the concessions offered in a plea bargain. When the price of a trial becomes this clear, few defendants will ever risk going to trial. In such systems, for all the apparent involvement of multiple actors and rule-based equality, to a considerable extent the true sentencer becomes the prosecutor. See George Fisher, Plea Bargaining's Triumph 205-230 (2003).

2. *Prosecutorial accountability to community priorities.* Should prosecutors also be able to make charging decisions on the basis of local needs? Should prosecutorial needs and resources then be allowed to affect sentences? An important illustration of these questions arises in the courts in southern California. The U.S. Attorney's office in San Diego receives far more immigration cases than it can prosecute. Of the 565,581 illegal aliens apprehended in fiscal year 1992, the U.S. Attorney prosecuted 245 felony immigration cases and another 5,000 misdemeanors. Because the San Diego district attorney, as a matter of policy, will not prosecute any cases related to the border, these cases must be prosecuted in federal court or not at all. William Braniff, Local Discretion, Prosecutorial Choices and the Sentencing Guidelines, 5 Fed. Sent'g Rep. 309 (1993). If every alien apprehended at the border were prosecuted for felony reentry (most are reentering), the size of the entire federal prison system would need to quadruple in a single year based on cases in this one district alone. Of course, the local U.S. Attorney's office has the resources to prosecute only a fraction of these cases—as the numbers indicate. How should a sentencing judge respond to the limited prosecutorial resources that sometimes force unpleasant choices on prosecutors? Should the judge enhance a sentence when she knows that an unusually large number of offenders are going unpunished? Should the judge reduce the sentence out of concern for selective and discriminatory treatment or ignore prosecutorial priorities entirely? How should a judge in a neighboring district react to the nonprosecution or lesser sentencing in the adjacent area? See United States v. Banuelos-Rodriguez, 215 F.3d 969 (9th Cir. 2000) (rejecting sentencing disparities arising from different charging and plea bargaining policies of different U.S. Attorneys as a basis for departure from presumptive sentencing range); Linda Drazga Maxfield & Keri Burchfield, Immigration Offenses Involving Unlawful Entry: Is Federal Practice Comparable Across Districts?, 15 Fed. Sent'g Rep. 260 (2002).

3. *Prosecutorial punishment: critical yet hidden.* The regulation (or lack thereof) of prosecutorial discretion is one of the great puzzles of the criminal justice system. The puzzle is hidden beneath the surface whenever analysts study

whether offenders *convicted* of the same offense are treated similarly: These analyses ignore whether similar offenders were not charged at all or were charged or convicted of a different offense. The impact of a prosecutor's sorting decisions may also be felt when prosecutorial office policy assigns a case to one of two or more possible screening or trial attorneys. Although these kinds of decisions are hard to study, any full assessment of sentencing or the equal treatment of individuals must address these preconviction sorting decisions.

PROBLEM 2-5.   LOW-HANGING FRUIT

The purposes of prosecution take on additional levels of complexity when multiple jurisdictions might prosecute for the offense, whether those jurisdictions are the federal and one state government, or multiple state governments. In a speech to law enforcement officers on May 13, 2003, U.S. Attorney General John Ashcroft asserted that the Department of Justice was "taking gun-toting thugs off the streets." The next day, the Justice Department echoed his assertion with the following statement:

> This Justice Department has made the aggressive prosecution of those who violate our nation's gun laws a priority, and the 38% increase in prosecutions demonstrates we have been very busy taking criminals who misuse guns off the streets. Last year, the Department had the largest recorded increase in prosecuting and convicting defendants for violating our nation's gun laws. [We have] seen increases in prosecutions of many firearms crimes over the last year, including a 100% increase in gun trafficking prosecutions, [and] a 25% increase in obliterated serial number cases. . . .
>   There should be no doubt: the Justice Department is working hard to enforce all federal firearms laws and lock up those who criminally misuse guns. We are also working in very close coordination with our state and local partners, who are also prosecuting gun crimes at higher rates. Our message is clear: gun crime means hard time. . . .

In the same week, a policy group seeking more federal prosecutions, Americans for Gun Safety, released a study with more uneven findings:

> ### Conclusion #1 — There is a vast enforcement gap between the level of federal gun crimes and the number of federal prosecutions.

> Over the past three fiscal years, prosecutors have filed 25,002 federal gun crime cases. During the same period:

> - More than 330,000 guns used in violent gun crimes showed telltale signs of black market trafficking;
> - 420,000 firearms were stolen;
> - 450,000 individuals lied on the federal background check form used to determine eligibility for a gun;
> - 93,000 gun crimes were committed by those under the age of 18; and
> - Thousands of guns with obliterated serial numbers were recovered by law enforcement.

It is a violation of federal law to traffic in firearms, steal guns, lie on the background check form, sell to minors, and obliterate serial numbers. This translates into well over a million crimes where it is likely or certain that a federal law was broken. The 25,002 prosecutions represent a ratio of about 2 federal prosecutions for every 100 federal gun crimes.

Conclusion #2 — Twenty of twenty-two of the major federal gun statutes are rarely enforced.

Of the 25,002 federal firearms cases over the past three years, 85% of the prosecutions were for violations of just two federal statutes: the illegal possession of a firearm by a felon or other prohibited buyer, and the possession of a firearm while in the commission of a violent or drug-related federal crime. During both the Clinton and Bush Administrations, the other twenty statutes went virtually unenforced. For example, only 2% of prosecutions were for crimes associated with illegal gun trafficking and less than 1% for illegally selling a gun to a minor. . . . [T]he paucity of prosecutions under the other twenty statutes mean[s] that the federal government is doing little or nothing to break up the vast black market in illegal guns.

The Enforcement Gap: Federal Gun Laws Ignored (May 2003). Can you determine whether the federal government is prosecuting too much gun crime, too little gun crime, or the wrong gun crimes? Criminologist Alfred Blumstein described current gun prosecutions as aimed at the "low-hanging fruit." See Eric Lichtblau, Justice Dept. Plans to Step Up Gun-Crime Prosecutions, N.Y. Times, May 14, 2003. Given the very large number of crimes that might be prosecuted under firearms statutes and that typically can be prosecuted by federal or state authorities, how can the federal government or a state government decide how best to allocate prosecutorial gun crime resources? What priority should gun crimes take compared with violent offenses against the person, drug crimes, stock fraud, environmental crimes, or immigration offenses? Should Congress authorize and fund new prosecutorial lines solely to prosecute gun crimes? In general, who should make the policy judgments about which crimes to prosecute, how should those policies be articulated, and what institution should see that the policies are consistently applied?

D. APPELLATE COURT GUIDANCE

In indeterminate sentencing systems, appellate courts play almost no role, and appellate sentencing law before 1980 is almost impossible to find. Appellate courts typically have the simple task of determining whether the sentence of the trial court falls between the statutory minimum and maximum for the charged crime — a very limited notion of legality. In some states, statutes affirmatively limit appellate courts to this measly role. In states that do not explicitly constrain appellate sentencing authority, appellate judges avoid developing sentencing rules, perhaps because they believe that there is little "law" for them to apply. But this explanation is inadequate: in other areas with little law to apply, courts have exercised either interpretive or common law powers and developed rules to guide important discretionary decisions. Why have appellate courts shied away from developing a common law of sentencing?

In a more modern trend in the United States, especially in structured sentencing systems, legislatures provide for more searching appellate review of sentences. In such a system, the appellate court confirms both the legality and the "reasonableness" or "proportionality" of the sentence. An illustration comes from section 244.11 of the Minnesota statutes:

> An appeal to the court of appeals may be taken by the defendant or the state from any sentence imposed or stayed by the district court. . . . On an appeal pursuant to this section, the court may review the sentence imposed or stayed to determine whether the sentence is inconsistent with statutory requirements, unreasonable, inappropriate, excessive, unjustifiably disparate, or not warranted by the findings of fact issued by the district court. . . .

When appellate courts have broader authority to review sentences, they are more likely to come up with sentencing guidance as part of statutory interpretation (an entire legal regime can be created by allowing review for "reasonableness" of sentences) or as part of a common law of sentencing.

In addition to sentencing individuals, there are other ways that judges in general, and appellate judges in particular, might help set the sentencing rules. Judges might be called to testify before a legislature or sentencing commission, or a judge might serve on a sentencing commission. Judges might gather together formally (in a judicial conference) or informally (say, over lunch) and issue nonbinding sentencing recommendations.

Another approach, with its strongest illustration in England, finds appellate courts issuing "guideline judgments" that are announced in specific cases. English appellate courts have become one of the main institutions for developing sentencing policy, because those courts establish benchmark sentences and sentencing principles to operate within broad statutory ranges.

In R. v. Aramah, 76 Crim. App. R. 190 (1983), the Court of Appeal, Criminal Division, first set out a framework for sentencing in drug cases. Aramah was convicted of importing 59 kilograms of cannabis valued between £100,000 and £135,000. The defendant was a 50-year-old man of Nigerian origin who had two previous convictions for drug offenses, one involving the importation of 88 kilograms of cannabis in 1972, for which he had been sentenced to three years' imprisonment. He was sentenced in this most recent case to six years' imprisonment. After stating the facts, the court began its decision by making "some general observations about the level of sentences for drug offences, since our list, as will have been observed, is entirely composed of such crimes." The court then gave the following guidelines:

Class "A" Drugs and Particularly Heroin and Morphine

> It is common knowledge that these are the most dangerous of all the addictive drugs for a number of reasons: first of all, they are easy to handle. Small parcels can be made up into huge numbers of doses. Secondly, the profits are so enormous that they attract the worst type of criminal. Many of such criminals may think, and indeed do think, that it is less dangerous and more profitable to traffic in heroin or morphine than it is to rob a bank. [The] heroin taker, once addicted[, may require] anything up to hundreds of pounds a week to buy enough heroin to satisfy the craving, depending upon the degree of addiction of the person involved. The [person might

obtain these sums by] trafficking in the drug itself and disseminating accordingly its use still further.

[Lastly], and we have purposely left it for the last, because it is the most horrifying aspect, comes the degradation and suffering and not infrequently the death which the drug brings to the addict. It is not difficult to understand why in some parts of the world traffickers in heroin in any substantial quantity are sentenced to death and executed. Consequently anything which the courts of this country can do by way of deterrent sentences on those found guilty of crimes involving these class "A" drugs should be done.

[With large-scale importation of heroin, morphine, and so on], where the street value of the consignment is in the order of £100,000 or more, sentences of seven years and upwards are appropriate. There will be cases where the values are of the order of £1 million or more, in which case the offence should be visited by sentences of 12 to 14 years. It will seldom be that an importer of any appreciable amount of the drug will deserve less than four years.

This, however, is one area in which it is particularly important that offenders should be encouraged to give information to the police, and a confession of guilt, coupled with considerable assistance to the police, can properly be marked by a substantial reduction in what would otherwise be the proper sentence.

Next, supplying heroin, morphine, etc.: it goes without saying that the sentence will largely depend on the degree of involvement, the amount of trafficking and the value of the drug being handled. It is seldom that a sentence of less than three years will be justified and the nearer the source of supply the defendant is shown to be, the heavier will be the sentence. There may well be cases where sentences similar to those appropriate to large scale importers may be necessary. It is, however, unhappily all too seldom that those big fish amongst the suppliers get caught.

Possession of heroin, morphine, etc. (simple possession): it is at this level that the circumstances of the individual offender become of much greater importance. Indeed the possible variety of considerations is so wide, including often those of a medical nature, that we feel it impossible to lay down any practical guidelines. On the other hand the maximum penalty for simple possession of class "A" drugs is seven years' imprisonment and/or a fine, and there will be very many cases where deprivation of liberty is both proper and expedient.

Class "B" Drugs, Particularly Cannabis

[Importation] of very small amounts [of cannabis] for personal use can be dealt with as if it were simple possession, with which we will deal later. Otherwise importation of amounts up to about 20 kilograms of herbal cannabis, or the equivalent in cannabis resin or cannabis oil, will, save in the most exceptional cases, attract sentences of between 18 months and three years, with the lowest ranges reserved for pleas of guilty in cases where there has been small profit to the offender. The good character of the courier (as he usually is) is of less importance than the good character of the defendant in other cases. The reason for this is, it is well known that the large scale operator looks for couriers of good character and for people of a sort which is likely to exercise the sympathy of the court if they are detected and arrested. . . . There are few, if any, occasions when anything other than an immediate custodial sentence is proper in this type of importation.

Medium quantities over 20 kilograms will attract sentences of three to six years' imprisonment, depending upon the amount involved, and all the other circumstances of the case. Large scale or wholesale importation of massive quantities will justify sentences in the region of 10 years' imprisonment for those playing other than a subordinate role.

Supply of cannabis: here again the supply of massive quantities will justify sentences in the region of 10 years for those playing anything more than a subordinate role. Otherwise the bracket should be between one to four years' imprisonment, depending upon the scale of the operation. Supplying a number of small sellers — wholesaling if you like — comes at the top of the bracket. At the lower end will be the retailer of a small amount to a consumer. Where there is no commercial motive (for example, where cannabis is supplied at a party), the offence may well be serious enough to justify a custodial sentence.

Possession of cannabis: when only small amounts are involved being for personal use, the offence can often be met by a fine. If the history shows, however, a persisting flouting of the law, imprisonment may become necessary.

The court then applied its own guidelines to the case before it and upheld the six-year sentence, finding that there was a "very large quantity of cannabis" and no "mitigating feature," including the absence of a plea of guilty, and prior convictions for drug offenses.

Four years later, the same court reconsidered its *Aramah* guidelines in light of subsequent developments.

R. v. Edward Bilinski
86 Crim. App. R. 146 (1987)

THE LORD CHIEF JUSTICE

On February 20, 1987 in the Crown Court at Chelmsford the appellant pleaded guilty to importing 3.036 kilograms of heroin into the United Kingdom. He was sentenced to 12 years' imprisonment. Against that sentence he now appeals by leave of the single judge.

The material facts are as follows. On November 7, 1986 the M.V. *Gdansk II* was searched at Tilbury by Customs officers. They discovered three packages containing white powder subsequently found to be heroin hidden behind a wiring duct 30 feet above the deck. Suspicion fell on the appellant who was a senior member of the crew. He was questioned in Polish through an interpreter. He denied all knowledge of the packages. However, his fingerprints were found on the sticky side of adhesive tape binding the packages. At first he said that he did not know "by what miracle" his prints had been placed there. The following day on further questioning, however, he admitted that he was responsible for the packages being on board. He had been approached by two Polish men at a time when his finances were at a low ebb. They had suggested he should assist them in transporting drugs from Hamburg to Sydney via Tilbury. He was to be paid the equivalent of some £3,500 in U.S. dollars. The size of the reward, he said, clouded his judgment. He was given the packages in Hamburg. According to his story, he was told that the drugs were cannabis. When they were handed to him the packages were malleable and wrapped in transparent plastic. He could see a white powder inside. He had later wrapped and secured them in further plastic material (hence the fingerprints) in order to protect the contents from the damp, because he had been told to be careful to prevent them from coming to any harm. He said he did not recognize the powder as heroin; he had never seen heroin before; the two men had told him the drug had come from the Far East, but even then he did not realize it might be heroin. Amongst other items found in the appellant's cabin was a book entitled "Heroina," which we are told is the Polish for heroin. Surprisingly this volume had come from the ship's library.

The heroin was of very high purity—90 per cent. Its street value in this country was in the region of £600,000. The mitigation was in essence based on four matters:

(1) The appellant thought he was smuggling cannabis not heroin.
(2) He had pleaded guilty and given what assistance he could to the authorities in the shape of the names of his suppliers.
(3) He was only a courier whose reward as it transpires was to be a minute fraction of the value of the drugs.
(4) He was of hitherto good character.

Steyn J., in the course of passing sentence, said this: . . . "It is said that you did not know that it was heroin. I regard that (and I make that clear) as irrelevant. . . . If it had been relevant, I would have directed an issue to be tried on it, but I find that it is irrelevant." [Defense counsel] makes two submissions to this Court: (1) That the judge was in error in regarding the appellant's belief as to the nature of the drug as irrelevant so far as sentence was concerned. (2) That the sentence of 12 years was in any event too long. . . .

Is it relevant? On the one hand is the argument that anyone who chooses to engage in smuggling prohibited drugs must accept the risk that the drug is of a kind different from that which he believes or has been told it is. . . . On the other hand, submits [defense counsel], if a defendant genuinely has been misled as to the type of drug, then in light of the fact that the maximum sentence for importing heroin is imprisonment for life as against the 12 years maximum for importation of cannabis, it would be unjust not to allow some mitigation at least of the punishment. . . .

We are of the view that the defendant's belief in these circumstances is relevant to punishment and that the man who believes he is importing cannabis is indeed less culpable than he who knows it to be heroin. . . . To what extent the punishment should be mitigated by this factor will obviously depend upon all the circumstances, amongst them being the degree of care exercised by the defendant.

How should the issue be determined? In some cases no doubt it will be necessary for the judge to hear evidence. . . . If that procedure had been adopted in the present case . . . the appellant would probably have been the only witness, apart perhaps from someone to speak as to the street value of these packages had they contained cannabis rather than heroin. It is difficult to see what the appellant could have said other than that which he had already stated in his interviews with the Customs officers. If so, it is scarcely likely that the judge would have been in any doubt but that the appellant must have known that the substance was heroin. . . . Where the defendant's story is manifestly false the judge is entitled to reject it out of hand without hearing evidence. Whether that is so or not, we take the view that the exercise of only a small degree of curiosity, enquiry or care would have revealed the true nature of the drug in this case and that accordingly the mitigating effect of the belief, if held, was small.

The next question is what the proper sentence should be for the carrier/importer of this quantity of 90 per cent pure heroin. The guidelines in

Aramah ... must be updated to take account of the fact that the maximum sentence for the importation of Class A drugs has now been increased by the Controlled Drugs (Penalties) Act 1985, from 14 years to life imprisonment. It was suggested in *Aramah* that where the street value of the consignment is in the order of £100,000 or more, sentences of seven years and upwards are appropriate, and that 12 to 14 years' imprisonment is appropriate where the value of the drugs involved is £1 million or more. The former figure should now be increased to 10 years and upwards and the latter to 14 years and upwards.

Thus a term of 12 years or thereabouts would have been appropriate for this level of importation in the absence of any mitigating features. There are, however, these matters to be taken into account in mitigation of the penalty. First, the plea of guilty. Secondly, the fact that the appellant gave all the help which he could to the authorities by naming his suppliers and, thirdly, for what it is worth, the possibility (in the absence of a finding to the contrary by the judge) that the appellant may have believed the drugs to be cannabis. We think that in the light of those factors, and taking into account all the circumstances of the case a term of 8 years' imprisonment would have been appropriate. . . .

NOTES

1. *Appellate court guideline sentencing rules.* The English experiment with appellate guideline judgments has been under way for about 25 years. The guideline judgments have not kept Parliament from enacting additional sentencing legislation, including harsher punishments for drug offenses. See Aaron Rappaport, Sentencing in England: The Rise of Populist Punishment, 10 Fed. Sent'g Rep. 247 (1998). What sorts of reasons might persuade an appellate court to change its own sentencing guidelines? Based on the drug guidelines in *Aramah* as modified by *Bilinski*, what advantages do you think appellate judges have over legislators in developing sentencing rules? Over sentencing experts such as sentencing commission members? Over trial judges?

In R. v. Barrick, 81 Crim. App. R. 78 (1985), the English Court of Appeal set out guidelines for fraud cases. The defendant in *Barrick* was convicted on four counts of false accounting, four counts of obtaining by deception, and two counts of theft. He was sentenced to two years' imprisonment on each count, to run concurrently. The defendant handled the accounting for a small finance company, and in that capacity he created imaginary borrowers and stole around £9,000. The court used the case as "an opportunity to make some observations upon the proper sentence to be passed in respect of certain types of theft and fraud":

> The type of case with which we are concerned is where a person in a position of trust, for example, an accountant, solicitor, bank employee or postman, has used that privileged and trusted position to defraud his partners or clients or employers or the general public of sizeable sums of money. He will usually, as in this case, be a person of hitherto impeccable character. It is practically certain, again as in this case, that he will never offend again. . . . It was not long ago that this type of offender might expect to receive a term of imprisonment of three or four years, and indeed a great deal more if the sums involved were substantial. More recently, however, the sentencing climate in this area has changed. . . .

In *Jacob* (1981), . . . a solicitor who had over a period of some three years stolen money from clients and his partners to the tune of between £40,000 and £57,000 had his sentence of four years' imprisonment reduced by this Court to eighteen months. . . . On the other hand postmen do not seem to have fared quite so well. In *Eagleton* (1982), a postman had been sentenced to five years' imprisonment for three offences of theft of packets in transit by mail with 80 offences taken into consideration. A sentence of thirty months' imprisonment was substituted. *Briggs* (1982) was another postman case. The defendant had stolen from the mail goods worth about £1,300, most of which were recovered. On appeal a term of two years' imprisonment was substituted for the three years which had been imposed by the trial judge. We can see no proper basis for distinguishing between cases of this kind simply on the basis of the defendant's occupation. . . .

It is, we appreciate, dangerous to generalize where the circumstances of the offender and the offence may vary so widely from case to case. In the hope that they may be helpful to sentencers generally, and may lead to a little more uniformity, we make the following suggestions.

In general a term of immediate imprisonment is inevitable, save in very exceptional circumstances or where the amount of money obtained is small. Despite the great punishment that offenders of this sort bring upon themselves, the Court should nevertheless pass a sufficiently substantial term of imprisonment to mark publicly the gravity of the offence. The sum involved is obviously not the only factor to be considered, but it may in many cases provide a useful guide. Where the amounts involved cannot be described as small but are less than £10,000 or thereabouts, terms of imprisonment ranging from the very short up to about eighteen months are appropriate. Cases involving sums of between about £10,000 and £50,000 will merit a term of about two to three years' imprisonment. Where greater sums are involved, for example those over £100,000, then a term of three and a half years to four and a half years would be justified. . . .

The following are some of the matters to which the Court will no doubt wish to pay regard in determining what the proper level of sentence should be: (i) the quality and degree of trust reposed in the offender including his rank; (ii) the period over which the fraud or the thefts have been perpetrated; (iii) the use to which the money or property dishonestly taken was put; (iv) the effect upon the victim; (v) the impact of the offences on the public and public confidence; (vi) the effect on fellow-employees or partners; (vii) the effect on the offender himself; (viii) his own history; (ix) those matters of mitigation special to himself such as illness; being placed under great strain by excessive responsibility or the like; where, as sometimes happens, there has been a long delay, say over two years, between his being confronted with his dishonesty by his professional body or the police and the start of his trial; finally, any help given by him to the police.

The court found that Barrick had committed "mean offences" from people of modest means and had given "no help to the police," so the court upheld the two-year sentence. See also R. v. Billam, 8 Crim. App. R. (S.) 48 (1986) (guidelines for sexual assault); D. A. Thomas, Sentencing Sex Offenders — English Law, 10 Fed. Sent'g Rep. 74 (1997) (reviewing interaction of legislation and English guideline decisions); Andrew Ashworth, Three Techniques for Reducing Sentencing Disparity, in Principled Sentencing 282 (Andrew von Hirsch and Andrew Ashworth eds., 1992).

2. *Judges and rule making in the United States.* Could appellate courts make rules for sentencing in the United States? Or would this violate the separation of powers, because rule making would be either a legislative or executive function? See State v. Wentz, 805 P.2d 962 (Alaska 1991) (limiting use of judicially created

"benchmark" sentence for assault). Appellate courts play a more substantial role in modern U.S. structured sentencing systems, such as the federal and many state guideline systems. Sentencing issues generate lots of work for appellate courts. In the federal system in 2001, 51% of the appeals in criminal cases raised sentencing issues alone, and another 22% challenged the sentence along with the conviction.

Given that judges see so many individual cases and develop such expertise in sentencing, shouldn't judges develop sentencing rules rather than just apply rules that others create? Statutes establishing sentencing commissions often reserve some commission posts for judges. Are there other ways to involve judges in the creation of general sentencing rules? Under the federal guidelines and in many structured state systems, courts that sentence outside the recommended range must explain the decision. The sentencing commission collects data on these sentences and in theory uses the feedback to amend the sentencing rules. We consider the judicial power to depart from sentencing guidelines more thoroughly in Chapter 3.

3. *Regional appellate tribunals.* National criminal courts traditionally handle criminal trials and sentencing, even if the offenses involve foreign nationals who committed crimes on their territory. While criminal jurisdiction is primarily territorial (the territoriality principle), countries also have the right to try their nationals who commit crimes abroad (the nationality principle), offenders who commit crimes against their territory or political and judicial structure (the protective principle), and offenders who run afoul of universal prohibitions (the universality principle). Some courts have also exercised jurisdiction if the victim was one of its nationals (the passive personality principle). As regional human rights organizations evolved in Europe and the Americas, regional tribunals, such as the European Court of Human Rights (ECHR) and the Inter-American Court of Human Rights, acquired limited appellate jurisdiction over criminal cases tried in the courts of the member nations.

Sentencing appeals have come to the ECHR under Article 3 of the European Convention on Human Rights, which protects individuals against inhuman or degrading treatment or punishment, and Article 5, which guarantees the right to liberty and security of persons. The ECHR has decided what practices constitute torture and whether discretionary decisions as to the release of life prisoners must be subject to judicial control.

4. *The ICTR and the ICTY.* In the wake of the conflicts in Yugoslavia and Rwanda, the U.N. Security Council established two ad hoc tribunals in 1993 and 1994, respectively: the International Criminal Tribunal for Yugoslavia (ICTY), with its seat in The Hague, Netherlands, and the International Criminal Tribunal for Rwanda (ICTR), located in Arusha, Tanzania. Both courts have jurisdiction over genocide, crimes against humanity, war crimes, and select breaches of the Geneva Conventions. Their jurisdiction is complementary to that of national courts, but they have the primary right to prosecute and try war criminals. As of February 2002 the ICTY has filed charges in more than 70 cases. As of early 2003 the ICTR had tried nine individuals, resulting in eight convictions and one acquittal. Those convicted in the ICTR include Jean Kambanda, the prime minister of Rwanda during the genocide, who was the first head of government

to be indicted and subsequently convicted for genocide. See www.un.org/icty or www.ictr.org.

The maximum sentence either tribunal can hand down is life imprisonment, with the sentence to be served in countries that have entered into agreements with the ad hoc tribunals. The jurisprudence developed by the two tribunals will shape the definition and prosecution of international crimes and has already affected the decision making of national courts. See Mark Drumbl & Kenneth S. Gallant, Sentencing Policies and Practices in the International Criminal Tribunals, 15 Fed. Sent'g Rep. 140 (2002).

5. *Sentencing in the International Criminal Court.* Even though attempts were made immediately after World War II to establish an international criminal tribunal, it took more than 50 years to become a reality. The International Criminal Court (ICC) came into existence in 2002 and opened for business in 2003. By February 2003, 89 countries had ratified the Statute of Rome, which set up the ICC, and 139 countries had signed the treaty. The United States withdrew its signature in May 2002, because of concerns about the treaty's applicability to its military personnel, and has since negotiated a number of bilateral treaties intended to shield U.S. nationals from prosecution by the ICC.

The ICC has jurisdiction over genocide, crimes against humanity, war crimes, and the yet undefined crime of aggression. The ICC's jurisdiction complements that of national courts, with trials occurring only if national courts are unwilling or unable to prosecute suspects. The maximum sentence is a life term "when justified by the extreme gravity of the crime and the individual circumstances of the convicted person," with a 30-year maximum for all other offenders (Art. 77, Statute of Rome). A list of aggravating and mitigating circumstances is set out in the Rules of Procedure and Evidence. In addition to imprisonment, the ICC may order a fine, restitution, and forfeiture of property and proceeds received from the crime committed. See www.un.org/law/icc.

=3=
‖ *Regulating Discretion* ‖

Prior to a conviction, discretion plays a key role in the criminal justice system. Victims exercise discretion in reporting crimes, police exercise discretion in investigations, and prosecutors exercise discretion in charging, plea bargaining, and trial decisions. The exercise of sentencing discretion following a defendant's conviction is also common, and it is also sometimes controversial. Indeed, many modern sentencing reforms have been prompted by concern over the discretion granted to judges and juries in their sentencing.

Sentencing discretion has both positive and negative aspects. Because, in the words of the Supreme Court, "every convicted person [is] an individual and every case [is] a unique study in human failings," Koon v. United States, 518 U.S. 81, 113 (1996), it has long been thought essential that sentencers possess some discretion to fine-tune punishments to fit the specific circumstances of particular cases. Yet discretion exercised across a set of cases can result in sentencing disparity: different judges and juries, even when exercising their discretion soundly, may reach different sentencing judgments in seemingly similar cases. And sentencing disparity may reflect a form of discrimination if irrelevant or illegitimate factors influence the outcomes.

This chapter presents two case studies in efforts to regulate sentencing discretion. First is the emergence of guideline systems to structure the exercise of noncapital sentencing discretion. Second is the development of constitutional rules to structure the exercise of capital sentencing discretion.

A. SENTENCING GUIDELINE STRUCTURES: REGULATING DISCRETION THROUGH ADMINISTRATIVE RULES

1. *Origins and Foundation*

Beginning in the late nineteenth and continuing through most of the twentieth century, a highly discretionary, rehabilitative "medical" model dominated criminal sentencing. Trial judges in federal and state systems had nearly unfettered discretion to impose on defendants any sentence selected from wide statutory ranges. Such broad judicial discretion — complemented by similar discretion of parole officials concerning prison release dates — was viewed as necessary to ensure that sentences were tailored to the rehabilitative prospects and progress of each offender.

But by the 1970s criminal justice researchers and scholars had become concerned about the unpredictable and widely disparate sentences that indeterminate sentencing systems produced. Empirical and anecdotal evidence revealed that sentencing judges' discretionary choices created substantial and undue differences in both the lengths and types of sentences meted out to similar defendants. Even more worrisome, some studies found that purportedly irrelevant personal factors such as an offender's race, gender, or socioeconomic status were affecting sentencing outcomes.

Troubled by the disparity and discrimination resulting from highly discretionary sentencing practices — and fueled by concerns over increasing crime rates and powerful criticisms of the entire rehabilitative model of punishment and corrections — many criminal justice experts proposed reforms to bring greater consistency and certainty to the sentencing enterprise. Perhaps the most powerful and influential criticism of then prevailing sentencing practices was delivered by Judge Marvin Frankel, who drew on his personal experiences as a federal district judge to author one of the most influential books in American criminal justice.

Criminal Sentences: Law Without Order, Marvin E. Frankel
Pages 3-10, 16-19, 39-41, 47, 89-123 (1973)

We boast that ours is a "government of laws, not of men." We do not mean . . . that men make no difference in the administration of law. Among the basic things we do mean is that all of us, governors and governed alike, are or ought to be bound by laws of general and equal application. We mean, too, that in a just legal order, the laws should be knowable and intelligible so that, to the fullest extent possible, a person meaning to obey the law may know his obligations and predict within decent limits the legal consequences of his conduct. . . .

As to the penalty that may be imposed, our laws characteristically leave to the sentencing judge a range of choice that should be unthinkable in a "government of laws, not of men." . . . The almost wholly unchecked and sweeping powers we give to judges in the fashioning of sentences are terrifying and intolerable for a society that professes devotion to the rule of law.

For examples of such unbounded "discretion" [consider that] the federal kidnapping law authorizes "imprisonment for any term of years or for life." To take some of our most common federal crimes — driving a stolen car across state lines may result in a term of "not more than five years," robbing a federally insured bank "not more than twenty-five years." [Federal] trial judges, answerable only to their varieties of consciences, may and do send people to prison for terms that may vary in any given case from none at all up to five, ten, thirty, or more years. . . .

The result . . . is a wild array of sentencing judgments without any sem-
blance of the consistency demanded by the ideal of equal justice. . . . The
broad statutory ranges might approach a degree of ordered rationality if
there were prescribed any standards for locating a particular case within any
range. But neither our federal law nor that of any state I know contains meaningful criteria for this purpose. [Our] legislators have not done the most rudimentary job of enacting meaningful sentencing "laws" when they have
neglected even to sketch democratically determined statements of basic
purpose. Left at large, wandering in deserts of uncharted discretion, the judges
suit their own value systems insofar as they think about the problem at all. . . .

The prevalent thesis of the last hundred years or so has been that the treatment of criminals must be "individualized." [But] we ought to recall that individualized justice is prima facie at war with such concepts, at least as fundamental,
as equality, objectivity, and consistency in the law. It is not self-evident that the
flesh-and-blood judge coming (say) from among the white middle classes will
inevitably achieve admirable results when he individualizes the narcotics sentences of the suburban college youth and the street-wise ghetto hustler.

[Judges] have expressed misgivings — about their own and (perhaps more
strongly) about their colleagues' handling of [sentencing] powers so huge and
so undefined over the lives of their fellow men. . . . Everyone connected with this
grim business has his own favorite atrocity stories. . . . One story concerns a
casual anecdote over cocktails in a rare conversation among judges touching
the subject of sentencing. Judge X, to designate him in a lawyerlike way, told of a
defendant for whom the judge, after reading the presentence report, had
decided tentatively upon a sentence of four years' imprisonment. At the sentencing hearing in the courtroom, after hearing counsel, Judge X invited the
defendant to exercise his right to address the court in his own behalf. The
defendant [read] from a sheaf of papers . . . excoriating the judge, the "kanga-
roo court" in which he'd been tried, and the legal establishment in general.
Completing the story, Judge X said, "I listened without interrupting. Finally,
when he said he was through, I simply gave the son of a bitch five years instead of
the four." None of the three judges listening to that (including me) tendered a
whisper of dissent, let alone a scream of outrage. But think about it. . . . A year in
prison for speaking disrespectfully to a judge. . . . Would we tolerate an act of
Congress penalizing such an outburst by a year in prison? The question, however
rhetorical, misses one truly exquisite note of agony: that the wretch sentenced by
Judge X never knew, because he was never told, how the fifth year of his sentence
came to be added. . . .

WALLS OF SILENCE

[The] swift ukase, without explanation, is the tyrant's way. The despot is
not bound by rules. He need not justify or account for what he does. Criminal
sentences, as our judges commonly pronounce them, are in these vital respects
tyrannical. Largely unfettered by limiting standards, and thus having neither
occasion nor meaningful terms for explaining, the judge usually supplies nothing in the way of a coherent and rational judgment when he informs the
defendant of his fate.

[The] parties (especially the loser) are, on deep principles, not merely entitled to a decision; they are entitled to an explanation. . . . The duty to give an account of the decision is to promote thought by the decider, to compel him to cover the relevant points, to help him eschew irrelevancies — and, finally, to make him show that these necessities have been served. The requirement of reasons expressly stated is not a guarantee of fairness. The judge or other official may give good reasons while he acts upon outrageous ones. However, given decision-makers who are both tolerably honest and normally fallible, the requirement of stated reasons is a powerful safeguard against rash and arbitrary decisions. Knowing this to be so, we apply it to affairs of lesser consequence, yet we place no burden of explanation upon the judge who decides that the defendant before him must be locked up for ten years rather than five or one or none. . . .

Improvements in communications are less perceptible — they are practically nonexistent — when we move on to the parole stage. [Parole] boards, like judges and prison officials, for the most part neglect altogether to supply information or explanations. . . . Parole boards don't explain. They confer miracles or they refuse. . . . The general fact [is] that most parole boards, subject to no precise rules of any kind, decree secretly and silently how tens and hundreds of thousands of convict-years shall be passed.

INDETERMINATE SENTENCES

The case for the indeterminate sentence rests, initially, upon a laudable concern for each unique individual, coupled with a frequently baseless assumption that we are able effectively to understand and uniquely to "treat" the individual. The offender is "sick," runs the humane thought, and/or dangerous. He needs to be helped and "cured." Nobody, certainly not the sentencing judge, can know when he will be well and no more dangerous than the masses of us who are lucky enough not to have been convicted. Hence, those charged with "treatment" must be left to decide the time for release.

This "rehabilitative ideal" [is based on] the fallacious — or, at least, far too broad — assumption that criminals are "sick" in some way that calls for "treatment." . . . We sentence many people every day who are not "sick" in any identifiable respect and are certainly not candidates for any form of therapy or "rehabilitation" known thus far. Many convicted criminals . . . are not driven by, or "acting out," neurotic or psychotic impulses. Instead, they have coldly and deliberately figured the odds, risked punishment for rewards large enough (in their view) to justify the risk, but then had the misfortune to be caught. It seems likely that many of those in organized crime fall within this category. The same is true for large numbers (though by no means all) of those who scheme to defraud, to evade taxes, to counterfeit the currency, or to commit other varieties of acquisitive crime. . . .

The apostles of rehabilitation and indeterminate sentences posit "sickness" without identifying its character and then urge "treatment" no better defined or specified. The absence of treatment or facilities is by itself a fatal defect [as] there is no justification for a regime of rehabilitation through indeterminate sentences unless we have some substantial hope or prospect of rehabilitating. Our subject is, after all, the confinement of people for long and uncertain periods of time. It is an evil to lock people up. There may be compensating goods that warrant it. But a mythical goal of rehabilitation is no good at all. . . .

Believing, then, that there is need for broad and drastic reform of the law, I [offer these] legislative proposals. . . . To begin at the elementary beginning, we have an almost entire absence in the United States of legislative determinations — of "law" — governing the basic questions as to the purposes and justifications of criminal sanctions. Without binding guides on such questions, it is inevitable that individual sentencers will strike out on a multiplicity of courses chosen by each decision-maker for himself. The result is chaos. . . .

Along with the declaration of sentencing purposes, the legislature would — certainly it should — provide that the judge (or sentencing tribunal) must state which among the allowable purposes were the supposed bases for each particular sentence. The simple requirement would compel the judge to think connectedly about his reasons and to justify explicitly decisions now taken on unarticulated hunches. . . . And it would open the way for intelligent scrutiny on appeal since an appellate court can function usefully only when it knows the grounds of the decision brought to it for review. . . .

TOWARD CODIFIED WEIGHTS AND MEASURES

[We allow the sentencing judge] not merely to "weigh" the various elements that go into a sentence [but also] leave to his unfettered (and usually unspoken) preferences the determination as to what factors ought to be considered at all, and in what direction. . . . We do not allow each judge to make up the law for himself on other questions. We should not allow it with respect to sentencing. . . .

Beyond codifying the numerous factors affecting the length or severity of sentences, an acceptable code of penal law should, in my judgment, prescribe guidelines for the application and assessment of these factors. While it may seem dry, technical, unromantic, and "mechanical," I have in mind the creation eventually of a detailed chart or calculus — to be used (1) by the sentencing judge in weighing the many elements that go into the sentence; (2) by lawyers, probation officers, and others undertaking to persuade or enlighten the judge; and (3) by appellate courts in reviewing what the judge has done.

[The sentencing judge] will presumably consider a host of factors in the case: the relative seriousness of the particular offense — the degree of danger threatened, cruelty, premeditation; the prior record of the defendant; situational factors — health, family disturbance, drug use; the defendant's work history, skills, potential; etc. In the existing mode of handling the sentence, the judge is under no pressure — and is without guidelines — toward systematic, exhaustive, detailed appraisal of such things one by one. He probably does not list them even for himself. He certainly does not record or announce the analysis. Probably, in most cases, he broods in a diffuse way toward a hunch that becomes a sentence. . . .

The partial remedy I propose is a kind of detailed profile or checklist of factors that would include, wherever possible, some form of numerical or other objective grading. Still being crude and cursory, I suggest that "gravity of offense" could be graded along a scale from, perhaps, 1 to 5. Other factors could be handled in the same way. The overall result might be a score — or, possibly, an individual profile of sentencing elements — that would make it feasible to follow the sentencer's estimates, criticize them, and compare the sentence in the given case with others.

The justification for such a technique does not require that we accept delusions of precision. Admittedly, "gravity of offense" does not lend itself to weighing with the mechanical simplicity of grocery or jewelers' scales. But we know from sufficiently analogous fields that numerical statements may serve, for obviously non-quantifiable subjects, as useful implements for clarification of thought, comparisons, and criticism. . . . The physician who speaks of a grade-three heart murmur may not be reporting a measurement as precise as the number of feet in a yard. But he says a meaningful thing that informs and guides others professionally trained. . . . It is not necessary, or desirable, to imagine that sentencing can be completely computerized. . . .

A Commission on Sentencing

Using the jargon of our time, entirely apt in this instance, there are huge needs for organized research and development in the field of sentencing. . . . There must be a commitment to change, to application of the learning as it is acquired. . . . Since we deal with the law, the normal agency of change is, increasingly, the legislature. But the subject of sentencing is not steadily exhilarating to elected officials. There are no powerful lobbies of prisoners, jailers, or, indeed, judges, to goad and reward. Thus, accounting in good part for our plight, legislative action tends to be sporadic and impassioned, responding in haste to momentary crises, lapsing then into the accustomed state of inattention. . . .

These thoughts . . . lead to my proposed "Commission on Sentencing" [which] would be a permanent agency responsible for (1) the study of sentencing, corrections, and parole; (2) the formulation of laws and rules to which the studies pointed; and (3) *the actual enactment of rules*, subject to traditional checks by Congress and the courts. . . . The commission would require prestige and credibility. It would be necessary to find for it people of stature, competence, devotion, and eloquence. The kinds of people . . . could include lawyers, judges, penologists, and criminologists. They should also include sociologists, psychologists, business people, artists, and, lastly for emphasis, former or present prison inmates.

[The] commission would have the function of actually enacting rules — i.e., making law. This suggestion would presumably generate controversy; legislators do not (and should not) lightly delegate their authority. Nevertheless, there is both precedent and good reason for delegating in this instance. As I have said, the subjects of sentencing, corrections, and parole are going to need ongoing study and an indefinite course of revision. Sweeping changes of policy, touching basic principles and institutions, will naturally remain for the legislature to determine from time to time. But relative details, numerous and cumulatively important, neither require nor are likely to receive from the legislature the necessary measure of steady attention. Thinking along such lines, Congress has delegated in a variety of fields — e.g., securities, transportation, communications — rulemaking powers with substantial day-to-day impact upon the affected areas. The suggestion here contemplates an analogous arrangement. . . .

The uses of a commission, if one is created, will warrant volumes of debate and analysis. For this moment and this writer, the main thing is to plead for an instrumentality, whatever its name or detailed form, to marshal full-time wisdom and power against the ignorance and the barbarities that characterize sentencing for crimes today. . . .

NOTES

1. *Rise and fall of the rehabilitative ideal.*   As highlighted by Judge Frankel, the grant of broad discretion to sentencing judges and parole officials was linked to a rehabilitative "medical" model of sentencing and corrections in which authority to individualize punishments seemed essential. This model of punishment emerged in the United States from the early development of the modern penitentiary in the late 1800s. See David Rothman, Perfecting the Prison, in The Oxford History of the Prison 111-129 (Norval Morris & David Rothman eds., 1995). The rehabilitative model grew in prominence throughout the 1900s, finding expression in state statutes and model codes, Supreme Court opinions, and major governmental reports. See, e.g., Model Penal Code §6.10 ("An offender sentenced to an indefinite term of imprisonment in excess of one year . . . shall be released conditionally on parole at or before the expiration of the maximum of such term."); §7.04 ("The Court may sentence a person who has been convicted of a misdemeanor or petty misdemeanor to an extended term of imprisonment if it finds [that the defendant] is a chronic alcoholic, narcotic addict, prostitute or person of abnormal mental condition who requires rehabilitative treatment for a substantial period of time."); Williams v. New York, 337 U.S. 241 (1949) (explaining that "reformation and rehabilitation of offenders have become important goals of criminal jurisprudence" and noting the "prevalent modern philosophy that the punishment should fit the offender and not merely the crime"); President's Commission on Law Enforcement and Administration of Justice, The Challenge of Crime in a Free Society 159-166, 171-177 (1967) (discussing the new "reform model" in which an offender is a "patient" and the system follows "a new maxim — 'Let the treatment fit the needs of the individual offender'").

As the excerpt highlights, Judge Frankel questioned both the effectiveness and the appropriateness of a purely rehabilitative model of corrections within his broader criticisms of discretionary sentencing practices. Writing around the same time, many other commentators across the political spectrum — liberals stressing concerns about inequitable and uncertain treatment of offenders, and conservatives highlighting increased crime rates and the apparent ineffectiveness of rehabilitative efforts — developed similar criticisms about indeterminate sentencing and the "rehabilitative ideal." See American Friends Service Committee, Struggle for Justice (1971); James Q. Wilson, Thinking About Crime (1975); Francis A. Allen, The Decline of the Rehabilitative Ideal 3-20 (1981) (discussing the "dominance" of the rehabilitative ideal through the late 1960s and the subsequent "wide and precipitous decline of penal rehabilitationism" as a foundational theory for the criminal justice system).

2. *Evidence of disparity and other calls for reform.*   Judge Frankel was not alone in identifying the problem of sentencing disparity and the consequent need for sentencing reform. An influential 1976 report of the Twentieth Century Fund Task Force on Criminal Sentencing lamented that discretionary sentencing schemes were creating "unexplained and seemingly inexplicable sentencing disparity," and it marshaled some of the evidence of this disparity:

> One recent study . . . of felony sentences imposed by judges in one Ohio county [showed that] one judge granted probation to 26% of convicted offenders; another judge imposed probationary terms upon 51% of convicted offenders. . . . One judge imprisoned 56% of black defendants but only 35% of white defendants. . . . A South Carolina sample of sentencing [showed] in two marijuana cases, the same judge sentenced a white youth to one year's probation and a $400 fine; a black male received a two-year sentence. . . . A recent study commissioned by the judges of the U.S. Court of Appeals for the Second Circuit involved 50 federal judges who were given 20 identical files drawn from actual cases and asked what sentence they would impose on each defendant. In [an extortion case], one judge proposed a sentence of 20 years' imprisonment plus a $65,000 fine [while] another judge proposed a 3-year sentence with no fine.

Fair and Certain Punishment: Report of the Twentieth Century Fund Task Force on Criminal Sentencing 3-29 (1976). For similar expressions of concern about sentencing disparity and uncertainty in discretionary sentencing systems, see National Conference of Commissioners on Uniform State Laws, Model Sentencing and Corrections Act (1979); David Fogel, "We Are the Living Proof": The Justice Model for Corrections (1976).

3. *Frankel's impact on federal and state reforms.*   Because Judge Frankel provided a provocative blueprint for change, his book served as a major catalyst for modern sentencing reforms. Most tangibly, Judge Frankel's work became the centerpiece of a series of policy workshops at Yale Law School, which culminated in a book proposing federal legislation for sentencing reform. See Pierce O'Donnell et al., Toward a Just and Effective Sentencing System (1977). The findings of the Yale workshops and accompanying book in turn provided the foundation for a federal sentencing reform bill introduced by Senator Edward Kennedy of Massachusetts. In addition, many states looked directly to Judge Frankel's suggestions when embarking on their own sentencing reform efforts. Professor Kevin Reitz has effectively summarized the importance and impact of Judge Frankel's work:

> Judge Frankel's *Criminal Sentences* may be the single most influential work of criminal justice scholarship in the last 20 years. It stands as the best indictment of traditional, indeterminate sentencing practices in the literature. Its proposals have charted the general outline of sentencing reform through the 1980s and into the 1990s [and] the ABA adopted a new edition of its Sentencing Standards modeled largely on Judge Frankel's early plan for commission-based regulation of sentencing discretion.

Kevin R. Reitz, Sentencing Reform in the States: An Overview of the Colorado Law Review Symposium, 64 U. Colo. L. Rev. 645, 650 n.21 (1993). Current drafts of the American Law Institute's project to revise the sentencing provisions of the Model Penal Code also endorse the use of sentencing commissions to develop coherent sentencing policy.

2. Development and Structure of State Guideline Systems

Through the late 1970s and early 1980s, legislatures in a few states — most notably California and North Carolina — passed determinate sentencing statutes that abolished parole and created presumptive sentencing ranges for various classes of offenses. Minnesota became the first state to turn Judge Frankel's ideas into a full-fledged reality when in 1978 the state legislature established the Minnesota Sentencing Guidelines Commission to develop comprehensive sentencing guidelines. Pennsylvania and Washington soon thereafter created their own distinctive forms of sentencing commissions and sentencing guidelines, and the federal government followed suit through the passage of the Sentencing Reform Act of 1984, which created the U.S. Sentencing Commission to develop guidelines for federal sentencing. By the year 2000, nearly every state in the country had adopted some form of structured sentencing; though a number of states did so only through a few mandatory sentencing statutes, many states created sentencing commissions to develop comprehensive guideline schemes.

Because so many states have now adopted some form of sentencing guidelines and because each state's system has some unique features, it is difficult to summarize the development and fundamental characteristics of all state guideline systems. One state worth examining closely is Minnesota, the first to create comprehensive sentencing guidelines through the work of a sentencing commission. Minnesota has enjoyed a quarter-century of success with its reforms and stands as a trailblazer for state guideline systems.

Structuring Criminal Sentencing, Dale Parent
Pages 51-53, 57-60 (1988)

In at least three major respects, Minnesota's venture altered traditional institutions and concepts in the realm of criminal sentencing:

- It substituted a new system — guided discretion — for the more extreme methods of dividing authority over the punishment process between legislatures and courts.
- It inserted a new governmental entity — the sentencing commission — between the legislature and the judiciary, and authorized the commission to monitor and continuously adjust criminal sentences.
- And it established an unprecedented conceptual connection — known as capacity constraint — between the degree of severity with which guidelines could specify prison sentences and the extent to which state prison resources were available to carry such sentences into effect. . . .

Minnesota's innovation [conferred] on guidelines the force of law. The former system of indeterminate prison sentences set by a judge, subject to the possibility of early release in the discretion of a parole board, was abolished. In its place came a system of determinate sentences, set by the judge under guidance from the sentencing commission, with review by an appellate court. Five key elements were incorporated into this plan:

- First, sentences would be scaled to take account of differences both in the gravity of crimes and the prior records of offenders. Guidance would be specified in the form of sentencing ranges, rather than precise sentences.

- Second, factors relevant to the individualization process would be standardized and weighted in advance. Clear rules would encourage similar outcomes in similar cases. Proportionality among different cases would be facilitated by a carefully constructed hierarchy of offense seriousness.

- Third, a set of departure principles would define the circumstances under which judges could deviate from the guideline sentencing range with good reasons. Judges would thus retain discretion to set the actual sentence, to do justice on a case-by-case basis.

- Fourth, sentencing judges would be required to state reasons for each sentence that differed from the applicable guideline, to assure accountability and reviewability.

- Fifth, all sentences would be subject to review by an appellate court whose written opinions could, over time, evolve finely tuned principles to guide future sentencers. . . .

The [1978 Minnesota] law created a nine-member Sentencing Guidelines Commission, consisting of the chief justice or his designee, two district court judges appointed by the chief justice, the Commission of Corrections, the chairman of the Minnesota Corrections Board, and four gubernatorial appointees — a prosecutor, a public defender, and two citizens. . . . The [Commission's] guidelines . . . were to recommend when state imprisonment was appropriate and to recommend presumptive sentencing durations. . . . Judges had to give written reasons for sentences that departed from the guidelines recommendation. The state or the defense could appeal any sentence. . . . The Commission sought to assure that guideline punishments would be proportional to the seriousness of offenders' crimes. To achieve that proportionality, it was necessary for the Commission to rank crimes in the order of their seriousness. The seriousness of a crime varies according to the gravity of the offense and the blameworthiness of the offender. Gravity is determined by the harm caused, directly or as a consequence of the crime. Blameworthiness is determined by the offender's motivation, intent, and behavior in the crime and is enhanced if the offender previously has been convicted of and sentenced for criminal acts. . . .

Although most of us have an intuitive sense of offense seriousness, the concept is highly complex. [Judgments] about the seriousness of criminal events may involve facts about offenders, victims, and criminal acts. Some factors can be dismissed because all would agree they are irrelevant to assessing gravity or ascribing blame — for example, that the victim was a Mason or the offender was a Methodist. Some facts are both irrelevant and invidious — such as that the offender and the victim were of the same or different races. But there is a long list of factors that some would consider relevant to assessing harm or ascribing blame.

The victim may be a normal healthy adult or a person who may be especially vulnerable due to age or infirmity. In violent crimes the extent of physical injury may vary from a scratch to death. Some victims may recover fully from physical injuries, while others suffer permanent damage or impairment. In property crimes, the victim's loss could range from a small amount to a fortune.

The consequences of property loss may vary greatly with the economic status of the victim. The crime may involve one victim or many. A crime might involve an offender acting alone or in concert with others. . . .

Given events as complex and diverse as criminal acts, how was the Commission to go about judging their seriousness? [The Commission created a subcommittee to divide the task into more manageable components. The subcommittee grouped] crimes into 6 categories — violent, arson, sex, drug, property, and miscellaneous — 5 of which contained 20 or fewer crimes. . . . The subcommittee instructed the Commission to focus on the usual or typical case in [a] ranking exercise. . . . In phase one, individual Commission members ranked crimes within each of the six categories. . . . Phases two, three, and four relied on identification of differences among members, on the articulation of reasons for those differences, and on debate about those reasons. . . . When differences existed it assured that the basis of the differences would be discovered and scrutinized and that the final rankings would reflect a majority opinion. [The] Commission divided the overall ranking into ten seriousness levels. . . . [The accompanying table] shows the most common types of offenses within each of the ten seriousness levels.

Most Frequent Offenses in Seriousness Scale

Seriousness Level	Most Frequent Offenses
1.	Aggravated forgery, less than $100
	Possession of marijuana (more than 1.5 ounces)
	Unauthorized use of a motor vehicle
2.	Aggravated forgery, $150 to $2,500
	Sale of marijuana . . .
3.	Aggravated forgery, over $2,500
	Arson, third-degree . . .
	Theft crimes, $150 to $2,500
	Sale of cocaine
	Possession of LSD, PCP
4.	Burglary, nondwellings and unoccupied dwellings
	Theft crimes, over $2,500
	Receiving stolen goods, $150 to $2,500
	Criminal sexual assault, fourth-degree
	Assault, third-degree (injury)
5.	Criminal negligence (resulting in death)
	Criminal sexual conduct, third-degree
	Manslaughter, second-degree . . .
	Witness tampering
	Simple (unarmed) robbery . . .
6.	Assault, second-degree (weapon)
	Burglary (occupied dwelling)
	Criminal sexual conduct, second-degree . . .
	Kidnapping (released in a safe place)
	Sale, LSD or PCP
	Sale, heroin and remaining hard narcotics
	Receiving stolen goods, over $2,500

Most Frequent Offenses in Seriousness Scale *(Cont'd)*

Seriousness Level	Most Frequent Offenses
7.	Aggravated (armed) robbery
	Arson, first-degree
	Burglary (victim injured) ...
	Kidnapping (not released in a safe place)
	Manslaughter, first-degree ...
8.	Assault, first-degree (great bodily harm)
	Kidnapping (great bodily harm)
	Criminal sexual conduct, first-degree
9.	Murder, third-degree
10.	Murder, second-degree

NOTES

1. *Voluntary and presumptive sentencing guidelines in the states.*   Though the federal sentencing guidelines garner the most attention from courts and commentators, nearly half the states regulate their sentencing judges' discretion through their own guidelines. In most states, a sentencing commission drafts an initial set of guidelines on behalf of the state legislature, which then enacts it as an integrated package of sentencing reforms. But in a few states, the judiciary adopts a package of guidelines as procedural rules or as informal guidance to judges. Some guidelines are only voluntary: there is no review of a judge's application of the guidelines or decision to sentence outside the range recommended in the guidelines so long as the judge remains within the statutory maximum and minimum for the crime. Other guidelines are presumptive: a judge who misapplies the guidelines or sentences outside the presumed range for sentences without an adequate justification can be overturned on appeal.

If you were a legislator in a state considering the adoption of sentencing guidelines, would you create a sentencing commission or instead look for mechanisms through which the judiciary might develop sentencing structures on its own? Regardless of the institution used to develop guidelines, would you prefer a voluntary or a presumptive approach? What do you see as the potential benefits and drawbacks of each approach to the development of sentencing guidelines?

The Supreme Court's interpretation of the Sixth Amendment in Blakely v. Washington and United States v. Booker appears to endow juries with an expanded factfinding role in presumptive guidelines systems, but it also permits judges to engage in factfinding within voluntary guideline systems. As a result, a number of jurisdictions, either through judicial rulings or legislative changes, have adjusted their systems away from presumptive guidelines systems toward voluntary guideline systems. Do you think judges operating within a presumptive guideline system are likely to follow the guidelines with the same rigor if a judicial decision or new legislation suddenly converts the system to a voluntary one?

2. *Policy authority given to sentencing commissions.*   As highlighted above, the Minnesota Sentencing Commission was given broad authority to assess the seriousness of various offenses when developing sentencing guidelines. Indeed, as

Professor Michael Tonry has noted, the Minnesota Sentencing Commission initially made many "bold policy decisions":

> First, it decided to be "prescriptive" and to establish its own explicit sentencing priorities [rather than] to be "descriptive," to attempt to replicate existing sentencing patterns. Second, the commission decided to de-emphasize imprisonment as a punishment for property offenders and to emphasize imprisonment for violent offenders. . . . Third, in order to attack sentencing disparities, the commission decided to establish narrow sentencing ranges (for example, 30 to 34 months, or 50 to 58 months) and to authorize departures from guideline ranges only when "substantial and compelling" reasons were present. Fourth, the commission elected to adopt "just deserts" as the governing premise of its policies concerning who receives prison sentences. Fifth, the commission chose to interpret an ambiguous statutory injunction that it take correctional resources into "substantial consideration" as a mandate that its guidelines not increase prison populations beyond existing capacity constraints. . . . Sixth, the commission forbade consideration at sentencing of many personal factors — such as education, employment, marital status, living arrangements — that many judges believed to be legitimate. This decision resulted from a policy that sentencing decisions not be based on factors that might directly or indirectly discriminate against minorities, women, or low-income groups. . . .

Michael Tonry, Sentencing Guidelines and Their Effects 16-20 (1987). If you were a legislator who had voted in favor of (or against) establishing the Minnesota Sentencing Commission, would you override any of the commission's important policy decisions? How and to what extent should legislatures and sentencing commissions interact in making key policy decisions about the structure and content of guideline systems? Should certain policy decisions be made only by elected legislatures as opposed to appointed commissions?

   3. *Discretion within ranges and departure authority.*   Even in guideline systems that are presumptive, judges typically retain a measure of sentencing discretion through their power to select a specific sentence within the ranges set forth in the guidelines, as well as through their more limited authority to depart from those ranges. In a few states, guidelines provide fairly broad ranges from which judges make their sentencing decisions, although these states tend to be more restrictive concerning departures from the ranges. Representing the most extreme example, North Carolina's guidelines establish ranges in which the longest available sentence is often twice the shortest available sentence, but they do not permit departures from these ranges for any reason. See http://www. nccourts.org/Courts/CRS/Councils/spac/Documents/felonypunishmentchart. pdf. In most states, the ranges provided in the guidelines are fairly narrow, but authority to depart is given to sentencing judges. In Kansas, for example, the longest sentence within a prescribed range is usually no more than 20% higher than the shortest sentence, but judges can depart from these ranges on numerous grounds.

   Departures may affect either the disposition of the sentence (active prison term or nonprison sanctions) or the duration of the sentence (the number of months to be served), and statutes generally require the judge to explain in writing any departure. In most jurisdictions, the selection of a particular sentence from the applicable guidelines sentencing range is not subject to appeal, but departure decisions are appealable, and reliance on improper grounds or inadequate explanations for a departure can lead to reversal. Although appellate courts in many jurisdictions have developed extensive case law approving or disapproving various grounds for departure, rarely do they examine a sentencing judge's decision not to depart. Should defendants' and prosecutors' opportunities to appeal a decision *not* to depart be equivalent to their opportunities to appeal a decision to depart from the guidelines?

4. *Amending the rules.*   States with sentencing guidelines sometimes need to amend those guidelines over time, in response to the passage of new criminal prohibitions or to problematic judicial interpretations of certain guidelines, or when particular guidelines provisions do not work well. States typically give the leading role in the amendment process to a permanent sentencing commission, although the commission's power to amend the guidelines varies. In the largest group of states, the commission only recommends changes to the guidelines, and the legislature (and sometimes the state supreme court) must approve the changes before they become law. See Kan. Stat. Ann. §74-9101(b)(2), (6), (7); N.C. Gen. Stat. §§164-36, 164-43. Elsewhere, amendments to the guidelines take effect at the end of the commission's administrative rule-making process or after a waiting period to give the legislature a chance to pass a statute disapproving of the changes. See Minn. Stat. Ann. §244.09(11); 42 Pa. Cons. Stat. §2153(a)(1). Would you expect these procedural variations to make any difference in the content of sentencing guidelines?

PROBLEM 3-1.   THE MINNESOTA MACHINE

Clayton James Hanks broke into a home outside Minneapolis one night and stole some stereo equipment, worth about $1,000. He also went into the backyard of the home and took some tools. The prosecutor charged Hanks with residential burglary and theft; Hanks pled guilty to both charges. Hanks has no prior arrests or convictions on his record.

At sentencing, the trial court calculated the outcome prescribed under the Minnesota sentencing guidelines. The presumptive sentence for any felon is determined by locating the appropriate cell of the Sentencing Guidelines Grid, reprinted below. The vertical axis of the grid represents the severity level of the offense of conviction. When an offender is convicted of two or more felonies, the severity level is determined by the most severe offense of conviction. The most frequently occurring offenses within a severity level are listed on the vertical axis of the grid.

The horizontal axis of the grid looks to the offender's criminal history. The offender is assigned a particular score for every prior criminal or juvenile sentence, with the more severe prior crimes assigned a larger number of points.

The guidelines remind judges that "the capacities of state and local correctional facilities are finite" and that "incarcerative sanctions should be limited to those convicted of more serious offenses or those who have longer criminal histories." In general, the "sanctions used in sentencing convicted felons should be the least restrictive necessary to achieve the purposes of the sentence."

Sentencing Guidelines Grid
Presumptive Sentence Lengths in Months

Italicized numbers within the grid denote the range within which a judge may sentence without the sentence being deemed a departure. Offenders with nonimprisonment felony sentences are subject to jail time according to law.

SEVERITY LEVEL OF CONVICTION OFFENSE (Common offenses listed in italics)		**CRIMINAL HISTORY SCORE**						
		0	1	2	3	4	5	6 or more
Murder, 2nd Degree (intentional murder; drive-by-shootings)	XI	306 *299-313*	326 *319-333*	346 *339-353*	366 *359-373*	386 *379-393*	406 *399-413*	426 *419-433*
Murder, 3rd Degree Murder, 2nd Degree (unintentional murder)	X	150 *144-156*	165 *159-171*	180 *174-186*	195 *189-201*	210 *204-216*	225 *219-231*	240 *234-246*
Criminal Sexual Conduct, 1st Degree[2] Assault, 1st Degree	IX	86 *81-91*	98 *93-103*	110 *105-115*	122 *117-127*	134 *129-139*	146 *141-151*	158 *153-163*
Aggravated Robbery 1st Degree	VIII	48 *44-52*	58 *54-62*	68 *64-72*	78 *74-82*	88 *84-92*	98 *94-102*	108 *104-112*
Felony DWI	VII	36	42	48	54 *51-57*	60 *57-63*	66 *63-69*	72 *69-75*
Criminal Sexual Conduct, 2nd Degree (a) & (b)	VI	21	27	33	39 *37-41*	45 *43-47*	51 *49-53*	57 *55-59*
Residential Burglary Simple Robbery	V	18	23	28	33 *31-35*	38 *36-40*	43 *41-45*	48 *46-50*
Nonresidential Burglary	IV	12[1]	15	18	21	24 *23-25*	27 *26-28*	30 *29-31*
Theft Crimes (Over $2,500)	III	12[1]	13	15	17	19 *18-20*	21 *20-22*	23 *22-24*
Theft Crimes ($2,500 or less) Check Forgery ($200-$2,500)	II	12[1]	12[1]	13	15	17	19	21 *20-22*
Sale of Simulated Controlled Substance	I	12[1]	12[1]	12[1]	13	15	17	19 *18-20*

☐ Presumptive commitment to state imprisonment. First Degree Murder is excluded from the guidelines by law and continues to have a mandatory life sentence. See section II.E. **Mandatory Sentences** for policy regarding those sentences controlled by law, including minimum periods of supervision for sex offenders released from prison.

 Presumptive stayed sentence; at the discretion of the judge, up to a year in jail and/or other non-jail sanctions can be imposed as conditions of probation. However, certain offenses in this section of the grid always carry a presumptive commitment to state prison. These offenses include Third Degree Controlled Substance Crimes when the offender has a prior felony drug conviction, Burglary of an Occupied Dwelling when the offender has a prior felony burglary conviction, second and subsequent Criminal Sexual Conduct offenses and offenses carrying a mandatory minimum prison term due to the use of a dangerous weapon (e.g., Second Degree Assault). See sections II.C. **Presumptive Sentence** and II.E. **Mandatory Sentences**.

The Minnesota guidelines are presumptive, meaning that any sentence selected from outside the designated range is subject to appeal. The guidelines say that departures from the presumptive sentences established in the guidelines "should be made only when substantial and compelling circumstances exist."

As a judge, what arguments from the prosecution or the defense might be persuasive as you decide whether to depart from the presumptive outcome under the guidelines? What facts would be important to you?

> *Sentencing Guidelines in Minnesota, Other*
> *States, and the Federal Courts: A Twenty-Year*
> *Retrospective, Richard S. Frase*
> 12 Fed. Sent'g Rep. 69 (1999)

As of 1999, about one-third of the states had sentencing guidelines in effect, and guidelines reforms were being considered in a number of other states. But guidelines systems are not all alike. . . . Although state guidelines systems are very diverse, they have a couple of things in common which distinguish them from the federal guidelines. Without exception, state systems are more flexible than the federal guidelines. There is a range; some state systems are so flexible that they are hardly "guidelines" at all, others are much more restrictive. . . .

Another thing that distinguishes state guidelines is that they are relatively simple to apply. The federal guidelines are quite ambitious; they try to regulate every decision. This is related to the flexibility point, but it goes beyond that. State guidelines are generally relatively short documents; sometimes very short. [It] is important to keep guidelines relatively easy to apply and easy for courts, defendants, and the public to understand. That is an important point which was lost in the federal system.

[There are some] important structural differences among guidelines systems. . . . For instance, Delaware, Florida, and Ohio don't use a grid (although their "narrative" or "point-system" guidelines could be translated into a grid). State and federal grids vary considerably in such things as: whether certain offenses have a separate grid; the number of grid cells; the breadth of cell ranges; and whether the ranges of adjoining cells overlap. Guidelines systems also differ in the number of disposition options permitted for a given case (e.g., prison, jail, restrictive intermediate sanctions, etc.); whether any guidance is offered as to the choice among sentencing purposes; how criminal history is defined; how multiple offenses are sentenced; and the extent to which the sentencing commission has made independent judgments about appropriate sentences (so-called "prescriptive" rules), rather than simply compiling guidelines which are descriptive of past judicial and paroling practices. . . .

THE CHANGING PURPOSES OF SENTENCING GUIDELINES

The original goals of sentencing guidelines reforms were two-fold. First, to reduce sentencing discretion and its resulting disparities; and second, to promote more rational sentencing policy developed and monitored by a specialized sentencing commission. . . . Since Minnesota's Guidelines first became effective, sentencing goals and values in Minnesota and other guidelines jurisdictions have evolved considerably. [I]t appears that the goal of disparity reduction has become somewhat less important, while other goals have become more important. . . . Almost every guidelines system which was adopted or revised since the mid-1980s has included resource-impact assessments, in an attempt to avoid prison overcrowding and control the growth of prison populations. More recent guideline reforms are also more likely to regulate and attempt to encourage the use of intermediate sanctions. Broader use of such sanctions

is intended to reduce unnecessary prison use — thus avoiding prison overcrowding and reducing prison costs — and also to better promote public safety. . . .

WHAT HAVE GUIDELINES ACCOMPLISHED?

How well have state guidelines [worked]? Any such assessment must begin
with a frank admission: no "expert" on sentencing guidelines can say very much
about how most state guidelines systems have worked in practice. In some cases,
this is because a state's system is too new to have generated enough data for
evaluation. In other cases, the guidelines commission has not published or
commissioned any evaluations, nor is there some professor or other outside
researcher who takes a special interest in that state's guidelines. So much of
what follows is based on a few, well-documented systems, and some "educated
guesswork" about the rest.

Disparity Reduction.   Since most guidelines systems have abolished parole,
they have eliminated that form of disparity. Judicial sentencing disparities have
also been reduced, at least in the states which have been evaluated. Minnesota is
the only system to have been subjected to extensive outside evaluation, but data
reported by sentencing commissions or their staff suggest that disparity has also
been reduced in Delaware, Oregon, Pennsylvania and Washington. Two of these
five jurisdictions do not have legally-binding guidelines (Delaware's are formally
voluntary, and Pennsylvania's lack effective appellate review). . . .

More Rational Sentencing Policy.   [Most] guidelines systems include a
permanent sentencing commission. Although some are more active than others,
all of these commissions have begun to develop useful sentencing policy expertise, a comprehensive state-wide view of punishment priorities, better management of resources, and a long-term perspective. Even in states with fairly weak
guidelines, sentencing commissions can play an important role, not just in drafting guidelines but also by advising the legislature as to various sentencing policy
matters of current concern.

As for the increasingly important goal of resource-impact assessment, there
is considerable evidence that sentencing guidelines can help to avoid prison
overcrowding and the kinds of dramatic (and very expensive) escalation in
prison populations which has occurred in many non-guidelines states in the
past 20 years. Minnesota pioneered this concept, and has successfully avoided
major prison overcrowding problems for almost two decades — a period in
which most non-guidelines states experienced both overcrowding and court
intervention. Although Minnesota's prison population has increased substantially since 1979, the average annual rate of growth (about 5 percent per year)
has only been about two-thirds the rate for the nation as a whole (8 percent per
year). Other guidelines jurisdictions which emphasized resource-management
goals have also had low average annual growth rates. . . .

Truth in Sentencing.   Any system which has abolished parole release
discretion — as the majority of guidelines systems have done — has achieved
a greater degree of "truth in sentencing." Of course, this goal has also been

achieved in a number of states which abolished parole without adopting judicial sentencing guidelines. However, there is reason to believe that the abolition of parole works much better in a system with such guidelines. [Systems] with judicial guidelines have less need to rely on state-wide parole standards as a means of reducing disparity in the sentences imposed by local judges. [Further,] systems with guidelines and a permanent sentencing commission are in a better position to predict the effects abolition of parole will have on prison populations; such systems can then either build more prisons, modify the guidelines to lower prison commitment or duration rates, or pursue a combination of these strategies. In contrast, the abolition of parole, in a system without judicial guidelines, eliminates a means of counteracting judicial disparity and prison overcrowding at the "back end" of the sentencing process, without providing any means of controlling these problems from the "front end."

Public Safety.   States with sentencing guidelines have generally had stable or falling crime rates since their guidelines became effective. However, crime rates have recently been stable or falling in most states, with or without guidelines. And, of course, crime rates depend on many social and economic factors in addition to sentencing policy; a thorough examination of the relationship between guidelines and public safety would thus be very complex (and has not been attempted by quantitative criminologists). But the stable or falling pattern of crime rates, noted above, at least suggests that sentencing guidelines do not threaten public safety. . . .

Two Persistent Challenges

Despite the accomplishments of many state guidelines, there are a number of legitimate criticisms which can be leveled at even the best of these systems. Two of the most important problems are the failure to effectively regulate prosecutorial discretion and plea bargaining; and the limited efforts to regulate and encourage the use of non-custodial ("intermediate") sanctions. Although each of these "gaps" in guidelines coverage is a problem, neither is a major problem in well-designed systems; indeed they may even be strengths, helping these systems accommodate important contemporary sentencing goals and values.

Prosecutorial Discretion and Plea Bargaining.   . . . Since guidelines limit the range of sentences available for a given offense, the power to drop or not drop charges is the power to select the sentence range available to the court (that is, what "box" on the grid the case ends up in). Thus, any disparity in charging translates into disparity in sentencing. Unregulated charging and plea bargaining also make it more difficult for the sentencing commission to predict future resource needs. Yet no guidelines system has come up with an effective way of structuring prosecutorial sentencing power, and its potential for disparity and unpredictability. Washington has state-wide charging guidelines, but they are not legally enforceable. The federal Guidelines tried to mitigate this problem by requiring trial courts to consider certain alleged criminal acts ("relevant conduct") whether or not such acts were included in any conviction offense. But this essentially lawless approach goes too far in the opposite direction — allowing sentences to be based on weak charges which were properly dismissed, resulted in acquittal, or were never even filed.

What should be done? Clearly efforts to structure prosecutorial discretion and plea bargaining should continue, especially by means of internal, administrative measures within prosecutor's offices, such as written policies and review of decisions by supervising staff. [But it will be very difficult to enforce controls,] especially to impose lower limits on charge and recommended-sentence severity (since, in most cases, neither prosecutors nor defendants will appeal cases of prosecution leniency).

However, I believe that most state guidelines systems are valuable reforms even if prosecutorial decisions remain substantially unregulated. I have two reasons for this belief. First, the absence of widespread complaints about prosecutorial dominance in state guidelines systems is an important sign, suggesting that closer regulation may not be needed. Specifically, I am suggesting that, in a properly balanced guidelines system — that is, one with reasonable sentence severity levels and few mandatory minimum statutes, in which courts retain substantial sentencing discretion for any given offense (due to broad guidelines ranges, limited appellate scrutiny, and/or flexible departure powers) — it is rare that prosecutorial decisions will produce sentences which judges strongly disapprove, yet are powerless to prevent (as often seems to occur in federal courts). Second, prosecutorial charging and plea bargaining are valuable sources of flexibility and moderation in sentencing. These discretionary powers permit systems to consider individual offense and offender factors which may not fit squarely within formal statutory and guidelines rules. And of course, prosecutorial discretion also allows systems to tailor sentencing severity to the available resources and evidence.

Intermediate Sanctions. Only a few guidelines jurisdictions have attempted to regulate the conditions of non-custodial sanctions, or even to encourage broader use of such sanctions. Even the few jurisdictions which have attempted to address these issues have not gone very far. Several systems authorize judges, in certain cases, to substitute specified amounts of certain intermediate sanctions for custody; for example, sixteen hours of community service, or a day of home detention, might be substituted for a day of custody. Two states, Pennsylvania and North Carolina, have attempted to define large groups of offenders for whom various kinds of intermediate sanctions are appropriate. These guidelines first classify penalties into three types: incarceration (prison or jail), severe intermediate sanctions (such as residential treatment), and mild intermediate sanctions (such as community service). . . . But the Pennsylvania and North Carolina Guidelines provide no guidance as to the choice to be made, when more than one sanction type is allowed in a given cell, or (when a non-custodial option is chosen), how much of that option to impose (for instance, what length of home detention or community service). . . .

CONCLUSION

After two decades of guidelines reforms, what have we learned? Here is a short list of the most important lessons which a review of this experience teaches:

First: guidelines in a number of states have succeeded in improving sentencing policy and practice — reducing bias and disparity in sentencing; avoiding serious prison overcrowding; and ensuring that adequate prison space is available for the most serious offenders. State guidelines regulate but do not eliminate discretion. . . . Most state guidelines systems have abolished parole release discretion, which serves to achieve Truth in Sentencing; offenders serve most of the sentence imposed by the trial court, and there is no pretense that sentences are longer than they really are. State guidelines have achieved more rational sentencing policy because they are developed and monitored by an independent, non-partisan agency charged with the responsibility of collecting detailed data on sentencing practices and resources, evaluating sentencing policy from a long-term perspective, setting priorities for use of limited resources, and developing a comprehensive approach to the sentencing of all crimes, thereby avoiding the problems of piecemeal reforms. [Yet] other major public and private stakeholders . . . have significant input into the development and implementation of state sentencing policy. The Legislature maintains oversight and ultimate control over major policy issues, and important roles are also played by trial and appellate judges, the defense and prosecution, victims, community representatives, and correctional officials. And yet — most state guidelines systems remain relatively simple to understand and apply.

Second: the best state guidelines work better, in all of the ways described above, than any other sentencing system which has yet been tried or even proposed. Quite simply, there is no realistic alternative as a means of accommodating all of the many important values and principles which we want sentences to serve. The prior indeterminate sentencing system permitted intolerable extremes of disparity; the unpredictable nature of indeterminate sentencing also prevented effective resource-management, and violated the public's desire for Truth in Sentencing. . . .

Third: state sentencing guidelines are politically viable. They have been successfully implemented in many states, and have survived — in some cases for almost 20 years, which is a very long time, given the extreme political salience and volatility of sentencing issues in recent years. These systems have survived because they work. . . .

Fourth: state guidelines continue to evolve and improve. Newer systems are more likely to take advantage of the potential which guidelines provide for resource-management and the promotion and structuring of intermediate sanctions. Most older systems are better today than when they began, not only because they have added desirable features (a permanent commission; resource-management; intermediate sanctions) which they originally lacked, but also because these system[s] now openly recognize and incorporate a wide variety of sentencing goals and values. . . .

Fifth: the development of sentencing guidelines remains an area of state, not federal, leadership. This reform began in the states; state guidelines have improved over time more than the federal version. [The] great diversity of guidelines systems provides a rich menu of reform options and experience to guide sentencing reformers in other states — and in the federal system — in their efforts to design, implement, improve, and preserve guidelines systems.

NOTES

1. *Evolving goals for state guideline system.*   The principal goal of early sentencing reforms was to regulate sentencing discretion and thereby limit sentencing disparities. As Professor Frase explains, however, the goals of sentencing reform in many states transformed over time to emphasize controlling the growth of prison populations and encouraging the use of intermediate sanctions. What forces do you think prompted this evolution in the goals of modern sentencing reform? Do you think a sentencing guideline system managed by a sentencing commission is better suited to effectuate these changed goals than the legislature?

2. *Developing guidelines in the shadow of the federal system.*   Though Minnesota and a few other states adopted guideline systems before the creation of the federal sentencing guidelines, most states with guidelines began their reform efforts afterward. Many states have expressly rejected the federal sentencing guidelines as a model for their own reforms. Professor Michael Tonry has noted that in numerous states considering sentencing reforms, "commissions at early meetings adopted resolutions expressly repudiating the federal guidelines as a model for anything they might develop." Michael Tonry, Sentencing Matters 134 (1996); see Paul J. Hofer, Immediate and Long-Term Effects of United States v. Booker: More Discretion, More Disparity, or Better Reasoned Sentences?, 38 Ariz. St. L.J. 425, 463 (2006) (ALI's review of Model Penal Code sentencing provisions "takes pain to distance itself from the pre-*Booker* federal guidelines"); Kevin R. Reitz & Curtis R. Reitz, Building a Sentencing Reform Agenda: The ABA's New Sentencing Standards, 78 Judicature 189, 189-192 (1995) (explaining that during the American Bar Association's drafting of model standards, "the federal system was held out repeatedly as a bad example," requiring the proposed standards "to be defended as very different than the federal guidelines").

3. Development and Structure of the Federal Sentencing Guidelines

a. Statutory Foundations

Though Judge Marvin Frankel's ideas were the catalyst for many reforms, Senator Edward Kennedy was the central political figure who turned Judge Frankel's ideas into a specific proposal for federal sentencing reform. Throughout the 1970s, Senator Kennedy championed Judge Frankel's ideas, as shown in the following excerpt:

> The absence in the federal criminal code of any articulated purposes or goals of sentencing has led to a situation where different judges often mete out different sentences to similar defendants convicted of similar crimes, depending on the sentencing attitudes of the particular judge. [Some] convicted offenders (including repeat offenders) escape jail altogether while others — convicted of the same crime — go to jail for excessively long periods. . . .
>
> An important prerequisite of any effective crime-fighting program — certainty of punishment — is absent. In addition, the criminal justice system

appears arbitrary and unjust, a game of chance in which the offender may "gamble" on receiving not just a lenient term of imprisonment but no jail sentence at all. . . . Sentencing disparity also strikingly demonstrates the fallacy of fighting crime by increasing maximum sentences which can be imposed. Counterfeiting carries a maximum penalty of fifteen years imprisonment; not only is the average sentence actually imposed less than five years, but almost 50% of convicted counterfeiters receive no imprisonment at all. Simply increasing maximum penalties is an exercise in futility. . . .

What can be done? I have introduced legislation in the U.S. Senate, [entitled] the Sentencing Guidelines bill, [which] would bring welcome uniformity to the sentencing process by articulating for the first time the general purposes and goals of sentencing that a judge should consider before imposing a sentence of imprisonment. The bill also provides for appellate review of sentences and creates a United States Commission on Sentencing to establish specific, fixed sentencing ranges for similar defendants who commit similar crimes. . . .

Edward M. Kennedy, Criminal Sentencing: A Game of Chance, 60 Judicature 208, 210-212 (1976).

Despite the force of Senator Kennedy's advocacy, it took nearly a decade before a version of his reform bill was passed into law as the Sentencing Reform Act of 1984 (SRA). In an account of the SRA's legislative history, Kate Stith and Steve Koh observed that the "legislative history of federal sentencing reform [reveals a] subtle transformation of sentencing reform legislation: conceived by liberal reformers as an anti-imprisonment and antidiscrimination measure, but finally born as part of a more conservative law-and-order crime control measure." Kate Stith & Steve Koh, The Politics of Sentencing Reform: The Legislative History of the Federal Sentencing Guidelines, 28 Wake Forest L. Rev. 223, 226 (1993). Cf. Marc L. Miller & Ronald F. Wright, Your Cheatin' Heart(land): The Long Search for Administrative Sentencing Justice, 2 Buff. Crim. L. Rev. 723 (1999) (providing a somewhat different account of the SRA's legislative history). What might appeal to a political conservative, such as Senator Orrin Hatch, about presumptive sentencing guidelines?

Though the passage of the SRA in 1984 created the U.S. Sentencing Commission and provided the statutory foundation for federal sentencing guidelines, the commission struggled to fulfill the SRA's mandates, and its initial set of mandatory guidelines did not become effective until November 1987. In a decision challenging the constitutionality of the guidelines on separation of powers grounds, Justice Blackmun described the new legislation:

The Act, as adopted, revises the old sentencing process in several ways:

1. It rejects imprisonment as a means of promoting rehabilitation, and it states that punishment should serve retributive, educational, deterrent, and incapacitative goals.
2. It consolidates the power that had been exercised by the sentencing judge and the Parole Commission to decide what punishment an offender should suffer. This is done by creating the United States Sentencing Commission, directing that Commission to devise guidelines to be used for sentencing, and prospectively abolishing the Parole Commission.
3. It makes all sentences basically determinate. A prisoner is to be released at the completion of his sentence reduced only by any credit earned by good behavior while in custody.
4. It makes the Sentencing Commission's guidelines binding on the courts, although it preserves for the judge the discretion to depart from the

guideline applicable to a particular case if the judge finds an aggravating or mitigating factor present that the Commission did not adequately consider when formulating guidelines. The Act also requires the court to state its reasons for the sentence imposed and to give "the specific reason" for imposing a sentence different from that described in the guideline.

5. It authorizes limited appellate review of the sentence. It permits a defendant to appeal a sentence that is above the defined range, and it permits the Government to appeal a sentence that is below that range. It also permits either side to appeal an incorrect application of the guideline. . . .

Mistretta v. United States, 488 U.S. 361, 367-68 (1989).

The guidelines did not become fully operational until 1989 because many of the first guideline cases focused primarily on constitutional challenges to the SRA's entire approach to sentencing reform. In *Mistretta* the Court addressed the question of whether the creation of the U.S. Sentencing Commission, as "an independent commission in the judicial branch of the United States," was constitutional. The commission, as set out in the SRA, has seven voting members who are appointed by the president with the advice of the Senate. They serve for six years and may not serve more than two full terms. Initially, at least three of its members had to be federal judges, selected by the president from a list of six judges recommended by the Judicial Conference. The members of the commission are subject to removal by the president "only for neglect of duty or malfeasance in office or for other good cause shown."

Initially the commission had to promulgate determinate sentencing guidelines. Congress had charged it with meeting the purposes of sentencing set out in the SRA, to provide "certainty and fairness in meeting the purposes of sentencing, avoiding unwarranted sentencing disparities among defendants with similar records . . . while maintaining sufficient flexibility to permit individualized sentences," where appropriate; and to "reflect, to the extent practicable, advancement in knowledge of human behavior as it relates to the criminal justice process." Congress further specified four "purposes" of sentencing that the commission was required to pursue in carrying out its mandate: "to reflect the seriousness of the offense, to promote respect for the law, and to provide just punishment for the offense"; "to afford adequate deterrence to criminal conduct"; "to protect the public from further crimes of the defendant"; and "to provide the defendant with needed . . . correctional treatment." In describing the desired guidelines, Congress directed the commission to develop a system of "sentencing ranges" applicable "for each category of offense involving each category of defendant." For imprisonment sentences, Congress mandated that "the maximum of the range established for such a term shall not exceed the minimum of that range by more than the greater of 25 percent or 6 months." Moreover, it directed the commission to use current average sentences "as a starting point" for structuring the sentencing ranges.

To guide the commission in its formulation of offense categories, Congress directed it to consider seven factors: the grade of the offense; the aggravating and mitigating circumstances of the crime; the nature and degree of the harm caused by the crime; the community view of the gravity of the offense; the public concern generated by the crime; the deterrent effect that a particular sentence may have on others; and the current incidence of the offense. Congress also set forth 11 factors for the commission to consider in establishing categories of defendants. These include the offender's age, education, vocational skills, mental and emotional condition, physical condition (including drug dependence), previous employment record, family ties and responsibilities, community ties, role in the offense, criminal history, and degree of dependence on crime for a livelihood. Congress also prohibited the commission from considering the "race, sex, national origin, creed, and socioeconomic status of offenders" and instructed that the guidelines should reflect the "general inappropriateness" of considering certain other factors, such as current unemployment, that might serve as proxies for forbidden criteria.

The Sentencing Reform Act laid out even more detailed guidance for the commission concerning categories of offenses and offender characteristics. Congress directed that guidelines specify a term of confinement at or near the statutory maximum for certain crimes and ensure a substantial term of imprisonment for various other offenses. On the other hand, Congress directed that guidelines reflect the general inappropriateness of imposing a sentence of imprisonment for certain first-time offenders.

Following promulgation of the guidelines, the statute called for the commission to continually review and revise them and report to Congress any amendments; the commission must also provide an annual analysis of the operation of the guidelines and issue "general policy statements" regarding their application.

In *Mistretta* the Court was asked to address the question of whether Congress granted the commission excessive legislative discretion, in violation of the nondelegation doctrine. Because Congress had provided detailed direction to the commission, the Court found no such violation. The Court also addressed the issue of whether the commission, which was placed in the judicial branch, violated the principles of separation of powers by undermining the independence of the judiciary. It likened the commission's role to that of the Supreme Court

> in establishing rules of procedure under the various enabling Acts. . . . Just as the rules of procedure bind judges and courts in the proper management of the cases before them, so the Guidelines bind judges and courts in the exercise of their uncontested responsibility to pass sentence in criminal cases. In other words, the Commission's functions, like this Court's function in promulgating procedural rules, are clearly attendant to a central element of the historically acknowledged mission of the Judicial Branch. . . .

Justice Scalia dissented, referring to the commission as a "junior-varsity Congress," an expert body with the right to make laws. This he viewed as undemocratic.

NOTES

1. *Judicial resistance to federal sentencing reform.* Though *Mistretta* ultimately found the constitutional challenges to be unavailing, more than 200 district judges and one circuit court had ruled the SRA unconstitutional on various grounds. Commentators have suggested that federal judges' apparent eagerness to strike down the SRA regime revealed their distaste for the entire agenda of

guideline sentencing. See Michael Tonry, Sentencing Matters 73-74 (1996). More tellingly, federal judges were among the most vocal critics of the federal sentencing guidelines following their enactment. See, e.g., Jose A. Cabranes, Sentencing Guidelines: A Dismal Failure, N.Y. L.J. 2 (February 11, 1992); Marc Miller, Rehabilitating the Federal Sentencing Guidelines, 78 Judicature 180, 180-183 (1995) (detailing widespread judicial hostility to the federal guidelines). Some commentators and members of the commission suggested that these complaints simply represented judges' displeasure over losing some of their broad sentencing powers. Others, however, believed that these judicial criticisms were sound indicators of serious problems with the SRA's overall approach to sentencing reform. See Kate Stith & Jose A. Cabranes, Fear of Judging: Sentencing Guidelines in the Federal Courts (1998).

2. *Congress's mandatory sentencing provisions and their impact on the guidelines.* In the very same legislative session in which it enacted the SRA, Congress began relying on mandatory sentencing laws to restrict judicial sentencing discretion. In 1984 Congress created a set of general minimum sentences for certain felonies and enacted a mandatory five-year sentence increase for crimes of violence involving a gun. Additional sentencing mandates followed nearly every two years — synchronized, not coincidentally, with the federal election cycle. Of most consequence, in 1986 Congress enacted a five-year mandatory enhancement for use of a firearm in a drug crime and created a broad set of mandatory minimum penalties for drug trafficking that linked the minimum sentence to the amount of drugs involved in the offense.

Though mandatory sentencing statutes have proved consistently popular with Congress, they have been assailed by judges, researchers, and commentators. In a speech about federal sentencing reform, Justice Stephen Breyer, a member of the original U.S. Sentencing Commission, effectively summarized the many criticisms of mandatory sentencing provisions:

> [Statutory] mandatory sentences prevent the Commission from carrying out its basic, congressionally mandated task: the development, in part through research, of a rational, coherent set of punishments. Mandatory minimums will sometimes make it impossible for the Commission to adjust sentences in light of factors that its research shows to be directly relevant. . . . They will sometimes prevent the application of Guidelines that would reduce a sentence in light of, for example, a minimal role in a drug offense, thereby sentencing similarly offenders who are very different, perhaps like a drug lord and a mule. Most seriously, they skew the entire set of criminal punishments, for Congress rarely considers more than the criminal behavior directly at issue when it writes these provisions. . . .
>
> Moreover, mandatory minimums . . . may permit the prosecutor, not the judge, to select the sentence by choosing . . . to charge, or not to charge, a violation of a statute that carries a mandatory prison term. [A] 1991 Commission study indicates that in nearly 40% of the cases involving conduct to which a mandatory minimum attached, the offender received a sentence lower than the minimum, perhaps because the prosecutor charged a different crime. . . . In sum, Congress, in simultaneously requiring Guideline sentencing and mandatory minimum sentencing, is riding two different horses. And those horses, in terms of coherence, fairness, and effectiveness, are traveling in opposite directions.

Speech of Associate Justice Stephen Breyer, University of Nebraska College of Law (November 18, 1998), 11 Fed. Sent'g Rep. 180, 184-185 (1999).

In addition to their direct consequences, the mandatory sentencing laws enacted in 1984 and 1986 skewed the initial development of the federal sentencing guidelines. Especially in the creation of the guidelines' drug sentencing provisions, the U.S. Sentencing Commission felt it had to alter its standard approach to guideline development to harmonize its provisions with Congress's sentencing mandates, which focused almost exclusively on drug quantities. See William W. Wilkins Jr. et al., Competing Sentencing Policies in a "War on Drugs" Era, 28 Wake Forest L. Rev. 305, 319-321 (1993).

3. *Composition of a sentencing commission.*   Recall that Judge Frankel encouraged broad-based membership in a sentencing commission to ensure the establishment of a well-rounded and knowledgeable group that could insulate sentencing rules from political pressures. In many states, the formation of sentencing commissions lived up to Frankel's ideals. In the words of Professor Michael Tonry, "sentencing commissions in [many states] have operated much as Judge Frankel hoped they would[; they] have achieved and sustained specialized institutional competence, insulated sentencing policy from short-term 'crime of the week' political pressures, and maintained a focus on comprehensive system-wide policymaking." Michael Tonry, The Success of Judge Frankel's Sentencing Commission, 64 U. Colo. L. Rev. 713, 713 (1993).

In the federal system, however, the U.S. Sentencing Commission has, more often than not, reflected the "tough on crime" stance of appointing presidents and confirming Congresses, and commentators have noted that commission deliberations generally reflect a prosecutorial orientation. See Douglas A. Berman, Common Law for This Age of Federal Sentencing: The Opportunity and Need for Judicial Lawmaking, 11 Stan. L. & Pol'y Rev. 93, 108-109 (1999). The statutory structure might explain this turn of events: the SRA provides for a designee of the attorney general to be an ex officio member of the commission, but provides no equivalent representation to a member of the defense bar. See 28 U.S.C. §991(a). And in 2003, apparently in response to concerns that the U.S. Sentencing Commission was not controlling judicial sentencing tightly enough, Congress altered the commission's judicial representation. The SRA's initial mandate that "at least three" of the commission's seven voting members be federal judges was changed to provide that the commission is to be composed of "not more than three" federal judges. Pub. L. 108-21, 117 Stat. 650, §401(n). It is now possible for the commission to have no judicial representation at all.

b. Basic Guideline Structure

Though the SRA in 1984 created a basic statutory framework as well as a general direction for the development of federal sentencing guidelines, it still left the U.S. Sentencing Commission with sweeping authority and many difficult decisions about how best to regulate judicial discretion through sentencing guidelines. After three years of deliberation and drafting in which the U.S. Sentencing Commission considered a range of approaches to reform, in 1987 the commission finally produced the initial sentencing guidelines. The following excerpt from the introduction to the Guidelines Manual gives important background on many of the structural and policy choices the commission made in forming its first guidelines.

> ## U.S. Sentencing Guidelines Manual,
> ## Chapter One — Introduction and
> ## General Application Principles
> ### U.S. Sentencing Commission (1987)

... The initial sentencing guidelines and policy statements were developed after extensive hearings, deliberation, and consideration of substantial public comment. The Commission emphasizes, however, that it views the guideline-writing process as evolutionary. It expects, and the governing statute anticipates, that continuing research, experience, and analysis will result in modifications and revisions to the guidelines through submission of amendments to Congress. To this end, the Commission is established as a permanent agency to monitor sentencing practices in the federal courts. ...

THE BASIC APPROACH (POLICY STATEMENT)

The [Sentencing Reform Act's] basic objective was to enhance the ability of the criminal justice system to combat crime through an effective, fair sentencing system. To achieve this end, Congress first sought honesty in sentencing. It sought to avoid the confusion and implicit deception that arose out of the pre-guidelines sentencing system, which required the court to impose an indeterminate sentence of imprisonment and empowered the parole commission to determine how much of the sentence an offender actually would serve in prison. ... Second, Congress sought reasonable uniformity in sentencing by narrowing the wide disparity in sentences imposed for similar criminal offenses committed by similar offenders. Third, Congress sought proportionality in sentencing through a system that imposes appropriately different sentences for criminal conduct of differing severity.

Honesty is easy to achieve: the abolition of parole makes the sentence imposed by the court the sentence the offender will serve, less approximately 15 percent for good behavior. There is a tension, however, between the mandate of uniformity and the mandate of proportionality. Simple uniformity — sentencing every offender to five years — destroys proportionality. Having only a few simple categories of crimes would make the guidelines uniform and easy to administer, but might lump together offenses that are different in important respects. [But] a sentencing system tailored to fit every conceivable wrinkle of each case would quickly become unworkable and seriously compromise the certainty of punishment and its deterrent effect. For example: a bank robber with (or without) a gun, which the robber kept hidden (or brandished), might have frightened (or merely warned), injured seriously (or less seriously), tied up (or simply pushed) a guard, teller, or customer, at night (or at noon), in an effort to obtain money for other crimes (or for other purposes), in the company of a few (or many) other robbers, for the first (or fourth) time. ...

The larger the number of subcategories of offense and offender characteristics included in the guidelines, the greater the complexity and the less workable the system. [Probation] officers and courts, in applying a complex system having numerous subcategories, would be required to make a host of decisions regarding whether the underlying facts were sufficient to bring the case within a particular subcategory. The greater the number of decisions required and the greater their complexity, the greater the risk that different courts would apply the guidelines differently to situations that, in fact, are similar, thereby reintroducing the very disparity that the guidelines were designed to reduce. . . .

In the end, there was no completely satisfying solution to this problem. The Commission had to balance the comparative virtues and vices of broad, simple categorization and detailed, complex subcategorization, and within the constraints established by that balance, minimize the discretionary powers of the sentencing court. Any system will, to a degree, enjoy the benefits and suffer from the drawbacks of each approach.

A philosophical problem arose when the Commission attempted to reconcile the differing perceptions of the purposes of criminal punishment. . . . Some argue that appropriate punishment should be defined primarily on the basis of the principle of "just deserts." Under this principle, punishment should be scaled to the offender's culpability and the resulting harms. Others argue that punishment should be imposed primarily on the basis of practical "crime control" considerations. This theory calls for sentences that most effectively lessen the likelihood of future crime, either by deterring others or incapacitating the defendant.

Adherents of each of these points of view urged the Commission to choose between them and accord one primacy over the other. As a practical matter, however, this choice was unnecessary because in most sentencing decisions the application of either philosophy will produce the same or similar results.

In its initial set of guidelines, the Commission sought to solve both the practical and philosophical problems of developing a coherent sentencing system by taking an empirical approach that used as a starting point data estimating pre-guidelines sentencing practice. It analyzed data drawn from 10,000 presentence investigations, the differing elements of various crimes as distinguished in substantive criminal statutes, the United States Parole Commission's guidelines and statistics, and data from other relevant sources in order to determine which distinctions were important in pre-guidelines practice. After consideration, the Commission accepted, modified, or rationalized these distinctions. . . .

The Commission did not simply copy estimates of pre-guidelines practice as revealed by the data. . . . Rather, it departed from the data at different points for various important reasons. Congressional statutes, for example, suggested or required departure, as in the case of the Anti-Drug Abuse Act of 1986 that imposed increased and mandatory minimum sentences. In addition, the data revealed inconsistencies in treatment, such as punishing economic crime less severely than other apparently equivalent behavior.

Despite these policy-oriented departures from pre-guidelines practice, the guidelines represent an approach that begins with, and builds upon, empirical data. The guidelines will not please those who wish the Commission to adopt a single philosophical theory and then work deductively to establish a simple and perfect set of categorizations and distinctions. The guidelines may prove acceptable, however, to those who seek more modest, incremental improvements in the status quo, who believe the best is often the enemy of the good, and who recognize that these guidelines are, as the Act contemplates, but the first step in an evolutionary process. . . .

DEPARTURES

The sentencing statute permits a court to depart from a guideline-specified sentence only when it finds "an aggravating or mitigating circumstance of a kind, or to a degree, not adequately taken into consideration by the Sentencing Commission in formulating the guidelines that should result in a sentence different from that described." 18 U.S.C. §3553(b). The Commission intends the sentencing courts to treat each guideline as carving out a "heartland," a set of typical cases embodying the conduct that each guideline describes. When a court finds an atypical case, one to which a particular guideline linguistically applies but where conduct significantly differs from the norm, the court may consider whether a departure is warranted. Section 5H1.10 (Race, Sex, National Origin, Creed, Religion, and Socio-Economic Status), §5H1.12 (Lack of Guidance as a Youth and Similar Circumstances), the third sentence of §5H1.4 (Physical Condition, Including Drug or Alcohol Dependence or Abuse), and the last sentence of §5K2.12 (Coercion and Duress) list several factors that the court cannot take into account as grounds for departure. With those specific exceptions, however, the Commission does not intend to limit the kinds of factors, whether or not mentioned anywhere else in the guidelines, that could constitute grounds for departure in an unusual case.

The Commission has adopted this departure policy for two reasons. First, it is difficult to prescribe a single set of guidelines that encompasses the vast range of human conduct potentially relevant to a sentencing decision. The Commission also recognizes that the initial set of guidelines need not do so. The Commission is a permanent body, empowered by law to write and rewrite guidelines, with progressive changes, over many years. By monitoring when courts depart from the guidelines and by analyzing their stated reasons for doing so and court decisions with references thereto, the Commission, over time, will be able to refine the guidelines to specify more precisely when departures should and should not be permitted.

Second, the Commission believes that despite the courts' legal freedom to depart from the guidelines, they will not do so very often. This is because the guidelines, offense by offense, seek to take account of those factors that the Commission's data indicate made a significant difference in pre-guidelines sentencing practice. Thus, for example, where the presence of physical injury made an important difference in pre-guidelines sentencing practice (as in the case of robbery or assault), the guidelines specifically include this factor to enhance the sentence. . . .

SENTENCING RANGES

. . . While the Commission has not considered itself bound by pre-guidelines sentencing practice, it has not attempted to develop an entirely new system of sentencing on the basis of theory alone. Guideline sentences, in many instances, will approximate average pre-guidelines practice and adherence to the guidelines will help to eliminate wide disparity. . . . In some instances, short sentences of incarceration for all offenders in a category have been substituted for a pre-guidelines sentencing practice of very wide variability in which some defendants received probation while others received several years in prison for the same offense. Moreover, inasmuch as those who pleaded guilty under pre-guidelines practice often received lesser sentences, the guidelines permit the court to impose lesser sentences on those defendants who accept responsibility for their misconduct. For defendants who provide substantial assistance to the government in the investigation or prosecution of others, a downward departure may be warranted. . . .

The Commission has also examined its sentencing ranges in light of their likely impact upon prison population. Specific legislation, such as the Anti-Drug Abuse Act of 1986 and the career offender provisions of the Sentencing Reform Act of 1984, required the Commission to promulgate guidelines that will lead to substantial prison population increases. These increases will occur irrespective of the guidelines. The guidelines themselves, insofar as they reflect policy decisions made by the Commission (rather than legislated mandatory minimum or career offender sentences), are projected to lead to an increase in prison population . . . estimated at approximately 10 percent over a period of ten years. . . .

THE SENTENCING TABLE

The Commission has established a sentencing table that for technical and practical reasons contains 43 levels. Each level in the table prescribes ranges that overlap with the ranges in the preceding and succeeding levels. By overlapping the ranges, the table should discourage unnecessary litigation. Both prosecution and defense will realize that the difference between one level and another will not necessarily make a difference in the sentence that the court imposes. Thus, little purpose will be served in protracted litigation trying to determine, for example, whether $10,000 or $11,000 was obtained as a result of a fraud. At the same time, the levels work to increase a sentence proportionately. A change of six levels roughly doubles the sentence irrespective of the level at which one starts. The guidelines, in keeping with the statutory requirement that the maximum of any range cannot exceed the minimum by more than the greater of 25 percent or six months (28 U.S.C. §994(b)(2)), permit courts to exercise the greatest permissible range of sentencing discretion. . . .

A CONCLUDING NOTE

The Commission emphasizes that it drafted the initial guidelines with considerable caution [by relying] upon pre-guidelines sentencing practice as revealed by its own statistical analyses based on summary reports of some 40,000 convictions, a sample of 10,000 augmented presentence reports, the parole guidelines, and policy judgments. The Commission recognizes that some will criticize this approach as overly cautious, as representing too little a departure from pre-guidelines sentencing practice. Yet, it will cure wide disparity. The Commission is a permanent body that can amend the guidelines each year. Although the data available to it, like all data, are imperfect, experience with the guidelines will lead to additional information and provide a firm empirical basis for consideration of revisions.

NOTES

1. *Theoretical choices (or lack thereof).*   Many of the early calls for sentencing reform urged that reforms be driven by a specific theoretical commitment to a "just deserts" or "limiting retributivism" philosophy. See Andrew von Hirsch, Doing Justice: The Choice of Punishments (1976); Norval Morris, The Future of Imprisonment (1974). As noted before, Minnesota's sentencing commission heeded this recommendation when it adopted just deserts as the governing premise of its policies concerning who receives prison sentences. The American Law Institute (ALI) in its current redrafting of the sentencing provisions in the Model Penal Code has focused on utilitarian goals but mandates that these be pursued within proportionality constraints. As explained in the introduction to the federal sentencing guidelines, however, the U.S. Sentencing Commission concluded that as a "practical matter" any choice between crime control and retributivist philosophies of punishment in the construction of the guidelines "was unnecessary because in most sentencing decisions the application of either philosophy will produce the same or similar results." Do you agree with this assertion?

2. *Training exercises.*   One of the functions of the U.S. Sentencing Commission is to train the judges, probation officers, and attorneys who work with the guidelines daily. The extensive website for the commission, at http://www.ussc.gov, includes training exercises and detailed study papers on how to apply the guidelines in various situations. It is easier to appreciate the design choices the commission made in constructing the guidelines machine after having at least glimpsed that machine in operation. Now, or after reviewing the following overview of the federal guidelines in operation, would be a good time to use the worksheets at the commission's website and step through one or more of the training exercises (perhaps the Robbery Exercise, available at http://www.ussc.gov/training/ws_ex_rob.pdf (hypothetical facts) and http://www.ussc.gov/training/sent_ex_rob.pdf (completed worksheet)). The worksheets are helpful in pointing the way through the tangles of the guidelines.

|| *Overview of the Federal Sentencing Guidelines* ||
|| U.S. Sentencing Commission (2001) ||

HOW THE SENTENCING GUIDELINES WORK

The sentencing guidelines take into account both the seriousness of the offense and the offender's criminal history.

Offense Seriousness.   The sentencing guidelines provide 43 levels of offense seriousness — the more serious the crime, the higher the offense level. . . . Each type of crime is assigned a base offense level, which is the starting point for determining the seriousness of a particular offense. More serious types of crimes have higher base offense levels (for example, a trespass has a base offense level of 4, while kidnapping has a base offense level of 24).

In addition to base offense levels, each offense type typically carries with it a number of specific offense characteristics. These are factors that vary from offense to offense, but that can increase or decrease the base offense level and, ultimately, the sentence an offender receives. Some examples:

- One of the specific base offense characteristics for theft (which has a base offense level of 6) increases the offense level based on the amount of loss involved in the offense. If a theft involved a $6,000 loss, there is to be a 2-level increase to the base offense level, bringing the level up to 8. If a theft involved a $50,000 loss, there is to be a 6-level increase, bringing the total to 12.
- One of the specific offense characteristics for robbery (which has a base offense level of 20) involves the use of a firearm. If a firearm was displayed during the robbery, there is to be a 5-level increase, bringing the level to 25; if a firearm was actually discharged during the robbery, there is to be a 7-level increase, bringing the level to 27.

Adjustments.   Adjustments are factors that can apply to any offense. Like specific offense characteristics, they increase or decrease the offense level. Categories of adjustments include: victim-related adjustments, the offender's role in the crime, and obstruction of justice. Examples of adjustments are as follows:

- If the offender was a minimal participant in the offense, the offense level is decreased by 4 levels.
- If the offender knew that the victim was unusually vulnerable due to age or physical or mental condition, the offense level is increased by 2 levels.
- If the offender obstructed justice, the offense level is increased by 2 levels. . . .
- [The judge may decrease the offense level by two levels if, in the judge's opinion, the offender accepted responsibility for his offense.]

When there are multiple counts of conviction, the sentencing guidelines provide instructions on how to achieve a "combined offense level." These rules provide incremental punishment for significant additional criminal conduct. The most serious offense is used as a starting point. The other counts determine whether to and how much to increase the offense level. . . .

Criminal History.   The guidelines assign each offender to one of six criminal history categories based upon the extent of an offender's past misconduct and how recently these crimes took place. Criminal History Category I is assigned to the least serious criminal record and includes many first-time offenders. Criminal History Category VI is the most serious category and includes offenders with lengthy criminal records.

Determining the Guideline Range.   The final offense level is determined by taking the base offense level and then adding or subtracting from it any specific offense characteristics and adjustments that apply. The point at which the final offense level and the criminal history category intersect on the Commission's sentencing table determines the defendant's sentencing guideline range.

[An] offender with a Criminal History Category of I and a final offense level of 20 would have a guideline range of 33 to 41 months. . . .

Sentencing Options. In addition to providing a guideline range, there are a series of rules that determine the availability of non-imprisonment sentencing options for offenders. For example, if the applicable guideline range is 0-6 months, the judge has a number of options, including a guideline sentence of probation only, or a sentence of up to six months' imprisonment.

Departures. After the guideline range is determined, if the court determines that there is a factor that the guidelines did not adequately consider, it may "depart" from the guideline range. That is, the judge may sentence the offender above or below the range. When departing, the judge must state the reason for the departure. If the sentence is an upward departure, the offender may appeal the sentence; if it is a downward departure, the government may appeal. One special kind of departure is the "substantial assistance" departure. This downward departure may be granted if the offender has provided substantial assistance in the investigation or prosecution of another offender. A motion to depart for substantial assistance must be made by the prosecution, but it is the judge who decides whether to grant it and, if so, to what extent.

Commentary to Sentencing Table [reprinted on page 172]

The Offense Level (1-43) forms the vertical axis of the Sentencing Table. The Criminal History Category (I-VI) forms the horizontal axis of the Table. The intersection of the Offense Level and Criminal History Category displays the Guideline Range in months of imprisonment. "Life" means life imprisonment. For example, the guideline range applicable to a defendant with an Offense Level of 15 and a Criminal History Category of III is 24-30 months of imprisonment.

NOTES

1. *Guideline commentary.* In addition to the detailed instructions set forth in guideline provisions, most guidelines are accompanied by official commentary from the U.S. Sentencing Commission in the form of "application notes" and "background." This commentary is designed to aid courts in applying specific provisions by defining key terms or providing insights into the development and purpose of the provision. In Stinson v. United States, 508 U.S. 36 (1993), the Supreme Court unanimously ruled that "commentary in the *Guidelines Manual* that interprets or explains a guideline is authoritative unless it violates the Constitution or a federal statute, or is inconsistent with, or a plainly erroneous reading of, that guideline." In other words, courts and others interpreting and applying the guidelines must generally treat the commentary as binding and having the same force as the actual guideline provisions.

Sentencing Table
(in months of imprisonment)

	Offense Level	I (0 or 1)	II (2 or 3)	III (4, 5, 6)	IV (7, 8, 9)	V (10, 11, 12)	VI (13 or more)
		Criminal History Category (Criminal History Points)					
	1	0-6	0-6	0-6	0-6	0-6	0-6
	2	0-6	0-6	0-6	0-6	0-6	1-7
	3	0-6	0-6	0-6	0-6	2-8	3-9
	4	0-6	0-6	0-6	2-8	4-10	6-12
Zone A	5	0-6	0-6	1-7	4-10	6-12	9-15
	6	0-6	1-7	2-8	6-12	9-15	12-18
	7	0-6	2-8	4-10	8-14	12-18	15-21
	8	0-6	4-10	6-12	10-16	15-21	18-24
Zone B	9	4-10	6-12	8-14	12-18	18-24	21-27
	10	6-12	8-14	10-16	15-21	21-27	24-30
Zone C	11	8-14	10-16	12-18	18-24	24-30	27-33
	12	10-16	12-18	15-21	21-27	27-33	30-37
	13	12-18	15-21	18-24	24-30	30-37	33-41
	14	15-21	18-24	21-27	27-33	33-41	37-46
	15	18-24	21-27	24-30	30-37	37-46	41-51
	16	21-27	24-30	27-33	33-41	41-51	46-57
	17	24-30	27-33	30-37	37-46	46-57	51-63
	18	27-33	30-37	33-41	41-51	51-63	57-71
	19	30-37	33-41	37-46	46-57	57-71	63-78
	20	33-41	37-46	41-51	51-63	63-78	70-87
	21	37-46	41-51	46-57	57-71	70-87	77-96
	22	41-51	46-57	51-63	63-78	77-96	84-105
	23	46-57	51-63	57-71	70-87	84-105	92-115
	24	51-63	57-71	63-78	77-96	92-115	100-125
	25	57-71	63-78	70-87	84-105	100-125	110-137
	26	63-78	70-87	78-97	92-115	110-137	120-150
Zone D	27	70-87	78-97	87-108	100-125	120-150	130-162
	28	78-97	87-108	97-121	110-137	130-162	140-175
	29	87-108	97-121	108-135	121-151	140-175	151-188
	30	97-121	108-135	121-151	135-168	151-188	168-210
	31	108-135	121-151	135-168	151-188	168-210	188-235
	32	121-151	135-168	151-188	168-210	188-235	210-262
	33	135-168	151-188	168-210	188-235	210-262	235-293
	34	151-188	168-210	188-235	210-262	235-293	262-327
	35	168-210	188-235	210-262	235-293	262-327	292-365
	36	188-235	210-262	235-293	262-327	292-365	324-405
	37	210-262	235-293	262-327	292-365	324-405	360-life
	38	235-293	262-327	292-365	324-405	360-life	360-life
	39	262-327	292-365	324-405	360-life	360-life	360-life
	40	292-365	324-405	360-life	360-life	360-life	360-life
	41	324-405	360-life	360-life	360-life	360-life	360-life
	42	360-life	360-life	360-life	360-life	360-life	360-life
	43	life	life	life	life	life	life

2. *Conflicting judicial interpretations of guideline provisions.* As with any other intricate set of legal rules, the federal sentencing guidelines are often interpreted in conflicting ways by different judges. In Braxton v. United States, 500 U.S. 344 (1991), the Supreme Court unanimously ruled that the U.S. Sentencing Commission is to have the initial and primary responsibility of responding to

circuit conflicts over guideline interpretations. According to the Court in *Braxton*, "in charging the Commission 'periodically [to] review and revise' the guidelines, Congress necessarily contemplated that the Commission would periodically review the work of the courts, and would make whatever clarifying revisions to the guidelines conflicting judicial decisions might suggest." Though the Supreme Court in *Braxton* said that it should be more "restrained and circumspect" in using its certiorari power to resolve circuit conflicts for guidelines issues, the Court has still played a role in the development of federal sentencing law by deciding more than two dozen significant sentencing cases in the past decade. The most important of these decisions was United States v. Booker in which the Court declared the federal guidelines advisory only.

3. *Guideline complexity.* Though simplified in the summary above, the federal sentencing guidelines are quite complex. The complexity of the federal guideline system has been a concern since the U.S. Sentencing Commission promulgated its initial guidelines in 1987: there were more than 100 multisection guidelines filling more than 200 pages in the first Guidelines Manual, and they included an intricate nine-step process for determining a defendant's applicable sentencing range using a 258-box grid known as the "sentencing table." Judicial decisions have since increased the corpus of federal sentencing law and thus complicated an already intricate sentencing process: confronted with numerous interpretive questions in applying the guidelines, district and circuit courts issue hundreds of guideline sentencing opinions each year. Meanwhile, the U.S. Sentencing Commission, honoring its statutory obligation to review and revise the guidelines, has passed almost 700 amendments to the guidelines over the past 18 years. The U.S. Sentencing Guidelines Manual now runs more than 650 pages and has an even lengthier, separate appendix that chronicles the amendments. Tens of thousands of federal court opinions have interpreted these guidelines.

Many judges, practitioners, and commentators have lamented the system's complexity, in part because complex guidelines increase the risk that the sentencing rules will be misunderstood or misapplied. Thus, complexity undercuts the goals of sentencing predictability and certainty. Justice Stephen Breyer, a member of the original Sentencing Commission, identifies a link between complexity and judicial discretion:

> The original 1987 Guidelines draft was just over 200 pages long, and many criticized that draft as too lengthy and too complex. The Guidelines are now twice as long[, and] the greatest obstacle to [simplification] is, I believe, the legal mind itself. We judges and lawyers love to make distinctions. For sentencing purposes, distinctions about how a crime was carried out are important in order to assure sentencing proportionality. . . . But it is important to know when to stop. [The] Commission should review the present Guidelines, acting forcefully to diminish significantly the number of offense characteristics attached to individual crimes. The characteristics that remain should be justified for the most part by data that shows their use by practicing judges to change sentences. . . . The Commission originally stated that each Guideline was to cover only the "heartland" of the offense at issue. That concept — the "heartland" — should remain our guiding principle. Less typical cases may be left to departures imposed by the sentencing judge, and perhaps guided, though not directly mandated, by the Commission. . . . The result would be an increase in the discretionary authority of the sentencing judge.

Speech of Associate Justice Stephen Breyer, 11 Fed. Sent'g Rep. at 185-186 (1999). The U.S. Sentencing Commission has often indicated that simplifying the guidelines is an institutional goal, but it has failed so far to engineer such simplification. In addition to other impacts, the guidelines' complexity also creates serious problems for the defense bar in providing effective representation for federal defendants. See Alan J. Chaset, A Teacher at the Top: Another Reason to Have a Representative of the Criminal Defense Bar on the Sentencing Commission, 11 Fed. Sent'g Rep. 309, 309-310 (1999) (suggesting that guidelines may "involve too much law for the average practitioner to keep current with"); Douglas A. Berman, From Lawlessness to Too Much Law? Exploring the Risk of Disparity from Differences in Defense Counsel Under Guidelines Sentencing, 87 Iowa L. Rev. 435 (2002).

4. *Offender characteristics.*   Although the characteristics of an *offense* play a central role in establishing applicable sentencing ranges under the federal sentencing guidelines, characteristics of an offender (other than past criminal history) play almost no role in the determination of applicable guideline ranges. Such matters are addressed in the federal guidelines only through policy statements that seek to regulate departures, and these provisions state that many such offender characteristics are "not relevant" or "not ordinarily relevant" to a departure decision. See, e.g., U.S. Sentencing Guidelines Manual §5H1.12 ("Lack of guidance as a youth and similar circumstances indicating a disadvantaged upbringing are not relevant grounds for imposing a sentence outside the applicable guideline range."); §5H1.2 ("Education and vocational skills are not ordinarily relevant in determining whether a sentence should be outside the applicable guideline range."); §5H1.4 ("Drug or alcohol dependence or abuse is not a reason for imposing a sentence below the guidelines."); §5H1.6 ("Family ties and responsibilities and community ties are not ordinarily relevant in determining whether a sentence should be outside the applicable guideline range.").

Many judges and commentators have been especially critical of the guidelines' failure to account for offender characteristics, such as disadvantaged background or family circumstances, that judges often used as mitigating considerations in pre-guidelines sentencing practice. See, e.g., Kate Stith & Jose A. Cabranes, Judging Under the Federal Sentencing Guidelines, 91 Nw. U. L. Rev. 1247 (1997); Daniel J. Freed, Federal Sentencing in the Wake of Guidelines: Unacceptable Limits on the Discretion of Sentencers, 101 Yale L.J. 1681 (1992); Charles J. Ogletree, The Death of Discretion? Reflections on the Federal Sentencing Guidelines, 101 Harv. L. Rev. 1938 (1988). Congress and the U.S. Sentencing Commission have not generally heeded these criticisms. In fact, Congress in 2003 passed legislation that further curtailed the ability of sentencing judges in certain cases to depart from the guidelines based on offender characteristics, and it also directed the commission to review critically how judges were using their departure authority to take into account offender characteristics.

c.   Departures and Discretion

Although the Sentencing Reform Act significantly altered the judicial role in sentencing, it did not remove the judge's discretion entirely from the federal sentencing process. Despite the strictures of mandatory sentencing laws and complex guidelines, the SRA and the guidelines guaranteed an important role for the sentencing judge.

First and foremost, the guidelines preserve a judicial role simply through the adoption of sentencing ranges. Like most state guideline systems, the federal guidelines do not specify an exact sentence for each offense and offender; they establish a range from which sentencing judges select a specific sentence. Notably, Congress specifically mandated in the SRA that sentencing ranges in the federal guidelines be fairly narrow by providing that "the maximum of the range established for [any imprisonment] term shall not exceed the minimum of that range by more than the greater of 25 percent or 6 months." 28 U.S.C. §994(b)(2). Because district judges have complete discretion to select a sentence from within this range, and because this decision is not subject to appeal, the independent determination and judgment of district judges still, in effect, controls at least one-quarter of every federal guideline sentence.

The SRA also gives judges express authority to depart from the guidelines whenever there is a "circumstance of a kind, or to a degree, not adequately taken into consideration by the Sentencing Commission in formulating the guidelines that should result in a sentence different from that described." 18 U.S.C. §3553(b). How the U.S. Sentencing Commission and courts should interpret this provision has been intensely debated since the guidelines' inception, and for good reason. The rules governing departures are the focal point of the guideline system's efforts to achieve greater sentencing consistency without sacrificing necessary flexibility. If departure authority too readily allows judges to deviate from the guidelines' presumptive sentences, then the system will be too pliant and unwarranted sentencing disparity may persist. Yet if departure authority too rarely allows judges to depart from the guidelines' presumptive sentences, then the system will be too rigid, judicial discretion will be overly limited, and unwarranted sentencing uniformity may occur.

Departure authority technically takes two different forms in the federal guideline system. The commission used the departure mechanism in U.S.S.G. §5K1.1 to implement Congress's directive that judges generally impose lower sentences "to take into account a defendant's substantial assistance in the investigation and prosecution" of others. 28 U.S.C. §994(n). This provision for departures based on a prosecutor's motion plays a critical role not only in the sentence imposed but also in plea negotiations, in which prosecutors use their authority to recommend departures as a way to persuade defendants to cooperate in further criminal investigations. Commentators have noted that section 5K1.1 and other guideline provisions enhance the sentencing discretion of prosecutors; the uneven application of section 5K1.1 and prosecutorial discretion more generally is discussed below.

Even more fundamental to the operation of the guidelines and the preservation of judicial discretion is the district judge's distinct power to depart from the guidelines without a motion from the prosecutor. According to the Guidelines Manual, a sentencing court may depart if the case at issue is "atypical," which means that certain factors differ significantly from the norm and were therefore not considered by the drafters of the guidelines. While some factors, such as race, sex, national origin, creed, religion, socioeconomic status, lack of guidance as a youth, drug or alcohol dependence, and economic hardship, may never serve as reasons for downward departures, the Guidelines Manual sets out some factors as encouraged or discouraged bases for departure — with the latter to be used to justify a departure only "in exceptional cases." If a factor is not mentioned in the guidelines, the sentencing court must determine whether the factor takes the case out of the "heartland" of other cases, after considering the structure and theory of both relevant individual guidelines and the guidelines taken as a whole.

In Koon v. United States, 518 U.S. 81 (1993), the Supreme Court addressed the level of appellate review that was appropriate for assessing a sentencing court's decision to depart. The Court held that a district court judge's decision to depart from the guidelines

> will in most cases be due substantial deference, for it embodies the traditional exercise of discretion by a sentencing court. . . . Whether a given factor is present to a degree not adequately considered by the Commission, or whether a discouraged factor nonetheless justifies departure because it is present in some unusual or exceptional way, are matters determined in large part by comparison with the facts of other Guidelines cases. District courts have an institutional advantage over appellate courts in making these sorts of determinations, especially as they see so many more Guidelines cases than appellate courts do. In 1994, for example, 93.9% of Guidelines cases were not appealed. . . .
>
> This does not mean that district courts do not confront questions of law in deciding whether to depart. . . . The Government is quite correct that whether a factor is a permissible basis for departure under any circumstances is a question of law, and the court of appeals need not defer to the district court's resolution of the point. . . .

As the Court applied this holding to the facts of the case, it found that the district court had abused its discretion by considering the defendants' collateral employment consequences in granting a downward departure. It found that career loss "is not unusual for a public official who is convicted of using his governmental authority to violate a person's rights to lose his or her job and to be barred from future work in that field." In addition, the Court held that "the low likelihood of petitioners' recidivism was not an appropriate basis for departure," as criminal history category I already indicates a low likelihood of repeat offending. On the other hand, the Court determined that the sentencing court acted within its discretion in considering susceptibility to abuse in prison and successive prosecutions as grounds for a downward departure.

NOTES

1. *Departure patterns before and after* Koon.   Prior to the Supreme Court's decision in *Koon*, federal district judges used their departure authority rather sparingly, perhaps because many circuit courts reviewed decisions to depart de novo while refusing to review any discretionary decision *not* to depart from the guidelines. Before *Koon*, district judges exercised their independent authority to depart from the guidelines in only about 10% of cases (although, during the same period, prosecutors requested and judges granted departures based on defendants' substantial assistance in about twice as many cases). The *Koon* decision, perhaps responding to judicial and academic complaints about guideline rigidity, seemed designed through its adoption of an "abuse of discretion"

review standard to enhance sentencing courts' departure authority. If this was indeed the Supreme Court's goal, *Koon* has proved to be a very effective ruling. The total number of departures has increased by nearly 20% every year following the *Koon* decision, and in 2001 there were roughly twice as many departures as in 1995.

Notably, almost all departures involve decisions by sentencing judges to impose a sentence *below* the applicable guideline range. Since the start of guideline sentencing, upward departures have never constituted much more than 1% of all sentenced cases, and in 2001 there were 30 times more downward departures than upward departures. By 2006 the number of upward departures had slightly increased, as had the number of downward departures. Did these trends occur because federal sentencing judges generally disapprove of the severity of sentences under the guidelines, or is some other dynamic at work?

Though consistent in direction, judicial departure rates have not been uniform across federal districts and circuits. The U.S. Sentencing Commission reported in 2001 that among districts with more than 100 cases, the percentage of downward departures ranged from a low of 1.4% in the Eastern District of Kentucky to a high of 62.8% in the District of Arizona; among the circuits that same year, the Ninth Circuit had the highest downward departure rate, at 38.7%, while the Fourth Circuit had the lowest, at 5.2%. See United States Sentencing Commission, 2001 Annual Report. A high rate of non-guideline sentences in certain southwestern border districts, such as Southern California and Arizona, can be traced in part to "fast track" departure programs adopted in districts with a high volume of immigration cases; these programs were designed to encourage the prompt disposition of cases in which a defendant would ultimately be deported following any term of imprisonment. Should statistics revealing significant regional variations in the use of departure authority be a source of particular concern?

2. *Congressional reaction to* Koon: *the Feeney Amendment.*   Despite the occasional expression of concerns by the Department of Justice and a few commentators over the increased use of downward departure authority after *Koon*, many judges and most commentators welcomed the increased sentencing flexibility that *Koon* seemed to endorse through its expanded view of departure authority. In 2003, however, Congress decreed through a provision known as the Feeney Amendment that the use of departure authority had to be reined in. The statute required circuit courts to apply de novo review of departures (effectively overruling the *Koon* decision) and directed the commission to amend the guidelines to "substantially reduce" the number of downward departures. Pub. L. 108-21, 117 Stat. 650, §401(m). Congress has provided no specific guidance to the commission on how to interpret or effectuate this directive.

3. *Extent of departures.*   Although the SRA defines a standard for the decision to depart, and the commission and courts have expounded upon this standard at length, neither the SRA nor the commission specifies the "extent" of departure. The SRA simply states in 18 U.S.C. §3742 that the extent of any departure must be "reasonable," and the commission has not elaborated on what qualifies as "reasonable." Given the emphasis on the decision to depart, the failure to be concerned with the extent of departure is somewhat curious in the federal system; because the commission constructed its sentencing table

with overlapping sentencing ranges, departures of one or two levels are of limited consequence, and it is really only *large* departures that pose a significant threat of serious sentencing disparity under the guidelines. Notably, the Minnesota Supreme Court, early in the history of the Minnesota sentencing guidelines, held that any upward departure duration should generally not exceed twice the presumptive duration. See State v. Evans, 311 N.W.2d 481 (Minn. 1981).

4. *State approaches to departure authority.* As in the federal system, most state guidelines allow the judge to depart from the sentence range designated in the guidelines. In some states, the departures are categorized according to whether they affect either the disposition of the sentence or the duration of the sentence. Departure standards in most states are generally not as detailed or restrictive as in the federal system: state systems providing for departures typically permit the sentencing court to depart for any "substantial" or "compelling" reasons, or they set forth nonexclusive lists of reasons for departures. The departure statutes generally require the judge to explain any departure, and an inadequate explanation can lead to reversal on appeal. Appellate courts in these jurisdictions have developed extensive case law approving or disapproving various grounds for departure. The case law in some states, such as Pennsylvania, gives the trial judge much wider latitude than that in other states, such as Minnesota.

Despite more permissive departure standards, the number of departures in state systems has remained well below the number of cases sentenced within the state guidelines. For instance, in Minnesota dispositional departures have occurred in around 10% of total cases sentenced, while durational departures have occurred in about 25% of cases involving an active prison term. See Richard Frase, Implementing Commission-Based Sentencing Guidelines: The Lessons of the First Ten Years in Minnesota, 2 Cornell J.L. & Pub. Pol'y 279 (1993). By what criteria could a sentencing commission decide how many departures are too many?

> *Substantial Assistance: An Empirical Yardstick*
> *Gauging Equity in Current Federal Policy*
> *and Practice, Linda Drazga Maxfield and*
> *John H. Kramer*
> Pages 2-4, 19-21 (1999)

THE UNDEFINED SUBSTANCE OF SUBSTANTIAL ASSISTANCE

Congress directed the Commission to create [a method to] decrease sentences below the guideline range for offenders who assist in the investigation or prosecution of another person committing a criminal offense. The Sentencing Commission's response to this congressional mandate took the form of guideline policy statement 5K1.1 — Substantial Assistance to Authorities:

> Upon motion of the government stating that the defendant has provided substantial assistance in the investigation or prosecution of another person who has committed an offense, the court may depart from the guidelines. . . .

Issues raised in the substantial assistance policy statement, but left unanswered elsewhere . . . include [several] that are cited below.

First, the factors to be used by the prosecutor prior to sentencing to determine whether the cooperation of a given defendant is "substantial" — and therefore warrants a substantial assistance departure motion — are unaddressed. . . . What objective and equitable parameters distinguish between "substantial" assistance and "non-substantial" assistance?

Second, the authority to move for a §5K1.1 departure is limited to the prosecution. This exclusivity has resulted in spirited debate in the criminal justice community. Government prosecutors defend the appropriateness of their substantial assistance monopoly by citing the government's unique capability to judge accurately the benefit obtained from the type and extent of assistance provided. The critical response is that predicating a substantial assistance departure on a government motion is a potential source of disparity because the unilateral government decision whether to make the substantial assistance motion is not subject to challenge by the defense and is not reviewable by the court (unless constitutional grounds are cited). . . .

Finally, apparently not all substantial assistance is equal. The policy statement places no conditions on the magnitude of the sentence reduction to be given. Consequently, extensive cooperation theoretically would deserve a larger sentence reduction than less extensive (but still substantial) cooperation. What is the link between assessing the value of a defendant's substantial assistance and deciding on the magnitude of the sentence reduction? . . . Achieving equity in the substantial assistance process has major ramifications for the overall equity of the guidelines system; 19 percent of federal criminal convictions — roughly 7,500 cases per year — were granted downward departures under §5K1.1 over the past three fiscal years (1994 through 1996). . . .

SUMMARY AND IMPLICATIONS

[A] working group was established to explore the policies and procedures across the judicial districts, and to study the factors associated with §5K1.1 sentence reductions and the magnitudes of the departures [through] a diversity of research methodologies. . . . The data reported were not able to find direct correlations between type of cooperation provided, type of benefit or result received by the government, the making of a §5K1.1 motion, and the extent of the substantial assistance departure received. [The] consistency of the findings across methodologies reveals . . . an equity problem requiring subsequent research.

First, this analysis uncovered that the definition of "substantial assistance" was not being consistently applied across the federal districts. Not only were some districts considering cooperation that was not being considered by other districts, but the components of a given behavior that classified it as "substantial" were unclear.

Second, while the U.S. attorney offices are required to record the reason for making a substantial assistance motion, there is no provision that this information be made available for review. It is exactly such a lack of review, inherent in preguideline judicial discretion, that led to charges of unwarranted sentencing disparity and passage of the SRA. Under the SRA, the court is now compelled to report a reason for the sentence imposed and a reason for a departure. . . . A comparable §5K1.1 "statement of reasons" appears appropriate for a guideline process affecting nearly one in every five federal defendants. DOJ information on district charging practices, plea bargaining practices, degree and type of cooperation, and usefulness of information to the prosecution is crucial in an assessment of §5K1.1. . . .

Third, the evidence consistently indicated that factors that were associated with either the making of a §5K1.1 motion and/or the magnitude of the departure were not consistent with principles of equity. Expected factors (e.g., type of cooperation, benefit of cooperation, defendant culpability or function, relevant conduct, offense type) generally were found to be inadequate in explaining §5K1.1 departures. Even more worrisome, legally irrelevant factors (e.g., gender, race, ethnicity, citizenship) were found to be statistically significant in explaining §5K1.1 departures. . . .

Data indicate that currently judges relate the magnitude of departure to the length of the predeparture sentence: higher predeparture guideline ranges bring more absolute months of departure. However, no evidence supports the conclusion that defendants facing higher sentences, in fact, provide absolutely more cooperation, or absolutely more beneficial cooperation, to warrant a larger relative departure. The issue is whether the magnitude of a substantial assistance departure should be an absolute amount (all defendants who cooperate at a given substantial assistance level receive a set and absolute number of months reduction in sentence) or a relative amount (all defendants who cooperate at a given substantial assistance level receive a proportional . . . reduction in sentence). The philosophical debate that addresses the assumptions and ramifications of the absolute versus proportional approach is long overdue.

NOTES

1. *Prosecutorial discretion under the guidelines.* In part because §5K1.1 of the federal guidelines requires a government motion before the court can reduce the sentence based on the defendant's cooperation (and because 18 U.S.C. §3553(e) requires the same before a court can reduce a sentence below a statutory mandatory minimum), many commentators lament that prosecutors ultimately possess more sentencing discretion than judges within the federal sentencing system. For instance, Professor Kate Stith and Judge Jose Cabranes contend that mandatory sentencing schemes "inevitably shift power toward prosecutors":

> Because the sentencing rules are known in advance, prosecutors may greatly influence the ultimate sentence through their decisions on charges, plea agreements, and motions to depart for substantial assistance to law enforcement authorities. Although prosecutors have always had significant discretion in charging and plea bargaining, the prosecutor's decisions on these matters have far greater significance for sentencing in the Guidelines regime; they determine not only the maximum term of a sentence (as provided in the statute prohibiting the conduct), but, in many cases, the precise sentence range that a sentencing court may consider. . . .

Kate Stith & Jose A. Cabranes, To Fear Judging No More: Recommendations for the Federal Sentencing Guidelines, 11 Fed. Sent'g Rep. 187-188 (1999). Though few dispute that prosecutors possess considerable power and discretion within the federal system, some question whether the guidelines themselves are responsible for shifting power to the prosecutors. For example, Justice Stephen Breyer has argued that the guidelines have actually "shifted the power to determine sentences away from prosecutors in at least some ways":

> Prosecutors should find it more difficult than under pre-Guideline practice to control the sentence by manipulating the charge. For, within broad limits, the offender's actual conduct, not the charge, will determine the sentence. For this same reason plea bargaining over charges should have diminished, because again within broad limits, a defendant's promise to plead guilty to a particular, perhaps less serious, charge likely will not affect the sentence. . . . This is not to deny the prosecutor's considerable bargaining power. The prosecutor still may choose to charge an offense that carries a lower statutory maximum penalty (and statutory maximum penalties trump the Guidelines). He may enter into a plea agreement for a fixed sentence, an agreement that will carry significant weight with the judge. He can simply ignore certain conduct, believing that the probation officer will not discover it. And he can ask the judge to depart from a Guideline sentence. But the prosecutor possessed all these powers before the Guidelines as well — and to a greater extent. . . .
>
> I recognize, however, other sources of special prosecutor power. Upon recommendation of the prosecutor, a court may depart downward from a Guideline sentence, and below even a statutory mandatory minimum, where there is "substantial assistance in the investigation or prosecution of another person who has committed an offense." U.S.S.G. §5K1.1. Moreover, statutory mandatory minimum sentences and Guideline sentences written to reflect those mandatory minimums — particularly in respect to drug crimes — may increase the pressure upon a defendant to provide "substantial assistance" in order to obtain a downward departure, or to plead guilty to an offense with a low statutory maximum (e.g., simple possession).
>
> Both factors — "substantial assistance" and "mandatory minimum" — rest upon special provisions in the Guideline statute. Moreover, those two factors play a particularly important role in federal drug prosecutions, which account for about 40% of all federal sentencing. Viewed in light of Guideline history, however, these two special "power-shifting" factors are nonessential, peripheral features of the Guidelines. And, for that reason, I believe it promotes accuracy in analysis, and leads to more constructive recommendations, to point to these two special statutory provisions, rather than the Guidelines themselves, as having increased prosecutorial power. . . .

Speech of Associate Justice Stephen Breyer, 11 Fed. Sent'g Rep. at 182-183 (1999).

2. *Departures, disparity, and discrimination.* Although departure authority provides judges with an opportunity to adjust sentences in light of unique circumstances in particular cases, it also provides a means for disparity and even discrimination to work their way back into a guideline system. Consider again the U.S. Sentencing Commission report on substantial-assistance departures, which stated that "legally irrelevant factors (e.g., gender, race, ethnicity, citizenship) were found to be statistically significant in explaining §5K1.1 departures." Does this conclusion, and data that show significant circuit-by-circuit discrepancies in the use of departure authority, suggest that guideline systems must more carefully circumscribe and more closely monitor any retained areas of

discretion? What roles should Congress, the U.S. Sentencing Commission, and appellate courts play in response to such evidence of disparity in the application of departure authority? May disparity between districts perhaps reflect different charging patterns that ultimately lead to similar sentences? See Laura Storto, Getting Behind the Numbers: A Report on Four Districts and What They Do "Below the Radar Screen," 15 Fed. Sent'g Rep. 204 (2003).

3. *Unavoidable tensions between equal justice and individual justice?* One could summarize the entire guideline sentencing movement as just another chapter in an endless struggle to calibrate the unavoidable tension between efforts to achieve equal justice across cases and those to achieve individual justice in specific cases. Kate Stith and Jose Cabranes, leading critics of the federal sentencing guidelines, argue that in the federal system this effort has inappropriately prioritized equal justice over individual justice:

> Grounded in a fear of judging, the Guidelines seek not to channel the exercise of informed judicial discretion, but to repress judgment and replace it with a calculus of justice. . . . This structure ignores the most important capacity that judges bring to criminal sentencing: the ability to pronounce moral judgment that takes into account all aspects of the crime and the offender. . . . It is not that the idea of equal treatment is unworthy; rather, this ideal cannot be, and should not be, pursued through complex, mandatory guidelines. . . . Uniform treatment ought to be one objective of sentencing, to be sure, but not the sole or overriding objective.
>
> In the traditional ritual of sentencing, the judge pronounced not only a sentence but society's condemnation as well. . . . The sentencing ritual was predicated on the fundamental understanding that only a person can pass moral judgment, and only a person can be morally judged. In emphasizing the human face of justice, we are not blind to the limitations of the traditional sentencing hearing. Human judgment is fallible. Unfortunately, this is a fact of our existence for which there can be no easy technological solution. By replacing the case-by-case exercise of human judgment with a mechanical calculus, we do not judge better or more objectively, nor do we judge worse. Instead, we cease to judge at all. We process individuals according to a variety of purportedly objective criteria. But genuine judgment, in the sense of moral reckoning, cannot be inscribed in a table of offense levels and criminal history categories. . . .

Stith & Cabranes, 11 Fed. Sent'g Rep. at 187-188 (1999).

d.   *Advisory Guidelines: The Aftermath of* Booker

In Blakely v. Washington, 542 U.S. 296 (2004), the Supreme Court held that a jury rather than a judge must find any fact that becomes necessary to authorize a new sentence. Although *Blakely* was a state case that formally addressed only one state sentencing system, its broad statement of the constitutional principles safeguarded by the Sixth Amendment raised questions about any guideline sentencing system that relied on judicial factfinding. Because the federal system relies heavily on judicial factfinding for guideline calculations, litigation began immediately after *Blakely* to determine whether the federal sentencing guidelines could possibly stand after the Court's decision. The Supreme Court gave its answer in January 2005.

United States v. Freddie J. Booker
125 S. Ct. 738 (2005)

STEVENS, J., delivered the opinion of the Court in part.

The question presented in each of these cases is whether an application of the Federal Sentencing Guidelines violated the Sixth Amendment. . . . In both cases the courts rejected, on the basis of our decision in Blakely v. Washington, 542 U.S. 296 (2004), the Government's recommended application of the Sentencing Guidelines because the proposed sentences were based on additional facts that the sentencing judge found by a preponderance of the evidence. We hold that both courts correctly concluded that the Sixth Amendment as construed in *Blakely* does apply to the Sentencing Guidelines. In a separate opinion authored by Justice Breyer, the Court concludes that in light of this holding, two provisions of the Sentencing Reform Act of 1984 (SRA) that have the effect of making the Guidelines mandatory must be invalidated in order to allow the statute to operate in a manner consistent with congressional intent.

Respondent Booker was charged with possession with intent to distribute at least 50 grams of cocaine base (crack). . . . Based upon Booker's criminal history and the quantity of drugs found by the jury, the Sentencing Guidelines required the District Court Judge to select a "base" sentence of not less than 210 nor more than 262 months in prison. See USSG §§2D1.1(c)(4), 4A1.1. The judge, however, held a post-trial sentencing proceeding and concluded by a preponderance of the evidence that Booker had possessed an additional 566 grams of crack and that he was guilty of obstructing justice. Those findings mandated that the judge select a sentence between 360 months and life imprisonment; the judge imposed a sentence at the low end of the range. Thus, instead of the sentence of 21 years and 10 months that the judge could have imposed on the basis of the facts proved to the jury beyond a reasonable doubt, Booker received a 30-year sentence. . . .

It has been settled throughout our history that the Constitution protects every criminal defendant against conviction except upon proof beyond a reasonable doubt of every fact necessary to constitute the crime with which he is charged. It is equally clear that the Constitution gives a criminal defendant the right to demand that a jury find him guilty of all the elements of the crime with which he is charged. These basic precepts, firmly rooted in the common law, have provided the basis for recent decisions interpreting modern criminal statutes and sentencing procedures. . . .

In Blakely v. Washington, 542 U.S. 296 (2004), we dealt with a determinate sentencing scheme similar to the Federal Sentencing Guidelines. There the defendant pleaded guilty to kidnaping, a class B felony punishable by a term of not more than 10 years. Other provisions of Washington law, comparable to the Federal Sentencing Guidelines, mandated a "standard" sentence of 49 to 53 months, unless the judge found aggravating facts justifying an exceptional sentence. Although the prosecutor recommended a sentence in the standard range, the judge found that the defendant had acted with "deliberate cruelty" and sentenced him to 90 months. . . .

The application of Washington's sentencing scheme violated the defendant's right to have the jury find the existence of "any particular fact" that the

law makes essential to his punishment. That right is implicated whenever a judge
seeks to impose a sentence that is not solely based on "facts reflected in the jury
verdict or admitted by the defendant." . . . The determination that the
defendant acted with deliberate cruelty . . . increased the sentence that the
defendant could have otherwise received. Since this fact was found by a judge
using a preponderance of the evidence standard, the sentence violated Blakely's
Sixth Amendment rights.

[There] is no distinction of constitutional significance between the
Federal Sentencing Guidelines and the Washington procedures at issue in
that case. This conclusion rests on the premise, common to both systems,
that the relevant sentencing rules are mandatory and impose binding requirements on all sentencing judges.

If the Guidelines as currently written could be read as merely advisory
provisions that recommended, rather than required, the selection of particular
sentences in response to differing sets of facts, their use would not implicate the
Sixth Amendment. We have never doubted the authority of a judge to exercise
broad discretion in imposing a sentence within a statutory range. See Williams v.
New York, 337 U.S. 241 (1949). . . . For when a trial judge exercises his discretion to select a specific sentence within a defined range, the defendant has no
right to a jury determination of the facts that the judge deems relevant.

The Guidelines as written, however, are not advisory; they are mandatory
and binding on all judges. [Subsection (b) of §3553] directs that the court "shall
impose a sentence of the kind, and within the range" established by the Guidelines, subject to departures in specific, limited cases. [Departures] are not available in every case, and in fact are unavailable in most. In most cases, as a matter
of law, the Commission will have adequately taken all relevant factors into
account, and no departure will be legally permissible. In those instances, the
judge is bound to impose a sentence within the Guidelines range. . . .

Booker's case illustrates the mandatory nature of the Guidelines. The jury
convicted him of possessing at least 50 grams of crack in violation of 21 U.S.C.
§841(b)(1)(A)(iii) based on evidence that he had 92.5 grams of crack in his
duffel bag. Under these facts, the Guidelines specified an offense level of 32,
which, given the defendant's criminal history category, authorized a sentence of
210 to 262 months. See USSG §2D1.1(c)(4). Booker's is a run-of-the-mill drug
case, and does not present any factors that were inadequately considered by the
Commission. The sentencing judge would therefore have been reversed had he
not imposed a sentence within the level 32 Guidelines range. . . .

We recognize . . . that in some cases jury factfinding may impair the
most expedient and efficient sentencing of defendants. But the interest in fairness and reliability protected by the right to a jury trial—a common-law right
that defendants enjoyed for centuries and that is now enshrined in the Sixth
Amendment—has always outweighed the interest in concluding trials swiftly.
As Blackstone put it:

> However convenient these [new methods of trial] may appear at first (as
> doubtless all arbitrary powers, well executed, are the most convenient) yet let
> it be again remembered, that delays, and little inconveniences in the forms of
> justice, are the price that all free nations must pay for their liberty in more
> substantial matters; that these inroads upon this sacred bulwark of the nation

are fundamentally opposite to the spirit of our constitution; and that, though begun in trifles, the precedent may gradually increase and spread, to the utter disuse of juries in questions of the most momentous concerns. 4 Commentaries on the Laws of England 343-344 (1769).

Accordingly, [any] fact (other than a prior conviction) which is necessary to support a sentence exceeding the maximum authorized by the facts established by a plea of guilty or a jury verdict must be admitted by the defendant or proved to a jury beyond a reasonable doubt.

BREYER, J., delivered the opinion of the Court in part.

. . . We answer the question of remedy by finding the provision of the federal sentencing statute that makes the Guidelines mandatory, 18 U.S.C. §3553(b)(1), incompatible with today's constitutional holding. We conclude that this provision must be severed and excised, as must one other statutory section, §3742(e), which depends upon the Guidelines' mandatory nature. So modified, the Federal Sentencing Act makes the Guidelines effectively advisory. It requires a sentencing court to consider Guidelines ranges, but it permits the court to tailor the sentence in light of other statutory concerns as well.

I

We answer the remedial question by looking to legislative intent. We seek to determine what "Congress would have intended" in light of the Court's constitutional holding. Denver Area Ed. Telecommunications Consortium, Inc. v. FCC, 518 U.S. 727, 767 (1996) (plurality opinion) ("Would Congress still have passed" the valid sections had it known about the constitutional invalidity of the other portions of the statute?). In this instance, we must determine which of the two following remedial approaches is the more compatible with the legislature's intent as embodied in the 1984 Sentencing Act.

One approach, that of Justice Stevens' dissent, would retain the Sentencing Act (and the Guidelines) as written, but would engraft onto the existing system today's Sixth Amendment "jury trial" requirement. The addition would change the Guidelines by preventing the sentencing court from increasing a sentence on the basis of a fact that the jury did not find (or that the offender did not admit).

The other approach, which we now adopt, would (through severance and excision of two provisions) make the Guidelines system advisory while maintaining a strong connection between the sentence imposed and the offender's real conduct — a connection important to the increased uniformity of sentencing that Congress intended its Guidelines system to achieve. . . .

In today's context — a highly complex statute, interrelated provisions, and a constitutional requirement that creates fundamental change — we cannot assume that Congress, if faced with the statute's invalidity in key applications, would have preferred to apply the statute in as many other instances as possible. . . . It is, of course, true that the numbers show that the constitutional jury trial requirement would lead to additional decisionmaking by juries in only a minority of cases. Prosecutors and defense attorneys would still resolve the lion's share of criminal matters through plea bargaining, and plea bargaining takes place without a jury. Many of the rest involve only simple issues calling for no upward Guidelines adjustment. And in at least some of the remainder, a judge may find adequate room to adjust a sentence within the single Guidelines range to which the jury verdict points, or within the overlap between that range and the next highest.

But the constitutional jury trial requirement would nonetheless affect every case. It would affect decisions about whether to go to trial. It would affect the content of plea negotiations. It would alter the judge's role in sentencing. Thus we must determine likely intent not by counting proceedings, but by evaluating the consequences of the Court's constitutional requirement in light of the Act's language, its history, and its basic purposes. While reasonable minds can, and do, differ about the outcome, we conclude that the constitutional jury trial requirement is not compatible with the Act as written and that some severance and excision are necessary.

II

Several considerations convince us that, were the Court's constitutional requirement added onto the Sentencing Act as currently written, the requirement would so transform the scheme that Congress created that Congress likely would not have intended the Act as so modified to stand. First, the statute's text states that "the court" when sentencing will consider "the nature and circumstances of the offense and the history and characteristics of the defendant." 18 U.S.C. §3553(a)(1). In context, the words "the court" mean "the judge without the jury," not "the judge working together with the jury." The Act's history confirms it. See, e.g., S. Rep. No. 98-225, p. 51 (1983) (the Guidelines system "will guide the judge in making" sentencing decisions). . . .

This provision makes it difficult to justify Justice Stevens' approach, for that approach requires reading the words "the court" as if they meant "the judge working together with the jury." Unlike Justice Stevens, we do not believe we can interpret the statute's language to save its constitutionality, because we believe that any such reinterpretation, even if limited to instances in which a Sixth Amendment problem arises, would be plainly contrary to the intent of Congress. . . .

Second, Congress' basic statutory goal — a system that diminishes sentencing disparity — depends for its success upon judicial efforts to determine, and to base punishment upon, the real conduct that underlies the crime of conviction. That determination is particularly important in the federal system where crimes defined as, for example, "obstructing, delaying, or affecting commerce or the movement of any article or commodity in commerce, by . . . extortion," 18 U.S.C. §1951(a), or, say, using the mail "for the purpose of executing" a "scheme or artifice to defraud," §1341, can encompass a vast range of very different kinds of underlying conduct. But it is also important even in respect to ordinary crimes, such as robbery, where an act that meets the statutory definition can be committed in a host of different ways. Judges have long looked to real conduct when sentencing. Federal judges have long relied upon a presentence report, prepared by a probation officer, for information (often unavailable until after the trial) relevant to the manner in which the convicted offender committed the crime of conviction. . . .

To engraft the Court's constitutional requirement onto the sentencing statutes, however, would destroy the system. It would prevent a judge from relying upon a presentence report for factual information, relevant to sentencing, uncovered after the trial. In doing so, it would, even compared to pre-Guidelines sentencing, weaken the tie between a sentence and an offender's real conduct. It would thereby undermine the sentencing statute's basic aim of ensuring similar sentences for those who have committed similar crimes in similar ways.

[An example can] illustrate the point. Imagine Smith and Jones, each of whom violates the Hobbs Act in very different ways. See 18 U.S.C. §1951(a) (forbidding "obstructing, delaying, or affecting commerce or the movement of any article or commodity in commerce, by . . . extortion"). Smith threatens to injure a co-worker unless the co-worker advances him a few dollars from the interstate company's till; Jones, after similarly threatening the co-worker, causes far more harm by seeking far more money, by making certain that the co-worker's family is aware of the threat, by arranging for deliveries of dead animals to the co-worker's home to show he is serious, and so forth. The offenders' behavior is very different; the known harmful consequences of their actions are different; their punishments both before, and after, the Guidelines would have been different. But, under the dissenters' approach, unless prosecutors decide to charge more than the elements of the crime, the judge would have to impose similar punishments. . . .

This point is critically important. Congress' basic goal in passing the Sentencing Act was to move the sentencing system in the direction of increased uniformity. See 28 U.S.C. §991(b)(1)(B); see also §994(f). That uniformity does not consist simply of similar sentences for those convicted of violations of the same statute — a uniformity consistent with the dissenters' remedial approach. It consists, more importantly, of similar relationships between sentences and real conduct, relationships that Congress' sentencing statutes helped to advance and that Justice Stevens' approach would undermine. In significant part, it is the weakening of this real-conduct/uniformity-in-sentencing relationship . . . that leads us to conclude that Congress would have preferred no mandatory system to the system the dissenters envisage.

Third, the sentencing statutes, read to include the Court's Sixth Amendment requirement, would create a system far more complex than Congress could have intended. How would courts and counsel work with an indictment and a jury trial that involved not just whether a defendant robbed a bank but also how? Would the indictment have to allege, in addition to the elements of robbery, whether the defendant possessed a firearm, whether he brandished or discharged it, whether he threatened death, whether he caused bodily injury, whether any such injury was ordinary, serious, permanent or life threatening, whether he abducted or physically restrained anyone, whether any victim was unusually vulnerable, how much money was taken, and whether he was an organizer, leader, manager, or supervisor in a robbery gang? See USSG §§2B3.1, 3B1.1. If so, how could a defendant mount a defense against some or all such specific claims should he also try simultaneously to maintain that the Government's evidence failed to place him at the scene of the crime? . . . How would the court take account, for punishment purposes, of a defendant's contemptuous behavior at trial—a matter that the Government could not have charged in the indictment? See §3C1.1.

Fourth, plea bargaining would not significantly diminish the consequences of the Court's constitutional holding for the operation of the Guidelines. Rather, plea bargaining would make matters worse. Congress enacted the sentencing statutes in major part to achieve greater uniformity in sentencing, i.e., to increase the likelihood that offenders who engage in similar real conduct would receive similar sentences. The statutes reasonably assume that their efforts to move the trial-based sentencing process in the direction of greater sentencing uniformity would have a similar positive impact upon plea-bargained sentences, for plea bargaining takes place in the shadow of (i.e., with an eye towards the hypothetical result of) a potential trial. . . .

The Court's constitutional jury trial requirement, however, if patched onto the present Sentencing Act, would move the system backwards in respect both to tried and to plea-bargained cases. In respect to tried cases, it would effectively deprive the judge of the ability to use post-verdict-acquired real-conduct information; it would prohibit the judge from basing a sentence upon any conduct other than the conduct the prosecutor chose to charge; and it would put a defendant to a set of difficult strategic choices as to which prosecutorial claims he would contest. The sentence that would emerge in a case tried under such a system would likely reflect real conduct less completely, less accurately, and less often than did a pre-Guidelines, as well as a Guidelines, trial.

Because plea bargaining inevitably reflects estimates of what would happen at trial, plea bargaining too under such a system would move in the wrong direction. That is to say, in a sentencing system modified by the Court's constitutional requirement, plea bargaining would likely lead to sentences that gave greater weight, not to real conduct, but rather to the skill of counsel, the policies of the prosecutor, the caseload, and other factors that vary from place to place, defendant to defendant, and crime to crime. Compared to pre-Guidelines plea bargaining, plea bargaining of this kind would necessarily move federal sentencing in the direction of diminished, not increased, uniformity in sentencing. It would tend to defeat, not to further, Congress' basic statutory goal.

Such a system would have particularly troubling consequences with respect to prosecutorial power. Until now, sentencing factors have come before the judge in the presentence report. But in a sentencing system with the Court's constitutional requirement engrafted onto it, any factor that a prosecutor chose not to charge at the plea negotiation would be placed beyond the reach of the judge entirely. Prosecutors would thus exercise a power the Sentencing Act vested in judges: the power to decide, based on relevant information about the offense and the offender, which defendants merit heavier punishment.

In respondent Booker's case, for example, the jury heard evidence that the crime had involved 92.5 grams of crack cocaine, and convicted Booker of possessing more than 50 grams. But the judge, at sentencing, found that the crime had involved an additional 566 grams, for a total of 658.5 grams. A system that would require the jury, not the judge, to make the additional "566 grams" finding is a system in which the prosecutor, not the judge, would control the sentence. That is because it is the prosecutor who would have to decide what drug amount to charge. He could choose to charge 658.5 grams, or 92.5, or less.

It is the prosecutor who, through such a charging decision, would control the sentencing range. . . .

For all these reasons, Congress, had it been faced with the constitutional jury trial requirement, likely would not have passed the same Sentencing Act. It likely would have found the requirement incompatible with the Act as written. Hence the Act cannot remain valid in its entirety. Severance and excision are necessary.

III

We now turn to the question of which portions of the sentencing statute we must sever and excise as inconsistent with the Court's constitutional requirement. [We] do not believe that the entire statute must be invalidated. Most of the statute is perfectly valid. See, e.g., 18 U.S.C. §3551 (describing authorized sentences as probation, fine, or imprisonment); §3552 (presentence reports); §3554 (forfeiture); §3555 (notification to the victims); §3583 (supervised release). And we must refrain from invalidating more of the statute than is necessary.

[We] must sever and excise two specific statutory provisions: the provision that requires sentencing courts to impose a sentence within the applicable Guidelines range (in the absence of circumstances that justify a departure), see 18 U.S.C. §3553(b)(1), and the provision that sets forth standards of review on appeal, including de novo review of departures from the applicable Guidelines range, see §3742(e). With these two sections excised (and statutory cross-references to the two sections consequently invalidated), the remainder of the Act satisfies the Court's constitutional requirements.

The remainder of the Act functions independently. Without the "mandatory" provision, the Act nonetheless requires judges to take account of the Guidelines together with other sentencing goals. See 18 U.S.C. §3553(a). The Act nonetheless requires judges to consider the Guidelines "sentencing range established for . . . the applicable category of offense committed by the applicable category of defendant," §3553(a)(4), the pertinent Sentencing Commission policy statements, the need to avoid unwarranted sentencing disparities, and the need to provide restitution to victims, §§3553(a)(1), (3), (5)-(7). And the Act nonetheless requires judges to impose sentences that reflect the seriousness of the offense, promote respect for the law, provide just punishment, afford adequate deterrence, protect the public, and effectively provide the defendant with needed educational or vocational training and medical care. §3553(a)(2).

Moreover, despite the absence of §3553(b)(1), the Act continues to provide for appeals from sentencing decisions (irrespective of whether the trial judge sentences within or outside the Guidelines range in the exercise of his discretionary power under §3553(a)). See §3742(a) (appeal by defendant); §3742(b) (appeal by Government). We concede that the excision of §3553(b)(1) requires the excision of a different, appeals-related section, namely §3742(e), which sets forth standards of review on appeal. That section contains critical cross-references to the (now-excised) §3553(b)(1) and consequently must be severed and excised for similar reasons.

Excision of §3742(e), however, does not pose a critical problem for the handling of appeals. That is because . . . a statute that does not explicitly set forth a standard of review may nonetheless do so implicitly. We infer appropriate review standards from related statutory language, the structure of the statute, and the sound administration of justice. And in this instance those factors, in addition to the past two decades of appellate practice in cases involving departures, imply a practical standard of review already familiar to appellate courts: review for "unreasonableness." 18 U.S.C. §3742(e)(3).

Until 2003, §3742(e) explicitly set forth that standard. In 2003, Congress modified the pre-existing text, adding a de novo standard of review for departures. . . . Prosecutorial Remedies and Other Tools to End the Exploitation of Children Today Act of 2003, Pub. L. 108-21, §401(d)(1), 117 Stat. 670. In light of today's holding, the reasons for these revisions — to make Guidelines sentencing even more mandatory than it had been — have ceased to be relevant. [The text of §3742(e)(3) in effect before 2003 directed appellate courts to review sentences outside the guidelines range to determine whether the sentence was] "unreasonable, having regard for . . . the factors to be considered in imposing a sentence, as set forth in [§3553(a)]." Section 3553(a) remains in effect, and sets forth numerous factors that guide sentencing. Those factors in turn will guide appellate courts, as they have in the past, in determining whether a sentence is unreasonable. . . .

Nor do we share the dissenters' doubts about the practicality of a "reasonableness" standard of review. "Reasonableness" standards are not foreign to sentencing law. The Act has long required their use in important sentencing circumstances — both on review of departures, see 18 U.S.C. §3742(e)(3), and on review of sentences imposed where there was no applicable Guideline, see §§3742(a)(4), (b)(4), (e)(4). Together, these cases account for about 16.7% of sentencing appeals. That is why we think it fair . . . to assume judicial familiarity with a "reasonableness" standard. And that is why we believe that appellate judges will prove capable of . . . applying such a standard across the board.

[The] remedial question we must ask here (as we did in respect to §3553(b)(1)) is, which alternative adheres more closely to Congress' original objective: (1) retention of sentencing appeals, or (2) invalidation of the entire Act, including its appellate provisions? The former, by providing appellate review, would tend to iron out sentencing differences; the latter would not. Hence we believe Congress would have preferred the former to the latter — even if the former means that some provisions will apply differently from the way Congress had originally expected.

[The] Sentencing Commission remains in place, writing Guidelines, collecting information about actual district court sentencing decisions, undertaking research, and revising the Guidelines accordingly. See 28 U.S.C. §994. The district courts, while not bound to apply the Guidelines, must consult those Guidelines and take them into account when sentencing. See 18 U.S.C. §§3553(a)(4), (5). The courts of appeals review sentencing decisions for unreasonableness. These features of the remaining system, while not the system Congress enacted, nonetheless continue to move sentencing in Congress' preferred direction, helping to avoid excessive sentencing disparities while maintaining flexibility sufficient to individualize sentences where necessary. We can find no feature of the remaining system that tends to hinder, rather than to further, these basic objectives. Under these circumstances, why would Congress not have preferred excision of the "mandatory" provision to a system that engrafts today's constitutional requirement onto the unchanged pre-existing statute — a system that, in terms of Congress' basic objectives, is counterproductive? . . .

Ours, of course, is not the last word: The ball now lies in Congress' court. The National Legislature is equipped to devise and install, long-term, the sentencing system, compatible with the Constitution, that Congress judges best for the federal system of justice. . . .

STEVENS, J., dissenting in part.

[Neither] 18 U.S.C. §3553(b)(1), which makes application of the Guidelines mandatory, nor §3742(e), which authorizes appellate review of departures from the Guidelines, is even arguably unconstitutional. . . . While it is perfectly clear that Congress has ample power to repeal these two statutory provisions if it so desires, this Court should not make that choice on Congress' behalf. . . .

When one pauses to note that over 95% of all federal criminal prosecutions are terminated by a plea bargain, and the further fact that in almost half of the cases that go to trial there are no sentencing enhancements, the extraordinary overbreadth of the Court's unprecedented remedy is manifest. . . .

It is a fundamental premise of judicial review that all Acts of Congress are presumptively valid. [It] is abundantly clear that the fact that a statute, or any provision of a statute, is unconstitutional in a portion of its applications does not render the statute or provision invalid, and no party suggests otherwise. The Government conceded at oral argument that 45% of federal sentences involve no enhancements. And, according to two U.S. Sentencing Commissioners who testified before Congress shortly after we handed down our decision in *Blakely*, the number of enhancements that would actually implicate a defendant's Sixth Amendment rights is even smaller. Simply stated, the Government's submissions to this Court and to Congress demonstrate that the Guidelines could be constitutionally applied in their entirety, without any modifications, in the majority of the cases sentenced under the federal guidelines. On the basis of these submissions alone, this Court should have declined to find the Guidelines, or any particular provisions of the Guidelines, facially invalid. . . .

Rather than engage in a wholesale rewriting of the SRA, I would simply allow the Government to continue doing what it has done since this Court handed down *Blakely*— prove any fact that is required to increase a defendant's sentence under the Guidelines to a jury beyond a reasonable doubt. [A] requirement of jury factfinding for certain issues can be implemented without difficulty in the vast majority of cases.

Indeed, this already appears to be the case. The Department of Justice already has instituted procedures which would protect the overwhelming majority of future cases from *Blakely* infirmity. The Department of Justice has issued detailed guidance for every stage of the prosecution from indictment to final sentencing, including alleging facts that would support sentencing enhancements and requiring defendants to waive any potential *Blakely* rights in plea agreements. Given this experience, I think the Court dramatically overstates the difficulty of implementing this solution. . . .

The majority's remedy was not the inevitable result of the Court's holding that *Blakely* applies to the Guidelines. [*Blakely* did not render] determinate sentencing unconstitutional.[17] . . . No judicial remedy is proper if it is "not commensurate with the constitutional violation to be repaired." Hills v. Gautreaux, 425 U.S. 284, 294 (1976). The Court's system fails that test, frustrates Congress' principal goal in enacting the SRA, and violates the tradition of judicial restraint that has heretofore limited our power to overturn validly enacted statutes. I respectfully dissent.

SCALIA, J., dissenting in part.

The remedial majority takes as the North Star of its analysis the fact that Congress enacted a "judge-based sentencing system." That seems to me quite misguided. Congress did indeed expect judges to make the factual determinations to which the Guidelines apply, just as it expected the Guidelines to be mandatory. But which of those expectations was central to the congressional purpose is not hard to determine. No headline describing the Sentencing Reform Act of 1984 would have read "Congress reaffirms judge-based sentencing" rather than "Congress prescribes standardized sentences." Justice Breyer's opinion for the Court repeatedly acknowledges that the primary objective of the Act was to reduce sentencing disparity. Inexplicably, however, the opinion concludes that the manner of achieving uniform sentences was more important to Congress than actually achieving uniformity — that Congress was so attached to having judges determine "real conduct" on the basis of bureaucratically prepared, hearsay-riddled presentence reports that it would rather lose the binding nature of the Guidelines than adhere to the old-fashioned process of having juries find the facts that expose a defendant to increased prison time. The majority's remedial choice is thus wonderfully ironic: In order to rescue from nullification a statutory scheme designed to eliminate discretionary sentencing, it discards the provisions that eliminate discretionary sentencing. . . .

As frustrating as this conclusion is to the Act's purpose of uniform sentencing, it at least establishes a clear and comprehensible regime — essentially the regime that existed before the Act became effective. That clarity is eliminated, however, by the remedial majority's surgery on 18 U.S.C. §3742, the provision governing appellate review of sentences. Even the most casual reading of this section discloses that its purpose — its only purpose — is to enable courts of appeals to enforce conformity with the Guidelines. All of the provisions of that section that impose a review obligation beyond what existed under prior law are related to the district judge's obligations under the Guidelines. If the Guidelines are no longer binding, one would think that the provision designed to ensure compliance with them would, in its totality, be inoperative. The Court holds otherwise. Like a black-robed Alexander cutting the Gordian knot, it simply severs the purpose of the review provisions from their text, holding that only subsection (e), which sets forth the determinations that the court of

---

17. Moreover, even if the change to an indeterminate system were necessary, the Court could have minimized the consequences to the system by limiting the application of its holding to those defendants on direct review who actually suffered a Sixth Amendment violation. Griffith v. Kentucky, 479 U.S. 314 (1987), does not require blind application of every part of this Court's holdings to all pending cases, but rather, requires that we apply any new "rule to all similar cases pending on direct review." For obvious reasons, not all pending cases are made similar to Booker and Fanfan's merely because they involved an application of the Guidelines.

appeals must make, is inoperative, whereas all the rest of §3742 subsists. . . . This is rather like deleting the ingredients portion of a recipe and telling the cook to proceed with the preparation portion.

[The Court] announces that the standard of review for all [sentencing] appeals is "unreasonableness." This conflates different and distinct statutory authorizations of appeal and elides crucial differences in the statutory scope of review. Section 3742 specifies four different kinds of appeal,[7] [and it creates] no one-size-fits-all "unreasonableness" review. The power to review a sentence for reasonableness arises only when the sentencing court has departed from "the applicable guideline range." §3742(f)(2).

[Thus, we] have before us a statute that does explicitly set forth a standard of review. The question is, when the Court has severed that standard of review (contained in §3742(e)), does it make any sense to look for some congressional "implication" of a different standard of review in the remnants of the statute that the Court has left standing? Only in Wonderland. . . .

The worst feature of the scheme is that no one knows — and perhaps no one is meant to know — how advisory Guidelines and "unreasonableness" review will function in practice. . . . What I anticipate will happen is that "unreasonableness" review will produce a discordant symphony of different standards, varying from court to court and judge to judge. . . .

BREYER, J., dissenting in part.

. . . I find nothing in the Sixth Amendment that forbids a sentencing judge to determine (as judges at sentencing have traditionally determined) the manner or way in which the offender carried out the crime of which he was convicted. . . . I continue to disagree with the constitutional analysis the Court set forth . . . in *Blakely*. But even were I to accept that analysis as valid, I would disagree with the way in which the Court applies it here.

[The] Court's opinion today illustrates the historical mistake upon which its conclusions rest. The Court reiterates its view that the right of "trial by jury has been understood to require" a jury trial for determination of "the truth of every accusation." This claim makes historical sense insofar as an "accusation" encompasses each factual element of the crime of which a defendant is accused. But the key question here is whether that word also encompasses sentencing facts — facts about the offender (say, recidivism) or about the way in which the offender committed the crime (say, the seriousness of the injury or the amount stolen) that help a sentencing judge determine a convicted offender's specific sentence.

History does not support a "right to jury trial" in respect to sentencing facts. Traditionally, the law has distinguished between facts that are elements of crimes and facts that are relevant only to sentencing. Traditionally, federal law has looked to judges, not to juries, to resolve disputes about sentencing facts. Traditionally, those familiar with the criminal justice system have found

---

7. The four kinds of appeal arise when, respectively, (1) the sentence is "imposed in violation of law," §§3742(a)(1), (b)(1), (e)(1), (f)(1); (2) the sentence is "imposed as a result of an incorrect application of the sentencing guidelines," §§3742(a)(2), (b)(2), (e)(2), (f)(1); (3) the sentence is either above or below "the applicable guideline range," §§3742(a)(3), (b)(3), (e)(3), (f)(2); and (4) no guideline is applicable and the sentence is "plainly unreasonable," §§3742(a)(4), (b)(4), (e)(4), (f)(2).

separate, postconviction judge-run sentencing procedures sensible given the difficulty of obtaining relevant sentencing information before the moment of conviction. They have found those proceedings practical given the impracticality of the alternatives, say, two-stage (guilt, sentence) jury procedures. And, despite the absence of jury determinations, they have found those proceedings fair as long as the convicted offender has the opportunity to contest a claimed fact before the judge, and as long as the sentence falls within the maximum of the range that a congressional statute specifically sets forth. . . .

The upshot is that the Court's Sixth Amendment decisions . . . deprive Congress and state legislatures of authority that is constitutionally theirs. The sentencing function long has been a peculiarly shared responsibility among the Branches of Government. Congress' share of this joint responsibility has long included not only the power to define crimes (by enacting statutes setting forth their factual elements) but also the power to specify sentences, whether by setting forth a range of individual-crime-related sentences (say, 0 to 10 years' imprisonment for bank robbery) or by identifying sentencing factors that permit or require a judge to impose higher or lower sentences in particular circumstances. . . .

NOTES

1. *Understanding the essence of* Booker. The decisions in *Booker* run 118 pages, and the unique "split" majority opinion, which can be separated in a "merits" and a "remedial" majority, defies neat summarization. One group of five Justices — the same five Justices that composed the majority in *Blakely* — declared that the federal sentencing guidelines violate the Sixth Amendment because they rely on judicial factfinding to enhance sentences; another group of five Justices — the *Blakely* dissenters plus Justice Ginsburg — declared the guidelines advisory, and in so doing sought to ensure that the guidelines system would continue to operate in a manner as close to the old system as possible.

The remedy in *Booker* strikes down only two parts of the Sentencing Reform Act — 18 U.S.C. §3553(b)(1), the provision that requires trial courts to impose a sentence within the applicable Guidelines range (in the absence of circumstances that justify a departure), and §3742(e), the provision that sets forth standards of appellate review, including de novo review of departures from the applicable guideline range — and stresses that other parts of the Act are still to play a central role in federal sentencing. The remedial majority requires judges "to take account of the Guidelines together with other sentencing goals." This means that they must consider the sentencing ranges set out in the Guidelines, Sentencing Commission policy statements, and other provisions, such as those governing victim restitution. On the other hand, courts are to consider general sentencing goals, such as proportionality, just punishment, deterrence, protection of the public, respect for the law, and rehabilitation, all of which are set out in §3553(a)(2), in fashioning a sentence.

To ensure that judges follow these requirements, the remedial majority reinforced the availability of appellate review for "unreasonable" sentences in all cases. The standard of review, even though no longer explicitly set out in the statute, could be inferred, according to the remedial majority.

However surprising the remedy in *Booker*, what is the real effect of converting the federal sentencing guidelines from mandatory to advisory sentencing rules for the 1,200 cases sentenced in federal court each week? What is the real meaning and likely impact of Justice Breyer's assertion in *Booker* that "district courts, while not bound to apply the Guidelines, must consult those Guidelines and take them into account when sentencing"?

2. *Defining a remedy.* In their remedial opinion five Justices concluded that the best response to the constitutional problem flowing from *Blakely*'s application to the federal guidelines would be to make the system advisory. Nevertheless, Justice Breyer stressed that the Sentencing Reform Act still "requires judges to consider the Guidelines" and that "district courts, while not bound to apply the Guidelines, must consult those Guidelines and take them into account when sentencing." Moreover, the Court stressed that federal judges imposing sentences after *Booker* remain fully bound by the dictates of 18 U.S.C. §3553(a), which "sets forth numerous factors that guide sentencing," including the need to avoid disparities and traditional purposes of punishment.

3. *Rule by judges?* According to the merits majority opinion by Justice Stevens, the *Booker* decision is designed to "preserve Sixth Amendment substance" so as to guarantee "in a meaningful way . . . that the jury would still stand between the individual and the power of the government under the new sentencing regime." And yet, because of the remedy crafted by the remedial majority opinion of Justice Breyer, judges may still make all sentencing determinations under the federal sentencing system. How are lower courts to decipher and give effect to a seemingly inconsistent ruling concerning the roles of judges and juries in sentencing factfinding?

4. *Section 5K1.1 motions in the wake of* Booker. Before *Booker*, §5K1.1 motions were the primary avenue for defendants to obtain below-guideline sentences. Such a motion is no longer required for a *Booker* variance. Some courts have held that a defendant may receive credit for cooperation where the government does not file a motion for substantial assistance. Such cooperation might shed light on the defendant's "history and circumstances." United States v. Fernandez, 443 F.3d 19 (2d Cir. 2006). Will *Booker* break the influence of §5K1.1 motions? As a criminal defense lawyer, how would you explain the role of cooperation in sentencing to your client post-*Booker*?

5. *Applying* Booker. Immediately after the decision was released, leading sentencing judges attempted to explain the relevance of the guidelines in a post-*Booker* world. Within 24 hours of the *Booker* ruling, U.S. District Judge Paul Cassell—an insightful and articulate conservative, former prosecutor, and law professor—detailed the post-*Booker* relationship between sentencing judges and the guidelines in United States v. Wilson, 350 F. Supp. 2d 910 (D. Utah 2005):

> In light of the Supreme Court's holding [in *Booker*], this court must now consider just how "advisory" the Guidelines are. . . .
>   Having reviewed the applicable congressional mandates in the Sentencing Reform Act, the court concludes that considerable weight should be given to the Guidelines in determining what sentence to impose. The Sentencing

Reform Act requires the court to impose sentences that "reflect the seriousness of the offense, promote respect for the law, provide just punishment, afford adequate deterrence, [and] protect the public." The court must also craft a sentence that affords "adequate deterrence to criminal conduct" and "protect[s] the public from further crimes of the defendant." 18 U.S.C. §3553(a)(2)(B), (C). Finally, the court should "avoid unwarranted sentence disparities among defendants with similar records who have been found guilty of similar conduct." 18 U.S.C. §3553(a)(6).

Over the last 16 years, the Sentencing Commission has promulgated and honed the Guidelines to achieve these congressional purposes. Congress, too, has approved the Guidelines and indicated its view that Guidelines sentences achieve its purposes. Indeed, with respect to the congressionally mandated goal of achieving uniformity, the Guidelines are the only way to create consistent sentencing as they are the only uniform standard available to guide the hundreds of district judges around the country. Therefore, in all future sentencings, the court will give heavy weight to the Guidelines in determining an appropriate sentence. In the exercise of its discretion, the court will only depart from those Guidelines in unusual cases for clearly identified and persuasive reasons. . . .

While *Booker* renders the Guidelines advisory, the court is still obligated to consider the need to avoid unwarranted sentencing disparities among defendants with similar records who have been found guilty of similar conduct. The only way of avoiding gross disparities in sentencing from judge to judge and district to district is for sentencing courts to apply some uniform measure in all cases. The only standard currently available is the Sentencing Guidelines. . . .

Only a few days after *Wilson* was issued, Judge Adelman provided a much different account of federal sentencing after *Booker* in United States v. Ranum, 353 F. Supp. 2d 984 (E.D. Wis. 2005):

The directives of *Booker* and §3553(a) make clear that courts may no longer uncritically apply the guidelines and, as one court suggested, "only depart . . . in unusual cases for clearly identified and persuasive reasons." United States v. Wilson, 2005 WL 78552 (D. Utah Jan. 13, 2005). The approach espoused in *Wilson* is inconsistent with the holdings of the merits majority in *Booker*, rejecting mandatory guideline sentences based on judicial fact-finding, and the remedial majority in *Booker*, directing courts to consider all of the §3353(a) factors, many of which the guidelines either reject or ignore. For example, under §3553(a)(1) a sentencing court must consider the "history and characteristics of the defendant." But under the guidelines, courts are generally forbidden to consider the defendant's age, U.S.S.G. §5H1.1, his education and vocational skills, §5H1.2, his mental and emotional condition, §5H1.3, his physical condition including drug or alcohol dependence, §5H1.4, his employment record, §5H1.5, his family ties and responsibilities, §5H1.6, his socio-economic status, §5H1.10, his civic and military contributions, §5H1.11, and his lack of guidance as a youth, §5H1.12. The guidelines' prohibition of considering these factors cannot be squared with the §3553(a)(1) requirement that the court evaluate the "history and characteristics" of the defendant. The only aspect of a defendant's history that the guidelines permit courts to consider is criminal history. Thus, in cases in which a defendant's history and character are positive, consideration of all of the §3553(a) factors might call for a sentence outside the guideline range.

Further, §3553(a)(2)(D) requires a sentencing court to evaluate the need to provide the defendant with education, training, treatment or medical care in the most effective manner. This directive might conflict with the guidelines, which in most cases offer only prison. *See* U.S.S.G. §5C1.1 (describing limited circumstances in which court can impose sentence other than imprisonment). In some cases, a defendant's educational, treatment or medical needs may be better served by a sentence which permits the offender to remain in the community.

In addition, §3553(a)(7) directs courts to consider "the need to provide restitution to any victims of the offense." In many cases, imposing a sentence of no or only a short period of imprisonment will best accomplish this goal by allowing the defendant to work and pay back the victim. The guidelines do not account for this. In fact, the mandatory guideline regime forbids departures to facilitate restitution. United States v. Seacott, 15 F.3d 1380, 1388-89 (7th Cir. 1994).

Finally, in some cases the guidelines will clash with §3553(a)'s primary directive: to "impose a sentence sufficient, but not greater than necessary to comply with the purposes" of sentencing.

In sum, in every case, courts must now consider all of the §3553(a) factors, not just the guidelines. And where the guidelines conflict with other factors set forth in §3553(a), courts will have to resolve the conflicts.

Is it relevant that Judge Cassell's view of the guidelines as nearly mandatory came in a case that involved a violent crime committed by a person with a long criminal history in which no "*Blakely* facts" were in dispute, whereas *Ranum* involved a first offender who committed a nonviolent crime in which some "*Blakely* facts" were at issue?

6. *The "new" §3553(a) sentencing factors.* Judge Cassell considers the statutory parsimony mandate of §3553(a) and acknowledges that it played virtually no role in federal sentencing before *Booker*. The same point could be made about all of the elements of §3553(a) other than the requirement that judges consider the guideline sentence. Does §3553(a) become the heart of the federal sentencing system after *Booker*? If this provision is so important, why has it not played a major role in federal sentencing cases over the past 15 years? See United States v. Davern, 937 F.2d 1041 (6th Cir. 1991) (holding that §3553(a) justifies approaching the guidelines as "general principles of sentencing" in order to "transform mandatory rules into the more modest name guidelines"), *rev'd*, 970 F.2d 1490 (6th Cir. 1992) (en banc) (rejecting broad reading of the role of §3553(a)).

The disagreement between Judge Cassell and Judge Adelman over the nature of federal sentencing after *Booker* might be viewed as a disagreement concerning the relationship between the guidelines and the goals articulated in the various provisions of §3553(a). Judge Cassell's opinion in *Wilson* suggests that the guidelines themselves reflect the factors articulated in §3553(a), while Judge Adelman suggests in *Ranum* that the guidelines may, as applied in individual cases, actually conflict with other factors set forth in §3553(a).

7. *Do judges monitor the political winds?* Shortly after Judge Cassell issued his decision in *Wilson*, a respected Arkansas trial judge apparently e-mailed the decision to all federal judges, asking them to consider whether Judge Cassell's approach might encourage Congress to leave the federal sentencing system alone. Should protection of the federal judiciary or protection of judicial discretion be a factor in how a judge decides a case? Should systemic concerns trump individual justice? Is there anything objectionable in a judge sharing publicly available judicial decisions with other judges?

8. *Guideline sentences and* Booker *variances.* As the appellate courts began to review lower court decisions, it became clear that sentencing courts had to apply the guidelines and determine applicable guideline ranges before

determining whether a non-guideline sentence would be appropriate. Sentencing courts could impose either a guideline sentence, with or without a departure, or a so-called *Booker* variance.

In the imposition of a post-*Booker* sentence, a sentencing court could commit the following procedural errors:

> First, and most obviously, a sentencing judge would violate the Sixth Amendment by making factual findings and mandatorily enhancing a sentence above the range applicable to facts found by a jury or admitted by a defendant. That is the error that occurred in Booker's case, as the Supreme Court in its Substantive Opinion made clear.
>
> Second, and less obviously, a sentencing judge would commit procedural error by mandatorily applying the applicable Guidelines range that was based solely on facts found by a jury or admitted by a defendant. The Court in its Remedy Opinion made clear that, even though the resulting sentence would not violate the Sixth Amendment, the judge would have erred by mandatorily acting under the now-excised requirement of subsection 3553(b)(1). A sentence explicitly based upon a non-existent statutory provision, even if "reasonable" in length, constitutes error (although possibly "harmless error" or not "plain error"), because of the unlawful method by which it was selected. . . .
>
> Third, a sentencing judge would commit a statutory error in violation of section 3553(a) if the judge failed to "consider" the applicable Guidelines range (or arguably applicable ranges) as well as the other factors listed in section 3553(a), and instead simply selected what the judge deemed an appropriate sentence without such required consideration.
>
> Fourth, a sentencing judge would also violate section 3553(a) by limiting consideration of the applicable Guidelines range to the facts found by the jury or admitted by the defendant, instead of considering the applicable Guidelines range, as required by subsection 3553(a)(4), based on the facts found by the court. . . . All of these potential errors, if available for review on appeal, would render a sentence unreasonable, regardless of length, because of the unlawfulness of the method of selection.

United States v. Crosby, 397 F.3d 103 (2d Cir. 2005).

9. *The meaning of reasonableness review.*   Critical to any assessment of the impact of *Booker* is the meaning of the new appellate review standard. Justice Breyer, in the remedy portion of the decision, says that courts are "familiar" with applying reasonableness (or, rather, "unreasonableness") review. What other kinds of appellate review are most analogous to the review of the exercise of sentencing discretion? How would you compare a reasonableness standard of review to other, more familiar standards, such as de novo review or review for clear error or abuse of discretion? Predict what changes in sentencing patterns, if any, will arise from the requirement that district courts "consult" and "take account" of the guidelines and that circuit courts review for "reasonableness."

10. *Circuit courts and reasonableness.*   After *Booker,* most federal circuit courts began to develop general rules of thumb in asking about the reasonableness of sentences. Many circuits stressed that district courts are required to "consult" and "consider" the guidelines, and have thus indicated directly or indirectly that a district court's sentencing judgment will likely be declared unreasonable if the sentencing judge fails to calculate a defendant's applicable guideline sentencing range, even though these guideline ranges are now only advisory. As judges will necessarily have to find facts, including facts not found by

a jury or admitted by the defendant, in the course of calculating an advisory guideline range, this element of guideline calculation spotlights the tension between the merits and remedy portions of *Booker*. District judges can no longer find facts that raise sentencing ranges within a mandatory guidelines system, as this would violate the Sixth Amendment; but they apparently still must find facts that raise sentencing ranges within an advisory guidelines system, because failing to do so would be unreasonable.

While some circuit courts view reasonableness review as "a concept of flexible meaning," United States v. Crosby, 397 F.3d 103 (2d Cir. 2005), other circuits have intimated that any sentence within the guidelines would likely in nearly every case be deemed reasonable.

‖ *Victor Rita v. United States* ‖
‖ 551 U.S. __ (2007) ‖

BREYER, J.

The federal courts of appeals review federal sentences and set aside those they find "unreasonable." See, e.g., United States v. Booker, 543 U.S. 220 (2005). Several Circuits have held that, when doing so, they will presume that a sentence imposed within a properly calculated United States Sentencing Guidelines range is a reasonable sentence. The most important question before us is whether the law permits the courts of appeals to use this presumption. We hold that it does.

I

The basic crime in this case concerns two false statements which Victor Rita, the petitioner, made under oath to a federal grand jury. The jury was investigating a gun company called InterOrdnance. Prosecutors believed that buyers of an InterOrdnance kit, called a "PPSH 41 machinegun 'parts kit,'" could assemble a machinegun from the kit, that those kits consequently amounted to machineguns, and that InterOrdnance had not secured proper registrations for the importation of the guns.

Rita had bought a PPSH 41 machinegun parts kit. Rita, when contacted by the Bureau of Alcohol, Tobacco, and Firearms and Explosives (ATF), agreed to let a federal agent inspect the kit. But before meeting with the agent, Rita called InterOrdnance and then sent back the kit. He subsequently turned over to ATF a different kit that apparently did not amount to a machinegun.

The investigating prosecutor brought Rita before the grand jury, placed him under oath, and asked him about these matters. Rita denied that the Government agent had asked him for the PPSH kit, and also denied that he had spoken soon thereafter about the PPSH kit to someone at InterOrdnance. The Government claimed these statements were false, charged Rita with perjury, making false statements, and obstructing justice, and, after a jury trial, obtained convictions on all counts.

[The presentence report describes] other "Offender Characteristics." . . .
It states that [Rita] served in the Armed Forces for over 25 years, on active duty and
in the Reserve. During that time he received 35 commendations, awards, or
medals of different kinds. . . .

Ultimately, the report calculates the Guidelines sentencing range. The
Guidelines specify for base level 20, criminal history category I, a sentence of
33-to-41 months' imprisonment. The report adds that there "appears to be no
circumstance or combination of circumstances that warrant a departure from
the prescribed sentencing guidelines."

At the sentencing hearing, both Rita and the Government presented their
sentencing arguments. Each side addressed the report. Rita argued for a
sentence outside (and lower than) the recommended Guidelines 33-to-41
month range.

The judge made clear that Rita's argument for a lower sentence could take
either of two forms. First, Rita might argue within the Guidelines' framework, for
a departure from the applicable Guidelines range on the ground that his circumstances present an "atypical case" that falls outside the "heartland" to
which the United States Sentencing Commission intends each individual Guideline to apply. USSG §5K.0(a)(2). Second, Rita might argue that, independent of
the Guidelines, application of the sentencing factors set forth in 18 U.S.C.
§3553(a) warrants a lower sentence.

[Counsel for Rita] said that he rested his claim for a lower sentence on "just
[those] three" special circumstances, "physical condition, vulnerability in
prison and the military service." . . . The Government [did not ask] for a
sentence higher than the report's recommended Guidelines range. . . .

After hearing the arguments, the judge concluded that he was "unable to
find that the [report's recommended] sentencing guideline range . . . is an
inappropriate guideline range for that, and under 3553 . . . the public needs
to be protected if it is true, and I must accept as true the jury verdict." The court
concluded: "So the Court finds that it is appropriate to enter" a sentence at the
bottom of the Guidelines range, namely a sentence of imprisonment "for a
period of 33 months."

On appeal, Rita argued that his 33-month sentence was "unreasonable"
because (1) it did not adequately take account of "the defendant's history and
characteristics," and (2) it "is greater than necessary to comply with the purposes of sentencing set forth in 18 U.S.C. §3553(a)(2)." The Fourth Circuit . . .
stated that "a sentence imposed within the properly calculated Guidelines
range . . . is presumptively reasonable." It added that "while we believe that the
appropriate circumstances for imposing a sentence outside the guideline range
will depend on the facts of individual cases, we have no reason to doubt that most
sentences will continue to fall within the applicable guideline range." The Fourth
Circuit then rejected Rita's arguments and upheld the sentence.

II

The first question is whether a court of appeals may apply a presumption of
reasonableness to a district court sentence that reflects a proper application of
the Sentencing Guidelines. We conclude that it can.

A

For one thing, the presumption is not binding. It does not, like a trial-related evidentiary presumption, insist that one side, or the other, shoulder a particular burden of persuasion or proof lest they lose their case. Nor does the presumption reflect strong judicial deference of the kind that leads appeals courts to grant greater factfinding leeway to an expert agency than to a district judge. Rather, the presumption reflects the fact that, by the time an appeals court is considering a within-Guidelines sentence on review, both the sentencing judge and the Sentencing Commission will have reached the same conclusion as to the proper sentence in the particular case. That double determination significantly increases the likelihood that the sentence is a reasonable one.

Further, the presumption reflects the nature of the Guidelines-writing task that Congress set for the Commission and the manner in which the Commission carried out that task. In instructing both the sentencing judge and the Commission what to do, Congress referred to the basic sentencing objectives that the statute sets forth in 18 U.S.C. §3553(a). That provision tells the sentencing judge to consider (1) offense and offender characteristics; (2) the need for a sentence to reflect the basic aims of sentencing, namely (a) "just punishment" (retribution), (b) deterrence, (c) incapacitation, (d) rehabilitation; (3) the sentences legally available; (4) the Sentencing Guidelines; (5) Sentencing Commission policy statements; (6) the need to avoid unwarranted disparities; and (7) the need for restitution. The provision also tells the sentencing judge to "impose a sentence sufficient, but not greater than necessary, to comply with" the basic aims of sentencing as set out above.

Congressional statutes then tell the Commission to write Guidelines that will carry out these same §3553(a) objectives. . . . The provision adds that the Commission must seek to "provide certainty and fairness" in sentencing, to "avoid unwarranted sentencing disparities," to "maintain sufficient flexibility to permit individualized sentences when warranted by mitigating or aggravating factors not taken into account in the establishment of general sentencing practices," and to "reflect, to the extent practicable [sentencing-relevant] advancement in [the] knowledge of human behavior." . . .

The upshot is that the sentencing statutes envision both the sentencing judge and the Commission as carrying out the same basic §3553(a) objectives, the one at retail, the other at wholesale.

The Commission has made a serious, sometimes controversial, effort to carry out this mandate. The Commission, in describing its Guidelines-writing efforts, refers to these same statutory provisions. It says that it has tried to embody in the Guidelines the factors and considerations set forth in §3553(a). . . .

The Guidelines as written reflect the fact that the Sentencing Commission examined tens of thousands of sentences and worked with the help of many others in the law enforcement community over a long period of time in an effort to fulfill this statutory mandate. They also reflect the fact that different judges (and others) can differ as to how best to reconcile the disparate ends of punishment.

The Commission's work is ongoing. The statutes and the Guidelines themselves foresee continuous evolution helped by the sentencing courts and courts of appeals in that process. The sentencing courts, applying the Guidelines in individual cases, may depart (either pursuant to the Guidelines or, since *Booker*, by imposing a non-Guidelines sentence). The judges will set forth their reasons. The Courts of Appeals will determine the reasonableness of the resulting sentence. The Commission will collect and examine the results. . . . The result is a set of Guidelines that seek to embody the §3553(a) considerations, both in principle and in practice. Given the difficulties of doing so, the abstract and potentially conflicting nature of §3553(a)'s general sentencing objectives, and the differences of philosophical view among those who work within the criminal justice community as to how best to apply general sentencing objectives, it is fair to assume that the Guidelines, insofar as practicable, reflect a rough approximation of sentences that might achieve §3553(a)'s objectives.

An individual judge who imposes a sentence within the range recommended by the Guidelines thus makes a decision that is fully consistent with the Commission's judgment in general. Despite Justice Souter's fears to the contrary, the courts of appeals' "reasonableness" presumption, rather than having independent legal effect, simply recognizes the real-world circumstance that when the judge's discretionary decision accords with the Commission's view of the appropriate application of §3553(a) in the mine run of cases, it is probable that the sentence is reasonable. . . .

B

Rita and his supporting amici make two further arguments against use of the presumption. First, Rita points out that many individual Guidelines apply higher sentences in the presence of special facts, for example, brandishing a weapon. In many cases, the sentencing judge, not the jury, will determine the existence of those facts. A pro-Guidelines "presumption of reasonableness" will increase the likelihood that courts of appeals will affirm such sentences, thereby increasing the likelihood that sentencing judges will impose such sentences. For that reason, Rita says, the presumption raises Sixth Amendment "concerns."

In our view, however, [a] nonbinding appellate presumption that a Guidelines sentence is reasonable does not require the sentencing judge to impose that sentence. Still less does it forbid the sentencing judge from imposing a sentence higher than the Guidelines provide for the jury-determined facts standing alone. As far as the law is concerned, the judge could disregard the Guidelines and apply the same sentence (higher than the statutory minimum or the bottom of the unenhanced Guidelines range) in the absence of the special facts (say, gun brandishing) which, in the view of the Sentencing Commission, would warrant a higher sentence within the statutorily permissible range. Thus, our Sixth Amendment cases do not forbid appellate court use of the presumption. . . .

Rita may be correct that the presumption will encourage sentencing judges to impose Guidelines sentences. But we do not see how that fact could change the constitutional calculus. Congress sought to diminish unwarranted sentencing disparity. It sought a Guidelines system that would bring about greater fairness in sentencing through increased uniformity. The fact that the presumption might help achieve these congressional goals does not provide cause for holding the presumption unlawful as long as the presumption remains constitutional.

And, given our case law, we cannot conclude that the presumption itself violates the Sixth Amendment.

The fact that we permit courts of appeals to adopt a presumption of reasonableness does not mean that courts may adopt a presumption of unreasonableness. Even the Government concedes that appellate courts may not presume that every variance from the advisory Guidelines is unreasonable.

Second, Rita and his amici claim that use of a pro-Guidelines presumption on appeal conflicts with Congress' insistence that sentencing judges apply the factors set forth in 18 U.S.C. §3553(a) (and that the resulting sentence be "sufficient, but not greater than necessary, to comply with the purposes" of sentencing set forth in that statute). We have explained above, however, why we believe that, where judge and Commission both determine that the Guidelines sentences is an appropriate sentence for the case at hand, that sentence likely reflects the §3553(a) factors (including its "not greater than necessary" requirement). This circumstance alleviates any serious general conflict between §3553(a) and the Guidelines, for the purposes of appellate review. And, for that reason, we find that nothing in §3553(a) renders use of the presumption unlawful.

III

We next turn to the question whether the District Court properly analyzed the relevant sentencing factors. In particular, Rita argues that the court took inadequate account of §3553(c), a provision that requires a sentencing judge, "at the time of sentencing," to "state in open court the reasons for its imposition of the particular sentence." In our view, given the straightforward, conceptually simple arguments before the judge, the judge's statement of reasons here, though brief, was legally sufficient.

The statute does call for the judge to "state" his "reasons." And that requirement reflects sound judicial practice. Judicial decisions are reasoned decisions. Confidence in a judge's use of reason underlies the public's trust in the judicial institution. A public statement of those reasons helps provide the public with the assurance that creates that trust.

That said, we cannot read the statute (or our precedent) as insisting upon a full opinion in every case. The appropriateness of brevity or length, conciseness or detail, when to write, what to say, depends upon circumstances. Sometimes a judicial opinion responds to every argument; sometimes it does not; sometimes a judge simply writes the word "granted" or "denied" on the face of a motion while relying upon context and the parties' prior arguments to make the reasons clear. The law leaves much, in this respect, to the judge's own professional judgment.

In the present context, a statement of reasons is important. The sentencing judge should set forth enough to satisfy the appellate court that he has considered the parties' arguments and has a reasoned basis for exercising his own legal decisionmaking authority. Nonetheless, when a judge decides simply to apply the Guidelines to a particular case, doing so will not necessarily require lengthy explanation. . . .

Where the defendant or prosecutor presents nonfrivolous reasons for imposing a different sentence, however, the judge will normally go further and explain why he has rejected those arguments. Sometimes the circumstances will call for a brief explanation; sometimes they will call for a lengthier explanation. Where the judge imposes a sentence outside the Guidelines, the judge will explain why he has done so. To our knowledge, an ordinary explanation of judicial reasons as to why the judge has, or has not, applied the Guidelines triggers no Sixth Amendment "jury trial" requirement. . . .

In the present case the sentencing judge's statement of reasons was brief but legally sufficient. Rita argued for a downward departure from the 33-to-41 month Guidelines sentence on the basis of three sets of special circumstances. [The judge] simply found these circumstances insufficient to warrant a sentence lower than the Guidelines range of 33 to 45 months. . . .

We acknowledge that the judge might have said more. He might have added explicitly that he had heard and considered the evidence and argument; that (as no one before him denied) he thought the Commission in the Guidelines had determined a sentence that was proper in the mine run of roughly similar perjury cases; and that he found that Rita's personal circumstances here were simply not different enough to warrant a different sentence. But context and the record make clear that this, or similar, reasoning underlies the judge's conclusion. Where a matter is as conceptually simple as in the case at hand and the record makes clear that the sentencing judge considered the evidence and arguments, we do not believe the law requires the judge to write more extensively. . . .

Like the District Court and the Court of Appeals, we simply cannot say that Rita's special circumstances are special enough that, in light of §3553(a), they require a sentence lower than the sentence the Guidelines provide. . . .

STEVENS, J., concurring.

. . . Simply stated, *Booker* replaced the de novo standard of review required by 18 U.S.C. §3742(e) with an abuse-of-discretion standard that we called " 'reasonableness' " review. . . . Critically, we did not touch the portions of §3742(e) requiring appellate courts to "give due regard to the opportunity of the district court to judge the credibility of the witnesses," to "accept the findings of fact of the district court unless they are clearly erroneous," and to "give due deference to the district court's application of the guidelines to the facts." By leaving those portions of the statute intact while severing the portion mandating a de novo standard of review, *Booker* restored the abuse-of-discretion standard [adopted in Koon v. United States, 518 U.S. 81 (1996)].

[In *Koon* we held] unanimously that a district court's decision to depart from the Guidelines "will in most cases be due substantial deference, for it embodies the traditional exercise of discretion by a sentencing court." [We] added that "district courts have an institutional advantage over appellate courts" because they "must make a refined assessment of the many facts bearing on the outcome, informed by its vantage point and day-to-day experience in criminal sentencing." . . . After *Booker*, appellate courts are now to assess a district court's exercise of discretion "with regard to §3553(a)." . . .

Guided by these §3553(a) factors, *Booker*'s abuse-of-discretion standard directs appellate courts to evaluate what motivated the District Judge's individualized sentencing decision. While reviewing courts may presume that a sentence within the advisory Guidelines is reasonable, appellate judges must still always defer to the sentencing judge's individualized sentencing determination. As we stated in *Koon*, "it has been uniform and constant in the federal judicial tradition for the sentencing judge to consider every convicted person as an individual and every case as a unique study in the human failings that sometimes mitigate, sometimes magnify, the crime and the punishment to ensue." The Commission has not developed any standards or recommendations that affect sentencing ranges for many individual characteristics. Matters such as age, education, mental or emotional condition, medical condition (including drug or alcohol addiction), employment history, lack of guidance as a youth, family ties, or military, civic, charitable, or public service are not ordinarily considered under the Guidelines. These are, however, matters that §3553(a) authorizes the sentencing judge to consider. As such, they are factors that an appellate court must consider under *Booker*'s abuse-of-discretion standard.

My disagreement with Justice Scalia and Justice Souter rests on the above understanding of *Booker*'s standard of appellate review. I do not join Justice Scalia's opinion because I believe that the purely procedural review he advocates is inconsistent with our remedial opinion in *Booker*, which plainly contemplated that reasonableness review would contain a substantive component. . . .

As to Justice Souter's opinion, I think he overestimates the "gravitational pull" towards the advisory Guidelines that will result from a presumption of reasonableness. *Booker*'s standard of review allows — indeed, requires — district judges to consider all of the factors listed in §3553(a) and to apply them to the individual defendants before them. Appellate courts must then give deference to the sentencing decisions made by those judges, whether the resulting sentence is inside or outside the advisory Guidelines range, under traditional abuse-of-discretion principles. As the Court acknowledges, moreover, presumptively reasonable does not mean always reasonable; the presumption, of course, must be genuinely rebuttable. . . . Our decision today makes clear . . . that the rebuttability of the presumption is real. It should also be clear that appellate courts must review sentences individually and deferentially whether they are inside the Guidelines range (and thus potentially subject to a formal "presumption" of reasonableness) or outside that range. Given the clarity of our holding, I trust that those judges who had treated the Guidelines as virtually mandatory during the post-*Booker* interregnum will now recognize that the Guidelines are truly advisory.

. Applying this standard, I would affirm the sentence imposed by the District Court. . . . I agree that he did not abuse his discretion in making the particular decision that he did. I also agree with the Court that his decision is entitled to added respect because it was consistent with the advice in the Guidelines. . . .

SCALIA, J., concurring in part and concurring in the judgment.
. . . As a matter of statutory stare decisis, I accept *Booker*'s remedial holding that district courts are no longer bound by the Guidelines and that appellate courts should review the sentences imposed for reasonableness. As should be clear from our need to decide the case today, however, precisely what "reasonableness" review entails is not dictated by *Booker*. . . .

No explanation is given because no explanation is possible. The Court has reintroduced the constitutional defect that *Booker* purported to eliminate. I cannot acquiesce in this course. If a sentencing system is permissible in which some sentences cannot lawfully be imposed by a judge unless the judge finds certain facts by a preponderance of the evidence, then we should have left in place the compulsory Guidelines that Congress enacted, instead of imposing this jerry-rigged scheme of our own. In order to avoid the possibility of a Sixth Amendment violation, which was the object of the *Booker* remedy, district courts must be able, without finding any facts not embraced in the jury verdict or guilty plea, to sentence to the maximum of the statutory range. Because, therefore, appellate courts cannot reverse within-range sentences for being too high; and because no one would contend that Congress intended that sentences be reviewed only for being too low; I would hold that reasonableness review cannot contain a substantive component at all. I believe, however, that appellate courts can nevertheless secure some amount of sentencing uniformity through the procedural reasonableness review made possible by the *Booker* remedial opinion.

I

... Two hypotheticals will suffice to reveal why the notion of excessive sentences within the statutory range, and the ability of appellate courts to reverse such sentences, inexorably produces, in violation of the Sixth Amendment, sentences whose legality is premised on a judge's finding some fact (or combination of facts) by a preponderance of the evidence.

First, consider two brothers with similar backgrounds and criminal histories who are convicted by a jury of respectively robbing two banks of an equal amount of money. Next assume that the district judge finds that one brother, fueled by racial animus, had targeted the first bank because it was owned and operated by minorities, whereas the other brother had selected the second bank simply because its location enabled a quick getaway. Further assume that the district judge imposes the statutory maximum upon both brothers, basing those sentences primarily upon his perception that bank robbery should be punished much more severely than the Guidelines base level advises, but explicitly noting that the racially biased decisionmaking of the first brother further justified his sentence. Now imagine that the appellate court reverses as excessive only the sentence of the nonracist brother. Given the dual holdings of the appellate court, the racist has a valid Sixth Amendment claim that his sentence was reasonable (and hence lawful) only because of the judicial finding of his motive in selecting his victim.

Second, consider the common case in which the district court imposes a sentence within an advisory Guidelines range that has been substantially enhanced by certain judge-found facts. For example, the base offense level for robbery under the Guidelines is 20, which, if the defendant has a criminal history of I, corresponds to an advisory range of 33-41 months. If, however, a judge finds that a firearm was discharged, that a victim incurred serious bodily injury, and that more than $5 million was stolen, then the base level jumps by 18, producing an advisory range of 235-293 months. When a judge finds all of those facts to be true and then imposes a within-Guidelines sentence of 293 months, those judge-found facts, or some combination of them, are not merely facts that the judge finds relevant in exercising his discretion; they are the legally essential predicate for his imposition of the 293-month sentence. His failure to find them would render the 293-month sentence unlawful. That is evident because, were the district judge explicitly to find none of those facts true and nevertheless to impose a 293-month sentence (simply because he thinks robbery merits seven times the sentence that the Guidelines provide) the sentence would surely be reversed as unreasonably excessive.

These hypotheticals are stylized ways of illustrating the basic problem with a system in which district courts lack full discretion to sentence within the statutory range. Under such a system, for every given crime there is some maximum sentence that will be upheld as reasonable based only on the facts found by the jury or admitted by the defendant. Every sentence higher than that is legally authorized only by some judge-found fact, in violation of the Sixth Amendment. Appellate courts' excessiveness review will explicitly or implicitly accept those judge-found facts as justifying sentences that would otherwise be unlawful. The only difference between this system and the pre-*Booker* mandatory Guidelines is that the maximum sentence based on the jury verdict or guilty plea was specified under the latter but must be established by appellate courts, in case-by-case fashion, under the former. This is, if anything, an additional constitutional disease, not a constitutional cure.

To be clear, I am not suggesting that the Sixth Amendment prohibits judges from ever finding any facts. We have repeatedly affirmed the proposition that judges can find facts that help guide their discretion within the sentencing range that is authorized by the facts found by the jury or admitted by the defendant. But there is a fundamental difference . . . between facts that must be found in order for a sentence to be lawful, and facts that individual judges choose to make relevant to the exercise of their discretion. The former, but not the latter, must be found by the jury beyond a reasonable doubt in order "to give intelligible content to the right of jury trial." *Blakely*, 542 U.S. at 305.

I am also not contending that there is a Sixth Amendment problem with the Court's affirmation of a presumption of reasonableness for within-Guidelines sentences. I agree with the Court that such a presumption never itself makes judge-found facts legally essential to the sentence imposed, since it has no direct relevance to whether the sentence would have been unreasonable in the absence of any judge-found facts.[3] Nor is my claim that the Sixth Amendment was violated in this case, for petitioner cannot demonstrate that his relatively low sentence would have been unreasonable if the District Court had relied on nothing but jury-found or admitted facts.

Rather, my position is that there will inevitably be some constitutional violations under a system of substantive reasonableness review, because there

---

3. For this reason, I do not join Justice Souter's dissent. He wishes to give "district courts [assurance] that the entire sentencing range set by statute is available to them." That is a proper goal — indeed, an essential one to prevent the *Booker* remedy from effectively overturning . . . *Blakely*. But eliminating the presumption of reasonableness will not achieve it. In those Circuits that already decline to employ the presumption, a within-Guidelines sentence has never been reversed as substantively excessive, Brief for New York Council of Defense Lawyers as Amicus Curiae 5, refuting the belief that mere elimination of the presumption will destroy the "gravitational pull" (Souter, J., dissenting) to stay safely within the Guidelines. The only way to assure district courts that they can deviate from the advisory Guidelines, and to ensure that judge-found facts are never legally essential to the sentence, is to prohibit appellate courts from reviewing the substantive sentencing choices made by district courts.

will be some sentences that will be upheld as reasonable only because of the existence of judge-found facts. [If] the contours of reasonableness review must be narrowed in some cases because of constitutional concerns, then they must be narrowed in all cases in light of Congress's desire for a uniform standard of review. . . .

II

Abandoning substantive reasonableness review does not require a return to the pre-SRA regime that the *Booker* remedial opinion sought to avoid. As I said at the outset, I believe it is possible to give some effect to the *Booker* remedial opinion and the purposes that it sought to serve while still avoiding the constitutional defect identified in the *Booker* merits opinion. Specifically, I would limit reasonableness review to the sentencing procedures mandated by statute.

A central feature of the *Booker* remedial opinion was its conclusion that the SRA was not completely inseverable. As a result, the Sentencing Commission "remains in place, writing Guidelines, collecting information about actual district court sentencing decisions, undertaking research, and revising the Guidelines accordingly." Likewise, sentencing courts remain obligated to consider the various factors delineated in 18 U.S.C. §3553(a), including the now-advisory Guidelines range. And they are still instructed by that subsection to "impose a sentence sufficient, but not greater than necessary, to comply with the purposes set forth in paragraph (2) of [that] subsection." Significantly, §3553(c) continues to require that district courts give reasons for their sentencing decisions, a requirement the requisite detail of which depends on whether the sentence is: (1) within the advisory Guidelines range; (2) within an advisory Guidelines range that spans more than 24 months; or (3) outside the advisory Guidelines range. These explanations, in turn, help the Commission revise the advisory Guidelines to reflect actual sentencing practices consistent with the statutory goals.

Booker's retention of these statutory procedural provisions furthered the congressional purpose of "ironing out sentencing differences," and "avoiding excessive sentencing disparities." It is important that appellate courts police their observance. *Booker* excised the provision of the SRA containing the standards for appellate review, but the remedial majority's creation of reasonableness review gave appellate courts the necessary means to reverse a district court that: appears not to have considered §3553(a); considers impermissible factors; selects a sentence based on clearly erroneous facts; or does not comply with §3553's requirement for a statement of reasons.[6] In addition to its direct effect on sentencing uniformity, this procedural review will indirectly produce, over time, reduction of sentencing disparities. By ensuring that district courts give reasons for their sentences, and more specific reasons when they decline to

---

6. "Substance" and "procedure" are admittedly chameleon-like terms. As the text indicates, my use of the term "procedure" here includes the limiting of sentencing factors to permissible ones — as opposed to using permissible factors but reaching a result that is "substantively" wrong. . . .

follow the advisory Guidelines range, appellate courts will enable the Sentencing Commission to perform its function of revising the Guidelines to reflect the desirable sentencing practices of the district courts. And as that occurs, district courts will have less reason to depart from the Commission's recommendations, leading to more sentencing uniformity.

One possible objection to procedural review that the *Booker* remedial opinion appears not to have considered is 18 U.S.C. §3742(f), which limits appellate courts to reversing sentences that are imposed "in violation of law" or "as a result of an incorrect application of the sentencing guidelines," or that fall in certain categories and are either "too high" or "too low." But, as I noted in *Booker*, §3742(e) and §3742(f) are inextricably intertwined: Having excised §3742(e)'s provisions setting forth the standards for appellate review, it is nonsensical to continue to apply §3742(f)'s provisions governing the "Decision and Disposition" of appeals, which clearly track those now-excised standards. I would hold that §3742(f) is "incapable of functioning independently" of the provisions excised in *Booker*, and is thus inseverable from them. . . .

The Court's decision today leaves unexplained why the mandatory Guidelines were unconstitutional, but the Court-created substantive-review system that contains the same potential for Sixth Amendment violation is not. It is irresponsible to leave this patent inconsistency hanging in the air, threatening in the future yet another major revision of Guidelines practices to which the district courts and courts of appeals will have to adjust. Procedural review would lay the matter to rest, comporting with both parts of the *Booker* opinion and achieving the maximum degree of sentencing uniformity on the basis of judge-found facts that the Constitution permits.

SOUTER, J., dissenting.

Applying the Sixth Amendment to current sentencing law has gotten complicated, and someone coming cold to this case might wonder how we reached this point. . . .

In United States v. Booker, 543 U.S. 220 (2005), a majority of the Court . . . held that the Federal Guidelines [] subjected defendants to unconstitutional sentences in upper subranges, absent a jury finding or waiver. So far, so good for the Sixth Amendment, but there was the further issue of remedy, and at that step consistency began to falter. If statutory Guidelines were to survive, there were two serious alternatives. One was already in place in courts with the foresight to apply *Apprendi* to the Guidelines: require any additional facts necessary for a possible high subrange sentence to be charged and submitted to the jury. [The] mandatory character of the Guidelines would be preserved, the goal of consistency would continue to be served, and the practical value of the jury right would not face erosion.

The second remedial alternative was a declaration by the Court that the Guidelines were not mandatory but discretionary, so that finding extraverdict facts was not strictly necessary for sentencing in a high subrange under the Guidelines. . . .

But that second alternative could not be so simple: . . . If district judges treated the now-discretionary Guidelines simply as worthy of consideration but open to rejection in any given case, the *Booker* remedy would threaten a return to the old sentencing regime and would presumably produce the apparent disuniformity that convinced Congress to adopt Guidelines sentencing in the first place. But if sentencing judges attributed substantial gravitational pull to the now-discretionary Guidelines, if they treated the Guidelines result as persuasive or presumptively appropriate, the *Booker* remedy would in practical terms preserve the very feature of the Guidelines that threatened to trivialize the jury right. For a presumption of Guidelines reasonableness would tend to produce Guidelines sentences almost as regularly as mandatory Guidelines had done, with judges finding the facts needed for a sentence in an upper subrange. This would open the door to undermining *Apprendi* itself, and this is what has happened today.

Without a powerful reason to risk reversal on the sentence, a district judge faced with evidence supporting a high subrange Guidelines sentence will do the appropriate factfinding in disparagement of the jury right and will sentence within the high subrange. This prediction is weakened not a whit by the Court's description of within-Guidelines reasonableness as an "appellate" presumption. What works on appeal determines what works at trial, and if the Sentencing Commission's views are as weighty as the Court says they are, a trial judge will find it far easier to make the appropriate findings and sentence within the appropriate Guideline, than to go through the unorthodox factfinding necessary to justify a sentence outside the Guidelines range. The upshot is that today's decision moves the threat to the practical value of the Sixth Amendment jury right closer to what it was . . . , and it seems fair to ask just what has been accomplished in real terms by all the judicial labor imposed by *Apprendi* and its associated cases.

Taking the *Booker* remedy (of discretionary Guidelines) as a given, however, the way to avoid further risk to *Apprendi* and the jury right is to hold that a discretionary within-Guidelines sentence carries no presumption of reasonableness. Only if sentencing decisions are reviewed according to the same standard of reasonableness whether or not they fall within the Guidelines range will district courts be assured that the entire sentencing range set by statute is available to them. And only then will they stop replicating the unconstitutional system by imposing appeal-proof sentences within the Guidelines ranges determined by facts found by them alone.

I would therefore reject the presumption of reasonableness adopted in this case, not because it is pernicious in and of itself, but because I do not think we can recognize such a presumption and still retain the full effect of *Apprendi* in aid of the Sixth Amendment guarantee. . . . Neither my preferred course nor the choice of today's majority can avoid being at odds to some degree with the intent of Congress; there is no question that Congress meant to impose mandatory Guidelines as the means of bringing greater uniformity to sentencing. So I point out that the congressional objective can still be attained, but that *Booker*'s remedial holding means that only Congress can restore the scheme to what it had in mind, and in a way that gives full measure to the right to a jury trial. If Congress has not had a change of heart about the value of a Guidelines system, it can reenact the Guidelines law to give it the same binding force it originally had, but with provision for jury, not judicial, determination of any fact necessary for a sentence within an upper Guidelines subrange. At this point, only Congress can make good on both its enacted policy of mandatory Guidelines sentencing and the guarantee of a robust right of jury trial. I respectfully dissent.

NOTES

1. *Presumption of reasonableness.* Does *Rita* require all appellate courts to presume that within-guidelines sentences are reasonable, or does the Court rather declare such review permissible, without ruling on the reverse? The *Rita* decision does not resolve the circuit split as to whether a within-guidelines sentence must be presumed reasonable, but rather merely permits such a presumption. The courts of appeals had been almost evenly split on the question of whether to afford such a presumption. The Supreme Court sided with the circuits which had held that any properly calculated guideline sentence is entitled to a rebuttable presumption of reasonableness.

What does the Court mean when it says the presumption is nonbinding? Does it imply that the presumption is rebuttable, or does it rather assume that the appellate court may, or may not, apply it in the appropriate case?

The Court based much of its decision on the interplay between the commission and the district courts. Since the commission implements the guidelines based on the SRA and district courts apply it to individual situations, courts of appeals are justified in assuming that these decisions are presumptively correct. Why does a general application make a specific one more reasonable?

What are the pros and cons of adopting firm rules concerning reasonableness and sentencing within the guidelines? Might the debate about presumptions of reasonableness be merely academic in an appellate court system in which only a precious few within-guidelines sentences have been declared "unreasonable" on appeal? Keep in mind that the first declaration to that effect came from a circuit that had adopted the presumption of reasonableness. See United States v. Lazenby, 439 F.3d 928 (8th Cir. 2006). In light of this reality, is it really possible that appellate courts adhere yet more closely to the guidelines, and continue as the primary protectors of the guidelines? Would a different decision have made a difference? What signal, if any, would it have sent to the appellate courts? Were appellate courts in presumption circuits more likely to uphold guideline sentences, would the decision in *Rita* not substantially undermine the Sentencing Reform Act's goal of national uniformity?

The Court left unresolved the question of whether outside-guidelines sentences are presumptively unreasonable. At the time the Court granted the petition for certiorari in the *Rita* case, it had also granted certiorari in United States v. Claiborne, which squarely raised the question of whether a sentence outside the otherwise applicable guideline range would be presumptively unreasonable. Since Claiborne was killed in a robbery-murder before the decision was rendered, the Court dismissed certiorari. Subsequently, it granted certiorari in Gall v. United States, which presents the same issue.

2. *Reasonableness review in light of* Booker. Justice Scalia challenges the majority as unfaithful to the entire line of Sixth Amendment cases beginning with *Apprendi.* He advocates a solely procedural, rather than a substantive, reasonableness review. Do you find his argument that substantive reasonableness review constitutes a violation of the Sixth Amendment tenable? Does procedural review solve this problem?

3. *The intersection of §3553(a) and reasonableness review.* Presumably, since all of the elements of §3553(a) now govern sentencing decisions in federal courts,

these same elements ought to play a central role in appellate determinations of reasonableness. Justice Breyer painstakingly goes through all the factors the presentence report detailed and the sentencing court presumably considered.

The trial court's decision, however, appears to be relatively devoid of argument. Justice Breyer notes that it was not necessary to address every argument in such a straightforward case. Nevertheless, *Rita* seems to provide sentencing courts with relatively limited requirements with respect to the justification and explanation they owe to the defendant, the appellate court, and the Sentencing Commission.

This is yet more curious as the Supreme Court in *Rita* appears to have clarified some of the discretion sentencing courts gained after *Booker*. It confirms that sentencing courts may sentence outside the guidelines in atypical cases and appears to indicate that policy disagreements with the commission are sufficient grounds for a *Booker* variance. Nevertheless, the Court seems to impose only limited obligations on district courts to explain their sentencing decisions.

Is there reason to fear that *Booker* will fail to facilitate a renaissance for all the elements of §3553(a), and that the guidelines will still serve as the central and dominant consideration in most if not all federal sentencing cases? Will limited requirements for explanations for within-guidelines sentences guarantee the perpetuation of the existing system, as a result of the inability to develop a common law of sentencing as well as the commission's inability to take action based on sufficient information from sentencing judges?

Final Quarterly Data Report, Fiscal Year 2006 U.S. Sentencing Commission

National Comparison of Sentences Imposed and Position Relative to the Guideline Range[1]

	N	%
Total cases	70,187	100.0
Within guideline range	43,307	61.7
Above guideline range	1,129	1.6
Departure above guideline range	589	0.9
Upward departure from guideline range	412	0.6
Upward departure with *Booker*/18 USC §3553	177	0.3
Otherwise above the guideline range	540	0.7
Above guideline range with *Booker*/18 USC §3553	455	0.6
All remaining cases above guideline range	85	0.1
Government sponsored below range[6]	17,244	24.6
§5K1.1 Substantial assistance departure	10,139	14.4
§5K3.1 Early disposition program departure	5,166	7.4
Other gov't sponsored below range departure	1,939	2.8

National Comparison of Sentences Imposed and Position Relative to the Guideline Range[1] (Cont'd)

	N	%
Non-government sponsored below range	8,507	12.0
Departure below guideline range	3,335	4.7
Downward departure from the guideline range	1,903	2.7
Downward Departure with *Booker*/18 USC §3553	1,432	2.0
Otherwise below the guideline range	5,172	7.3
Below guideline range with *Booker*/18 USC §3553	4,243	6.0
All remaining cases below guideline range	929	1.3

1. This table reflects the 72,585 cases sentenced in Fiscal Year 2006. Of these, 2,389 cases were excluded for one of two general reasons. Some involved certain Class A misdemeanors or other offenses which do not reference a sentencing guideline. In others, information was missing from the submitted documents that prevented the comparison of the sentence and the guideline range. . . .

6. Cases in which a reason for the sentence indicated that the prosecution initiated, proposed, or stipulated to a sentence outside of the guideline range, either pursuant to a plea agreement or as part of a non-plea negotiation with the defendant.

U.S. Sentencing Commission, Special Post-*Booker* Coding Project: Cases Sentenced Subsequent to United States v. Booker (July 6, 2006)

National Guideline Application Trends

Position of Sentence Relative to Guideline Range	FY2001	FY2002	FY2003	FY2004 (Pre-Blakely)	FY 2005 (Post-Booker)	FY 2006
Within range	64.0%	65.0%	69.4%	72.2%	61.6%	61.9%
Upward departures	0.6%	0.8%	0.8%	0.8%	0.3%	0.9%
Otherwise above range	—	—	—	—	1.4%	0.8%
Substantial assistance departures	17.1%	17.4%	15.9%	15.5%	14.7%	14.3%
Other gov't sponsored departures	—	—	6.3%	6.4%	9.1%	9.9%
Other departures downward	18.3%	16.8%	7.5%	5.2%	3.2%	5.2%
Departures otherwise below range	—	—	—	—	9.7%	7.2%

NOTES

1. *Sentences within the guidelines.*   The yearly comparison data reveals a downturn in the number of within-guidelines sentences after *Booker*, which follows a notable increase in the number of within-guidelines sentences before *Blakely* and *Booker*. Even after *Booker*, more than 60% of all sentences are within the guidelines, and nearly two-thirds of all sentences outside the guidelines are the result of a motion by the prosecution. How should policymakers in Congress, in the Sentencing Commission, and in the Department of Justice respond to this information? Are the guidelines still "working well" after *Booker*? Given the long-standing criticism of the guidelines before *Booker* and the constitutional issues raised in *Booker*, are the guidelines perhaps working surprisingly well after *Booker*? What factors may account for the continuing judicial faithfulness to the guideline system?

2. *Sentences outside the guidelines.*   As the data indicate, even after *Booker*, nearly two-thirds of all sentences outside the guidelines are the result of a motion by the prosecution. Does this suggest that the entire guidelines movement is too focused on the regulation of judicial discretion and not sufficiently concerned with the exercise of prosecutorial discretion? One issue that has been robustly debated in the wake of *Booker* is whether judges ought to sentence outside the guideline range on grounds such as the defendant's cooperation with authorities or agreement to a rapid guilty plea disposition when the prosecutor does not recommend a sentence below the guidelines on these grounds. See Testimony of James E. Felman, Esq., before the Subcommittee on Crime, Terrorism, and Homeland Security of the Judiciary Committee of the United States House of Representatives, March 16, 2006, Oversight Hearing, United States v. Booker: One Year Later — Chaos or Status Quo?, 19-21 (available at sentencing.typepad.com/sentencing_law_and_policy/files/felman_testimony.pdf).

Replicating patterns that have developed since the origins of the federal sentencing guidelines, judges, even after *Booker*, are nearly ten times more likely to exercise their discretion to sentence outside the applicable guideline range in order to impose a below-guideline sentence rather than to go above the applicable guideline range. What do these numbers suggest about the overall severity of the sentences set forth in the guidelines? Should the U.S. Sentencing Commission consider lowering guideline sentencing ranges in an effort to achieve greater parity between above- and below-guideline sentences? Should it matter in what types of cases the courts sentence below the guidelines? Whose decision is more democratic, that of the judiciary or that of the commission? Whose is fairer?

3. *Sentence length.*   Even though post-*Booker* data reveals a downturn in the number of sentences within the guideline range, other data released by the Sentencing Commission indicates that average and median sentence lengths appear to be stable (or even rising a bit) post-*Booker*. Thus, even if we may be seeing a (slight) drift away from the guidelines, the data does not (yet?) reveal a dramatic shift toward more lenient sentences overall. How do you account for the fact that there are now more below-guidelines sentences than before *Booker*

while the sentence lengths are holding steady? Is it likely that the mix of the types of cases coming up for sentencing has changed?

4. *Increased disparity?*   The circuit-by-circuit data indicates that the rates of judicial variation from the guidelines are distinctly different in different circuits. In the Second Circuit, for example, judges are initiating departures or *Booker* variances in almost one of every four cases, while in the Fifth Circuit, judges are doing so in less than one-tenth of cases. The rates of prosecutorial variation from the guidelines also differ distinctly among the different circuits. In the Ninth Circuit, prosecutors initiate departures in almost half of all cases, while in the First Circuit prosecutors do so in roughly one of every eight cases. See U.S. Sentencing Commission, 2006 Sourcebook of Federal Sentencing Statistics. (Of course, significant circuit-by-circuit variations were also common in the pre-*Booker* era.)

5. *How to assess a new sentencing system.*   Should the distribution of sentences reflected in the data be a central concern in assessing the changes *Booker* has made to the federal sentencing system? More generally, can data patterns ever serve as a measure of the justice of any individual sentence, or of any sentencing system?

PROBLEM 3-2. ASYMMETRICAL GUIDELINES

In the aftermath of the *Blakely* decision, staff working for the Sentencing Commission and for various members of Congress began exploring options for a revised federal sentencing system that could overcome those Sixth Amendment violations described in *Blakely*.

One leading option, first conceived by Professor Frank Bowman, a former prosecutor, defense attorney, and staff attorney for the Sentencing Commission, called for asymmetrical guidelines. The proposal asked Congress to pass a statute redefining the "guideline maximum" to be the current statutory maximum for the crime of conviction. However, the existing sentencing guidelines would remain in place for the bottom of the range. Any guideline adjustments that raise the bottom of the guideline range would continue to bind the sentencing judge. Bowman described the justification for and likely effect of this revision as follows:

> The practical effect of such an amendment would be to preserve current federal practice almost unchanged. Guidelines factors would not be elements. They could still constitutionally be determined by post-conviction judicial findings of fact. No modifications of pleading or trial practice would be required. The only theoretical difference would be that judges could sentence defendants above the top of the current guideline ranges without the formality of an upward departure. However, given that the current rate of upward departures is 0.6%, and that judges sentence the majority of all offenders at or below the midpoint of existing sentencing ranges, the likelihood that judges would use their newly granted discretion to increase the sentences of very many defendants above now-prevailing levels seems, at best, remote.
>
> This proposal could not be effected without an amendment of the SRA because it would fall afoul of the so-called "25% rule," 28 U.S.C. §994(b)(2),

which mandates that the top of any guideline range be no more than six months or 25% greater than its bottom. The ranges produced by this proposal would ordinarily violate that provision. . . .

In addition, if such a statute were passed, the Commission might think it proper to enact a policy statement recommending that courts not impose sentences more than 25% higher than the guideline minimum in the absence of one or more of the factors now specified in the Guidelines as potential grounds for upward departure. Failure to adhere to this recommendation would not be appealable, and thus such a provision would not fall foul of *Blakely*. A few modifications to the Guidelines themselves would also be required to bring them into conformity with *Blakely* and the new statute. . . . But otherwise, very little would have to change. . . .

Frank Bowman, Memorandum Presenting a Proposal for Bringing the Federal Sentencing Guidelines into Conformity with Blakely v. Washington, 16 Fed. Sent'g Rep. 364 (2004).

You serve on the staff of a member of Congress, and you specialize in criminal justice issues. Your boss wants to know how various groups are likely to respond to the "asymmetrical guidelines" proposal, both as a response to *Booker* and as a longer-term restructuring of the system. What is the likely reaction from the leadership of the Department of Justice? See Federal Sentencing Guidelines Speech by Attorney General Alberto Gonzalez, 17 Fed. Sent'g Rep. 324 (2005). What about the National Association of Federal Defenders, and the federal judges as represented by the Judicial Conference of the United States?

What suggestions do you have for any longer-term solutions for the federal sentencing system? Here are several options:

- Congress picks some high-priority crimes and designates mandatory minimum sentences for those crimes.
- Congress leaves judges the discretion to impose a sentence anywhere between the statutory minimum and maximum, perhaps relying on guidelines for voluntary guidance (and eliminating any appellate review of sentences based on application of the guidelines).
- Congress creates "inverted guidelines" that designate the presumptive sentence as the statutory maximum and use guideline factors (and judicial factfinding) to justify any downward movement from that statutory maximum.
- Congress designates a few critical "enhancement factors," such as use of a weapon, and authorizes prosecutors to allege such factors in the indictment and prove them to a jury, either during the trial or in a bifurcated sentencing proceeding.

For details on legislative proposals issued in response to *Blakely* and *Booker*, see Defending America's Most Vulnerable: Safe Access to Drug Treatment and Child Protection Act of 2005, H.R 1528, 109th Cong. 12 (2005); Albert W. Alschuler, To Sever or Not to Sever? Why *Blakely* Requires Action by Congress, 17 Fed. Sent'g Rep. 11 (2004); Rachel E. Barkow, The Devil You Know: Federal Sentencing After *Blakely*, 17 Fed. Sent'g Rep. 312 (2004);

Stephanos Bibas, *Blakely*'s Federal Aftermath, 16 Fed. Sent'g Rep. 333 (2004); James Felman, How Should the Congress Respond If the Supreme Court Strikes Down the Federal Sentencing Guidelines? 17 Fed. Sent'g Rep. 97 (2004); Nancy J. King & Susan R. Klein, Beyond *Blakely*, 16 Fed. Sent'g Rep. 316 (2004); Mark Osler, The *Blakely* Problem and the 3x Solution, 16 Fed. Sent'g Rep. 344 (2004); Kevin R. Reitz, The Enforceability of Sentencing Guidelines, 58 Stan. L. Rev. 155 (2005); Ian Weinstein & Nathaniel Z. Marmur, Federal Sentencing During the Interregnum: Defense Practice as the *Blakely* Dust Settles, 17 Fed. Sent'g Rep. 51 (2004).

B.   CAPITAL PUNISHMENT: REGULATING DISCRETION THROUGH CONSTITUTIONAL RULES

Though many view capital punishment as markedly distinct from other types of sentencing, the regulation of sentencing *discretion* in the modern death penalty closely parallels its regulation in modern noncapital sentencing. As detailed throughout this section, the modern administration of the death penalty has been centrally concerned with the limitation of sentencing discretion. Two features differentiate the death penalty from other sentencing: the actors targeted for regulation are usually jurors, and the catalyst of reform has been the U.S. Supreme Court. In nondeath sentencing it has been sentencing commissions that have operated as the main innovators in structuring the exercise of judges' discretion.

1.   Origins and Foundations

The death penalty once occupied the center of attention in criminal justice; it was the penalty most commonly authorized and imposed under English law before the American colonial period. In part because prison systems did not develop fully until the end of the nineteenth century, the death penalty was a central component of the American criminal justice system during the colonial period and through the eighteenth and early nineteenth centuries. By some counts, there were as many as 15,000 authorized executions (and perhaps as many lynchings) during this period, many of which took place in Southern states and disproportionately involved African Americans. An abolitionist movement took root soon after the nation's founding and gained force through the nineteenth century. This movement combined with the creation of penitentiaries to diminish the reliance on capital punishment, although 100 to 150 executions still took place each year between the Civil War and World War II.

As explained in the following excerpt, discretion claimed a central role long ago in the American story of the death penalty. The late nineteenth and early twentieth centuries saw most states move away from statutes mandating death as the punishment for certain crimes toward new laws that gave juries discretion to choose which defendants would be sentenced to die.

The Death Penalty in America,
Hugo Adam Bedau
Pages 9-12 (3d ed. 1982)

Traditionally, under English law, death penalties were mandatory; once the defendant was found guilty of a capital offense, the court had no alternative but a death sentence. Thus the jury could avoid a death penalty in a capital case only by acquitting the defendant or by a finding of guilt on a lesser offense (e.g., manslaughter rather than murder). Remission of the death sentence in favor of transportation to the colonies, or some lesser punishment . . . remained a prerogative of the Crown. But as long as the death penalty was a mandatory punishment, there was always the possibility of acquitting a clearly guilty defendant in order to avoid a death sentence, especially in rare cases where the defendant was unusually pitiable or his conduct was thought to be morally excusable. This threat of "jury nullification," as it has come to be called, on the one side, and the undemocratic character of unbridled executive power to pardon, on the other, encouraged the American colonies to reject the traditional mandatory death penalty in favor of some alternative. What eventually developed was the characteristically American practice that divided murder into degrees and gave the court some sentencing discretion in capital cases. . . .

The first of the [Massachusetts] Bay Colony's capital statutes to authorize an alternative penalty to the death sentence was for the crime of rape. Under a law enacted in 1642, rape was punishable by death or by some "other grievous punishment," at the discretion of the court. A severe whipping and the humiliation of standing on the gallows with a rope around one's neck quickly became the most common punishment for the convicted rapist (unless he was a Negro or an Indian, in which case his punishment was likely to be sale into slavery). The heritage of sentencing discretion did not carry over into the post-Revolutionary period, however. [By] 1780 Massachusetts's seven capital felonies (including rape) were subject to a mandatory death penalty. . . .

Elsewhere in the nation, discretionary capital laws slowly replaced mandatory death penalties. . . . In Maryland, where the jury already had the power to fix degrees of murder, the death penalty became optional in 1809 for treason, rape, and arson, but not for homicide. Tennessee (1838) and Alabama (1841) were the first to authorize a discretionary death sentence for murder, and Louisiana (1846) appears to have been the first jurisdiction to make all its capital crimes optionally punishable by life imprisonment. Between 1886 and 1900, twenty states and the federal government followed suit; by 1926, the practice had been adopted in 33 jurisdictions[, and] seven more . . . introduced this procedure for the punishment of murder [by 1963].

No doubt the development of jury sentencing-discretion in capital cases was seen in part in some jurisdictions as an effective compromise with forces that might otherwise continue to press for complete abolition. . . . In other jurisdictions, however, a very different motivation prevailed. In the postbellum South, research has shown that where the number of capital statutes increased dramatically, as they did in Virginia, they tended to be enacted in a discretionary rather than a mandatory form. With black Americans newly freed from slavery, but disqualified from testifying against whites, excluded by law from serving on juries, and lacking in trained counsel of their own race, the dominant white class could comfortably place their trust in the judgment of white judges and white juries to administer these discretionary death penalty statutes in the desired manner.

NOTES

1. *Legislative control of the death penalty.*   Before the U.S. Supreme Court's significant involvement in capital punishment administration starting in the 1970s, America's history with the death penalty had been primarily about statutes and legislative debate. State legislatures were responsible for the evolution (and even sometimes the abandonment) of capital punishment in the American criminal justice system from the colonial era through the twentieth century. A number of colonial legislative enactments, though influenced by England's embrace of the death penalty, defined for themselves a subset of crimes that were to be subject to capital punishment. State legislatures further narrowed the reach of the death penalty through the early nineteenth century as states, led by developments in Pennsylvania, divided the offense of murder into degrees and provided that only the most aggravated murderers would be subject to punishment of death. And, as highlighted above, this period also saw a slow but steady evolution in the death penalty from a mandatory punishment to a discretionary one. As Hugo Adam Bedau further explained, these legislative developments reflect "the struggle between abolitionists and retentionists, as well as larger social forces shaping the pattern and institutions of criminal justice." Hugo Adam Bedau, The Death Penalty in America 4 (3d ed. 1982).

2. *Parallel paths in Europe and the United States.*   The path followed by the death penalty in Europe paralleled that in the United States. Although a few countries abolished it during the nineteenth and early twentieth centuries, capital punishment saw a resurgence during and after World War I. With the end of World War II, however, a number of European countries abolished the death penalty in their constitutions, largely as a reaction to the abuse of capital punishment during the war. Others accomplished the same result judicially or through legislation. Most countries gradually reduced the use of the death penalty, and by the late 1960s it was virtually no longer employed. In England, for example, though all first-degree murders remained subject to the death penalty until the 1960s, executive clemency commuted most death sentences to life imprisonment until Parliament changed the law.

3. *Constitutional text and capital punishment.*   Capital punishment was a well-established and well-accepted practice during the nation's founding, and the drafters of the Constitution apparently contemplated that it would be a lawful practice in the United States. For instance, the Fifth Amendment

says that "[n]o person shall be held to answer for a capital, or otherwise infamous crime, unless on a presentment or indictment of a Grand Jury. . . ." The Amendment's double jeopardy clause provides that no person shall "be twice put in jeopardy of life or limb," and its due process clause declares that no person shall be "deprived of life . . . without due process of law." Do you think this text conclusively establishes the constitutionality of capital punishment so long as appropriate procedural rules are followed? Does the Eighth Amendment's prohibition of "cruel and unusual punishments" change the textual analysis in any way?

Despite the U.S. Constitution's apparent acceptance of capital punishment, the seemingly arbitrary use of discretion in capital cases led lawyers in the 1950s to start questioning the constitutionality of the penalty. Legal challenges to the death penalty took many forms in lower courts through the 1960s, and this litigation helped produce a de facto moratorium on the death penalty as courts stayed executions while they considered various constitutional objections. Broad constitutional challenges to the death penalty first came before the Supreme Court in cases from California and Ohio in which defendants challenged as a violation of due process the discretionary systems under which they were sentenced to death.

Dennis McGautha v. California
402 U.S. 183 (1971)

HARLAN, J.

. . . McGautha and his codefendant Wilkinson were charged with committing two armed robberies and a murder. . . . In accordance with California procedure in capital cases, the trial was in two stages, a guilt stage and a punishment stage. [Based on testimonial and physical evidence, the jury found both defendants guilty at the guilt stage.] At the penalty trial, which took place on the following day but before the same jury, the State . . . presented evidence of McGautha's prior felony convictions and sentences, and then rested. [Wilkinson and McGautha thereafter both testified, each claiming that his accomplice fired the fatal shot. Wilkinson also called character witnesses, who testified that he had] a good reputation and was honest and peaceable. The jury was instructed in the following language:

> In this part of the trial the law does not forbid you from being influenced by pity for the defendants and you may be governed by mere sentiment and sympathy for the defendants in arriving at a proper penalty in this case; however, the law does forbid you from being governed by mere conjecture, prejudice, public opinion or public feeling.
>
> [You] should consider all of the evidence received here in court presented by the People and defendants throughout the trial before this jury. You may also consider all of the evidence of the circumstances surrounding the crime, of each defendant's background and history, and of the facts in aggravation or mitigation of the penalty which have been received here in court. However, it is not essential to your decision that you find mitigating

circumstances on the one hand or evidence in aggravation of the offense on the other hand. . . . Notwithstanding facts, if any, proved in mitigation or aggravation, in determining which punishment shall be inflicted, you are entirely free to act according to your own judgment, conscience, and absolute discretion. . . .

Now, beyond prescribing the two alternative penalties [of death or life imprisonment], the law itself provides no standard for the guidance of the jury in the selection of the penalty, but, rather, commits the whole matter of determining which of the two penalties shall be fixed to the judgment, conscience, and absolute discretion of the jury. In the determination of that matter, if the jury does agree, it must be unanimous as to which of the two penalties is imposed.

The jury returned verdicts fixing Wilkinson's punishment at life imprisonment and McGautha's punishment at death.

[In a companion case on this appeal, John] Crampton was indicted for the murder of his wife. . . . He pleaded not guilty and not guilty by reason of insanity. [Physical evidence linked Crampton to his wife's killing, although his attorney submitted evidence suggesting her shooting was accidental.] In accordance with the Ohio practice which Crampton challenges, his guilt and punishment were determined in a single unitary proceeding. The jury was instructed that: "If you find the defendant guilty of murder in the first degree, the punishment is death, unless you recommend mercy, in which event the punishment is imprisonment in the penitentiary during life." The jury was given no other instructions specifically addressed to the decision whether to recommend mercy, but was told in connection with its verdict generally:

You must not be influenced by any consideration of sympathy or prejudice. It is your duty to carefully weigh the evidence, to decide all disputed questions of fact, to apply the instructions of the court to your findings and to render your verdict accordingly. In fulfilling your duty, your efforts must be to arrive at a just verdict.

Consider all the evidence and make your finding with intelligence and impartiality, and without bias, sympathy, or prejudice, so that the State of Ohio and the defendant will feel that their case was fairly and impartially tried.

The jury deliberated for over four hours and returned a verdict of guilty, with no recommendation for mercy.

[McGautha and Crampton both] claim that the absence of standards to guide the jury's discretion on the punishment issue is constitutionally intolerable. [They] contend that to leave the jury completely at large to impose or withhold the death penalty as it sees fit is fundamentally lawless and therefore violates the basic command of the Fourteenth Amendment that no State shall deprive a person of his life without due process of law. Despite the undeniable surface appeal of the proposition, we conclude that the courts below correctly rejected it. . . .

The history of capital punishment . . . reveals continual efforts, uniformly unsuccessful, to identify before the fact those homicides for which the slayer should die. [Jurors on occasion took the law into their own hands when facing cases that seemed] clearly inappropriate for the death penalty. In such cases they simply refused to convict of the capital offense. [To] meet the problem of jury nullification, legislatures . . . adopted the method of forthrightly granting juries the discretion which they had been exercising in fact. [Our precedents have consistently suggested the lawfulness of] standardless jury sentencing in capital cases, [stressing that juries] express the conscience of the community on the ultimate question of life or death. . . .

In recent years academic and professional sources have suggested that jury sentencing discretion should be controlled by standards of some sort. The American Law Institute first published such a recommendation in 1959. Several States have enacted new criminal codes in the intervening 12 years, some adopting features of the Model Penal Code. Other States have modified their laws with respect to murder and the death penalty in other ways. None of these States have followed the Model Penal Code and adopted statutory criteria for imposition of the death penalty. In recent years, challenges to standardless jury sentencing have been presented to many state and federal appellate courts. No court has held the challenge good. . . .

Those who have come to grips with the hard task of actually attempting to draft means of channeling capital sentencing discretion have confirmed the lesson taught by the history recounted above. To identify before the fact those characteristics of criminal homicides and their perpetrators which call for the death penalty, and to express these characteristics in language which can be fairly understood and applied by the sentencing authority, appear to be tasks which are beyond present human ability.

Thus the British Home Office, which [selected] the cases from England and Wales which should receive the benefit of the Royal Prerogative of Mercy, observed: "No simple formula can take account of the innumerable degrees of culpability, and no formula which fails to do so can claim to be just or satisfy public opinion. . . . Discretionary judgment on the facts of each case is the only way in which they can be equitably distinguished." . . .

The draftsmen of the Model Penal Code [declared] "that it is within the realm of possibility to point to the main circumstances of aggravation and of mitigation that should be weighed and weighed against each other when they are presented in a concrete case." The circumstances the draftsmen selected . . . were not intended to be exclusive. The Code provides simply that the sentencing authority should "take into account the aggravating and mitigating circumstances enumerated . . . and any other facts that it deems relevant," and that the court should so instruct when the issue was submitted to the jury.

It is apparent that such criteria do not purport to provide more than the most minimal control over the sentencing authority's exercise of discretion. They do not purport to give an exhaustive list of the relevant considerations or the way in which they may be affected by the presence or absence of other circumstances. They do not even undertake to exclude constitutionally impermissible considerations. And, of course, they provide no protection against the jury determined to decide on whimsy or caprice. In short, they do no more than suggest some subjects for the jury to consider during its deliberations, and they bear witness to the intractable nature of the problem of "standards" which the history of capital punishment has from the beginning reflected. Thus, they indeed caution against this Court's undertaking to establish such standards itself, or to pronounce at large that standards in this realm are constitutionally required.

In light of history, experience, and the present limitations of human knowledge, we find it quite impossible to say that committing to the untrammeled discretion of the jury the power to pronounce life or death in a capital case is offensive to anything in the Constitution. The States are entitled to assume that jurors confronted with the truly awesome responsibility of decreeing death for a fellow human will act with due regard for the consequences of their decision and will consider a variety of factors, many of which will have been suggested by the evidence or by the arguments of defense counsel. For a court to attempt to catalog the appropriate factors in this elusive area could inhibit rather than expand the scope of consideration, for no list of circumstances would ever be really complete. The infinite variety of cases and facets to each case would make general standards either meaningless "boiler-plate" or a statement of the obvious that no jury would need. . . .

It may well be, as the American Law Institute and the National Commission on Reform of Federal Criminal Laws have concluded, that bifurcated trials and criteria for jury sentencing discretion are superior means of dealing with capital cases if the death penalty is to be retained at all. But the Federal Constitution, which marks the limits of our authority in these cases, does not guarantee trial procedures that are the best of all worlds, or that accord with the most enlightened ideas of students of the infant science of criminology, or even those that measure up to the individual predilections of members of this Court. The Constitution requires no more than that trials be fairly conducted and that guaranteed rights of defendants be scrupulously respected. . . .

NOTES

1. *Meaning of due process.* Dennis McGautha and John Crampton based their constitutional objection to standardless jury sentencing in capital cases on the Fourteenth Amendment's guarantee that no state shall "deprive any person of life . . . without due process of law." Do you agree with Justice Harlan's core conclusion that the jury instructions used in the trials of McGautha and Crampton provided due process? Do you think the requirements concerning what process is "due" should be heightened in death penalty cases?

2. *Establishing jury standards and the institutions for reform.* Do you concur with Justice Harlan's assertion in *McGautha* that to "identify before the fact those characteristics of criminal homicides and their perpetrators which call for the death penalty, and to express these characteristics in language which can be fairly understood and applied by the sentencing authority, appear to be tasks which are beyond present human ability"? Notably, the drafters of the Model Penal Code, though they took "no position on the desirability of the death penalty," developed a detailed set of possible aggravating and mitigating circumstances that could be used by states adopting the death penalty to guide juries in deciding whether to sentence a particular offender to death. See Model Penal Code §210.6(3) and (4). Justice Harlan's opinion does seem on firmer ground when he states that the history of capital reforms "caution against this Court's

undertaking to establish [death penalty] standards itself, or to pronounce at large that standards in this realm are constitutionally required." In other words, though Justice Harlan's assertion about the impossibility of developing jury standards seems questionable, his apparent unwillingness for the Supreme Court to constitutionally mandate such standards seems much more sound.

2.   Constitutional Regulation of Capital Sentencing Systems

Right after its decision in *McGautha*, the Supreme Court revisited the constitutionality of the death penalty through three cases posing challenges based on the Eighth Amendment's prohibition of "cruel and unusual punishments." This strategy seemed unlikely to succeed since, in Trop v. Dulles, 356 U.S. 86 (1958), a noncapital case in which the defendant raised an Eighth Amendment claim, Chief Justice Warren suggested in dicta that the death penalty, by dint of tradition, must be a constitutionally permissible punishment:

> Whatever the arguments may be against capital punishment, both on moral grounds and in terms of accomplishing the purposes of punishment—and they are forceful—the death penalty has been employed throughout our history, and, in a day when it is still widely accepted, it cannot be said to violate the constitutional concept of cruelty.

In the same opinion, however, Chief Justice Warren further elaborated on how courts should interpret the Eighth Amendment's vague restriction on government power, suggesting that even historically accepted punishments could be subjected to renewed constitutional scrutiny. In an oft-quoted passage, Chief Justice Warren stressed: "The basic concept underlying the Eighth Amendment is nothing less than the dignity of man. [T]he words of the Amendment are not precise, and their scope is not static. The Amendment must draw its meaning from the evolving standards of decency that mark the progress of a maturing society."

In Furman v. Georgia and companion cases, Justices Potter Stewart and Byron White joined three of the dissenters in *McGautha* to hold that existing capital punishment statutes were applied in a manner that violated the Eighth Amendment's prohibition on "cruel and unusual punishments." There was no majority opinion in *Furman*, just the per curiam order set forth below, and each Justice authored a separate—and lengthy—opinion. (*Furman* still ranks among the longest decisions in U.S. Supreme Court history, occupying 233 pages in the Supreme Court Reporter.)

How can the outcome in *Furman* be explained in light of *McGautha*? Did McGautha and Crampton merely stake their claims on the wrong amendment?

|| **William Henry Furman v. Georgia** ||
|| **408 U.S. 238 (1972)** ||

PER CURIAM
[Appeals were consolidated here from convictions in three cases. Furman was convicted of murder in Georgia; Jackson was convicted of rape in Georgia;

Branch was convicted of rape in Texas. All three were sentenced to death.]
Certiorari was granted limited to the following question: "Does the imposition
and carrying out of the death penalty in [these cases] constitute cruel and
unusual punishment in violation of the Eighth and Fourteenth Amendments?"
The Court holds that the imposition and carrying out of the death penalty in
these cases constitute cruel and unusual punishment in violation of the Eighth
and Fourteenth Amendments. The judgment in each case is therefore reversed
insofar as it leaves undisturbed the death sentence imposed, and the cases are
remanded for further proceedings. So ordered. . . .

STEWART, J., concurring.
The constitutionality of capital punishment in the abstract is not . . . before
us in these cases. . . . Instead, the death sentences now before us are the product
of a legal system that brings them, I believe, within the very core of the Eighth
Amendment's guarantee against cruel and unusual punishments, a guarantee
applicable against the States through the Fourteenth Amendment. In the first
place, it is clear that these sentences are "cruel" in the sense that they excessively
go beyond, not in degree but in kind, the punishments that the state legislatures
have determined to be necessary. In the second place, it is equally clear that
these sentences are "unusual" in the sense that the penalty of death is infrequently imposed for murder, and that its imposition for rape is extraordinarily
rare. But I do not rest my conclusion upon these two propositions alone.
These death sentences are cruel and unusual in the same way that being
struck by lightning is cruel and unusual. For, of all the people convicted of rapes
and murders in 1967 and 1968, many just as reprehensible as these, the petitioners are among a capriciously selected random handful upon whom the
sentence of death has in fact been imposed. My concurring Brothers have demonstrated that, if any basis can be discerned for the selection of these few to be
sentenced to die, it is the constitutionally impermissible basis of race. But racial
discrimination has not been proved, and I put it to one side. I simply conclude
that the Eighth and Fourteenth Amendments cannot tolerate the infliction of a
sentence of death under legal systems that permit this unique penalty to be so
wantonly and so freakishly imposed. . . .

WHITE, J., concurring.
The narrower question to which I address myself concerns the constitutionality of capital punishment statutes under which (1) the legislature
authorizes the imposition of the death penalty for murder or rape; (2) the
legislature does not itself mandate the penalty in any particular class or kind
of case (that is, legislative will is not frustrated if the penalty is never imposed),
but delegates to judges or juries the decisions as to those cases, if any, in which
the penalty will be utilized; and (3) judges and juries have ordered the death
penalty with such infrequency that the odds are now very much against imposition and execution of the penalty with respect to any convicted murderer or
rapist. . . .
The [death] penalty has not been considered cruel and unusual punishment in the constitutional sense because it was thought justified by the social
ends it was deemed to serve. At the moment that it ceases realistically to further
these purposes, [it] would violate the Eighth Amendment . . . for its imposition

would then be the pointless and needless extinction of life with only marginal contributions to any discernible social or public purposes. A penalty with such negligible returns to the State would be patently excessive and cruel and unusual punishment violative of the Eighth Amendment.

It is also my judgment that this point has been reached with respect to capital punishment as it is presently administered under the statutes involved in these cases. . . . I cannot avoid the conclusion that as the statutes before us are now administered, the penalty is so infrequently imposed that the threat of execution is too attenuated to be of substantial service to criminal justice. [It is clear that] the death penalty is exacted with great infrequency even for the most atrocious crimes and that there is no meaningful basis for distinguishing the few cases in which it is imposed from the many cases in which it is not. . . .

DOUGLAS, J., concurring.

. . . Juries (or judges, as the case may be) have practically untrammeled discretion to let an accused live or insist that he die. . . . Former Attorney General Ramsey Clark has said, "It is the poor, the sick, the ignorant, the powerless and the hated who are executed." One searches our chronicles in vain for the execution of any member of the affluent strata of this society. . . .

Jackson, a black, convicted of the rape of a white woman, was 21 years old. . . . Furman, a black, killed a householder while seeking to enter the home at night. . . . Branch, a black, entered the rural home of a 65-year-old widow, a white, while she slept and raped her, holding his arm against her throat. . . . We cannot say from facts disclosed in these records that these defendants were sentenced to death because they were black. Yet our task is not restricted to an effort to divine what motives impelled these death penalties. Rather, we deal with a system of law and of justice that leaves to the uncontrolled discretion of judges or juries the determination whether defendants committing these crimes should die or be imprisoned. Under these laws no standards govern the selection of the penalty. People live or die, dependent on the whim of one man or of 12. . . .

The high service rendered by the "cruel and unusual" punishment clause of the Eighth Amendment is to require legislatures to write penal laws that are evenhanded, nonselective, and nonarbitrary, and to require judges to see to it that general laws are not applied sparsely, selectively, and spottily to unpopular groups. A law that stated that anyone making more than $50,000 would be exempt from the death penalty would plainly fall, as would a law that in terms said that blacks, those who never went beyond the fifth grade in school, those who made less than $3,000 a year, or those who were unpopular or unstable should be the only people executed. A law which in the overall view reaches that result in practice has no more sanctity than a law which in terms provides the same. . . .

Thus, these discretionary statutes are unconstitutional in their operation. They are pregnant with discrimination and discrimination is an ingredient not compatible with the idea of equal protection of the laws that is implicit in the ban on "cruel and unusual" punishments. . . .

BRENNAN, J., concurring.

[The] Cruel and Unusual Punishments Clause prohibits the infliction of uncivilized and inhuman punishments. The State, even as it punishes, must treat its members with respect for their intrinsic worth as human beings. A punishment is "cruel and unusual," therefore, if it does not comport with human dignity. . . .

The primary principle is that a punishment must not be so severe as to be degrading to the dignity of human beings. Pain, certainly, may be a factor in the judgment. . . . More than the presence of pain, however, is comprehended in the judgment that the extreme severity of a punishment makes it degrading to the dignity of human beings. The barbaric punishments condemned by history, "punishments which inflict torture, such as the rack, the thumbscrew, the iron boot, the stretching of limbs and the like," . . . have been condemned [because] they treat members of the human race as nonhumans, as objects to be toyed with and discarded. They are thus inconsistent with the fundamental premise of the Clause that even the vilest criminal remains a human being possessed of common human dignity.

[A] second principle inherent in the Clause [is] that the State must not arbitrarily inflict a severe punishment [because] the State does not respect human dignity when, without reason, it inflicts upon some people a severe punishment that it does not inflict upon others. Indeed, the very words "cruel and unusual punishments" imply condemnation of the arbitrary infliction of severe punishments. [W]hen a severe punishment is inflicted in the great majority of cases in which it is legally available, there is little likelihood that the State is inflicting it arbitrarily. If, however, the infliction of a severe punishment is something different from that which is generally done in such cases, there is a substantial likelihood that the State, contrary to the requirements of regularity and fairness embodied in the Clause, is inflicting the punishment arbitrarily. This principle is especially important today. There is scant danger, given the political processes in an enlightened democracy such as ours, that extremely severe punishments will be widely applied. The more significant function of the Clause, therefore, is to protect against the danger of their arbitrary infliction.

A third principle inherent in the Clause is that a severe punishment must not be unacceptable to contemporary society. Rejection by society, of course, is a strong indication that a severe punishment does not comport with human dignity. In applying this principle, however, we must make certain that the judicial determination is as objective as possible. Thus, for example, . . . one factor that may be considered is the existence of the punishment in jurisdictions other than those before the Court. [Another] factor to be considered is the historic usage of the punishment. . . . Accordingly, the judicial task is to review the history of a challenged punishment and to examine society's present practices with respect to its use. Legislative authorization, of course, does not establish acceptance. The acceptability of a severe punishment is measured, not by its availability, for it might become so offensive to society as never to be inflicted, but by its use.

The final principle inherent in the Clause is that a severe punishment must not be excessive. A punishment is excessive under this principle if it is unnecessary: The infliction of a severe punishment by the State cannot comport with human dignity when it is nothing more than the pointless infliction of suffering. If there is a significantly less severe punishment adequate to achieve the purposes for which the punishment is inflicted, the punishment inflicted is unnecessary and therefore excessive. . . .

The outstanding characteristic of our present practice of punishing criminals by death is the infrequency with which we resort to it. . . . There has been a

steady decline in the infliction of this punishment in every decade since the
1930's, the earliest period for which accurate statistics are available. In the
1930's, executions averaged 167 per year; in the 1940's, the average was 128;
in the 1950's, it was 72; and in the years 1960-1962, it was 48. There have been a
total of 46 executions since then, 36 of them in 1963-1964. Yet our population
and the number of capital crimes committed have increased greatly over the past
four decades. The contemporary rarity of the infliction of this punishment is
thus the end result of a long-continued decline. . . . When the punishment of
death is inflicted in a trivial number of the cases in which it is legally available,
the conclusion is virtually inescapable that it is being inflicted arbitrarily.
Indeed, it smacks of little more than a lottery system.

[The] punishment of death is inconsistent with all four principles: Death is
an unusually severe and degrading punishment; there is a strong probability that
it is inflicted arbitrarily; its rejection by contemporary society is virtually total;
and there is no reason to believe it serves any penal purpose more effectively
than the less severe punishment of imprisonment. The function of these principles is to enable a court to determine whether a punishment comports with
human dignity. Death, quite simply, does not. . . .

MARSHALL, J., concurring.

[A] penalty may be cruel and unusual because it is excessive and serves no
valid legislative purpose. [There are several] purposes conceivably served by
capital punishment: retribution, deterrence, prevention of repetitive criminal
acts . . . and economy. . . .

The fact that the State may seek retribution against those who have broken
its laws does not mean that retribution may then become the State's sole end in
punishing. . . . If retribution alone could serve as a justification for any
particular penalty, then all penalties selected by the legislature would by definition be acceptable means for designating society's moral approbation of a
particular act. . . .

The most hotly contested issue regarding capital punishment is whether it
is better than life imprisonment as a deterrent to crime. [Thorsten Sellin, one of
the leading authorities on capital punishment, compiled statistics to] demonstrate that there is no correlation between the murder rate and the presence or
absence of the capital sanction. He compares States that have similar characteristics and finds that irrespective of their position on capital punishment, they
have similar murder rates. . . . Sellin also concludes that abolition and/or rein-
troduction of the death penalty had no effect on the homicide rates of the
various States involved. This conclusion is borne out by others who have
made similar inquiries and by the experience of other countries. . . .

Much of what must be said about the death penalty as a device to prevent
recidivism is obvious — if a murderer is executed, he cannot possibly commit
another offense. The fact is, however, that murderers are extremely unlikely to
commit other crimes either in prison or upon their release. For the most part,
they are first offenders, and when released from prison they are known to
become model citizens. Furthermore, most persons who commit capital crimes
are not executed. With respect to those who are sentenced to die, it is critical to
note that the jury is never asked to determine whether they are likely to be
recidivists. In light of these facts, if capital punishment were justified purely

on the basis of preventing recidivism, it would have to be considered to be excessive; no general need to obliterate all capital offenders could have been demonstrated, nor any specific need in individual cases. . . .

As for the argument that it is cheaper to execute a capital offender than to imprison him for life, even assuming that such an argument, if true, would support a capital sanction, it is simply incorrect. A disproportionate amount of money spent on prisons is attributable to death row. Condemned men are not productive members of the prison community, although they could be, and executions are expensive. Appeals are often automatic, and courts admittedly spend more time with death cases. . . . When all is said and done, there can be no doubt that it costs more to execute a man than to keep him in prison for life.

[Even] if capital punishment is not excessive, it nonetheless violates the Eighth Amendment because it is morally unacceptable to the people of the United States at this time in their history. In judging whether or not a given penalty is morally acceptable, most courts have said that the punishment is valid unless "it shocks the conscience and sense of justice of the people." [But] whether or not a punishment is cruel and unusual depends, not on whether its mere mention shocks the conscience and sense of justice of the people, but on whether people who were fully informed as to the purposes of the penalty and its liabilities would find the penalty shocking, unjust, and unacceptable. . . . In other words, the question with which we must deal is not whether a substantial proportion of American citizens would today, if polled, opine that capital punishment is barbarously cruel, but whether they would find it to be so in the light of all information presently available. . . .

It has often been noted that American citizens know almost nothing about capital punishment [and much that I have propounded in this opinion is] critical to an informed judgment on the morality of the death penalty: e.g., that the death penalty is no more effective a deterrent than life imprisonment, that convicted murderers are rarely executed, but are usually sentenced to a term in prison; that convicted murderers usually are model prisoners, and that they almost always become law-abiding citizens upon their release from prison; that the costs of executing a capital offender exceed the costs of imprisoning him for life; that while in prison, a convict under sentence of death performs none of the useful functions that life prisoners perform; that no attempt is made in the sentencing process to ferret out likely recidivists for execution; and that the death penalty may actually stimulate criminal activity.

This information would almost surely convince the average citizen that the death penalty was unwise, but [the] desire for retribution . . . might influence the citizenry's view of the morality of capital punishment. [Yet] no one has ever seriously advanced retribution as a legitimate goal of our society. Defenses of capital punishment are always mounted on deterrent or other similar theories. This should not be surprising. It is the people of this country who have urged in the past that prisons rehabilitate as well as isolate offenders, and it is the people who have injected a sense of purpose into our penology. I cannot believe that at this stage in our history, the American people would ever knowingly support purposeless vengeance. Thus, I believe that the great mass of citizens would conclude on the basis of the material already considered that the death penalty is immoral and therefore unconstitutional.

But, if this information needs supplementing, I believe that the following facts would serve to convince even the most hesitant of citizens to condemn death as a sanction: capital punishment is imposed discriminatorily against certain identifiable classes of people; there is evidence that innocent people have been executed before their innocence can be proved; and the death penalty wreaks havoc with our entire criminal justice system. . . .

Regarding discrimination, it . . . is usually the poor, the illiterate, the under-privileged, the member of the minority group—the man who, because he is without means, and is defended by a court-appointed attorney—who becomes society's sacrificial lamb. . . . Indeed, a look at the bare statistics regarding executions is enough to betray much of the discrimination. A total of 3,859 persons have been executed since 1930, of whom 1,751 were white and 2,066 were Negro. . . .

Assuming knowledge of all the facts presently available regarding capital punishment, the average citizen would, in my opinion, find it shocking to his conscience and sense of justice. For this reason alone capital punishment can-not stand.

BURGER, C.J., dissenting.

. . . Counsel for petitioners properly concede that capital punishment was not impermissibly cruel at the time of the adoption of the Eighth Amendment. Not only do the records of the debates indicate that the Founding Fathers were limited in their concern to the prevention of torture, but it is also clear from the language of the Constitution itself that there was no thought whatever of the elimination of capital punishment. . . .

In the 181 years since the enactment of the Eighth Amendment, not a single decision of this Court has cast the slightest shadow of a doubt on the constitutionality of capital punishment. . . . Today the Court has not ruled that capital punishment is per se violative of the Eighth Amendment; nor has it ruled that the punishment is barred for any particular class or classes of crimes. The substantially similar concurring opinions of Mr. Justice Stewart and Mr. Justice White, which are necessary to support the judgment setting aside petitioners' sentences, stop short of reaching the ultimate question. The actual scope of the Court's ruling, which I take to be embodied in these concurring opinions, is not entirely clear. This much, however, seems apparent: if the legislatures are to continue to authorize capital punishment for some crimes, juries and judges can no longer be permitted to make the sentencing determination in the same manner they have in the past. . . .

Real change could clearly be brought about if legislatures provided mandatory death sentences in such a way as to deny juries the opportunity to bring in a verdict on a lesser charge; under such a system, the death sentence could only be avoided by a verdict of acquittal. If this is the only alternative that the legislatures can safely pursue under today's ruling, I would have preferred that the Court opt for total abolition.

It seems remarkable to me that with our basic trust in lay jurors as the keystone in our system of criminal justice, it should now be suggested that we take the most sensitive and important of all decisions away from them. I could more easily be persuaded that mandatory sentences of death, without the inter-vening and ameliorating impact of lay jurors, are so arbitrary and doctrinaire that they violate the Constitution. The very infrequency of death penalties imposed by jurors attests their cautious and discriminating reservation of that penalty for the most extreme cases. I had thought that nothing was clearer in history, as we noted in *McGautha* one year ago, than the American abhorrence of "the common-law rule imposing a mandatory death sentence on all convicted murderers." 402 U.S. at 198. [The] nineteenth century movement away from mandatory death sentences marked an enlightened introduction of flexibility into the sentencing process. It recognized that individual culpability is not always measured by the category of the crime committed. I do not see how this history can be ignored and how it can be suggested that the Eighth Amendment demands the elimination of the most sensitive feature of the sentencing system. . . .

BLACKMUN, J., dissenting.
. . . Cases such as these provide for me an excruciating agony of the spirit. I yield to no one in the depth of my distaste, antipathy, and, indeed, abhorrence, for the death penalty, with all its aspects of physical distress and fear and of moral judgment exercised by finite minds. . . . Were I a legislator, I would do all I could to sponsor and to vote for legislation abolishing the death penalty. [However, as judges we] should not allow our personal preferences as to the wisdom of legislative and congressional action, or our distaste for such action, to guide our judicial decision in cases such as these. . . . Although personally I may rejoice at the Court's result, I find it difficult to accept or to justify as a matter of history, of law, or of constitutional pronouncement. I fear the Court has overstepped. It has sought and has achieved an end.

POWELL, J., dissenting.
[A] comment on the racial discrimination problem seems appropriate. The possibility of racial bias in the trial and sentencing process has diminished in recent years. The segregation of our society in decades past, which contributed substantially to the severity of punishment for interracial crimes, is now no longer prevalent in this country. Likewise, the day is past when juries do not represent the minority group elements of the community. The assurance of fair trials for all citizens is greater today than at any previous time in our history. Because standards of criminal justice have "evolved" in a manner favorable to the accused, discriminatory imposition of capital punishment is far less likely today than in the past.
. . . It is important to keep in focus the enormity of the step undertaken by the Court today. Not only does it invalidate hundreds of state and federal laws, it deprives those jurisdictions of the power to legislate with respect to capital punishment in the future, except in a manner consistent with the cloudily outlined views of those Justices who do not purport to undertake total abolition. Nothing short of an amendment to the United States Constitution can reverse the Court's judgments. Meanwhile, all flexibility is foreclosed. The normal democratic process, as well as the opportunities for the several States to respond to the will of their people expressed through ballot referenda . . . is now shut off. . . .

REHNQUIST, J., dissenting.
The Court's judgments today strike down a penalty that our Nation's legislators have thought necessary since our country was founded. My Brothers

Douglas, Brennan, and Marshall would at one fell swoop invalidate laws enacted by Congress and 40 of the 50 state legislatures, and would consign to the limbo of unconstitutionality under a single rubric penalties for offenses as varied and unique as murder, piracy, mutiny, highjacking, and desertion in the face of the enemy. My Brothers Stewart and White, asserting reliance on a more limited rationale — the reluctance of judges and juries actually to impose the death penalty in the majority of capital cases, join in the judgments in these cases. Whatever its precise rationale, today's holding necessarily brings into sharp relief the fundamental question of the role of judicial review in a democratic society. . . .

The task of judging constitutional cases [cannot] be avoided, but it must surely be approached with the deepest humility and genuine deference to legislative judgment. Today's decision to invalidate capital punishment is, I respectfully submit, significantly lacking in those attributes. . . . I conclude that this decision holding unconstitutional capital punishment is not an act of judgment, but rather an act of will.

NOTES

1. *Meaning of "cruel and unusual."*   Do you agree with the *Furman* majority's core holding that William Furman's punishment was cruel and unusual? Does your answer hinge, as it did for the Court, on the fact that Furman was sentenced through a system of standardless jury discretion that allowed, in the words of Justice Stewart, "this unique penalty to be so wantonly and so freakishly imposed"?

Considering these issues more generally, by what standards should a judge or other official assess whether a punishment inflicted is cruel and unusual? Or, drawing on Chief Justice Warren's famous discussion of the Eighth Amendment in Trop v. Dulles quoted earlier, how should judges or other officials assess "the evolving standards of decency that mark the progress of a maturing society"?

What impact, if any, should international developments — such as the abolition of capital punishment in Great Britain or the European Union — have on the interpretation of the Eighth Amendment's prohibition of cruel and unusual punishments? Notably, when the European Convention for the Protection of Human Rights and Fundamental Freedoms was adopted in the early 1950s, the death penalty was still widely in use. Therefore, its prohibition on "torture or . . . inhuman or degrading treatment or punishment" in Article 3 did not apply to capital punishment. Protocol 6, in force since 1988, however, explicitly abolishes the death penalty in peacetime. Signature of this protocol has become a virtual prerequisite for membership in the European human rights regime. Consequently, when considered against the backdrop of the near universal abolition of the death penalty in other Western nations, the use of capital punishment in the United States is now unusual. When and how should international human rights norms influence interpretations of U.S. constitutional provisions that implicate human rights concerns?

2. *Discretion, disparity, and discrimination.*   What seems to have been the central concern of the Justices voting in the majority in *Furman*? Was it the

fact that the juries exercised discretion without having any standards to guide life-and-death decisions? Was it the disparity in outcomes (that is, who was sentenced to die) that resulted from the exercise of standardless jury discretion? Was it the discriminatory judgments seemingly reflected by the results of standardless jury discretion in capital cases? Justice Douglas's opinion makes clear that the potentially discriminatory application of standardless jury discretion was his chief concern, suggesting that the constitutional provision transgressed was actually the Fourteenth Amendment's equal protection clause rather than the Eighth Amendment: "The [discretionary statutes] are pregnant with discrimination and discrimination is an ingredient not compatible with the idea of equal protection of the laws."

3. *The Marshall hypothesis.*   In one of the more famous passages from the *Furman* opinions, Justice Marshall argues that the more fully informed people become about the operation of the death penalty, the less likely they are to support its use. (Indeed, Justice Marshall justified his vote in *Furman* by contending that the average citizen, with "knowledge of all the facts presently available regarding capital punishment, would . . . find it shocking to his conscience and sense of justice.") This argument has come to be known as "the Marshall hypothesis." Is it appropriate (or even sensible) for legislators or executive branch officials to defer especially to the judgment of those with the most knowledge or expertise in an area? Is there anything in the role of a judge that should prevent reliance on such arguments? As you work through the remainder of the materials in this chapter and throughout this book, watch for other examples of this argument at work and try to gauge whether your own (or others') opinions about the death penalty change as you become more informed about its application.

4. *State responses to* Furman.   The Supreme Court's holding in *Furman* effectively declared unconstitutional the death penalty statutes then in place in 40 states and commuted the sentences of 629 death row inmates around the country.

Because only Justices Brennan and Marshall asserted that the death penalty was per se unconstitutional, the opinions of Justices Stewart, White, and Douglas suggested that states could rewrite their death penalty statutes to remedy the constitutional problems. Led by Florida, which enacted a new death penalty statute five months after *Furman*, 35 states reacted to the decision by passing new death penalty statutes: ten states addressed the unconstitutionality of standardless jury discretion by making the death penalty mandatory for all offenders convicted of certain capital crimes; 25 other states sought to limit discretion by setting forth aggravating and mitigating factors for judge and jury to consider.

5. *The tide turns in 1976.*   The nationwide ban on capital punishment that the Court created in 1972 with its opinion in *Furman* did not last long. In 1976 the Court decided a set of five cases testing the constitutionality of various state death penalty statutes passed in reaction to *Furman*. In the lead case, Gregg v. Georgia, 428 U.S. 153 (1976), Justice Stewart authored the opinion of the Court, which held that "the punishment of death does not invariably violate the

Constitution." First the Court took note of the widespread debate about capital punishment in state legislatures:

> Despite the continuing debate, dating back to the nineteenth century, over the morality and utility of capital punishment, it is now evident that a large proportion of American society continues to regard it as an appropriate and necessary criminal sanction.
>
> The most marked indication of society's endorsement of the death penalty for murder is the legislative response to *Furman.* The legislatures of at least 35 States have enacted new statutes that provide for the death penalty for at least some crimes that result in the death of another person. And the Congress of the United States, in 1974, enacted a statute providing the death penalty for aircraft piracy that results in death. [The] post-*Furman* statutes make clear that capital punishment itself has not been rejected by the elected representatives of the people.
>
> [The] actions of juries in many States since *Furman* are fully compatible with the legislative judgments, reflected in the new statutes, as to the continued utility and necessity of capital punishment in appropriate cases. At the close of 1974 at least 254 persons had been sentenced to death since *Furman,* and by the end of March 1976, more than 460 persons were subject to death sentences.

428 U.S. at 179-182.

The Court also accepted both deterrence and retribution as appropriate social purposes justifying the use of the death penalty:

> In part, capital punishment is an expression of society's moral outrage at particularly offensive conduct. This function may be unappealing to many, but it is essential in an ordered society that asks its citizens to rely on legal processes rather than self-help to vindicate their wrongs. . . . Retribution is no longer the dominant objective of the criminal law, but neither is it a forbidden objective nor one inconsistent with our respect for the dignity of men. . . . Indeed, the decision that capital punishment may be the appropriate sanction in extreme cases is an expression of the community's belief that certain crimes are themselves so grievous an affront to humanity that the only adequate response may be the penalty of death.
>
> Statistical attempts to evaluate the worth of the death penalty as a deterrent to crimes by potential offenders have occasioned a great deal of debate. The results simply have been inconclusive. Although some of the studies suggest that the death penalty may not function as a significantly greater deterrent than lesser penalties, there is no convincing empirical evidence either supporting or refuting this view. We may nevertheless assume safely that there are murderers, such as those who act in passion, for whom the threat of death has little or no deterrent effect. But for many others, the death penalty undoubtedly is a significant deterrent. There are carefully contemplated murders, such as murder for hire, where the possible penalty of death may well enter into the cold calculus that precedes the decision to act. . . . The value of capital punishment as a deterrent of crime is a complex factual issue the resolution of which properly rests with the legislatures, which can evaluate the results of statistical studies in terms of their own local conditions and with a flexibility of approach that is not available to the courts.

Id. at 183-186.

Finally, the Court considered the procedural devices that the Georgia statute used to guide the discretion of the sentencing jury:

> Jury sentencing has been considered desirable in capital cases in order "to maintain a link between contemporary community values and the penal

system. . . ." But it creates special problems. Much of the information that is relevant to the sentencing decision may have no relevance to the question of guilt, or may even be extremely prejudicial to a fair determination of that question. This problem, however, is scarcely insurmountable. Those who have studied the question suggest that a bifurcated procedure, one in which the question of sentence is not considered until the determination of guilt has been made, is the best answer. [And though] members of a jury will have had little, if any, previous experience in sentencing, [this] problem will be alleviated if the jury is given guidance regarding the factors about the crime and the defendant that the State, representing organized society, deems particularly relevant to the sentencing decision. . . .

While some have suggested that standards to guide a capital jury's sentencing deliberations are impossible to formulate, the fact is that such standards have been developed. When the drafters of the Model Penal Code faced this problem, they concluded "that it is within the realm of possibility to point to the main circumstances of aggravation and of mitigation that should be weighed and *weighed against each other* when they are presented in a concrete case." While such standards are by necessity somewhat general, they do provide guidance to sentencing authority and thereby reduce the likelihood that it will impose a sentence that fairly can be called capricious or arbitrary. Where the sentencing authority is required to specify the factors it relied upon in reaching its decision, the further safeguard of meaningful appellate review is available to ensure that death sentences are not imposed capriciously or in a freakish manner.

[To] guard further against a situation comparable to that presented in *Furman*, the Supreme Court of Georgia compares each death sentence with the sentences imposed on similarly situated defendants to ensure that the sentence of death in a particular case is not disproportionate. On their face these procedures seem to satisfy the concerns of *Furman*. No longer should there be "no meaningful basis for distinguishing the few cases in which [the death penalty] is imposed from the many cases in which it is not."

The basic concern of *Furman* centered on those defendants who were being condemned to death capriciously and arbitrarily. Under the procedures before the Court in that case, sentencing authorities were not directed to give attention to the nature or circumstances of the crime committed or to the character or record of the defendant. Left unguided, juries imposed the death sentence in a way that could only be called freakish. The new Georgia sentencing procedures, by contrast, focus the jury's attention on the particularized nature of the crime and the particularized characteristics of the individual defendant. While the jury is permitted to consider any aggravating or mitigating circumstances, it must find and identify at least one statutory aggravating factor before it may impose a penalty of death. In this way the jury's discretion is channeled. No longer can a jury wantonly and freakishly impose the death sentence; it is always circumscribed by the legislative guidelines. In addition, the review function of the Supreme Court of Georgia affords additional assurance that the concerns that prompted our decision in *Furman* are not present to any significant degree in the Georgia procedure applied here. [The] statutory system under which Gregg was sentenced to death does not violate the Constitution.

Id. at 190-198, 206-207.

6. *Key features of approved death penalty schemes.*   Two of the other cases decided the same day as *Gregg* also upheld newly revised statutory schemes to impose the death penalty for some murders. See Jurek v. Texas, 428 U.S. 262 (1976); Proffitt v. Florida, 428 U.S. 242 (1976). The statutes involved in these three cases shared some important features. Each called for bifurcated proceedings, with a jury hearing the evidence relevant to the choice of punishment only

after deliberating and delivering a guilty verdict after trial. The statutes also specified aggravating factors for the jury to find as a prerequisite to the death penalty and provided for automatic review of the case in the state's appellate courts. While the Court stopped short of saying that any of these features was absolutely essential to the judgment that they satisfied the Eighth Amendment, each feature drew positive comment in the opinions. Ultimately, the Court's language in *Gregg* about the importance of "a carefully drafted statute that ensures that the sentencing authority is given adequate information and guidance," combined with the Court's rejection of a mandatory death sentencing scheme (detailed below), made it clear that a state's development of a system of "guided discretion" was central to the constitutionality of its use of the death penalty.

7. *Strategic litigation.*   Numerous commentators expected *Furman* to end the death penalty in the United States. Instead, the opposite occurred: the Court's decision reinvigorated capital punishment. To what extent is this a cautionary tale about using the Court to bring about social change? Compare Brown v. Board of Education, 349 U.S. 294 (1954) (striking down the existence of segregated elementary schools), and Roe v. Wade, 410 U.S. 113 (1973) (striking down Texas's absolute prohibition of abortions in cases where the mother's life was not at stake).

James Tyrone Woodson v. North Carolina
428 U.S. 280 (1976)

STEWART, J.

The question in this case is whether the imposition of a death sentence for the crime of first-degree murder under the law of North Carolina violates the Eighth and Fourteenth Amendments.

The petitioners, James Tyrone Woodson and Luby Waxton, were convicted of first-degree murder as the result of their participation in an armed robbery of a convenience food store, in the course of which the cashier was killed and a customer was seriously wounded. There were four participants in the robbery: the petitioners Woodson and Waxton and two others, Leonard Tucker and Johnnie Lee Carroll. At the petitioners' trial Tucker and Carroll testified for the prosecution after having been permitted to plead guilty to lesser offenses. . . . The petitioners were found guilty on all charges, and, as was required by statute, sentenced to death.

The North Carolina General Assembly in 1974 [after the invalidation of its death penalty statute in the wake of *Furman*] enacted a new statute that was essentially unchanged from the old one except that it made the death penalty mandatory. . . . It was under this statute that the petitioners were tried, convicted, and sentenced to death.

North Carolina, unlike Florida, Georgia, and Texas, has thus responded to the *Furman* decision by making death the mandatory sentence for all persons convicted of first-degree murder. . . . Although it seems beyond dispute that, at the time of the *Furman* decision in 1972, mandatory death penalty statutes had been renounced by American juries and legislatures, there remains the question whether the mandatory statutes adopted by North Carolina and a number of other States following *Furman* evince a sudden reversal of societal values regarding the imposition of capital punishment. In view of the persistent and unswerving legislative rejection of mandatory death penalty statutes beginning in 1838 and continuing for more than 130 years until *Furman*, it seems evident that the post-*Furman* enactments reflect attempts by the States to retain the death penalty in a form consistent with the Constitution, rather than a renewed societal acceptance of mandatory death sentencing. The fact that some States have adopted mandatory measures following *Furman* while others have legislated standards to guide jury discretion appears attributable to diverse readings of this Court's multi-opinioned decision in that case. . . .

It is now well established that the Eighth Amendment draws much of its meaning from "the evolving standards of decency that mark the progress of a maturing society." [One] of the most significant developments in our society's treatment of capital punishment has been the rejection of the common-law practice of inexorably imposing a death sentence upon every person convicted of a specified offense. North Carolina's mandatory death penalty statute for first-degree murder departs markedly from contemporary standards respecting the imposition of the punishment of death and thus cannot be applied consistently with the Eighth and Fourteenth Amendments' requirement that the State's power to punish "be exercised within the limits of civilized standards."

A separate deficiency of North Carolina's mandatory death sentence statute is its failure to provide a constitutionally tolerable response to *Furman*'s rejection of unbridled jury discretion in the imposition of capital sentences. Central to the limited holding in *Furman* was the conviction that the vesting of standardless sentencing power in the jury violated the Eighth and Fourteenth Amendments.

It is argued that North Carolina has remedied the inadequacies of the death penalty statutes held unconstitutional in *Furman* by withdrawing all sentencing discretion from juries in capital cases. But when one considers the long and consistent American experience with the death penalty in first-degree murder cases, it becomes evident that mandatory statutes enacted in response to *Furman* have simply papered over the problem of unguided and unchecked jury discretion. . . .

Instead of rationalizing the sentencing process, a mandatory scheme may well exacerbate the problem identified in *Furman* by resting the penalty determination on the particular jury's willingness to act lawlessly. While a mandatory death penalty statute may reasonably be expected to increase the number of persons sentenced to death, it does not fulfill *Furman*'s basic requirement by replacing arbitrary and wanton jury discretion with objective standards to guide, regularize, and make rationally reviewable the process for imposing a sentence of death.

A third constitutional shortcoming of the North Carolina statute is its failure to allow the particularized consideration of relevant aspects of the character and record of each convicted defendant before the imposition upon him of a sentence of death. In *Furman*, members of the Court acknowledged what cannot fairly be denied — that death is a punishment different from all other sanctions in kind rather than degree. A process that accords no significance to relevant facets of the character and record of the individual offender or the circumstances of the particular offense excludes from consideration in fixing the ultimate punishment of death the possibility of compassionate or mitigating factors stemming from the diverse frailties of humankind. It treats all persons convicted of a designated offense not as uniquely individual human beings, but as members of a faceless, undifferentiated mass to be subjected to the blind infliction of the penalty of death. . . .

Consideration of both the offender and the offense in order to arrive at a just and appropriate sentence has been viewed as a progressive and humanizing development. While the prevailing practice of individualizing sentencing determinations generally reflects simply enlightened policy rather than a constitutional imperative, we believe that in capital cases the fundamental respect for humanity underlying the Eighth Amendment requires consideration of the character and record of the individual offender and the circumstances of the particular offense as a constitutionally indispensable part of the process of inflicting the penalty of death.

This conclusion rests squarely on the predicate that the penalty of death is qualitatively different from a sentence of imprisonment, however long. Death, in its finality, differs more from life imprisonment than a 100-year prison term differs from one of only a year or two. Because of that qualitative difference, there is a corresponding difference in the need for reliability in the determination that death is the appropriate punishment in a specific case.

For the reasons stated, we conclude that the death sentences imposed upon the petitioners under North Carolina's mandatory death sentence statute violated the Eighth and Fourteenth Amendments and therefore must be set aside. . . .

REHNQUIST, J., dissenting.

[The plurality's holding] will result in the invalidation of a death sentence imposed upon a defendant convicted of first-degree murder under the North Carolina system, and the upholding of the same sentence imposed on an identical defendant convicted on identical evidence of first-degree murder under the Florida, Georgia, or Texas systems, a result surely as "freakish" as that condemned in the separate opinions in *Furman*. . . .

In any event, while the imposition of such unlimited consideration of mitigating factors may conform to the plurality's novel constitutional doctrine that a "jury must be allowed to consider on the basis of all relevant evidence not only why a death sentence should be imposed, but also why it should not be imposed," the resulting system seems as likely as any to produce the unbridled discretion which was condemned by the separate opinions in *Furman*. The plurality seems to believe that provision for appellate review will afford a check upon the instances of juror arbitrariness in a discretionary system. But it is not at all apparent that appellate review of death sentences, through a process of comparing the facts of one case in which a death sentence was imposed with the facts of another in which such a sentence was not imposed, will afford any meaningful protection against whatever arbitrariness results from jury discretion. . . .

The plurality's insistence on "standards" to "guide the jury in its inevitable exercise of the power to determine which . . . murderers shall live and which shall die" is squarely contrary to the Court's opinion in *McGautha*. . . . So is the plurality's latter-day recognition . . . that *Furman* requires "objective standards to guide, regularize, and make rationally reviewable the process for imposing a sentence of death." . . . The plurality's insistence on individualized consideration of the sentencing . . . does not depend upon any traditional application of the prohibition against cruel and unusual punishment contained in the Eighth Amendment. . . . What the plurality opinion has actually done is to import into the Due Process Clause of the Fourteenth Amendment what it conceives to be desirable procedural guarantees where the punishment of death, concededly not cruel and unusual for the crime of which the defendant was convicted, is to be imposed. . . .

NOTES

1. *Mandatory death penalty.* In Louisiana v. Roberts, 428 U.S. 325 (1976), a companion case decided the same day as *Woodson* and *Gregg*, the Court struck down another capital sentencing statute that made the death penalty mandatory for five narrowly defined categories of first-degree murder (and also required juries to be instructed on manslaughter and second-degree murder even if there was no evidence to support such a verdict). Together, *Woodson* and *Roberts* established that the Supreme Court would not let states respond to *Furman's* concerns about standardless jury discretion by creating mandatory death penalty systems that simply eliminated jury discretion. In subsequent cases, the Supreme Court ultimately ruled that no form of mandatory death penalty could be constitutional. See Sumner v. Shuman, 483 U.S. 66 (1987) (invalidating a mandatory death penalty statute for life-term inmates convicted of murder).

Isn't a mandatory sentencing system the best way to deal with *Furman's* concerns about arbitrary and potentially discriminatory exercise of juries' capital sentencing discretion? Is the requirement of individualization propounded in *Woodson* and *Roberts* really a constitutional necessity, or just a good idea? Compare the decision of the Judicial Committee of the English Privy Council upholding Singapore's mandatory death penalty statute for certain drug offenses, in which it distinguished legal guilt and moral guilt. The Privy Council did not find Singapore in violation of its equality and due process provisions because "the Constitution is not concerned with equal punitive treatment for equal moral blameworthiness; it is concerned with equal punitive treatment for similar legal guilt." Ong Ah Chuan v. Public Prosecutor, [1981] A.C. 648, 674 (P.C.). Subsequent Privy Council decisions, however, superseded that case. By 2006 the Privy Council had rejected the mandatory death sentence for murder in almost all the cases that came before it, so that it is now outlawed in all the English-speaking countries in the Caribbean, with the exception of two.

2. *Categorical exclusion of certain offenses.* In Coker v. Georgia, 433 U.S. 584 (1977), the Supreme Court struck down the death penalty as a sentencing option in the rape of an adult woman; as in *Furman*, the constitutional basis for the decision was the Eighth Amendment's prohibition of cruel and unusual punishments. Since then only murder convictions have led to death sentences. In addition, through a series of cases culminating in Tison v. Arizona, 481 U.S. 137 (1987), the Supreme Court held that only killers with a mens rea of reckless

indifference to human life or worse are sufficiently culpable to be constitutionally subject to the death penalty.

If no crime can trigger a mandatory death sentence, on what basis should a court hold categorically that certain crimes can never be eligible for the death penalty? By what yardstick can and should the Supreme Court determine whether a particularly heinous crime, such as the rape of a young child or attempted murder of a police officer, can justify the death penalty? Some states believe there are offenses other than murder for which death might be the appropriate sanction; at present five states, for example, permit death as punishment for the rape of a minor. See La. Rev. Stat. §14:42(D)(2)(a). The Louisiana Supreme Court upheld the statute in State v. Kennedy, 957 So. 2d 757 (La. 2007). Should such proportionality determinations be the province of the legislature? Do you see any link between the concerns expressed in *Furman* about the arbitrary imposition of the death penalty and the categorical exclusion of certain offenses from capital punishment?

The federal system allows for the death penalty in cases of treason and terrorism, as do some of the states. During wartime the death penalty may be imposed in cases of desertion. Many European states that have otherwise abolished capital punishment have retained the death penalty during times of war. Almost 40 countries, however, have already ratified Protocol 13 of the European Convention of Human Rights (effective in 2002), which outlaws capital punishment even during wartime. Why should there be an exception to the prohibition on capital punishment during wartime?

3. *Categorical exclusion of certain offenders.* In 2002 the Supreme Court outlawed execution of the mentally retarded because it violates the Eighth Amendment's prohibition of cruel and unusual punishments. The decision in Atkins v. Virginia, 536 U.S. 304 (2002), reversed the Court's prior decision in Penry v. Lynaugh, 492 U.S. 302 (1989), which had held that the Constitution did allow the execution of mentally retarded individuals. The Court's reversal in *Atkins* reflected the shift in legislative thinking since the *Penry* decision in 1989: during those years, nearly half the states that authorize capital punishment had removed offenders with mental retardation from the reach of the death penalty. Researchers estimate that since the death penalty was reinstated in 1976, at least 35 people with mental retardation had been executed in the United States before the Supreme Court declared this punishment unconstitutional in *Atkins*. The *Atkins* Court found mentally retarded offenders categorically less culpable than others, and therefore ineligible for capital punishment.

Do you see any link between the concerns expressed in *Furman* about the arbitrary imposition of the death penalty and the categorical exclusion of certain offenders from capital punishment? Is there any risk that the definition of "mental retardation" could lead to further inequities in the application of capital punishment? The Supreme Court in *Atkins* left it to states to define which individuals are mentally retarded and thus exempt from capital punishment. As a legislator, how might you draft a definition of mental retardation to minimize disparate application of the death penalty? See People v. Superior Court (Vidal), 155 P.3d 259 (Cal. 2007).

Through another pair of cases in the late 1980s, the Supreme Court held that the Constitution does not permit the execution of an offender who was age

15 or younger at the time of his or her crime, but that it does allow the execution
of an offender who was 16 or older at the time of the crime. See Stanford v.
Kentucky, 492 U.S. 362 (1989) (allowing execution of 16- and 17-year-old killers); Thompson v. Oklahoma, 487 U.S. 815 (1988) (prohibiting execution of
killers age 15 or younger). Between 1976 and the beginning of 2003, 22 men
were executed for crimes committed as juveniles; by 2004 there were 80 inmates
on death row (all male) who were sentenced as juveniles, constituting about 2%
of the total death row population. At that point the United States was one of the
few countries in the world that still executed juvenile offenders. Article 6(5) of
the International Covenant on Civil and Political Rights—which the United
States ratified with a reservation to Article 6(5)—requires that a sentence
of death "not be imposed for crimes committed by persons below eighteen
years of age."

In its decision in Roper v. Simmons, 543 U.S. 551 (2005), discussed more
fully in Chapter 5, the Supreme Court overruled *Stanford* and declared unconstitutional the execution of those who committed capital offenses while under
the age of 18. The Court found, as it had in *Atkins*, that for juveniles the death
penalty "is a disproportionate punishment" and that a national consensus, supported by international law, had developed against such executions.

Does the categorical exclusion of 17-year-olds not deprive juries of the
individualized decision making that the Court demands in its case law? Why
should juries not be permitted to decide whether individual offenders who
were under 18 at the time they committed their crimes are sufficiently culpable
and depraved to deserve the death penalty? Is the difference between a 17- and
an 18-year-old sufficient to justify such differential treatment?

Sandra Lockett v. Ohio
438 U.S. 586 (1978)

Burger, C.J.

We granted certiorari in this case to consider, among other questions,
whether Ohio violated the Eighth and Fourteenth Amendments by sentencing
Sandra Lockett to death pursuant to a statute that narrowly limits the sentencer's discretion to consider the circumstances of the crime and the record and
character of the offender as mitigating factors. . . .

Lockett [suggested to acquaintances Al Parker and Nathan Earl Dew] that
they could get some money by robbing a grocery store and a furniture store in
the area[, and she] also volunteered to get a gun from her father's basement to
aid in carrying out the robberies. . . . Lockett's brother [later] suggested a plan
for robbing a pawnshop. . . . No one planned to kill the pawnshop operator in
the course of the robbery. Because she knew the owner, Lockett was not . . .
among those entering the pawnshop, though she did guide the others to the
shop that night. The robbery proceeded according to plan until the pawnbroker
grabbed the gun when Parker announced the "stickup." The gun went off . . .
firing a fatal shot into the pawnbroker, and Parker went back to the car where
Lockett waited with the engine running. . . .

Parker was subsequently apprehended and charged with aggravated
murder with specifications, an offense punishable by death, and aggravated

robbery. Prior to trial, he pleaded guilty to the murder charge and agreed to testify against Lockett, her brother, and Dew. In return, the prosecutor dropped the aggravated robbery charge and the specifications to the murder charge, thereby eliminating the possibility that Parker could receive the death penalty. . . . Two weeks before Lockett's separate trial, the prosecutor offered to permit her to plead guilty to voluntary manslaughter and aggravated robbery (offenses which each carried a maximum penalty of 25 years' imprisonment and a maximum fine of $10,000) if she would cooperate with the State, but she rejected the offer. . . .

Once a verdict of aggravated murder with specifications had been returned, the Ohio death penalty statute required the trial judge to impose a death sentence unless, after "considering the nature and circumstances of the offense" and Lockett's "history, character, and condition," he found by a preponderance of the evidence that (1) the victim had induced or facilitated the offense, (2) it was unlikely that Lockett would have committed the offense but for the fact that she "was under duress, coercion, or strong provocation," or (3) the offense was "primarily the product of [Lockett's] psychosis or mental deficiency." . . . After considering the reports and hearing argument on the penalty issue, the trial judge concluded that the offense had not been primarily the product of psychosis or mental deficiency. Without specifically addressing the other two statutory mitigating factors, the judge said that he had "no alternative, whether [he liked] the law or not" but to impose the death penalty. He then sentenced Lockett to death. . . .

Lockett challenges the constitutionality of Ohio's death penalty statute [based on the fact that it] did not permit the sentencing judge to consider, as mitigating factors, her character, prior record, age, lack of specific intent to cause death, and her relatively minor part in the crime. . . .

Prior to Furman v. Georgia, 408 U.S. 238 (1972), every State that authorized capital punishment had abandoned mandatory death penalties, and instead permitted the jury unguided and unrestrained discretion regarding the imposition of the death penalty in a particular capital case. . . . The constitutional status of discretionary sentencing in capital cases changed abruptly, however, as a result of the separate opinions supporting the judgment in Furman. . . . In the last decade, many of the States have been obliged to revise their death penalty statutes in response to the various opinions supporting the judgments in Furman and Gregg and its companion cases. The signals from this Court have not, however, always been easy to decipher. The States now deserve the clearest guidance that the Court can provide; we have an obligation to reconcile previously differing views in order to provide that guidance. With that obligation in mind we turn to Lockett's attack on the Ohio statute. Essentially she contends that the Eighth and Fourteenth Amendments require that the sentencer be given a full opportunity to consider mitigating circumstances in capital cases and that the Ohio statute does not comply with that requirement. She relies, in large part, on the plurality opinions in Woodson. . . .

Although legislatures remain free to decide how much discretion in sentencing should be reposed in the judge or jury in noncapital cases, the plurality opinion in Woodson, after reviewing the historical repudiation of mandatory sentencing in capital cases, concluded that "in capital cases the fundamental respect for humanity underlying the Eighth Amendment . . . requires consideration of the character and record of the individual offender and the circumstances of the particular offense as a constitutionally indispensable part of the process of inflicting the penalty of death." That declaration rested "on the predicate that the penalty of death is qualitatively different" from any other sentence. We are satisfied that this qualitative difference between death and other penalties calls for a greater degree of reliability when the death sentence is imposed. The mandatory death penalty statute in *Woodson* was held invalid because it permitted *no* consideration of "relevant facets of the character and record of the individual offender or the circumstances of the particular offense." The plurality did not attempt to indicate, however, which facets of an offender or his offense it deemed "relevant" in capital sentencing or what degree of consideration of "relevant facets" it would require.

We are now faced with those questions and we conclude that the Eighth and Fourteenth Amendments require that the sentencer, in all but the rarest kind of capital case, not be precluded from considering, *as a mitigating factor*, any aspect of a defendant's character or record and any of the circumstances of the offense that the defendant proffers as a basis for a sentence less than death. We recognize that, in noncapital cases, the established practice of individualized sentences rests not on constitutional commands, but on public policy enacted into statutes. The considerations that account for the wide acceptance of individualization of sentences in noncapital cases surely cannot be thought less important in capital cases. Given that the imposition of death by public authority is so profoundly different from all other penalties, we cannot avoid the conclusion that an individualized decision is essential in capital cases. The need for treating each defendant in a capital case with that degree of respect due the uniqueness of the individual is far more important than in noncapital cases. A variety of flexible techniques — probation, parole, work furloughs, to name a few — and various postconviction remedies may be available to modify an initial sentence of confinement in noncapital cases. The nonavailability of corrective or modifying mechanisms with respect to an executed capital sentence underscores the need for individualized consideration as a constitutional requirement in imposing the death sentence.

There is no perfect procedure for deciding in which cases governmental authority should be used to impose death. But a statute that prevents the sentencer in all capital cases from giving independent mitigating weight to aspects of the defendant's character and record and to circumstances of the offense proffered in mitigation creates the risk that the death penalty will be imposed in spite of factors which may call for a less severe penalty. When the choice is between life and death, that risk is unacceptable and incompatible with the commands of the Eighth and Fourteenth Amendments. . . .

NOTES

1. *Access to mitigating evidence.* In a series of cases, the Court elaborated on the basic holding of *Lockett*, that a capital jury must have access to a wide range of information about the crime and the offender's character and background. Just as the statutory language at issue in *Lockett* unduly limited access, jury instructions or evidentiary rulings could create the same problem. See Eddings v.

Oklahoma, 455 U.S. 104 (1982) (court's instructions wrongly told jury to ignore nonstatutory mitigating evidence); Skipper v. South Carolina, 476 U.S. 1 (1986) (defendant can put in evidence of good behavior in prison to demonstrate nondangerousness). Defense counsel must also have access to the aggravating evidence that the prosecutor plans to present, to prepare for cross-examination or other testing of its accuracy. See Gardner v. Florida, 430 U.S. 349 (1977) (defense counsel must have access to all information in the presentence investigation report provided to the sentencer, based on right to confrontation).

2. *Instructions to underscore mitigating evidence.*   Some Supreme Court rulings have required the trial judge not only to give the jury access to mitigating evidence but also to instruct the jury to take special care in considering certain kinds of mitigating evidence, such as the youth of the offender. See Penry v. Lynaugh, 492 U.S. 302 (1989) (stressing the necessity of instructions that inform the jury how to "consider and give effect" to mitigating evidence so that the jury is "provided with a vehicle for expressing its reasoned moral response to that evidence"); Abdul-Kabir v. Quarterman, 127 S. Ct. 1654 (2007) (special instructions to jury necessary when defendant's mitigation evidence may have meaningful relevance to defendant's moral culpability and jury could not otherwise give meaningful effect to such evidence). Another series of cases provides that trial judges in capital cases have a special obligation to instruct the jury on lesser included offenses. See Beck v. Alabama, 447 U.S. 625 (1980) (court must instruct on lesser included offense whenever a jury issue as to that offense is present); Schad v. Arizona, 501 U.S. 624 (1991) (enough to instruct on second-degree murder but not theft; jury not faced with all-or-nothing choice).

3. *Access to aggravating evidence.*   After having established that defendants have a broad right to present all sorts of mitigating evidence to the capital sentencing decision maker, the Supreme Court faced cases in which prosecutors argued that they should have similarly broad rights to present all sorts of aggravating evidence. These dynamics had perhaps their greatest impact in Payne v. Tennessee, 501 U.S. 808 (1991), in which the Supreme Court overruled two prior holdings that had limited victim impact evidence in capital cases. Following *Payne,* capital sentencing juries are allowed to receive victim impact evidence relating to the personal characteristics of the murder victim and the emotional impact of the death on the victim's family, and prosecutors are allowed to make statements about the personal qualities of the victim.

4. *Impact of individualization on women.*   Capital prosecutions involving women are extremely rare, and the execution of women rarer still. Though women account for about 1 in 10 murder arrests, they account for only 1 in 52 death sentences imposed at the trial level; of more than 850 persons executed since *Furman,* only 10 have been women. See Victor L. Streib, Gendering the Death Penalty: Countering Sex Bias in a Masculine Sanctuary, 63 Ohio St. L.J. 433 (2002). Usually, such capital cases involve women who killed their children or who are serial killers. The execution in Texas in 1999 of Karla Faye Tucker — who was involved in a brutal double murder when under the influence of a drug addiction, but then became a model prisoner after more than a decade on death row — led to widespread national and international protests. Though it usually does not join international agreements that restrict the use of the death penalty,

the United States has signed on to the global ban on executing pregnant women.

What factors may account for the apparent gender disparity in executions? Are female offenders presumed to be less threatening? Is the execution of a woman viewed as particularly repulsive? Or does the execution of women perhaps pose different issues compared with the execution of men, differences that might come to light when we consider the battered-spouse syndrome or the presence of young children?

5. *Inevitability of failure?* Many observers have noted a tension in the Supreme Court's capital punishment cases decided under the Eighth Amendment. On one hand, cases such as *Furman* and *Gregg* emphasize the importance of guiding or structuring the sentencing jury's discretion through the use of statutory aggravating factors, bifurcated proceedings, appellate review, and other legal controls. On the other hand, cases such as *Woodson* and *Lockett* insist that the decision to impose the death penalty must be individualized, and legal rules must not unduly restrict the information the jury receives about the case or the ability of individual jurors to act on that information. Does the current Eighth Amendment jurisprudence reconcile these competing ambitions? If such a goal is beyond reach, how should judges and other decision makers in the legal system respond? Justices Blackmun and Scalia debated this question in Callins v. Collins, 510 U.S. 1141 (1994). Although the Court denied the petition for writ of certiorari in the case, Justice Blackmun dissented and explained the dilemma he faced in death cases:

> [The] problems that were pursued down one hole with procedural rules and verbal formulas have come to the surface somewhere else, just as virulent and pernicious as they were in their original form. Experience has taught us that the constitutional goal of eliminating arbitrariness and discrimination from the administration of death can never be achieved without compromising an equally essential component of fundamental fairness — individualized sentencing.

Blackmun returned to themes explored in the "partly prophetic" opinion of Justice Harlan in *McGautha*, agreeing that to "identify before the fact those characteristics of criminal homicides and their perpetrators which call for the death penalty" appears to be a task "beyond human ability." Blackmun noted the varying efforts states made to address *Furman*'s constitutional barrier by guiding jury discretion but found that none could balance "fairness to the individual . . . without sacrificing the consistency and rationality promised in *Furman*." Although *Furman, Gregg,* and *Lockett* attempted to strike a balance between consistent sentencing and individualized sentencing in the capital context, Blackmun declared that effort a failure:

> In the first stage of capital sentencing, the demands of *Furman* are met by "narrowing" the class of death-eligible offenders according to objective, fact-bound characteristics of the defendant or the circumstances of the offense. Once the pool of death-eligible defendants has been reduced, the sentencer retains the discretion to consider whatever relevant mitigating evidence the defendant chooses to offer.
>
> Over time, I have come to conclude that even this approach is unacceptable: It simply reduces, rather than eliminates, the number of people subject to

arbitrary sentencing. It is the decision to sentence a defendant to death — not merely the decision to make a defendant eligible for death — that may not be arbitrary. While one might hope that providing the sentencer with as much relevant mitigating evidence as possible will lead to more rational and consistent sentences, experience has taught otherwise. It seems that the decision whether a human being should live or die is so inherently subjective — rife with all of life's understandings, experiences, prejudices, and passions — that it inevitably defies the rationality and consistency required by the Constitution.

Summarizing his views, Blackmun explained that "[e]xperience has shown that the consistency and rationality promised in *Furman* are inversely related to the fairness owed the individual when considering a sentence of death. A step toward consistency is a step away from fairness." And this failure to reconcile the requirements of consistency and individualized fairness, in Blackmun's view, caused the Court to "retreat" from its earlier ambitious efforts to regulate discretion, "allowing relevant mitigating evidence to be discarded, vague aggravating circumstances to be employed, and providing no indication that the problem of race in the administration of death will ever be addressed." Blackmun declared himself unwilling to continue to play a part in this enterprise:

> From this day forward, I no longer shall tinker with the machinery of death. For more than 20 years I have endeavored — indeed, I have struggled — along with a majority of this Court, to develop procedural and substantive rules that would lend more than the mere appearance of fairness to the death penalty endeavor. Rather than continue to coddle the Court's delusion that the desired level of fairness has been achieved and the need for regulation eviscerated, I feel morally and intellectually obligated simply to concede that the death penalty experiment has failed. . . .

Justice Scalia agreed with Justice Blackmun that the competing aspirations of the Court's Eighth Amendment jurisprudence could not be reconciled, but he argued for a different response to this dilemma. Because the text of the Constitution, in the Fifth and Eighth Amendments, indicates that the use of the death penalty is a legitimate criminal punishment, he argued that the Court had no business blocking the government from using this sanction. Instead of declaring that the death penalty cannot be administered in accord with the Constitution, Scalia urged the Court to reach a different conclusion:

> Though Justice Blackmun joins those of us who have acknowledged the incompatibility of the Court's *Furman* and *Lockett* lines of jurisprudence, he unfortunately draws the wrong conclusion for the acknowledgment. [At] least one of these judicially announced irreconcilable commands which cause the Constitution to prohibit what its text explicitly permits must be wrong. Convictions in opposition to the death penalty are often passionate and deeply held. That would be no excuse for reading them into a Constitution that does not contain them, even if they represented the convictions of a majority of Americans. . . . If the people conclude that . . . brutal deaths may be deterred by capital punishment — indeed, if they merely conclude that justice requires such brutal deaths to be avenged by capital punishment — the creation of false, untexual, and unhistorical contradictions within "the Court's Eighth Amendment jurisprudence" should not prevent them.

Do you agree with Justice Blackmun's reasoning, or is Justice Scalia's resolution of this conundrum more satisfactory? Or are both Justices wrong to conclude that the competing aspirations of consistency and individualized sentencing cannot be balanced in an acceptable way? Does not much, if not all, of what Justice Blackmun says about the tensions between consistency and individualized fairness in the application of the death penalty also apply to other sanctions?

3. Capital Discretion in Operation

There is often a profound gap between the law on paper and the law in practice. The same is true of capital punishment, for two important reasons: (1) the constitutional rules established by the Supreme Court provide only broad parameters for the structure of capital sentencing, so particular capital statutes in individual states determine the rules under which death penalty systems actually operate; and (2) although statutory provisions structure how states apply the death penalty, the way these provisions are understood and applied by prosecutors, defense counsel, juries, and judges determine the day-to-day operation of the death penalty.

Both legal and social factors have significantly affected the operation of the death penalty since the Supreme Court's 1976 decision in *Gregg*. Most tangibly, 12 states (nearly all in the northern parts of the United States) and the District of Columbia do not authorize capital punishment, and thus the law precludes the operation of the death penalty in these jurisdictions. In the 38 other states (and in the federal system), the use of capital punishment varies dramatically in terms of both the number of persons sentenced to death and the number of executions carried out. Applying either metric, Southern states — particularly Texas and Florida — have been national leaders. Between 1976 and mid-2007, Texas executed almost 400 persons, almost four times more than any other state, and had another 400 defendants on death row. Some states, notably California, Pennsylvania, and Ohio, have sentenced many offenders to death but have carried out relatively few executions. Other states, such as Virginia and Missouri, have carried out a large number of executions but have relatively small death row populations. Overall, the number of death sentences imposed has been declining over the last few years in every state, including Texas.

The impact of appellate review in capital cases can explain some of the differences among states in the number of death sentences imposed and the number of executions carried out. As detailed more fully in Chapter 11, typically both state and federal courts review every death sentence imposed, although the rigor of this review varies greatly by court and region. In total, since *Gregg*, over 7,000 death sentences have been imposed, and more than half of these sentences have been reversed on appeal. Since 1999 the number of death sentences imposed has declined dramatically every year. As of January 2007, 3,350 defendants were on death row and almost 1,100 persons have been executed since 1976.

When state legislatures during the years after 1976 created acceptable systems of capital punishment, they based their decisions on some speculation about how prosecutors, jurors, defense lawyers, defendants, judges, and the public would respond. In other words, efforts by courts and legislatures to regulate capital sentencing discretion often relied on a variety of assumptions about how this discretion is exercised. As you review the material in the rest of this chapter, consider whether the capital sentencing structures that emerged as a result of the Supreme Court's regulatory efforts have effectively addressed the problems of arbitrariness that the Court identified in *Furman.*

a.   Statutory Schemes

State legislatures responded to the various opinions in *Furman* with different strategies for limiting the sentencer's discretion to choose a lengthy prison term or death. As detailed above, the Supreme Court ultimately ruled unconstitutional the efforts by some states to make the death penalty mandatory for certain crimes, and it also required states to allow the consideration of nearly all mitigating circumstances. Other than these basic requirements, however, states have fairly broad latitude in deciding how to structure death penalty decisions. Some states reserve the decision exclusively to a jury, while others allow the judge to make the choice after the jury renders an advisory verdict. Some statutes provide lengthy lists of aggravating and mitigating factors, while others set forth much shorter lists or none at all.

The statutes in operation throughout the various states generally adopt two or three distinct strategies to guide sentencing discretion. Some states, including Georgia, are known as "threshold" states. Their statutes require jurors to find beyond a reasonable doubt at least one aggravating factor from the list included in the statute; after crossing that threshold, the jurors are free to impose life or death without further instructions. The largest group of states, including Florida, use "balancing" statutes. These laws require jurors to determine the presence or absence of aggravating and mitigating factors specified in the statute, and then to balance the aggravating factors against the mitigating factors. In some of these states, the jury is instructed to impose a death penalty if the aggravating factors outweigh the mitigating factors; in others, the jury remains free to impose a life term even if the aggravating factors weigh more heavily than the mitigating factors. Finally, a third group of "directive" or "limiting" states, including Texas, give further structure to the jury's decision by presenting a sequence of special questions to the jury (often related to the future dangerousness of the offender) that supposedly determine the jury's decision on death or life.

The following problem provides an opportunity to observe how different capital sentencing statutes operate in the context of a specific case. As you work through the problem, consider whether these death penalty statutes sufficiently address the problems and other issues that lay behind the Supreme Court's decisions and reasoning in *Furman, Gregg,* and the other early constitutional cases.

PROBLEM 3-3.   CHOOSE YOUR POISON

During the 1980s and 1990s, Theodore Kaczynski sent a series of bombs through the mail, and a number of them exploded and killed the recipients of the packages. Kaczynski selected as his victims key figures in universities and in transportation, advertising, and high-technology firms because he believed that the reliance on computers and other technological devices was a disastrous trend for modern society, a trend he hoped his bombs would reverse. Kaczynski became known as the "Unabomber." Using this name, he wrote lengthy letters to major newspapers from time to time, explaining his views on the evils of technology and modern life and his reasons for sending the bombs. After years of investigation, authorities found the Unabomber in a small cabin in Montana, and the federal government charged him with several counts of murder. As the proceedings moved along, it became clear that there was some question about Kaczynski's sanity, and prosecutors decided to accept a guilty plea in exchange for a sentence of life in prison without possibility of parole.

This outcome proved unsatisfactory to some prosecutors in states where victims were killed; they still want a piece of the action. Imagine now that prosecutors from Texas and Florida can establish jurisdiction in their states and have contacted the U.S. Attorney General, asking for custody of Kaczynski to try him for murder in their states. (The law of double jeopardy allows states to prosecute a person for a crime even after the federal government has obtained a conviction for that same crime, but the state authorities must have physical custody of Kaczynski before proceeding with a murder trial.)

Lawyers serving on Kaczynski's appointed defense team have asked for your advice about which jurisdiction they should choose to assume custody. (The team has explained to you that the Attorney General feels obliged to allow one state to try Kaczynski but is eager to minimize legal battles over this case now that the federal charges have been resolved. Consequently, the Attorney General wants a transfer decision to have defense counsel's acquiescence in order to avoid any legal challenges.) Read the two statutes that follow, then give the defense lawyers your best advice about the prospects for the government in obtaining a death sentence under each statute. Do the different statutes impact aggravating and mitigating evidence that will be considered or emphasized at trial?

‖ Texas Code of Criminal Procedure, Art. 37.071 ‖

Section 1. If a defendant is found guilty in a capital felony case in which the state does not seek the death penalty, the judge shall sentence the defendant to life imprisonment without parole.

Section 2. (a) (1) If a defendant is tried for a capital offense in which the state seeks the death penalty, on a finding that the defendant is guilty of a capital offense, the court shall conduct a separate sentencing proceeding to determine whether the defendant shall be sentenced to death or life imprisonment without parole. The proceeding shall be conducted in the trial court and . . . before the trial jury as soon as practicable. In the proceeding, evidence may be presented by the state and the defendant or the defendant's counsel as to any matter that the court deems relevant to sentence, including evidence of the defendant's background or character or the circumstances of the offense that mitigates against the imposition of the death penalty. This subdivision shall not be construed to authorize the introduction of any evidence secured in violation of the Constitution of the United States or of the State of Texas. The state and the defendant or the defendant's counsel shall be permitted to present argument for or against sentence of death. . . . The court, the attorney representing the state, the defendant, or the defendant's counsel may not inform a juror or a prospective juror of the effect of a failure of a jury to agree on issues submitted under Subsection (c) or (e). . . .

(b) On conclusion of the presentation of the evidence, the court shall submit the following issues to the jury:

(1) whether there is a probability that the defendant would commit criminal acts of violence that would constitute a continuing threat to society; and

(2) in cases in which the jury charge at the guilt or innocence stage permitted the jury to find the defendant guilty as [an accomplice], whether the defendant actually caused the death of the deceased or did not actually cause the death of the deceased but intended to kill the deceased or another or anticipated that a human life would be taken.

(c) The state must prove each issue submitted under Subsection (b) of this article beyond a reasonable doubt, and the jury shall return a special verdict of "yes" or "no" on each issue submitted under Subsection (b) of this Article.

(d) The court shall charge the jury that:

(1) in deliberating on the issues submitted under Subsection (b) of this article, it shall consider all evidence admitted at the guilt or innocence stage and the punishment stage, including evidence of the defendant's background or character or the circumstances of the offense that militates for or mitigates against the imposition of the death penalty;

(2) it may not answer any issue submitted under Subsection (b) of this article "yes" unless it agrees unanimously and it may not answer any issue "no" unless 10 or more jurors agree; and

(3) members of the jury need not agree on what particular evidence supports a negative answer to any issue submitted under Subsection (b) of this article.

(e)(1) The court shall instruct the jury that if the jury returns an affirmative finding to each issue submitted under Subsection (b), it shall answer the following issue:

Whether, taking into consideration all of the evidence, including the circumstances of the offense, the defendant's character and background, and the personal moral culpability of the defendant, there is a sufficient mitigating circumstance or circumstances to warrant that a sentence of life imprisonment rather than a death sentence be imposed. . . .

(2) The court shall:

(A) instruct the jury that if the jury answers that a circumstance or circumstances warrant that a sentence of life imprisonment without parole rather than a death sentence be imposed, the court will sentence the defendant to imprisonment . . . for life without parole; and

(B) charge the jury that a defendant sentenced to confinement for life without parole under this article is ineligible for release. . . .

(f) The court shall charge the jury that in answering the issue submitted under Subsection (e) of this article, the jury:

(1) shall answer the issue "yes" or "no";

(2) may not answer the issue "no" unless it agrees unanimously and may not answer the issue "yes" unless 10 or more jurors agree;

(3) need not agree on what particular evidence supports an affirmative finding on the issue; and

(4) shall consider mitigating evidence to be evidence that a juror might regard as reducing the defendant's moral blameworthiness.

(g) If the jury returns an affirmative finding on each issue submitted under Subsection (b) of this article and a negative finding on an issue submitted under Subsection (e)(1) of this article, the court shall sentence the defendant to death. If the jury returns a negative finding on any issue submitted under Subsection (b) of this article or an affirmative finding on an issue submitted under Subsection (e)(1) or is unable to answer any issue submitted under Subsection (b) or (e), the court shall sentence the defendant to confinement in the institutional division of the Texas Department of Criminal Justice for life imprisonment without parole.

(h) The judgment of conviction and sentence of death shall be subject to automatic review by the Court of Criminal Appeals.

‖ *Florida Statutes Annotated §921.141* ‖

(1) *Separate proceedings on issue of penalty.* Upon conviction or adjudication of guilt of a defendant of a capital felony, the court shall conduct a separate sentencing proceeding to determine whether the defendant should be sentenced to death or life imprisonment. . . . The proceeding shall be conducted by the trial judge before the trial jury as soon as practicable. . . . If the trial jury has been waived, or if the defendant pleaded guilty, the sentencing proceeding shall be conducted before a jury impaneled for that purpose, unless waived by the defendant. In the proceeding, evidence may be presented as to any matter that the court deems relevant to the nature of the crime and the character of the defendant and shall include matters relating to any of the aggravating or mitigating circumstances enumerated in subsections (5) and (6). Any such evidence which the court deems to have probative value may be received, regardless of its admissibility under the exclusionary rules of evidence, provided the defendant is accorded a fair opportunity to rebut any hearsay statements. However, this subsection shall not be construed to authorize the introduction of any evidence secured in violation of the Constitution of the United States or the Constitution of the State of Florida. The state and the defendant or the defendant's counsel shall be permitted to present argument for or against sentence of death.

(2) *Advisory sentence by the jury.* After hearing all the evidence, the jury shall deliberate and render an advisory sentence to the court, based upon the following matters:

(a) Whether sufficient aggravating circumstances exist as enumerated in subsection (5);

(b) Whether sufficient mitigating circumstances exist which outweigh the aggravating circumstances found to exist; and

(c) Based on these considerations, whether the defendant should be sentenced to life imprisonment or death.

(3) *Findings in support of sentence of death.*   Notwithstanding the recommendation of a majority of the jury, the court, after weighing the aggravating and mitigating circumstances, shall enter a sentence of life imprisonment or death, but if the court imposes a sentence of death, it shall set forth in writing its findings upon which the sentence of death is based as to the facts:

(a) That sufficient aggravating circumstances exist as enumerated in subsection (5), and

(b) That there are insufficient mitigating circumstances to outweigh the aggravating circumstances.

In each case in which the court imposes the death sentence, the determination of the court shall be supported by specific written findings of fact based upon the circumstances in subsections (5) and (6) and upon the records of the trial and the sentencing proceedings. If the court does not make the findings requiring the death sentence within 30 days after the rendition of the judgment and sentence, the court shall impose sentence of life imprisonment. . . .

(4) *Review of judgment and sentence.*   The judgment of conviction and sentence of death shall be subject to automatic review by the Supreme Court of Florida and disposition rendered within 2 years after the filing of a notice of appeal. Such review by the Supreme Court shall have priority over all other cases and shall be heard in accordance with rules promulgated by the Supreme Court.

(5) *Aggravating circumstances.*   Aggravating circumstances shall be limited to the following:

(a) The capital felony was committed by a person previously convicted of a felony and under sentence of imprisonment or placed on community control or on felony probation.

(b) The defendant was previously convicted of another capital felony or of a felony involving the use or threat of violence to the person.

(c) The defendant knowingly created a great risk of death to many persons.

(d) The capital felony was committed while the defendant was engaged, or was an accomplice, in the commission of, or an attempt to commit, or flight after committing or attempting to commit, any: robbery; sexual battery; aggravated child abuse; abuse of an elderly person or disabled adult resulting in great bodily harm, permanent disability, or permanent disfigurement; arson; burglary; kidnapping; aircraft piracy; or unlawful throwing, placing, or discharging of a destructive device or bomb.

(e) The capital felony was committed for the purpose of avoiding or preventing a lawful arrest or effecting an escape from custody.

(f) The capital felony was committed for pecuniary gain.

(g) The capital felony was committed to disrupt or hinder the lawful exercise of any governmental function or the enforcement of laws.

(h) The capital felony was especially heinous, atrocious, or cruel.

(i) The capital felony was a homicide and was committed in a cold, calculated, and premeditated manner without any pretense of moral or legal justification.

(j) The victim of the capital felony was a law enforcement officer engaged in the performance of his or her official duties.

(k) The victim of the capital felony was an elected or appointed public official engaged in the performance of his or her official duties if the motive for the capital felony was related, in whole or in part, to the victim's official capacity.

(l) The victim of the capital felony was a person less than 12 years of age.

(m) The victim of the capital felony was particularly vulnerable due to advanced age or disability, or because the defendant stood in a position of familial or custodial authority over the victim.

(n) The capital felony was committed by a criminal street gang member. . . .

(o) The capital felony was committed by a person designated as a sexual predator . . . or a person previously designated as a sexual predator who had the sexual predator designation removed.

(6) *Mitigating circumstances.*   Mitigating circumstances shall be the following:

(a) The defendant has no significant history of prior criminal activity.

(b) The capital felony was committed while the defendant was under the influence of extreme mental or emotional disturbance.

(c) The victim was a participant in the defendant's conduct or consented to the act.

(d) The defendant was an accomplice in the capital felony committed by another person and his or her participation was relatively minor.

(e) The defendant acted under extreme duress or under the substantial domination of another person.

(f) The capacity of the defendant to appreciate the criminality of his or her conduct or to conform his or her conduct to the requirements of law was substantially impaired.

(g) The age of the defendant at the time of the crime.

(h) The existence of any other factors in the defendant's background that would mitigate against imposition of the death penalty.

(7) *Victim impact evidence.*   Once the prosecution has provided evidence of the existence of one or more aggravating circumstances as described in subsection (5), the prosecution may introduce, and subsequently argue, victim impact evidence to the jury. Such evidence shall be designed to demonstrate the victim's uniqueness as an individual human being and the resultant loss to the community's members by the victim's death. Characterizations and opinions about the crime, the defendant, and the appropriate sentence shall not be permitted as a part of victim impact evidence.

NOTES

1. *Impact of legal standards.*   In terms of the decision whether to sentence a defendant to death, do the standards that the sentencing jury employs make a difference? Consider the likely outcome for two infamous defendants. Would Timothy McVeigh, the Oklahoma City bomber who killed 168 people in 1995, have received a death sentence under either or both of these statutes? How about John Allen Mohammad, one of the two Washington-area sniper suspects apprehended in 2002?

To prevent the execution of an innocent person, some have proposed that the jury be required at the sentencing stage to find "no doubt" as to the defendant's guilt. Massachusetts Governor's Council on Capital Punishment, at www.lawlib.state.ma.us/5-3-04Governorsreportcapitalpunishment.pdf. Do you find this helpful? See Erik Lillquist, Absolute Certainty and the Death Penalty, 42 Am. Crim. L. Rev. 45 (2005).

2. *Impact of procedural rules.*   Can and should the procedures used at a standard criminal trial apply during a capital sentencing hearing? Consider, for example, the traditional rules of evidence, and the possibility that strict adherence to them might significantly limit the ability of prosecutors and defense counsel to present all the evidence they might consider important at a sentencing hearing. How, if at all, might these rules or other traditional trial procedures influence the outcome of a capital sentencing hearing?

3. *Weighing aggravating and mitigating circumstances.*   Both of the preceding statutes stipulate that the jury weigh specific aggravating and mitigating circumstances. How should the jury decide when aggravating and mitigating factors are in equipoise? In Kansas v. Marsh, 126 S. Ct. 2516 (2006), the Supreme Court held that a state statute may direct imposition of the death penalty "when the State has proved beyond a reasonable doubt that mitigators do not outweigh aggravators, including where [they] are in equipoise." In its decision, the Court relied on Walton v. Arizona, 497 U.S. 639 (1990), where it held that a state death penalty statute may place the burden on the defendant to prove that mitigating circumstances outweigh aggravators. In addition, the Court found the Kansas statute to "rationally narrow the class of death-eligible defendants" and to allow the jury to "render a reasoned, individualized sentencing determination," which is required under *Furman* and *Gregg.*

4. *The availability of "life without parole" as a sentencing option.* Almost all states now provide life without parole as a sentencing option. Public opinion polls have indicated that a slightly larger proportion of the American public would chose life without parole rather than the death penalty as the appropriate punishment for murder. May this sanction give jurors who are concerned about public safety the opportunity to avoid imposing a death sentence? Might the decrease in the number of death sentences be connected to the availability of this sanction? The New Jersey Death Penalty Study Commission recommended that the death penalty be abolished in New Jersey since "life without parole" provides sufficient guarantees of public safety and also addresses other penological concerns. New Jersey Death Penalty Study Commission Report 1-2 (January 2007), at www.njleg.state.nj.us/committees/dpsc_final.pdf.

b.   Jury Selection and Decision Making

Although very few states rely on juries for noncapital sentencing decisions, nearly all states that authorize the death penalty give juries a central role in capital sentencing. This raises a number of important and interesting questions: Why do states believe that juries are the appropriate decision makers in capital cases where life and death are at stake, but exclude juries from other sentencing decisions? Should the jury determining a defendant's guilt also decide whether the defendant receives the death penalty, or should two different juries make these respective decisions? Can we be confident that any system of jury decision making in capital cases will be free of the problems that prompted the Supreme Court's decision in *Furman*?

Beyond these broad questions, the reliance on juries to make capital punishment decisions raises a host of more intricate legal and practical issues that can greatly influence the operation of death penalty systems. For example, should a jury have to render a unanimous verdict to impose a death sentence? What standard of proof should a jury apply when making a death penalty decision? Should a defendant have a right to request that a judge instead of a jury make the death sentencing decision? Can we be confident that jurors will understand and follow the detailed instructions in a death penalty statute?

As we have seen, the thrust of the constitutional rules that regulate capital punishment is to channel and preserve the discretion of the sentencing authority, usually a jury. Whenever the law assigns discretion to someone, it becomes critical to know *who* will exercise that discretion. Thus, the method of selecting the jury members in a capital case is a crucial element of this system, which depends so much on guided discretion. When life is at stake, both prosecutors and defense counsel are very concerned about the jury's composition, especially since determining whether to sentence a person to death is fundamentally a moral decision rather than a factual one. As the following case highlights, there is good reason to fear that in the operation of capital sentencing systems, the very processes used in jury selection may prompt some of the same concerns that troubled the Supreme Court in *Furman*.

Thomas Joe Miller-El v. Janie Cockrell
537 U.S. 322 (2003)

KENNEDY, J.

In 1986 two Dallas County assistant district attorneys used peremptory strikes to exclude 10 of the 11 African-Americans eligible to serve on the jury which tried Thomas Joe Miller-El. During the ensuing 17 years, petitioner has been unsuccessful in establishing, in either state or federal court, that his conviction and death sentence must be vacated because the jury selection procedures violated the Equal Protection Clause and our holding in Batson v. Kentucky, 476 U.S. 79 (1986). The claim now arises in a federal petition for writ of habeas corpus [and we consider whether the federal habeas corpus statute precludes further consideration of Miller-El's claim].

Petitioner, his wife Dorothy Miller-El, and one Kenneth Flowers robbed a Holiday Inn in Dallas, Texas. They emptied the cash drawers and ordered two employees, Doug Walker and Donald Hall, to lie on the floor. Walker and Hall were gagged with strips of fabric, and their hands and feet were bound. Petitioner asked Flowers if he was going to kill Walker and Hall. When Flowers hesitated or refused, petitioner shot Walker twice in the back and shot Hall in the side. Walker died from his wounds.

The State indicted petitioner for capital murder. He pleaded not guilty, and jury selection took place during five weeks in February and March 1986. When voir dire had been concluded, petitioner moved to strike the jury on the grounds that the prosecution had violated the Equal Protection Clause of the

Fourteenth Amendment by excluding African-Americans through the use of peremptory challenges. . . .

A comparative analysis of the venire members demonstrates that African-Americans were excluded from petitioner's jury in a ratio significantly higher than Caucasians were. Of the 108 possible jurors reviewed by the prosecution and defense, 20 were African-American. Nine of them were excused for cause or by agreement of the parties. Of the 11 African-American jurors remaining, however, all but 1 were excluded by peremptory strikes exercised by the prosecutors. On this basis 91% of the eligible black jurors were removed by peremptory strikes. In contrast the prosecutors used their peremptory strikes against just 13% (4 out of 31) of the eligible nonblack prospective jurors qualified to serve on petitioner's jury.

These numbers, while relevant, are not petitioner's whole case. During voir dire, the prosecution questioned venire members as to their views concerning the death penalty and their willingness to serve on a capital case. Responses that disclosed reluctance or hesitation to impose capital punishment were cited as a justification for striking a potential juror for cause or by peremptory challenge [based upon this Court's decision in] Wainwright v. Witt, 469 U.S. 412 (1985). The evidence suggests, however, that the manner in which members of the venire were questioned varied by race. . . .

Most African-Americans (53%, or 8 out of 15) were first given a detailed description of the mechanics of an execution in Texas:

> If those three [sentencing] questions are answered yes, at some point Thomas Joe Miller-El will be taken to Huntsville, Texas. He will be placed on death row and at some time will be taken to the death house where he will be strapped on a gurney, an IV put into his arm and he will be injected with a substance that will cause his death . . . as the result of the verdict in this case if those three questions are answered yes.

Only then were these African-American venire members asked whether they could render a decision leading to a sentence of death. Very few prospective white jurors (6%, or 3 out of 49) were given this preface prior to being asked for their views on capital punishment. Rather, all but three were questioned in vague terms: "Would you share with us . . . your personal feelings, if you could, in your own words how you do feel about the death penalty and capital punishment and secondly, do you feel you could serve on this type of a jury and actually render a decision that would result in the death of the Defendant in this case based on the evidence?"

There was an even more pronounced difference, on the apparent basis of race, in the manner the prosecutors questioned members of the venire about their willingness to impose the minimum sentence for murder. Under Texas law at the time of petitioner's trial, an unwillingness to do so warranted removal for cause. This strategy normally is used by the defense to weed out pro-state members of the venire, but, ironically, the prosecution employed it here. The prosecutors first identified the statutory minimum sentence of five years' imprisonment to 34 out of 36 (94%) white venire members, and only then asked: "If you hear a case, to your way of thinking [that] calls for and warrants and justifies five years, you'll give it?" In contrast, only 1 out of 8 (12.5%) African-American prospective jurors were informed of the statutory minimum before being asked what minimum sentence they would impose. The typical questioning of the other seven black jurors was as follows:

> [Prosecutor]: Now, the maximum sentence for [murder] . . . is life under the law. Can you give me an idea of just your personal feelings what you feel a minimum sentence should be for the offense of murder the way I've set it out for you?
> [Juror]: Well, to me that's almost like it's premeditated. But you said they don't have a premeditated statute here in Texas. . . .
> [Prosecutor]: Again, we're not talking about self-defense or accident or insanity or killing in the heat of passion or anything like that. We're talking about the knowing—
> [Juror]: I know you said the minimum. The minimum amount that I would say would be at least twenty years.

Furthermore, petitioner points to the prosecution's use of a Texas criminal procedure practice known as jury shuffling. This practice permits parties to rearrange the order in which members of the venire are examined so as to increase the likelihood that visually preferable venire members will be moved forward and empaneled. With no information about the prospective jurors other than their appearance, the party requesting the procedure literally shuffles the juror cards, and the venire members are then reseated in the new order. Tex. Code Crim. Proc. Ann., Art. 35.11. Shuffling affects jury composition because any prospective jurors not questioned during voir dire are dismissed at the end of the week, and a new panel of jurors appears the following week. So jurors who are shuffled to the back of the panel are less likely to be questioned or to serve.

On at least two occasions the prosecution requested shuffles when there were a predominate number of African-Americans in the front of the panel. On yet another occasion the prosecutors complained about the purported inadequacy of the card shuffle by a defense lawyer but lodged a formal objection only after the postshuffle panel composition revealed that African-American prospective jurors had been moved forward.

[As additional evidence to support his claims,] petitioner subpoenaed a number of current and former Dallas County assistant district attorneys, judges, and others who had observed firsthand the prosecution's conduct during jury selection over a number of years. Although most of the witnesses denied the existence of a systematic policy to exclude African-Americans, others disagreed. A Dallas County district judge testified that, when he had served in the District Attorney's Office from the late 1950s to early 1960s, his superior warned him that he would be fired if he permitted any African-Americans to serve on a jury. Similarly, another Dallas County district judge and former assistant district attorney from 1976 to 1978 testified that he believed the office had a systematic policy of excluding African-Americans from juries.

Of more importance, the defense presented evidence that the District Attorney's Office had adopted a formal policy to exclude minorities from jury service. A 1963 circular by the District Attorney's Office instructed its prosecutors to exercise peremptory strikes against minorities: "Do not take Jews, Negroes, Dagos, Mexicans or a member of any minority race on a jury, no matter how rich or how well educated." A manual entitled "Jury Selection in a Criminal

Case" was distributed to prosecutors. It contained an article authored by a former prosecutor (and later a judge) under the direction of his superiors in the District Attorney's Office, outlining the reasoning for excluding minorities from jury service. Although the manual was written in 1968, it remained in circulation until 1976, if not later, and was available at least to one of the prosecutors in Miller-El's trial.

Some testimony casts doubt on the State's claim that these practices had been discontinued before petitioner's trial. For example, a judge testified that, in 1985, he had to exclude a prosecutor from trying cases in his courtroom for race-based discrimination in jury selection. Other testimony indicated that the State, by its own admission, once requested a jury shuffle in order to reduce the number of African-Americans in the venire. Concerns over the exclusion of African-Americans by the District Attorney's Office were echoed by Dallas County's Chief Public Defender.

[The] State now concedes that petitioner satisfied step one [under the standards established in Batson v. Kentucky, 476 U.S. 79 (1986)]: "There is no dispute that Miller-El presented a prima facie claim" that prosecutors used their peremptory challenges to exclude venire members on the basis of race. Petitioner, for his part, acknowledges that the State proceeded through step two [of the *Batson* analysis] by proffering facially race-neutral explanations for these strikes. Under *Batson*, then, the question remaining is step three: whether Miller-El "has carried his burden of proving purposeful discrimination." . . .

In this case, the statistical evidence alone raises some debate as to whether the prosecution acted with a race-based reason when striking prospective jurors. The prosecutors used their peremptory strikes to exclude 91% of the eligible African-American venire members, and only one served on petitioner's jury. In total, 10 of the prosecutors' 14 peremptory strikes were used against African-Americans. Happenstance is unlikely to produce this disparity. . . .

In this case, three of the State's proffered race-neutral rationales for striking African-American jurors pertained just as well to some white jurors who were not challenged and who did serve on the jury. The prosecutors explained that their peremptory challenges against six African-American potential jurors were based on ambivalence about the death penalty; hesitancy to vote to execute defendants capable of being rehabilitated; and the jurors' own family history of criminality. In rebuttal of the prosecution's explanation, petitioner identified two empaneled white jurors who expressed ambivalence about the death penalty in a manner similar to their African-American counterparts who were the subject of prosecutorial peremptory challenges. One indicated that capital punishment was not appropriate for a first offense, and another stated that it would be "difficult" to impose a death sentence. Similarly, two white jurors expressed hesitation in sentencing to death a defendant who might be rehabilitated; and four white jurors had family members with criminal histories. As a consequence, even though the prosecution's reasons for striking African-American members of the venire appear race neutral, the application of these rationales to the venire might have been selective and based on racial considerations. Whether a comparative juror analysis would demonstrate the prosecutors' rationales to have been pretexts for discrimination is an unnecessary determination at this stage, but the evidence does make debatable the District Court's conclusion that no purposeful discrimination occurred.

We question the Court of Appeals' and state trial court's dismissive and strained interpretation of petitioner's evidence of disparate questioning. . . . Disparate questioning did occur. Petitioner submits that disparate questioning created the appearance of divergent opinions even though the venire members' views on the relevant subject might have been the same. It follows that, if the use of disparate questioning is determined by race at the outset, it is likely a justification for a strike based on the resulting divergent views would be pretextual. In this context the differences in the questions posed by the prosecutors are some evidence of purposeful discrimination. . . .

We agree with petitioner that the prosecution's decision to seek a jury shuffle when a predominate number of African-Americans were seated in the front of the panel, along with its decision to delay a formal objection to the defense's shuffle until after the new racial composition was revealed, raise a suspicion that the State sought to exclude African-Americans from the jury. Our concerns are amplified by the fact that the state court also had before it, and apparently ignored, testimony demonstrating that the Dallas County District Attorney's Office had, by its own admission, used this process to manipulate the racial composition of the jury in the past. Even though the practice of jury shuffling might not be denominated as a *Batson* claim because it does not involve a peremptory challenge, the use of the practice here tends to erode the credibility of the prosecution's assertion that race was not a motivating factor in the jury selection. . . .

Finally, in our threshold examination, we accord some weight to petitioner's historical evidence of racial discrimination by the District Attorney's Office. . . . Irrespective of whether the evidence could prove sufficient to support a charge of systematic exclusion of African-Americans, it reveals that the culture of the District Attorney's Office in the past was suffused with bias against African-Americans in jury selection. Both prosecutors [in Miller-El's case] joined the District Attorney's Office when assistant district attorneys received formal training in excluding minorities from juries. The supposition that race was a factor could be reinforced by the fact that the prosecutors marked the race of each prospective juror on their juror cards. . . .

To secure habeas relief, petitioner must demonstrate that a state court's finding of the absence of purposeful discrimination was incorrect by clear and convincing evidence, 28 U.S.C. §2254(e)(1), and that the corresponding factual determination was "objectively unreasonable" in light of the record before the court. The State represents to us that petitioner will not be able to satisfy his burden. That may or may not be the case. It is not, however, the question before us [as we are considering only whether his claim may proceed under the federal habeas statute, and that] inquiry asks only if the District Court's decision was debatable. Our threshold examination convinces us that it was.

NOTES

1. *Death qualification and life qualification of jurors.* As briefly mentioned in the *Miller-El* decision, the Supreme Court developed special rules to govern the selection and exclusion of jurors in death penalty cases. Through its decisions in Witherspoon v. Illinois, 391 U.S. 510 (1968), and Wainwright v. Witt, 469 U.S.

412 (1985), the Supreme Court established that jurors may be excused for cause when they indicate they are so opposed to capital punishment that they would not find the defendant guilty regardless of the evidence, or would not consider death as a possible sentence regardless of the circumstances of the crime. In Uttecht v. Brown, 127 S. Ct. 2218 (2007), the Supreme Court held that a juror may be excused for cause if he indicates during voir dire that a death sanction was an option for him only if the defendant could be released to re-offend. A contrary decision would substantially impact the state's ability to impose the death penalty.

Many commentators have assailed the practice of excluding jurors who express sincere misgivings about capital punishment — a process known as "death qualifying" a juror — arguing that it biases the decision making of capital juries and denies capital defendants their constitutional rights to an impartial jury and to a jury drawn from a fair cross-section of the community. See Craig Haney, Aida Hurtado & Luis Vega, Modern Death Qualification: New Data on Its Biasing Effects, 18 Law & Hum. Behav. 619, 624-631 (1994); Stephen Gillers, Deciding Who Dies, 129 U. Pa. L. Rev. 1 (1980).

Following the same principles it applied in *Witt*, the Supreme Court subsequently held in Morgan v. Illinois, 504 U.S. 719 (1992), that a defendant could seek to "life qualify" a capital jury by excluding for cause any juror who indicates he or she will automatically vote for the death penalty regardless of any presented mitigating circumstances. The efficacy of the Supreme Court's rules regulating the selection of capital jurors has been repeatedly questioned, with a number of commentators raising serious concerns based on data collected by the Capital Jury Project (see below) about the decisions of actual capital jurors. See John H. Blume et al., Probing "Life Qualification" Through Expanded Voir Dire, 29 Hofstra L. Rev. 1209 (2001); William J. Bowers et al., Foreclosed Impartiality in Capital Sentencing: Jurors' Predispositions, Guilt-Trial Experience, and Premature Decision Making, 83 Cornell L. Rev. 1476 (1998).

2. *Review of death sentencing procedures.*   The Supreme Court in *Miller-El* was not asked to resolve the merits of the defendant's constitutional claim because the case was enmeshed in the complicated procedural issues that surround federal habeas review of state death sentences. Because state courts rejected Miller-El's claims on their merits, and because the federal district court denied relief, the specific question before the Supreme Court was whether Miller-El's claim was sufficiently "debatable" to permit further appellate review in the federal courts. Given the force of the factual evidence presented by Miller-El, why do you think the state courts rejected his claims of equal protection violation? Given the concerns expressed by the Supreme Court in *Furman*, do you think capital cases warrant a higher standard of appellate review?

On remand from the Supreme Court after its initial ruling in *Miller-El*, the Fifth Circuit held that defendant Miller-El failed to show by clear and convincing evidence that the state court's finding of no discrimination was wrong. In June 2005, through a 6-3 decision, the Supreme Court once again reversed the Fifth Circuit and ruled that Miller-El was entitled to a new trial in light of strong evidence of racial bias during jury selection at his original trial and general historical evidence of the racially biased policies of the Dallas County District Attorney's office. Miller-El v. Dretke, 545 U.S. 231 (2005). The Supreme Court said the prosecutors' supposedly race-neutral reasons for the strikes were so far at odds with the evidence that pretext is the fair conclusion. The Court stated that the Texas court's finding of no discrimination "blinks reality," and was both unreasonable and erroneous.

3. *Potential sources of racial bias.* As highlighted earlier, a clear concern for certain justices who voted in the majority in *Furman* was not just the possibility of arbitrary death sentencing but the real potential for discriminatory decisions in capital cases. Do the racial realities revealed in the *Miller-El* case suggest that unique safeguards against racial bias are needed in capital cases? The Supreme Court's struggles with racial discrimination in the administration of the death penalty are covered more fully in Chapter 9.

> ## The Capital Jury Project: Rationale, Design, and Preview of Early Findings,
> ### William J. Bowers
> #### 70 Ind. L.J. 1043 (1995)

Now underway in fourteen states, the Capital Jury Project ("CJP") is a multidisciplinary study of how jurors make their life or death sentencing decisions. Drawing upon three-to-four-hour interviews with 80 to 120 capital jurors in each of the participating states, the CJP is examining the extent to which jurors' exercise of capital sentencing discretion is still infected with, or now cured of, the arbitrariness which the United States Supreme Court condemned in Furman v. Georgia, and the extent to which the principal kinds of post-*Furman* guided discretion statutes are curbing arbitrary decision-making — as the Court said they would in Gregg v. Georgia and its companion cases. . . .

THE GUILT PHASE

Jurors' responses to questions about the guilt phase of the trial suggest that many of them began considering aggravation and punishment while they were still deciding on the defendant's guilt, and indeed, that many began to take a stand on what the defendant's punishment should be well before being exposed to the statutory guidelines for this decision. We see these indications in their responses to questions about topics they discussed during the jury's guilt deliberations and in their answers to a question about what they thought the punishment should be prior to the punishment phase of the trial.

Considerations of Aggravation and Punishment

When the questioning turned to the jury's deliberations at the guilt phase of the trial, we asked jurors about a number of specific topics they might have discussed, including some that are legally irrelevant or impermissible in determining guilt, such as the defendant's likely future dangerousness and jurors' feelings about the appropriate punishment — considerations explicitly reserved for the later punishment phase of the trial. . . .

Jurors were evidently concerned with the defendant's future dangerousness and the punishment to be imposed during their deliberation on the
defendant's guilt. More than six out of ten said the jury's guilt deliberations
focused on each of these topics a "great deal" or a "fair amount." One-half
of the jurors said that there was a great deal of discussion about the "right
punishment."

Conscious that jurors might not clearly distinguish between the guilt and
punishment deliberations in response to this question, and that some topics
discussed during guilt deliberations might not have actually figured in the
decision-making about guilt, we asked a further question explicitly worded to
focus the juror's attention exclusively on the defendant's punishment as a relevant consideration in the jury's decision about the defendant's guilt. [We
asked]: In deciding guilt, did jurors talk about whether or not the defendant
would, or should, get the death penalty? Here, too, a sizable number (over 30%)
of jurors recall that in deciding guilt, there was explicit discussion of what the
defendant's punishment would or should be.

Timing of the Punishment Decision

In addition to these questions about what the jury did as a group, CJP
investigators also asked the individual jurors about their own personal thinking
and decision-making with respect to the defendant's punishment prior to the
sentencing phase of the trial. In particular, we asked whether they had come to a
decision on punishment, what they thought the punishment should be, and how
convinced they were of their decision. . . .

One-half of the jurors were undecided, but the other one-half said that they
had chosen (more or less firmly) between a life or death sentence at the guilt
stage of the trial. A second follow-up question, addressed only to those who, at
this stage, thought that the defendant should be given a life or death sentence,
asked: How strongly did you think so? [M]ost of the jurors who had decided what
the punishment should be before the sentencing phase of the trial were "absolutely convinced" of their punishment decision, and nearly all the rest were at
least "pretty sure." In effect, it appears that three out of ten jurors had essentially
made up their minds, and another two in ten were leaning one way or the other,
before hearing from the judge about the standards that should guide their
sentencing decisions.

THE PUNISHMENT PHASE

Guidelines and Instructions

If statutory standards are to guide the exercise of sentencing discretion,
they must, of course, be understood and applied in the course of actually making
the sentencing decision. Among the various questions we asked to tap jurors'
understanding of sentencing guidelines, the responses to the question regarding the substance of the statutory standards were unsettling. . . .

Contrary to the laws of their states, four out of ten capital jurors believed that they were required to impose the death penalty if they found that the crime was heinous, vile, or depraved, and three out of ten thought that the death penalty was required if they found that the defendant would be dangerous in the future. . . .

Three out of four participating jurors said that the evidence proved that the crime was heinous, vile, or depraved, and that the defendant would be dangerous in the future. In combination with the percentages of those who believed that the death penalty was required if these factors were proved, it appears that between 21% and 33% of the jurors mistakenly believed that the state's proof of heinousness required them to vote for the death penalty. In addition, between 8% and 24% of jurors wrongly believed that evidence of the defendant's dangerousness required them to vote in favor of death. . . .

Responsibility for the Punishment

One criticism of guided discretion capital statutes is that they tend to allay jurors' sense of responsibility for their life or death sentencing decisions by appearing to provide them with an authoritative formula that yields the "correct" or "required" punishment. . . . To see where capital jurors located responsibility for punishment, we asked them to: *Rank the following from "most" through "least" responsible for [the defendant's] punishment.*

Unmistakably, jurors placed responsibility for the defendant's punishment elsewhere. Eight out of ten jurors feel that the defendant or the law is the most responsible for the defendant's punishment. More jurors believe that the greatest responsibility lies with the defendant rather than with the law. . . .

CONCLUSION

The early indications in our research . . . sketch out a picture of the exercise of capital sentencing discretion that differs from that found in current Supreme Court precedent. [The] emerging picture is noteworthy for the questions it raises concerning the Supreme Court's presumptions about the exercise of capital sentencing discretion. . . .

[We] find that many jurors appear to make their decisions apart from, and indeed prior to, sentencing instructions on the bases of their unguided feelings or reactions to the crime. The findings also show that sentencing guidelines provide "legal cover" to many who have already made up their minds, and "legal leverage" for persuading the undecided. In either case, the guidelines appear to lessen the sense of responsibility for imposing an awful punishment. Yet, these are still early soundings of what the jurors have to tell us about how they think about the crimes, the defendants, the victims, and how they decide what the defendant's punishment should be. The yet unanswered critical questions, of course, are how standardless is this decision-making process; how widespread is such standardless decision-making; and — for the Court to answer — does it represent a constitutionally unacceptable level or risk of arbitrariness?

NOTES

1. *Challenges to jurors' life-or-death decision.*   Is it surprising that jurors typically do not fully understand or adhere to the instructions that are designed to guide their decisions? After comparing the modern capital sentencing statutes used in Texas and Florida (reprinted above) with the instructions used in pre-*Furman* cases in California and Ohio (discussed in *McGautha* above), it is easy to appreciate how the detailed instructions to jurors in capital cases today recast capital sentencing as a legal issue rather than a moral issue for the jury to decide. Should a death sentencing decision be recast in these terms? Whether it is a legal or a moral decision, are you confident that juries are the best sentencers in capital cases? For a dynamic discussion of the psychology surrounding capital jury decision making, see Craig Haney, Violence and the Capital Jury: Mechanisms of Moral Disengagement and the Impulse to Condemn to Death, 49 Stan. L. Rev. 1447 (1997).

Justice John Paul Stevens, in an August 2005 speech to the American Bar Association, made some pointedly critical remarks about the abilities of jurors to make appropriate decisions in capital cases: "In many of these cases the outrageously brutal facts cry out for retribution. . . . Gruesome facts pose a danger that emotion will play a larger role in the decisional process than dispassionate analysis." For the full text of Justice Stevens' address, see http://www.supremecourtus.gov/publicinfo/speeches/sp_08-06-05.html.

2. *Judicial decisions to impose death sentences.*   A few jurisdictions have given some sentencing discretion to judges in capital cases. In some states, this discretion is secondary to the discretion exercised by a capital jury; in Ohio, for example, the trial judge may decide that a defendant does not deserve to die even if the jury recommends death, but the judge may not impose a death sentence if a jury does not so recommend. See Ohio Rev. Code §2929.03. In other states (such as Florida, whose statute is reprinted above), judges can "override" a jury recommendation of either death or life.

The Supreme Court's decision in Ring v. Arizona, 536 U.S. 584 (2002), which partially overruled its prior decision in Walton v. Arizona, 497 U.S. 639 (1990), threw into question the constitutionality of capital sentencing systems in which judges exercise substantial sentencing authority. In *Ring* the Court held that the Sixth Amendment's right to trial by jury in criminal prosecutions requires a jury to determine the presence of those aggravating factors necessary for a sentence of death. Though *Ring* still allows the judge to be the final decision maker as to whether to impose a death sentence, it precludes judges from finding those facts that can form the basis for a death sentence under a state's statutory scheme.

c.   Executive Discretion

Although the discretion exercised by a jury deciding whether to sentence a defendant to death is the most tangible and visible discretionary decision in capital cases, many other actors make discretionary judgments about the availability and imposition of a death sentence. Prosecutors possess wide (and essentially unreviewable) discretion when initially deciding whether to charge certain murders as capital crimes and whether to reduce capital charges as part of a plea agreement. In addition, nearly every state grants its governor or board of pardons, or both, the authority to commute death sentences. As you review the following materials, think about whether these sorts of discretionary decisions are likely to aggravate or ameliorate the concerns expressed by the Supreme Court in *Furman*.

Speech at Northwestern University College of Law, Illinois Governor George Ryan
January 11, 2003

Four years ago I was sworn in as the 39th Governor of Illinois. That was just four short years ago; that's when I was a firm believer in the American System of Justice and the death penalty. I believed that the ultimate penalty for the taking of a life was administrated in a just and fair manner. Today, three days before I end my term as Governor, I stand before you to explain my frustrations and deep concerns about both the administration and the penalty of death. . . .

During my time in public office I have always reserved my right to change my mind if I believed it to be in the best public interest, whether it be about taxes, abortions or the death penalty. But I must confess that the debate with myself has been the toughest concerning the death penalty. I suppose the reason the death penalty has been the toughest is because it is so final — the only public policy that determines who lives and who dies. In addition it is the only issue that attracts most of the legal minds across the country. I have received more advice on this issue than any other policy issue I have dealt with in my 35 years of public service. I have kept an open mind on both sides of the issues of commutation for life or death. . . .

The other day, I received a call from former South African President Nelson Mandela, who reminded me that the United States sets the example for justice and fairness for the rest of the world. Today the United States is not in league with most of our major allies: Europe, Canada, Mexico, most of South and Central America. These countries rejected the death penalty. We are partners in death with several third world countries. Even Russia has called a moratorium. . . .

I never intended to be an activist on this issue. I watched in surprise as freed death row inmate Anthony Porter was released from jail. A free man, he ran into the arms of Northwestern University Professor Dave Protess, who poured his heart and soul into proving Porter's innocence with his journalism students. He was 48 hours away from being wheeled into the execution chamber where the state would kill him. It would all be so antiseptic and most of us would not have even paused, except that Anthony Porter was innocent of the double murder for which he had been condemned to die.

After Mr. Porter's case there was the report by *Chicago Tribune* reporters Steve Mills and Ken Armstrong documenting the systemic failures of our capital punishment system. Half of the nearly 300 capital cases in Illinois had been reversed for a new trial or resentencing. Nearly Half! Thirty-three of the death row inmates were represented at trial by an attorney who had later been disbarred or at some point suspended from practicing law.

Of the more than 160 death row inmates, 35 were African American defendants who had been convicted or condemned to die by all-white juries. More than two-thirds of the inmates on death row were African American. Forty-six inmates were convicted on the basis of testimony from jailhouse informants. . . .

Then over the next few months, there were three more exonerated men, freed because their sentence hinged on a jailhouse informant or new DNA technology proved beyond a shadow of doubt their innocence. We then had the dubious distinction of exonerating more men than we had executed: 13 men found innocent, 12 executed. As I reported yesterday, there is not a doubt in my mind that the number of innocent men freed from our Death Row stands at 17, with the pardons of Aaron Patterson, Madison Hobley, Stanley Howard and Leroy Orange. That is an absolute embarrassment. Seventeen exonerated death row inmates is nothing short of a catastrophic failure. But the 13, now 17 men, is just the beginning of our sad arithmetic in prosecuting murder cases. During the time we have had capital punishment in Illinois, there were at least 33 other people wrongly convicted on murder charges and exonerated. Since we reinstated the death penalty there are also 93 people — 93 — where our criminal justice system imposed the most severe sanction and later rescinded the sentence or even released them from custody because they were innocent. How many more cases of wrongful conviction have to occur before we can all agree that the system is broken?

In the United States the overwhelming majority of those executed are psychotic, alcoholic, drug addicted or mentally unstable. They frequently are raised in an impoverished and abusive environment. Seldom are people with money or prestige convicted of capital offenses, even more seldom are they executed. . . .

At stake throughout the clemency process was whether some, all or none of these inmates on death row would have their sentences commuted from death to life without the possibility of parole. One of the things discussed with family members was [that] life without parole was seen as a life filled with perks and benefits. Some inmates on death row don't want a sentence of life without parole. Danny Edwards wrote me and told me not to do him any favors because he didn't want to face a prospect of a life in prison without parole. They will be confined in a cell that is about 5-feet-by-12 feet, usually double-bunked. Our prisons have no air conditioning, except at our supermax facility, where inmates are kept in their cell 23 hours a day. In summer months, temperatures in these prisons exceed one hundred degrees. It is a stark and dreary existence. They can think about their crimes. Life without parole has even, at times, been described by prosecutors as a fate worse than death. . . .

I started with this issue concerned about innocence. But once I studied, once I pondered what had become of our justice system, I came to care above all about fairness. Fairness is fundamental to the American system of justice and our way of life. The facts I have seen in reviewing each and every one of these cases raised questions not only about the innocence of people on death row, but about the fairness of the death penalty system as a whole. If the system was making so many errors in determining whether someone was guilty in the first place, how fairly and accurately was it determining which guilty defendants deserved to live and which deserved to die? What effect was race having? What effect was poverty having?

And in almost every one of the exonerated 17, we not only have break-downs in the system with police, prosecutors and judges, we have terrible cases of shabby defense lawyers. There is just no way to sugar coat it. There are defense attorneys that did not consult with their clients, did not investigate the case and were completely unqualified to handle complex death penalty cases. They often didn't put much effort into fighting a death sentence. If your life is on the line, your lawyer ought to be fighting for you. As I have said before, there is more than enough blame to go around.

In Illinois, I have learned, we have 102 decision makers. Each of them [is] politically elected, each beholden to the demands of their community and, in some cases, to the media or especially vocal victims' families. In cases that have the attention of the media and the public, are decisions to seek the death penalty more likely to occur? What standards are these prosecutors using?

Some people have assailed my power to commute sentences. . . . But prosecutors in Illinois have the ultimate commutation power, a power that is exercised every day. They decide who will be subject to the death penalty, who will get a plea deal or even who may get a complete pass on prosecution. By what objective standards do they make these decisions? We do not know, they are not public. There were more than 1,000 murders last year in Illinois. There is no doubt that all murders are horrific and cruel. Yet, less than 2 percent of those murder defendants will receive the death penalty. . . . Moreover, if you look at the cases, as I have done — both individually and collectively — a killing with the same circumstances might get 40 years in one county and death in another county. [You are five times more likely to get a death sentence for first-degree murder in the rural area of Illinois than you are in Cook County.] I have also seen where co-defendants who are equally or even more culpable get sentenced to a term of years, while another less culpable defendant ends up on death row.

In my case-by-case review, I found three people that fell into this category: Mario Flores, Montel Johnson and William Franklin. Today I have commuted their sentences to a term of 40 years to bring their sentences into line with their co-defendants and to reflect the other extraordinary circumstances of these cases.

Supreme Court Justice Potter Stewart has said that the imposition of the death penalty on defendants in this country is as freakish and arbitrary as who gets hit by a bolt of lightning. . . . What are we to make of the studies that showed that more than 50% of Illinois jurors could not understand the confusing and obscure sentencing instructions that were being used? What effect did that problem have on the trustworthiness of death sentences? A review of the cases shows that often even the lawyers and judges are confused about the instructions — let alone the jurors sitting in judgment. Cases still come before the Supreme Court with arguments about whether the jury instructions were proper. . . .

As I prepare to leave office, I had to ask myself whether I could really live with the prospect of knowing that I had the opportunity to act, but that I failed to do so because I might be criticized. Could I take the chance that our capital punishment system might be reformed, that wrongful convictions might not occur, that enterprising journalism students might free more men from death row? . . . Our own study showed that juries were more likely to sentence to death if the victim were white than if the victim were black — three-and-a-half times more likely to be exact. . . . Is our system fair to all? Is justice blind? These are important human rights issues. . . .

In 1994, near the end of his distinguished career on the Supreme Court of the United States, Justice Harry Blackmun wrote an influential dissent in the body of law on capital punishment. Twenty years earlier he was part of the court that issued the landmark *Furman* decision. . . . But 20 years later, after affirming hundreds of death penalty decisions, Justice Blackmun came to the realization, in the twilight of his distinguished career, that the death penalty remains "fraught with arbitrariness, discrimination, caprice and mistake." He expressed frustration with a 20-year struggle to develop procedural and substantive safeguards. In a now famous dissent he wrote in 1994, "From this day forward, I no longer shall tinker with the machinery of death." . . . The Governor has the constitutional role in our state of acting in the interest of justice and fairness. Our state constitution provides broad power to the Governor to issue reprieves, pardons and commutations. Our Supreme Court has reminded inmates petitioning them that the last resort for relief is the governor.

At times the executive clemency power has perhaps been a crutch for courts to avoid making the kind of major change that I believe our system needs. Our systemic case-by-case review has found more cases of innocent men wrongfully sentenced to death row. Because our three year study has found only more questions about the fairness of the sentencing; because of the spectacular failure to reform the system; because we have seen justice delayed for countless death row inmates with potentially meritorious claims; because the Illinois death penalty system is arbitrary and capricious — and therefore immoral — I no longer shall tinker with the machinery of death. I cannot say it more eloquently than Justice Blackmun.

The legislature couldn't reform it. Lawmakers won't repeal it. But I will not stand for it. I must act. Our capital system is haunted by the demon of error, error in determining guilt, and error in determining who among the guilty deserves to die. Because of all of these reasons today I am commuting the sentences of all death row inmates. . . .

NOTES

1. *Executive clemency.*   Although it was common early in the twentieth century for governors to pardon offenders and to commute many death sentences to life terms, most governors have not used this discretionary power extensively since the courts became actively involved in constitutional regulation and review of capital sentencing. From 1955 to 1965, more than 200 death sentences were commuted and roughly the same number of executions were carried out; from 1985 to 1995, about 20 death sentences were commuted and roughly *ten times* as many executions were carried out. As detailed in the excerpt above, in January 2003 Governor George Ryan of Illinois followed up his 2000 decision to impose a moratorium on executions in his state with the decision, as one of his last acts in office, to empty death row by pardoning four persons and commuting the sentences of the remaining 156 to life imprisonment.

Anti–death penalty advocates hailed Governor Ryan's decision. Those opposed to his decision accused him of a cheap political ploy designed to divert attention away from his own legal problems stemming from a large-scale corruption investigation. Governor Ryan's action again brought to light cases in which factually innocent prisoners were held on death row, some for decades.

2. *Abolition and the innocence movement.* Some opponents of the death penalty have questioned whether the innocence movement is a viable strategy to achieve abolition. If the state can develop a system virtually guaranteeing that the death penalty will be imposed only on the guilty, how can one defend the abolition of the death penalty entirely? Might the innocence movement not ensure that the death penalty is reserved for the truly heinous, and thus strengthen the argument of the retentionist?

3. *Abolition and the mode of execution.* A new strategy in anti–death penalty litigation is to attack the mode of execution. In some states appellate courts have questioned the constitutionality of procedures used. In Hill v. McDonough, 126 S. Ct. 2096 (2006), the Supreme Court halted Hill's execution by lethal injection, ruling that lethal injection challenges could be raised in federal court under civil rights laws.

4. *European involvement in capital sanctions.* Increasingly, European countries have waged a multi-front battle against capital punishment in the United States and Japan. One prong of their strategy had been to support the litigation efforts of those who aimed to exempt juveniles and the mentally retarded from execution. With the Court's decisions in *Atkins* and *Roper,* they have successfully concluded that phase. Europe's opposition to the death penalty has caused serious problems for U.S. diplomats in conducting foreign policy. See Nora V. Demleitner, The Death Penalty in the United States: Following the European Lead?, 81 Or. L. Rev. 131 (2002). To what extent should the determination of common standards of decency depend on international developments? Should a traditionally domestic issue, such as criminal sanctions, be influenced by international bodies or concerns?

5. *The death row phenomenon.* Many death row inmates spend a decade or more awaiting their execution. Although inmate appeals are frequently the source of this delay, a number of foreign countries have declared the so-called death row phenomenon — years spent under the restrictive conditions imposed by death row confinement — an unjust punishment in its own right. See, e.g., Soering v. United Kingdom, 11 Eur. H.R. Rep. 439 (Eur. Ct. H.R. 1989); Pratt v. Attorney General for Jamaica, Privy Council Appeal No. 10 of 1993 (1993); United States v. Burns [2001] 1 S.C.R. 283, 2001 SCC 7. Countries operating under the European human rights system as well as Canada no longer extradite individuals to the United States unless they are given explicit guarantees that the prosecution will not request a death sentence at trial. Any defendant who is successful in escaping to one of these countries effectively insulates herself from the death penalty. Should a prosecutor promise not to seek a death sentence so that the defendant can be tried in the United States? Or is it preferable to avoid entering into such agreements?

6. *Consular notification.* Foreign nationals in the United States have the right to have their consulate notified of their arrest. Some foreign countries provide counsel free of charge to their nationals. With many foreign countries

willing and able to furnish excellent capital counsel, the foreign-national defendant whose home country is not notified of the need for trial counsel is at a severe disadvantage. Because U.S. law enforcement officials frequently fail to notify the representatives of foreign governments of such arrests, a number of such countries, including Paraguay, Germany, and Mexico, have filed suit before the International Court of Justice (ICJ) against the United States for violation of the consular convention.

In the case of the LaGrand brothers, two German nationals, the ICJ found that by not informing them of their convention rights and subsequently by not permitting review and reconsideration of their convictions and sentences, the United States violated their rights as well as Germany's rights. It also held the United States in breach for failing to take all measures to prevent Walter LaGrand's execution after the ICJ issued a stay order. The court accepted the United States' assurance that it would implement specific measures to comply with its obligations under the convention. Nevertheless, the ICJ required that should German nationals be sentenced to "severe penalties, without their rights under Article 36, paragraph 1(b), of the Convention having been respected, the United States, by means of its own choosing, shall allow the review and reconsideration of the conviction and sentence by taking account of the violation of the rights set forth in that Convention." LaGrand Case (Germany v. United States of America), 40 I.L.M. 1069 (I.C.J. 2001).

In the later *Avena* case, the ICJ again held the United States in breach of its treaty obligations and asked that the United States provide judicial review and reconsideration of the convictions and sentences of 51 Mexicans who were being held on death row. Case Concerning Avena and Other Mexican Nationals (Mexico v. U.S.) I.C.J (2004). The United States subsequently withdrew from the Optional Protocol to the Convention, which had provided the United States' consent to ICJ jurisdiction over cases arising under the Consular Convention. At the same time the president issued a memorandum to the attorney general indicating that the United States would discharge its obligations under the *Avena* decision. The cases of the 51 Mexicans on death row continue to engage state and federal court systems. In Sanchez-Llamas v. Oregon, 126 S. Ct. 2669 (2006), the Supreme Court held that a violation of the Consular Convention does not automatically require suppression of a defendant's statements and that a state may apply standard procedural default rules to that claim.

The Texas Court of Criminal Appeals, in Ex parte Medellin, 2006 Tex. Crim. App. LEXIS 2236 (Tex. Crim. App. 2006), *cert. granted*, Medellin v. Texas, 127 S. Ct. 2129 (2007), decided not to provide the defendant with the review he sought following the *Avena* decision. The decision stated that neither the ICJ's decision nor the president's memorandum constituted binding federal law that could preempt a state statute limiting habeas relief. The decision has set the stage for a clash between state and federal powers, in particular between presidential authority and the power of the state judiciary.

PROBLEM 3-4.   MORATORIUM

You are the state governor's chief advisor on criminal justice issues. She has asked for your opinion about whether she should declare a moratorium on the use of capital punishment in the state. She raised the question with you after hearing about the actions of Illinois Governor George Ryan and then receiving a copy of a report from the American Bar Association about the administration of capital punishment. In 1997 the ABA recommended that states not carry out the death penalty "until the jurisdiction implements policies and procedures that are consistent with ... longstanding American Bar Association policies intended to (1) ensure that death penalty cases are administered fairly and impartially, in accordance with due process, and (2) minimize the risk that innocent persons may be executed. . . ."

The ABA pointed to inadequate defense counsel (and insufficient funding for those lawyers) as one of the central flaws in the system:

Jurisdictions that employ the death penalty have proven unwilling to establish the kind of legal services system that is necessary to ensure that defendants charged with capital offenses receive the defense they require. Many death penalty states have no working public defender programs, relying instead upon scattershot methods for selecting and supporting defense counsel in capital cases. For example, some states simply assign lawyers at random from a general list—a scheme destined to identify attorneys who lack the necessary qualifications and, worse still, regard their assignments as a burden. Other jurisdictions employ "contract" systems, which typically channel indigent defense business to attorneys who offer the lowest bids. Other states use public defender schemes that appear on the surface to be more promising, but prove in practice to be just as ineffective.

It is scarcely surprising that the results of poor lawyering are often literally fatal for capital defendants. Systematic studies reveal ... the inexperience of lawyers appointed to represent capital clients. In [many instances, state trial courts have] assigned capital cases to young lawyers who had passed the bar only a few months earlier; [to] a lawyer who had never finished a criminal trial of any kind; and [even] allowed a third-year law student to handle most of a capital trial. . . . Even when experienced and competent counsel are available in capital cases, they often are unable to render adequate service for want of essential funding to pay the costs of investigations and expert witnesses. In some rural counties in Texas, an appointed attorney receives no more than $800 to represent a capital defendant. Similar limits are in place in other states. In Virginia, the hourly rate for capital defense services works out to about $13. In an Alabama case, the lawyer appointed to represent a capital defendant in a widely publicized case was allowed a total of $500 to finance his work, including any investigations and expert services needed. With that budget, it is hardly surprising that the attorney conducted no investigation at all. . . .

Another systematic problem cited by the ABA was more recent: restrictions on the procedures available for capital defendants to obtain judicial review of legal and factual errors in their trials. The report noted that in 1996 Congress amended the federal habeas corpus statutes to make it "even more difficult for the federal courts to adjudicate federal claims in capital cases."

Finally, the ABA report pointed to race discrimination in the administration of capital punishment:

Numerous studies have demonstrated that defendants are more likely to be sentenced to death if their victims were white rather than black. Other studies have shown that in some jurisdictions African Americans tend to receive the death penalty more often than do white defendants. And in countless cases, the poor legal services that capital clients receive are rendered worse still by racist attitudes of defense counsel. . . .

As you formulate your advice to the governor, what sources will you consult? What sorts of arguments or evidence will be relevant to her decision? Which of the issues raised are solvable, and at what cost?

=4=

Sentencing Inputs: The Crime and Its Effects

Chapter 1 introduced the social purposes of punishment, Chapter 2 surveyed the groups and individuals who create sentencing rules and impose sentences, and Chapter 3 offered two case studies of sentencing systems designed to control discretion. Along the way, you became familiar with the basic contours of sentencing guidelines and the capital punishment system. Building on this foundation, we now turn to the substantive components of sentencing decisions, starting in this chapter with the relevance of the crime and its effects. In Chapter 5 we consider the background and characteristics of the criminal offender. Together, these two chapters address the raw materials of the sentencing decision, what we call "sentencing inputs."

Sentencing practice always informs sentencing theory. Hence, our discussion of the crime and its effects begins with an introductory sentencing exercise. The exercise calls on you to sentence a mythical criminal offender, Rob Anon, and introduces you to the difficulties of selecting a criminal punishment, even in this seemingly simple case. Throughout the next two chapters, we return to Rob's case periodically to see whether our detailed study of sentencing systems changes your initial perspective on Rob's status.

PROBLEM 4-1. ROB ANON

A jury found Rob Anon guilty of one count of armed bank robbery. The evidence at trial proved that Rob planned the robbery and then recruited his two co-defendants to participate. According to the testimony of co-defendant Zweite (who pled guilty to the charge pursuant to a plea agreement with the government), Rob gave each participant in the robbery a firearm and a ski mask. Rob also provided a getaway car, although the origins and current location of the car remain unknown.

According to the testimony at trial, the activities of the three defendants inside the bank were as follows: Rob disabled the surveillance cameras and alarms; co-defendant Tercero kept his firearm pointed at the teller while Zweite vaulted the counter and collected more than $200,000 in cash. As the threesome hurried out of the bank, Tercero pushed to the ground an elderly man who walked into the bank during the robbery. The man broke his hip when he fell. In dividing the loot, Rob gave Zweite and Tercero one-fourth of the proceeds each, keeping half for himself.

The government's evidence at Rob's trial included surveillance photos, eyewitness accounts, physical evidence, and testimony by Zweite and Tercero. From the moment of his indictment and throughout his prosecution, Rob denied responsibility for the robbery and claimed he was "set up."

Rob is 22 years old and has produced a spotty employment record since dropping out of high school at age 16. Rob was last employed in a series of construction projects with a local landscaping company; he previously worked for a shoe store as a salesman on a part-time basis. Reared by a single mother in an economically depressed urban area and the second youngest of five children, Rob seems to have few friends and mostly keeps to himself. Rob's mother recalls that Rob's siblings taunted and teased him because of his small stature. She believes that Rob became addicted to cocaine in the past year.

Rob's criminal record includes two prior offenses. Six years ago, a juvenile court convicted Rob for shoplifting and sentenced him to 100 hours of community service. Two years ago, Rob was convicted of receipt of stolen goods and sentenced to three years' probation. Rob was still serving that term of probation at the time of the bank robbery. Armed bank robbery carries a maximum penalty of 25 years in prison or a fine of $250,000 or both. Compare http://www.ussc.gov/training/ws_ex_rob.pdf.

1. Assume you are the sentencing judge for Rob in a jurisdiction that places no limits on your discretion to choose a sentence ranging anywhere from probation to the statutory maximum. What sentence would you impose? If you feel you need more information before choosing a sentence, what additional information would you seek?
2. If the robbers had taken less money (say, only $500), would your sentencing decision change?
3. If the elderly man had not been injured, would your sentencing decision change?
4. If you knew that Zweite received a sentence of 5 years' probation as a result of a plea agreement, would your sentencing decision change?

A.   WHICH CRIME?

It is often said that the punishment must fit the crime. This is a true statement, but radically incomplete. Sentencing judges consider more than the crime; they also consider other wrongdoing by the offender, some of it proven during the criminal trial and some of it not mentioned until the presentence investigation or the sentencing hearing. Some conduct constitutes a separate crime, while some of the wrongdoing is not criminal at all. What guidance does the law give to the sentencing judge, who must sort out the defendant's various forms of wrongdoing?

1. Real Offense Versus Conviction Offense

It might seem obvious (to lawyers, at any rate) that defendants can be punished only for the crimes of which they have been *convicted*. Obvious, perhaps, but that is not the law in most jurisdictions. To varying degrees, sentencing laws allow judges to impose punishments based on the "real offense" and not just for the offense of conviction.

Uses for Uncharged Conduct

How can defendants be punished for acts that are not the basis for a conviction? Under an indeterminate sentencing system, the sentencing judge can consider any evidence of the offender's wrongdoing, regardless of whether the conduct formed the basis of the criminal charges. The statutory floor and ceiling for punishing the crime of conviction leave the judge with plenty of latitude to set a punishment, even if it is based in part on uncharged conduct. It is difficult to define offenses in sufficient detail to capture the facts that intuition suggests should affect the sentence. According to the Supreme Court in Williams v. New York, 337 U.S. 241 (1949) (reprinted in Chapter 2), the importance of "individualizing punishments" supports the "age-old practice of seeking information from out-of-court sources" and means that sentencing judges should "not be denied an opportunity to obtain pertinent information by a requirement of rigid adherence to restrictive rules of evidence properly applicable to the trial."

Even structured sentencing systems tend to allow a *range* of presumptive sentences, and when choosing a sentence within that range, a judge may account for circumstances that the elements of the crime cannot cover. Structured systems also usually allow judges to depart up or down from the range of preferred sentences, based on specified details of the crime such as the use of a weapon or the amount of loss or harm inflicted. In death penalty cases, facts about the "real offense" can determine life or death, as capital statutes make murderers eligible for the death penalty only if the killing involved specific "aggravating circumstances."

Types of Uncharged Conduct

Judges receive information about conduct beyond the offense itself from several sources: in plea agreements or during trial, in presentence investigation reports, and from prosecutors during the sentencing hearing. Even if a prosecutor ignores or is unaware of some wrongdoing, a probation officer or other presentence investigator may discover this conduct and the judge may still take it into account.

The defendant's uncharged conduct might be an *element* of an offense other than the one charged. For instance, the defendant may have used a gun during the robbery, even though the charge was robbery and not armed robbery. Other facts about the offense, such as the defendant's role in a multiparty offense, may receive no mention in the statutory framework. The extra information could involve criminal conduct that is *conceptually connected* to the charged crime, such as uncharged criminal conduct that happened during the same time period as the charged crime, or uncharged conduct that was part of the same overarching criminal scheme. Finally, the court might rely on the defendant's past *noncriminal* conduct that is nevertheless blameworthy.

When a judge looks at the defendant's behavior beyond the facts necessary to prove the offense of conviction, the judge is said to be considering (to use the vernacular of the federal sentencing guidelines) "relevant conduct." Under indeterminate sentencing, it has always been possible for a judge to consider all this information, though judges could reject some of it as irrelevant or unreliable. Structured sentencing brought the issue of relevant conduct to a more formal and visible level. Legislatures, sentencing commissions, and judges must now decide explicitly which additional facts a sentencing judge may or may not consider and how much impact the uncharged relevant conduct should have. The sentencing laws that allow the judge to consider uncharged conduct are sometimes called "real offense" systems (as opposed to "charge offense" systems) because the judge sentences based on the "real" criminal behavior, independent of the prosecutor's charging decisions.

Practical Impact of Limiting Use of Uncharged Conduct

The key fact to remember about relevant conduct is the difference in methods of proof at trial and at sentencing. At trial, the prosecution must prove all elements of the crime to a jury, beyond a reasonable doubt. At a noncapital sentencing hearing, the prosecution proves any additional relevant facts to the sentencing judge by a preponderance of the evidence. Thus, any decision to restrict the judge's consideration of relevant conduct for sentencing also makes it harder for the prosecutor to use facts proven by a preponderance of evidence at the sentencing hearing. At the same time, rules that limit the use of uncharged conduct make the charges that the prosecutor selects all the more important; such rules make it more difficult for the judge to "correct" any perceived problems with the prosecutor's selection of charges. As you consider the material below sketching various approaches to the problem of uncharged conduct, keep in mind the effects of the rules on prosecutors, in a world where the law places few limits on the prosecutor's choice among potential criminal charges.

|| *U.S. Sentencing Guidelines Manual* ||

§1B1.3(a)   Relevant Conduct (Factors that Determine the Guideline Range)

[The seriousness of the offense] shall be determined on the basis of the following:

(1) (A) all acts and omissions committed, aided, abetted, counseled, commanded, induced, procured, or willfully caused by the defendant; and

(B) in the case of a jointly undertaken criminal activity (a criminal plan ... undertaken by the defendant in concert with others, whether or not charged as a conspiracy), all reasonably foreseeable acts and omissions of others in furtherance of the jointly undertaken criminal activity,

that occurred during the commission of the offense of conviction, in preparation for that offense, or in the course of attempting to avoid detection or responsibility for that offense. ...

(3) all harm that resulted from the acts and omissions specified in [subsection (a)(1)], and all harm that was the object of such acts and omissions. ...

United States v. Vernon Watts
519 U.S. 148 (1997)

PER CURIAM

[The] Court of Appeals for the Ninth Circuit held that sentencing courts could not consider conduct of the defendants underlying charges of which they had been acquitted. Every other Court of Appeals has held that a sentencing court may do so, if the Government establishes that conduct by a preponderance of the evidence. [Because the Ninth Circuit's holding conflicts with] the clear implications of 18 U.S.C. §3661, the Sentencing Guidelines, and this Court's decisions, particularly Witte v. United States, 515 U.S. 389 (1995), we grant the petition and reverse.

[Police] discovered cocaine base in a kitchen cabinet and two loaded guns and ammunition hidden in a bedroom closet of Watts' house. A jury convicted Watts of possessing cocaine base with intent to distribute, in violation of 21 U.S.C. §841(a)(1), but acquitted him of using a firearm in relation to a drug offense, in violation of 18 U.S.C. §924(c). Despite Watts' acquittal on the firearms count, the District Court found by a preponderance of the evidence that Watts had possessed the guns in connection with the drug offense. In calculating Watts' sentence, the court therefore added two points to his base offense level under [the federal sentencing guidelines. The court of appeals held that a sentencing judge may not, under any standard of proof, rely on facts of which the defendant was acquitted].

We begin our analysis with 18 U.S.C. §3661, which codifies the longstanding principle that sentencing courts have broad discretion to consider various kinds of information. The statute states: "No limitation shall be placed on the information concerning the background, character, and conduct of a person convicted of an offense which a court of the United States may receive and consider for the purpose of imposing an appropriate sentence."

We reiterated this principle in Williams v. New York, 337 U.S. 241 (1949), in which a defendant convicted of murder and sentenced to death challenged the sentencing court's reliance on information that the defendant had been involved in 30 burglaries of which he had not been convicted. We contrasted the different limitations on presentation of evidence at trial and at sentencing: "Highly relevant—if not essential—to [the judge's] selection of an appropriate sentence is the possession of the fullest information possible concerning the defendant's life and characteristics." Neither the broad language of §3661 nor our holding in *Williams* suggests any basis for the courts to invent a blanket prohibition against considering certain types of evidence at sentencing. Indeed, under the pre-Guidelines sentencing regime, it was well established that a sentencing judge may take into account facts introduced at trial relating to other charges, even ones of which the defendant has been acquitted.

The Guidelines did not alter this aspect of the sentencing court's discretion. Very roughly speaking, relevant conduct corresponds to those actions and circumstances that courts typically took into account when sentencing prior to the Guidelines' enactment. Section 1B1.4 of the Guidelines reflects the policy set forth in 18 U.S.C. §3661: "In determining the sentence to impose within the guideline range, or whether a departure from the guidelines is warranted, the court may consider, without limitation, any information concerning the background, character and conduct of the defendant, unless otherwise prohibited by law."

Section 1B1.3, in turn, describes in sweeping language the conduct that a sentencing court may consider in determining the applicable guideline range. The commentary to that section states: "Conduct that is not formally charged or is not an element of the offense of conviction may enter into the determination of the applicable guideline sentencing range." With respect to certain offenses, . . . USSG §1B1.3(a)(2) requires the sentencing court to consider "all acts and omissions . . . that were part of the same course of conduct or common scheme or plan as the offense of conviction." Application Note 3 . . . gives the following example: "Where the defendant engaged in three drug sales of 10, 15, and 20 grams of cocaine, as part of the same course of conduct or common scheme or plan, subsection (a)(2) provides that the total quantity of cocaine involved (45 grams) is to be used to determine the offense level even if the defendant is convicted of a single count charging only one of the sales." Accordingly, the Guidelines conclude that "relying on the entire range of conduct, regardless of the number of counts that are alleged *or on which a conviction is obtained,* appears to be the most reasonable approach to writing workable guidelines for these offenses."

Although the dissent concedes that a district court may properly consider "evidence adduced in a trial that resulted in an acquittal" when choosing a particular sentence within a guideline range, it argues that the court must close its eyes to acquitted conduct at earlier stages of the sentencing process because the "broadly inclusive language of §3661" is incorporated only into §1B1.4 of the Guidelines. This argument ignores §1B1.3 which, as we have noted, directs sentencing courts to consider all other related conduct, whether or not it resulted in a conviction. The dissent also contends that because Congress instructed the Sentencing Commission, in 28 U.S.C. §994(l), to ensure that the Guidelines provide incremental punishment for a defendant who is convicted of multiple offenses, it could not have meant for the Guidelines to increase a sentence based on offenses of which a defendant has been acquitted. The statute is not, however, cast in restrictive or exclusive terms. Far from limiting a sentencing court's power to consider uncharged or acquitted conduct, §994(l) simply ensures that, at a minimum, the Guidelines provide additional penalties when defendants are convicted of multiple offenses. . . . In short, we are convinced that a sentencing court may consider conduct of which a defendant has been acquitted.

As we explained in Witte v. United States, 515 U.S. 389 (1995), . . . sentencing enhancements do not punish a defendant for crimes of which he was not convicted, but rather increase his sentence because of the manner in which he committed the crime of conviction. In *Witte*, we held that a sentencing court could, consistent with the Double Jeopardy Clause, consider uncharged cocaine importation in imposing a sentence on marijuana charges that was within the statutory range, without precluding the defendant's subsequent prosecution for the cocaine offense. We concluded that "consideration of information about the defendant's character and conduct at sentencing does not result in 'punishment' for any offense other than the one of which the defendant was convicted." Rather, the defendant is "punished only for the fact that the *present* offense was carried out in a manner that warrants increased punishment."

The Court of Appeals failed to appreciate the significance of the different standards of proof that govern at trial and sentencing. [Acquittal] on criminal charges does not prove that the defendant is innocent; it merely proves the existence of a reasonable doubt as to his guilt. [It] is impossible to know exactly why a jury found a defendant not guilty on a certain charge. Thus, contrary to the Court of Appeals' assertion . . . , the jury cannot be said to have "necessarily rejected" any facts when it returns a general verdict of not guilty.

For these reasons, an acquittal in a criminal case does not preclude the Government from relitigating an issue when it is presented in a subsequent action governed by a lower standard of proof. The Guidelines state that it is "appropriate" that facts relevant to sentencing be proved by a preponderance of the evidence, USSG §6A1.3 commentary, and we have held that application of the preponderance standard at sentencing generally satisfies due process. McMillan v. Pennsylvania, 477 U.S. 79, 91-92 (1986). . . . We therefore hold that a jury's verdict of acquittal does not prevent the sentencing court from considering conduct underlying the acquitted charge, so long as that conduct has been proved by a preponderance of the evidence.

[In this case], the jury acquitted the defendant of using or carrying a firearm during or in relation to the drug offense. That verdict does not preclude a finding by a preponderance of the evidence that the defendant did, in fact, use or carry such a weapon, much less that he simply *possessed* the weapon in connection with a drug offense.

Stevens J., dissenting.

The Sentencing Reform Act of 1984 revolutionized the manner in which district courts sentence persons convicted of federal crimes. . . . Strict mandatory rules have dramatically confined the exercise of judgment based on a totality of the circumstances. . . .

In 1970, during the era of individualized sentencing, Congress enacted the statute now codified as 18 U.S.C. §3661 to make it clear that otherwise inadmissible evidence could be considered by judges in the exercise of their sentencing discretion. The statute, however, did not tell the judge how to weigh the significance of any of that evidence. The judge was free to rely on any information that might shed light on a decision to grant probation, to impose the statutory maximum, or to determine the precise sentence within those extremes. Wisdom and experience enabled the judge to give appropriate weight to uncorroborated hearsay or to evidence of criminal conduct that had not resulted in a conviction. . . . Like a jury in a capital case, the judge could exercise discretion to dispense mercy on the basis of factors too intangible to write into a statute.

Although the Sentencing Reform Act of 1984 has cabined the discretion of sentencing judges, the 1970 statute remains on the books. As was true when it was enacted, §3661 does not speak to questions concerning the relevance or the weight of any item of evidence. That statute is not offended by provisions in the Guidelines that proscribe reliance on evidence of economic hardship, drug or alcohol dependence, or lack of guidance as a youth, in making certain sentencing decisions. Conversely, that statute does not command that any particular weight—or indeed that any weight at all—be given to evidence that a defendant may have committed an offense that the prosecutor failed to prove beyond a reasonable doubt. . . .

A closer examination of the interaction among §3661, the other provisions of the Sentencing Reform Act, and the Guidelines demonstrates that the role played by §3661 is of a narrower scope than the Court's opinion suggests. The Sentencing Reform Act was enacted primarily to address Congress' concern that similar offenders convicted of similar offenses were receiving an unjustifiably wide range of sentences. . . . The [statute requires] that for any sentence of imprisonment in the Guidelines, "the maximum of the range established for such a term shall not exceed the minimum of that range by more than the greater of 25 percent or 6 months," 28 U.S.C. §994(b)(2). The determination of which of these narrow ranges a particular sentence should fall into is made by operation of mandatory rules, but within the particular range, the judge retains broad discretion to set a particular sentence.

By their own terms, the Guidelines incorporate the broadly inclusive language of §3661 only into those portions of the sentencing decision in which the judge retains discretion. [The] Guidelines Manual §1B1.4 provides: "In determining the sentence to impose within the guideline range, or whether a departure from the guidelines is warranted, the court may consider, without limitation, any information concerning the background, character and conduct of the defendant, unless otherwise prohibited by law. See 18 U.S.C. §3661."

Thus, as in the pre-Guidelines sentencing regime, it is in the area in which the judge exercises discretion that §3661 authorizes unlimited access to information concerning the background, character, and conduct of the defendant. When the judge is exercising such discretion, I agree that he may consider otherwise inadmissible evidence, including evidence adduced in a trial that resulted in an acquittal. But that practice, enshrined in §3661 and USSG §1B1.4, sheds little, if any, light on the appropriateness of the District Courts' application of USSG §1B1.3, which defines relevant conduct for the purposes of determining the Guidelines range within which a sentence can be imposed. . . .

In 28 U.S.C. §994(l) Congress specifically directed the Commission to ensure that the Guidelines included incremental sentences for multiple offenses. That subsection provides: "The Commission shall insure that the Guidelines promulgated [reflect] the appropriateness of imposing an incremental penalty for each offense in a case in which a defendant is convicted of (A) multiple offenses committed in the same course of conduct . . . and (B) multiple offenses committed at different times. . . ." It is difficult to square this explicit statutory command to impose incremental punishment for each of the "multiple offenses" of which a defendant "is convicted" with the conclusion that Congress intended incremental punishment for each offense of which the defendant has been acquitted. . . .

In my opinion the statute should be construed in the light of the traditional requirement that criminal charges must be sustained by proof beyond a reasonable doubt. That requirement has always applied to charges involving multiple offenses as well as a single offense. Whether an allegation of criminal conduct is the sole basis for punishment or merely one of several bases for punishment, we should presume that Congress intended the new sentencing Guidelines that it authorized in 1984 to adhere to longstanding procedural requirements enshrined in our constitutional jurisprudence. The notion that a charge that cannot be sustained by proof beyond a reasonable doubt may give rise to the same punishment as if it had been so proved is repugnant to that jurisprudence. I respectfully dissent.

Charles Frederick Barr v. State
674 So. 2d 628 (Fla. 1996)

HARDING, J.

. . . Charles Frederick Barr stole a car at gunpoint. Thereafter, when a police officer spotted the stolen car and attempted to pull the car over, Barr fled. A high speed chase followed in heavy traffic, nearly causing several accidents. Barr was charged with armed robbery and possession of a firearm by a convicted felon.

A jury convicted Barr of armed robbery. He was sentenced to twenty-five years in prison, which was an upward departure from Barr's recommended guideline sentence of seven to nine years, with a permitted range of five and one-half to twelve years. The trial court entered a written departure order, reasoning that Barr displayed a flagrant disregard for the safety of others by recklessly driving during the chase with the police and endangering the lives of numerous innocent citizens. . . .

Barr argues that Florida Rule of Criminal Procedure 3.701(d)(11) . . . prohibits upward departure sentences when the conduct can be separately charged as another crime. Barr further argues that a contrary holding would eliminate a defendant's constitutional right to a trial as it would permit sentencing for a crime for which the defendant has not been convicted. Thus, he contends, a defendant must be charged and convicted for each instance of criminal conduct.

The State argues, however, that Florida Statutes §921.0016, which includes endangering the lives of many persons as a valid reason for upward departure sentences, controls the instant case instead of Rule 3.701(d)(11). Section 921.0016 addresses recommended sentences and departure sentences. [The statute lists a number of aggravating circumstances that reasonably justify departure from the sentencing guidelines, such as the creation of a "substantial risk of death or great bodily harm to many persons."]

We find that §921.0016 is not applicable to the instant case as it only applies to offenses committed on or after January 1, 1994. Barr was arrested and charged on November 24, 1993. Instead, we look to the language of Rule 3.701(d)(11) to determine whether departure was proper in this case. Rule 3.701(d)(11) provides that "[r]easons for deviating from the guidelines shall not include factors relating to . . . the instant offenses for which convictions have not been obtained."

As this Court explained in State v. Tyner, 506 So. 2d 405 (Fla. 1987), the language of Rule 3.701(d)(11) is "plain" and specifically provides that judges "may consider only that conduct of the defendant relating to an element of the offense for which he has been convicted." *Tyner* involved a defendant originally charged with two counts of first-degree murder and one count of armed burglary. After the murder counts were dismissed, the defendant was convicted of armed burglary. The defendant's departure sentence was invalidated because it was based upon the murders for which Tyner had not yet been found guilty. We concluded that "[to] hold otherwise would effectively circumvent the basic requirement of obtaining a conviction before meting out punishment."

We adhered to this position in State v. Varner, 616 So. 2d 988 (Fla. 1993), and specifically held that "departure may not be based on conduct that could have, but has not yet, resulted in criminal conviction." Varner was convicted of shooting into a building, shooting into a vehicle, and aggravated assault. Prior to his trial, Varner allegedly threatened a witness and the trial court entered a departure sentence based in part upon that threat. On appeal, the district court found this to be an invalid reason for departure. In our review of the case, we approved the district court's decision and explained that "[if] the State wishes to punish such collateral misconduct, the proper method is to separately charge and convict." . . .

Relying upon the reasoning in . . . *Tyner* and *Varner,* a departure sentence based on flagrant disregard for the safety of others is not valid where the conduct at issue could be separately charged and convicted. See, e.g., Felts v. State, 537 So. 2d 995 (Fla. App. 1988) (finding that high speed chase and resulting fatal accident were not valid basis for departure because they involved circumstances surrounding the offense for which convictions were not obtained). However, where the conduct evincing such disregard involves a situation where the conduct could not be separately charged as another crime it can be a valid reason for departure. See, e.g., *Felts* (finding that gun battle with Georgia police officers which posed unnecessary risk of harm was valid basis for departure where the subsequent Georgia convictions for aggravated assault could not be factored into scoresheet); Burgess v. State, 524 So. 2d 1132 (Fla. App. 1988) (upholding departure based on flagrant disregard for safety of others where defendant shot two victims who were standing in an alley while three bystanders stood nearby).

In the instant case, the auto chase that ensued after the officer attempted to stop Barr constituted criminal conduct. Barr could have been charged either with fleeing or attempting to elude a law enforcement officer pursuant to Florida Statutes §316.1935(1), or with reckless driving pursuant to Florida Statutes §316.192(1). Thus, this criminal conduct for which Barr was neither charged nor convicted cannot be a valid reason for a departure sentence. Moreover, while it is not determinative of our conclusion here, we note that Barr's departure sentence far exceeds any sentence that could have been imposed if he had been convicted of the uncharged offenses of eluding a police officer or reckless driving. [At the time of Barr's arrest, fleeing or attempting to elude an officer was punishable by imprisonment for a period not to exceed one year. Reckless driving is punishable for up to 90 days' imprisonment for a first offense and up to six months' imprisonment for a second offense.] Accordingly, we quash the decision below and remand for imposition of an appropriate guideline sentence. . . . It is so ordered.

NOTES

1. *Relevant conduct in state sentencing: majority position.* Sentencing judges in indeterminate sentencing systems have the power (but not the obligation) to consider any conduct of the defendant, whether charged or uncharged. This conduct might influence the judge's choice of a maximum or minimum sentence from within the broad statutory range. See State v. O'Donnell, 495 A.2d 798, 803 (Me. 1985) ("we find nothing objectionable in treating trial evidence of a defendant's uncharged conduct regarding other victims as relevant information for sentencing purposes on the ground that it indicates a continuing course of conduct over a substantial period of time"); Anderson v. People, 337 P.2d 10 (Colo. 1959) (conviction for forgery; evidence at sentencing of forgeries submitted to six additional victims); see also Williams v. New York, 337 U.S. 961 (1949) (death sentence imposed by judge based on presentence report suggesting defendant had been involved in "30 other burglaries" in area of murder).

States with more structured sentencing systems place more restrictions on the use of the defendant's uncharged conduct. Formally, the structured state systems adopt charge offense rather than real offense sentencing. The charged offense determines a fairly small range of options available to the judge in the normal case. But real and charge offense concepts define the ends of a spectrum, and all systems allow some amount of real offense conduct to affect the sentencing determination. At a minimum, the uncharged conduct is available to influence the judge's selection of a sentence *within* the narrow range that the guidelines designate for typical cases. Some states go further and allow judges to use uncharged conduct as a basis for a departure from the designated normal range of sentences. Other structured sentencing states (such as Florida) prevent the judge from using some types of uncharged conduct to depart from the guideline sentence. Commentary to the Minnesota sentencing guidelines states that "departures from the guidelines should not be permitted for elements of alleged offender behavior not within the definition of the offense of conviction." Minn. Stat. Ann. §244 cmt. II.D.103. The ABA Standards for Criminal Justice, Sentencing 18-3.6 (3d ed. 1994), also opts for an offense-of-conviction model.

2. *Relevant conduct in federal sentencing.* In contrast to the states, the federal guidelines create a modified real offense system. In a 1995 self-study report, the U.S. Sentencing Commission described the trade-offs at stake in framing a relevant conduct provision:

> If uncharged misconduct is considered, punishment is based on facts proven outside procedural protections constitutionally defined for proving criminal charges, introducing an argument of unfairness. . . . The scope of conduct considered at sentencing will also affect, at least to some extent, the complexity of a sentencing system. The scope can be as limited as the conduct defined by the elements of the offense or as broad as any wrongdoing ever committed by the

defendant or the defendant's partners in crime. All things being equal, a large scope of considered conduct will require more fact-finding than a more limited scope. . . . Besides fairness and complexity, the scope of conduct considered at sentencing may have serious implications for the balance between prosecutorial and judicial power in sentencing. For example, if the scope of considered conduct is confined to the offense of conviction, many argue that the sentencing system will provide relatively more power to prosecutors to control sentences. . . . Finding the right balance among fairness, complexity, and the role of the prosecutor has been a struggle for sentencing commissions generally. . . .

Discussion Paper, Relevant Conduct and Real Offense Sentencing (1995) (available at http://www.ussc.gov/simple/relevant.htm). The federal system uses the offense of conviction as a starting point for guideline calculations but then requires many adjustments (and permits a few discretionary adjustments) to the offense level based on other relevant conduct.

The commission explained its support for real-offense factors on several grounds. First, such a system mirrored prior practices in the indeterminate system. It also gave judges a means to refine and rationalize the chaotic federal criminal code. Finally, the real-offense features of the system gave judges a way to check the prosecutor's power to dictate a sentence based on the selection of charges. When the rules allow the trial judge to look behind the charged offense to select a sentence based on the real-offense conduct, the judge serves as a counterweight to the prosecutor. See Julie R. O'sullivan, In Defense of the U.S. Sentencing Guidelines' Modified Real-Offense System, 91 Nw. U. L. Rev. 1342 (1997).

The use of relevant conduct to enhance sentences in the federal system has come under sharp attack from scholars. See Kate Stith & Jose A. Cabranes, Fear of Judging: Sentencing Guidelines in the Federal Courts 66-77 (1998); Elizabeth Lear, Is Conviction Irrelevant?, 40 UCLA L. Rev. 1179 (1993); David Yellen, Illusion, Illogic and Injustice: Real-Offense Sentencing and the Federal Sentencing Guidelines, 78 Minn. L. Rev. 403 (1993). Critics have attacked the uses of uncharged or dismissed conduct as bad policy because of the uncertain proof of the uncharged conduct during the sentencing hearing. They also point out the difficulty of remaining consistent from case to case in deciding how much uncharged conduct is relevant. They also have raised constitutional questions about whether reliance on such information violates due process (by punishing a person for conduct that is not proven beyond a reasonable doubt) or undermines the investigative and charging functions of the grand jury.

3. *Acquitted conduct versus uncharged conduct.*   Although indeterminate sentencing systems typically allow judges to consider prior misconduct when setting a sentence, many states make an exception for acquitted conduct — conduct that formed the basis for a charge resulting in an acquittal at trial. Judges in many states have developed common law rules preventing the use of acquitted conduct at sentencing. See State v. Cobb, 732 A.2d 425 (N.H. 1999); Bishop v. State, 486 S.E.2d 887 (Ga. 1997); Anderson v. State, 448 N.E.2d 1180 (Ind. 1983). On the other hand, a roughly equal number of states approve the use of acquitted conduct. State v. Huey, 505 A.2d 1242 (Conn. 1986); State v. Woodlief, 90 S.E. 137 (N.C. 1916); State v. Leiter, 646 N.W.2d 341 (Wis. 2002). Why do so many states limit the use of acquitted conduct but permit sentencing judges to consider prior convictions and prior uncharged conduct more generally?

The Supreme Court in *Watts* confirmed that neither the Constitution nor the federal sentencing statutes or guidelines bar a judge from using acquitted conduct. See also Edwards v. United States, 523 U.S. 511 (1998) (sentencing judge can determine that defendants were trafficking in both crack and powder, even if jury believed defendants were trafficking only in powder). But the Court did not resolve the policy issue of whether the guidelines *should* limit the use of acquitted conduct. Justices Breyer and Scalia, in separate opinions in *Watts* not reprinted above, disagreed about whether 18 U.S.C. §3661 blocks the U.S. Commission from creating such a rule. The statute says that "no limitation shall be placed on the information concerning the background, character, and conduct of a person convicted" that the sentencing judge may "receive and consider." Can the commission limit the use of acquitted conduct, consistent with this statute?

Just before the Court decided *Watts,* the commission did in fact consider several options for limiting the use of acquitted conduct. One option would have excluded "the use of acquitted conduct as a basis for determining the guideline range" but would have allowed upward departures based on acquitted conduct. Another option would have allowed acquitted conduct only if it was proved at sentencing by clear and convincing evidence (rather than the usual preponderance standard). A third option would have allowed judges to use acquitted conduct in setting the guideline range but also would have authorized downward departures from the range to avoid fundamental unfairness. 62 Fed. Reg. 151, 161 (Jan. 2, 1997). In the end, the commission did not adopt any of these options. Why do you suppose the commission kept the status quo? Are sentencing commissions better situated than judges to create limits on the use of acquitted conduct?

As discussed fully in Chapter 6, not long after the *Watts* decision, the Supreme Court started to give new attention to the jury's role in sentencing determinations through a revised interpretation of the Sixth Amendment in the *Apprendi-Blakely-Booker* line of cases. Many defendants have argued to lower courts that the Supreme Court's recent Sixth Amendment rulings essentially abrogate *Watts.* The federal circuit courts have so far generally rejected this claim and have consistently ruled that *Watts* remains good law. See, e.g., United States v. Gobbi, 471 F.3d 302 (1st Cir. 2006); United States v. Farias, 469 F.3d 393 (5th Cir. 2006); United States v. Mercado, 474 F.3d 654 (9th Cir. 2007); United States v. Dorcely, 454 F.3d 366, 371 (D.C. Cir. 2006). Some district courts have, however, relied on the Supreme Court's new Sixth Amendment jurisprudence to resist consideration of acquitted conduct at sentencing. See United States v. Wendelsdorf, 423 F. Supp. 2d 927, 937-938 (N.D. Iowa 2006) (rejecting as "an abomination" the government's proposed sentence increase based on acquitted conduct "for two, distinct and separate, criminal acts from the offense of conviction"); United States v. Pimental, 367 F. Supp. 2d 143 (D. Mass. 2005) ("It makes absolutely no sense to conclude that the Sixth Amendment is violated whenever facts essential to sentencing have been determined by a judge rather than a jury, and also conclude that the fruits of the jury's efforts can be ignored with impunity by the judge in sentencing.").

4. *Criminal elements versus noncriminal wrongdoing.* As *Barr* shows, some states prevent sentencing judges from considering the defendant's wrongdoing

if that conduct could form the basis for additional criminal charges or more serious criminal charges. Other conduct, while blameworthy, does not affect the charging options available to the prosecutor. For example, under the federal criminal code, a mail fraud that nets $10,000 is eligible for the same punishment as a mail fraud that nets $100,000. Should it matter to a sentencing judge (or to a sentencing commission creating sentencing guidelines) whether the conduct in question is an element of some crime for which the defendant was not charged? Consider this approach to the problem in Kan. Stat. §21-4716(b)(3): "If a factual aspect of a crime is a statutory element of the crime . . . that aspect of the current crime of conviction may be used as an aggravating or mitigating factor only if [it] is significantly different from the usual criminal conduct captured by the aspect of the crime."

Review again the provisions of Fla. R. Crim. Proc. 3.701(d)(11) and Fla. Stat. §921.0016, discussed in the *Barr* case. Why did Florida lawmakers generally prohibit sentencing judges from increasing the sentence above the normal guideline range based on "factors relating to . . . the instant offenses for which convictions have not been obtained"? Did the Florida legislature meaningfully change the system when it passed §921.0016(3)(i), which authorizes a departure to a more serious sentence when the offense of conviction "created a substantial risk of death or great bodily harm to many persons"? Should it matter to a sentencing judge whether the defendant's relevant (but uncharged) conduct is recent? What should Florida judges do in cases involving uncharged criminal conduct that is not part of the same transaction or series of events as the crime of conviction?

5. *Conduct after charging.*   Sometimes the defendant's relevant conduct occurs after the government files charges, perhaps during or after the trial. For instance, the law in about 30 states authorizes the sentencing judge to select a higher sentence from within the authorized range if the judge believes the defendant committed perjury at trial. See People v. Redmond, 633 P.2d 976 (Cal. 1981); see also People v. Stewart, 473 N.E.2d 840 (Ill. 1984) (allowing consideration of conduct in jail awaiting trial); Alabama v. Smith, 490 U.S. 794 (1989) (allowing judge who imposes sentence after guilty plea to impose higher sentence on same defendant after appeal and retrial based on information about crime and postconviction conduct). In the federal system, U.S. Sentencing Guidelines Manual §3C1.1 increases the offense level when a defendant obstructs the administration of justice during the prosecution of the offense; this rule can be applied whenever a court finds that the defendant committed perjury at trial. The Supreme Court in United States v. Dunnigan, 507 U.S. 87 (1993), upheld the constitutionality of this provision against a claim that it undermines a defendant's right to testify on his own behalf. But compare Mitchell v. United States, 526 U.S. 314 (1999) (Fifth Amendment privilege against self-incrimination bars judge from drawing inferences about details of crime from defendant's silence at sentencing).

6. *Double jeopardy for enhancing sentences based on prior crimes.*   When criminal conduct gives a sentencing judge the basis for increasing a sentence against a defendant charged with some separate crime, would a later sentence for the original crime constitute multiple punishment for double jeopardy purposes? In

Witte v. United States, 515 U.S. 389 (1995), the defendant raised such a claim. Witte was involved in two illegal drug transactions, one in 1990 and the other in 1991. The judge sentencing Witte for the 1991 sale increased the sentence based on the amount of drugs involved in the 1990 sale, because the judge considered the two sales to be part of a single continuing conspiracy. Later, a grand jury indicted Witte for the 1990 sale, and Witte raised a double jeopardy objection because the judge in the earlier proceeding had already punished him for that conduct. The Supreme Court rejected the challenge, noting that sentencing courts have traditionally "considered a defendant's past criminal behavior, even if no conviction resulted from that behavior." The opinion also concluded that the same practice is acceptable under the federal sentencing guidelines: "Regardless of whether particular conduct is taken into account by rule or as an act of discretion, the defendant is still being punished only for the offense of conviction." The state high courts that have addressed a double jeopardy challenge on similar facts have reached the same result. See, e.g., Traylor v. State, 801 S.W.2d 267 (Ark. 1990).

In capital punishment cases, extensive appeals and habeas corpus proceedings lead to the reversal of many convictions. A retrial on the charges can raise some double jeopardy issues. If the jury in the first capital trial imposes a life sentence rather than the death penalty, double jeopardy prevents the prosecutor from seeking a death penalty in the later retrial. But if the jury in the first trial deadlocks on the question of the proper penalty and the judge imposes a life term, the prosecutor remains free to seek the death penalty during a later retrial after the conviction is reversed on appeal. See Sattazahn v. Pennsylvania, 537 U.S. 101 (2003).

7. *Checks on prosecutorial power at sentencing.* Criminal codes typically give prosecutors several options when deciding which (if any) charges to file based on a given set of acts. As the Supreme Court explained in Bordenkircher v. Hayes, 434 U.S. 357, 364 (1978), other institutions generally do not review the prosecutor's choices: "In our system, so long as the prosecutor has probable cause to believe that the accused committed an offense defined by statute, the decision whether or not to prosecute, and what charge to file or bring before a grand jury, generally rests entirely in his discretion." While courts might overturn charging decisions based on racial or other invidious discrimination, the decision in United States v. Armstrong, 517 U.S. 456 (1996), established that defendants face a heavy burden in obtaining pretrial discovery to prove that their prosecutions were racially motivated.

Sentencing rules, at least in theory, can expand the effects of the prosecutor's charging decisions. Guidelines that instruct judges to set the sentence based largely on charge of conviction give the prosecutor more power to influence the sentence, especially since the vast majority of convictions are secured through plea bargains. Do real-offense elements in a sentencing system offer sentencing judges a realistic method of reviewing the prosecutor's charging and plea bargaining decisions after conviction? Can a real-offense system constrain prosecutorial discretion if it authorizes the prosecutor to prove some conduct at the sentencing hearing under a lower standard of proof? The workloads of prosecutors may affect their willingness to manipulate charges to obtain different sentencing results, since prosecutors with heavy dockets might simply carry forward traditional charging patterns.

8. *The importance of presentence investigations.*   Judges often rely heavily on the investigatory work of probation officers or other court personnel, embodied in a presentence report. Historically, in indeterminate sentencing systems that expressly pursued rehabilitative goals, such presentence investigations and reports focused on defendants' character and background to assess their amenability to various rehabilitative possibilities. With structured sentencing systems now considering real-offense conduct more formally, these presentence investigations sometimes have been transformed into initial evaluations of defendants' relevant conduct. Especially in the federal system, commentators have expressed concerns about the role of probation officers' efforts in guidelines calculations. See, e.g., Kate Stith & Jose A. Cabranes, Fear of Judging: Sentencing Guidelines in the Federal Courts 87-91 (1998). Some defense attorneys have complained that probation officers often act as a sort of "second prosecutor" by uncovering aggravating facts or additional wrongdoing by defendants that did not come to light at trial or in plea negotiations. See, e.g., Felicia Sarner, "Fact Bargaining" Under the Sentencing Guidelines: The Role of the Probation Department, 8 Fed. Sent'g Rep. 328 (1996).

PROBLEM 4-2.   ROB ANON REVISITED

Recall the case of Rob Anon, described in Problem 4-1. As a probation officer assigned to prepare a presentence report before Rob's sentencing, would you spend any time investigating the background and status of the getaway car used in the robbery? As a sentencing judge in an indeterminate sentencing jurisdiction, would evidence that the getaway car had been reported stolen influence the sentence you select? Suppose this evidence comes to light right before sentencing, when the prosecutor reports that the car had just been recovered. Should a sentencing judge in such a situation hold an evidentiary hearing to give Rob and his lawyer a chance to respond to the car theft allegation? As a member of a state sentencing commission, would you want to draft guidelines that instruct judges to consider (or not to consider) facts such as these? Should such a commission also draft procedural rules to govern this sort of factfinding?

2.   Multiple Convictions

Many defendants are convicted of more than one crime at trial, and the judge imposes sentences for the multiple convictions during a single sentencing hearing. The judge might impose sentences on the different convictions to run concurrently (all the terms begin at the same time) or consecutively (a second sentence starts after the first one ends). Even if the judge imposes concurrent sentences, he might increase the sentence for the most serious charge to reflect the fact that the defendant committed multiple crimes. States have created a variety of rules to guide sentencing judges as they account for multiple convictions.

Justice (then Judge) Stephen Breyer used the following example to illustrate traditional practices involving multiple convictions:

Column A	Column B
1. *D*, in a brawl, injures one person seriously.	1. *D*, in a brawl, injures six persons seriously.
2. *D* sells 100 grams of cocaine.	2. *D* sells 600 grams of cocaine.
3. *D* robs one bank.	3. *D* robs six banks.

Most persons react to these examples in accordance with two principles: [First, the] behavior in Column B warrants more severe punishment with respect to each example than the behavior in . . . Column A. [Second, the] punishment for behavior in Column B . . . should not be six times as severe as that in Column A. . . . These two widely held principles, or perceptions, make it difficult to write rules that properly treat "multiple counts."

Some state commissions have dealt with this problem by giving the trial judge considerable discretion as to whether to sentence defendants convicted of several counts consecutively or concurrently. A moment's thought suggests, however, that this approach leaves the prosecutor and the judge free to construct almost any sentence whatsoever. . . .

Other guidelines have distinguished among types of crimes, requiring, for example, concurrent sentences for multiple counts charging property crimes but consecutive sentences for crimes against the person. This approach, however, violates both principles. It violates the first principle with respect to property crimes, since it would treat the Column B defendants no more severely than the Column A defendants; it violates the second principle with respect to crimes against the person, because it is too severe. The federal Commission has tried to satisfy both principles through a system that treats additional counts as warranting additional punishment but in progressively diminishing amounts. . . . The upshot is that a bank robber who robs six banks will receive roughly twice as much (not six times as much punishment) as the robber who robs one bank.

The Federal Sentencing Guidelines and the Key Compromises upon Which They Rest, 17 Hofstra L. Rev. 1, 25-28 (1988). Read the statutes below carefully, and consider how they would guide a sentencing judge in Problem 4-3. Each statute offers judges distinctive guidance in choosing between consecutive and concurrent sentences. The North Carolina statute leaves the decision entirely in the judge's hands. The Indiana statute directs the judge's attention to particular considerations that are relevant to this choice, while the Kansas statute offers no substantive guidance but caps the possible impact of consecutive sentences.

PROBLEM 4-3. TAKE TWO

Review the facts of Problem 4-1. In addition to the bank robbery (which occurred in early December), Rob Anon and his co-defendants pled guilty to two other armed robberies. The first, committed on November 12, involved an evening holdup of Joru's Tavern. When Anon, Zweite, and Tercero entered the tavern about 9:00 p.m., Anon acted as lookout while the others took $240 from the tavern cash register. Tercero was armed with a shotgun, and the robbers took wallets and jewelry from three tavern patrons. The proceeds totaled $600.

The second robbery occurred on November 26. It involved the late evening holdup of Mike and Ginny's Tap. Anon, Zweite, and Tercero entered the tavern at 11:20 p.m. Anon was armed with a long-bladed knife, which he held to the throat of tavern owner Virginia Brown, stating, "Where's the money? Give me all of it or I'll slit your throat." Brown sustained a small cut on her right hand when she tried to push the knife away from her throat. One of the other robbers pointed a handgun at tavern patrons. The proceeds this time totaled $225.

Recall that armed robbery is punishable by a prison term of up to 25 years or a fine of up to $250,000 or both. The judge will impose sentences for the bank robbery and the two other robberies at the same time. What sentences are available to a judge applying each of the statutes below?

‖ *North Carolina General Statutes §15A-1340.15* ‖

(a) *Consecutive Sentences.* This Article [setting penalty ranges for particular crimes] does not prohibit the imposition of consecutive sentences. Unless otherwise specified by the court, all sentences of imprisonment run concurrently with any other sentences of imprisonment.

(b) *Consolidation of Sentences.* If an offender is convicted of more than one offense at the same time, the court may consolidate the offenses for judgment and impose a single judgment for the consolidated offenses. The judgment shall contain a sentence disposition specified for the class of offense and prior record level of the most serious offense, and its minimum sentence of imprisonment shall be within the ranges specified for that class of offense and prior record level, unless applicable statutes require or authorize another minimum sentence of imprisonment.

‖ *Indiana Code §35-38-1-7.1(b)* ‖

The court may consider the following factors as aggravating circumstances or as favoring imposing consecutive terms of imprisonment:

(1) The person has recently violated the conditions of any probation, parole, or pardon granted to the person.

(2) The person has a history of criminal or delinquent activity.

(3) The person is in need of correctional or rehabilitative treatment that can best be provided by commitment of the person to a penal facility.

(4) Imposition of a reduced sentence or suspension of the sentence and imposition of probation would depreciate the seriousness of the crime.

(5) The victim of the crime was less than twelve years of age or at least sixty-five years of age.

(6) The victim of the crime was mentally or physically infirm. . . .

(14) The person committed the offense in the presence or within hearing of a person who is less than eighteen years of age who was not the victim of the offense.

‖ *Kansas Statutes §21-4720* ‖

(b) The sentencing judge shall . . . have discretion to impose concurrent or consecutive sentences in multiple conviction cases. . . . In cases where consecutive sentences may be imposed by the sentencing judge, the following shall apply: . . .

(2) The sentencing judge must establish a base sentence for the primary crime. The primary crime is the crime with the highest crime severity ranking. . . .

(4) The total prison sentence imposed in a case involving multiple convictions arising from multiple counts within an information, complaint or indictment cannot exceed twice the base sentence. . . .

(c) The following shall apply for a departure from the presumptive sentence based on aggravating factors within the context of consecutive sentences:

(1) The court may depart from the presumptive limits for consecutive sentences only if the judge finds substantial and compelling reasons to impose a departure sentence for any of the individual crimes being sentenced consecutively.

(2) When a departure sentence is imposed for any of the individual crimes sentenced consecutively, the imprisonment term of that departure sentence shall not exceed twice the maximum presumptive imprisonment term that may be imposed for that crime.

(3) The total imprisonment term of the consecutive sentences, including the imprisonment term for the departure crime, shall not exceed twice the maximum presumptive imprisonment term of the departure sentence following aggravation.

PROBLEM 4-4. PREDISPOSED TO PRISON

Anthony Soto met an informant and a police officer who was working undercover. The informant asked Soto about drugs, but Soto replied that he was not involved in the sale of drugs at that time. After this conversation, the informant called Soto three times to discuss a purchase of cocaine. Soto finally agreed to locate some cocaine for the informant because Soto was in bad financial shape.

Soto later agreed to meet the informant and the undercover police officer in a parking lot on February 8, where the undercover officer informed Soto that he had $1,300 for an ounce of cocaine. Soto left the area for five minutes and returned with a bag containing 27 grams of cocaine, which he exchanged with the officer for the money. At that meeting, the officer asked Soto if he could buy two or three more ounces of cocaine from him at a later time. Soto responded that it would be no problem. On February 11 Soto again met with the informant and the undercover police officer in the same parking lot to sell two ounces of cocaine for $2,600. Once again, the officer asked Soto at this meeting if he could buy a larger amount later, and Soto again replied that it was no problem.

After the February 11 sale, the informant and the undercover police officer called Soto at least three times a week to arrange a larger sale of cocaine. On March 11 the officer met Soto and asked to buy eight ounces of cocaine. The officer agreed to buy ten ounces for $1,150 per ounce and they arranged a time to meet later in the day. When the officer arrived at a shopping center to meet with Soto, he was wired with a body microphone and had several officers in the area monitoring him. Soto arrived and gave the officer ten ounces of cocaine in exchange for $11,500. After the exchange was completed, Soto was arrested by the backup officers.

Soto was charged with one count of sale of cocaine in the first degree, and the state offered not to charge him with two additional counts if he would testify against two of his accomplices. Soto declined the offer, and the prosecutors amended their complaint by adding two counts. At trial, Soto asserted the defense of entrapment, but the jury found him guilty of three counts of sale of cocaine in the first degree. The sentencing judge imposed concurrent sentences on the three convictions, with the most serious sentence attached to the March 11 sale, count 3, because of the large amount of drugs involved. The judge also increased the sentence for count 3 based on the fact that Soto engaged in multiple sales.

Soto argues on appeal that the sentencing court should not use the fact that the government charged multiple counts of drug violations as a reason to enhance the guideline sentence for some of the counts. He says that such a sentencing rule would permit police officers and prosecutors to manipulate investigative or charging procedures to achieve a specific sentence. For instance, Soto argues that police officers could manipulate the amount of drugs or the number of sales involved, while prosecutors could separate the drug sales into multiple charges to ensure that a higher sentence would be imposed. Soto further argues that permitting police officers and prosecutors to have such discretion creates the potential for racially biased decisions and perpetuates racial disparities in the prosecution of drug crimes. How would you rule? Compare State v. Soto, 562 N.W.2d 299 (Minn. 1997).

NOTES

1. *Multiple counts, indeterminate systems.* Defendants are often convicted of multiple offenses arising from the same transaction or course of conduct. The sentencing judge in an indeterminate system typically has the discretion to impose separate sentences for the multiple convictions and to decide whether those sentences will be served concurrently or consecutively. The sentencing judge faces such a choice if the defendant was convicted of multiple crimes at one trial, or if the defendant is serving some other criminal sentence at the time of sentencing for the current conviction. As the Indiana Supreme Court put it in Williams v. State, 690 N.E.2d 162, 172 (Ind. 1997), "[i]t is within the trial court's discretion to determine . . . whether multiple sentences are to be concurrent or consecutive. The trial court will be reversed only upon a showing of a manifest abuse of discretion." Judges with complete power over the concurrent or con-secutive nature of sentences have tended to give what might be termed a

"volume discount." Additional convictions will increase the total sentence served, but in decreasing amounts for each extra conviction. Is there any reason to favor either consecutive or concurrent sentences as the presumptive or normal outcome? Cf. ABA Standards Relating to Sentencing Alternatives and Procedures 18-6.5 (3d ed. 1994) (sentencing court "ordinarily should designate" sentences to be served concurrently).

2. *Multiple counts, structured systems.* Some state systems limit the judge's ability to adjust a sentence based on multiple convictions. The Kansas statute above offers one example. The grouping rules of the federal sentencing guidelines, designed to address this issue, are particularly complex. The basic strategy of the grouping rules of Chapter 3D of the federal guidelines is to increase the sentence for the most serious crime by diminishing amounts for each extra conviction. You might want to practice using the federal grouping rules; try completing Worksheet B at http://www.ussc.gov/training/worksheets01.pdf and the online exercise at http://www.ussc.gov/training/quizmc.pdf.

But controls over sentences for multiple counts are not a necessary part of sentencing guidelines. Some states start with a presumption of concurrent sentences but direct the sentencing judge to consider specific factors that might lead to a consecutive sentence instead. See Utah Code §76-3-401(1). North Carolina has adopted a highly structured sentencing system, yet judges retain all of their traditional authority to choose between consecutive and concurrent sentences. Does a rule such as North Carolina's undermine the predictability and uniformity of sentences, which are the underlying purposes of many guideline sentencing systems?

In sentencing systems that require the finding of some predicate fact before a consecutive sentence is allowed to replace the presumptive concurrent sentence, defendants have often argued that Blakely v. Washington, 542 U.S. 296 (2004), requires a jury to find the relevant fact before a judge may order the sentences to run consecutively. Most courts addressing this issue, however, have concluded that *Blakely* applies to the selection of the proper sentence for each crime of conviction, but not to the interaction among those sentences. See, e.g., Smylie v. State, 823 N.E.2d 679 (Ind. 2005); State v. Cubias, 120 P.3d 929 (Wash. 2005). But see State v. Foster, 845 N.E.2d 470 (Ohio 2006) (finding *Blakely* applicable to factfinding required for consecutive sentencing).

3. *Special rules for special crimes.* From time to time, a legislature specifies in a criminal statute that any sentence imposed under the statute must be consecutive rather than concurrent. For instance, under Idaho Code §18-2502(1), a sentence for escape by a prisoner "shall commence at the time [the prisoner] would otherwise have been discharged." Similarly, the Supreme Court in United States v. Gonzales, 520 U.S. 1 (1997), interpreted 18 U.S.C. §924(c) to prevent the federal firearm enhancement from being imposed concurrently with an existing state or federal sentence. Are there general criteria that legislatures might follow in selecting crimes to receive consecutive sentences automatically? See also 11 Del. C. §1447(c). Should sentencing courts set consecutive or concurrent sentences based on what they believe was the legislative intent of the criminal statute violated by the defendant?

4. *Multiplicity and sentencing.*   The rules growing out of the constitutional bar on double jeopardy for the same offense help determine whether the prosecutor can charge multiple crimes based on a single set of related acts. In most states, so long as two crimes each require proof of an element that the other does not require, the prosecutor can file distinct charges, even if they are based on essentially the same conduct. Blockburger v. United States, 284 U.S. 299 (1932). Indeed, so long as the legislature intended to create separate criminal statutes punishing the same conduct, multiple convictions and punishments do not create double jeopardy problems. Missouri v. Hunter, 459 U.S. 359 (1983). Does the law guiding the sentencing judge's choice of consecutive or concurrent sentences supplement these minimal double jeopardy rules aimed at preventing multiple punishments?

The International Criminal Tribunal for Yugoslavia (ICTY) and the International Criminal Tribunal for Rwanda (ICTR) have both addressed the double jeopardy question in connection with multiple charges. The ICTR held that under national and international law "it is acceptable to convict the accused of two offences in relation to the same set of facts in the following circumstances: (1) where the offences have different elements; or (2) where the provisions creating the offences protect different interests; or (3) where it is necessary to record a conviction for both offences in order fully to describe what the accused did." The Prosecutor v. Akayesu, Case No. ICTR-96-4-T, Judgement of Sept. 2, 1998, at para. 468. The court found genocide, crimes against humanity, and war crimes to have different elements and to protect different interests so as to justify multiple convictions arising from the same underlying conduct.

5. *Sentence entrapment and manipulation: majority position.*   Entrapment, like other complete criminal defenses, is an all-or-nothing doctrine, allowing no subtlety or gradation in the analysis of government behavior or its effect. Sentencing, defendants claim, is an appropriate time to make more carefully graded judgments about both the offender's relative culpability (compared with offenders not subject to government encouragement) and the harms more properly attributed to government actions. Claims of sentencing entrapment or sentencing manipulation often arise in drug cases, in which the amount of drugs in a transaction can have a major impact on the likely sentence.

Indeterminate sentencing statutes do not tell a judge whether to take corrective action if she believes that government agents attempted to manipulate a sentence. Likewise, most sentencing guidelines do not address the issue of sentencing entrapment or manipulation. A few courts have refused to recognize government behavior as a potential factor at sentencing. See Commonwealth v. Garcia, 659 N.E.2d 741 (Mass. 1996).

More courts have recognized the possibility of accounting for government behavior but have not found facts that support a departure in a particular case. See United States v. Barth, 990 F.2d 422 (8th Cir. 1993); Leech v. State, 66 P.3d 987 (Okla. Crim. App. 2003). A few lower state courts in structured sentencing systems have altered sentences because of investigators' choices. For instance, in State v. Sanchez, 848 P.2d 208 (Wash. Ct. App. 1993), the government arranged a series of three small drug transactions between the defendant and one confidential informant, and the trial court departed downward to a sentence greater than the norm for one buy but less than the norm for three independent buys. Compare Graham

v. State, 608 So. 2d 123 (Fla. Dist. Ct. App. 1992) (undercover officer selects location for drug sale at night within 650 feet of school, increasing penalties).

6. *Developing rules for sentence manipulation.*   "Reverse buys"—in which the government agent sells to the target of the investigation and can choose the amount and price to offer—highlight claims about sentencing manipulation, especially in the federal system, where the type and amount of drugs involved in the offense have a significant and specified impact on final sentencing ranges. The federal sentencing guidelines instruct judges facing this situation: "If, in a reverse sting operation . . . , the court finds that the government agent set a price for the controlled substance that was substantially below the market value of the controlled substance, thereby leading to the defendant's purchase of a significantly greater quantity of the controlled substance than his available resources would have allowed him to purchase . . . a downward departure may be warranted." U.S. Sentencing Guidelines Manual §2D1.1, cmt. n.17. Is this policy an adequate response to potential government manipulation of the sentence? Perhaps government agents could be required to arrest a suspect whenever they have enough proof to make conviction at trial likely. A court might require the government to state its reasons for continuing its investigation after obtaining enough evidence for a conviction. What reasons might the government give?

7. *Inadequate self-defense and other "partial" substantive criminal law defenses.* Should courts develop refined or modified versions of substantive criminal law defenses other than entrapment, such as self-defense or duress? For instance, a defendant's self-defense argument may not result in an acquittal, but the court may nevertheless rely on the argument to reduce a sentence. Some state sentencing statutes explicitly recognize "partial" or "near-miss" defenses at sentencing: In Tennessee, the court may reduce a sentence if "substantial grounds exist tending to excuse or justify the defendant's criminal conduct, though failing to establish a defense." Tenn. Code §40-35-113(3); see also United States v. Whitetail, 956 F.2d 857 (8th Cir. 1992) (battered woman defense); United States v. Cheape, 889 F.2d 477 (3d Cir. 1989) (duress; defendant participated in robbery at gunpoint). Does the lack of a more refined set of "partial" defenses undermine the purposes of punishment?

8. *Pro-defendant sentencing manipulation and plea bargaining.*   How should a sentencing judge respond if the terms of a plea agreement suggest that the prosecution and defense have not fully disclosed to the court all of the defendant's relevant conduct? See U.S. Sentencing Guidelines Manual §5K2.21 (court may increase sentence above the guideline range to reflect "actual seriousness of the offense" based on conduct underlying a dismissed charge or a charge not pursued, if that conduct did not enter into the selection of the applicable guideline range). Especially in the federal system, there is evidence to suggest that, in perhaps as many as one-third of all cases, prosecutors underreport offense facts that could aggravate a defendant's guideline sentence in order to secure a guilty plea. See Stephen J. Schulhofer & Ilene H. Nagel, Plea Negotiations Under the Federal Sentencing Guidelines: Guidelines Circumvention and Its Dynamics in the Post-*Mistretta* Period, 91 Nw. U. L. Rev. 1284 (1997). Should such pro-defendant manipulation of sentencing outcomes concern us as much as (or perhaps even more than) manipulation of offense facts that potentially harm defendants?

3. Role in a Group Offense

The language of crime recognizes that the pecking order in a group crime matters. We often speak of kingpins and bosses, henchmen and mules. To what extent should a sentencing judge consider the relative blameworthiness of defendants who have different roles in the same offense?

|| *U.S. Sentencing Guidelines Manual* ||

§3B1.1   AGGRAVATING ROLE

Based on the defendant's role in the offense, increase the offense level as follows:

(a) If the defendant was an organizer or leader of a criminal activity that involved five or more participants or was otherwise extensive, increase by 4 levels.

(b) If the defendant was a manager or supervisor (but not an organizer or leader) and the criminal activity involved five or more participants or was otherwise extensive, increase by 3 levels.

(c) If the defendant was an organizer, leader, manager, or supervisor in any criminal activity other than described in (a) or (b), increase by 2 levels.

§3B1.2   MITIGATING ROLE

Based on the defendant's role in the offense, decrease the offense level as follows:

(a) If the defendant was a minimal participant in any criminal activity, decrease by 4 levels.

(b) If the defendant was a minor participant in any criminal activity, decrease by 2 levels.

In cases falling between (a) and (b), decrease by 3 levels.

|| *United States v. Donald Carpenter* ||
252 F.3d 230 (2d Cir. 2001)

MESKILL, J.

This appeal arises out of defendant-appellee Donald Carpenter's plea of guilty to conspiring to steal firearms from two Dick's Clothing and Sporting Goods (Dick's) stores located near Syracuse, New York. . . . The mechanics of the conspiracy's firearm theft and resale scheme are not complicated. [Marty Wise, a sales associate at Dick's,] initially approached Carpenter with the plan to steal firearms from Dick's. As part of their scheme, Wise would contact Carpenter and inform him when a specific theft should occur. When Carpenter arrived at Dick's, Wise handed Carpenter a pre-selected firearm. Carpenter then completed the Alcohol, Tobacco and Firearms (ATF) Form 4473 transferring the firearm from Dick's to himself, and Wise signaled to the cashier that Carpenter "was all set" and could leave without paying for the firearm. . . . Carpenter was in charge of disposing of the firearms stolen from Dick's. As a partner in a business named "The Gun Room," which possessed a federal firearms license, Carpenter was able regularly to acquire firearms and subsequently resell them to Dick's and other businesses. . . .

The thefts were discovered by David Murano, the store manager at Dick's, after Carpenter was unable to produce the sales receipt for one of the firearms he allegedly purchased from Dick's. After being confronted by Murano, Carpenter confessed to his and Wise's involvement in numerous firearm thefts from Dick's. A few months later, Carpenter and Wise made a similar confession to ATF agents. [An] ATF audit revealed that between October 1993 and March 1997, the period the conspiracy was active, Carpenter and Wise engaged in fifty separate firearm thefts from Dick's. . . . Wise kept the proceeds from nineteen guns; Carpenter kept the proceeds from nineteen guns; Wise and Carpenter split the proceeds from three guns; and one firearm actually was purchased by Carpenter.

On July 2, 1998, Carpenter pleaded guilty to an information charging him with one count of conspiring to steal firearms from a licensed firearms dealer. . . . At sentencing, the district court heard extensive argument from both parties on the issue of whether Carpenter was entitled to a mitigating role adjustment. The district court then reduced Carpenter's base offense level by three levels pursuant to U.S.S.G. §3B1.2 for his role in the firearm theft conspiracy. . . .

The base offense level for Carpenter's offense was twelve. Because the offense involved 25-49 firearms, the offense level was increased by five levels. The district court then departed downward three levels for a mitigating role adjustment, and two levels for acceptance of responsibility. This resulted in a total offense level of twelve. This offense level, combined with a criminal history category of I, resulted in a guideline imprisonment range of 10 to 16 months. [T]he district court sentenced Carpenter at the lowest end of that range, and ordered him to serve a term of imprisonment of five months, followed by five months in home detention. The district court also ordered Carpenter to pay restitution in the amount of $17,975.04. . . . Wise, who also pleaded guilty to one count of conspiracy to steal firearms from a licensed firearms dealer, was sentenced to a term of imprisonment of fifteen months and ordered to pay restitution in the amount of $18,975.04. . . .

On appeal, the government argues that the district court misapplied U.S.S.G. §3B1.2 as a matter of law when it held that Carpenter was entitled to a mitigating role adjustment on the ground that his conduct was less culpable than that of Wise, his co-conspirator. We agree that the district court erred. . . . We review factual findings underlying the district court's application of the Sentencing Guidelines for clear error, giving due deference to the district court's application of the guidelines to the facts. In applying [this standard], we are mindful that a sentencing court's assessment of the defendant's role in criminal activity is highly fact-specific and depends upon the nature of the defendant's relationship to other participants, the importance of the defendant's actions to the success of the venture, and the defendant's awareness of the nature and scope of the criminal enterprise. . . .

Section 3B1.2 of the Sentencing Guidelines provides for a four-level downward adjustment if the defendant was a "minimal participant" in criminal activity, and a two-level downward adjustment where the defendant was a "minor participant." The commentary to the Guidelines provides that a "minimal role" adjustment applies to a defendant who is "plainly among the least culpable of those involved in the conduct of a group." U.S.S.G. §3B1.2, commentary (n.1). "Under this provision, the defendant's lack of knowledge or understanding of the scope and structure of the enterprise and of the activities of others is indicative of a role as minimal participant." The Guidelines make clear that the "minimal role" adjustment should be used "infrequently." In comparison, a "minor role" adjustment applies to "any participant who is less culpable than most other participants, but whose role could not be described as minimal." U.S.S.G. §3B1.2, commentary (n.3). The Guidelines further provide that a mitigating role adjustment is appropriate if the defendant is "substantially less culpable than the *average participant*." ...

On numerous occasions we have reiterated that a reduction pursuant to U.S.S.G. §3B1.2 will not be available simply because the defendant played a lesser role than his co-conspirators; to be eligible for a reduction, the defendant's conduct must be "minor" or "minimal" as compared to the average participant in such a crime. Accordingly, the fact that a defendant played a minimal or minor role in his offense vis-à-vis the role of his co-conspirators is insufficient, in and of itself, to justify a mitigating role reduction.

The rationale for such a rule is self-evident. [If] participation in the offense were measured solely in relation to the co-defendants, the anomaly would arise that a deeply involved participant would be rewarded with a downward adjustment, just because his co-defendants were even more culpable. Further, such a result runs contrary to the statutory purposes of sentencing, which are aimed at reducing unwarranted sentencing disparities among defendants with similar records who have been found guilty of similar criminal conduct. ...

In ruling that Carpenter's base offense level should be reduced by three levels pursuant to §3B1.2 for his role in the conspiracy, the district court found that

> Carpenter's role in the offense is much less culpable than that of Marty Wise, the co-defendant. It's clear from the record that Wise initiated the offense and recruited Carpenter to take part in the thefts and that [Wise] was the one that had unlimited access to the guns, decided which guns would be stolen, when the thefts would take place, et cetera. Wise used Carpenter and four other individuals to accomplish these thefts and reaped the most from the crimes. ...

Because the district court compared Carpenter's role to that of Wise, rather than to the *average* participant in a similar firearm theft conspiracy, the sentence imposed by the district court must be vacated.

The government next argues that Carpenter's role in the conspiracy and his knowledge of the scope and structure of the conspiracy render him ineligible as a matter of law for a mitigating role adjustment under U.S.S.G. §3B1.2. ... Because the relevant facts on this issue are clear from the record, we choose to decide the question of Carpenter's entitlement to a mitigating role adjustment in the first instance, rather than remand that determination to the district court for additional factfinding.

Carpenter's active involvement in stealing the firearms from Dick's and reselling them to various third parties confirms that he played an important and significant part in the conspiracy to violate federal firearms laws to which he pleaded guilty. . . . As a partner in a business that was a federally licensed dealer, Carpenter was able to regularly purchase and transfer firearms without drawing suspicion. This fact was critical to the success of the conspiracy. Further, Carpenter falsely executed the ATF forms that were designed to conceal the thefts of the firearms. Given these facts, we conclude that Carpenter possessed an intimate "knowledge or understanding of the scope and structure of the enterprise" for which he pleaded guilty. U.S.S.G. §3B1.2, commentary (n.1).

The fact that Wise recruited Carpenter for the *first* of fifty firearm thefts does not render Carpenter an unwitting participant in the two and one-half year conspiracy during which he actively and systematically stole firearms and illegally resold them for personal profit. This is not a situation involving the isolated theft of a single firearm; instead, this case involved a scheme designed to deal in stolen firearms. The continuing nature of the conspiracy, coupled with Carpenter's repeated involvement in the firearm thefts and resales, further render Carpenter ineligible for a mitigating role adjustment. . . .

Finally, Carpenter argues . . . that he is entitled to a mitigating role adjustment because the firearms were not used for unlawful purposes. Specifically, Carpenter contends that "the firearms Carpenter obtained were used primarily by him for hunting and target shooting. . . . Unlike many, if not most people involved in gun thefts, Carpenter did not knowingly act as a conduit for supplying weapons in reckless disregard of whether they were to be used in the commission of other illegal acts." Even accepting Carpenter's facts as true, they are irrelevant to our determination of whether Carpenter is entitled to a mitigating role adjustment and, specifically, to the issue of Carpenter's knowledge of the scope and structure of the conspiracy and the scope of his role within that conspiracy. . . .

The judgment imposed by the district court is vacated as to the sentence only and the matter is remanded to the district court with instructions to resentence Carpenter at a base offense level of 15 and a criminal history category of I, which carries a sentencing range of 18-24 months. . . .

NOTES

1. *Impact of role in offense.* As we saw in the *Carpenter* case, the federal sentencing guidelines decrease the sentence by specific amounts for those who take relatively small roles in an offense carried out by a group. In an indeterminate sentencing system, the judge also traditionally considers the defendant's relative culpability in the group offense. The extent of any decrease or increase based on this factor is impossible to judge. More structured guideline systems in some states may mention the offender's relative culpability in a group offense as one possible reason to depart from the ordinary sentence range. See Md. Sentencing Guidelines §9.2 (departure below guideline range allowed

based on "offender's minor role in the offense"); N.C. Gen. Stat. §15A-1340.16(d)(1), (e)(2) (listing as an aggravating factor the fact that defendant "occupied a position of leadership or dominance over other participants" and listing as a mitigating factor the fact that defendant "was a passive participant or played a minor role in the commission of the offense"). Under the capital punishment statutes in some states, the defendant's role in the offense can mean the difference between life and death. Ohio and Florida, among others, include the defendant's relatively minor role as a mitigating factor that could lead a jury to recommend a life sentence rather than capital punishment. See Ohio Rev. Code §2929.04(B)(6); Fla. Stat. Ann. §921.141(6)(d).

The federal provision flushes out several questions that are not explicitly addressed in the typical state system (either indeterminate or guideline). What is the proper amount to decrease or increase a sentence based on this factor? In judging the relative culpability of a defendant, what is the proper comparison point: others involved in the current crime, or those involved in similar crimes around the country? Note that your answer to these questions might change depending on the size of the group involved or the seriousness of the crime committed. See United States v. Almanza, 225 F.3d 845 (7th Cir. 2000) (Posner, J.) ("The 'mule' who transports one kilogram of cocaine is a more minor participant in a conspiracy to distribute 1,000 kilograms of cocaine than in a conspiracy to distribute 10 kilograms of cocaine, because the potential punishment of a member of the first conspiracy is so much greater, even though his conduct is identical.").

2. *Co-defendant's sentence as a basis for departure.* How should a judge respond when the sentencing rules indicate a sentence for one defendant that is higher than the sentence already imposed on a more culpable co-defendant? In the federal system, courts have usually refused to depart from the sentencing guidelines in an effort to give comparable sentences to co-defendants in the same crime. See United States v. Joyner, 924 F.2d 454, 460-461 (2d Cir. 1991) (consideration of the sentences given to co-defendants "creates a new and entirely unwarranted disparity between the defendant's sentence and that of all similarly situated defendants throughout the country"). The sentencing judge could impose a sentence out of line with the sentence already received by other participants in the present crime, or a sentence out of line with the lesser participants in similar crimes from other districts. Which is the greater (and more visible) threat to the principle of equal treatment at sentencing?

3. *Relative culpability and cooperation with the government.* Conspirators who plead guilty and cooperate with the government in prosecutions against other members of the conspiracy often receive sentence discounts, both in federal and state systems. Recall U.S. Sentencing Guidelines Manual §5K1.1 (allowing departure for substantial assistance). This often means that some higher-ranking conspiracy members — those who know the most about the operation — receive lesser sentences than some lower-ranking conspiracy members who have less to offer the government. Especially in the federal system, in which a substantial assistance departure is authorized only upon a motion by the prosecutor, defendants who cooperate on a similar basis could receive different sentences because of different practices of prosecutors in different districts. Can a sentencing judge counteract these sources of unequal sentences? If a

judge learns that prosecutors in the local district deal with some co-conspirators differently than prosecutors in other districts (for instance, by offering immunity under U.S. Sentencing Guidelines Manual §1B1.8 in exchange for information about the conspiracy), should the judge adjust the sentence to equalize outcomes in different districts? See United States v. Buckendahl, 251 F.3d 753 (8th Cir. 2001).

PROBLEM 4-5. ROB ANON REVISITED

Look again at §3B1.1 of the federal guidelines, reprinted above. The application notes to this guideline do not define the key terms such as "leader" or "manager." How would these provisions apply to the sentence of Rob Anon, based on the facts described in Problem 4-1? Was this enterprise "otherwise extensive" within the meaning of §3B1.1(a)? The commentary offers some hope for the prosecution here: "In assessing whether an organization is 'otherwise extensive,' all persons involved during the course of the entire offense are to be considered. Thus, a fraud that involved only three participants but used the unknowing services of many outsiders could be considered extensive." Where might the prosecutor find evidence about other "persons involved"?

As explained in Chapter 3, the Supreme Court's decision in United States v. Booker, 543 U.S. 220 (2005), made the federal sentencing guidelines "effectively advisory." In the context of Rob Anon's case, does §3B1.1 provide sound advice that you would likely follow when considering Rob's role in the offense at his sentencing? Do the categories and labels used in §3B1 provide a helpful framework for the consideration of these issues? Can you conceive of another means or a distinct approach to assessing and distinctly weighing a defendant's aggravating or mitigating role?

B. ASSESSING OFFENSE SERIOUSNESS

Deciding the scope of behavior that will form the basis for a sentence is only one step in choosing an appropriate sentence. Sentencing authorities must also judge the *seriousness* of the defendant's offense.

In all sentencing systems, legislatures make initial judgments about offense seriousness through the grading of offenses. They decide which crimes to label as felonies or misdemeanors and further subdivide these broad categories by using degrees or classes to specify appropriate punishment ranges. These decisions can sometimes raise constitutional concerns, because the Supreme Court has interpreted the Eighth Amendment's prohibition of cruel and unusual punishments to preclude grossly disproportionate punishments (see Chapter 7). More fundamentally, these legislative decisions always implicate policy choices, because legislatures must decide which aspects of an offense should be categorized as more or less serious.

Basic legislative grading choices are only one component of the many judgments made about the seriousness of offense behavior in the sentencing process. Legislatures also authorize or require specific sentencing enhancements based on particular aspects of offense behavior, such as gun possession. And other sentencing decision makers — including sentencing commissions, prosecutors, judges, and parole officials — measure the seriousness of offense behavior in ways that change final sentencing outcomes.

The following excerpt from the Senate report supporting the Sentencing Reform Act of 1984 instructs the U.S. Sentencing Commission how to establish sentencing rules for different categories of offenses. The report mentions the numerous offense-related elements that become relevant in passing judgment on the overall seriousness of criminal behaviors.

‖ *U.S. Senate Report No. 98-225* ‖
Pages 169-171 (1984)

[Title 28 U.S.C. §994(c) of the Sentencing Reform Act] lists a number of offense characteristics that the sentencing commission is required to examine [in the establishment of sentencing guidelines. This provision] specifies that the commission consider the degree of relevance of the grade of the offense to the sentencing decision. [All] offenses are graded according to their relative seriousness. [The grading provides] some guide as to the congressional view of the relative seriousness of similar offenses. The rough approximations practical for statutory purposes are expected . . . to be refined considerably by the sentencing guidelines.

[This provision further] specifies that the commission consider the relevance to the sentencing decision of the circumstances under which the offense was committed that might aggravate or mitigate the seriousness of the offense. Among the considerations the commission might examine under this factor are whether the offense was particularly heinous; whether the offense was committed on the spur of the moment or after substantial planning; whether the offense was committed in reckless disregard of the safety of others; whether the offense involved a threat with a weapon or use of a weapon; whether the offense was committed in a manner plainly designed to limit the danger to the victims; whether the defendant was acting under a form of duress not rising to the level of a defense; etc.

[This provision further] specifies that the commission consider the relevance to the sentencing decision of the nature and degree of the harm caused by the offense, including whether it involved property, irreplaceable property, a person, a number of persons, or a breach of public trust. The commission might include in this consideration, or in policy statements, an evaluation of the role that unusual vulnerability of the victim that is known to the defendant should play in the sentencing decision.

[This provision further] specifies that the commission consider the relevance of the community view of the gravity of the offense to the sentencing decision, . . . public concern generated by an offense, . . . the deterrent effect a particular sentence may have on the commission of the offense by others [, and] the current incidence of the offense in the community and in the nation as a whole.

NOTES

1. *The centrality of harm and culpability on legislative grading of offenses.*   Most criminal codes state that the fundamental requirements for criminal liability are a voluntary act (the objective component) and a mens rea, or culpable mental state (the subjective component). See, e.g., N.Y. Penal Code §15.10; Ohio Rev. Code §2901.21; Tex. Penal Code §§6.01-6.04. Similarly, the initial grading of a criminal offense by the legislature typically depends on the objective seriousness of the harm or threat of harm resulting from the defendant's behavior and on the defendant's subjective culpability. Certain classes of crimes share a common objective harm, leading to offense grades that turn entirely on the defendant's subjective mental state. For instance, homicides are usually defined in terms of causing another person's death; the grade of offense depends on whether the killing was intentional, provoked, unintentional, or accidental. See, e.g., Cal. Penal Code §§187-192; Kan. Stat. Ann. §§21-3401B to 21-3404. Other crimes share a common subjective mental state, leading to offense grades that depend on the objective harm inflicted. For example, most forms of theft require the intent to deprive others of property; the grade principally depends on the value of the property stolen.

2. *Institutional roles in judging offense seriousness.*   Historically, legislatures made only general assessments of offense seriousness through grading choices, juries applied offense grades to the facts of specific cases, and sentencing judges made more particularized judgments about the seriousness of the defendant's crime when ascribing specific sentences. Professor Paul Robinson has suggested that this traditional allocation of responsibility is fundamentally sound:

> The amount of punishment to be imposed is in large measure a function of the value of the interest injured or threatened and the culpability of the act. In a democracy, . . . the relative value of the interest is a judgment uniquely within the authority of a legislative body[, and] the actor's culpability, which necessarily requires an inferential judgment, is a judgment within the expertise of a jury of peers. [Because] a criminal code cannot take account of every factor that contributes to the amount of punishment a defendant deserves . . . codes generally give only an approximation of the amount of punishment that should be imposed. The judge must determine the exact amount on the facts of the particular case, which requires exercise of judicial discretion to refine the code's "first cut," or to account for relevant factors not taken into account by the code.

Paul H. Robinson, Are Criminal Codes Irrelevant?, 68 S. Cal. L. Rev. 159, 183 (1994). How should a sentencing commission fit into Professor Robinson's taxonomy of institutional roles? Should the work of sentencing commissions be conceived primarily in traditional legislative terms, focusing on developing sentencing rules that provide only a "first cut" as to the amount of punishment a court ought to impose? Or should the work of sentencing commissions be conceived instead in traditional judicial terms, focusing on developing sentencing rules to account for factors appearing less often in individual cases?

1. Qualitative Assessments of Harm

The harm or threat of harm that arises from a defendant's behavior profoundly influences final sentencing choices, perhaps even more than it affects legislative grading of criminal offenses. Various legal structures and rules translate judgments about the seriousness of harm into final sentencing outcomes.

When legislatures, sentencing commissions, and judges think about the seriousness of offenses, they sometimes consider the *type* of harm the crime causes or threatens rather than the *amount* of harm. Which types of harm deserve the most serious punishments? As you read the following cases and materials, think about the inherent challenge of making qualitative judgments about the relative seriousness of violent crimes versus drug crimes versus sex crimes versus economic crimes. Consider also how judges, legislatures, and commissions make these rankings.

|| *Ehrlich Anthony Coker v. Georgia* ||
433 U.S. 584 (1977)

WHITE, J.

Georgia Code §26-2001 provides that "(a) person convicted of rape shall be punished by death or by imprisonment for life, or by imprisonment for not less than one nor more than 20 years." Petitioner Coker was convicted of rape and sentenced to death. Coker [contends] that the punishment of death for rape violates the Eighth Amendment.

While serving various sentences for murder, rape, kidnaping, and aggravated assault, petitioner escaped from [prison. Petitioner] entered the house of Allen and Elnita Carver through an unlocked kitchen door. Threatening the couple with a "board," he tied up Mr. Carver in the bathroom, obtained a knife from the kitchen, and took Mr. Carver's money and the keys to the family car. Brandishing the knife and saying "you know what's going to happen to you if you try anything, don't you," Coker then raped Mrs. Carver. Soon thereafter, petitioner drove away in the Carver car, taking Mrs. Carver with him. Mr. Carver, freeing himself, notified the police; and not long thereafter petitioner was apprehended. Mrs. Carver was unharmed.

Petitioner was charged with [various offenses, including] rape. . . . The jury returned a verdict of guilty, rejecting his general plea of insanity. A sentencing hearing was then conducted in accordance with [our decision in] Gregg v. Georgia, 428 U.S. 153 (1976), where this Court sustained the death penalty for murder when imposed pursuant to [certain] procedures. . . . The jury's verdict on the rape count was death by electrocution.

Furman v. Georgia, 408 U.S. 238 (1972), and the Court's decisions last Term in Gregg v. Georgia, 428 U.S. 153 (1976) [and companion cases] settled that the death penalty is not invariably cruel and unusual punishment within the meaning of the Eighth Amendment; it is not inherently barbaric or an unacceptable mode of punishment for crime; neither is it always disproportionate to the crime for which it is imposed. In sustaining the imposition of the death penalty in *Gregg*, however, the Court firmly embraced the holdings and dicta from prior cases to the effect that the Eighth Amendment bars not only those punishments that are "barbaric" but also those that are "excessive" in relation to the crime committed. Under *Gregg*, a punishment is "excessive" and unconstitutional if it (1) makes no measurable contribution to acceptable goals of punishment and hence is nothing more than the purposeless and needless imposition of pain and suffering; or (2) is grossly out of proportion to the severity of the crime. . . . We have concluded that a sentence of death is grossly disproportionate and excessive punishment for the crime of rape and is therefore forbidden by the Eighth Amendment as cruel and unusual punishment.

[We] seek guidance in history and from the objective evidence of the country's present judgment concerning the acceptability of death as a penalty for rape of an adult woman. At no time in the last 50 years have a majority of the States authorized death as a punishment for rape. In 1925, 18 States, the District of Columbia, and the Federal Government authorized capital punishment for the rape of an adult female. By 1971 just prior to the decision in *Furman*, that number had declined, but not substantially, to 16 States plus the Federal Government. *Furman* then invalidated most of the capital punishment statutes in this country, including the rape statutes. . . .

In reviving death penalty laws to satisfy *Furman*'s mandate, none of the States that had not previously authorized death for rape chose to include rape among capital felonies. Of the 16 States in which rape had been a capital offense, only three provided the death penalty for rape of an adult woman in their revised statutes, Georgia, North Carolina, and Louisiana. . . . It should be noted that Florida, Mississippi, and Tennessee also authorized the death penalty in some rape cases, but only where the victim was a child and the rapist an adult. . . . The current judgment with respect to the death penalty for rape is not wholly unanimous among state legislatures, but it obviously weighs very heavily on the side of rejecting capital punishment as a suitable penalty for raping an adult woman.

It was also observed in *Gregg* that "the jury . . . is a significant and reliable objective index of contemporary values because it is so directly involved," and that it is thus important to look to the sentencing decisions that juries have made in the course of assessing whether capital punishment is an appropriate penalty for the crime being tried. [Out] of all rape convictions in Georgia since 1973, . . . 63 cases had been reviewed by the Georgia Supreme Court as of the time of oral argument; and of these, 6 involved a death sentence. [Recent] experience surely does not prove that jurors consider the death penalty to be a disproportionate punishment for every conceivable instance of rape, no matter how aggravated. Nevertheless, it is true that in the vast majority of cases, at least 9 out of 10, juries have not imposed the death sentence.

These recent events evidencing the attitude of state legislatures and sentencing juries do not wholly determine this controversy, for the Constitution contemplates that in the end our own judgment will be brought to bear on the question of the acceptability of the death penalty under the Eighth Amendment. . . .

We do not discount the seriousness of rape as a crime. It is highly reprehensible, both in a moral sense and in its almost total contempt for the personal integrity and autonomy of the female victim and for the latter's privilege of choosing those with whom intimate relationships are to be established. Short of homicide, it is the "ultimate violation of self." It is also a violent crime because it normally involves force, or the threat of force or intimidation, to overcome the will and the capacity of the victim to resist. Rape is very often accompanied by physical injury to the female and can also inflict psychological damage. Because it undermines the community's sense of security, there is public injury as well.

Rape is without doubt deserving of serious punishment; but in terms of moral depravity and of the injury to the person and to the public, it does not compare with murder, which does involve the unjustified taking of human life. Although it may be accompanied by another crime, rape by definition does not include the death of or even the serious injury to another person. The murderer kills; the rapist, if no more than that, does not. Life is over for the victim of the murderer; for the rape victim, life may not be nearly so happy as it was, but it is not over and normally is not beyond repair. We have the abiding conviction that the death penalty, which is unique in its severity and irrevocability, is an excessive penalty for the rapist who, as such, does not take human life. . . .

POWELL, J., concurring in the judgment in part and dissenting in part.

I concur in the judgment of the Court on the facts of this case, and also in the plurality's reasoning supporting the view that ordinarily death is disproportionate punishment for the crime of raping an adult woman. Although rape invariably is a reprehensible crime, there is no indication that petitioner's offense was committed with excessive brutality or that the victim sustained serious or lasting injury.

[However], the plurality draws a bright line between murder and all rapes regardless of the degree of brutality of the rape or the effect upon the victim. I dissent because I am not persuaded that such a bright line is appropriate. [T]here is extreme variation in the degree of culpability of rapists. The deliberate viciousness of the rapist may be greater than that of the murderer. Rape is never an act committed accidentally. Rarely can it be said to be unpremeditated. There also is wide variation in the effect on the victim. . . . Some victims are so grievously injured physically or psychologically that life is beyond repair. . . .

BURGER, C.J., dissenting.

. . . On December 5, 1971 Ehrlich Anthony Coker raped and then stabbed to death a young woman. Less than eight months later Coker kidnaped and raped a second young woman. After twice raping this 16-year-old victim, he stripped her, severely beat her with a club, and dragged her into a wooded area where he left her for dead. He was apprehended and pleaded guilty to offenses stemming from these incidents. He was sentenced by three separate courts to three life terms, two 20-year terms, and one 8-year term of imprisonment. Each judgment specified that the sentences it imposed were to run consecutively rather than concurrently. Approximately one and a half years later, on September 2, 1974, petitioner escaped from the state prison where he was serving these sentences. He promptly raped another 16-year-old woman in the presence of her husband, abducted her from her home, and threatened her with death and serious bodily harm. It is this crime for which the sentence now under review was imposed.

The Court today holds that Georgia may not impose the death penalty on Coker. In so doing, it prevents the State from imposing any effective punishment upon Coker for his latest rape. The Court's holding, moreover, bars Georgia from guaranteeing its citizens that they will suffer no further attacks by this habitual rapist . . . who has shown total and repeated disregard for the welfare, safety, personal integrity, and human worth of others, and who seemingly cannot be deterred from continuing such conduct. . . .

A rapist not only violates a victim's privacy and personal integrity, but inevitably causes serious psychological as well as physical harm in the process. The long-range effect upon the victim's life and health is likely to be irreparable; it is impossible to measure the harm which results. Volumes have been written by victims, physicians, and psychiatric specialists on the lasting injury suffered by rape victims. Rape is not a mere physical attack, it is destructive of the human personality. The remainder of the victim's life may be gravely affected, and this in turn may have a serious detrimental effect upon her husband and any children she may have. . . . Victims may recover from the physical damage of knife or bullet wounds, or a beating with fists or a club, but recovery from such a gross assault on the human personality is not healed by medicine or surgery. To speak blandly . . . of rape victims who are "unharmed," or to classify the human outrage of rape . . . in terms of "excessively brutal," versus "moderately brutal," takes too little account of the profound suffering the crime imposes upon the victims and their loved ones.

The question of whether the death penalty is an appropriate punishment for rape is surely an open one. It is arguable that many prospective rapists would be deterred by the possibility that they could suffer death for their offense; it is also arguable that the death penalty would have only minimal deterrent effect. It may well be that rape victims would become more willing to report the crime and aid in the apprehension of the criminals if they knew that community disapproval of rapists was sufficiently strong to inflict the extreme penalty; or perhaps they would be reluctant to cooperate in the prosecution of rapists if they knew that a conviction might result in the imposition of the death penalty. Quite possibly, the occasional, well-publicized execution of egregious rapists may cause citizens to feel greater security in their daily lives; or, on the contrary, it may be that members of a civilized community will suffer the pangs of a heavy conscience because such punishment will be perceived as excessive. We cannot know which among this range of possibilities is correct, but today's holding forecloses the very exploration we have said federalism was intended to foster.

[Rape] is not a crime "light years" removed from murder in the degree of its heinousness; it certainly poses a serious potential danger to the life and safety of innocent victims apart from the devastating psychic consequences. . . . Whatever our individual views as to the wisdom of capital punishment, I cannot agree that it is constitutionally impermissible for a state legislature to make the "solemn judgment" to impose such penalty for the crime of rape. Accordingly, I would leave to the States the task of legislating in this area of the law.

NOTES

1. *Constitutional proportionality between harm and severity of punishment.* As *Coker* reveals, the Supreme Court has placed some substantive constitutional limitations on the use of capital punishment for certain crimes. In addition to *Coker*'s preclusion of capital punishment for the crime of adult rape, the Supreme Court has held through a line of decisions culminating in Tison v.

Arizona, 481 U.S. 137 (1987), that the death penalty is permissible in homicide cases only for offenders who acted at least with the culpable mental state of reckless indifference to human life. As detailed in Chapter 7, the Supreme Court has also held that noncapital sentences can be unconstitutional if they are "grossly disproportionate" to the offender's crime.

Consider all the people who had to agree that Ehrlich Anthony Coker should die for his crime: the Georgia legislature had to authorize the death penalty for certain rapes; the local prosecutor (influenced perhaps by the victim's input) had to charge and pursue Coker's case as a capital crime; the sentencing jury had to conclude not only that Coker was guilty but also that he deserved to die for his crime; the Georgia state courts had to decide, pursuant to their own state laws, that Coker's sentence was proportionate to the crime. Does the U.S. Supreme Court bring something to the job of measuring the seriousness of Coker's crime that the other actors were missing?

2. *Child rape as a capital offense. Coker* precluded the use of capital punishment only in cases of adult rape. After the decision, at least a few states left on their books laws allowing for the death penalty for rape of a child, and a few states subsequently amended laws to make child rape a potential capital offense. In Louisiana a statute provides that defendants convicted of "aggravated rape" can be subject to the death penalty if "the victim was under the age of twelve years." La. Rev. Stat. §14:42. In State v Wilson, 685 So. 2d 1063 (La. 1996), the Louisiana Supreme Court upheld the facial constitutionality of this statute, and in 2003 defendant Patrick Kennedy was sentenced to death under this statute for raping an eight-year-old girl. His sentence was recently affirmed by the Louisiana Supreme Court in State v. Kennedy, 957 So. 2d 757 (La. May 22, 2007), and some commentators predict that this case will be considered by the U.S. Supreme Court.

Driven by high-profile abductions and public concerns about child predators, a small but growing number of states have passed new legislation in recent years making certain pedophiles eligible for the death penalty. Some of these new statutes make death an eligible punishment only for a repeat offense of child rape, but a few make even a first offense of child rape with certain aggravating circumstances a potential capital offense. Compare Mont. Code Ann. §45-5-503 (providing death penalty eligibility only for offender with a previous aggravated child rape conviction) with 21 Okla. Stat. §1114 (providing that rape in the first degree is potentially punishable by death). Both the constitutionality and appropriateness of imposing the death penalty on child rapists has generated significant academic commentary. See, e.g., Corey Rayburn, Better Dead Than R(ap)ed?: The Patriarchal Rhetoric Driving Capital Rape Statutes, 78 St. John's L. Rev. 1119 (2004); J. Richard Broughton, "On Horror's Head Horrors Accumulate": A Reflective Comment on Capital Child Rape Legislation, 39 Duq. L. Rev. 1 (2000); Annaliese Flynn Fleming, Louisiana's Newest Capital Crime: The Death Penalty for Child Rape, 89 J. Crim. L. & Criminology 717 (1999).

Does rape of a child create a different *type* of harm than rape of an adult? Is there a sound (or potential constitutional) argument that a second offense of child rape is itself qualitatively worse than a first offense?

3. *Nonjudicial assessments of harm and severity of punishment.* Distinct from any constitutional questions about permissible punishments are the policy questions concerning appropriate punishments. As to the death penalty, 38 states along with the federal government permit the imposition of capital punishment for certain aggravated homicides, although there is some notable variation in these jurisdictions as to exactly which sorts of aggravating factors make a particular killer eligible for capital punishment. See the Death Penalty Information Center website at http://www.deathpenaltyinfo.org/capitaloffenses.html; Va. Code §18.2-31(12) ("killing of a person under the age of fourteen by a person age twenty-one or older"); Ala. Code §13A-5-40(a)(11) ("when the victim is a state or federal public official or former public official and the murder stems from or is caused by or is related to his official position"); Ind. Code §35-50-2-9(b) ("killing the victim while committing or attempting to commit any of the following [crimes]: arson, burglary, child molesting, criminal deviate conduct, kidnapping, rape, robbery, carjacking, criminal gang activity, dealing in cocaine or a narcotic drug"). Do these aggravating factors speak to the same basic types of harm?

Although varying in their use and application of the death penalty, nearly all jurisdictions deem aggravated forms of homicide to be the most serious of crimes. In states without the death penalty, this means the crime is punished by life imprisonment without the possibility of parole. Similarly, though *Coker* makes the death penalty unavailable for the crime of adult rape, most jurisdictions still provide severe sanctions for serious sexual offenses, especially when these crimes include additional physical harm to the victim or when the victim is young or especially vulnerable. See Ohio Rev. Code §2907.02.

How do legislatures and commissions make judgments about the relative seriousness of offenses less obvious than murder or rape? Consider again Dale Parent's description, reprinted in Chapter 3, of the efforts of the Minnesota Sentencing Commission to rank different offenses. What other methods might you recommend?

Although legislatures and commissions must grade offenses in comparison with other offenses, they also guide sentencing judges in how to distinguish among offenders convicted of the same crime. The following materials highlight two ways that sentencing rules can specifically respond to various harms and threats of harms.

State v. Stanley Royster
590 N.W.2d 82 (Minn. 1999)

STRINGER, J.

On February 12, 1997, the Minneapolis Police executed a search warrant at Royster's residence [searching for illegal drugs]. Police found Royster and another man inside. Items recovered in Royster's search included cash in his pocket and some pre-recorded buy money from the Minneapolis Narcotics Unit. In the premises search, specifically of Royster's bedroom, the police recovered additional pre-recorded buy money, a bag of crack-cocaine in a boot, and a fully-loaded .22 revolver from underneath his mattress located approximately three feet from the boot containing the crack-cocaine. After his arrest Royster admitted to the police that he was selling cocaine out of his home and claimed that his father had given him the revolver for protection because he lived in a dangerous neighborhood. . . .

When Minnesota Statute §609.11, subdivision 5, was enacted in 1981, it originally provided in relevant part [that any defendant convicted of specified offenses] in which "the defendant or an accomplice, at the time of the offense, used, whether by brandishing, displaying, threatening with, or otherwise employing, a firearm" [must receive a minimum prison term of at least three years.] Another subdivision pertaining to commission of a predicate offense while "in possession of a firearm," mandated a minimum sentence of one year. . . . In 1994 the Minnesota Legislature [consolidated these subdivisions to provide that] both *possession* and *use* while committing a predicate felony offense triggered the three-year mandatory minimum sentence.

Royster argues that [the "possession" term in the 1994 amendment] must be read in conjunction with "brandishing, displaying, threatening with, or otherwise employing" [the firearm] to trigger the mandatory minimum sentence and because his firearm was not so employed but rather lay dormant under his mattress, he did not have the "possession" contemplated by the legislature. Clearly the statute cannot be read to reach such a conclusion however, for it is obvious that in 1994 the legislature intended to increase the sentence for those who possess a firearm while committing a crime even though they do not actually use a firearm. To conclude that "possession" must be accompanied by some kind of "brandishing" would render the 1994 amendment meaningless. . . . We hold that "brandishing" is not required as an element of proof of possession to trigger the [three-year] mandatory minimum sentence. . . .

Finally, we consider what should be the test for determining when constructive possession while committing the predicate offense should trigger the mandatory minimum sentence. The sentence enhancement amendment reflects the obvious reality that possession of a firearm while committing a predicate felony offense substantially increases the risk of violence, whether or not the offender actually uses the firearm. The firearm in possession was recognized by the legislature as an "insurance policy . . . to be used to further the crime if need be" and clearly raises the stakes of severe injury or death as a result of the commission of the predicate offenses. It seems reasonable then to examine all aspects of the firearm in possession to determine whether it was reasonable to assume that its presence increased the risk of violence and to what degree the risk is increased: the nature, type and condition of the firearm, its ownership, whether it was loaded, its ease of accessibility, its proximity to the drugs, why the firearm was present and whether the nature of the predicate offense is frequently or typically accompanied by use of a firearm, to name a few of the considerations.

Applying these standards to the present case, we hold that the state presented sufficient evidence to prove beyond a reasonable doubt that Royster's possession of a firearm while committing the predicate felony offense met the requisites of section 609.11, subdivision 5. Because Royster's .22 caliber pistol, fully loaded, was found under Royster's mattress within 3 feet of 2.9 grams of crack-cocaine, the trial court could reasonably infer that possession of the firearm substantially increased the risk of violence related to his drug trafficking.

|| *U.S. Sentencing Guidelines Manual* ||

§2B3.1   ROBBERY

(a) Base Offense Level: 20

(b) Specific Offense Characteristics

(1) If the property of a financial institution or post office was taken, or if the taking of such property was an object of the offense, increase by 2 levels.

(2) (A) If a firearm was discharged, increase by 7 levels; (B) if a firearm was otherwise used, increase by 6 levels; (C) if a firearm was brandished or possessed, increase by 5 levels; (D) if a dangerous weapon was otherwise used, increase by 4 levels; (E) if a dangerous weapon was brandished or possessed, increase by 3 levels; or (F) if a threat of death was made, increase by 2 levels.

(3) If any victim sustained bodily injury, increase the offense level according to the seriousness of the injury:

Degree of Bodily Injury	Increase in Level
(A) Bodily Injury	add 2
(B) Serious Bodily Injury	add 4
(C) Permanent or Life-Threatening Bodily Injury	add 6
(D) If the degree of injury is between that specified in subdivisions (A) and (B), add 3 levels; or	
(E) If the degree of injury is between that specified in subdivisions (B) and (C), add 5 levels.	

Provided, however, that the cumulative adjustments from (2) and (3) shall not exceed 11 levels.

NOTES

1. *Legislative and commission roles in defining offense seriousness.* Sometimes legislative bodies decide for themselves the specific increases in sentences that must occur when particular harms or threats are present. The *Royster* case gives one example of legislatively enacted mandatory sentencing laws that have proven popular at both the federal and state levels, especially in the context of narcotics and weapons offenses. In the federal system, more than 75 statutes now establish fixed prison terms or minimum sentences that judges must impose based on certain offense factors. Over the past two decades, nearly every state has also adopted some form of mandatory sentencing provisions. See, e.g., Dale Parent et al., National Institute of Justice, Mandatory Sentencing

(January 1997). As we saw in Chapter 2, legislators often embrace mandatory sentencing laws primarily for immediate political benefits, even though studies have generally shown that these laws are not applied uniformly and thus have limited deterrent impact and produce sentencing disparities. Indeed, the consensus within the criminal justice community is that, in practice, mandatory sentencing laws are ineffectual and often produce unjust outcomes. See, e.g., Jonathan P. Caulkins et al., Rand Corporation, Mandatory Minimum Drug Sentences: Throwing Away the Key or the Taxpayer's Money (1997); Barbara S. Vincent & Paul J. Hofer, Federal Judicial Center, The Consequences of Mandatory Minimum Prison Terms: A Summary of Recent Findings (1994); Gary T. Lowenthal, Mandatory Sentencing Laws: Undermining the Effectiveness of Determinate Sentencing Reform, 81 Cal. L. Rev. 61 (1993).

Judges also tend to have a low regard for mandatory minimum sentences set by legislatures. In August 2003 Justice Anthony Kennedy delivered a speech to the American Bar Association that was frankly critical of mandatory sentencing laws in the federal system: "Our resources are being misspent. Our punishments are too severe. Our sentences are too long." He urged the ABA to tell Congress, "Don't take discretion away from the courts. . . . Let judges be judges." Although he agreed with the need for federal sentencing guidelines to set uniform sentences, he contrasted guidelines with mandatory minimum sentences: "I can accept neither the wisdom, the justice nor the necessity of mandatory minimums. . . . In all too many cases, they are unjust. . . . A country which is secure in its institutions and confident in its laws should not be ashamed of the concept of mercy."

Section 2B3.1 of the federal sentencing guidelines illustrates an important alternative to mandatory minimum sentences. Structured sentencing jurisdictions can employ a more refined approach to assessing offense seriousness. In the federal system, determinations of an offense's overall seriousness can be highly detailed; for example, in addition to the portion reprinted above, §2B3.1 has four additional subsections and incorporates three pages of application notes. In state guideline systems, the computation is less complex but the idea is similar. The guidelines list particularly serious harms or threats as grounds for increasing the presumptive sentence. See N.C. Gen. Stat. §15A-1340.16(d)(8), (13) (aggravating factor if the defendant "knowingly created a great risk of death to more than one person" or "involved a person under the age of 16 in the commission of the crime").

2. *Sentencing enhancements based on "use" of firearm or weapon.* Federal criminal law and the laws of many states increase criminal penalties and sometimes mandate certain minimum sentences when the offense behavior involves use of a firearm or other weapon. See, e.g., 18 U.S.C. §924(c) (mandating five years' imprisonment consecutive to the sentence for the underlying offense whenever a defendant "uses or carries" a firearm "during and in relation to" any crime of violence or drug trafficking offense); 42 Pa. Cons. Stat. Ann. §9712 (mandating five-year minimum sentence for "visibly possessing a firearm or a replica of a firearm during the commission of a crime of violence").

As *Royster* highlights, statutes that include such weapons enhancements often raise legal questions about the "use" or "possession" that is sufficient to trigger the special sanctions. For example, in Bailey v. United States, 516 U.S. 137 (1995), the Supreme Court narrowed application of the "uses" provision in the federal firearms enhancement, overturning a conviction of a defendant who possessed a loaded pistol that police found inside a bag in his locked car trunk after they arrested him for possession of cocaine that they found in the passenger compartment. Congress soon amended the statute to cover all forms of possession of a firearm "in furtherance of" the crime and also introduced even higher mandatory penalties for brandishing or discharging a weapon, for repeat offenders, and for using certain types of dangerous guns. As a legislator, would you attach use of a weapon to particular crimes, or would you use it as a sentence enhancement for any crime? Are certain kinds of crimes categorically more blameworthy or more harmful by the presence or use of a gun?

3. *Bodily harm and other aggravating factors.*   Federal criminal law and the laws of many states increase criminal penalties or mandate certain minimum sentences, or both, when offenses result in bodily harm. Sometimes these enhancements are codified as elements of other crimes. For example, many kidnapping statutes increase the penalty when the offender harms the seized victims. See, e.g., 18 U.S.C. §1201; Cal. Penal Code §209. Especially in states with guidelines, it is common to place such enhancements in general sentencing instructions. See, e.g., Fla. Stat. Ann. §921.0016(3)(l) (allowing departure from guideline sentence if the victim "suffered extraordinary physical or emotional trauma or permanent physical injury"). Courts have addressed many issues under these statutes, including whether certain injuries are severe enough to constitute harm within the statutory meaning and whether harm inflicted by an accomplice or accessory can be attributed to the defendant for sentencing purposes.

Many other indicators of serious harms or threats can operate just like use of a firearm or bodily injury. Legislatures or sentencing commissions designate these factors as a basis for increased sentences. Sometimes the increase is defined, and in other instances the judge is allowed to increase the sentence in her discretion. See, e.g., U.S. Sentencing Guidelines Manual §3B1.4 (increasing offense level by 2 if defendant used a minor to commit crime); Utah Sentencing Guidelines Form 4 (listing as an aggravating sentencing factor the fact that the "offense was characterized by extreme cruelty or depravity").

PROBLEM 4-6.   ROB ANON REVISITED

Recall again Rob Anon, described in Problem 4-1, and then reexamine the specifics of §2B3.1 of the federal guidelines. Based on that provision, how many offense levels should be added to the base offense level of 20? Though it appears that at least 9 levels must be added, interpretation of the provision's key terms might suggest that as many as 13 levels should be added; the difference between adding 9 and adding 13 levels could mean a sentencing range for Rob as low as 8 to 10 years or as high as 12 to 15 years.

2. *Quantitative Assessments of Harm*

Certain types of offenses—particularly drug crimes and economic crimes—lend themselves to quantitative measures of offense seriousness. For drug crimes, offense harms are defined in terms of the type and quantity of the drugs involved. For economic crimes, offense harms are defined in terms of the quantity of money taken. Larger quantities of drugs or a larger amount of money mean a more severe sentence.

As the following case highlights, the amount of "quantified harm," especially in drug cases under federal law, can have a dramatic impact on sentence length, eclipsing the impact of all other sentencing factors. For example, even for a first-time offender, the amount of drugs involved in a drug distribution offense could mean the difference between a sentence of life imprisonment (for very large quantities) and a sentence of probation (for very small quantities). See U.S. Sentencing Guidelines Manual §2D1.1(c). As you read the following case, consider why jurisdictions rely so heavily on quantifiable measures of offense seriousness in drug crimes and financial crimes, and also consider whether there can and should be other ways to judge offense seriousness in these settings.

Richard Chapman v. United States
500 U.S. 453 (1991)

REHNQUIST, C.J.

Section 841(b)(1)(B)(v) of Title 21 of the United States Code calls for a mandatory minimum sentence of five years for the offense of distributing more than one gram of a "mixture or substance containing a detectable amount of lysergic acid diethylamide (LSD)." We hold that it is the weight of the blotter paper containing LSD, and not the weight of the pure LSD, which determines eligibility for the minimum sentence.

Petitioner Richard L. Chapman [was] convicted of selling 10 sheets (1,000 doses) of blotter paper containing LSD. The District Court included the total weight of the paper and LSD in determining the weight of the drug to be used in calculating petitioners' sentences. . . . [Chapman and his co-petitioner claim] that the blotter paper is only a carrier medium, and that its weight should not be included in the weight of the drug for sentencing purposes. Alternatively, [they argue] that, if the statute and Sentencing Guidelines were construed so as to require inclusion of the blotter paper or other carrier medium when calculating the weight of the drug, this would violate the right to equal protection incorporated in the Due Process Clause of the Fifth Amendment. . . .

Title 21 U.S.C. §841(b)(1)(B) provides that [a person who distributes one gram or more of a "mixture or substance containing a detectable amount" of LSD must be sentenced to a prison term of at least five years; §841(b)(1)(A)(v) calls for a mandatory minimum of ten years' imprisonment for a violation involving ten grams or more]. Section 2D1.1(c) of the Sentencing Guidelines parallels the statutory language and requires the base offense level to be determined based upon the weight of a "mixture or substance containing a detectable amount of" LSD.

According to the Sentencing Commission, the LSD in an average dose weighs 0.05 milligrams; there are therefore 20,000 pure doses in a gram. The pure dose is such an infinitesimal amount that it must be sold to retail customers in a "carrier" [such as] paper or gel . . . cut into "one-dose" squares and sold by the dose. . . . Although gelatin and paper are light, they weigh much more than the LSD. The ten sheets of blotter paper carrying the 1,000 doses sold by petitioners weighed 5.7 grams; the LSD by itself weighed only about 50 milligrams, not even close to the one gram necessary to trigger the 5-year mandatory minimum.

Petitioners argue that §841(b) should not require that the weight of the carrier be included when computing the appropriate sentence for LSD distribution, for the words "mixture or substance" are ambiguous, and should not be construed to reach an illogical result. Because LSD is sold by dose, rather than by weight, the weight of the LSD carrier should not be included when determining a defendant's sentence, because it is irrelevant to culpability. They argue that including the weight of the carrier leads to anomalous results, viz: a major wholesaler caught with 19,999 doses of pure LSD would not be subject to the five-year mandatory minimum sentence, while a minor pusher with 200 doses on blotter paper, or even one dose on a sugar cube, would be subject to the mandatory minimum sentence. Thus, they contend, the weight of the carrier should be excluded, the weight of the pure LSD should be determined, and that weight should be used to set the appropriate sentence.

We think that petitioners' reading of the statute — a reading that makes the penalty turn on the net weight of the drug, rather than the gross weight of the carrier and drug together — is not a plausible one. The statute refers to a "mixture or substance containing a detectable amount." So long as it contains a detectable amount, the entire mixture or substance is to be weighed when calculating the sentence.

This reading is confirmed by the structure of the statute. With respect to various drugs, including heroin, cocaine, and LSD, it provides for mandatory minimum sentences for crimes involving certain weights of a "mixture or substance containing a detectable amount" of the drugs. With respect to other drugs, however, namely phencyclidine (PCP) or methamphetamine, it provides for a mandatory minimum sentence based either on the weight of a mixture or substance containing a detectable amount of the drug, or on lower weights of pure PCP or methamphetamine. . . . Thus, with respect to these two drugs, Congress clearly distinguished between the pure drug and a "mixture or substance containing a detectable amount of" the pure drug. But with respect to drugs such as LSD, which petitioners distributed, Congress declared that sentences should be based exclusively on the weight of the "mixture or substance." Congress knew how to indicate that the weight of the pure drug was to be used to determine the sentence, and did not make that distinction with respect to LSD. . . .

The history of Congress's attempts to control illegal drug distribution shows why Congress chose the course that it did with respect to sentencing. The Comprehensive Drug Abuse Prevention and Control Act of 1970 . . . did not link penalties to the quantity of the drug possessed; penalties instead depended upon whether the drug was classified as a narcotic or not. The Controlled Substances Penalties Amendments Act of 1984 . . . first made punishment dependent upon the quantity of the controlled substance involved [and was] intended "to provide a more rational penalty structure for the major drug trafficking offenses," by eliminating sentencing disparities caused by classifying drugs as narcotic and non-narcotic. Penalties were based instead upon the weight of the pure drug involved.

The current penalties for LSD distribution originated in the Anti–Drug Abuse Act of 1986. Congress adopted a "market-oriented" approach to punishing drug trafficking, under which the total quantity of what is distributed, rather than the amount of pure drug involved, is used to determine the length of the sentence. To implement that principle, Congress set mandatory minimum sentences corresponding to the weight of a "mixture or substance containing a detectable amount of" the various controlled substances, including LSD. It intended the penalties for drug trafficking to be graduated according to the weight of the drugs in whatever form they were found—cut or uncut, pure or impure, ready for wholesale or ready for distribution at the retail level. Congress did not want to punish retail traffickers less severely, even though they deal in smaller quantities of the pure drug, because such traffickers keep the street markets going. . . .

Petitioners argue that the due process of law guaranteed them by the Fifth Amendment is violated by determining the lengths of their sentences in accordance with the weight of the LSD "carrier," a factor which they insist is arbitrary. . . . We find that Congress had a rational basis for its choice of penalties for LSD distribution. The penalty scheme set out in the Anti-Drug Abuse Act of 1986 is intended to punish severely large-volume drug traffickers at any level. . . . That is a rational sentencing scheme.

This is as true with respect to LSD as it is with respect to other drugs. Although LSD is not sold by weight, but by dose, and a carrier medium is not, strictly speaking, used to "dilute" the drug, that medium is used to facilitate the distribution of the drug. Blotter paper makes LSD easier to transport, store, conceal, and sell. It is a tool of the trade for those who traffic in the drug, and therefore it was rational for Congress to set penalties based on this chosen tool. Congress was also justified in seeking to avoid arguments about the accurate weight of pure drugs which might have been extracted from blotter paper had it chosen to calibrate sentences according to that weight. . . .

Petitioners argue that those selling different numbers of doses, and, therefore, with different degrees of culpability, will be subject to the same minimum sentence because of choosing different carriers. The same objection could be made to a statute that imposed a fixed sentence for distributing any quantity of LSD, in any form, with any carrier. Such a sentencing scheme—not considering individual degrees of culpability—would clearly be constitutional. Congress has the power to define criminal punishments without giving the courts any sentencing discretion. Determinate sentences were found in this country's penal codes from its inception, and some have remained until the present. . . . That distributors of varying degrees of culpability might be subject to the same sentence does not mean that the penalty system for LSD distribution is unconstitutional. . . .

STEVENS, J., dissenting.

The consequences of the majority's construction of 21 U.S.C. §841 are so bizarre that I cannot believe they were intended by Congress. [There] is no evidence that Congress intended the weight of the carrier to be considered in the sentence determination in LSD cases, and that there is good reason to believe Congress was unaware of the inequitable consequences of the Court's interpretation of the statute. . . .

In light of the ambiguity of the phrase "mixture or substance" and the lack of legislative history to guide us, it is necessary to examine the congressional purpose behind the statute. [The] majority's construction will lead to anomalous sentences that are contrary to one of the central purposes of the Sentencing

Guidelines, which was to eliminate disparity in sentencing. [Widely] divergent sentences may be imposed for the sale of identical amounts of a controlled substance simply because of the nature of the carrier. If 100 doses of LSD were sold on sugar cubes, the sentence would range from 188-235 months, whereas if the same dosage were sold in its pure liquid form, the sentence would range only from 10-16 months. The absurdity and inequity of this result is emphasized in Judge Posner's dissent:

> . . . A person who sells five doses of LSD on sugar cubes is not a worse person than a manufacturer of LSD who is caught with 19,999 doses in pure form, but the former is subject to a ten-year mandatory minimum no-parole sentence, while the latter is not even subject to the five-year minimum. If defendant Chapman, who received five years for selling a thousand doses of LSD on blotter paper, had sold the same number of doses in pure form, his Guidelines sentence would have been fourteen months. . . . In none of these computations, by the way, does the weight of the LSD itself make a difference — so slight is its weight relative to that of the carrier — except of course when it is sold in pure form. Congress might as well have said: if there is a carrier, weigh the carrier and forget the LSD. . . .

Sentencing disparities that have been described as "crazy" and "loony" could well be avoided if the majority did not insist upon stretching the definition of "mixture" to include the carrier along with the LSD. It does not make sense to include a carrier in calculating the weight of the LSD because LSD, unlike drugs such as cocaine or marijuana, is sold by dosage, rather than by weight. Thus, whether one dose of LSD is added to a glass of orange juice or to a pitcher of orange juice, it is still only one dose that has been added. But if the weight of the orange juice is to be added to the calculation, then the person who sells the single dose of LSD in a pitcher, rather than in a glass, will receive a substantially higher sentence. If the weight of the carrier is included in the calculation, not only does it lead to huge disparities in sentences among LSD offenders, but also it leads to disparities when LSD sentences are compared to sentences for other drugs. [The severity of the sentences in LSD cases would be comparable with those in other drug cases only if the weight of the LSD carrier were disregarded. Congress] did not express any intention to treat those who sell LSD differently from those who sell other dangerous drugs. . . .

NOTES

1. *Quantity-based measures of harm in drug offenses.*   Federal statutes and guidelines make sentences for most drug convictions depend primarily on the type and amount of drugs involved in the offense. Section 2D1.1(c) of the federal guidelines provides that the base offense level for most drug convictions depends on the type and amount of drugs involved. Much of the wrangling at sentencing hearings in drug cases (the largest single category of crimes now charged in the federal system) revolves around the amount of drugs actually involved in the sale or the amount "reasonably foreseeable" to the defendant. Courts must determine how to calculate specific drug quantities and the requisite mens rea for attributing drug amounts to particular offenders so as to quantify the harm created by a particular offender.

As intimated in *Chapman,* federal drug sentencing has not always relied on drug quantities. In 1956 Congress mandated minimum sentences for drug importation and distribution offenses through the Narcotic Control Act, but in the Comprehensive Drug Abuse Prevention and Control Act of 1970 Congress repealed these mandates and returned significant discretion to judges in setting drug sentences. Through a series of statutory enactments in the mid-1980s, however, Congress directly linked mandatory minimum penalties and sentencing ranges to the type and quantity of drugs involved in the offense. When it first created the federal sentencing guidelines, the U.S. Sentencing Commission also adopted a quantity-based scheme for drug sentencing in an effort to harmonize its guidelines with Congress's sentencing mandates. See William W. Wilkins Jr. et al., Competing Sentencing Policies in a "War on Drugs" Era, 28 Wake Forest L. Rev. 305 (1993).

Many state jurisdictions in the 1970s and 1980s joined the trend of using quantity-based measures of culpability and mandatory sentencing terms for drug crimes. New York began this trend in 1973 with the passage of the "Rockefeller drug laws" (named for Governor Nelson Rockefeller) requiring mandatory 15-year prison sentences for possession or sales of relatively small amounts of narcotics. The New York Court of Appeals interpreted the statute to require proof that a defendant knew about the amount of drugs involved, but the state legislature later eliminated this requirement. See People v. Ryan, 626 N.E.2d 51 (N.Y. 1993). In 1978 Michigan enacted the so-called 650 lifer law, which required mandatory life imprisonment for possession or sale of 650 grams of cocaine or heroin. See Harmelin v. Michigan, 501 U.S. 957 (1991) (upholding this sanction against a constitutional challenge). A number of states that have adopted guideline systems (including Virginia and Kansas) have separate sentencing grids for drug offenses, and these systems also rely heavily on drug types and quantities.

In more recent years, some states have reduced sentence lengths based on drug quantity triggers. In Michigan, for example, legislation that became effective in 2003 eliminated mandatory minimum sentences for certain controlled-substance violations. Similarly, in December 2004 the New York legislature made some modest amendments to the Rockefeller drug laws. Some first-time drug offenders who were eligible for sentences ranging from 15 years to life under the prior law now face reduced terms of 8 to 20 years in prison. Though these sorts of legislative changes can often ameliorate the sentencing consequences of particular drug quantities, the type and weight of illegal narcotics involved in an offense will still frequently play a central role in sentencing outcomes in many jurisdictions.

2. *Quantification of crack versus powder cocaine.* The use of quantity measures for assessing the seriousness of drug offenses has proved most controversial in the context of cocaine, especially in the federal system. Since the inception of modern sentencing reforms in the mid-1980s, federal statutes and guidelines incorporated a "100-to-1 ratio" between powder cocaine and crack — that is, an offense must involve 500 grams of powder cocaine, but only 5 grams of crack, to trigger a five-year minimum penalty. As discussed more fully in Chapter 9, this 100-to-1 ratio has been the subject of heated debate for a number of years, primarily because of its disparate impact on minority

defendants. After the Supreme Court in United States v. Booker, 543 U.S. 220 (2005), made the federal sentencing guidelines "effectively advisory," lower courts have struggled to determine whether and when the severe crack guidelines should be followed. As discussed more fully in Chapter 9, the United States Sentencing Commission in May 2007 issued a report reiterating the Commission's position that the 100-to-1 powder-crack drug quantity ratio significantly undermines various congressional objectives set forth in the Sentencing Reform Act and recommending to Congress modifications to the statutory penalties for crack cocaine offenses. Nevertheless, despite urging significant reform, the Commission's report did not seriously question the basic choice to use quantity measures in drug sentencing rules.

3. *Quantity-based measures of harm for economic offenses.* Under the federal sentencing guidelines, sentence severity for economic offenses such as fraud increases with the value of the property involved. For losses greater than $5,000, §2B1.1 calls for incremental increases in the offense level as the amount of loss rises. The sentencing judge adds two levels for losses over $5,000, four levels for losses over $10,000, and so on, to the top of the scale: 26 levels added for losses of more than $100 million. Because the U.S. Sentencing Commission made the concept of "loss" the centerpiece for setting sentence length in fraud and theft cases, loss calculations have generated lots of litigation and numerous doctrinal splits within the federal circuits. As a result, the commission in 2001 made a considered effort to reform the guidelines' "loss table" to create a doctrinally coherent, easy-to-apply set of rules. The old rules defined "loss" to mean "the value of the property taken, damaged or destroyed." The current, amended rules give more specific guidance on the question of causation. The sentence turns on the actual or intended loss, whichever is greater, and actual loss is defined as "the reasonably foreseeable pecuniary harm that resulted from the offense." This definition requires, at a minimum, that the defendant's offense be a cause-in-fact of the economic harm. But it also limits losses to those foreseeable by a reasonable person. See Frank O. Bowman III, The 2001 Economic Crime Sentencing Reform: An Analysis and Legislative History, 35 Ind. L. Rev. 5 (2001).

In the federal system, all fraud and theft offenses use the same loss table, and the amount of loss determines the bulk of the punishment (for fraud, the base offense is 6 and the loss could add up to 26 levels to that base). Robbery, under §2B3.1, uses a separate loss table and the loss determines a smaller proportion of the sentence: the base offense is 20, and the amount of loss could add only 7 further levels. Why does loss account for relatively more of the sentence in fraud or theft than in robbery cases? Are there recurring features of frauds or thefts that should figure more heavily in the sentence? Think again about the robberies described in Problems 4-1 and 4-3. To what extent does the amount of money lost in each robbery determine in your mind the seriousness of the crime?

4. *Quantity-based measures of harm for child pornography offenses.* The growth of online technology has been accompanied by the growth of online pornography and of new sentencing laws targeting illegal child pornography disseminated or accessed via the Internet. Federal sentencing guidelines and some state sentencing laws rely heavily on the number of images of child pornography distributed or downloaded. See, e.g., U.S. Sentencing Guidelines §2G2.2(b)(7)

(providing progressively enhanced punishment if the offense involves more than 10 images, more than 150 images, more than 300 images, or more than 600 images). In Arizona, which treats the possession of each image of child pornography as a separate offense with a 10-year mandatory minimum sentencing term that must be imposed consecutively, the state Supreme Court recently affirmed over an Eighth Amendment objection a 200-year sentence imposed on a high school teacher convicted of possessing 20 images of child pornography. See State v. Berger, 134 P.3d 378 (Ariz. 2006), *cert. denied,* 127 S. Ct. 1370 (2007).

5. *Statutory interpretation: absurd results.* As the dissenting opinion in *Chapman* argues, the LSD punishment scheme based on weight of the carrier can produce absurd results. How can judges best respond to such a statute? Two distinguished federal judges, Frank Easterbrook and Richard Posner, debated this question in the lower court opinions in this case. Judge Easterbrook suggested that judges ordinarily must enforce what they believe to be an unwise sentencing scheme:

> A preference for giving statutes a constitutional meaning is a reason to construe, not to rewrite or "improve." Canons are doubt-resolvers, useful when the language is ambiguous and a construction of the statute is fairly possible by which the question may be avoided. "Substance or mixture containing a detectable quantity" is not ambiguous. . . . The canon about avoiding constitutional decisions, in particular, must be used with care, for it is a closer cousin to invalidation than to interpretation. It is a way to enforce the constitutional penumbra, and therefore an aspect of constitutional law proper. Constitutional decisions breed penumbras, which multiply questions. Treating each as justification to construe laws out of existence too greatly enlarges the judicial power.

United States v. Marshall, 908 F.2d 1312, 1318 (7th Cir. 1990). Judge Posner's dissent described a more active form of statutory interpretation for judges:

> Well, what if anything can we judges do about this mess? The answer lies in the shadow of a jurisprudential disagreement . . . between the severely positivistic view that the content of law is exhausted in clear, explicit, and definite enactments . . . from legislatures, and the natural lawyer's or legal pragmatist's view that the practice of interpretation and the general terms of the Constitution (such as "equal protection of the laws") authorize judges to enrich positive law with the moral values and practical concerns of civilized society. Judges who in other respects have seemed quite similar, such as Holmes and Cardozo, have taken opposite sides of this issue. Neither approach is entirely satisfactory. The first buys political neutrality and a type of objectivity at the price of substantive injustice, while the second buys justice in the individual case at the price of considerable uncertainty and, not infrequently, judicial willfulness. It is no wonder that our legal system oscillates between the approaches. The positivist view, applied unflinchingly to this case, commands the affirmance of prison sentences that are exceptionally harsh by the standards of the modern Western world, dictated by an accidental, unintended scheme of punishment nevertheless implied by the words (taken one by one) of the relevant enactments. The natural law or pragmatist view leads to a freer interpretation, one influenced by norms of equal treatment.

908 F.2d at 1334-1335. Is it possible to generalize as to when judges should use each of these approaches to statutory interpretation?

PROBLEM 4-7.   GETTING TOUGH ON DRUNK DRIVERS

The National Commission Against Drunk Driving reports that state laws "frequently fail to reflect the seriousness" of driving while intoxicated. "Courts frequently impose lenient sentences without regard for the offender's driving and criminal record, alcohol problems, or the damage caused to the victims. This undercuts any general deterrent effect of the laws regulating the drinking driver."

You are a senator in a state where a number of serious, well-publicized accidents have occurred recently involving intoxicated drivers with a history of drinking and driving. Your state law currently provides for a maximum sentence of six months' imprisonment for a first drunk-driving offense and a three-year maximum for a repeat offender. Bills are circulating to increase the statutory penalties for driving while intoxicated.

One bill — entitled Responding to Inebriated Drivers (RID) — increases the range of available punishment for driving under the influence. The RID bill proposes raising the maximum sentence for a first offense to 5 years and the maximum sentence for repeat offenders to 20 years. The bill gives sentencing judges broad discretion to individualize punishments while suggesting that higher sentences are more fitting for offenders with high blood-alcohol content at the time of arrest.

Another bill — entitled Taking on Utterly Grotesque Harmers (TOUGH) — mandates minimum sentences for those who cause property or bodily harm while drinking and driving. Specifically, the TOUGH bill requires at least a 1-year imprisonment term for anyone who causes more than $500 of property damage, at least 5 years' imprisonment for anyone who causes serious physical harm, and 20 years' imprisonment for anyone who causes a death while driving under the influence.

Which bill would you support? Why?

3.   *The Role of Mens Rea and Motive*

a.   **Strict Liability Sentencing Factors**

Legal philosopher H. L. A. Hart, in his renowned text on criminal law and punishment theory *Punishment and Responsibility,* referred to this fundamental principle of just punishment: "causing harm intentionally must be punished more severely than causing the same harm unintentionally." Though legislatures have usually taken this advice to heart when grading offenses, they do not give mens rea concepts so much weight at sentencing.

|| *United States v. Ana Marin de Velasquez* ||
|| 28 F.3d 2 (2d Cir. 1994) ||

McLAUGHLIN, J.
Ana Marin de Velasquez arrived at New York's John F. Kennedy International Airport from Colombia. During a customs inspection, she appeared to be

extremely nervous and was sweating profusely. A search of the soles of the shoes she was wearing revealed that the shoes contained 167.8 grams of heroin. Customs agents also determined that she was transporting 636.3 grams of heroin internally, for a total of 804.1 grams.

After her arrest, the defendant admitted to agents that she was transporting drugs internally, but disclaimed all knowledge of the drugs found in the soles of her shoes. She claimed that Colombian drug traffickers gave her a pair of shoes that would identify her to her New York contact but she never knew the shoes contained heroin. Eventually, defendant pled guilty to importing heroin. During the plea allocution, defendant stated that she knew she was importing narcotics, although she did not know what kind. . . . In calculating the total quantity of heroin defendant possessed for sentencing purposes, the court included the heroin in defendant's shoes.

Defendant argues that the mens rea doctrine and considerations of due process required the district court to exclude the heroin in her shoes when calculating the total amount of drugs she possessed for sentencing purposes. In the alternative, she argues that the heroin in her shoes should have been included only if it was reasonably foreseeable that her shoes contained heroin.

[We have previously] held that neither due process nor the doctrine of mens rea requires that a defendant actually know the total quantity of drugs in his possession to be sentenced for the full amount under the Sentencing Guidelines. We reaffirm that holding here. We now [also] hold that in a possession case the sentence should be based on the total amount of drugs in the defendant's possession, without regard to foreseeability. [Federal law] makes it a crime to "knowingly" import certain illicit drugs into the United States [and] makes it a crime to "knowingly" manufacture, distribute, or otherwise possess illicit drugs. Quantity is not part of the corpus delicti, i.e., forms no part of the substantive offense under any of these statutes. Conviction rests solely on the knowing possession of some quantity, however large or small, of illicit drugs.

Quantity comes into play only at the sentencing stage, where it determines the minimum or maximum penalty the defendant may receive. It is settled that the minimum and maximum sentences are to be strictly imposed, regardless of the defendant's state of mind concerning the total quantity of drugs in his possession. Mens rea and due process concerns are fully satisfied at the conviction stage, where the defendant must be found guilty of, or plead to, "knowingly" possessing some amount of drugs. . . .

Particularly in drug offense cases, it is by no means unusual to peg the sentence to factors that were not known—or even foreseeable—to the defendant at the time the crime was committed. For example, a defendant who distributes drugs within 1000 feet of a school is subject to twice the maximum penalties for drug distribution. This is true, regardless of whether he knew or could foresee that he was within the proscribed distance. Similarly, a defendant who distributes drugs to a minor is subject to twice the maximum penalty, regardless of whether he knew or could foresee that the buyer was a minor. Thus, there is nothing startling, or even notable, in the conclusion that a defendant who knows she is carrying some quantity of illicit drugs should be sentenced for the full amount on her person. This remains true even where, as here, defendant claims she did not know she was carrying an additional quantity of drugs—additional to the packet she agreed to carry.

A fertile imagination can conjure bizarre situations where the defendant's possession is tenuous and fleeting. The statute has yet to be drafted that could not be unconstitutionally applied in some extraordinary case, and these cases will have to be dealt with if they arise. Here, however, the defendant was wearing the very shoes that contained the heroin. Clearly, her possession was not ephemeral, and the statute properly applied to her. . . .

There is no requirement under the Guidelines that the defendant know or foresee the total quantity of drugs in his possession to be sentenced for the full amount — just as there is no such requirement under the statutes. [The] Guidelines provide that defendants are accountable for "all quantities" of drugs with which they are "directly involved."

The Guidelines contain two enlightening illustrations. In the first, a hypothetical defendant is arrested while assisting in offloading a ship containing a large amount of marijuana. In the second, a defendant transports a suitcase knowing that it contains some quantity of drugs. In both cases, the Guidelines conclude, the defendant's sentence should be based on the full amount of drugs involved, "without regard to the issue of reasonable foreseeability" and "regardless of his knowledge or lack of knowledge." Thus, the Guidelines make clear that a defendant who knowingly possesses some quantity of illicit drugs cannot disclaim "direct involvement" with the full amount on the ground that the full amount was not foreseeable. . . .

In a possession case, . . . we see no reason why a defendant who knowingly traffics in drugs should not bear the risk that his conduct may be more harmful to society than he intends or foresees. We decline to fashion a rule that would permit a defendant to avoid the consequences of that risk because of a fortuitous lack of knowledge or foreseeability — fortuities which apparently occur with some frequency. See United States v. Ekwunoh, 12 F.3d 368, 369 (2d Cir. 1993) (defendant thought she possessed 400 grams of heroin instead of one kilogram); United States v. Obi, 947 F.2d 1031, 1032 (2d Cir. 1991) (defendant thought he was importing cocaine rather than heroin). In the drug trade, there is always the chance, as is alleged in most of these cases, that the supplier will not recognize "the punctilio of an honor the most sensitive." Meinhard v. Salmon, 164 N.E. 545, 546 (N.Y. 1928) (Cardozo, J.). . . .

It is certainly possible, of course, to imagine a situation where the gap between belief and actuality was so great as to make the Guideline grossly unfair in application. In such cases, a downward departure may be appropriate. The Guidelines, however, were designed to apply to the ordinary mine-run case. This is such a case. Applying the foregoing principles, we believe Ana Marin de Velasquez was properly sentenced for the total amount of heroin in her possession, without regard to whether she knew or could foresee the heroin concealed in her shoes.

NOTES

1. *The role (or lack thereof) of mens rea at sentencing.* Though mens rea concepts are usually integral to legislative grading of offenses, mens rea issues are secondary or altogether ignored at sentencing. In the federal system, drug type

and quantity (along with a number of other increases to the offense level) apply as a matter of strict liability. See United States v. Litchfield, 986 F.2d 21 (2d Cir. 1993) (guideline increasing sentence for possession of stolen firearm did not require knowledge that firearm was stolen); United States v. Lewin, 900 F.2d 145 (8th Cir. 1990) (upholding penalty enhancement for distribution of drugs when sale occurs within 1,000 feet of school, regardless of defendant's knowledge of proximity); United States v. Schnell, 982 F.2d 216 (7th Cir. 1992) (upholding enhancement for possession of firearm with an altered or obliterated serial number regardless of knowledge about obliteration). Jack B. Weinstein, a federal district court judge, laments the lowly place of mens rea in federal sentencing:

> Mens rea, a principle central to our criminal law, is crucial in linking punishment to individual culpability. It is the bridge between morality and law. Yet, in the guidelines era, mens rea has been all but eliminated from the sentencing of drug offenders. This development is a disastrous departure from the great traditions of Anglo-American law. . . .
>
> Courts have defended the absence of mens rea protections in sentencing as not "in any way criminaliz[ing] otherwise innocent activity." Is this really so? In *de Velasquez*, the defendant effectively committed a second crime of which she had no knowledge. Had the drugs in her shoes been the only contraband on her, mens rea principles dictate that she could not have been convicted.

Jack B. Weinstein & Fred A. Bernstein, The Denigration of Mens Rea in Drug Sentencing, 7 Fed. Sent'g Rep. 121, 121-122 (1994). The authors illustrate their point with a "simple hypothetical":

> Your daughter is packing up her car to return home after her first year of college. A friend who is helping her pack asks her to carry a parcel home to a mutual friend, Steven. To your daughter's query, "What's in it?" her friend answers, "Some Stephen King novels and a couple of joints." In fact, there is more than a kilogram of cocaine in the box, which is discovered when your daughter is pulled over for a traffic violation. Your daughter is properly charged with possession with intent to distribute (to Steven). Her intent related to two marijuana cigarettes, yet the government contends that she should be punished for transporting a kilogram of cocaine. The sentence? Years in prison. Despite this frightening prospect, the government insists that your daughter's contention — that she was unaware that she was carrying cocaine — is irrelevant "at the sentencing stage."

Weinstein & Bernstein, 7 Fed. Sent'g Rep. at 123. Is the government's argument in this hypothetical case a necessary logical consequence of the holding in *de Velasquez*?

2. *Reasonable foreseeability in conspiracy cases.* Though mens rea does not have a guaranteed place in sentencing determinations, the federal sentencing guidelines do provide in commentary to the relevant conduct rules that a defendant charged with conspiracy will be sentenced only for conduct that was reasonably foreseeable by the individual defendant. See U.S. Sentencing Guidelines Manual §1B1.3, cmt. n.1 ("In the case of criminal activity undertaken in concert with others . . . the conduct for which the defendant 'would be otherwise accountable' also includes conduct of others in furtherance of the

execution of the jointly-undertaken criminal activity that was reasonably fore-seeable by the defendant."). Though it is akin to a test of a defendant's subjective mens rea, federal courts in sentencing cases have stressed that the "test as to whether conduct is reasonably foreseeable is an objective one." United States v. Cochran, 14 F.3d 1128, 1133 (6th Cir. 1994).

b. Hate Crimes and the Relevance of Motive

Whereas mens rea matters *less* at sentencing than for the substantive crime, a defendant's motives (that is, her reasons for committing the crime) tend to matter *more* at sentencing. Sentencing statutes and rules allow judges to consider motives. Indeed, for some particular motives, the rules call for mandatory increases in the sentence.

|| *Wisconsin v. Todd Mitchell* ||
|| 508 U.S. 476 (1993) ||

REHNQUIST, C.J.

Respondent Todd Mitchell's sentence for aggravated battery was enhanced because he intentionally selected his victim on account of the victim's race. The question presented in this case is whether this penalty enhancement is prohibited by the First and Fourteenth Amendments. We hold that it is not.

On the evening of October 7, 1989, a group of young black men and boys, including Mitchell, gathered at an apartment complex in Kenosha, Wisconsin. Several members of the group discussed a scene from the motion picture "Mississippi Burning," in which a white man beat a young black boy who was praying. The group moved outside and Mitchell asked them: "Do you all feel hyped up to move on some white people?" Shortly thereafter, a young white boy approached the group on the opposite side of the street where they were standing. As the boy walked by, Mitchell said: "You all want to fuck somebody up? There goes a white boy; go get him." Mitchell counted to three and pointed in the boy's direction. The group ran toward the boy, beat him severely, and stole his tennis shoes. The boy was rendered unconscious and remained in a coma for four days.

After a jury trial in the Circuit Court for Kenosha County, Mitchell was convicted of aggravated battery. That offense ordinarily carries a maximum sentence of two years' imprisonment. But because the jury found that Mitchell had intentionally selected his victim because of the boy's race, the maximum sentence for Mitchell's offense was increased to seven years under [a Wisconsin statutory provision that] enhances the maximum penalty for an offense whenever the defendant "[i]ntentionally selects the person against whom the crime . . . is committed . . . because of the race, religion, color, disability, sexual orientation, national origin or ancestry of that person. . . ." The Circuit Court sentenced Mitchell to four years' imprisonment for the aggravated battery. Mitchell . . . appealed his conviction and sentence, challenging the constitutionality of Wisconsin's penalty-enhancement provision on First Amendment grounds. The Wisconsin . . . Supreme Court held that the statute "violates the

First Amendment directly by punishing what the legislature has deemed to be offensive thought." . . .

The State argues that the statute does not punish bigoted thought, as the Supreme Court of Wisconsin said, but instead punishes only [the conduct of intentional selection of a victim]. While this argument is literally correct, it does not dispose of Mitchell's First Amendment challenge. To be sure, . . . a physical assault is not by any stretch of the imagination expressive conduct protected by the First Amendment. But the fact remains that under the Wisconsin statute the same criminal conduct may be more heavily punished if the victim is selected because of his race or other protected status than if no such motive obtained. . . . Because the only reason for the enhancement is the defendant's discriminatory motive for selecting his victim, Mitchell argues (and the Wisconsin Supreme Court held) that the statute violates the First Amendment by punishing offenders' bigoted beliefs.

Traditionally, sentencing judges have considered a wide variety of factors in addition to evidence bearing on guilt in determining what sentence to impose on a convicted defendant. The defendant's motive for committing the offense is one important factor. See 1 W. LaFave & A. Scott, Substantive Criminal Law §3.6(b) (1986) ("Motives are most relevant when the trial judge sets the defendant's sentence, and it is not uncommon for a defendant to receive a minimum sentence because he was acting with good motives, or a rather high sentence because of his bad motives"). Thus, in many States the commission of a murder, or other capital offense, for pecuniary gain is a separate aggravating circumstance under the capital sentencing statute.

[M]otive plays the same role under the Wisconsin statute as it does under federal and state antidiscrimination laws, which we have previously upheld against constitutional challenge. Title VII of the Civil Rights Act of 1964, for example, makes it unlawful for an employer to discriminate against an employee "*because of* such individual's race, color, religion, sex, or national origin." 42 U.S.C. §2000e-2(a)(1) (emphasis added). [We have] rejected the argument that Title VII infringed employers' First Amendment rights. . . .

Nothing in our decision last Term in R.A.V. v. St. Paul, 505 U.S. 377 (1992), compels a different result here. That case involved a First Amendment challenge to a municipal ordinance prohibiting the use of "fighting words" that insult, or provoke violence, "on the basis of race, color, creed, religion or gender." Because the ordinance only proscribed a class of "fighting words" deemed particularly offensive by the city—i.e., those "that contain . . . messages of bias-motivated hatred," we held that it violated the rule against content-based discrimination. But whereas the ordinance struck down in *R.A.V.* was explicitly directed at expression (i.e., "speech" or "messages"), the statute in this case is aimed at conduct unprotected by the First Amendment.

Moreover, the Wisconsin statute singles out for enhancement bias-inspired conduct because this conduct is thought to inflict greater individual and societal harm. For example, according to the State and its amici, bias-motivated crimes are more likely to provoke retaliatory crimes, inflict distinct emotional harms on their victims, and incite community unrest. The State's desire to redress these perceived harms provides an adequate explanation for its penalty-enhancement provision over and above mere disagreement with offenders' beliefs or biases. As Blackstone said long ago, "it is but reasonable that among crimes of different natures those should be most severely punished, which are the most destructive of the public safety and happiness." 4 W. Blackstone, Commentaries.

Finally, there remains to be considered Mitchell's argument that the Wisconsin statute is unconstitutionally overbroad because of its "chilling effect" on free speech. Mitchell argues (and the Wisconsin Supreme Court agreed) that the statute is "overbroad" because evidence of the defendant's prior speech or associations may be used to prove that the defendant intentionally selected his victim on account of the victim's protected status. . . .

The sort of chill envisioned here is far more attenuated and unlikely than that contemplated in traditional "overbreadth" cases. [T]he prospect of a citizen suppressing his bigoted beliefs for fear that evidence of such beliefs will be introduced against him at trial if he commits a more serious offense against person or property . . . is simply too speculative a hypothesis to support Mitchell's overbreadth claim. . . .

NOTES

1. *Hate crimes legislation.* States have passed an array of hate crimes laws that either create new crimes based on the offender's motives or enhance penalties for existing crimes if the government proves that the offender committed the crime because of characteristics of the victim. See, e.g., Fla. Stat. Ann. §921.0016(3); Haw. Rev. Stat. §706-662(6). In addition to statutes prohibiting violence or intimidation toward persons based on certain characteristics, some state laws prohibit vandalism of religious sites, the wearing of masks, and the burning of crosses. States still differ as to the size of the penalty enhancement, the types of biases that trigger these sentence enhancements, and the predicate offenses that may qualify as hate crimes. Congress has often debated but never passed federal hate crimes legislation. It did in 1994 enact the Hate Crime Statistics Act, 28 U.S.C. §534, which requires the federal government to collect and publish information concerning crimes that "manifest evidence of prejudice based on race, religion, disability, sexual orientation, or ethnicity."

Following the lead of Wisconsin v. Mitchell, most state courts hold that sentencing enhancements for hate crimes are consistent with their state constitutions. See, e.g., In re M.S., 896 P.2d 1365 (Cal. 1995); State v. McKnight, 511 N.W.2d 389 (Iowa 1994); State v. Wyant, 624 N.E.2d 722 (Ohio 1994). Though broad consensus exists concerning the constitutionality of most hate crimes legislation, considerable dispute remains over the soundness of these politically popular provisions. Scholarly commentary on the functioning of hate crimes has been dynamic and varied. See James B. Jacobs & Kimberly Potter, Hate Crimes: Criminal Law and Identity Politics 4 (1998). Apart from worries about the free speech and association rights of a defendant, can you think of any potential negative effects of a sentencing enhancement for offenders who select their victims based on race? On religion? On sex? On sexual orientation?

2. *Economic motives as an aggravating factor.* As the *Mitchell* Court notes, sentencing judges and juries have a long tradition of considering various motives at sentencing. In capital cases in particular, many jurisdictions have statutes that call for the judge or jury to consider whether a murder was committed for "pecuniary gain." See, e.g., 18 U.S.C. §3952(c)(8); Ariz. Rev. Stat.

Ann. §13-703(F)(5). In addition, a number of sentencing guideline states provide that an economic motivation aggravates the offense in ways calling for an enhanced sentence. See N.C. Gen. Stat. §15A-1340.16(d)(4) (aggravating factor present when "defendant was hired or paid to commit the offense").

3. *Making motives matter more.*   In a recent article, Motive's Role in Criminal Punishment, 80 S. Cal. L. Rev. 89 (2006), Professor Carissa Byrne Hessick has argued that motive should play a more prominent and formal role in sentencing determinations. Her article's conclusion sums up her main contentions:

> Motive plays an important role in criminal law. But its present role does not reflect its centrality to the relative culpability of different defendants. Because our system of criminal punishment is predicated on the moral assessment of a defendant and her actions, motive should play an expanded role in criminal punishment. The most efficient and effective method to accomplish this integration is to identify and classify various motives *ex ante* and then incorporate an individual defendant's reasons for committing a crime into the amount of her punishment. Accounting for motives at sentencing will help to ensure that a defendant receives the punishment she deserves and that criminal punishment accurately expresses the appropriate amount of moral condemnation for the defendant's actions. Because a punishment system that reflects shared values is more effective at deterring crime, and because motives are perceived as relevant to a defendant's blameworthiness, a punishment system that accounts for motives may also result in less crime.

In her article, Hessick recognizes "the challenge of classifying motives" but asserts that this challenge "should not prevent motive from playing a larger role in criminal punishment." If you were a legislator or a member of a sentencing commission convinced by Hessick's arguments, what first steps would you pursue to give motives a larger and more formal role in sentencing determinations? Are motives best assessed ex ante by legislatures and sentencing commissions or ex post by individual judges deciding particular sentences?

PROBLEM 4-8.   ROB ANON (aka JEAN VALJEAN?) REVISITED

Although it is common for statutes or guidelines to provide expressly that certain "bad" motives will increase a sentence, rarely are there provisions expressly stating that "good" motives can reduce a sentence. An exception might be provisions that encourage a mitigated sentence when a defendant commits an offense because of serious coercion, blackmail, or duress. These rules might well be understood as reducing the defendant's sentence because his reason for doing wrong was not so bad. The provision of the federal sentencing guidelines that encourages a reduced sentence based on coercion or duress, U.S. Sentencing Guidelines Manual §5K2.12, goes on to state that "personal financial difficulties and economic pressures upon a trade or business do not warrant a decrease in sentence."

Do you agree with the U.S. Sentencing Commission that personal financial pressures should not warrant a decrease in sentence? Consider again the case of Rob Anon, described in Problem 4-1, and now imagine that he had a profound personal motivation for his crime: his fiancée was in a car accident and lacked medical insurance or the personal funds needed to pay for a life-saving operation. In light of this "personal financial difficulty," would you be willing to decrease his sentence? Cf. *John Q.* (New Line Cinema 2002).

C.   THE ROLE OF VICTIMS AND THE COMMUNITY

One key source of information about the harm that a crime causes is the victim of the crime. In a traditional indeterminate sentencing system, victims do not formally address the sentencing court. Of course, the prosecutor attempts in many cases to bring the victim's concerns or information to the court's attention, and the judge may account for this in imposing a sentence. But until recently, the victim had little opportunity to speak directly to the sentencing court.

In recent decades, most jurisdictions have created a formal role for victims at sentencing. But what impact should victims have on individual sentences? Should the victim's personal or family circumstances matter? Will these factors, if considered, become a cover for invidious factors such as wealth and race?

|| *State v. Rasheed Muhammad* ||
|| 678 A.2d 164 (N.J. 1996) ||

GARIBALDI, J.

Defendant is charged with the kidnapping, rape, and murder of an eight-year-old child, Jakiyah McClain. On the afternoon of April 1, 1995, Jakiyah received permission from her mother to visit a friend, Ah-Tavia Maxey, who lived only a few blocks away. Jakiyah arrived at her friend's apartment between 4:00 p.m. and 5:00 p.m. . . .

While Jakiyah and Ah-Tavia were talking, defendant entered the apartment building. He volunteered to walk Jakiyah upstairs. He knew Jakiyah's mother. Ah-Tavia watched defendant take Jakiyah's hand and lead her upstairs. Ah-Tavia apparently remained on the ground floor. Shortly after, Ah-Tavia heard kicking, banging, and the sound of Jakiyah's screams. [The next day, the] police found Jakiyah's body, curled in a fetal position with her underpants around one ankle, under a pile of clothes in the bedroom closet [of Muhammad's apartment]. Ah-Tavia Maxey identified defendant as the man she saw the day before with Jakiyah.

Defendant was taken into custody. He gave a statement to the police in which he admitted to kidnapping, sexually assaulting, and murdering Jakiyah. An autopsy of the victim indicated that the cause of death was asphyxiation and that the victim was sexually assaulted. On June 27, 1995, an Essex County Grand Jury indicted defendant for the capital murder of Jakiyah McClain. . . . Defendant brought a pretrial motion, challenging the constitutionality of the victim impact statute under both the New Jersey and United States Constitutions. The trial court granted defendant's motion and declared the statute unconstitutional under both Constitutions. . . .

In 1985, the Legislature enacted the Crime Victim's Bill of Rights, which granted crime victims and witnesses certain rights, including the right to be treated with dignity, the right to be informed about the criminal justice process, and the right to be told about available remedies and social services. The following year, the Legislature [allowed] family members of murder victims to include a written statement in the defendant's presentence report. In 1991, the Legislature amended the Crime Victim's Bill of Rights to provide victims with the opportunity to submit to a representative of the county prosecutor's office a written statement about the impact of the crime on the family and to allow victims to make in-person victim impact statements in non-capital cases directly to the sentencing court.

Finally, on November 5, 1991, the New Jersey electorate overwhelmingly approved Article I, paragraph 22 of the New Jersey Constitution, which is better known as the Victim's Rights Amendment. . . . The Victim's Rights Amendment explicitly authorizes the Legislature to provide victims with "those rights and remedies" that are deemed appropriate to effectuate the purpose of that amendment. On the basis of that constitutional authority . . . the New Jersey Legislature enacted the victim impact statute [in 1995].

The various victims' statutory rights enacted in this State are the product of a "victims' rights" movement that has swept through this nation over the last two decades. Historically, the legal system did not view crime victims as having any rights. Because criminal attacks were viewed as attacks and threats on the entire community, and were prosecuted by the state on behalf of "the people," the actual victim was treated as merely another piece of evidence. Although victims were expected to cooperate with authorities and to testify as part of the state's case-in-chief, little attention was paid to the financial, physical, and emotional needs of victims. [Crime] victims are largely excluded from the criminal justice system, and . . . those who are able to participate suffer a "second victimization" at the hands of the system. That feeling of isolation from the system causes many victims and their families to report widespread dissatisfaction with the criminal system. . . .

The victim impact statute provides that if the defendant presents evidence of his character or record pursuant to [a "catch-all" statutory provision allowing introduction of any mitigating evidence during his capital sentencing trial], the State may present evidence of the murder victim's character and background and of the impact of the murder on the victim's survivors. . . . Defendant alleges that the admission of victim impact statements in a capital case is likely to confuse and impassion the jury, and thus creates an impermissible risk that the penalty decision will be made in an arbitrary and capricious manner rather than on the basis of the relevant evidence. . . . The State contends that victim impact evidence is relevant to the sentencing decision because it illustrates each victim's uniqueness as a human being and the nature of the harm caused by the defendant's criminal conduct. . . .

The victim impact statute does not violate the United States Constitution. [In Payne v. Tennessee, 501 U.S. 808 (1991), the] Supreme Court overruled the prior holdings of Booth v. Maryland, 482 U.S. 496 (1987), in which the Court held that the Eighth Amendment prohibits a capital sentencing jury from receiving victim impact evidence relating to the personal characteristics of the murder victim and the emotional impact of the death on the victim's family, and South

Carolina v. Gathers, 490 U.S. 805 (1989), in which the Supreme Court extended the rule adopted in *Booth* to statements made by the prosecutor about the personal qualities of the victim.

In reevaluating the exclusion of victim impact evidence, the Court [in *Payne*] rejected two of the premises underlying *Booth* and *Gathers:* first, that evidence of the personal characteristics of the victim and of the emotional impact of the crimes on the family does not in general reflect on the defendant's blameworthiness, and second, that only evidence of moral culpability is relevant to a capital sentencing decision. . . . The Court opined that . . . *Booth* had "unfairly weighted the scales in a capital trial" because it allowed the defendant to introduce virtually all mitigating evidence concerning his own circumstance, but barred the State from offering any victim impact evidence. . . .

The *Payne* Court thus held that if a "State chooses to permit the admission of victim impact evidence and prosecutorial argument on that subject, the Eighth Amendment erects no per se bar." The majority opined that "[v]ictim impact evidence is simply another form or method of informing the sentencing authority about the specific harm caused by the crime in question, evidence of a general type long considered by sentencing authorities." *Payne* left undisturbed the holding in *Booth* that the admission of a victim's family members' characterizations and opinions about the crime, the defendant, and the appropriate sentence violates the Eighth Amendment.

[Our] State Constitution explicitly provides victims of crimes with more rights than the Federal Constitution. The Victim's Rights Amendment expressly authorizes the Legislature to provide crime victims with "those rights and remedies" as it determines are necessary. Even if we were inclined to diverge from the holding in *Payne* and interpret the Cruel and Unusual Punishment Clause of our State Constitution as providing greater protections against the arbitrary imposition of the death penalty, the text of the New Jersey Constitution demands that we not pursue such an independent course. . . . To hold the victim impact statute unconstitutional would require us to ignore the Victim's Rights Amendment and the will of the electorate that overwhelmingly approved the constitutional amendment. . . .

Defendant asserts that, to the extent that a victim impact statement presents evidence about conditions that the defendant was unaware [of] when he committed the criminal act, such as the victim's occupation and marital status, the statement is irrelevant and impermissibly diverts the jury from making its sentencing decision on the character of the defendant and the circumstances of the crime. However, [while] it is clear that a defendant's foreknowledge of the specific consequences that his acts are likely to have is relevant to sentencing, the foreseeable consequences of a defendant's actions are equally relevant. Murder has foreseeable consequences. . . . Defendants who intentionally choose to kill know that their actions will destroy a unique individual who is likely to be a parent, child, spouse, brother, or sister.

While a defendant might be unaware of the specific characteristics of his victim or of the particular survivors that the victim will leave behind, it is completely foreseeable that the killing will eliminate a unique person and destroy a web of familial relationships. That conclusion is buttressed by the facts of this case. When the killer brutally attacked eight-year-old Jakiyah, it was completely foreseeable that the homicidal behavior would eliminate a uniquely individual human being and cause great harm to the survivors of the little girl. Although the killer might have been ignorant of the details about Jakiyah and her family, it does not violate the Constitution if the jury is permitted to take into account such obviously foreseeable consequences.

Although victim impact evidence when offered to rebut a defendant's presentation of catch-all mitigation evidence is not prohibited by the New Jersey Constitution, it must nevertheless be relevant and reliable. The admission of evidence relating to the victim's character or the impact of the murder on the victim's family requires a balancing of the probative value of the proffered evidence against the risk that its admission may pose the danger of undue prejudice or confusion to the jury. . . .

Although the decision to admit specific victim impact statements will typically be in the discretion of the trial court, certain statements are clearly impermissible. For example, the State will not be permitted to elicit testimony concerning the victim's family members' characterizations and opinions about the defendant, the crime, or the appropriate sentence. . . . Victim impact evidence should be limited to statements designed to show the impact of the crime on the victim's family and to statements that demonstrate that the victim was not a faceless stranger, but was a unique individual human being. There is no place in a capital case for unduly inflammatory commentary. . . .

The Legislature has taken appropriate steps to reduce the possibility that jurors will misuse victim impact evidence. Under the victim impact statute, the admission of victim impact evidence is limited to a clearly delineated course. Only if the jury finds that the State has proven at least one aggravating factor beyond a reasonable doubt and the jury finds the existence of a [catch-all] mitigating factor may the jury consider victim impact evidence. Even if these requirements are met, the victim impact statements can be used solely for the purpose of determining how much weight to attach to the catch-all mitigating factor. Victim impact testimony may not be used as a general aggravating factor or as a means of weighing the worth of the defendant against the worth of the victim. Our law does not regard a crime committed against a particularly virtuous person as more heinous than one committed against a victim whose moral qualities are perhaps less noteworthy or apparent. . . . While legislatures in other states have enacted statutes that allow victim impact evidence to be admitted for any purpose, . . . the New Jersey Legislature was very careful not to allow victim impact evidence to be used as a general aggravating factor. . . .

To harmonize the victim impact statute with the due process clauses of the Federal and State Constitutions, the Attorney General and County Prosecutors Association have both urged us to devise additional procedural safeguards to reduce the possibility that victim impact evidence is admitted for improper purposes or is used inappropriately. As a matter of fairness, we hold that certain additional procedures must be followed before victim impact statements can be entered into evidence. The defendant should be notified prior to the commencement of the penalty phase that the State plans to introduce victim impact evidence if the defendant asserts the catch-all factor. The State shall also provide the defendant with the names of the victim impact witnesses that it plans to call so that defense counsel will have an opportunity to interview the witnesses prior to their testimony. The greater the number of survivors who are permitted to present victim impact evidence, the greater the potential for the victim impact evidence to unduly prejudice the jury against the defendant. Thus, absent special circumstances, we expect that the victim impact testimony of one survivor will be adequate to provide the jury with a glimpse of each victim's uniqueness as a human being and to help the jurors make an informed assessment of the defendant's moral culpability and blameworthiness. Further, minors should not be permitted to present victim impact evidence except under circumstances where there are no suitable adult survivors and thus the child is the closest living relative.

Before a family member is allowed to make a victim impact statement, the trial court should ordinarily conduct a hearing, outside the presence of the jury, to make a preliminary determination as to the admissibility of the State's proffered victim impact evidence. The witness's testimony should be reduced to writing to enable the trial court to review the proposed statement to avoid any prejudicial content. The testimony can provide a general factual profile of the victim, including information about the victim's family, employment, education, and interests. The testimony can describe generally the impact of the victim's death on his or her immediate family. The testimony should be factual, not emotional, and should be free of inflammatory comments or references.

The trial court should weigh each specific point of the proffered testimony to ensure that its probative value is not substantially outweighed by the risk of undue prejudice or misleading the jury. N.J.R.E. 403. Determining the relevance of the proffered testimony is particularly important because of the potential for prejudice and improper influence that is inherent in the presentation of victim impact evidence. However, in making that determination, there is a strong presumption that victim impact evidence that demonstrates that the victim was a unique human being is admissible. During the preliminary hearing, the trial court should inform the victim's family that the court will not allow a witness to testify if the person is unable to control his or her emotions. That concern should be alleviated by our requirement that the witness be permitted only to read his or her previously approved testimony. . . . Finally, the trial court should inform the prosecutor that any comments about victim impact evidence in his or her summation should be strictly limited to the previously approved testimony of the witness. . . .

Even though we hold that the introduction of victim impact statements during the sentencing phase of a capital case does not violate the New Jersey Constitution, we recognize that under certain circumstances victim impact statements could render a defendant's sentencing fundamentally unfair and could lead to the arbitrary imposition of the death penalty. . . . We have confidence in the ability of the courts to determine whether a defendant has been impermissibly prejudiced by the admission of unduly inflammatory victim impact evidence. . . .

HANDLER, J., dissenting.

[Expanding] "relevant evidence" to include victim-impact evidence will effectively prevent a jury from rendering a death penalty verdict based on the defendant's character and the circumstances of the crime. Evidence about the crime victim has always been admissible in a capital prosecution when it is relevant to guilt or innocence. Victim-impact evidence, as now authorized, however, is not relevant to criminal guilt or innocence. A death sentence must be based on a determination of the defendant's deathworthiness in terms of his or her character and the circumstances of the case. The constitutionality of the death penalty based on that determination hinges on the requirement that clear standards guide jury discretion. A jury's consideration of victim-impact evidence, as now authorized by the Court, cannot be controlled by any standards. Jurors will not be capable of disregarding victim-impact evidence's extreme prejudicial effects or avoiding its distorting and devastating impact. Thus, victim-impact evidence will inevitably derail the jury's function and purpose, resulting in the unconstitutional imposition of the death penalty. . . .

The introduction of victim-impact evidence unacceptably exacerbates the racial disparities evident in capital sentencing. Victim-impact evidence encourages jurors to examine and use, both consciously and unconsciously, the comparative worth of the defendant and the victim. Race unquestionably influences our perceptions. . . . Jurors will utilize their unconscious impressions of the victim's worth when considering whether the credibility of the victim-impact evidence and the degree to which the survivors' suffering will counter the weight of the [general mitigating] evidence. First, jurors will consider whether the victim-impact evidence correlates to what the jurors believe is the appropriate impact for the victim's death. Second, jurors will make a moral determination of the gravity of the victim's death. Such steps accentuate disparate capital sentencing on the basis of the victim's race. For these reasons, victim-impact evidence raises the foreboding possibility that death-penalty sentencing decisions influenced by victim-impact evidence will be based on the same invidious motives as race-based discrimination. . . .

NOTES

1. *Victim input at sentencing.*   Over the past 20 years nearly every state has increased victim involvement at sentencing. See generally National Victim Center, The 1996 Victims' Rights Sourcebook: A Compilation and Comparison of Victims' Rights Laws (1996). Almost all states now permit victim input through the presentence report. Many state laws allow victims a separate opportunity to make a written or oral statement regarding sentencing, often detailing the kinds of information victims may offer. A few states have retained sharper limits, such as those allowing judges to choose whether to admit or refuse victim impact information; Texas allows a victim to make a personal statement in court only *after* sentencing, Tex. Code Crim. Proc. art. 42.03. The Victim and Witness Protection Act of 1982 amended the Federal Rules of Criminal Procedure to require the inclusion of a victim impact statement as a part of the presentence investigation report in federal court. See Fed. R. Crim. P. 32 (presentence report must contain "verified information, stated in a nonargumentative style, containing an assessment of the financial, social, psychological, and medical impact on any individual against whom the offense has been committed"). Why do some jurisdictions (such as New Jersey) accept the victim's statements about the impact of the crime but not the victim's opinion about an appropriate sentence? Cf. Fryer v. State, 68 S.W.2d 628 (Tex. 2002) (law allows sentencing court to consider victim's opinion about proper punishment, as recorded in presentence

report; here, victim recommends that defendant in sexual assault case not receive probation).

Victim impact information is supposed to influence the judge; indeed, many statutes require the judge to take account of victim information. The rich variety of statutes has not produced detailed case law regarding victim impact statements outside the capital sentencing context. Is victim impact evidence a less difficult issue in the noncapital setting because a judge rather than a jury selects the sentence? Is a judge more likely to ignore any "emotional" aspects of the victim's testimony? Is it even *possible* to distinguish, as the *Muhammad* court attempted to do, between emotional and informational statements from victims?

2. *Sentencing provisions in federal victim rights legislation.*   In October 2004 Congress enacted a comprehensive Crime Victims Rights Act (CVRA), codified at 18 U.S.C. §3771. Among its comprehensive list of rights, the act gives victims "the right to be reasonably heard at any public proceeding in the district court involving . . . sentencing." This act thus seems to codify in federal law the right of crime victims to provide what is known as a "victim impact statement" to the court. This new act does not, however, limit the right of victims to providing just impact information. The rights conferred by the act are designed to be broad and to allow victims to be "reasonably heard" at all sentencing proceedings.

In the first major test of the sentencing reach of the CVRA, the Ninth Circuit in Kenna v. U.S. District Court for the Central District of California, 435 F.3d 1011 (9th Cir. 2006), indicated that Congress sought to confer broad rights on victims and granted a writ of mandamus to ensure that victims could speak at a defendant's sentencing hearing. In a subsequent ruling, however, the Ninth Circuit summarily rejected a crime victim's claim that the CVRA provided victims the right to obtain disclosure of a full presentence report. See Kenna v. U.S. District Court for the Central District of California, 453 F.3d 1136 (9th Cir. 2006).

The particulars of working victims into the sentencing process presents various challenges, and requires preliminary resolution of who exactly qualifies as a victim under applicable laws. In the context of some offenses, the victims as so defined will be obvious; but are there any "victims" in drug and firearm possession offenses, and are there not hundreds of thousands of victims in large corporate frauds that impact financial markets? Though many policymakers embrace the basic idea of granting victims rights in the criminal justice system, in practice victims can sometimes disrupt the traditional operation of the system. For a fuller review of these and related issues, see generally Victim Impact Evidence, the Crime Victims' Rights Act and *Kenna*, 19 Fed. Sent'g Rep. no. 1 (October 2006).

3. *Support services for victims.*   Although the law in many jurisdictions now allows a victim to provide formal input to the sentencer (whether jury or judge), most victims in noncapital cases do not take advantage of the opportunity. What practical hurdles might block the routine participation of victims at sentencing? What support services might a prosecutor's office (or some other government agency) offer to victims that could increase the number of victims who take an active role at sentencing? Do prosecutors have incentives to provide such services?

4. *Vulnerable victims.*   Structured sentencing rules often instruct a judge to enhance a sentence if the victim of the crime was vulnerable or otherwise worthy of exceptional protection. The Minnesota sentencing guidelines authorize the judge to decrease a sentence if "the victim was an aggressor in the incident" and to increase the sentence if the "victim was particularly vulnerable due to age, infirmity, or reduced physical or mental capacity, which was known or should have been known to the offender" or if the "victim was treated with particular cruelty for which the individual offender should be held responsible." Minn. Sentencing Guidelines II.D.2.a.1, II.D.2.b.1 to II.D.2.b.2. The federal guidelines contain a similar provision for enhancement of the sentence by a designated amount if "the defendant knew or should have known that a victim of the offense was unusually vulnerable due to age, physical or mental condition, or that a victim was otherwise particularly susceptible to criminal conduct." U.S. Sentencing Guidelines Manual §3A1.1. A specified increase is also required when the victim is "a government officer or employee" or a law enforcement officer.

5. *Community perspectives at sentencing.*   Crimes rarely have only one victim. Indeed, many crimes affect an entire community. How can the sentencing judge learn about such wide-ranging effects? The Sentencing Reform Act requires the U.S. Sentencing Commission to consider, when creating the federal sentencing guidelines, "the community view of the gravity of the offense." 28 U.S.C. §944(c)(4). Should the commission interpret that instruction to require polls on the views of the national "community" to create one set of guidelines, or does it instead call for the creation of guideline provisions that are uniquely attentive to the various communities that make up the United States? Since the commission chose to create uniform federal guidelines, would it be appropriate for judges in different federal jurisdictions to weigh community impact differently? Federal judge Reena Raggi argues that federal guidelines should allow local variation among federal districts because particular crimes may create special harms in some localities and because the judges in that area develop special expertise on certain topics:

> I first began to question [the nationally uniform approach of the sentencing guidelines] when I had to impose sentences on a number of defendants who had unlawfully transported firearms into New York from other states. Almost daily my fellow New Yorkers and I would read in the press of the senseless shooting of young children, on the streets, even in their own homes, all victims of random gun fire. . . . Almost invariably the guns used in these crimes, as well as most others unlawfully possessed in this area, had come from out of state.
>
> This sort of interstate transportation of guns into the New York area is big business. In the two years between 1990 and 1992, a joint federal-state task force operating in New York arrested 260 people for such trafficking. And yet, when it came time for me to impose sentences in my cases that summer of 1990, I was confronted by a guideline range that rarely exceeded six months' incarceration. When I voiced my concern to the Sentencing Commission about these guidelines for gun trafficking as they applied in New York, I was told that other parts of the country viewed gun crimes differently and that the guidelines were meant to reflect an average. . . .
>
> The insight judges have about crimes in their particular districts goes beyond simply recognizing which conduct is more destructive to a community. It also reaches the question of how different levels of conduct contribute to an

area's crime problems. For example, . . . few judges have as broad an experience dealing with drug importation and large-scale distribution as my colleagues in the Eastern District of New York. The piers and airports of the district make it . . . the entry point for a large percentage of the contraband entering this country. . . . The fact that a sentencing factor . . . does not pertain nationwide, indeed, the fact that it may be unique to the case at hand, does not make the factor irrelevant to the imposition of a just sentence. District judges should enjoy more discretion — indeed they should be encouraged — to depart from the guidelines to reflect specific local concerns.

Reena Raggi, Local Concerns, Local Insights, 5 Fed. Sent'g Rep. 306-308 (1993). As a member of the U.S. Sentencing Commission, how might you respond?

= 5 =

Sentencing Inputs:
The Offender's Record and Background

In Chapter 4 we reviewed how various features of the crime can affect sentencing outcomes. But that review covered only one side of the substantive components of sentencing decisions—the offense. In this chapter we turn to another major sentencing input, the background and characteristics of the criminal offender. A prior criminal record, cooperation with the government in other investigations, and other aspects of the offender's personal history and prospects can all play a role in the sentencing decision. The foundational question to consider throughout this chapter is why sentence determinations should turn on *who* the offender is in addition to *what* the offender did.

As we stressed at the outset of Chapter 4, sentencing practice always informs sentencing theory, and thus it is again appropriate to begin our discussion of offender characteristics with an introductory sentencing exercise—indeed, the same basic exercise that started Chapter 4. Below we supplement the facts relating to the fictitious offender Rob Anon. The questions following the facts highlight the relevance of Rob's personal characteristics rather than his crime. As before, you should be prepared to return to Rob's case periodically to see whether our detailed study of sentencing systems changes your initial perspective on Rob's status.

PROBLEM 5-1. ROB ANON

A jury found Rob Anon guilty of one count of armed bank robbery. The evidence at trial proved that Rob planned the robbery and then recruited his two co-defendants to participate. According to the testimony of co-defendant Zweite (who pled guilty to the charge pursuant to a plea agreement with the government), Rob gave each participant in the robbery a firearm and a ski mask. Rob also provided a getaway car, although the origins and current location of the car remain unknown.

According to the testimony at trial, the activities of the three defendants inside the bank were as follows: Rob disabled the surveillance cameras and alarms; co-defendant Tercero kept his firearm pointed at the teller while Zweite vaulted the counter and collected more than $200,000 in cash. As the threesome hurried out of the bank, Tercero pushed to the ground an elderly man who walked into the bank during the robbery. The man broke his hip when he fell. In dividing the loot, Rob gave Zweite and Tercero one-fourth of the proceeds each, keeping half for himself.

The government's evidence at Rob's trial included surveillance photos, eyewitnesses, physical evidence, and testimony by Zweite and Tercero. From the moment of his indictment and throughout his prosecution, Rob denied responsibility for the robbery and claimed he was "set up."

Rob is 22 years old and has produced a spotty employment record since dropping out of high school at age 16. Rob was last employed in a series of construction projects with a local landscaping company; he previously worked for a shoe store as a salesman on a part-time basis. Reared by a single mother in an economically depressed urban area and the second youngest of five children, Rob seems to have few friends and mostly keeps to himself. Rob's mother recalls that Rob's siblings taunted and teased him because of his small stature. She believes that Rob became addicted to cocaine in the past year.

Rob's criminal record includes two prior offenses. Six years ago, a juvenile court convicted Rob of one count of shoplifting and sentenced him to 100 hours of community service. Two years ago, Rob was convicted of receipt of stolen goods and sentenced to three years' probation. Rob was still serving that term of probation at the time of the bank robbery. In the federal system, armed bank robbery carries a maximum penalty of 25 years in prison or a fine of $250,000 or both. Compare http://www.ussc.gov/training/ws_ex_rob.pdf.

1. You are the sentencing judge for Rob in a jurisdiction that places no limits on your discretion to choose a sentence from probation to the statutory maximum of 25 years. What sentence would you impose? If you need more information before choosing a sentence, what additional information would you seek?

2. If this had been Rob's first offense rather than his third, would your sentencing decision change?

3. If Rob accepted responsibility for his action, pled guilty to the charged offense, and agreed to testify against his co-conspirators, would your sentencing decision change?

4. If Rob was 45 years old with a Ph.D. and had been raised in an affluent home, would your sentencing decision change?

5. If Rob (and an expert testifying on his behalf) claimed that his criminal behavior was the product of his cocaine addiction and Rob was now voluntarily enrolled in an intensive drug treatment program, would your sentencing decision change?

A. PRIOR CRIMINAL RECORD

At sentencing, the court learns about the defendant's life before the crime of conviction took place. Probation officers collect some of this information; attorneys for either the prosecution or the defense present facts about the offender's personal background and history as well. Often the offender's past includes prior convictions or other encounters with the criminal justice system. In an unstructured sentencing system, the judge gives the prior criminal record whatever weight she thinks appropriate. Sentencing statutes and guidelines, however, instruct judges in some systems more precisely about the effect that a prior criminal record must have on a sentence.

1. "Strikes" Laws and Other Mandatory Rules

|| *People v. Jerry Garcia* ||
|| 976 P.2d 831 (Cal. 1999) ||

CHIN, J.

In this case, we consider whether a trial court, when applying the "Three Strikes" law, Penal Code §§667(b)-(i), 1170.12(a)-(d), may exercise its discretion under Penal Code §1385(a), so as to dismiss a prior conviction allegation with respect to one count but not another. We conclude that a court may exercise its discretion in this way and that the trial court did not abuse its discretion in doing so here. . . .

On June 19, 1996, Barbara Gantt left her home suddenly to go to the hospital and inadvertently left a window open. She returned home less than two hours later and found the place ransacked. Various items were missing, including a translating machine, jewelry, and a videocassette recorder. As she was cleaning up, she found a wallet with defendant's driver's license on the floor among some of her papers.

On September 4, 1996, Grace Kobel returned home to find defendant bicycling out of her driveway. A window was broken, the screen was lying on the ground, and her front door was open. Kobel called the police, who arrived a few minutes later. She entered the house with the police and found various items missing, including a telephone, jewelry, and a toy airplane. About the same time, police officers spotted defendant riding a bicycle several blocks away and stopped him. Defendant was holding two plastic bags that contained many of the items missing from Kobel's home. He also had jewelry in his pockets. . . .

The court found defendant guilty on [two counts of burglary]. The court also found true an allegation that defendant had five prior serious felony convictions qualifying as "strikes" for purposes of the Three Strikes law.[1] These

---

1. Penal Code §667(e)(2) provides:

> (A) If a defendant has two or more prior felony convictions [qualifying as serious or violent felonies under this law], the term for the current felony conviction shall be an indeterminate term of life imprisonment with a minimum term of the indeterminate

convictions, all on July 17, 1991, were for five burglaries that took place on separate occasions during a short crime spree. The court also found that the same five burglary convictions qualified as one prior serious felony conviction for purposes of the five-year enhancement set forth in §667(a)(1).[2] Finally, for purposes of the one-year enhancement set forth in §667.5(b),[3] the court found true an allegation that defendant had served three prior prison terms. The first of these terms was for a January 10, 1985, conviction for receiving stolen property, the second for a February 19, 1987, conviction for possession of heroin, and the third for the five 1991 burglary convictions already mentioned.

At the sentencing hearing, the court considered a probation report indicating defendant had a history of burglarizing homes and then trading stolen property for drugs. Barbara Gantt and Grace Kobel then described the impact defendant's crimes had on them and asked the court to give defendant the maximum sentence. Next, defendant's girlfriend described defendant's difficult life, saying he grew up in foster homes and was addicted to heroin by age 12. Finally, defendant expressed remorse about the burglaries and asked for forgiveness.

Defense counsel then asked the court to exercise its discretion under §1385(a),[4] and dismiss, or "strike," four of the five prior conviction allegations as to both counts, thereby making the case a "second strike" case and reducing defendant's sentence to a term of twenty-two years and eight months. The court responded that "the interests of justice would not be served by striking four strikes in this case," and to do so "would be for the sole purpose of avoiding the sentence I'm required to hand down by law." The court noted that defendant

---

sentence calculated as the greater of [three] times the term otherwise provided as punishment for each current felony conviction subsequent to the two or more prior felony convictions [or] imprisonment in the state prison for 25 years. . . .

(B) The indeterminate term described in subparagraph (A) shall be served consecutive to any other term of imprisonment for which a consecutive term may be imposed by law. Any other term imposed subsequent to any indeterminate term described in subparagraph (A) shall not be merged therein but shall commence at the time the person would otherwise have been released from prison. — EDS.

2. Penal Code §667(a)(1) provides as follows: "[Any] person convicted of a serious felony who previously has been convicted of a serious felony in this state or of any offense committed in another jurisdiction which includes all of the elements of any serious felony, shall receive, in addition to the sentence imposed by the court for the present offense, a five-year enhancement for each such prior conviction on charges brought and tried separately. The terms of the present offense and each enhancement shall run consecutively." — EDS.

3. Penal Code §667.5(b) provides: "[Where] the new offense is any felony for which a prison sentence is imposed, in addition and consecutive to any other prison terms therefor, the court shall impose a one-year term for each prior separate prison term served for any felony; provided that no additional term shall be imposed under this subdivision for any prison term served prior to a period of five years in which the defendant remained free of both prison custody and the commission of an offense which results in a felony conviction." — EDS.

4. Penal Code §1385(a) provides: "The judge or magistrate may, either of his or her own motion or upon the application of the prosecuting attorney, and in furtherance of justice, order an action to be dismissed. The reasons for the dismissal must be set forth in an order entered upon the minutes. . . ." — EDS.

committed five separate residential burglaries, went to state prison, and then, shortly after his release and while still on parole, committed two more residential burglaries. "[I]f the Three Strikes law was meant for anyone it was meant for Mr. Garcia," the court said. [The] court agreed that defendant's drug addiction was "a factor in mitigation." The court also noted that all defendant's prior serious felony convictions arose from a single period of aberrant behavior for which he served a single prison term. The court commented that defendant had cooperated with police both in 1991 and when they arrested him for the current offenses. Finally, the court stated that defendant had no record of violence.

As to the Kobel burglary, the court sentenced defendant to a term of 30 years to life in state prison. This sentence included 25 years to life under the Three Strikes law plus the mandatory 5-year enhancement under §667(a)(1). The court initially imposed three 1-year enhancements under §667.5(b), for the prior prison terms, but then exercised its discretion under §1385(a), and struck these enhancements. As to the Gantt burglary, the court exercised its discretion under §1385(a), and struck all the prior conviction allegations. In a minute order, the court stated it was striking the prior conviction allegations because they "all refer [to] one case, defendant has cooperated with police in both cases, is addicted to drugs and has not suffered any violent priors." The court calculated a sentence of 16 months, which was one-third the middle term of 4 years. The court ordered that this sentence be served consecutive to the sentence on the Kobel burglary, because the two counts reflected "two separate incidents on two separate dates." Nevertheless, the court stated that a sentence of 30 years to life was "appropriate" and that, but for the constraints of the Three Strikes law, it would have ordered that the 16-month sentence on the Gantt burglary be served concurrently. Defendant's total sentence on both counts was 31 years and 4 months to life. The court imposed a $200 restitution fine, and also ordered $400 restitution to Grace Kobel and $20,000 restitution to Barbara Gantt, less the value of any property returned.

[On appeal, the Attorney General] asserted that the trial court lacked authority under §1385(a) to strike the prior conviction allegations as to the Gantt burglary while not striking them as to the Kobel burglary, claiming that therefore defendant's sentence was unauthorized. [He argued] that striking prior conviction allegations as to some, but not all, current counts was inconsistent with the requirement in the Three Strikes law that sentences be consecutive for current felonies relating to separate criminal episodes. . . .

Section 1385(a) authorizes a trial court to act on its own motion to dismiss a criminal action "in furtherance of justice." We have long held that this power includes the ability to strike prior conviction allegations that would otherwise increase a defendant's sentence. People v. Burke, 301 P.2d 241 (Cal. 1956). Our reasoning in *Burke* is particularly relevant to the issue in this case. In *Burke*, the defendant had been convicted of possession of marijuana . . . , and he admitted a prior conviction for the same offense. At that time, Health and Safety Code former §11712 provided: "Any person convicted . . . for having in possession any narcotic [if] such a person has been previously convicted [of the same offense] shall be imprisoned in the state prison for not less than two years. . . ." Nevertheless, the trial court struck the prior conviction allegation and sentenced the defendant to county jail. . . . We concluded that this power to strike a sentencing allegation fell within the broader power to dismiss an entire action under section

1385. More importantly, however, we also concluded that "[the] striking or dismissal of a charge of prior conviction . . . is not the equivalent of a determination that defendant did not in fact suffer the conviction [citations]; such judicial action is taken . . . for the purpose of sentencing only and any dismissal of charges of prior convictions . . . does not wipe out such prior convictions or prevent them from being considered in connection with later convictions." Thus, we acknowledged that a court might strike a prior conviction allegation in one context, but use it in another.

In People v. Superior Court (Romero), 928 P.2d 1171 (Cal. 1996), we held that the Three Strikes law did not remove or limit this §1385 power to strike sentencing allegations. The defendant in *Romero* pleaded guilty to possession of 0.13 grams of cocaine base. . . . The information also alleged five prior felony convictions, two of which — attempted burglary and first degree burglary of an inhabited dwelling — qualified as strikes for purposes of the Three Strikes law. The trial court struck the prior conviction allegations and imposed a sentence of six years in state prison. This sentence represented three years (the upper term) for possession of a controlled substance plus three consecutive one-year enhancements for prior prison terms. [We] concluded that, in a Three Strikes case, the trial court can, on its own motion and over the prosecutor's objection, strike a prior conviction allegation in furtherance of justice.

Our holding in *Romero* flowed directly from the plain language of the Three Strikes law, which expressly authorizes prosecutors to move to strike prior conviction allegations "pursuant to" §1385(a). We reasoned that, because the Three Strikes law makes express reference to §1385 and does not anywhere bar courts from acting pursuant to that section, the drafters of the law must have intended that section to apply without limitation in Three Strikes cases. . . .

Nevertheless, we stressed that "[a] court's discretion to strike prior felony conviction allegations in furtherance of justice is limited." [A] court may not strike a sentencing allegation solely "to accommodate judicial convenience or because of court congestion." Nor may a court strike a sentencing allegation "simply because a defendant pleads guilty." Finally, we stated that a court may not strike a sentencing allegation "guided solely by a personal antipathy for the effect that the three strikes law would have on [a] defendant," while ignoring defendant's background, the nature of his present offenses, and other individualized considerations.

In People v. Williams, 948 P.2d 429 (Cal. 1998), we further delineated the parameters that govern a trial court's discretion under §1385(a), to strike prior conviction allegations in a Three Strikes case. *Williams* involved a defendant who pleaded guilty to driving a vehicle under the influence of phencyclidine (PCP). . . . The defendant had a 19-year criminal history, including convictions for attempted robbery, rape, and spousal battery, and a series of convictions for firearm possession and driving under the influence. The attempted robbery and rape convictions, which the defendant admitted, qualified as strikes for purposes of the Three Strikes law. However, because those convictions were about 13 years old and because of "the lack of any kind of violence related crimes from then until now," the trial court vacated its finding with respect to the prior attempted robbery conviction, leaving only the prior rape conviction. [We] concluded that the trial court had abused its discretion by vacating one of its prior conviction findings [and] discussed the factors a trial court may legitimately consider when exercising its §1385 discretion in a Three Strikes case. We said that the trial court could give "no weight whatsoever . . . to factors extrinsic to the [Three Strikes] scheme." On the other hand, the court must accord "preponderant weight . . . to factors intrinsic to the scheme, such as the nature and circumstances of the defendant's present felonies and prior serious and/or violent felony convictions, and the particulars of his background, character, and prospects." Ultimately, a court must determine whether "the defendant may be deemed outside the scheme's spirit, in whole or in part."

The reasoning of *Romero* and the standards we enunciated in *Williams* logically support the trial court's action in this case. In *Romero,* we concluded that, by referencing §1385, the Three Strikes law incorporated that section without limitation. [The] standards we enunciated in *Williams* indicate that a trial court has discretion in a Three Strikes case to strike prior conviction allegations on a count-by-count basis. In *Williams,* we instructed trial courts to consider among other things, "individualized considerations" such as the nature and circumstances of the defendant's present felonies and his "prospects." In many cases, "the nature and circumstances" of the various felonies described in different counts will differ considerably. A court might therefore be justified in striking prior conviction allegations with respect to a relatively minor current felony, while considering those prior convictions with respect to a serious or violent current felony.

The Attorney General argues, however, that in a case such as this one, where both current felonies are for the same or similar crimes, the "individualized considerations" we enumerated in *Williams* do not provide a "principled basis" for treating the felonies differently. We disagree. Even if the current offenses are virtually identical, a defendant's "prospects" will differ greatly from one count to another because a Three Strikes sentence on one count will itself radically alter those prospects. Here, for example, once the trial court had sentenced defendant to a term of 30 years to life for the Kobel burglary, his "prospects" for committing future burglaries diminished significantly. [A] defendant's sentence is . . . a relevant consideration when deciding whether to strike a prior conviction allegation; in fact, it is the overarching consideration because the underlying purpose of striking prior conviction allegations is the avoidance of unjust sentences. . . .

The Attorney General, however, points to the requirement in the Three Strikes law that sentencing on distinct current offenses be consecutive, §§667(c)(6)-(8), 1170.12(a)(6)-(8), and without any aggregate term limitation, §§667(c)(1), 1170.12(a)(1). The Attorney General argues that striking prior conviction allegations with respect to one count, but not with respect to another, undermines this principle of consecutive Three Strikes sentences. Again, we disagree. A requirement that a defendant serve the individual sentences for different current felonies consecutively does not indicate how the trial court should determine the lengths of those individual sentences. Here, for example, the trial court conformed to the consecutive sentencing requirement by ordering that the 16-month sentence for the Gantt burglary be served consecutively to the 30-year-to-life sentence for the Kobel burglary. . . .

The Attorney General also argues that the trial court here "eviscerated" the Three Strikes law, the purpose of which was to restrict the discretion of "soft-on-crime judges" and "ensure longer prison sentences." We agree with the

Attorney General that a primary purpose of the Three Strikes law was to restrict judicial discretion, but the Attorney General's argument merely begs the question of *how* judicial discretion was to be restricted. The answer to that question can be found only by examining the language of the act. The Three Strikes law expressly incorporates the power to strike prior conviction allegations under §1385(a). Therefore, rather than eviscerating the Three Strikes law, the trial court in this case *applied* that law, which expressly contemplates the trial court's action.

[Appellate] review of a trial court's §1385 decision is not de novo. [The abuse of discretion] standard is deferential. But it is not empty. Although variously phrased in various decisions, it asks in substance whether the ruling in question falls outside the bounds of reason under the applicable law and the relevant facts. Here, we cannot say that the trial court's decision to strike the prior conviction allegations as to count 3 "falls outside the bounds of reason." The court sentenced defendant to 31 years and 4 months to life in state prison. This sentence is not lenient. . . . Moreover, as the trial court noted, defendant's prior convictions all arose from a single period of aberrant behavior for which he served a single prison term. Defendant cooperated with police, his crimes were related to drug addiction, and his criminal history does not include any actual violence. Cumulatively, all these circumstances indicate that "defendant may be deemed outside the [Three Strikes] scheme's spirit," at least in part, and that the trial court acted within the limits of its §1385 discretion. . . .

BROWN, J., dissenting.

I respectfully dissent. This case asks the age-old question: does judicial commitment to principle matter? The majority gives the modern answer. Not if it gets in the way of expediency.

The "Three Strikes" law reflects the public's long-simmering frustration with perceived laxity in a criminal justice system that allowed repeatedly convicted felons to be released after serving modest sentences with time off for good behavior. All too often, this revolving door led to more crimes, new victims, and greater tragedies. The public saw "soft on crime" judges who were more solicitous of criminal defendants than public safety as the problem; they viewed Three Strikes as the solution. . . .

Under our precedents, the trial court retains discretion under Penal Code §1385 or §17(b), to remove a case from the reach of the law. But, until today, in choosing to rely upon these latter statutes, a trial court had to make a principled determination that the defendant did not come within the spirit of the Three Strikes law and therefore should not be subject to its letter. Thus, I disagree that a court can dismiss prior convictions on a count-by-count basis. Moreover, even if in rare cases a court has that power, the principles we articulated in our recent precedents bar the trial court from doing so here.

[Unless] carefully circumscribed, the power to strike prior felony conviction allegations "in furtherance of justice" . . . carries with it the real potential for undermining the intent of the Three Strikes law itself—namely, to restrict courts' discretion in sentencing repeat offenders. In *Williams,* we . . . undertook to "render §1385(a)'s concept of 'furtherance of justice' somewhat more determinate." We concluded that "in ruling whether to strike or vacate a prior serious and/or violent felony conviction allegation or finding under the Three Strikes law, on its own motion, 'in furtherance of justice' pursuant to §1385(a), or in reviewing such a ruling, the court in question must consider whether, in light of the nature and circumstances of his present felonies and prior serious and/or violent felony convictions, and the particulars of his background, character, and prospects, the defendant may be deemed outside the scheme's spirit, in whole or in part, and hence should be treated as though he had not previously been convicted of one or more serious and/or violent felonies. If it is striking or vacating an allegation or finding, it must set forth its reasons in an order entered on the minutes, and if it is reviewing the striking or vacating of such allegation or finding, it must pass on the reasons so set forth." We emphasized that "no weight whatsoever may be given to factors extrinsic to the [Three Strikes] scheme, such as the mere desire to ease court congestion or, a fortiori, bare antipathy to the consequences for any given defendant."

While professing to follow *Williams,* in reality, the majority tosses aside its carefully crafted limits on judicial discretion. [Notwithstanding] *Williams's* unequivocal holding that "bare antipathy to the consequences for any given defendant" should be given "no weight whatsoever," the majority now concludes that the "overarching consideration" in determining whether to strike prior felony conviction allegations with respect to some, but not all, counts is the total length of a defendant's sentence "because the underlying purpose of striking prior conviction allegations is the avoidance of unjust sentences." In other words, the "overarching consideration" in determining whether to strike prior felony conviction allegations "in furtherance of justice" under §1385(a) is the trial court's antipathy to the sentence the law would otherwise require. . . .

One need only compare the facts of this case to the facts of *Williams* to see how standardless things have become. In *Williams,* in concluding that the trial court had abused its discretion in striking one of Williams's prior felony convictions, we pointed to his failure to "follow through in efforts to bring his substance abuse problem under control." Here, in upholding the trial court's decision to strike, the majority points to the fact defendant's crimes were related to drug addiction. In *Williams,* in concluding that the trial court had abused its discretion in striking one of Williams's prior felony convictions, we noted that "as to his present felony: It is a conviction of driving under the influence that followed three other convictions of driving under the influence; the existence of such convictions reveals that he had been taught, through the application of formal sanction, that such criminal conduct was unacceptable — but had failed or refused to learn his lesson." Here, in upholding the trial court's decision to strike, the majority glosses over the fact defendant's two present convictions for burglary followed quickly on the heels of five previous convictions for exactly the same offense. . . .

The real effect of today's decision is to make the defendant's eligibility for punishment under Three Strikes a factor in mitigation. When a defendant receives a lengthy Three Strikes term on the first of multiple counts, the trial court may disregard the law as to all other counts. . . . *Romero* is no longer reserved for the rare case involving a particularly harsh sentence for a relatively minor offense. Courts may now routinely apply *Romero* to the benefit of recidivists for whom such solicitude is not appropriate. That is not what I heard the voters demand when they enacted the Three Strikes law. Three Strikes was not about judicial discretion; it was about accountability. It was not about "just" sentences; it was about swift, certain, and harsh retribution. Moreover, by encouraging courts to impose only a single Three Strikes sentence regardless of the circumstances, the majority's decision rewards the industrious career criminal—after the first count, the rest are virtually free. . . .

The sentence imposed here was lengthy. But that is beside the point. It was still less than the law required. When the Legislature enacted, and the voters passed, the Three Strikes law, they intended to restrict trial courts' discretion in sentencing. The trial court here had it right when it initially observed that striking defendant's prior felony convictions "would be for the sole purpose of avoiding the sentence I'm required to hand down by law" and that "if the Three Strikes law was meant for anyone it was meant for Mr. Garcia." Today's holding eviscerates the intent of the Three Strikes law. . . .

NOTES

1. *Habitual-offender statutes: the three-strikes variety.*   The provision under which Garcia was sentenced, California Penal Code §667, is an example of a habitual-offender law popularly known as "three strikes and you're out." Almost all states have habitual-felon statutes, which increase sentences by designated amounts for offenders with a particular prior felony record. The three-strikes variety is distinctive for the type of prior record necessary and the amount of increase in the sentence. California's three-strikes law is the most severe in the nation for several reasons: many types of prior convictions qualify as "serious" or "violent" and thus count as a strike, a third felony results in a minimum sentence of 25 years to life even if the third felony is neither violent nor serious, and sentences are doubled even for offenders with only one strike. As detailed more fully in Chapter 7, the U.S. Supreme Court in 2003 upheld the application of California's three-strikes law to two shoplifters with extended criminal histories who claimed that their lengthy imprisonment terms violated the Eighth Amendment's prohibition of cruel and unusual punishments. See Ewing v. California, 538 U.S. 11 (2003) (reprinted in Chapter 7); Lockyer v. Andrade, 538 U.S. 63 (2003).

About half the states have enacted three-strikes laws, but they vary considerably in reach and impact. A few states have two-strikes provisions for particularly serious felonies, while others have adopted four-strikes provisions. See, e.g., Ga. Code Ann. §17-10-7 (providing a sentence of life without parole for two serious violent felonies); Fla. Stat. Ann. §775.084 (requiring three prior felonies to trigger sentence of life imprisonment). See generally Michael Vitiello, Three Strikes: Can We Return to Rationality?, 87 J. Crim. L. & Criminology 395, 463-481, tbls. 1-2 (1997) (reviewing key features of three-strikes laws enacted in various states). The federal three-strikes law imposes a mandatory sentence of life imprisonment on defendants convicted of a serious federal violent felony if they have been previously convicted in state or federal court of two or more serious violent felonies or one serious violent felony and one serious drug offense. See 18 U.S.C. §3559.

2. *Impact of three-strikes law in California and elsewhere.*   Because of its broad reach, California's three-strikes law has had the biggest impact of any jurisdiction's, although that impact is certain only with respect to increased prison rolls.

There is a robust debate over whether decreases in crime rates in California through the 1990s could be attributed to the deterrent or incapacitation effects of California's three-strikes law. Critics of the law note that some states with no comparable three-strikes law had crime drops equal to or greater than California's. Compare Scott Ehlers et al., Still Striking Out: Ten Years of California's Three Strikes (Justice Policy Institute, March 2004) (arguing based on statistical analysis that California's three-strikes law had no measurable impact on the crime rate) with Bill Jones, Why the Three Strikes Law Is Working in California, 11 Stan. L. & Pol'y Rev. 23 (1999) (claiming that significant decreases in California's crime rates could be attributed to three-strikes law). Studies offer vastly different assessments of how potential offenders might respond to the three-strikes law's harsh sanctions. Compare Thomas B. Marvell & Carlisle E. Moody, The Lethal Effects of Three-Strikes Laws, 30 J. Legal Stud. 89 (2001) (contending that three-strikes laws actually increase homicides because a few criminals, fearing the enhanced penalties, will murder victims and witnesses to limit resistance and identification), with Joanna Shepherd, Fear of the First Strike: The Full Deterrent Effect of California's Two- and Three-Strikes Legislation, 31 J. Legal Stud. 159 (2002) (suggesting pronounced deterrent impact from three-strikes laws as potential criminals diligently endeavor to avoid a *first* strike).

A recent work suggests that while the three-strikes law probably provides some deterrent effect, it will have its most significant and tangible long-term impact on California's future prison population. Frank Zimring, Gordon Hawkins & Sam Kamin, Punishment and Democracy: Three Strikes and You're Out in California (2001). Indeed, researchers at the Sentencing Project, a public advocacy group, report that as of May 31, 2001, more than 50,000 prisoners were serving additional time because of California's three-strikes law—nearly 7,000 were serving 25 years to life in prison on three-strikes convictions, and more than 43,000 were serving double time under the law's two-strike provisions. See Ryan S. King & Marc Mauer, Aging Behind Bars: "Three Strikes" Seven Years Later (August 2001). By mid-2005 the number of inmates serving sentences of 25 years to life in prison under the three-strikes law had increased by another 10%. California's prisons now house more than 166,000 offenders, and its rate of imprisonment (456 per 100,000 residents as of June 30, 2005) ranks in the top third among all states. See Chapter 7.

While California's three-strikes law is having a significant impact on that state's criminal justice system, this is not true in other states with similarly named but less sweeping habitual-offender provisions. As a National Institute of Justice paper explains, these states have experienced no major repercussions from enacting such laws:

> With the noted exception of California, there has been virtually no impact on the courts, local jails, or State prisons; nor does there appear to have been an impact on crime rates. [The] projected effects of the law have not been realized as . . . local criminal justice system[s] (the courts in particular) have found ways to circumvent the law. [It seems that in most instances] this form of legislation was carefully crafted to be largely symbolic.

James Austin, John Clark, Patricia Hardyman & D. Alan Henry, Abstract, Three Strikes and You're Out: The Implementation and Impact of Strike Laws (National Institute of Justice, NCJ 181297, 1999).

In 2004 a voter initiative appeared on the November ballot in California to amend the state's three-strikes law. Known as Proposition 66, and prompted by concerns about racial disparity and rising prison costs, this ballot initiative would have limited the reach of the law by preventing nonviolent felonies from triggering the law's tough sentencing provisions. Though early polls registered broad support for Proposition 66, a last-minute advertising campaign against the law featuring Governor Arnold Schwarzenegger shifted the proposition's focus from images of drug addicts and petty thieves serving unfairly harsh prison sentences to hardened criminals receiving leniency and suddenly becoming eligible for release. In a close vote, Proposition 66 was ultimately defeated, with 53% of voters opposed. Subsequent attempts to change the law by requiring that the third offense be a "serious" or "violent" felony, despite strong support by individual district attorneys, have also failed. However, another ballot initiative is very likely to follow. Who would you expect to support California's three-strikes law most vigorously, and why? See Ben Carrasco, Assessing the CCPOA's Political Influence and Its Impact on Efforts to Reform the California Corrections System (January 27, 2006) (available at papers.ssrn.com/sol3/papers.cfm?abstract_id=977005).

3. *Prosecutors and habitual felons.* Although habitual-felon laws in California and elsewhere empower the prosecutor to file additional charges that result automatically in increased sentences, the laws usually do not *require* the prosecutor to file the habitual-felon charge for every qualifying defendant. Not many California citizens appreciate how much prosecutorial discretion remains in this law and how much its use varies around the state. Steve Cooley won election in 2000 as the new district attorney in Los Angeles on a platform of increasing screening of three-strikes cases by focusing on those who have committed serious or violent felonies. Cooley appealed both to the public's perception that the law was creating unjust outcomes and to the need to concentrate resources on truly serious offenses. See Special Directive 00-02 (December 19, 2000) (available at da.co.la.ca.us/3strikes.htm); Twila Decker, Lawyers Say D.A. Breaking Three-Strikes Pledge, L.A. Times, Jan. 22, 2001, at B1 (policy described as means of reserving mandatory sentences for most serious felonies). Since Los Angeles is the primary source of three-strikes cases in California, Cooley's policy has made an enormous difference in the state's crime budget.

Habitual-felon laws in other states (not just the three-strikes variety) also give prosecutors the critical power to choose which among the eligible defendants will be charged as habitual felons. See North Carolina Sentencing and Policy Advisory Commission, Sentencing Practices Under North Carolina's Structured Sentencing Laws 39-41 (March 2002) (available at http://www.nccourts.org/Courts/CRS/Councils/spac/Documents/disparityreportforweb.pdf). (One practical concern that traditionally limited how often prosecutors invoked habitual-felon laws — the need to collect formal documentation establishing the prior convictions — is fast disappearing in a world of electronic records.) If you were the chief prosecutor for a county, what instructions would you give your trial attorneys about which defendants to charge under the habitual-felon law?

4. *Politics surrounding passage of three-strikes laws.* A high-profile crime by a repeat offender often serves as the catalyst for the enactment of three-strikes

laws. In California, the drive for a three-strikes ballot initiative was instigated by Mike Reynolds, a Fresno photographer whose 18-year-old daughter was murdered in 1992 by a parolee. The three-strikes movement became a national phenomenon the following year after 12-year-old Polly Klaas was kidnapped and murdered by Richard Allen Davis, a repeat violent criminal. Though headline-making crimes gave the public the impression that tougher criminal sanctions were needed for repeat offenders, most jurisdictions already had laws in place that provided lengthy terms of imprisonment for serious recidivists.

Of course, the distorting influences of politics and symbolism in the criminal justice system are not new. As discussed in Chapter 2, the development of sentencing commissions was driven in large part by the hope that this sort of institution — consisting of knowledgeable experts, insulated from short-term political pressures, who would have the time and opportunity to study sentencing — would avoid these influences while developing sound criminal justice laws and policies. But in the face of politicians and the public clamoring for tough habitual-offender laws, most sentencing commissions have been unsuccessful in limiting the impact of this legislation. See Ronald F. Wright, Three Strikes Legislation and Sentencing Commission Objectives, 20 Law & Pol'y 429, 437 (1998). What features of a three-strikes law might create special problems for a sentencing commission advocating cautious changes in sentencing laws?

2. Long Records

An offender's criminal past played a central role in sentencing well before the enactment of modern three-strikes laws. The law rarely mandated a particular sentence based on an offender's criminal history in the era of indeterminate sentencing, but judges still used their discretion to impose longer sentences on defendants who had a lengthy criminal record. Modern sentencing reforms have focused on systematizing the effect that a criminal record has on the sentence imposed.

|| **United States v. Anthony Croom** ||
|| 50 F.3d 433 (7th Cir. 1995) ||

EASTERBROOK, J.

Anthony Croom is a punk who grew up to be a thug. His first juvenile conviction was for battery. Next came a conviction for child molestation: when 13 years old, Croom had sexual intercourse with an 11 year old girl. Later Croom was convicted of burglary and other offenses. The burglary conviction disqualified Croom from possessing guns, but he thumbed his nose at the law. One day, while attired like a refugee from a gangster movie, with gloves and a hat pulled down to cover his face, Croom bolted from a meal into the arms of police, who recovered a semi-automatic weapon. He was charged with violating 18 U.S.C. §922(g)(1) and released pending trial. Ten days later Croom invaded a fast food restaurant, drew a gun, ordered the staff into the meat locker (threatening them with death if they did not cooperate), and emptied the till. He did not get far, and his capture led to another federal weapons charge.

Croom pleaded guilty to both; another, similar charge was dismissed as part of a plea bargain. His sentence of 160 months' imprisonment exceeds the guideline range of 110-137 months for a level 28 offense by someone with a criminal history category of IV, and he appeals from the upward departure.

A district judge may give a sentence exceeding the range specified by the Sentencing Guidelines only on account of circumstances "not adequately taken into consideration" by the Sentencing Commission. 18 U.S.C. §3553(b). The district judge gave this explanation of his decision:

> [C]onsidering the offenses which did not count for criminal history score points . . . as well as the . . . short period of time which elapsed between the defendant's last incarceration and the first of these offenses and [the fast food robbery committed after the initial gun arrest], and considering the nature of the offenses reflected in [the presentence investigation report plus the charges to which Croom pleaded guilty], I find . . . that the criminal history category IV does not adequately reflect the seriousness of the defendant's past criminal conduct, and perhaps more so the likelihood that the defendant will commit other crimes. I think there is a clearly ascertainable and projectable pattern here by this defendant of ever increasing in ever more dangerous offenses as he proceeds through life. . . . So I will depart upward to a criminal history category of VI. . . .

The judge did not reveal which of these factors he believed the Sentencing Commission has "not adequately taken into consideration" or why he increased the criminal history category from IV to VI rather than V. Croom has earned a substantial sentence, but 137 months' imprisonment—more than 11 years without possibility of parole—is stern punishment. The stated rationale for tacking on two years is problematic under §3553(b).

The judge's explanation starts with the observation that the Guidelines did not count two of Croom's juvenile convictions. Under U.S.S.G. §4A1.2(d)(2) juvenile convictions the sentences for which ended more than five years before the commission of the latest offense do not contribute any criminal history points. Far from representing an aspect of criminal history that the Sentencing Commission overlooked or did not consider adequately, this exclusion is a conscious decision, one a district judge may not override by the mechanism of an upward departure. The Sentencing Commission believed that old juvenile convictions should be "forgiven" in assigning criminal history points; that the district judge is less forgiving than the Commission does not authorize him to strike out on a different path. To forgive is not necessarily to forget, however; as we explain below the judge may consider the juvenile convictions as part of the larger picture when deciding whether to depart under the criteria of U.S.S.G. §4A1.3.

After remarking on the juvenile convictions, the judge observed that Croom committed the first federal gun offense shortly after release from his most recent state imprisonment, then committed the second gun offense while on pretrial release from the first. These are surely grounds for increasing a sentence—but the Sentencing Commission took them into consideration. Croom received two criminal history points under §4A1.1(d) for committing the first gun offense while on parole from a state sentence, and one point under §4A1.1(e) for committing that offense within two years after leaving prison. He paid for the close relation between the first and second gun offenses by forfeiting the three-level reduction for acceptance of responsibility that otherwise would have been available to one who entered a prompt plea of guilty. The judge did not explain why these adjustments are an insufficient recognition of the circumstances.

The district court's final observation — that Croom has led a life of essentially continual crime, of increasing violence — is a sound reason for a departure. Croom not only has a long record but also admitted that he possessed guns all the time between 1991 and 1993. That amounts to many additional offenses under §922(g). He scarcely gets out of the jail's shadow before committing another crime. The Guidelines are designed for normal cases; a defendant who has demonstrated criminal propensities that make him more dangerous than the ordinary person with the same criminal history score may receive a higher sentence. So the Commission said in §4A1.3, describing some situations that it has not fully considered and that therefore authorize departures. Thus, for example, the fact that Croom committed his second gun offense while on release from the first led to the denial of a reduction for acceptance of responsibility; but the fact that he committed the second, more serious, gun offense swiftly after release on the first also shows that he is incorrigible — an armed career criminal in fact if not technically one under 18 U.S.C. §924(e)(1). His juvenile convictions may not be counted directly, but they may be considered as part of the pattern of recidivism. U.S.S.G. §4A1.2 Application Note 8. Meeting most of the criteria for designation as an armed career criminal (or "career offender" under the Guidelines) does not permit the judge to impose the penalties designed for those who meet all of the criteria, but it does permit a departure in the *direction* of those penalties.

What we have, then, is a good reason for departure coupled with two bad ones. The district court must reconsider Croom's sentence but need not necessarily lower it. On remand the court should hew to the considerations approved in §4A1.3 and choose the offense level that best approximates the seriousness of Croom's record and the threat of future crimes it portends. How much to increase the sentence is a judgment call, which if thoughtfully explained will not be disturbed on any later appeal. . . .

ROVNER, J., concurring.

Although I concur in the result and rationale of the majority, I believe that the appropriate exercise of our judicial function requires restraint in the language we use to describe the people who come before us, regardless of how dreadful their transgressions.

NOTES

1. *Considering prior convictions at sentencing.* In all U.S. sentencing systems, the offender's prior convictions are among the most important determinants of the sentence imposed. Most sentencing guideline systems place onto a severity scale the number and seriousness of prior convictions. The federal sentencing guidelines, for example, convert prior offenses into criminal history points, which are then grouped into criminal history categories ranging from I (for first offenders) to VI (for offenders with lengthy records); these categories

are then used to determine the offender's applicable sentencing range. In most sentencing guideline systems, more-serious prior offenses increase the sentence more than less-serious prior offenses; prior convictions for the same type of crime as the current offense often increase a sentence more than prior convictions for unrelated wrongdoing. Minnesota, for example, assigns prior felony offenses from $1/2$ to 2 points depending on the offense's "severity level." Similarly, Pennsylvania assigns 4 criminal history points, the maximum amount available, for the most serious prior convictions such as murder, voluntary manslaughter, kidnapping, rape, involuntary deviate intercourse, arson, and robbery.

2. *Theoretical foundations for considering criminal history.* Why increase a defendant's sentence for the current offense based on *past* criminal behavior? Are such enhanced sentences designed to deter the offender, or other offenders, from committing future crimes? Are they designed to select a sentence proportionate to the crime committed (that is, to give the offender her just deserts)? Consider this excerpt from a U.S. Sentencing Commission report discussing the philosophy behind using criminal history to help determine sentencing outcomes:

> Those who argue that retribution is a key principle in sentencing [contend] that criminal history is inappropriate to consider at sentencing because the defendant has already been punished for the previous offense [and] that a defendant has no greater culpability (blameworthiness) because of having committed the prior offense; nor is victimization greater in the current offense as a result of the prior offense. . . . A contrary theory of the role of criminal justice is incapacitation. This approach advocates the expanded use of imprisonment to incapacitate offenders[, assuming] that while offenders are incarcerated they will not be able to engage in additional criminal behavior. [S]elective incapacitation seeks to prevent crime by using certain criteria to identify for restraint a smaller number of offenders who are predicted to commit more crime and/or serious crime. . . . Society and its elected representatives have reached a level of frustration with crime so that current policies more frequently tend to reflect the selective incapacitation philosophy in sentencing practices in general and criminal history in particular.

U.S. Sentencing Commission, Simplification Draft Paper (1995) (see http://www.ussc.gov/simple/crimhist.htm). What role would criminal records play for those who emphasize the rehabilitative power of criminal sentences? Would it be more or less appropriate to use the prior criminal record if it could predict recidivism accurately?

3. *Intricacies and complexities in assessing criminal history.* As the decision in *Croom* suggests, the federal guidelines that quantify a defendant's criminal history are complex, in large part because the U.S. Sentencing Commission decided to base its criminal history points on the *length* of prior sentences imposed. Consequently, the federal guidelines include intricate application notes and commentary that address the myriad of possible state court dispositions and instruct judges how to assess each prior sentence, including the custodial component, sentence type, and length. State sentencing rules typically group prior convictions into only a few categories (such as felonies and misdemeanors), which simplifies the criminal history calculation. Nevertheless,

quantifying the variations in offenders' criminal records is always intricate. In Maryland, for example, calculation of the offender score has four primary components (relationship to criminal justice system when instant offense occurred, juvenile delinquency, prior adult criminal record, and prior adult criminal justice violation), each of which has multiple subparts with detailed application instructions. See Md. Sentencing Guidelines §7.1.

4. *Stale offenses.*   Older convictions tell us less about an offender than more recent ones. Should older convictions have less of an impact (or no impact at all) on the sentence for the current crime? Guideline systems often consider the time period of a prior conviction when assessing criminal history. The federal guidelines use five different time periods for calculating criminal history points, based on the length of the sentence imposed and the age of the defendant when the prior offense was committed. State rules that discount or ignore older convictions generally set one applicable expiration date for all offenses (say, all convictions more than ten years old). Instead of setting an expiration date for older crimes, some states allow defendants to benefit from "crime free" periods. In these states, if the defendant was conviction free for a certain length of time (usually 10 or 15 years, not including periods of imprisonment, probation, or parole) prior to the instant offense, the sentencing judge does not count any convictions prior to that period. Other states leave this item as a departure consideration.

5. *Unreliable prior convictions.*   The use of prior convictions to enhance the sentence for the current offense becomes more controversial when there are reasons to question the accuracy of the earlier conviction. This is true especially when the earlier conviction occurred without the involvement of defense counsel. The Constitution bars the use at sentencing of some uncounseled prior convictions, but only if the government obtained the prior conviction by violating the defendant's constitutional right to counsel. See Nichols v. United States, 511 U.S. 738 (1994) (sentencing court may consider defendant's previous uncounseled misdemeanor conviction in sentencing him for subsequent offense); United States v. Tucker, 404 U.S. 443 (1972) (conviction obtained in violation of Sixth Amendment rights cannot enhance later sentence). These questions often arise when the prior conviction took place in the juvenile system or when the earlier case dealt with charges of driving while intoxicated. See Thompson v. State, 583 S.E.2d 14 (Ga. 2003) (explaining that prior uncounseled DUI convictions could not be used to enhance a sentence for a later offense). Compare United States v. Huggins, 467 F.3d 359 (2006) (adjudication as a delinquent under Pennsylvania law not a "prior conviction" for purposes of a sentencing enhancement under federal law, as "an adjudication of delinquency is not the same as an adult conviction") with State v. LaMunyon, 911 P.2d 151 (Kan. 1996) (finding no constitutional or statutory bar to using juvenile adjudication in calculating criminal history status).

How should a sentencing court react if a conviction is vacated while the defendant awaits sentencing on a new offense? Must the court disregard the prior conviction and its underlying criminal conduct? See United States v. Marsh, 486 F. Supp.2d 150 (D. Mass., 2007) (determining that even after the Supreme Court's decision in Shepard v. United States, 544 U.S. 13 (2005), criminal conduct underlying vacated conviction can be considered at sentencing).

6. *Foreign convictions.*   While the federal guidelines do not factor foreign convictions into the calculation of a defendant's prior criminal record, such convictions may be considered for departure purposes. Federal courts have used foreign convictions to enhance the sentence for drug convictions. See United States v. Kole, 164 F.3d 164 (3d Cir. 1998) (sentence enhancement granted based on prior drug trafficking conviction in the Philippines that did not violate due process requirements). Courts can consider only foreign convictions that were not obtained in violation of the Constitution. What types of violations should lead a court not to consider a foreign conviction? Violations of the right to jury trial? Violations of the right to counsel?

Not all federal statutes permit foreign convictions to be treated like state convictions for sentence enhancement purposes. See Small v. United States, 544 U.S. 385 (2005) (for purpose of felon-in-possession statute, foreign conviction is not a predicate offense). Failure to consider foreign convictions in sentencing, however, may lead to inappropriately low sentences for foreign nationals or immigrants in particular. A study by the U.S. Sentencing Commission found that noncitizens have disproportionately fewer criminal history points, possibly because their foreign convictions do not count. Yet the process of ascertaining foreign convictions may create logistical problems for probation offices and lead the court into difficult considerations concerning the fairness of convictions in foreign systems. See Michael Edmund O'Neill, Abraham's Legacy: An Empirical Assessment of (Nearly) First-Time Offenders in the Federal System, 42 B.C. L. Rev. 291 (2001) (discussing consideration of foreign convictions); Magdeline E. Jensen, Reflections of a Southwest Border Probation Chief, 14 Fed. Sent'g Rep. 255, 258 (2002) (noting difficulties in getting criminal records from Mexico).

7. *Prior criminal record exception.*   As a result of the decision in Almendarez-Torres v. United States, 523 U.S. 224 (1998), a "prior conviction" exception has been built into the Sixth Amendment's application of the jury trial right to sentence enhancements in *Apprendi* and *Blakely*. Both *Apprendi* and *Blakely* state that its rule requiring sentence-enhancing facts to be proven to a jury beyond a reasonable doubt or admitted by the defendant applies only to facts "other than the fact of a prior conviction." The theoretical soundness of this exception has been widely questioned. See Kyron Huigens & Danielle Chinea, "Three Strikes" Laws and *Apprendi*'s Irrational, Inequitable Exception for Recidivism, 37 Crim. L. Bull. 575 (2001). Justice Thomas's comments about *Almendarez-Torres* in his *Apprendi* concurrence suggest that there are no longer five votes on the High Court in support of this exception; Justice Scalia's opinion for the *Blakely* Court did not even deign to mention *Almendarez-Torres*. Justice O'Connor, now retired from the Court, was one of the supporters of the "prior record" exception.

In the wake of *Blakely*, lower state and federal courts have split over the scope and application of the "prior conviction" exception, debating whether only the fact of a prior conviction or other, related facts (such as a defendant's status on probation) fall within the exception. The Supreme Court's decision in

Shepard v. United States, 544 U.S. 13 (2005), has added further uncertainty to this area of the law. *Shepard* technically concerned a narrow issue of federal law: which offenses qualify as "crimes of violence" for a particular statutory sentence enhancement. The Court ruled that judges must confine their review of evidence regarding prior convictions to the charging document, the terms of the plea agreement, or admissions by the defendant in an exchange with the trial judge. In dicta in the majority opinion, however, Justice Souter hinted that the Court may eventually eliminate the "prior conviction" exception established by *Almendarez-Torres*; Justice Thomas, in a separate opinion, expressly called for the Court to overrule *Almendarez-Torres* as soon as possible.

3. The First-Time Offender

Since all sentencing systems increase punishment levels for repeat offenders, they conversely and necessarily provide lesser sentences for first-time offenders. But is there something special about first-time offenders compared with those with a limited previous criminal record? Should special rules be in place to further mitigate the sentences of first-time offenders?

‖ *Washington Revised Code §9.94A.650* ‖

FIRST-TIME OFFENDER WAIVER

(1) This section applies to offenders who have never been previously convicted of a felony in this state, federal court, or another state, and who have never participated in a program of deferred prosecution for a felony, and who are convicted of a felony that is not:

(a) Classified as a violent offense or a sex offense under this chapter;

(b) Manufacture, delivery, [sale] or possession with intent to manufacture or deliver [various] controlled substance[s]. . . .

(2) In sentencing a first-time offender the court may waive the imposition of a sentence within the standard sentence range and impose a sentence which may include up to ninety days of confinement in a [local jail] facility. . . . The sentence may also include a term of community supervision or community custody [and] may include requirements that the offender perform any one or more of the following:

(a) Devote time to a specific employment or occupation;

(b) Undergo available outpatient treatment . . . , or inpatient treatment not to exceed the standard range of confinement for that offense;

(c) Pursue a prescribed, secular course of study or vocational training;

(d) Remain within prescribed geographical boundaries and notify the community corrections officer prior to any change in the offender's address or employment;

(e) Report as directed to a community corrections officer; or

(f) Pay all court-ordered legal financial obligations . . . and/or perform community service work.

|| *State v. Joshua Fowler* ||
|| 38 P.3d 335 (Wash. 2002) ||

ALEXANDER, C.J.

On October 30, 1997, Joshua Fowler joined friends . . . at "Fast Freddy's Tavern" in Kent. Fowler, who had gone without sleep for three days while drinking alcohol and using methamphetamine, ingested additional alcohol and methamphetamine at the tavern. Fowler [later] departed the tavern [with companions] to collect a debt he believed [Ken] Carroll owed to him, . . . armed with a handgun and knife. Once inside [Carroll's] apartment, an argument ensued between Fowler and Carroll. This led to Fowler hitting Carroll in the head with the gun that Fowler was carrying. Carroll was then taken to a back bedroom where . . . he was threatened and beaten by Fowler. As Fowler administered the beating, he told Carroll that he would "cut him" in order to "teach him a lesson." Carroll's roommate, Thomas Gochanour . . . was struck in the face by Fowler with the flat side of the knife that Fowler was carrying. Fowler also threatened to cut Gochanour's throat with the knife. After engaging in this activity, Fowler and his accomplices fled taking some videotapes, a cellular phone, a wallet, and some money from the apartment.

Eighteen months after the above-described incident, Fowler turned himself in to the police. He was thereafter charged with and pleaded guilty to first degree robbery. At sentencing, the trial court determined that because Fowler had no prior criminal history, the standard sentencing range for the offense was 31 to 41 months, plus a mandatory 60 month firearm enhancement penalty. Fowler sought an exceptional sentence of six months, exclusive of the firearm enhancement, basing his request on what he claimed was the presence of three statutory mitigating factors. Although the trial court did not find any of those factors present, it nevertheless imposed a 15 month exceptional sentence based on its determination that Fowler: (1) had no history of violent behavior and no pertinent criminal history; (2) was experiencing symptoms of extreme sleep deprivation at the time of the offense; (3) exhibited behavior at the time of the offense that was aberrational and represented an isolated incident of violence; (4) had strong family support; and (5) was a low to moderate risk to reoffend. . . .

A court must generally impose a sentence within the standard sentence range. It may, however, impose a sentence above or below the standard range for reasons that are "substantial and compelling." [Washington's Sentencing Reform Act] contains a list of aggravating and mitigating factors "which the court may consider in the exercise of its discretion to impose an exceptional sentence." Although this list is not exclusive, any such reasons must relate to the crime and make it more, or less, egregious. . . . A sentencing court may not, in imposing an exceptional sentence, take into account the defendant's criminal history and the seriousness level of the offense because those are considered in computing the presumptive range for the offense. . . .

The first factor the sentencing court relied on in imposing an exceptional sentence was that the "defendant [had] no history of violent behavior and no pertinent criminal history." Although Fowler concedes that a defendant's lack of criminal history alone is an insufficient ground for a sentence below the standard range, he asserts that a clean record combined with a complete absence of police contacts may be a substantial and compelling reason for imposing an exceptional sentence.

This argument is without merit. Saying that the defendant had no history of violent behavior and no pertinent criminal history is essentially equivalent to saying that he has no criminal record. [A] lack of a criminal history is not a mitigating factor because criminal history is already encompassed in the sentencing guidelines. The only exception to this general rule is that a lack of criminal history may be considered "in combination with the finding that the defendant was 'induced' to commit the crime" or lacked a predisposition to commit the crime. State v. Ha'mim, 132 Wash. 2d 834, 842-843 (1997). Here, the trial court rejected a finding that Fowler was either induced by others to commit the crime or that he lacked a predisposition to commit the crime. . . .

The trial court also found that a downward exceptional sentence was justified on the basis that Fowler's behavior during the commission of the crime was aberrational and represented an isolated incident of violence. Specifically the trial court stated:

> I have absolutely no trouble believing the defendant when he said and his family said that the behavior that occurred on the night of this incident was an aberration. It was unusual. It was out of character for him. . . . I believe the defendant when he says that his behavior was fueled by some form of chemical imbalance, whether it was chronic depression I can't say. I certainly think there is every indication that it was fueled by sleep deprivation, ingestion of methamphetamines, ingestion of alcohol.

. . . Fowler argues here that federal case law supports the proposition that aberrant behavior is a valid mitigating factor. [However, the] fact that a defendant's criminal conduct is exceptional or aberrant does not distinguish the defendant's crime from others in the same category. Furthermore, to say that conduct is an aberration is tantamount to saying that the defendant "has not done anything like this before." That, in our view, is yet another way of saying that the defendant has little or no history of criminal behavior. . . .

Even if we were inclined to follow the lead of the federal circuit courts that have recognized that aberrational behavior may justify a departure from the standard range, Fowler's conduct does not resemble the type of conduct that those courts have found to be aberrational. The act Fowler committed was not committed without forethought and planning, and thus fails the spontaneity test enunciated in [federal cases on this subject]. Indeed, the record shows that Fowler's motivation in going to Ken Carroll's house was to collect a debt. To aid himself in that endeavor he armed himself with a handgun and knife, items that he subsequently used in the commission of the robbery. This was hardly a spontaneous act. Neither can it be said that any of the factors [are present] evidencing aberrational behavior under the "totality of the circumstance test," . . . i.e., that the defendant suffered from a psychological disorder, that he was under external pressure, that his motivation was other than pecuniary gain, or that he took steps to mitigate the effects of his acts. In short, Fowler's conduct was not aberrational, even under the case law or federal guidelines. . . .

Fowler also contends that . . . what the trial court described as his low to moderate risk to reoffend is . . . a substantial and compelling reason for imposing an exceptional sentence. Specifically, he argues that a low risk of reoffense is a valid factor when a court finds by clear and convincing evidence that a standard range disposition would be detrimental to the goal of rehabilitating the offender. . . . The sentencing court's finding that Fowler was a low to moderate risk to reoffend was based upon an evaluation and report of the Washington State Department of Corrections. [However, our prior cases establish] that the risk of reoffense is not a substantial and compelling reason for an exceptional sentence. State v. Estrella, 798 P.2d 289 (Wash. 1990). [Protection] of the public has already been considered by the legislature in computing the presumptive sentencing range.

MADSEN, J., dissenting.
 . . . The defendant, Joshua Fowler, urges the court to follow federal cases recognizing aberrant behavior as a mitigating factor in sentencing. The majority summarily concludes that calling a defendant's criminal conduct aberrational is simply another way of saying that the defendant has little or no history of criminal behavior. . . . Federal courts agree that a lack of criminal history is not a basis for a downward sentence under the federal scheme. They conclude, however, that "aberrational behavior" is not equivalent to a lack of criminal history. . . . All of the federal circuits have recognized aberrational behavior as a factor that may, in the appropriate case, justify an exceptional sentence downward. A split developed in the circuits, however, as to what constitutes aberrational behavior. Some courts concluded that "a spontaneous and seemingly thoughtless act, rather than one which was the result of substantial planning" was a single act of aberrant behavior. Others applied a totality of circumstances approach, considering a number of factors. . . . In November 2000, the federal sentencing commission added §5K2.20 to the guidelines, defining "aberrant behavior" as "a single criminal occurrence or single criminal transaction that (A) was committed without significant planning; (B) was of limited duration; and (C) represents a marked deviation by the defendant from an otherwise law-abiding life." The commission directed that in deciding whether to depart from the guideline sentences on the basis of aberrant behavior, a court could consider the defendant's "(A) mental and emotional conditions; (B) employment record; (C) record of prior good works; (D) motivation for committing the offense; and (E) efforts to mitigate the effects of the offense."
 [Some] crimes represent the truly unusual behavior of individuals who are generally nonviolent, law-abiding citizens [and were committed] under unusual circumstances. Similar to the federal approach, this court should hold that a trial court may, in its discretion, impose an exceptional sentence downward based upon aberrant behavior. . . .
 The majority also rejects the trial court's reliance on a low to moderate risk of reoffending as supporting a downward sentence. [The sentencing statutes do not currently account for this factor.] A presumptive sentencing range is based upon the seriousness level of the current offense and the defendant's offender score. Whether the individual defendant has a low, moderate, or high risk of reoffending is not part of the calculation. . . . Further, this court has in the past accepted the premise that future dangerousness is an appropriate nonstatutory aggravating factor under certain circumstances involving offenders convicted of sex offenses. If future dangerousness can justify an upward sentence, albeit in

limited cases, why should a low risk of reoffending be rejected as a mitigating factor? At least two of the goals of the SRA favor allowing sentencing discretion to impose a downward sentence where there is a low risk of reoffending: the promotion of respect for the law by provision of just punishment, and making frugal use of the state's resources. . . .

NOTES

1. *Treatment of first-time offenders at sentencing.* In indeterminate sentencing systems, sentencing informally reflects the maxim that everyone deserves a second chance. With the exception of the most serious and violent offenses, most first-time offenders can expect a sentencing judge to impose a relatively brief sentence of imprisonment or suspend any incarceration and place the offender on probation. As the statute from Washington highlights, this tendency to cut first-time offenders a break has been codified in many structured sentencing systems. The Sentencing Reform Act requires the U.S. Sentencing Commission to "insure that the [federal] guidelines reflect the general appropriateness of imposing a sentence other than imprisonment in cases in which the defendant is a first offender who has not been convicted of a crime of violence or an otherwise serious offense. . . ." 28 U.S.C. §994(j).

More generally, all structured sentencing systems provide for first-time offenders to receive no criminal history points or the lowest possible offender score, which in turn limits the upper level of the sentencing range designated for the offense. Many of these systems, however, group the true first-time offender with other offenders who have some minor criminal history. In the federal system, for example, criminal history category I treats a wide range of defendants the same; defendants who have no prior record (no prior arrests, no pending charges, no dismissed charges, no prior convictions) fall into category I, along with defendants who have one prior conviction and received a sentence of imprisonment of as long as 60 days. This category also includes defendants who may have had contact with the criminal justice system, such as arrests or dismissed charges, and defendants with convictions not counted under the guidelines for a variety of reasons, such as the "age" of the conviction, the locality where the conviction occurred, or the minor nature of the offense. What reasons might support such a structure for considering criminal history, which seems to allow defendants "one free bite at the apple"?

In its recent research report on "Recidivism and the 'First Offender,'" the U.S. Sentencing Commission's staff found different recidivism rates for those with no prior arrests, those with prior arrests but no prior convictions, and those with prior convictions that do not count toward criminal history under the federal guidelines. See www.ussc.gov/publicat/Recidivism-FirstOffender.pdf. Is there any explanation as to why the group with prior arrests but no prior convictions has the highest recidivism rate, almost twice as high as that of offenders with prior but uncounted convictions? What would be the impact — in terms of information collection and length of sentence by offender and offense categories — if Congress approved the creation of a "no prior connection with the criminal justice system" category?

2. *Departures for first-time offenders and "aberrant behavior."*   In part because many guideline systems group true first-time offenders with other offenders who have some minor criminal history, cases like *Fowler* arise in many jurisdictions in which a sentencing judge departs below the applicable guideline sentence because the offender's wrongdoing seems truly exceptional and the judge believes the offender is unlikely to engage in criminal activity again. Most appellate courts rule that first-time offender status and related concerns have already been considered in the guideline scheme and thus cannot serve as the basis for a departure. See, e.g., Koon v. United States, 518 U.S. 81, 110-112 (1996) (holding that district court could not depart based on defendant's "low likelihood of recidivism" because the U.S. Sentencing Commission took that factor into account in formulating the lowest criminal history category); cf. State v. Grady, 258 Kan. 72, 87-88 (1995) ("While generally criminal history is an improper departure factor because criminal history has already been used to set the presumptive sentence, we believe the legislature intended in the interest of justice that a trial court have discretion to impose a downward dispositional departure where a defendant has no prior criminal history and has a failed common-law or statutory defense that is not meritless.").

As noted in *Fowler,* the federal system developed a way to reduce sentences in exceptional cases based on the concept of "aberrational behavior." A federal sentencing judge may depart downward when the defendant's background and the nature of the offense show that the offense grew out of peculiar circumstances not likely to be repeated. The rationale has been common among downward departures that do not mention *Booker,* with a total of 205 offenders receiving reduced sentences on this basis in 2006. As noted in the *Fowler* dissent, the federal courts of appeals were initially divided over when to allow an aberrant behavior departure. Some required the offense to be a single "spontaneous and seemingly thoughtless act"; others allowed sentencing judges more latitude under a "totality of the circumstances" approach. The U.S. Sentencing Commission's policy statement in §5K2.20 adopted a compromise view of what constitutes aberrant behavior, going beyond a "single act" to include "a single criminal *occurrence* or single criminal *transaction* that (A) was committed without significant planning; (B) was of limited duration; and (C) represents a marked deviation by the defendant from an otherwise law-abiding life" (emphasis added). The policy statement also barred departures on this basis for certain crimes, including serious drug trafficking offenses, those that cause "serious bodily injury or death," and crimes in which the defendant uses a dangerous weapon. Does the fact that a defendant used a gun make a crime any less aberrational?

3. *Safety valve to ameliorate mandatory sentences.*   One common complaint lodged against mandatory sentencing statutes is that by requiring a particular sentence based only on the offense, the provisions fail to allow for mitigated sentences for first-time offenders. Congress responded to these concerns in the context of federal mandatory minimum drug sentences by enacting a "safety valve" provision as part of the Violent Crime Control and Law Enforcement Act of 1994. This provision instructs judges to apply the federal guidelines, rather than the often harsher mandatory minimum drug sentencing statutes, when five criteria are satisfied: "(1) the defendant does not have more than one criminal

history point, as determined under the [federal] sentencing guidelines; (2) the defendant did not use violence . . . or possess . . . a dangerous weapon . . . in connection with the offense; (3) the offense did not result in death or serious bodily injury . . . ; (4) the defendant was not an organizer, leader, manager, or supervisor of others in the offense . . . ; and (5) . . . the defendant . . . provided to the Government [complete] information [about the crime and related offenses]." 18 U.S.C. §3553(f). For a detailed empirical analysis of the impact of this safety valve provision, see Celesta A. Albonetti, The Effects of the "Safety Valve" Amendment on Length of Imprisonment for Cocaine Trafficking/ Manufacturing Offenders: Mitigating the Effects of Mandatory Minimum Penalties and Offender's Ethnicity, 87 Iowa L. Rev. 401 (2002).

B.   THE COOPERATIVE DEFENDANT

By the time a convicted defendant faces a sentencing judge, several months or even years may have passed since the crime occurred. During that time, the defendant performs many acts that can have some bearing on the sentence. For a sentencing judge who emphasizes retributive purposes of a criminal sentence, with a focus on the harm created by the crime, this postcrime behavior might have little effect. But for a sentencing judge (or a sentencing system) placing more weight on utilitarian goals such as incapacitation or rehabilitation, post-crime behavior plays a significant role. This recent conduct offers important clues about how the defendant will act in the near future. In this section, we explore postcrime conduct that signals the defendant's willingness to cooperate with the authorities, both in her own case and in other cases.

1.   Acceptance of Responsibility and Plea Bargains

Most courtroom veterans believe that a guilty plea produces big advantages at sentencing, and empirical research confirms this belief. Defendants pleading guilty tend to receive substantially lower sentences than defendants who go to trial (in some studies the "plea discount" has been more than one-third off post-trial sentences).

In structured sentencing systems, the rules give sentencing judges different instructions about the impact of a plea agreement. Some rules say that plea agreements should not change the sentence at all; other rules allow the judge to accept the parties' recommendations within certain broad limits. For instance, under the Minnesota sentencing guidelines, judges must impose the sentence indicated in the guideline grid unless there is a valid ground for departure. A plea agreement, standing alone, is not a sufficient reason to depart from the guidelines. In Washington state, statutory guidelines tell the judge to "determine if the agreement is consistent with the interests of justice and with the [statutory] prosecuting standards" and to reject the agreement if it is not. Wash. Rev. Code §9.94A.431(1). The federal sentencing guidelines also advise judges to limit the impact of a guilty plea at sentencing. The court may accept sentencing recommendations offered in a plea agreement "if the court is satisfied either that (1) the recommended sentence is within the applicable guideline range; or (2) (A) the recommended sentence departs from the applicable guideline range for justifiable reasons; and (B) those reasons are specifically set forth in writing in the statement of reasons or judgment and commitment order." U.S. Sentencing Guidelines Manual §6B1.2(b).

If it is true that sentencing judges in most systems reward defendants who plead guilty, does that mean that sentencing judges punish a defendant for exercising the right to a trial? Do sentencing rules discourage judges from honestly explaining what they are doing?

State v. David Tiernan
645 A.2d 482 (R.I. 1994)

WEISBERGER, Acting C.J.

... The precise issue we confront in this appeal is the question of whether the trial justice improperly considered either defendant's exercise of his privilege against self-incrimination under the Fifth Amendment to the United States Constitution or his exercise of his right to a public trial guaranteed by the Sixth Amendment to the United States Constitution and article 1, section 10, of the Rhode Island Constitution. We answer this question in the negative. . . .

In November 1990 defendant was convicted of two counts of second-degree child molestation after a trial by jury in Superior Court. At the sentencing hearing defendant argued that in light of his background, the absence of any prior record, and the nature of the crime involved, he should be given a sentence involving only treatment and counseling rather than imprisonment. The prosecutor disagreed, arguing that such treatment would not be effective unless defendant acknowledged his wrongdoing, which defendant refused to do. As a matter of deterrence and punishment, the prosecutor urged the court to impose a lengthy jail sentence.

The trial justice agreed with the prosecutor, citing five factors that were considered in formulating his decision — "the nature of the offense and the offender, punishment, rehabilitation and deterrence." The trial justice explained that "some program of counseling could be effective if culpability is accepted, but the problem is defendant's continued protestations of innocence." The trial justice explained this comment, stating that "it is my understanding from everybody knowledgeable in this area that treatment is not effective unless and until the person being treated, the defendant, acknowledges guilt, and the defendant still protests his innocence, and has done so here in court." Therefore, the trial justice reasoned that since rehabilitation was improbable, . . . "punishment and deterrence are most important to the Court in this case when determining an appropriate sentence." In light of the aforementioned factors, the trial justice sentenced defendant to two terms of twenty years, eight years to serve and twelve years suspended on each count, to be served concurrently.

[The] defendant filed a timely Rule 35 motion to reduce sentence. At the hearing on the motion, defendant presented the court with an admission of guilt and a profession of remorse — the key ingredients that the trial justice had found lacking at the time of the original sentencing with respect to defendant's potential for rehabilitation. The defendant attempted to justify his delayed acknowledgment of his crime by explaining that at the time of the sentencing hearing he had not yet come to terms with the sexual molestation that, he revealed to the court, he himself had endured in his own childhood. After hearing from defendant, the trial justice was presented with testimony from the victim's mother who painfully recounted the traumatic effect that the molestation and the trial had had upon her daughter.

After considering the testimony presented, the trial justice denied defendant's motion to reduce sentence and made the following observations:

> [I observed] that little girl testify. The defendant sat there and required her to testify. She did, and although she was a little girl, she was believed by the jury and by me; and yet he stood up and indicated to me that he intended to pursue all of his rights of appeal, again, which I believe he had his right to do, everybody does. He did that knowing full well that what that little girl said from the stand was absolutely true and he let her go through it. While I am somewhat moved by defense counsel's argument and even the defendant's own statements, I am not persuaded by them, not in the least. . . .

On appeal defendant challenges his sentence on the grounds that at both the sentencing hearing and the Rule 35 hearing the trial justice violated defendant's constitutional rights by considering improper factors. First, defendant claims that at the sentencing hearing the trial justice's decision was tainted by his consideration of the fact that defendant invoked his Fifth Amendment privilege against self-incrimination and he used that fact to justify the imposition of a lengthy sentence upon defendant. Then at the Rule 35 hearing, when defendant waived his Fifth Amendment right and admitted his guilt, defendant claims that the trial justice justified defendant's lengthy sentence with an alternative, but equally objectionable, fact — that defendant had exercised his right to stand trial and thereby forced his child victim to endure a painful court experience. The defendant cites to us in support of his assertions a plethora of cases from other jurisdictions. . . .

A motion to reduce sentence under Rule 35 is basically a plea by a defendant for leniency and, as such, is addressed to the sound discretion of the trial justice. Because of our strong policy against interfering with a trial justice's exercise of discretion with respect to such motions, we shall interfere with the lower court's decision only in the rarest of cases. With this deferential standard of review in mind, we now turn to the applicable substantive law.

A judge has no more difficult duty nor awesome responsibility than the pronouncement of sentence in a criminal case. To guide trial justices in carrying out this responsibility, we have identified the following factors as falling within the scope of constitutionally permissible sentencing considerations: (1) the severity of the crime, (2) the defendant's personal, educational, and employment background, (3) the potential for rehabilitation, (4) the element of societal deterrence, and (5) the appropriateness of the punishment. State v. Bertoldi, 495 A.2d 247 (R.I. 1985); State v. Upham, 439 A.2d 912 (R.I. 1982).

Most of these factors are multidimensional and require a trial justice to reflect upon a variety of subsidiary factors. For example, with respect to the element of rehabilitation, a trial justice may consider a defendant's attitude toward society, his sense of remorse, as well as his inclination and capacity to take his place as an honest and useful member of society. Likewise, a defendant's giving of false testimony may be probative of his attitude toward society and consequently his prospects for rehabilitation.

In addition to the above five factors, a trial justice may also take into consideration a corollary factor to justify reducing a sentence — that a defendant exhibited contrition and consideration for the victims of his or her criminal activity and pled guilty to the crime charged. See Brady v. United States, 397 U.S. 742 (1970) ("encouraging a guilty plea by opportunity or promise of leniency" does not violate Fifth Amendment). We are mindful that a defendant, by pleading guilty, waives a broad array of rights, including the right to trial by jury, the presumption of innocence, the state's burden to prove one guilty beyond a reasonable doubt, the privilege against self-incrimination, the right to confront and cross-examine one's accusers, the right to testify and call witnesses in one's defense, and the right to appeal one's conviction to this court. By waiving these rights, a defendant, first, has spared the state from expending considerable time, money and other precious judicial and law enforcement resources and, second, has prevented the public scrutiny of and embarrassment to the victim that derives from recounting his or her victimization in a public forum. In exchange therefor a defendant may properly be extended a certain amount of leniency in sentencing.

Although we have recognized the propriety of extending leniency when a defendant pleads guilty, we have specifically prohibited the lengthening of a sentence on the basis of a defendant's refusal to plead guilty or his or her insistence on holding the state to its burden of proving guilt beyond a reasonable doubt at trial. State v. Rollins, 359 A.2d 315, 320 (R.I. 1976). [The] rights implicated when a defendant chooses to stand trial . . . are some of the most jealously guarded and deeply embedded rights of our criminal justice jurisprudence, rights that both the Federal and our State Constitutions unconditionally extend to criminal defendants. To exact a price or impose a penalty upon a defendant in the form of an enhanced sentence for invoking such rights would amount to a deprivation of due process of law, and that we shall not condone. . . .

FIFTH AMENDMENT PRIVILEGE AGAINST SELF-INCRIMINATION CLAIM

Reviewing the transcript of the original sentencing hearing, we cannot say that the trial justice improperly considered in his sentencing decision defendant's exercise of his Fifth Amendment privilege against self-incrimination. In making the sentencing determination, the trial justice articulated and applied the very five factors we condoned in *Upham* and *Bertoldi*: the nature of the offense and of the offender, punishment, rehabilitation, and deterrence. [The trial justice] considered defendant's refusal to acknowledge guilt for the limited purpose of assessing defendant's potential for rehabilitation. Underlying rehabilitation is the thesis that the offender needs assistance in making behavioral and/or psychological changes. In order for that assistance to be effective, a defendant must be open and receptive to the proffered treatment. A defendant's adamant denial of engaging in any wrongful conduct — the very conduct that necessitates the treatment—cannot be said to be indicative of any receptiveness to rehabilitation. Accordingly we hold that the trial justice properly considered defendant's refusal to admit perpetrating the molestation in his assessment of defendant's rehabilitative potential. Other courts have similarly recognized the probative value of a defendant's refusal to acknowledge wrongdoing with respect to assessing the element of rehabilitative capacity. See Gallucci v. State, 371 So. 2d 148, 150 (Fla. App. 1979). . . .

After evaluating defendant's questionable potential for rehabilitation, the trial justice properly determined that "example type" sentencing was demanded. [Defendant] was not penalized for refusing to waive his Fifth Amendment right; rather he was simply not extended a benefit which he might have enjoyed had he waived his rights and pled either guilty or nolo to the charges.

THE RIGHT TO STAND TRIAL

. . . In considering defendant's motion to reduce his sentence, the trial justice remarked that defendant had "required" the child to testify by exercising his right to stand trial, after which defendant indicated his intention to appeal while "knowing full well that what that little girl said from the stand was absolutely true." The defendant claims that these remarks evidence an intent to penalize him for standing trial. We cannot agree.

At the outset we are compelled to point out that the right guaranteed to defendant by the Sixth Amendment to the United States Constitution and article 1, section 10, of the Rhode Island Constitution is the right to stand trial and *truthfully* testify in his own behalf. This defendant did not do. Rather defendant exercised his right and took the opportunity to present false testimony to the court in the hopes of escaping conviction and punishment.

The trial justice's remarks clearly related to the fact that defendant had, while under a solemn oath and in a court of law, knowingly and intentionally perpetrated a falsehood. The trial justice proceeded to identify the impact upon the victim of defendant's decision to stand trial and tell a falsehood—namely, that she was forced to endure the trauma of testifying about embarrassing and intimate sexual details and to undergo an intense cross-examination.

[T]he trial justice's consideration of defendant's false testimony and the impact of the trial upon the victim was proper as these factors related to his prospects for rehabilitation. With respect to defendant's falsehood, we stated in *Bertoldi* that a defendant's willingness to take the stand and lie "not only demonstrates a disrespect for the law and the judicial system, but also evidences an important character trait. It reveals that the defendant is perfectly willing to commit a crime in an attempt to conceal an earlier crime. . . ." The fact that defendant claimed to have lied because of an event he endured in his childhood does not cast a different light onto his falsehood or justify in any way, shape, or form his decision to give false testimony while under a solemn judicial oath to tell the truth.

Likewise, consideration of the impact of the trial upon the child victim, especially in the face of a posttrial confession, is proper as it reflects a defendant's attitude toward his victim and society. In State v. Farnham, 479 A.2d 887

(Me. 1984), the Supreme Judicial Court of Maine upheld consideration of this factor in circumstances very similar to those in the case at hand. [As the court noted, although the defendant] "had an absolute right to a trial and to conduct vigorous cross-examination in connection with a crime for which he soon after admitted his guilt, he cannot escape the fact that his exercise of those rights are probative of his attitude towards the victim and society." . . .

We note that this was not a case in which the trial justice threatened pretrial to impose a harsher sentence if defendant opted to stand trial, see United States v. Stockwell, 472 F.2d 1186 (9th Cir. 1973), or one in which the trial justice stated posttrial that a more severe sentence was warranted because defendant wasted time, public funds, and resources by insisting on a trial, see United States v. Hutchings, 757 F.2d 11 (2d Cir. 1985). . . .

The length of the sentence imposed was well within the parameters set forth by the Legislature in G.L. 1956 (1981 Reenactment) §11-37-8.4 ("every person who shall commit second degree child molestation sexual assault shall be imprisoned for not less than six years nor more than thirty years"). Given our limited scope of review, we hold that the trial justice remained soundly within the bounds of his discretion. . . .

Charles Hynes v. Albert Tomei
706 N.E. 2d 1202 (N.Y. 1991)

KAYE, C.J.

Thirty years ago, the United States Supreme Court struck down the death penalty provision of the Federal Kidnaping Act, which allowed a defendant to be sentenced to death only after a jury trial. The Supreme Court invalidated the provision because, by needlessly encouraging guilty pleas and jury waivers to avoid death sentences, it impermissibly burdened defendants' Fifth Amendment right against self-incrimination and Sixth Amendment right to a jury trial. United States v. Jackson, 390 U.S. 570 (1968). Despite the passage of three decades, a plethora of decisions involving the death penalty and a sea change in plea bargaining, the Supreme Court has never overruled *Jackson*, which binds this Court. Indeed, every other death penalty State has fit its capital murder plea-bargaining procedures within the rationale of *Jackson*.

Three years ago, the New York State Legislature enacted a capital punishment statute that—like the Federal Kidnaping Act—allows a defendant to be sentenced to death only after a jury trial. Bench trials are not permitted in capital cases, N.Y. Const., art. I, §2, and the statute bars imposition of a death sentence upon a guilty plea. The New York law thus explicitly provides two levels of penalty for the same offense, imposing death only on those who assert innocence and proceed to trial. . . . We are convinced that *Jackson* compels [us to] declare CPL §§220.10(5)(e) and 220.30(3)(b)(vii) unconstitutional. . . .

The Federal Kidnaping Act considered in *Jackson* provided [that whoever knowingly transports in interstate commerce a kidnaped person] "shall be punished (1) by death if the kidnaped person has not been liberated unharmed, and if the verdict of the jury shall so recommend, or (2) by imprisonment for any term of years or for life, if the death penalty is not imposed." Because the Act authorized the death penalty only on the recommendation of a jury, while a defendant convicted of the same offense on a guilty plea or by a Judge escaped the threat of capital punishment, the Supreme Court concluded that the Act "needlessly" encouraged guilty pleas and jury waivers. The Court acknowledged that restricting the death penalty to cases in which a jury recommends it is a legitimate goal, and that such a restriction would likely decrease the frequency of capital punishment. However, the Court concluded these considerations did not save the Act from constitutional infirmity. While the Act's chilling effect on a defendant's exercise of the Fifth Amendment right against self-incrimination and Sixth Amendment right to a jury trial may have been incidental, the effect was also "unnecessary and therefore excessive," since Congress could have achieved its goals by allowing juries to sentence defendants to the full range of punishments regardless of how guilt was determined.

Shortly after *Jackson*, this Court invalidated two provisions of the former Code of Criminal Procedure that required waiver of a jury trial in order to receive the benefit of youthful offender treatment. See People v. Michael A.C., 261 N.E.2d 620 (N.Y. 1970). Although respondents who refused to waive a jury trial were not subject to the death penalty, they were exposed to longer prison sentences than those prosecuted as youthful offenders. Drawing a parallel to *Jackson*, this Court held that "a procedure which offers an individual a reward for waiving a fundamental constitutional right, or imposes a harsher penalty for asserting it, may not be sustained."

New York's death penalty statute authorizes a District Attorney to file a notice of intent to seek the death penalty against a defendant charged with murder in the first degree. Upon conviction by a jury, a capital defendant faces a separate sentencing proceeding before a jury to determine whether the penalty imposed will be death or life imprisonment without parole. The statute affords a defendant the opportunity to ensure a maximum sentence of life without parole by pleading guilty pursuant to the following provisions:

> A defendant may not enter a plea of guilty to the crime of murder in the first degree . . . ; provided, however, that a defendant may enter such a plea with both the permission of the court and the consent of the people when the agreed upon sentence is either life imprisonment without parole or a term of imprisonment for . . . murder in the first degree other than a sentence of life imprisonment without parole. CPL §§220.10(5)(e); 220.30(3)(b)(vii).
>
> A defendant who has entered a plea of not guilty to an indictment may, with both the permission of the court and the consent of the people, withdraw such plea at any time before the rendition of a verdict and enter . . . a plea of guilty to part of the indictment . . . but subject to the limitation in subdivision five of section 220.10. CPL §220.60(2)(a). . . .

Thus, like the invalidated Federal Kidnaping Act provision, New York's death penalty statute explicitly provides for the imposition of the death penalty only upon a jury verdict. As a result, under the New York statute, only those defendants who exercise the Fifth Amendment right against self-incrimination and Sixth Amendment right to a jury trial put themselves at risk of death.

[Respondents] argue that the challenged New York provisions are distinguishable from the Federal Kidnaping Act because they merely codify permissible plea bargaining, which was not at issue in *Jackson*. Subsequent to *Jackson*, both the Supreme Court and this Court have acknowledged the legitimacy and desirability—indeed, the necessity—of plea bargaining.

See Santobello v. New York, 404 U.S. 257 (1971); People v. Selikoff, 318 N.E.2d 784 (N.Y. 1974). Plea bargaining serves important functions for both prosecutors and defendants, such as individualized justice, leniency and economy. A State clearly may encourage guilty pleas by offering benefits to defendants in return for a guilty plea. Furthermore, plea bargaining becomes no less lawful or desirable when it is codified in statutory form.

While plea bargaining is permissible, the Supreme Court in *Jackson* prohibited statutes that "needlessly" encourage guilty pleas, which are not constitutionally protected, by impermissibly burdening constitutional rights. Given the availability of alternatives that do not impermissibly burden defendants' constitutional rights, the plea provisions of the statute before us cannot be justified by an ostensible purpose such as the facilitation of plea bargaining.

Respondents rely heavily on Corbitt v. New Jersey, 439 U.S. 212 (1978), in which the Supreme Court held that it is constitutionally permissible to offer a defendant the possibility of escaping the most severe penalty by pleading guilty. The New Jersey statute at issue in *Corbitt*, however, provided for the same maximum sentence — life imprisonment — regardless of a defendant's plea. While a lesser sentence was permitted for those defendants who pleaded guilty, it was not guaranteed. Thus, the statute survived constitutional scrutiny because it did "not reserve the maximum punishment for murder for those who insist on a jury trial." This situation is readily distinguishable from the challenged New York provisions, which indeed prescribe a lesser agreed-upon sentence for those who plead guilty. . . .

In sum, respondents' attempts to distinguish New York's death penalty statute from the death penalty invalidated by the Supreme Court in *Jackson* fail. [By] statutory mandate, the death penalty hangs over only those who exercise their constitutional rights to maintain innocence and demand a jury trial. Thus, *Jackson* compels us to invalidate these provisions, just as it has compelled other State high courts to invalidate their capital plea provisions with the same constitutional infirmity. See State v. Johnson, 595 A.2d 498 (N.H. 1991); Commonwealth v. Colon-Cruz, 470 N.E.2d 116 (Mass. 1984); State v. Frampton, 627 P.2d 922 (Wash. 1981); State v. Funicello, 286 A.2d 55 (N.J. 1972). By contrast, the death penalty statutes of States that have rejected a *Jackson* challenge, with one exception, provide for the possibility of a death sentence upon a guilty plea. See State v. Mann, 959 S.W.2d 503 (Tenn. 1996); Conger v. Warden, 510 P.2d 1359 (Nev. 1973). The exception, Arkansas, avoided a *Jackson* problem because the Trial Judge, not the jury, made the final determination of whether the death penalty would be imposed, and because guilty pleas were permitted only after the prosecutor waived the death penalty. See Ruiz v. State, 630 S.W.2d 44 (Ark. 1982).

[Invalidation of the death penalty is not] necessary to obviate the *Jackson* problem: excision of the capital pleading provisions eliminates the burden on constitutional rights prohibited by *Jackson*, since without those provisions there is only one maximum penalty for first degree murder. [While] CPL §§221.10(5)(e) and 220.30(3)(b)(vii) relate exclusively to pleas in first degree murder cases and "needlessly" encourage guilty pleas in violation of *Jackson*, CPL §220.60(2)(a) is not limited to first degree murder cases, nor does it, in the absence of CPL §220.10(5)(e), violate *Jackson*. Therefore, only CPL §§220.10(5)(e) and 220.30(3)(b)(vii) must be stricken. Under the resulting statute, a defendant may not plead guilty to first degree murder while a notice of intent to seek the death penalty is pending.

We realize this result will reduce the flexibility of both prosecutors and defendants who wish to plea bargain in capital cases. Indeed, our reversal in these cases may well have an ironic twist in that capital defendants will have fewer opportunities to avoid the possibility of the death penalty. . . . While reducing the flexibility of plea bargaining in capital cases, excision of the unconstitutional provisions does not prevent pleas of guilty to first degree murder when no notice of intent to seek the death penalty is pending, since defendants in that situation face the same maximum sentence regardless of how they are convicted. Nor does the resulting statute prevent a defendant from pleading guilty to another offense not punishable by death, even when a notice of intent to seek the death penalty is pending, since nothing in *Jackson* prohibits imposing different penalties for different crimes. . . . Thus, while a defendant may not plead guilty to first degree murder while a notice of intent to seek the death penalty is pending, plea bargaining to lesser offenses even when a notice of intent is pending, or to first degree murder in the absence of a notice of intent, remains unaffected. . . .

‖ U.S. Sentencing Guidelines Manual ‖

§3E1.1 ACCEPTANCE OF RESPONSIBILITY

(a) If the defendant clearly demonstrates acceptance of responsibility for his offense, decrease the offense level by 2 levels.

(b) If the defendant qualifies for a decrease under subsection (a), the offense level determined prior to the operation of subsection (a) is level 16 or greater, and upon motion of the government stating that the defendant has assisted authorities in the investigation or prosecution of his own misconduct by timely notifying authorities of his intention to enter a plea of guilty, thereby permitting the government to avoid preparing for trial and permitting the government and the court to allocate their resources efficiently, decrease the offense level by 1 additional level.

‖ Powers of Criminal Courts (Sentencing) Act 2000 (United Kingdom), Ch. 6, Pt. VIII, §152 ‖

(1) In determining what sentence to pass on an offender who has pleaded guilty to an offence in proceedings before that or another court, a court shall take into account—

(a) the stage in the proceedings for the offence at which the offender indicated his intention to plead guilty; and

(b) the circumstances in which this indication was given.

(2) If, as a result of taking into account any matter referred to in subsection (1) above, the court imposes a punishment on the offender which is less severe than the punishment it would otherwise have imposed, it shall state in open court that it has done so.

(3) In the case of an offence the sentence for which falls to be imposed under subsection (2) of section 110 or 111 above [dealing with minimum sentences for drug and burglary crimes], nothing in that subsection shall prevent the court, after taking into account any matter referred to in subsection (1) above, from imposing any sentence which is not less than 80 per cent of that specified in that subsection.

NOTES

1. *The guilty plea discount and the trial penalty at sentencing.*   Courts walk a fine line when talking about the effect of a guilty plea on a sentence. On the one hand, they routinely say that a sentencing court may not penalize a defendant for exercising the constitutional rights that go along with a criminal trial. On the other hand, courts declare that a sentencing judge may reward a defendant for pleading guilty. State v. Balfour, 637 A.2d 1249 (N.J. 1994) (defendant's agreement to plead guilty can appropriately be weighed in the decision to downgrade an offense to a lower degree at sentencing). The defendant who pleads guilty saves the resources of the system for other cases; the administrative reasons for rewarding this choice are obvious. Is there a meaningful difference between penalizing a defendant and refusing to reward a defendant who insists on a trial? Do these rules encourage judges to do anything more than choose their words carefully?

The sentencing judge often reasons that a defendant's decision to go to trial reveals a lack of remorse or a refusal to accept responsibility for the crime. These facts have some bearing on the defendant's prospects for rehabilitation, or perhaps on the chances that he will commit crimes in the future. Cf. Ohio Rev. Code §2929.12(D)(5) (providing that judges should consider the fact that "offender shows no genuine remorse for the offense" as a factor indicating a greater likelihood of recidivism). Thus, the judges say, an enhanced penalty after trial merely responds to this relevant information and does not directly punish the exercise of rights. Jennings v. State, 664 A.2d 903 (Md. 1995). Similarly, the judge might believe that the impact of a trial on a victim (particularly a vulnerable victim who must testify at trial) justifies a more severe sentence. Does this reasoning apply to most (or all) defendants who go to trial? See Michael O'Hear, Remorse, Cooperation and "Acceptance of Responsibility": The Structure, Implementation and Reform of Section 3E1.1 of the Federal Sentencing Guidelines, 91 Nw. U. L. Rev. 1507 (1997).

2. *Legislative and commission rules on the guilty plea discount.*   The New York court in the *Tomei* case discussed the constitutional limits on the use of incentives to plead guilty in death penalty cases. The court looked for guidance in United States v. Jackson, 312 U.S. 275 (1968), but distinguished another case, Corbitt v. New Jersey, 439 U.S. 212 (1978). In *Corbitt* a statute required the sentencing judge in first-degree murder cases to impose a life sentence when the defendant was convicted after trial. Should the defendant plead guilty, however, the judge could choose either a life term or a 30-year term (the punishment for second-degree murder). How do you explain the difference in the outcomes in *Jackson* and *Corbitt?* See Joseph L. Hoffmann, Marcy L.

Kahn & Steven W. Fisher, Plea Bargaining in the Shadow of Death, 63 Fordham
L. Rev. 2313 (2001).

Are plea negotiations conducted differently when legislatures or sentencing commissions set the possible bargaining terms for all cases rather
than when the prosecutor sets possible terms for a particular case? Many
jurisdictions with structured sentencing rules provide for some form of guilty
plea discount, either directly or indirectly. The Massachusetts sentencing
guidelines list the plea agreement as a mitigating factor for a court to consider
at sentencing. North Carolina law lists two mitigating factors: that the
defendant accepted responsibility for the crime or that "prior to arrest or
at an early stage of the criminal process, the defendant voluntarily acknowledged wrongdoing in connection with the offense to a law enforcement
officer." N.C. Gen. Stat. §15A-1340.16(e)(11), (15). Sentence discounts
may also differ between jury trials and bench trials. See Nancy J. King et
al., When Process Affects Punishment: Differences in Sentences After Guilty
Plea, Bench Trial, and Jury Trial in Five Guidelines States, 105 Colum. L. Rev.
959 (2005).

Section 3E1.1 of the federal sentencing guidelines (reprinted above)
allows courts to reduce a sentence for a defendant who accepts responsibility.
The application notes indicate that pleading guilty operates as a close proxy for
accepting responsibility:

> This adjustment is not intended to apply to a defendant who puts the govern-
> ment to its burden of proof at trial by denying the essential factual elements of
> guilt, is convicted, and only then admits guilt and expresses remorse. Convic-
> tion by trial, however, does not automatically preclude a defendant from con-
> sideration for such a reduction. In rare situations a defendant may clearly
> demonstrate an acceptance of responsibility for his criminal conduct even
> though he exercises his constitutional right to a trial. This may occur, for
> example, where a defendant goes to trial to assert and preserve issues that do
> not relate to factual guilt. . . .

The commentary goes on to remind courts that pleading guilty will not
necessarily lead to a lower sentence: "A defendant who enters a guilty plea is
not entitled to an adjustment under this section as a matter of right." Yet historically, well over 90% of offenders who plead guilty get this reduction. Is
section 3E1.1 significantly different from a sentencing guideline provision
that sets a uniform discount for the sentences of all defendants who plead guilty?
Does it reward cooperation that produces administrative savings or remorse for
the crime or both?

The international tribunals adjudging crimes committed in Rwanda and
Yugoslavia have given sentence discounts for defendants who showed sincere
remorse, but they have not done so in all cases. According to the rules of procedure for those tribunals, counseling in favor of a sentence decrease are the
enormous costs of these trials and the ability of guilty pleas to add to national
reconciliation and truth-finding. Still, in some cases the gravity of the offense has
caused the courts to discount the value of the guilty plea.

3. *Prevalence and size of the discount.* In discretionary sentencing systems,
judges give different discounts to defendants for pleading guilty (or for
accepting responsibility or expressing remorse, if you prefer). Those studying

sentences in the aggregate have estimated that a guilty plea can reduce a sentence by 15-40%.

Under the federal guidelines section 3E1.1, if a defendant "clearly demonstrates acceptance of responsibility," her "offense level" can be reduced by two or three levels. The three-level discount was once available to any defendant charged with the most serious crimes who pled guilty early or who cooperated in the investigation of her own crimes. But Congress amended the guidelines in 2003 to condition this greater discount on a motion by the prosecution stating that the defendant's early plea or cooperation was beneficial to the government. What was Congress's goal in specifying a motion by the government as a prerequisite to an increased reduction for acceptance of responsibility? A three-level discount could mean a reduction of as much as 50% of the sentence for lesser crimes or as little as 20% for more serious offenses.

The structured sentencing rules in most states do not specify how much the judge should discount the sentence of a defendant who pleads guilty. Compare this with the cap specified in the legislation from the United Kingdom, reprinted above. It does appear that early guilty pleas in the Crown Court lead to more nonprison sentences and to shorter prison terms. See Ralph J. Henham, Sentence Discounts and the Criminal Process (2001). If a state were to pass a statute identical to the UK legislation, would it survive constitutional challenge? Some state statutes in the United States do specify the maximum discount that a court may grant for pleading guilty. See Iowa Code §901.10(3) (in sentencing certain drug defendants otherwise subject to a mandatory minimum sentence, "the court may, at its discretion, reduce the maximum sentence by up to one-third" for a defendant who pleads guilty).

In a world where more than 90% of all felony defendants plead guilty, how many defendants fail to receive a discount? In only 7% of cases did offenders fail to receive some discount for acceptance of responsibility in 2006 (with almost 65% receiving three-level discounts and 28% receiving two-level discounts). Only 4.3% of the defendants convicted in federal court in 2006 actually went to trial. Does this pattern undermine the claim that courts are not punishing defendants who exercise their trial rights?

4. *Silence, perjury, and sentencing.* As the Rhode Island court in *Tiernan* mentioned, defendants have a right to trial, but they have no right to perjury. A defendant who testifies at trial might receive a stiffer punishment if the judge believes that the testimony was not truthful. See United States v. Dunnigan, 507 U.S. 87, 97 (1993) (sentencing court can enhance defendant's sentence by designated amount under federal guidelines if the court finds that the defendant committed perjury at trial; court must make "findings to support all the elements of a perjury violation in the specific case").

But the trial is not the only setting in which it is dangerous for the defendant to speak. The probation officer who prepares a presentence investigation report might ask to interview the defendant. If the officer believes that the defendant lied during the interview, he might recommend against any discount for acceptance of responsibility. Cf. People v. Hicks, N.E.2d 205 (N.Y. 2002) (approving imposition of an enhanced sentence after defender lied about crime to probation officer). At the same time, the Fifth Amendment's privilege against self-incrimination limits the consequences of a defendant's decision to remain silent. In Mitchell v. United States, 526 U.S. 314 (1999), the defendant faced a sentence of anywhere from one year to life depending on the quantity of drugs involved in her offense. Mitchell did not testify at the sentencing hearing, but contended that the evidence established the presence of only a small amount of cocaine. The Supreme Court held that the trial court could not consider Mitchell's silence as a basis for a factual finding that higher amounts of drugs were involved in the case. Drawing such inferences from her silence impermissibly burdened her exercise of the constitutional right against compelled self-incrimination. Would the same reasoning apply to a defendant who declines a probation officer's invitation to discuss the case? Consider this application note to section 3E1.1: "[A] defendant is not required to volunteer, or affirmatively admit, relevant conduct beyond the offense of conviction in order to obtain a reduction. . . ."

5. *"Vindictive" sentencing after retrial.* Just as courts insist that a sentence may not be increased to punish a defendant for exercising the right to trial, federal and state courts say that a trial judge may not punish a defendant for exercising the statutory right to appeal. If a defendant successfully appeals a conviction and is convicted again after retrial, a sentence higher than the original sentence imposed is presumed to be a product of vindictiveness by the sentencing judge. A sentence motivated by such vindictiveness violates federal due process. The judge must rebut this presumption by placing on the record her reasons for increasing the sentence after the second conviction. See North Carolina v. Pearce, 395 U.S. 711, 726 (1969). The Court in *Pearce* stated that those reasons could be based on "objective information concerning identifiable conduct on the part of the defendant occurring after the time of the original sentence proceeding." In a latter case, the Court held that a trial judge could rebut the presumption of vindictiveness by pointing to any "objective information" that the judge did not consider during the first sentencing proceeding. See Texas v. McCullough, 475 U.S. 134 (1986).

6. *Plea bargaining and structured sentencing rules.* When sentencing rules place a specified weight on the charges, offense facts, and criminal history, the prosecutor has greater influence over the sentence to be imposed. Through investigations, indictments, and plea bargains, the prosecutor can often specify exactly what charges, facts, and history get admitted by the defendant and become known to the sentencing court. Interestingly, early research has suggested that prosecutors do not tend to change their customary charging or plea bargaining practices to exploit their power to influence sentences in structured-sentencing states. Specifically, this research shows that structured systems are not characterized by dramatically longer sentences or different rates of guilty pleas. See Terance Miethe, Charging and Plea Bargaining Practices Under Determinate Sentencing: An Investigation of the Hydraulic Displacement of Discretion, 78 J. Crim. L. & Criminology 155 (1987). Why do you suppose that structured sentencing rules have affected guilty plea rates so little?

This is not to say that plea bargains have no effect on either the plea process or the uniformity of individual sentences in structured systems. Available evidence suggests that in a significant number of cases (perhaps as many as one-third) prosecutors and defendants use plea bargains to circumvent the strictures of the guidelines by agreeing to charges and to factual and guideline stipulations that place the sentence outside the range that would ordinarily be prescribed—without asking the judge to depart from the guidelines. See Ilene Nagel & Stephen Schulhofer, A Tale of Three Cities: An Empirical Study of Charging and Bargaining Practice Under the Federal Sentencing Guidelines, 66 S. Cal. L. Rev. 501 (1992); Frank O. Bowman, To Tell the Truth: The Problem of Prosecutorial "Manipulation" of Sentencing Facts, 8 Fed. Sent'g Rep. 324 (1996); Linda Drazgo Maxfield & Keri Burchfield, Immigration Offenses Involving Unlawful Entry: Is Federal Practice Comparable Across Districts?, 14 Fed. Sent'g Rep. 260 (2002).

2.   Substantial Assistance

Sometimes it takes a crook to catch a crook. A defendant can tell investigators about crimes that others committed in the past or can agree to take part in future sting operations. In the federal system, substantial assistance to the government is by far the most common single reason judges give for departing downward from the sentencing range specified in the guidelines. Judges relied on substantial-assistance departures in more than 14% of all federal cases in 2006.

It is clear that all sentencing systems allow trial judges to reduce a defendant's sentence based on cooperation. What is less clear is exactly *who* can determine whether the defendant should benefit from an effort to cooperate and how large the benefit should be.

|| ***United States v. Amanda Williams***
474 F.3d 1130 (8th Cir. 2007) ||

COLLOTON, J.

The Sentencing Reform Act provides that a district court has "limited authority to impose a sentence below a statutory minimum," upon motion of the government, "so as to reflect a defendant's substantial assistance in the investigation or prosecution of another person who has committed an offense." 18 U.S.C. §3553(e). This case presents the question whether a district court, after reducing a sentence based on substantial assistance pursuant to §3553(e), may reduce the sentence further based on factors, other than assistance, set forth in 18 U.S.C. §3553(a). We hold that it may not. Where a court has authority to sentence below a statutory minimum only by virtue of a government motion under §3553(e), the reduction below the statutory minimum must be based exclusively on assistance-related considerations.

Amanda Williams pled guilty to conspiracy to distribute more than 500 grams of methamphetamine within 1000 feet of a protected location. At sentencing, the government filed motions under USSG §5K1.1 and 18 U.S.C. §3553(e) to reduce her sentence based on the provision of substantial assistance to authorities in the investigation or prosecution of other persons. A motion under §5K1.1 authorizes the sentencing court to depart below the applicable advisory guideline range in determining the advisory guideline sentence, and a

§3553(e) motion permits the court to sentence below a statutory minimum. See Melendez v. United States, 518 U.S. 120 (1996).

Prior to any reduction for assistance, the advisory guideline sentence for Williams was 120-121 months' imprisonment, and the applicable statutory minimum was 120 months. The district court granted the substantial-assistance motions and announced that it would reduce the term of imprisonment to 78 months based on Williams's assistance. The court then invoked §3553(a) to reduce the sentence further, to a final term of 60 months' imprisonment, based on Williams's young age, medical history, drug use, and limited criminal history. The government does not challenge the district court's reduction of the sentence to 78 months based on substantial assistance, but argues that the additional reduction to 60 months was legally impermissible, because the court relied on factors other than substantial assistance. This is a legal question that we review *de novo*.

We have said that a reduction in sentence based on §3553(e) may be based only on assistance-related considerations, but we have twice reserved deciding whether, in light of United States v. Booker, 543 U.S. 220 (2005), a district court may also rely on §3553(a) to reduce a sentence further below the statutory minimum once the government has filed a motion under §3553(e). In [an earlier case], we implied strongly — if we did not explicitly hold — that a district court in that situation is limited to assistance-related considerations. . . . The clear implication of [that case] is that factors unrelated to assistance were not "permissible" considerations in determining the extent of a reduction below the statutory minimum.

To the extent the question remains open . . . , we conclude that the text of §3553(e) provides a clear answer, and that *Booker* does not expand the district court's authority to impose a sentence below a statutory minimum. Section 3553(e) provides:

> **(e) Limited authority to impose a sentence below a statutory minimum.** — Upon motion of the Government, the court shall have the authority to impose a sentence below a level established by statute as a minimum sentence so as to reflect a defendant's substantial assistance in the investigation or prosecution of another person who has committed an offense. Such sentence shall be imposed in accordance with the guidelines and policy statements issued by the Sentencing Commission pursuant to section 994 of title 28, United States Code.

Two aspects of the text are particularly instructive. First is the title, which states that the section provides only "limited authority" to impose a sentence below the statutory minimum. Congress evidently wanted statutory minimum sentences to be firmly enforced, subject only to carefully "limited" exceptions. The body of §3553(e) specifies precisely how a sentencing court's authority is limited. It may impose a sentence below the statutory minimum only "*so as to reflect a defendant's substantial assistance.*" 18 U.S.C. §3553(e) (emphasis added). If a district court imposes a sentence below the statutory minimum in part so as to reflect the history and characteristics of the defendant, see §3553(a)(1), then the court exceeds the limited authority granted by §3553(e). The second textual sentence of §3553(e) refers back to the penal sentence contemplated in the first textual sentence, and thus "restricts the court's reference to those guidelines and policy statements that bear directly upon the desirability and extent of a substantial assistance departure." United States v. Ahlers, 305 F.3d 54, 61 (1st Cir. 2002).

Nothing in the reasoning of *Booker* expands the authority of a district court to sentence below a statutory minimum. The Court's remedial holding provided that to cure the constitutional infirmity of the mandatory guidelines system, a district court is authorized to consider the factors set forth in §3553(a), and to vary from the sentence otherwise indicated by the sentencing guidelines. But *Booker* did not question the constitutionality of statutory minimum sentences, and while the Court excised §§3553(b)(1) and 3742(e) from the Code, §3553(e) was unmentioned in the opinion. The Court deviated from the mandatory guidelines system adopted by Congress only insofar as the deviation was necessary to make the remaining advisory system consistent with the Sixth Amendment. Because statutory minimum sentences remain constitutional, and it is constitutional for Congress to limit a court's authority to sentence below such minimums, the remedial holding of *Booker* does not impact the pre-existing limitations embodied in §3553(e).

In this case, the district court reduced Williams's sentence below the statutory minimum in two increments—one based on substantial assistance and one based on other factors. Because the second increment was impermissible for the reasons explained above, we vacate the sentence and remand for resentencing consistent with this opinion.

‖ *Nevada Revised Statutes §453.3405(2)* ‖

The judge, upon an appropriate motion, may reduce or suspend the sentence of any person convicted of violating any of the [code provisions dealing with trafficking in controlled substances] if he finds that the convicted person rendered substantial assistance in the identification, arrest or conviction of any of his accomplices, accessories, coconspirators or principals or of any other person involved in trafficking in a controlled substance. . . . The arresting agency must be given an opportunity to be heard before the motion is granted. Upon good cause shown, the motion may be heard in camera.

PROBLEM 5-2.   HELPING OTHERS

The County Police Department of Nassau, New York, and the U.S. Bureau of Alcohol, Tobacco and Firearms (BATF) conducted a joint investigation of Lancelotte Kaye's illegal trafficking in narcotics and firearms. During this investigation, Kaye sold both marijuana and illegal firearms to an undercover Nassau County detective. The state authorities arrested Kaye for selling marijuana; the federal authorities arrested him for illegal possession of firearms. Soon after his indictments on these charges, Kaye agreed to cooperate with both state and federal authorities in the identification and conviction of other wrongdoers.

His efforts for the state investigators proved fruitful. Kaye covertly recorded conversations with various individuals, at some personal risk. As a result of these recordings, the Nassau P.D. arrested two individuals, one of whom pleaded guilty to a misdemeanor. In Nassau County Court, Kaye pleaded guilty to a lesser drug felony and was sentenced to time served. Unfortunately, Kaye's efforts on behalf of the federal authorities were unproductive. Kaye recorded phone conversations with the individual who sold him weapons. He also met with that individual and provided the BATF with his first name, telephone number, and home address. Nevertheless, the BATF made no arrests.

In federal district court, Kaye pleaded guilty to possession of firearms with obliterated serial numbers. The prosecutor declined to move for a downward departure pursuant to section 5K1.1. In a letter to the court, the prosecutor acknowledged that Kaye had cooperated in Nassau County but noted that he had received the benefit of a light sentence in return. The letter went on: "The federal effort was ultimately unsuccessful. As such, the government cannot certify that the defendant has provided substantial assistance."

As defense counsel for Kaye in federal court, how might you construct arguments for a downward departure based on Kaye's cooperation in the state and federal investigations? How is Kaye's case different from the typical refusal by federal prosecutors to request a departure under section 5K1.1? How might you use section 5K2.0, which empowers a sentencing judge to depart downward from a sentence designated under the guidelines if the case presents a factor that the U.S. Sentencing Commission did not "adequately consider" as it formulated the guidelines? Compare United States v. Kaye, 140 F.3d 86 (2d Cir. 1998).

PROBLEM 5-3. EARNED TIME

Return your attention to the robbery case involving Rob Anon and his accomplices. Suppose that during pretrial negotiations, the prosecutor made the same plea offer to Anon, Zweite, and Tercero: the government would move for a downward departure from the presumptive sentence under the sentencing guidelines, based on substantial assistance to the government, if one of the defendants would plead guilty and testify against the other defendants. The prosecutor told all three defendants that he did not care which of them received the downward departure motion, but that the government would make the motion for only one defendant.

Several weeks passed. Tercero finally accepted the offer and entered a plea agreement. He pled guilty and testified at the trial of Anon and Zweite; the jury convicted the two defendants on all charges. At the sentencing hearing, the prosecutor recommended a sentence of 12 months for Tercero, which was a downward departure from the presumptive sentence under the guidelines. The government recommended sentences within the relevant guideline range for Anon and Zweite, 108-135 months. The sentencing guidelines in the jurisdiction would make it difficult for the sentencing judge to depart downward (below 108 months) for Anon or Zweite.

As a law clerk to the sentencing judge, what sentence would you recommend for the three defendants? As a member of a sentencing commission, would you draft rules placing any limits on the use of substantial assistance as a basis for a departure? Any limits on the size of such a departure? Compare United States v. Maddox, 48 F.3d 791 (4th Cir. 1995).

NOTES

1. *Assisting in other investigations.*   In the unstructured sentencing states, cooperation with the government in investigating and trying other criminal cases is generally believed to have some positive effect both on the sentencing court's disposition of the case and on the duration of the sentence imposed. See State v. Johnson, 630 N.W.2d 583 (Iowa 2001). Even in highly discretionary sentencing systems, statutes commonly state that the sentencing court may give a sentencing discount to a defendant who provides assistance to the government. See Brugman v. State, 339 S.E.2d 244 (Ga. 1986) (discussing statute). The states with more structured sentencing systems have followed the same route, instructing the judge that cooperation with the government can serve as a basis for departing from the guideline range and imposing some lesser sentence. See Or. Admin. R. 213-008-0002(1)(F) (2007).

Is this reduction of the sentence a necessary evil, the price that prosecutors pay for creating additional criminal cases? Or would courts adjust a sentence in light of a defendant's cooperation even in an ideal world? Michael Simons argues that "cooperating" defendants are ostracized from their communities, so they have already been punished to some extent, and the criminal sanction should be reduced accordingly. He also suggests that cooperation encourages the defendant's atonement, increasing the odds that she will eventually reintegrate into the community. See Michael Simons, Retribution for Rats: Cooperation, Punishment, and Atonement, 56 Vand. L. Rev. 1 (2003). Should prosecutors consider the defendant's prospects for atonement through cooperation when recommending a reduced sentence for that defendant, or should the recommendation simply turn on the value of the help the defendant provided? If the latter, consider this irony: the "biggest fish" in any criminal organization is likely to know the most and to offer the most value to the government's investigators. Thus, the largest sentence reductions might go to the most important (and most culpable) defendants. Barry Tarlow, The Moral Conundrum of Representing the Rat, 30 Champion 64, 66-67 (March 2006) (describing some cases in which high-level offenders ended up with low sentences in exchange for providing information to the government). But see United States v. Duhon, 440 F.3d 711, 720-722 (5th Cir. 2006) (Congress intended for sentencing disparity based on substantial assistance).

2. *Substantial in whose eyes?*   There is some variation in the amount of control the prosecution has over the use of the "substantial assistance" sentencing factor. If the prosecution refuses to accept a defendant's offer of cooperation, then the sentence usually will not be affected. See Matos v. State, 878 P.2d 288 (Nev. 1994). But what happens if the government accepts the cooperation and later determines that it was not valuable or complete?

As we have seen in *Williams,* section 5K1.1 of the federal guidelines requires a government motion before the court can reduce the sentence based on the defendant's cooperation. Since the Supreme Court's decision in *Booker,* however, sentencing courts may also adjust a guideline sentence downward based on their independent assessment of whether the defendant offered or provided assistance. 18 U.S.C. §3553(e), on the other hand, mandates a governmental motion before a court can reduce a sentence below a statutory mandatory minimum. *Booker* did not change this statutory requirement. Should the court have an independent power to reduce a sentence on these grounds, even in the absence of a government motion? State legislatures and courts have been debating this issue for years, although the state debate has not figured in the federal discussions of this question. See State v. Sarabia, 875 P.2d 227 (Idaho 1994) (declaring unconstitutional on state grounds a statute allowing sentence below mandatory minimum only when prosecutor moves for reduction based on substantial assistance).

3. *Arbitrary and inconsistent prosecutor decisions.* According to the U.S. Supreme Court in Wade v. United States, 504 U.S. 181 (1992), the Constitution places some boundaries on the prosecutor's power to refuse to request a reduced sentence based on a defendant's substantial assistance. But only when the defendant makes a "substantial threshold showing" of a prosecutor's unconstitutional motive can the trial judge adjust the sentence without a government motion. Besides a refusal based on race or religion, what else might qualify as a constitutionally improper reason for a prosecutor to withhold a motion? How can a defendant gather evidence that an unconstitutional motive influenced the prosecutor's decision? If the defendant and the government enter into a plea agreement in which the government promises to file a substantial-assistance motion, and the government fails to do so, the sentencing court may review the agreement to see whether the prosecutor acted in bad faith. United States v. Roe, 445 F.3d 202 (2d Cir. 2006).

The real debate over limiting prosecutorial power in this sphere takes place at the nonconstitutional level. Legislatures and sentencing commissions must decide whether to make a prosecutor's motion a necessary precondition to this sort of sentence reduction. The concern, of course, is that an unsupervised prosecutor's grounds for making or refusing to make the recommendations may be arbitrary or inconsistent. With the ruling in *Booker*, federal courts may impose a non-guideline sentence based on substantial assistance even without a governmental motion; the same does not hold for sentences below a mandatory minimum, for which a governmental motion is still required. Are other institutions, such as sentencing courts, able to evaluate the prosecutor's decisions about which defendants provided substantial assistance? What advantages does a prosecutor have in making this choice? See Daniel Richman, The Challenge of Investigating Section 5K1.1 In Practice, 11 Fed. Sent'g Rep. 75 (1998).

In the federal system, prosecutors have attempted to regulate themselves by creating written policies concerning which defendants should receive a reduced sentence for substantial assistance. About 80% of the federal districts have adopted written guidelines on the subject, and their content is fairly consistent. A study sponsored by the U.S. Sentencing Commission (known as the Maxfield-Kramer Study), however, found great variety among the 94 federal districts in their granting of substantial assistance motions. See Linda Drazga Maxfield & John Kramer, Substantial Assistance: Empirical Yardstick Gauging Equity in Federal Policy and Practice (1998). Nationwide, less than 40% of defendants who provided assistance to the government have received substantial-assistance motions. Defendants who testified at trial, participated in undercover investigations, or provided tangible evidence such as documents received the motions most often. Defendants at various levels in drug conspiracies (high-level traffickers, street-level dealers, or lower-level support functionaries) received the motions at comparable rates. The study found that the demographic characteristics of defendants had some influence on whether they received a motion:

> Holding constant important variables such as offense type, guideline range, mitigating and/or aggravating factors, weapon involvement, and a host of other possible explanatory concepts, [we] found that personal characteristics remained significant predictors of who received substantial assistance departures. [Defendants who were male, black, Hispanic, non-citizens, and older were all less likely to receive a motion. Controlling] for all other personal, judicial, and guideline factors in the model, a Hispanic defendant was seven percentage points less likely than a non-Hispanic defendant to receive a substantial assistance departure.

As a chief prosecutor, how would you react to this news? Could you create guidelines within your office that would promote more consistent decisions about sentence discounts for cooperating defendants? See Frank Bowman, Substantial Assistance: An Old Prosecutor's Meditation on *Singleton, Sealed Case,* and the Maxfield-Kramer Report, 12 Fed. Sent'g Rep. 45 (1999).

4. *Magnitude and type of discount.*   The federal guidelines do not instruct the sentencing judge on how much of a departure to grant to a cooperating defendant, but section 5K1.1 does list a few factors to consider: the "usefulness of the defendant's assistance," the "truthfulness, completeness, and reliability of any information or testimony provided," and "any injury suffered, or any danger or risk of injury to the defendant or his family resulting from his assistance." The Maxfield-Kramer Study found that judges gave larger departures in the cases involving the highest sentences, not necessarily for the defendants who provided the most valuable cooperation or who cooperated under the most dangerous circumstances. It also found that demographic features of defendants affected the size of the discount awarded. After controlling for various features of the crime and the type of cooperation, "female defendants received departures that were nine percentage points higher than did similar male defendants. Smaller, but still significant, differences were measured for ethnicity and citizenship (five percentage points), age (four percentage points), and race and education (two percentage points)." As a U.S. Sentencing Commission member, would you favor the imposition of limits on the magnitude of a departure expressed in absolute terms (say, two years or two offense levels) or in relative terms (say, 20% of the sentence)? In recent cases courts have reversed sentencing decisions because of the magnitude of the substantial-assistance departure. United States v. Desselle, 450 F.3d 179 (5th Cir. 2006); United States v. McVay, 447 F.3d 1348 (11th Cir. 2006).

Defendants can receive not just different amounts of discounts but different *types* of benefits other than sentence adjustments for their cooperation with government investigations. These include a reduction of charges during plea negotiations or favorable treatment for immigration purposes. See Nora V. Demleitner, Immigration Threats and Rewards: Effective Law Enforcement Tools in the War on Terrorism?, 51 Emory L.J. 1059 (2002).

C. THE OFFENDER'S CHARACTER AND CIRCUMSTANCES

A criminal defendant is not merely the sum of his or her contacts with the criminal justice system; there is, of course, much more to every offender than simply a criminal record and some post-offense behavior. Indeed, many people think that personal characteristics — ethnicity, gender, age, family context, educational background, and social and economic history — define not only who we are but also how we ought to be judged by others. Sentencing judges usually learn facts about an offender's personal background and circumstances, and historically they have adjusted sentences in light of the offender's overall character, often giving particular attention to facts relating to the offender's family, physical or mental health, and prospects for rehabilitation. A persistent challenge in modern sentencing reform efforts has been to identify and regulate the appropriate role of so-called offender characteristics.

PROBLEM 5-4. TURNING GUIDANCE INTO GUIDELINES

It is spring 1985 and you have been appointed as one of the U.S. Sentencing Commission's first seven commissioners. Your institution has the enormous task of turning all the mandates of the recently passed Sentencing Reform Act (SRA) into sentencing guidelines for use by federal courts. The commissioners agreed to subdivide the work ahead, with each taking responsibility for drafting one part of the guidelines. You are assigned the section dealing with offender characteristics, and your work is guided by the following provisions of 28 U.S.C. §994, part of the SRA:

> (d) The U.S. Sentencing Commission in establishing [sentencing guidelines for federal offenses] shall consider whether the following matters, among others with respect to a defendant, have any relevance to the nature, extent, place of service, or other incidents of an appropriate sentence . . . : (1) age; (2) education; (3) vocational skills; (4) mental and emotional condition . . . ; (5) physical condition, including drug dependence; (6) previous employment record; (7) family ties and responsibilities; (8) community ties; . . . .
>
> The Commission shall assure that the guidelines and policy statements are entirely neutral as to the race, sex, national origin, creed, and socioeconomic status of offenders.
>
> (e) The Commission shall assure that the guidelines and policy statements, in recommending a term of imprisonment or length of a term of imprisonment, reflect the general inappropriateness of considering the education, vocational skills, employment record, family ties and responsibilities, and community ties of the defendant.

How will you turn the SRA's guidance into specific guidelines for courts to follow in sentencing individual offenders? Will you leave all these questions to the sentencing judge, or will you instead try to encourage or require judges to adjust a sentence up or down in light of some of these factors? Is it a good idea to specify the amount of adjustment that the judge should use in a normal case? Should you instruct judges only to move sentences *down* based on these personal characteristics of the offender? Cf. U.S. Sentencing Guidelines

Manual §5H1.1 (age), §5H1.2 (education and vocational skills), §5H1.3 (mental and emotional conditions), §5H1.4 (physical condition, including drug or alcohol dependence or abuse), §5H1.5 (employment record), §5H1.6 (family ties and responsibilities and community ties).

NOTES

1. *Offender characteristics at sentencing: majority rule.*   Every U.S. jurisdiction allows judges at sentencing to consider various aspects of the defendant's life, including events occurring far before the offense, matters that do not bear directly on guilt or innocence, and post-offense activities. In unstructured sentencing systems, it is difficult to establish or measure just how much an offender's personal background and characteristics tend to influence the sentence, although anecdotal reports suggest that the influence can be sizable. Most structured systems do not directly integrate personal characteristics into the calculation of offenders' presumptive guideline sentences; instead, they often allow (and even encourage in some instances) sentencing judges to depart from the guidelines to impose a higher or lower sentence than prescribed based on these factors. In addition, legislatures as well as sentencing commissions sometimes instruct judges *not* to consider certain offender characteristics. The Minnesota sentencing guidelines, for example, state that the following factors "should not be used as reasons for departing from the presumptive sentences" provided in their sentencing guidelines:

   (a)   Race
   (b)   Sex
   (c)   Employment factors, including: (1) occupation or impact of sentence on profession or occupation; (2) employment history; (3) employment at time of offense; (4) employment at time of sentencing, [and]
   (d)   Social factors, including: (1) educational attainment; (2) living arrangements at time of offense or sentencing; (3) length of residence; (4) marital status.

Minn. Sentencing Guidelines II.D.1.

2. *Theory and concerns behind considering offender characteristics.*   What is the theoretical justification for altering a defendant's sentence based on certain personal characteristics? Could one argue from a retributivist perspective that certain personal characteristics, such as mental condition, education, and drug dependence, are not only relevant but fundamental to determining what sentence is needed to give an offender his just deserts? Could one argue from a utilitarian perspective that certain other personal characteristics, such as age, employment circumstances, and family background, are not only relevant but fundamental to determining what sentence is needed to effectively incapacitate, deter, or rehabilitate an offender?

Many modern structured-sentencing reforms were prompted by concerns that personal factors such as an offender's ethnicity, gender, and socioeconomic status were influencing judges' exercise of their broad sentencing discretion, resulting in unwarranted sentencing disparities. As detailed in Problem 5-4 above, Congress addressed this concern in federal sentencing reform by mandating that the federal sentencing guidelines be "entirely neutral as to the race, sex, national origin, creed, and socioeconomic status of offenders." Do you think this mandate is realistic or merely aspirational — that is, is it truly possible for a sentencing system to be "entirely neutral" with respect to all these factors? Can a principled argument be made that at least some of these listed factors ought to be considered at sentencing?

A number of other personal factors are closely associated with these forbidden factors. Employment and education, for example, are highly correlated with socioeconomic class; pregnancy is associated with gender, as can be some child-rearing realities. To the extent that gender and socioeconomic status are deemed per se illegitimate as sentencing considerations, should rules also bar any consideration of these related factors at sentencing? Consider the commentary to the Minnesota guidelines provision discussed above in note 1:

> The [Minnesota Sentencing] Commission believes that sentencing should be neutral with respect to offenders' race, sex, and income levels. Accordingly, the Commission has listed several factors which should not be used as reasons for departure from the presumptive sentence, because these factors are highly correlated with sex, race, or income levels. Employment is excluded as a reason for departure not only because of its correlation with race and income levels, but also because this factor is manipulable — offenders could lessen the severity of the sentence by obtaining employment between arrest and sentencing.

Minn. Sentencing Guidelines II.D.101, cmt. Do you agree that consideration of employment history and status should be prohibited at sentencing? Is such a prohibition the best way to address the concerns raised by the Minnesota Sentencing Commission?

1. Immutable Characteristics

Should the treatment of certain personal characteristics at sentencing depend on whether they are within the offender's control? The immutability of certain factors that seem irrelevant to an offender's culpability and future prospects — factors such as race or creed — might suggest firm rules forbidding their consideration at sentencing. However, the immutability of other factors that seem quite relevant to an offender's culpability and future prospects — factors such as mental or physical condition — might suggest the need for rules requiring judges to consider them at sentencing.

‖ **ABA Standards for Criminal Justice,** ‖
Sentencing 18-3.4(d)
(3d ed. 1994)

The legislature should specify that the following personal characteristics shall not, in and of themselves, be used for [any] purpose with regard to sentencing: (i) Race, (ii) Gender or sexual orientation, (iii) National origin, (iv) Religion or creed, (v) Marital status, (vi) Political affiliation or belief.

|| *Donald Roper v. Christopher Simmons* ||
543 U.S. 551 (2005)

KENNEDY, J.

This case requires us to address, for the second time in a decade and a half, whether it is permissible under the Eighth and Fourteenth Amendments to the Constitution of the United States to execute a juvenile offender who was older than 15 but younger than 18 when he committed a capital crime. In Stanford v. Kentucky, 492 U.S. 361 (1989), a divided Court rejected the proposition that the Constitution bars capital punishment for juvenile offenders in this age group. We reconsider the question.

I

At the age of 17, when he was still a junior in high school, Christopher Simmons, the respondent here, committed murder. About nine months later, after he had turned 18, he was tried and sentenced to death. There is little doubt that Simmons was the instigator of the crime. Before its commission Simmons said he wanted to murder someone. In chilling, callous terms he talked about his plan, discussing it for the most part with two friends, Charles Benjamin and John Tessmer, then aged 15 and 16 respectively. Simmons proposed to commit burglary and murder by breaking and entering, tying up a victim, and throwing the victim off a bridge. Simmons assured his friends they could "get away with it" because they were minors.

The three met at about 2 A.M. on the night of the murder, but Tessmer left before the other two set out. . . . Simmons and Benjamin entered the home of the victim, Shirley Crook, after reaching through an open window and unlocking the back door. Simmons turned on a hallway light. Awakened, Mrs. Crook called out, "Who's there?" In response Simmons entered Mrs. Crook's bedroom, where he recognized her from a previous car accident involving them both. Simmons later admitted this confirmed his resolve to murder her.

Using duct tape to cover her eyes and mouth and bind her hands, the two perpetrators put Mrs. Crook in her minivan and drove to a state park. They reinforced the bindings, covered her head with a towel, and walked her to a railroad trestle spanning the Meramec River. There they tied her hands and feet together with electrical wire, wrapped her whole face in duct tape and threw her from the bridge, drowning her in the waters below.

By the afternoon of September 9, Steven Crook had returned home from an overnight trip, found his bedroom in disarray, and reported his wife missing. On the same afternoon fishermen recovered the victim's body from the river. Simmons, meanwhile, was bragging about the killing, telling friends he had killed a woman "because the bitch seen my face."

The next day, after receiving information of Simmons' involvement, police arrested him at his high school and took him to the police station in Fenton,

Missouri. . . . The State charged Simmons with burglary, kidnaping, stealing, and murder in the first degree. As Simmons was 17 at the time of the crime, he was outside the criminal jurisdiction of Missouri's juvenile court system. He was tried as an adult. . . . The jury having returned a verdict of murder, the trial proceeded to the penalty phase. The State sought the death penalty. . . .

During closing arguments, both the prosecutor and defense counsel addressed Simmons' age, which the trial judge had instructed the jurors they could consider as a mitigating factor. Defense counsel reminded the jurors that juveniles of Simmons' age cannot drink, serve on juries, or even see certain movies, because "the legislatures have wisely decided that individuals of a certain age aren't responsible enough." Defense counsel argued that Simmons' age should make "a huge difference to [the jurors] in deciding just exactly what sort of punishment to make." In rebuttal, the prosecutor gave the following response: "Age, he says. Think about age. Seventeen years old. Isn't that scary? Doesn't that scare you? Mitigating? Quite the contrary I submit. Quite the contrary."

The jury recommended the death penalty after finding the State had proved each of the three aggravating factors submitted to it. Accepting the jury's recommendation, the trial judge imposed the death penalty.

[In a hearing on his postconviction motion to set aside the conviction and sentence, Simmons called several clinical psychologists as witnesses, who testified] that Simmons was "very immature," "very impulsive," and "very susceptible to being manipulated or influenced." The experts testified about Simmons' background including a difficult home environment and dramatic changes in behavior, accompanied by poor school performance in adolescence. Simmons was absent from home for long periods, spending time using alcohol and drugs with other teenagers or young adults. The contention by Simmons' postconviction counsel was that these matters should have been established in the sentencing proceeding. The trial court found no constitutional violation by reason of ineffective assistance of counsel and denied the motion for postconviction relief. . . .

After these proceedings in Simmons' case had run their course, this Court held that the Eighth and Fourteenth Amendments prohibit the execution of a mentally retarded person. Atkins v. Virginia, 536 U.S. 304 (2002). Simmons filed a new petition for state postconviction relief, arguing that the reasoning of *Atkins* established that the Constitution prohibits the execution of a juvenile who was under 18 when the crime was committed. The Missouri Supreme Court agreed. . . . We granted certiorari and now affirm.

II

The Eighth Amendment provides: "Excessive bail shall not be required, nor excessive fines imposed, nor cruel and unusual punishments inflicted." [Our cases] have established the propriety and affirmed the necessity of referring to "the evolving standards of decency that mark the progress of a maturing society" to determine which punishments are so disproportionate as to be cruel and unusual. Trop v. Dulles, 356 U.S. 86, 100-101 (1958) (plurality opinion).

In Thompson v. Oklahoma, 487 U.S. 815 (1988), a plurality of the Court determined that our standards of decency do not permit the execution of any offender under the age of 16 at the time of the crime. The plurality opinion explained that no death penalty State that had given express consideration to a minimum age for the death penalty had set the age lower than 16. The plurality also observed that "[t]he conclusion that it would offend civilized standards of decency to execute a person who was less than 16 years old at the time of his or her offense is consistent with the views that have been expressed by respected professional organizations, by other nations that share our Anglo-American heritage, and by the leading members of the Western European community." The opinion further noted that juries imposed the death penalty on offenders under 16 with exceeding rarity; the last execution of an offender for a crime committed under the age of 16 had been carried out in 1948, 40 years prior.

Bringing its independent judgment to bear on the permissibility of the death penalty for a 15-year-old offender, the *Thompson* plurality stressed that "[t]he reasons why juveniles are not trusted with the privileges and responsibilities of an adult also explain why their irresponsible conduct is not as morally reprehensible as that of an adult." According to the plurality, the lesser culpability of offenders under 16 made the death penalty inappropriate as a form of retribution, while the low likelihood that offenders under 16 engaged in "the kind of cost-benefit analysis that attaches any weight to the possibility of execution" made the death penalty ineffective as a means of deterrence. . . .

The next year, in Stanford v. Kentucky, 492 U.S. 361 (1989), the Court, over a dissenting opinion joined by four Justices, referred to contemporary standards of decency in this country and concluded the Eighth and Fourteenth Amendments did not proscribe the execution of juvenile offenders over 15 but under 18. The Court noted that 22 of the 37 death penalty States permitted the death penalty for 16-year-old offenders, and, among these 37 States, 25 permitted it for 17-year-old offenders. These numbers, in the Court's view, indicated there was no national consensus "sufficient to label a particular punishment cruel and unusual." . . .

The same day the Court decided *Stanford,* it held that the Eighth Amendment did not mandate a categorical exemption from the death penalty for the mentally retarded. Penry v. Lynaugh, 492 U.S. 302 (1989). In reaching this conclusion it stressed that only two States had enacted laws banning the imposition of the death penalty on a mentally retarded person convicted of a capital offense. According to the Court, "the two state statutes prohibiting execution of the mentally retarded, even when added to the 14 States that have rejected capital punishment completely, [did] not provide sufficient evidence at present of a national consensus."

Three Terms ago the subject was reconsidered in *Atkins.* We held that standards of decency have evolved since *Penry* and now demonstrate that the execution of the mentally retarded is cruel and unusual punishment. The Court noted objective indicia of society's standards, as expressed in legislative enactments and state practice with respect to executions of the mentally retarded. When *Atkins* was decided only a minority of States permitted the practice, and even in those States it was rare. On the basis of these indicia the Court determined that executing mentally retarded offenders "has become truly unusual, and it is fair to say that a national consensus has developed against it."

The inquiry into our society's evolving standards of decency did not end there. [The] Constitution contemplates that in the end our own judgment will be brought to bear on the question of the acceptability of the death penalty under the Eighth Amendment. Mental retardation, the Court said, diminishes personal culpability even if the offender can distinguish right from wrong. The impairments of mentally retarded offenders make it less defensible to impose the death penalty as retribution for past crimes and less likely that the death penalty will have a real deterrent effect. Based on these considerations and on the finding of national consensus against executing the mentally retarded, the Court ruled that the death penalty constitutes an excessive sanction for the entire category of mentally retarded offenders, and that the Eighth Amendment places a substantive restriction on the State's power to take the life of a mentally retarded offender.

Just as the *Atkins* Court reconsidered the issue decided in *Penry*, we now reconsider the issue decided in *Stanford*. The beginning point is a review of objective indicia of consensus, as expressed in particular by the enactments of legislatures that have addressed the question. This data gives us essential instruction. We then must determine, in the exercise of our own independent judgment, whether the death penalty is a disproportionate punishment for juveniles.

III

A

The evidence of national consensus against the death penalty for juveniles is similar, and in some respects parallel, to the evidence *Atkins* held sufficient to demonstrate a national consensus against the death penalty for the mentally retarded. When *Atkins* was decided, 30 States prohibited the death penalty for the mentally retarded. This number comprised 12 that had abandoned the death penalty altogether, and 18 that maintained it but excluded the mentally retarded from its reach. By a similar calculation in this case, 30 States prohibit the juvenile death penalty, comprising 12 that have rejected the death penalty altogether and 18 that maintain it but, by express provision or judicial interpretation, exclude juveniles from its reach. *Atkins* emphasized that even in the 20 States without formal prohibition, the practice of executing the mentally retarded was infrequent. . . . In the present case, too, even in the 20 States without a formal prohibition on executing juveniles, the practice is infrequent. Since *Stanford*, six States have executed prisoners for crimes committed as juveniles. In the past 10 years, only three have done so: Oklahoma, Texas, and Virginia. . . .

There is, to be sure, at least one difference between the evidence of consensus in *Atkins* and in this case. Impressive in *Atkins* was the rate of abolition of the death penalty for the mentally retarded. Sixteen States that permitted the execution of the mentally retarded at the time of *Penry* had prohibited the practice by the time we heard *Atkins*. By contrast, the rate of change in reducing the incidence of the juvenile death penalty, or in taking specific steps to abolish it, has been slower. Five States that allowed the juvenile death penalty at the time of *Stanford* have abandoned it in the intervening 15 years — four through legislative enactments and one through judicial decision.

Though less dramatic than the change from *Penry* to *Atkins* . . . we still consider the change from *Stanford* to this case to be significant. As noted in *Atkins*, with respect to the States that had abandoned the death penalty for the mentally retarded since *Penry*, "it is not so much the number of these States that is significant, but the consistency of the direction of change." . . . The number of States that have abandoned capital punishment for juvenile offenders since *Stanford* is smaller than the number of States that abandoned capital punishment for the mentally retarded after *Penry*; yet we think the same consistency of direction of change has been demonstrated. Since *Stanford*, no State that previously prohibited capital punishment for juveniles has reinstated it. This fact, coupled with the trend toward abolition of the juvenile death penalty, carries special force in light of the general popularity of anticrime legislation, and in light of the particular trend in recent years toward cracking down on juvenile crime in other respects. Any difference between this case and *Atkins* with respect to the pace of abolition is thus counterbalanced by the consistent direction of the change.

The slower pace of abolition of the juvenile death penalty over the past 15 years, moreover, may have a simple explanation. When we heard *Penry*, only two death penalty States had already prohibited the execution of the mentally retarded. When we heard *Stanford*, by contrast, 12 death penalty States had already prohibited the execution of any juvenile under 18, and 15 had prohibited the execution of any juvenile under 17. If anything, this shows that the impropriety of executing juveniles between 16 and 18 years of age gained wide recognition earlier than the impropriety of executing the mentally retarded. . . .

Petitioner cannot show national consensus in favor of capital punishment for juveniles but still resists the conclusion that any consensus exists against it. Petitioner supports this position with, in particular, the observation that when the Senate ratified the International Covenant on Civil and Political Rights (ICCPR), Dec. 19, 1966, 999 U.N.T.S. 171 (entered into force Mar. 23, 1976), it did so subject to the President's proposed reservation regarding Article 6(5) of that treaty, which prohibits capital punishment for juveniles. This reservation at best provides only faint support for petitioner's argument. First, the reservation was passed in 1992; since then, five States have abandoned capital punishment for juveniles. Second, Congress considered the issue when enacting the Federal Death Penalty Act in 1994, and determined that the death penalty should not extend to juveniles. The reservation to Article 6(5) of the ICCPR provides minimal evidence that there is not now a national consensus against juvenile executions. . . .

B

. . . There are a number of crimes that beyond question are severe in absolute terms, yet the death penalty may not be imposed for their commission. Coker v. Georgia, 433 U.S. 584 (1977) (rape of an adult woman); Enmund v. Florida, 458 U.S. 782 (1982) (felony murder where defendant did not kill, attempt to kill, or intend to kill). The death penalty may not be imposed on certain classes of offenders, such as juveniles under 16, the insane, and the mentally retarded, no matter how heinous the crime. These rules vindicate the underlying principle that the death penalty is reserved for a narrow category of crimes and offenders.

Three general differences between juveniles under 18 and adults demonstrate that juvenile offenders cannot with reliability be classified among the worst offenders. First, as any parent knows and as the scientific and sociological studies respondent and his amici cite tend to confirm, a lack of maturity and an underdeveloped sense of responsibility are found in youth more often than in adults and are more understandable among the young. These qualities often result in impetuous and ill-considered actions and decisions. . . . In recognition of the comparative immaturity and irresponsibility of juveniles, almost every State prohibits those under 18 years of age from voting, serving on juries, or marrying without parental consent.

The second area of difference is that juveniles are more vulnerable or susceptible to negative influences and outside pressures, including peer pressure. This is explained in part by the prevailing circumstance that juveniles have less control, or less experience with control, over their own environment. The third broad difference is that the character of a juvenile is not as well formed as that of an adult. The personality traits of juveniles are more transitory, less fixed. . . .

From a moral standpoint it would be misguided to equate the failings of a minor with those of an adult, for a greater possibility exists that a minor's character deficiencies will be reformed. Indeed, the relevance of youth as a mitigating factor derives from the fact that the signature qualities of youth are transient; as individuals mature, the impetuousness and recklessness that may dominate in younger years can subside. . . .

Once the diminished culpability of juveniles is recognized, it is evident that the penological justifications for the death penalty apply to them with lesser force than to adults. We have held there are two distinct social purposes served by the death penalty: retribution and deterrence of capital crimes by prospective offenders. . . . Whether viewed as an attempt to express the community's moral outrage or as an attempt to right the balance for the wrong to the victim, the case for retribution is not as strong with a minor as with an adult. Retribution is not proportional if the law's most severe penalty is imposed on one whose culpability or blameworthiness is diminished, to a substantial degree, by reason of youth and immaturity.

As for deterrence, it is unclear whether the death penalty has a significant or even measurable deterrent effect on juveniles, as counsel for the petitioner acknowledged at oral argument. In general we leave to legislatures the assessment of the efficacy of various criminal penalty schemes. Here, however, the absence of evidence of deterrent effect is of special concern because the same characteristics that render juveniles less culpable than adults suggest as well that juveniles will be less susceptible to deterrence. In particular, as the plurality observed in *Thompson*, the likelihood that the teenage offender "has made the kind of cost-benefit analysis that attaches any weight to the possibility of execution is so remote as to be virtually nonexistent."

[Petitioner and his amici] assert that even assuming the truth of the observations we have made about juveniles' diminished culpability in general, jurors nonetheless should be allowed to consider mitigating arguments related to youth on a case-by-case basis, and in some cases to impose the death penalty if justified. . . . Given this Court's own insistence on individualized consideration, petitioner maintains that it is both arbitrary and unnecessary to adopt a categorical rule barring imposition of the death penalty on any offender under 18 years of age.

We disagree. The differences between juvenile and adult offenders are too marked and well understood to risk allowing a youthful person to receive the death penalty despite insufficient culpability. An unacceptable likelihood exists that the brutality or cold-blooded nature of any particular crime would overpower mitigating arguments based on youth as a matter of course, even where the juvenile offender's objective immaturity, vulnerability, and lack of true depravity should require a sentence less severe than death. In some cases a defendant's youth may even be counted against him. In this very case, as we noted above, the prosecutor argued Simmons' youth was aggravating rather than mitigating. . . .

It is difficult even for expert psychologists to differentiate between the juvenile offender whose crime reflects unfortunate yet transient immaturity, and the rare juvenile offender whose crime reflects irreparable corruption. As we understand it, this difficulty underlies the rule forbidding psychiatrists from diagnosing any patient under 18 as having antisocial personality disorder, a disorder also referred to as psychopathy or sociopathy, and which is characterized by callousness, cynicism, and contempt for the feelings, rights, and suffering of others. If trained psychiatrists with the advantage of clinical testing and observation refrain, despite diagnostic expertise, from assessing any juvenile under 18 as having antisocial personality disorder, we conclude that States should refrain from asking jurors to issue a far graver condemnation — that a juvenile offender merits the death penalty. . . .

Drawing the line at 18 years of age is subject, of course, to the objections always raised against categorical rules. The qualities that distinguish juveniles from adults do not disappear when an individual turns 18. By the same token, some under 18 have already attained a level of maturity some adults will never reach. For the reasons we have discussed, however, a line must be drawn. . . . The age of 18 is the point where society draws the line for many purposes between childhood and adulthood. It is, we conclude, the age at which the line for death eligibility ought to rest. . . .

IV

Our determination that the death penalty is disproportionate punishment for offenders under 18 finds confirmation in the stark reality that the United States is the only country in the world that continues to give official sanction to the juvenile death penalty. This reality does not become controlling, for the task of interpreting the Eighth Amendment remains our responsibility. Yet at least from the time of the Court's decision in Trop v. Dulles, the Court has referred to the laws of other countries and to international authorities as instructive for its interpretation of the Eighth Amendment's prohibition of "cruel and unusual punishments." 356 U.S., at 102-103 (plurality opinion) ("The civilized nations of the world are in virtual unanimity that statelessness is not to be imposed as punishment for crime").

As respondent and a number of amici emphasize, Article 37 of the United Nations Convention on the Rights of the Child, which every country in the world has ratified save for the United States and Somalia, contains an express prohibition on capital punishment for crimes committed by juveniles under 18. No ratifying country has entered a reservation to the provision prohibiting the execution of juvenile offenders. Parallel prohibitions are contained in other significant international covenants. See ICCPR, Art. 6(5), 999 U.N.T.S., at 175 (prohibiting capital punishment for anyone under 18 at the time of offense) (signed and ratified by the United States subject to a reservation regarding Article 6(5)); American Convention on Human Rights: Pact of San Jose, Costa Rica, Art. 4(5), Nov. 22, 1969, 1144 U.N.T.S. 146 (entered into force July 19, 1978); African Charter on the Rights and Welfare of the Child, Art. 5(3), OAU Doc. CAB/LEG/24.9/49 (1990) (entered into force Nov. 29, 1999).

Respondent and his amici have submitted, and petitioner does not contest, that only seven countries other than the United States have executed juvenile offenders since 1990: Iran, Pakistan, Saudi Arabia, Yemen, Nigeria, the Democratic Republic of Congo, and China. Since then each of these countries has either abolished capital punishment for juveniles or made public disavowal of the practice. In sum, it is fair to say that the United States now stands alone in a world that has turned its face against the juvenile death penalty. . . . The opinion of the world community, while not controlling our outcome, does provide respected and significant confirmation for our own conclusions. . . .

It does not lessen our fidelity to the Constitution or our pride in its origins to acknowledge that the express affirmation of certain fundamental rights by other nations and peoples simply underscores the centrality of those same rights within our own heritage of freedom. . . .

O'CONNOR, J., dissenting.

[The] rule decreed by the Court rests, ultimately, on its independent moral judgment that death is a disproportionately severe punishment for any 17-year-old offender. I do not subscribe to this judgment. Adolescents as a class are undoubtedly less mature, and therefore less culpable for their misconduct, than adults. But the Court has adduced no evidence impeaching the seemingly reasonable conclusion reached by many state legislatures: that at least some 17-year-old murderers are sufficiently mature to deserve the death penalty in an appropriate case. Nor has it been shown that capital sentencing juries are incapable of accurately assessing a youthful defendant's maturity or of giving due weight to the mitigating characteristics associated with youth.

On this record — and especially in light of the fact that so little has changed since our recent decision in *Stanford*—I would not substitute our judgment about the moral propriety of capital punishment for 17-year-old murderers for the judgments of the Nation's legislatures. . . .

II

. . . . In determining whether the juvenile death penalty comports with contemporary standards of decency, our inquiry begins with the clearest and most reliable objective evidence of contemporary values — the actions

of the Nation's legislatures. As the Court emphasizes, the overall number of
jurisdictions that currently disallow the execution of under-18 offenders is
the same as the number that forbade the execution of mentally retarded
offenders when *Atkins* was decided. At present, 12 States and the District of
Columbia do not have the death penalty, while an additional 18 States and
the Federal Government authorize capital punishment but prohibit the execution of under-18 offenders. And here, as in *Atkins*, only a very small fraction
of the States that permit capital punishment of offenders within the relevant
class has actually carried out such an execution in recent history: Six States
have executed under-18 offenders in the 16 years since *Stanford*, while five
States had executed mentally retarded offenders in the 13 years prior to
Atkins.

    While the similarities between the two cases are undeniable, the objective
evidence of national consensus is marginally weaker here. Most importantly, in
Atkins there was significant evidence of opposition to the execution of the mentally retarded, but there was virtually no countervailing evidence of affirmative
legislative support for this practice. The States that permitted such executions
did so only because they had not enacted any prohibitory legislation. Here, by
contrast, at least eight States have current statutes that specifically set 16 or 17 as
the minimum age at which commission of a capital crime can expose the offender to the death penalty. Five of these eight States presently have one or more
juvenile offenders on death row (six if respondent is included in the count), and
four of them have executed at least one under-18 offender in the past 15 years.
In all, there are currently over 70 juvenile offenders on death row in 12 different
States (13 including respondent). This evidence suggests some measure of
continuing public support for the availability of the death penalty for 17-year-
old capital murderers.

    Moreover, the Court in *Atkins* made clear that it was not so much the
number of States forbidding execution of the mentally retarded that was significant, but the consistency of the direction of change. In contrast to the trend in
Atkins, the States have not moved uniformly towards abolishing the juvenile
death penalty. Instead, since our decision in *Stanford*, two States have expressly
reaffirmed their support for this practice by enacting statutes setting 16 as the
minimum age for capital punishment. See Mo. Rev. Stat. §565.020.2 (2000); Va.
Code Ann. §18.2-10(a) (Lexis 2004). Furthermore, . . . the pace of legislative
action in this context has been considerably slower than it was with regard to
capital punishment of the mentally retarded. In the 13 years between our decisions in *Penry* and *Atkins*, no fewer than 16 States banned the execution of
mentally retarded offenders. By comparison, since our decision 16 years ago
in *Stanford*, only four States that previously permitted the execution of under-18
offenders, plus the Federal Government, have legislatively reversed course.
[The] extraordinary wave of legislative action leading up to our decision in
Atkins provided strong evidence that the country truly had set itself against
capital punishment of the mentally retarded. Here, by contrast, the halting
pace of change gives reason for pause.

    [The] compelling moral proportionality argument against capital punish-
ment of mentally retarded offenders played a decisive role in persuading the
Court that the practice was inconsistent with the Eighth Amendment. Indeed,
the force of the proportionality argument in *Atkins* significantly bolstered the

Court's confidence that the objective evidence in that case did, in fact, herald the emergence of a genuine national consensus. Here, by contrast, the proportionality argument against the juvenile death penalty is so flawed that it can be given little, if any, analytical weight—it proves too weak to resolve the lingering ambiguities in the objective evidence of legislative consensus or to justify the Court's categorical rule. . . .

First, the Court adduces no evidence whatsoever in support of its sweeping conclusion that it is only in "rare" cases, if ever, that 17-year-old murderers are sufficiently mature and act with sufficient depravity to warrant the death penalty. . . . At most, the Court's argument suggests that the average 17-year-old murderer is not as culpable as the average adult murderer. But an especially depraved juvenile offender may nevertheless be just as culpable as many adult offenders considered bad enough to deserve the death penalty. Similarly, the fact that the availability of the death penalty may be less likely to deter a juvenile from committing a capital crime does not imply that this threat cannot effectively deter some 17-year-olds from such an act. Surely there is an age below which no offender, no matter what his crime, can be deemed to have the cognitive or emotional maturity necessary to warrant the death penalty. But at least at the margins between adolescence and adulthood— and especially for 17-year-olds such as respondent—the relevant differences between "adults" and "juveniles" appear to be a matter of degree, rather than of kind. It follows that a legislature may reasonably conclude that at least some 17-year-olds can act with sufficient moral culpability, and can be sufficiently deterred by the threat of execution, that capital punishment may be warranted in an appropriate case.

Indeed, this appears to be just such a case. Christopher Simmons' murder of Shirley Crook was premeditated, wanton, and cruel in the extreme. Well before he committed this crime, Simmons declared that he wanted to kill someone. . . . Simmons [also] said they could " 'get away with it' " because they were minors. . . . Whatever can be said about the comparative moral culpability of 17-year-olds as a general matter, Simmons' actions unquestionably reflect a consciousness materially more "depraved" than that of the average murderer. And Simmons' prediction that he could murder with impunity because he had not yet turned 18—though inaccurate—suggests that he did take into account the perceived risk of punishment in deciding whether to commit the crime. . . .

For purposes of proportionality analysis, 17-year-olds as a class are qualitatively and materially different from the mentally retarded. . . . [A] mentally retarded offender is one whose demonstrated impairments make it so highly unlikely that he is culpable enough to deserve the death penalty or that he could have been deterred by the threat of death, that execution is not a defensible punishment. There is no such inherent or accurate fit between an offender's chronological age and the personal limitations which the Court believes make capital punishment excessive for 17-year-old murderers. Moreover, it defies common sense to suggest that 17-year-olds as a class are somehow equivalent to mentally retarded persons with regard to culpability or susceptibility to deterrence. Seventeen-year-olds may, on average, be less mature than adults, but that lesser maturity simply cannot be equated with the major, lifelong impairments suffered by the mentally retarded. . . .

The Court argues that sentencing juries cannot accurately evaluate a youthful offender's maturity or give appropriate weight to the mitigating characteristics related to youth. But, again, the Court presents no real evidence—and the record appears to contain none supporting this claim. Perhaps more importantly, the Court fails to explain why this duty should be so different from, or so much more difficult than, that of assessing and giving proper effect to any other qualitative capital sentencing factor. I would not be so quick to conclude that the constitutional safeguards, the sentencing juries, and the trial judges upon which we place so much reliance in all capital cases are inadequate in this narrow context. . . .

Reasonable minds can differ as to the minimum age at which commission of a serious crime should expose the defendant to the death penalty, if at all. . . . Indeed, were my office that of a legislator, rather than a judge, then I, too, would be inclined to support legislation setting a minimum age of 18 in this context. But a significant number of States, including Missouri, have decided to make the death penalty potentially available for 17-year-old capital murderers such as respondent. Without a clearer showing that a genuine national consensus forbids the execution of such offenders, this Court should not substitute its own "inevitably subjective judgment" on how best to resolve this difficult moral question for the judgments of the Nation's democratically elected legislatures. I respectfully dissent.

SCALIA, J., dissenting.

In urging approval of a constitution that gave life-tenured judges the power to nullify laws enacted by the people's representatives, Alexander Hamilton assured the citizens of New York that there was little risk in this, since the judiciary has "neither FORCE nor WILL but merely judgment." The Federalist No. 78, p. 465 (C. Rossiter ed. 1961). But Hamilton had in mind a traditional judiciary, "bound down by strict rules and precedents which serve to define and point out their duty in every particular case that comes before them." Bound down, indeed. What a mockery today's opinion makes of Hamilton's expectation, announcing the Court's conclusion that the meaning of our Constitution has changed over the past 15 years—not, mind you, that this Court's decision 15 years ago was wrong, but that the Constitution has changed. The Court reaches this implausible result by purporting to advert, not to the original meaning of the Eighth Amendment, but to "the evolving standards of decency" of our national society. It then finds, on the flimsiest of grounds, that a national consensus which could not be perceived in our people's laws barely 15 years ago now solidly exists. Worse still, the Court says in so many words that what our people's laws say about the issue does not, in the last analysis, matter: "In the end our own judgment will be brought to bear on the question of the acceptability of the death penalty under the Eighth Amendment." The Court thus proclaims itself sole arbiter of our Nation's moral standards—and in the course of discharging that awesome responsibility purports to take guidance from the views of foreign courts and legislatures. Because I do not believe that the meaning of our Eighth Amendment, any more than the meaning of other provisions of our Constitution, should be determined by the subjective views of five Members of this Court and like-minded foreigners, I dissent.

I

[The Court] claims halfheartedly that a national consensus has emerged since our decision in *Stanford*, because 18 States — or 47% of States that permit capital punishment — now have legislation prohibiting the execution of offenders under 18, and because all of four States have adopted such legislation since *Stanford*. Words have no meaning if the views of less than 50% of death penalty States can constitute a national consensus. Our previous cases have required overwhelming opposition to a challenged practice, generally over a long period of time. . . . In Enmund v. Florida, 458 U.S. 782, 792 (1982), we invalidated capital punishment imposed for participation in a robbery in which an accomplice committed murder, because 78% of all death penalty States prohibited this punishment. . . . By contrast, agreement among 42% of death penalty States in *Stanford*, which the Court appears to believe was correctly decided at the time, was insufficient to show a national consensus. . . .

None of our cases dealing with an alleged constitutional limitation upon the death penalty has counted, as States supporting a consensus in favor of that limitation, States that have eliminated the death penalty entirely. And with good reason. Consulting States that bar the death penalty concerning the necessity of making an exception to the penalty for offenders under 18 is rather like including old-order Amishmen in a consumer-preference poll on the electric car. Of course they don't like it, but that sheds no light whatever on the point at issue. That 12 States favor no executions says something about consensus against the death penalty, but nothing — absolutely nothing — about consensus that offenders under 18 deserve special immunity from such a penalty. In repealing the death penalty, those 12 States considered none of the factors that the Court puts forth as determinative of the issue before us today — lower culpability of the young, inherent recklessness, lack of capacity for considered judgment, etc. What might be relevant, perhaps, is how many of those States permit 16- and 17-year-old offenders to be treated as adults with respect to noncapital offenses. (They all do; indeed, some even require that juveniles as young as 14 be tried as adults if they are charged with murder.) The attempt by the Court to turn its remarkable minority consensus into a faux majority by counting Amishmen is an act of nomological desperation.

. . . Now, the Court says a legislative change in four States is "significant" enough to trigger a constitutional prohibition. It is amazing to think that this subtle shift in numbers can take the issue entirely off the table for legislative debate. I also doubt whether many of the legislators who voted to change the laws in those four States would have done so if they had known their decision would (by the pronouncement of this Court) be rendered irreversible. After all, legislative support for capital punishment, in any form, has surged and ebbed throughout our Nation's history. . . .

Relying on such narrow margins is especially inappropriate in light of the fact that a number of legislatures and voters have expressly affirmed their support for capital punishment of 16- and 17-year-old offenders since *Stanford*. Though the Court is correct that no State has lowered its death penalty age, both the Missouri and Virginia Legislatures — which, at the time of *Stanford*, had no minimum age requirement — expressly established 16 as the minimum. Mo. Rev. Stat. §565.020.2 (2000); Va. Code Ann. §18.2-10(a) (Lexis 2004).

The people of Arizona and Florida have done the same by ballot initiative. Thus, even States that have not executed an under-18 offender in recent years unquestionably favor the possibility of capital punishment in some circumstances.

The Court's reliance on the infrequency of executions for under-18 murderers credits an argument that this Court considered and explicitly rejected in *Stanford.* That infrequency is explained . . . . both by the undisputed fact that a far smaller percentage of capital crimes are committed by persons under 18 than over 18, and by the fact that juries are required at sentencing to consider the offender's youth as a mitigating factor. . . . It is, furthermore, unclear that executions of the relevant age group have decreased since we decided *Stanford.* Between 1990 and 2003, 123 of 3,599 death sentences, or 3.4%, were given to individuals who committed crimes before reaching age 18. By contrast, only 2.1% of those sentenced to death between 1982 and 1988 committed the crimes when they were under 18. As for actual executions of under-18 offenders, they constituted 2.4% of the total executions since 1973. In *Stanford,* we noted that only 2% of the executions between 1642 and 1986 were of under-18 offenders and found that that lower number did not demonstrate a national consensus against the penalty. Thus, the numbers of under-18 offenders subjected to the death penalty, though low compared with adults, have either held steady or slightly increased since *Stanford.* These statistics in no way support the action the Court takes today.

II

Of course, the real force driving today's decision is not the actions of four state legislatures, but the Court's own judgment that murderers younger than 18 can never be as morally culpable as older counterparts. . . . If the Eighth Amendment set forth an ordinary rule of law, it would indeed be the role of this Court to say what the law is. But the Court having pronounced that the Eighth Amendment is an ever-changing reflection of "the evolving standards of decency" of our society, it makes no sense for the Justices then to prescribe those standards rather than discern them from the practices of our people. On the evolving-standards hypothesis, the only legitimate function of this Court is to identify a moral consensus of the American people. By what conceivable warrant can nine lawyers presume to be the authoritative conscience of the Nation? . . .

Today's opinion provides a perfect example of why judges are ill equipped to make the type of legislative judgments the Court insists on making here. To support its opinion that States should be prohibited from imposing the death penalty on anyone who committed murder before age 18, the Court looks to scientific and sociological studies, picking and choosing those that support its position. It never explains why those particular studies are methodologically sound; none was ever entered into evidence or tested in an adversarial proceeding. . . .

We need not look far to find studies contradicting the Court's conclusions. As petitioner points out, the American Psychological Association (APA), which claims in this case that scientific evidence shows persons under 18 lack the ability to take moral responsibility for their decisions, has previously taken precisely the opposite position before this very Court. In its brief in

Hodgson v. Minnesota, 497 U.S. 417 (1990), the APA found a "rich body of research" showing that juveniles are mature enough to decide whether to obtain an abortion without parental involvement. . . . Given the nuances of scientific methodology and conflicting views, courts — which can only consider the limited evidence on the record before them — are ill equipped to determine which view of science is the right one. Legislatures are better qualified to weigh and evaluate the results of statistical studies in terms of their own local conditions and with a flexibility of approach that is not available to the courts.

Even putting aside questions of methodology, the studies cited by the Court offer scant support for a categorical prohibition of the death penalty for murderers under 18. At most, these studies conclude that, on average, or in most cases, persons under 18 are unable to take moral responsibility for their actions. Not one of the cited studies opines that all individuals under 18 are unable to appreciate the nature of their crimes. Moreover, the cited studies describe only adolescents who engage in risky or antisocial behavior, as many young people do. Murder, however, is more than just risky or antisocial behavior. It is entirely consistent to believe that young people often act impetuously and lack judgment, but, at the same time, to believe that those who commit premeditated murder are — at least sometimes — just as culpable as adults. [The] studies the Court cites in no way justify a constitutional imperative that prevents legislatures and juries from treating exceptional cases in an exceptional way — by determining that some murders are not just the acts of happy-go-lucky teenagers, but heinous crimes deserving of death.

That "almost every State prohibits those under 18 years of age from voting, serving on juries, or marrying without parental consent," is patently irrelevant. [It is] absurd to think that one must be mature enough to drive carefully, to drink responsibly, or to vote intelligently, in order to be mature enough to understand that murdering another human being is profoundly wrong, and to conform one's conduct to that most minimal of all civilized standards. Serving on a jury or entering into marriage also involve decisions far more sophisticated than the simple decision not to take another's life.

Moreover, the age statutes the Court lists "set the appropriate ages for the operation of a system that makes its determinations in gross, and that does not conduct individualized maturity tests." The criminal justice system, by contrast, provides for individualized consideration of each defendant. In capital cases, this Court requires the sentencer to make an individualized determination, which includes weighing aggravating factors and mitigating factors, such as youth. In other contexts where individualized consideration is provided, we have recognized that at least some minors will be mature enough to make difficult decisions that involve moral considerations. For instance, we have struck down abortion statutes that do not allow minors deemed mature by courts to bypass parental notification provisions. It is hard to see why this context should be any different. Whether to obtain an abortion is surely a much more complex decision for a young person than whether to kill an innocent person in cold blood.

The Court concludes, however, that juries cannot be trusted with the delicate task of weighing a defendant's youth along with the other mitigating and aggravating factors of his crime. This startling conclusion undermines the very foundations of our capital sentencing system, which entrusts juries with making the difficult and uniquely human judgments that defy codification and that build discretion, equity, and flexibility into a legal system. The Court says that juries will be unable to appreciate the significance of a defendant's youth when faced with details of a brutal crime. This assertion is based on no evidence; to the contrary, the Court itself acknowledges that the execution of under-18 offenders is "infrequent" even in the States "without a formal prohibition on executing juveniles," suggesting that juries take seriously their responsibility to weigh youth as a mitigating factor.

Nor does the Court suggest a stopping point for its reasoning. If juries cannot make appropriate determinations in cases involving murderers under 18, in what other kinds of cases will the Court find jurors deficient? We have already held that no jury may consider whether a mentally deficient defendant can receive the death penalty, irrespective of his crime. Why not take other mitigating factors, such as considerations of childhood abuse or poverty, away from juries as well? . . .

The Court's contention that the goals of retribution and deterrence are not served by executing murderers under 18 is also transparently false. The argument that "retribution is not proportional if the law's most severe penalty is imposed on one whose culpability or blameworthiness is diminished" is simply an extension of the earlier, false generalization that youth always defeats culpability. The Court claims that "juveniles will be less susceptible to deterrence" [but the] facts of this very case show the proposition to be false. Before committing the crime, Simmons encouraged his friends to join him by assuring them that they could "get away with it" because they were minors. . . .

III

Though the views of our own citizens are essentially irrelevant to the Court's decision today, the views of other countries and the so-called international community take center stage. [The United States never ratified Article 37 of the United Nations Convention on the Rights of the Child, which prohibits capital punishment for crimes committed by juveniles under 18. The Senate ratified the International Covenant on Civil and Political Rights (ICCPR), subject to a reservation that reserves the right for the United States to impose capital punishment on persons less than 18 years of age.]

Unless the Court has added to its arsenal the power to join and ratify treaties on behalf of the United States, I cannot see how this evidence favors, rather than refutes, its position. That the Senate and the President—those actors our Constitution empowers to enter into treaties, see Art. II, §2— have declined to join and ratify treaties prohibiting execution of under-18 offenders can only suggest that our country has either not reached a national consensus on the question, or has reached a consensus contrary to what the Court announces. That the reservation to the ICCPR was made in 1992 does not suggest otherwise, since the reservation still remains in place today. It is also worth noting that, in addition to barring the execution of under-18 offenders, the United Nations Convention on the Rights of the Child prohibits punishing them with life in prison without the possibility of release. If we are truly going to get in line with the international community, then the Court's reassurance that the death penalty is really not needed, since "the punishment of life imprisonment without the possibility of parole is itself a severe sanction," gives little comfort.

[The Court does not] inquire into how many of the countries that have the death penalty, but have forsworn (on paper at least) imposing that penalty on offenders under 18, have what no State of this country can constitutionally have: a mandatory death penalty for certain crimes, with no possibility of mitigation by the sentencing authority, for youth or any other reason. I suspect it is most of them. To forbid the death penalty for juveniles under such a system may be a good idea, but it says nothing about our system, in which the sentencing authority, typically a jury, always can, and almost always does, withhold the death penalty from an under-18 offender except, after considering all the circumstances, in the rare cases where it is warranted. The foreign authorities, in other words, do not even speak to the issue before us here.

More fundamentally, however, the basic premise of the Court's argument—that American law should conform to the laws of the rest of the world—ought to be rejected out of hand. In fact the Court itself does not believe it. In many significant respects the laws of most other countries differ from our law—including not only such explicit provisions of our Constitution as the right to jury trial and grand jury indictment, but even many interpretations of the Constitution prescribed by this Court itself. The Court-pronounced exclusionary rule, for example, is distinctively American. . . .

Most other countries—including those committed to religious neutrality—do not insist on the degree of separation between church and state that this Court requires. . . . And let us not forget the Court's abortion jurisprudence, which makes us one of only six countries that allow abortion on demand until the point of viability. The Court should either profess its willingness to reconsider all these matters in light of the views of foreigners, or else it should cease putting forth foreigners' views as part of the reasoned basis of its decisions. To invoke alien law when it agrees with one's own thinking, and ignore it otherwise, is not reasoned decisionmaking, but sophistry. . . .

IV

. . . . In a system based upon constitutional and statutory text democratically adopted, the concept of "law" ordinarily signifies that particular words have a fixed meaning. Such law does not change, and this Court's pronouncement of it therefore remains authoritative until (confessing our prior error) we overrule. The Court has purported to make of the Eighth Amendment, however, a mirror of the passing and changing sentiment of American society regarding penology. The lower courts can look into that mirror as well as we can; and what we saw 15 years ago bears no necessary relationship to what they see today. Since they are not looking at the same text, but at a different scene, why should our earlier decision control their judgment? . . .

Allowing lower courts to reinterpret the Eighth Amendment whenever they decide enough time has passed for a new snapshot leaves this Court's decisions without any force—especially since the "evolution" of our Eighth

Amendment is no longer determined by objective criteria. To allow lower courts to behave as we do, "updating" the Eighth Amendment as needed, destroys stability and makes our case law an unreliable basis for the designing of laws by citizens and their representatives, and for action by public officials. The result will be to crown arbitrariness with chaos.

NOTES

1. *Treatment of immutable characteristics: majority position.* Driven by constitutional concerns and also policy considerations, every jurisdiction has either expressly or implicitly adopted the ABA's recommendation to bar the consideration at sentencing of factors such as race, gender, religion, and national origin. But as Chapter 9 details, many sentencing practices have a disproportionate impact on these groups despite the formal legal rules.

Statutory and guideline provisions take different approaches when it comes to certain other immutable personal factors such as mental condition, physical disability, and age. See, e.g., U.S. Sentencing Guidelines Manual §§5H1.1, 5H1.3, 5H1.4 (deeming age, mental condition, and physical condition "not ordinarily relevant" at federal sentencing); N.C. Gen. Stat. §15A-1340.16(e)(3), (4) (providing that defendant's "mental or physical condition" and defendant's "age, immaturity, or limited mental capacity" can serve as the basis for a mitigated sentence).

2. *Age as mitigating (aggravating?) factor.* Under common law rules and throughout modern times, very young children have generally been exempted from all criminal responsibility. And because of the view that even older children are less responsible for their actions and have more potential to be redeemed even after doing wrong, every jurisdiction has special courts and legal rules for juvenile offenders. Because the punishments imposed under these special rules tend to be less severe than those imposed under the rules for adults, age serves as a mitigating factor at sentencing for young offenders who are eligible for specialized juvenile systems. Jurisdictions vary considerably in defining the exact age and circumstances when an offender will be handled as a juvenile rather than as an adult.

The Supreme Court's ruling in *Roper* includes much interesting discussion of the "diminished culpability of juveniles" and the "mitigating force of youth," due in part to the "immaturity" and "vulnerability" of juveniles. Is the majority's argumentation persuasive in light of the dissents by Justices O'Connor and Scalia? May it not indicate that the decision whether a 17-year-old is death eligible should either be made by a jury on an individual basis or be left to the legislature?

If the Constitution now demands a categorical bar on the death penalty for crimes committed before age 18 because of some offenders' "immaturity" and "vulnerability" and the general mitigating force of youth, should these same realities and concerns come to bear in at least some noncapital sentencing cases? See United States v. Naylor, 359 F. Supp. 2d 521 (W.D. Va. 2005) (citing *Roper* to justify reduced emphasis at sentencing on prior offenses committed when defendant was a juvenile).

State laws vary concerning the age at which offenders are eligible to be sentenced to life without parole. While most states permit such a sentence even for offenders below the age of 18, in eight states and the District of Columbia the sentence of life without parole is either not available at all or not a sentencing option for those under 18. See Hillary J. Massey, Disposing of Children: The Eighth Amendment and Juvenile Life without Parole after *Roper,* 46 B.C. L. Rev. 1083 (2006). Currently there is a petition pending before the Inter-American Commission on Human Rights asking that the commission declare the imposition of life without parole on juveniles in violation of universal human rights principles.

Once an offender comes within the jurisdiction of the adult criminal justice system, her age rarely serves as a definitive or formal criterion for a reduced sentence. Social science data reveals, however, that recidivism rates for older offenders are much lower than for offenders in their teens and 20s. See, e.g., U.S. Dept. of Justice, Recidivism of Prisoners Released in 1994 (June 2002) (detailing a much lower recidivism rate for older prisoners upon their release). Consequently, a sentencing system or sentencing judge concerned particularly with incapacitation goals might reasonably assign longer sentences to younger offenders and shorter sentences to older offenders. Indeed, anecdotal evidence suggests that in unstructured systems, judges and parole officials do grant a "senior sentencing discount." Structured-sentencing systems, however, have not consistently codified such sentencing discounts based on the offender's age. Compare U.S. Sentencing Guidelines Manual §5H1.1 ("Age (including youth) is not ordinarily relevant in determining whether a sentence should be outside the applicable guideline range [but] may be a reason to impose a sentence below the applicable guideline range when the defendant is elderly and infirm and where a form of punishment such as home confinement might be equally efficient as and less costly than incarceration") with N.C. Gen. Stat. §15A-1340.16(e)(4) (authorizing a mitigated sentence if the "defendant's age [or] immaturity . . . at the time of commission of the offense significantly reduced the defendant's culpability for the offense").

3. *Mental impairments in noncapital sentencing.* The *Roper* Court repeatedly cites its decision in Atkins v. Virginia, 536 U.S. 304 (2002), in which it declared the execution of the mentally retarded unconstitutional. In *Roper* the Court parallels much of the argument it presented in *Atkins.*

If reduced mental capacity in the form of mental retardation justifies a categorical reduction in the available sentence in capital cases, does it likewise justify an automatic sentence reduction in noncapital cases? The Supreme Court's opinion in *Atkins* viewed the decision by many states to exempt mentally retarded persons from the death penalty as "powerful evidence that today our society views mentally retarded offenders as categorically less culpable than the average criminal." Does this suggest that mentally retarded offenders also ought to be exempt from the strictures of mandatory sentencing provisions or guideline sentencing systems altogether? Cf. Mont. Code Ann. §46-18-222(2) (2005) (mandatory minimum sentences do not apply if "the offender's mental capacity at the time of the commission of the offense for which the offender is to be sentenced, was significantly impaired, although not so impaired as to constitute a defense to the prosecution"); People v. Watters, 595 N.E.2d 1369 (Ill. App. Ct.

1992) (finding that Illinois law authorized sentencing below an applicable mandatory minimum imprisonment term based on a defendant's mental retardation).

At common law those with severe mental impairments could be excused from guilt altogether, but offenders with lesser impairments would usually be subject to the same punishments as mentally sound offenders. In more recent times, judges in unstructured-sentencing jurisdictions have had discretion to consider the defendant's mental condition in setting the sentence, while judges in structured-sentencing systems face varying instructions concerning the way mental retardation or mental condition ought to be considered at sentencing. See, e.g., N.C. Gen. Stat. §15A-1340.16(e)(3), (4) (authorizing a mitigated sentence when the defendant "was suffering from a mental . . . condition" or had "limited mental capacity" that "significantly reduced the defendant's culpability for the offense"); Or. Sentencing Guidelines §213-008-0002(1)(a)(C) (providing that a mitigating departure factor can be that the "defendant's mental capacity was diminished").

In the federal system, section 5H1.3 of the federal sentencing guidelines provides that mental and emotional conditions "are not ordinarily relevant in determining whether a sentence should be outside the applicable guideline range [but] may be relevant in determining the conditions of probation or supervised release; e.g., participation in a mental health program." But another federal guidelines provision, section 5K2.13, states that a "sentence below the applicable guideline range may be warranted if the defendant committed the offense while suffering from a significantly reduced mental capacity." While making diminished capacity an "encouraged" basis for a departure, the federal guidelines further state that a court may not depart if "(1) the significantly reduced mental capacity was caused by the voluntary use of drugs or other intoxicants; (2) the facts and circumstances of the defendant's offense indicate a need to protect the public because the offense involved actual violence or a serious threat of violence; or (3) the defendant's criminal history indicates a need to incarcerate the defendant to protect the public." Similarly, the Oregon sentencing guidelines provide that a mitigating departure factor can be that the "defendant's mental capacity was diminished," but this provision expressly excludes "diminished capacity due to voluntary drug or alcohol abuse." Or. Sentencing Guidelines §213-008-0002(1)(a)(C).

4. *Procedures to determine mental retardation in capital cases.* The unique severity of capital punishment explains in large part why many jurisdictions have statutes prohibiting the execution of the mentally retarded, and why *Atkins* drew from these legislative decisions to find in the Eighth Amendment a constitutional ban against applying the death penalty to the mentally retarded. In *Atkins* the Supreme Court did not suggest specific procedures for determining which offenders are mentally retarded and thus exempt from the death penalty. The Court left to individual states "the task of developing appropriate ways to enforce" the rule announced in *Atkins*. If you were a legislator or a sentencing commissioner or a judge in a state that had not previously addressed this issue, what sorts of procedures would you propose? Should it be for a judge or for a jury to decide whether an offender is mentally retarded? Should an

offender have the burden of proving mental retardation by a preponderance of the evidence to avoid execution, or should a prosecutor have to disprove any claim of retardation beyond a reasonable doubt? Should an inquiry about an offender's mental status occur before any indictment on a capital charge, or only after an offender has been convicted of a crime that qualifies for the death penalty? See State v. Jimenez, 908 A.2d 181 (N.J. 2006) (requiring defendant to prove to the jury a claim of mental retardation by a preponderance of the evidence at the close of the guilt phase of the trial); Cal. Pen. Code §1376 (2007) (setting out procedures for mental retardation hearing).

What indicia of mental retardation should suffice to prove its existence? How should standardized intelligence testing be weighed as opposed other evidence? See People v. Superior Court (Vidal), 155 P.3d 259 (Cal. 2007) (trial court may weigh evidence other than standardized intelligence tests more heavily in making a finding on mental retardation); James W. Ellis, Mental Retardation and the Death Penalty: A Guide to State Legislative Issues (2002) (providing suggestions to legislatures for implementing *Atkins*).

Mental retardation may also impact a prisoner's competency to be executed. In Panetti v. Quarterman, 127 S. Ct 2842 (2007), the Court held that a prisoner may not be executed if his mental illness deprives him of the mental capacity to understand that he is being executed as a punishment for a crime. The Court noted that "[g]ross delusions stemming from a severe mental disorder may put an awareness of a link between a crime and its punishment in a context so far removed from reality that the punishment can serve no proper purpose."

5. *Does immutability matter?* Is the immutability of certain personal characteristics a significant consideration in whether that characteristic should play a role at sentencing, or is the only relevant question whether the factor is related to the offender's culpability and future prospects? If immutability is an important and influential consideration, should certain conditions such as drug dependency, treatable mental illness, or socioeconomic class be deemed immutable?

6. *Consideration of foreign laws and practices.* Since foreign nations do not permit the execution of juvenile offenders, at least de jure, *Roper* was closely watched as a litmus test for the Supreme Court's concern with foreign laws and practices,. Some considered *Roper* controversial because the final section of Justice Kennedy's majority opinion includes an extended discussion of foreign laws and practices as part of the Court's justification for its ruling. Much of the debate about the use of non-U.S. legal sources in Supreme Court cases has taken place in the context of sentencing decisions, with Justices Scalia and Thomas forcefully denouncing references to foreign laws and practices as undemocratic. Even though Justice O'Connor dissented in *Roper*, in a part of the opinion not reprinted above, she forcefully defended the Court's reference to foreign and international law since international opinion reflects the values of a civilized society, so important to the development of the Eighth Amendment. For an interesting defense of the usage of international and comparative materials from an originalist perspective, see David C. Gray, Why Justice Scalia Should Be a Constitutional Comparativist . . . Sometimes, 59 Stan. L. Rev. 1249 (2007);

David C. Gray, A Prayer for Constitutional Comparativism in Eighth Amendment Cases, 18 Fed. Sent'g Rep. 234 (2006).

2.   Circumstances Within the Defendant's Control

A criminal conviction holds a defendant responsible for the criminal act; the criminal sentence carries the ideal of responsibility one step further. Sentencing allows the judge to fine-tune the clumsy notions of responsibility, such as those embodied in the insanity defense. A defendant who is guilty, but who is less clearly responsible than some other defendants convicted of similar crimes, will often receive a lesser sentence.

Moreover, the concept of responsibility at sentencing extends to events that happen after the crime. Some defendants take actions after their crime or even after their arrest—such as enrolling in treatment programs or making restitution to victims—to show they are amenable to rehabilitation and will not present a danger in the future. Do sentencing rules and sentencing judges treat these notions of responsibility during the crime and after the crime similarly? Do they react consistently to the various ways that defendants signal their prospects for rehabilitation?

|| *State v. Vickie Keith* ||
|| 995 P.2d 966 (Mont. 2000) ||

NELSON, J.

... On the evening of May 7, 1998, [Vickie] Keith, her boyfriend Dean Yates, and a mutual friend, Richard Wolde, went out to a local tavern to drink and dance. They returned to Keith's apartment around midnight. Keith lay down on a mattress on the living room floor and took a short nap. According to Yates, Keith was very inebriated. When Keith awoke from her nap, she was angry and hostile towards Yates and started saying "crazy sounding things." ... Keith told Yates that she wanted him out of her life and she ordered him to leave. Yates agreed and began gathering his things while Keith went into her bedroom and locked the door.

As Yates and Wolde were leaving the apartment, they heard a gun shot from Keith's bedroom. Yates was attempting to break the lock on the door when they heard a second shot. When they entered the room, they found Keith sitting in a corner holding a .357 caliber handgun. Before they could reach her, Keith fired the gun a third time in the direction of the window. Yates grabbed the gun in an attempt to disarm Keith, but before he could get it away from her, a fourth shot was fired. This shot went through a desk and into a wall that separated Keith's apartment from the apartment next door. In the next apartment, Keith's neighbor, Mary Snyder, awoke to the sounds of gun fire and muffled screams. Snyder called 911 and, while talking to the dispatcher, she heard the fourth shot hit her bedroom wall. When the officers arrived at the scene, they arrested Keith, who proceeded to scream obscenities at the officers.

On May 19, 1998, the State charged Keith by Information with criminal endangerment, a felony. ... The Information also contained notice that Keith could receive an additional sentence for the use of a weapon pursuant to [Mont. Code Ann.] §46-18-221. On August 27, 1998, Keith filed a motion to add her psychiatrist, Dr. Noel Hoell, as a witness. Keith had been undergoing treatment with Dr. Hoell since 1990. . . . In an affidavit in support of the motion, Keith's counsel stated that the combination of stress, a change in Keith's medication, and the consumption of alcohol may have precluded Keith from knowingly committing the crime. Counsel stated that while he did not believe that Keith had a mental disease or defect, "her mental thoughts and processes were impaired." The District Court granted Keith's motion. . . .

At trial, Dr. Hoell testified that Keith had been under a great deal of stress the past year because her daughter had been molested and because of the molestation trial that followed. He explained that Keith was suffering from anxiety and depression and "general emotional turmoil" during this time. Dr. Hoell also testified that Keith was suffering considerable pain and discomfort because, a few months before the shooting incident, Keith had an altercation with someone in which her neck and shoulder were injured.

Dr. Hoell further testified that he had prescribed three medications for Keith; Prozac, Doxepin, and Valium. He stated that on the day of the shooting, Keith had contacted him regarding her Valium prescription. She told him that the generic Valium she was taking was not as effective as the brand name and she requested a different medication. Dr. Hoell gave Keith a new prescription. According to Wolde, although he was unsure whether Keith took any of this new medication, he was with Keith when she filled the prescription later that day.

As to the physiological effects of these drugs when taken in conjunction with alcoholic beverages, Dr. Hoell testified that while Prozac does not have any specific interaction with alcohol, alcohol mixed with Doxepin could cause sleepiness and confusion, and the combination of Valium and alcohol could cause sedation, confusion and agitation. Dr. Hoell also testified that he prescribed the Valium for Keith with the understanding that she would refrain from using alcohol. [The] jury found Keith guilty of criminal endangerment. The District Court ordered a presentence investigation report.

[Prior to the sentencing hearing itself, the court declared that it would entertain argument on exceptions to the mandatory minimum sentence. During the hearing, the court heard Keith's claim that her mental capacity was impaired at the time of the offense. In support of this argument, Keith pointed to portions of Dr. Hoell's trial testimony regarding the stress she was under at the time of the crime and that she had taken drugs and alcohol prior to the offense. The court also questioned Keith regarding her claim. Defense counsel argued that the mandatory minimum sentence under the weapon enhancement statute] did not apply here because Keith was under a great deal of stress and she had ingested drugs and alcohol prior to the offense. The court responded that in order to waive the mandatory minimum sentence, there would have to be some evidence that Keith's mental capacity was significantly impaired. The court explained that under §46-18-222(2), it could not give Keith the benefit of any type of voluntarily induced intoxicated or drugged state. The court concluded that there was no evidence of mental impairment in this case sufficient to require waiving the mandatory minimum sentence. The District Court sentenced Keith to 10 years in the Women's State Prison in Billings for the offense of criminal endangerment plus an additional

10 years for the use of a weapon in connection with that offense. The court subsequently suspended 15 years of Keith's sentence. . . .

This Court reviews a criminal sentence only for legality (i.e., whether the sentence is within the parameters provided by the statute). Section 46-18-221 [of the Montana Code Annotated], the weapon enhancement statute, provides that a person who uses a weapon in the commission of an offense "shall, in addition to the punishment provided for the commission of such offense, be sentenced to a term of imprisonment in the state prison of not less than 2 years or more than 10 years, except as provided in 46-18-222." Section 46-18-222(2) provides, in pertinent part,

> Mandatory minimum sentences prescribed by the laws of this state [do not apply if] the offender's mental capacity, at the time of the commission of the offense for which the offender is to be sentenced, was significantly impaired, although not so impaired as to constitute a defense to the prosecution. However, a voluntarily induced intoxicated or drugged condition may not be considered an impairment for the purposes of this subsection.

Keith contends that, at the time of the crime, her mental capacity was impaired due to physical pain, mental anguish, high levels of stress, and the taking of prescription drugs and alcohol. She argues that although her mental state was not so diminished as to support a claim for mental disease or defect under §46-14-312,* her mental condition was "significantly impaired," thus she falls within the exceptions to mandatory minimum sentences as provided for in §46-18-222(2).

While §46-18-222(2) does permit the sentencing court to reject the mandatory minimum sentence if it determines that the defendant's mental capacity was significantly impaired during the commission of the offense, this Court has repeatedly held that this statute does not apply in cases where the maximum sentence or any sentence greater than the mandatory minimum is imposed. State v. Zabawa 928 P.2d 151, 157 (Mont. 1996).

As the State points out, Keith's argument would only have merit if the District Court had intended to sentence Keith to less than the two-year mandatory minimum sentence and was prevented from doing so because it found that the exceptions under §46-18-222 did not apply. In this case, there is no indication that the District Court ever intended to sentence Keith to either the two-year mandatory minimum or to a period of time less than the two-year mandatory minimum, therefore, the exceptions are not applicable in this case.

[Keith's mental] impairment was based in part on the alcohol and drugs she voluntarily consumed. Moreover, as the District Court noted, being under stress is not the same as having your mental capacity significantly impaired. Accordingly, we hold that the District Court did not err in failing to apply the exceptions to mandatory minimum sentences, as set forth in §46-18-222, in this case. . . .

---

* Section 46-14-312(2) provides: "If the court finds that the defendant at the time of the commission of the offense suffered from a mental disease or defect . . . any mandatory minimum sentence prescribed by law for the offense need not apply and the court shall sentence the defendant to be committed to . . . an appropriate correctional or mental health facility for custody, care, and treatment for a definite period of time not to exceed the maximum term of imprisonment that could be imposed [in the absence of the mental disease or defect]." — Eds.

PROBLEM 5-5.   TREATMENT AND TIMING

Review again the facts from State v. Joshua Fowler, reprinted earlier in this chapter. Suppose that Fowler's abuse of alcohol and methamphetamines during the three days before the crime was typical. The day after he committed the crime, Fowler realized that his addictions had become a major problem, and he sought help by enrolling in a treatment program. During the 18 months between the crime and the time he turned himself in to authorities, Fowler made real progress in the program.

You are the judge who must sentence Fowler for first-degree armed robbery. In Washington, the standard sentencing range for the offense is 31 to 41 months, plus a mandatory 60-month firearm enhancement penalty. Fowler asks for an exceptional sentence of 6 months, given that he voluntarily enrolled in a treatment program before his arrest and has nearly completed the program. If the relevant law leaves you with discretion on this question, would you impose a sentence below the standard range based on this factor?

Now suppose that federal authorities charged Fowler with illegal possession of a weapon, and the guidelines produce an adjusted offense level of 9, resulting in a presumptive prison term of 4 to 10 months for somebody with no prior criminal history. As a federal judge, would you depart below the guideline range and grant a probationary sentence based on Fowler's enrollment in the treatment program?

Finally, let us consider the timing of Fowler's decision to undertake treatment. As a sentencing judge, would you still consider Fowler's treatment in setting the criminal sentence if he began his treatment after arrest but before prosecution? After conviction but before sentencing? Would you grant a motion to reconsider the sentence if he began treatment after you imposed the original sentence?

A policy statement in the federal guidelines addresses the last question. Section 5K2.19 provides that "post-sentencing rehabilitative efforts, even if exceptional" are not an appropriate basis for a downward departure when resentencing the defendant for the original offense. But post-sentencing rehabilitation can give corrections authorities reason to shorten the defendant's period of "supervised release" to be served at the end of a prison term. Note also that the federal policy statement does not restrict departures based on extraordinary post-offense rehabilitation that occurs *before* the original sentencing, even if it begins after arrest or after conviction. Appellate courts often view post-offense rehabilitative efforts as part of acceptance of responsibility under §3E1.1. In post-*Booker* cases courts may deem post-offense rehabilitation a §3553(a) factor in sentencing below the otherwise applicable guideline range. See United States v. Clay, 483 F.3d 739 (11th Cir. 2007). Should the federal guidelines discourage or prohibit judges from reducing sentences based on any post-arrest rehabilitation efforts?

PROBLEM 5-6.   RESTITUTION AND REHABILITATION

Cattle rancher William Oligmueller misrepresented the number of cattle he owned in an application for a loan from First State Bank. The bank discovered the fraud when bank officers arrived at the ranch to inspect the collateral. At the time the officers discovered the fraud, Oligmueller owed the bank approximately $894,000 on the loan, which was secured by livestock, feed, and machinery.

Oligmueller began liquidating his assets in September 1997 to initiate repayment to the bank. He tended the crops until harvest, and the livestock until sale, increasing the price that the bank ultimately received through the sales. He often worked 16-hour days. He loaded the hay trucks for the bank. Oligmueller pledged assets not previously pledged to the bank, including his ranch. He turned over to the bank his life insurance policy and his wife's certificate of deposit, and he and his wife sold their home and moved in with their daughter. Oligmueller also took a job with a farm supply company and set up a lawn mower repair business. In addition, he sent to the bank approximately half of his Social Security check each month to pay his debts.

By October 1998, through asset liquidation, Oligmueller had repaid the bank approximately $808,000. The bank also received $28,000 in cash payments directly from Oligmueller. This brought the bank's loss down to approximately $58,000.

A federal grand jury indicted Oligmueller in August 1998 for making false statements to the bank. He pled guilty. You are the district court judge who will preside at the upcoming sentencing hearing.

Under section 2F1.1 of the U.S. Sentencing Guidelines, the amount of loss used to determine a sentence for a fraudulent loan application is the greater of the actual loss to the victim or the intended loss. In determining the amount of actual loss, the application notes to the guidelines say that a sentencing court cannot consider payments made to the bank after the fraud is discovered unless the payments are the result of the sale of pledged assets. Of the $808,000 paid to the bank from the sale of assets, only $65,000 resulted from the sale of pledged assets. The sentencing guidelines also allow either a downward or an upward departure if the amount of loss significantly overstates or understates the risk to the lending institution. See U.S. Sentencing Guidelines Manual §2F1.1, cmt. n.8(b).

Oligmueller argues that his offense level should be reduced based on his "acceptance of responsibility." Commentary to the sentencing guidelines lists "post-offense efforts to rehabilitate" and "voluntary payment of restitution before adjudication of guilt" as two factors that tend to show when a defendant qualifies for a two-level reduction for "acceptance of responsibility." U.S. Sentencing Guidelines Manual §3E1.1, cmt. n.1. Oligmueller also requests a downward departure from the guideline sentence based on his extraordinary efforts at rehabilitation.

As a sentencing judge, how will you calculate the amount of loss (and thus the initial offense level) involved in this fraud? Will you reduce the offense level based on Oligmueller's acceptance of responsibility? Will you grant any further downward departure? How much restitution will you order him to pay? Cf. United States v. Oligmueller, 198 F.3d 669 (8th Cir. 1999). Would you deem Oligmueller's conduct sufficient to lead to a sentence outside the guidelines in light of §3553(a)?

NOTES

1. *Addiction at sentencing.*   The fact that a defendant was extremely intoxicated at the time of the crime can, in some states and for some crimes, lead to

an acquittal because the intoxication may have prevented the defendant from forming a criminal intent. But this argument rarely succeeds as a complete defense to criminal charges. Cf. Montana v. Egelhoff, 518 U.S. 37 (1996) (finding constitutionally permissible Montana's statute barring consideration of intoxication as a defense). Intoxication or addiction at the time of an offense matters more often at the sentencing stage. In unstructured sentencing jurisdictions, the judge usually has discretion (and little direction) concerning how to consider the defendant's addiction in setting the sentence. Does substance abuse share any features with mental impairments such as those considered in the previous section? Should the law insist on the same sentence for two defendants, one whose addiction contributed to the crime and another who faced no substance abuse problems?

In most jurisdictions with more structured sentencing rules, the law instructs a sentencing judge to give limited or no consideration to substance abuse. Under the federal guidelines, section 5H1.4 states that drug or alcohol dependence or abuse "is not a reason for imposing a sentence below the guidelines. Substance abuse is highly correlated to an increased propensity to commit crime." Substance abuse can lead a judge to order treatment during a prison term or a period of supervised release. See U.S. Sentencing Guidelines Manual §5D1.3(d)(4). While the law in Florida at one time provided that addiction was a valid ground for a downward departure, the legislature amended the law in 1997 to remove this basis for a reduced sentence. See 1997 Fla. Laws ch. 97-194, §41, at 3728 (codified at Fla. Stat. Ann. §921.0026(3)); Jones v. State, 813 So. 2d 22 (Fla. 2002) (drug offender probation not precluded by guideline provision, as special statutory scheme applies only to chronic substance abusers who commit specific drug-related crimes). In other jurisdictions, this result has been reached through case law. See, e.g., State v. Gaines, 859 P.2d 36, 42 (Wash. 1993) (holding that "drug addiction and its casual role in an addict's criminal offense may not properly serve as justification for a durational departure from the standard range").

Can an argument be made that sentencing rules should authorize (or even require) judges to treat addiction as an aggravating factor that can (or must) increase a sentence? See Ariz. Stat. §41-1604.15 ("Notwithstanding any law to the contrary, any person who is convicted of a violent crime . . . that is committed while the person is under the influence of marijuana, a dangerous drug or a narcotic drug . . . is not eligible for probation or release on any basis until the entire sentence has been served"; statute passed by voter initiative also providing for nonprison treatment sanctions for drug possession offenses). Alaska law provides that "voluntary alcohol or other drug intoxication or chronic alcoholism or other drug addiction may not be considered an aggravating or mitigating factor." Alaska Stat. §12.55.155(g).

2. *Post-arrest efforts at rehabilitation.*   Defendants with substance abuse problems sometimes enroll themselves in treatment programs before the time of conviction or sentencing. Does this action suggest an effort to manipulate the sentence or a genuine willingness to fix the root problem behind the crime? In the federal courts, it is clear that truly "extraordinary" rehabilitation efforts could create a basis for a downward departure and may now be considered as a possible justification for a sentence outside the guidelines. See United

States v. Clay, 483 F.3d 739 (11th Cir. 2007) (district court's consideration of extraordinary post-offense rehabilitation from drug addiction found reasonable); United States v. Newlon, 212 F.3d 423 (8th Cir. 2000) (departure for drug addiction treatment). A number of state systems also allow drug treatment or even amenability to treatment as a basis for a mitigated sentence. See Md. Sentencing Guidelines §13.2(7) (providing as a reason for a departure an "offender's commitment to substance abuse treatment or other therapeutic program"); Or. Sentencing Guidelines §213-008-0002(I) (providing for a mitigated sentence when "offender is amenable to treatment and an appropriate treatment program is available to which the offender can be admitted within a reasonable period of time; the treatment program is likely to be more effective than the presumptive prison term in reducing the risk of offender recidivism; and the probation sentence will serve community safety interests by promoting offender reformation").

3. *Education and employment.* There is an obvious correlation between employment and crime. A person with a steady job is less likely to commit a crime. Further, education can create skills that make a person easier to employ. Should a sentencing judge consider the defendant's education, vocational skills, and employment record as a basis for choosing a lower sentence? As a sentencing judge, would you find post-arrest *changes* in education or employment status to be more significant than education or employment at the time of the crime?

In the federal system, sections 5H1.2 and 5H1.5 of the sentencing guidelines provide that education, vocational skills, and employment record are "not ordinarily relevant in determining whether a sentence should be outside the applicable guideline range," but they can be relevant in selecting appropriate conditions for probation or community service activities. What reasons could explain the reluctance to consider education, vocational skills, and employment record in the federal system? The consideration of these factors in state systems varies considerably. Compare Minn. Sentencing Guidelines II.D.1 (precluding departures based on "employment factors" or "educational attainment") with Delaware Sentencing Accountability Commission, Benchbook 2006 (providing for an exceptional sentence below the presumptive range if the "offender is gainfully employed and will more than likely lose his/her job if the sentencing standard is imposed") and State v. Murphy, 19 P.3d 80 (Kan. 2001) (while good employment record alone would not justify a departure, it could be a factor combined with others that would allow departure).

4. *Voluntary restitution before sentencing.* Most state systems allow the judge to consider voluntary restitution as a basis for reducing a sentence. See Wash. Code §9.94A.535(1)(b) (mitigating circumstance present if "[b]efore detection, the defendant compensated, or made a good faith effort to compensate, the victim of the criminal conduct for any damage or injury sustained"); Fla. Stat. Ann. §921.0016(4)(h) (authorizing a departure if "[b]efore the identity of the defendant was determined, the victim was substantially compensated"). Is it realistic, as many of these statutes require, to expect an offender to make restitution before his crime is detected? As Problem 5-6 indicates, the federal system allows a judge to consider voluntary restitution in several contexts. What features does voluntary restitution share with post-offense addiction treatment

as a mitigating factor? Does voluntary restitution give more affluent defendants a chance to "buy" a lower sentence?

3. Social Context of the Offender

Even offenders who might be described as loners have a lifetime of social history and interpersonal connections. Should such social contexts play a role in sentencing decision making? Consider what theoretical grounds might support consideration or exclusion of such factors at sentencing.

|| **United States v. Fadya Husein** ||
478 F.3d 318 (6th Cir. 2007)

GILMAN, J.

Fadya Husein pled guilty to federal charges relating to her role in the distribution of 763 pills of ecstasy, a controlled substance. A probation officer calculated her advisory Guidelines range to be between 37 and 46 months in prison. Prior to sentencing, Husein moved the district court to grant a downward departure based on extraordinary family circumstances. Husein alleged that her father was totally incapacitated due to the effects of several strokes that he had recently suffered, and that the round-the-clock care that she provided both to him and to her three younger minor siblings was "irreplaceable." A court-ordered home visit by Husein's probation officer subsequently confirmed these allegations.

Acting pursuant to United States Sentencing Guidelines (U.S.S.G.) §§5H1.6 and 5K2.0, as well as 18 U.S.C. §3553(a), the district court concluded that Husein's family circumstances were in fact extraordinary, and therefore granted her motion for a downward departure. The result was a noncustodial sentence of 3 years' supervised release, which included an initial term of 270 days of home confinement. As a formality, the district court also imposed a one-day term of custodial imprisonment, but Husein was given credit for already having served that time.

The government argues on appeal that certain post-sentencing . . . developments undermine the basis for Husein's sentence and, in the alternative, that even based on the facts in the record alone, the departure granted by the district court was an abuse of discretion and/or unreasonable in light of *Booker*. For the reasons set forth below, we affirm the judgment of the district court.

I. BACKGROUND

A. Factual Background

In August and September of 2004, Fadya Husein participated in two transactions involving the sale of ecstasy near her home in Dearborn, Michigan. She was physically present for both transactions, which took place in or around the cars of the other individuals who were indicted along with her. Husein was neither a buyer nor a seller in either transaction, and she was not the source of the ecstasy pills exchanged. But she did help to arrange the meetings by putting Mohammed Nasser, "the number one Defendant in this case" according to the government, in contact with the other indicted individuals. In her guilty plea, Husein admitted these basic facts.

Husein is 25 years of age and the oldest of five children. She has three brothers and one sister, who were 21, 15, 11, and 17 years of age, respectively, at the time of sentencing. All of the siblings live together in Dearborn, Michigan, with the exception of Husein's eldest brother Fady, who resides in Florida. Husein married Tarek Hussein in 2001, but they separated in 2003 and have had no contact since. She stayed in school through the eleventh grade and is currently pursuing a GED. Husein works as a packager at a factory in Sterling Heights, Michigan. Until her father's death in February of 2006, she and her 46-year-old mother had alternated shifts at the factory to ensure that at all times an adult would be at home to attend to her father.

This appeal principally concerns the healthcare needs of Husein's father, as well as the overall financial condition of the Husein household, at the time of sentencing. The district court provided a thorough summary of the relevant facts during the October 2005 sentencing hearing:

> The Defendant's father suffered a stroke seven years ago, after which various organs began to fail. He was placed on dialysis to treat chronic kidney failure. Mr. Husein also suffers from coronary artery disease, diabetes, hypertension and cardiomyopathy. Several weeks ago he suffered another stroke. He was taken to the hospital on September 14th due to complications from renal failure, dementia and fluid on the brain. These conditions, according to Mr. Weidemeyer's [Husein's probation officer] visit to the family on September 15th, 2005, have left Mr. Husein paralyzed on his right side, unable to use the restroom without assistance, unable to walk, barely able to talk. He is to be fed via a feeding tube attached to his stomach. During the home visit, Mr. Weidemeyer observed Mr. Husein's bedroom which contained a hospital bed, a breathing machine and a feeding machine. . . .
>
> Mr. Husein does not receive financial assistance from Social Security. Therefore, Defendant says that she and her mother provide for all of the family's financial and other needs. . . .
>
> Additionally, Defendant Husein is the only member of the household with a valid driver's license and says that she is responsible for transporting her siblings as necessary and performing all other functions that require an automobile. Defendant also says that she helps the youngest child with homework and assists in cooking, cleaning and shopping. There is an older brother who has lived outside of the state of Michigan and per investigation does not assist the family financially or otherwise. . . .
>
> The Court wants to place more in the record of Mr. Husein — Mr. Weidemeyer's findings from his September 15th home visit, where it appears that Miss Husein's day begins as early as six a.m. and ends at 11 p.m. each day. At six [a.m.], she and her mother work or depart for work at [Volt] Services in Sterling Heights. At 10 a.m., Miss Husein drives home everyday to administer her father's medicine and feed him through his feeding tube. I believe she returns to work at 2:30 [p.m.], picks up her younger siblings from middle school, drives them home and returns to work again. At 4:30 [p.m.], the Defendant drives her mother home from work and then returns to work until 11 p.m. She reports that she works approximately 65 hours per week and that she's responsible for 50% of the family income; that all of her

income is used to pay the home mortgage and the mortgage is in her name. The 50% — she provides 50% of the family income and [t]he income is used to pay the mortgage, utilities, food and supplies for her siblings.

B. Procedural Background

... Husein pled guilty to all three counts[— conspiracy to possess and distribute ecstasy and two counts of unlawfully aiding and abetting in the distribution of ecstasy — with which she was charged]. Prior to sentencing, she filed a motion requesting that the district court grant a downward departure in light of Husein's extraordinary family circumstances, specifically the condition of her dying father. The government opposed the motion, arguing, among other things, that Husein and the care that she provided to her father were not "irreplaceable."

A probation officer prepared a Presentence Report (PSR) in which he calculated Husein's advisory Guidelines range to be between 37 and 46 months in prison. This was based on a total offense level of 21, which reflected a 3-level reduction for acceptance of responsibility. Husein was not assessed any criminal-history points. ...

[T]he district court concluded that Husein "has presented sufficient facts to warrant a departure under [U.S.S.G. §] 5H1.6, and the Court will grant the [defendant's] motion." The court based this conclusion in large part on its earlier finding that Husein was irreplaceable to her family:

> Assuming that the Defendant's representations here are true, the Court finds that she has established that she is personally responsible to a significant extent for the physical and financial support of her father. She also provides significant financial and other support to her mother and minor siblings. *It appears that there is no one else available to fill Defendant's role if she were incarcerated.*

(Emphasis added.)

The district court then imposed a noncustodial sentence of 3 years' supervised release, which included an initial 270-day term of home confinement. During the period of home confinement, Husein was required to wear an electronic monitoring device as directed by her probation officer. The district court also imposed a one-day term of custodial imprisonment, but Husein was given credit for already having served that time. At the conclusion of the sentencing hearing, the district court offered Husein the following words of advice:

> Miss Husein, the sentence is imposed in large part because the Court has reviewed the Presentence Investigation Report and believes that you — your family is going to benefit more by your presence than society is going to benefit from your incarceration. But the sentence in no way is meant to minimize what you did and your participation in this crime, and we hope that this is an adequate enough deterrent to you so that you don't engage in criminal activity in the future.
>
> You have a family that obviously depends on you a great deal and if you do anything that is violative of the conditions that are set on you, you could find yourself back here or in front of some other Court and another Judge may not give you this break that you are asking for and that we granted today.

The government timely appealed the district court's ruling in regard to Husein's sentence.

II. ANALYSIS

We read the government's briefs as presenting two distinct arguments: (1) that certain facts discovered by the government after sentencing would have necessarily altered the district court's conclusion that Husein's family circumstances were extraordinary, and (2) that, even ignoring these new facts, the lengthy downward departure granted by the court on account of extraordinary family circumstances was still an abuse of discretion and/or unreasonable in light of 18 U.S.C. §3553(a). These arguments will be addressed in reverse order. We do this because if we were to conclude that the district court erred in granting the family-circumstances departure based on the facts known to the court at the time of sentencing, then we would obviously have no need to reach the alternative question of whether the district court erred based on what the government discovered only after sentencing.

A. Standard of Review

The Prosecutorial Remedies and Tools Against the Exploitation of Children Today Act of 2003 ("PROTECT Act"), Pub. L. No. 108-21, 117 Stat. 650, changed the standard for reviewing a district court's application of the Guidelines, including available departures, to the facts of a given case [from an abuse-of-discretion standard] to the less deferential de novo standard. . . .

But after the Supreme Court's decision in United States v. Booker, 543 U.S. 220 (2005), which changed the status of the Guidelines from mandatory to advisory, the continuing validity of the de novo standard has been called into question. The few courts to have considered this issue have all ruled that, post-*Booker*, the abuse-of-discretion standard is once again the proper standard for reviewing a district court's decision to depart downward under the Guidelines. . . .

The rationale offered by these courts, and the one that we now adopt, is that the Supreme Court in *Booker* explicitly severed the statutory provision mandating the de novo review of departures, 18 U.S.C. §3742(e), from the Sentencing Reform Act of 1984 in order to uphold the Act's constitutionality. Of course, we must still review the overall sentence for reasonableness.

B. Husein's Family Circumstances

1. The District Court Did Not Abuse Its Discretion

The government correctly notes that even though the Guidelines are no longer mandatory, sentencing courts still must consider "any pertinent policy statement" contained therein. See 18 U.S.C. §3553(a)(5). And, to be sure, §5H1.6 is one such statement. It provides in pertinent part that "family ties and responsibilities are not ordinarily relevant in determining whether a departure may be warranted." This, in turn, makes family circumstances a "discouraged" factor under the Guidelines. See *Koon*, 518 U.S. at 95 ("Discouraged factors . . . are those not ordinarily relevant to the determination of whether a sentence should be outside the applicable guideline range.") (quotation marks omitted).

But this policy statement alone does not render the district court's decision to grant Husein a downward departure based on family circumstances an abuse of discretion. *Booker* in part accounts for why. As the First Circuit recently explained:

> Under the Guidelines, courts are discouraged from taking family circumstances into account, and before *Booker* the court would have been unlikely to take them into account in imposing sentence. After *Booker*, however, the fact that a factor is discouraged or forbidden under the guidelines does not automatically make it irrelevant when a court is weighing statutory factors apart from the guidelines.

United States v. Aitoro, 446 F.3d 246, 255 n.9 (1st Cir. 2006).

Nevertheless, when a district court departs downward on the basis of a discouraged factor such as family circumstances, those circumstances must be "exceptional." *Koon*, 518 U.S. 96 (noting that a district court should consider a downward departure based on a discouraged factor "only if the factor is present to an exceptional degree or in some other way makes the case different from the ordinary case where the factor is present"); U.S.S.G. §5K2.0(a)(4) ("An offender characteristic or other circumstance identified in . . . the guidelines as not ordinarily relevant in determining whether a departure is warranted may be relevant to this determination only if such offender characteristic or other circumstance is present to an exceptional degree.").

This court has not yet articulated a set of factors to consider in determining what constitutes "exceptional" or "extraordinary" family circumstances. It has instead resorted to a less structured comparative approach that takes the facts of a given case and compares them to the facts and holdings of other cases also involving departures for family circumstances. Fortunately, the recent commentary added to §5H1.6 offers substantial guidance by requiring the presence of the following four "circumstances" before a determination of extraordinariness may be made:

> (i) The defendant's service of a sentence within the applicable guideline range will cause a substantial, direct, and specific loss of essential caretaking, or essential financial support, to the defendant's family.
>
> (ii) The loss of caretaking or financial support substantially exceeds the harm ordinarily incident to incarceration for a similarly situated defendant. For example, the fact that the defendant's family might incur some degree of financial hardship or suffer to some extent from the absence of a parent through incarceration is not in itself sufficient as a basis for departure because such hardship or suffering is of a sort ordinarily incident to incarceration.
>
> (iii) *The loss of caretaking or financial support is one for which no effective remedial or ameliorative programs reasonably are available, making the defendant's caretaking or financial support irreplaceable to the defendant's family.*
>
> (iv) The departure effectively will address the loss of caretaking or financial support.

U.S.S.G. §5H1.6, ct. 1(B) (emphasis added).

The only factor that the government challenged in the district court was the third factor: Husein's irreplaceability. . . .

The government argues [on appeal] that because "there were untapped resources available to the family," Husein was not irreplaceable. Specifically, the government refers to Husein's oldest sister Shadya, Husein's mother Fizan, Husein's oldest brother Fady, and unnamed "friends, other extended family members, or neighbors [who] *might have been* able to render assistance in Mr. Husein's care." (Emphasis added.) But the mere existence of potential alternative sources of assistance or care is not sufficient to undermine a claim of irreplaceability. Instead, as the wording of the Guidelines makes clear, the alternatives must also be "reasonably available," which has been understood to mean "feasible" and "relatively comparable" to the defendant.

None of the alternatives suggested by the government meets this standard. Although the government is correct in noting that Shadya Husein "was only three months shy of her eighteenth birthday at the time of sentencing," she was also a full-time high-school student at the time. Fizan Husein was an even less feasible option. She alternated shifts with Fadya at the factory in Sterling Heights in order to ensure that one adult would be home at all times to attend to Husein's father. If the district court had sent Fadya to jail, her mother Fizan would have been forced to quit her job and stay home. But Fizan was the family's only source of income aside from Fadya, because Fadya's father was not receiving any Social Security benefits. Jailing Fadya, in other words, not only would have forced her mother to remain at home, but would have put the entire family on welfare. This fact alone strongly suggests infeasibility. See United States v. Norton, 218 F. Supp. 2d 1014, 1019 (E.D. Wis. 2002) (noting that one of the principal considerations to "have emerged from the cases reviewing §5H1.6 departures" is "whether the defendant's absence would force the family onto public assistance"); United States v. Owens, 145 F.3d 923, 926 (7th Cir. 1998) (affirming a downward departure where the defendant supported his family financially and the family would therefore be forced into public housing and/or welfare if he were incarcerated).

Finally, Fady Husein lived in Florida, did not have a job, and was unwilling to "step up to the plate" to help his family in Michigan. Fizan herself said that her son "does not help the family in any way. He visits us on occasion, but he doesn't have a job. *He will not come back to live here no matter what happens to Fadya.*" (Emphasis added.) In any event, the district court's conclusion that Fady was not a feasible alternative "financially or otherwise" was based not only on the evidence offered by Husein, but also on the court's own investigation.

The one obvious nonfamilial alternative that neither party mentions—and that the district court failed to consider at sentencing—was for Husein's father to have gone to a hospital for professional care. This omission is especially glaring because Husein's father had already received treatment for the same symptoms on several occasions at a nearby hospital. A return to that hospital, accordingly, would seem to have presented precisely the type of alternative that the district court should have considered in determining whether Husein was truly "irreplaceable."

Husein's case, however, survives this omission in the district court's analysis for the same reason that Husein's mother did not present a feasible alternative. Simply stated, the Huseins would not have been able to afford the hospital bills.

We recognize that the options of Medicaid and/or hospice treatment might have been available, but the government never suggested them as alternatives. Nor has the government raised the possibility on appeal. As defense counsel noted at oral argument, moreover, Fizan Husein possessed limited "life skills" and likely would not have thought of or even known how to pursue such options in Fadya's absence.

.... [T]he record is replete with references to the fact that the Huseins were hovering barely above the poverty line. . . .

If the stricter de novo standard of review were still applicable, we might be more inclined to conclude that Husein had failed to prove her irreplaceability. But under the — again — prevailing abuse-of-discretion standard, we hesitate to "second guess" the determination of the district court. . . . Deference is especially appropriate where, as here, the court "clearly explains the basis for its finding of an extraordinary family circumstance." United States v. Owens, 145 F.3d 923, 929 (7th Cir. 1998).

We acknowledge that United States v. Reed, 264 F.3d 640 (6th Cir. 2001), which has been declared the "leading case in the Sixth Circuit on the propriety of a downward departure for family responsibilities," was also decided under the abuse-of-discretion standard, albeit in its pre–PROTECT Act incarnation. The *Reed* court held that the district court had in fact abused its discretion in departing downward 13 levels to account in part for the money-laundering defendant's role in helping to care for her sister's five children. A psychiatrist-prepared assessment had deemed *Reed* "the glue that holds this family together" for her role in supervising her "dysfunctional" sister and raising her sister's children.

But *Reed* [] is distinguishable from the present case because Reed, unlike Husein, was not living with or financially supporting the nieces and nephews there in question, and in fact took extended, sometimes several-months-long vacations to Jamaica every year. . . .

We therefore conclude that the district court did not abuse its discretion by departing downward under §5H1.6. As noted, however, we must still review the resulting one-day prison sentence for reasonableness within the meaning of *Booker* and 18 U.S.C. §3553(a).

2. Husein's Sentence Was Both Procedurally and Substantively Reasonable

In the sentencing memorandum that she submitted to the district court, Husein argued that she was entitled to the noncustodial sentence that she ultimately received with or "even without a downward departure from the guidelines" under §5H1.6. Post-*Booker* caselaw confirms Husein's understanding that family circumstances can form the basis of either a Guidelines-authorized departure or a non-Guidelines, §3553(a)-based departure, also known as a variance.

This point was well stated by the Ninth Circuit in United States v. Merryweather:

> In the broader appraisal[] available to district courts after *Booker*, courts can justify consideration of family responsibilities, an aspect of the defendant's history and characteristics, 18 U.S.C. §3553(a)(1), for reasons extending

beyond the Guidelines. District courts now have the discretion to weigh a multitude of mitigating and aggravating factors that existed at the time of mandatory Guidelines sentencing, but were deemed not ordinarily relevant, such as age, education and vocational skills, mental and emotional conditions, employment record, *and family ties and responsibilities.*

431 F.3d 692, 700 (9th Cir. 2005), *amended on other grounds*, 447 F.3d 625 (9th Cir. 2006) (emphasis in original) (ellipses, footnotes, and quotation marks omitted).

    a.   Procedural Reasonableness   We review sentences post-*Booker* for reasonableness. Under the law of this circuit, reasonableness has both procedural and substantive components. United States v. Caver, 479 F.3d 220, 248 (6th Cir. 2006). A sentence is procedurally unreasonable "if the district judge fails to 'consider' the applicable Guidelines range or neglects to 'consider' the other factors listed in 18 U.S.C. §3553(a), and instead simply selects what the judge deems an appropriate sentence without such required consideration."

    In the present case, the district court explicitly mentioned §3553(a) only once in the course of Husein's entire sentencing hearing. Even then the reference was only to the statute as a whole, as opposed to one or more of its seven individual subsections. In some sense, the lack of an explicit §3553(a) analysis is understandable. The bulk of the sentencing hearing revolved around Husein's motion for a downward departure based on extraordinary family circumstances, which the district court treated almost exclusively as a motion for a Guidelines departure as discussed above. Nevertheless, *Booker* requires us to determine whether the overall sentence, of which the downward departure is only a part, is reasonable within the parameters set by §3553(b).

    The district court need not discuss each and every §3553(a) factor, but the reasons that it does provide for the sentence must sufficiently reflect considerations akin to those enumerated in the statute. . . . That the district court treated Husein's motion almost exclusively as one for a Guidelines departure, accordingly, does not necessarily render the resulting sentence procedurally unreasonable. The issue is not how the district court considered the relevant factors, but simply whether it considered them at all.

    A review of the record in the present case compels the conclusion that Husein's one-day sentence was procedurally reasonable. In arriving at this sentence, the district court considered facts that correspond to five of the seven §3553(a) factors. And the seventh §3553(a) factor — "the need to provide restitution to any victims of the offense" — was inapplicable to Husein's case because, as the PSR makes clear, "there is no identifiable victim."

    Regarding the first factor, the district court amply considered the "nature and circumstances" of Husein's offense as well as her "history and characteristics." At various points during the sentencing hearing, the court addressed the degree of Husein's participation in the ecstasy transactions, the nature of her relationship with the relevant buyers and sellers, and the amount of ecstasy involved. The district court also considered Husein's background, including her financial and employment record, her lack of a criminal record, and, obviously, her family circumstances.

Despite the government's argument to the contrary, the district court also considered the second §3553(a) factor, which directs the sentencing court to consider, among other things, "the seriousness of the offense" and the need "to afford adequate deterrence to criminal conduct," including "further crimes of the defendant." The court explicitly determined that the sentence of 3 years' supervised release, which included an initial 270-day term of home confinement, would act as a sufficient deterrent to Husein despite the seriousness of her crime. . . .

Regarding the third, fourth, and fifth factors, the district court considered the availability of both custodial and noncustodial sentencing options, the applicable Guidelines range of 37 to 46 months in prison, and also, as noted above, the Sentencing Commission's stated policy of discouraging the invocation of family circumstances as a ground for a downward departure.

The only applicable factor that the district court appears not to have considered is the sixth factor, which references "the need to avoid unwarranted sentence disparities among defendants with similar records who have been found guilty of similar conduct." To be sure, as this court recently emphasized in United States v. Davis, 458 F.3d 491, 499 (6th Cir. 2006), drastic departures from the applicable Guidelines range typically "leav[e] no room to make reasoned distinctions" between the fortunate defendant and others who might be more deserving. But, as discussed in the substantive-reasonableness analysis below, affirming Husein's sentence in the present case would not be contrary to the goal of allowing for "reasoned distinctions" that §3553(a)(6) codifies. We thus conclude that the sentence imposed by the district court, which considered at least five of the six relevant §3553(a) factors, was procedurally reasonable.

b. Substantive Reasonableness   "[E]ven if a sentence is calculated properly, i.e., the Guidelines were properly applied and the district court clearly considered the §3553(a) factors and explained its reasoning, a sentence can yet be unreasonable." United States v. Cage, 451 F.3d 585, 591 (10th Cir. 2006). A sentence is substantively unreasonable if the district court "selects the sentence arbitrarily, bases the sentence on impermissible factors, fails to consider pertinent §3553(a) factors or gives an unreasonable amount of weight to any pertinent factor." *Caver*, 479 F.3d at 248 (brackets and quotation marks omitted).

Although within-Guidelines sentences receive a presumption of reasonableness in this circuit, "a sentence outside of the Guidelines range — either higher or lower — is [not] presumptively *un*reasonable. . . . Rather, our reasonableness review is in light of the §3553(a) factors which the district court felt justified such a variance." United States v. Collington, 461 F.3d 805, 808 (6th Cir. 2006) (emphasis in original) (citation and quotation marks omitted). In reviewing outside-the-Guidelines sentences such as the one imposed in the present case, accordingly, "we apply a form of proportionality review: the farther the judge's sentence departs from the guidelines sentence[,] the more compelling the justification based on factors in section 3553(a) must be." *Davis*, 458 F.3d at 496 (quotation marks omitted).

To be sure, *Davis*'s emphasis on the distinction between a §3553(a), multifactor variance (at issue there) and a Guidelines-authorized departure (at issue here) leaves open the question of whether the proportionality test applies to both. We will simply assume without deciding that the answer is "yes" because, as set forth below, we believe that the downward departure granted to Husein in the present case passes muster even under *Davis*.

As an initial matter, the offense to which Husein pled guilty, 21 U.S.C. §841(b)(1)(C), does not mandate a minimum sentence. (The statutory range is 0 to 20 years in prison.) Congress thus not only envisioned, but accepted, the possibility that some defendants found guilty of that subsection of the statute would receive no jail time at all. This is especially significant in the area of drug-related crimes, where mandatory-minimum sentences . . . are most common. . . .

As both this court and the Supreme Court have recognized, moreover, the existence of a mandatory minimum directly affects the discretion of a sentencing judge. Accordingly, if a mandatory minimum denies discretionary authority to a sentencing judge, then that authority is a fortiori restored where, as here, no mandatory minimum exists.

Sentences must nonetheless comport with prevailing standards of reasonableness, of course, and we recognize that Husein's one-day sentence in the present case represents an exponentially large departure from the applicable advisory Guidelines range of 37 to 46 months in prison. Expressed as a percentage, the departure is 99.91% below the low end of the range. This makes it even more extraordinary than the 99.89% variance (from a 30-to-37-month range to a one-day sentence) held to be unreasonably and unjustifiably low under the "proportionality" standard of review first articulated and employed by this court in *Davis*. But in judging the extent of the departure granted by the district court in this case, we bear in mind the departure's primary purpose of allowing Husein to provide the assistance that her father needed to survive. Any time that Husein would have spent in jail necessarily would have defeated this purpose. This distinguishes the present case from *Davis*, which instead dealt with a multifactor-based variance whose only discernible purpose was, and generally is, leniency.

In *Davis*, the court's principal concern with the one-day sentence imposed by the district court was that it represented "the most extreme variance possible, leaving no room to make reasoned distinctions between Davis's variance and the variances that other, more worthy defendants may deserve." To be sure, Husein's one-day sentence in the present case also represents "the most extreme [departure] possible." But unlike in *Davis*, it leaves fairly ample "room to make reasoned distinctions" between Husein's Guidelines departure and what other defendants with extraordinary family circumstances might receive. These distinctions will be based not only on the exigency or seriousness of the family circumstances in each individual case, but also on the relative "worthiness" of each individual defendant. No judge, for example, would likely reduce the sentence of a convicted mass murderer due to family circumstances, and we do not intend to suggest otherwise. The extent of a downward departure or variance, in other words, should bear an inversely proportional relationship to the "evilness" of the crime, and criminal, at issue.

In *Davis*, the court belabored the defendant's considerable unworthiness: "The record shows that the fraud [perpetrated by Davis] caused over $900,000 in loss; Davis did not repay the lost money; he did not accept responsibility for the crimes; and he has yet to show remorse for the crimes." If such a defendant received what amounted to the lowest sentence possible, the court worried, how could sentencing courts confronted with far more worthy defendants possibly grant greater, more deserved departures? And would those courts necessarily also have to award the bare minimum sentence that Davis had received? . . .

In the present case, however, "more worthy defendants" than Husein are difficult to imagine, short of those found to be not guilty. Her actions — namely, helping to arrange the sale of ecstasy between several of her acquaintances — caused no immediate harm to the individuals involved, much less the type of harm for which restitution was available as in *Davis*. In addition, Husein fully accepted responsibility for her actions, a fact that the district court credited by adopting the portion of the PSR that had reduced Husein's base offense level by three levels. . . .

She further appears to have expressed remorse for her actions, as several handwritten letters from family members and coworkers attest. Husein was also found to have no prior criminal history, thereby placing her in Category I for the purpose of calculating her advisory Guidelines range.

. . . But in the world of convicted and guilty defendants . . . Husein appears to be precisely the type of defendant most worthy of the one-day sentence that she received. Affirming her sentence therefore would not, as the court feared in *Davis*, "leav[e] no room to make reasoned distinctions" for other, similarly situated defendants. To the contrary, the drawing of such distinctions would be facilitated by establishing a concrete example of the circumstances that render a defendant eligible for the lowest end of the statutory range. . . .

. . . For all of the reasons set forth above, we conclude that Husein's sentence is substantively reasonable under the proportionality test of *Davis*.

C.   *The Effect of the Post-Sentencing Discoveries and Developments*

2.   Death of Husein's Father

Finally, the government argues that because of the death of Husein's father four months after sentencing, Husein is currently enjoying a "windfall" by remaining at home as opposed to being in prison. . . .

The finality of judgments is a key element of the American system of justice. This is especially true for defendants in criminal cases, where the enhancement of a sentence in a subsequent proceeding can violate the defendant's rights to the due process of law. As the Supreme Court has held, "when the Government has already imposed a criminal penalty and seeks to impose additional punishment in a second proceeding, the Double Jeopardy Clause protects against the possibility that the Government is seeking the second punishment because it is dissatisfied with the sanction obtained in the first proceeding." United States v. Halper, 490 U.S. 435, 451 n.10 (1989), abrogated on other grounds by United States v. Ursery, 518 U.S. 267 (1996).

The relevant question is "whether the addition[al sentence] upsets the defendant's legitimate 'expectation of finality in the original sentence.'" Jones v. Thomas, 491 U.S. 376, 394 (1989) (Scalia, J., dissenting) (quoting United States v. DiFrancesco, 449 U.S. 117 (1980)). "If a defendant has a legitimate expectation of finality, then an increase in that sentence is prohibited. . . ." United States v. Fogel, 829 F.2d 77, 87 (D.C. Cir. 1987). "A defendant has a legitimate expectation in the finality of a sentence *unless he is or should be aware at sentencing that the sentence may permissibly be increased.*" *Id.* (emphasis added).

In the present case, nothing in the record indicates that Husein was aware at the time of sentencing that her sentence could "permissibly be increased" or otherwise transformed from noncustodial to imprisonment. The district court, to be sure, did warn Husein that "if you do anything that is violative of the conditions [of home confinement and supervised release] that are set on you, you could find yourself back here or in front of some other Court and another Judge may not give you this break that you are asking for and that we granted today." But the court did not mention that a change in Husein's family circumstances, the relevant issue here, also might result in an increased sentence.

. . . .

The government further argues that "[a]s events unfolded, a mere four-month delay in the defendant's sentencing or her report date would have obviated the need for any departure whatsoever." In its reply brief, the government clarifies its position as follows:

> Clearly, the district court could not have known that the defendant's father would die only four months later, and we do not suggest as much. However, given the fact that the defendant's father suffered from multiple and worsening ailments and a "drastically reduced life expectancy," we do submit that the district court could, and should, have at least *considered* the possibility of either delaying sentencing or granting a delayed report date as part of the sentencing equation.

(Emphasis in original.)

But the fact remains that the district court did not do so, and that the government, more tellingly, never asked the court to do so. The government cites no authority for the proposition that a district court should sua sponte consider such possibilities in analogous circumstances. If the government had even the faintest visions of appealing Husein's sentence on this ground—a likely possibility in light of the government also having been well aware of Husein's father's "drastically reduced life expectancy"—at the very least it should have made that view known to the district court and thus part of the record.

Finally, although the health of Husein's father was the primary family circumstance on which the district court based its downward departure, it was not the only circumstance. The court also took note of Husein's "significant" responsibilities to her siblings and mother. Accordingly, the likelihood that waiting for Husein's father to die would have resulted in the district court's imposing an entirely different sentence is not as certain as the government seems to imply. Several of the extraordinary circumstances would still have existed, and Husein presumably would have had the added responsibility of helping her mother and siblings cope with the loss of their husband and father.

For all of these reasons, the government's windfall argument is without merit. It is also shortsighted. What if, instead of "getting better," Husein's family situation had actually become worse? Suppose, for example, that both Husein's father and mother had died in the several months after sentencing, leaving Husein alone to care for her three younger siblings. Also suppose that Husein had timely appealed on other grounds and, upon learning of this unfortunate news, argued for the first time that even her term of home confinement and supervised release was too harsh of a punishment. Would this court have accepted her argument and further reduced her sentence? Almost certainly not.

We see no reason why we should respond to the government's argument in the present appeal any differently. To hold to the contrary, after all, would mainly harm the government by subjecting it to a flood of post-sentencing litigation brought by unforeseeably worse-off defendants. . . .

The essence of the problem in this case is the government's failure to ask the district court to fashion a sentence that would take into account the likelihood that Husein's father would die in the immediate future. Its afterthought on appeal simply comes too late.

We also recognize that, as in *Fuson*, this case "approach[es] the boundary of the district court's broader sentencing discretion under *Booker*." United States v. Fuson, 215 Fed. Appx. 468 , 475 (6th Cir. 2007). But the plain import of *Booker* is that a 1-day, below-the-Guidelines sentence, no less than a 7,300-day, above-the-Guidelines sentence, is now a viable sentence for a district court to impose so long as it is authorized by statute and reasonable within the meaning of 18 U.S.C. §3553(a). Because Husein's sentence both falls within the statutory range and survives reasonableness review as defined by the law of this circuit in *Davis*, we find no abuse of the district court's *Booker* discretion under the unique facts of this case. . . .

NOTES

1. *Consideration of social context factors: majority position.* Historically, in indeterminate sentencing systems, social context factors such as family history and situation, educational background, and employment record have been of great importance to sentencing judges (and parole officials) when exercising their discretion to individualize sentences with the offender's rehabilitation in mind. Presentence reports have often provided considerable detail on each offender's social history, education, and employment, and they have suggested how these background factors might affect the offender's rehabilitative prospects and progress.

Anecdotal and empirical research suggests that undue sentencing disparity, and the apparent disfavoring of certain minority offenders, can be traced back to the emphasis on these sorts of social context factors. As a result, many modern sentencing reforms have precluded or greatly restricted the consideration of these factors. The U.S. Sentencing Commission has excluded these social context factors from sentencing calculations for the most part and has further declared most social context matters "not ordinarily relevant" to a departure determination. See, e.g., U.S. Sentencing Guidelines Manual §§5H1.2 (education and vocational skills), 5H1.5 (employment record), 5H1.6 (family ties and responsibilities and community ties), and 5H1.11 (military, civic, charitable, or public service). Federal case law, however, has interpreted these instructions to mean that social context factors can be the basis for a departure in "extraordinary" cases. In the advisory guideline system, courts may also consider such factors in fashioning a reasonable sentence. Likewise, in many state structured sentencing systems, social context factors are not directly incorporated into most sentencing determinations, but they can on occasion serve as a basis for a departure. See, e.g., Utah 2007 Adult Sentencing and Release Guidelines Form 2 (providing that a mitigating factor to be considered at sentencing is that "offender has exceptionally good employment and/or family relationships").

2. *Relevance (or irrelevance) of offenders' social context*   In some cases, certain social context factors might directly bear on the offender's culpability; an offender with many children who steals in order to feed his family, for example, seems less culpable than a thief who lacks any such family needs. Such factors might seem important considerations in light of the traditional purposes of sentencing. But should consideration of such social context factors be permitted at sentencing when they do not directly bear on an offender's culpability or future prospects? Consider ABA Standard for Criminal Justice, Sentencing 18-3.4 (3d ed. 1994), which suggests the following approach for allowing limited consideration of the offender's personal characteristics at sentencing:

> (a) The legislature and [sentencing commission] should authorize sentencing courts, sentencing individual offenders, to consider their physical, mental, social and economic characteristics, even though not material to their culpability for the offense, only as provided in this Standard.
>
> (b) The legislature and [sentencing commission] should permit sentencing courts to use information about offenders' financial circumstances for the purpose of determination of the amount or terms of fines or other economic sanctions.
>
> (c) Except as provided in (b), the legislature and the agency should provide that sentencing courts may take into account personal characteristics of offenders not material to their culpability to determine the appropriate types of sanctions to impose or, if the characteristics are indicative of circumstances of hardship, deprivation, or handicap, to lessen the severity of sentences that would have been imposed.

What uses of personal history are permitted and not permitted under this standard? Why, if an offender's "physical, mental, social and economic characteristics" are "not material to [his or her] culpability for the offense," should these characteristics be considered at all at sentencing? The commentary to the standards explains its compromise position:

> Many determinate jurisdictions have sought to restrict or prohibit the sentencing consideration of personal characteristics unrelated to culpability on the theory that such consideration can act to preserve or exacerbate preexisting class and race disparities in sentencing patterns. At least in the federal system such restrictions have prompted criticism that the sentencing process has been dehumanized, that the life history of defendants can no longer be argued to show extenuating circumstances, and that desirable individualization of sentences cannot occur. The Standards attempt to find a balance between the need to avoid class and race disparities and the need to preserve a meaningful level of individualization in sentences.

3. *Family circumstances.*   Especially because offenders at sentencing will often highlight family situations when pleading for leniency, sentencing judges are frequently asked to consider the impact of a proposed sentence on the defendant's family. As detailed in *Husein,* the federal sentencing guidelines attempt to limit this practice by declaring that "family ties and responsibilities" are "not ordinarily relevant" to a sentence, and appellate courts have upheld departure sentences based on such circumstances only when they are present to an "extraordinary" degree. The federal circuits were less than perfectly consistent in assessing what sorts of family situations qualify as extraordinary. Compare United States v. Johnson, 964 F.2d 124 (2d Cir. 1992) (departure allowed for female offender who was sole support for three children under 7 years, institutionalized adult daughter, 17-year-old son, and 6-year-old granddaughter), with United States v. Sweeting, 213 F.3d 95 (3d Cir. 2000) (departure reversed for mother of six children, including one suffering from Tourette's syndrome), and compare United States v. Haverstat, 22 F.3d 790 (8th Cir. 1994) (upholding departure on grounds that caring for ill family member was "extraordinary" family circumstance), with United States v. Allen, 87 F.3d 1224 (11th Cir. 1996) (disallowing departure on similar grounds). Even greater disparity is likely to occur in the advisory guideline system.

Because of the number of cases and families affected, this is a high-stakes decision for every sentencing system. Consider the following excerpt from an opinion by Judge Patricia Wald, dissenting from the denial of a motion for rehearing in United States v. Dyce, 91 F.3d 1462, 1472-1478 (D.C. Cir. 1996), a case in which a panel of the U.S. Court of Appeals for the D.C. Circuit decided that the mother of three young children, including a three-month-old still being breastfed, did not warrant a downward departure based on family circumstances:

> The question of when family obligations rise to [the level of a departure ground] is an issue affecting tens of thousands of federal offenders and their families. More than half of all female prisoners and more than one-quarter of all male prisoners are caring for minor children at the time they enter prison. Other prisoners have primary responsibility for the care of parents, siblings, spouses, or grandchildren. In these cases, the impact of imprisonment on a defendant's family is profound; it imposes not just financial and emotional hardship, but in some cases, loss of children to foster care or even complete severance of parental rights. [In] light of the significant detriment experienced by children as a result of a parent's incarceration, the Commission's initial presumption against considering family ties is unwarranted, short-sighted, and unwise. . . .
>
> In reviewing §5H1.6 departures, courts are asked (mistakenly, I believe) to undertake a "mission impossible" of identifying where the ephemeral line between "ordinary" and "extraordinary" lies in the tragic realm of family breakup and disruption of children's lives. Obviously no bright-line rule is reasonable, or even feasible — for example, "single parent with two or more children and dependent parent," or "single parent with young child and infant"; the variety of family structures, attachments, personalities, and track records in fulfilling responsibilities defies any such easy categorization. . . .
>
> I believe rehearing en banc is [needed] to define for the district court some comprehensible parameters for departure under §5H1.6. The cumulation of rulings by our sister circuits provides only suggestions, not a great deal of firm guidance. . . . Several circuits have refused to sanction departures simply

because incarceration will jeopardize the parental ties of a young child, where a relative is available to care for the children during the parent's incarceration. But other circuits have affirmed departures in circumstances markedly less compelling than this defendant's. The First Circuit — though denying departures in several earlier cases . . . involving dependent minor children — did permit a departure based on a showing of a strong relationship between a defendant and his lover's son, even though the child's mother had custody of her son. In other cases, departures have been authorized on the grounds that the defendant has several young children, in many cases without discussion of whether other relatives can or will care for the children. One circuit left open the possibility that a departure would be permissible based solely on defendant's role as a "good father" to "three exemplary children." . . .

The precedent is admittedly conflicting, perhaps because the task assigned by the Guidelines is so frustrating and counterintuitive — that is, where on the spectrum we should draw the line between "ordinary" and "extraordinary" family tragedies? But the fact remains that our trial judges must wrestle with the problem every day. . . .

In your view, what are extraordinary family circumstances? In 1999, 63% of all federal prisoners and 55.5% of all state prisoners had children under age 18. Among female prisoners, the comparable numbers were 59% and 65%. An estimated 722,000 state and federal prisoners in 1999 were parents to almost 1.5 million children under the age of 18. Christopher J. Mumola, Bureau of Justice Statistics, Incarcerated Parents and Their Children (National Institute of Justice, NCJ 182335, August 2000). In light of Judge Wald's criticisms of the existing approach, if you were a judicial clerk, how would you help your judge develop a principled but individualized approach to determining in which cases a sentence outside the guidelines is appropriate based on family circumstances? If you were a member of the U.S. Sentencing Commission, do you think a more structured approach to this issue — for example, one that depends on the number of children affected or the likely home for the children if the parent is incarcerated — would provide for more sensible and consistent results than the current prescription of not ordinarily considering family circumstances? Do you think the ABA approach would be an improvement?

In *Husein* the court also focused on the defendant and her family's economic situation. Would it have been justifiable for the court to deny the departure had Husein been the sole caretaker rather than the caretaker and breadwinner for the household? Should it matter to the court whether the incarceration of a defendant leads the family to resort to public assistance?

PROBLEM 5-7.   PILLAR OF THE COMMUNITY

John Morken owned and operated a cattle brokerage business based in a small town in Minnesota. When the company's cash flow began to suffer, Morken began "kiting" checks (shifting funds to create the illusion of larger bank accounts), thus inflating his purchasing power in the cattle market. He used the nonexistent funds to buy more cattle, and then cattle prices fell. Ultimately, Morken put the business into bankruptcy. A federal grand jury indicted Morken for bank fraud and making false statements to a financial institution. He pled guilty to one count of bank fraud, and the government dropped the remaining charges. The applicable provisions of the U.S. Sentencing Guidelines call for a prison term of between 63 and 78 months.

Many citizens of Morken's hometown (with a population just over 1,000) wrote to the sentencing judge, asking him to impose a lenient sentence. The letters portrayed Morken as a hard-working and honest businessman, the owner of a once-thriving operation. Morken's father started the business in the 1930s. Morken joined it in 1964 and assumed leadership of the company in 1992. The letters to the judge also praised Morken for his community service. They spoke of him as an accommodating neighbor and a good friend. He advised local business owners, hired young people, served on his church council, and raised money for charity.

In addition to the family cattle brokerage business, Morken owned and operated the All Phase Arena, which hosted horse shows, farm and home shows, and the like. This operation provided dozens of jobs for local workers and generated revenue for local businesses. The All Phase Arena was unaffected by the bankruptcy of Morken's cattle operation, but it likely would not survive if Morken were to serve a lengthy prison term.

The federal sentencing guidelines advise judges that "community ties are not ordinarily relevant in determining whether a sentence should be outside the applicable guideline range." U.S. Sentencing Guidelines Manual §5H1.6. They also say that "[m]ilitary, charitable, or public service; employment-related contributions; and similar prior good works are not ordinarily relevant in determining whether a sentence should be outside the applicable guideline range." U.S. Sentencing Guidelines Manual §5H1.11. As the district court judge in this case, what sentence would you impose? How would you explain your decision? Cf. United States v. Morken, 133 F.3d 628 (8th Cir. 1998).

NOTES

1. *The significance of prior good works.* As noted earlier in this chapter, every jurisdiction views an offender's criminal history as an aggravating factor justifying an enhanced sentence for the current offense. Because these criminal history rules essentially mandate an increased sentence based on the defendant's past *bad* acts, logic would seem to dictate that jurisdictions should also have sentencing rules that mandate a reduced sentence based on the defendant's past *good* works. In other words, if defendants are to be penalized for prior bad behavior, shouldn't they also be rewarded for prior good behavior? A few jurisdictions follow this logic. North Carolina, for example, provides that a mitigated sentence could be appropriate when the defendant "has been a person of good character or has had a good reputation in the community" or when the defendant "has been honorably discharged from the United States armed services." N.C. Gen. Stat. §15A-1340.16(e)(12), (14). As noted in Problem 5-7, however, the federal sentencing guidelines provide that "[m]ilitary, charitable, or public service; employment-related contributions; and similar prior good works are not ordinarily relevant in determining whether a sentence should be outside the applicable guideline range." U.S. Sentencing Guidelines Manual §5H1.11. Why do you think the U.S. Sentencing Commission deemed these

factors inappropriate as the basis for a departure in the ordinary case? Should service to the country through participation in the military merit some consideration in sentencing? See United States v. Lett, 483 F.3d 782 (11th Cir. 2007).

2. *The significance of third-party impact.* The criminal conviction and potential incarceration of an offender almost always affect various third parties — most commonly the offender's immediate family and dependents, but often also the offender's employer or employees. As part of a plea for leniency, sentencing judges will almost invariably hear from the defendant or defense counsel about the hardships that third parties may suffer if the defendant is incarcerated. Should sentencing judges reduce sentences to try to minimize the harm to third parties, or does that unfairly reward defendants who are fortunate enough to have others depend on them? Professor Darryl Brown has noted that both prosecutors and judges have historically considered third-party interests in their charging and sentencing decisions, even though traditional criminal law theories do not suggest the consideration of such interests. See Darryl K. Brown, Third-Party Interests in Criminal Law, 80 Tex. L. Rev. 1383 (2002). However, not all agree that family ties are appropriate for consideration at sentencing. Dan Markel et al., Criminal Justice and the Challenge of Family Ties, U. Ill. L. Rev. (forthcoming August 2007) (available at papers.srrn. com/sol3/papers.cfm?abstract_id=933427#).

At least a few states have codified in their structured-sentencing reforms the idea that judges should consider third-party concerns at sentencing. See Utah 2007 Adult Sentencing and Release Guidelines Form 2 (providing that a mitigating factor to be considered at sentencing is that "imprisonment would entail excessive hardship on offender or dependents"). In the federal system, the appropriateness of and place for considering third-party interests are less defined and less clear although a number of commentators have asked federal courts to consider family interests. See Myrna S. Raeder, Rethinking Sentencing Post-*Booker:* Gender-Related Issues in a Post-*Booker* Federal Guidelines World, 37 McGeorge L. Rev. 691 (2006).

3. *The significance of upbringing and social environment.*   Criminologists, psychologists, and other social scientists trace the roots of much crime to deep social causes relating to the offender's childhood social environment and upbringing. Recognizing that a poor childhood environment is not the offender's fault, should sentencing judges consider reducing an offender's sentence when her wrongdoing can be linked to childhood abuse or an otherwise unfortunate early social history? Not long after the federal sentencing guidelines were enacted, one federal circuit held that a downward departure was permissible based on the defendant's "youthful lack of guidance." United States v. Floyd, 945 F.2d 1096 (9th Cir. 1991). Fearing the potentially expansive reach of this ground for departing from the guidelines, the U.S. Sentencing Commission amended the sentencing guidelines to provide that "lack of guidance as a youth and similar circumstances indicating a disadvantaged upbringing are not relevant grounds for imposing a sentence outside the applicable guideline range." U.S. Sentencing Guidelines Manual §5H1.12. If you had been a commissioner during this period, would you have favored or opposed this amendment? See United States v. Collington,

461 F.3d 805 (6th Cir. 2006). For a more general discussion of social environment theories and criminal law, see Patricia J. Falk, Novel Theories of Criminal Defense Based upon the Toxicity of the Social Environment: Urban Psychosis, Television Intoxication, and Black Rage, 74 N.C. L. Rev. 731 (1996). The defendant's unsupportive or abusive family of origin often figures into capital murder trials as defendants attempt to establish mitigating circumstances for the crime.

=6=

Procedure and Proof at Sentencing

Chapter 1 explored *why* society punishes, Chapters 2 and 3 focused on *who* holds the power and discretion to set sentences, and Chapters 4 and 5 together examined *what* elements factor into sentencing decisions (offense and offender characteristics). This chapter looks at *how* sentencing and punishment decisions are made.

The possible application of trial rights at sentencing is the focus of the first half of this chapter. The Fifth and Sixth Amendments to the United States Constitution lay down some foundational rules for the prosecution of criminal offenses. These provisions include both relatively specific commands (for example, "presentment or indictment" is required for "capital, or otherwise infamous" crimes) and some that are notoriously abstract (no person shall be "deprived of life, liberty, or property, without due process of law"). The constitutional amendments are conspicuously silent on the subject of sentencing.

Until recently this had been the subject of an interesting but largely academic discussion. No longer. The decisions in *Apprendi* and *Blakely* have made the issue of procedural rights in the sentencing process the most debated topic in sentencing law.

While the constitutional doctrine has changed the procedures used in the courtroom to determine sentences, the procedural realities take place mostly outside the courtroom. Criminal justice is far more commonly negotiated than adjudicated. In other words, defendants and their attorneys care more about the charging and plea bargaining practices of prosecutors and the presentence investigations of probation offices than they do about the sentencing procedures of judges or juries. The second part of this chapter explores these less visible presentence practices and policies.

A.   CONSTITUTIONAL SENTENCING PROCEDURES: TRIAL VERSUS SENTENCING

The substantive distinction between criminal trials and criminal sentencing is fairly obvious: trials determine a defendant's legal guilt and sentencing determines how a guilty defendant will be treated. Far less obvious is what this substantive distinction means in procedural terms. Should the rights typically afforded criminal defendants at a trial also apply at sentencing? Should the answer to this question be influenced by the reality that very few criminal defendants ever experience trial procedures because so many defendants plead guilty?

If you believe that different procedures are appropriate (or inevitable) at a criminal trial and at a criminal sentencing, who gets to decide which issues and facts are resolved at trial and which will be considered only at sentencing? Should legislatures—the institutions typically responsible for defining crimes and for authorizing punishments—have sole authority to define what "elements" are subject to resolution at trial and what "sentencing factors" are subject to consideration only at sentencing?

1.   Formal Trial, Informal Sentencing

The Fifth and Sixth Amendments to the Constitution provide rules for the prosecution and trial of criminal offenses. Read the text of the amendments closely. Do you find these commands specific or abstract compared with other rights specified in the Bill of Rights?

U.S. Const. Amend. V

No person shall be held to answer for a capital, or otherwise infamous crime, unless on a presentment or indictment of a grand jury . . . ; nor shall any person be subject for the same offense to be twice put in jeopardy of life or limb, nor shall be compelled in any criminal case to be a witness against himself, nor be deprived of life, liberty, or property, without due process of law. . . .

U.S. Const. Amend. VI

In all criminal prosecutions, the accused shall enjoy the right to a speedy and public trial, by an impartial jury . . . , and to be informed of the nature and cause of the accusation; to be confronted with the witnesses against him; to have compulsory process for obtaining witnesses in his favor, and to have the assistance of counsel for his defense.

Noticeably absent from these amendments are explicit procedural rights at sentencing. When the Constitution speaks of punishment, it mentions the legislative obligation to define crimes before they occur and to give them general application (the ex post facto and bill of attainder clauses), or it limits the available sanctions (the prohibition of "cruel and unusual punishments"), or it recognizes that convicted criminals have qualified civil rights (the Thirteenth Amendment's decree that "[n]either slavery nor involuntary servitude, except as a punishment for crime whereof the party shall have been duly convicted, shall exist within the United States").

The silence on sentencing process is perhaps not surprising given the sentencing dynamics at the time of the founding. Following English traditions, during the founding era each particular criminal offense had a distinct sentencing consequence, and thus the results of a criminal trial conclusively determined an offender's sentence. See Report of the Twentieth Century Fund Task Force on Criminal Sentencing, Fair and Certain Punishment 83-85 (1976). In other words, the Constitution's failure to regulate procedures at sentencing simply reflects the fact that at the time of the founding there were no distinct sentencing procedures to be regulated.

But with the emergence of the penitentiary and a shift in punishment theory toward a rehabilitative model in the late nineteenth century, the direct connection between the criminal verdict and the sentence was severed and distinct sentencing proceedings emerged. Trial judges were given discretion to impose on defendants any sentence among the broad statutory ranges and were permitted to consider any and all evidence when crafting a sentence. Judge and commentator Nancy Gertner summarized this evolution:

> [In] colonial times verdict and sentencing were closely linked. Felony conviction led to a definite punishment, often death, unless the defendant could offer a legal reason to excuse it. The jury's verdict was the pivotal event. Pronouncement of the sentence by the judge was an essentially ministerial task.
>
> By the nineteenth century, tradition and changes in penology dramatically altered the function of sentencing, while the jury's functions changed little. The sentencing model was now a therapeutic one, seeking to rehabilitate the offender. Each offense carried a very broad range of potential sentences; the judge had the discretion to pick any sentence within the range.

Nancy Gertner, *Apprendi* and the Return of the Criminal Code, 37 Crim. L. Bull. 553, 557 (2001).

The emergence of a distinct sentencing proceeding raised questions about whether traditional trial rights ought to apply at sentencing. These questions came before the Supreme Court most dramatically in Williams v. New York, 337 U.S. 241 (1949), after the progressive rehabilitative model of sentencing had already been operating for nearly half a century. As we saw in Chapter 2, the trial judge in *Williams* sentenced to death a defendant convicted of first-degree murder, despite a jury recommendation of life imprisonment, relying on allegations in the presentence report about illegal and unsavory activities by the defendant. Williams appealed and claimed that he had a right at sentencing—just as he did at trial—to confront and cross-examine the witnesses against him.

The Supreme Court in *Williams* approved the reliance on informal procedures at sentencing. The Court stressed rehabilitation of offenders as an important goal of criminal jurisprudence and spoke approvingly of the "prevalent modern philosophy of penology that the punishment should fit the offender and not merely the crime." To deprive sentencing judges of "the fullest information possible concerning the defendant's life and characteristics" would undermine "modern penological procedural policies." In other words, the rehabilitative ideal not only justified entrusting judges with enormous sentencing discretion, but it also freed sentencing judges from any procedural trial rules that might limit the sound exercise of their discretion.

Williams was decided before the Supreme Court began "revolutionizing" criminal procedure by interpreting the Constitution expansively to provide criminal defendants with an array of procedural rights. Nevertheless, throughout the 1960s and 1970s, as the Supreme Court established numerous pretrial and trial rights for defendants, the Court continued to cite *Williams* favorably and continued to suggest that sentencing was to be treated differently — and should be far less procedurally regulated — than a traditional criminal trial. See North Carolina v. Pearce, 395 U.S. 711, 723 (1969) (favorably citing *Williams* while stressing "the freedom of a sentencing judge" to consider a defendant's postconviction conduct in imposing a sentence).

The Supreme Court did hold that defendants had a right to an attorney at sentencing hearings in Mempa v. Rhay, 389 U.S. 128 (1967), and suggested that defendants also had a right to discovery of evidence that could affect a sentence in Brady v. Maryland, 373 U.S. 83 (1963). Nevertheless, the Court did not formally extend other Bill of Rights protections to the sentencing process.

As the Supreme Court continued to cite *Williams* favorably and to sanction informal sentencing procedures, the theory supporting the rehabilitative model of sentencing itself came under attack. Through the 1960s and 1970s, criminal justice researchers and scholars grew increasingly concerned about the unpredictable and disparate sentences produced by highly discretionary sentencing systems. During the last quarter of the twentieth century, jurisdictions started to adopt more structured sentencing laws. Some states tried determinate sentencing statutes, which abolished parole and created presumptive sentencing ranges, while others created full-fledged sentencing guideline systems.

These new sentencing laws attached specific sentencing effects to particular factual findings. Conspicuously absent from modern sentencing reform, however, has been a concern for factfinding procedures at sentencing. Despite creating a significant body of substantive sentencing law, lawmakers and commissions have largely ignored fundamental issues such as notice to parties, burdens of proof, appropriate factfinders, evidentiary rules, and hearing processes. Some critics of lax sentencing procedures blame this neglect on the Supreme Court's decision in McMillan v. Pennsylvania, litigated during the early development of structured sentencing reforms.

Dynel McMillan v. Pennsylvania
477 U.S. 79 (1986)

REHNQUIST, J.

Pennsylvania's Mandatory Minimum Sentencing Act, 42 Pa. Cons. Stat. 9712, . . . was adopted in 1982. It provides that anyone convicted of certain enumerated felonies is subject to a mandatory minimum sentence of five years' imprisonment if the sentencing judge finds, by a preponderance of the evidence, that the person "visibly possessed a firearm" during the commission of the offense. At the sentencing hearing, the judge is directed to consider the evidence introduced at trial and any additional evidence offered by either the defendant or the Commonwealth. The Act operates to divest the judge of discretion to impose any sentence of less than five years for the underlying felony; it does not authorize a sentence in excess of that otherwise allowed for that offense. . . .

McMillan, who shot his victim in the right buttock after an argument over a debt, was convicted by a jury of aggravated assault. [The Commonwealth sought an enhanced sentence under the Act, but McMillan and his co-defendants argued] that visible possession of a firearm is an element of the crimes for which they were being sentenced and thus must be proved beyond a reasonable doubt under In re Winship, 397 U.S. 358 (1970). . . . Petitioners also contended that even if visible possession is not an element of the offense, due process requires more than proof by a preponderance of the evidence. . . .

Winship held that "the Due Process Clause protects the accused against conviction except upon proof beyond a reasonable doubt of every fact necessary to constitute the crime with which he is charged." In Mullaney v. Wilbur, 421 U.S. 684 (1975), we held that the Due Process Clause "requires the prosecution to prove beyond a reasonable doubt the absence of the heat of passion on sudden provocation when the issue is properly presented in a homicide case." But in Patterson v. New York, 432 U.S. 197 (1977), we rejected the claim that whenever a State links the "severity of punishment" to "the presence or absence of an identified fact" the State must prove that fact beyond a reasonable doubt. In particular, we upheld against a due process challenge New York's law placing on defendants charged with murder the burden of proving the affirmative defense of extreme emotional disturbance. *Patterson* stressed that in determining what facts must be proved beyond a reasonable doubt the state legislature's definition of the elements of the offense is usually dispositive. [The] Pennsylvania Legislature has expressly provided that visible possession of a firearm is not an element of the crimes enumerated in the mandatory sentencing statute, but instead is a sentencing factor that comes into play only after the defendant has been found guilty of one of those crimes beyond a reasonable doubt. . . .

As *Patterson* recognized, of course, there are constitutional limits to the State's power in this regard; in certain limited circumstances *Winship*'s reasonable-doubt requirement applies to facts not formally identified as elements of the offense charged. Petitioners argue that Pennsylvania has gone beyond those limits and that its formal provision that visible possession is not an element of the crime is therefore of no effect. We do not think so. While we have never attempted to define precisely the constitutional limits [on] the extent to which due process forbids the reallocation or reduction of burdens of proof in criminal cases, and do not do so today, we are persuaded by several factors that Pennsylvania's Mandatory Minimum Sentencing Act does not exceed those limits.

We note first that the Act plainly does not . . . discard the presumption of innocence [nor] relieve the prosecution of its burden of proving guilt; §9712 only becomes applicable after a defendant has been duly convicted of the crime for which he is to be punished. [Further], §9712 neither alters the maximum penalty for the crime committed nor creates a separate offense calling for a separate penalty; it operates solely to limit the sentencing court's discretion in selecting a penalty within the range already available to it without the special finding of visible possession of a firearm. Section 9712 "ups the ante" for the defendant only by raising to five years the minimum sentence which may be imposed within the statutory plan. The statute gives no impression of having been tailored to permit the visible possession finding to be a tail which wags the dog of the substantive offense. . . .

Finally, we note that the specter raised by petitioners of States restructuring existing crimes in order to "evade" the commands of *Winship* just does not appear in this case. As noted above, §9712's enumerated felonies retain the same elements they had before the Mandatory Minimum Sentencing Act was passed. The Pennsylvania Legislature did not change the definition of any existing offense. It simply took one factor that has always been considered by sentencing courts to bear on punishment — the instrumentality used in committing a violent felony — and dictated the precise weight to be given that factor if the instrumentality is a firearm. Pennsylvania's decision to do so has not transformed against its will a sentencing factor into an "element" of some hypothetical "offense." . . .

Having concluded that States may treat "visible possession of a firearm" as a sentencing consideration rather than an element of a particular offense, we now turn to petitioners' subsidiary claim that due process nonetheless requires that visible possession be proved by at least clear and convincing evidence. Like the court below, we have little difficulty concluding that in this case the preponderance standard satisfies due process. [Petitioners] do not and could not claim that a sentencing court may never rely on a particular fact in passing sentence without finding that fact by "clear and convincing evidence." Sentencing courts have traditionally heard evidence and found facts without any prescribed burden of proof at all. See Williams v. New York, 337 U.S. 241 (1949). . . .

Petitioners apparently concede that Pennsylvania's scheme would pass constitutional muster if only it did not remove the sentencing court's discretion, i.e., if the legislature had simply directed the court to consider visible possession in passing sentence. We have some difficulty fathoming why the due process calculus would change simply because the legislature has seen fit to provide sentencing courts with additional guidance. Nor is there merit to the claim that a heightened burden of proof is required because visible possession is a fact concerning the crime committed rather than the background or character of the defendant. Sentencing courts necessarily consider the circumstances of an offense in selecting the appropriate punishment, and we have consistently approved sentencing schemes that mandate consideration of facts related to the crime, without suggesting that those facts must be proved beyond a reasonable doubt.

In light of the foregoing, petitioners' final claim — that the Act denies them their Sixth Amendment right to a trial by jury — merits little discussion. Petitioners again argue that the jury must determine all ultimate facts concerning the offense committed. Having concluded that Pennsylvania may properly treat visible possession as a sentencing consideration and not an element of any offense, we need only note that there is no Sixth Amendment right to jury sentencing, even where the sentence turns on specific findings of fact. . . .

STEVENS, J., dissenting.

. . . In my view, a state legislature may not dispense with the requirement of proof beyond a reasonable doubt for conduct that it targets for severe criminal penalties. Because the Pennsylvania statute challenged in this case describes conduct that the Pennsylvania Legislature obviously intended to prohibit, and because it mandates lengthy incarceration for the same, I believe that the conduct so described is an element of the criminal offense to which the proof beyond a reasonable doubt requirement applies.

Once a State defines a criminal offense, the Due Process Clause requires it to prove any component of the prohibited transaction that gives rise to both a special stigma and a special punishment beyond a reasonable doubt. . . . Nothing in *Patterson* or any of its predecessors authorizes a State to decide for itself which of the ingredients of the prohibited transaction are "elements" that it must prove beyond a reasonable doubt at trial. . . .

A legislative definition of an offense named "assault" could be broad enough to encompass every intentional infliction of harm by one person upon another, but surely the legislature could not provide that only that fact must be proved beyond a reasonable doubt and then specify a range of increased punishments if the prosecution could show by a preponderance of the evidence that the defendant robbed, raped, or killed his victim "during the commission of the offense." . . .

It is true, as the Court points out, that the enhanced punishment is within the range that was authorized for any aggravated assault. That fact does not, however, minimize the significance of a finding of visible possession of a firearm whether attention is focused on the stigmatizing or punitive consequences of that finding. The finding identifies conduct that the legislature specifically intended to prohibit and to punish by a special sanction. . . .

NOTES

1. *Standard of proof at sentencing.* In *McMillan,* the Court noted that sentencing courts "have traditionally heard evidence and found facts without any prescribed burden of proof at all." What does it mean to have no prescribed burden of proof? Can sentencing judges rely on whatever facts tickle their fancy? A more plausible reading of the *McMillan* holding is that the Constitution's due process clause allows states to treat some facts relevant to the sentence as "sentencing factors" subject only to proof by a preponderance of the evidence at sentencing. Only when an extreme increase in punishment attaches to a sentencing factor — or, to use the Court's terms, when the "tail" of the sentencing factor "wags the dog" of the substantive offense — will a federal court overturn the legislature's choices.

Virtually all states use the preponderance standard for facts to be proven at sentencing, although this issue has not been litigated (or even expressly considered) as often as one might expect. When the question does arise, most state courts have held that their state constitutions allow the prosecution to prove certain facts to increase a sentence using the lower standard of proof at sentencing. See, e.g., People v. Williams, 599 N.E.2d 913 (Ill. 1992). In a discretionary sentencing system, when judges pronounce sentences from the bench without any written opinion, how can a defendant know what standard of proof the judge applied? Are the judges making *factual* determinations that can be regulated through standards of proof or are they making legal judgments?

Structured sentencing systems, which distinctly define the factual determinations that can have an impact on sentencing outcomes, often expressly establish preponderance of the evidence as the standard of proof at sentencing. In the federal system, the U.S. Sentencing Commission, in commentary to a policy statement on resolution of disputed factors, stated that "use of a preponderance of the evidence standard is appropriate to meet due process requirements and policy concerns in resolving disputes regarding application of the guidelines to the facts of a case." U.S. Sentencing Guidelines Manual §6A1.3. Why shouldn't the traditional standard of proof beyond a reasonable doubt apply at sentencing? How about some other heightened standard, such as clear and convincing evidence?

In guideline systems, not only can certain aggravating factors lead to an increase in the applicable sentence, but certain mitigating factors can lead to a decrease in the applicable sentence. For example, in the federal system, the sentencing guidelines provide that a defendant's sentence will be less severe if the defendant establishes that her role in a large criminal enterprise was minor or minimal. Should the Constitution require different standards of proof depending on whether a fact is raised by prosecutors seeking an increase in the applicable sentence or by defendants seeking a decrease in the applicable sentence? Should legislatures and sentencing commissions develop different procedural rules and evidence standards for aggravating and mitigating facts?

2. *Formative doctrinal legacy of* McMillan.   It is important to remember that in 1986, when *McMillan* was decided, only a few states had guideline systems in place and the federal guideline system was in its developmental stages. Since then, as many more jurisdictions have adopted forms of structured sentencing, two contrasting developments have emerged. State courts and lower federal courts, citing *McMillan* and *Williams* as controlling authority, have consistently rejected constitutional challenges to structured sentencing systems that impose punishment without affording defendants at sentencing the procedural protections of a criminal trial. See, e.g., State v. Rettinghaus, 591 N.W.2d 15 (Iowa 1999); Farris v. McKune, 911 P.2d 177 (Kan. 1996); United States v. Mergerson, 995 F.2d 1285 (5th Cir. 1993). At the same time, individual judges and academic commentators have regularly lamented the continued adherence to *McMillan* and *Williams* as controlling authority, citing the unfairness of subjecting defendants to fact-driven guideline sentencing determinations without significant procedural rights. See, e.g., United States v. Concepcion, 983 F.2d 369, 389, 396 (2d Cir. 1992) (Newman, C.J., concurring); Sara Sun Beale, Procedural Issues Raised by Guidelines Sentencing: The Constitutional Significance of the "Elements of the Sentence," 35 Wm. & Mary L. Rev. 147 (1993).

3. *Tails wagging dogs.*   Most state courts have upheld legislative decisions that allow the government to prove some facts as "sentencing enhancements" at the sentencing hearing. See Vega v. People, 893 P.2d 107 (Colo. 1995). Only rarely have courts found that a fact introduced at sentencing was so important that it required proof by some standard higher than a preponderance. In United States v. Kikumura, 918 F.2d 1084 (3d Cir. 1990), the federal sentencing guidelines prescribed a sentence between 27 and 33 months for explosives and passport violations. The sentencing court, however, departed from this range to impose a 30-year sentence based on evidence that the defendant was engaged in terrorist activities for the Japanese Red Army. Although the appeals court

acknowledged that most sentencing facts could be proven under a preponderance standard, it held that a clear and convincing standard should apply to this case: "[Here] we are dealing with findings that would increase Kikumura's sentence from about 30 months to 30 years. . . . This is perhaps the most dramatic example imaginable of a sentencing hearing that functions as 'a tail which wags the dog of the substantive offense.' "

4. *Informal procedures and rules of evidence at sentencing.* Most states allow sentencing judges to consider evidence inadmissible under the rules of evidence. See Tex. Crim. Proc. Code Ann. §37.07(3). Particularly in states with an indeterminate sentencing system, the informal presentation of evidence supposedly enables to judge to make an individualized (perhaps even clinical) decision about the best response to the case and the offender at hand. More than half of the states use such an indeterminate sentencing system for large groups of cases, although many of these same states use more narrowly circumscribed sentencing rules for some crimes.

Most states indicate that evidence presented at sentencing must be relevant and reliable. According to one court, the Constitution prohibits sentencing only on "materially untrue information." State v. Ramsay, 499 A.2d 15, 20 (Vt. 1985). Reliable hearsay is often allowed, and many sentences are based mostly or entirely on hearsay. The federal courts do not apply the rules of evidence at sentencing: "the rules (other than with respect to privileges) do not apply in . . . sentencing." Fed. R. Evid. 1101(d)(3). The federal sentencing guidelines adopt the following standard: "any information may be considered, so long as it has sufficient indicia of reliability to support its probable accuracy." U.S. Sentencing Guidelines Manual §6A1.3(a). Is the federal guideline standard higher or lower than the New York practice challenged in *Williams*?

Those who argue in favor of the current federal position (and a similar position in many states) explain that rules of evidence do not apply because of the burden they would place on sentencing judges, converting the sentencing hearing into a second trial. Should Congress or the U.S. Sentencing Commission change positions and apply the rules of evidence to sentencing hearings? Professor Deborah Young favors use of the rules of evidence over other methods of increasing the reliability of factfinding at sentencing because it corrects both potential errors that benefit the prosecution and those that benefit the defense. She argues that evenhanded factfinding rules make sense at sentencing since an offender has already been convicted and should no longer be given the benefit of the presumption of innocence. Deborah Young, Fact-Finding at Federal Sentencing: Why the Guidelines Should Meet the Rules, 79 Cornell L. Rev. 299 (1994).

5. *Confrontation of witnesses.* Although the evidentiary rules governing hearsay do not apply to sentencing hearings in federal or state courts, the overlapping protections of the Sixth Amendment's confrontation clause (and the equivalent provisions of a state constitution) still might require that a defendant be allowed to cross-examine witnesses at the sentencing hearing. The Supreme Court interpreted the confrontation clause in Crawford v. Washington, 541 U.S. 36 (2004), to bar admission during trial of "testimonial" hearsay unless the declarant is unavailable and the defendant had a prior opportunity for cross-examination of the declarant. Would the same reasoning apply to the testimony and evidence used at sentencing?

Before *Crawford,* courts mostly concluded that the confrontation clause did not apply to the evidence presented during a sentencing hearing. See United States v. Wise, 976 F.2d 393 (8th Cir. 1992); State v. DeSalvo, 903 P.2d 202 (Mont. 1995). After *Crawford,* the lower federal courts and state courts reopened the question of whether the use of testimonial hearsay during noncapital sentencing proceedings violates the defendant's confrontation rights. Most concluded that it does not. See Summers v. State, 148 P.3d 778 (Nev. 2006).

Might the courts rule differently in capital sentencing proceedings? The imposition of a death sentence based on information that a defendant does not have the opportunity to deny or explain may run afoul of the confrontation clause, but this does not necessarily require full confrontation rights. See Gardner v. Florida, 430 U.S. 349 (1977); United States v. Brown, 441 F.3d 1330, 1361 n.12 (11th Cir. 2006) (applying *Crawford* to capital sentencing); United States v. Fields, 483 F.3d 313 (5th Cir. 2007) (declining to apply *Crawford*); State v. McGill, 140 P.3d 930 (Ariz. 2006) (full confrontation rights do not apply to rebuttal testimony at capital sentencing hearing).

It is clear that the sentencing hearing is part of the "criminal proceedings" and that the right to counsel applies at that stage of the proceedings. Mempa v. Rhay, 389 U.S. 128 (1967) (establishing right to counsel at sentencing). If the Sixth Amendment's right to counsel (granted to "the accused") applies at sentencing, why doesn't the same conclusion apply to the Sixth Amendment's right to confront witnesses?

6. *Right to remain silent.*   In Mitchell v. United States, 526 U.S. 314 (1999), the Supreme Court held that a defendant, after pleading guilty to a specific offense, can assert her Fifth Amendment privilege against self-incrimination at the sentencing hearing and not have a judge draw an adverse inference from the defendant's silence. Mitchell refused to testify at a sentencing hearing about her involvement in a cocaine conspiracy. The sentencing judge drew a negative inference from the defendant's refusal to discuss the amount of drugs involved in the offense and sentenced her to ten years' imprisonment. The Supreme Court reversed, holding that neither the defendant's guilty plea nor her statements at a plea colloquy functioned as a waiver of her right to remain silent at sentencing. Furthermore, relying on Griffin v. California, 380 U.S. 609 (1995), which held that it is constitutionally impermissible for the prosecutor or judge to comment at trial on a criminal defendant's refusal to testify, the Court concluded that the defendant should have been allowed to remain silent without paying the price of a longer sentence.

7. *Other rights at sentencing.*   Although many academic commentators focus on (and lament) the courts' refusal to extend to sentencing traditional trial rights and procedures relating to proof and evidence standards, Professor Alan Michaels has pointed out that many more trial rights apply at sentencing than one might expect. Michaels systematically examined judicial decisions regarding the applicability of constitutional trial rights to sentencing proceedings and produced a comprehensive taxonomy of sentencing rights. Summarizing the cases relating to 25 trial rights "from employing an attorney to not having inferences drawn from one's silence, from bail and *Brady* to presence and proceeding pro se," Michaels concluded that that the Supreme Court "has found roughly one quarter apply at sentencing and one quarter do not" and has

not ruled definitively on the other half. The lower federal courts have reached a similar pattern of outcomes. Alan C. Michaels, Trial Rights at Sentencing, 81 N.C. L. Rev. 1771, 1775 (2003). According to Michaels, the Court's decisions tend to follow what he calls a "best estimate" principle: trial rights that are "directed primarily at determining the correct result apply at sentencing, whereas those rights designed to offer special protection to a defendant's liberty or autonomy interests do not." Id. at 1771.

2. *The Resurgent Jury Trial Right*

When jurisdictions began to develop structured reforms in which sentencing determinations turned on particular facts, sentencing became a more trial-like enterprise and the justification for having limited procedural rights at sentencing lost a key foundation. Yet legislators and sentencing commissions enacting structured sentencing reforms paid little attention to procedural rules and generally failed to justify their continued use of lax procedures. As a result, the soundness and stability of *Williams* and *McMillan* became ever more questionable.

After offering a series of clues pointing in different directions, the Supreme Court in 2004 finally laid out a new vision of constitutional limits on sentencing procedures. The following opinion represents an alternative to the model of informal sentencing procedures, creating stronger constitutional limits on the power of legislatures to sort factual issues into a formal trial process and an informal sentencing process.

|| *Ralph Blakely, Jr. v. Washington* ||
542 U.S. 296 (2004)

SCALIA, J.

Petitioner Ralph Howard Blakely, Jr., pleaded guilty to the kidnaping of his estranged wife. The facts admitted in his plea, standing alone, supported a maximum sentence of 53 months. Pursuant to state law, the court imposed an "exceptional" sentence of 90 months after making a judicial determination that he had acted with "deliberate cruelty." We consider whether this violated petitioner's Sixth Amendment right to trial by jury.

I

Petitioner married his wife Yolanda in 1973. He was evidently a difficult man to live with, having been diagnosed at various times with psychological and personality disorders including paranoid schizophrenia. His wife ultimately filed for divorce. In 1998, he abducted her from their orchard home in Grant County, Washington, binding her with duct tape and forcing her at knifepoint into a wooden box in the bed of his pickup truck. In the process, he implored her to dismiss the divorce suit and related trust proceedings.

When the couple's 13-year-old son Ralphy returned home from school, petitioner ordered him to follow in another car, threatening to harm Yolanda with a shotgun if he did not do so. Ralphy escaped and sought help when they stopped at a gas station, but petitioner continued on with Yolanda to a friend's house in Montana. He was finally arrested after the friend called the police.

The State charged petitioner with first-degree kidnaping. Upon reaching a plea agreement, however, it reduced the charge to second-degree kidnaping involving domestic violence and use of a firearm. Petitioner entered a guilty plea admitting the elements of second-degree kidnaping and the domestic-violence and firearm allegations, but no other relevant facts.

The case then proceeded to sentencing. In Washington, second-degree kidnaping is a class B felony. State law provides that [a person convicted of a class B felony faces a maximum punishment of ten years confinement]. Other provisions of state law, however, further limit the range of sentences a judge may impose. Washington's Sentencing Reform Act specifies, for petitioner's offense of second-degree kidnaping with a firearm, a "standard range" of 49 to 53 months. A judge may impose a sentence above the standard range if he finds "substantial and compelling reasons justifying an exceptional sentence." §9.94A.120(2). The Act lists aggravating factors that justify such a departure, which it recites to be illustrative rather than exhaustive. . . . When a judge imposes an exceptional sentence, he must set forth findings of fact and conclusions of law supporting it. A reviewing court will reverse the sentence if it finds that under a clearly erroneous standard there is insufficient evidence in the record to support the reasons for imposing an exceptional sentence.

Pursuant to the plea agreement, the State recommended a sentence within the standard range of 49 to 53 months. After hearing Yolanda's description of the kidnaping, however, the judge rejected the State's recommendation and imposed an exceptional sentence of 90 months — 37 months beyond the standard maximum. He justified the sentence on the ground that petitioner had acted with "deliberate cruelty," a statutorily enumerated ground for departure in domestic-violence cases.

Faced with an unexpected increase of more than three years in his sentence, petitioner objected. The judge accordingly conducted a 3-day bench hearing featuring testimony from petitioner, Yolanda, Ralphy, a police officer, and medical experts. After the hearing, he issued 32 findings of fact, [reaffirming] his initial determination of deliberate cruelty. Petitioner appealed, arguing that this sentencing procedure deprived him of his federal constitutional right to have a jury determine beyond a reasonable doubt all facts legally essential to his sentence.

II

This case requires us to apply the rule we expressed in Apprendi v. New Jersey, 530 U.S. 466, 490 (2000): "Other than the fact of a prior conviction, any fact that increases the penalty for a crime beyond the prescribed statutory maximum must be submitted to a jury, and proved beyond a reasonable doubt." This rule reflects two longstanding tenets of common-law criminal jurisprudence: that the "truth of every accusation" against a defendant "should afterwards be confirmed by the unanimous suffrage of twelve of his equals and neighbours," 4 W. Blackstone, Commentaries on the Laws of England 343 (1769), and that "an accusation which lacks any particular fact which the

law makes essential to the punishment is . . . no accusation within the requirements of the common law, and it is no accusation in reason," 1 J. Bishop,
Criminal Procedure §87, p. 55 (2d ed. 1872). These principles have been
acknowledged by courts and treatises since the earliest days of graduated sentencing. . . .

Apprendi involved a New Jersey hate-crime statute that authorized a 20-year
sentence, despite the usual 10-year maximum, if the judge found the crime to
have been committed "with a purpose to intimidate . . . because of race, color,
gender, handicap, religion, sexual orientation or ethnicity." . . .

In this case, petitioner was sentenced to more than three years above the
53-month statutory maximum of the standard range because he had acted with
"deliberate cruelty." The facts supporting that finding were neither admitted by
petitioner nor found by a jury. The State nevertheless contends that there was no
Apprendi violation because the relevant "statutory maximum" is not 53 months,
but the 10-year maximum for class B felonies in §9A.20.021(1)(b). . . . Our precedents make clear, however, that the "statutory maximum" for *Apprendi* purposes is the maximum sentence a judge may impose solely on the basis of the
facts reflected in the jury verdict or admitted by the defendant. In other words,
the relevant "statutory maximum" is not the maximum sentence a judge may
impose after finding additional facts, but the maximum he may impose without
any additional findings. When a judge inflicts punishment that the jury's verdict
alone does not allow, the jury has not found all the facts "which the law makes
essential to the punishment," Bishop, *supra*, §87, at 55, and the judge exceeds
his proper authority.

The judge in this case could not have imposed the exceptional 90-month
sentence solely on the basis of the facts admitted in the guilty plea. Those facts
alone were insufficient because, as the Washington Supreme Court has explained,
"[a] reason offered to justify an exceptional sentence can be considered only if it
takes into account factors other than those which are used in computing
the standard range sentence for the offense," State v. Gore, 21 P.3d 262,
277 (Wash. 2001), which in this case included the elements of second-degree
kidnaping and the use of a firearm. Had the judge imposed the 90-month
sentence solely on the basis of the plea, he would have been reversed. . . .

The State defends the sentence by drawing an analogy to those we upheld
in McMillan v. Pennsylvania, 477 U.S. 79 (1986), and Williams v. New York, 337
U.S. 241 (1949). Neither case is on point. *McMillan* involved a sentencing
scheme that imposed a statutory minimum if a judge found a particular fact.
We specifically noted that the statute "does not authorize a sentence in excess
of that otherwise allowed for [the underlying] offense." *Williams* involved an
indeterminate-sentencing regime that allowed a judge (but did not compel
him) to rely on facts outside the trial record in determining whether to sentence
a defendant to death. The judge could have sentenced the defendant to death
giving no reason at all. Thus, neither case involved a sentence greater than what
state law authorized on the basis of the verdict alone. . . .

III

Our commitment to *Apprendi* in this context reflects not just respect for
longstanding precedent, but the need to give intelligible content to the right of

jury trial. That right is no mere procedural formality, but a fundamental reservation of power in our constitutional structure. Just as suffrage ensures the people's ultimate control in the legislative and executive branches, jury trial is meant to ensure their control in the judiciary. *Apprendi* carries out this design by ensuring that the judge's authority to sentence derives wholly from the jury's verdict. Without that restriction, the jury would not exercise the control that the Framers intended.

Those who would reject *Apprendi* are resigned to one of two alternatives. The first is that the jury need only find whatever facts the legislature chooses to label elements of the crime, and that those it labels sentencing factors—no matter how much they may increase the punishment—may be found by the judge. This would mean, for example, that a judge could sentence a man for committing murder even if the jury convicted him only of illegally possessing the firearm used to commit it—or of making an illegal lane change while fleeing the death scene. Not even *Apprendi*'s critics would advocate this absurd result. The jury could not function as circuit-breaker in the State's machinery of justice if it were relegated to making a determination that the defendant at some point did something wrong, a mere preliminary to a judicial inquisition into the facts of the crime the State actually seeks to punish.

The second alternative is that legislatures may establish legally essential sentencing factors within limits—limits crossed when, perhaps, the sentencing factor is a "tail which wags the dog of the substantive offense." *McMillan*, 477 U.S., at 88. What this means in operation is that the law must not go too far—it must not exceed the judicial estimation of the proper role of the judge.

The subjectivity of this standard is obvious. Petitioner argued below that second-degree kidnaping with deliberate cruelty was essentially the same as first-degree kidnaping, the very charge he had avoided by pleading to a lesser offense. . . . Petitioner's 90-month sentence exceeded the 53-month standard maximum by almost 70 percent; the Washington Supreme Court in other cases has upheld exceptional sentences 15 times the standard maximum. Did the court go too far in any of these cases? There is no answer that legal analysis can provide. . . .

Whether the Sixth Amendment incorporates this manipulable standard rather than *Apprendi*'s bright-line rule depends on the plausibility of the claim that the Framers would have left definition of the scope of jury power up to judges' intuitive sense of how far is too far. We think that claim not plausible at all, because the very reason the Framers put a jury-trial guarantee in the Constitution is that they were unwilling to trust government to mark out the role of the jury.

IV

. . . This case is not about whether determinate sentencing is constitutional, only about how it can be implemented in a way that respects the Sixth Amendment. . . .

Justice O'Connor argues that, because determinate sentencing schemes involving judicial factfinding entail less judicial discretion than indeterminate schemes, the constitutionality of the latter implies the constitutionality of the former. This argument is flawed on a number of levels. First, the Sixth Amendment by its terms is not a limitation on judicial power, but a reservation of jury power. It limits judicial power only to the extent that the claimed judicial power infringes on the province of the jury. Indeterminate sentencing does not do so. It increases judicial discretion, to be sure, but not at the expense of the jury's traditional function of finding the facts essential to lawful imposition of the penalty. . . . In a system that says the judge may punish burglary with 10 to 40 years, every burglar knows he is risking 40 years in jail. In a system that punishes burglary with a 10-year sentence, with another 30 added for use of a gun, the burglar who enters a home unarmed is entitled to no more than a 10-year sentence — and by reason of the Sixth Amendment the facts bearing upon that entitlement must be found by a jury.

But even assuming that restraint of judicial power unrelated to the jury's role is a Sixth Amendment objective, it is far from clear that *Apprendi* disserves that goal. Determinate judicial-factfinding schemes entail less judicial power than indeterminate schemes, but more judicial power than determinate jury-factfinding schemes. Whether *Apprendi* increases judicial power overall depends on what States with determinate judicial-factfinding schemes would do, given the choice between the two alternatives. Justice O'Connor simply assumes that the net effect will favor judges, but she has no empirical basis for that prediction. Indeed, what evidence we have points exactly the other way: When the Kansas Supreme Court found *Apprendi* infirmities in that State's determinate-sentencing regime in State v. Gould, 23 P.3d 801, 809-814 (Kan. 2001), the legislature responded not by reestablishing indeterminate sentencing but by applying *Apprendi*'s requirements to its current regime. The result was less, not more, judicial power.

Justice Breyer argues that *Apprendi* works to the detriment of criminal defendants who plead guilty by depriving them of the opportunity to argue sentencing factors to a judge. But nothing prevents a defendant from waiving his *Apprendi* rights. When a defendant pleads guilty, the State is free to seek judicial sentence enhancements so long as the defendant either stipulates to the relevant facts or consents to judicial factfinding. . . . Even a defendant who stands trial may consent to judicial factfinding as to sentence enhancements, which may well be in his interest if relevant evidence would prejudice him at trial. We do not understand how *Apprendi* can possibly work to the detriment of those who are free, if they think its costs outweigh its benefits, to render it inapplicable.

Nor do we see any merit to Justice Breyer's contention that *Apprendi* is unfair to criminal defendants because, if States respond by enacting "17-element robbery crimes," prosecutors will have more elements with which to bargain. Bargaining already exists with regard to sentencing factors because defendants can either stipulate or contest the facts that make them applicable. If there is any difference between bargaining over sentencing factors and bargaining over elements, the latter probably favors the defendant. Every new element that a prosecutor can threaten to charge is also an element that a defendant can threaten to contest at trial and make the prosecutor prove beyond a reasonable doubt. Moreover, given the sprawling scope of most criminal codes, and the power to affect sentences by making (even nonbinding) sentencing recommendations, there is already no shortage of in terrorem tools at prosecutors' disposal.

Any evaluation of *Apprendi*'s "fairness" to criminal defendants must compare it with the regime it replaced, in which a defendant, with no warning in either his indictment or plea, would routinely see his maximum potential sentence balloon from as little as five years to as much as life imprisonment . . . based not on facts proved to his peers beyond a reasonable doubt, but on facts extracted after trial from a report compiled by a probation officer who the judge thinks more likely got it right than got it wrong. . . .

Justice Breyer's more general argument—that *Apprendi* undermines alternatives to adversarial factfinding—is not so much a criticism of *Apprendi* as an assault on jury trial generally. . . . Ultimately, our decision cannot turn on whether or to what degree trial by jury impairs the efficiency or fairness of criminal justice. One can certainly argue that both these values would be better served by leaving justice entirely in the hands of professionals; many nations of the world, particularly those following civil-law traditions, take just that course. There is not one shred of doubt, however, about the Framers' paradigm for criminal justice: not the civil-law ideal of administrative perfection, but the common-law ideal of limited state power accomplished by strict division of authority between judge and jury. . . .

Petitioner was sentenced to prison for more than three years beyond what the law allowed for the crime to which he confessed, on the basis of a disputed finding that he had acted with "deliberate cruelty." The Framers would not have thought it too much to demand that, before depriving a man of three more years of his liberty, the State should suffer the modest inconvenience of submitting its accusation to "the unanimous suffrage of twelve of his equals and neighbours," 4 Blackstone, Commentaries, at 343, rather than a lone employee of the State. . . .

O'CONNOR, J., dissenting.

The legacy of today's opinion, whether intended or not, will be the consolidation of sentencing power in the State and Federal Judiciaries. The Court says to Congress and state legislatures: If you want to constrain the sentencing discretion of judges and bring some uniformity to sentencing, it will cost you— dearly. Congress and States, faced with the burdens imposed by the extension of *Apprendi* to the present context, will either trim or eliminate altogether their sentencing guidelines schemes and, with them, 20 years of sentencing reform. . . .

I

. . . Prior to 1981, Washington, like most other States and the Federal Government, employed an indeterminate sentencing scheme. . . . This system of unguided discretion inevitably resulted in severe disparities in sentences received and served by defendants committing the same offense and having similar criminal histories. . . . To counteract these trends, the state legislature passed the Sentencing Reform Act of 1981. The Act had the laudable purposes of making the criminal justice system "accountable to the public," and ensuring that "the punishment for a criminal offense is proportionate to the seriousness of the offense [and] commensurate with the punishment imposed on others committing similar offenses." Wash. Rev. Code Ann. §9.94A.010. The Act neither increased any of the statutory sentencing ranges for the three types of felonies . . . nor reclassified any substantive offenses. It merely placed meaningful constraints on discretion to sentence offenders within the statutory ranges, and eliminated parole. There is thus no evidence that the legislature was attempting to manipulate the statutory elements of criminal offenses or to circumvent the procedural protections of the Bill of Rights. . . .

II

Far from disregarding principles of due process and the jury trial right, as the majority today suggests, Washington's reform has served them. Before passage of the Act, a defendant charged with second degree kidnaping, like petitioner, had no idea whether he would receive a 10-year sentence or probation. The ultimate sentencing determination could turn as much on the idiosyncrasies of a particular judge as on the specifics of the defendant's crime or background. A defendant did not know what facts, if any, about his offense or his history would be considered relevant by the sentencing judge or by the parole board. After passage of the Act, a defendant charged with second degree kidnaping knows what his presumptive sentence will be; he has a good idea of the types of factors that a sentencing judge can and will consider when deciding whether to sentence him outside that range; he is guaranteed meaningful appellate review to protect against an arbitrary sentence. . . .

While not a constitutional prohibition on guidelines schemes, the majority's decision today exacts a substantial constitutional tax. [Facts] that historically have been taken into account by sentencing judges to assess a sentence within a broad range — such as drug quantity, role in the offense, risk of bodily harm — all must now be charged in an indictment and submitted to a jury simply because it is the legislature, rather than the judge, that constrains the extent to which such facts may be used to impose a sentence within a pre-existing statutory range. . . . The majority may be correct that States and the Federal Government will be willing to bear some of these costs. But simple economics dictate that they will not, and cannot, bear them all. To the extent that they do not, there will be an inevitable increase in judicial discretion with all of its attendant failings.

[The] guidelines served due process by providing notice to petitioner of the consequences of his acts; they vindicated his jury trial right by informing him of the stakes of risking trial; they served equal protection by ensuring petitioner that invidious characteristics such as race would not impact his sentence. Given these observations, it is difficult for me to discern what principle besides doctrinaire formalism actually motivates today's decision. . . .

The consequences of today's decision will be as far reaching as they are disturbing. Washington's sentencing system is by no means unique. Numerous other States have enacted guidelines systems, as has the Federal Government. Today's decision casts constitutional doubt over them all and, in so doing, threatens an untold number of criminal judgments. Every sentence imposed under such guidelines in cases currently pending on direct appeal is in jeopardy. . . . What I have feared most has now come to pass: Over 20 years of sentencing reform are all but lost, and tens of thousands of criminal judgments are in jeopardy. I respectfully dissent.

KENNEDY, J., dissenting.

. . . The Court, in my respectful submission, disregards the fundamental principle under our constitutional system that different branches of government converse with each other on matters of vital common interest. . . . Case-by-case judicial determinations often yield intelligible patterns that can be refined by legislatures and codified into statutes or rules as general standards. As these legislative enactments are followed by incremental judicial interpretation, the legislatures may respond again, and the cycle repeats. This recurring dialogue, an essential source for the elaboration and the evolution of the law, is basic constitutional theory in action.

Sentencing guidelines are a prime example of this collaborative process. Dissatisfied with the wide disparity in sentencing, participants in the criminal justice system, including judges, pressed for legislative reforms. In response, legislators drew from these participants' shared experiences and enacted measures to correct the problems. [Because] the Constitution does not prohibit the dynamic and fruitful dialogue between the judicial and legislative branches of government that has marked sentencing reform on both the state and the federal levels for more than 20 years, I dissent.

BREYER, J., dissenting.

[The] difference between a traditional sentencing factor and an element of a greater offense often comes down to a legislative choice about which label to affix. [One might ask why it should matter for jury trial purposes whether the statute (or guideline) labels a fact as a sentencing factor or a crime element. But] the conclusion that the Sixth Amendment always requires identical treatment of the two scenarios [carries] consequences that threaten the fairness of our traditional criminal justice system; it distorts historical sentencing or criminal trial practices; and it upsets settled law on which legislatures have relied in designing punishment systems. . . .

As a result of the majority's rule, sentencing must now take one of three forms, each of which risks either impracticality, unfairness, or harm to the jury trial right the majority purports to strengthen. This circumstance shows that the majority's Sixth Amendment interpretation cannot be right.

A

A first option for legislators is to create a simple, pure or nearly pure "charge offense" or "determinate" sentencing system. In such a system, an indictment would charge a few facts which, taken together, constitute a crime, such as robbery. Robbery would carry a single sentence, say, five years' imprisonment. . . .

Such a system assures uniformity, but at intolerable costs. First, simple determinate sentencing systems impose identical punishments on people who committed their crimes in very different ways. When dramatically different conduct ends up being punished the same way, an injustice has taken place. Simple determinate sentencing has the virtue of treating like cases alike, but it simultaneously fails to treat different cases differently. . . .

Second, in a world of statutorily fixed mandatory sentences for many crimes, determinate sentencing gives tremendous power to prosecutors to manipulate sentences through their choice of charges. Prosecutors can simply charge, or threaten to charge, defendants with crimes bearing higher mandatory sentences. Defendants, knowing that they will not have a chance to argue for a lower sentence in front of a judge, may plead to charges that they might otherwise contest. . . .

B

A second option for legislators is to return to a system of indeterminate sentencing. . . . When such systems were in vogue, they were criticized, and rightly so, for producing unfair disparities, including race-based disparities, in the punishment of similarly situated defendants. [Under] such a system, the judge could vary the sentence greatly based upon his findings about how the defendant had committed the crime — findings that might not have been made by a "preponderance of the evidence," much less "beyond a reasonable doubt." Returning to such a system would . . . do little to ensure the control of what the majority calls "the people," i.e., the jury, "in the judiciary," since "the people" would only decide the defendant's guilt, a finding with no effect on the duration of the sentence. . . .

C

A third option is that which the Court seems to believe legislators will in fact take. That is the option of retaining structured schemes that attempt to punish similar conduct similarly and different conduct differently, but modifying them to conform to *Apprendi*'s dictates. Judges would be able to depart downward from presumptive sentences upon finding that mitigating factors were present, but would not be able to depart upward unless the prosecutor charged the aggravating fact to a jury and proved it beyond a reasonable doubt. . . .

This option can be implemented in one of two ways. The first way would be for legislatures to subdivide each crime into a list of complex crimes, each of which would be defined to include commonly found sentencing factors such as drug quantity, type of victim, presence of violence, degree of injury, use of gun, and so on. A legislature, for example, might enact a robbery statute, modeled on robbery sentencing guidelines, that increases punishment depending upon (1) the nature of the institution robbed, (2) the (a) presence of, (b) brandishing of, (c) other use of, a firearm, (3) making of a death threat, (4) presence of (a) ordinary, (b) serious, (c) permanent or life threatening, bodily injury, (5) abduction, (6) physical restraint, (7) taking of a firearm, (8) taking of drugs, (9) value of property loss, etc.

[Under this option, the] prosecutor, through control of the precise charge, controls the punishment, thereby marching the sentencing system directly away from, not toward, one important guideline goal: rough uniformity of punishment for those who engage in roughly the same real criminal conduct. . . .

This "complex charge offense" system . . . prejudices defendants who seek trial, for it can put them in the untenable position of contesting material aggravating facts in the guilt phases of their trials. Consider a defendant who is charged, not with mere possession of cocaine, but with the specific offense of possession of more than 500 grams of cocaine. Or consider a defendant charged, not with murder, but with the new crime of murder using a machete. Or consider a defendant whom the prosecution wants to claim was a "supervisor," rather than an ordinary gang member. How can a Constitution that guarantees due process put these defendants, as a matter of course, in the position of arguing, "I did not sell drugs, and if I did, I did not sell more than 500 grams" or, "I did not kill him, and if I did, I did not use a machete," or "I did not engage in gang activity, and certainly not as a supervisor" to a single jury? . . .

The majority announces that there really is no problem here because "States may continue to offer judicial factfinding as a matter of course to all defendants who plead guilty" and defendants may stipulate to the relevant facts or consent to judicial factfinding. [The] fairness problem arises because States may very well decide that they will not permit defendants to carve subsets of facts out of the new, *Apprendi*-required 17-element robbery crime, seeking a judicial determination as to some of those facts and a jury determination as to others. . . .

The second way to make sentencing guidelines *Apprendi*-compliant would be to require at least two juries for each defendant whenever aggravating facts are present: one jury to determine guilt of the crime charged, and an additional jury to try the disputed facts that, if found, would aggravate the sentence. Our experience with bifurcated trials in the capital punishment context suggests that requiring them for run-of-the-mill sentences would be costly, both in money and in judicial time and resources. . . . The Court can announce that the Constitution requires at least two jury trials for each criminal defendant — one for guilt, another for sentencing — but only because it knows full well that more than 90% of defendants will not go to trial even once, much less insist on two or more trials.

What will be the consequences of the Court's holding for the 90% of defendants who do not go to trial? The truthful answer is that we do not know. . . . At the least, the greater expense attached to trials and their greater complexity, taken together in the context of an overworked criminal justice system, will likely mean, other things being equal, fewer trials and a greater reliance upon plea bargaining — a system in which punishment is set not by judges or juries but by advocates acting under bargaining constraints. At the same time, the greater power of the prosecutor to control the punishment through the charge would likely weaken the relation between real conduct and real punishment as well. . . .

For more than a century, questions of punishment (not those of guilt or innocence) have reflected determinations made, not only by juries, but also by judges, probation officers, and executive parole boards. Such truth-seeking determinations have rested upon both adversarial and non-adversarial processes. The Court's holding undermines efforts to reform these processes, for it means that legislatures cannot both permit judges to base sentencing upon real conduct and seek, through guidelines, to make the results more uniform. . . .

Now, let us return to the question I posed at the outset. Why does the Sixth Amendment permit a jury trial right (in respect to a particular fact) to depend upon a legislative labeling decision, namely, the legislative decision to label the fact a sentencing fact, instead of an element of the crime? The answer is that the fairness and effectiveness of a sentencing system, and the related fairness and effectiveness of the criminal justice system itself, depend upon the legislature's possessing the constitutional authority (within due process limits) to make that labeling decision. To restrict radically the legislature's power in this respect, as the majority interprets the Sixth Amendment to do, prevents the legislature from seeking sentencing systems that are consistent with, and indeed may help to advance, the Constitution's greater fairness goals. . . . Whatever the faults of guidelines systems—and there are many—they are more likely to find their cure in legislation emerging from the experience of, and discussion among, all elements of the criminal justice community, than in a virtually unchangeable constitutional decision of this Court. . . .

NOTES

1. Blakely *and sentencing guideline systems.* The sweeping language that Justice Scalia used in *Blakely* suggested to most readers that many nondiscretionary sentencing procedures were constitutionally suspect. Most immediately, the *Blakely* decision cast doubt on the constitutionality of the federal sentencing guidelines. As we saw in Chapter 3, the second shoe did drop for the federal system: a few months after *Blakely,* the Supreme Court ruled in United States v. Booker, 543 U.S. 220 (2005), that the presumptive guideline system in the federal courts violated the Sixth Amendment jury trial guarantee. The Court remedied this constitutional error in a surprising way, by excising only those portions of the federal statutes that gave the guidelines binding force on the sentencing judge.

In the states, the courts responded to *Blakely* in a variety of ways. Some declared that their determinate sentencing systems violated jury trial rights as described in *Blakely.* See Smylie v. State, 823 N.E.2d 679 (Ind. 2005); State v. Natale, 878 A.2d 724 (N.J. 2005). Others labored to demonstrate that their statutes governing sentencing leave enough discretion to the trial judge to avoid any *Blakely* problems. See People v. Black, 113 P.3d 534, 543, 548 (Cal. 2005); State v. Lopez, 123 P.3d 754, 768 (N.M. 2005).

The Supreme Court reaffirmed the impact of the *Blakely* rule on a variety of structured sentencing laws in Cunningham v. California, 127 S. Ct. 856 (2007). The California sentencing laws gave judges a choice among three sentencing outcomes in many cases, and designated the "middle term" as the presumptively correct sentence, but allowed the judge to select the upper term after finding "circumstances in aggravation" of the offense. Justice Ginsburg's opinion declared that the California determinate sentencing law violated the "bright-line rule" of *Apprendi*: "Except for a prior conviction, any fact that increases the penalty for a crime beyond the prescribed statutory maximum must be submitted to a jury, and proved beyond a reasonable doubt."

To what extent do the *Blakely* and *Apprendi* cases cast doubt on earlier holdings about sentencing procedure? In Nichols v. United States, 511 U.S. 738 (1994), the Court held that a sentencing court may consider a defendant's previous uncounseled misdemeanor conviction when sentencing him for a subsequent offense, and it cited both *Williams* and *McMillan* when stressing that the "traditional understanding of the sentencing process [is] less exacting than the process of establishing guilt." Recall also from Chapter 5 the decision in Witte v. United States, 515 U.S. 389 (1995), where the Court held that there was no double jeopardy violation when a prior conviction increased punishment through sentence calculations under the federal sentencing guidelines. In United States v. Watts, 519 U.S. 148 (1997), the Court stressed the "significance of the different standards of proof that govern at trial and sentencing" in holding that courts sentencing under the federal guidelines could consider conduct relating to charges of which defendants had been acquitted. Do any of these decisions survive *Blakely*?

2. *Glimpses of broader jury rights before* Apprendi.   Though now overshadowed by the *Apprendi* and *Blakely* decisions, the Supreme Court's decisions in Almendarez-Torres v. United States, 523 U.S. 224 (1998), and Jones v. United States, 526 U.S. 227 (1999), showed that the traditional approach to sentencing procedures was near the breaking point. In *Almendarez-Torres,* the Supreme Court interpreted the federal alien reentry statute, which imposed punishment of up to two years in prison if a deported alien reentered the United States without permission, but raised the maximum sentence to 20 years if the alien had been convicted of an aggravated felony before deportation. Although the government asked for the enhanced sentence for Almendarez-Torres, prosecutors did not allege his prior felony in the indictment or prove it at trial but instead submitted proof of his record at sentencing. On appeal, Almendarez-Torres argued that the recidivism issue could not be treated as a mere sentencing enhancement but rather constituted an element of the separate aggravated felony authorizing the 20-year sentence. In a 5-4 decision, the Supreme Court interpreted the reentry statute to provide for a recidivism enhancement only as a sentencing factor, and thus the facts about his prior record were not subject to the procedural rules of proof at trial. The majority opinion, authored by Justice Breyer, emphasized that recidivism long has been a sentencing factor not needed to be proven to the jury.

When a similar issue arose the following term in Jones v. United States, there were five votes to recast what looked like a sentencing factor into a traditional element of an offense. The majority in *Jones* concluded that the federal carjacking statute created distinct crimes with distinct elements, because several related subsections defined increasing maximum penalty levels if the offense resulted in serious bodily injury or death. In a revealing footnote, the *Jones* Court suggested an emerging due process principle that "any fact (other than prior conviction) that increases the maximum penalty for a crime must be charged in an indictment, submitted to a jury, and proven beyond a reasonable doubt." The majority reinterpreted *Almendarez-Torres* to create a recidivism "exception" to this rule.

Despite these early clues in the cases, the decisions in *Apprendi* and *Blakely* took most observers by surprise. Even after the Court decided *Apprendi,* most observers believed that the decision was limited to factual findings that moved a sentence higher than the original statutory maximum, not findings that changed the relevant maximum under the sentencing guidelines. Among the persistent critiques of the federal sentencing system over the years, almost nobody claimed that the key problem was its failure to rely on juries for factual findings.

3. *The Swiss cheese* Blakely *holding.* Despite the breadth of *Blakely*'s holding and dicta, the ruling still allows judicial factfinding in an array of sentencing settings. The *Blakely* decision formally distinguished United States v. Harris, 536 U.S. 545 (2002), which permits judges to find those facts that increase *minimum* sentences. The *Blakely* decision also formally distinguished Williams v. New York, 337 U.S. 241 (1949), which permits judges to find facts in the course of making discretionary sentencing determinations. In addition, the *Apprendi* and *Blakely* rulings apply only to those facts that *increase* sentences; judges may still find those facts that the law provides as the basis for decreasing sentences. As we have seen, the decision in Almendarez-Torres v. United States, 523 U.S. 224 (1998), built a "prior conviction" exception into the Sixth Amendment's jury requirements for sentencing facts. Both *Apprendi* and *Blakely* stated that the jury must find sentence-enhancing facts "other than the fact of a prior conviction." See generally Kevin Reitz, The New Sentencing Conundrum: Policy and Constitutional Law at Cross-Purposes, 105 Colum. L. Rev. 1082 (2005) ("As things stand, there are so many exceptions to the new safeguards announced in *Apprendi* and *Blakely*—and many of them are important exceptions—that we are left with a kind of constitutional 'Swiss cheese.'"). Could a jurisdiction, drawing on these gaps in the reach of the *Blakely* rule, construct a sound sentencing system that is still administered principally through judicial factfinding?

4. *Jury rights and plea bargaining.* Because the *Apprendi* and *Blakely* decisions established that defendants are entitled to a fuller set of trial procedures for facts that raise the applicable maximum sentence, the cases appear to give a big victory to defendants. It is worth asking, however, how this grant of trial rights will play out in a world that only rarely sees criminal cases go to trial. Professor Stephanos Bibas argued that the trial right protected by *Apprendi* does little good and much harm for most defendants, because the rule gave prosecutors an incentive to pressure defendants into admitting as part of a plea agreement those facts that would support a higher sentence. See Stephanos Bibas, Judicial Fact-Finding and Sentence Enhancements in a World of Guilty Pleas, 110 Yale L.J. 1097, 1100 (2001). Professors Nancy King and Susan Klein, responded, however, that prosecutors have no more leverage over defendants after *Apprendi* than they did before, while defendants have the additional bargaining chip of forcing a prosecutor to prove certain facts to a jury beyond a reasonable doubt. Nancy J. King & Susan R. Klein, *Apprendi* and Plea Bargaining, 54 Stan. L. Rev. 295, 297 (2001). How might you resolve such conflicting claims about bargaining behavior? Is there a practical empirical test you might perform? A relevant theoretical model that makes one account more plausible than the other?

5. *Retroactivity and cases in the pipeline.* The *Blakely* holding could call into question the validity of hundreds of thousands of existing sentences that were imposed without input from a jury. In Teague v. Lane, 489 U.S. 288 (1989), the Supreme Court set out the modern ground rules for the retroactive application of its constitutional pronouncements. Reduced to their essence, these rules suggest that *Blakely* applies to all cases that were not yet "final" (meaning that direct appeals were still pending) on the date the decision was rendered (June 24, 2004), but *Blakely* likely will not apply to any cases that were final on that date.

Despite viable arguments about *Blakely*'s retroactivity, most commentators take the (slightly cynical) view that courts will seek to limit retroactivity simply because the consequences of giving *Blakely* retroactive effect could be so extreme. (Justice O'Connor's dissent in *Blakely* suggested, in a footnote, that well over 200,000 cases in the federal system alone could be impacted if *Blakely* were to be made retroactive to the date *Apprendi* was decided in 2000.) From a legal realist perspective, it seems quite unsurprising that courts so far have not applied *Blakely* retroactively. In United States v. Cotton, 536 U.S. 625 (2002), the Supreme Court effectively limited the retroactive impact of *Apprendi* by ruling that indictments rendered defective by the *Apprendi* rule should be reviewed only for plain error and do not require automatic reversal of a conviction or sentence.

As for cases pending at the time of the *Blakely* decision, the Supreme Court has given lower courts the means to sustain most sentences despite any errors. The Court declared in Washington v. Recuenco, 126 S. Ct. 2546 (2006), that the failure to submit a sentencing factor to a jury does not qualify as "structural error" requiring the automatic reversal of an enhanced sentence. Instead, explained the Court, *Blakely* errors should be reviewed on appeal and can be excused as "harmless error."

Do other branches of government bear some responsibility for devising a remedy for those prisoners who may be serving decades of additional jail time based on a judicial factfinding that the Supreme Court has now deemed unconstitutional? Should the clemency power be reinvigorated to address this situation?

6. *Principle versus pragmatism.*   Do the *Blakely* dissenters provide any strong constitutional arguments against the majority's interpretation of the Sixth Amendment, or might it be fair to characterize their complaints as providing only pragmatic arguments against the Court's holding? An old Roman maxim, "Let justice be done though the heavens fall," is meant to suggest that a decision's adverse practical consequences should not keep a court from rendering justice. Can this maxim, though inspiring, really be practiced?

PROBLEM 6-1. MOVING VIOLATIONS OF *BLAKELY*

Responding to concerns expressed by the National Commission Against Drunk Driving and to a recent rise in alcohol-related accidents, the state legislature passed a bipartisan package of bills amending the Penal Code. The new laws include the following provisions:

- Operating a motor vehicle with a Blood Alcohol Concentration (BAC) greater than .08% constitutes the offense of Driving Under the Influence (DUI), requiring, in addition to license revocation and other administrative sanctions, a mandatory minimum sentence of no less than 5 days' imprisonment and a maximum sentence of no more than 1 year's imprisonment.
- Operating a motor vehicle with a BAC greater than .15% constitutes the offense of Driving While Intoxicated (DWI), requiring, in addition to administrative sanctions, a mandatory minimum sentence of no less than 3 months and a maximum sentence of no more than 2 years.

- Operating a motor vehicle with a BAC greater than .25% constitutes the offense of Aggravated Driving While Intoxicated (ADWI), requiring, in addition to administrative sanctions, a mandatory minimum sentence of no less than 2 years and a maximum sentence of no more than 5 years.
- If a defendant has previously been convicted of one drunk-driving–related charge, the required minimum and allowed maximum sentences for these crimes shall be doubled. If the defendant has previously been convicted of two or more drunk-driving–related charges, the required minimum and allowed maximum sentences shall be multiplied by a factor of 10.
- A sentencing judge may sentence a defendant below the applicable mandatory minimum sentence if the defendant shows, by clear and convincing evidence, that the incident of drunk driving involved a completely aberrant act or was the result of an unavoidable and compelling necessity.
- A sentencing judge may sentence a defendant above the otherwise applicable maximum if the prosecution shows, by clear and convincing evidence, that the incident of drunk driving resulted in serious physical harm or death to any innocent persons.

Adam Even, the first person prosecuted under the state's new drunk-driving laws, comes to you for legal advice. This past weekend he drove to a friend's house (which was only two miles from his home) to watch a big football game on television. After drinking beer throughout the evening, Adam realized he was not fit to drive home after the game ended.

Upon calling his wife to tell her he planned to stay at his friend's house until the morning, Adam learned that his young daughter was ill and that he was needed at home as soon as possible. Unable to secure a ride from his friends (who themselves were intoxicated), Adam quickly downed a few cups of coffee and convinced himself that he would now be able to navigate the ride home.

Adam managed to drive safely and without incident until he reached the traffic light at the entrance to his subdivision. Feeling sleepy from the alcohol in his system, Adam momentarily dozed off while waiting for the light to turn from red to green. He awoke to the sound of car horns and breaking glass, and saw that two cars had collided in the intersection in front of him. (Adam's car remained untouched, idling in front of the traffic light.) Before Adam could take in what was going on, the police and an ambulance arrived at the scene. The ambulance quickly drove away with a passenger from one of the smashed cars, who appeared to have a broken leg.

Adam and the other motorists on the scene were given Breathalyzer tests. To Adam's surprise, he registered a BAC of .254%, while the other drivers tested fully sober. The police interviewed the drivers involved in the collision. One driver told the police that, after sitting a while behind Adam's car at the green light, she tried to navigate her car around his vehicle, but apparently did not get through the intersection before the light changed, and a car coming the other way drove into hers. After hearing this story, the police arrested Adam for Aggravated DWI; he was processed that night and released on bail.

The district attorney has now informed Adam that he plans to prosecute fully. This DA told Adam that he planned to introduce evidence establishing that Adam had pled guilty to two prior DUIs: one 15 years ago, when Adam was a high school junior, and another 10 years ago, when Adam was a college senior.

What would be the longest sentence Adam could face under the new drunk-driving laws? What procedural rights might Adam have if he pleads guilty to DWI but wants to contest some of the facts that seem to be the basis for an enhanced sentence? What procedure should the prosecutor follow to make sure the new law complies with *Apprendi* and *Blakely*?

PROBLEM 6-2.   THE CAPITAL JURY

Timothy Ring was convicted of felony murder in the course of an armed robbery but acquitted of premeditated murder. As required by Arizona law, the trial judge then held "a separate sentencing hearing to determine the existence or nonexistence" of certain enumerated circumstances "for the purpose of determining the sentence to be imposed." According to Arizona law, the "court alone shall make all factual determinations required by this section or the constitution of the United States or this state." The statute authorized the judge to sentence the defendant to death only if there was at least one aggravating circumstance and there were "no mitigating circumstances sufficiently substantial to call for leniency." The trial judge sentenced Ring to death.

Because Ring was convicted of felony murder, not premeditated murder, the judge recognized that Ring was eligible for the death penalty only if he was the victim's actual killer or if he was "a major participant in the armed robbery that led to the killing and exhibited a reckless disregard or indifference for human life." Based on evidence at the sentencing hearing, the judge concluded that Ring "is the one who shot and killed Mr. Magoch" and then found two aggravating factors: (1) Ring committed the offense in expectation of receiving something of "pecuniary value," and (2) the offense was committed "in an especially heinous, cruel or depraved manner."

On appeal, Ring argued that Arizona's capital sentencing scheme violated the Sixth and Fourteenth Amendments to the U.S. Constitution because it entrusted to a judge the finding of a fact raising the defendant's maximum penalty. If *Apprendi* were the most recent relevant authority, how would you rule on Ring's argument? What if *Blakely* were the most recent case?

NOTES

1. *The* Harris *retreat.*   There was a serious tension between *Apprendi*'s "elements" rule for facts that raise maximum sentences and *McMillan*'s holding that facts triggering mandatory minimum sentences can be found by a judge based on a preponderance standard of proof. In Harris v. United States, 536 U.S. 545 (2002), the Court addressed this tension and came down on the side of *McMillan.* The opinion significantly restricted the reach of *Apprendi,* holding that facts that increase mandatory minimum penalties can still be treated as sentencing factors and thus do not require submission to a jury or proof beyond

a reasonable doubt. The holding seemed, at the time, to endorse a narrow reading of *Apprendi*; it remains a puzzling (and perhaps unstable) limit on the broader *Blakely* rule.

2. *Capital sentencing procedures and the Sixth Amendment.*   The constitutional and statutory sentencing procedures that apply in death penalty cases have filled many textbooks and treatises. The Supreme Court's landmark decisions in Furman v. Georgia, 408 U.S. 238 (1972), and Gregg v. Georgia, 428 U.S. 153 (1976), initiated a series of reforms that transformed capital sentencing into perhaps the most procedurally intricate and complicated area of any legal field. To what extent does the *Apprendi-Blakely* vision of the jury's functions for sentencing facts influence capital sentencing?

On the same day the U.S. Supreme Court significantly restricted the reach of *Apprendi* through Harris v. United States, 536 U.S. 545 (2002), the Court also significantly expanded *Apprendi* through its opinion in Ring v. Arizona, 536 U.S. 584 (2002). The Court held that facts establishing eligibility for the death penalty must be treated as "elements" and thus require submission to a jury and proof beyond a reasonable doubt. Although the Court had upheld Arizona's system in the past, that outcome was no longer tenable. Writing for the majority, Justice Ginsberg explained:

> In Walton v. Arizona, 497 U.S. 639 (1990), we upheld Arizona's scheme against a charge that it violated the Sixth Amendment. [We now] overrule *Walton* to the extent that it allows a sentencing judge, sitting without a jury, to find an aggravating circumstance necessary for imposition of the death penalty. Because Arizona's enumerated aggravating factors operate as "the functional equivalent of an element of a greater offense," the Sixth Amendment requires that they be found by a jury. . . .
>
> The right to trial by jury guaranteed by the Sixth Amendment would be senselessly diminished if it encompassed the factfinding necessary to increase a defendant's sentence by two years, but not the factfinding necessary to put him to death. We hold that the Sixth Amendment applies to both.

Justice Scalia (joined by Justice Thomas) concurred. While disagreeing with the capital jurisprudence that requires findings of aggravating factors to justify a capital sentence, he stated that "the fundamental meaning of the jury-trial guarantee of the Sixth Amendment is that all facts essential to imposition of the level of punishment that the defendant receives — whether the statute calls them elements of the offense, sentencing factors, or Mary Jane — must be found by the jury beyond a reasonable doubt."

Justice O'Connor and Chief Justice Rehnquist dissented. While they agreed that *Apprendi* and *Walton* were inconsistent, the experience of two years suggested to them that *Apprendi* should be reversed. Justice O'Connor wrote:

> Not only was the decision in *Apprendi* unjustified in my view, but it has also had a severely destabilizing effect on our criminal justice system. I predicted in my dissent that the decision would "unleash a flood of petitions by convicted defendants seeking to invalidate their sentences in whole or in part on the authority of [*Apprendi*]." As of May 31, 2002, less than two years after *Apprendi* was announced, the United States Courts of Appeals had decided approximately 1,802 criminal appeals in which defendants challenged their sentences, and in some cases even their convictions, under *Apprendi*. These federal appeals

are likely only the tip of the iceberg, as federal criminal prosecutions represent a tiny fraction of the total number of criminal prosecutions nationwide. The number of second or successive habeas corpus petitions filed in the federal courts also increased by 77% in 2001, a phenomenon the Administrative Office of the United States Courts attributes to prisoners bringing *Apprendi* claims. . . .

The decision today is only going to add to these already serious effects. The Court effectively declares five States' capital sentencing schemes unconstitutional [by] identifying Colorado, Idaho, Montana, and Nebraska as having sentencing schemes like Arizona's. There are 168 prisoners on death row in these States, each of whom is now likely to challenge his or her death sentence. . . . In addition, I fear that the prisoners on death row in Alabama, Delaware, Florida, and Indiana, which the Court identifies as having hybrid sentencing schemes in which the jury renders an advisory verdict but the judge makes the ultimate sentencing determination, may also seize on today's decision to challenge their sentences. There are 529 prisoners on death row in these States. By expanding on *Apprendi,* the Court today exacerbates the harm done in that case.

3. *The implications of juries for other trial procedures.*   The Sixth Amendment jury trial right now requires jury involvement in finding the facts that authorize certain sentence increases. Based on passing statements in the *Apprendi* and *Blakely* opinions, it appears that the standard of proof for the criminal trial — beyond a reasonable doubt — also applies to those facts that are relevant to sentencing.

What other aspects of trial procedure are implicated in the finding of these facts? Does *Blakely* mean that defendants now have a constitutional right to testify in their own behalf at a sentencing hearing? To present favorable witnesses or other evidence at sentencing? To cross-examine witnesses at the sentencing hearing? Procedural rules already provide many of these opportunities, but will practices change once these procedures gain constitutional status?

3.   Rebuilding Guideline Procedures

The Supreme Court's new vision of the role of juries in sentencing disrupted the operation of many sentencing procedures. The cases have required legislators, judges, prosecutors, defense attorneys, sentencing commissioners, and many other criminal justice players to think creatively and to rebuild systems in light of the new requirements. The following materials — an appellate opinion and a report from a sentencing commission — show this creative rebuilding at work.

|| *State v. Abdul Abdullah* ||
|| **878 A.2d 746 (N.J. 2005)** ||

ALBIN, J.
The Sixth Amendment's jury trial guarantee forbids a judge from imposing a sentence beyond the range authorized by either a jury's verdict or a defendant's admissions at a plea hearing. To conform the Code of Criminal Justice to that constitutional principle, today, in State v. Natale, we struck down the Code's system of presumptive term sentencing. 878 A.2d 724 (N.J. 2005) (*Natale II*).

Under the Code, the maximum sentence that a judge may impose based on a jury verdict alone is the statutory presumptive term. Without being bound by the verdict, however, the judge is empowered by the Code to sentence a defendant above the presumptive term based on a finding of one or more aggravating factors listed in N.J.S.A. 2C:44-1(a). It is the delegation of that authority to a judge to impose a sentence above the presumptive based on judicial factfinding that runs afoul of the Sixth Amendment. In *Natale II* we removed the presumptive terms from N.J.S.A. 2C:44-1(f) to bring the Code into compliance with the Sixth Amendment.

We now must decide whether other sentencing procedures under the Code intrude on the authority reserved to the jury under the Constitution. In this case, we conclude that the powers given to a judge by the Code to sentence a defendant to a period of life imprisonment for murder, to a period of parole disqualification pursuant to N.J.S.A. 2C:43-6(b), and to consecutive sentences for multiple convictions do not run counter to the Sixth Amendment.

[Catrina Lark and Abdul Aleem Abdullah] were involved in a two-year romantic relationship that ended in December 1998. During that period, defendant spent daytime hours with Lark and his evenings with his girlfriend Joan Robinson, the mother of his two children. Around January 1999, while incarcerated in the Atlantic County jail for a parole violation, defendant learned that Lark was involved in a relationship with his cousin, Robert Boswell, who also was detained in that jail facility. . . .

In April 1999, defendant was released from jail. On May 2, 1999, [a neighbor discovered Lark's body on the kitchen floor of her apartment.] Upon arriving in Lark's apartment, the police observed blood on the walls and the scene in total disarray. Lark was found lying naked from the waist down in a pool of her own blood on the kitchen floor. She had no pulse and had suffered "multiple lacerations, contusions, and cutting wounds" and "blunt force injuries" over her entire upper body and head. . . .

The police retrieved from the area near Lark's body a bloody rolling pin, a broken clothes iron, an electric skillet, a cast-iron frying pan, and a ceramic lamp. The police also recovered a variety of broken, bent, and blood-stained knives scattered throughout the apartment, and a bloody weightlifting glove. The physical evidence pointed to defendant as the killer. Defendant's fingerprints were discovered on the skillet's broken handle.

[The] police arrested defendant at his home. At the time of his arrest, defendant was bleeding from a cut on his hand that he claimed occurred when he fell from his bicycle the previous day. In response to questioning, defendant maintained that he had been home with his girlfriend, Robinson, on the morning of the killing. However, Robinson testified that defendant got up and left their apartment at around 2:40 A.M., and returned sometime between 3:00 and 3:30 A.M., making "a lot of noise when he came in." . . .

The jury found defendant guilty of all counts in the indictment, [including murder, second-degree burglary, third-degree possession of a weapon for an unlawful purpose, and fourth-degree unlawful possession of a weapon]. At sentencing, the trial court identified four aggravating factors: "the nature and circumstances of the offense . . . including whether or not it was committed in an especially heinous, cruel, or depraved manner"; "the risk that . . . defendant will commit another offense"; the extent and seriousness of defendant's prior criminal record; and the need to deter defendant and others from violating the law. Finding the aggravating factors to be "overwhelming" and no mitigating factors, the court sentenced defendant to life imprisonment with a thirty-year parole disqualifier on the murder conviction and to a consecutive ten-year prison term with a five-year parole disqualifier on one of the second-degree burglary convictions. The remaining charges were merged into the murder conviction.

The court detailed its reasons for imposing sentence:

> This is the most brutal murder the court has seen in over 23 years on the bench. Defendant stabbed and bludgeoned the victim. Six knives were either bent or broken. A cast iron frying pan, an electric frying pan, a wooden rolling pin, an electric iron and a ceramic lamp were also smashed and broken over the victim's head and body. Defendant has a prior history of domestic violence. He has previously violated parole. This is a vicious dangerous defendant. Society needs to be protected from him. . . . An 18-year prison term imposed on a prior offense did not deter defendant. He violated parole on that offense and committed this murder shortly after being released when he "maxed out." . . . [He] is the same man who laughed and smirked at the victim's family during trial. His sympathy at sentencing rings hollow.

On appeal, defendant argued that because the jury did not determine the essential facts necessary for the imposition of maximum terms for murder and second-degree burglary, for the burglary parole disqualifier, and for consecutive sentences, defendant was denied his Sixth Amendment jury trial right as articulated in Blakely v. Washington. . . .

We first consider the constitutionality of defendant's sentence for second-degree burglary. . . . Under the Code of Criminal Justice, a second-degree crime is punishable by a term of imprisonment between five and ten years, with a presumptive term of seven years. In *Natale II* we held that the maximum sentence that can be imposed based on a jury verdict alone is the presumptive term. [A] sentence *above the presumptive term* premised on a judge's finding of aggravating factors, other than the fact of a prior criminal conviction, is incompatible with the holdings in *Apprendi* [and] *Blakely*. . . .

In this case, the trial court imposed a ten-year sentence for second-degree burglary based on its finding four aggravating factors in N.J.S.A. 2C:44-1(a): (1) nature of the offense, (3) risk of recidivism, (6) prior criminal record, and (9) need to deter. Apparently, based on facts not found by the jury, defendant received a sentence three years above the presumptive term for second-degree burglary. . . . On the spare record before us, it appears that the sentencing court used the "especially heinous, cruel, or depraved nature of the crime" — a fact not specifically found by the jury — as a basis for increasing the burglary sentence above its presumptive term. Moreover, we cannot tell from the record whether the court used that factfinding to support only aggravating factor (1) or whether it also was used to support aggravating factors (3) and (9). In other words, the sentencing court may have concluded that the "especially heinous, cruel, or depraved manner" of the killing indicated a risk of recidivism and a need to deter. In light of *Blakely* and our decision in *Natale II* only a jury finding of that fact would justify increasing a sentence above the presumptive.

Accordingly, we are compelled to remand for resentencing on the burglary conviction.[2]

[On] remand, without the presumptive term as the required starting point, the court will consider all applicable aggravating and mitigating factors in determining the appropriate sentence within the range for second-degree burglary. Unlike almost every crime enumerated in the Code, murder has no presumptive term. N.J.S.A. 2C:11-3(b)(1) provides in relevant part:

> Murder is a crime of the first degree but a person convicted of murder shall be sentenced . . . by the court to a term of 30 years, during which the person shall not be eligible for parole, or be sentenced to a specific term of years *which shall be between 30 years and life imprisonment* of which the person shall serve 30 years before being eligible for parole. [Emphasis added.]

The provision of the Code that implements presumptive term sentencing specifically exempts murder from its sweep: "*Except for the crime of murder,* unless the preponderance of aggravating or mitigating factors . . . weighs in favor of a higher or lower term" within the sentencing ranges for the four degrees of crimes, the court "shall impose" the presumptive term. N.J.S.A. 2C:44-1(f)(1) (emphasis added). Accordingly, the standard range for murder is a sentence between thirty years and life imprisonment. In contrast with defendant's burglary conviction, in which the upper sentencing limit based on the jury's verdict alone was the presumptive term, defendant's murder conviction did not impose a *de facto* ceiling below life imprisonment. Therefore, the trial court had discretion to impose a sentence within the statutory range of thirty years to life based on its consideration of the applicable sentencing factors. This state's sentencing scheme for murder is almost identical to the example of an indeterminate sentencing scheme depicted with approval in *Blakely.* . . .

Based on its finding of four aggravating factors and no mitigating factors, the trial court imposed the maximum parole disqualifier — five years — on the ten-year burglary sentence in accordance with N.J.S.A. 2C:43-6(b). That statute provides sentencing judges with the authority to impose a period of parole ineligibility on the four graded crimes enumerated in the Code:

> As part of a sentence for any crime, *where the court is clearly convinced that the aggravating factors substantially outweigh the mitigating factors,* as set forth in subsections a. and b. of N.J.S.A. 2C:44-1, *the court may fix a minimum term not to exceed one-half of the term set pursuant to subsection a.,* or one-half of the term set pursuant to a maximum period of incarceration for a crime set forth in any statute other than this code, during which the defendant shall not be eligible for parole. . . .

---

2. We note that had the trial court specifically found that aggravating factors (3), (6), and (9) related to defendant's prior convictions as the basis for increasing defendant's sentence above the presumptive, we might have come to a different result. "[T]he fact of a prior conviction" may be used to increase the "penalty for a crime beyond the prescribed statutory maximum." *Apprendi,* 530 U.S. at 490; see also Almendarez-Torres v. United States, 523 U.S. 224, 243 (1998) ("[Recidivism] is a traditional, if not the most traditional, basis for a sentencing court's increasing an offender's sentence"). Aggravating factors (3), (6), and (9), *arguably,* are inextricably linked to the recidivism exception. . . .

In making the discretionary decision whether to impose a parole disqualifier, the court balances the same aggravating and mitigating factors used to determine the length of the sentence, but applies a stricter standard that reflects the serious impact that a parole disqualifier will have on the "real time" a defendant serves on his sentence.

Both the United States Supreme Court and this Court have upheld the constitutionality of statutes that allow judges to impose mandatory-minimum parole ineligibility terms within the sentencing range authorized by the jury verdict. See, e.g., Harris v. United States, 536 U.S. 545, 568 (2002); McMillan v. Pennsylvania, 477 U.S. 79, 84-86 (1986); State v. Stanton, 820 A.2d 637 (N.J. 2003). [For] Sixth Amendment purposes, facts used to extend the sentence beyond the statutory maximum are deemed different from facts used to set the minimum sentence. Within the range authorized by the jury's verdict, . . . the political system may channel judicial discretion — and rely upon judicial expertise — by requiring defendants to serve minimum terms after judges make certain factual findings. . . .

In State v. Stanton, this Court upheld the constitutionality of the vehicular homicide statute that required the sentencing judge to impose a mandatory-minimum sentence if he found by a preponderance of the evidence that the defendant drove while under the influence of alcohol or drugs. In that case, the defendant was convicted by a jury of second-degree vehicular homicide. . . . Based on evidence presented at trial that the defendant was driving while under the influence, the sentencing court imposed a three-year parole disqualifier. This Court determined that the under-the-influence sentencing factor was not an element of vehicular homicide necessitating a jury determination.

[The aggravating and mitigating factors that the judge weighs under N.J.S.A. 2C:43-6(b)] are the traditional factors that courts always have considered in determining an appropriate sentence. They were neither intended by the Legislature to constitute elements of a crime nor were they transformed into constitutional elements when the judge used them to justify imposing a parole disqualifier. In light of the outcomes in *McMillan, Harris* and *Stanton* and the constitutional principles that undergird them, we hold that N.J.S.A. 2C:43-6(b) does not violate the federal or state constitutional rights to due process and trial by jury.

[Because] of our earlier holding requiring a remand for resentencing on the burglary conviction, the remand court again will consider the appropriate parole disqualifier based on its weighing of the applicable factors. We note that the court must articulate on the record whether it was clearly convinced that the aggravating factors substantially outweighed the mitigating factors. . . .

Last, defendant claims that *Blakely* requires that the jury, not the judge, make the findings of fact necessary for the imposition of consecutive sentences. On that basis, he challenges the judicially-imposed consecutive sentences that he received for murder and burglary. We find no constitutional impediment to a judge's deciding whether a defendant should serve consecutive sentences under the standards governing sentencing in this state. N.J.S.A. 2C:44-5(a) provides in relevant part that when "multiple sentences of imprisonment are imposed on a defendant for more than one offense, . . . such multiple sentences shall run concurrently or consecutively as the court determines at the time of sentence." The discretion given to sentencing courts to impose consecutive sentences by the Code of Criminal Justice was the continuation of a long-standing common-law principle. The Code, however, does not set forth any standards to guide the court's discretion in deciding whether to impose consecutive or concurrent sentences when a defendant is convicted of multiple offenses. To bring rationality to the process and to further the goal of sentencing uniformity, this Court, in State v. Yarbough, 498 A.2d 1239 (N.J. 1985), developed criteria to be applied by the courts in making those decisions. The *Yarbough* criteria are:

(1) there can be no free crimes in a system for which the punishment shall fit the crime;

(2) the reasons for imposing either a consecutive or concurrent sentence should be separately stated in the sentencing decision;

(3) some reasons to be considered by the sentencing court should include facts relating to the crimes, including whether or not:

   (a) the crimes and their objectives were predominantly independent of each other;

   (b) the crimes involved separate acts of violence or threats of violence;

   (c) the crimes were committed at different times or separate places, rather than being committed so closely in time and place as to indicate a single period of aberrant behavior;

   (d) any of the crimes involved multiple victims;

   (e) the convictions for which the sentences are to be imposed are numerous;

(4) there should be no double counting of aggravating factors;

(5) successive terms for the same offense should not ordinarily be equal to the punishment for the first offense; and

(6) there should be an overall outer limit on the cumulation of consecutive sentences for multiple offenses not to exceed the sum of the longest terms (including an extended term, if eligible) that could be imposed for the two most serious offenses.

In 1993, the Legislature eliminated the cap on the number of consecutive sentences that could be imposed pursuant to the sixth factor by amending N.J.S.A. 2C:44-5(a)(2) to provide that "[t]here shall be no overall outer limit on the cumulation of consecutive sentences for multiple offenses." The amendment granted greater discretion to judges in determining the overall length of a sentence.

Under our sentencing scheme, there is no presumption in favor of concurrent sentences and therefore the maximum potential sentence authorized by the jury verdict is the aggregate of sentences for multiple convictions. See N.J.S.A. 2C:44-5(a). In other words, the sentencing range is the maximum sentence for each offense added to every other offense. The *Yarbough* factors serve much the same purpose that aggravating and mitigating factors do in guiding the court toward a sentence within the statutory range. . . .

In that vein, consecutive sentences do not invoke the same concerns that troubled the Supreme Court in *Apprendi* [and] *Blakely*. . . . As in any indeterminate sentencing scheme, the jury verdict in this case allowed the judge to impose a consecutive or concurrent sentence within the maximum range based on the sentencing court's discretionary findings. Unlike a trial court that engages in factfinding as the basis for exceeding the sentence authorized by a jury's verdict, the court here imposed consecutive sentences that were supported by the jury's separate guilty verdicts for each offense. With the exception of merged offenses, defendant knew that he potentially could be sentenced to the sum of the maximum sentences for all of the offenses combined.

We therefore conclude that imposing a consecutive sentence for murder and burglary in this case did not exceed the statutory maximum for *Blakely* or *Apprendi* purposes. However, because the trial court did not explain why it imposed consecutive sentences, we are compelled to remand for the court to place its reasons on the record. We remind our courts that when imposing either consecutive or concurrent sentences, the focus should be on "the fairness of the overall sentence," and that they should articulate the reasons for their decisions with specific reference to the *Yarbough* factors. . . .

PROBLEM 6-3.   PRIOR JUVENILE ADJUDICATIONS

Charles Weber was at a friend's apartment with several people drinking beer, when Weber started to argue with Gabriel Manzo. During the argument, Weber pulled a gun on Manzo, who escaped the apartment by jumping out of a bedroom window and running to his motorcycle. Weber followed Manzo outside and fired multiple shots at Manzo. One of the bullets grazed Manzo's side, causing a slight injury. When the police investigated the incident, Manzo told them that a man he knew as "Guero Loco" (or "crazy white guy") shot him. He identified Weber from a photo lineup.

The prosecuting attorney charged Weber with first-degree attempted murder with a firearm, first-degree assault with a firearm, first-degree unlawful possession of a firearm, and possession of cocaine with intent to manufacture or deliver. Weber pleaded guilty to possession of cocaine with intent to deliver. A jury acquitted Weber of first-degree attempted murder and instead found him guilty of second-degree attempted murder with a firearm, as well as first-degree assault with a firearm and first-degree unlawful possession of a firearm.

At sentencing, the trial court declined to count a prior juvenile adjudication for first-degree attempted robbery against Weber in his offender score. The judge reasoned that enough years had passed since the juvenile adjudication that it now "washed out" under the state's sentencing guideline rules. The trial court also noted that Weber's second juvenile adjudication, for taking a motor vehicle without permission, only counted half a point and therefore did not factor into his offender score.

The state appealed the trial court's finding that Weber's juvenile attempted robbery adjudication "washed out." Weber replied that the inclusion of his prior juvenile adjudications in his offender score would violate his due process rights under the Fifth and Fourteenth Amendments and his right to a jury trial under the Sixth Amendment.

Assume that you serve as a judge on the state's intermediate appellate court. You are convinced that the sentencing guidelines, correctly interpreted, do not prevent the sentencing judge from considering Weber's two prior juvenile adjudications because they happened too long ago. In other words, they do not "wash out."

Inclusion of Weber's juvenile adjudications in his offender score would increase his maximum sentence above the sentence supported by the jury's verdict. Weber argues, therefore, that the Sixth Amendment blocks the judge from considering his juvenile adjudications as part of the guidelines calculation.

The U.S. Supreme Court has suggested in a few cases that an offender's prior criminal record is one aggravating factor at sentencing that need not be proven to a jury beyond a reasonable doubt. It described the basis for this exception to the *Apprendi* rule as follows: "One basis for that possible constitutional distinctiveness is not hard to see: unlike virtually any other consideration used to enlarge the possible penalty for an offense, . . . a prior conviction must itself have been established through procedures satisfying the fair notice, reasonable doubt, and jury trial guarantees." Jones v. United States, 526 U.S. 227, 249 (1999).

Because juvenile adjudications do not carry the right to a jury trial, Weber argues that they do not fall within the prior-conviction exception. Weber further points out that juvenile adjudications are not convictions. The focus of the juvenile justice system is on rehabilitation and individualized treatment of the juvenile rather than assigning criminal responsibility and punishment. The state argues that juvenile adjudications carry sufficient procedural safeguards to qualify them as prior convictions under the *Apprendi* exception.

What would you need to know about Weber's juvenile adjudications, and about the state's juvenile system more generally, to decide this case? Compare State v. Weber, 149 P.3d 646 (Wash. 2006) with State v. Harris, 118 P.3d 236 (Oregon 2005).

NOTES

1. *State* Blakely *challenges.*   As many as 20 states have statutory or guideline structured sentencing systems or provisions that have been subject to new constitutional questions in the wake of *Blakely*. The amount of *Blakely* litigation in the states is staggering: within a year of the decision, there were already more than 2500 state judicial opinions appearing in online databases grappling with the impact of *Blakely*, and these opinions likely represent the proverbial tip of the *Blakely* iceberg. Interestingly, the pace of *Blakely* litigation in the states is varied even in those jurisdictions in which structured sentencing rules clearly needed reexamination in light of *Blakely*. In a few states (such as Minnesota and Oregon), litigation over *Blakely* issues produced a major state supreme court ruling less than six months after the *Blakely* decision was handed down by the Supreme Court; in other states (such as New Jersey and Ohio), over a year passed before the state's highest court addressed *Blakely*'s local impact.

2. *Judicial determination of concurrent versus consecutive sentences.*   In systems that require the finding of some predicate fact before a consecutive sentence can replace the presumptive concurrent sentence, judicial determination of the facts supporting the application of consecutive sentencing has the functional impact of extending a defendant's sentence. Don't such factual determinations to support the application of consecutive sentences necessarily implicate the Sixth Amendment concerns raised in *Blakely*? Most courts addressing this question to date have held, like the New Jersey Supreme Court in *Abdullah*, that *Blakely* applies only to the selection of the proper sentence for

each crime of conviction, and not to the interaction among those sentences. But see In re VanDelft, 147 P.3d 573 (Wash. 2006) (*Blakely* applies to findings needed to support imposition of exceptional consecutive sentence when statute creates presumption of concurrent offenses). The common law efforts in New Jersey (embodied in the *Yarbough* factors) to structure the choice between consecutive and concurrent sentences were not enough to trigger *Blakely*. Which efforts to structure this choice will bring Sixth Amendment rights into play?

3. *Reach of the prior-conviction exception.*   Many sentencing laws call for the sentencing judge to consider some aspects of the defendant's past dealings with the criminal justice system, and yet the consideration involves something more than the mere "fact" of a prior conviction. For instance, the state of Washington asks the sentencing judge to consider whether the defendant was serving a "community placement" sentence at the time he committed the new crime. See State v. Jones, 149 P.3d 636 (Wash. 2006) (community placement status included within prior-conviction exception). North Carolina law increases the sentence if the defendant committed the current offense while serving probation for a previous crime. N.C.G.S. §15A-1340.14(b)(7). Can you resolve these issues through a functional assessment of the types of facts that juries and judges are well suited to find?

4. *Juveniles and prior convictions.*   There is a split on the issue of whether a juvenile adjudication is "the functional equivalent" of a prior conviction for purposes of *Apprendi*. The legal debate about whether juvenile adjudications fall within the prior-conviction exception is fascinating for a number of reasons. First, the exception itself is both doctrinally and theoretically shaky. Second, because juveniles are not afforded the right to a jury trial, juvenile proceedings do not employ the sorts of safeguards that may give adult prior convictions the added reliability justifying an exception to the *Apprendi-Blakely* rule. The lower federal courts and the state courts are split on this issue. Compare United States v. Smalley, 294 F.3d 1030 (8th Cir. 2002), and State v. McFee, 721 N.W.2d 607 (Minn. 2006), with United States v. Tighe, 266 F.3d 1187 (9th Cir. 2001), and State v. Brown, 879 So. 2d 1276 (La. 2004). See also Colleen P. Murphy, The Use of Prior Convictions after *Apprendi*, 37 U.C. Davis L. Rev. 973 (2004).

5. *Jury rights and back-end punishments.*   Think about Justice Scalia's breathtakingly bold assertion in *Blakely* that "every defendant has the right to insist that the prosecutor prove to a jury all facts legally essential to the punishment." Could this apply to decisions other than the judge's selection of the length of a prison term, and decisions that took place after the initial sentencing hearing? For instance, what if the judge can order the defendant to pay restitution only after finding certain relevant "circumstances" to be present in the case? And if the judge orders a suspended sentence, and then some months (or years) later is asked to revoke the probation and send the offender back to prison, will jury findings be necessary to establish the probation violation conditions that are the necessary precursor to a revocation? See Laura Appleman, Retributive Justice and Hidden Sentencing After Blakely, 68 Ohio St. L.J. (forthcoming 2007) (available at ssrn.com/abstract=956405).

The Impact of Blakely v. Washington on Sentencing in Minnesota: Short Term Recommendations Minnesota Sentencing Guidelines Commission (August 6, 2004)

... The recent *Blakely v. Washington* decision directly impacts neither the constitutionality nor the structure of the Minnesota Sentencing Guidelines. However, the decision does affect certain sentencing procedures pertaining to aggravated departures and specific sentence enhancements that will need to be modified to meet the constitutionality issues identified under *Blakely*. ...

Aggravated departures resulting in enhanced sentences under the Minnesota Sentencing Guidelines are outside the structure of the guidelines. Unlike the federal guidelines, there are no points assigned for aggravating factors, nor are judges mandated by the guidelines to impose an aggravated departure or enhanced sentence. The sentencing guidelines determine presumptive sentences for offenses on the sentencing grid. Departures are viewed as sentences outside or apart from presumptive sentences set forth on the sentencing grid and are available for judges to use when deciding a case that is atypical or when the factors surrounding a specific case sets it apart from the norm. A departure/enhanced sentence is not controlled by the guidelines regarding the length of the enhancement other than not exceeding the statutory maximum for a specific offense. ...

The Sentencing Guidelines Commission strongly believes that preserving aggravated departures is necessary to ensure public safety and provide for appropriate sentencing when aggravating factors related to an offense are present and an enhanced sentence is in the interest of justice. ... In Minnesota, aggravated departures accounted for approximately 7.7% (1,002) of a total of 12,978 felony sentences in 2002. Aggravated departures can occur in two ways under sentencing guidelines. The first type of aggravated departure is an aggravated dispositional departure in which the defendant should have received a presumptive stayed sentence under the guidelines but the court instead imposes a prison sentence. The second type of aggravated departure is an aggravated durational departure that occurs when the offender receives a sentence length that is longer than the sentence recommended by the sentencing grid, regardless of whether the sentence is a presumptive stay or a presumptive prison sentence. Listed below is the distribution of aggravated departures for 2002.

Total Aggravated Departures For 2002

Type of Departure	# Cases	% Overall Cases
Aggravated Disposition	481	3.7%
Agg. Disposition and Agg. Duration	50	0.4%
Aggravated Duration — Prison	224	1.7%
Aggravated Duration — Probation	247	1.9%
Total	1,002	7.7% (of 12,978)

From the data available, approximately 1,000 cases per year involve aggravated departures and would be subject to the constitutional issues raised in *Blakely*. When this data is further examined by method of conviction, approximately 92% (923) of the cases involved a guilty plea and only 8% (79) of the cases involved a trial. The data would indicate that a very small number of cases resulting in aggravated departures actually involve a criminal trial. [The largest number of trials occurred for defendants who received an aggravated duration in a prison term: 46 of 224 (21%) of those cases were resolved by trial rather than guilty plea.]

It would be reasonable to assume that there will be a slight increase in the number of trials in the future since a certain percentage of offenders who currently plead guilty may request a jury trial in the future to have the aggravating factors determined by a jury. There would be corresponding costs to the courts for these additional trials. However, it should be noted that 67% of the offenders who pled guilty in 2002, either agreed to the departure in the guilty plea or the defendant requested the aggravated dispositional departure. . . .

There are four potential situations that could result when pursuing aggravated departures:

(1)   the defendant pleads not guilty to the offense and does not admit to any of the aggravating factors;
(2)   the defendant pleads not guilty to the offense but admits to the aggravating factors;
(3)   the defendant pleads guilty to the offense but does not admit the aggravating factors; and
(4)   multiple offenses involve any combination of the above.

The issue of whether a defendant can waive a jury trial on guilt or innocence but request a jury to determine the presence of aggravating factors is an issue that will have to be addressed. The Kansas statute relevant to bifurcated trials states that if a defendant waives the right to a jury trial he also waives the right to have a jury determine the presence of aggravating factors. This is an issue that will need further legislative or judicial consideration. . . .

Although the plea bargaining process is permitted when aggravated departures are involved, the defendant must stipulate to the aggravating factors or consent to judicial fact finding. Neither of these options is currently being required in pleas involving aggravated departures, thus, our current plea process would need to be modified to bring the state into compliance with the *Blakely v. Washington* ruling.

RECOMMENDATIONS:

(1)   Notice Procedures should be modified when there is an intent to seek an aggravated departure . . .
(3)   Procedures will need to be developed to permit juries to determine aggravating factors
    a.   Develop bifurcated trial policies and procedures . . .
    d.   Develop special jury verdict forms to be used in bifurcated jury trial situations . . .
    e.   Incorporate Special Interrogatories on the jury verdict form

In Minnesota, there are several specific statutory enhancements for certain offenses that result in an aggravated departure or an enhanced sentence above the presumptive sentence for the offense due to the determination of one or more aggravating factors, other than prior convictions. Currently, the court makes the determination of additional factors that increase the length of sentence for a conviction under these statutes. They include sentencing enhancements for heinous crimes; certain pattern and predatory sex offenders; mandatory sentences for repeat sex offenders; dangerous offenders; career offenders; and depriving of custodial or parental rights. . . .

A very small number of offenders are sentenced under these statutes per year. The number averages 50 to 60 offenders per year, with only a total of 420 offenders sentenced since 1991.

RECOMMENDATION:

Due to the public safety issues and seriousness of the offenses in this category, bifurcated trials should be used when sentencing under these specific statutes. . . .

. . . The commission recommends that the state move cautiously and thoughtfully as it explores potential changes to the current sentencing system. It may be counter productive to begin developing solutions before the nature of the problem is fully understood. Before embarking on a series of statutory responses to the *Blakely* decision, it may be more prudent for the judiciary, prosecutors and defense attorneys to develop temporary interim policies and procedures that are advisory in nature for conducting bifurcated jury trials, plea negotiations, and sentencing procedures that impact the areas of sentencing that have previously been identified as most likely be affected by this decision. . . .

Although advisory policies and procedures will carry no legal force, they will provide for some consistency in sentencing throughout the state as the legal issues work their way through the courts at both the state and federal levels. In addition, they will help to limit the number of future of appeals that could result from every judicial district interpreting and responding to *Blakely* in a different manner. . . .

PROBLEM 6-4. INDICTING *BLAKELY*

Kevin Badoni was initially charged in 1998 with one count of murder, two counts of attempted murder "by any of the means with which death may be caused," aggravated battery, and tampering with evidence for disposing of a .380 handgun. All the charges resulted from a confrontation between two groups of young men during which one man was killed and two men were seriously wounded by gunshots. Badoni was convicted of second-degree murder and aggravated battery.

Through a special verdict, the jury found that Badoni used a firearm in the commission of these offenses. Badoni's attorney had opposed the use of the special verdict because the use of a firearm was not pled in the murder and attempted murder charges. Badoni was sentenced to 15 years in prison for the murder conviction, three years for aggravated battery, and 18 months for tampering with evidence. The murder and aggravated battery sentences were each enhanced by one year because of the application of an enhancement statute based on the use of a firearm.

Badoni argues that, under *Apprendi* and *Blakely*, the state must give formal notice in the criminal information or indictment that Badoni used a firearm in the commission of the offense before the state may seek to enhance Badoni's sentence under the statute.

As an appellate court judge, how would you rule? See State v. Badoni, 62 P.3d 348 (N.M. Ct. App. 2002).

As a prosecutor, would you encourage the use of indictments even if you had no constitutional obligation to include the enhancement factor in the indictment? Assuming that you would oppose a constitutional requirement of indictment, would you take a different posture toward a proposed amendment to the state rules of criminal procedure to require notice of enhancement facts before trial?

NOTES

1. *Number of cases affected.*   The central claim of the report from the Minnesota Sentencing Commission is that *Blakely* does not require a fundamental restructuring of the sentencing guidelines because it affects so few "contested" enhancement cases. As the commission put it, "The impact of *Blakely* on sentencing in Minnesota, while temporarily disruptive, is limited in scope and can be addressed within the current sentencing guidelines scheme." This limited impact applies to most state systems because the number of enhancement-related factual findings to be made at sentencing is small. In contrast with the federal system's use of "relevant conduct" to increase the upper available guideline boundary, most state systems rely more heavily on "charge offense conduct" — that is, conduct already alleged in the indictment and proven at trial (or admitted in the guilty plea).

Are courts or sentencing commissions best suited to estimate the number of cases affected by the new Sixth Amendment jurisprudence? Does the commission have an incentive to minimize its estimate of the impact? The Minnesota Commission report mentions only in passing two loudly ticking time bombs that could lead to an explosion in the number of cases affected. First, *Blakely* might affect all cases involving a "custody status point" (an additional criminal history point added if the current offense was committed while the defendant was still on probation or parole status from a previous crime). Second, *Blakely* could affect all probation revocations. These two categories could overwhelm the small number of cases with *Blakely* effects noted elsewhere in the report.

2. *Guilty pleas and the scope of waiver.*   When a defendant pleads guilty, she waives the right to a jury trial. As *Blakely* makes clear, this waiver does not necessarily include the right to a jury determination of sentencing factors. Does the use of a jury for sentencing factors undermine the value of the defendant's guilty plea? In People v. Lopez, 148 P.3d 121 (Colo. 2006), the defendant pled guilty to

vehicular homicide and vehicular assault. The trial court impaneled a jury solely to determine the facts surrounding the commission of the crime, which the court then considered to be aggravating circumstances justifying an enhanced sentence. The Colorado Supreme Court held that the trial court erred in impaneling a jury at sentencing, because the defendant's guilty plea set a statutory maximum, and the jury findings created the "functional equivalent of elements of a greater offense." The state must abide by the plea, and courts must enforce the state's concessions. As the lead prosecutor in a jurisdiction that views guilty pleas in this way, how would you adjust office policy to allow enhanced sentencing based on aggravating circumstances?

3. *Minimum and maximum starting points.*   If only the facts that increase the penalty for a crime beyond the prescribed statutory maximum must be submitted to a jury and proved beyond a reasonable doubt, legislatures could avoid procedural safeguards by raising the statutory maximum sentences for all crimes and then listing facts that could authorize *reduced* sentences. Justice O'Connor's dissent in *Apprendi* assailed this apparent formalism and suggested that it rendered the constitutional rule "meaningless." Yet at least a few academic commentators have suggested that there is value in even such a formalistic reading of *Apprendi*. See Benjamin J. Priester, Constitutional Formalism and the Meaning of *Apprendi v. New Jersey*, 38 Am. Crim. L. Rev. 281 (2001); Alan C. Michaels, Truth in Convicting: Understanding and Evaluating *Apprendi*, 12 Fed. Sent'g Rep. 320 (2000).

In footnote 16 of his opinion for the Court, Justice Stevens responded to the formalism charge:

> [Structural] democratic constraints exist to discourage legislatures from enacting penal statutes that expose *every* defendant convicted of, for example, weapons possession, to a maximum sentence exceeding that which is, in the legislature's judgment, generally proportional to the crime. This is as it should be. Our rule ensures that a State is obliged to make its choices concerning the substantive content of its criminal laws with full awareness of the consequence, unable to mask substantive policy choices of exposing all who are convicted to the maximum sentence it provides. So exposed, the political check on potentially harsh legislative action is then more likely to operate.
>
> In all events, if such an extensive revision of the State's entire criminal code were enacted for the purpose the dissent suggests, or if New Jersey simply reversed the burden of the hate crime finding (effectively assuming a crime was performed with a purpose to intimidate and then requiring a defendant to prove that it was not), we would be required to question whether the revision was constitutional under this Court's prior decisions.
>
> Finally, the principal dissent ignores the distinction the Court has often recognized between facts in aggravation of punishment and facts in mitigation. If facts found by a jury support a guilty verdict of murder, the judge is authorized by that jury verdict to sentence the defendant to the maximum sentence provided by the murder statute. If the defendant can escape the statutory maximum by showing, for example, that he is a war veteran, then a judge that finds the fact of veteran status is neither exposing the defendant to a deprivation of liberty greater than that authorized by the verdict according to statute, nor is the Judge imposing upon the defendant a greater stigma than that accompanying the jury verdict alone. Core concerns animating the jury and burden-of-proof requirements are thus absent from such a scheme.

530 U.S. at 490 n.16.

4. *Translation of jury functions to a new context.*   The criminal justice system changed enormously between the eighteenth and twenty-first centuries. Consider, for example, the increased role of guilty pleas and the enormous innovations in sentencing rules. How can courts in the twenty-first century give meaning to the constitutional vision of a criminal adjudication process that gives juries the real power to apply the criminal law reasonably? Judge Jack Weinstein offered the following long-term historical perspective on the subject:

> [In the eighteenth century], the discretionary function in sentencing was shared by judge and jury. . . . Juries decided questions of law and fact in criminal and civil cases. . . . The authors known to the founders had a high respect for the wide powers of the jury over law, fact and punishment. In a sense, the jury was, and remains, the direct voice of the sovereign, in a collaborative effort with the judge. It expresses the view of a sometimes compassionate free people faced with an individual miscreant in all of his or her tainted humanity, as opposed to the abstract cruelties of a more theoretical and doctrinaire distant representative government. . . . Clemency was widespread. The jury could exercise its charity. . . .
>
> [The use of advisory juries for sentencing questions] cannot be said to be out of character for a colonial judge faced with the kind of sentencing dilemmas a federal judge now confronts under the Guidelines. It is not aberrational to suggest that use of a jury on sentencing issues of fact — and perhaps on severity — is consistent with history, practice and the inherent role of federal courts and juries.
>
> Reliance on the jury represents a reflection of our government's dependence on the ultimate and residual sovereignty of the people. That foundation for all power — executive, legislative and judicial — is reflected in the preamble to the Constitution beginning, "We the People . . . do ordain and establish this Constitution."

United States v. Khan, 325 F. Supp. 2d 218 (E.D.N.Y. 2004).

5. *Possible structures for jury involvement in sentencing.*   Despite its broad language, *Blakely* technically mandates that juries have a role in factfinding only to support sentence enhancements. Especially in light of Judge Weinstein's comments in *Khan* noted above, we might want to think more dynamically about how to construct a new sentencing world with significant jury participation. Consider just some of the ways juries might be involved in sentencing decision making that go beyond *Blakely*'s mandate:

Juries as comprehensive fact finders. We might require juries to be the finders of all (or at least all significant) sentencing facts. Notably, *Blakely* requires juries to be finders only of aggravating facts, allowing judges still to find mitigating facts. But though the Constitution apparently permits this distinction, a sounder system might be one in which juries decide all these facts.

Juries as fact finders and sentence advisors. We might prefer that juries not only find facts, but also advise judges on appropriate punishments. Though the Constitution may not require juries to do anything more than find (aggravating) sentencing facts, we might still envision a sounder system to be one where juries also recommend sentences based on these facts.

Juries as fact finders and sentencers. We might want juries not only to find facts, but also to impose specific punishments. Again, though the Constitution may not require juries to do anything more than find (aggravating) sentencing facts, we might still think a sounder system would have juries impose specific sentences based on these facts.

In this context, it is worth remembering that jury participation in death penalty sentencing is the norm; in that setting, juries typically find and weigh aggravating and mitigating facts and also recommend or impose the ultimate sentence. In addition, six states allow jury sentencing in noncapital cases. See Ronald F. Wright, Rules for Sentencing Revolutions, 108 Yale L.J. 1355 (1999). In foreign countries professional judges often sit with lay jurors, and together they decide on guilt and the appropriate sentence.

6. *Jury findings and the purposes of sentencing.*   Is there a natural fit between the functions of a jury and particular purposes of sentencing? Consider the possibility that the Blakely line of cases is an outgrowth of shifting purposes for sentencing. In an era of indeterminate sentencing, when rehabilitation and other consequentialist theories dominated our thinking, the jury was not especially well suited to the clinical determinations necessary to impose a successful sentence. On the other hand, in an era when limited retributivism has become the leading rationale for determinate sentencing laws, the jury's findings about historical facts have become more important to the enterprise. Cf. Laura Appleman, Retributive Justice and Hidden Sentencing After *Blakely*, 68 Ohio St. L.J. (forthcoming 2007) (available at ssrn.com/abstract=956405).

7. *Indictments and negotiating strength.*   While the Sixth Amendment cases address the right to a jury trial, there are related rights that require the government to begin proving its facts before the time of sentencing. Must the government allege any aggravating facts that affect the authorized sentence in the indictment before trial? See State v. Davis, 141 S.W.3d 600 (Tenn. 2004) (*Apprendi* and *Blakely* do not require aggravating circumstances that enhance first-degree murder punishment to be alleged in the indictment; primary function of indictment is to offer defendant notice of issues, and current procedural rules provide notice of issues in other formats). Some states have resolved this question through statute or procedural rule, requiring the state to notify the defendant about the issues before trial, but not necessarily in the indictment. How will the relevant state rules on indictments and other disclosure of aggravating facts influence the timing and outcome of plea negotiations?

B. PROCEDURAL REALITIES

Defendants' concerns about the sentence they may receive shape the entire criminal process. Sentencing "process" might reach back to include each stage of criminal proceedings that has a distinct impact on the sentence determination. While in some situations, constitutional rights (including any developing rights under *Apprendi* and *Blakely*) may be an essential part of sentencing process, in most cases the principal procedures will be nonconstitutional, guided by statute and, to an even greater extent, by rules of procedure, prosecutorial policies, and local judicial culture.

The dominant procedural reality for all defendants is this: the overwhelming majority of cases in both state and federal systems are resolved by guilty pleas, and those pleas generally reflect bargaining between prosecution and defense. The contents of guilty pleas, going well beyond simply the offense of conviction, are likely to have a significant effect on the sentence.

After an exploration of the connection between plea negotiations and sentencing, the latter part of this chapter considers two procedures unique to sentencing — sentencing hearings and the creation of presentence investigation (PSI) reports — along with the special institutional role of probation officers who write the PSI reports.

1.   Plea Practices and Sentencing

Given the importance of guilty pleas and the underlying plea bargains, it might seem that there should be a constitutional jurisprudence to match. There is not; indeed, there is surprisingly little case law or doctrine governing guilty pleas or plea bargains. There is, however, quite a bit of relevant law governing plea bargains and guilty pleas in statutes and rules.

Decisions whether to offer or accept plea bargains are also governed by executive branch policies. These policies vary in their level of detail; in many smaller offices, prosecutors follow consistent plea practices that may reflect unwritten (but explicit) guidelines, or they may simply reflect shared office culture and experience. Sometimes prosecutors develop formal plea review standards, describing substantively the types of bargains that are acceptable. Other times they create procedural review mechanisms, such as supervisory review or committee review of possible plea bargains.

Federal prosecutors, under the central control of the attorney general, have developed a detailed set of written plea bargaining policies. In addition to the nationwide guidelines set out below, many of the U.S. Attorneys' offices in the federal districts around the country have developed guidance to reflect the distinctive caseloads, resources, and other factors in each district.

The following policies require slow and careful reading. Note that some reverse earlier policies, while others add new standards or procedures. The following questions applied to each policy may help to reveal the dynamics at work.

- What are the goals of the policy, and are they explicitly stated? Do the goals relate to authorizing statutes, general principles of justice (such as sentencing purposes), or internal administrative aims?
- Is the link between plea bargains and sentencing explicitly stated?
- Does the policy use substantive limitations (rules about the content of acceptable agreements) or procedures (written decisions, internal review and approval) to achieve its goals?

The first policy below was promulgated before the legislation that created the federal guidelines, when the federal system (and most state systems) still operated under an indeterminate sentencing model. To what extent were these original principles (developed in 1980) concerned with sentencing?

Federal Rule of Criminal Procedure 11, Pleas

(a) Entering a Plea.

(1) *In General.* A defendant may plead guilty, not guilty, or (with the court's consent) nolo contendere. . . .

(b) Considering and Accepting a Guilty or Nolo Contendere Plea.

(1) *Advising and Questioning the Defendant.* Before the court accepts a plea of guilty or nolo contendere, the defendant may be placed under oath, and the court must address the defendant personally in open court. During this address, the court must inform the defendant of, and determine that the defendant understands, the following:

(A) the government's right, in a prosecution for perjury or false statement, to use against the defendant any statement that the defendant gives under oath;

(B) the right to plead not guilty, or having already so pleaded, to persist in that plea;

(C) the right to a jury trial;

(D) the right to be represented by counsel — and if necessary have the court appoint counsel — at trial and at every other stage of the proceeding;

(E) the right at trial to confront and cross-examine adverse witnesses, to be protected from compelled self-incrimination, to testify and present evidence, and to compel the attendance of witnesses;

(F) the defendant's waiver of these trial rights if the court accepts a plea of guilty or nolo contendere;

(G) the nature of each charge to which the defendant is pleading;

(H) any maximum possible penalty, including imprisonment, fine, and term of supervised release;

(I) any mandatory minimum penalty;

(J) any applicable forfeiture;

(K) the court's authority to order restitution;

(L) the court's obligation to impose a special assessment;

(M) the court's obligation to apply the Sentencing Guidelines, and the court's discretion to depart from those guidelines under some circumstances; and

(N) the terms of any plea-agreement provision waiving the right to appeal or to collaterally attack the sentence.

(2) *Ensuring that a Plea Is Voluntary.* Before accepting a plea of guilty or nolo contendere, the court must address the defendant personally in open court and determine that the plea is voluntary and did not result from force, threats, or promises (other than promises in a plea agreement).

(3) *Determining the Factual Basis for a Plea.* Before entering judgment on a guilty plea, the court must determine that there is a factual basis for the plea.

(c) Plea Agreement Procedure.

(1) *In General.* An attorney for the government and the defendant's attorney, or the defendant when proceeding pro se, may discuss and reach a plea agreement. The court must not participate in these discussions. If the defendant pleads guilty or nolo contendere to either a charged offense or a lesser or related offense, the plea agreement may specify that an attorney for the government will:

(A) not bring, or will move to dismiss other charges;

(B) recommend, or agree not to oppose the defendant's request, that a particular sentence or sentencing range is appropriate or that a particular provision of the Sentencing Guidelines, or policy statement, or sentencing factor does or does not apply (such a recommendation or request does not bind the court); or

(C) agree that a specific sentence or sentencing range is the appropriate disposition of the case, or that a particular provision of the Sentencing Guidelines, or policy statement, or sentencing factor does or does not apply (such a recommendation or request binds the court once the court accepts the plea agreement).

(2) *Disclosing a Plea Agreement.* The parties must disclose the plea agreement in open court when the plea is offered, unless the court for good cause allows the parties to disclose the plea agreement in camera.

(3) *Judicial Consideration of a Plea Agreement.*

(A) To the extent the plea agreement is of the type specified in Rule 11(c)(1)(A) or (C), the court may accept the agreement, reject it, or defer a decision until the court has reviewed the presentence report.

(B) To the extent the plea agreement is of the type specified in Rule 11(c)(1)(B), the court must advise the defendant that the defendant has no right to withdraw the plea if the court does not follow the recommendation or request.

(4) *Accepting a Plea Agreement.* If the court accepts the plea agreement, it must inform the defendant that to the extent the plea agreement is of the type specified in Rule 11(c)(1)(A) or (C), the agreed disposition will be included in the judgment.

(5) *Rejecting a Plea Agreement.* If the court rejects a plea agreement containing provisions of the type specified in Rule 11(c)(1)(A) or (C), the court must do the following on the record and in open court (or, for good cause, in camera):

(A) inform the parties that the court rejects the plea agreement;

(B) advise the defendant personally that the court is not required to follow the plea agreement and give the defendant the opportunity to withdraw the plea; and

(C) advise the defendant personally that if the plea is not withdrawn, the court may dispose of the case less favorably toward the defendant than the plea agreement contemplated.

(d) Withdrawing a Guilty or Nolo Contendere Plea. A defendant may withdraw a plea of guilty or nolo contendere:

(1) before the court accepts the plea, for any reason or no reason; or

(2) after the court accepts the plea, but before it imposes sentence if:

(A) the court rejects a plea agreement under Rule 11(c)(5); or

(B) the defendant can show a fair and just reason for requesting the withdrawal.

(e) Finality of a Guilty or Nolo Contendere Plea. After the court imposes sentence, the defendant may not withdraw a plea of guilty or nolo contendere, and the plea may be set aside only on direct appeal or collateral attack.

	U.S. Department of Justice,	
	Principles of Federal Prosecution	
	(1980)	

Entering into Plea Agreements

1. The attorney for the government may, in an appropriate case, enter into an agreement with a defendant that, upon the defendant's plea of guilty or nolo contendere to a charged offense or to a lesser or related offense, he will move for dismissal of other charges, take a certain position with respect to the sentence to be imposed, or take other action.

2. In determining whether it would be appropriate to enter into a plea agreement, the attorney for the government should weigh all relevant considerations, including:

(a) the defendant's willingness to cooperate in the investigation or prosecution of others;

(b) the defendant's history with respect to criminal activity;

(c) the nature and seriousness of the offense or offenses charged;

(d) the defendant's remorse or contrition and his willingness to assume responsibility for his conduct;

(e) the desirability of prompt and certain disposition of the case;

(f) the likelihood of obtaining a conviction at trial;

(g) the probable effect on witnesses;

(h) the probable sentence or other consequences if the defendant is convicted;

(i) the public interest in having the case tried rather than disposed of by a guilty plea;

(j) the expense of trial and appeal; and

(k) the need to avoid delay in the disposition of other pending cases.

Comment: . . . The provision is not intended to suggest the desirability or lack of desirability of a plea agreement in any particular case or to be construed as a reflection on the merits of any plea agreement that actually may be reached; its purpose is solely to assist attorneys for the government in exercising their judgment as to whether some sort of plea agreement would be appropriate in a particular case. Government attorneys should consult the investigating agency involved in any case in which it would be helpful to have its views concerning the relevance of particular factors or the weight they deserve. . . .

A plea disposition in one case may facilitate the prompt disposition of other cases, including cases in which prosecution might otherwise be declined. This may occur simply because prosecutorial, judicial, or defense resources will become available for use in other cases, or because a plea by one of several defendants may have a "domino effect," leading to pleas by other defendants. In weighing the importance of these possible consequences, the attorney for the government should consider the state of the criminal docket and the speedy trial requirements in the district, the desirability of handling a larger volume of criminal cases, and the workloads of prosecutors, judges, and defense attorneys in the district.

3. If a prosecution is to be concluded pursuant to a plea agreement, the defendant should be required to plead to a charge or charges:

(a) that bears a reasonable relationship to the nature and extent of his criminal conduct;

(b) that has an adequate factual basis;

(c) that makes likely the imposition of an appropriate sentence under all the circumstances of the case; and

(d) that does not adversely affect the investigation or prosecution of others.

Comment: [T]he considerations that should be taken into account in selecting the charge or charges to which a defendant should be required to plead guilty . . . are essentially the same as those governing the selection of charges to be included in the original indictment or information.

(a) Relationship to criminal conduct — The charge or charges to which a defendant pleads guilty should bear a reasonable relationship to the defendant's criminal conduct, both in nature and in scope. . . . In many cases, this will probably require that the defendant plead to the most serious offense charged. . . . The requirement that a defendant plead to a charge that bears a reasonable relationship to the nature and extent of his criminal conduct is not inflexible. There may be situations involving cooperating defendants in which [lesser charges may be appropriate].

(b) Factual basis — The attorney for the government should also bear in mind the legal requirement that there be a factual basis for the charge or charges to which a guilty plea is entered. This requirement is intended to assure against conviction after a guilty plea of a person who is not in fact guilty. . . .

(c) Basis for sentencing — [T]he prosecutor should take care to avoid a "charge agreement" that would unduly restrict the court's sentencing authority. [I]f restitution is appropriate under the circumstances of the case, a sufficient number of counts should be retained under the agreement to provide a basis for an adequate restitution order. . . .

(d) Effect on other cases — . . . Among the possible adverse consequences to be avoided are the negative jury appeal that may result when relatively less culpable defendants are tried in the absence of a more culpable defendant or when a principal prosecution witness appears to be equally culpable as the defendants but has been permitted to plead to a significantly less serious offense. . . .

5. If a prosecution is to be terminated pursuant to a plea agreement, the attorney for the government should ensure that the case file contains a record of the agreed disposition, signed or initialed by the defendant or his attorney. . . .

NOTES

1. *Plea procedures and sentencing.* Federal Rule of Criminal Procedure 11 has been a model for many states. The types of pleas in Rule 11 were identified before the implementation of the federal guideline system; one of those types

allows for plea agreements to particular sentences. Such binding sentence pleas are quite rare — most prosecutors refuse to make such pleas and some courts refuse to accept them.

Rule 11 was amended and reorganized effective December 1, 2002. Most of the cases and literature before that date and some (by force of habit) afterward use a reference to the prior rule — with "(e)(1)(A)" pleas being the prior form of current "(c)(1)(A)" (charge bargains), "(e)(1)(B)" pleas the earlier form of "(c)(1)(B)" (sentence recommendation bargains), and "(e)(1)(C)" the earlier form of "(c)(1)(C)" (binding pleas to a specific sentence).

2. *The federal guidelines and plea agreements.* What did the Sentencing Commission do about plea bargains, which account for roughly 90% of all convictions in the federal system? When the Sentencing Commission created its initial set of guidelines, it included a "policy statement" about plea agreements, which is reprinted below. At the time, it was generally assumed that policy statements had less binding effect than the guidelines themselves, although later events have all but erased this distinction. What was the commission trying to accomplish with regard to plea agreements?

3. *Guidance from Main Justice.* The U.S. Department of Justice realized that this new system of guideline sentencing was complicated. Thus, it issued special guidance to prosecutors that appeared simultaneously with the guidelines. Excerpts from the 1987 "Redbook" are reprinted below. Is this internal guidance to prosecutors consistent with the statute and with the policy statements? What changes does it make to the 1980 Principles of Federal Prosecution?

After the first few months of practice under the new sentencing and plea bargaining rules, officials in the Department of Justice believed that federal prosecutors in the field were not adhering closely enough to the department's plea bargaining policies. Consequently, the leadership of the department (housed in "Main Justice" in Washington, D.C.) revised the 1987 Redbook by issuing the 1989 "Thornburgh Bluesheet," also reprinted below. The revision of the policy was aimed at increasing compliance with the plea practices that the leadership of the department wanted. What elements of the policy did the revisers focus on? What were the likely effects of the revisions?

4. *Change of administrations.* After the 1992 elections, the incoming Clinton administration appointed new leadership to the Department of Justice. The new attorney general, Janet Reno, reviewed plea bargaining policies and issued a "Bluesheet" of her own. It too is reprinted below. In most districts, this policy was carried out by newly appointed U.S. Attorneys, along with many career attorneys who had also served under the previous administration. What prior statements does the Reno Bluesheet hark back to? What, if anything, is new in the policy?

‖ *28 U.S.C. §994(a)(2)(E)* ‖

The Commission . . . shall promulgate . . . general policy statements regarding application of the guidelines or any other aspect of sentencing or sentence implementation . . . including the appropriate use of . . . the authority granted under Rule 11(c)(2) of the Federal Rules of Criminal Procedure to accept or reject a plea agreement. . . .

U.S. Sentencing Guidelines §§6B1.2, 6B1.4 (Policy Statements)

§6B1.2 STANDARDS FOR ACCEPTANCE OF PLEA AGREEMENTS

(a) In the case of a plea agreement that includes the dismissal of any charges or an agreement not to pursue potential charges [under Rule 11(c)(1)(A)], the court may accept the agreement if the court determines, for reasons stated on the record, that the remaining charges adequately reflect the seriousness of the actual offense behavior and that accepting the agreement will not undermine the statutory purposes of sentencing or the sentencing guidelines. Provided, that a plea agreement that includes the dismissal of a charge or a plea agreement not to pursue a potential charge shall not preclude the conduct underlying such charge from being considered under the provisions of §1B1.3 (Relevant Conduct) in connection with the count(s) of which the defendant is convicted.

(b) In the case of a plea agreement that includes a nonbinding recommendation [under Rule 11(c)(1)(B)], the court may accept the recommendation if the court is satisfied either that: (1) the recommended sentence is within the applicable guideline range; or (2) the recommended sentence departs from the applicable guideline range for justifiable reasons.

(c) In the case of a plea agreement that includes a specific sentence [under Rule 11(c)(1)(C)], the court may accept the agreement if the court is satisfied either that: (1) the agreed sentence is within the applicable guideline range; or (2) the agreed sentence departs from the applicable guideline range for justifiable reasons.

§6B1.4 STIPULATIONS

(a) A plea agreement may be accompanied by a written stipulation of facts relevant to sentencing. [S]tipulations shall: (1) set forth the relevant facts and circumstances of the actual offense conduct and offender characteristics; (2) not contain misleading facts; and (3) set forth with meaningful specificity the reasons why the sentencing range resulting from the proposed agreement is appropriate.

(b) To the extent that the parties disagree about any facts relevant to sentencing, the stipulation shall identify the facts that are in dispute. . . .

(d) The court is not bound by the stipulation, but may with the aid of the presentence report, determine the facts relevant to sentencing.

Prosecutors' Handbook on Sentencing Guidelines ("The Redbook")
William Weld, Assistant Attorney General (1987)

[T]he validity and use of the Commission's policy statements by prosecutors should depend upon whether the agreement reflects charge bargaining or sentence bargaining under [Rule 11(c)].

SENTENCE BARGAINING

A significant problem with the Commission's policy statements on plea bargains which include a specific sentence under [Rule 11(c)(1)(B) and (C)], §6B1.2(b) and (c), is that the standard they set forth for acceptance or rejection of a sentence that departs from the guidelines appears to be of doubtful validity under the Sentencing Reform Act (SRA). The standard for departure from the guidelines is set forth in the Act and requires a finding that an aggravating or mitigating circumstance exists that was not adequately taken into consideration by the Commission in formulating the guidelines. Yet the Commission's policy statements relating to sentence bargains authorize departure "for justifiable reasons." We do not believe it is possible to argue that the Commission has not adequately taken into consideration the value of a plea agreement as a mitigating factor so as to support a departure. . . . We recognize, nonetheless, that many judges might be tempted to take a realistic approach; a sentence outside the guidelines in the context of a plea agreement is unlikely to result in an appeal of the sentence. Therefore, if urged to accept a plea agreement that departs from the guidelines, they will follow the policy statements despite their questionable basis.

Nevertheless, the Criminal Division has concluded that the apparent authority for a judge to depart from the guidelines pursuant to the Commission's policy statements, §6B1.2(b) and (c), for plea agreements involving a particular sentence under [Rule 11(c)(1)(B) and (C)] is at variance with the more restrictive departure language of [the statute] and that, consequently, these policy statements should not be used as a basis for recommending a sentence that departs from the guidelines. [P]rosecutors should not recommend or agree to a lower-than-guideline sentence merely on the basis of a plea agreement. They may, however, recommend or agree to a sentence at the low end of an applicable sentencing range [within the guidelines].

In addition to the above-described legitimate guideline reductions that may be used in sentence-type negotiations, a departure from the guidelines may be warranted and may be included in the recommended or agreed-upon sentence if the [statutory] standard . . . is met. That is, a mitigating circumstance must exist (other than the reaching of a plea agreement) that was not adequately taken into consideration by the Commission in formulating the guidelines and that should result in a sentence different from that described. Moreover, a departure from the guidelines may also be reflected in a plea agreement if the defendant provided substantial assistance in the investigation or prosecution of another person who has committed an offense. . . . Therefore, even though plea-bargained sentences must accord with the law and the guidelines, there is considerable room for negotiating.

The basic reason for rejecting the Commission's policy statements on sentence bargains and treating sentences which are the subject of a sentence bargain in the same manner as sentences which result from conviction after trial is that any other result could seriously thwart the purpose of the SRA to reduce unwarranted disparity in sentencing [among defendants with similar records who have been found guilty of similar criminal conduct]. Congress could not have expressed the concerns reflected in the SRA and the legislative history with unwarranted disparity and uncertainty in sentencing but have intended the

484

reforms enacted to be limited to the small percentage of cases that go to trial. The legislative history of the SRA indeed indicates that Congress was concerned with the potential shift of discretion in sentencing from the court to the prosecutor through plea agreements and the unwarranted disparity that could result. . . .

CHARGE BARGAINING

The policy statement on charge bargaining addresses agreements that include the dismissal of any charges under [Rule 11(c)(1)(A)] or an agreement not to pursue potential charges. It authorizes the court to accept such an agreement if it determines, "for reasons stated on the record, that the remaining charges adequately reflect the seriousness of the actual offense behavior and that accepting the agreement will not undermine the statutory purposes of sentencing." §6B1.2(a). The requirement that the "remaining charges adequately reflect the seriousness of the actual offense behavior" in charge bargaining is important since the charge of conviction itself is the most significant factor in establishing the guideline sentence. . . .

Although Congress intended that courts exercise "meaningful" review of charge reduction plea agreements, it is our view that moderately greater flexibility legally can and does attach to charge bargains than to sentence bargains. While, as indicated previously, the Commission's quite liberal policy statements on sentence bargaining appear to be inconsistent with the controlling (and stricter) statutory departure standard, the statutory departure standard is not applicable in the charge-bargain context. . . .

Nevertheless, in order to fulfill the objectives of the Sentencing Reform Act prosecutors should conduct charge bargaining in a manner consistent with the direction in the applicable policy statement, §6B1.2(a), i.e., subject to the policy statement's instruction that the "remaining charges [should] adequately reflect the seriousness of the actual offense behavior" and that the agreement not undermine the statutory purposes of sentencing. In our view, this translates into a requirement that readily provable serious charges should not be bargained away. The sole legitimate ground for agreeing not to pursue a charge that is relevant under the guidelines to assure that the sentence will reflect the seriousness of the defendant's "offense behavior" is the existence of real doubt as to the ultimate provability of the charge.

Concomitantly, however, the prosecutor is in the best position to assess the strength of the government's case and enjoys broad discretion in making judgments as to which charges are most likely to result in conviction on the basis of the available evidence. For this reason, the prosecutor entering into a charge bargain may enjoy a degree of latitude that is not present when the plea bargain addresses only sentencing aspects. . . .

It is appropriate that the sentence for an offender who agrees to plead guilty to relatively few charges should be different from the sentence for an offender convicted of many charges since guilt has not been determined as to the dismissed charges. At the same time, however, sentence bargaining should not result in a vastly different sentence as compared to a sentence following trial. . . .

The overriding principle governing the conduct of plea negotiations is that plea agreements should not be used to circumvent the guidelines. This principle is in accordance with the policies set forth in the Principles of Federal Prosecution. . . . For example, charges should not be filed simply to exert leverage to induce a plea. Rather, the prosecutor should charge the most serious offense consistent with the defendant's provable conduct. . . .

A subsidiary but nonetheless important issue concerns so-called "fact" bargaining or stipulations. [The policy statement §6B1.4] attaches certain conditions to such stipulations. The most important condition, with which the Department concurs, is that stipulations shall "not contain misleading facts." Otherwise, the basic purpose of the SRA to reduce unwarranted sentence disparity will be undermined. Thus, if the defendant can clearly be proved to have used a weapon or committed an assault in the course of the offense, the prosecutor may not stipulate, as part of a plea agreement designed to produce a lower sentence, that no weapon was used or assault committed. If, on the other hand, certain facts surrounding the offense are not clear, e.g., the extent of the loss or injury resulting from the defendant's fraud, the prosecutor is at liberty to stipulate that no loss or injury beyond that clearly provable existed. Prosecutors may not, however, instruct investigators not to pursue leads, or make less than ordinary efforts to ascertain facts, simply to be in a position to say that they are unable clearly to prove a sentencing fact and thereby increase the latitude for bargaining. . . . Subject to the above constraints, however, the Department encourages the use of stipulations accompanying plea agreements to the extent practicable. . . .

Plea Policy for Federal Prosecutors ("Thornburgh Bluesheet")
Richard Thornburgh, Attorney General (1989)

. . . Should a prosecutor determine in good faith after indictment that, as a result of a change in the evidence or for another reason (e.g., a need has arisen to protect the identity of a particular witness until he testifies against a more significant defendant), a charge is not readily provable or that an indictment exaggerates the seriousness of an offense or offenses, a plea bargain may reflect the prosecutor's reassessment. There should be a record, however, in a case in which charges originally brought are dropped. . . .

Department policy requires honesty in sentencing; federal prosecutors are expected to identify for U.S. District Courts departures when they agree to support them. For example, it would be improper for a prosecutor to agree that a departure is in order, but to conceal the agreement in a charge bargain that is presented to a court as a fait accompli so that there is neither a record of nor judicial review of the departure. . . .

The basic policy is that charges are not to be bargained away or dropped, unless the prosecutor has a good faith doubt as to the government's ability readily to prove a charge for legal or evidentiary reasons. It would serve no purpose here to seek to further define "readily provable." The policy is to bring cases that the government should win if there were a trial. There are, however, two exceptions.

First, if the applicable guideline range from which a sentence may be imposed would be unaffected, readily provable charges may be dismissed or dropped as part of a plea bargain. . . . Second, federal prosecutors may drop readily provable charges with the specific approval of the United States Attorney or designated supervisory level official for reasons set forth in the file of the case. This exception recognizes that the aims of the Sentencing Reform Act must be sought without ignoring other, critical aspects of the federal criminal justice system. For example, approval to drop charges in a particular case might be given because the United States Attorney's office is particularly overburdened, the case would be time-consuming to try, and proceeding to trial would significantly reduce the total number of cases disposed of by the office. . . .

The Department's policy is only to stipulate to facts that accurately represent the defendant's conduct. If a prosecutor wishes to support a departure from the guidelines, he or she should candidly do so and not stipulate to facts that are untrue. Stipulations to untrue facts are unethical. If a prosecutor has insufficient facts to contest a defendant's effort to seek a downward departure or to claim an adjustment, the prosecutor can say so. If the presentence report states facts that are inconsistent with a stipulation in which a prosecutor has joined, it is desirable for the prosecutor to object to the report or to add a statement explaining the prosecutor's understanding of the facts or the reason for the stipulation. . . .

Charging and Plea Decisions ("Reno Bluesheet")
Janet Reno, Attorney General (1993)

As first stated in the preface to the original 1980 edition of the Principles of Federal Prosecution, "they have been cast in general terms with a view to providing guidance rather than to mandating results. The intent is to assure regularity without regimentation, to prevent unwarranted disparity without sacrificing flexibility."

It should be emphasized that charging decisions and plea agreements should reflect adherence to the Sentencing Guidelines. However, a faithful and honest application of the Sentencing Guidelines is not incompatible with selecting charges or entering into plea agreements on the basis of an individualized assessment of the extent to which particular charges fit the specific circumstances of the case, are consistent with the purposes of the federal criminal code, and maximize the impact of federal resources on crime. Thus, for example, in determining "the most serious offense that is consistent with the nature of the defendant's conduct, that is likely to result in a sustainable conviction," it is appropriate that the attorney for the government consider, inter alia, such factors as the sentencing guideline range yielded by the charge, whether the penalty yielded by such sentencing range (or potential mandatory minimum charge, if applicable) is proportional to the seriousness of the defendant's conduct, and whether the charge achieves such purposes of the criminal law as punishment, protection of the public, specific and general deterrence, and rehabilitation. Note that these factors may also be considered by the attorney for the government when entering into the plea agreements.

To ensure consistency and accountability, charging and plea agreement decisions must be made at an appropriate level of responsibility and documented with an appropriate record of the factors applied.

NOTES

1. *The 1992 Terwilliger Bluesheet.* After a few years of experience with the new system, officials in the Department of Justice remained dissatisfied with the plea bargaining practices of its attorneys in the field. In a 1992 revision of the plea bargaining policy, known as the "Terwilliger Bluesheet," the department moved away from an emphasis on describing the types of bargains that are acceptable. Instead, the revised policy strengthened the procedural review process for plea agreements:

> All negotiated plea agreements to felonies or misdemeanors negotiated from felonies shall be in writing and filed with the court. . . . There shall be within each office a formal system for approval of negotiated pleas. The approval authority shall be vested in at least a supervisory criminal Assistant United States Attorney . . . who will have the responsibility of assessing the appropriateness of the plea agreement under the policies of the Department of Justice pertaining to pleas, including those set forth in the Thornburgh Memo.

The 1992 policy allowed for categorical review of certain plea bargains. Fact situations that "arise with great frequency and are given identical treatment" could be handled through a "written instruction" that "describes with particularity the standard plea procedure to be followed, so long as that procedure is otherwise within Departmental guidelines." The policy listed as an example "a border district which routinely deals with a high volume of illegal alien cases daily." What do you suppose were the effects of these 1992 policy changes?

2. *Prosecutorial discretion and control.* How would you describe these DOJ policies in terms of the degree of control each policy exerted over federal prosecutorial plea practices? Did all of these policies move toward increasing control over individual prosecutorial decisions? For further background on the creation of these federal policies, see David Robinson, The Decline and Potential Collapse of Federal Guideline Sentencing, 74 Wash. U. L.Q. 881 (1996). Are executive plea bargaining policies a good idea? What problems could they solve? What problems might they create?

3. *Policies and political accountability.* In response to the Reno Bluesheet, on January 13, 1994, Senator Orrin Hatch (R-Utah), the ranking minority member on the Judiciary Committee, sent Attorney General Janet Reno a letter strongly opposing her directive:

> The Department's new policy now permits prosecutors to make independent decisions about whether a prescribed guideline sentence or mandatory minimum charge is not "proportional to the seriousness of the defendant's

conduct." In other words, this new policy increases the potential for the unwarranted softening of sentences for violent offenders. . . .

I do not support the Department's announcement to drug traffickers and violent criminals that certain illegal conduct may not be charged because a Department employee may find the prescribed punishment too severe. If the Administration believes that existing sentences for drug cases and violent criminals are too severe, then it should seek to change the law or the relevant sentencing guidelines — not ignore them. I strongly urge you to reconsider your action in this matter.

Reno responded on March 8, 1994:

Let me reiterate, as set forth in the clarifying bluesheet to which you allude, that it remains the directive of the Department of Justice that prosecutors charge the most serious offense that is consistent with the nature of the defendant's conduct, that is likely to result in a sustainable conviction; that prosecutors adhere to the Sentencing Guidelines; and that charging and plea agreements be made at an appropriate level of responsibility with appropriate documentation. In short, contrary to what you suggest, individual prosecutors are not free to follow their own lights or to ignore legislative directives. . . . We are steadfast in our opposition to unwarranted softening of sentences for violent offenders or drug traffickers. . . .

4. *Congress reasserts control over federal sentencing.*   In 2003 Congress enacted the USA PROTECT Act, Public Law 108-21, 117 Stat. 650. Although the statute dealt primarily with crimes involving child abuse, it also changed several features of federal sentencing law more generally, making downward departures from the sentencing prescribed by the federal guidelines more difficult for judges to invoke. Congress also asked the attorney general to submit a report to the House and Senate judiciary committees, detailing the policies the department would follow to discourage downward departures.

5. *The Ashcroft Memos.*   The USA PROTECT Act requested a report from the Department of Justice within 90 days of the statute's passage. If such a report did not appear by that deadline, the law imposed a more onerous set of reporting requirements for the attorney general to follow. The statute was signed into law on April 30, 2003. On July 28, Attorney General John Ashcroft issued a set of policies concerning "sentencing recommendations and sentencing appeals." The policies emphasized "honesty in sentencing, both with respect to the facts and the law." A prosecutor's sentencing recommendations to the court "must honestly reflect the totality and seriousness of the defendant's conduct and must be fully consistent with the Guidelines," regardless of whether the individual prosecutor agrees with the policy embodied in the sentencing guidelines. Under the policy, prosecutors may not agree to "stand silent" while a defendant requests a downward adjustment to a sentence, "unless the prosecutor determines in good faith that the adjustment is supported by facts and the law."

Two months later, Attorney General Ashcroft issued a second policy statement, this one dealing with selection of charges and plea agreements. The policy is reprinted below. How does Ashcroft's policy compare with those of Reno, Terwilliger, Thornburgh, and Weld?

Department Policy Concerning Charging Criminal Offenses, Disposition of Charges, and Sentencing
John Ashcroft, Attorney General
(September 22, 2003)

... The fairness Congress sought to achieve by the Sentencing Reform Act and the PROTECT Act can be attained only if there are fair and reasonably consistent policies with respect to the Department's decisions concerning what charges to bring and how cases should be disposed. Just as the sentence a defendant receives should not depend upon which particular judge presides over the case, so too the charges a defendant faces should not depend upon the particular prosecutor assigned to handle the case. ...

I. DEPARTMENT POLICY CONCERNING CHARGING AND PROSECUTION OF CRIMINAL OFFENSES

A. General Duty to Charge and to Pursue the Most Serious, Readily Provable Offense in All Federal Prosecutions

It is the policy of the Department of Justice that, in all federal criminal cases, federal prosecutors must charge and pursue the most serious, readily provable offense or offenses that are supported by the facts of the case, except as authorized by an Assistant Attorney General, United States Attorney, or designated supervisory attorney in the limited circumstances described below. The most serious offense or offenses are those that generate the most substantial sentence under the Sentencing Guidelines, unless a mandatory minimum sentence or count requiring a consecutive sentence would generate a longer sentence. A charge is not "readily provable" if the prosecutor has a good faith doubt, for legal or evidentiary reasons, as to the Government's ability readily to prove a charge at trial. Thus, charges should not be filed simply to exert leverage to induce a plea. Once filed, the most serious readily provable charges may not be dismissed except to the extent permitted in Section B.

B. Limited Exceptions

The basic policy set forth above requires federal prosecutors to charge and to pursue all charges that are determined to be readily provable and that, under the applicable statutes and Sentencing Guidelines, would yield the most substantial sentence. There are, however, certain limited exceptions to this requirement:

1. *Sentence would not be affected.* First, if the applicable guideline range from which a sentence may be imposed would be unaffected, prosecutors may decline to charge or to pursue readily provable charges. However, if the most serious readily provable charge involves a mandatory minimum sentence that exceeds the applicable guideline range, counts essential to establish a

mandatory minimum sentence must be charged and may not be dismissed, except to the extent provided elsewhere below.

2. *"Fast-track" programs.*   With the passage of the PROTECT Act, Congress recognized the importance of early disposition or "fast-track" programs [to handle the high volume of cases (particularly immigration cases) in some districts. As a matter of Department policy, Attorney General authorization is necessary for] any fast-track program that relies on "charge bargaining" — *i.e.*, an expedited disposition program whereby the Government agrees to charge less than the most serious, readily provable offense. Such programs are intended to be exceptional and will be authorized only when clearly warranted by local conditions within a district. . . .

3. *Post-indictment reassessment.*   In cases where post-indictment circumstances cause a prosecutor to determine in good faith that the most serious offense is not readily provable, because of a change in the evidence or some other justifiable reason (*e.g.*, the unavailability of a witness or the need to protect the identity of a witness until he testifies against a more significant defendant), the prosecutor may dismiss the charge(s) with the written or otherwise documented approval of an Assistant Attorney General, United States Attorney, or designated supervisory attorney.

4. *Substantial assistance.*   The preferred means to recognize a defendant's substantial assistance in the investigation or prosecution of another person is to charge the most serious readily provable offense and then to file an appropriate motion or motions under U.S.S.G. §5K1.1, 18 U.S.C. §3553(e), or Federal Rule of Criminal Procedure 35(b). However, in rare circumstances, where necessary to obtain substantial assistance in an important investigation or prosecution, and with the written or otherwise documented approval of an Assistant Attorney General, United States Attorney, or designated supervisory attorney, a federal prosecutor may decline to charge or to pursue a readily provable charge as part of plea agreement that properly reflects the substantial assistance provided by the defendant in the investigation or prosecution of another person.

5. *Statutory enhancements.*   The use of statutory enhancements is strongly encouraged, and federal prosecutors must therefore take affirmative steps to ensure that the increased penalties resulting from specific statutory enhancements [such as use of a weapon] are sought in all appropriate cases. . . . In many cases, however, the filing of such enhancements will mean that the statutory sentence exceeds the applicable Sentencing Guidelines range, thereby ensuring that the defendant will not receive any credit for acceptance of responsibility and will have no incentive to plead guilty. Requiring the pursuit of such enhancements to trial in every case could therefore have a significant effect on the allocation of prosecutorial resources within a given district. Accordingly, an Assistant Attorney General, United States Attorney, or designated supervisory attorney may authorize a prosecutor to forgo the filing of a statutory enhancement, but *only* in the context of a negotiated plea agreement. . . .

6. *Other exceptional circumstances.*   Prosecutors may decline to pursue or may dismiss readily provable charges in other exceptional circumstances with the written or otherwise documented approval of an Assistant Attorney General, United States Attorney, or designated supervisory attorney. This exception

recognizes that the aims of the Sentencing Reform Act must be sought without ignoring the practical limitations of the federal criminal justice system. For example, a case-specific approval to dismiss charges in a particular case might be given because the United States Attorney's Office is particularly over-burdened, the duration of the trial would be exceptionally long, and proceeding to trial would significantly reduce the total number of cases disposed of by the office. However, such case-by-case exceptions should be rare; otherwise the goals of fairness and equity will be jeopardized.

II. DEPARTMENT POLICY CONCERNING PLEA AGREEMENTS

[It] remains Department policy that the sentencing court should be informed if a plea agreement involves a "charge bargain." Accordingly, a nego-tiated plea that uses any of the options described in Section I(B)(2), (4), (5), or (6) must be made known to the court at the time of the plea hearing and at the time of sentencing, *i.e.*, the court must be informed that a more serious, readily provable offense was not charged or that an applicable statutory enhancement was not filed. . . . Charges may be declined or dismissed pursuant to a plea agreement only to the extent consistent with the principles set forth in Section I of this Memorandum.

[As for sentence bargains], prosecutors may enter into a plea agreement for a sentence that is within the specified guideline range. For example, when the Sentencing Guidelines range is 18-24 months, a prosecutor may agree to recommend a sentence of 18 or 20 months rather than to argue for a sentence at the top of the range. Similarly, a prosecutor may agree to recommend a downward adjustment for acceptance of responsibility under U.S.S.G. §3E1.1 if the prosecutor concludes in good faith that the defendant is entitled to the adjustment. . . .

In passing the PROTECT Act, Congress has made clear its view that there have been too many downward departures from the Sentencing Guidelines, and it has instructed the Commission to take measures "to ensure that the incidence of downward departures [is] substantially reduced." The Department has a duty to ensure that the circumstances in which it will request or accede to downward departures in the future are properly circumscribed.

Accordingly, federal prosecutors must not request or accede to a downward departure except in the limited circumstances specified in this mem-orandum and with authorization from an Assistant Attorney General, United States Attorney, or designated supervisory attorney. . . .

Federal criminal law and procedure apply equally throughout the United States. As the sole federal prosecuting entity, the Department of Justice has a unique obligation to ensure that all federal criminal cases are prosecuted according to the same standards. . . .

NOTES

1. *Prosecutor plea policies and legislative oversight.* In what ways do the Ashcroft Memos reveal their intended function as responses to Congress's request to push sentencing practices in a particular direction? What do you

make of the policy decision to equate the criteria for initial selection of charges (Section I of the Memos) and the criteria for evaluating charge bargains (Section II of the Memos)?

2. *Policies and practice.*   Do "line" attorneys follow directives from their boss? The most complete studies of federal plea practices during the early implementation of the guidelines concluded that prosecutors manipulated the guidelines in 20-35% of all cases. Stephen Schulhofer & Ilene Nagel, A Tale of Three Cities: An Empirical Study of Charging and Bargaining Practice Under the Federal Sentencing Guidelines, 66 S. Cal. L. Rev. 501 (1992). Sentencing Commission studies found charge manipulation in 17% of all cases and 26% of drug cases. U.S. Sentencing Commission, The Federal Sentencing Guidelines: A Report on the Operation of the Guidelines System and Short-Term Impacts on Disparity in Sentencing, Use of Incarceration, and Prosecutorial Discretion and Plea Bargaining, Executive Summary 31-54 (December 1991). Why might line attorneys not follow plea guidelines? Why might different U.S. Attorneys' offices develop different patterns of plea bargaining?

3. *Written and unwritten guidance.*   A striking feature of the plea bargaining policies in the federal system is the fact that they are written. Many other prosecutors' offices in state systems have pursued goals similar to those of the Department of Justice in creating its plea policies. They hope to maintain adequate control over prosecutors in the field and to send appropriate public signals about sentencing and plea bargaining. Nonetheless, within the state systems, such policies are rarely written, even when they are explicit. Why might a supervising prosecutor choose to keep such a critical office policy unwritten? See William Pizzi, Understanding Prosecutorial Discretion in the United States: The Limits of Comparative Criminal Procedure as an Instrument of Reform, 54 Ohio St. L.J. 1325 (1993) (discussing reasons that offices keep their plea bargaining policies informal and unwritten, including ill effects on deterrent value of criminal law, unfavorable public impressions related to policies perceived as lenient, need for flexibility in unusual cases, need to avoid judicial review of prosecutorial decisions); but compare Kim Banks Mayer, Applying Open Records Policy to Wisconsin District Attorneys: Can Charging Guidelines Promote Public Awareness? 1996 Wis. L. Rev. 295 (giving examples of prosecutorial charging and plea bargaining guidelines made public with no apparent ill effects, and arguing generally for public availability of policies). Is there any reason not to create a written office policy, given that all plea agreements in individual cases will become a matter of public record?

4. *Sentencing guidelines and the shift to charge bargains.*   A large number of states have changed their sentencing laws over the past few decades to reduce the discretion of judges in selecting a sentence and to restrict the discretion of corrections or parole officials in releasing offenders before the end of their announced sentences. These more "determinate" sentencing systems make the selection of the criminal charge more important than it was under more discretionary sentencing systems. Unlike the federal system, state guideline systems reject the use of uncharged conduct when setting a sentence. As a result, prosecutors and defendants in these jurisdictions have shifted away from sentence bargains toward charge bargains and "fact" bargains. In Minnesota,

which adopted a more determinate sentencing guideline system in 1980, studies focusing on the first few years of practice under the new laws revealed an increase in charge negotiations and a decrease in sentence negotiations. Terance Miethe, Charging and Plea Bargaining Practices Under Determinate Sentencing: An Investigation of the Hydraulic Displacement of Discretion, 78 J. Crim. L. & Criminology 155 (1987) (describing earlier studies).

5. *Uniformity within a jurisdiction.*   The federal plea bargaining policies reprinted above apply to U.S. Attorneys' offices throughout the country. While these offices still have a great deal of independence and vary from one another in their plea bargaining practices, they are still subject to more centralized control than the various prosecutors' offices located throughout a given state. Since prosecutors often create plea bargaining policies for their own offices, shouldn't there be great variety in plea bargaining practices among the different prosecutors within a state? Or are there institutions or incentives that produce similar prosecutorial plea policies throughout a state or even across different states?

6. *Waivers of the right to appeal: federal policy.*   One question about potential limits on the substantive content of pleas is whether defendants may waive the right to appeal or collaterally attack their sentences. This is an especially significant issue because of the importance of appellate decisions in providing law and norms for some structured sentencing systems, including the federal system. At the same time, sentencing appeals have made up a very significant proportion of criminal appeals, and indeed of all appeals in the federal system.

In 1995 the Department of Justice circulated a memo to all U.S. Attorneys to provide guidance on the drafting and use of sentencing appeal waivers in plea agreements. Though each of the U.S. Attorneys' offices sets its own policies — with some refusing to make use of these waivers and others using them regularly — the memorandum made a determined argument for waivers. The "Keeney memo" stated that the use of appeal waivers is "helpful in reducing the burden of appellate and collateral litigation involving sentencing issues," though it also cautions that the use of broad sentencing appeal waivers "could result in guideline-free sentencing of defendants in guilty plea cases, and it could encourage a lawless district court to impose sentences in violation of the guidelines."

Noting the increased use of appeal waivers in plea agreements, the Committee on Criminal Law of the Judicial Conference of the United States issued a memorandum in July 1996 to aid district judges and probation officers in their consideration of such provisions. This memo noted that "waivers have been consistently upheld as legal, primarily because it is well established that a defendant can waive any right, even a constitutional right, as long as the waiver is knowing and voluntary." The committee suggested that courts provide all defendants with a "qualified, yet informative, advisement of the right to appeal at sentencing," followed by a specific oral colloquy about the terms of any appeal waiver provision to which a defendant has agreed.

As the use of appeal waivers has become more common in the federal system, judges have expressed concerns that such waivers, especially in their broadest forms, can be unlawful, inappropriate, and dangerous. A number of circuit courts have expressed concerns about broad appeal waivers that eliminate all appellate rights concerning any guideline sentence that is imposed. These courts have indicated that they would look closely at the particular facts of each case to ensure that a defendant fully understood and voluntarily accepted such a waiver. See United States v. Rosa, 123 F.2d 94 (2d Cir. 1997) (affirming appeal waiver while observing that a broad waiver "presents grave dangers and implicates both constitutional questions and ordinary principles of fairness and justice"). More dramatically, a number of district judges have refused to accept pleas that include broad appeal waivers. Will such positions by district judges lead to different outcomes in their courts? Will it create disparities in substance and sentence, or only in process?

7. *Waivers of the right to appeal: state practices.*   Prosecutors in many systems will try to include explicit waivers of the right to appeal a conviction or sentence as part of the plea agreement. Most state courts have concluded that a defendant may explicitly waive the right to appeal a conviction as part of a plea agreement. See State v. Hinners, 471 N.W.2d 841 (Iowa 1991); People v. Seaberg, 541 N.E.2d 1022 (N.Y. 1989). A few courts maintain that public policy forbids prosecutors from insulating themselves from review by bargaining away a defendant's appeal rights. Cf. State v. Ethington, 592 P.2d 768 (Ariz. 1979) (defendant can appeal conviction, notwithstanding agreement not to appeal).

Is it necessary for a defendant to waive the right to appeal explicitly, or does it go without saying that a defendant who pleads guilty will not attack the conviction on appeal? If a defendant wants to appeal some aspect of a conviction based on a guilty plea, should she explicitly condition the guilty plea on the outcome of the planned appeal? How might we decide what must be explicit in a plea agreement and what will be implied? Does this depend on what the parties are likely to have contemplated, even if they did not address the issue specifically? See Peter Westen, Away from Waiver: A Rationale for the Forfeiture of Constitutional Rights in Criminal Procedure, 75 Mich. L. Rev. 1214 (1977).

8. *Substantive limits on bargains.*   There are a few types of legal challenges to a conviction that some courts say a defendant may not waive, even if the waiver appears explicitly in a plea agreement. Courts have taken this position on constitutional speedy trial rights, see People v. Callahan, 604 N.E.2d 108 (N.Y. 1992), and for sentences more severe than the statutory maximum allowable sentence, see Lanier v. State, 635 So. 2d 813 (Miss. 1994). Courts are split on whether the parties can agree to a sentence outside the statutorily authorized range of punishments; often they enforce illegal sentences falling below the authorized range of punishments but not illegal sentences set above the authorized range. See Ex parte Johnson, 669 So. 2d 205 (Ala. 1995) (enforces prosecutor's agreement to two-year prison term, even though prosecutor failed to account for sentencing enhancements requiring additional minimum sentences); but see Patterson v. State, 660 So. 2d 966 (Miss. 1995) (holding plea bargain to life without possibility of parole invalid because no statute authorizes such a sentence for murder).

When defendants attempt to raise challenges that they waived in plea agreements, claiming that the agreement is unenforceable, it is far more common for courts to refuse to hear the challenge. Courts allow defendants to bargain away rights of all sorts. See United States v. Mezzanatto, 513 U.S. 196

(1995) (allowing defendant to waive protections of Rule 11(e)(6), which prevented later introduction into evidence of statements made during plea negotiations); People v. Stevens, 610 N.W.2d 881 (Mich. 2000) (statements made during plea negotiations are admissible in prosecution's case-in-chief); Cowan v. Superior Court, 926 P.2d 438 (Cal. 1996) (allowing waiver of statute of limitations); People v. Allen, 658 N.E.2d 1012 (N.Y. 1995) (allowing waiver of double jeopardy); Joseph A. Colquitt, Ad Hoc Plea Bargaining, 75 Tul. L. Rev. 695 (2001). Is there a pattern that separates the waivable from the nonwaivable rights? Are the waivable rights the lesser ones? Professor Nancy King notes the increasing willingness of courts to allow waivers. She favors keeping as nonwaivable rights only constitutional claims that have an impact on third parties, since legislatures can decide whether to protect statutory rights from waiver. See Nancy J. King, Priceless Process, 47 UCLA L. Rev. 113 (1999). Should courts allow defendants to waive their right to effective assistance of counsel?

9. *Waiving discovery.* If defendants must know about the nature of the charges and the direct consequences of a guilty plea, must they also know about the basic facts the prosecutor could present against them at trial? In United States v. Ruiz, 536 U.S. 622 (2002), the Court held that the Fifth and Sixth Amendments did not "require federal prosecutors, before entering into a binding plea agreement with a criminal defendant, to disclose 'impeachment information relating to any informants or other witnesses.'" The Supreme Court's decision in *Ruiz* is typical in its refusal to declare a per se rule against bargaining away discovery rights. A few courts, however, have concluded that in some cases, accepting a guilty plea based on a plea agreement that prevents the defendant from engaging in discovery violates due process. See State v. Draper, 784 P.2d 259 (Ariz. 1989) (due process and right to counsel sometimes may prohibit plea agreement conditioned on defendant not interviewing victim of alleged crime; remand to determine defendant's access to state's evidence through other witnesses). Can you identify circumstances in which a defendant could make a knowing waiver of the right to a jury trial without discovery? The *Ruiz* Court found it significant that the condition relating to discovery was nonmandatory — the defendant could choose to go forward with discovery and forgo the plea agreement. Are there any terms that prosecutors simply may not offer because they prevent the defendant from making a knowing waiver?

10. *Are plea bargains contracts?* Some scholars have accepted the essentially contractual nature of plea bargaining — a position that largely supports the right of defendants to bargain for whatever they want. Critics of plea bargaining, such as Professor Stephen Schulhofer, have rejected the notion that plea bargains are fair simply because the defendant agreed to the terms and because the agreement puts the defendant in a better position than if the defendant had gone to trial. Stephen Schulhofer, Plea Bargaining as Disaster, 101 Yale L.J. 1979 (1992). Schulhofer and other critics focus on the public interest in criminal justice that the contract model obscures. Does plea bargaining undermine public confidence in the criminal justice system? See Stanley Cohen & Anthony Doob, Public Attitudes to Plea Bargaining, 32 Crim. L.Q. 85 (1989-1990) (1988 survey found that more than two-thirds of Canadians disapprove of plea bargaining). What other public interests are at stake in plea bargains? In sentences?

2.   *Presentence Reports and the Role of Probation Officers*

Sentencing systems for the most part encourage judges to consider additional information that was not presented at trial. The defense might want to provide additional information about the defendant. The prosecution might want to illuminate aspects of the crime or criminal record. A victim might want to speak about the harm the crime inflicted. As noted in Chapters 4 and 5, the scope of information that might be considered at sentencing can be extremely wide, especially in the federal system, which constructed its guidelines in reliance on the availability of additional facts about the defendant's "real offense" and "relevant conduct" (uncharged acts). 18 U.S.C. §3661, promulgated before the guidelines, remains in effect:

> No limitation shall be placed on the information concerning the background, character, and conduct of a person convicted of an offense which a court of the United States may receive and consider for the purpose of imposing an appropriate sentence.

Where do judges get the additional information that might inform their sentencing judgments? Who gathers the information?

The short answer in most sentencing systems is twofold. First, the parties may present additional evidence, and second, the judge will receive a presentence investigation report, typically prepared by a probation officer who works for the court. In the federal system, the presentence investigation report includes the probation officer's assessment of the applicable guidelines and a sentence recommendation to the judge.

Many issues are generated by these odd procedures, documents, and actors — odd, at least, in comparison with the model of an adversarial system in which advocates present and challenge information and arguments to a neutral judge. The issues surrounding presentence reports include the following:

- What will be included in the report?
- Do the attorneys have access to the report?
- Is there an opportunity to challenge the report?
- What deference or independent assessment does the judge bring to the report?

The first part of this section considers rules on the content and access to presentence investigation reports. The second part considers the role of the probation officer, with a focus on the federal system.

a.   Presentence Investigation Reports

How are the purposes of presentence reports (or of the sentencing system as a whole) served by the procedures used to produce and contest those reports? Consider the following rules.

|| *Federal Rules of Criminal Procedure 32(c)-(h),* ||
Sentencing and Judgment

(c) Presentence Investigation.

   (1) *Required Investigation.*

      (A) *In General.* The probation officer must conduct a presentence investigation and submit a report to the court before it imposes sentence unless: . . .

         (ii) the court finds that the information in the record enables it to meaningfully exercise its sentencing authority under 18 U.S.C. §3553, and the court explains its finding on the record.

      (B) *Restitution.* If the law requires restitution, the probation officer must conduct an investigation and submit a report that contains sufficient information for the court to order restitution.

   (2) *Interviewing the Defendant.* The probation officer who interviews a defendant as part of a presentence investigation must, on request, give the defendant's attorney notice and a reasonable opportunity to attend the interview.

(d) Presentence Report.

   (1) *Applying the Sentencing Guidelines.* The presentence report must:

      (A) identify all applicable guidelines and policy statements of the Sentencing Commission;

      (B) calculate the defendant's offense level and criminal history category;

      (C) state the resulting sentencing range and kinds of sentences available;

      (D) identify any factor relevant to:

         (i) the appropriate kind of sentence, or

         (ii) the appropriate sentence within the applicable sentencing range; and

      (E) identify any basis for departing from the applicable sentencing range.

   (2) *Additional Information.* The presentence report must also contain the following information:

      (A) the defendant's history and characteristics, including:

         (i) any prior criminal record;

         (ii) the defendant's financial condition; and

         (iii) any circumstances affecting the defendant's behavior that may be helpful in imposing sentence or in correctional treatment;

      (B) verified information, stated in a nonargumentative style, that assesses the financial, social, psychological, and medical impact on any individual against whom the offense has been committed;

      (C) when appropriate, the nature and extent of nonprison programs and resources available to the defendant;

      (D) when the law provides for restitution, information sufficient for a restitution order; . . .

      (F) any other information that the court requires.

(3) *Exclusions.* The presentence report must exclude the following:

(A) any diagnoses that, if disclosed, might seriously disrupt a rehabilitation program;

(B) any sources of information obtained upon a promise of confidentiality; and

(C) any other information that, if disclosed, might result in physical or other harm to the defendant or others.

(e) Disclosing the Report and Recommendation.

(1) *Time to Disclose.* Unless the defendant has consented in writing, the probation officer must not submit a presentence report to the court or disclose its contents to anyone until the defendant has pleaded guilty or nolo contendere, or has been found guilty.

(2) *Minimum Required Notice.* The probation officer must give the presentence report to the defendant, the defendant's attorney, and an attorney for the government at least 35 days before sentencing unless the defendant waives this minimum period.

(3) *Sentence Recommendation.* By local rule or by order in a case, the court may direct the probation officer not to disclose to anyone other than the court the officer's recommendation on the sentence.

(f) Objecting to the Report.

(1) *Time to Object.* Within 14 days after receiving the presentence report, the parties must state in writing any objections, including objections to material information, sentencing guideline ranges, and policy statements contained in or omitted from the report.

(2) *Serving Objections.* An objecting party must provide a copy of its objections to the opposing party and to the probation officer.

(3) *Action on Objections.* After receiving objections, the probation officer may meet with the parties to discuss the objections. The probation officer may then investigate further and revise the presentence report as appropriate.

(g) Submitting the Report. At least 7 days before sentencing, the probation officer must submit to the court and to the parties the presentence report and an addendum containing any unresolved objections, the grounds for those objections, and the probation officer's comments on them.

(h) Notice of Possible Departure from Sentencing Guidelines. Before the court may depart from the applicable sentencing range on a ground not identified for departure either in the presentence report or in a party's prehearing submission, the court must give the parties reasonable notice that it is contemplating such a departure. The notice must specify any ground on which the court is contemplating a departure.

U.S. Sentencing Guidelines Manual
§§6A1.1, 6A1.2 (Policy Statements)

§6A1.1 PRESENTENCE REPORT

A probation officer shall conduct a presentence investigation and report to the court before the imposition of sentence unless the court finds that there is information in the record sufficient to enable the meaningful exercise of sentencing authority pursuant to 18 U.S.C. §3553, and the court explains this finding on the record. Rule 32(b)(1), Fed. R. Crim. P. The defendant may not waive preparation of the presentence report.

§6A1.2 DISCLOSURE OF PRESENTENCE REPORT; ISSUES IN DISPUTE

Courts should adopt procedures to provide for the timely disclosure of the presentence report; the narrowing and resolution, where feasible, of issues in dispute in advance of the sentencing hearing; and the identification for the court of issues remaining in dispute. Rule 32(b)(6), Fed. R. Crim. P.

Pennsylvania Rules of Criminal Procedure 702, 703

RULE 702. AIDS IN IMPOSING SENTENCE

(A) Pre-sentence investigation report.

1. The sentencing judge may, in the judge's discretion, order a presentence investigation report in any case.

2. The sentencing judge shall place on the record the reasons for dispensing with the pre-sentence investigation report if the judge fails to order a pre-sentence report in any of the following instances:

(a) where incarceration for one year or more is a possible disposition under the applicable sentencing statutes;

(b) where the defendant is less than twenty-one years old at the time of conviction or entry of a plea of guilty; or

(c) where a defendant is a first offender in that he or she has not heretofore been sentenced as an adult.

3. The pre-sentence investigation report shall include information regarding the circumstances of the offense and the character of the defendant sufficient to assist the judge in determining sentence.

4. The pre-sentence investigation report shall also include a victim impact statement as provided by law. . . .

RULE 703. DISCLOSURE OF PRE-SENTENCE REPORTS

(A) All pre-sentence reports and related psychiatric and psychological reports shall be confidential, and not of public record. They shall be available to the sentencing judge, and to:

1. an examining professional or facility appointed to assist the court in sentencing . . . ;

2. the attorney for the Commonwealth and counsel for the defendant, for inspection and copying, unless the sentencing judge orders that they be available for inspection only.

(B) If the defendant or the Commonwealth alleges any factual inaccuracy in a report under this rule, the sentencing judge shall, as to each inaccuracy found, order that the record be corrected accordingly. . . .

| *Use of Pre-sentence Investigations in Maryland Circuit Courts, January 1999-June 2002, Jill Farrell* **Sentencing Fax (Maryland State Commission on Criminal Sentencing Policy), Mar. 28, 2003** |

In Maryland, pre-sentence investigation reports (PSIs) are prepared by the Division of Parole and Probation in an effort to provide background information on defendant and case characteristics. The information contained within PSIs is designed to assist the courts in the sentencing process. According to the Maryland statute, a PSI may be requested in, but not limited to, cases in which the defendant is (1) convicted of a felony or misdemeanor that resulted in serious physical injury or death to the victim or (2) being referred to Patuxent Institution.[*]

Between January 1999 and June 2002, 26% of all valid cases sentenced in Maryland circuit courts indicated the existence of a PSI report. PSIs were nearly three times more likely to be completed for felony offenses (72%) than for misdemeanors (28%). With respect to offense types (Fig. 1), PSI reports were most likely completed for property offenses (68%), followed closely by person offenses (62%). Drug offenses were the least likely offense type (16%) to have a PSI report submitted.

As indicated in Figure 2, there was substantial variation between circuits. Eighty percent of cases in Circuit 2 had PSI reports submitted, while only 6% of

FIGURE 1
Cases with PSIs by Offense Type

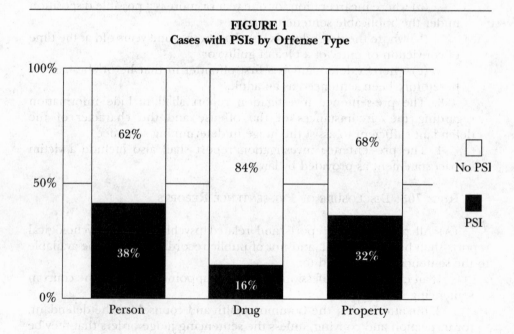

---

[*] The Patuxent Institution is a facility in the Maryland system that focuses on offender remediation and treatment, and includes mental health and substance abuse populations. — Eds.

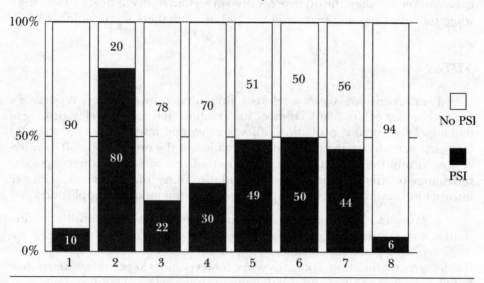

FIGURE 2
Cases with PSIs by Circuit 2

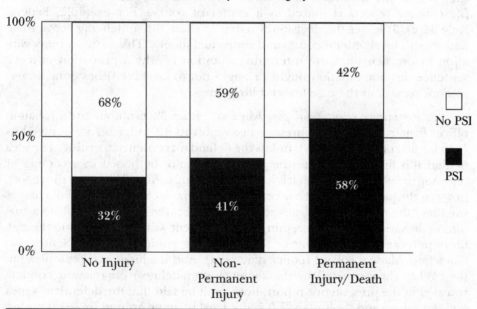

FIGURE 3
Cases with PSIs by Victim Injury Status

cases submitted reports in Circuit 8. This may be due in part to a disproportionate number of drug cases in Circuit 8, thus minimizing the necessity for a PSI
report. On average, 25% of circuit court cases in Maryland included PSI reports
(75% did not).

With regard to victim injury, Figure 3 shows a gradual increase in the presence of PSI reports. In cases where there was a victim, a PSI was more likely to be completed when the offense resulted in serious injury or death (58%) than when the injury was non-permanent (41%) or when there was no injury (32%).

NOTES

1. *Presentence investigation reports.*   Presentence investigation reports are the focal point of the many kinds of information that may be relevant to sentencing. Traditionally, probation officers expended much effort on offender facts that had no bearing on the determination of the offender's guilt or innocence. Now in the federal system probation officers include in their reports a wide range of offense information (beyond the offense of conviction), offender information, and information impacting sentencing guideline application.

2. *Presentence reports and secrecy.*   One of the critical issues involving presentence reports is who gets to see them and when. Confidentiality in presentence reports is generally considered important to allow for a full exploration of the defendant's situation. For many years, however, rules kept not only the public but also defense counsel and the defendant from seeing the report. Questions about the processes for challenging reports and the standards of proof at sentencing fade in importance when such critical information is hidden.

The modern view is that the presentence report should (indeed, must) be shared with the defendant and defense counsel. But not all information in presentence reports is shared as a matter of course. For example, Federal Rule 32(e)(3) leaves the decision whether to share the sentencing recommendation with local federal courts and individual judges. This extraordinary variation in practice (and the interesting question of why a probation officer's sentence recommendation ought or ought not to be shared) has gone largely without remark in the case law and literature.

3. *Presentence reports and plea bargains.*   Rule 32 prohibits the probation officer from submitting the presentence report to the judge before guilty pleas (or a finding of guilt by a jury), unless the defendant consents in writing. The idea behind this limitation is that the judge should not be biased in accepting or rejecting the plea based on what is in the report. But without first seeing the report, how can the judge know when accepting a plea that includes dismissal of charges whether "the remaining charges adequately reflect the seriousness of the actual offense behavior and that accepting the agreement will not undermine the statutory purposes of sentencing or the sentencing guidelines"? U.S. Sentencing Guidelines Manual §6B1.2 (policy statement). And if a judge accepts a plea but then relies (as instructed by the sentencing guidelines) on relevant conduct revealed in the presentence report, how can it be said that the defendant's plea was "knowing" and "voluntary"? It is not hard to argue around these questions: The defendant knows what the presentence report is likely to say, and therefore what the judge might rely on, so the defendant takes the risks of sentence calculations, departures, and possible ranges into account in deciding whether to plea.

But this technical answer leaves the deeper issue unaddressed: Either pleas are made with a full understanding of the consequences, or they are not; either the pleas are accepted with a full picture of the offense and offender, or they are not.

4. *Challenging presentence reports.*   Notice the timing requirements in Rule 32. The probation officer must give the presentence report to the defendant and both attorneys at least 35 days before sentencing unless the defendant waives this minimum period. The defendant then has 14 days to assess and challenge the report in writing. Is 14 days enough time? Should the same strict time frame apply to objections by the government? Compare United States v. Young, 140 F.3d 453 (2d Cir. 1998) (allowing untimely objections to presentence report by the government if defendant is given the opportunity to respond), with United States v. Chung, 261 F.3d 536 (5th Cir. 2001) (upholding refusal to consider supplemental objections by defendant to presentence report filed after 14-day limit). Rule 32 suggests that defendants and their counsel may object to information relevant to sentencing guideline application. As noted above, however, courts are left with the decision whether to share the probation officer's sentencing recommendation with the defendant. Can defendants fully appreciate the calculus of federal sentencing and judgment that underlies guilty pleas when they do not know what recommendation the judge will receive?

b.   The Special Role of Probation Officers

In 1989 federal defender Judy Clarke foresaw the important role that probation officers would play in the federal guideline sentencing era:

> The federal probation officer has emerged as the guardian of the guidelines. The probation officer not only collects the factual data important to the sentencing decisions but also makes recommendations regarding application of the guidelines. The Sentencing Commission has one or more federal probation officers on assignment to provide training for probation officers. There is a Commission staffed hotline for probation officers to call for help with application problems. Federal probation officers send to the Commission copies of presentence reports which reflect the officer's application decisions as well as how the court imposed sentence. In a practical sense, federal probation officers have become guardians, a role which results from the probation officer being closely connected with the Commission's training efforts and becoming well versed in the Commission's view of the guidelines. Whether the prosecutor, defense attorney or sentencing court agree with the guardian's conclusion is insignificant — the guardian reports the result to the Commission and moves on to the next presentence report. All's well that ends.

Judy Clarke, Ruminations on Restrepo, 2 Fed. Sent'g Rep. 131 (1989). The phrase "guardians of the guidelines" and the ideas raised by Clarke caught on. Chief probation officer Charlie Varnon, however, begged to differ:

> I find it very interesting that some members of the defense bar are so hostile to the role of the probation officer in the guideline sentencing process. The probation officer's report to the court has no impact on the defendant whatsoever

unless the judge adopts the recommended findings and guideline calculations. The defense and the prosecution have the opportunity to present their own recommended findings and calculations to the court. Under these circumstances, I might assume the real complaint is that the court too often adopts the recommendations of the probation officers and not those of the lawyers. It is more politic, I assume, to criticize the probation officer for making the recommendation than to criticize the court for adopting the recommendation.

Charlie E. Varnon, Response to Judy Clarke, 2 Fed. Sent'g Rep. 202, 202 (1990).

Probation officers may act below the radar of most scholars and many policymakers, but careful observers and participants agree that they are a central part of the guideline sentencing process. Consider the account of the probation officer's role — central or supportive, heroic or tragic — in the following report, written by a member of the U.S. Sentencing Commission, as well as in the subsequent commentary, written by a former supervising probation officer.

> ## The Independent Role of the Probation Officer
> ## at Sentencing and in Applying
> ## Koon v. United States,
> ### Catharine M. Goodwin
> ### 60 Fed. Probation 71 (Sept. 1996)

The question of the nature of the role of the probation officer in federal guidelines sentencing is a fundamental and recurring one. . . .

There are various ways the independent role of the probation officer at sentencing is challenged or impeded. The probation officer is sometimes impeded from doing a complete investigation by the parties' withholding information, and, for various reasons, plea agreements do not always accurately reflect the facts of the case. Critics of the guideline system have periodically complained about probation officer "advocacy" and called for restricting probation officers to computing the "matrix calculations" or restricting them from making recommendations on "discretionary decisions" such as departures. In addition, a court will sometimes ask the probation office to restrict its investigation to the parties' stipulations, and others may be tempted to do so, in order to avoid objections to the presentence report and disputed issues.

As an initial matter, it must be noted that the probation officer is an officer of the court. Ultimately, the court determines the scope of the probation officer's role in sentencing in any particular district or courtroom. . . .

I. THE ROLE OF THE PROBATION OFFICER IN GUIDELINE SENTENCING

The legal authorities which define the role of the probation officer in federal guideline sentencing consistently define it as an integral, independent function, apart from party stipulations.

A. Rule 32. Rule 32, Federal Rules of Criminal Procedure (F.R.Cr.P.), indicates that the presentence report must contain:

> (B) the classification of the offense and of the defendant under the categories established by the Sentencing Commission under 28 U.S.C. §994(a), as the probation officer believes to be applicable to the defendant's case; the kinds of sentence and the sentencing range suggested for such a category of defendant as set forth in the guidelines issued by the Sentencing Commission under 28 U.S.C. §994(a)(1); and the probation officer's explanation of any factors that may suggest a different sentence — within or without the applicable guideline — that would be more appropriate, given all the circumstances.

Rule 32(b)(4)(B). Thus, the probation officer has a duty directed by the federal rules to compute and describe what the officer believes to be the appropriate sentence under the guidelines, as well as what, if any, departure the officer believes is appropriate. . . .

B. Sentencing Reform Act, Its Legislative History, and the Guidelines. The Sentencing Reform Act provided that the probation officer would conduct an "investigation" of the defendant, pursuant to Rule 32 F.R.Cr.P. and report that investigation to the court. In addition, it is clear that Congress intended sentencing courts to actively exercise their discretion to accept or reject plea agreements to ensure that the resulting sentences meet the purposes of sentencing.

However, Congress recognized that the potential for prosecutorial charging and plea practices to effectively determine the sentence "could well reduce the benefits otherwise to be expected from the bill's guideline sentencing system." It directed the Sentencing Commission to promulgate policy statements for district courts to use in determining whether to accept plea agreements, in order "to provide an opportunity for meaningful judicial review of proposed charge-reduction plea agreements, as well as other forms of plea agreements, while at the same time to guard against improper judicial intrusion upon the responsibilities of the Executive Branch."

Accordingly, the Commission promulgated the Chapter Six Policy Statements to guide courts in accepting plea agreements. Those Policy Statements describe an active, independent role for the probation officer because, "[a] thorough presentence investigation is essential in determining the facts relevant to sentencing." . . . While the guidelines provide for "stipulations," which are points upon which the parties agree or disagree, "[the] court is not bound by the stipulation, but may with the aid of the presentence report, determine the facts relevant to sentencing." Further: Even though stipulations are expected to be accurate and complete, the court cannot rely exclusively upon stipulations in ascertaining the factors relevant to the determination of the sentence. Rather, in determining the factual basis for the sentence, the court will consider the stipulation, together with the results of the presentence investigation, and any other relevant information. . . .

Clearly, the presentence report prepared by the probation officer is the only source of information outside the stipulations of the parties which the court can use to decide whether or not to accept those stipulations in fashioning the sentence. . . . This is also true regarding the court's determination whether to accept a plea agreement. For example, where the plea agreement includes a dismissal of charges or an agreement not to pursue potential charges, the court is asked to evaluate whether the remaining charges "adequately reflect the seriousness of the actual offense behavior," and whether the agreement will support the statutory purposes of sentencing or the sentencing guidelines. Therefore, it is easy to see that Congress intended that "[t]he probation officers will be a crucial link in the effectiveness of both sentencing guidelines and policy statement."

    C. Publication 107.   There are numerous provisions to support the independent role of the probation officer in Publication 107. For example:

> A primary role of the probation officer is to prepare a presentence report of the highest quality for the court that will assist in sentencing a defendant. Under guideline sentencing, the probation officer's role as *the court's independent investigator* is critical, although the scope of the investigation may be determined by the court. . . . [In determining a tentative guideline range, the officer must] *thoroughly explore and analyze the circumstances of the offense and the offender.* (emphasis added)

The officer is to provide the court ". . . with relevant, objective, and verifiable information that will assist in the selection of a proper sentence"; and ". . . it is crucial that a probation officer exercise independence as an agent of the court by developing factual and rule-related assertions."

    To underscore the fact that the monograph envisions the probation officer doing more than providing sentence calculations based on the parties' stipulations, it says that where the parties' stipulations differ from the results of the officer's investigation, the officer should "display the range that would have resulted if there had been no plea agreement" under the "Impact of the Plea Agreement" section of the PSR, to assist "the court in evaluating the impact of the plea agreement on the ultimate sentence." Finally, to further underscore the independent nature of the probation officer's investigation, the monograph also envisions that the probation officer will discuss any potential bases for departure, and possibly make a recommendation on departure in the "Factors That May Warrant Departure" section of the presentence report. . . .

    D. Case Law.   Not surprisingly, the courts have uniformly endorsed and upheld the independent role of the probation officer in federal guideline sentencing. . . .

    E. The Officer's Investigation in the Presentence Report.   The "Impact of the Plea Agreement" section of the presentence report should provide a comparison of the sentencing range which results from the independent investigation, where different, with that which results from the parties' stipulations. . . . The most important thing is that the court is provided with the maximum amount of information upon which to make the sentencing determination.

    F. Practical and Logical Necessity for Independent Investigation.   Realistically, the court has the ultimate authority to determine the "scope" of the probation officer's role at sentencing. And, to the extent that the officer's role is limited, the potential for objections to the presentence report is admittedly minimized. . . .

There are strong practical and logical needs for an independent probation officer at sentencing. The reason the court needs "objective" information, which may go beyond and differ from the stipulation of the parties, is that the court has the discretion, and, indeed, the responsibility, to determine whether to accept the plea agreement, pursuant to Rule 11(c)(1)(A) and (C), and whether to impose a sentence in accord with any non-binding recommendations ("stipulations") of the parties, pursuant to Rule 11(c)(1)(B). [The] sentencing process must provide the court with the information necessary to perform its duty to supervise the plea process and to make a sentence determination.

To the extent that the court relies on stipulations and agreements, practical problems and concerns arise. The court is denied information on sentencing factors which the parties may not have anticipated or agreed upon. Stipulations sometimes omit, either intentionally or inadvertently, key facts necessary to apply the guidelines. Familiarity with the guidelines varies considerably among practitioners and prosecutors, and the parties cannot always identify and adequately address all pertinent sentencing factors or bases for departure at the plea stage. For example, if the parties do not stipulate to adequate facts to determine role, or do not anticipate what ultimately appears to be a meritorious basis for departure, a court that does not receive such information, or limits itself to the stipulations of the parties, loses the ability to employ its sentencing discretion in a fully knowledgeable manner.

Aside from such practical problems, larger, institutional concerns arise if the role of the probation officer in sentencing is limited. . . . Without the "check" on the system that the probation officer provides, we would still have a complicated, resource intensive guideline system, but without the measure of proportionality and uniformity in sentencing which the guidelines were created to achieve. This would primarily be because the court's ability to supervise the plea bargaining process and to sentence based on all the relevant information would be significantly diluted. . . .

G. Procedural Suggestions to Narrow the Gap and to Enhance Fact Finding and Dispute Resolution at Sentencing.   Critics periodically complain that the probation officer's independent investigation results in the probation officer recommending a sentence different than that recommended by the parties, thereby converting the officer into a "third advocate." There are many reasons that the officer may arrive at a different calculation than the parties, including the fact that the officer is not subject to the same negotiation pressures of the parties, and the fact that the officer does not always have the same perspective of the strength of some of the evidence as, for example, the government may have, given that the officer often receives merely a written summary of that evidence.

While some of these differences can be minimized with better communication . . . , wherever differences exist between the sentence calculations of the officer and the parties, the existence of an independent probation investigation does not eliminate nor diminish the opportunity for advocacy by the parties. On the contrary, it highlights and enhances the need for advocacy of the parties, and enriches the information given the court, thereby helping to ensure the best sentence determination possible by the court. Parties still have the opportunity to convince the court of the validity of their positions. The courts have denied any claim that the role of the probation officer improperly influences the court, finding that, in spite of recommendations made by probation officers on sentencing factors, the court is still required to resolve any and all disputes, and that the court has the ability to read a presentence report without being improperly influenced. . . .

1. Some districts have found it beneficial to require, or offer as a possibility, some form of pre-plea advisory conference with a probation officer for a non-binding computation of guidelines relevant to computing at least the offense level, or sometimes even an estimated range (with appropriate waivers that it is non-binding and subject to change upon preparation of a full presentence report). A few districts provide for a Magistrate, or non-sentencing district court judge, to conduct the conference, which becomes in essence a settlement conference. All pre-plea computations or conferences, if they are to be meaningful, depend on full discovery from the government, which is perhaps their primary value, which in turn assists plea negotiations and presentencing disclosure.

2. Some districts require that the government (and defense, optionally) submit within so many days after a plea or trial, an early statement of the facts, disputed issues, and applicable sentencing and guideline factors, in order to focus attention early on sentencing factors and to assist the probation officer.

3. Rule 32(6)(B) F.R.Cr.P. suggests, after the parties submit objections to the presentence report, that the probation officer "may meet with the defendant, the defendant's counsel, and the attorney for the government to discuss those objections." While this is no doubt helpful, some districts find it useful, in addition to this requirement, to require or urge both counsel to meet with the probation officer earlier, during the preparation of the draft presentence report, in order to provide maximum assistance to the officer, to avoid misunderstandings regarding the evidence, and to focus the parties' attention on sentencing factors early in the process.

4. Rule 32 F.R.Cr.P. directs that objections, if any, to the draft presentence report be submitted to the probation officer. It does not specify what form the objection should take. . . .

5. [U.S. Court of Appeals Judge Edward R.] Becker suggests that courts provide an opportunity for a presentence conference with the court (at least in more complicated cases) in order to narrow issues, plan evidence, minimize delay and avoid last-minute submissions.

Obviously, most of these measures require court initiation, but probation officers can implement some on their own, such as requesting early conferences with the parties and asking parties to submit their sentencing positions (and legal authorities for those positions) prior to the issuance of the draft presentence report. Some probation offices may wish to . . . seek the court's endorsement of their requests for meetings and early submissions.

> ### Looking at the Federal Sentencing Process One Judge at a Time, One Probation Officer at a Time, Leslie A. Cory
> 51 Emory L.J. 379 (2002)

Probation officers are employees of the court, hired and fired by the sentencing judges for whom they write presentence reports. While 18 U.S.C. §3603 sets out the duties of the probation officer in regard to the court, 28 U.S.C. §995(a) authorizes the Sentencing Commission to "monitor the performance of probation officers with regard to sentencing recommendations, including application of the Sentencing Commission guidelines and policy statements"; and to "issue instructions to probation officers concerning the application of Commission guidelines and policy statements. . . ." If the instructions of the Sentencing Commission and the judge for whom the probation officer works diverge, the officer will be forced to choose whose instructions take precedence.

[How] do probation officers view their role? One study found that probation officers' perceptions of their role varied from one district to another. Some officers viewed their role as enforcers of the sentencing guidelines. Others viewed themselves as employees of the court, gathering whatever information on sentencing factors, including offender characteristics, the judges will want to evaluate at sentencing. In that study, neither group of officers acknowledged that the particular officer writing the presentence report might have a significant impact on the sentencing outcome. The officers did comment upon an informal policy in each district, set by the judges, of either giving offender characteristics significant consideration in sentencing decisions or of disregarding offender characteristics as a sentencing consideration.

Because the probation officer stands between the sentencing judge and the other parties, the other parties may regard the officer as an obstacle to the achievement of their purposes. From some officers' perspective, the source of the conflict is that, unlike defense attorneys and prosecutors, the probation officer is required to make an "impartial" determination of the guidelines. And unlike the judge, the probation officer is not insulated from ex parte communications. The officer is required to meet with the parties and to develop relationships with them. The positive implication of the probation officer's availability is that the parties have far more of an opportunity to persuade the officer than they do the judge.

The parties involved in the sentencing process often consider the probation officer the sentencing expert. Probation officers ought to be sentencing experts. However, because they have so much discretion in interpreting and applying the guidelines, probation officer error can have a powerful impact upon sentences. A study conducted by the Federal Judicial Center . . . demonstrated the possible impact on sentencing of probation officer error in interpreting the guidelines.[78] In this study, forty-seven probation officers were given the same crime scenario, dealing with three defendants involved in a drug conspiracy. The officers' assignment was to determine the quantity of drugs

---

78. Pamela B. Lawrence & Paul J. Hofer, An Empirical Study of the Application of the Relevant Conduct Guideline 1B1.3, 10 Fed. Sent'g Rep. 16 (1997).

attributable to each defendant. Based upon the same set of facts, the officers came up with widely varying offense levels, depending upon how the officers interpreted the provisions of the Relevant Conduct guideline. Over-reliance on probation officer expertise, by defense attorneys, prosecutors, or judges, can be disastrous for defendants.

How a judge uses a presentence report varies according to the judge's assessment of the Sentencing Commission and its sentencing guidelines, and according to how much control the judge chooses to exercise over the sentencing process. . . .

The use a judge makes of the presentence report will also vary according to the judge's attitude toward plea agreements. A judge who believes sentencing outcomes should be determined by the parties (defendant, defense attorney, and prosecutor) may forego inquiry into whether the plea agreement adequately reflects the statutory purposes of sentencing. . . .

When a probation officer presents to a judge the facts that the officer believes are relevant to sentencing, the officer exercises great informal discretion — it is the officer alone who decides which facts are relevant. Policy may guide, but the officer decides. When a judge disregards facts that are arguably relevant under the guidelines, to achieve a lower offense level, the judge is exercising her discretion. Whether that exercise is legitimate depends upon the judge's motivation. Whether it appears legitimate depends upon the care with which she frames her explanation. Each participant in the sentencing process exercises the discretion accorded to him or her in a unique manner. A passive prosecutor may defer to an aggressive defense attorney. A laissez-faire judge may defer to whatever compromises the prosecution and defense are prepared to accept. An inexperienced probation officer may rely heavily on the input of the prosecutor. . . .

The study suggests the following conclusions . . . :

3. Some probation officers are more inclined to recommend sentences that cover the entire spectrum of the guideline range. Others are more inclined to recommend sentences toward the bottom. Judges frequently rely on these recommendations, with the result that where within the guideline range a defendant's sentence is imposed will depend in part upon who the probation officer is. . . .

5. Although judges depart [less often than probation officers recommend], judges do rely on the information supplied by probation officers for making the departure decision. Some probation officers are more inclined than others to suggest possible grounds for departure.

6. Defendants who object to the presentence report experience no adverse consequences, and have a relatively good record of success. . . .

NOTES

1. *Probation officers as officers of the court.*   As these readings indicate, the role of the probation officer in the federal system, while long important to the administration of justice, has taken on a more central and contested role under the sentencing guidelines. The probation officer, when drafting the presentence investigation report for the judge, does not simply serve as a conduit for the competing claims of the parties. The officer makes preliminary factual findings and recommendations to the judge.

Criminal procedures are adversarial in the pretrial and trial phases with the two sides guarding the interests of the client or the government by introducing information for the court's consideration and debating whether it is admissible. At sentencing, on the other hand, the primary source of information is the presentence investigation report, a document submitted from the vantage of a third party. The notion is that the investigation should be conducted by one who has not been a party to the case prior to conviction, is theoretically neutral, and is strictly responsible to the court. In this role, the probation officer acts as an "arm" of the court. . . .

In the past, an officer could collect facts from several sources and present various renditions of the facts of the offense (the prosecution version, the defendant's version, and the victim's version). Under the guidelines, however, the officer is required to sort out and analyze the facts with the goal of determining, on the best available information, what happened during the course of the offense. This investigation is necessary in order to apply the facts to the guideline provisions. Because a specific fact, such as the presence of a gun, or the dimension of a fact, such as the amount of drugs, may translate to a difference in exposure to a prison term, effective advocates will challenge the officer's guideline application in order to protect the interest of the defendant or government. This process may bring the officer into conflict with the attorneys. Although the officer does not have an adversarial role in the sentencing process, he may find himself in the gunsight of one attorney or be caught in the crossfire of both. . . .

Magdeline E. Jensen, Has the Role of the U.S. Probation Officer Really Changed?, 4 Fed. Sent'g Rep. 94 (1991).

2. *Probation officers as advocates.* Once the probation officer makes preliminary judgments about various guideline calculations, the parties inevitably agree, and the officer is drawn into an advocacy role, defending the conclusions of the report in court. As one supervising probation officer put it:

[As] a group we generally abhor being placed in an adversarial position. Probation officers traditionally were attracted to the job to have personal contact with the clients — to get into their lives. We are, by profession, nosey. We get into the client's home, figure out what went wrong and then are paid to fix it. The way it is fixed can vary from pure social work to investigation and surveillance. But it all amounts to the same thing — access to other people's lives. Our mindset, therefore, differs substantially from that of lawyers, who are always ready for a good fight, and from judges, who have left the good fight and now do referee work.

With the adoption of the guidelines, we found ourselves thrown into the fight with the professional heavyweights. At first we objected, but as we found ourselves sparring, the great American competitive spirit prevailed and it turned out to be not only interesting, but challenging — even fun. To the government, we have become a thorny contender; to the defense, we are accused of being more cutthroat than the government. For our part, it is all done in the name of being true to the guidelines. And we have been scrupulous.

Francesca D. Bowman, The Greening of Probation Officers in Their New Role, 4 Fed. Sent'g Rep. 99 (1991).

3. *Probation officers as deal busters.* The role of the probation officer is especially precarious when he or she disagrees with the stipulations of both parties about the proper resolution of various guideline findings and calculations.

In applying the guidelines, particularly to cases in which the parties have agreed to certain facts or guideline applications which are at odds with the officer's perception of the matter at hand, does the officer strictly adhere to his guideline manual and cause a further independent and time-consuming investigation, provoke argument, create the need to prepare a presentence addendum in defense of his position, and ultimately find that no one will argue his view at the time of the sentencing hearing? Or, will the officer pursue the path of least resistance and prepare the computations based upon the parties' agreement? While one might hope that this never occurs, a perfunctory understanding of human behavior suggests otherwise.

At the time of the sentencing hearing, the court is frequently faced with an agreement between the parties which produces a much different guideline computation than the one presented by the probation officer. This situation poses the potential for lengthy fact-finding hearings. Not infrequently, the prosecutor may take the position that the government cannot prove those facts contained in the probation officer's report by a preponderance of evidence standard. How is an already overburdened court—inundated by increasing numbers of drug related crimes—to respond?

Frank S. Gilbert, A Probation Officer's Perception of the Allocation of Discretion, 4 Fed. Sent'g Rep. 109 (1991).

3.   Sentencing Hearings

After prosecutors and defense counsel strike a plea bargain (or after the jury returns a guilty verdict in those rare cases that go to trial), and after a probation officer has completed a presentencing investigation report, the sentencing drama moves to its most public setting, the courtroom, for a sentencing hearing. Do sentencing hearings resemble trials? What is the standard for admission of evidence? What rules and procedures are used to test evidence? Should the sentencing hearing be a minitrial?

|| *Federal Rule of Criminal Procedure 32(i),* ||
|| *Sentencing and Judgment* ||

(i) Sentencing.

(1) *In General.* At sentencing, the court:

(A) must verify that the defendant and the defendant's attorney have read and discussed the presentence report and any addendum to the report;

(B) must give to the defendant and an attorney for the government a written summary of—or summarize in camera—any information excluded from the presentence report . . . on which the court will rely in sentencing, and give them a reasonable opportunity to comment on that information;

(C) must allow the parties' attorneys to comment on the probation officer's determinations and other matters relating to an appropriate sentence; and

(D) may, for good cause, allow a party to make a new objection at any time before sentence is imposed.

(2) *Introducing Evidence; Producing a Statement.* The court may permit the parties to introduce evidence on the objections. . . .

(3) *Court Determinations.* At sentencing, the court:

(A) may accept any undisputed portion of the presentence report as a finding of fact;

(B) must—for any disputed portion of the presentence report or other controverted matter—rule on the dispute or determine that a ruling is unnecessary either because the matter will not affect sentencing, or because the court will not consider the matter in sentencing; . . .

(4) *Opportunity to Speak.*

(A) *By a Party.* Before imposing sentence, the court must:

(i) provide the defendant's attorney an opportunity to speak on the defendant's behalf;

(ii) address the defendant personally in order to permit the defendant to speak or present any information to mitigate the sentence; and

(iii) provide an attorney for the government an opportunity to speak equivalent to that of the defendant's attorney.

(B) *By a Victim.* Before imposing sentence, the court must address any victim of a crime of violence or sexual abuse who is present at sentencing and must permit the victim to speak or submit any information about the sentence. Whether or not the victim is present, a victim's right to address the court may be exercised by the following persons if present:

(i) a parent or legal guardian, if the victim is younger than 18 years or is incompetent; or

(ii) one or more family members or relatives the court designates, if the victim is deceased or incapacitated.

(C) *In Camera Proceedings.* Upon a party's motion and for good cause, the court may hear in camera any statement made under Rule 32(i)(4).

U.S. Sentencing Guidelines Manual
§6A1.3 (Policy Statement)

§6A1.3   RESOLUTION OF DISPUTED FACTORS

(a) When any factor important to the sentencing determination is reasonably in dispute, the parties shall be given an adequate opportunity to present information to the court regarding that factor. In resolving any dispute concerning a factor important to the sentencing determination, the court may consider relevant information without regard to its admissibility under the rules of evidence applicable at trial, provided that the information has sufficient indicia of reliability to support its probable accuracy.

(b) The court shall resolve disputed sentencing factors at a sentencing hearing in accordance with Rule 32(c)(1), Fed. R. Crim. P.

COMMENTARY

In pre-guidelines practice, factors relevant to sentencing were often determined in an informal fashion. The informality was to some extent explained by the fact that particular offense and offender characteristics rarely had a highly specific or required sentencing consequence. This situation no longer exists under sentencing guidelines. The court's resolution of disputed sentencing factors usually has a measurable effect on the applicable punishment. More formality is therefore unavoidable if the sentencing process is to be accurate and fair.

Although lengthy sentencing hearings seldom should be necessary, disputes about sentencing factors must be resolved with care. When a dispute exists about any factor important to the sentencing determination, the court must ensure that the parties have an adequate opportunity to present relevant information. Written statements of counsel or affidavits of witnesses may be adequate under many circumstances. An evidentiary hearing may sometimes be the only reliable way to resolve disputed issues. The sentencing court must determine the appropriate procedure in light of the nature of the dispute, its relevance to the sentencing determination, and applicable case law.

In determining the relevant facts, sentencing judges are not restricted to information that would be admissible at trial. See 18 U.S.C. §3661; see also United States v. Watts, 117 S. Ct. 633, 635 (1997) (holding that lower evidentiary standard at sentencing permits sentencing court's consideration of acquitted conduct); Witte v. United States, 515 U.S. 389 (1995) (noting that sentencing courts have traditionally considered wide range of information without the procedural protections of a criminal trial, including information concerning criminal conduct that may be the subject of a subsequent prosecution); Nichols v. United States, 511 U.S. 738 (1994) (noting that district courts have traditionally considered defendant's prior criminal conduct even when the conduct did not result in a conviction). Any information may be considered, so long as it has sufficient indicia of reliability to support its probable accuracy. Out-of-court declarations by an unidentified informant may be considered where there is good cause for the non-disclosure of the informant's identity and there is sufficient corroboration by other means.

The Commission believes that use of a preponderance of the evidence standard is appropriate to meet due process requirements and policy concerns in resolving disputes regarding application of the guidelines to the facts of a case.

NOTES

1. *Sentencing hearings.*   How much do the federal sentencing guidelines have to say about the procedures that should govern sentencing hearings? What are the key procedural questions that should be determined by statute or rule? For example, do the federal rules determine what proof and procedure will be allowed at sentencing hearings? Questions raised by the constitutional debate over *Apprendi* arise again in the context of sentencing hearings. What does it mean for a judge to accept testimony with "sufficient indicia of reliability"? How does that standard relate to the more familiar standards and evidentiary rules at trial? See Susan N. Herman, The Tail that Wagged the Dog: Bifurcated Fact-Finding and the Limits of Due Process Under the Federal Sentencing Guidelines, 66 S. Cal. L. Rev. 289 (1992); Deborah Young, Fact-Finding at Federal Sentencing: Why the Guidelines Should Meet the Rules, 79 Cornell L. Rev. 299 (1994); David Adair, House Built on Weak Foundation — Sentencing Guidelines and the Preponderance Standard of Proof, 10 Fed. Sent'g Rep. 41 (1997).

2. *Exclusionary rule at the sentencing hearing.* Most jurisdictions allow sentencing judges to consider evidence obtained in violation of a defendant's constitutional rights, even when that evidence is suppressed at trial. See Elson v. State, 659 P.2d 1195 (Alaska 1983) (allowing evidence obtained illegally at sentencing unless violation was for purpose of obtaining facts to enhance sentencing); Smith v. State, 517 A.2d 1081 (Md. 1986). The federal courts are split on whether the exclusionary rule applies in sentencing proceedings. The U.S. Supreme Court held in Estelle v. Smith, 451 U.S. 454 (1981), that a sentencing judge in a capital case could not consider a statement obtained in violation of the Fifth Amendment, but the Court has never addressed whether the exclusionary rule applies in noncapital sentencing proceedings. Some state statutes and cases allow the introduction of illegally obtained evidence in capital cases, at least within the boundaries of Estelle v. Smith. See, e.g., Utah Code §76-3-207(2) ("Any evidence the court deems to have probative force may be received regardless of its admissibility under the exclusionary rules of evidence."); Stewart v. State, 549 So. 2d 171 (Fla. 1989). Most lower federal courts have decided that the exclusionary rule does not apply at sentencing in noncapital proceedings. See, e.g., United States v. Torres, 926 F.2d 321 (D.C. Cir. 1991). A smaller group apply the exclusionary rule at sentencing. See Pens v. Bail, 902 F.2d 1464 (9th Cir. 1991).

3. *The right of allocution.* Federal Rule of Criminal Procedure 32 gives the defendant the right to speak at sentencing, which is often known as a right of allocution. As *Black's Law Dictionary* explains, an allocution is "an unsworn statement from a convicted defendant to the sentencing judge or jury in which the defendant can ask for mercy, explain his or her conduct, apologize for the crime, or say anything else in an effort to lessen the impending sentence. This statement is not subject to cross-examination." *Black's Law Dictionary* 75 (7th ed. 1999).

Perhaps in part because most states, like the federal system, expressly grant defendants the right to speak at sentencing, the Supreme Court has never squarely addressed whether the constitution protects the right of allocution. The Court has, however, spoken grandly of the history and importance of this right:

> [Rule 32's] legal provenance was the common-law right of allocution. As early as 1689, it was recognized that the court's failure to ask the defendant if he had anything to say before sentence was imposed required reversal. . . . Taken in the context of its history, there can be little doubt that the drafters of Rule 32 intended that the defendant be personally afforded the opportunity to speak before imposition of sentence. We are not unmindful of the relevant major changes that have evolved in criminal procedure since the seventeenth century — the sharp decrease in the number of crimes which were punishable by death, the right of the defendant to testify on his own behalf, and the right to counsel. But we see no reason why a procedural rule should be limited to the circumstances under which it arose if reasons for the right it protects remain. None of these modern innovations lessens the need for the defendant, personally, to have the opportunity to present to the court his plea in mitigation. The most persuasive counsel may not be able to speak for a defendant as the defendant might, with halting eloquence, speak for himself.

Green v. United States, 365 U.S. 301, 303 (1961). And yet, in Hill v. United States, 368 U.S. 424 (1962), the Court held that a trial judge's failure to expressly ask a defendant represented by counsel whether he wished to make a statement at sentencing was not an error of constitutional dimension and therefore provided no basis for a collateral attack.

Lower state and federal courts split over whether a right of allocution is constitutionally protected, although most of these cases turn on whether defendants were fully afforded their statutory right to speak at sentencing and what the appropriate remedy should be for statutory violations. See, e.g., Michigan v. Petit, 648 N.W.2d 193 (Mich. 2002); In re Personal Restraint of Echeverria, 6 P.3d 573 (Wash. 2000).

The practical importance of the right of allocution may be as debatable as its legal standing. Especially in sentencing systems with structured sentencing rules, it is far more likely for a defendant's statement to have symbolic value than to present information directly relevant to a judge's or jury's sentencing determination. Even if allocution is likely to be only symbolic most of the time, is there anything wrong with symbolic rights? Allocution can have tangible costs for a defendant: an admission made during an allocution might be used against the defendant at retrial or re-sentencing. If concerns about the possible future use of an allocution statement might chill the practice, should jurisdictions adopt rules limiting the later use of allocution statements against defendants?

4. *Victims' right to speak at sentencing.* Is the right of victims or their representatives to speak also merely symbolic? The inclusion of victim statements is now widespread throughout the United States in response to the victims' rights movement that emerged in the 1980s. The Victim and Witness Protection Act of 1982 amended the Federal Rules of Criminal Procedure to require the inclusion of a victim impact statement as part of the presentence report in federal court. Proposed federal legislation and constitutional amendments would increase victim participation at sentencing.

Over the past 20 years, nearly every state has decided to allow victim involvement at sentencing. See generally National Victim Center, The 1996 Victims' Rights Sourcebook: A Compilation and Comparison of Victims' Rights Laws (1996). It is difficult to capture the depth, range, and impact of this dramatic change in sentencing practice. Almost all states allow victim input through the presentence report. Many allow victims a separate opportunity to make a written or oral statement regarding sentencing, often specifying the kinds of information victims may offer. A few states have retained sharper limits: several allow judges to choose whether to admit or refuse victim impact information; Texas allows victim to make a statement only after sentencing, Tex. Code Crim. Proc. art. 42.03.

The rich variety of statutes has not produced a substantial case law regarding victim impact statements in the noncapital context. Challenges to such statements often assert that the judge was biased or unduly influenced by the information. Should judges rely on their own sense of the unique nature of harm imposed in particular cases? Does victim impact information differ in kind from other types of new information, such as information about the offender?

=7=

Sentencing Outcomes: The Scale of Imprisonment

We have reviewed the typical "inputs" that influence the choice of sentences in a particular case and the procedural setting for the sentencing decision. Now we turn to the typical outcomes of the sentencing decision, beginning with imprisonment.

We start with prison, although it is not the most common sentencing outcome. Very few misdemeanors result in a prison term, and many of the least serious felonies (which account for the greatest number of felonies) also result in a nonprison punishment. Yet prison is the sentence that occupies a large place in public debates and the largest place in public budgets. In the United States, it is the expected sentence for the most serious felonies. Gustave du Beaumont and Alexis de Tocqueville, who toured prisons in the United States on behalf of the French government in 1831, noted the emphasis that Americans placed on the prison early in its history: "they have caught the monomania of the penitentiary system, which to them seems the remedy for all the evils of society." Gustave de Beaumont & Alexis de Tocqueville, On the Penitentiary System in the United States and Its Application in France 80 (Francis Lieber trans., 1833).

In this chapter we consider why criminal justice in the United States relies as much as it does on the prison sanction. What do governments hope to accomplish when they use prison rather than other punishments for crimes? Which of the limits on the use of prison are legal, and which are political or cultural?

A. INCARCERATION TRENDS

Prison began as a distinctly American contribution to criminal justice, and today the United States is unmatched in its use of prison as a criminal punishment. But our reliance on prison has changed in interesting ways over time. In the following passage, Norval Morris briefly summarizes the history of prison as a sanction for crimes, emphasizing its American origins. He then evokes a moment that is now difficult to reconstruct: a time in the 1960s and 1970s when a serious debate occurred in the United States about whether to abolish or seriously limit the use of prison.

That moment has passed. Since the early 1980s, governments in the United States have embraced prison as never before. The tables following the Morris excerpt track the increasing rate of imprisonment in the United States since 1970; of particular significance are the differences among various regions and states.

The Future of Imprisonment, Norval Morris
Pages 3-9 (1974)

[Until] quite recently the serious offender, other than the political criminal, was not imprisoned as a penal sanction. He may have been penned for other purposes but not imprisoned as a punishment. Felons were dealt with by exile, banishment, transportation, and a diversity of demeaning and painful corporal punishments—the "cat," the ear and nose cropper, the branding iron, and that reliable standby, capital punishment. Prisons for felons arose as a reaction to the excesses and barbarisms of earlier punishments; imprisonment was one of the early "diversions" from traditional criminal sanctions.

The jail, the workhouse, the almshouse, the reformatory, and the convict ship all antedate the prison. The castle keep for the political personage out of favor or office and the church's cell for retreat and penance were part of the genesis of the prison, but they were established for different social classes and different political purposes. What is sometimes forgotten . . . is that the prison is an American invention, an invention of the Pennsylvania Quakers of the last decade of the eighteenth century, though one might also note the confining "People Pen" put up by the Massachusetts Pilgrims nearly two centuries earlier. In their "penitentiary" the Quakers planned to substitute the correctional specifics of isolation, repentance, and the uplifting effects of scriptural injunctions and solitary Bible reading for the brutality and inutility of capital and corporal punishments. These three treatments—removal from corrupting peers, time for reflection and self-examination, the guidance of biblical precepts—would no doubt have been helpful to the reflective Quakers who devised the prison, but relatively few of them ever became prisoners. The suitability of these remedies for the great mass of those who subsequently found their way to the penitentiary is more questionable. . . .

At all events, in 1790 a cell block was opened in the Walnut Street Jail of Philadelphia as the "penitentiary" for the Commonwealth of Pennsylvania. In 1796, Newgate began service as the penitentiary for the State of New York, modeled on the Walnut Street Jail but taking its name from an earlier English institution serving a different clientele (civil and criminal debtors and those awaiting trial or punishment).

Prisons grew and flourished throughout America and later throughout the world; they are a pervasive American export, like tobacco in their international acceptance and perhaps also in their adverse consequences. The Pennsylvania Quakers must be praised or blamed for the invention or reinvention of the prison. Their vision and initiative gave us our hulking penal institutions, our "edifice complex." It was a gift born of benevolence not malevolence, of philanthropy not punitiveness, so that the most important contemporary lesson of this historical sketch may well be a deeper appreciation of the truth that benevolent intentions do not necessarily produce beneficent results.

ABOLITION OR ABATEMENT OF IMPRISONMENT

Contemporary Quakers in the American Friends Service Committee's book, *Struggle for Justice,* recognize that "the horror that is the American prison system grew out of an eighteenth century reform" proposed by their ideological forebears. Their criticism is of a cruelty characteristic of intrafamilial disputes, but they are by no means alone in their castigation of imprisonment. . . . Both national crime commissions of the past decade recommended the swift abatement of imprisonment, and the 1973 commission urged a moratorium on the construction of all new institutions for adult or juvenile offenders, a position also adopted by the National Council on Crime and Delinquency. Judge James E. Doyle, a federal district judge of the Western District of Wisconsin, was formidably direct in the matter. In Morales v. Schmidt, 340 F. Supp. 544, 548-549 (W.D. Wis. 1972), a prison mail censorship case, he said: "I am persuaded that the institution of prison probably must end. In many respects it is as intolerable within the United States as was the institution of slavery, equally brutalizing to all involved, equally toxic to the social system, equally subversive of the brotherhood of man, even more costly by some standard, and probably less rational."

The 1973 national commission, the National Advisory Commission on Criminal Justice Standards and Goals, recommended that "the institution should be the last resort for correctional problems," gave their reasons — failure to reduce crime, success in punishing but not in deterring, providing only temporary protection to the community, changing the offender but mostly for the worse — and concluded that "the prison . . . has persisted, partly because a civilized nation could neither turn back to the barbarism of an earlier time nor find a satisfactory alternative." . . .

Imprisonment has been too much used, it has discriminated against races and classes, sentences imposed have been too long, and too many of them have been served in degrading and brutalizing circumstances. There is widespread advocacy of the swift abatement if not an abolition of imprisonment. How is this to be achieved?

THE PATHS TO ABATEMENT OF IMPRISONMENT

[Several] paths are believed to lead to the abatement of imprisonment. First, the "overreach" of the criminal law is to be reduced. . . . Regulatory systems, backed by the criminal sanctions if regulations are flouted, should be substituted for the mass of prohibitory propositions at present brought to bear on a wide swath of behavior. Though much of what now busies the criminal justice system may be immoral or troublesome or distasteful or unseemly or injurious to the actor and those who love him or depend on him, it does not represent a serious threat to the physical safety of others nor a major depredation to property nor a serious challenge to governmental authority. . . .

Just as there has been an overemphasis on the use of the prohibitory sanctions of the criminal law, so there has been an overemphasis on custody.

It is widely recognized that we have locked up too many social nuisances who are not social threats, too many petty offenders and minor thieves, severing such few social ties as they have and pushing them further toward more serious criminal behavior. This excessive use of incarceration, the prison and the jail, the reformatory and the detention center, has been expensive, criminogenic, and unkind. Hence, increasingly we try to "divert" different categories of offenders from the criminal justice system and from penal institutions.

Diversions from the criminal justice system and from prisons grow apace at the police, prosecutorial, and judicial levels. Police diversions to mental health, social welfare, and addiction treatment units reduce the flow to prison as do judicial and prosecutorial diversions to probationary and similar supervisory and supportive services. There is also support for increased reliance on the fine and on restitution and compensation payments to the victims of crime as an alternative to imprisonment. . . .

Despite these movements, the prison population remains stable at about the 200,000 mark (I do not count the jails), though an increased proportion of convicted offenders are on probation, in "halfway" houses and probation hostels, and in other community-based treatments. . . .

Rate (per 100,000 residents) of Sentenced Prisoners under Jurisdiction of State and Federal Correction Authorities

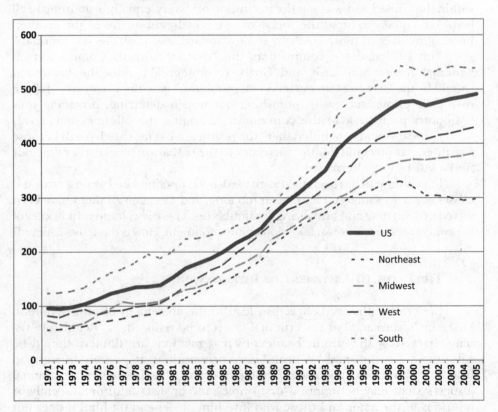

Source: Sourcebook of Criminal Justice Statistics, U.S. Dept. of Justice, Bureau of Justice Statistics.

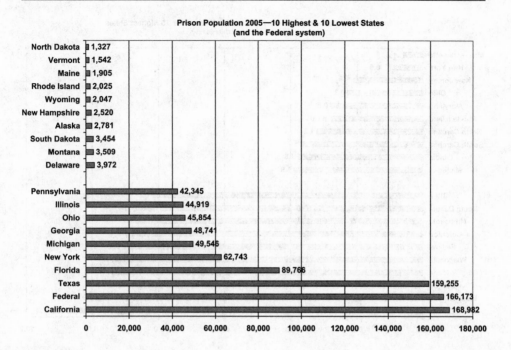

Prison Population 2005—10 Highest & 10 Lowest States (and the Federal system)

North Dakota	1,327
Vermont	1,542
Maine	1,905
Rhode Island	2,025
Wyoming	2,047
New Hampshire	2,520
Alaska	2,781
South Dakota	3,454
Montana	3,509
Delaware	3,972
Pennsylvania	42,345
Illinois	44,919
Ohio	45,854
Georgia	48,741
Michigan	49,546
New York	62,743
Florida	89,766
Texas	159,255
Federal	166,173
California	168,982

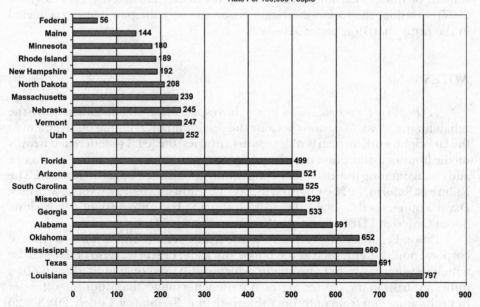

Incarceration Rates (2005)—10 Highest & 10 Lowest States (and the Federal system)
Rate Per 100,000 People

Federal	56
Maine	144
Minnesota	180
Rhode Island	189
New Hampshire	192
North Dakota	208
Massachusetts	239
Nebraska	245
Vermont	247
Utah	252
Florida	499
Arizona	521
South Carolina	525
Missouri	529
Georgia	533
Alabama	591
Oklahoma	652
Mississippi	660
Texas	691
Louisiana	797

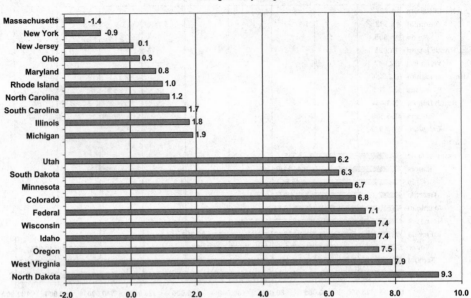

Prison Population Growth Since 1995—10 Lowest & 10 Highest States
Average % Yearly Change

As Norval Morris noted, for much of the 20th century the total U.S. prison population was stable. So too were the prison populations of the federal system, and of some of the biggest states, such as California. Starting in the mid 1970s that stability unraveled, and the U.S. prison population has now reached well over 2 million. See William J. Sabol, Todd D. Minton & Paige M. Harrison, Bureau of Justice Statistics, Prison and Jail Inmates, 2006, NCJ 217675 (June 2007). Consider the variation in state prison use over the past decade, reflected in the prior charts on pages 520–522.

NOTES

1. *Origins of the prison.* The prison has especially strong historical ties to the rehabilitative ideal. As prisons became the predominant criminal punishment in the late eighteenth and early nineteenth centuries, the legal system relied heavily on the hope or assumption that the penitentiary would create genuine penitence and change among the offenders living within its walls. See Edgardo Rotman, The Failure of Reform, in The Oxford History of the Prison 169-197 (Norval Morris & David Rothman eds., 1995); David J. Rothman, The Discovery of the Asylum: Social Order and Disorder in the New Republic (1971).

Prison began as an alternative to the death penalty and to various types of corporal punishment, such as the public stockade. Prison was also believed to be a humane alternative to banishment, which is still used on a limited (and often informal) basis in the United States. A sentencing judge "banishes" an offender by prohibiting him from entering the jurisdiction. See State v. Collett, 208 S.E.2d 472 (Ga. 1974) (banishment of the defendant from seven counties in Georgia, imposed as condition for suspension of 12-month sentence for drug offense, was not unconstitutional or violative of public policy); but see McCreary v. State, 582 So. 2d 425 (Miss. 1991) (banishment from state does not serve a rehabilitative function and dumps offenders on other states). In Germany, prison replaced exile as a sanction for serious crimes during the eighteenth century.

2. *Prison trends before 1970.*   Although our knowledge of crime rates before 1970 is a bit sketchy, we do have fairly complete information about the imprisonment rate in the twentieth century. The rate stayed within a reasonably stable range between 1925 and 1975, and increased above those earlier levels during the last quarter of the century. Criminologist Alfred Blumstein, writing in 1979, proposed a "stability of punishment" thesis, suggesting that states tend to reduce their arrests, convictions, and prison terms whenever the prison population goes too high and to increase the coverage of the criminal law when prison populations become too low. He found that about 20 states were trendless over the 50-year period of his study, while the states with long-term changes in rates of imprisonment showed relatively minor changes, and most showed a small decrease in the rate of imprisonment over time. Alfred Blumstein & Soumyo Moitra, An Analysis of Time Series of the Imprisonment Rate in the States of the United States: A Further Test of the Stability of Punishment Hypothesis, 70 J. Crim. L. & Criminology 376-390 (1979). As the data above reveal, prison populations have been anything but stable since 1980.

3. *Types of prisons.*   Prisons are not interchangeable. States run prisons with different levels of security, meaning different types of restrictions on liberty and different levels of staffing. For instance, the Bureau of Prisons in the federal system gives the following description of security levels:

> The Bureau operates institutions at four security levels (minimum, low, medium, and high) to meet the various security needs of its diverse inmate population and has one maximum-security prison for the less than 1 percent of the inmates who require that level of security. It also has administrative facilities, such as pretrial detention centers and medical referral centers, that have specialized missions and confine offenders of all security levels. The characteristics that help to define the security level of an institution are perimeter security measures (such as fences, patrol officers, and towers), the level of staffing, the internal controls for inmate movement and accountability, and the type of inmate living quarters (such as cells or open dormitories). The Bureau's graduated security scheme allows staff to assign an inmate to an institution in accordance with the inmate's individual security needs. Inmates who are able to function with relatively little supervision, without disrupting institution operations or threatening the safety of staff, other inmates, or the public, can be housed in lower security level institutions.

U.S. Department of Justice, About the Federal Bureau of Prisons (July 2001). The maximum-security prisons cost the most both to build and to operate. Keep in mind that prisons are not the only secure facilities that governments operate: other institutions serving similar functions include secure mental health facilities and immigration detention facilities.

Recent prison classifications include the "supermax" prison, in which the emphasis lies on incapacitation rather than rehabilitation. Supermax prisons have provoked international objections on human rights grounds, including critical reports from the United Nations Committee against Torture. See http://193.194.138.190/html/menu2/6/cat.htm.

4. *Prison capacity and overcrowding.*   Prisons in the United States are routinely said to operate above capacity, but the concept of capacity has several layers. Rated capacity is the maximum number of beds assigned to a particular facility by corrections accrediting bodies. Operational capacity is set by state officials based on the facility's staff and programs. Design capacity represents the number of inmates that the designers of the facility intended for it to hold. Overcrowding is a perennial complaint recorded by those who survey criminal justice systems in the United States, dating back to when prison populations were much lower. See National Commission on Law Observance and Enforcement (Wickersham Commission), Report on Penal Institutions, Probation and Parole 211, 231-238 (1931); President's Commission on Criminal Justice and the Administration of Justice, The Challenge of Crime in a Free Society 45 (1967).

Federal courts have occasionally ruled in favor of prison inmates who allege that overcrowded prisons violate the Eighth Amendment's prohibition of cruel and unusual punishments. See Malcolm M. Feeley & Edward L. Rubin, Judicial Policy Making and the Modern State: How the Courts Reformed America's Prisons (1998). Thus, constitutional law doctrine also has some influence on the definition of a prison's capacity.

5. *Demographic impact of incarceration rates.*   Many prisoners in the United States have committed nonviolent crimes, such as low-level drug trafficking. Over the long haul, their sentences affect the demographic makeup of the prison population. For instance, the prison population now includes more black inmates than it once did, because blacks are arrested and convicted more often for the drug crimes that receive the longest prison terms. Blacks account for about three-fourths of all those sentenced to prison for drug offenses, although about 13% of drug users in the United States are black. The prison population today also includes a larger number of older inmates — who require more expensive prison operations, such as health care — because prison terms have been getting longer in the United States for several decades. While the male prison population substantially surpasses the number of female inmates, the latter grew dramatically faster during the 1990s. We explore further the distribution of sentencing outcomes across race, class, and gender in Chapter 9.

B.   IS THE U.S. STORY UNIQUE?

Some scholars have made the claim that United States rates of imprisonment are "exceptional" and the factors that have driven the massive use of imprisonment are unique to United States culture and politics. A competing view has been expressed most prominently by legal sociologist David Garland in his 2001 book *The Culture of Control.* Garland identifies the following 12 factors as central and common "currents of change" across the United States and Britain: (1) the decline of the rehabilitative ideal; (2) the reemergence of punitive sanctions and expressive justice; (3) changes in the emotional tone of crime policy; (4) the return of the victim; (5) public protection as a predominant purpose of punishment; (6) politicization and a "new populism" in punishment policy (e.g., "three strikes and you're out," "truth in sentencing," "zero tolerance"); (7) the reinvention of prison; (8) the transformation of criminological thought from multifaceted theories of behavior and reform to "control theories"; (9) the expanding infrastructure of crime prevention and community safety; (10) civil society and the commercialization of crime control; (11) new management styles and working practices of major criminal justice organizations; and (12) a perpetual sense of crisis. See David Garland, The Culture of Control: Crime and Social Order in Contemporary Society (2001).

Consider the following descriptions of Canadian imprisonment rates and imprisonment rates around the world. Does the Canadian experience reinforce or undermine the claim of American exceptionalism? Does it provide lessons for other countries? If so, what are those lessons?

> ## Countering Punitiveness: Understanding Stability in Canada's Imprisonment Rate,
> ### Anthony N. Doob and Cheryl Marie Webster
> 40 Law & Soc'y Rev. 325-335, 337-349, 351,
> 354-356 (2006)

Canada's imprisonment rate has not changed appreciably since 1960. . . . Canada's anomalous imprisonment trend provides a contrast to patterns in nations generally considered to be similar in nature to Canada. The most obvious examples are England and Wales — to which Canada is historically and institutionally tied — and the United States — to which Canada is geographically, culturally, and economically linked. Despite these close affinities, Canadian criminal justice policies as they relate to imprisonment have diverged from those of these two comparators.[3]

INCREASING PUNITIVENESS: CANADA AMONG OTHER NATIONS

The explanations that have been offered for growth in imprisonment share the common starting point of a shift toward more punitive criminal justice responses to crime. Such policies as three-strikes sentencing, mandatory minimum penalties, habitual offender laws, and truth-in-sentencing are typically cited as evidence of increasing punitiveness, which is reflected in rising imprisonment rates.

---

3. The irony of the Canadian reality would not be lost on those familiar with Blumstein and Cohen (1973). They proposed that stable incarceration rates in the United States and Norway in the half-century preceding the writing of their article reflected the natural state of equilibrium maintained by modern societies. Blumstein et alia (1977) extended this analysis by including Canadian data. Ironically, it would seem that unlike Americans, Canadians (and Norwegians; Lappi-Seppälä 2005) took this "stability hypothesis" to heart, providing unexpected support for a theory whose ability to fit U.S. data ended almost simultaneous to its publication.

Indeed, the similarities among Canada, the United States, and England are not only historical, cultural, economic, or geographic in nature. They are also criminological. Canada has experienced a crime culture similar to that found in the United States and England since the 1960s. [B]oth the (police-recorded) total and the violent crime rates for Canada from 1962 to 2003[8] [show] a substantial increase in reported crime beginning in the early 1960s and only leveling off in the early 1990s. This pattern is similar to that found in the United States and — at least until the mid-1990s — the trend in England.

Even more convincing are the data on Canadian and U.S. homicide rates. . . . Although Canada's homicide rate (in absolute terms) is approximately one-third of that of the United States during this period, the shapes of the curves across time in the two countries are similar. . . .

Given these similarities, one might assume that the criminal justice responses of these countries would also be similar. . . . [S]cholars have been content simply to note that Canada's imprisonment rate (e.g., 103 per 100,000 in the general population in 2002) is comparable to that in some European countries (e.g., 101 in the Netherlands, and 92 in an unweighted average of the European Union countries) and English-speaking nations (e.g., 116 in Australia), while it is lower than that found in other countries (e.g., 137 in England and Wales, 126 in Scotland, 144 in New Zealand, and [the most obvious difference] 702 in the United States) for the same year.

Indeed, the focus of recent discussions surrounding levels of incarceration has been on the dramatic increase in the United States over the past 30 years, as well as a similar — albeit less dramatic — rise in England. While the recent increase in imprisonment rates in the Netherlands, the contrasting decreases in certain periods in other countries such as Germany and Finland, and the relative stability — at least until very recently — in such nations as Denmark, Norway, and Sweden have received sporadic attention, the United States and England continue to hold a near monopoly on scholarly inquiry in the English language academic literature.

[T]he increase . . . in American imprisonment rates since the mid-1970s justifies this focus. In striking contrast to the remarkable stability described by Blumstein and Cohen (1973) between 1930 and 1970, combined state and federal prison incarceration rates increased almost fivefold between 1970 and 2002. When the jail populations are included, the 2003 U.S. rate was 714 per 100,000 in the general population.

In contrast, Canadian imprisonment rates (comprising sentenced and all other — largely pretrial remand — prisoners) over the same period look quite different. The level of incarceration in Canada has been relatively stable since 1960. While there has been some fluctuation — with a low of 83 per 100,000 residents in 1974 to a high of 116 in 1995 — there is no consistent upward trend in Canada's imprisonment rate. . . .

Clearly, the data depict Canadian blandness: imprisonment rates have not changed dramatically since 1960. . . .

---

8. Unless otherwise noted, all Canadian statistics reported in this article are from publications of the Canadian Centre for Justice Statistics, Statistics Canada (previously the Dominion Bureau of Statistics), or from Statistics Canada's Web site, http://www.statcan.ca. Statistics Canada typically publishes annual reports on such matters as *Canadian Crime Statistics* or *Adult Correctional Services in Canada*. Rather than list each year that we accessed, we have listed a single illustrative instance of each series in the references.

CANADIAN PUNITIVENESS: TALK TOUGH — ACT SOFTLY

[I]t would be misguided to conclude from these data that Canada has been immune to pressure to adopt more punitive policies. On the contrary, an examination of several of the changes introduced in Canadian policy and legislation suggests that many of the forces behind higher incarceration rates in other countries have also impacted Canada.

Most obviously, Canada witnessed the introduction, in 1996, of mandatory minimum sentences for offenders found guilty of any of 10 serious violent crimes with a firearm. Similarly, the maximum sanctions for certain offenses were increased during the 1990s. Paralleling, to some extent, these changes in the adult criminal justice system, the maximum sentences for youths convicted of murder in youth court were increased both in 1992 (from three years to a total sentence length of five years less a day) and again in 1996 (to 10 years). This change in the youth system was also accompanied by changes in the rules governing the transfer of young offenders charged with serious crimes to adult court, rendering this process easier to accomplish by creating "presumptive transfers" to adult court of those over 16 years old charged with a serious violent offense. . . .

Clearly, Canada has not escaped many of the broader forces propelling countries toward more punitive responses to criminal behavior. The difference — it would seem — resides in the extent to which harsher policies and practices have been allowed to affect the level of punitiveness. Indeed, while the mandatory minimum sentence for violent crimes carried out with a firearm (four years in prison) did, in fact, increase the sentences that *some* offenders received, it is likely that the "new" sanction would not significantly differ from that which would have been handed down under the prior legislation for most offenders. Given the seriousness of the offense and the fact that those offenders falling under these new mandatory minimum sentences would frequently have criminal records — often serious in nature — it is probable that they would already have received a four-year sentence. Hence the legislation almost certainly contributed little to prison populations.

It is also noteworthy that previously legislated mandatory minimum sentences disappeared for drug offenses — a type of criminal activity responsible for a disproportionate proportion of the increase in the U.S. prison population during the 1980-1990s. Until 1987, Canada had a mandatory minimum sanction of seven years for importing narcotics. In that year, the Supreme Court of Canada ruled in *R. v. Smith* (34 C.C.C. (3d) 97) that this mandatory minimum penalty constituted cruel and unusual punishment under Section 12 of the Charter of Rights and Freedoms. . . . [T]he government of Canada never attempted to legislate a more selective mandatory minimum sanction for this offense. . . .

The pattern depicted in these examples is one of muted or limited expression of wider punitive trends. While Canada has obviously not been immune to the broader forces that compel other nations toward harsher responses to crime, it has been largely able to restrict or contain their impact. . . . Borrowing from the language of developmental psychology, it would seem that Canada has not only been able to escape several of the forces — or "risk factors" — producing higher imprisonment rates in other nations. Rather, there also appear to be certain "protective factors" that have restricted the extent to which Canada has adopted the punitive policies at the root of the U.S. and English levels of incarceration. . . .

RESISTING PUNITIVE TRENDS: REDUCED RISK FACTORS

In contrast with the United States and England, Canada has never given primacy to any one specific sentencing purpose. Rather, Canadian sentencing policies have historically been guided by the notion that multiple (and presumably equally acceptable) purposes of sentencing exist and that judges are responsible for choosing the most relevant purposes for each case (*R. v. Morrissette and two others*, 1 C.C.C. (2d) 307 [1970]). Indeed, Canadian judges have had—for the most part—wide discretion to sentence within a range determined largely by practice and by guidance from appeals courts. In fact, courts of appeal have not only developed the notion that judges should choose among all of the standard purposes of sentencing (i.e., denunciation, individual and general deterrence, incapacitation, and rehabilitation), but they have also reined in individual outliers.

Even when Parliament gave sentencing a legislated purpose and a set of principles in the Criminal Code in 1996, these provisions did not challenge the guiding notions in place for decades as a result of judicial decisions. The legislation stated that sentences were supposed to

> contribute, along with crime prevention initiatives, to respect for the law and the maintenance of a just, peaceful and safe society by imposing just sanctions that have one or more of the following objectives: [denunciation, general and individual deterrence, incapacitation, rehabilitation, reparations to victim and community, promoting a sense of responsibility and acknowledgment of harm by offenders] (Criminal Code, Section 718). While there was also a new requirement that "[a] sentence [be] proportionate to the gravity of the offence and the degree of responsibility of the offender" (Criminal Code, Section 718.1), we can find no important discernible changes or shifts in sentencing *practices* in Canada as reflected in imprisonment levels since 1996.

Within this context, Canada—unlike the United States—has never experienced a crisis of principles in sentencing whereby disillusionment with one predominant objective leads to the wholesale adoption of another. Hence, the radical shift in American courts from an indeterminate model based on a rehabilitative paradigm to one of determinate sentencing rooted in principles of denunciation, deterrence, and incapacitation was averted. . . .

Second, Canada has lacked the enthusiasm of the United States and England (primarily since the 1990s) toward harsher sanctions. Indeed, the tough-on-crime movement adopted by the United States and England appears to have permeated and propelled a number of key players—the general public, the media, the politicians, and the judiciary—toward support for increased punitiveness. While the causal relationships among these groups are unclear, the introduction of more punitive practices and policies has gone largely unchallenged in these countries. Indeed, politicians from the two main political parties in the United States and England have positioned themselves as tough on crime, neither wanting to be associated with "softer" responses. Similarly, judges—either voluntarily or through increasingly punitive sentencing guidelines—have begun showing a greater propensity to send more people to prison and for longer periods of time. Coupled with the "institutionalization" of the experience of crime through the mass media and an increasingly punitive public mood, these countries have lacked powerful inhibiting forces that would challenge or moderate punitive enthusiasm.

In contrast, the tough-on-crime movement has not caught on to the same extent within the Canadian imagination. While the media and the general public have not been immune to calls for tougher policies and practices, recent research shows that most Canadians do not strongly support "get tough" strategies as a solution to crime (Public Safety and Emergency Preparedness Canada 2001). More important, the government and the opposition rarely make crime issues a central part of their political platform. Rather, the role of the governing party tends to be one of quiet acceptance of a more balanced response to crime. As an illustration, the federal ministry responsible for federal penitentiaries recently concluded on its official Web site that

> [m]ost Canadians feel safe in their communities. Conveying these findings to the public is important to counter-balance media portrayals of crime as a pervasive problem. Compared to other issues, the majority of Canadians do not view crime as a priority issue for the government. This information is helpful in ensuring that the government's response to the crime problem is kept in perspective (Public Safety and Emergency Preparedness Canada 2001:2) Canadian judges have also demonstrated a lack of enthusiasm for more punitive responses to crime. Despite legislative freedom to increase the punitiveness of sentences, there was no notable change in the proportion of convicted cases sentenced to prison or in the overall mean prison sentence length handed down over the most recent 10-year period of available national data, from 1994-1995 to 2003-2004. Further, court decisions — like legislation more generally — have resisted many of the exclusionary practices adopted by other countries toward offenders. . . .

Canada's response to issues of race and sentencing also differs from that of the Americans. In the United States, the "war on drugs" arguably reflected a period of intolerance toward African Americans who were labeled as "bad people" — a view rooted in the individual rather than in social forces that may have produced the original criminal behavior. While Canada — and its justice system — have certainly not been immune to racist attitudes, with disadvantaged groups such as African Americans and Aboriginal Canadians continuing to be overrepresented in Canada's prisons (*Report of the Commission on Systemic Racism in the Ontario Criminal Justice System* 1995), its response — at least in terms of its expression through laws related to imprisonment — has clearly been different. Indeed, the government of Canada has attempted, through targeted legislation, to *reduce* the incarceration level of its most disadvantaged and imprisoned group: Aboriginal Canadians. In particular, a sentencing principle was included in the 1996 Criminal Code amendments requiring that "[a]ll available sanctions other than imprisonment that are reasonable in the circumstances should be considered for all offenders, with particular attention to the circumstances of aboriginal offenders" (Section 718.2[e]). Further, the constitutionality of this section was challenged and upheld by the Supreme Court of Canada (*R. v. Gladue*, 1 S.C.R. 688 [1999]). In fact, specialized courts in some locations deal exclusively with Aboriginal people in an attempt to give meaning to this provision.

HISTORICAL PROTECTIVE FACTORS

In striking contrast with the United States and England, Canada has shown deep skepticism about imprisonment as an appropriate response to crime.

Canada's caution in the use of imprisonment was written into legislation in 1996. Section 718.2 of Canada's Criminal Code states that "[a]n offender should not be deprived of liberty, if less restrictive sanctions may be appropriate in the circumstances," and "All available sanctions other than imprisonment that are reasonable in the circumstances should be considered for all offenders. . . ."

However, these statements constitute only part of a long history of recognition by the government and government-appointed commissions of the overuse of incarceration. In 1969, the Canadian Committee on Corrections stressed the importance of dealing with the offender in the community and explicitly suggested "changes in sentencing policy to provide for the use of alternatives to prison. . . ." It noted that "through these measures a major decrease in Canada's prison population would prove possible, without increased danger to the public and with greater success in terms of rehabilitated offenders." Despite never succeeding in reducing incarceration levels, the committee's views set the tone and theme for the rest of the century.

The first report of the federal Law Reform Commission of Canada in 1976 also promotes restraint in the use of the criminal law generally and of imprisonment in particular. In fact, it urges Parliament to employ prison sentences "sparingly" as a penalty of last resort. This recommendation is reiterated in the Government of Canada's 1982 statement of policy on criminal law. It concludes that "it seems justifiable and appropriate to endorse the general philosophy of restraint in criminal law. . . ." In particular, it suggests that "[i]n awarding sentences, preference should be given to the least restrictive alternative adequate and appropriate in the circumstances." This same sentiment was quoted with approval 20 years later by the then Minister of Justice. In a speech to the Canadian Bar Association, he reaffirmed that the criminal law should be used "only as a last resort" and that "there may be other ways to achieve positive social outcomes." . . .

Similarly, a policy paper entitled *Sentencing* (Government of Canada 1984) notes that Canada's imprisonment rate "looks relatively restrained only in comparison to that of the U.S., and such other countries as the Soviet Union and South Africa." Like its predecessors, this document recommends that judges consider prison only after rejecting other choices. Similarly, the Canadian Sentencing Commission (1987) notes under the subheading "An Over-Reliance on Imprisonment" (in a section on the "Effects of the Structural Deficiencies in Sentencing" (1987) that "much concern over the years has been expressed concerning Canada's level of dependence on incarceration as the 'standard' penalty for criminal offences. In the submissions to this Commission, most groups and individuals called for restraint in the use of custodial sentences and advocated a greater use of community sanctions." Although the recommendations of the Canadian Sentencing Commission were never adopted, they serve as another indicator of the degree to which the notion of restraint in the recourse to custody is entrenched in Canada's formal statements of criminal justice policy. . . .

In response to a 1995 request made by the federal, provincial, and territorial ministers responsible for justice to "identify options to deal effectively with the growing prison populations," proposals by deputies symptomatically focused on noncustodial measures (*Corrections Population Growth* 1996:i). Suggestions were made for the expanded use of diversion programs, the nonincarceration of low-risk offenders, and the increased use of restorative and mediation approaches. A screening mechanism to divert cases from the justice system as well as legislated principles encouraging nonprison sanctions were made part of the Criminal Code in 1996. As a direct attempt to respond to provincial concerns about their levels of incarceration, a "conditional sentence of imprisonment" was also introduced to reduce the use of custodial sentences of less than two years.

Clearly, the value of Canada's long history of official statements urging caution in the use of imprisonment does not reside in any real impact that it has had on the government's actions or in changing criminal justice practices. Indeed, there is no empirical evidence demonstrating any appreciable *reduction* in Canadian incarceration rates since 1960. Rather, this official culture of restraint would seem to be important in protecting Canada from some of the broader forces that have propelled other nations toward more punitive policies. Certainly in comparison with the United States or England, the simple maintenance of the status quo in imprisonment rates may be seen as an accomplishment.

STRUCTURAL-POLITICAL PROTECTIVE FACTORS

This politicization of crime policy has been identified as a powerful force in the trend toward more punitive approaches to criminal behavior. Hence, it is noteworthy that Canada has largely escaped this phenomenon. . . .

Unlike England with its unitary criminal justice jurisdiction and the United States with its 51 separate criminal justice jurisdictions, the Canadian federal government is responsible for criminal law while the provinces have responsibility for the administration of criminal justice. Therefore, Canadian provincial governments have no direct power to modify the criminal law despite the fact that they play the largest role in the administration of justice. This distinction is crucial in creating and maintaining a two-tiered political structure that distances the federal government — with the power to increase punitiveness within the criminal justice realm — from provincial and public demands.

Indeed, provincial governments, which tend to be susceptible to populist punitive talk, have no legislative power over sentencing. The federal government appoints all appeals court judges. Hence, no structural mechanism is available for local (grassroots) citizens' groups to create laws that have a direct impact on imprisonment policies, as has been the case in some U.S. states (e.g., California's three-strikes legislation). . . .

This division of responsibility between the federal and provincial/territorial governments also ensures that changes to the criminal law require extensive consultation between the two "partners." . . . Not surprisingly, this process is typically time-consuming, virtually (albeit not entirely) eliminating the possibility of introducing quick-fix, politically motivated legislation in response to unusual circumstances that arise from isolated cases. . . .

Beyond these structural benefits of the two-tiered political system whereby the federal government is both insulated from public petitions for harsher sentences and strategically positioned to moderate provincial demands, many of the key players in the decisionmaking processes involving criminal justice issues also have the advantage of being insulated — to some degree — from swings in public opinion. Potentially most important is the fact that Canadian judges are appointed rather than elected, with no need for them to be confirmed or examined by any formal process. . . .

Further, criminal justice reforms in Canada are typically written by non-elected bureaucrats, civil servants, and nongovernmental experts—not politicians—who are less susceptible to public pressure, as they almost always remain in their positions independent of changes in government. Unlike citizens of the United States and England, Tonry notes that Canadians continue to demonstrate considerable confidence "in both the appropriateness and the competence of professionals to determine policy," entrusting these nonpartisan, non-elected authorities with significant power to guide criminal justice policy in Canada. Indeed, while the Minister of Justice and the federal cabinet ultimately determine any modifications of criminal law introduced into Parliament, specialists tend to define the need for changes, the nature of those changes, and the specific means of accomplishing them. . . .

In contrast with the American and English power struggles during the 1990s between sentencing judges on the one hand and governments and prosecutors on the other, sentencing power has always remained firmly in the hands of Canadian judges. Even when the Canadian Sentencing Commission recommended that the government of Canada adopt a system of very permissive presumptive guidelines that would be established by a permanent sentencing commission and confirmed by Parliament, the proposal was rejected—in part because guidelines of any kind were seen as a radical departure from traditional policy. Indeed, despite the fact that these presumptive guidelines would have left enormous power to sentence with the sentencing judge in particular, and with judges (including appeals judges) more generally, the historically entrenched model in which judges are given almost complete responsibility for sentencing prevailed. . . .

PROTECTIVE FACTORS: CULTURAL VALUES

Canadians also seem to possess cultural values that have limited enthusiasm for increased imprisonment. These beliefs have permeated both the political and popular culture. Indeed, Canadians appear to lack the moral taste for harshness—on an individual level—and faith—at the political level—regarding the effectiveness of more-punitive sanctions in solving the crime problem.

Unlike Canada, the United States and England (since the 1990s) have shown a belief in the possibility of legislating away the crime problem. The history of crime control in the United States reflects characteristically American optimism in the ability of the state to reduce crime rates through sentencing. Whether the solution resides in the belief that rehabilitation works or—more currently—that deterrence and incapacitation are effective in solving crime, the United States has been continually lured by the utilitarian purposes of sentencing. . . .

In contrast, Canadian politicians have shown skepticism about the effectiveness of criminal punishment in reducing criminal activity. The federal government's 1982 policy statement sets the tone of Canadian political culture related to sentencing by affirming that "[i]t is now generally agreed that the [criminal justice] system cannot realistically be expected to eliminate or even significantly reduce crime . . ." (Government of Canada 1982:28). . . .

This rejection of the "punishment stops crime" argument was reiterated a decade later in the political realm. The Canadian Minister of Justice affirmed publicly that just as "war is too important to be left to the generals . . . [c]rime prevention is too important to be left to the lawyers, or the justice ministers, or even the judges. . . . In the final analysis, crime prevention has as much to do with the [Minister of] . . . Finance, [the Minister of] . . . Industry, and [the Minister of] . . . Human Resources Development, as it does with [the Minister of] Justice" (Rock 1996:191-2). While this message has not always been expressed in such clear terms — as Canadian politicians have always had highly developed abilities to support both sides of a criminal justice policy issue — the lack of general endorsement from politicians of the notion that judges are well-placed to solve the problem of crime seems to have ensured ambivalence within Canadian political culture vis-à-vis tough-on-crime measures. . . .

Indeed, some have suggested that Canadian identity is often constructed in opposition to its American neighbor. . . . Many Canadian policy makers have shown a desire to shun an Americanized approach to criminal justice. In particular, Canada has been especially vocal in its rejection of U.S. imprisonment policies and practices. As a Conservative-dominated 1993 Parliamentary committee noted, "[i]f locking up those who violate the law contributed to safer societies, then the United States should be the safest country in the world. In fact, the United States affords a glaring example of the limited impact that criminal justice responses may have on crime" (Standing Committee on Justice and the Solicitor General 1993:2). . . .

Incarceration Rates Across the World, Andre Kuhn
10 Overcrowded Times, no. 2 (April 1999)

[The number of prison inmates per 100,000 inhabitants in different countries] varies today from about 20 in Indonesia to about 685 in the Russian Federation. In Western Europe it varies between 35 (Cyprus) and 145 (Portugal) and in the United States there were at midyear 1998 about 668 inmates per 100,000 population. [This] article tries to show national trends in prison population rather than to analyze differences between countries. A number of generalizations emerge from examination of penal patterns in the countries discussed. First, though crime rates increased substantially in most industrialized countries in the 1970s and 1980s, there is no standard of incarceration rate patterns. Finland and Japan have experienced declining rates for several decades, the U.S. has experienced unbroken increases since 1973, and other countries' patterns vary between those extremes. Second, . . . prison population trends are powerfully shaped by countries' cultures and histories and by contemporary politics and ideologies; whether imprisonment-use changes inevitably must follow or can themselves lead penal attitudes, remains to be seen.

The Netherlands illustrates the recent increase in incarceration rates in many European countries. Although the Netherlands is well known for its low incarceration rate, its prison population increased from 28 prisoners per 100,000 population in 1983 to about 74 in 1997, an increase of 164 percent. The increase is attributable largely to longer sentences for sentenced offenders rather than to growth in the numbers of sentenced or pretrial inmates.

[The] Swiss incarceration rate fell by half between the 1930s and 1980s, suggesting that the contemporary criminal justice system is less severe than formerly. Between 1982 and 1997, however, the average length of sentences increased by 132 percent, from 74 to 172 days, while the median term increased by only 50 percent, from 28 to 42 days. This suggests that [most] sentences stayed short but that longer ones became substantially longer.

[In Italy between] 1991 and 1997, the total incarceration rate increased significantly, from 56 to 86 per 100,000. This seems to be an effect of illegal Albanian immigration, enlargement of the anti-Mafia fight after the assassination of judges, and anticorruption operations led by the magistrates. . . .

Between 1983 and 1991, the German incarceration rate fell significantly from 93.3 to 69.2 per 100,000. This phenomenon has not been fully explained by criminal policy specialists, although it may be attributable, in part, to change in judges' and prosecutors' attitudes. Nonetheless, . . . the German incarceration rate increased between 1990 and 1997 by 15.7 percent [to reach] ninety prisoners per 100,000 inhabitants. This remains, however, below the 1983 level. . . .

Finland, unlike any other European country discussed here, has long had a decreasing incarceration rate. . . . Twenty years ago, the Finnish incarceration rate was one of the highest in Europe. Today, with about 60 inmates per 100,000 population, Finland has one of the lowest. . . . Finland has moved gradually toward a criminal justice system based on general prevention, which holds that it is important that criminals are caught and punished, but that the severity of the sanction is, in comparison, a minor issue. The Finnish criminal justice system therefore emphasizes the *certainty* of the sanction rather than its *severity*. That philosophy, according to which it is not useful to sentence an offender to several months of deprivation of liberty if several weeks will equally effectively demonstrate society's condemnation, has affected incarceration rates.

[Japan] has experienced decreasing incarceration rates since 1950 and has one of the lowest incarceration rates (37 per 100,000 in 1995) among the industrialized countries. . . . Notions of a hierarchical social order remain important in Japan today: knowing one's place in the societal scheme, fulfilling the Confucian obligations that the ruler be benevolent and the ruled be obedient, and holding the respect of others by maintaining social harmony, even at the expense of self-interest, remain widely held norms. The law breaker is expected to be repentant and to undertake self correction. It is therefore understandable that the criminal justice system is "lenient" toward offenders who express repentance and show willingness and capacity for self correction. Legal standards and procedures permit diversion extensively of defendants from trials and suspended prison sentences. . . . Japan decreased its prison population principally by reducing the number of entries into prison from 64,112 in 1951 to 31,122 in 1989. The incarceration rate dropped despite growth in the mean length of sentence from 17.5 months in 1970 to 20.9 months in 1990 and despite a rising crime rate. . . .

The differences [in incarceration rates] between Europe and the United States are largely ideological. Americans tend to accept the proposition that human beings are possessed of free will and are capable of making rational choices. They are generally receptive to the idea that people succeed or fail as a result of their own initiative. That ideology views crimes as the moral failure of individuals who freely elect to commit crimes, and who can therefore be held to account for their behavior. In this light, punishment ought to be designed to increase the costs of crime to such an extent that rationally acting individuals will no longer have incentives to commit crimes. Europeans more often view human behavior as more than just a function of free will. Human behavior is influenced by social circumstances such as education, peer relationships, and many other variables. All are important factors in the progression of events that lead to crime. Viewing crime as the product of both social and individual circumstances inclines Europeans more readily to accept responses to crime that include rehabilitative measures. That reflects the moral understanding that if individuals cannot be held solely responsible for what they become and what they do, society has an obligation to try to correct the influences or the conditions which may have led an individual into crime.

NOTES

1. *Imprisonment rates abroad.* Imprisonment rates in the United States are on average much higher than those in most other industrialized countries. There is some question as to whether that difference derives from shorter prison terms in other countries or a lower rate of imprisonment or some combination of the two. Sheryl Van Horne & Graham Farrell, Drug Offenders in the Global Criminal Justice System (European Institute for Crime Prevention and Control affiliated with the United Nations, HEUNI Paper No. 13, 1999, available at www.heuni.fi/uploads/jh0bv0x.pdf) (larger number of drug prosecutions rather than severity of drug sentences is the primary contributor to the difference between United States and Western Europe); Michael Tonry, Prisons and Imprisonment, in 18 International Encyclopedia of the Social and Behavioral Sciences 12,062 (2001). Do any of the differences in prison trends in industrialized nations surprise you? Are you convinced by the explanation provide by Doob and Webster for the striking difference in imprisonment rates in Canada compared with the United States—in the face of similar crime trends? In the end does the Canadian story undermine or reinforce the theory of exceptionalism (unique circumstances) for the United States? For Canada? Looking farther abroad, can you explain why imprisonment rates in Finland fell over time while rates in Italy increased? For more detailed accounts of the evolution of sentencing policies in other nations, see Michael Tonry & Richard Frase, Sentencing and Sanctions in Western Countries (2001); James Q. Whitman, Harsh Justice: Criminal Punishment and the Widening Divide Between America and Europe (2003).

2. *An imaginary future.* Imagine a world without prison. Such a world did exist, and in historical perspective it was not so long ago—only a few hundred years. The Norval Morris passage reprinted above appears as part of a larger effort to consider whether modern society could get along without prisons. Could such a world be established again today? What would it look like? Cf. John Braithwaite, A Future Where Punishment Is Marginalized: Realistic or Utopian?, 46 UCLA L. Rev. 1727 (1999).

PROBLEM 7-1. THE COMPANY WE KEEP

The Centre for Prison Studies at King's College, London, reports that as of October 2006 the United States boasts the highest imprisonment rates in the world (reported at 738 per 100,000), followed by Russia (611), St Kitts–Nevis (547), U.S. Virgin Islands (521), Turkmenistan (ca. 489), Belize (487), Cuba (ca. 487), Palau (478), British Virgin Islands (464), Bermuda (463), Bahamas (462), Cayman Islands (453), American Samoa (446), Belarus (426), and Dominica (419). See Centre for Prison Studies, World Prison Population List (Jan. 2007). Current U.S. imprisonment rates appear to exceed rates from apartheid-era South Africa, the former Soviet Union, and China. Comparison of the imprisonment rate of black males between apartheid-era South Africa and the United States today makes the discrepancy even more stark. But are such comparisons useful?

C. COMPETING EXPLANATIONS FOR GROWTH

A massive change in practice such as the enormous increase in American incarceration rates over the last 30 years begs for some explanation. There is likely no single reason, but many criminologists, political scientists, and criminal law scholars have offered theories. The materials that follow begin with one of the more straightforward theories: prison rates go up as a rational governmental response to increases in crime (or increases in certain serious crimes). The later materials point out some difficulties in linking crime rates and imprisonment rates, and explain our increased use of prison as a product of our national politics and our social psyche.

> ## The Social Benefits of Confining Habitual Criminals, Kent Scheidegger and Michael Rushford
> ### 11 Stan. L. & Pol'y Rev. 59 (1999)

. . . The cycle of rising and dropping crime rates appears to correspond to the level of public and political resolve to aggressively capture and incapacitate criminal offenders. In periods when crime rates and public concern about crime have been relatively low, the premium on aggressive law enforcement appears to diminish, while programs attempting to socialize rather than punish offenders enjoy popularity in political and academic circles. Later, as crime rates and public concern about crime increase, such increases are accompanied by political pressure for a return to aggressive law enforcement and the incapacitation of criminals.

The simple truth is that imprisonment works. Locking up more criminals for longer periods reduces the level of crime. The benefits of doing so far offset the costs.

THE CURRENT CYCLE

The national reduction in crime over the past eight years (1990-1998) is rooted in a crime policy cycle that began in the mid-1970s, with the public's response to a doubling of the rate of serious crimes between 1965 and 1975. The initial indicators in California, which played a leading role in this cycle, included a ballot initiative to reinstate capital punishment in 1972, the Legislature's adoption of the "Use a Gun, Go to Prison" law in 1975, the override of the Governor's veto of another death penalty law in 1977, and the adoption of strict sentencing increases for habitual criminals as part of the "Victims' Bill of Rights" initiative in 1982.

The sentence increases in the 1982 initiative represented a major statewide policy shift toward lengthened incarceration of habitual felons. In accordance with the new law, a California judge could sentence a convicted felon to an additional five years in prison for each prior felony conviction. A 1995 study led by Berkeley law professor Franklin Zimring, a well-known opponent of tough sentencing, credited increased incarceration with a marked drop in burglary and larceny crimes between 1980 and 1991, but found the evidence more ambiguous for violent offenses. . . .

In the early 1990s, several states began to adopt sentence increases for habitual criminals. Washington State's adoption of Initiative 593 in November of 1993, which mandated life in prison without parole upon conviction of a third violent felony, set a standard duplicated in some form by several other states. California's "Three Strikes and You're Out" law modified this approach by providing increased sentences for all repeat felons and a top term of 25 years to life for those convicted of any felony if they had two prior convictions for violent or serious felonies. While California's earlier sentencing and procedural reforms corresponded with a 10 percent reduction in the crime rate between 1991 and 1994, after adoption of the Three Strikes in 1994 the crime rate plummeted over 21 percent during the next 3 years. . . .

During the 15-year period between 1982 and 1997, as the state more than tripled its prison commitment rate with a focus on incarcerating habitual felons, the number of California victims of serious crime dropped from 4,777.1 per 100,000 in 1982 to 2,381.4 per 100,000 in 1997, less than half the previous figure. . . . The increase of young males in the population may well have contributed to the growth in the rate of incarceration, especially over the past 7 years, but it appears that the correct criminal justice policies were in place to prevent the predicted rise in crime.

COMMON SENSE AND EMPIRICAL EVIDENCE

The idea that increased incarceration of criminals will reduce the rate of crime has two bases in common sense. First, incentives matter. When the incentives to engage in or refrain from a particular behavior change, the number of people who choose to engage in that behavior also changes. In criminology, this effect is called deterrence. Second, the crime rate is determined by the number of criminals, not by the availability of victims, and removing a criminal from the street to prison prevents him from committing crimes against the general public. Reducing crime by direct restraint is called incapacitation.

The anti-incarceration hypothesis that neither effect is significant, i.e., that prison neither deters nor incapacitates, is extremely difficult to swallow. There will always be some people who cannot be deterred because they act without thinking. There will always be some who do not need to be deterred because their character and conscience would prevent them from committing crimes even if they could do so with impunity. Between the wild beasts and the saints, though, there will always be a large segment of the population that refrains from crime out of fear of the consequences, i.e., that is deterrable, and the size of that segment naturally depends on the severity of the consequences. For incapacitation, the often-heard notion that if we incarcerate one criminal another will take his place assumes that there are a fixed number of places. This assumption makes no sense. As high as the rates of burglary and robbery are, there are still far more targets than crimes each year.

The anti-incarceration hypothesis is so strongly contrary to common sense that it would take powerful empirical evidence to support it. In fact, there is substantial empirical reason to believe that imprisonment works.

For an initial, admittedly simplistic overview, Figure 1 plots incarceration versus crime. The solid line represents the FBI crime index per 100,000 population. The dotted line represents prisoners in custody per 1000 index crimes. As imprisonment fell sharply in the 1960s, the crime rate more than doubled. As imprisonment remained low in the 1970s, the crime rate continued its rise. As imprisonment rose in the 1980s, the crime rate fluctuated, dropping in the early part of the decade then rising during the crack epidemic of 1985-1990. Finally, as imprisonment rose sharply in the 1990s, the crime rate went steadily down, although the rate still remains far above where it was in 1960.

These time-line data provide an indication, but not proof. There is a possibility that other changes occurring in society could account for the crime rate changes. The claim is often made, for example, that the sharp increase in crime in the 1960s was due primarily, if not entirely, to the young males of the "baby boom" reaching their peak crime-prone years. There can be no doubt that punishment is only one of many factors affecting crime rates. The simple time-line data need to be confirmed by other methods that control, at least partially, for these other variables. . . .

Figure 1

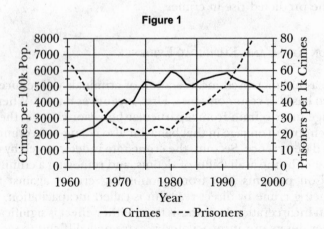

— Crimes   --- Prisoners

A more sophisticated cross-jurisdictional comparison was done by University of Chicago economist Steven Levitt. See Steven D. Levitt, The Effect of Prison Population Size on Crime Rates: Evidence from Prison Overcrowding Litigation, 109 Q. J. Econ. 319 (1996). Levitt grappled with the problem of separating cause from effect in the connection between crime rates and incarceration rates. "Increased incarceration is likely to reduce the amount of crime, but there is also little question that increases in crime will translate into larger prison populations." This creates a measurement problem called "simultaneity bias." To control this effect, Levitt compared states where statewide prison overcrowding litigation had capped the use of incarceration with states not subject to such caps.

Levitt found that an adverse decision in prison overcrowding litigation slowed the growth of the prison population by 13.7-19.7 percent. This caused an increase in violent crime of 7.9-8.3 percent, and an increase in property crime of 5.7-6.2 percent. Applying the rates derived from this study to the 272 percent increase in per capita incarceration in the United States from 1971 to 1993, Levitt concluded that violent crime would be 70 percent higher and property crime would be 50 percent higher without that increase. . . .

COSTS AND BENEFITS

Is the benefit of reducing crime through tough sentencing worth the cost? The answer, we believe, is quite clearly yes. In 1994, during the debate over Three Strikes, RAND Corporation produced a study predicting a 22-34 percent reduction in crime at a cost of $4.5-6.5 billion. The law appears to have a much lower cost than predicted.

RAND's cost figures were based on prison population projections showing, for example, about 250,000 prisoners by 1999 under Three Strikes, compared with about 120,000 under prior law. The actual prison population at present is 159,706, closer to RAND's "prior law" figure than its Three Strikes figure. In part, the lower cost is the result of court decisions implementing Three Strikes less severely than RAND anticipated. It is also likely, though, that tougher sentencing is simply more effective than anticipated at bringing down the crime rate and thus reducing the number of repeat felons who need to be imprisoned. RAND's projections were based on an assumption of a zero deterrent effect, a highly doubtful assumption. . . .

Tough sentencing is effective and economically efficient. We can and should investigate crime prevention and operate pilot programs to find out what works on the front end of criminal careers. We should not, however, turn career criminals loose on the streets to prey upon innocent people.

Why Are U.S. Incarceration Rates So High?, Michael Tonry
45 Crime & Delinq. 419 (1999)

American imprisonment rates, 668 per 100,000 residents behind bars in mid-1998, have reached unprecedented levels compared with other times in

United States history or with current times in other Western democracies. . . . Only in the United States are prison sentences longer than 1 or 2 years common; in most countries, fewer than 5 percent of sentences are for a year or longer. In the United States, in 1994, the average sentence among people sent to state prisons for felonies was 71 months. Among those in prison, more than half were serving terms exceeding 10 years.

All of this is a drastic change from earlier times. In the 1930s, for example, the United States had incarceration rates comparable to or lower than European countries such as England, France, Switzerland, and Finland. More recently, in the 1960s, the United States was in the mainstream. The death penalty was withering away, the incarceration rate was dropping and comparable to those in other Western countries, the courts were establishing and refining defendants' procedural protections, and crime control was not generally viewed as a partisan or ideological issue.

Now, of course, the United States is unique. The aim of this article is to offer and assess alternate explanations for why American policies have diverged so far from our own past practices and from the practices of other Western countries. . . .

CRUDE EMPIRICISM

The first explanation for why so many Americans are in prison, that our crime rates are higher or faster rising than other countries', has virtually no validity. Crime rates in the United States in the 1990s are, for the most part, no higher than in other Western countries. . . . For property crimes, the United States is in the middle of the pack. Chances of being burglarized, having your pocket picked, or having your car stolen are considerably higher in England and several other European countries. For most violent crimes, American rates are among the highest, along with Australia, Canada, Spain, and France, but not the highest. Chances of being robbed, being assaulted, or being a victim of a stranger rape are higher in several other Western countries.

[Trends] in American imprisonment, homicide, and violent crime rates from 1960 to 1993 . . . suggest that violent crime and imprisonment at least initially rose together (more recently, however, imprisonment rates have continued their steep climb whereas violence rates have dropped sharply). However, . . . data for Finland and Germany during the same period indicate that there is no [necessary connection between crime rates and imprisonment rates]. Although the homicide and violent crime curves in Finland and Germany rose as steeply as the U.S. curves . . . the imprisonment rate in Germany fell throughout the 1960s and remained roughly level thereafter, and the incarceration rate in Finland fell sharply and steadily throughout the entire period. The reasons for those two countries' patterns are somewhat different, but the important point is that they reflect policy decisions that are based on the belief that increased incarceration is neither an appropriate nor an effective response to rising crime rates. American politicians decided otherwise. American imprisonment rates did not rise simply because crime rates rose. They rose because American politicians wanted them to rise.

Something was not working, and deterrence and incapacitation were chosen as strategies to lower crime rates. The only problem with this is that the most drastic such strategies were adopted long after crime rates began to fall. [Crime] rates for most crimes peaked around 1980, fell through the mid-1980s, rose for awhile for reasons largely associated with the crack cocaine epidemic, and have since fallen sharply. However, the first three-strikes law was enacted in 1993, and the federal truth-in-sentencing law, which authorized $8 billion for state prison construction, was passed in 1994. The meanings of these data are complex, but whatever else they show, they do not show any simple interaction between crime trends and imprisonment patterns.

PUBLIC OPINION

The second explanation for the high imprisonment rate is that public opinion survey results sometimes show that crime and drugs come in first as America's most pressing problem, that large majorities often express the view that sentencing is too lenient, and that people demand that criminal punishment be made tougher. On this account, elected officials have merely respected the public will, and imprisonment rates have risen as a result.

There are two serious deficiencies in this story. [First,] ordinary citizens base their opinions on what they know about crime from the mass media. Consequently, they regard heinous crimes and bizarre sentences as the norms, they believe sentences are much softer than they are, and they believe crime rates are rising when they are falling. As a result, majorities nearly always report that judges' sentences are too lenient; yet, when they are asked to propose sentences appropriate for individual cases, they generally propose sentences that are shorter than those actually imposed. . . .

The second point is more important. Public nomination of crime as the nation's most pressing problem and public support for harsh laws typically follow, not precede, media and political preoccupation with crime. Although politicians who attempt to win favor by demonstrating their toughness nearly always say that they are honoring citizens' wishes, the evidence is that harping by politicians and the media on crime issues is what causes citizens to become concerned. . . .

PARTISAN POLITICS

Crime and punishment have been high on American political agendas since the late 1960s. Before Republican presidential candidate Barry Goldwater raised crime in the streets as a partisan issue in his unsuccessful 1964 campaign, public safety was generally seen as one among several important, but unglamorous, core functions of government, like public health, public transit, and public education. Public officials were expected to do their work conscientiously and well. . . . Reasonable people differed over the best approaches for addressing particular problems, but the debates were seldom partisan or ideological. Criminal justice policy was a subject for practitioners and technocrats, and sentencing was the specialized case-by-case business of judges and corrections officials.

In recent decades, however, crime control has been at the center of partisan politics, and policies have been shaped more by symbols and rhetoric than by substance and knowledge. [During the 1960s, a fissure developed] within the Democratic Party between racial and social policy liberals and racial and social policy conservatives. This occurred initially in the South, and eventually nationwide. Republican strategists seized the opportunity to appeal to Nixon (later Reagan) Democrats by defining sharp differences between the parties on three wedge issues: crime control, welfare, and affirmative action. On crime control, conservatives blamed rising crime rates on lenient judges and soft punishments, and demanded toughness. . . .

Crime's role as a wedge issue has had important consequences. Issues that are debated on television and examined in 15- and 30-second commercials necessarily are presented in simplistic and emotional terms. Matters judges and prosecutors agonize over in individual cases are addressed in slogans and symbols, which often leads to the adoption of ham-fisted and poorly considered policies. Notable recent examples include widespread adoption of broadly defined three-strikes laws, mandatory minimum-sentence laws, sexual psychopath laws, and the federal sentencing guidelines. . . . When issues are defined in polar terms of morality and immorality, or responsibility and irresponsibility, few elected officials are prepared to be found at the wrong pole. . . .

What is needed is an explanation for why crime and punishment served so nicely as a wedge issue, and why so many elected officials were prepared, in recent decades, to behave in ways that their opponents and many observers often perceived as demagogic. [One such explanation] comes from the work of historian David Musto, which suggests that crime policies, political sensibilities, and the nature of public attitudes about crime are determined by cyclical trends in criminality and responses to it. David Musto, The American Disease: Origins of Narcotic Control (1987).

HISTORICAL CYCLES

Historians have long known that crime rates rise and fall over extended periods for reasons that have little to do with crime control policies. The three most influential scholars of the subject—historian Roger Lane and political scientists Ted Robert Gurr and James Q. Wilson—concur in the view that crime rates in the United States, England, Germany, France, and other Western countries have followed a U-shaped or a backwards J-shaped curve, falling from the second quarter of the nineteenth century through the middle of the twentieth century and rising until late in the twentieth century. . . .

More recently, there is evidence that crime rates in Western countries may be in another long-term decline. In the United States, for example, data from the National Crime Victimization Survey show that rates for many crimes fell steadily from 1973 to the 1980s, after which, they increased or stabilized for a few years and resumed a downward path. Police data from the Federal Bureau of Investigation's Uniform Crime Reports show a somewhat different (but reconcilable) pattern of crime rates that rose through 1981, fell through 1986, rose again through 1991, and have plummeted since then to levels that, for some crimes, have not been seen since the 1960s. English, Dutch, Swedish, and Norwegian data likewise show significant victimization-rate declines in the 1990s. . . .

Yale historian David Musto has shown that antidrug policies interact in predictable ways with patterns of drug use. Seemingly perverse but, on reflection understandable, the harshest policies are adopted and the most vigorous prosecutions are carried out after drug use has begun to decline. In our era, for example, self-reported use of marijuana, heroin, and amphetamines peaked for every age group in 1979 to 1980 (for cocaine, in 1984 to 1985) and fell steadily thereafter, but the harshest federal antidrug laws were not enacted until 1986 and 1988, and the first federal drug czar was not named until 1989. If reduced drug use was its aim, the war was being won a decade before it was declared.

The reason all this is understandable is that recreational drug use during prohibitionistic periods is widely seen as immoral and socially destructive. Such attitudes explain why an increasing number of people stop using and experimenting with drugs and why, after drug use begins falling, comparatively few voices are raised in opposition to harsh policies. Few people, especially elected public officials, are comfortable speaking out on behalf of immorality. . . . In more tolerant periods, by contrast, many more people celebrate Enlightenment ideals of moral autonomy and individuals' rights to make choices about their own lives, and comfortably oppose harsh laws and policies on those grounds.

I mention the recurrent interaction between drug-use patterns and drug abuse policy because similar patterns may characterize interactions between contemporary crime patterns and crime-control policies. [The] harshest crime control policies — three-strikes laws; lengthy mandatory minimum sentence laws; truth-in-sentencing laws; and increased use of the death penalty — date from the early and mid-1990s, long after crime rates began their steep decline.

[Enhancing] people's predisposition to believe that harsh measures work, harsh laws are often enacted when crime rates are already falling. People who want to make year-to-year comparisons can easily show that the new, tougher policies have worked, because crime rates have fallen in the years immediately after the change when compared with the year immediately before. This happened in relation to New York City's adoption in the early 1990s of zero-tolerance policing, California's adoption in 1994 of a broadly defined three-strikes law, and many states' passage in the mid-1990s of truth-in-sentencing laws. These may be plausible claims on the part of people who are unaware of long-term crime trends, but for people who are, they are disingenuous. The year-to-year crime-rate declines are at least as likely merely to be a continuation of long-term trends as they are to be effects of policy changes. . . .

As a hypothesis, Musto's paradigm provides a richer account of American exceptionalism in the past quarter century than do any of the other accounts that I have attempted. It explains why public attitudes are harsher when crime rates are falling than when they are rising and, consequently, why law-and-order appeals fell on fertile electoral ground. It explains why politicians feel comfortable appealing to base instincts and proposing policies that, in other times, would have seemed demagogic and cruel. It explains not only why so few voices were raised in opposition to those policies but also why few people felt a need to speak out in opposition. It explains why people were inclined to believe that declining crime and drug-use rates showed that harsh policies worked. . . .

America's unprecedented and unmatched taste for imprisonment and harsh criminal justice policies has little to do with them — the offenders who get dealt with one way or another — and everything to do with us. If we took the historical lessons to heart, we might be less quick to adopt harsh crime policies. In our private lives, we know these things, and our folk wisdom celebrates it — do not strike in anger; sit down and count to 10; do not take your frustrations out on your child, your spouse, or your employee; and write the angry letter, but put it aside until tomorrow and see if you still want to send it. Whether those private insights will soon shape our public policies remains to be seen. . . .

NOTES

1. *Crime control through deterrence.*   The most straightforward way to explain why U.S. legal systems rely so heavily on prison relates to crime control. Prison, the argument goes, both deters crimes and incapacitates criminals better than the alternatives, so the heavy use of prison in the United States is a rational effort to reduce crime. There are powerful theoretical reasons to believe that at least some use of prison can deter crime. For instance, one could analogize potential criminals to rational economic actors, who weigh the benefits of crime against the likelihood of conviction and the severity of the punishment. Longer prison terms, in this model, increase the cost of crime and encourage more people to avoid it. See Gary S. Becker, Crime and Punishment: An Economic Approach, 76 J. Pol. Econ. 169 (1968).

The difficulty arises in the gap between theory and experience. While many agree that at least some use of prison deters crime, there is intense debate over whether marginal increases in the use of prison translate into marginal increases in deterrence. See Cassia Spohn & David Holleran, The Effect of Imprisonment on Recidivism Rates of Felony Offenders: A Focus on Drug Offenders, 40 Criminology 329 (2002) (comparison of drug offenders in Missouri sentenced to prison and probation; prison increases rather than reduces likelihood of recidivism); Richard A. Wright, The Evidence in Favor of Prisons, in Crime and Criminals (Frank R. Scarpitti & Amiel Nelsen eds., 1999). What specific claims do Scheidegger and Rushford make about deterrence, and what specific evidence do they use? Does Tonry address their evidence?

2. *Crime control through incapacitation.*   There is no question that prison incapacitates some offenders from committing new crimes during their prison term. Given the number of career criminals and the short span of years that constitutes the criminal "career" for many offenders, it should be possible in theory to reduce crime through heavier use of prison. One practical difficulty is deciding how to target the offenders who are most likely to commit new crimes, a practice known as "selective incapacitation." See James Q. Wilson, Thinking About Crime 193-194 (1977); Shlomo Shinnar & Reuel Shinnar, The Effects of the Criminal Justice System on the Control of Crime: A Quantitative Approach, 9 Law & Soc'y Rev. 581 (1975). Given the difficulty of predicting which offenders are the best targets, some argue for general incapacitation, claiming that higher levels of incapacitation will generally reduce crime even if we cannot know which offenders would have committed the extra crimes. Apart from the costs of this approach (both in human and in economic terms), it is doubtful that it works across all categories of crimes. For some crimes

(perhaps narcotics sales), new criminals may simply step forward to fill the positions vacated by those sentenced to prison.

3. *Economics and demographics.*   We could also explain imprisonment rates not as a product of deliberate policy but as a natural outcome of a slowdown in the economy and a corresponding increase in crime. Similarly, levels of imprisonment might be driven by demographics (such as the number of young males in the population at a given time). How would you go about testing these hypotheses? See Frank Zimring & Gordon Hawkins, The Scale of Imprisonment 119-136 (1991) (reviewing potential explanations for prison rates in the United States, including crime rates, public opinion, demographics, economics, and drug use).

4. *Politics and public opinion.*   Michael Tonry and others have argued that U.S. politics is uniquely pathological when it comes to crime. The political rhetoric in the United States has remained partisan and "tough on crime" for several generations. The debate has marginalized rehabilitation as a purpose of criminal sanctions and has suggested that prison is the only "real" sanction. What in particular about the U.S. political system produces these results? Sara Sun Beale traces the influence to the news media's focus on crime for purposes of attracting high ratings: the coverage affects public perceptions of the level of serious crime, and it shapes the political agenda that gets a positive response from the public. Beale, What's Law Got to Do with It? The Political, Social, Psychological and Other Non-legal Factors Influencing the Development of (Federal) Criminal Law, 1 Buff. Crim. L. Rev. 23 (1997). See also Katherine Beckett, Making Crime Pay: Law and Order in Contemporary American Politics (1997); Bert Useem, Raymond V. Liedka & Anne Morrison Piehl, Popular Support for the Prison Build-up, 5 Punishment & Soc'y 5 (2003).

5. *Social control or social cohesion.*   Some accounts of prison look beyond the instrumental reasons such as deterrence or incapacitation and emphasize the prison's place in struggles among social groups or in creating social solidarity. Some of these "social control" arguments draw generally on Marxist theory. For instance, Georg Rusche and Otto Kirchheimer, in Punishment and Social Structure (1939), suggest that the demands of the labor market shape the penal system and determine its transformation over time. In years of high employment, prisons must shrink to provide more workers for society, while in years of lower employment, prisons expand to maintain control over the unemployed. Cf. Christian Parenti, Lockdown America: Police and Prisons in the Age of Crisis (1998). Social theorist Michel Foucault's famous work, Discipline and Punish: The Birth of the Prison (1977) (excerpted in Chapter 1), describes the prison as one among many tools used in modern societies to exert more minute control over the human body as a way of making the masses more useful and docile.

"Social cohesion" theories, in contrast, stress the role of prison in creating agreement and shared ideologies across social groups rather than in controlling unruly social orders. Sociologist Émile Durkheim pointed to criminal law and punishment as a method of expressing and creating social consensus. As traditional communities give way to complex economic arrangements and societies that celebrate individual freedom, criminal law becomes an especially important source of social solidarity. See Émile Durkheim, The Division of Labor (1933); cf. Joseph Kennedy, Monstrous Offenders and the Search for Solidarity Through Modern Punishment, 51 Hastings L.J. 829 (2000). For an overview of the different perspectives that social theory brings to questions of punishment, see Jonathan Simon, Sanctioning Government: Explaining America's Severity Revolution, 56 U. Miami L. Rev. 217 (2001).

Earlier we considered social and political forces that could explain the remarkable growth in U.S. prisons over the past quarter-century. Now we examine the other side of the coin: what political forces or institutions might operate to *check* the growth of prisons?

One of those limiting forces might be money. Prisons are more expensive to build and operate than any other criminal sanction. In difficult economic times, as Marc Miller explains, budgetary considerations become especially powerful at the state and local levels of government:

> Criminal justice expenditures, and spending on corrections in particular, increasingly occupy a noticeable chunk of total state budgets. The growth of corrections budgets is so great that they have come to threaten other major categories of government expenditure. In California, for example, the corrections budget equaled 85 percent of the higher education budget in 1994, and by 1995 corrections had surpassed higher education. (A few years earlier, in the late 1980s, corrections cost only one-half the total spent on higher education.) [State] governments spend almost all of their funds on a handful of areas — education, health and welfare, transportation, housing, and crime. When criminal justice expenditures go up, they compete with these other basic services, not with the purchase of aircraft carriers or with foreign aid.
>
> [Policy] and budget changes are much harder to hide at the local government level. [The] smaller size of the budgets and political playing fields makes the budget [effect] more likely to be noticed for all budget expenditures. It is more likely that a county hospital or city clinic or board of education (in states where local funds support primary education) will feel that dollars put into corrections are dollars out of their pockets than will health care or educational representatives at state and federal levels. At higher levels of government, with bigger budgets and more abstract debates, a decision about prisons will rarely seem like a choice about schools or hospitals. At local levels, even modest proposed expenditures will be seen to compete with the full range of social services provided by local government. . . .

Marc Miller, Cells vs. Cops vs. Classrooms, in The Crime Conundrum 127 (Lawrence M. Friedman & George Fisher eds., 1997).

The following two statutes build on the observation that prison growth can be slowed if the relevant decision makers are forced to consider long-term budgets when making choices that would expand the use of prisons. Note the differences between the budgetary mechanisms at work in these two statutes. Can you devise similar strategies that might apply to other sentencing actors, such as judges or prosecutors? The following statistical study by David Greenberg and Valerie West examines the larger political and social context to identify factors limiting prison growth.

North Carolina General Statutes §120-36.7(d)

Every bill and resolution introduced in the General Assembly proposing any change in the law that could cause a net increase in the length of time for which persons are incarcerated or the number of persons incarcerated, whether by increasing penalties for violating existing laws, by criminalizing behavior, or by any other means, shall have attached to it at the time of its consideration by the General Assembly a fiscal note prepared by the Fiscal Research Division. The fiscal note shall be prepared in consultation with the Sentencing Policy and Advisory Commission and shall identify and estimate, for the first five fiscal years the proposed change would be in effect, all costs of the proposed net increase in incarceration, including capital outlay costs if the legislation would require increased cell space. . . . No comment or opinion shall be included in the fiscal note with regard to the merits of the measure for which the note is prepared. . . .

The sponsor of each bill or resolution to which this subsection applies shall present a copy of the bill or resolution with the request for a fiscal note to the Fiscal Research Division. . . . The Fiscal Research Division shall prepare the fiscal note and transmit it to the sponsor within two weeks after the request is made, unless the sponsor agrees to an extension of time. . . .

Kansas Statutes §74-9101(b)

(1) . . . In developing its recommended sentencing guidelines, the [Kansas sentencing] commission shall take into substantial consideration current sentencing and release practices and correctional resources, including but not limited to the capacities of local and state correctional facilities. . . .

(6) [The commission shall] advise and consult with the secretary of corrections and members of the legislature in developing a mechanism to link guidelines sentence practices with correctional resources and policies, including but not limited to the capacities of local and state correctional facilities. Such linkage shall include a review and determination of the impact of the sentencing guidelines on the state's prison population. . . .

(15) [The commission shall] produce official inmate population projections annually on or before six weeks following the date of receipt of the data from the department of corrections. When the commission's projections indicate that the inmate population will exceed available prison capacity within two years of the date of the projection, the commission shall identify and analyze the impact of specific options for (A) reducing the number of prison admissions; or (B) adjusting sentence lengths for specific groups of offenders. . . .

State Prison Populations and Their Growth, 1971-1991,
David F. Greenberg and Valerie West
39 Criminology 615 (2001)

. . . Between 1970 and midyear 2000, the federal and state imprisonment rate increased by a factor of almost five, from 98 per 100,000 to 476 per 100,000.

These national figures disguise much variation among states in the rates of growth. In Oklahoma, for example, the imprisonment rate in 1981 was just 17% higher than it had been ten years earlier, whereas in Montana, it was 196% higher. . . .

Previous research on state differences in imprisonment rates . . . has focused on a small number of explanatory variables — state crime rates, racial composition, and economic conditions (unemployment or labor force participation, income level). . . . In so doing, this work slights the policy choices that structure a state's response to its circumstances. Our work extends the theoretical scope of this body of research by [examining] the importance of a state's culture and political arrangements to policy outcomes in a number of different domains, such as welfare. . . .

|| *Theorizing Imprisonment Rates* ||

[We expect] institutional responses to law violations to be determined at least in part by the volume of crime in that state, but only in part. We expect a state's responses to be conditioned by its ability to finance their cost, and by its political culture. The anxieties and fears that lead residents and politicians to support the expanded use of imprisonment can be heightened or moderated by factors other than crime. . . .

Crime Rates. If imprisonment is a strategy for coping with crime, one would expect states with more crime to make more extensive use of imprisonment. We expect imprisonment to be more strongly related to violent crime than to property crime because violent crimes are considered more serious than are nonviolent crimes of acquisition. Defendants convicted of violent crimes are more likely to be sentenced to prison terms than are those convicted of stealing. Nevertheless, substantial numbers of prisoners are serving sentences for property offenses. . . . We thus consider the violent crime rate and the property crime rate as two measures of the "problem" to which the prison is supposedly a response. . . .

Drug law violations are expected to influence imprisonment rates because publicity about arrests contributes to public perceptions about the seriousness of crime as a social problem and thus influences public punitiveness. Drug arrestees also represent a caseload burden: if convicted, many drug arrestees will be sentenced to a term of imprisonment. . . .

Fiscal Constraint. Prison construction and maintenance are expensive. Costs of prison construction have been estimated at $23,000 to $54,000 per bed, and operating costs from $9500 to $39,000 per prisoner each year. . . . Less affluent states may have to restrict spending on criminal justice in order to repair potholes, plant trees, pay teachers, and shelter the homeless. For this reason, we predict a positive relationship between imprisonment rates and the state's capacity to tax its citizens and business enterprises.

Perceived Threat. Students of penality have argued that imprisonment can be a response to anxiety-provoking conditions other than crime. In particular, it may be targeted at "the dangerous classes" — populations perceived as threatening because of their economic circumstances, race, or ethnicity, independently of their involvement in crime. . . . We introduce the percentage of families below the poverty line as an alternative measure of the population that might be seen as having little to lose and who must, therefore, be dealt with through imprisonment.

The numerical overrepresentation of blacks in prison is high. Even though blacks make up about 12 percent of the population, slightly more than half of all new court commitments to prison are black, a rate that is approximately 6.5 times as high as that of whites. . . . By looking at the effect of a state's racial composition on the prison population controlling for crime rates, we should be able to clarify the relationship between race and imprisonment. . . .

Cultural Influences.   . . . Social structural theories of social control suggest that urbanized polities will make greater use of formal methods of control, such as courts and prisons, to make up for deficiencies in informal social control. The anonymity and heterogeneity of large urban populations linked by impersonal market transactions supposedly impair informal social control, leading to the compensatory strengthening of governmental control. Rural regions, on the other hand, are presumed to require less vigorous formal social control because they can rely on personal ties based on kinship and multiplex patterns of informal association. On this basis, one would expect imprisonment rates to be higher in states whose populations are highly urbanized. On the other hand, urban criminal courts may face especially heavy caseloads, necessitating more generous concessions in plea bargaining to induce guilty pleas. This should slow prison growth. Moreover, urban populations, exposed as they are to greater cultural diversity, should be more tolerant of rule breakers and, thus, less punitive. . . .

Historically, welfare benefits were instituted as alternatives to human institutions for poor and marginalized populations. . . . If imprisonment indeed reflects an exclusionary stance toward those who have broken the law, . . . it should be used with greater reluctance in those states that are relatively generous toward the poor by providing greater welfare benefits, [and] cuts in welfare should be accompanied by increases in imprisonment. . . .

Political Factors.   . . . We examine the influence of officeholders' party affiliation at the state level. We focus on the governor because it is the governor who prepares budgets, making decisions about prison construction that should ultimately impact on prison populations. It is also the governor who appoints parole board members. . . .

A number of policy analysts have attributed growth in prison populations to determinate sentencing legislation that severely restricts judicial discretion to impose a sentence and eliminates release on parole for prison inmates. [Ten] states adopted fixed sentencing legislation ending release on parole between the mid-1970s and mid-1980s. Because the adoption of determinate sentencing legislation was often accompanied by "get tough" rhetoric, one might expect that states with determinate sentencing legislation will have higher prison populations and experience more rapid growth in these rates. . . .

METHODS AND RESULTS

[We used a statistical technique known as regression analysis to measure the impact of each of these variables on a state's imprisonment rate between 1971 and 1991. We used a second model to estimate the impact of these variables on the *changes* in rates of imprisonment that each state experienced during these two decades.]

Consistent with public choice theory, states with high violent crime rates have higher levels of imprisonment. An increase in the violent crime rate of 1 per 100,000 is associated with an increase of .12 per 100,000 in the imprisonment rate, whereas the increase associated with the property crime rate is smaller and not statistically significant. An increase in the narcotics arrest rate of 1 per 100,000 increases the imprisonment rate by about .11 per 100,000.

As expected, states with higher revenues have higher prison populations. Although economic inequality and urbanization are unrelated to imprisonment, there are more people in prison in states with higher unemployment rates and where there is a higher percentage of blacks in the population. Other things being equal, an increase in the unemployment rate of 5% corresponds to an imprisonment rate that is higher by about 16.5 per 100,000. A state with a population that is 10% black will have an imprisonment rate higher than that of a state that has no blacks by . . . 91 per 100,000, a substantial amount. The presence of Latinos, however, does not raise imprisonment rates. . . .

Several measures of a state's political culture are related to its imprisonment rate. States that are more generous with welfare payments had lower prison populations. An increase of $30 per person in welfare spending is associated with an imprisonment rate that is smaller by about 19 per 100,000. . . .

In states where there were more conservatives, imprisonment rates were not only higher, but also grew more rapidly. . . . If cultural differences are associated with the South, they did not contribute to high rates of imprisonment growth; quite the contrary, growth rates were significantly slower in the South than elsewhere, so that by 1991, regional disparities in imprisonment rates were substantially smaller than in 1971. In other words, in recent years regions outside the South have been catching up to the South in imprisonment. . . .

Contrary to popular opinion, the adoption of determinate sentencing legislation did not increase imprisonment rates; it moderately reduced them. The adoption of these laws may have helped to placate a punitive public, reducing pressure on state officials to impose harsh sentences. [Perhaps] these laws were carefully crafted to be largely symbolic and, in many states, had little effect because prosecutors and judges took steps to minimize their impact.

Some of the most striking findings concern state economic and demographic characteristics. Unemployment was associated with higher rates of prison population growth, as was change in unemployment. Economic inequality was not. Growth in imprisonment rates was also related to the size of the black population and its increase. It cannot be stressed too strongly that the coefficients for unemployment and race are direct effects, with crime rates controlled, and so they cannot be explained away by claims that crime rates are higher where there is more unemployment or where more blacks live.

Consistent with much research showing that party control of state government has little or no impact on state policy and is unrelated to the liberalism or conservatism of the state's voters, the political party of a state's governor failed to make a significant contribution to prison populations or their growth. It appears that the political incentives for an expansive prison policy transcend party affiliations. States governed by Democrats responded to the crime issue no differently from states governed by Republicans. . . .

Our results are equally consistent with the presence and absence of racial discrimination. [A] positive relationship between percent black in a state and the state's imprisonment rate could occur in the absence of racial discrimination. [At the same time, our] results are consistent with the "racial threat" hypothesis. Blacks — black males in particular — appear to have become "symbolic assailants" whose presence in a city evokes fear of crime independently of the actual level of crime. . . . That the presence of Latinos is not associated with imprisonment rate growth indicates that it is not minorities in general, but blacks in particular, who are perceived as threatening. Our results also point to unemployment as a separate, distinct source of threat or anxiety. . . . We think that welfare is important to imprisonment not because it directly restrains legislators, prosecutors, and judges; rather, we see the comparative leniency in high-welfare states as reflecting a more general policy of avoiding excessively harsh treatment of the poor, who make up the bulk of criminal court defendants. . . .

NOTES

1. *Prisons and state budget cycles.*   From time to time, budgetary constraints restrict further prison expansions. For examples, see Robin Campbell, Dollars and Sentences: Legislators' Views on Prisons, Punishment, and the Budget Crisis (Vera Institute, July 2003, available at http://www.vera.org).

Traditional legislative debates do not make the connection between setting criminal penalties and funding adequate space in the prison. Some extraordinary debates, however, do underscore the connection, and yet legislators are still sometimes willing to change the penalties without funding the prisons that new sentencing laws will require. See Franklin Zimring, The New Politics of Criminal Justice: Of "Three Strikes," Truth-in-Sentencing, and Megan's Laws (Earl Warren Legal Institute, University of California–Berkeley, Dec. 8, 1999).

Sentencing commissions are considered one of the most important institutions in state government to highlight the connection between corrections budgets and sentencing rules. According to a 2003 survey by the National Association of Sentencing Commissions, 12 of the 19 responding states gave their commissions responsibility to create impact statements for at least some criminal justice bills after their introduction in the state legislature. Note the distinction, however, between a commission advocating a smaller prison system and a commission advocating a fully funded prison system.

2. *More on costs and benefits of prison.*   The balance between the costs and benefits of longer prison terms could shift if one considers as a benefit the

crimes prevented through detention. Economists have employed statistical techniques to estimate the number of crimes prevented and the monetary value of the harm that would have occurred if those crimes had happened. See Edwin W. Zedlewski, Making Confinement Decisions (National Institute of Justice, Research in Brief, 1987); Joanna Mehlhop Shepherd, Police, Prosecutors, Criminals, and Determinate Sentencing: The Truth About Truth-in-Sentencing Laws, 45 J.L. & Econ. 509 (2002) (estimating that sentencing laws requiring violent offenders to serve at least 85% of their prison sentences decrease murders by 16%, aggravated assaults by 12%, robberies by 24%, rapes by 12%, and larcenies by 3%; however, violent offenders shift to property crimes, meaning that burglaries increase by 20% and auto thefts by 15%). What types of data are used to make estimates of these sorts? What uncertainties are involved in constructing the estimates?

D. THE HUMAN EXPERIENCE OF PRISON

Part of understanding the nature of prison is to recognize the size of the institution and its functions over the years. The statistics and trends we have discussed thus far address these aspects, but they miss the profound human experience of prison. The offenders who fill prisons in large numbers, for long periods of time, are individuals who experience the daily routines and restrictions of life in prison. The victims of their crimes are individuals who remain aware of their stay in prison and (sometimes) of the moment of their release. The officers who run the prisons work under extraordinarily tough conditions.

The law surrounding conditions in prison is complex and deserves far more attention than we can offer here. See Michael B. Mushlin, Rights of Prisoners (2d ed. 1993). Instead, we aim for a more personal glimpse into prison life as a way to place the law of sentencing in context. In the following excerpt, Norval Morris presents a rewritten version of a diary, recording the mundane events in the day of an inmate, Sam Gutierrez, incarcerated in Stateville Prison in Illinois.

	The Contemporary Prison, 1965-Present,	
	Norval Morris	
	The Oxford History of the Prison: The Practice	
	of Punishment in Western Society	
	202, 203-211 (1998)	

... It is not easy to describe a day of monotony and boredom other than as monotonous and boring. Before I start on the diary, let me say this: if you expect the usual prison tale of constant violence, brutal guards, gang rapes, daily escape efforts, turmoil, and fearsome adventures, you will be deeply disappointed. ...

6:00 A.M.:

... As F House came to life, the noise began — radios, TVs, shouting from cell to cell — and so it would go on till night, with an occasional scream of rage or fear through the night. Tyrone and I did our best to keep out of each other's way in the space of nine feet by six in our cell while we used our toilet and washed and dressed and pulled up the blankets on our steel bunks. We change our outer clothes sometimes twice a week, sometimes once a week, and our socks and underwear every other day. If you have money, or influence, or a friend in the laundry, you can do better than this. Our dress in summer is blue jeans and a blue shirt or a white T-shirt; in winter we wear blue jeans, a blue shirt, and one of those heavy, lined, blue jackets. Our sartorial flourish is our sneakers, with Nike outranking Reebok and so on down the line; they cost a lot, but in this place they are worth it. . . .

6:30 A.M.:
F House began to be unlocked, with the loudspeaker from the tower guards bellowing, "Three and four galleries: in the tunnel for chow." I turned off the radio and flipped the light switch at the back of the cell, on and off, on and off, the flickering light being my request to the tower guard to open the door to this cell, which he does. . . .

Food is served cafeteria style. We pick up our trays and wait in line. The food is either waiting in bowls for us to pick up, as we file by, or is served onto our plates by the kitchen detail. Knives and forks and spoons are of plastic, not particularly useful for making weapons, though they are sometimes smuggled back to the cells and narrowed and sharpened for this purpose. . . .

They serve meals here, three times a day, to over two thousand prisoners each meal, 365 times a year, on a twelve-day repeating menu. I calculate that this comes to more than two million meals a year. I suppose I should expect it to be dull and lifeless food — and it is. But guys mostly tend to put on weight in prison; I know I do. The meals are not light on carbohydrates. The cartons of milk cannot be spoiled by our prison cooks, and I usually manage to collect two of them with whatever else is handed to me. I did this today.

After you get your food you walk back to the seating area, metal tables with six metal seats fixed to them. You have to be careful where you sit; there are "regulars" who sit together and expect this to be known. And, of course, the blacks and Hispanics don't welcome a white guy joining their tables. The prison is more than 90 percent black and Hispanic, but this causes no great problem — the whites tend to congregate with one another in the mess hall and in the yard. . . .

8:30 A.M.:
[I went to the yard to] get a workout, bench-pressing some weights. . . . The yard is of playing-field size and of rounded, triangular shape, with a rough baseball diamond, with other areas of grass and of packed earth, surrounded by a running track and a fence. Some sparse outdoor gym equipment is in one corner. There are two telephones, protected a little from the weather by steel surrounds; a small line formed. Guys ran around the track or walked around in twos or small groups. Five or six of us worked out on the equipment.

The telephones here and in F House are monitored, and every few minutes a voice interrupts telling you and whomever you are speaking to that this is a call from a "state correctional facility." And the time you are allowed for any one call is limited, depending on whatever the prison authorities have arranged with the telephone company. Of course, only collect calls can be made, so that no one outside has to talk to a prisoner on the telephone, and this makes the telephone expensive for the person you are calling, particularly long-distance calls.

10:30 A.M.:

[I showered after my workout.] The showers are dangerous places; gangs tend to shower together as a protective measure; only a very few prisoners shower alone and without security, as I do. I am known as a loner and dangerous to cross and tend therefore to be left alone. . . .

When you come to prison it is wise to leave all shyness behind. But I am not anxious for myself in the showers. Here in Stateville there aren't gang rapes or even rapes that I hear about, though they are reputed to take place occasionally, and they are certainly more frequent in the jails. . . . Prisoners taking showers need security from gang attacks, not from sexual attacks. Still, I suppose I am always a little anxious in the showers; I avoid being alone in the showers with any one or more who might have some particular reason to dislike me. Even if violence is not all that common, still there is often tension and anxiety and, I suppose, fear.

11:30 A.M.:

I looked for some semi-clean socks, got dressed, and started typing a letter. I was waiting for the call to lunch, though I hate the mess hall at lunchtime. It is chaos at lunch; the prisoners refuse to act "orderly," and the guards do not take the trouble to enforce order. The gang element is definitely in control. Nevertheless, to the sound of "Chow going out the door," I joined the mass of prisoners heading for the tunnel. . . .

1:00 P.M.:

I joined the "school" detail and with six others from F House went off to a course on computers run in the school area. Unlike all but a few prisoners in Stateville, I am a genuine high school graduate. [The] majority of my fellow prisoners in Stateville are functionally illiterate, and only a handful have any sort of a record of high school academic achievement. In earlier years in Stateville I worked in the furniture factory and in the tailor shop, earning more than I can earn at school; but the computer course interested me, and I applied for it and got it. I have now been in it for three months and am beginning to be able to write programs. The course is taught by an Indian who speaks strangely but knows what he is doing. It fills my afternoons, three days a week, two hours each day.

The better-educated have the pick of the jobs in Stateville. Though it is poorly paid, the library, particularly the law library, is probably the best job, passing prison time more swiftly than other prison jobs, having influence in the prison, and being left alone by the guards; but the computer class seems to me in some ways even better. In the distant years when I am free I may be able to use what I am learning about computer programming, but I doubt it; the point is that it helps to keep me alive here. . . .

3:30 P.M.:

Two guards escorted the school detail back to F House. I went back to my cell. Tyrone was showering, his work in the tailor shop finished. While he was away I turned on the TV. It is my set, but I cannot control what we watch, since his friends outside could afford to give him a set if he wanted it. So, if we are to share this cell, we have to strike some bargain about what we watch. I am fortunate; he mostly falls in with my preferences, and when he doesn't, I yield.

I've never watched so much TV as I do here. My set is a thirteen-inch RCA color TV. . . . The TV is on a little table we have rigged up beside the toilet; it is best watched by lying on one's bunk. Tyrone came in and lay down on his bunk without speaking. It's the best way; avoid useless chatter. I got sleepy and dozed. I was awakened by the mailman rapping on the bars of our cell and giving a small package of mail to Tyrone. Nothing for me; after a year or two in prison, incoming mail dries up to a trickle, even if you write regularly. . . .

7:00 P.M.:

[After dinner at 5:25, the evening count of inmates] went smoothly. Most everyone was by now back in the cell houses, and there were fewer places — schoolroom, gym, yard, industry, barbershop, kitchen, and so on — to be counted.

It was F House's turn for evening gym. Many, including Tyrone, went to throw basketballs around. I stayed in the cell and followed a batch of my favorite TV programs — they passed the time well for me, and I had had my exercise for that day.

And so the evening went: TV, reading a little in my computer training manual, TV again, and by nine o'clock Tyrone was back in the cell, and I got out of my clothes, except my undershorts, and got into my bunk. The central lights in F House stay on through the night. I wondered if perhaps we should put up some sort of curtains, and with that thought the day ended for me.

[Let me comment a bit on my diary.] Yesterday was unusually uneventful. Often in prison something happens to disturb the dull flow of the day. . . . There are times to go to the library and to the law library for those of us still appealing our convictions or pursuing prisoners' rights litigation, which they tell me is a good way to "do time" but rarely produces any success in the courts. And then there are the hard-to-avoid confrontations with some of the guards — leading to tickets and segregation and loss of "good time." Even worse are the collective punishments of the "lockdown," when cells are locked for all twenty-four hours, sometimes for months, with only one shower a week out of the cell; time moves even slower then.

Neither Tyrone nor I use prison hooch [alcohol] or drugs to get through the days and nights, but many prisoners do, and the disorder of prison, the frequency of punishments and of lockdowns, is increased because of it. Drugs, all drugs, are readily available at about twice their street price, payable inside or outside the prison. . . .

There are regular and intermittent shakedowns of all the cells and other areas for shanks and other contraband. It is a violent place, but most prisoners do their time without being victimized physically unless they are looking to prove something to themselves or unless they get into trouble with betting, or hooch, or drugs, or with the gangs.

[This diary] fails to capture the constant unhappiness of prison life and the constant sense of danger. [It] misses the relentless, slow-moving routine, the dull repetitiveness, the tension mixed with occasional flashes of fear and rage; it misses the consuming stupidity of living this way. I am sorry; it is not easy. . . .

NOTES

1. *Prisoners and correctional officers.*   The officers who maintain order in a prison have a complex relationship with the inmates they monitor every day. The stereotype of the brutal prison guard is a staple of literature and movies such as *Cool Hand Luke* (1967) and *The Shawshank Redemption* (1994). The following passage from a prison memoir (written by a former middle manager at a telephone company, convicted in Nevada for manslaughter) summarizes the nature of this relationship from the vantage point of the inmate:

> The sergeant glared down at the benches till the dawgs hushed. "Rule number one," he continued, "y'all got *nothin'* coming! Rules number two to two thousand—see rule number one." The sergeant paused to let us bask in this bit of penological cleverness.
> "My name is Sergeant Grafter. I am a correctional officer—not a fucking prison guard and not a cop. You will address me as 'C.O.' or 'Sergeant.' . . . cause you're *convicts!* Your job here is to lie, cheat, steal, extort, get tattoos, take drugs, sell drugs, shank, sock, fuck, and suck each other. Just don't let us catch you—that's *our* job." . . .
> "The warden and prison medical director have asked me to pass along a . . . health advisory. This prison has a combined HIV and hepatitis C infection rate of 60 percent. If you choose to just say yes, and use drugs, and you will— that's your job—then snort them, smoke them, or swallow them, but don't shoot them." Grafter irritably perused the rest of the memo before crushing it into a ball and tossing it over the rail. . . .
> "Finally, don't cross the red lines unless you like getting shot. Above all, *don't get caught!* We catch you, you got nothin' comin'."

Jimmy A. Lerner, You Got Nothing Coming: Notes from a Prison Fish 37-38 (2002).

The relationship looks different from the perspective of the correctional officer. Writer Ted Conover worked for a year as a correctional officer in New York's legendary Sing Sing prison; his account of that year emphasizes the combination of boredom and danger in the atmosphere: "I always thought of an assembly line in a poorly run explosives factory. Tedium, tedium, tedium, then—*bang*—you'd be missing your hands." Conover describes the tension between inmates and officers in these terms:

> A consequence of putting men in cells and controlling their movements is that they can do almost nothing for themselves. For their various needs they are dependent on one person, their gallery officer. Instead of feeling like a big, tough guard, the gallery officer at the end of the day often feels like a waiter serving a hundred tables or like the mother of a nightmarishly large brood of sullen, dangerous, and demanding children. When grown men are infantilized, most don't take to it nicely.
> That morning, I decided to count the number of times I said no before lunch. . . .

— CO, can you find out when my disciplinary hearing is?
— CO, can you call to see why my laundry bag didn't come back? . . .
— CO, do all you guys get your hair cut in the same place? (a joke) . . .
— CO, do you got any more state soap?
— CO, can I go on the W side and borrow a belt from my homey? I got
a visit. . . .

Not all of these were improper requests; but the others were mainly favors, to be done when I had spare time, which was seldom. You had to get good at saying no. . . .

Ted Conover, Newjack: Guarding Sing Sing 234-235, 250 (2000).

2. *Violence, gangs, and race in prison.*   One constant in the fictional and non-fictional accounts of prison life is violence and — more commonly — the threat of violence. In 2003 Congress passed the Prison Rape Elimination Act, which funds a study of sexual assaults in male and female prisons and creates preventive programs.

Many inmates, including female inmates, join gangs in prison for a sense of security, and the gangs tend to break down along racial lines and to deepen racial tensions in prisons. See American History X (1998). Jimmy Lerner's prison memoirs chronicle the racial tension at the center of prison life, observing that the correctional officers assigned cell mates on the basis of race: "Following some unwritten rule, he scrupulously placed blacks with the blacks, the white dawgs with the white dawgs."

Racial injustice in society spills over into the views of inmates about the legitimacy of their own punishment. Consider this classic passage from Eldridge Cleaver:

One thing that the judges, policemen, and administrators of prisons seem never to have understood, and for which they certainly do not make any allowances, is that Negro convicts, basically, rather than see themselves as criminals and perpetrators of misdeeds, look upon themselves as prisoners of war, the victims of a vicious, dog-eat-dog social system that is so heinous as to cancel out their own malefactions: in the jungle there is no right or wrong.
Rather than owing and paying a debt to society, Negro prisoners feel that they are being abused, that their imprisonment is simply another form of the oppression which they have known all their lives. Negro inmates feel that they are being robbed, that it is "society" that owes them, that should be paying them, a debt. America's penology does not take this into account. . . .

Eldridge Cleaver, Soul on Ice 58-59 (1968).

3. *Women in prison.*   The female prison population differs from the male in several respects. Women tend to be incarcerated for nonviolent offenses, such as prostitution and theft, or for drug crimes. Women tend to be economically worse off than male offenders. Drug usage of women admitted into state prisons is substantially higher than that of men. More women than men test HIV-positive upon admission, usually because of intravenous drug use or work in the sex industry.

Female inmates often enter prison with a different background from that of male prisoners. Almost 60% of female state prisoners have a history of physical or sexual abuse or both.

One late afternoon as we sit in [Delia's] room, she tells me that her stepfather had sexually molested her at the age of eleven. She hoped that by telling her mother the man would be thrown out of the house. Instead she was sent from her home to live with an aunt. At twelve, she had her first child. From that point on, her life revolved around a series of violent relationships with men.

Andi Rierden, The Farm: Life Inside a Women's Prison 81 (1997). Often the abuse continues in prison, as male correctional officers and other prison employees sexually assault female prisoners or coerce them into sexual relationships. See Human Rights Watch Women's Rights Project, Human Rights Watch, All Too Familiar: Sexual Abuse of Women in U.S. State Prisons (1996).

The most important differences between female and male inmates are related to reproduction and parenting. Five to 10% of women who enter prisons are pregnant, but only three prisons in the country permit women to spend time with their newborns.

Sixty-four percent of state inmates lived with their minor children prior to incarceration. In contrast to the children of male prisoners, the children of female inmates do not usually end up living with their other parent but with other close family members. Because of the smaller number of female prisons, women are often incarcerated far from their families. Not seeing their children during incarceration is difficult, but seeing them can be equally excruciating. The excerpt below is taken from the 1995 inmate handbook of the Edna Mahon Correctional Facility for Women:

> All visits will be conducted in a quiet, orderly and dignified manner. Handshaking, embracing and kissing by the immediate family members and close friends are permitted within the bounds of good taste at the beginning and at the end of the visit only. Hand holding, in full view, is the only body contact allowed between a visitor and their inmate during a visit. Visitors and inmates must sit facing each other. Visiting children must remain under the inmate's supervision. Failure to properly supervise visiting children will be cause to terminate the visit.

Kathryn Watterson, Women in Prison: Inside the Concrete Womb 215 (rev. ed. 1996). Visiting with children is particularly difficult:

> Two weeks in segregation, with no visitors, nothing but stone-cold walls, a window to a parking lot, a pot to pee in, and thoughts, thoughts, thoughts. . . . Two weeks later [BeBe] emerges from segregation, from the cell block of her mind, raw, humiliated, shamed. Her two children visit. They are very young, under ten. They still think they are visiting their mommy in the hospital. It is the lie a lot of inmates spin. BeBe prays they never learn the truth. "When will you be better, mommy?" they ask her. Soon babies, soon.

Rierden, The Farm at 125. For a fictionalized but realistic account of life in prison, see Olivia Goldsmith, Pen Pals (2002).

4. *Release.* Especially for inmates who have served long sentences, release is both joyful and stressful, according to an inmate:

> You just come out *bam.* . . . And you don't know how to deal with it. You don't have a family to go to, half the time. You don't have a home or a job. All this time you've been fantasizing about the way things are and the way things are going to be when you really have no way of knowing how they are. You can

imagine the shock. A lot of times the only thing left for a person to do is commit a new crime.

Besides that, prisons really help produce crime. You take away any human being and put them out of contact and take away all their responsibility and you're denying them an opportunity to grow. So to expect a person to leave here being grown and responsible, you're making an impossible demand, because all her sense of responsibility and her ability to interact has been brutalized.

To deal with society you have to interact with society. We only know how to interact with one society — and that's prison society.

Watterson, Women in Prison at 311.

E. LIMITING IMPRISONMENT UNDER THE EIGHTH AMENDMENT

The Supreme Court and lower courts have spent much effort explicating the meaning of the Eighth Amendment to guide states in imposing the death penalty. To a lesser extent, courts interpreting the Eighth Amendment have also restricted the imposition of other sentences, especially imprisonment. A series of Supreme Court cases sets out the type of proportionality review needed to assess the constitutionality of a prison sentence.

|| *John Albert Ewing v. California* ||
538 U.S. 11 (2003)

O'CONNOR, J.

In this case, we decide whether the Eighth Amendment prohibits the State of California from sentencing a repeat felon to a prison term of 25 years to life under the State's "Three Strikes and You're Out" law.

I

California's three strikes law reflects a shift in the State's sentencing policies toward incapacitating and deterring repeat offenders who threaten the public safety. The law was designed "to ensure longer prison sentences and greater punishment for those who commit a felony and have been previously convicted of serious and/or violent felony offenses." Cal. Penal Code §667(b). . . .

California's current three strikes law consists of two virtually identical statutory schemes designed to increase the prison terms of repeat felons. When a defendant is convicted of a felony, and he has previously been convicted of one or more prior felonies defined as "serious" or "violent" in Cal. Penal Code Ann. §§667.5 and 1192.7, sentencing is conducted pursuant to the three strikes law. . . . If the defendant has one prior "serious" or "violent" felony conviction, he must be sentenced to twice the term otherwise provided as punishment for the current felony conviction. If the defendant has two or more prior "serious" or "violent" felony convictions, he must receive an indeterminate term of life imprisonment. Defendants sentenced to life under the three strikes law become eligible for parole on a date calculated by reference to a "minimum term," which is the greater of (a) three times the term otherwise provided for the current conviction, (b) 25 years, or (c) the term determined by the court pursuant to §1170 for the underlying conviction, including any enhancements.

Under California law, certain offenses may be classified as either felonies or misdemeanors. These crimes are known as "wobblers." Some crimes that would otherwise be misdemeanors become "wobblers" because of the defendant's prior record. For example, petty theft, a misdemeanor, becomes a "wobbler" when the defendant has previously served a prison term for committing specified theft-related crimes. Other crimes, such as grand theft, are "wobblers" regardless of the defendant's prior record. Both types of "wobblers" are triggering offenses under the three strikes law only when they are treated as felonies. Under California law, a "wobbler" is presumptively a felony and remains a felony except when the discretion is actually exercised to make the crime a misdemeanor.

In California, prosecutors may exercise their discretion to charge a "wobbler" as either a felony or a misdemeanor. [Trial] courts may avoid imposing a three strikes sentence in two ways: first, by reducing "wobblers" to misdemeanors (which do not qualify as triggering offenses), and second, by vacating allegations of prior "serious" or "violent" felony convictions.

On parole from a 9-year prison term, petitioner Gary Ewing walked into the pro shop of the El Segundo Golf Course in Los Angeles County on March 12, 2000. He walked out with three golf clubs, priced at $399 apiece, concealed in his pants leg. A shop employee, whose suspicions were aroused when he observed Ewing limp out of the pro shop, telephoned the police. The police apprehended Ewing in the parking lot.

Ewing is no stranger to the criminal justice system. In 1984, at the age of 22, he pleaded guilty to theft. The court sentenced him to six months in jail (suspended), three years' probation, and a $300 fine. In 1988, he was convicted of felony grand theft auto and sentenced to one year in jail and three years' probation. After Ewing completed probation, however, the sentencing court reduced the crime to a misdemeanor, permitted Ewing to withdraw his guilty plea, and dismissed the case. In 1990, he was convicted of petty theft with a prior and sentenced to 60 days in the county jail and three years' probation. In 1992, Ewing was convicted of battery and sentenced to 30 days in the county jail and two years' summary probation. One month later, he was convicted of theft and sentenced to 10 days in the county jail and 12 months' probation. In January 1993, Ewing was convicted of burglary and sentenced to 60 days in the county jail and one year's summary probation. In February 1993, he was convicted of possessing drug paraphernalia and sentenced to six months in the county jail and three years' probation. In July 1993, he was convicted of appropriating lost property and sentenced to 10 days in the county jail and two years' summary probation. In September 1993, he was convicted of unlawfully possessing a firearm and trespassing and sentenced to 30 days in the county jail and one year's probation.

In October and November 1993, Ewing committed three burglaries and one robbery at a Long Beach, California, apartment complex over a 5-week period. [During the robbery], Ewing accosted a victim in the mailroom of the apartment complex. Ewing claimed to have a gun and ordered the victim to hand over his wallet. When the victim resisted, Ewing produced a knife and forced the victim back to the apartment itself. While Ewing rifled through the bedroom, the victim fled the apartment screaming for help. Ewing absconded with the victim's money and credit cards. . . . A jury convicted Ewing of first-degree robbery and three counts of residential burglary. Sentenced to nine years and eight months in prison, Ewing was paroled in 1999.

Only 10 months later, Ewing stole the golf clubs at issue in this case. He was charged with, and ultimately convicted of, one count of felony grand theft of personal property in excess of $400. As required by the three strikes law, the prosecutor formally alleged, and the trial court later found, that Ewing had been convicted previously of four serious or violent felonies for the three burglaries and the robbery in the Long Beach apartment complex. . . .

Before sentencing Ewing, the trial court took note of his entire criminal history, including the fact that he was on parole when he committed his latest offense. . . . As a newly convicted felon with two or more "serious" or "violent" felony convictions in his past, Ewing was sentenced under the three strikes law to 25 years to life. . . .

II

The Eighth Amendment, which forbids cruel and unusual punishments, contains a narrow proportionality principle that applies to noncapital sentences. We have most recently addressed the proportionality principle as applied to terms of years in a series of cases beginning with Rummel v. Estelle, 445 U.S. 263 (1980).

In *Rummel,* we held that it did not violate the Eighth Amendment for a State to sentence a three-time offender to life in prison with the possibility of parole. Like Ewing, Rummel was sentenced to a lengthy prison term under a recidivism statute. Rummel's two prior offenses were a 1964 felony for "fraudulent use of a credit card to obtain $80 worth of goods or services," and a 1969 felony conviction for "passing a forged check in the amount of $28.36." His triggering offense was a conviction for felony theft— "obtaining $120.75 by false pretenses."

This Court ruled that having twice imprisoned him for felonies, Texas was entitled to place upon Rummel the onus of one who is simply unable to bring his conduct within the social norms prescribed by the criminal law of the State. The recidivism statute is nothing more than a societal decision that when such a person commits yet another felony, he should be subjected to the admittedly serious penalty of incarceration for life, subject only to the State's judgment as to whether to grant him parole. We noted that this Court has on occasion stated that the Eighth Amendment prohibits imposition of a sentence that is grossly disproportionate to the severity of the crime. But outside the context of capital punishment, successful challenges to the proportionality of particular sentences have been exceedingly rare. Although we stated that the proportionality principle would "come into play in the extreme example . . . if a legislature made overtime parking a felony punishable by life imprisonment," we held that the mandatory life sentence imposed upon this petitioner does not constitute cruel and unusual punishment under the Eighth and Fourteenth Amendments. . . .

Three years after *Rummel,* in Solem v. Helm, 463 U.S. 277, 279 (1983), we held that the Eighth Amendment prohibited "a life sentence without possibility of parole for a seventh nonviolent felony." The triggering offense in *Solem* was uttering a "no account" check for $100. We . . . explained that three factors may be relevant to a determination of whether a sentence is so disproportionate that it violates the Eighth Amendment: "(i) the gravity of the offense and the harshness of the penalty; (ii) the sentences imposed on other criminals in the same jurisdiction; and (iii) the sentences imposed for commission of the same crime in other jurisdictions."

Applying these factors in *Solem,* we struck down the defendant's sentence of life without parole. We specifically noted the contrast between that sentence and the sentence in *Rummel,* pursuant to which the defendant was eligible for parole. Indeed, we explicitly declined to overrule *Rummel.* . . .

Eight years after *Solem,* we grappled with the proportionality issue again in Harmelin v. Michigan, 501 U.S. 957 (1991). *Harmelin* was not a recidivism case, but rather involved a first-time offender convicted of possessing 672 grams of cocaine. He was sentenced to life in prison without possibility of parole. A majority of the Court rejected Harmelin's claim that his sentence was so grossly disproportionate that it violated the Eighth Amendment. The Court, however, could not agree on why his proportionality argument failed. Justice Scalia, joined by the Chief Justice, wrote that the proportionality principle was "an aspect of our death penalty jurisprudence, rather than a generalizable aspect of Eighth Amendment law." He would thus have declined to apply gross disproportionality principles except in reviewing capital sentences.

Justice Kennedy, joined by two other Members of the Court, concurred in part and concurred in the judgment. Justice Kennedy specifically recognized that "the Eighth Amendment proportionality principle also applies to noncapital sentences." He then identified four principles of proportionality review—"the primacy of the legislature, the variety of legitimate penological schemes, the nature of our federal system, and the requirement that proportionality review be guided by objective factors"—that inform the final one: "The Eighth Amendment does not require strict proportionality between crime and sentence. Rather, it forbids only extreme sentences that are 'grossly disproportionate' to the crime." . . .

The proportionality principles in our cases . . . guide our application of the Eighth Amendment in the new context [of California's three strikes law] that we are called upon to consider.

For many years, most States have had laws providing for enhanced sentencing of repeat offenders. Yet between 1993 and 1995, three strikes laws effected a sea change in criminal sentencing throughout the Nation. These laws responded to widespread public concerns about crime by targeting the class of offenders who pose the greatest threat to public safety: career criminals. . . .

Throughout the States, legislatures enacting three strikes laws made a deliberate policy choice that individuals who have repeatedly engaged in serious or violent criminal behavior, and whose conduct has not been deterred by more conventional approaches to punishment, must be isolated from society in order to protect the public safety. Though three strikes laws may be relatively new, our tradition of deferring to state legislatures in making and implementing such important policy decisions is longstanding.

Our traditional deference to legislative policy choices finds a corollary in the principle that the Constitution does not mandate adoption of any one penological theory. A sentence can have a variety of justifications, such as incapacitation, deterrence, retribution, or rehabilitation. Some or all of these justifications may play a role in a State's sentencing scheme. Selecting the sentencing rationales is generally a policy choice to be made by state legislatures, not federal courts.

When the California Legislature enacted the three strikes law, it made a judgment that protecting the public safety requires incapacitating criminals who have already been convicted of at least one serious or violent crime. Nothing in the Eighth Amendment prohibits California from making that choice. To the contrary, our cases establish that States have a valid interest in deterring and segregating habitual criminals. Recidivism has long been recognized as a legitimate basis for increased punishment.

California's justification is no pretext. Recidivism is a serious public safety concern in California and throughout the Nation. According to a recent report, approximately 67 percent of former inmates released from state prisons were charged with at least one "serious" new crime within three years of their release. See U.S. Dept. of Justice, Bureau of Justice Statistics, Special Report: Recidivism of Prisoners Released in 1994, p. 1 (June 2002). In particular, released property offenders like Ewing had higher recidivism rates than those released after committing violent, drug, or public-order offenses. . . .

In 1996, when the *Sacramento Bee* studied 233 three strikes offenders in California, it found that they had an aggregate of 1,165 prior felony convictions, an average of 5 apiece. The prior convictions included 322 robberies and 262 burglaries. About 84 percent of the 233 three strikes offenders had been convicted of at least one violent crime. In all, they were responsible for 17 homicides, 7 attempted slayings, and 91 sexual assaults and child molestations. . . .

The State's interest in deterring crime also lends some support to the three strikes law. . . . Four years after the passage of California's three strikes law, the recidivism rate of parolees returned to prison for the commission of a new crime dropped by nearly 25 percent. California Dept. of Justice, Office of the Attorney General, "Three Strikes and You're Out" — Its Impact on the California Criminal Justice System After Four Years 10 (1998). Even more dramatically:

> an unintended but positive consequence of "Three Strikes" has been the impact on parolees leaving the state. More California parolees are now leaving the state than parolees from other jurisdictions entering California. This striking turnaround started in 1994. It was the first time more parolees left the state than entered since 1976. This trend has continued and in 1997 more than 1,000 net parolees left California.

To be sure, California's three strikes law has sparked controversy. Critics have doubted the law's wisdom, cost-efficiency, and effectiveness in reaching its goals. This criticism is appropriately directed at the legislature, which has primary responsibility for making the difficult policy choices that underlie any criminal sentencing scheme. We do not sit as a "superlegislature" to second-guess these policy choices. It is enough that the State of California has a reasonable basis for believing that dramatically enhanced sentences for habitual felons advances the goals of its criminal justice system in any substantial way.

III

... Against this backdrop, we consider Ewing's claim that his three strikes sentence of 25 years to life is unconstitutionally disproportionate to his offense of "shoplifting three golf clubs." We first address the gravity of the offense compared to the harshness of the penalty. At the threshold, we note that Ewing incorrectly frames the issue. The gravity of his offense was not merely "shoplifting three golf clubs." Rather, Ewing was convicted of felony grand theft for stealing nearly $1,200 worth of merchandise after previously having been convicted of at least two "violent" or "serious" felonies. Even standing alone, Ewing's theft should not be taken lightly. . . . Theft of $1,200 in property is a felony under federal law, 18 U.S.C. §641, and in the vast majority of States.

That grand theft is a "wobbler" under California law is of no moment. Though California courts have discretion to reduce a felony grand theft charge to a misdemeanor, it remains a felony for all purposes unless and until the trial court imposes a misdemeanor sentence [because] the rehabilitation of the convicted defendant either does not require or would be adversely affected by, incarceration in a state prison as a felon. . . .

In weighing the gravity of Ewing's offense, we must place on the scales not only his current felony, but also his long history of felony recidivism. Any other approach would fail to accord proper deference to the policy judgments that find expression in the legislature's choice of sanctions. . . . To give full effect to the State's choice of this legitimate penological goal, our proportionality review of Ewing's sentence must take that goal into account.

. . . To be sure, Ewing's sentence is a long one. But it reflects a rational legislative judgment, entitled to deference, that offenders who have committed serious or violent felonies and who continue to commit felonies must be incapacitated. . . . Ewing's is not the rare case in which a threshold comparison of the crime committed and the sentence imposed leads to an inference of gross disproportionality. We hold that Ewing's sentence of 25 years to life in prison, imposed for the offense of felony grand theft under the three strikes law, is not grossly disproportionate and therefore does not violate the Eighth Amendment's prohibition on cruel and unusual punishments. . . .

SCALIA, J., concurring.

[The] Eighth Amendment's prohibition of "cruel and unusual punishments" was aimed at excluding only certain *modes* of punishment, and was not a guarantee against disproportionate sentences. . . . Proportionality — the notion that the punishment should fit the crime — is inherently a concept tied to the penological goal of retribution. It becomes difficult even to speak intelligently of "proportionality," once deterrence and rehabilitation are given significant weight — not to mention giving weight to the purpose of California's three strikes law: incapacitation. In the present case, the game is up once the plurality has acknowledged that "the Constitution does not mandate adoption of any one penological theory." . . . That acknowledgment having been made, it no longer suffices merely to assess the gravity of the offense compared to the harshness of the penalty . . . ; that classic description of the proportionality principle (alone and in itself quite resistant to policy-free, legal analysis) now becomes merely the "first" step of the inquiry. . . . Having completed that step (by a discussion which, in all fairness, does not convincingly establish that 25-years-to-life is a "proportionate" punishment for stealing three golf clubs), the plurality must then *add* an analysis to show that "Ewing's sentence is justified by the State's public-safety interest in incapacitating and deterring recidivist felons." . . .

Which indeed it is — though why that has anything to do with the principle of proportionality is a mystery. Perhaps the plurality should revise its terminology, so that what it reads into the Eighth Amendment is not the unstated proposition that all punishment should be reasonably proportionate to the gravity of the offense, but rather the unstated proposition that all punishment should reasonably pursue the multiple purposes of the criminal law. That formulation would make it clearer than ever, of course, that the plurality is not applying law but evaluating policy. . . .

STEVENS, J., dissenting.

. . . The Eighth Amendment succinctly prohibits "excessive" sanctions. See U.S. Const., Amdt. 8 ("Excessive bail shall not be required, nor excessive fines imposed, nor cruel and unusual punishments inflicted"). Faithful to the Amendment's text, this Court has held that the Constitution directs judges to apply their best judgment in determining the proportionality of fines, bail, and other forms of punishment, including the imposition of a death sentence, see, e.g., Coker v. Georgia, 433 U.S. 584 (1977). It would be anomalous indeed to suggest that the Eighth Amendment makes proportionality review applicable in the context of bail and fines but not in the context of other forms of punishment, such as imprisonment. . . .

Throughout most of the Nation's history — before guideline sentencing became so prevalent — federal and state trial judges imposed specific sentences pursuant to grants of authority that gave them uncabined discretion within broad ranges. . . . In exercising their discretion, sentencing judges wisely employed a proportionality principle that took into account all of the justifications for punishment — namely, deterrence, incapacitation, retribution and rehabilitation. . . . Likewise, I think it clear that the Eighth Amendment's prohibition of "cruel and unusual punishments" expresses a broad and basic proportionality principle that takes into account all of the justifications for penal sanctions. It is this broad proportionality principle that would preclude reliance on any of the justifications for punishment to support, for example, a life sentence for overtime parking. Accordingly, I respectfully dissent.

BREYER, J., dissenting. . . .

[Courts] faced with a "gross disproportionality" claim must first make "a threshold comparison of the crime committed and the sentence imposed." *Harmelin,* 501 U.S., at 1005 (Kennedy, J., concurring). If a claim crosses that threshold — itself a *rare* occurrence — then the court should compare the sentence at issue to other sentences imposed on other criminals in the same, or in other, jurisdictions. The comparative analysis will validate or invalidate an initial judgment that a sentence is grossly disproportionate to a crime. . . . I believe that the case before us is a "rare" case — one in which a court can say with reasonable confidence that the punishment is "grossly disproportionate" to the crime.

Ewing's claim crosses the gross disproportionality "threshold." [Precedent] makes clear that Ewing's sentence raises a serious disproportionality question. Ewing is a recidivist. Hence the two cases most directly in point are those in which the Court considered the constitutionality of recidivist sentencing: *Rummel* and *Solem*. Ewing's claim falls between these two cases. It is stronger than the claim presented in *Rummel*, where the Court upheld a recidivist's sentence as constitutional. It is weaker than the claim presented in *Solem*, where the Court struck down a recidivist sentence as unconstitutional.

Three kinds of sentence-related characteristics define the relevant comparative spectrum: (a) the length of the prison term in real time, i.e., the time that the offender is likely actually to spend in prison; (b) the sentence-triggering criminal conduct, i.e., the offender's actual behavior or other offense-related circumstances; and (c) the offender's criminal history. . . .

In *Rummel*, the Court held constitutional (a) a sentence of life imprisonment *with parole available within 10 to 12 years*, (b) for the offense of obtaining $120 by false pretenses, (c) committed by an offender with two prior felony convictions (involving small amounts of money). . . . In *Solem*, the Court held unconstitutional (a) a sentence of life imprisonment *without parole*, (b) for the crime of writing a $100 check on a nonexistent bank account, (c) committed by an offender with six prior felony convictions (including three for burglary). . . . Which of the three pertinent comparative factors made the constitutional difference? . . .

The one critical factor that explains the difference in the outcome is the length of the likely prison term measured in real time. In *Rummel*, where the Court upheld the sentence, the state sentencing statute authorized parole for the offender, Rummel, after 10 or 12 years. In *Solem*, where the Court struck down the sentence, the sentence required the offender, Helm, to spend the rest of his life in prison.

Now consider the present case. The third factor, *offender characteristics* — i.e., prior record — does not differ significantly here from that in *Solem*. Ewing's prior record consists of four prior felony convictions (involving three burglaries, one with a knife) contrasted with Helm's six prior felony convictions (including three burglaries, though none with weapons). The second factor, *offense behavior*, is worse than that in *Solem*, but only to a degree. It would be difficult to say that the actual behavior itself here (shoplifting) differs significantly from that at issue in *Solem* (passing a bad check) or in *Rummel* (obtaining money through false pretenses). Rather the difference lies in the *value* of the goods obtained. That difference, measured in terms of the most relevant feature (loss to the victim, i.e., wholesale value) and adjusted for the irrelevant feature of inflation, comes down (in 1979 values) to about $379 here compared with $100 in *Solem*, or (in 1973 values) to $232 here compared with $120.75 in *Rummel*. . . .

The difference in *length* of the real prison term — the first, and critical, factor in *Solem* and *Rummel* — is considerably more important. Ewing's sentence here amounts, in real terms, to at least 25 years without parole or good-time credits. That sentence is considerably shorter than Helm's sentence in *Solem*, which amounted, in real terms, to life in prison. Nonetheless Ewing's real prison term is more than twice as long as the term at issue in *Rummel*, which amounted, in real terms, to at least 10 or 12 years. And, Ewing's sentence, unlike Rummel's (but like Helm's sentence in *Solem*), is long enough to consume the productive remainder of almost any offender's life. (It means that Ewing himself, seriously ill when sentenced at age 38, will likely die in prison.) The upshot is that the length of the real prison term — the factor that explains the *Solem/Rummel* difference in outcome — places Ewing closer to *Solem* than to *Rummel*. . . .

Believing Ewing's argument a strong one, sufficient to pass the threshold, I turn to the comparative analysis. A comparison of Ewing's sentence with other sentences requires answers to two questions. First, how would other jurisdictions (or California at other times, i.e., without the three strikes penalty) punish the *same offense conduct?* Second, upon what other conduct would other jurisdictions (or California) impose the *same prison term?* Moreover, since hypothetical punishment is beside the point, the relevant prison time, for comparative purposes, is *real* prison time, i.e., the time that an offender must *actually serve.* . . .

As to California itself, we know the following: First, between the end of World War II and 1994 (when California enacted the three strikes law, . . .), *no one* like Ewing could have served more than *10* years in prison. . . . Second, statistics suggest that recidivists *of all sorts* convicted during that same time period in California served a small fraction of Ewing's real-time sentence. On average, recidivists served three to four additional (recidivist-related) years in prison, with 90 percent serving less than an additional real seven to eight years. Third, we know that California has reserved, and still reserves, Ewing-type prison time, i.e., at least 25 real years in prison, for criminals convicted of crimes far worse than was Ewing's. Statistics for the years 1945 to 1981, for example, indicate that typical (nonrecidivist) male first-degree murderers served between 10 and 15 real years in prison, with 90 percent of all such murderers serving less than 20 real years. . . .

As to other jurisdictions, we know the following: The United States, bound by the federal Sentencing Guidelines, would impose upon a recidivist, such as Ewing, a sentence that, in any ordinary case, would not exceed 18 months in prison. USSG §2B1.1(a) (assuming a base offense level of 6, a criminal history of VI, and no mitigating or aggravating adjustments). The Guidelines, based in part upon a study of some 40,000 actual federal sentences . . . reserve a Ewing-type sentence for Ewing-type *recidivists* who currently commit such crimes as murder, §2A1.2; air piracy, §2A5.1; robbery (involving the discharge of a firearm, serious bodily injury, and about $1 million), §2B3.1; drug offenses involving more than, for example, 20 pounds of heroin, §2D1.1; aggravated theft of more than $100 million, §2B1.1; and other, similar offenses. . . .

[We] do not have before us information about actual time served by Ewing-type offenders in other States. We do know, however, that the law would make it legally impossible for a Ewing-type offender to serve more than 10 years in prison in 33 jurisdictions, as well as the federal courts, . . . more than 15 years in 4 other States, . . . and more than 20 years in 4 additional States, . . . In nine other States, the law *might* make it legally possible to impose a sentence of 25 years or more, [but that] does not mean that judges have actually done so. . . .

The upshot is that comparison of other sentencing practices, both in other jurisdictions and in California at other times (or in respect to other crimes), validates what an initial threshold examination suggested. . . . Outside the California three strikes context, Ewing's recidivist sentence is virtually unique in its harshness for his offense of conviction, and by a considerable degree.

This is not the end of the matter. [It] is important to consider whether special criminal justice concerns related to California's three strikes policy might justify including Ewing's theft within the class of triggering criminal conduct (thereby imposing a severe punishment), even if Ewing's sentence would otherwise seem disproportionately harsh.

I can find no such special criminal justice concerns that might justify this sentence. The most obvious potential justification for bringing Ewing's theft within the ambit of the statute is administrative. California must draw some kind of workable line between conduct that will trigger, and conduct that will not trigger, a "three strikes" sentence. . . . The administrative line that the statute draws separates "felonies" from "misdemeanors." [However], California uses those words in a way unrelated to the seriousness of offense conduct in a set of criminal statutes called "wobblers," . . . one of which is at issue in this case. . . .

"Wobbler" statutes cover a wide variety of criminal behavior, ranging from assault with a deadly weapon, §245, vehicular manslaughter, §193(c)(1), and money laundering, §186.10(a), to the defacement of property with graffiti, §594(b)(2)(A), or stealing more than $100 worth of chickens, nuts, or avocados, §487(b)(1)(A); §489. Some of this behavior is obviously less serious, even if engaged in twice, than other criminal conduct that California statutes classify as pure misdemeanors. . . .

There is no obvious reason why the statute could not enumerate, consistent with its purposes, the relevant triggering crimes. Given that possibility and given the anomalies that result from California's chosen approach, I do not see how California can justify on *administrative* grounds a sentence as seriously disproportionate as Ewing's.

. . . Given the omission of vast categories of property crimes—including grand theft (unarmed)—from the "strike" definition, one cannot argue, on *property-crime-related incapacitation grounds,* for inclusion of Ewing's crime among the triggers.

. . . No one argues for Ewing's inclusion within the ambit of the three strikes statute on grounds of "retribution." [I]n terms of "deterrence," Ewing's 25-year term amounts to overkill. And "rehabilitation" is obviously beside the point. The upshot is that, in my view, the State cannot find in its three strikes law a special criminal justice need sufficient to rescue a sentence that other relevant considerations indicate is unconstitutional. . . .

People v. Leon Miller
781 N.E.2d 300 (Ill. 2002)

FITZGERALD, J.

Defendant, Leon Miller, a 15-year-old juvenile, was charged with two counts of first degree murder based upon accountability. Defendant was transferred to the criminal division of the Cook County circuit court and prosecuted as an adult. Following a jury trial, defendant was convicted of both counts, and the State requested that the circuit court sentence defendant to natural life imprisonment under the multiple-murder provision of the Unified Code of Corrections. The circuit court declined to impose the statutorily mandated sentence, holding that application of the statute to defendant would offend the proportionate penalties clause of the Illinois Constitution (Ill. Const. 1970, art. I, §11) and the eighth amendment of the United States Constitution. Instead, the circuit court sentenced defendant to a term of 50 years in prison. The State appealed directly to this court. . . .

According to defendant, on the night of the murders, Arthur Beckom and Kentrell Stoutmire observed people walking through their neighborhood that they believed belonged to a rival gang. Beckom and Stoutmire approached defendant, who was standing outside on a corner in the neighborhood, and asked him to stand as a lookout. Defendant saw that both Beckom and Stoutmire had guns in their possession, and although defendant never handled or touched the guns, he agreed to stand as a lookout. One minute later, Beckom and Stoutmire fired gunshots in the direction of [Tommy Jones and Keith Alexander], who both died as a result of their injuries. Once the shooting began, defendant ran to his girlfriend's house.

Four individuals were charged for their participation in the shooting. The first degree murder indictment charged Stoutmire and Beckom as the alleged shooters and defendant and another 15-year-old male, Douglas Baskerville, for their participation as lookouts. At separate jury trials, Beckom and Baskerville were acquitted. Stoutmire, who was 17 years old at the time of the murders, was convicted and sentenced to natural life in prison. Defendant was also convicted of the murders. At sentencing, however, [Miller] argued that a sentence of natural life imprisonment, pursuant to the multiple-murder sentencing statute, violated the proportionate penalties clause of the Illinois Constitution, the prohibition against cruel and unusual punishment contained within the federal constitution, as well as international law, which prohibits the imposition of a natural life sentence on a juvenile. Conversely, the State argued that the circuit court was obligated by the statute to impose a sentence of natural life imprisonment.

At the conclusion of the sentencing hearing, the circuit court discussed its inability to sentence defendant pursuant to the terms of the multiple-murder sentencing statute:

> I have from the moment that the Jury came back with their findings been very concerned about what this meant [to this defendant] as a 15-year-old child, what this meant to society at large, to be part of a society where a 15-year-old child on a theory of accountability only, passive accountability, would suffer a sentence of life in the Penitentiary without the possibility of parole. . . . I feel that it is clear that in my mind this is blatantly unfair and highly unconscionable, and let me state that I do not believe for a second that Mr. Miller is innocent of these charges. . . . I am concerned that a person under the age of 18 under Illinois law can do everything that John Gacy did, can torture and abuse and murder over 30 people, and would be in the same boat as [defendant] right now looking at a sentence of a minimum and maximum of life without the possibility of parole. . . . I have a 15-year-old child who was passively acting as a look-out for other people, never picked up a gun, never had much more than — perhaps less than a minute — to contemplate what this entire incident is about, and he is in the same situation as a serial killer for sentencing purposes.

... Defendant was sentenced to a term of 50 years' imprisonment.

[Our] review begins with the presumption that the statute is constitutional. Because of this presumption, the party challenging the statute bears the burden of showing its invalidity. A circuit court's finding that a statute is unconstitutional is reviewed de novo.

The multiple-murder sentencing statute provides, in pertinent part:

> [For] first degree murder . . . the court shall sentence the defendant to a term of natural life imprisonment when the death penalty is not imposed if the defendant . . . is a person who, at the time of the commission of the murder, had attained the age of 17 or more and is found guilty of murdering an individual under 12 years of age; or, irrespective of the defendant's age at the time of the commission of the offense, is found guilty of murdering more than one victim.

730 ILCS 5/5-8-1(a)(1)(c)(ii).

We have repeatedly recognized that the legislature has discretion to prescribe penalties for defined offenses. The legislature's discretion necessarily includes the power to prescribe mandatory sentences, even if these mandatory sentences restrict the judiciary's discretion in imposing sentences. However, the power to impose sentences is not without limitation; the penalty must satisfy constitutional constrictions. . . .

The State . . . argues that Illinois courts have previously upheld the constitutionality of the multiple-murder sentencing statute as applied to juveniles against proportionate penalty challenges. See People v. Cooks, 648 N.E.2d 190 (Ill. App. Ct. 1995) (holding that the multiple-murder sentencing statute did not violate the United States or Illinois Constitutions as applied to a 14-year-old principal offender).

We reject the State's assertion that the question at issue in this appeal has been decided. Illinois courts have only upheld application of the statute to juvenile principals and adult accomplices. The issue we address — the application of the statute to a *juvenile* convicted upon a theory of *accountability* — is an issue of first impression. We begin with a discussion of the proportionate penalties clause of the Illinois Constitution.

The proportionate penalties clause of the Illinois Constitution declares that "all penalties shall be determined . . . according to the seriousness of the offense." Ill. Const. 1970, art. I, §11. While courts of review are generally reluctant to override the judgment of the General Assembly with respect to criminal penalties, it is also true that when defining crimes and their penalties, the legislature must consider the constitutional goals of restoring an offender to useful citizenship and of providing a penalty according to the seriousness of the offense. With regard to the statute at issue, we have recognized that the legislature considered the possible rehabilitation of an offender who commits multiple murder, and the seriousness of that offense, in determining that a mandatory minimum sentence of natural life imprisonment is appropriate for the offense of multiple murders. People v. Taylor, 464 N.E.2d 1059 (Ill. 1984).

However, the instant matter concerns a different type of challenge under the proportionate penalties clause and a different set of circumstances not addressed in *Taylor*. We have recognized three different forms of proportionality review. A statute may be deemed unconstitutionally disproportionate if (1) the punishment for the offense is cruel, degrading, or so wholly disproportionate to the offense as to shock the moral sense of the community; (2) similar offenses are compared and the conduct that creates a less serious threat to the public health and safety is punished more harshly; or (3) identical offenses are given different sentences. Here, the circuit court ruled that application of the multiple-murder sentencing statute to defendant was "highly unconscionable," and, therefore, we first consider whether the statute as applied to defendant is shocking to the moral sense of the community. . . .

We have never defined what kind of punishment constitutes "cruel," "degrading," or "so wholly disproportioned to the offense as to shock the moral sense of the community." This is so because, as our society evolves, so too do our concepts of elemental decency and fairness which shape the "moral sense" of the community. Similarly, our United States Supreme Court has stated in the context of the eighth amendment that "proportionality review under those evolving standards should be informed by objective factors to the maximum possible extent." Atkins v. Virginia, 536 U.S. 304 (2002). However, this objective evidence, though of great importance, does not wholly determine the controversy, for the Constitution contemplates that in the end our own judgment will be brought to bear on the question.

We review the gravity of the defendant's offense in connection with the severity of the statutorily mandated sentence within our community's evolving standard of decency. Here, a sentence of natural life imprisonment would be the result of three converging statutes. Section 5-4(6)(a) of the Juvenile Court Act of 1987 (705 ILCS 405/5-4(6)(a)) mandates that all 15- or 16-year-old offenders charged with murder be automatically transferred and prosecuted as adults in criminal court. The accountability statute (720 ILCS 5/5-2(c)) effectively bars courts from considering the offender's degree of participation in the crime by making all persons who participate in a common criminal design equally responsible. Finally, the multiple-murder sentencing statute (730 ILCS 5/5-8-1(a)(1)(c)(ii)) does not allow a court to consider the age of the offender or the offender's participation in the crime at the time of sentencing. . . . When these three statutes converge, a court never considers the actual facts of the crime, including the defendant's age at the time of the crime or his or her individual level of culpability.

Accordingly, we hold that the penalty mandated by the multiple-murder sentencing statute as applied to this defendant is particularly harsh and unconstitutionally disproportionate. We agree with defendant that a mandatory sentence of natural life in prison with no possibility of parole grossly distorts the factual realities of the case and does not accurately represent defendant's personal culpability such that it shocks the moral sense of the community. This moral sense is particularly true, as in the case before us, where a 15-year-old with one minute to contemplate his decision to participate in the [incident, who] stood as a lookout during the shooting, but never handled a gun, is subject to life imprisonment with no possibility of parole — the same sentence applicable to the actual shooter. Our decision does not imply that a sentence of life imprisonment for a juvenile offender convicted under a theory of accountability is never appropriate. It is certainly possible to contemplate a situation where a juvenile offender actively participated in the planning of a crime resulting in the death of two or more individuals, such that a sentence of natural life imprisonment without the possibility of parole is appropriate. . . .

Our decision is consistent with the longstanding distinction made in this state between adult and juvenile offenders, a distinction underscored by the reality that our state was the first to create a court system dedicated exclusively to juveniles. 1899 Ill. Laws 131. Illinois led the nation with our policy towards the treatment of juveniles in first forming the juvenile court, and, traditionally, as a society we have recognized that young defendants have greater rehabilitative potential. . . . Therefore, in many cases courts have discretion to grant leniency to a juvenile even if he or she is prosecuted as an adult. See, e.g., People v. Kolakowski, 745 N.E.2d 62 (Ill. App. Ct. 2001) (noting that defendant's sentence was less than her codefendant's because of her age and potential for rehabilitation). [As] with juvenile offenders, courts in some cases may grant leniency in sentencing to offenders guilty by accountability. Disparate sentences between an offender convicted by accountability and a principal offender reflect the different degrees of participation in the crime. See, e.g., People v. Godinez, 434 N.E.2d 1121 (Ill. 1982) (finding that a defendant who stood as a lookout deserved a lesser sentence than his codefendant who was convicted as the principal). . . . A life sentence without the possibility of parole implies that under any circumstances a juvenile defendant convicted solely by accountability is incorrigible and incapable of rehabilitation for the rest of his life. The trial judge in this case did not agree with such a blanket proposition. We also decline to find that the sentence mandated by the multiple-murder sentencing statute in this case satisfies the proportionate penalties clause of the Illinois Constitution. . . . We affirm the circuit court's imposition of a term of 50 years' imprisonment. . . .

PROBLEM 7-2.   FAMILY BUSINESS

Angela Thompson was reared in Jamaica by her grandmother and then lived with a variety of family members in Jamaica and later in the United States. Her uncle, Norman Little, ran a major drug-selling operation in Harlem, and he employed Thompson in his illegal enterprise when she was 17 years old. One summer afternoon, an undercover police officer bought 200 vials of cocaine from her for $2,000 on the street outside Little's residence. The officer claimed that it was customary in a sale of this size for him to receive a bonus of 20 additional vials. Thompson, however, gave him only 14 extra vials and promised to "take care" of him personally the next time he made a purchase.

On that same day, officers also made five separate purchases from Little, and one purchase from another of Little's employees, a young woman known as "Shorty." Uniformed officers later arrested Thompson and Little. They decided, however, not to arrest Shorty because they were afraid that an arrest would reveal the identity of an undercover officer. Thompson had no previous encounters with law enforcement officials.

Thompson was indicted for the sale of 2.13 ounces of cocaine, a class A-I felony that carries a mandatory prison sentence. Under the New York statute, the judge must impose a minimum prison term of between 15 and 25 years and a maximum term of life. If Thompson had not awarded the bonus vials to the undercover officer, the government could have charged her only with an A-II sale (less than two ounces), whose mandatory minimum sentence is three years.

Little was indicted for five criminal sales of a controlled substance in the first degree. He had three prior felony and seven prior misdemeanor convictions; Little pleaded guilty to one illicit sale in exchange for dismissal of the remaining four counts and a sentence of 15 years to life imprisonment. The prosecutor offered Thompson a plea bargain carrying a sentence of three years to life, but she rejected the offer and went to trial. The jury convicted her of the A-I felony.

As defense counsel, how would you convince the sentencing judge that a minimum sentence of 15 years for Angela Thompson is cruel and unusual punishment, under either the federal or state constitution? Compare People v. Thompson, 633 N.E.2d 1074 (N.Y. 1994).

NOTES

1. *Eighth Amendment limits on legislative choice of sanctions.*   The language of Eighth Amendment and similar provisions in state constitutions goes back to the English Bill of Rights of 1689, which prohibited "cruel and unusual punishments." This provision arose from concerns about the unwarranted infliction of pain through unlimited state power.

The Supreme Court's proportionality analysis in imprisonment situations has been limited. The truncated review of prison sentences may indicate the degree to which the death penalty drives the entire sentencing structure in the United States. After all, if death is available as the ultimate sanction, how can life without parole be disproportionate? The *Ewing* opinion summarizes the cases in this area, including the three-part test in Solem v. Helm, 463 U.S. 277 (1983), and the modified version of that test developed by Justice Kennedy in Harmelin v. Michigan, 501 U.S. 957 (1991). In a companion case to *Ewing*, Lockyer v. Andrade, 538 U.S. 63 (2003), the defendant stole videotapes worth $154 from two Kmart stores. Andrade also had a criminal record with several convictions for misdemeanor theft, residential burglary, and transportation of marijuana. Although Andrade was sentenced under California's three-strikes law to a life term lasting at least 50 years, the Court upheld the sentence. How can the Court assess the first prong of its test — the gravity of the offense and the harshness of the penalty — other than by relying on prongs 2 and 3 to provide an answer?

Does the decision in *Ewing* reflect merely the predilections of the majority of the Court rather than a principled assessment of the sentence? Would it have been more honest for the Court to decline proportionality review in imprisonment cases generally? Cf. Henderson v. Norris, 258 F.3d 706 (8th Cir. 2001) (life sentence for first offense of delivery of .238 grams of cocaine base held cruel and unusual punishment).

The Canadian Supreme Court's proportionality test requires an assessment of the circumstances of the particular conduct involved in an individual case and the defendant's personal characteristics. A sentence would have to fall if it either "outraged decency" or was grossly disproportionate in some reasonably imaginable hypothetical situation. R. v. Goltz, [1991] S.C.R. 485.

In the International Criminal Court (ICC), the maximum penalties under the Statute of Rome are a term of 30 years or a life sentence; the latter must be justified in light of the "extreme gravity of the crime" and the personal circumstances of the defendant. The ICC's governing statute explicitly grants prosecutors and the convicted person the right to appeal "on the ground of disproportion between the crime and the sentence." Statute of Rome, Art. 81(2)(a). Should the Appeals Chamber find the sentence disproportionate, it may vary the sentence. Art. 83(3). What test, if any, should the ICC adopt in determining whether a sentence is disproportionate?

2. *Deference to the legislature.*   In the Supreme Court proportionality opinions, the Justices have emphasized their deference to legislative decisions. In *Ewing* Justices Scalia and Thomas concluded that federal courts should never inquire into the proportionality of noncapital offenses because this concern is purely a legislative issue. Nevertheless, state and federal courts still insist that they can engage in an abbreviated proportionality review. Is it appropriate for courts to defer substantially to the legislature in defining the Eighth Amendment? Would such deference be more justified if a sentencing commission developed the sentence range?

The Judicial Committee of the Privy Council rejected a constitutional challenge to a statute from the former Southern Rhodesia, which imposed a mandatory death sentence for assisting in an arson attempt. The Judicial Committee noted that "[it] can hardly be for the courts, unless clearly so empowered or directed to rule as to the necessity or propriety of particular legislation. The provision [barring inhuman or degrading punishment] enables the court to adjudicate as to whether some form or type or description of punishment, . . . is inhuman or degrading, but it does not enable the Court to declare an enactment imposing a punishment to be ultra vires on the ground that the court considers that the punishment laid down by the enactment is inappropriate or excessive for the particular offence." Runyowa v. R. [1967] A.C. 26 (P.C.). In a recent decision, the Privy Council questioned the authority of *Runyowa*, noting that the international jurisprudence on human rights was rudimentary at the time of the decision. Reyes v. R. [2002] 2 A.C. 235 (P.Q.).

3. *Multiple charges and the Eighth Amendment.*   In Close v. People, 48 P.3d 528 (Colo. 2002), the Colorado court upheld a 60-year term for a teenager charged with multiple offenses arising from a single incident. In its review of consecutive sentences, the Colorado court relied on O'Neil v. Vermont, 144 U.S. 323 (1892), in which the Supreme Court analyzed the severity of a defendant's sentence in light of the number of crimes he had committed. The *Close* court concluded that a proportionality review can be applied only to each conviction, not to the sum of the consecutive prison terms imposed. This approach gives prosecutors room to increase the maximum available sentence by adding counts to the indictment, without running into Eighth Amendment problems. Typically, judges counter this prosecutorial power by imposing concurrent rather than consecutive sentences. Is it possible to craft a constitutional rule here that would still ordinarily allow a defendant who commits more offenses to receive a more severe punishment?

4. *Life is different?*   In *Solem* and *Harmelin*, the defendants received life-without-parole terms. In *Miller*, the trial court refused to impose this sanction. The *Solem* Court contrasted the sentence facing the defendant with the life

sentence in *Rummel,* which allowed for parole after 12 years. Should a life-without-parole term change the parameters of the proportionality review employed? In proportionality decisions, the courts frequently refer to the more searching proportionality review used in death cases, under the notion that "death is different." Does the impact of a life-without-parole sanction also justify a different approach?

Many countries in Latin America and Europe, including Portugal and Mexico, prohibit the imposition of life-without-parole sentences. They view such a penalty as violating human dignity and as inherently inhumane because it denies an individual the opportunity to rehabilitate herself. What purpose does the life-without-parole sentence serve? For an in-depth discussion of life imprisonment around the world, see Dirk van Zyl Smit, Taking Life Imprisonment Seriously in National and International Law (2002).

5. *Juveniles and proportionality.* In *Miller* a juvenile was the defendant; the court emphasized his age but stated explicitly that the defendant's youth alone would not have rendered the sentence disproportionate. A 1998 study indicates that most U.S. courts refuse to consider a defendant's age when engaging in a proportionality analysis under the Eighth Amendment. See Wayne A. Logan, Proportionality and Punishment: Imposing Life Without Parole on Juveniles, 33 Wake Forest L. Rev. 681 (1998).

In State v. Green, 502 S.E.2d 819, 833-834 (N.C. 1998), the Supreme Court of North Carolina upheld a life sentence imposed on a 13-year-old repeat offender convicted of first-degree sexual offense, attempted first-degree rape, and first-degree burglary. It considered the sentence to comport with "evolving standards of decency" in light of public and legislative concern about violent juvenile crime. In addition, it found the sentence not excessive in the constitutional sense in light of the violent nature of the crime, the defendant's culpability, his prior record, and the potential maximum sentence of 4 years that could have been imposed under the juvenile system. Finally, the court addressed the question whether the sentence was "unusual," as the defendant was the only 13-year-old offender who was convicted and sentenced under the legislative scheme that mandated a life term under similar circumstances:

> The fact that a particular punishment is "unusual," in the sense that few defendants fall within its purview, is largely irrelevant to our inquiry. . . . This Court and the United States Supreme Court traditionally have not afforded separate treatment to the words "cruel" and "unusual," but have looked only to whether a particular punishment involves basic inhuman treatment. . . . The suggestion that an equally applicable punishment is rendered unconstitutional by virtue of the fact that few choose to commit the crime underlying it, or that only one of many who commit such crime is the one caught and convicted, does not fall within the bounds of any reasonable constitutional discourse.

6. *The jurisprudence of state courts.* State courts have applied the *Harmelin* test under the Eighth Amendment to bar some disproportionate sentences. See Crosby v. State, 824 A.2d 894 (Del. 2003) (life sentence of 45-year fixed term for second-degree forgery was excessive, even for defendant with prior felony convictions). It is more common for state courts to uphold a legislative choice of sanctions in the case at hand, even if they recognize that a proportionality

challenge might succeed in theory. State v. Moss-Dwyer, 686 N.E.2d 109 (Ind. 1997) (recognizing possible proportionality challenges under state constitution, but refusing to declare a sentence disproportionate where statute made misinformation on a handgun permit application a greater crime than carrying a handgun without a license).

A few state courts have been willing to insist, under various provisions of their state constitutions, that the legislature select a punishment that is proportionate to the crime. The *Miller* court, for example, rested its decision solely on the Illinois constitution, without reaching the federal constitutional question. Whose standards—those of a state, of the nation, of a local community—should apply in determining what shocks the conscience?

Nonconstitutional limitations on imprisonment provide more meaningful day-to-day controls than do constitutional limitations. Sentencing guidelines, for example, set out presumptive sentencing ranges for specific offenses. While guideline regimes allow for departures, they require detailed justifications and are open to appellate challenges. Another statutory limitation on imprisonment is the federal safety valve program, which allows for the sentencing of low-level, nonviolent drug offenders to prison terms below the mandatory minimum. Other limitations may be imposed by state statutes mandating that certain offenders not be sentenced to prison. Among such legislation is the 2002 California referendum requiring drug treatment rather than imprisonment for first-time, nonviolent drug offenders. For discussion of a similar statute, see State v. DePiano, 926 P.2d 494 (Ariz. 1996) (despondent mother's unsuccessful attempt to commit suicide and infanticide by asphyxiation was punished by 34-year prison term; court reduced sentence under statute allowing reduction if "the punishment imposed is greater than under the circumstances of the case ought to be inflicted").

7. *Internal consistency: similar statutes, similar safety threats.* In People v. Walden, 769 N.E.2d 928 (Ill. 2002), the court struck down a 15-year sentencing enhancement for the carrying of a firearm during an armed robbery as violating the proportionate penalties clause of the Illinois constitution. David Walden was charged with one count of armed robbery while in possession of a firearm. He challenged his sentence as disproportionate under the state constitution, because it punished him more severely than a related crime in the state code, armed violence predicated upon aggravated robbery. The appellate court reviewed the legislative history of the two provisions and concluded that they share a statutory purpose—the more severe punishment of violent crimes when committed with firearms:

> Having concluded that the two offenses share an identical statutory purpose, we next must determine whether one offense is more serious than the other. This is not a difficult inquiry, as armed violence predicated upon aggravated robbery is clearly the more serious offense. [Armed] violence predicated upon aggravated robbery . . . requires that the offender, while using or threatening the imminent use of force, inform the victim that he or she is presently armed with a firearm. Thus, armed robbery while in possession of a firearm may be committed while carrying a concealed firearm that is neither revealed nor even mentioned to the victim. . . .
> Our final inquiry, then, is whether armed robbery while in possession of a firearm is punished more or less severely than armed violence predicated upon aggravated robbery. [Armed] robbery while in possession of a firearm is punishable by 21 to 45 years in prison. Armed violence predicated upon aggravated robbery is a Class X felony punishable by either 10 to 30 or 15 to 30 years in

prison, depending upon the type of firearm used in the offense. Thus, it is the less serious offense — armed robbery while in possession of a firearm — that is punished more severely. The 15-year enhancement for armed robbery while in possession of a firearm therefore violates the proportionate penalties clause of the Illinois Constitution and is unenforceable.

769 N.E.2d at 931-932. *Walden* is reminiscent of People v. Stewart (reprinted in Chapter 2), in which the Colorado court addressed an equal protection challenge to Stewart's conviction of reckless second-degree assault rather than vehicular assault, which carried a lesser sentence. The court denied the claim since it found a sufficient rational basis for distinguishing the offenses so as to justify the different penalties attached to them.

Should courts engage in a proportionality review of the internal consistency of state sentencing laws? How would you expect a state legislator to react to the *Walden* decision?

8. *Expanding on the prohibition of cruel and unusual punishments.* Human rights law has borrowed heavily from U.S. legal principles, but the Eighth Amendment analogues have been drawn more broadly in the international arena. The International Covenant for Civil and Political Rights, which the United States has ratified, prohibits "cruel, inhuman or degrading treatment or punishment." The United States has taken a reservation to Article 7, interpreting this provision to reach no further than the Fifth, Eighth, and Fourteenth Amendments. Article 3 of the European Convention on Human Rights prohibits "inhuman or degrading treatment or punishment." On their face, do these provisions differ with regard to proportionality of prison terms? How important should the drafters' intent be in reviewing sentences under these provisions?

9. *Proportionality analysis in extraditions.* National courts have employed proportionality analysis to assess the penalty threatening an individual upon extradition. In 2002 the German courts, for example, rejected a Turkish extradition request based on a 1996 conviction for trafficking of .05 gram of heroin. The alleged offender was threatened with a sentence of three years and four months, which could be reduced to one year and four months upon good behavior. The court considered the penalty inappropriate because the defendant was a first offender and the Turkish authorities had waited five years to request extradition. If required to assess the proportionality of the penalty in extradition cases, courts frequently attempt to determine possible justifications for a particular sentence under the laws of the country requesting the extradition and then compare the sentence with penalties for comparable offenses in their home countries.

In a potential death penalty case involving extradition to the United States, the European Court of Human Rights held that a Council of Europe member state has "an inherent obligation not to extradite [where] the fugitive would be faced in the receiving State by a real risk of exposure to inhuman or degrading treatment or punishment" in violation of Article 3 of the European Convention on Human Rights. Soering v. United Kingdom, 11 Eur. H.R. Rep. 439, para. 88 (Eur. Ct. H.R. 1989). The court held that conditions on Virginia's death row (the so-called death row phenomenon) amounted to "inhuman or degrading treatment" under the convention. In other cases, the court has also applied the phrase "inhuman or degrading treatment or punishment" to prison sentences, depending on their length and conditions.

In 2002 the Mexican Supreme Court rejected extradition to the United States in cases in which the alleged offenders faced life-without-parole terms. Such sentences are prohibited under the Mexican constitution and therefore constitute a total barrier to extradition. How can U.S. prosecutors make successful extradition requests in cases in which the indictment charges offenses that carry life without parole as a sentencing option or as a mandatory sentence? Is it appropriate for national courts to hold the potential sentences of foreign countries as disproportionate under their own laws and therefore as grounds for refusal to extradite?

F.   RECONSIDERING MASS INCARCERATION

Is the trend toward mass incarceration likely to continue? What are the consequences if it does? Is there any idea, fact, or policy that might change the trend toward mass incarceration? Or, when change comes, will it be the result of some long-term "natural" cycle or perhaps of some subtle, complex, and possibly unpredictable combination of factors? Is the strongest argument against mass imprisonment that it may fail to achieve a meaningful social benefit while entailing a great cost? Would a shift from "purposes of punishment" to "principles of public safety" lead to a significant reduction in the use of imprisonment as a tool by either the criminal justice system or society in general?

Reconsidering Incarceration: New Directions for Reducing Crime, Don Stemen
Vera Institute of Justice (Jan. 2007)

Research has consistently shown crime rates to be affected by many factors, including economics, social and demographic characteristics, culture, politics, and incarceration rates. . . . [T]hanks to rapid increases in crime and imprisonment through the 1970s and 1980s, followed by a sharp decrease in crime in the 1990s, we now have a large body of recent empirical work on the effects of incarceration to draw on as well. . . .

[R]esearchers have found that a 10 percent higher incarceration rate is associated with anywhere from a 9 percent to a 22 percent lower crime rate. In contrast, analyses using state-level data found a weaker association, concluding that a 10 percent increase in incarceration is associated with a crime rate that is anywhere from 0.11 percent to 4 percent lower. Similar estimates have been generated from studies using county-level data, ranging from a 2 percent to a 4 percent crime-rate difference. Moreover, several studies have found no relationship between incarceration rates and crime rates. One study even found that higher incarceration rates were associated with *higher* crime rates in states with already high incarceration rates (incarceration rates above 325 inmates per 100,000 population).

As these disparate findings suggest, the impact of incarceration on crime is inconsistent from one study to the next. . . .

APPLYING THE RESEARCH FINDINGS: PERILS FOR POLICY

. . . Research only provides an estimate of *average* relationships between incarceration and crime rates across jurisdictions. Thus, such findings are a blunt instrument whose applicability to any specific jurisdiction is dubious.

Research, therefore, cannot predict the impact of future prison increases in a given state. . . .

THE SIZE OF STATE PRISON POPULATIONS

The size of a state's prison population and crime rate will influence the impact of increases in incarceration rates. . . . [F]or a state with an already high incarceration rate the costs of increasing incarceration by 10 percent to achieve a 2 to 4 percent reduction in crime could be tremendous. For example, California and Nebraska had very similar crime rates in 2003 of approximately 4,000 index offenses per 100,000 people in the population. To achieve a 2 to 4 percent reduction, California, with a prison population of 162,678 inmates, would have to incarcerate an additional 16,089 inmates. To achieve the same rate of reduction, Nebraska, with a prison population of 3,976, would have to incarcerate just 400 additional inmates. If the average cost to incarcerate an offender for one year is $22,650, California would spend $355 million *more* than Nebraska to achieve the same level of public safety. . . . Thus, increases in incarceration rates are associated with lower crime rates at low levels of imprisonment, but the size of that association shrinks as incarceration rates get bigger. Eventually, they say, there is an "inflection point" where increases in incarceration rates are associated with *higher* crime rates. This inflection point occurs when a state's incarceration rate reaches some point between 325 and 492 inmates per 100,000 people. In other words, states with incarceration rates above this range can expect to experience higher crime rates with future increases in incarceration rates. . . .

THE CONTENT OF PUNISHMENT

Incarceration is not the only punishment that may reduce crime rates. Other types of punishment, including fines, probation, community service, drug treatment, or other sanctions, have also been shown to suppress crime. These alternative sanctions are not considered in the crime control studies noted above, however. Had they increased at the same time as the expansion of imprisonment, these sanctions may have contributed—in part or even completely—to the effects found in those studies. Similarly, the content of incarceration—the quality of inmates' experience in prison—may matter greatly as well. Studies so far have only considered how the size of prison populations affects crime rates. . . .

THE TYPES OF OFFENDERS IN PRISON

The type of offenders a state decides to incarcerate may also be a relevant factor. . . . By 2004, 419,000 drug possessors were incarcerated in state prisons or local jails at a cost of nearly $8.3 billion annually. Ilyana Kuziemko and Steven D. Levitt argue that the continued increase in the number of drug offenders in prisons may lead to a "crowding out" effect, in which the high number of incarcerated drug offenders prevents the incarceration of offenders prone to more serious crime, thereby reducing the effectiveness of incarceration to reduce crime. Analysts agree with apparent unanimity that future increases in incarceration rates for such offenders will do less and cost more. Washington State, for example, . . . concluded that while incarcerating violent and high-volume property offenders continued to generate more benefits than costs, in the future each additional person incarcerated will result in fewer prevented crimes. Washington even found that increasing the incarceration rate for drug offenders in the 1990s actually had a negative impact overall, as it now costs more to incarcerate additional drug offenders than the average value of the crimes prevented by the imprisonment. . . .

ESTIMATING THE IMPACT OF OTHER FACTORS ON CRIME

Between 1990 and 2005, the crime rate in the United States fell dramatically to its lowest point in 30 years. However, . . . according to Spelman only 25 percent of this crime drop through the 1990s could be explained by increasing incarceration rates. The remaining 75 percent, therefore, must be due to factors other than incarceration. Indeed, researchers have identified a number of such factors including, for example, fewer young persons in the population, smaller urban populations, decreases in crack cocaine markets, lower unemployment rates, higher wages, more education and high school graduates, more police per capita, and more arrests for public order offenses. An examination of just a few of these indicates that future investment in other policy areas may be not only more effective but also more cost effective than continued investment in increased prison populations. . . .

Policing.   Several authors have found an association between increases in the number of police per capita and lower crime rates. For example, using city-level data, Levitt found that a 10 percent increase in the size of a city's police force was associated with an 11 percent lower violent crime rate and a 3 percent lower property crime rate. . . . [W]e can imagine how a crime reduction policy focusing on policing might operate in, say, New York City, where the 2004 index crime rate was 2,800 offenses per 100,000 people in the population. To achieve a 3 percent reduction in the crime rate by increasing incarceration, New York City — with a prison population of 33,564 inmates — would have to incarcerate an additional 3,300 inmates at a cost of approximately $121.5 million per year. With a police force of 39,110 sworn police officers, the city could achieve the same reduction in crime by hiring 3,911 more police officers at a cost of $97.2 million per year. Compared to policing, then, incarceration would cost the city $24.3 million more to achieve the same level of public safety. . . .

Unemployment and Wages.   . . . Research has shown that men with criminal records experience no growth in earnings and, therefore, have few choices other than day labor. At the community level, neighborhoods with high incarceration rates may be shunned by employers. Further, as John Hagan argues, incarceration can generate social connections to illegal rather than legal employment, thus, potentially increasing crime. . . .

Using state-level data, Steven Raphael and Rudolf Winter-Ebmer found that a 10 percent decrease in a state's unemployment rate corresponded with a 16 percent reduction in property crime rates; the researchers concluded that, between 1992 and 1997, "slightly more than 40 percent of the decline [in the overall property crime rate] can be attributed to the decline in unemployment." . . .

Research has also considered the relationship between real wages and crime. Using national-level data, Gould, Weinberg, and Mustard determined that a 10 percent increase in real wages saw a 13 percent lower index crime rate — specifically, a 12 percent lower property crime rate and a 25 percent lower violent crime rate. . . .

Education. . . . Lance Lochner and Enrico Moretti . . . have shown an increase in citizens' education levels to be associated with lower crime rates: specifically, a one-year increase in the average education of citizens results in a 1.7 percent lower index crime rate. In addition, they associated a 10 percent increase in graduation rates with a 9.4 percent lower index crime rate. Combined with Gould and his colleagues' findings on the link between wages and crime, Lochner and Moretti argue that "a 10 percent increase in high school graduation rates should reduce arrest rates by 5 to 10 percent through increased wages alone." "[A] 1 percent increase in male high school graduation rates would save as much as $1.4 billion" nationally through crime reduction, they conclude. Moreover, prison-based education programs have been found to significantly reduce recidivism rates for offenders after release. . . .

BEYOND INCARCERATION

. . . As William Spelman has cautioned, "It is no longer sufficient, if it ever was, to demonstrate that prisons are better than nothing. Instead, they must be better than the next-best use of the money."

Yet, in the past two decades, spending on these other factors has been cut. Corrections expenditures were the only state budget category other than Medicaid to increase as a percentage of total state spending over the past 20 years. Between 1985 and 2004, states increased corrections spending by 202 percent. By comparison, spending on higher education grew by just 3 percent, Medicaid by 47 percent, and secondary and elementary education by 55 percent; spending on public assistance decreased by more than 60 percent during the same period (see Figure 1). . . .

. . . But a broader approach would require a shift in criminal justice policy away from reactive responses to criminal offending and toward a proactive attempt to address the underlying causes of criminal offending. . . .

Moreover, the public favors a policy that addresses the underlying causes of crime rather than simply responds to crime after it occurs. Polling by Peter D. Hart Research Associates, for example, shows the public questioning whether incarceration is the best crime control policy. In 1994, 42 percent of Americans favored responding to crime with stricter sentencing; by 2001, this had decreased to just 32 percent. Conversely, in 1994, only 48 percent of Americans said they favored addressing the underlying causes of crime; by 2001, this had increased to 65 percent.

Percent Change in State Spending, 1985-2004

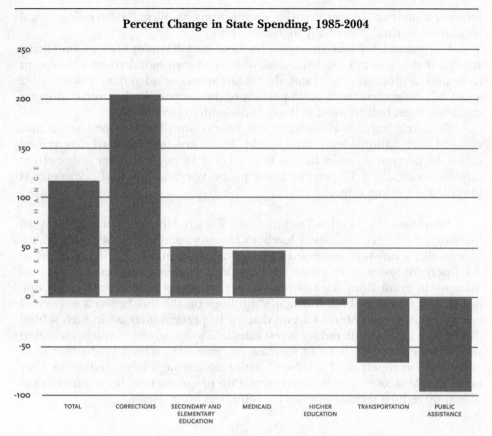

Source: National Association of State Budget Officers, State Expenditure Reports annual series.

Toward a New Approach to Public Safety

After 15 years of declining crime rates, many analysts are claiming that "prison works." But, as Elliot Currie notes, "if 'prison works' is the answer, what was the question?" If the question is whether it is possible to prevent individuals from committing crimes by putting them in prison, then prison certainly works; it works to punish and incapacitate those who have committed crimes. But if the question is what is the best way to reduce crime, "prison works" may not be the most helpful response. Does a five-year prison sentence "work" better to reduce crime than a two-year prison sentence? Does a two-year prison sentence for nonviolent offenders "work" as well as a two-year prison sentence for violent offenders?

The most salient question of all may be, Do the resources devoted to prison "work" better to ensure public safety than if those resources were devoted to something else? Prisons are not the only way to fight crime. Policymakers could spend money on more judges, better staffed or equipped law enforcement, or better-trained probation and parole officers. They could invest, as this paper indicates, in other, non-criminal-justice areas shown to affect crime: education, employment, economic development, etc. The impact of incarceration on crime is limited and diminishing. The public's support for reactive crime control is also in decline. It is therefore fitting that we reconsider the continued emphasis on and dedication of resources to incarceration.

Public safety cannot be achieved only by responding to crime after it occurs; research shows that it may also depend on protecting people against those factors that have been shown to be associated with high crime rates, such as unemployment, poverty, and illiteracy. By pursuing crime reduction chiefly through incarceration, states are forgoing the opportunity to invest in these other important areas. As state policymakers continue to feel pressure to introduce measures to keep crime rates low, they would therefore do well to look beyond incarceration for alternative policies that not only may be able to accomplish the important task of protecting public safety, but may do so more efficiently and more effectively.

NOTES

1. *Slowing growth as a victory.*   The increasing rate of incarceration cannot continue forever. But at what point will it level off? When will it decline? And how far? Will there come a time when the United States is no longer the unqualified leader in world imprisonment rates? A return to a time like the early 1970s, when many scholars and policy actors believed imprisonment was fading as a social tool, is unlikely on any short or moderate time horizon. But perhaps the leveling of imprisonment rates in the new millennium, reductions in imprisonment numbers in some states, and increasing attention by state actors and voters to the substantial social and economic costs of mass imprisonment may together signal a turning point in United States punishment policy. As a policymaker, what strategies might you suggest to speed or magnify this change? Should responsibility for criminal justice policy be shifted more to local levels? Professor Marc Miller suggests that in a time of central and abstract punitiveness, liberals ought to reconsider their fears of control at the local level, where resources are more limited and choices among competing social policies often more stark. See Marc Miller, Cells vs. Cops vs. Classrooms, in The Crime Conundrum: Essays on Criminal Justice 127 (Lawrence Friedman & George Fisher eds., 1997).

2. *The possible shift to public safety.*   Don Stemen identifies a possible shift from crime control (or some mix of current purposes) to public safety as the governing rationale for the criminal justice system. Of course, such a shift would necessarily involve more than the criminal justice system; the system would become more emphatically a part of a larger enterprise (public safety). But what would such a shift mean if it were taken seriously and made the defining justification for criminal justice actors? How would police act in a system defined by public safety? How would prosecutors act? How is a shift to public safety as a governing rationale related to policies of "community prosecution" and "problem-oriented prosecution"? See Walter Dickey & Peggy McGarry, The Search for Justice and Safety Through Community Engagement: Community Justice and Community Prosecution, 42 Idaho L. Rev. 313 (2006). What would a shift to public safety mean for sentencing systems and sentencing purposes?

3. *Does mass incarceration obscure consistent mass social control?*   Professor Bernard makes the claim that a focus on dramatically increasing imprisonment

rates in the United States obscures a longer and more consistent level of mass social control. Harcourt points to the deinstitutionalization of mental health institutions in the 1960s and 1970s and claims that when populations of psychiatric institutions and prisons are combined, the United States' level of incarceration has remained relatively stable.

> [T]he empirical data on mental hospitalization reflect extraordinarily high rates of institutionalization at mid-century. Simply put, when the data on mental hospitalization rates are combined with the data on prison rates for the years 1928 through 2000, the incarceration revolution of the late twentieth century barely reaches the level of aggregated institutionalization that the United States experienced at mid-century. The highest rate of aggregated institutionalization during the entire twentieth century occurred in 1955 when almost 640 persons per 100,000 adults over age fifteen were institutionalized in asylums, mental hospitals, and state and federal prisons. Throughout almost the entire period from 1938 to 1960, the U.S. population experienced rates of institutionalization in excess of 600 inmates per 100,000 adults. Figure 1 shows the aggregate rate of institutionalization in the United States for the period 1928 to 2000, as well as the disaggregated trend lines for mental hospitalization on the one hand and state and federal prisons on the other.
>
> Aggregating mental hospitalization and imprisonment rates into a combined institutionalization rate significantly changes the trend line for confinement over the twentieth century. We are used to thinking of confinement through the lens of incarceration only, and to referring to the period prior to the mid-1970s as one of "relative stability" followed by an exponential rise. . . . As a literal matter, this is of course right. If all we are describing is the specific variable in our study and the source of the data, then indeed the observations are relatively stable over the five decades. But the truth is, what we are trying to capture when we use the variable of imprisonment is something about confinement in an institutional setting — confinement that renders the population in question incapacitated or unable to work, pursue educational opportunities, and so forth. And from this larger perspective, the period before 1970 — in fact, the entire twentieth century — reflects remarkable instability.

Bernard Harcourt, From the Asylum to the Prison: Rethinking the Incarceration Revolution, 84 Tex. L. Rev. 1751, 1754-1755 (2006). Harcourt describes a relationship between the rate of homicides and total social control. But his work also forces scholars and policy advocates to step back and ask what "real" social forces and phenomena explain the use of incarceration in the United States. If Harcourt's analysis is correct, what impact should this have on the law and politics of incarceration? Does Harcourt's analysis encourage the proposed shift to a central goal of public safety, or should it lead to concern that under various rubrics the United States may favor very high levels of confinement and that deeper forces are at work?

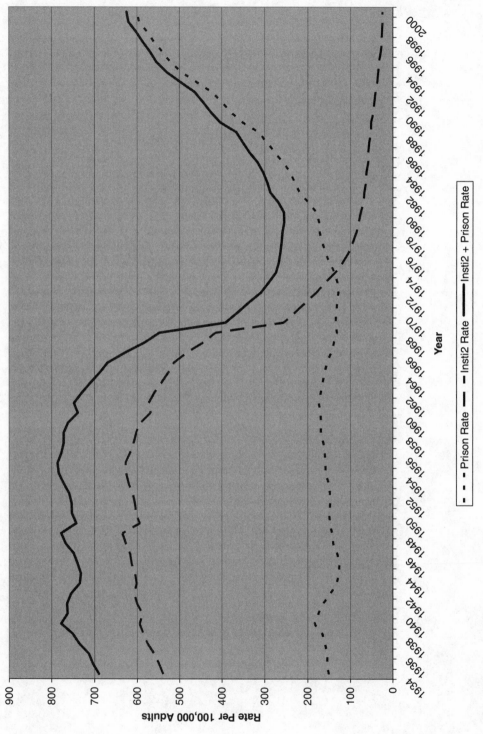

Year

- - - - Prison Rate — — Insti2 Rate —— Insti2 + Prison Rate

Rate Per 100,000 Adults

Source: Chart courtesy of Harcourt.

=8=

Sentencing Outcomes: Nonprison Punishments

In the United States, the dominant criminal sanction appears to be imprisonment (see Chapter 7), but appearances can be deceiving: In reality, the majority of criminal defendants receive nonprison sentences. Nevertheless, policymakers typically speak as if prison were the only penalty worth discussing, and much of the criminal justice system operates in an imprisonment mindset. Other countries and some U.S. jurisdictions, however, seek other options or operate under different punishment presumptions.

The terms "nonprison sanctions" and "alternatives to imprisonment" are revealing. Since imprisonment is frequently viewed as the default option, the implication is that such sanctions are acceptable only if they resemble prison in some way. Excellent examples are boot camp, which mimics the conditions of prison, and home confinement.

The United Nations Global Report on Crime and Justice distinguishes countries by the primary form of punishment they use. Some countries focus on imprisonment, others on fines, and still others on a combination of deprivation of liberty and probation. In most of the countries that responded to the U.N. survey, a fine is the most common noncustodial sentence. For example, more than 95% of Japanese offenders are assessed a fine. Noncustodial sanctions are little used in Latin America, Africa, and Asia—with the exception of Japan and South Korea—but are popular in Europe and North America.

The prevalence of noncustodial sanctions does not necessarily indicate a systematically low use of imprisonment. It may reflect a shift away from custody or an increase in the proportion of the population being criminally sanctioned. It may also be a response to other developments in the criminal justice arena, such as a focus on the risk certain offenders pose, increased opportunities to combine criminal with administrative sanctions, the development of new sentencing options, and the prosecution of new criminal actors such as organizations.

Noncustodial sanctions can serve a variety of purposes. Some sanctions, such as probation and annulment of licenses, are intended to provide some degree of control and supervision over offenders, if less than imprisonment. Other sanctions, such as fines and confiscation, are meant to punish without individual corporal control.

This chapter outlines the use of noncustodial sanctions in the United States. The first part addresses the dominant nonprison sanctions of probation and fines. The second part discusses modern alternative sanctions that have received much public attention but relatively little use. The third section considers a set of punishments labeled "collateral sanctions" that are applied in addition to other sanctions, including imprisonment.

A. TRADITIONAL ALTERNATIVES

The most common and best-established nonprison sanctions are fines and probation. Much of the public debate over punishment turns on the little-used but severe and highly symbolic imposition of capital punishment and the dominant coin of the realm — imprisonment. Yet most criminal sentences use some combination of fines and probation. The use of fines, both alone and especially in conjunction with prison or other sanctions, is far more prevalent than public debate and, indeed, much of the scholarly literature would suggest. Even among felons, straight probation (with no time in jail or prison) is used in about one-third of all cases.

Sanctions often have several components, but the public takes note of only the most severe aspects of the punishment. Among all felons sentenced in 2002 to either incarceration or probation, a fine was imposed on 25%, restitution on 12%, community service on 4%, and treatment for 3%. See Bureau of Justice Statistics, Felony Sentences in State Courts, 2002 (NCJ 206916, December 2004).

For all sanctions, one key but often implicit issue is the purpose of punishment that the sanction is intended to fulfill. When can fines and probation serve purposes similar to those served by prison — that is, when can they "replace" imprisonment? How do constitutional and political considerations limit the use of nonprison sanctions?

1. Fines

Fines have been used extensively in some European countries, where the amount of the penalty is keyed to the type of offense and the offender's income. This approach has not caught on in the United States, but the use of fines here has been increasing generally, even though judges often express reluctance to levy them. Like many European countries, the United States has also seen a steady increase in statutory or guideline requirements for restitution by criminal offenders to their victims. Only in the United States are offenders asked to pay for some or all of the costs of punishment, though it is not clear how often such fines are in fact imposed or paid.

Some of the recurring issues with fines are whether they are fair to the poor and whether they impose a proportional punishment on either the poor or the rich. In the following case, the Mississippi Supreme Court addresses one of these issues.

Mary Ann Moody v. State
716 So. 2d 562 (Miss. 1998)

BANKS, J.

Here we consider the question of whether a standard practice of extracting a set fine from persons accused of writing bad checks on the pain of suffering a full criminal prosecution for failure to do so comports with the Equal Protection Clause of the Fourteenth Amendment to the Constitution of the United States. We answer that it does not. . . .

On or about October 12, 1991, Mary Ann Moody wrote a check to the order of City Salvage for $123.89. The check was written in exchange for two doors for Moody's mother's house. The check was returned to City Salvage for "non-sufficient funds." On February 24, 1993, she was indicted by a Jones County Grand Jury, for the crime of False Pretense. Moody was appointed counsel as an indigent defendant. After indictment the district attorney's office assessed a levy of $500 plus restitution. Moody was given the option of paying a $500 fine plus restitution and having the case nolle prossed, or not paying the fine and being subjected to prosecution. Jeanne Jefcoat of the district attorney's office testified that this fine is imposed automatically once a defendant is indicted. . . . Moody testified that she could not pay all the fine, restitution and other costs at one time. Moody's motion to dismiss the action was denied and the case proceeded to trial.

. . . She was subsequently convicted of the crime of false pretense [and sentenced to three years in the Mississippi Department of Corrections and fined $1,000, which was ordered one year suspended and $500 suspended] and appeals, raising a violation of the Fourteenth Amendment to the Constitution of the United States as her sole ground on appeal.

Moody claims that the district attorney's office lacks statutory or constitutional authority to automatically impose a set fine of $500 on all defendants indicted under the Mississippi Bad Check Law. Furthermore, she claims that such a fine violates an indigent's right to equal protection under the Fourteenth Amendment. The State argues that the fine is merely a plea bargain, and as such is in the discretion of the district attorney. This is a case of first impression before this Court. We are unable to find any cases directly on point in any other jurisdiction. . . .

In Bearden v. Georgia, 461 U.S. 660 (1983), the United States Supreme Court considered whether a sentencing court can revoke a defendant's probation for failure to pay the imposed fine and restitution. The *Bearden* Court stated:

> This Court has long been sensitive to the treatment of indigents in our criminal justice system. Over a quarter-century ago, Justice Black declared that "[t]here can be no equal justice where the kind of trial a man gets depends on the amount of money he has."

Bearden, 461 U.S. at 664 (quoting Griffin v. Illinois, 351 U.S. 12 (1956) (plurality opinion)). The Court held that before revocation of an indigent's probation, the court must inquire into the reasons for failure to pay. In holding such, the Court opined:

> If the probationer willfully refused to pay or failed to make sufficient bona fide efforts legally to acquire the resources to pay, the court may revoke probation and sentence the defendant to imprisonment within the authorized range of its sentencing authority. If the probationer could not pay despite sufficient bona fide efforts to acquire the resources to do so, the court must consider alternative measures of punishment other than imprisonment. Only if alternative measures are not adequate to meet the State's interests in punishment and deterrence may the court imprison a probationer who has made sufficient bona fide efforts to pay. To do otherwise would deprive the probationer of his conditional freedom simply because, through no fault of his own, he cannot pay the fine. Such a deprivation would be contrary to the fundamental fairness required by the Fourteenth Amendment.

See also Tate v. Short, 401 U.S. 395 (1971) (holding that a State cannot convert a fine imposed under a fine-only statute into a jail term solely because the defendant is indigent and cannot immediately pay the fine in full).

Moody cites Cassibry v. State, 453 So. 2d 1298 (Miss. 1984), where this Court held that an indigent may not be incarcerated because he is financially unable to comply with an otherwise lawfully imposed sentence of a fine. *Cassibry* is distinguishable in that, the defendant had failed to pay a fine and was subsequently imprisoned for failure to pay the fine while in this case, Moody was sentenced to an appropriate statutory prison term for her crime. But see Lee v. State, 457 So. 2d 920 (Miss. 1984) (stating *Cassibry* requires consideration of statutory alternatives to imprisonment for indigents financially unable to pay a fine). . . .

In a case similar to this one, the Oklahoma Criminal Court of Appeals considered whether a defendant was deprived of equal protection in plea bargaining. Gray v. State, 650 P.2d 880 (Okla. Crim. App. 1982). In *Gray* the defendant claimed that he was denied an opportunity to plea bargain because he was unable to contribute to a special community relations fund. The *Gray* court opined:

> The recognition of plea bargaining as an essential component of the administration of justice, however, does not elevate it to a constitutional right. That is not to say, that a prosecutor can accept or refuse plea negotiations in a way that discriminates against defendants on account of their race, religion, economic status or other arbitrary classification.

The court found that there was no violation of the defendant's equal protection rights, because he did not attempt to seek a plea bargain.

The State argues that Moody is confusing this fine with a plea bargain. There is no constitutional right to a plea bargain. Allman v. State, 571 So. 2d 244, 254 (Miss. 1990). The State argues that since there is no constitutional right to a plea bargain there can be no violation in this case. Furthermore, the State claims that since the fine or plea offer is offered to everyone who is indicted, there can be no equal protection violation, because it is treating everyone the same.

The record clearly indicates that after a defendant is indicted under the Bad Check Law, an automatic $500 plus restitution is charged to drop the prosecution. The amount is due immediately. The defendant then has the option of paying the $500 and have the indictment nolle prossed or proceeding to trial. Thus, one who is unable to pay will always be in a position of facing a felony conviction and jail time, while those with adequate resources will not. The automatic nature of the fine is what makes it discriminating to the poor, in that only the poor will face jail time. We hold that an indigent's equal protection rights are violated when all potential defendants are offered one way to avoid prosecution and that one way is to pay a fine, and there is no determination as to an individual's ability to pay such a fine. Subjecting one to a jail term merely because he cannot afford to pay a fine, due to no fault of his own, is unconstitutional.

Additionally, we note that this procedure does not involve a plea bargain at all because the only charge is nolle prosequi. There is no plea at all. What and all that happens is that a $500 fee is extracted in order to avoid prosecution. Thus the scheme is both procedurally and constitutionally flawed.

[W]e conclude that the only way to put Moody on a footing roughly equivalent to those able to purchase a nolle prosequi is to remand for new sentencing in which the trial court can withhold adjudication and place her on probation requiring restitution plus reasonable efforts to pay a reasonable fine and costs. This remedy does not restrict the trial judges where one complains of indigency. There are methods in use today which allow for indigent status where the penalty to be imposed is a fine. These include working out a payment schedule which is appropriate to the means of the offender. It is a proper solution for this case, granting Moody relief from an improper and unconstitutional practice subjecting her to disparate treatment based upon her indigency. In the future, it is to be hoped that this unconstitutional scheme will be abandoned and the matter of plea bargains will be handled in a proper manner which comports with the right to equal protection of the laws.

For the foregoing reasons, this matter is reversed and remanded to the circuit court for re-sentencing.

McRae, J., concurring in part and dissenting in part.

The Jones County District Attorney's approach to enforcing the Mississippi Worthless Check Law by charging a fine to avoid prosecution and incarcerating those who cannot pay discriminates against the poor in violation of the equal protection provisions of the United States Constitution and the Mississippi Constitution and offends the prohibition against imprisonment for civil debt found in art. 3, §30 of the Mississippi Constitution. It further allows the District Attorney's office to exercise powers well in excess of those afforded it by statute pursuant to the directive of art. 6, §174 of the Mississippi Constitution. The root of the problem, however, lies in our statutory framework that subjects one who "bounces" a check to criminal penalties. To remand Mrs. Moody's case for resentencing and merely "hope" that the practices used in her situation will be abandoned does nothing to remedy the larger problem.

Miss. Code Ann. §97-19-67(1)(d)(1994) sets the penalty for writing a bad check in excess of $100, regardless of whether a first or second offense, *upon conviction,* at a fine of not less than $100 and not more than $1000, *or* imprisonment for not more than three years *or* both, *in the discretion of the court.* Jeanne Jefcoat, the Worthless Check Director for the Jones County District Attorney's Office, however, testified that once an individual has been indicted by the grand jury for writing a bad check, he must immediately pay a set $500 fine, the amount of the check and a variety of fees, or else face trial. She stated that Mrs. Moody was told that to avoid prosecution, she would have to pay more than $800: the $123.89 check, the $500 fine, $163.50 court costs, a $40 processing fee levied by the District Attorney's Office and a $10 returned check fee. Thus, Mrs. Moody was fined before she was convicted and in essence, promised that if she paid the fine and costs, she wouldn't be convicted. Contrary to the State's argument, this cannot be construed as a "standard" plea bargain in any sense merely because Mrs. Moody was offered the opportunity to pay. . . .

Imprisonment may be an appropriate remedy for a defendant who refuses or neglects to pay a fine he can afford, or even when collection is unsuccessful despite the defendant's reasonable efforts to make payment. However, the imprisonment of an indigent defendant who cannot pay a fine imposed to avoid conviction is a violation of the fourteenth amendment to the United States Constitution as well as to art. 3, §30 of the Mississippi Constitution. . . .

Debtor's prison was abolished long ago. Our statutory system, nevertheless, allows for imprisonment of one who cannot pay all of the fines that may arise from "bouncing" a check. Further, while they may pursue actions for false pretenses, District Attorneys do not have the authority under our State Constitution or . . . Code . . . either to collect civil debts or to use criminal statutes to coerce payment of those debts and any fees and penalties which also might accrue. Moreover, the power to render fines and judgments belongs with the courts and not the District Attorney's Office. Accordingly, I do not think that the majority has gone far enough by recognizing only the fourteenth amendment problems or "hoping" that problematic debt collection practices are abandoned.

NOTES

1. *The use of fines.*   Straight fines (fines in the absence of other sanctions) are used most often for misdemeanants and other more minor offenders. Some states prohibit the use of fines for certain types of offenses. While only .5% of all those who committed felonies received a fine-only sentence, 26.8% of all misdemeanants did — with more than half of all traffic offenders receiving such a sentence. Fines are often only a part of the sentence imposed: They are used in about 21% of state felony cases, and 80% of all lower-court sentences include fines. The average fines in state courts are below $100. Straight fines are relatively uncommon in the federal system. In federal court 4% of all offenders sentenced between October 1, 1999, and September 30, 2000, received a fine-only sentence. Fines are also a component of other sentences; 13% of all

convicted federal offenders are fined. The federal sentencing guidelines mandate that the court impose a fine unless the offender shows that he is unable to pay a fine and it is unlikely that the situation will change.

2. *Who gets fined?*   Men are more likely to be fined than women; whites are more likely to be fined than blacks or Hispanics; employed offenders are significantly more likely to be fined than unemployed offenders; older offenders are more likely to be fined than younger offenders; nondrug offenders are more likely to be fined than drug offenders. In urban settings fines are imposed less frequently than in rural or suburban communities. In sum, fines are more likely to be used for low-level offenses and low-risk offenders, with judges considering the defendant's actual or perceived wealth and income.

3. *Fines in white-collar and corporate cases.*   The largest fines are generally imposed in antitrust prosecutions. The largest fine ever obtained in a federal criminal case was $500 million in the prosecution of an international vitamin cartel. Such fines are paid into the federal Crime Victims Fund and are available for disbursement to crime victims and to fund training programs during the following year.

4. *Restitution.*   In more than one-third of the states, courts are statutorily required to order restitution unless there are compelling or extraordinary circumstances to the contrary. Other states allow broad exceptions. More than a dozen states require courts to state on the record the reasons for failing to order restitution or for ordering only partial restitution. Some states have enacted specific directives to order restitution to victims of particular offenses.

Restitution is awarded for crime-related expenses incurred by the victim or, in homicide cases, the victim's family; it includes medical and counseling expenses, lost wages, and costs for lost or damaged property. Some states permit the award of future damages. Nevertheless, victims only infrequently receive restitution. The reasons for this include failure to request restitution, inability to demonstrate or calculate loss, the court's opinion that restitution is inappropriate in light of other penalties, and the defendant's inability to pay. Most states require courts to consider the defendant's financial resources and obligations when awarding restitution. Some states are beginning to move away from this requirement, instead merely considering the defendant's ability to pay when setting the payment schedule.

In 1996 Congress enacted the Mandatory Victims Restitution Act (MVRA), which mandates that restitution be ordered in full in certain cases to each victim, regardless of the offender's economic situation. In contrast to fines, restitution is not meant to be punitive but rather to make the victim whole. Despite the MVRA's mandate, of 48,000 federal offenders in fiscal year 1997, only about 20% were ordered to pay restitution while about 19% were ordered to pay fines. Factors used by courts in determining whether an offender was to be ordered to pay restitution included the offense of conviction, length and type of sentence imposed, and offender characteristics such as sex, race, education, and citizenship. But the most important factor was the judicial district or circuit in which the offender was sentenced. General Accounting Office, Federal Courts: Differences Exist in Ordering Fines and Restitution (May 1999).

The use of fines as the sole or primary sanction for offenses, both violent and nonviolent, raises two central questions. First, when can fines satisfy a sufficient mix of purposes to substitute for or improve on the use of imprisonment, and second, can fines be made relatively similar in impact for offenders with widely varying wealth? A related concern is whether people with more access to legitimate funds through family and friends will just "pay their way" out of a sanction, while poorer offenders may be induced to commit further crimes to pay their fines. Consider whether these issues are addressed in the following materials.

Day Fines, Sally T. Hillsman
Intermediate Sanctions in Overcrowded Times
(Michael Tonry and Kate Hamilton eds., 1995)

Day fines — fine sentences in which the amount is set in proportion to both the seriousness of the offense and the financial resources of the offender — have long been the sentence of choice in northern Europe for most offenses. The name derives from the practice of using the offender's daily income as the base for setting the fine amount.

Systematic day-fine systems typically rely upon flexible, written guidelines. They are increasingly attractive to American judges, prosecutors, and other criminal justice policymakers who look for a wider range of intermediate penalties that can be scaled to provide appropriate punishment for offenses of varying gravity, while reserving imprisonment for violent and predatory offenses.

The fine has always been an attractive sentence in American courts, and it is used more widely than is generally recognized. The fine's advantages are well known. Fines are unmistakably punitive; they deprive offenders of ill-gotten gain; they are inexpensive to administer; and they provide revenue to cover such things as the cost of collection or compensation to victims. Recent research has supported their deterrent impact: fines are associated with lower rates of recidivism than probation or jail for offenders with equivalent criminal records and current offenses.

Fines have not been used in the United States, particularly as a sole penalty, as frequently or for as wide a range of offenses as in European countries, which share many of our sentencing principles. In Germany, for example, 81 percent of adult offenses and 73 percent of crimes of violence are punished solely by fines. In England, 38 percent of offenses equivalent to our felonies and 39 percent of violent offenses result in fines.

A major impediment in American courts has been the widespread view that poor offenders cannot pay fines and that affluent offenders who do so are buying their way out of more punitive sanctions. Whatever truth there is in this view, however, stems largely from American use of "tariff" systems to set fine amounts. Tariff systems use informal "going rates" to guide judges in setting amounts. Because tariff systems tend to equate equity with consistency, they generally result in fines keyed to the lowest common economic denominator. This tends to limit judges' ability to adjust fines to an individual offender's financial means and to restrict their use of fines to less serious crimes or first offenders.

In contrast, day fines provide courts with greater capacity to vary fine amounts in a systematic and principled way. Day-fine systems accomplish this by a two-step process. First, the judge sentences an offender to a given number of fine units (e.g., 10, 15, or 90), which reflects the appropriate degree of punishment. Courts that rely on day fines have developed informal guidelines or benchmarks that suggest what number (or range) of units is appropriate for crimes of differing gravity.

The second step is to determine the monetary value of these units. Courts typically develop a rough but standardized method for calculating the proportion of a defendant's daily income that they view to be a "fair share" for the purposes of fining.

Using information routinely available from the police, a pretrial agency, probation, or (most often) the defendant, the judge will estimate the defendant's daily income and calculate the day-fine unit value. Multiplication of the number of units by this unit value produces the fine amount.

Since 1988, a day-fine system has been operating successfully in the Criminal Court of Richmond County, Staten Island, New York. A day-fine program has also been running successfully for over a year in the Maricopa Superior Court in Phoenix, Arizona. In Milwaukee, the day fine was introduced with considerable success as a strategy to reduce high levels of default among low-income offenders. Day-fine projects are under way in Oregon, Iowa, and Connecticut as part of a national demonstration project on "structured fines" sponsored by the Bureau of Justice Assistance. Numerous other jurisdictions are beginning to experiment with the concept, sometimes with encouragement from their state legislatures. In California, for example, legislation authorizes implementation of day-fine pilots.

Fines Reduce Use of Prison Sentences in Germany, Thomas Weigend
Intermediate Sanctions in Overcrowded Times
(Michael Tonry and Kate Hamilton eds., 1995)

Between 1968 and 1989, the former West Germany greatly reduced the proportion of convicted offenders sentenced to prison. In 1968, roughly a quarter of convicted offenders were sentenced to imprisonment. Two years later, the size of that group had dropped from 136,000 to 42,000, and the percentage of convicted offenders who were imprisoned had fallen from 24 percent to 7 percent. In 1989 (the latest year for which data are available), only 33,000 persons, less than 6 percent of adults convicted in West Germany, were sent directly to prison. . . .

The remarkable decline in prison use is due to a determined assault on use of short-term imprisonment. At the [start of the twentieth century], more than 50 percent of offenders received prison sentences of three months' duration or less. Legislation passed in 1921 obliged the courts to impose fines instead of short prison terms whenever the purpose of punishment could as well be achieved by a fine. Even so, the portion of short prison sentences among all prison sentences remained high; 83 percent of offenders sentenced to imprisonment in 1968 received sentences of six months or less. By that time, the German legislature had embraced the idea that short-term imprisonment does more harm than good: it disrupts the offender's ties with his family, job, and friends, introduces him into the prison subculture, and stigmatizes him for the rest of his life, but does not allow sufficient time for promising rehabilitative measures. Moreover, the data on the deterrent effectiveness of short-term imprisonment were inconclusive at best.

As a consequence, the German legislature in 1970 enacted section 47, sub. 1 of the Penal Code: "The court shall impose imprisonment below six months only if special circumstances concerning the offense or the offender's personality make the imposition of a prison sentence indispensable for reforming the offender or for defending the legal order." That amendment meant, in effect, that prison sentences below six months could be imposed only under exceptional circumstances for purposes of rehabilitation or general prevention. The number of such sentences dropped dramatically from 184,000 (1968) to 56,000 (1970); after some ups and downs, that figure reached a low of 48,000 in 1989 (and many of these were suspended).

At the same time, the German legislature extended the possibility of suspending short-term prison sentences (suspension being the German equivalent of probation). . . . .

The court can combine suspension with various conditions and restrictions, including the duty to make restitution to the victim or to pay a sum of money to the state or to a charitable organization. . . . .

German courts have made use of the suspension option with consistently increasing frequency. In 1968, the year before the reform, only 36 percent of prison sentences were suspended. By 1979, that portion had climbed to 65 percent, and it has not significantly changed since then (1989 — 67 percent). Prison sentences of six months or less have been suspended even more liberally (1989 — 77 percent). Revocations of suspension have diminished despite the more generous use of suspension. Whereas 46 percent of suspensions were revoked in 1986, less than a third (29 percent) were revoked in 1989.

For minor offenses, German law since 1975 offers an additional option of informal sanctioning. According to section 153a of the Code of Criminal Procedure, either the public prosecutor or the court can "invite" a suspect to pay a sum of money to the state, the victim, or a charitable organization in exchange for dismissal of the criminal prosecution. The theory of this quasi-sanction is that the suspect, by making the payment, eliminates the public interest in prosecuting the minor offense. The payment neither requires a formal admission of guilt nor implies a criminal conviction, but the (presumed) offender must pay an amount of money roughly equivalent to the fine that might be imposed if he were convicted. The use of this procedural option has greatly increased since its inception; prosecutors and courts employ it not only in petty cases but also for sanctioning fairly serious, especially economic, offenses without trial. Taking the quasi-sanction of section 153a into account, the distribution of criminal sanctions in Germany before and after the reforms of 1970 and 1975 is shown in figure 1.

FIGURE 1
Criminal Sanctions, 1968 and 1989

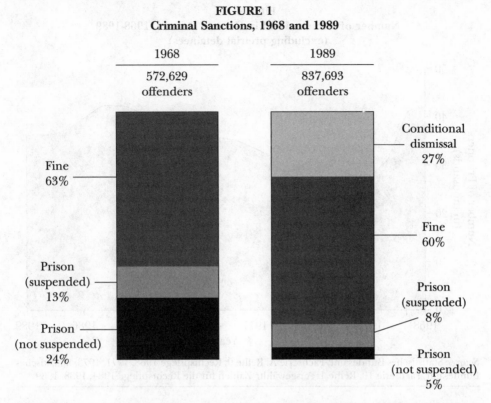

Sources: Statistisches Bundesamt, Fachserie A., Reihe 9: Rechtspflege 1968, p. 120; Statistisches Bundesamt, Fachserie 10, Reihe 3: Strafverfolgung 1989, p. 42; Statistisches Bundesamt Staatsanwaltschaften 1989, p. 14.

The de-emphasis of nonsuspended short prison sentences and the introduction of conditional dismissal produced a marked shift from custodial sentences (which, even in 1968, had a comparatively low incidence) to monetary sanctions. One might expect this shift to have led to a proportional depletion of German prisons. Curiously, that has failed to occur. Figure 2 shows the numbers of persons (excluding pretrial detainees) held in German prisons on March 31 of selected years.

[T]here are rational explanations for this development. First, the overall number of convicted offenders has increased, though not dramatically, from 573,000 (1968) to 609,000 (1989). More important, those who receive nonsuspended prison sentences tend to receive longer sentences than before: within fifteen years, the share of lengthy sentences (two to fifteen years) among all nonsuspended prison sentences increased from 9 percent (1974) to 15 percent. This change may be due to the increase in drug-related offenses, which tend to draw heavy sentences.

Moreover, the initial imposition of a noncustodial sentence does not necessarily mean that the offender can avoid prison, since about one third of suspended sentences are revoked (usually due to the commission of a new offense).

FIGURE 2
Number of Persons Held in German Prisons, 1968-1989
(excluding pretrial detainees)

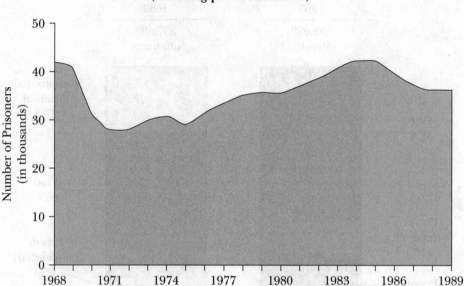

Sources: Statistisches Bundesamt, Fachserie A. Reihe 9: Rechtspflege 1968, 1971, 1973; Statistisches Bundesamt, Fachserie 10, Reihe 1: Ausgewählte Zahlen für die Rechtspflege 1984, 1988, 1989.

Offenders who receive fines can be sent to prison for nonpayment. Under German law, nonpayment can transform a fine into a prison term; the state need not show that the offender willfully refused to pay although he had the means to do so (section 43, Penal Code). Although only 6-7 percent of fined offenders eventually serve a prison term because of nonpayment, this group, due to the large absolute numbers involved, imposes a heavy burden on the corrections system: each year approximately 30,000 such persons enter prison.

In recent years, the German states have increasingly attempted to reduce that number by offering destitute offenders an alternative to prison. They can enter community service programs and thereby work off the fine instead of "sitting it off." These programs, though reaching only a limited number of offenders, have been described as fairly successful, especially when they are adequately staffed and organized. . . .

NOTES

1. *Day fines.* The underlying concept of day fines is that "punishment by a fine should be proportionate to the seriousness of the offense and should have roughly similar impact (in terms of economic sting) on persons with differing

financial resources who are convicted of the same offense." Bureau of Justice Assistance, How to Use Structured Fines (Day Fines) as an Intermediate Sanction (NCJ 156242, 1996). The concept was introduced in Sweden in the 1920s and then adopted in other Scandinavian and European countries. In Germany structured fines are used as the sole sanction for three-quarters of all offenders convicted of property crimes and two-thirds of offenders convicted of assaults. In the United States the first experiment with structured fines began on Staten Island, New York, in 1988. Fewer than a dozen U.S. jurisdictions have tried structured fine systems experimentally since that time. Why has the concept not (yet) taken off nationally?

2. *Structuring day fines.*   Day fines present structural and policy challenges. First the court must determine the number of fine units for each offense, based on offense seriousness. Then the court sets the dollar amount by multiplying the number of fine units by a portion of the defendant's daily income, subject to adjustment for taxes, dependents, and special circumstances. Both determinations — the relative seriousness of an offense and relative ability to pay — involve multiple policy choices. How should courts treat unemployed offenders? How should they calculate day fines on offenders working in the shadow economy, engaged in legal but untaxed activity?

3. *Constitutional limitations on fines.*   The Eighth Amendment to the Constitution prohibits "excessive fines." The provision's history can be traced back to the English Magna Carta, which gave judges the opportunity to overrule excessive penalties. In recent years the clause has been used most frequently to challenge punitive damage awards in civil cases as well as civil and criminal forfeitures, as discussed in more detail in Chapter 10. See, e.g., United States v. Bajakajian, 524 U.S. 321 (1998) (amount forfeited must be proportionate to the criminal offense); Austin v. United States, 509 U.S. 602 (1993). Might fines in criminal cases raise less of an Eighth Amendment question of absolute proportionality than an equal protection issue, given their disparate impact depending on a person's resources?

4. *Nonprison sanctions and crime rates.*   Do countries adopt nonprison sanctions only at times of decreasing crime (or decreasing fear of crime)? Note that the emphasis on fines described by Weigend occurred during a time of increasing crime rates.

> [O]fficial sentencing policy in Germany has responded in an anticyclical fashion by discouraging the imposition of prison sentences in the face of a growing crime rate. . . . German policies, and the faithful implementation of their directives by prosecutors and courts, . . . led to a "cushioning" of the crime wave of the 1970s. A greater percentage of offenses than before were resolved without conviction, and potential overcrowding of prisons was avoided by increased use of fines and suspended sentences. The crime wave ebbed after 1983, independent of any action or inaction on the part of criminal justice policymakers.

To what extent have concerns about the negative impact of short-term prison sentences (less than six months) driven the introduction of day fines in Germany? Current social science research in Europe indicates that such short prison terms do not have the feared negative impact, and some countries are moving back toward the imposition of short prison sentences.

May fines be viewed as categorically insufficient for some types of offenders and offenses? The Department of Justice, for example, has indicated that for high-level corporate officials involved in white-collar crime, prison is the only appropriate sanction because of its deterrent value, stigmatizing effect, and ability to highlight the seriousness of the offense. See, e.g., James B. Comey Jr., The Genesis of the Sentencing Provisions of the Sarbanes-Oxley Act, "Are We Getting Really Tough on White-Collar Crime?" Hearing Before the Subcomm. on Crime and Drugs, S. Judiciary Comm. (June 19, 2002), pt. 1, 15 Fed. Sent'g Rep. 234 (2002).

2. Probation

Probation, an outgrowth of the belief in rehabilitation, emerged during the second half of the nineteenth century. Probationary sentences typically release the offender into the community after sentencing but restrict the offender's freedom and actions. Usually a probation officer is assigned to supervise the offender. Probationary sentences are by far the most common type of criminal sanction imposed. At the end of 2005, more than 4 million adults were on probation in the United States. Just about half of them had been convicted of a felony, the others of misdemeanors and infractions. More than a quarter of them were drug offenders; 15% of them had been convicted of driving while intoxicated, and another 12% had been convicted of some form of larceny or theft offense. See Bureau of Justice Statistics, Probation and Parole in the United States, 2005 (NCJ 215091, November 2006).

Probationary sentences involve two closely related issues: first, what are acceptable conditions of probation, and second, what are the procedures and consequences for violation of those conditions?

a.   Probationary Conditions

The following case explores the foundations and limits of probationary conditions. Consider whether each judge's gender might have affected his or her view of the condition at issue.

|| *State v. David Oakley* ||
|| **629 N.W.2d 200 (Wis. 2001)** ||

WILCOX, J.

[W]e must decide whether as a condition of probation, a father of nine children, who has intentionally refused to pay child support, can be required to avoid having another child, unless he shows that he can support that child and his current children. We conclude that in light of Oakley's ongoing victimization of his nine children and extraordinarily troubling record manifesting his disregard for the law, this anomalous condition—imposed on a convicted felon facing the far more restrictive and punitive sanction of prison—is not overly broad and is reasonably related to Oakley's rehabilitation. Simply put, because Oakley was convicted of intentionally refusing to pay child support—a felony in Wisconsin—and could have been imprisoned for six years, which would have eliminated his right to procreate altogether during those six years, this probation condition, which infringes on his right to procreate during his term of probation, is not invalid under these facts. Accordingly, we hold that the circuit court did not erroneously exercise its discretion. . . .

David Oakley (Oakley), the petitioner, was initially charged with intentionally refusing to pay child support for his nine children he has fathered with four different women. The State subsequently charged Oakley with seven counts of intentionally refusing to provide child support as a repeat offender. His repeat offender status stemmed from intimidating two witnesses in a child abuse case—where one of the victims was his own child. . . .

Oakley . . . entered into [a] plea agreement in which he agreed to enter a no contest plea to three counts of intentionally refusing to support his children and have the other four counts read-in for sentencing. . . . The State, in turn, agreed that in exchange for his no contest plea, it would cap its sentencing recommendation to a total of six years on all counts. Oakley, however, was free to argue for a different sentence.

Oakley had paid no child support and there were arrears in excess of $25,000. Highlighting Oakley's consistent and willful disregard for the law and his obligations to his children, the State argued that Oakley should be sentenced to six years in prison. . . . Oakley, in turn, asked for the opportunity to maintain full-time employment, provide for his children, and make serious payment towards his arrears.

After taking into account Oakley's ability to work and his consistent disregard of the law and his obligations to his children, Judge Hazlewood observed that "if Mr. Oakley had paid something, had made an earnest effort to pay anything within his remote ability to pay, we wouldn't be sitting here," nor would the State argue for six years in prison. But Judge Hazlewood also recognized that "if Mr. Oakley goes to prison, he's not going to be in a position to pay any meaningful support for these children." Therefore, even though Judge Hazlewood acknowledged that Oakley's "defaults, are obvious, consistent, and inexcusable," he decided against sentencing Oakley to six years in prison . . . , as the State had advocated. Instead, Judge Hazlewood sentenced Oakley to three years in prison on the first count, imposed and stayed an eight-year term on the two other counts, and imposed a five-year term of probation consecutive to his incarceration. Judge Hazlewood then imposed the condition at issue here: while on probation, Oakley cannot have any more children unless he demonstrates that he has the ability to support them and that he is supporting the children he already has. After sentencing, Oakley filed for postconviction relief contesting this condition. . . .

Refusal to pay child support by so-called "deadbeat parents" has fostered a crisis with devastating implications for our children. Of those single parent households with established child support awards or orders, approximately one-third did not receive any payment while another one-third received only partial payment. For example, in 1997, out of $26,400,000,000 awarded by a court order to custodial mothers, only $15,800,000,000 was actually paid, amounting to a deficit of $10,600,000,000. These figures represent only a portion of the child support obligations that could be collected if every custodial parent had a support order established. Single mothers disproportionately bear the burden of nonpayment as the custodial parent. On top of the stress of being a single parent, the nonpayment of child support frequently presses single mothers below the poverty line. In fact, 32.1% of custodial mothers were below the poverty line in 1997, in comparison to only 10.7% of custodial fathers. . . .

The effects of the nonpayment of child support on our children are particularly troubling. In addition to engendering long-term consequences such as poor health, behavioral problems, delinquency and low educational attainment, inadequate child support is a direct contributor to childhood poverty. And childhood poverty is all too pervasive in our society. Over 12 million or about one out of every six children in our country lives in poverty. . . . Child support — when paid — on average amounts to over one-quarter of a poor child's family income. There is little doubt that the payment of child support benefits poverty-stricken children the most. Enforcing child support orders thus has surfaced as a major policy directive in our society.

In view of the suffering children must endure when their noncustodial parent intentionally refuses to pay child support, it is not surprising that the legislature has attached severe sanctions to this crime. . . . The legislature has amended this statute so that intentionally refusing to pay child support is now punishable by up to five years in prison.

But Wisconsin law is not so rigid as to mandate the severe sanction of incarceration as the only means of addressing a violation of §948.22(2). In sentencing, a Wisconsin judge can take into account a broad array of factors, including the gravity of the offense and need for protection of the public and potential victims. Other factors — concerning the convicted individual — that a judge can consider include:

> the past record of criminal offenses; any history of undesirable behavior patterns; the defendant's personality, character and social traits; the results of a presentence investigation; the vicious or aggravated nature of the crime; the degree of defendant's culpability; the defendant's demeanor at trial; the defendant's age, educational background and employment record; the defendant's remorse, repentance and cooperativeness; the defendant's need for close rehabilitative control; the rights of the public; and the length of pretrial detention.

After considering all these factors, a judge may decide to forgo the severe punitive sanction of incarceration and address the violation with the less restrictive alternative of probation coupled with specific conditions. Wisconsin Stat. §973.09(1)(a) provides:

> [I]f a person is convicted of a crime, the court, by order, may withhold sentence or impose sentence under s. 973.15 and stay its execution, and in either case place the person on probation to the department for a stated period, stating in

the order the reasons therefor. The court may impose any conditions which appear to be reasonable and appropriate.

The statute, then, grants a circuit court judge broad discretion in fashioning a convicted individual's conditions of probation. As we have previously observed, "[t]he theory of the probation statute is to rehabilitate the defendant and protect society without placing the defendant in prison. To accomplish this theory, the circuit court is empowered by Wis. Stat. §973.09(1)(a) to fashion the terms of probation to meet the rehabilitative needs of the defendant." While rehabilitation is the goal of probation, judges must also concern themselves with the imperative of protecting society and potential victims. On this score, we have explained:

> [Probation] involves a prediction by the sentencing court society will not be endangered by the convicted person not being incarcerated. This is risk that the legislature has empowered the courts to take in the exercise of their discretion. . . .
>   If the convicted criminal is thus to escape the more severe punishment of imprisonment for his wrongdoing, society and the potential victims of his anti-social tendencies must be protected.

State v. Evans, 252 N.W.2d 664, 666 (Wis. 1977). Thus, when a judge allows a convicted individual to escape a prison sentence and enjoy the relative freedom of probation, he or she must take reasonable judicial measures to protect society and potential victims from future wrongdoing. To that end — along with the goal of rehabilitation — the legislature has seen fit to grant circuit court judges broad discretion in setting the terms of probation. . . .

In the present case, the record indicates that Judge Hazlewood was familiar with Oakley's abysmal history prior to sentencing. The record reveals that Judge Hazlewood knew that Oakley had a number of support orders entered for his nine children, but he nevertheless continually refused to support them. He was aware that Oakley's probation for intimidating two witnesses in a child abuse case — where one of the witnesses was his own child and the victim — was in the process of being revoked. Judge Hazlewood was also apprised that Oakley had promised in the past to support his children, but those promises had failed to translate into the needed support. Moreover, he knew that Oakley had been employed and had no impediment preventing him from working. . . .

Judge Hazlewood asserted that some prison time coupled with conditional probation might convince Oakley to stop victimizing his children. With probation, Judge Hazlewood sought to rehabilitate Oakley while protecting society and potential victims — Oakley's own children — from future wrongdoing. The conditions were designed to assist Oakley in conforming his conduct to the law. . . . At the same time, Judge Hazlewood sought to protect the victims of Oakley's crimes — Oakley's nine children.

But Oakley argues that the condition imposed by Judge Hazlewood violates his constitutional right to procreate. This court, in accord with the United States Supreme Court, has previously recognized the fundamental liberty interest of a citizen to choose whether or not to procreate. Eberhardy v. Circuit Court for

Wood County, 307 N.W.2d 881 (Wis. 1981); Skinner v. Oklahoma ex rel. Williamson, 316 U.S. 535 (1942) (recognizing the right to procreate as "one of the basic civil rights of man"). Accordingly, Oakley argues that the condition here warrants strict scrutiny. That is, it must be narrowly tailored to serve a compelling state interest. Although Oakley concedes, as he must, that the State's interest in requiring parents to support their children is compelling, he argues that the means employed here is not narrowly tailored to serve that compelling interest because Oakley's "right to procreate is not restricted but in fact eliminated." . . . While Oakley's argument might well carry the day if he had not intentionally refused to pay child support, it is well-established that convicted individuals do not enjoy the same degree of liberty as citizens who have not violated the law. We emphatically reject the novel idea that Oakley, who was convicted of intentionally failing to pay child support, has an absolute right to refuse to support his current nine children and any future children that he procreates, thereby adding more child victims to the list. In an analogous case, Oregon upheld a similar probation condition to protect child victims from their father's abusive behavior in State v. Kline, 963 P.2d 697, 699 (Or. App. 1998). . . .

Oakley fails to note that incarceration, by its very nature, deprives a convicted individual of the fundamental right to be free from physical restraint, which in turn encompasses and restricts other fundamental rights, such as the right to procreate. Therefore, given that a convicted felon does not stand in the same position as someone who has not been convicted of a crime, we have previously stated that "conditions of probation may impinge upon constitutional rights as long as they are not overly broad and are reasonably related to the person's rehabilitation." Edwards v. State, 246 N.W.2d 109 (Wis. 1976). In Krebs v. State, 568 N.W.2d 26 (Wis. Ct. App. 1997), the court of appeals recently applied this established standard to uphold a condition of probation that required a defendant who sexually assaulted his own daughter to obtain his probation agent's approval before entering into an intimate or sexual relationship. The court found that although the condition infringed upon a constitutional right, it was reasonable and not overly broad.

Applying the relevant standard here, we find that the condition is not overly broad because it does not eliminate Oakley's ability to exercise his constitutional right to procreate. He can satisfy the condition of probation by making efforts to support his children as required by law. . . . If Oakley decides to continue his present course of conduct — intentionally refusing to pay child support — he will face eight years in prison regardless of how many children he has. Furthermore, this condition will expire at the end of his term of probation. He may then decide to have more children, but of course, if he continues to intentionally refuse to support his children, the State could charge him again under §948.22(2). Rather, because Oakley can satisfy this condition by not intentionally refusing to support his current nine children and any future children as required by the law, we find that the condition is narrowly tailored to serve the State's compelling interest of having parents support their children. It is also narrowly tailored to serve the State's compelling interest in rehabilitating Oakley through probation rather than prison. The alternative to probation with conditions—incarceration for eight years—would have further victimized his children. And it is undoubtedly much broader than this conditional impingement on his procreative freedom for it would deprive him of his fundamental right to be free from physical restraint. Simply stated, Judge Hazlewood preserved much of Oakley's liberty by imposing probation with conditions rather than the more punitive option of imprisonment.

Moreover, the condition is reasonably related to the goal of rehabilitation. A condition is reasonably related to the goal of rehabilitation if it assists the convicted individual in conforming his or her conduct to the law. See State v. Miller, 499 N.W.2d 215 (Wis. Ct. App. 1993) (ruling that condition on probationer convicted of making obscene telephone calls forbidding him to make calls to any woman other than a family member was reasonably related to his rehabilitation). Here, Oakley was convicted of intentionally refusing to support his children. The condition at bar . . . is narrowly tailored to serve the compelling state interest of requiring parents to support their children as well as rehabilitating those convicted of crimes. . . .

BABLITCH, J., concurring. . . .

The two dissents frame the issue in such a way that Oakley's intentional refusal to pay support evolves into an inability to pay support. This case is not at all about an inability to pay support; it is about the intentional refusal to pay support. . . .

The dissents conclude that the majority's means of advancing the state's interest is not narrowly tailored to advance the state's interest. The dissents fail to advance any realistic alternative solution to what they concede is a compelling state interest. As long as the defendant continues to intentionally refuse to pay support, the alternatives posed by the dissents will end up with incarceration—which of course accomplishes indirectly what the dissents say the state cannot do directly. . . .

I conclude that the harm to others who cannot protect themselves is so overwhelmingly apparent and egregious here that there is no room for question. Here is a man who has shown himself time and again to be totally and completely irresponsible. He lives only for himself and the moment, with no regard to the consequences of his actions and taking no responsibility for them. He intentionally refuses to pay support and has been convicted of that felony. The harm that he has done to his nine living children by failing to support them is patent and egregious. . . . Under certain conditions, it is overwhelmingly obvious that any child he fathers in the future is doomed to a future of neglect, abuse, or worse. That as yet unborn child is a victim from the day it is born.

I am not happy with this result, but can discern no other. And the dissents provide none. Accordingly, I join the majority opinion. . . .

BRADLEY, J., dissenting.

I begin by emphasizing the right that is at issue: the right to have children. The majority acknowledges this right, but certainly does not convey its significance and preeminence. The right to have children is a basic human right and an aspect of the fundamental liberty which the Constitution jealously guards for all Americans. See Skinner v. Oklahoma ex rel. Williamson, 316 U.S. 535 (1942).

Thus, the stakes are high in this case. The majority's decision allows, for the first time in our state's history, the birth of a child to carry criminal sanctions. Today's decision makes this court the only court in the country to declare constitutional a condition that limits a probationer's right to procreate based on his financial ability to support his children. Ultimately, the majority's decision may affect the rights of every citizen of this state, man or woman, rich or poor.

I wholeheartedly agree with the majority that the governmental interest at stake in this case is of great magnitude. . . . However, when fundamental rights are at issue, the end does not necessarily justify the means. The majority concludes that the means of effecting the state's interest are sufficiently narrow in light of this governmental interest. I disagree. . . .

The circuit court order forbids Oakley from fathering another child until he can first establish the financial ability to support his children. Oakley is not prohibited from having intercourse, either indiscriminately or irresponsibly. Rather, the condition of probation is not triggered until Oakley's next child is born. . . .

While on its face the order leaves room for the slight possibility that Oakley may establish the financial means to support his children, the order is essentially a prohibition on the right to have children. Oakley readily admits that unless he wins the lottery, he will likely never be able to establish that ability. The circuit court understood the impossibility of Oakley satisfying this financial requirement when it imposed the condition. . . . Stressing the realities of Oakley's situation, the circuit court explained:

> [Y]ou know and I know you're probably never going to make 75 or 100 thousand dollars a year. You're going to struggle to make 25 or 30. And by the time you take care of your taxes and your social security, there isn't a whole lot to go around, and then you've got to ship it out to various children.

In light of the circuit court's recognition of Oakley's inability to meet the condition of probation, the prohibition cannot be considered a narrowly drawn means of advancing the state's interest in ensuring support for Oakley's children. . . .

Let there be no question that I agree with the majority that David Oakley's conduct cannot be condoned. It is irresponsible and criminal. However, we must keep in mind what is really at stake in this case. The fundamental right to have children, shared by us all, is damaged by today's decision. Because I will not join in the majority's disregard of that right, I dissent.

SYKES, J., dissenting.

Can the State criminalize the birth of a child to a convicted felon who is likely to be unwilling or unable to adequately support the child financially? That is essentially the crux of the circuit court order in this case, or at least its apparent practical effect. . . .

Oakley must seek the court's permission and obtain the court's approval before bringing another child into the world. He is subject to probation revocation and imprisonment if he fathers a child without prior court approval.

While I sympathize with the circuit court's understandable exasperation with this chronic "deadbeat dad," I cannot agree that this probation condition survives constitutional scrutiny. It is basically a compulsory, state-sponsored, court-enforced financial test for future parenthood. . . .

NOTES

1. *Probation: the most common U.S. sanction.* At the end of 2005, more than 4 million adults were on probation in the United States. See Bureau of Justice Statistics, Probation and Parole in the United States, 2005 (NCJ 215091, November 2006). Of those sentenced to probation, the mean sentence length was 33.6 months, the median 36 months. The United States has the highest probation rate in the world, with 536 per 100,000 population, followed by Canada (269) and England and Wales (217).

In federal court 18.2% of all offenders sentenced between October 1, 1999, and September 30, 2000, received a probation-only sentence. About half of the misdemeanants received such a sentence, compared with only 13.3% of all felony offenders. Among those felons, however, a large disparity existed: only 5% of those convicted of drug trafficking received straight probation, but almost half of all larcenists and almost 90% of those convicted of gambling offenses received a probation sentence. Should certain types of offenders presumptively receive probationary sentences?

2. *Probationary conditions.* While the specific condition in *Oakley* is unusual, the more general question it raises is pervasive: what conditions may or should be imposed as part of probationary sentences? Probationary sentences are inherently more varied than imprisonment, and idiosyncratic probation conditions, such as the one in *Oakley,* are often challenged on appeal. For further examples and a critical review of such conditions, see Andrew Horwitz, Coercion, Pop-Psychology, and Judicial Moralizing: Some Proposals for Curbing Judicial Abuse of Probation Conditions, 57 Wash. & Lee L. Rev. 75 (2000). Is this flexibility always a virtue? Should lists of conditions be standardized? If so, by whom? See Demarce v. Willrich, 56 P.3d 76 (Ariz. Ct. App. 2002) (upholding lifetime probation for sex offender); People v. Kimbrell, 684 N.E.2d 443 (Ill. App. Ct. 1997) (upholding probation condition for theft offense forbidding contact with defendant's son's father).

3. *The nature and evolution of probationary sanctions.* Probationary sanctions are beginning to focus on the idea of "responsibilization," shifting more responsibility to offenders to solve their own problems. Is probation a privilege? What obligations flow from it? Some newer probationary sanctions have tended to emphasize greater control than regular probation. Among them are intensive supervised probation and house arrest, which often includes

electronic monitoring. Would it be more effective to move a smaller number of higher-risk offenders to increased supervision and decrease supervision for those considered a lesser or intermediate risk? Do the parallel trends of increasing "self-rescue" on the one hand and increasing intensive control on the other suggest differing conceptions of probation in general, or do they reflect the notion that probation may be structured to achieve different purposes for different offenders?

4. *The efficacy of probation.*   Research on the effectiveness of probation indicates that a high percentage of probationers either violate the conditions of probation or commit another offense while on probation. During 1990 17% of all persons arrested for felonies in large, urban counties were on probation. Nevertheless, risky behavior as well as criminal activity goes down during supervision. When the intensity of supervision increases, probation revocations also increase, largely because of technical violations.

b.   Probation Violations

Probation is violated when the offender acts contrary to the conditions of supervision established by the court or the probation department. The violation may be criminal, as in the commission of a new offense, or technical, as in the failure to meet a specific probation condition. Not all violations lead to automatic revocation of probation. While protection of the community is the guiding principle, after a violation other strategies to monitor and control offender behavior may be used.

Do the probation rules give probationers too many chances? Should all probation violations lead to immediate termination of probation?

Because probationary sentences involve substantially lower levels of social control than prison sentences and are served in the community, not only the specified conditions but also the processes for review and revocation reflect the essential qualities and purposes of such sentences. Consider the following policies and procedures in North Carolina.

Violations Policies — Procedures,
North Carolina Department of Correction
Division of Community Corrections
March 1, 2002

GENERAL PROVISIONS

A *violation* is any action by the offender that is contrary to the conditions of supervision established by the Court or Post-Release Supervision and Parole Commission. Violations may be criminal (involving the commission of a new offense) or technical (involving a failure to meet one or more specific conditions of the probation judgment or parole or post-release supervision agreement).

1. Violation Philosophy

All responses to violation behavior will be considered in light of the Department's mission and objectives, as well as the goals of the supervision process. While protection of the community must always be the primary consideration, it does not follow that revocation is always, or even usually, the most effective or efficient way of achieving this goal. The goal of community supervision is to selectively and proactively intervene with offenders to reduce the likelihood of future criminal activity and promote compliance with the supervision strategy. Strategies involve holding offenders accountable for their actions, monitoring and controlling offender behavior, and referring to rehabilitation programs specific to offender needs. Another significant piece of the supervision strategy is ensuring an appropriate and proportionate response to all violations of the conditions of probation, taking into account offender risk, the nature of the violation, and the objective of offender accountability.

The purpose of this policy is to provide a framework to guide officer decision-making when a violation of probation has occurred. . . . Technical violations of the conditions of probation are inevitable. It is unrealistic to believe offenders, even if they sincerely desire to develop drug-free, pro-social lifestyles, will immediately have the skills or abilities to do so. The issues and forces that brought them into the system will most likely continue to impact their behavior to some extent until they learn new skills and methods of dealing with these forces.

The basic expectations underlying the Division's policy regarding probation violations are:

- There will be a response to every detected violation;
- Responses to violations will be proportional to the risk to the community posed by the particular offender, the severity of the violation, and the current situational risk;
- The least restrictive response necessary to respond to the behavior will be used;
- There will be consistency in handling similar violation behavior given similar risk factors;
- Responses to violations will hold some potential for long-term positive outcomes in the context of the supervision strategy;
- While response to violation behavior is determined by considering both risk and needs, risk to the community is the overriding consideration; *and*
- Probationers who demonstrate a habitual unwillingness to abide by supervision requirements or who pose undue risk to the community will be subject to revocation of probation.

2. Violation Response Procedures

When a violation occurs the supervising officer will assess the type of violation (emergency or nonemergency) and take appropriate action.

A. Emergency Violations

Emergency violations involve behavior that *requires the immediate arrest of the offender* in order to ensure public safety. Emergency violations include, but are not limited to, the following:

- An imminent threat by the offender of physical harm to self or others;
- Electronic House Arrest violations such as equipment tampering;
- For probation cases only, possession of contraband necessitating an arrest incidental to search and/or seizure;
- Willful violations of residential facility rules; and/or
- For sex offenders, violations of specific conditions directly related to the crime. . . .

B. Non-emergency Violations

Non-emergency violations involve behavior that does not indicate the need for immediate arrest of the offender in order to ensure public safety. Non-emergency violations . . . include:

- A new conviction for any felony or a Class A1, 1 or 2 [or 3] misdemeanor;
- A new conviction for the same offense for which currently being supervised;
- Pending charges on a case about to expire;
- Being charged with a new offense in addition to [or without] one or more technical violations;
- Absconding;
- Financial arrearage of greater than six months for probation . . . cases . . . ;
- Lesser Electronic House Arrest violations that do not require immediate arrest;
- Possession of a weapon;
- Unwanted contact with the victim;
- Any violation related to substance abuse or any driving violation for DWI Level I or II cases;
- Pending technical violations at the expiration of the term of probation;
- Failure to comply with treatment;
- Notification of non-compliance with the rules of a Day Reporting Center, residential program, or the DART Program;
- Failure to report for jail time; . . .
- Non-compliance with community service requirement[;] . . .
- Verbal refusal to participate in substance abuse screening, not necessitating a Violation Report;
- Non-reporting for supervision; . . .
- Financial arrearage of less than six months for probation . . . cases . . . ; the Probation/Parole Officer may consider this violation an "A" violation for cases in which victim restitution is ordered;

- Curfew violation;
- Positive substance abuse screening;
- Unemployment, not seeking employment as ordered, or failure to notify the Probation [] Officer of employment loss;
- GED/school non-attendance;
- Leaving the jurisdiction or changing residence without permission;
- Going to restricted areas;
- Violating an order not to possess pagers or cellular phones;
- Failure to attend a prison tour; and
- Reporting in an unreasonable manner. . . .

Probation/Parole Officer will respond to non-emergency violations according to the Non-Emergency Violation Response Guidelines. The purpose for the Non-Emergency Violation Response Guidelines is to insure swift and certain response to every violation and to utilize the full continuum of sanctions prior to revocation. The Non-Emergency Response Guidelines apply to all technical violations except substance abuse testing violations. . . .

C. Non-emergency Violation Response Guidelines

a. Level I Violation Response — Officer Response

Upon detection of the offender's first violation(s), the supervising officer will warn the offender either verbally or in writing or seek the assistance of the Chief Probation [] Officer in warning the offender either verbally or in writing. The Probation [] Officer may also require the offender to report more frequently. Subsequent violation(s) may be addressed at Level I or Level II Response.

b. Level II Violation Response — Officer/Chief Response

If the supervising Probation [] Officer determines a Level II Response is needed, the officer will staff the case with the Chief Probation [] Officer. Level II Response includes override of supervision level and use of delegated authority sanctions available within community or intermediate punishment. . . .

c. Level III Violation Response — Court/Hearing Response

A Level III Violation Response may be initiated only after options from Level I and Level II have been used. Level III options, which may be pursued after staffing the case with the Chief Probation [] Officer, include a recommendation for an Intermediate Punishment, extending/modifying probation or contempt of court. . . .

d. Level IV Violation Response — Revocation

Revocation may be recommended only after staffing the case with the Chief Probation [] Officer and a Level III response has been used.

3. *Non-emergency Violation Response Charts*

The following [chart gives] non-emergency violation response guidelines for probation . . . cases.

Non-Emergency Violation Response Chart — Probation

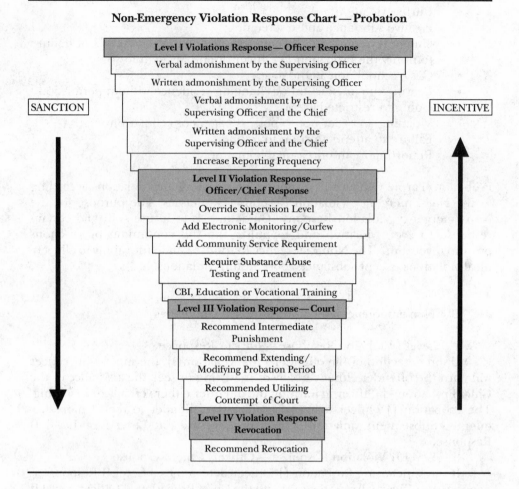

4.   Positive Substance Abuse Screening Guidelines

Following confirmation of the first positive screen result, the Probation []
Officer will confront the offender with the positive screen result within ten
(10) days:

A.   Procedure for First Positive Drug Screen Result

1. Offender Admits Illegal Drug Use
    a. If the offender agrees to seek treatment, make a referral to TASC
        where available for assessment and referral to treatment or to any
        licensed treatment program where TASC is unavailable.
    b. If the offender refuses to submit to assessment and/or treatment,
        the officer will staff the case with the Chief Probation [] Officer and
        will use delegated authority to have the offender submit to assess-
        ment and treatment. If delegated authority is not available issue
        a . . . Violation Report or . . . [a] Non-Compliance Report and

recommend a modification to the conditions of supervision requiring substance abuse assessment and compliance with the results.

2. Offender Denies Illegal Drug Use

    a. If the offender refuses to submit to a treatment assessment, . . .
obtain a confirmation test of the positive drug screen from the
substance abuse screening lab and forward with a . . . Violation
Report to the court of conviction or . . . to the Post-Release Supervision and Parole Commission; and,

    b. During the violation hearing, recommend a modification to the
conditions of supervision requiring substance abuse assessment
and compliance with the results.

B. Procedure for Second or Subsequent Positive Result

Following receipt of the second or subsequent positive screen result, the
Probation [] Officer will review the case with the Chief Probation [] Officer and
treatment provider, if applicable, to evaluate the offender's treatment needs and
determine an appropriate course of action, including but not limited to therapeutic sanctions. . . .

VIOLATION HEARINGS

Violation hearings may be held in the District Court or Superior Court
having original jurisdiction, the judicial district in which the offender resides, or
the judicial district in which he/she is alleged to have violated probation. . . .

NOTES

1. *Probation violations.*   The structure, purpose, and efficacy of probationary sentences turn as much on the procedures and consequences of violations as
on the terms of the sentence itself. One of the puzzles of probationary sentences
is that more aggressive enforcement and more rigid responses to conditions
such as drug screens can lead to very high rates of violation. Yet nonenforcement
may undermine the purposes and goals of the particular sentences. Does the
structured and graduated system in North Carolina respond to these concerns?
How would you define success in the North Carolina system? Should other states
adopt a similar system?

2. *Probation violators.*   The most recent statistics on probation violators in
state prisons are from 1991. They show a steady increase since the 1970s in the
incarceration of probation violators. As of 1991, almost one-quarter of probationers were incarcerated for probation violations. One-quarter of these had
probation revocation hearings because they had committed a new crime,
10% had failed a drug test, 36% did not report to their probation officer,
and 12% percent had failed to pay fines or restitution or to comply with
other financial commitments. See Robyn L. Cohen, Probation and Parole

Violators in State Prison, 1991 (NCJ 149076, August 1995). Is revocation of probation appropriate for any, or all, of these violations?

B.   MODERN ALTERNATIVE SANCTIONS

Appearing in the news much more often than probation and fines, but in reality much less common, are a range of new sentences — some creations of the postmodern mind and some resurrections of sentences long defunct (and perhaps justly so). The most significant of these are boot camp, home confinement, shaming sanctions, and community service.

While modern alternative sanctions are relatively rare, they appear to have captured the imagination of the public, politicians, and a fair number of legal scholars. They deserve attention here because of the public attention paid to them and because of the extent to which they reveal deeper symbolic aspects and needs of punishment (a point that may be made about capital sentences as well). Perhaps these unusual but dramatic sanctions highlight a demand for an "expressive" purpose distinct from (or perhaps a component of) the more traditional purposes of retribution and reinforcement of community norms. See Joel Feinberg, The Expressive Function of Punishment, reprinted in Joel Feinberg, Doing and Deserving 98 (1970).

These new sanctions also raise further concern about "net widening." Will they be applied to offenders who otherwise would go to prison? Or will they instead be imposed on those who would receive probationary sanctions, or even those whose cases would be dismissed? In the latter cases, intermediate sanctions have become supplements rather than alternatives to more traditional criminal justice sanctions.

In thinking about these new kinds of sentences, a useful distinction can be drawn between those that include some degree of physical detention, and that therefore either replace or mimic imprisonment, and those that do not.

1.   Nonprison Detention: Boot Camp and Home Confinement

In the mid-1990s, there were about 75 boot camps for adult offenders in more than 30 states and about 30 for juveniles, though since then the number of boot camps has declined. The adult state boot camps have a bed capacity of less than 7,000. The federal government recently eliminated its boot camp programs, which had been termed Intensive Confinement Centers (ICCs). According to statements from persons working with the U.S. Bureau of Prisons, the federal Intensive Confinement Program was discontinued after 14 years of operation because of the view of federal prison officials that the program was not cost-effective and was not successful in preventing people from becoming repeat offenders.

The first boot camps — originally designed for adult men — were developed in 1983 in Georgia and Oklahoma to contain rising confinement costs and alleviate prison overcrowding. Over the next decade boot camps began to serve women and juvenile offenders as well. The average age of state boot camp inmates is between 19 and 20.

Because boot camps are considered an intermediate sanction, only offenders convicted of less serious, nonviolent offenses are usually admitted, and for relatively short periods of time. While the first boot camps were modeled after military boot camps, they came to emphasize education, therapeutic and treatment services, and community aftercare, with the goal of reducing recidivism. Despite initially promising results and wide adoption, in recent years boot camps have fallen out of favor.

From reading the following study of boot camps, do you think they should be part of the array of available sanctions in your state? If so, for which offenders?

Correctional Boot Camps: Lessons from a Decade of Research, Dale G. Parent
(National Institute of Justice, NCJ 197018, July 2003)

In response to rising rates of serious crime, many correctional systems established boot camps as an alternative sanction that might reduce recidivism, prison populations, and operating costs. Despite a decade of popularity with policymakers and the public, boot camps have had difficulty meeting these objectives.

The National Institute of Justice (NIJ) sponsored an analysis of research conducted over a 10-year period beginning in the late 1980s. This analysis concluded that

- Boot camps generally had positive effects on the attitudes, perceptions, behavior, and skills of inmates during their confinement.
- With limited exceptions, these positive changes did not translate into reduced recidivism.
- Boot camps can achieve small relative reductions in prison populations and modest reductions in correctional costs under a narrow set of conditions (admitting offenders with a high likelihood of otherwise serving a conventional prison term and offering discounts in time served to those who complete boot camps).

The surveyed research identified three factors largely responsible for the failure of boot camps to reach goals related to prison population and recidivism:

- Mandates to reduce prison populations through early release made volunteering for boot camps unnecessary as a means of shortening sentences.
- Lack of a standard boot camp model.
- Insufficient focus on offenders' reentry into the community.

The camps' disciplined structure and therapeutic programs eliminated idleness and created a safer environment, which in turn improved inmate attitudes and behavior. Such structure, coupled with a therapeutic orientation, may apply to other correctional programs, especially those that target youthful offenders.

WHY BOOT CAMPS?

As the name implies, correctional boot camps are in-prison programs that resemble military basic training. They emphasize vigorous physical activity, drill and ceremony, manual labor, and other activities that ensure that participants have little, if any, free time. Strict rules govern all aspects of conduct and appearance. Correctional officers act as drill instructors, initially using intense verbal tactics designed to break down inmates' resistance and lead to constructive changes.

Three Generations of Camps.   Boot camps proliferated in the late 1980s and early 1990s. By 1995, State correctional agencies operated 75 boot camps for adults, State and local agencies operated 30 juvenile boot camps, and larger counties operated 18 boot camps in local jails.

The camps evolved over time. . . . Although first-generation camps stressed military discipline, physical training, and hard work, second-generation camps emphasized rehabilitation by adding such components as alcohol and drug treatment and prosocial skills training. Some also added intensive postrelease supervision that may include electronic monitoring, home confinement, and random urine tests. A few camps admitted females, but this proved somewhat controversial. Recently, some boot camps, particularly those for juveniles, have substituted an emphasis on educational and vocational skills for the military components to provide comparable structure and discipline.

After the mid-1990s, the number of boot camps declined. By 2000, nearly one-third of State prison boot camps had closed — only 51 camps remained. The average daily population in State boot camps also dropped more than 30 percent.

Boot Camps' Goals.   Boot camps had three main goals: reducing recidivism, reducing prison populations, and reducing costs.

Camps were expected to reduce recidivism by changing inmates' attitudes, values, and behaviors and by addressing factors that increase the likelihood of returning to prison (such as lack of job skills, addiction, and inability to control anger). Camps were expected to reduce prison populations by shortening time served. Reduced length of stay was expected to reduce costs.

Reducing Recidivism — An Unmet Goal.   NIJ evaluation studies consistently showed that boot camps did not reduce recidivism regardless of whether the camps were for adults or juveniles or whether they were first-generation programs with a heavy military emphasis or later programs with more emphasis on treatment. Most of the research suggested that the limitations of boot camps prevented them from reducing recidivism or prison populations, even as they achieved other goals. These limitations mostly resulted from —

- Low "dosage" effects. The length of stay in boot camps — usually from 90 to 120 days — was too brief to realistically affect recidivism.
- Insufficient preparation of boot camp inmates for reentry into the community. Many boot camps provided little or no postrelease programming to prepare graduates to lead productive lives. In addition,

the intensive supervision common to later generations of boot camps meant heightened surveillance levels for boot camp graduates. These factors combined to magnify the high rates of return for technical parole violations.

- Conflicting or unrealistic goals or mandates set by State legislatures. For example, most boot camp programs sought to reduce prison populations. Shorter programs more effectively meet this goal, but they also lower dosage effects and reduce the likelihood that treatment programs will work, thereby potentially increasing recidivism.
- The absence of a strong underlying treatment model. Pragmatism and local politics often affected boot camp structure more than theory and research results. . . .

Improving Behavior — A Success Story. Boot camps were almost universally successful in improving inmates' attitudes and behavior during the course of the program; they also produced safer environments for staff and residents, presumably due to their highly structured atmosphere and activities.

Several studies indicated that adult boot camp participants had better attitudes about their confinement experiences and had improved their prosocial attitudes more than comparison group members. One study concluded that inmates in adult boot camps had increased self-esteem, reduced antisocial attitudes, increased problem-solving skills, improved coping skills, and improved social support. In other studies, boot camp inmates improved their self-esteem and standardized education scores in reading and math more than comparison group members.

Anxiety and depression declined to a greater degree among juveniles in boot camps than among those in comparison facilities. Dysfunctional impulsivity (the inability to control one's impulses) increased among youths in comparison facilities but decreased among boot camp participants. Social attitudes improved among youths in boot camps, but worsened among those in comparison facilities.

Reducing Prison Population — Mixed Results. NIJ-sponsored boot camp researchers agree that correctional boot camps might achieve small relative[14] reductions in prison populations. Boot camps could reduce the number of prison beds needed in a jurisdiction, which would lead to modest reductions in correctional costs. . . .

However, restrictive entry criteria for boot camp participants often made it impossible to reduce prison populations. For example, some jurisdictions required that boot camp inmates be nonviolent offenders convicted of their first felony. This small pool of eligible candidates typically serves short prison terms before parole. These inmates had little incentive to volunteer for boot camps that would not shorten their terms. When inmates sentenced to longer

---

14. Boot camps were unlikely to lower absolute prison population levels. The camps opened during a time when major changes in sentencing policies and practices caused prison populations to soar. Even at the height of their popularity, the total capacity of boot camps was minuscule compared to the total prison population.

prison terms were recruited, however, a reduction in time served became a compelling incentive.

Efforts to meet the recidivism goal may work against meeting population and cost reduction goals. For example, lengthening a boot camp term to add more treatment programs in order to reduce the chances of recidivism would shorten the discount in time served and, thus, not reduce the population or prison bed costs.

NOTES

1. *Boot camps.* Has the 20-year experiment with boot camps failed? What lessons can be drawn about creative or modern sanctions more generally? Does the problem with boot camps lie in their conception? Their operation? Will there be any boot camps in operation in ten years? How could boot camps be reconfigured to fulfill their goals more effectively?

2. *Home confinement.* While it is relatively rare, many jurisdictions make some use of home confinement as a sanction, especially for short periods of time. For example, in the federal system in 1999 about 16,000 defendants and offenders had home confinement orders. The majority of home confinements, however, occur before trial. Home confinement does not necessarily mean 24-hour confinement: it can allow for specific periods of work or other reasons to leave the home. What purpose does home confinement serve? Do its goals differ from those of imprisonment?

3. *Electronic monitoring.* Electronic monitoring is often combined with home confinement, though the two concepts are distinct. Electronic monitoring adds a high-tech gloss by tracking the presence or absence of the offender at required locations (home, office, car). See People v. McNair, 642 N.Y.S.2d 597 (Ct. App. 1996) (sentence of one year of electronic monitoring for DUI defendant exceeded court's authority under general probation statutes). Is electronic monitoring efficient? Does it serve primarily an incapacitative function?

The latest high-tech monitoring innovation employs the technology used in the global positioning system (GPS). Especially for sex offenders, many states are adopting or considering GPS tracking for serious offenders after their release from prison. Consider this excerpt from a recent article in the technology magazine *Wired*:

> Just a few years ago, satellite tracking of convicts was a newfangled alternative to house arrest. Now, the number of American ex-offenders tracked through GPS-equipped ankle bracelets will likely triple to more than 30,000, thanks to the passage of a California ballot measure. California's Proposition 83, which easily passed . . . by a margin of 70 percent to 30 percent, requires many convicted sex offenders to be monitored by GPS for life. . . .
>
> At least 11 other states have recently considered GPS tracking legislation, with some inspired by the 2005 murder of a Florida girl, allegedly by a registered sex offender. Florida's high-profile legislation was named "Jessica's Law" in her honor, and talk-show host Bill O'Reilly has been pushing for passage of similar laws elsewhere.
>
> But there's a hitch: The ankle bracelets — usually accompanied by digital-pager-size transmitters — are hardly criminal-proof. Convicts can easily cut the bracelets off and run away as their probation officer gets an alarm and tries to

contact the local police. For health reasons, the bracelets aren't designed to be permanent.

"GPS will not prevent a crime," said Steve Chapin, CEO of Pro Tech Monitoring, a manufacturer of GPS tracking devices. "It's a crime deterrent. It has proven to be a good tool, but you can't oversell it—there's no physical barrier that it creates that can prevent a crime."

Randy Dotinga, Attack of the Perv Trackers, Wired (November 9, 2006). Although GPS monitoring is discussed mostly as a supplement to a period of incarceration, should jurisdictions start seriously exploring techno-tracking as an alternative to incarceration for certain types of offenders?

2. Nondetention Sanctions: Shaming and Community Service

During the past two decades, shame has emerged as an explicit and independent sanction. Many criminal sentences may convey or carry some shame for the convicted offender. Indeed, the shame associated with the fact of conviction alone for some offenders may, from their perspective or the perspective of friends, family, or fellow workers, be a substantial punishment in itself.

Academics have led the call for officially shaming offenders. John Braithwaite, an Australian scholar, called for greater use of shame in criminal penalties in his 1989 book *Crime, Shame and Reintegration*. Braithwaite distinguished "reintegrative" shaming, which reaffirms "the morality of the offender by expressing personal disappointment that the offender should do something so out of character" and invites the offender to rejoin the community, from "disintegrative" shaming, which further pushes the offender into outcast status. A leading academic proponent in the United States has been Professor Dan Kahan. A major critic of proposals to sanction through shame is Professor Toni Massaro, who questions the existence of the kind of societies and norms that would make social sanctions such as shame fair, consistent, and effective. See generally Note, Shame, Stigma and Crime: Evaluating the Efficacy of Shaming Sanctions in Criminal Law, 116 Harv. L. Rev. 2186 (2003).

While rare, shaming sanctions are starting to appear more often in statutes and in individual cases. Consider the purposes and wisdom of the shaming sanctions in the following statute and case. Should shaming sanctions become more widely used? If so, for what offenses and offenders? And which institutions should design, implement, and test such sanctions?

Ohio Revised Code §4503.231, Special Plates for Vehicles Registered to Persons Whose Registration Certificates and License Plates Have Been Impounded

No motor vehicle registered in the name of a person whose certificate of registration and identification license plates have been impounded . . . shall be operated or driven on any highway in this state unless it displays identification license plates which are a different color from those regularly issued and carry a special serial number that may be readily identified by law enforcement officers. The registrar of motor vehicles shall designate the color and serial number to be used on such license plates, which shall remain the same from year to year and shall not be displayed on any other motor vehicles. . . .

║ ***People v. Glenn Meyer*** ║
║ **680 N.E.2d 315 (Ill. 1997)** ║

McMorrow, J.

The sole question presented for our review in the instant case is whether section 5-6-3(b) of the Unified Code of Corrections (Code) (730 ILCS 5/ 5-6-3(b) (West 1994)) authorizes a trial court to order, as a condition of probation, that the defendant post a large sign at all entrances to his family farm which reads "Warning! A Violent Felon lives here. Enter at your own risk!" The appellate court affirmed the trial court's imposition of this condition. . . . We reverse, and hold that the trial court exceeded the scope of its sentencing authority because posting a sign of this type is not a reasonable condition of probation under section 5-6-3(b) of the Code. Therefore, we vacate the order of the circuit court in part.

Following a jury trial, the defendant, Glenn Meyer, was convicted of the aggravated battery of Gary Mason. The trial testimony showed that on February 25, 1995, Gary Mason visited the defendant's farm in order to return some vehicle parts that he purchased from the defendant. Mason and the defendant began to quarrel over whether the parts were functioning properly. During the argument the defendant swung one of the parts at Mason, striking him in the nose and eye, causing several injuries.

At the defendant's sentencing hearing, evidence was presented in aggravation and mitigation. On behalf of the State, Tim Belford testified that in September 1986, he went to the defendant's farm in order to collect monies for two insufficient fund checks issued by defendant to Belford's employer, the First National Bank of Pittsfield. Belford stated that the defendant eventually gave him the money, but then kicked him and ordered him off the farm. Belford acknowledged that a jury acquitted the defendant of aggravated battery charges stemming from this incident.

Next, Harry Dyel testified that in May of 1990, he went to the defendant's farm on behalf of his employer, Shelter Insurance Company, in order to investigate a claim filed by the defendant. Dyel testified that the defendant became hostile because he was annoyed by the company's failure to process his claim promptly. Dyel stated that after he attempted to comply with the defendant's demands for payment, the defendant pushed him down and kicked him several times, causing injuries to his torso, arms, face and head. The defendant was convicted of the aggravated battery of Dyel. Finally, Gary Mason, the victim in the present case, testified regarding the defendant's actions on February 25, 1995.

Several witnesses testified in mitigation. Kenwood Foster testified that he is a licensed clinical social worker who operates a private counselling service. The defendant began seeing Foster in the fall of 1991. Foster testified that doctors at several different clinics have diagnosed the defendant as having "major depressive disorder" or clinical depression. Foster further stated that he believes that the defendant may also suffer from a condition similar to a type of post-traumatic stress disorder. He indicated that the defendant has been taking prescription medication known as Zoloft, to control his illness.

Foster further testified that certain stresses, such as a perceived threat to the defendant or his family, could trigger a change in the defendant's behavior. Foster acknowledged that the defendant may perceive certain behavior as threatening, even if the average individual would not feel threatened under similar circumstances.

Friends of the defendant, Gregg Smith, David Gratton and Bruce Lightle, also testified. All three described the defendant's good character and reputation within the community.

Mary Meyer, the defendant's wife of 36 years, testified that the defendant's elderly mother relies on the defendant, her only child, for care and assistance. Mrs. Meyer stated that she teaches high school, and has always relied on the defendant to manage the farm. She indicated that her family would suffer great hardship if the defendant were incarcerated. Mrs. Meyer also testified regarding the defendant's prolonged psychological illness and his efforts to control his sickness with medication.

In addition to the testimony of the witnesses, 20 letters were submitted by individuals from throughout the defendant's community. These letters chronicle examples of the defendant's generosity and willingness to assist friends and neighbors in need. The letters contain many descriptions of the defendant's good character and reputation.

Additionally, the presentence investigation report contains a detailed description of the defendant's mental health history. Several psychological evaluations of the defendant, dating from 1989, show that he suffers from major depressive disorder and possibly an additional psychological malady.

Upon evaluating all of the evidence in mitigation and aggravation, the trial court sentenced the defendant to 30 months' probation. The court considered the defendant's family members and the adverse impact that incarceration would have upon them. The court stated that it considered that the defendant was 62 years old, his mother's age and ill-health, and Mary Meyer's need to have the defendant care for the farm, in deciding to sentence the defendant to probation instead of prison.

The court conditioned defendant's probation on the following: (1) payment of $9,615.95 in restitution, (2) payment of a $7,500 fine, (3) payment of a $25 monthly probation services fee, (4) psychological psychiatric evaluation and treatment, (5) one-year home confinement and (6) the placement of a "violent felon" warning sign at each entrance to the defendant's property for the duration of the probation period. With respect to the sign requirement, the court stated that it believed that "maybe [the sign] will protect society." The court's supplemental order regarding the sign provides:

> As a condition of probation defendant shall erect and maintain at each entrance of his property a 4' × 8' sign with clearly readable lettering at least 8" in height reading: "Warning! A Violent Felon lives here. Enter at your own Risk!" To be erected by 8-11-95. . . .

The sole issue presented to us for review is whether the trial court was authorized to order the violent felon warning sign as a condition of probation. The defendant maintains that the trial court acted outside of the scope of its sentencing authority because the sign is not a reasonable condition of probation within the meaning of the Unified Code of Corrections. Section 5-6-3(b) of the Code lists 16 permissible probation conditions that the trial court may impose "in addition to other *reasonable conditions* relating to the nature of the offense or the rehabilitation of the defendant as determined for each defendant in the proper discretion of the Court." (Emphasis added.) The defendant maintains that the warning sign is not a reasonable condition of probation because it does not comport with traditional notions of punishment or probation in Illinois, and instead is an unauthorized "shaming penalty" or a scarlet letter type of punishment. The defendant argues that nothing in the Code supports the subjection of probationers to public ridicule as a goal of probation.

The State responds that while the sign may embarrass the defendant, it is not intended to subject him to public ridicule. Rather, the State and the amicus curiae, the American Alliance for Rights and Responsibilities, contend that this condition of probation furthers the goals of probation because it protects the public and serves to rehabilitate the defendant.

The State maintains that the sign protects the public by warning against provoking the defendant and by reducing the number of guests or business invitees who visit the farm. The State and the amicus argue that the goal of rehabilitation is fostered by the sign because it reminds the defendant that society disapproves of his criminal conduct. The amicus further argues that because the sign reminds the defendant of his offense, the defendant will modify his behavior and will be less likely to commit acts of violence in the future. Finally, both the State and the amicus argue that the trial court acted within its discretion by carefully fashioning the conditions of probation to correspond to the needs of the defendant and the public.

Generally, the trial court is afforded wide discretion in fashioning the conditions of probation for a particular defendant. However, while the trial court has discretion to impose probation conditions which will foster rehabilitation and protect the public, the exercise of this discretion is not without limitation.

Section 5-6-3(b) of the Code contains 16 permitted conditions of probation which may be imposed "in addition to other *reasonable* conditions." (Emphasis added.) Requiring the defendant to erect a sign on his property, proclaiming his status as a violent convicted felon, is not statutorily identified as one of the conditions of probation. The statute gives the trial court the discretion to impose additional conditions of probation provided that they are reasonable. In People v. Ferrell 659 N.E.2d 992 (Ill. App. 1995), the court determined that a probation condition not expressly enumerated in the statute may be imposed as long as it is (1) reasonable and (2) relates to (a) the nature of the offense or (b) the rehabilitation of the defendant as determined by the trial court. We must, therefore, determine whether compelling defendant to post a 4-foot by 8-foot sign in front of his residence which, in 8-inch-high letters, states that defendant is a violent felon is a reasonable condition under section 5-6-3 of the Code.

Section 1-1-2 of the Unified Code of Corrections provides:

> The purposes of this Code of Corrections are to:
> (a) prescribe sanctions proportionate to the seriousness of the offenses and permit the recognition of differences in rehabilitation possibilities among individual offenders;
> (b) forbid and prevent the commission of offenses;
> (c) prevent arbitrary or oppressive treatment of persons adjudicated offenders or delinquents; and
> (d) restore offenders to useful citizenship. 730 ILCS 5/1-1-2 (West 1994).

Consistent with this legislative intent, this court has recognized repeatedly that the purpose of probation is to benefit society by restoring a defendant to useful citizenship, rather than allowing a defendant to become a burden as an habitual offender. Probation simultaneously serves as a form of punishment and as a method for rehabilitating an offender. Protection of the public from the type of conduct that led to a defendant's conviction is one of the goals of probation. . . .

Although the sign may foster the goals of probation to the extent that it punishes the defendant and protects the public, furtherance of these two goals alone does not render the condition reasonable. Indeed, we are persuaded by defendant's contention that the sign, in fact, may hamper the goal of rehabilitation, and that the erection of the sign is inconsistent with the conditions of probation listed in section 5-6-3(b). We recognize that the trial court labored arduously and sincerely to develop a sentence which would serve the needs of society and simultaneously avoid incarceration of the defendant. Nonetheless, we hold the sign condition of probation imposed in this case was unreasonable and did not serve the purposes of section 5-6-3(b).

The Tennessee Supreme Court in State v. Burdin, 924 S.W.2d 82 (Tenn. 1996), considered and rejected a comparable "shaming sign," finding that it was unreasonable. The Tennessee court held that the Tennessee statute at issue there did not authorize a condition of probation which required the defendant to erect a sign in the front yard of his residence which read, "Warning, all children. [Defendant] is an admitted and convicted child molester. Parents beware."

In Burdin, the defendant pleaded guilty to sexual battery of a 16-year-old victim. As a condition of probation, the court ordered the defendant to place the warning sign in front of his residence where he lived with his mother. . . .

The Burdin court stated:

> The consequences of imposing such a condition without the normal safeguards of legislative study and debate are uncertain. Posting a sign in the defendant's yard would dramatically affect persons other than the defendant and those charged with his supervision. . . . [C]ompliance with the condition would have consequences in the community perhaps beneficial, perhaps detrimental, but in any event unforeseen and unpredictable.

Similarly, in People v. Johnson, 528 N.E.2d 1360 (Ill. App. 1988), the court cautioned against allowing trial courts to impose unconventional conditions of supervision, which may have unknown consequences. The defendant in Johnson was convicted of driving under the influence of alcohol. As a condition of supervision, the trial court in *Johnson* ordered the defendant to place an advertisement in the local daily newspaper, which contained her booking picture and an apology. The appellate court vacated this condition, finding it to be inconsistent with the overall intent of section 5-3-6.1. . . .

We are mindful of the distinctions in the case sub judice and the *Burdin* and *Johnson* cases. However, we agree with the specially concurring opinion in *Johnson*, which observed:

> [T]o uphold the condition imposed here would encourage other courts to impose other unusual, dramatic conditions, and the proliferation of these types of conditions would cause problems of a greater magnitude than their propensity to rehabilitate.

See also People v. Harris, 606 N.E.2d 392 (Ill. App. 1992) (banishing the defendant from the state of Illinois as a condition of probation was unreasonable because no valid purpose would be served); People v. Letterlough, 655 N.E.2d 146 (N.Y. 1995) (condition of probation requiring the defendant to affix a fluorescent sign reading "convicted dwi" to the license plate of any vehicle he drove was not authorized); People v. Hackler, 16 Cal. Rptr. 2d 681 (Cal. App. 1993) (court not authorized to require probationer to wear a T-shirt bearing bold printed statement proclaiming his felony status); but see Lindsay v. State, 606 So. 2d 652 (Fla. App. 1992) (condition of probation requiring defendant to place a newspaper advertisement showing a mug shot, name and caption "DUI-convicted" upheld under Florida statute); Goldschmitt v. State, 490 So. 2d 123 (Fla. App. 1986) (bumper sticker reading "Convicted D.U.I. — Restricted License" upheld); Ballenger v. State, 436 S.E.2d 793 (Ga. App. 1993) (court had the authority to require the defendant to wear a pink fluorescent bracelet reading "D.U.I. Convict").

We hold that section 5-6-3(b) of the Code did not authorize the trial court to require the sign as a condition of the defendant's probation. The sign contains a strong element of public humiliation or ridicule because it serves as a formal, public announcement of the defendant's crime. Thus, the sign is inconsistent with the conditions of probation listed in section 5-6-3(b), none of which identify public notification or humiliation as a permissible condition. Further, we determine that the sign may have unpredictable or unintended consequences which may be inconsistent with the rehabilitative purpose of probation.

Finally, the nature and location of the sign are likely to have an adverse effect on innocent individuals who may happen to reside with the defendant. At the time of sentencing in this case, the defendant's wife was living on the premises where the violent felon sign was to be displayed. The defendant's elderly mother also intended to live there. The record shows that the defendant has two adult children who visit the farm, as well as young grandchildren. We believe that the manner in which the sign affects others also renders it an impermissible condition of probation.

Conditions which label a defendant's person or property have a stigmatizing effect and are considered shaming penalties. D. Kahan, What Do Alternative Sanctions Mean? 63 U. Chi. L. Rev. 591 (1996). Although a probationer may experience a certain degree of shame from a statutorily identified condition of probation, shame is not the primary purpose of the enumerated conditions.

   The judicially developed condition in the case at bar does not reflect present penological policies of this state as evidenced by our Unified Code of Corrections. The authority to define and fix punishment is a matter for the legislature. The drastic departure from traditional sentencing concepts utilized in this case is not contemplated by our Code. Therefore, we determine that the erection of the sign as a condition of probation was unreasonable, and may be counterproductive to defendant's rehabilitative potential. . . .

NOTES

   1. *Shaming.* Shaming has been big news in academic circles since John Braithwaite's pioneering work in the late 1980s. Occasional shaming sanctions make news — sometimes national news — highly disproportionate to their modest character and infrequent use. Shaming sanctions raise many issues. As is so often the habit of lawyers and legal scholars, among the first questions to be addressed is whether shaming sanctions are "legal" or, in the more common and often distorting reaction, whether they are constitutional. The much more difficult and important questions, however, have received less attention. Are shaming sanctions moral? Effective? To what purpose? Which institutions should authorize, design, impose, and review them? See James Q. Whitman, What Is Wrong with Inflicting Shame Sanctions?, 107 Yale L.J. 1055 (1998). In People v. Letterlough, 631 N.Y.S.2d 105 (N.Y. 1995), the court rejected a condition of probation for a DUI offender that he affix to any car he drove a fluorescent sign stating "convicted DWI." In response to *Letterlough* and People v. McNair, 642 N.Y.S.2d 597 (N.Y. 1996) (rejecting a one-year electronic monitoring sentence as beyond statutory authority), the New York legislature amended the relevant statute in 1996 to expand the authorized purposes of probation:

> New York Penal Law §65.10. When imposing a sentence of probation the court may, in addition to any conditions imposed pursuant to [existing authority], require that the defendant comply with any other reasonable condition as the court shall determine to be necessary or appropriate to ameliorate the conduct which gave rise to the offense or to prevent the incarceration of the defendant.

Based on this statutory mandate, what review powers, if any, do New York appellate courts have over probation conditions?

   2. *Community service sanctions.* A more common alternative to detention is the community service order, either as a stand-alone sentence or in conjunction with fines or shorter periods of incarceration. Community service sanctions seem to be used most often for low-level offenders, perhaps as a more intensive substitute for straight probation. New York instituted a community service sentence program designed both to broaden the base of offenders punished and to reduce the number of offenders serving short jail terms. See Douglas Corry McDonald, Punishment Without Walls: Community Service Sentences in New York City (1986). Community service sentences are usually imposed under the general authority of probationary sanctions. It is very hard to determine how many community service sentences are imposed in the United States, whether they are stand-alone sentences, and how many are successful.

3. Alternative Courts

Sometimes alternative sentences have different purposes from those of traditional sanctions and call for different adjudicative or sentencing institutions. One prominent example of an alternative court that appears to seek traditional goals is drug court. The growth of drug courts has been dramatic. The first self-identified drug court was created in 1989 at the urging of Judge Herbert Klein in Miami. See Peter Finn and Andrew Newlyn, Miami's Drug Court: A Different Approach (NCJ 142412, 1996). As of May 2003 there were more than 1,000 reported drug courts in operation and more than 400 more in planning stages. See Summary of Drug Court Activity by State and County (2003) (cited at http://www.ncjrs.org/ drug_courts/summary.html). Part of this growth may be attributed to the federal Drug Courts Program Office (created and funded by the Violent Crime Control and Law Enforcement Act of 1994), which spent $56 million to support the creation of drug courts between 1995 and 1997.

Judges and reformers created drug courts in response to both the limited range of sentencing options in traditional criminal courts for drug users and concerns about the effectiveness and cost of punishment instead of — or at least in the absence of — drug treatment. Drug courts typically use a less adversarial approach that is aimed at ensuring public safety. In some states drug courts amount to a diversionary program, where offenders must perform successfully to prevent a criminal conviction. Increasingly, however, drug court programs form part of a probationary sentence or follow a guilty plea while sentencing is being deferred.

Drug courts have not only spread like wildfire, they have offered a model for breaking the heavily socialized punishment settings of traditional courts and the erosion of rehabilitation. For drug offenders and others the rehabilitative ideal remains, or is again vibrant as, a goal of "punishment" (though perhaps the goal of rehabilitation is in some important way different from punishment). The broader philosophical and practical labels used to describe this larger movement are "restorative justice" and "therapeutic courts." We already saw one illustration of restorative purposes in the sentencing circle examined in Chapter 1.

‖ **Therapeutic Justice in Alaska's Courts, Teresa Carns, Michael Hotchkin, and Elaine Andrews** ‖
19 Alaska L. Rev. 1 (2002)

I. Therapeutic Courts in Alaska: History, Development and Present Structures

Wellness Court ... Anchorage Felony Drug Court ... Mental Health Court ... Therapeutic Justice Courts. . . . Underlying these new projects is a growing change in the justice system's response to the difficult problems presented by defendants whose substance abuse or mental disabilities appear to be related inextricably to repeated criminal behavior. Justice professionals describe this approach as "therapeutic justice." . . .

Therapeutic justice emphasizes the need to address the root causes of a specific offender's criminality, to treat the offender to remove the problems and to return the offender to the community as a responsible citizen. Restorative justice emphasizes repair of the relationships between the victim, community and offender. Retributive justice, the model on which much of the United States' criminal justice system is based, emphasizes fairness and punishment as more important values than rehabilitation or other interests. Each model seeks to express community condemnation in order to protect public safety and deter or dissuade the specific offender and others from similar behavior in the future. . . .

C. *Therapeutic Courts: Assets and Liabilities*

[P]olicymakers and justice system professionals have identified a wide range of benefits and concerns based on their experiences [with therapeutic courts].

1. The Views of Judges and Court Administrators. Judges and court administrators differ strongly in their beliefs about the benefits of the therapeutic justice approach. Proponents of therapeutic justice courts believe that the therapeutic justice model has reduced recidivism and increased the chances that defendants can return to their communities as productive individuals. Judges are willing to see a defendant repeatedly in a structured setting for months if they believe that in the end they will not see that defendant back before them for sentencing on repeated offenses. . . . Some judges see the situation as particularly troublesome for misdemeanor offenders who receive at best minimal supervision and often little or no treatment. . . .

Some court administrators and other judges express concerns that the therapeutic courts will be of limited benefit to a few defendants while consuming scarce resources at a rapid rate. In the short term, the projects require extra time to (1) facilitate the frequent meetings among the professionals and court staff involved in each case, (2) hold regular hearings and (3) administer the network of services, sanctions and incentives required to make the therapeutic process work. Project funding often does not include resources to pay for the increased clerical burden on the courts or for the additional administrative time needed for judges to oversee the court's operations. Other justice system professionals are equally concerned about the lack of resources for the added work involved in each therapeutic justice project case.

Other concerns include worries that therapeutic courts may be coercive, may become more paternalistic and repressive than the existing system and may be "net-widening," i.e., they may impose harsher penalties or expectations on relatively less serious offenders rather than targeting more serious offenders. . . .

Perhaps the most serious concern is that courts will be unable to apply therapeutic justice concepts to more than a select few defendants. In a climate where all courts struggle for resources to address their caseloads' demands, resource-intensive therapeutic processes appear out of reach for most cases. Therapeutic courts typically serve only a fraction of potentially eligible defendants. . . . [Some o]bservers . . . believe that drug court procedures eventually may become abbreviated and perfunctory if they "go to scale" to serve a majority of the defendants with substance abuse problems. Under such a system, defendants will lose the benefits of individualized attention and therapeutic justice approaches will devolve into pro forma applications that would be no more effective than the court procedures they replaced.

2. The Views of Defendants.   One stated purpose of therapeutic justice projects is to provide defendants with the structure, resources and incentives to end their addictions or help them resolve the problems that prevent them from leading satisfying and productive lives. Some defendants in therapeutic projects participate because they share the belief that rehabilitation is possible. Other defendants may participate because they believe that the projects are a less onerous choice than incarceration.

Proponents of therapeutic justice cite substantial evidence that coercing treatment through structures such as drug courts may result in better outcomes. Evidence suggests that people in coerced or mandated treatment (as distinct from voluntary treatment) are more likely to complete the treatment. Completion of treatment is critical to significant reduction in the likelihood of relapse.

Conversely, defendants may assess the difficulties of therapeutic justice projects and decide that incarceration is preferable. They may believe that they would fail in any case and would prefer to serve time in custody and be done with it. Some do not believe that they have a problem that needs treatment or that is amenable to the treatment offered, and they may decline to participate on those grounds. Additionally, defense attorneys perceive incarceration as less damaging for some defendants than participation in programs in which the defendant can be repeatedly incarcerated for violations of program guidelines.

3. The Views of Prosecutors.   Prosecutors who favor drug courts tend to believe that their role is to "represent[ ] the community's interest in public order." Other prosecutors question that "broader vision" and suggest instead that the goal of the criminal justice system is for prosecutors to "put bad guys in jail" by winning individual cases. Supporters of the therapeutic approach suggest that prosecutors working in therapeutic courts are as zealous as those working in regular courts, but more accountable. . . .

Some prosecutors may object to specific ways of administering therapeutic justice programs. For example, many oppose pre-plea programs that preserve defendants' options for going back to trial. "As time passes I am in a weaker position as to my case and my expenditure of resources." For this reason, many prosecutors insist on a plea from the defendant as a condition of entry into a therapeutic justice project. Other prosecutors perceive therapeutic justice's collaborative, non-adversarial approach as incompatible with "the public safety- and punishment-oriented goals of the prosecution[.]" They may reserve use of this approach for specific types of defendants and consider it inappropriate for others.

4. Other Justice System Perspectives.   Departments of Corrections and the public have responded favorably to therapeutic justice projects in their current form and scope. They favor the projects' potential for reducing incarceration costs and for successfully treating addictions. . . .

Many treatment providers also are supportive, although some individuals believe that the process may be too coercive and that coerced treatment does not work. Thorny confidentiality issues may arise with therapeutic justice projects because the projects require agencies to share and discuss information that is otherwise protected by complex confidentiality laws and regulations. Another concern is the change in the role of treatment providers from serving "exclusively as the gatekeepers to treatment, as they have been accustomed to doing," to having "courts . . . decide who will be sent to treatment and when treatment can be terminated for poor performance."

D.   Effectiveness of Therapeutic Courts

. . . Although fewer than one hundred evaluations of therapeutic courts have been published in the last ten years, many are underway. A number of preliminary or partial evaluations have been completed and researchers have considered the effectiveness of many of the separate components of drug courts, particularly the use of monitoring and supervision, completion of treatment programs and use of coerced treatment.

1. Treatment of Addiction/Disease.   Various researchers have demonstrated that treatment, if completed, reduces recidivism. Partial completion of treatment often appears to be better than no treatment in reducing recidivism, but length of time in treatment generally predicts the addict's post-treatment success. Other studies have shown that some types of treatment correlate more significantly with reduced recidivism than others. . . .

Other components of drug or therapeutic courts also have proven effective when used separately or outside the context of the therapeutic court. In a Washington, D.C. study, monitoring and closely supervising offenders on probation by itself reduced the incidence of positive drug tests. A Florida program uses intensive supervision of probationers for DWI offenders . . . and has shown significant reduction in recidivism.

The combination of these separate effective elements into therapeutic justice courts has proven successful in many, though not all, instances. Published research shows that many drug courts have reduced recidivism during their existence. However, a few projects have not been able to demonstrate that the drug court population fared any better in terms of post-program recidivism rates than the control or comparison groups.

2. Recidivism.   Researchers have conducted very few follow-up evaluations analyzing re-arrest rates and experiences of participants and controls in drug court programs over the months or years after completion of the program. The difficulties posed by long-term evaluations include the added costs of more evaluations, the problem of finding former participants and control group subjects and the management of confidentiality issues. Since most drug court programs are relatively new, insufficient time has elapsed to make realistic follow-up evaluations possible. A similar situation exists for mental health courts and other therapeutic justice projects. . . .

E.   Costs of Therapeutic Justice

Therapeutic justice projects are resource intensive. Even the projects that have functioned for some period of time without outside funding have managed only by using substantial time volunteered by judges, attorneys and other persons and organizations in the community. . . . The resources needed for therapeutic justice projects include added time for judges, attorneys and clerical staff, increased treatment resources, increased monitoring and drug testing of defendants, and expenses (in most programs) for case managers and coordinators. . . .

A [ ] realistic analysis would compare the costs for a drug court to the costs of incarcerating the same defendant for at least a year (the typical length of many drug court programs) and the costs of releasing the defendant untreated (the typical situation for most defendants). In Alaska, the cost for an Anchorage Felony Drug Court participant is estimated at $16,950 annually, as compared to the cost of more than $40,000 per year for incarceration. One observer suggests that because many of the defendants are repeat offenders who face presumptive sentences of two years or more, the actual costs of incarceration usually would be double the $40,000. The cost of incarceration does not include any of the costs associated with investigating the crimes charged, the costs of court processing (clerical and judge time, prosecution and defense costs) or costs of pretrial incarceration or pre-sentence report preparation for felony defendants. The cost for the Anchorage Felony Drug Court does include some attorney time, but neither judge time nor clerical time for any of the participants.

Depending on the program, defendants bear some of the costs. . . .

These differences in practices highlight different philosophies underlying similar projects. Proponents of having defendants pay argue that even if some defendants cannot participate due to very limited resources, those defendants who can should participate. Others contend that requiring any payment unfairly limits the program to those who have the economic resources to participate. . . .

II.   THERAPEUTIC JURISPRUDENCE: LEGAL ISSUES

[T]he therapeutic justice projects discussed in this Article describe a well-defined approach that differs significantly from that embodied in the traditional American adversarial system. Most of the legal issues that therapeutic justice approaches raise have not been resolved by the courts, although a few courts have issued opinions addressing them. . . .

A.   Constitutional Issues

Courts that have considered cases involving drug courts have dealt with a fairly limited range of the possible constitutional issues that could arise. . . .

1. Separation of Powers.   Many drug court-related cases deal with the defendant's rights in plea bargaining situations and the balance of powers between the executive and judicial branches in determining who is eligible for drug court programs and who makes the final decisions on admission to them. Most of the courts deciding cases related to plea bargains appear to treat drug court agreements as any other plea bargain.

For example, the Alabama Court of Criminal Appeals decided, based on existing case law, that the defendant had a binding agreement with the district attorney that the district attorney could not subsequently repudiate. In a Florida case, the District Court of Appeal ruled that because the defendant successfully completed a pretrial program, the State was bound by the fact that it had offered the defendant the chance to participate in the program and was obliged to dismiss the charges. . . .

The other major separation of powers issue focuses on the prosecutor's exclusive right to decide initial eligibility for drug court admission versus the judge's right to make the final decision about admission to the drug court. Several state courts, including those in Oklahoma and Florida, have held that separation of powers requires that prosecutors be permitted to make the first determination of admission to drug courts. Judges are not allowed to admit defendants to drug courts over the objections of prosecutors. On the other hand, Iowa and Louisiana courts have held that judges have the power to make the final decision about admission to drug court and are under no obligation to accept the prosecutor's recommendation.

2. Due Process.   A few cases address due process issues that have arisen in drug courts. For example, a Washington case held that the defendant must have a meaningful opportunity to respond to allegations of non-compliance before being terminated from the program. An Oklahoma case held that the court must give written reasons for termination of a defendant. This opinion also held that the court must state why the program sanctions were inadequate or inappropriate for the defendant.

3. Equal Access to Courts (Equal Protection).   Several courts have decided that defendants have no right to be admitted to drug courts and that they can be excluded on a variety of grounds. Prior felonies often are mentioned as grounds for ineligibility. A Florida case held that a defendant does not have a constitutional right to participate in a drug court if one had not been established in the circuit in which he was charged. . . . One author has warned that therapeutic justice projects "need to be sensitive to class and race bias, real or apparent. Unless care is taken, diversion courts may tend disproportionately to work with white and middle-class substance abusers."

Several authors have discussed the question of equal access to drug courts when programs do not have enough slots to serve all of the eligible defendants, as well as the question of whether the costs of programs where defendants pay all or part of the costs prohibit indigent defendants from using them. These problems have often been addressed in the context of "going to scale" or expanding the programs to serve the estimated seventy to eighty percent of defendants who have substance abuse problems. One court commentator noted: "We must address the fact that we are providing more resources for a misdemeanor drug offense than we are for a non-capital murder offense or a rape offense. Most states can't afford to continue to do this—politically and fiscally—if problem-solving courts go to scale." . . .

NOTES

1. *Therapeutic courts and restorative justice.*   The concepts of therapeutic courts and restorative justice exploded in policy and scholarly debates in the 1990s, but these ideas, and the closely linked traditional purpose of rehabilitation, have deep historic roots.

The restorative justice movement has become very popular in developed countries in recent years, though it has existed for decades in African countries in the form of informal customary practices. The goal of restorative justice is to restore the victim and the community that has been harmed. While it has only recently become popular for street offenses, it has been used for decades to address business regulatory challenges. Business regulatory practices focus on restitution, victim empowerment, and the restoration of trust and relationships. Restorative justice can be viewed as an extension of the victim-offender mediation and restorative justice conferences used in business disputes.

2. *Judicial and prosecutorial discretion and power sharing.*   Legislatures have limited judicial discretion in recent years through the establishment of mandatory sentences and sentencing guidelines. As judicial discretion has narrowed, prosecutorial discretion has broadened. How has the tension between prosecutorial and judicial discretion been resolved in therapeutic courts? To what extent are legislative actions necessary to institute therapeutic courts? In what areas would legislative action be helpful in facilitating the work of therapeutic courts? See Daniel Van Ness & Pat Nolan, Legislating for Restorative Justice, 10 Regent U. L. Rev. 53 (1998).

3. *Drug courts.*   Drug courts have emerged as the most common example of therapeutic courts. They provide intensive, long-term treatment services to offenders with long histories of drug use and criminal justice contacts and high rates of health and social problems. Most drug court participants are men with poor employment and educational records, fairly extensive criminal histories, and prior treatment failures. Usually drug courts target offenders who constitute a medium risk to the community. Hallmarks of the program are access to treatment and rehabilitation services as well as frequent alcohol and drug testing, all under ongoing judicial supervision and interaction with each participant. Treatment programs generally run for one year and are outpatient services. The drug court judge is assisted by a team of social workers and substance abuse counselors. Occasional lapses are expected, and sanctions and rewards are built into the program. The penalty is designed to enforce the prescribed treatment regime rather than solely to punish.

Even though drug courts enjoy widespread popularity and substantial funding, their success in terms of long-term rehabilitation and recidivism is less clear. See generally Richard Gebelein, The Promise and Perils of Drug Courts (U.S. Dept. of Justice, Office of Justice Programs, May 2000). The graduation rate for drug court enrollees is slightly less than 50%, with almost 75,000 having graduated by the end of 2000. This result is better than those of other community-based offender treatment programs. During drug court enrollment, criminal activity and drug use are reduced, but the duration of such success following enrollment remains undetermined. Some program-specific studies have found beneficial longer-term results, notably a decrease in recidivism and a greater likelihood of employment. See, e.g., Denise C. Gottfredson & M. Lyn Exum, The Baltimore City Drug Treatment Court: One-Year Results from a Randomized Study, 39 J. Res. Crime & Delinq. 337 (2002); National Center on Addiction and Substance Abuse at Columbia University, Crossing the Bridge: An Evaluation of the Drug Treatment Alternative-to-Prison (DTAP) Program, A CASA White Paper (March 2003).

Some critics of drug courts believe the courts undermine the adversarial system, since offenders must waive some of their rights in order to be enrolled: courts have a right of access to all treatment records and are permitted ex parte communications with the prosecution. Another concern, documented in some individual studies, is that drug court participants receive harsher sentences than other offenders.

The drug court model has been exported. In 2001 Glasgow established the first drug court in Scotland. Canada and Ireland also have similar programs. While the U.S. programs are based on abstinence, this is not always true of drug courts in other countries.

An overview of the literature and research on existing drug courts can be found in Steven Belenko, Research on Drug Courts: A Critical Review — 2001 Update (June 2001; original study done in 1998).

4. *Drug courts and prosecutorial discretion.*   Should the imposition of a drug court probation sentence depend on the prosecutor's recommendation? In Louisiana v. Taylor, 769 So. 2d 535 (La. 2000), the Louisiana Supreme Court held that a trial court is not authorized to place a defendant in a drug court program absent the prosecutor's recommendation. How can such a limitation on judicial discretion be justified in this context?

5. *Confidentiality concerns.*   Therapeutic justice courts raise difficult confidentiality concerns, as Carns, Hotchkin, and Andrews observe:

> Drug and alcohol courts require access to participants' drug and alcohol abuse treatment records. . . . The program's treatment assessor uses this information in determining whether the defendant is diagnostically appropriate for inclusion in the program and in designing an appropriate case plan. Once a program has accepted a defendant, the drug or alcohol court team uses reports of that person's ongoing treatment compliance and prognosis to assess the person's progress. The judge uses the reports to award incentives, impose sanctions and determine whether the participant should graduate, continue in the program or be terminated from the program. . . .
>
> Drug and alcohol courts face two significant issues created by [the] federal regulatory scheme [protecting information about an individual's participation in drug or alcohol abuse treatment programs]. First, . . . [p]articipants consent to release treatment information, both past and future, when they first apply for the programs. . . .
>
> The second issue facing drug and alcohol courts stems from the fact that the regulatory definition of "program" encompasses virtually all of these courts. This subjects them to the regulatory restrictions on disclosure of information that might identify a patient as an alcohol or drug abuser. A problem arises because the courts conduct public proceedings. Although most interactions

among judges, attorneys and offenders in drug court do not go into significant
detail about a participant's treatment, the mere fact that a person is participating in a drug or alcohol court program indicates that the person has abused
alcohol or drugs. One author notes that part of drug court procedure is for the
judge to "hold[ ] the offender publicly accountable for the results of the [drug
use] test and the treatment progress." The regulations thus create a conflict
between public access to court proceedings and the court's duty not to identify
or discuss drug and alcohol court participants in a public setting. . . .
          . . . Drug court team members are permitted to use such information for
their "official duties with regard to the patient's conditional release or other
action in connection with which the consent was given." One authority states
that the federal regulations have been interpreted to allow team members to
mention confidential information in court. . . . The authority goes on to say
that drug court officials should be mindful that consent has not been given
to disclose confidential information to unnamed third party bystanders in the
courtroom (e.g., public, press and law enforcement). Therefore, courtroom
discussions should avoid specific, confidential details of a person's treatment
experience and, instead, focus on more general concerns such as the participant's progress.
          The same authority notes that the question of whether confidentiality
rules apply to drug courts has not been fully resolved. . . .

19 Alaska L. Rev. at 48-49. Should there be more concern about confidentiality
in other areas of sentencing?

C.   COLLATERAL SANCTIONS

Collateral sanctions, or "collateral consequences," as they are often called,
have been part of the U.S. criminal justice system for centuries, and in recent
years they have received renewed support from legislatures and policymakers.
The origin of collateral sanctions can be found in so-called civil death provisions,
prevalent in the nineteenth century and earlier in the United States and Europe.
Civil death, the deprivation of an offender's civil rights, made it impossible for
convicted felons to enter into contracts, arranged for automatic divorce from
their spouses, prevented them from making a will, and imposed a host of other
sanctions on them that amounted to legal death. While many of the most
offensive of these restrictions have been eliminated, others remain. Some
modern collateral sanctions are particularly restrictive in a regulatory welfare
state and, for some offenders, may have more dramatic and longer-term consequences than the sentence imposed in court.
          The offenders released from U.S. prisons every year — over 650,000 in
2006 — do not again become "free" citizens. To the contrary, they often face
such a large number of restrictions that some have called the postrelease period
a time of "invisible punishment." Offenders can be barred from a large number
of jobs, from bartender to barber, from securities trader to bail bondsperson,
from nurse to beautician. They may be automatically disqualified from such
positions by their felony conviction, the specific offense they committed, or
restrictions on necessary licenses or mobility. Ironically, in some prisons,
inmates continue to be trained for jobs they cannot hold after release.

With the expansion of the welfare state, limitations or outright bans on public benefits have become a new form of collateral sanction. Drug and sex offenders are not eligible for public housing; drug offenders are barred from welfare benefits and student loans. Political rights are also restricted. In many states offenders are barred from the voting booth, the jury box, and political office — sometimes forever.

For a general discussion of collateral consequences, see Nora V. Demleitner, Preventing Internal Exile: The Need for Restrictions on Collateral Sentencing Consequences, 11 Stan. L. & Pol'y Rev. 153 (1999); Invisible Punishment: The Collateral Consequences of Mass Incarceration (Marc Mauer & Meda Chesney-Lind eds., 2002). For a review of collateral sanctions imposed on drug offenders, see Nora V. Demleitner, "Collateral Damage": No Re-entry for Drug Offenders, 47 Vill. L. Rev. 1027 (2002).

There are so many collateral sanctions that judges, prosecutors, and criminal defense attorneys are unable to inform most defendants of all the sanctions that will apply to them. For that reason, the American Bar Association has demanded that such sanctions be cataloged and that defendants be informed of them before they plead guilty. American Bar Association, Criminal Justice Standards, ch. 19 (2003).

Courts have generally declared collateral sanctions civil rather than criminal sanctions. They are assumed to protect the public against risk rather than constituting further punishment of the offender. Because they are civil sanctions, they are typically applied and enforced without the traditional procedural protections that apply in criminal cases.

1. Automatic Disabilities

a. Disenfranchisement

All but two states — Maine and Vermont — prohibit prison inmates from voting. Most states also prevent offenders from voting while under a criminal justice sentence: 32 states prohibit felons from voting while they are on parole, and 28 of those also exclude felony probationers from the voting process. Some states prohibit only those who have committed certain crimes from voting; others do so for all felonies. Offenders automatically regain the right to vote in most states upon completion of their sentence. In a small number of states, a felon must apply for a pardon to be permitted to vote.

Currently more than 5 million U.S. citizens are denied the right to vote because of criminal convictions, and more than 1 million of these have completed their sentences but live in states that deny voting rights to anyone who has been convicted of a felony and has not received a gubernatorial pardon. State rather than federal law governs voting rights, including the right to vote in presidential and congressional elections.

The Washington state constitution denies persons the right to vote unless their civil rights have been restored. Civil rights are restored when offenders complete all aspects of their sentence, including paying fines and restitution. In the state of Washington, 45,000 offenders have not had their civil rights restored because of unpaid legal obligations and thus are denied the right to vote. Does this arrangement reinstitute monetary payment as a requisite for voting?

In recent years, the issue of felon disenfranchisement has received more public policy attention, and a few states have acted to ease restrictions on voting rights. In 2007, for example, Maryland's legislature repealed all provisions of the state's lifetime voting ban, including the three-year waiting period after sentence completion for certain categories of offenses, and instituted an automatic restoration policy for all persons upon completion of sentence. In Florida, the state's Office of Executive Clemency voted to amend the state's voting rights restoration procedure to automatically approve the reinstatement of rights for many persons who have been convicted of nonviolent offenses.

In 1974 the Supreme Court confronted the question whether denial of the right to vote for felons who had served their sentences violated the equal protection clause. Richardson v. Ramirez, 418 U.S. 24 (1974). In its decision the Court stated that the drafting history, historic practice, and language of section 2 of the Fourteenth Amendment, the apportionment clause, justified state disenfranchisement of felons. The clause reads in part:

> [W]hen the right to vote at any election . . . is denied to any of the male inhabitants of such State, being twenty-one years of age, and citizens of the United States, or in any way abridged, *except for participation in rebellion, or other crime,* the basis of representation therein shall be reduced in the proportion which the number of such male citizens shall bear to the whole number of male citizens twenty-one years of age in such State. [Emphasis added.]

In his dissent, Justice Marshall questioned the majority's analysis of section 2 and advocated addressing the disenfranchisement question under section 1 of the Fourteenth Amendment. He considered the state as having failed its burden of justifying felon disenfranchisement under the compelling interest standard. The state had advocated felon voting restrictions because it wished to prevent voting fraud and because the "likely voting pattern [of felons] might be subversive of the interests of an orderly society." Are these grounds valid?

About a decade later the Court revisited the issue of felon disenfranchisement in Hunter v. Underwood, 471 U.S. 222 (1985). There the Court struck down Alabama's constitutional provision barring felons convicted of "any crime [felony and misdemeanor] . . . involving moral turpitude" from voting. The Court found a violation of the equal protection clause because the state constitutional provision had been passed with a racially discriminatory motive — the exclusion of blacks (and poor whites) from the ballot box.

State courts and lower federal courts have heard numerous challenges on constitutional and statutory grounds to felon disenfranchisement provisions. The most recent state case challenging the disenfranchisement of imprisoned offenders, Fischer v. Governor, 749 A.2d 321 (N.H. 2000), denied voting rights to them. The most frequently cited objections to inmate voting are practical difficulties in arranging for in-prison voting and philosophical objections to granting those who have violated society's laws the right to participate in the making of laws. For a different perspective, one more characteristic of other Western democracies, consider the following case.

	Richard Sauvé v. Canada	
	(Chief Electoral Officer)	
	[2002] 3 S.C.R. 519, 2002 SCC 68	

McLACHLIN, C.J.

1. The right of every citizen to vote, guaranteed by s. 3 of the *Canadian Charter of Rights and Freedoms,* lies at the heart of Canadian democracy. The law at stake in this appeal denies the right to vote to a certain class of people — those serving sentences of two years or more in a correctional institution. The question is whether the government has established that this denial of the right to vote is allowed under s. 1 of the Charter as a "reasonable limit . . . demonstrably justified in a free and democratic society." I conclude that it is not. The right to vote, which lies at the heart of Canadian democracy, can only be trammeled for good reason. Here, the reasons offered do not suffice.

2. The predecessor to s. 51(e) of the Canada Elections Act, R.S.C. 1985, c. E-2, prohibited all prison inmates from voting in federal elections, regardless of the length of their sentences. This section was held unconstitutional as an unjustified denial of the right to vote guaranteed by s. 3 of the Charter. Parliament responded to this litigation by replacing this section with a new s. 51(e), which denies the right to vote to all inmates serving sentences of two years or more. . . .

7. To justify the infringement of a Charter right, the government must show that the infringement achieves a constitutionally valid purpose or objective, and that the chosen means are reasonable and demonstrably justified. This two-part inquiry — the legitimacy of the objective and the proportionality of the means — ensures that a reviewing court examine rigorously all aspects of justification. Throughout the justification process, the government bears the burden of proving a valid objective and showing that the rights violation is warranted — that is, that it is rationally connected, causes minimal impairment, and is proportionate to the benefit achieved. . . .

20. The objectives' analysis entails a two-step inquiry. First, we must ask what the objectives are of denying penitentiary inmates the right to vote. This involves interpretation and construction, and calls for a contextual approach. Second, we must evaluate whether the objectives as found are capable of justifying limitations on Charter rights. The objectives must not be "trivial," and they must not be "discordant with the principles integral to a free and democratic society." . . .

21. Section 51(e) denying penitentiary inmates the right to vote was not directed at a specific problem or concern. Prisoners have long voted, here and abroad, in a variety of situations without apparent adverse effects to the political process, the prison population, or society as a whole. In the absence of a specific problem, the government asserts two broad objectives as the reason for this denial of the right to vote: (1) to enhance civic responsibility and respect for the rule of law; and (2) to provide additional punishment, or "enhance the general purposes of the criminal sanction." . . .

22. This leaves the question of whether the objectives of enhancing respect for law and appropriate punishment are constitutionally valid and sufficiently

significant to warrant a rights violation. . . . However, precisely because they leave so little room for argument, vague and symbolic objectives make the justification analysis more difficult. Their terms carry many meanings, yet tell us little about why the limitation on the right is necessary, and what it is expected to achieve in concrete terms. The broader and more abstract the objective, the more susceptible it is to different meanings in different contexts, and hence to distortion and manipulation. . . .

26. Quite simply, the government has failed to identify particular problems that require denying the right to vote, making it hard to say that the denial is directed at a pressing and substantial purpose. Nevertheless, despite the abstract nature of the government's objectives and the rather thin basis upon which they rest, prudence suggests that we proceed to the proportionality analysis, rather than dismissing the government's objectives outright. The proportionality inquiry allows us to determine whether the government's asserted objectives are in fact capable of justifying its denial of the right to vote. At that stage, as we shall see, the difficulties inherent in the government's stated objectives become manifest.

27. At this stage the government must show that the denial of the right to vote will promote the asserted objectives (the rational connection test); that the denial does not go further than reasonably necessary to achieve its objectives (the minimal impairment test); and that the overall benefits of the measure outweigh its negative impact (the proportionate effect test). . . .

28. Will denying the right to vote to penitentiary inmates enhance respect for the law and impose legitimate punishment? The government must show that this is likely, either by evidence or in reason and logic.

29. The government advances three theories to demonstrate rational connection between its limitation and the objective of enhancing respect for law. First, it submits that depriving penitentiary inmates of the vote sends an "educative message" about the importance of respect for the law to inmates and to the citizenry at large. Second, it asserts that allowing penitentiary inmates to vote "demeans" the political system. Finally, it takes the position that disenfranchisement is a legitimate form of punishment, regardless of the specific nature of the offence or the circumstances of the individual offender. . . .

30. The first asserted connector with enhancing respect for the law is the "educative message" or "moral statement" theory. The problem here, quite simply, is that denying penitentiary inmates the right to vote is bad pedagogy. . . .

31. Denying penitentiary inmates the right to vote misrepresents the nature of our rights and obligations under the law and consequently undermines them. In a democracy such as ours, . . . the legitimacy of the law and the obligation to obey the law flow directly from the right of every citizen to vote. As a practical matter, we require all within our country's boundaries to obey its laws, whether or not they vote. But this does not negate the vital symbolic, theoretical and practical connection between having a voice in making the law and being obliged to obey it. This connection, inherited from social contract theory and enshrined in the Charter, stands at the heart of our system of constitutional democracy.

32. The government gets this connection exactly backwards when it attempts to argue that depriving people of a voice in government teaches them to obey the law. The "educative message" that the government purports to send by disenfranchising inmates is both anti-democratic and internally self-contradictory. Denying a citizen the right to vote denies the basis of democratic legitimacy. It says that delegates elected by the citizens can then bar those very citizens, or a portion of them, from participating in future elections. But if we accept that governmental power in a democracy flows from the citizens, it is difficult to see how that power can legitimately be used to disenfranchise the very citizens from whom the government's power flows. . . .

38. The theoretical and constitutional links between the right to vote and respect for the rule of law are reflected in the practical realities of the prison population and the need to bolster, rather than to undermine, the feeling of connection between prisoners and society as a whole. The government argues that disenfranchisement will "educate" and rehabilitate inmates. However, disenfranchisement is more likely to become a self-fulfilling prophecy than a spur to reintegration. Depriving at-risk individuals of their sense of collective identity and membership in the community is unlikely to instill a sense of responsibility and community identity, while the right to participate in voting helps teach democratic values and social responsibility. . . .

To deny prisoners the right to vote is to lose an important means of teaching them democratic values and social responsibility.

39. Even if these difficulties could be overcome, it is not apparent that denying penitentiary inmates the right to vote actually sends the intended message to prisoners, or to the rest of society. People may be sentenced to imprisonment for two years or more for a wide variety of crimes, ranging from motor vehicle and regulatory offences to the most serious cases of murder. The variety of offences and offenders covered by the prohibition suggest that the educative message is, at best, a mixed and diffuse one.

40. It is a message sullied, moreover, by negative and unacceptable messages likely to undermine civic responsibility and respect for the rule of law. Denying citizen law-breakers the right to vote sends the message that those who commit serious breaches are no longer valued as members of the community, but instead are temporary outcasts from our system of rights and democracy. More profoundly, it sends the unacceptable message that democratic values are less important than punitive measures ostensibly designed to promote order. If modern democratic history has one lesson to teach it is this: enforced conformity to the law should not come at the cost of our core democratic values. . . .

42. The government also argues that denying penitentiary inmates the vote will enhance respect for law because allowing people who flaunt the law to vote demeans the political system. The same untenable premises we have been discussing resurface here—that voting is a privilege the government can suspend and that the commission of a serious crime signals that the offender has chosen to "opt out" of community membership. But beyond this, the argument that only those who respect the law should participate in the political process is a variant on the age-old unworthiness rationale for denying the vote.

43. . . . Until recently, large classes of people, prisoners among them, were excluded from the franchise. The assumption that they were not fit or "worthy" of voting — whether by reason of class, race, gender or conduct — played a large role in this exclusion. We should reject the retrograde notion that "worthiness" qualifications for voters may be logically viewed as enhancing the political process and respect for the rule of law. . . .

45. This brings us to the government's final argument for rational connection — that disenfranchisement is a legitimate weapon in the state's punitive arsenal against the individual lawbreaker. Again, the argument cannot succeed. The first reason is that using the denial of rights as punishment is suspect. The second reason is that denying the right to vote does not comply with the requirements for legitimate punishment established by our jurisprudence.

46. . . . I do not doubt that Parliament may limit constitutional rights in the name of punishment, provided that it can justify the limitation. But it is another thing to say that a particular class of people for a particular period of time will completely lose a particular constitutional right. This is tantamount to saying that the affected class is outside the full protection of the Charter. It is doubtful that such an unmodulated deprivation, particularly of a right as basic as the right to vote, is capable of justification under s. 1. Could Parliament justifiably pass a law removing the right of all penitentiary prisoners to be protected from cruel and unusual punishment? I think not. What of freedom of expression or religion? Why, one asks, is the right to vote different? The government offers no credible theory about why it should be allowed to deny this fundamental democratic right as a form of state punishment.

47. The social compact requires the citizen to obey the laws created by the democratic process. But it does not follow that failure to do so nullifies the citizen's continued membership in the self-governing polity. Indeed, the remedy of imprisonment for a term rather than permanent exile implies our acceptance of continued membership in the social order. Certain rights are justifiably limited for penal reasons, including aspects of the right to liberty, security of the person, mobility, and security against search and seizure. But whether a right is justifiably limited cannot be determined by observing that an offender has, by his or her actions, withdrawn from the social compact. Indeed, the right of the state to punish and the obligation of the criminal to accept punishment is tied to society's acceptance of the criminal as a person with rights and responsibilities. . . .

52. When the facade of rhetoric is stripped away, little is left of the government's claim about punishment other than that criminals are people who have broken society's norms and may therefore be denounced and punished as the government sees fit, even to the point of removing fundamental constitutional rights. Yet, the right to punish and to denounce, however important, is constitutionally constrained. It cannot be used to write entire rights out of the Constitution, it cannot be arbitrary, and it must serve the constitutionally recognized goals of sentencing. On all counts, the case that s. 51(e) furthers lawful punishment objectives fails. . . .

60. The negative effects of s. 51(e) upon prisoners have a disproportionate impact on Canada's already disadvantaged Aboriginal population, whose over-representation in prisons reflects "a crisis in the Canadian criminal justice system." To the extent that the disproportionate number of Aboriginal people in penitentiaries reflects factors such as higher rates of poverty and institutionalized alienation from mainstream society, penitentiary imprisonment may not be a fair or appropriate marker of the degree of individual culpability. . . . Aboriginal people in prison have unique perspectives and needs. Yet, s. 51(e) denies them a voice at the ballot box and, by proxy, in Parliament. That these costs are confined to the term of imprisonment does not diminish their reality. The silenced messages cannot be retrieved, and the prospect of someday participating in the political system is cold comfort to those whose rights are denied in the present. . . .

62. . . . I leave for another day whether some political activities, like standing for office, could be justifiably denied to prisoners under s. 1. It may be that practical problems might serve to justify some limitations on the exercise of derivative democratic rights. Democratic participation is not only a matter of theory but also of practice, and legislatures retain the power to limit the modalities of its exercise where this can be justified. Suffice it to say that the wholesale disenfranchisement of all penitentiary inmates, even with a two-year minimum sentence requirement, is not demonstrably justified in our free and democratic society.

GONTHIER, J., dissenting.

67. . . . If the social or political philosophy advanced by Parliament reasonably justifies a limitation of the right in the context of a free and democratic society, then it ought to be upheld as constitutional. I conclude that this is so in the case at bar.

68. I am of the view that by enacting s. 51(e) of the Act, Parliament has chosen to assert and enhance the importance and value of the right to vote by temporarily disenfranchising serious criminal offenders for the duration of their incarceration. . . . The Chief Justice and I are in agreement that the right to vote is profoundly important, and ought not to be demeaned. Our differences lie principally in the fact that she subscribes to a philosophy whereby the temporary disenfranchising of criminals does injury to the rule of law, democracy and the right to vote, while I prefer deference to Parliament's reasonable view that it strengthens these same features of Canadian society. . . .

70. . . . While there is little logical correlation between maintaining a "decent and responsible citizenry" and any of the past discriminatory exclusions (such as land-ownership, religion, gender, ethnic background), there clearly is such a logical connection in the case of distinguishing persons who have committed serious criminal offences. "*Responsible* citizenship" does not relate to what gender, race, or religion a person belongs to, but is logically related to whether or not a person engages in serious criminal activity.

71. [S]erious criminal offenders are excluded from the vote for the reason that they are the *subjects of punishment.* The disenfranchisement only lasts as long

as the period of incarceration. Thus, disenfranchisement, as a dimension of punishment, is attached to and mirrors the fact of incarceration. This fact makes the Canadian experience significantly different from the situation in some American states which disenfranchise ex-offenders for life.

72. It is important to look at prisoner disenfranchisement from the perspective of each serious criminal offender rather than perceive it as a form of targeted group treatment. Disenfranchised prisoners can be characterized loosely as a group, but what is important to realize is that each of these prisoners has been convicted of a serious criminal offence and is therefore serving a personalized sentence which is proportionate to the act or acts committed. Punishment is guided by the goals of denunciation, deterrence, rehabilitation and retribution and is intended to be morally educative for incarcerated serious criminal offenders. Each prisoner's sentence is a temporary measure aimed at meeting these goals, while also being aimed at the long-term objective of reintegration into the community. . . .

116. Permitting the exercise of the franchise by offenders incarcerated for serious offences undermines the rule of law and civic responsibility because such persons have demonstrated a great disrespect for the community in their committing serious crimes: such persons have attacked the stability and order within our community. Society therefore may choose to curtail temporarily the availability of the vote to serious criminals both to punish those criminals and to insist that civic responsibility and respect for the rule of law, as goals worthy of pursuit, are prerequisites to democratic participation. . . .

119. . . . The disenfranchisement of serious criminal offenders serves to deliver a message to both the community and the offenders themselves that serious criminal activity will not be tolerated by the community. In making such a choice, Parliament is projecting a view of Canadian society which Canadian society has of itself. The commission of serious crimes gives rise to a temporary suspension of this nexus: on the physical level, this is reflected in incarceration and the deprivation of a range of liberties normally exercised by citizens and, at the symbolic level, this is reflected in temporary disenfranchisement. The symbolic dimension is thus a further manifestation of community disapproval of the serious criminal conduct.

120. From the perspective of the person whose criminal activity has resulted in their temporary disenfranchisement, their benefiting from society brought with it the responsibility to be subjected to the sanctions which the state decides will be attached to serious criminal activity such as they have chosen to undertake. This understanding is complemented by the rehabilitative view that those who are in jail will hope and expect to regain the exercise of the vote on their release from incarceration, just like they hope and expect to regain the exercise of the fullest expressions of their liberty. Once released from prison, they are on the road to reintegration into the community. Obtaining the vote once released or paroled is a recognition of regaining the nexus with the community that was temporarily suspended during the incarceration. . . .

159. [G]iven that, the objectives are largely symbolic, common sense dictates that social condemnation of criminal activity and a desire to promote civic responsibility are reflected in disenfranchisement of those who have committed

serious crimes. This justification is rooted in a reasonable and rational social and political philosophy which has been adopted by Parliament. Further, it can hardly be seen as "novel." . . . The view of the courts below is that generally supported by democratic countries. Countries including the United States, the United Kingdom, Australia, New Zealand, and many European countries such as France and Germany, have, by virtue of choosing some form of prisoner disenfranchisement, also identified a connection between objectives similar to those advanced in the case at bar and the means of prisoner disenfranchisement. . . .

NOTES

1. *Voting restrictions on felons in the United States.*   In the United States voting restrictions based on a prior criminal record go back to the beginning of the Republic. They did not begin to play a prominent role until after the Civil War, when Southern legislatures in particular used them to prevent blacks from voting. See Hunter v. Underwood, 471 U.S. 222 (1985) (striking down Alabama voting restriction because it was motivated by racial animus). Even though in recent years states have cut back on voting restrictions, currently 48 states prevent inmates from voting. Most states also bar felons from voting while on parole, and more than half deny the vote to probationers. Thirteen states deny offenders the right to vote even after they have been released from or have otherwise fully satisfied a criminal justice sanction. See generally Jeff Manza & Christopher Uggen, Locked Out: Felony Disenfranchisement and American Democracy (2006).

2. *Justifications for felon disenfranchisement.*   Felon disenfranchisement has been justified on a number of grounds. Some have claimed that felons violate the implicit social contract and should therefore be excluded from voting. Others have stated that civic virtues are necessary for participation in political decision making; in their absence, individuals should be excluded from the polity. Among the more practical and frequently raised arguments are potential election fraud by convicted felons (the "purity of the ballot box" argument), potential problems of arranging for voting in prisons, and in the past, racial arguments defending felon disenfranchisement as a way of excluding blacks (and sometimes also poor whites) from voting. For a discussion of the political philosophies underlying criminal disenfranchisement, see Alec Ewald, "Civil Death": The Ideological Paradox of Criminal Disenfranchisement Law in the United States, 2002 Wis. L. Rev. 1045. In light of the Canadian high court's decision, are there certain justifications that you consider particularly valid (or invalid)?

3. *Race and felon disenfranchisement.*   Despite challenges to disenfranchisement provisions on equal protection grounds, the Supreme Court has upheld state laws disenfranchising felons generally. See Richardson v. Ramirez, 418 U.S. 24 (1974). In a handful of subsequent cases, however, courts have struck down disenfranchisement provisions that were animated by racial bias, in violation of the equal protection clause.

A 1998 study published by Human Rights Watch and the Sentencing Project illuminated the racially disproportionate impact of the exclusion of felons from voting. The Sentencing Project & Human Rights Watch, Losing the Vote: The Impact of Felony Disenfranchisement in the United States (October 1998) (available at www.sentencingproject.org/pdfs/9080.pdf). Because of their overrepresentation among convicted felons and their large numbers in states that continue disenfranchisement after an offender's sentence has been served, 1.8 million African Americans are excluded from the franchise. Should the disproportionate racial impact on a fundamental constitutional right—the franchise—be a reason for striking down such legislation on equal protection grounds? How could a legislator use the study to argue for the abolition or at least the restriction of felon disenfranchisement?

4. *The impact of felon disenfranchisement in elections.* The 2000 presidential election, whose outcome hinged on the result in the state of Florida, focused national attention in part on felon disenfranchisement. The state, with its large inmate population, disenfranchises not only prison inmates but also ex-offenders released from any criminal justice sanction unless they have obtained a gubernatorial pardon—a difficult and protracted process. Many argued that felon disenfranchisement changed the outcome of the presidential election in Florida. For some empirical support for the possible impact of felon disenfranchisement on election outcomes, see Christopher Uggen & Jeff Manza, Democratic Contraction? The Political Consequences of Felon Disenfranchisement in the United States, 67 Am. Soc. Rev. 777 (2002). For an account of how a new movement to restore voting rights to felons may significantly influence the electoral map, see Emily Bazelon, The Secret Weapon of 2008: Felons Are Getting the Vote Back—and Republicans Aren't Stopping Them, Slate (April 27, 2007).

5. *Restoration of voting rights.* Most states automatically restore voting rights to all offenders after they have served their criminal justice sentence. Some, however, restrict automatic restoration provisions to first-time or nonviolent offenders. States that do not have automatic restoration provisions offer administrative, judicial, or legislative relief. The difficulty and cost of obtaining relief varies based on the procedure and the state:

> Alabama's voting rights restoration process is complex and potentially intimidating. Those seeking restoration must first obtain a pardon from the Board of Pardons and Paroles. Before applying for pardon, ex-felons must complete three years of permanent parole. Certain offenders must provide the Board with DNA samples before they are eligible for a pardon. Obtaining a pardon alone, however, is insufficient; the Board must next vote affirmatively to restore the applicant's voting rights. . . .
>
> In 2000, Virginia passed a measure that allows ex-felons not convicted of drug offenses to apply to circuit courts for restoration after a five-year waiting period; ex-felons convicted of drug offenses must wait seven years before they become eligible for restoration. The circuit court's decision is not final; the Governor must review and approve any favorable decision. Despite an active reform campaign in the state legislature and the press, felons remain subject to one of the nation's most cumbersome restoration regimes.

Developments in the Law — The Law of Prisons, Part VI. One Person, No Vote: The Laws of Felon Disenfranchisement, 115 Harv. L. Rev. 1939, 1944-1945, 1947-1948 (2002).

6. *Felon disenfranchisement — uniquely American?* In most other Western democracies, voting restrictions on convicted felons are very limited. Germany, for example, allows disenfranchisement only upon conviction of one of a very small number of offenses, including treason and voting fraud, for a maximum period of five years, and only if imposed by a judge at sentencing in open court. See Nora V. Demleitner, Continuing Payment on One's Debt to Society: The German Model of Felon Disenfranchisement as an Alternative, 84 Minn. L. Rev. 753 (2000). In *Sauvé*, the Supreme Court of Canada surveyed the practices in other Western democracies:

> European countries demonstrate a broad range of practices. Eighteen European countries have no form of electoral ban for incarcerated offenders: Bosnia, Croatia, Cyprus, Denmark, Iceland, Ireland, Finland, Latvia, Lithuania, Macedonia, Netherlands, Poland, Slovenia, Spain, Sweden, Switzerland and the Ukraine. In Greece, prisoners serving life sentences or indefinite sentences are disqualified; otherwise the matter is left to the discretion of the court. In some other European countries, electoral disqualification depends on the crime committed or the length of the sentence: Austria, Malta and San Marino ban all prisoners serving more than one year from voting; Belgium disqualifies all offenders serving sentences of four months or more; Italy disenfranchises based on the crime committed and/or the sentence length; Norway removes the vote for prisoners sentenced for specific offences; and in France and Germany, the disqualification of a prisoner is dependent upon the sentence handed down by the court specifically providing for disenfranchisement (in France, certain crimes are identified which carry automatic forfeiture of political rights; in Germany, prisoners convicted of offences which target the integrity of the German state or its democratic order lose the vote). Armenia, Bulgaria, the Czech Republic, Estonia, Hungary, Luxembourg, Romania and Russia all have complete bans for sentenced offenders.
> Australia, New Zealand and the United Kingdom all disenfranchise at least some of the inmate population. In Australia, prisoners vote in two of seven states. In federal elections, inmates serving sentences of five years or more are disqualified from voting. In New Zealand, prisoners serving sentences for three years or more, preventative detention or life imprisonment are not qualified to vote. In the United Kingdom, prisoners are completely disenfranchised for Parliamentary elections, elections to the European Assembly, and local government elections. The only exceptions are for remand prisoners, persons imprisoned for contempt of court and persons detained for default in complying with their sentence. . . .
> Certain international instruments also address the issue of prisoner voting. Article 25 of the International Covenant on Civil and Political Rights ("ICCPR") states that every citizen shall have the "right and the opportunity" to vote "without unreasonable restrictions": ICCPR, 999 U.N.T.S. 171, entered into force March 23, 1976. The United Nations Human Rights Committee, in a comment on Art. 25 of the ICCPR, stated that restrictions on the right to vote should be "objective and reasonable" and that "[i]f conviction for an offence is a basis for suspending the right to vote, the period of such suspension should be proportionate to the offence and the sentence": "General Comment Adopted by the Human Rights Committee Under Article 40, Paragraph 4 of the International Comment on Civil and Political Rights," General Comment No. 25(57), Annex V(1), CCPR/C/21, Rev. 1, Add. 7, August 27, 1996. It is likely caveats, such as the one in Art. 25 of the ICCPR, which led the

international non-governmental organization Penal Reform International, in their 1995 publication Making Standards Work — An International Handbook on Good Prison Practice, at pp. 13-14, to distinguish between "retained rights," which it advocated must be retained in a prison setting, and other rights which may be limited, amongst which was listed the right to vote.

Sauvé, 2002 SCC at ¶¶130, 131, and 133.

In a seminal opinion, the Constitutional Court of South Africa in August v. Electoral Commn., 1999 (3) SA 1 (CC), struck down the disenfranchisement of felons; the high court's rationale was followed most recently by the Supreme Court of Canada in *Sauvé*.

b. Notification, Registration, and Residency Restrictions

In recent years sanctions have increased dramatically against sex offenders as a class. State and federal legislatures and sentencing commissions have lengthened prison sentences; numerous states have passed civil confinement statutes that allow judges to commit sex offenders civilly after their release from prison, a development sanctioned by the Supreme Court in Hendricks v. Kansas, 521 U.S. 346 (1996), and discussed in Chapter 11.

These harsher sanctions came in response to assessments that sentences for sex offenses were disproportionately low compared to other violent and nonviolent crimes and in light of beliefs about the future danger such offenders pose. Incapacitative goals animate sex offender civil commitment statutes, which are based on risk assessments derived from the offender's prior criminal record and assumptions about whether he is likely to reoffend. In addition to civil commitment laws, registration statutes enacted in the mid-1990s require that sex offenders register with local police upon release so that their names can be entered into a database. Notification statutes also require police to alert neighbors, schools, and certain other institutions when a sex offender moves into the area. And a new wave of state and local laws have placed formal restrictions on where sex offenders may reside after their release.

As you review the next two cases, discussing constitutional challenges to registration rules and residency restrictions for sex offenders, consider more broadly whether these laws are sound from a policy perspective. If you think these types of collateral sanctions are potentially effective, should jurisdictions consider expanding their reach to cover other criminal offenders, such as drug dealers and thieves?

Delbert Smith v. John Doe I
538 U.S. 84 (2003)

KENNEDY, J.

The Alaska Sex Offender Registration Act requires convicted sex offenders to register with law enforcement authorities, and much of the information is made public. We must decide whether the registration requirement is a retroactive punishment prohibited by the Ex Post Facto clause.

The State of Alaska enacted the Alaska Sex Offender Registration Act (Act) on May 12, 1994. Like its counterparts in other States, the Act is termed a "Megan's Law." Megan Kanka was a 7-year-old New Jersey girl who was sexually assaulted and murdered in 1994 by a neighbor who, unknown to the victim's family, had prior convictions for sex offenses against children. The crime gave impetus to laws for mandatory registration of sex offenders and corresponding community notification. In 1994, Congress passed the Jacob Wetterling Crimes Against Children and Sexually Violent Offender Registration Act, 42 U.S.C. §14071, which conditions certain federal law enforcement funding on the States' adoption of sex offender registration laws and sets minimum standards for state programs. By 1996, every State, the District of Columbia, and the Federal Government had enacted some variation of Megan's Law.

The Alaska law . . . contains two components: a registration requirement and a notification system. Both are retroactive. The Act requires any "sex offender or child kidnapper who is physically present in the state" to register, either with the Department of Corrections (if the individual is incarcerated) or with the local law enforcement authorities (if the individual is at liberty). Prompt registration is mandated. . . . The sex offender must provide his name, aliases, identifying features, address, place of employment, date of birth, conviction information, driver's license number, information about vehicles to which he has access, and postconviction treatment history. He must permit the authorities to photograph and fingerprint him.

If the offender was convicted of a single, nonaggravated sex crime, he must provide annual verification of the submitted information for 15 years. If he was convicted of an aggravated sex offense or of two or more sex offenses, he must register for life and verify the information quarterly. The offender must notify his local police department if he moves. A sex offender who knowingly fails to comply with the Act is subject to criminal prosecution.

The information is forwarded to the Alaska Department of Public Safety, which maintains a central registry of sex offenders. Some of the data . . . is kept confidential. The following information is made available to the public: "the sex offender's or child kidnapper's name, aliases, address, photograph, physical description, description[,] license [and] identification numbers of motor vehicles, place of employment, date of birth, crime for which convicted, date of conviction, place and court of conviction, length and conditions of sentence, and a statement as to whether the offender or kidnapper is in compliance with [the update] requirements . . . or cannot be located." . . . Alaska has chosen to make most of the nonconfidential information available on the Internet.

Respondents John Doe I and John Doe II were convicted of sexual abuse of a minor, an aggravated sex offense. . . . Both were released from prison in 1990 and completed rehabilitative programs for sex offenders. Although convicted before the passage of the Act, respondents are covered by it. After the initial registration, they are required to submit quarterly verifications and notify the authorities of any changes. Both respondents, along with respondent Jane Doe, wife of John Doe I, brought an action . . . seeking to declare the Act void as to them under the Ex Post Facto Clause of Article I, §10, cl. 1, of the Constitution and the Due Process Clause of §1 of the Fourteenth Amendment. . . .

This is the first time we have considered a claim that a sex offender registration and notification law constitutes retroactive punishment forbidden by the

Ex Post Facto Clause. The framework for our inquiry, however, is well established. We must "ascertain whether the legislature meant the statute to establish 'civil' proceedings." Kansas v. Hendricks, 521 U.S. 346, 361 (1997). If the intention of the legislature was to impose punishment, that ends the inquiry. If, however, the intention was to enact a regulatory scheme that is civil and non-punitive, we must further examine whether the statutory scheme is "'so punitive either in purpose or effect as to negate [the State's] intention' to deem it 'civil.'" Because we "ordinarily defer to the legislature's stated intent," "'only the clearest proof' will suffice to override legislative intent and transform what has been denominated a civil remedy into a criminal penalty," Hudson v. United States, 522 U.S. 93, 100 (1997); United States v. One Assortment of 89 Firearms, 465 U.S. 354 (1984). . . .

Whether a statutory scheme is civil or criminal "is first of all a question of statutory construction." We consider the statute's text and its structure to determine the legislative objective. Flemming v. Nestor, 363 U.S. 603 (1960). A conclusion that the legislature intended to punish would satisfy an ex post facto challenge without further inquiry into its effects, so considerable deference must be accorded to the intent as the legislature has stated it.

The courts "must first ask whether the legislature, in establishing the penalizing mechanism, indicated either expressly or impliedly a preference for one label or the other." Here, the Alaska Legislature expressed the objective of the law in the statutory text itself. The legislature found that "sex offenders pose a high risk of reoffending," and identified "protecting the public from sex offenders" as the "primary governmental interest" of the law. The legislature further determined that "release of certain information about sex offenders to public agencies and the general public will assist in protecting the public safety." As we observed in *Hendricks,* where we examined an ex post facto challenge to a post-incarceration confinement of sex offenders, an imposition of restrictive measures on sex offenders adjudged to be dangerous is "a legitimate nonpunitive governmental objective and has been historically so regarded." In this case, as in *Hendricks,* "nothing on the face of the statute suggests that the legislature sought to create anything other than a civil . . . scheme designed to protect the public from harm."

Respondents seek to cast doubt upon the nonpunitive nature of the law's declared objective by pointing out that the Alaska Constitution lists the need for protecting the public as one of the purposes of criminal administration. As the Court stated in Flemming v. Nestor, rejecting an ex post facto challenge to a law terminating benefits to deported aliens, where a legislative restriction "is an incident of the State's power to protect the health and safety of its citizens," it will be considered "as evidencing an intent to exercise that regulatory power, and not a purpose to add to the punishment." [P]recedents instruct us that even if the objective of the Act is consistent with the purposes of the Alaska criminal justice system, the State's pursuit of it in a regulatory scheme does not make the objective punitive. . . .

The procedural mechanisms to implement the Act do not alter our conclusion. After the Act's adoption Alaska amended its Rules of Criminal Procedure concerning the acceptance of pleas and the entering of criminal judgments. The rule[s] on pleas [and written judgments for sex offenses and child kidnapping] now require[] the court to "inform the defendant in writing of the requirements of [the Act] and, if it can be determined by the court, the period of registration required." . . .

The policy to alert convicted offenders to the civil consequences of their criminal conduct does not render the consequences themselves punitive. When a State sets up a regulatory scheme, it is logical to provide those persons subject to it with clear and unambiguous notice of the requirements and the penalties for noncompliance. . . . Although other methods of notification may be available, it is effective to make it part of the plea colloquy or the judgment of conviction. Invoking the criminal process in aid of a statutory regime does not render the statutory scheme itself punitive.

Our conclusion is strengthened by the fact that, aside from the duty to register, the statute itself mandates no procedures. Instead, it vests the authority to promulgate implementing regulations with the Alaska Department of Public Safety—an agency charged with enforcement of both criminal *and* civil regulatory laws. The Act itself does not require the procedures adopted to contain any safeguards associated with the criminal process. That leads us to infer that the legislature envisioned the Act's implementation to be civil and administrative. . . .

We conclude . . . that the intent of the Alaska Legislature was to create a civil, nonpunitive regime.

In analyzing the effects of the Act we refer to the seven factors noted in Kennedy v. Mendoza-Martinez, 372 U.S. 144 (1963), as a useful framework. These factors, which migrated into our ex post facto case law from double jeopardy jurisprudence, have their earlier origins in cases under the Sixth and Eight Amendments, as well as the Bill of Attainder and the Ex Post Facto Clauses. . . . The factors most relevant to our analysis are whether, in its necessary operation, the regulatory scheme: has been regarded in our history and traditions as a punishment; imposes an affirmative disability or restraint; promotes the traditional aims of punishment; has a rational connection to a nonpunitive purpose; or is excessive with respect to this purpose.

A historical survey can be useful because a State that decides to punish an individual is likely to select a means deemed punitive in our tradition, so that the public will recognize it as such. . . . Respondents argue [ ] that the Act—and, in particular, its notification provisions—resemble shaming punishments of the colonial period.

Some colonial punishments indeed were meant to inflict public disgrace. Humiliated offenders were required "to stand in public with signs cataloguing their offenses." Hirsh, From Pillory to Penitentiary: The Rise of Criminal Incarceration in Early Massachusetts, 80 Mich. L. Rev. 1179 (1982); see also L. Friedman, Crime and Punishment in American History 38 (1993). At times the labeling would be permanent: A murderer might be branded with an "M," and a thief with a "T." R. Semmes, Crime and Punishment in Early Maryland 35 (1938); see also Massaro, Shame, Culture, and American Criminal Law, 89 Mich. L. Rev. 1880 (1991). The aim was to make these offenders suffer "permanent stigmas, which in effect cast the person out of the community." The most serious offenders were banished, after which they could neither return to their original community nor, reputation tarnished, be admitted easily into a new one. . . .

Any initial resemblance to early punishments is, however, misleading. Punishments such as whipping, pillory, and branding inflicted physical pain and staged a direct confrontation between the offender and the public. Even punishments that lacked the corporal component, such as public shaming, humiliation, and banishment, . . . either held the person up before his fellow citizens for face-to-face shaming or expelled him from the community. By contrast, the stigma of Alaska's Megan's Law results not from public display for ridicule and shaming but from the dissemination of accurate information about a criminal record, most of which is already public. Our system does not treat dissemination of truthful information in furtherance of a legitimate governmental objective as punishment. . . . In contrast to the colonial shaming punishments, however, the State does not make the publicity and the resulting stigma an integral part of the objective of the regulatory scheme.

The fact that Alaska posts the information on the Internet does not alter our conclusion. . . . Widespread public access is necessary for the efficacy of the scheme, and the attendant humiliation is but a collateral consequence of a valid regulation.

The State's Web site does not provide the public with means to shame the offender by, say, posting comments underneath his record. An individual seeking the information must take the initial step of going to the Department of Public Safety's Web site, proceed to the sex offender registry, and then look up the desired information. The process is more analogous to a visit to an official archive of criminal records than it is to a scheme forcing an offender to appear in public with some visible badge of past criminality. The Internet makes the document search more efficient, cost effective, and convenient for Alaska's citizenry.

We next consider whether the Act subjects respondents to an "affirmative disability or restraint." Here, we inquire how the effects of the Act are felt by those subject to it. If the disability or restraint is minor and indirect, its effects are unlikely to be punitive.

The Act imposes no physical restraint, and so does not resemble the punishment of imprisonment, which is the paradigmatic affirmative disability or restraint. The Act's obligations are less harsh than the sanctions of occupational debarment, which we have held to be nonpunitive. See [*Hudson*] (forbidding further participation in the banking industry); De Veau v. Braisted, 363 U.S. 144 (1960) (forbidding work as a union official); Hawker v. New York, 170 U.S. 189 (1898) (revocation of a medical license). The Act does not restrain activities sex offenders may pursue but leaves them free to change jobs or residences. . . .

Although the public availability of the information may have a lasting and painful impact on the convicted sex offender, these consequences flow not from the Act's registration and dissemination provisions, but from the fact of conviction, already a matter of public record. The State makes the facts underlying the offenses and the resulting convictions accessible so members of the public can take the precautions they deem necessary before dealing with the registrant.

. . . The Court of Appeals held that the registration system is parallel to probation or supervised release in terms of the restraint imposed. This argument has some force, but, after due consideration, we reject it. Probation and supervised release entail a series of mandatory conditions and allow the supervising officer to seek the revocation of probation or release in case of infraction. By contrast, offenders subject to the Alaska statute are free to move where they wish and to live and work as other citizens, with no supervision. Although registrants must inform the authorities after they change their facial features (such as growing a beard), borrow a car, or seek psychiatric treatment, they are not required to seek permission to do so. A sex offender who fails to comply with the reporting requirement may be subjected to a criminal prosecution for that failure, but any prosecution is a proceeding separate from the individual's original offense. [T]he registration requirements make a valid regulatory program effective and do not impose punitive restraints in violation of the Ex Post Facto Clause.

The State concedes that the statute might deter future crimes. Respondents seize on this proposition to argue that the law is punitive, because deterrence is one purpose of punishment. This proves too much. Any number of governmental programs might deter crime without imposing punishment. "To hold that the mere presence of a deterrent purpose renders such sanctions 'criminal' . . . would severely undermine the Government's ability to engage in effective regulation."

The Court of Appeals was incorrect to conclude that the Act's registration obligations were retributive because "the length of the reporting requirement appears to be measured by the extent of the wrongdoing, not by the extent of the risk posed." The Act, it is true, differentiates between individuals convicted of aggravated or multiple offenses and those convicted of a single nonaggravated offense. The broad categories, however, and the corresponding length of the reporting requirement, are reasonably related to the danger of recidivism, and this is consistent with the regulatory objective.

The Act's rational connection to a nonpunitive purpose is a "most significant" factor in our determination that the statute's effects are not punitive. . . . A statute is not deemed punitive simply because it lacks a close or perfect fit with the nonpunitive aims it seeks to advance. The imprecision respondents rely upon does not suggest that the Act's nonpunitive purpose is a "sham or mere pretext."

. . . Alaska could conclude that a conviction for a sex offense provides evidence of substantial risk of recidivism. The legislature's findings are consistent with grave concerns over the high rate of recidivism among convicted sex offenders and their dangerousness as a class. The risk of recidivism posed by sex offenders is "frightening and high." McKune v. Lile, 536 U.S. 24, 33 (2002) ("When convicted sex offenders reenter society, they are much more likely than any other type of offender to be rearrested for a new rape or sexual assault") (citing U.S. Dept. of Justice, Bureau of Justice Statistics, Sex Offenses and Offenders 27 (1997); U.S. Dept. of Justice, Bureau of Justice Statistics, Recidivism of Prisoners Released in 1983, p. 6 (1997)).

The Ex Post Facto Clause does not preclude a State from making reasonable categorical judgments that conviction of specified crimes should entail particular regulatory consequences. We have upheld against ex post facto challenges laws imposing regulatory burdens on individuals convicted of crimes without any corresponding risk assessment. . . . The State's determination to legislate with respect to convicted sex offenders as a class, rather than require individual determination of their dangerousness, does not make the statute a punishment under the Ex Post Facto Clause.

. . . Our examination of the Act's effects leads to the determination that respondents cannot show, much less by the clearest proof, that the effects of the law negate Alaska's intention to establish a civil regulatory scheme. The Act is nonpunitive, and its retroactive application does not violate the Ex Post Facto Clause. . . .

STEVENS, J., dissenting.

. . . The Court's opinion[ ] fail[s] to decide whether the statutes deprive the registrants of a constitutionally protected interest in liberty. . . .

The statutes impose significant affirmative obligations and a severe stigma on every person to whom they apply. . . .

The registration and reporting duties imposed on convicted sex offenders are comparable to the duties imposed on other convicted criminals during periods of supervised release or parole. And there can be no doubt that the "widespread public access," to this personal and constantly updated information has a severe stigmatizing effect. In my judgment, these statutes unquestionably affect a constitutionally protected interest in liberty.

It is also clear beyond peradventure that these unique consequences of conviction of a sex offense are punitive. They share three characteristics, which in the aggregate are not present in any civil sanction. The sanctions (1) constitute a severe deprivation of the offender's liberty, (2) are imposed on everyone who is convicted of a relevant criminal offense, and (3) are imposed only on those criminals. Unlike any of the cases that the Court has cited, a criminal conviction under these statutes provides both a *sufficient* and a *necessary* condition for the sanction.

[T]he Constitution prohibits the addition of these sanctions to the punishment of persons who were tried and convicted before the legislation was enacted. As the Court recognizes, "recidivism is the statutory concern" that provides the supposed justification for the imposition of such retroactive punishment. . . . Reliance on that rationale here highlights the conclusion that the retroactive application of these statutes constitutes a flagrant violation of the protections afforded by the Double Jeopardy and Ex Post Facto Clauses of the Constitution.

[T]he State may impose registration duties and may publish registration information as a part of its punishment of this category of defendants. Looking to the future, these aspects of their punishment are adequately justified by two of the traditional aims of punishment — retribution and deterrence. Moreover, as a matter of procedural fairness, Alaska requires its judges to include notice of the registration requirements in judgments imposing sentences on convicted sex offenders and in the colloquy preceding the acceptance of a plea of guilty to such an offense. Thus, I agree with the Court that these statutes are constitutional as applied to postenactment offenses. . . .

GINSBURG, J., dissenting.

[I]n resolving whether the Act ranks as penal for ex post facto purposes, I would not demand "the clearest proof" that the statute is in effect criminal rather than civil. Instead, guided by Kennedy v. Mendoza-Martinez, 372 U.S. 144 (1963), I would neutrally evaluate the Act's purpose and effects.

... What ultimately tips the balance for me is the Act's excessiveness in relation to its nonpunitive purpose. ... The Act applies to all convicted sex offenders, without regard to their future dangerousness. And the duration of the reporting requirement is keyed not to any determination of a particular offender's risk of reoffending, but to whether the offense of conviction qualified as aggravated. The reporting requirements themselves are exorbitant: The Act requires aggravated offenders to engage in perpetual quarterly reporting, even if their personal information has not changed. And meriting heaviest weight in my judgment, the Act makes no provision whatever for the possibility of rehabilitation: Offenders cannot shorten their registration or notification period, even on the clearest demonstration of rehabilitation or conclusive proof of physical incapacitation. However plain it may be that a former sex offender currently poses no threat of recidivism, he will remain subject to long-term monitoring and inescapable humiliation.

John Doe I, for example, pleaded nolo contendere to a charge of sexual abuse of a minor nine years before the Alaska Act was enacted. He successfully completed a treatment program, and gained early release on supervised probation in part because of his compliance with the program's requirements and his apparent low risk of re-offense. He subsequently remarried, established a business, and was reunited with his family. He was also granted custody of a minor daughter, based on a court's determination that he had been successfully rehabilitated. The court's determination rested in part on psychiatric evaluations concluding that Doe had "a very low risk of re-offending" and is "not a pedophile." Notwithstanding this strong evidence of rehabilitation, the Alaska Act requires Doe to report personal information to the State four times per year, and permits the State publicly to label him a "Registered Sex Offender" for the rest of his life.

Satisfied that the Act is ambiguous in intent and punitive in effect, I would hold its retroactive application incompatible with the Ex Post Facto Clause, and would therefore affirm the judgment of the Court of Appeals.

|| *John Doe v. Tom Miller* ||
|| 405 F.3d 700 (8th Cir. 2005) ||

COLLOTON, C.J.

In 2002, in an effort to protect children in Iowa from the risk that convicted sex offenders may reoffend in locations close to their residences, the Iowa General Assembly passed, and the Governor of Iowa signed, a bill that prohibits a person convicted of certain sex offenses involving minors from residing within 2000 feet of a school or a registered child care facility. The district court declared the statute unconstitutional on several grounds and enjoined the Attorney General of Iowa and the ninety-nine county attorneys in Iowa from enforcing the prohibition.

Because we conclude that the Constitution of the United States does not prevent the State of Iowa from regulating the residency of sex offenders in this manner in order to protect the health and safety of the citizens of Iowa, we reverse the judgment of the district court. We hold unanimously that the residency restriction is not unconstitutional on its face. ...

I

Iowa Senate File 2197, now codified at Iowa Code §692A.2A, took effect on July 1, 2002. It provides that persons who have been convicted of certain criminal offenses against a minor, including numerous sexual offenses involving a minor, shall not reside within 2000 feet of a school or registered child care facility. The law does not apply to persons who established a residence prior to July 1, 2002, or to schools or child care facilities that are newly located after July 1, 2002. . . .

Almost immediately after the law took effect, three named plaintiffs — sex offenders with convictions that predate the law's effective date — filed suit asserting that the statute is unconstitutional on its face. . . . The named plaintiffs, identified as various "John Does," had committed a range of sexual crimes, including indecent exposure, "indecent liberties with a child," sexual exploitation of a minor, assault with intent to commit sexual abuse, lascivious acts with a child, and second and third degree sexual abuse, all of which brought them within the provisions of the residency restriction. A defendant class, including all of Iowa's county attorneys, also was certified.

During a two-day bench trial, plaintiffs presented evidence concerning the enforcement of §692A.2A, including maps that had been produced by several cities and counties identifying schools and child care facilities and their corresponding restricted areas. After viewing these maps and hearing testimony from a county attorney, the district court found that the restricted areas in many cities encompass the majority of the available housing in the city, thus leaving only limited areas within city limits available for sex offenders to establish a residence. In smaller towns, a single school or child care facility can cause all of the incorporated areas of the town to be off limits to sex offenders. The court found that unincorporated areas, small towns with no school or child care facility, and rural areas remained unrestricted, but that available housing in these areas is "not necessarily readily available." Doe v. Miller, 298 F. Supp. 2d 844, 851 (S.D. Iowa 2004).

Plaintiffs also presented evidence of their individual experiences in seeking to obtain housing that complies with the 2000-foot restriction. Several of the plaintiffs . . . have friends or relatives with whom they would like to live, but whose homes are within 2000 feet of a school or child care facility. Many . . . live in homes that are currently compliant, either because they were established prior to July 1, 2002, or because the homes are outside the 2000-foot restricted areas. These plaintiffs, however, testified that they would like to be able to move into a restricted area. Still others . . . are living in noncompliant residences that they wish to maintain.

. . .

In addition to evidence regarding the burden that §692A.2A places on sex offenders, both plaintiffs and defendants presented expert testimony about the potential effectiveness of a residency restriction in preventing offenses against minors. The State presented the testimony of Mr. Allison, a parole and probation officer who specialized in sex offender supervision. Allison described the process of treating sex offenders and his efforts at preventing recidivism by identifying the triggers for the original offense, and then imposing restrictions on the residences or activities of the offender. According to Allison, restrictions on the proximity of sex offenders to schools or other facilities that might create temptation to reoffend are one way to minimize the risk of recidivism. In the parole and probation context, Allison also has authority to limit offenders' activities in more specific ways, and he testified that he attempts to remove temptation by preventing offenders from working in jobs where they would have contact with potential victims or from living near parks or other areas where children might spend time unsupervised. In addition to the limits that he imposes on offenders under his supervision, Allison also testified that there is "a legitimate public safety concern" in where unsupervised sex offenders reside. In Allison's view, reoffense is "a potential danger forever." . . .

The plaintiffs offered the testimony of Dr. Luis Rosell, a psychologist with experience in sex offender treatment. Dr. Rosell estimated that the recidivism rate for sex offenders is between 20 and 25 percent, and like Allison . . . stated his belief that the key to reducing the risk of recidivism is identifying the factors that led to the offender's original offense and then helping the offender to deal with or avoid those factors in the future. Dr. Rosell testified that reducing a specific sex offender's access to children was a good idea, and that "if you remove the opportunity, then the likelihood of reoffense is decreased." He did not believe, however, that "residential proximity makes that big of a difference." Moreover, Dr. Rosell thought that a 2000-foot limit was "extreme." Like Dr. McEchron, he worried that the law might be counterproductive to the offender's treatment goals by causing depression and potentially removing the offender from his "support system."

After hearing the testimony of all three experts and of the individual plaintiffs, the district court declared that §692A.2A was unconstitutional. . . . Having found the statute unconstitutional, the district court issued a permanent injunction against enforcement. Doe v. Miller, 298 F. Supp. 2d at 880.

II

We first address the contention that §692A.2A violates the rights of the covered sex offenders to due process of law under the Fourteenth Amendment. The appellees (to whom we will refer as "the Does") argue that the statute is unconstitutional because it fails to provide adequate notice of what conduct is prohibited, and because it does not require an individualized determination whether each person covered by the statute is dangerous. This claim relies on what is known as "procedural due process."

. . . The Does contend that they are deprived of notice required by the Constitution because some cities in Iowa are unable to provide sex offenders with information about the location of all schools and registered child care facilities, and because it is difficult to measure the restricted areas, which are measured "as the crow flies" from a school or child care facility. We disagree that these potential problems render the statute unconstitutional on its face. A criminal statute is not vague on its face unless it is impermissibly vague in all of its applications, and the possibility that an individual might be prosecuted in a particular case in a particular community despite his best efforts to comply with the restriction is not a sufficient reason to invalidate the entire statute. . . . Due process does not require that independently elected county attorneys enforce each criminal statute with equal vigor, and the existence of different priorities or prosecution decisions among jurisdictions does not violate the Constitution.

The Does also argue that §692A.2A unconstitutionally forecloses an "opportunity to be heard" because the statute provides no process for individual determinations of dangerousness. . . .

We . . . conclude that the Iowa residency restriction does not contravene principles of procedural due process under the Constitution. The restriction applies to all offenders who have been convicted of certain crimes against minors, regardless of what estimates of future dangerousness might be proved in individualized hearings. Once such a legislative classification has been drawn, additional procedures are unnecessary, because the statute does not provide a potential exemption for individuals. . . . Thus, the absence of an individualized hearing in connection with a statute that offers no exemptions does not offend principles of procedural due process.

III

The Does also assert that the residency restriction is unconstitutional under the doctrine of substantive due process. . . . The Does argue that several "fundamental rights" are infringed by Iowa's residency restriction, including the "right to privacy and choice in family matters," the right to travel, and "the fundamental right to live where you want." The district court agreed that §692A.2A infringed upon liberty interests that constitute fundamental rights, applied strict scrutiny to the legislative classifications, and concluded that the statute was unconstitutional.

The Does first invoke "the right to personal choice regarding the family." . . .

We do not believe that the residency restriction of §692A.2A implicates any fundamental right of the Does that would trigger strict scrutiny of the statute. . . . The Does' characterization of a fundamental right to "personal choice regarding the family" is so general that it would trigger strict scrutiny of innumerable laws and ordinances that influence "personal choices" made by families on a daily basis. . . .

Unlike the precedents cited by the Does, the Iowa statute does not operate directly on the family relationship. Although the law restricts where a residence may be located, nothing in the statute limits who may live with the Does in their residences. . . .

While there was evidence that one adult sex offender in Iowa would not reside with his parents as a result of the residency restriction, that another sex offender and his wife moved 45 miles away from their preferred location due to the statute, and that a third sex offender could not reside with his adult child in a restricted zone, the statute does not directly regulate the family relationship or prevent any family member from residing with a sex offender in a residence that is consistent with the statute. We therefore hold that §692A.2A does not infringe upon a constitutional liberty interest relating to matters of marriage and family in a fashion that requires heightened scrutiny.

The Does also assert that the residency restrictions interfere with their constitutional right to travel. The modern Supreme Court has recognized a right to interstate travel in several decisions [and has] explained that the federal guarantee of interstate travel "protects interstate travelers against two sets of burdens: 'the erection of actual barriers to interstate movement' and 'being treated differently' from intrastate travelers."Bray v. Alexandria Women's Health Clinic, 506 U.S. 263, 277 (1993)....

The Does argue that §692A.2A violates this right to interstate travel by substantially limiting the ability of sex offenders to establish residences in any town or urban area in Iowa. They contend that the constitutional right to travel is implicated because the Iowa law deters previously convicted sex offenders from migrating from other States to Iowa. The district court agreed, reasoning that the statute "effectively bans sex offenders from residing in large sections of Iowa's towns and cities."298 F. Supp. 2d at 874.

We respectfully disagree with this analysis. The Iowa statute imposes no obstacle to a sex offender's entry into Iowa, and it does not erect an "actual barrier to interstate movement." *Bray*, 506 U.S. at 277 (internal quotation omitted). There is "free ingress and regress to and from" Iowa for sex offenders, and the statute thus does not "directly impair the exercise of the right to free interstate movement." *Saenz*, 526 U.S. at 501. Nor does the Iowa statute violate principles of equality by treating nonresidents who visit Iowa any differently than current residents, or by discriminating against citizens of other States who wish to establish residence in Iowa. We think that to recognize a fundamental right to interstate travel in a situation that does not involve any of these circumstances would extend the doctrine beyond the Supreme Court's pronouncements in this area. That the statute may deter some out-of-state residents from traveling to Iowa because the prospects for a convenient and affordable residence are less promising than elsewhere does not implicate a fundamental right recognized by the Court's right to travel jurisprudence.

The Does also urge that we recognize a fundamental right "to live where you want." ... Some thirty years ago, our court said "we cannot agree that the right to choose one's place of residence is necessarily a fundamental right," Prostrollo v. Univ. of S.D., 507 F.2d 775, 781 (8th Cir. 1974), and we see no basis to conclude that the contention has gained strength in the intervening years. ... The Does have not developed any argument that the right to "live where you want" is "deeply rooted in this Nation's history and tradition," id. at 721 (quoting *Moore*, 431 U.S. at 503 (plurality opinion)).... We are thus not persuaded that the Constitution establishes a right to "live where you want" that requires strict scrutiny of a State's residency restrictions.

Because §692A.2A does not implicate a constitutional liberty interest that has been elevated to the status of "fundamental right," we review the statute to determine whether it meets the standard of "rationally advancing some legitimate governmental purpose." *Flores*, 507 U.S. at 306. ... The Does contend ... that the statute is irrational because there is no scientific study that supports the legislature's conclusion that excluding sex offenders from residing within 2000 feet of a school or child care facility is likely to enhance the safety of children.

We reject this contention because we think it understates the authority of a state legislature to make judgments about the best means to protect the health and welfare of its citizens in an area where precise statistical data is unavailable and human behavior is necessarily unpredictable....

We think the decision whether to set a limit on proximity of "across the street" (as appellees suggest), or 500 feet or 3000 feet (as the Iowa Senate considered and rejected, *see* S. Journal 79, 2d Sess., at 521 (Iowa 2002)), or 2000 feet (as the Iowa General Assembly and the Governor eventually adopted) is the sort of task for which the elected policymaking officials of a State, and not the federal courts, are properly suited. . . .

The record does not support a conclusion that the Iowa General Assembly and the Governor acted based merely on negative attitudes toward, fear of, or a bare desire to harm a politically unpopular group [and] . . . we are not persuaded that the means selected to pursue the State's legitimate interest are without rational basis.

IV

The Does next argue that the residency restriction, "in combination with" the sex offender registration requirements of §692A.2, unconstitutionally compels sex offenders to incriminate themselves in violation of the Fifth and Fourteenth Amendments. The district court concluded that a sex offender who establishes residence in a prohibited area must either register his current address, thereby "explicitly admitting the facts necessary to prove the criminal act," or "refuse to register and be similarly prosecuted." 298 F. Supp. 2d at 879. The court then held that *§692A.2A* "unconstitutionally requires sex offenders to provide incriminating evidence against themselves," and enjoined enforcement of the residency restriction on this basis as well.

We disagree that the Self-Incrimination Clause of the Fifth Amendment renders the residency restriction of §692A.2A unconstitutional. Our reason is straightforward: the residency restriction does not compel a sex offender to be a witness against himself or a witness of any kind. The statute regulates only where the sex offender may reside; it does not require him to provide any information that might be used against him in a criminal case. A separate section of the Iowa Code, §692A.2, requires a sex offender to register his address with the county sheriff. The Does have not challenged the constitutionality of the registration requirement, or sought an injunction against its enforcement, and whatever constitutional problem may be posed by the registration provision does not justify invalidating the residency restriction. . . .

V

A final, and narrower, challenge advanced by the Does is that §692A.2A is an unconstitutional ex post facto law because it imposes retroactive punishment on those who committed a sex offense prior to July 1, 2002. . . . In determining whether a state statute violates the Ex Post Facto Clause by imposing such punishment, we apply the framework outlined in Smith v. Doe, 538 U.S. 84, 92 (2003). . . .

The district court found that in passing the residency restriction of §692A.2A, the Iowa General Assembly intended to create "a civil, non-punitive statutory scheme to protect the public." 298 F. Supp. 2d at 868. The Does do not dispute this conclusion on appeal, and we agree that the legislature's intent was not punitive. . . .

We must next consider whether the Does have established that the law was nonetheless so punitive in effect as to negate the legislature's intent to create a civil, nonpunitive regulatory scheme. In this inquiry, we refer to what the Supreme Court described in Smith v. Doe as "useful guideposts" . . . five factors drawn from Kennedy v. Mendoza-Martinez, 372 U.S. 144, 168-69, (1963), as particularly relevant: whether the law has been regarded in our history and traditions as punishment, whether it promotes the traditional aims of punishment, whether it imposes an affirmative disability or restraint, whether it has a rational connection to a nonpunitive purpose, and whether it is excessive with respect to that purpose. Smith v. Doe, 538 U.S. at 97. These factors are "neither exhaustive nor dispositive," id. (quotation omitted). . . .

Turning first to any historical tradition regarding residency restrictions, the Does argue that §692A.2A is the effective equivalent of banishment, which has been regarded historically as a punishment. . . .

While banishment of course involves an extreme form of residency restriction, we ultimately do not accept the analogy between the traditional means of punishment and the Iowa statute. Unlike banishment, §692A.2A restricts only where offenders may reside. It does not "expel" the offenders from their communities or prohibit them from accessing areas near schools or child care facilities for employment, to conduct commercial transactions, or for any purpose other than establishing a residence. With respect to many offenders, the statute does not even require a change of residence: the Iowa General Assembly included a grandfather provision that permits sex offenders to maintain a residence that was established prior to July 1, 2002, even if that residence is within 2000 feet of a school or child care facility. Iowa Code §692A.2A(4)(c). . . . We thus conclude that this law is unlike banishment in important respects, and we do not believe it is of a type that is traditionally punitive.

The second factor that we consider is whether the law promotes the traditional aims of punishment — deterrence and retribution. Smith v. Doe, 538 U.S. at 102. . . . The primary purpose of the law is not to alter the offender's incentive structure by demonstrating the negative consequences that will flow from committing a sex offense. The Iowa statute is designed to reduce the likelihood of reoffense by limiting the offender's temptation and reducing the opportunity to commit a new crime. . . .

The statute's "retributive" effect is similarly difficult to evaluate. . . . The Supreme Court . . . emphasized that the reporting requirements were "reasonably related to the danger of recidivism" in a way that was "consistent with the regulatory objective." Smith v. Doe, 538 U.S. at 102. While any restraint or requirement imposed on those who commit crimes is at least potentially retributive in effect, we believe that §692A.2A, like the registration requirement in Smith v. Doe, is consistent with the legislature's regulatory objective of protecting the health and safety of children.

The next factor we consider is whether the law "imposes an affirmative disability or restraint." Imprisonment is the "paradigmatic" affirmative disability or restraint, Smith v. Doe, 538 U.S. at 100, but other restraints, such as probation or occupational debarment, also can impose some restriction on a person's activities. Id. at 100-01. While restrictive laws are not necessarily punitive, they are more likely to be so; by contrast, "if the disability or restraint is minor and indirect, its effects are unlikely to be punitive." Id. at 100. For example, sex offender registration laws, requiring only periodic reporting and updating of personal information, do not have a punitive restraining effect. Id. at 102. At the same time, civil commitment of the mentally ill, though extremely restrictive and disabling to those who are committed, does not necessarily impose punishment because it bears a reasonable relationship to a "legitimate nonpunitive objective," namely protecting the public from mentally unstable individuals. Kansas v. Hendricks, 521 U.S. 346, 363 (1997).

Iowa Code §692A.2A is more disabling than the sex offender registration law at issue in Smith v. Doe. . . . The residency restriction is certainly less disabling, however, than the civil commitment scheme at issue in *Hendricks*, which permitted complete confinement of affected persons. In both *Smith* and *Hendricks*, the Court considered the degree of the restraint involved in light of the legislature's countervailing nonpunitive purpose, and the Court in *Hendricks* emphasized that the imposition of an affirmative restraint "does not inexorably lead to the conclusion that the government has imposed punishment." 521 U.S. at 363 (internal quotation omitted). Likewise here, while we agree with the Does that §692A.2A does impose an element of affirmative disability or restraint, we believe this factor ultimately points us to the importance of the next inquiry: whether the law is rationally connected to a nonpunitive purpose, and whether it is excessive in relation to that purpose.

This final factor — whether the regulatory scheme has a "rational connection to a nonpunitive purpose" — is the "most significant factor" in the ex post facto analysis. Smith v. Doe, 538 U.S. at 102. The requirement of a "rational connection" is not demanding: A "statute is not deemed punitive simply because it lacks a close or perfect fit with the nonpunitive aims it seeks to advance." Id. at 103. The district court found "no doubt" that §692A.2A has a purpose other than punishing sex offenders, 298 F. Supp. 2d at 870, and we agree. In light of the high risk of recidivism posed by sex offenders, see Smith v. Doe, 538 U.S. at 103, the legislature reasonably could conclude that §692A.2A would protect society by minimizing the risk of repeated sex offenses against minors.

. . .

The Does also urge that the law is excessive in relation to its regulatory purpose because there is no scientific evidence that a 2000-foot residency restriction is effective at preventing sex offender recidivism. "The excessiveness inquiry of our ex post facto jurisprudence is not an exercise in determining whether the legislature has made the best choice possible to address the problem it seeks to remedy," but rather an inquiry into "whether the regulatory means chosen are reasonable in light of the nonpunitive objective." Smith v. Doe, 538 U.S. at 105. In this case, there was expert testimony that reducing the frequency of contact between sex offenders and children is likely to reduce temptation and opportunity, which in turn is important to reducing the risk of reoffense. None of the witnesses was able to articulate a precise distance that optimally balanced the benefit of reducing risk to children with the burden of the residency restrictions on sex offenders, and the Does' expert acknowledged that "there is nothing in the literature that has addressed proximity" (Appellee's App. 198; accord id. at 41, 47-48 (testimony of Dr. McEchron)). . . .

We believe the legislature's decision to select a 2000-foot restriction, as opposed to the other distances that were considered and rejected, is reasonably related to its regulatory purpose. . . .

* * *

The judgment of the district court is reversed, and the case is remanded with directions to enter judgment in favor of the defendants.

MELLOY, C.J., concurring and dissenting.

I join in the majority's opinion, sections I through IV. However, I dissent as to section V because I believe section 692A.2A is an unconstitutional ex post facto law.

. . . I agree with the majority that the purpose of section 692A.2A is to protect the public. This purpose is nonpunitive, so we must determine if the statute is so punitive either in purpose or effect as to negate the State's intention to deem it civil. . . .

Though I believe a rational connection exists between the residency restriction and a nonpunitive purpose, I would find that the restriction is excessive in relation to that purpose. The statute limits the housing choices of all offenders identically, regardless of their type of crime, type of victim, or risk of re-offending. The effect of the requirement is quite dramatic: many offenders cannot live with their families and/or cannot live in their home communities because the whole community is a restricted area. This leaves offenders to live in the country or in small, prescribed areas of towns and cities that might offer no appropriate, available housing. In addition, there is no time limit to the restrictions.

. . . The severity of residency restriction, the fact that it is applied to all offenders identically, and the fact that it will be enforced for the rest of the offenders' lives, makes the residency restriction excessive. . . . Because the imposition of the residency requirement "'changes the punishment, and inflicts a greater punishment, than the law annexed to the crime, when committed,'" *Stogner*, 539 U.S. at 612 (quoting *Calder*, 3 U.S. at 390), I would find section 692A.2A is an unconstitutional ex post facto law that cannot be applied to persons who committed their offenses before the law was enacted.

NOTES

1. *An array of constitutional challenges.* As detailed in Smith v. Doe and Doe v. Miller, sex offenders subject to new registration requirements and residency restrictions have attacked these laws in many state and federal courts by bringing constitutional challenges based on an array of different theories and constitutional provisions. Especially when the laws are applied to offenders originally convicted before the registration requirement or restriction was enacted, the most common challenge is based on the ex post facto clause. Notably, ex post fact challenges address only when, and not whether, these laws can be applied. Other, broader challenges to these laws include claims based on due process, both procedural and substantive, equal protection, cruel and unusual punishment, double jeopardy, and self-incrimination. Most registration and residency restrictions are upheld against these challenges, validated as civil

provisions that are generally justified by the state's interest in protecting public safety.

2. *Are registration and residency restrictions sound policy?*   Registration and residency laws are enacted purportedly to protect the health and safety of the public. In theory, knowing where sex offenders live helps law enforcement solve sex crimes and enables the public to protect themselves against known registered offenders. In theory, residency restrictions reduce the contacts offenders have with children, which may in turn reduce offenders' ability and temptation to commit offenses. However, critics of these laws have developed arguments and evidence suggesting that registration and residency restrictions are not as beneficial as legislators may hope.

First, 80-90% of sex offenders' victims are family members or people known to the offender. Most offenses are not committed against the random child walking down the street; therefore, while registration and residency restrictions may help curb random sex offenses, they are unlikely to operate in a manner that can effectively curtail the vast majority of sex offenses.

Second, registration and residency restrictions are at tension with each other. If an offender lives within a restricted zone, he may choose not to register his address for fear that he will be told to move. Consequently, neither law enforcement nor neighbors will know where the sex offender is living, a situation that will undermine the interests of public safety.

Third, both of these sex offender restrictions are a drain on law enforcement resources. Law enforcement departments must choose between hiring more people to enforce and administer the restrictions or requiring the personnel they have to take time away from the enforcement of other laws to enforce sex offender laws.

Fourth, the registration and residency restrictions have negative effects on sex offenders. The laws hinder the offender's rehabilitation when he is unable to get a job, unable to find a place to live, and unable to establish beneficial relationships with friends and neighbors. Often, offenders reoffend because they are not able to overcome the adversities that may have led them to offend in the first place.

Fifth, the laws not only harm the offender's ability to rehabilitate, but they also affect offenders' loved ones. Children may be pulled out of school and spouses may have to quit their jobs because an offender is required to relocate.

Sixth, many registration and residency restrictions last for the life of the offender. There is nothing an offender can do to get off the registration list or become exempt from residency restrictions. This leaves an offender with no incentive to change. Given a way to get off the list, offenders may be more willing to go through with counseling and rehabilitation, but when there is no legal way to avoid registration, there is no incentive to change.

Seventh, the restrictions affect law enforcement on the front end. When people are charged with a sex offense, they may be less likely to plead guilty or enter a plea agreement, knowing that if they do, they will be subject to registration and residency restrictions. With the reduction in guilty pleas, trials will not only crowd the docket but also require child victims to endure the trauma of a trial.

Emphasizing all these points, the Iowa County Attorneys Association issued a Statement on Sex Offender Residency Restrictions in Iowa (February 14, 2006) urging legislators to rework the broad restrictions in Iowa law. This important statement originating from law enforcement officials has led some jurisdictions, though not all, to question whether the benefits of these laws really outweigh the undesirable consequences. If you were a legislator in a state considering a sex offender residency restriction bill, how might you try to gather information about this public safety cost-benefit question?

3. *Risk assessment.*   The Supreme Court held that individual risk assessments were not needed for entry into sex offender databases. Thus, states can continue to classify offenders based on the offense of conviction. Different states take different offenses as predicate crimes for entry into the database. Recent research indicates that the prediction of whether an offender will commit another serious sex-based violent crime in the short term is most effective when it combines an actuarial risk assessment, based on prior record, type of sex offense, and similar factors, with a clinical prediction model. Eric S. Janus & Robert A. Prentky, Forensic Use of Actuarial Risk Assessment with Sex Offenders: Accuracy, Admissibility and Accountability, 40 Am. Crim. L. Rev. 1443 (2003).

4. *Recidivism and sex offenses.*   The Smith v. Doe Court relies in part on the substantial risk that convicted sex offenders pose to the public. It cites a study indicating that sex offenders are much more likely than other offenders to commit a sex crime. But the same holds true for other types of criminals, such as drug and property offenders, with respect to their general crime of conviction. Moreover, reconviction rates for sex offenders are the second lowest among all offenders. Does this indicate that the Court's analysis is incorrect? Or does it support a more limited sex offender registry?

5. *Conduct-based ban.*   May sanctions or limits be imposed on offenders based on noncriminal conduct after sentencing? In Doe v. City of Lafayette, Ind., 334 F.3d 606, *vacated and reh'g granted*, 2003 U.S. App. LEXIS 16563 (7th Cir. 2003), a panel of the Seventh Circuit struck down the city's decision to ban a sex offender from all park property for life after he had visited a park and admitted to having had sexual urges while observing the children playing there. In this case the offender's prior criminal record combined with his later conduct (or thoughts?) caused the city to act. Administrative agencies and courts may also impose sanctions based on criminal conduct, even if no criminal conviction occurs. See Department of Housing and Urban Development v. Rucker, 535 U.S. 125 (2002) (eviction from public housing upheld when a member of the household or a guest engaged in drug-related criminal activity, regardless of whether the tenant knew, or should have known, of the drug-related activity).

PROBLEM 8-1.   DON'T WORK IN MY BACKYARD

As detailed on the city's official website, the City of Upper Arlington, Ohio, has enacted a sex offender ordinance that "bars convicted sexual offenders from living *or working* within 1,000 feet of any school premises, licensed daycare facility, preschool, public park, swimming pool, library, or playground." In light of Smith v. Doe and Doe v. Miller, what kinds of constitutional arguments might you be able to make against this legislation if you were representing a person who, after having pled guilty to a sex offense while in college, has been working for

over a decade as a real estate agent in a professional office building in Upper
Arlington that happens to be 950 feet from a licensed daycare facility?

c.   Firearms

For convicted felons, the most common collateral sanction (sometimes
called a disability), which may be imposed for a term or for life, is the state
and federal prohibition of the possession of firearms. Some statutes single
out certain types of felony offenses or classes of offenses to trigger a firearms
ban. Typically, drug offenses are included in this category. What rationale justifies this collateral sanction?

Given the broad applicability of such prohibitions, the wide availability
of firearms, and the strong legal, cultural, and social traditions surrounding
gun ownership, it is not surprising that the desire to own firearms is among
the most common reasons former offenders request relief from collateral sanctions.

Ohio Revised Code §2923.13, Having Weapons While Under Disability

(A) [N]o person shall knowingly acquire, have, carry, or use any firearm or
dangerous ordnance, if any of the following apply:

(1) The person is a fugitive from justice.

(2) The person is under indictment for or has been convicted of any
felony offense of violence. . . .

(3) The person is under indictment for or has been convicted of any
offense involving the illegal possession, use, sale, administration, distribution,
or trafficking in any drug of abuse. . . .

(4) The person is drug dependent, in danger of drug dependence, or a
chronic alcoholic.

(5) The person is under adjudication of mental incompetence.

(B) No person who has been convicted of a felony of the first or second
degree shall violate division (A) of this section within five years of the date of the
person's release from imprisonment or from post-release control that is
imposed for the commission of a felony of the first or second degree.

(C) Whoever violates this section is guilty of having weapons while under
disability. A violation of division (A) of this section is a felony of the fifth degree
[punishable by six, seven, eight, nine, ten, eleven, or twelve months]. A violation
of division (B) of this section is a felony of the third degree [punishable by one,
two, three, four, or five years].

Ohio Revised Code §2923.14, Relief from Disability

(A) Any person who, solely by reason of the person's disability under division (A)(2) or (3) of section 2923.13 of the Revised Code, is prohibited from

acquiring, having, carrying, or using firearms, may apply to the court of common pleas in the county in which the person resides for relief from such prohibition.

(B) The application shall recite the following:

(1) All indictments, convictions, or adjudications upon which the applicant's disability is based, the sentence imposed and served, and any release granted under a community control sanction, post-release control sanction, or parole, any partial or conditional pardon granted, or other disposition of each case;

(2) Facts showing the applicant to be a fit subject for relief under this section.

(C) A copy of the application shall be served on the county prosecutor. . . .

(D) Upon hearing, the court may grant the applicant relief pursuant to this section, if all of the following apply:

(1) The applicant has been fully discharged from imprisonment, community control, post-release control, and parole, or, if the applicant is under indictment, has been released on bail or recognizance.

(2) The applicant has led a law-abiding life since discharge or release, and appears likely to continue to do so.

(3) The applicant is not otherwise prohibited by law from acquiring, having, or using firearms. . . .

NOTES

1. *Felon-in-possession statutes.*   State and federal law prohibits some convicted felons from owning and using firearms. Federal law prohibits a convicted felon whose crime was "punishable by a term exceeding one year" from possessing firearms. Do you believe felon-in-possession statutes are effective as law-enforcement tools? Are statutes such as Ohio's over- or underinclusive? As a state legislator, would you support such legislation? Why?

2. *Removal of firearms disabilities.*   Most states provide judicial or administrative relief from firearms disabilities, but no equivalent procedure exists at the federal level. A part of the federal felon-in-possession statute grants the secretary of the treasury the right to reinstate a former felon's firearms privileges if past good conduct indicates that the disability should be removed. Since 1992, however, Congress has failed to fund this portion of the secretary's work. Courts have split on whether federal district courts may review such petitions. See Rice v. United States Dep't of Alcohol, Tobacco and Firearms, 68 F.3d 702 (3d Cir. 1995). But see United States v. McGill, 74 F.3d 64 (5th Cir. 1996).

2.   Administrative Sanctions

While many collateral sanctions befall the offender automatically upon conviction, others are imposed in regulatory hearings. One of the most important and pervasive illustrations of such a collateral sanction is deportation, which is declared by an immigration judge or the immigration agency rather than by the criminal court. For a proposal to allow the criminal sanctioning and the deportation decisions to be made by the sentencing judge, see Margaret Taylor & Ronald Wright, The Sentencing Judge as Immigration Judge, 51 Emory L.J. 1131 (2002).

Since the 1996 immigration acts, the deportation of criminal offenders has expanded dramatically. In 1986 not quite 2,000 noncitizens were removed for criminal violations; in 2002 the figure had risen to almost 71,000, with 41% of the convictions that formed the basis for deportation involving drug offenses. Removal is now mandatory for all noncitizens convicted of "aggravated felonies," a large category of offenses that includes more than just the most heinous crimes that the term implies. Moreover, deportation can occur upon conviction of "crimes of moral turpitude." Not surprisingly, lower courts sometimes disagree on the definitions of some these terms.

Immediately upon the passage of the 1996 legislation, the Immigration and Naturalization Service enforced the deportation provisions retroactively. This means that individuals who had pled guilty to offenses many years, and often decades, in the past were detained and deported without having available to them the more generous discretionary relief provisions they had relied on in earlier legislation. In its 2001 decision in INS v. St. Cyr, 533 U.S. 289 (2001), the Supreme Court held that such discretionary relief remained available to these individuals since they had relied on them in working out plea bargains.

Whether criminal defendants need to be informed of the immigration consequences of a guilty plea by the court, the prosecutor, or their counsel has been an important question, with far-reaching consequences for other, albeit less dramatic, collateral sanctions.

|| *United States v. Marino Amador-Leal* ||
|| 276 F.3d 511 (9th Cir. 2002) ||

RYMER, J.

Marino Amador-Leal appeals his conviction and sentence pursuant to a guilty plea on one count of possession with intent to distribute cocaine base in violation of 21 U.S.C. §841(a)(1). The magistrate judge did not explain the potential immigration consequences of Amador-Leal's conviction when the plea was taken. The question presented here is whether immigration consequences are collateral, as we held in Fruchtman v. Kenton, 531 F.2d 946 (9th Cir.), *cert. denied*, 429 U.S. 895 (1976), or have become direct in light of the aggravated felony provisions of the Antiterrorism and Effective Death Penalty Act of 1996 (AEDPA), and the Illegal Immigration Reform and Immigrant Responsibility Act of 1996 (IIRIRA), such that a defendant must be advised of them in order for his plea to be voluntary. We . . . conclud[e] that *Fruchtman* is still good law, and that immigration consequences remain collateral. . . .

Amador-Leal is an illegal alien who was caught selling crack in February, 2000. . . .

Pursuant to a written plea agreement . . . , Amador-Leal entered a plea of guilty to [a] possession [with intent to distribute cocaine base] count on May 18, 2000. The magistrate judge reviewed the charges with Amador-Leal, explained his rights and the implications of his plea, and found that he knowingly and voluntarily agreed to the plea. Based on the plea agreement and Amador-Leal's cooperation, the district court accepted the government's recommendation for a two level downward departure and sentenced Amador-Leal to 87 months in custody. . . .

Amador-Leal submits that his plea neither conforms to Rule 11 nor comports with due process because, for a plea to be considered voluntary, district courts must inform defendants pleading guilty of the direct consequences of their plea and resulting conviction; immigration consequences are direct as they flow automatically from a statute; and United States v. Littlejohn, 224 F.3d 960 (9th Cir. 2000), requires advice about statutorily mandated ineligibility to apply for a benefit such as relief with respect to immigration status or removal. He distinguishes *Fruchtman* on the footing that he and Littlejohn are similarly situated in that both suffer statutorily mandated ineligibility to apply for certain federal benefits, and that *Fruchtman* faced only the potential of deportation whereas his own removal is "practically guaranteed" under immigration laws enacted since *Fruchtman* was decided in 1976. We should therefore, in his view, find *Fruchtman* no longer controlling.

To start with the obvious, guilty pleas must be knowing and voluntary. As we explained in Torrey v. Estelle, 842 F.2d 234 (9th Cir. 1988):

> A plea is voluntary only if it is entered by one fully aware of the direct consequences of his plea of guilty. . . . This court, in harmony with other circuits, has held that although a defendant is entitled to be informed of the direct consequences of the plea, the court need not advise him of all the possible collateral consequences.

District courts are obliged to advise a defendant of direct consequences even if the particular consequence is not listed among the issues that Rule 11(c) requires the court to cover. However, there is no obligation to advise of collateral consequences. "The distinction between a direct and collateral consequence of a plea turns on whether the result represents a definite, immediate and largely automatic effect on the range of the defendant's punishment."

As Amador-Leal recognizes, we decided in *Fruchtman* that immigration consequences are collateral. In *Fruchtman,* the defendant was an alien who also was not advised by the district court that his conviction would subject him to deportation proceedings. Fruchtman argued on appeal that his plea was not voluntary because deportation is a drastic measure of which he should have been advised before his plea was accepted. We recognized that administration of Rule 11 "requires the development of some limiting guide to define the nature of the consequences of which a defendant must be advised so that the requirements of the rule shall have been met," and that the "common distinction" drawn is between consequences that are direct and those that are collateral. Noting that other appellate courts had resolved the issue, we adopted the reasoning of the Court of Appeals for the Second Circuit that "when, as in the case of deportation, the consequence in issue 'was not the sentence of the court which accepted the plea but of another agency over which the trial judge has no control and for which he has no responsibility,' Rule 11 imposes no duty on the District Court to advise a defendant of such consequences."

We must, of course, follow *Fruchtman* unless it is distinguishable or undermined. First, relying on *Littlejohn,* Amador-Leal suggests that the proper inquiry for determining whether a statutorily created ineligibility to apply for some form

668 Chapter 8. Sentencing Outcomes: Nonprison Punishments

of government benefit is a direct or collateral consequence is not whether the benefit is denied later by some agency other than the court, but whether the ineligibility is an automatic consequence of a statute. However, . . . we decline to embrace the test that Amador-Leal proposes. No court has, and it would be totally unworkable in practice.

In *Littlejohn,* the defendant pled guilty to a drug offense. His conviction automatically rendered him ineligible for certain food stamp and social security benefits pursuant to 21 U.S.C. §§862(a) and 862a, but the court did not say so during the Rule 11 colloquy. On appeal, Littlejohn argued that his plea was involuntary because he had not been warned that he would suffer ineligibility, and we agreed. We contrasted direct consequences . . . as consequences that have

> "a definite, immediate and largely automatic effect on the range of the defen-
> dant's punishment," [with collateral consequences that] have included the
> possibility of a felony prosecution for reentry following deportation; imposition
> of a consecutive rather than concurrent sentence where the district court has
> discretion to choose between the two; the possibility of being resentenced to a
> maximum term if a state agency determines that the defendant is not amenable
> to treatment; exposure to potential civil tax litigation; revocation of parole from
> a separate conviction where such revocation is within the power of a parole
> board; and the potential of deportation, where a separate agency has authority
> over such deportation. . . .

Littlejohn, 224 F.3d at 965. We then concluded that the benefit-stripping effect of both sections 862(a) and 862a was a direct consequence of conviction because "the ineligibility itself is not a result of other governmental agencies' actions, and it is not dependent upon Littlejohn's own future conduct. It is an automatic product of Littlejohn's conviction." For this reason, we held that district courts must advise defendants of §862a ineligibility, although we went on to say that the error was harmless given that Littlejohn would have pled guilty anyway. We treated §862(a) differently, holding that courts have no obligation to inform defendants of §862(a) ineligibility because applicability of this section depends upon the existence of prior convictions about which the judge would be unaware when taking the plea.[3] *Littlejohn* itself puts the potential for deportation firmly within the category of collateral consequences. Indeed, our decision in *Littlejohn* turned on the rationale articulated by *Fruchtman* for determining whether a consequence is direct or collateral. As we summed up in *Littlejohn,* "where the consequence is contingent upon action taken by an individual or individuals other than the sentencing court — such as another governmental agency or the defendant himself — the consequence is generally 'collateral.'" Thus, the *Fruchtman* test remains intact.

Nevertheless, Amador-Leal maintains, *Fruchtman* can no longer control in the context of deportation because AEDPA and IIRIRA have changed the landscape for illegal aliens convicted of aggravated felonies. No doubt the landscape has changed, because it is now virtually certain that an aggravated felon will be removed. Yet whether an alien will be removed is still up to the INS.

---

3. The same feasibility concerns that animated this different treatment in *Littlejohn* are also present here: district courts generally have no information about a defendant's immigration status at the Rule 11 proceeding.

There is a process to go through, and it is wholly independent of the court imposing sentence. The Supreme Court has made this clear by describing deportation as a "purely civil action" separate and distinct from a criminal proceeding. INS v. Lopez-Mendoza, 468 U.S. 1032 (1984). Removal is not part of the sentence; future immigration consequences do not bear on the "range of the defendant's punishment" imposed by the court, and deportation is not punishment for the crime. By contrast, the statutes at issue in *Littlejohn* are part of the criminal code. Also unlike the removal statutes, §§862(a) and 862a are self-executing upon imposition of sentence. A defendant receiving government benefits is immediately and automatically ineligible for them once convicted; however, immigration consequences will not be felt until the court's sentence has been served, the INS assumes control of the defendant, and the process of removal has been initiated and executed. In short, no matter what changes have been wrought by AEDPA and IIRIRA, removal remains the result of another governmental agency's subsequent actions. . . .

Therefore, immigration consequences continue to be a collateral consequence of a plea and the resulting conviction. This means that district courts are not constitutionally required to warn defendants about potential removal in order to assure voluntariness of a plea; but it does not mean that they should not do so. Many district judges comment in their Rule 11 colloquy that a plea of guilty and resulting conviction may affect an alien's status in this country, and inquire whether the defendant understands the possible immigration consequences of his plea. Although not required by Rule 11 or due process, we commend this sort of dialogue for there is no question that immigration consequences of a conviction are important to aliens contemplating a plea. See [INS v.] St. Cyr, 121 S. Ct. at 2291; Magana Pizano v. INS, 200 F.3d 603, 612 (9th Cir. 1999).[4] However, because immigration consequences are collateral, neither Rule 11 nor Amador-Leal's right to due process was violated in this case. . . .

PROBLEM 8-2.   WHAT'S WORSE?

Juan Nico, a permanent resident alien who entered the United States at age three and has lived here since then, got caught up in a bar brawl. He admits to having been drunk when his sister's ex-boyfriend, Bob Friendly, came into the bar. His sister had told him about the abuse Bob had inflicted on her, and he decided to show Bob what it would be like to be beaten up. Bob had not fully sat down when Juan attempted to throw a beer mug at him but missed. Juan and

---

4. Many states have enacted statutes that require courts to advise a defendant of the immigration consequences of a plea, see *St. Cyr*, 121 S. Ct. at 2291 n.48 (listing states with statutory requirement), but the general rule post-AEDPA and IIRIRA remains that there is no due process requirement for defendants to be informed of immigration consequences because immigration consequences are collateral. See, e.g., State v. Ramirez, 636 N.W.2d 740, 2001 WL 1035928 at *1 (Iowa 2001); State v. Jamison, 105 Wn. App. 572, 20 P.3d 1010 (Wash. App. 2001); State v. Jimenez, 987 S.W.2d 886 (Tex. Crim. App. 1999); State v. Modi, 1998 Del. Super. LEXIS 331, 1998 WL 735881 (Del. Super. Sept. 25, 1998); People v. Agero, 234 A.D.2d 94, 651 N.Y.S.2d 430 (App. Div. 1996).

Bob got into a fight, which ended when other patrons separated them. Both had minor injuries, largely scrapes and bruises.

The district attorney suggests that Nico plead guilty to assault with a one-year suspended sentence. It is the local district attorney's policy to offer such pleas to noncitizens. Had Nico been a citizen, the district attorney would have insisted on some jail time.

If he accepts the plea, Nico will become automatically deportable as an aggravated felon since he committed a crime of violence. As Nico's attorney, what options do you have at your disposal? Could you attack the district attorney's policy offering different pleas to citizens and noncitizens?

NOTES

1. *Deportation as a civil sanction.*   A long line of cases defines deportation as a civil rather than a criminal sanction. The distinction has traditionally been that collateral sanctions are indirect, and in the case of deportation they are imposed by an agency outside the criminal justice system. None of the procedural protections that attach in criminal cases, therefore, apply in deportation hearings. See INS v. Lopez-Mendoza, 468 U.S. 1032 (1984). This is the case even though deportation for a criminal offense includes a long-term ban on reentry and often requires the offender to uproot his entire life and be separated from his family.

2. *Notification.*   After the 1996 immigration laws substantially expanded the category of crimes making aliens deportable, some state legislatures mandated that courts inform noncitizen criminal defendants of potential immigration consequences. See, e.g., Cal. Penal Code §1016.5 (West 2001). In some other states, courts have ruled to that effect. Chapter 19 of the ABA Standards on Collateral Sanctions (2003) recommends that judges inform criminal defendants before the guilty plea of the whole panoply of potential collateral sanctions. This would necessitate that courts compile a list of existing sanctions, many of which are currently unknown to judges, prosecutors, and defense counsel. In In re Resendiz, 19 P.3d 1171 (Cal. 2001), the California Supreme Court held that in certain cases affirmative misadvice regarding immigration consequences could constitute ineffective assistance of counsel in the criminal case.

3. *Prosecutorial manipulation of collateral sanctions.*   Prosecutors are able to influence the imposition of collateral consequences through charging decisions and plea offers. If a defendant refuses to accept an apparently generous plea offer because of a collateral consequence, and the judge both agrees with the defendant's decision and considers the collateral sanction too harsh, what options does the judge have?

4. *Welfare and financial aid benefits.*   Federal law gives sentencing courts discretion to bar drug offenders temporarily from access to benefits. 21 U.S.C. §862(a). Studies have shown that neither state nor federal courts take advantage of this provision. See Robert Musser Jr., Denial of Federal Benefits to Drug Traffickers and Drug Possessors: A Broad-Reaching but Seldom Used

Sanction, 12 Fed. Sent'g Rep. 252 (2000). Upon a third conviction for sale of illegal narcotics, the ban becomes mandatory. 21 U.S.C. §862a requires that states permanently deny certain welfare benefits and food stamps to people convicted of state or federal felony drug possession, use, or sale offenses, unless the state explicitly opts out of such a ban. Currently, 22 states retain the ban. The denial of welfare benefits has been found to have a particularly devastating impact on women released from prison, since they are more likely to suffer a relapse. See Amy E. Hirsch, Parents with Criminal Records and Public Benefits: "Welfare Helps Us Stay in Touch with Society," in Every Door Closed: Barriers Facing Parents with Criminal Records 27, 31 (Community Legal Services 2002). The first conviction for a drug possession or sale offense also carries with it a temporary denial of financial aid benefits for students applying to or enrolled in institutions of higher learning. The sponsor of the legislation wanted the provision to apply only for convictions occurring while the student receives such benefits, but currently it is being implemented to apply to anyone with a drug offense conviction, however far in the past. The third possession or second sale offense results in indefinite suspension of financial aid. Students may restore their eligibility if they complete a drug rehabilitation program that complies with certain criteria. See 20 U.S.C. §1091(r).

5. *Administrative sanctions based on criminal conduct.*   Collateral sanctions depend on a criminal conviction. Some administrative restrictions, however, are based not on a criminal conviction but rather on criminal conduct. For example, involvement in drug activity carries with it a ban from public housing, irrespective of whether the renter was convicted of a drug offense. Although criminal conduct is most easily proven through a criminal record, a formal conviction is not required.

6. *Extralegal collateral sanctions.*   Employers such as schools, long-term care facilities, and security services are statutorily obligated to investigate the criminal record of a job applicant. In addition to governmental disabilities imposed on offenders after they have served their criminal justice sentences, nongovernmental (private) disabilities apply as well. Many employers voluntarily check criminal records and refuse to hire ex-offenders. Licensing boards frequently deny ex-offenders licenses for employment positions ranging from attorney to beautician. Ex-offenders are also finding it increasingly difficult to rent apartments and homes. This is particularly problematic for sex offenders, but many other offenders are also denied housing by rental agencies and home owners. Should the government protect the civil rights of ex-offenders who have served their sentences? Would an ex-offender nondiscrimination act have any chance of being enacted?

Notably, in his 2004 State of the Union address, President George W. Bush spoke passionately about the importance of showing compassion (and providing job training and placement services) to convicted offenders because "America is the land of second chance." In the years following this speech, numerous bills seeking to live up to this mantra have been introduced in the House and Senate. Such bills often have sponsors from both parties and often receive vocal bipartisan support, but none have yet secured passage. Why do you think it has proven difficult for Congress to pass what has come to be known as the "Second Chance Act"?

=9=
Race, Class, and Gender

Fundamental constitutional and moral principles of equal treatment tell us that people should not be punished more or less severely because of their race (or ethnicity), social or economic class, or gender. These abstract principles quickly confront a dramatic reality of American criminal justice: criminal defendants, as a group, are overwhelmingly male and poor. Equally striking, African Americans and Native Americans are convicted of crimes at highly disproportionate levels. These unsettling facts of the American criminal justice system — disproportions shared in varying degrees by other countries — raise a profound question: why are men, members of (some) racial minority groups, and the poor convicted more frequently than others?

For a good part of U.S. history, state laws explicitly justified differential treatment on the basis of race and gender. But such laws have for some time been anathema to the U.S. legal system. See, e.g., Commonwealth v. Butler, 328 A.2d 851 (Pa. 1974) (statute requiring mandatory minimum sentence for men but not women declared unconstitutional). Now, the issue of whether people are sentenced more severely on the basis of their race, ethnicity, wealth, or gender has become more subtle and difficult to answer.

Studies conducted in the United States find little difference between races in their formal treatment by the criminal justice system after controlling for other differences among cases. Some of the racial disproportionality in prison sentences appears to be largely contextual: African American defendants are more likely to go to prison in areas of high unemployment, in places where blacks constitute a larger percentage of the population, and in the South. For other racial groups the data are more ambiguous and more difficult to explain. The few empirical studies done on inmate populations indicate that those sentenced to custodial terms are poorer than the rest of the population. The gender data are clear: despite rising imprisonment rates for women, they are dramatically underrepresented, and the offenses of which they are convicted tend to be less violent than those of male offenders.

This chapter considers the charge that racism, classism, and sexism are an inherent part of the criminal justice process and that their end product is highly disproportionate punishment. The chapter also raises the question whether the criminal justice system in general, and sentencing law in particular, is an appropriate place to remedy bias that may stem from more pervasive societal and historical forces.

A.   AFRICAN AMERICANS IN THE CRIMINAL JUSTICE SYSTEM

> There is nothing more painful to me at this stage in my life than to
> walk down the street and hear footsteps and start thinking about robbery
> — then look around and see somebody white and feel relieved.
>
> *Jesse Jackson, 1993*

Race is an unavoidable issue in modern American criminal procedure. Difficult questions arise at all stages of the criminal process: What is the role of race in police stops and investigations? When might racial disparities justify challenges to charging practices? What role should race play in jury selection? In arguments at trial? But perhaps the most common and visible questions about race arise at the end of the process, in the form of claims that black Americans and other minorities are punished more severely than whites. In some situations, the responsible decision makers may be identifiable; in other situations, the source of racial disparity may be hard to specify even when it clearly exists.

The first section of this chapter sets the stage by identifying the aggregate racial disparities in sanctioning and by presenting some preliminary arguments about the source of those disparities. The next part examines the 1987 decision of the U.S. Supreme Court in McCleskey v. Kemp, one of the most difficult and contentious racial cases of the past half century. *McCleskey* addresses a claim that the state of Georgia discriminates on the basis of the *victim's* race when it imposes the death penalty. The last section considers the link between early decisions made in investigations or charging and the later pattern of sentencing outcomes. Sometimes early decisions by police and by prosecutors become de facto decisions about punishment, and the entire criminal justice process can be said to be racially skewed. In what circumstances — and in what legal institutions — should challenges to entire systems be allowed based on claims of racial bias? Does the criminal justice system exacerbate or mitigate larger social problems? Can criminal justice systems respond to intentional or unintentional racial bias in society?

1.   An American Dilemma

It seems obvious to many that there is a relationship between race and punishment, but it is difficult to study or discuss. Problems with studying racial disparities include difficulties in defining race, the propriety and cost of collecting useful data, and the difficulties in knowing what conclusions to draw from the information. Does the very pervasiveness of racial tension, and the difficulty of frank discussion about race in the United States, make it impossible to explain the numbers satisfactorily? Much of the racial focus in the United States has been on the black-white disparity. In June 2005 the rate of imprisonment for black men ages 25 to 29 was about 11.9%, while the rate for Hispanic men of the same age group was 3.9% and the comparable rate for white men was 1.7%. Bureau of Justice Statistics, Prison and Jail Inmates at Midyear 2005 (NCJ 213133, 2006). When the number of young men on probation or parole are combined with the number in prison or jail, almost one-third of young black men are under criminal justice supervision on any given day. In some states 10-15% of the black male population are in prison. As was the case throughout the 1990s, African American women remain the fastest-growing group in prisons and jails. Drug offenses have contributed more than any other crime to the rapid growth in the imprisonment rate for African Americans.

> ## Malign Neglect: Race, Crime and Punishment
> ## in America, Michael Tonry
> ### Pages 4, 29-30, 49-52 (1995)

Crime by blacks is not getting worse. The proportions of serious violent crimes committed by blacks have been level for more than a decade. Since the mid-1970s, approximately 45 percent of those arrested for murder, rape, robbery, and aggravated assault have been black (the trend is slightly downward). Disproportionate punishment of blacks, however, [has] been getting worse, especially since Ronald Reagan became president. Since 1980, the number of blacks in prison has tripled. . . .

Black Americans are far more likely than whites to be in prison or jail. [In June 2005 4,682 black American men per 100,000 were in prison or jail; among white American men, 709 per 100,000 were in prison or jail. For women the comparable figures were 347 and 88.]

Another even more remarkable pattern of black-white disparities has been revealed by a series of studies attempting to determine the proportions of blacks under the control of the criminal justice system on a given day. Of all the people in prison or jail, on probation or parole, or released on bail or recognizance pending trial, what percentage are black? . . .

The Correctional Association of New York found that 23 percent of black males aged 20 to 29 were under justice system control in 1990. California's Center on Juvenile and Criminal Justice found in 1990 that 33 percent of black males aged 20 to 29 were under justice system control. . . .

Three findings about race, crime, and punishment stand out concerning blacks. First, at every criminal justice stage from arrest through incarceration, blacks are present in numbers greatly out of proportion to their presence in the general population. . . . Second, although black disproportions in the front of the system — as offenders and arrestees — are essentially stable, since the early 1980s they have steadily grown worse at the back [in sentencing and in prison populations]. Third, perhaps surprisingly, for nearly a decade there has been a near consensus among scholars and policy analysts that most of the black disproportions result not from racial bias or discrimination within the system but from patterns of black offending and of blacks' criminal records. Drug law enforcement is the conspicuous exception. . . .

Do not misunderstand. A conclusion that black overrepresentation among prisoners is not primarily the result of racial bias does not mean that there is no racism in the system. Virtually no one believes that racial bias and enmity are absent, that no police, prosecutors, or judges are bigots, or that some local courts or bureaucracies are not systematically discriminatory. The overwhelming weight of evidence, however, is that invidious bias explains much less of racial disparities than does offending by black offenders. Much offending is intraracial, which means that a failure by the state to take crimes by blacks seriously depreciates the importance of victimization of blacks — discrimination little less objectionable than bias against black offenders. Virtually every sophisticated review of social science evidence on criminal justice decision making has concluded, overall, that the apparent influence of the offender's race on official decisions concerning individual defendants is slight. . . .

How is it possible that black participation in serious crime has not increased while rising numbers and proportions of blacks are in prison or jail, and yet racial bias does not pervade the system? . . . There is an answer, and it lies not in the criminal justice system but in the . . . aggressive promotion of punitive crime control policies and a "War on Drugs." [These policies have] caused the ever harsher treatment of blacks by the criminal justice system, and it was foreseeable that they would do so. Just as the tripling of the American prison population between 1980 and 1993 was the result of conscious policy decisions, so also was the greater burden of punishment borne by blacks. Crime control politicians wanted more people in prison and knew that a larger proportion of them would be black.

NOTES

1. *Data and knowledge about race.*   Surprisingly little race data is available in the criminal justice system. In most states, "race data are virtually nonexistent with regard to victims; information on the race of the offender is limited. Race data on offenders are collected by law enforcement at arrest and maintained in the criminal history record for felons and gross misdemeanants. Race data on offenders are also collected by probation officers on sentencing worksheets. . . . There are no race data anywhere on misdemeanants." Debra Dailey, Minnesota's Continuing Efforts to Address Racial Disparities in Sentencing, 8 Fed. Sent'g Rep. 89, 89 (1995) (describing the situation in Minnesota as typical for most states). For a thorough discussion of the limited available data on the racial impact of the federal sentencing guidelines, see United States Sentencing Commission, Fifteen Years of Guidelines Sentencing, 113-135 (2004) (available at http://www.ussc.gov/15_year/chap4.pdf).

Are the social and financial costs of collecting additional race data likely to be worth the benefits? Should the United States follow the model of many

European states that do not collect racial data on offenders, or does its history make this impossible? Dailey provides this cautionary note:

> One reason for the paucity of data is ambivalence as to whether the race of individuals ought to be recorded at all. In 1993, for instance, the mayor of Minneapolis declared that "the use of race in crime statistics is an abomination and an outrage." The mayor questioned the purpose of reporting arrest data by race and expressed concern that such data can lead to improper inferences about the relationship between crime and race. . . .
>
> Racial or ethnic data must be treated with caution because [this data] may be recorded from observation or from self-identification. . . . Moreover, existing research on crime has generally shown that racial or ethnic identity is not predictive of crime behavior within data which has been controlled for social or economic factors such as education levels, family status, income, housing density, and residential mobility.

Id. at 89. Is race merely a proxy for other factors? With increasing rates of intermarriage and offspring with multiple racial identities, will collections of racial data become misleading or even irrelevant?

2. *Who takes action?* Even if we do understand the sources of some racial disparities in the criminal justice system, how can we best implement changes? In 1993 the Minnesota legislature created the Criminal and Juvenile Justice Information Policy Group to provide leadership and support for improving criminal justice. Made up of representatives from the state's sentencing commission, the judiciary, and other governmental bodies, the group is expected to recommend a framework for integrating criminal justice information, including information about race and ethnicity. Is the Minnesota legislature likely to defer to the group's recommendations? What institutions are most likely to make changes in law that will reduce disparate racial effects throughout the criminal justice system? Are courts the best avenue to bring about such changes? Sentencing commissions? If none of these institutions is the answer, then what should we do? Wait for society to improve?

2. Whose Race?

Our exploration of the influence of race on punishment begins where the issue has received the most sustained attention: in the context of capital punishment. On the morning of May 13, 1978, Warren McCleskey and three other men planned to rob a furniture store. McCleskey had a .38 caliber Rossi nickel-plated revolver, which he had stolen in an armed robbery of a grocery store a month earlier. The others carried a sawed-off shotgun and pistols. McCleskey, who was black, entered the front of the store, and the other three came through the rear. While the robbers tied up all the employees, Officer Frank Schlatt, who was white, answered a silent alarm and entered the store, where he was fatally shot. The robbers fled but, some time later McCleskey was arrested in Cobb County in connection with another armed robbery. He confessed to the furniture store robbery but denied the shooting. Ballistics showed that Schlatt had been shot by a .38 caliber Rossi revolver. The weapon was never recovered.

McCleskey was convicted in 1978. The jury found two aggravating circumstances that authorized the use of the death penalty: (1) the murder was committed while the offender was committing another capital felony (armed robbery), and (2) the murder was committed against a police officer engaged in the performance of his official duties. The jury sentenced McCleskey to death for murder. One co-defendant was sentenced to life imprisonment, while another received a 20-year sentence.

On direct appeal in the Georgia courts, McCleskey first raised the claim that the death penalty violates the due process and equal protection provisions of the federal and state constitutions because prosecutorial discretion permits the government to apply the penalty in a racially discriminatory way. The Georgia Supreme Court rejected this claim as follows: "Appellant's argument is without merit. Gregg v. Georgia, 428 U.S. 153 (1976); Moore v. State, 243 S.E.2d 1 (Ga. 1978)." McCleskey v. State, 263 S.E.2d 146, 148 (Ga. 1980). After his direct appeals were exhausted, McCleskey began to file a series of state and federal habeas challenges to his conviction and sentence, which culminated in a decision by the U.S. Supreme Court.

‖ *Warren McCleskey v. Ralph Kemp* ‖
481 U.S. 279 (1987)

POWELL, J.

This case presents the question whether a complex statistical study that indicates a risk that racial considerations enter into capital sentencing determinations proves that petitioner McCleskey's capital sentence is unconstitutional under the Eighth or Fourteenth Amendment.

THE BALDUS STUDY

[In support of his habeas claim], McCleskey proffered a statistical study performed by Professors David Baldus, Charles Pulaski, and George Woodworth (the Baldus study) that purports to show a disparity in the imposition of the death sentence in Georgia based on the race of the murder victim and, to a lesser extent, the race of the defendant. The Baldus study is actually two sophisticated statistical studies that examine over 2,000 murder cases that occurred in Georgia during the 1970's. The raw numbers collected by Professor Baldus indicate that defendants charged with killing white persons received the death penalty in 11% of the cases, but defendants charged with killing blacks received the death penalty in only 1% of the cases. . . . Baldus also divided the cases according to the combination of the race of the defendant and the race of the victim. He found that the death penalty was assessed in 22% of the cases involving black defendants and white victims; 8% of the cases involving white defendants and white victims; 1% of the cases involving black defendants and black victims; and 3% of the cases involving white defendants and black victims. . . .

Baldus subjected his data to an extensive analysis, taking account of 230 variables that could have explained the disparities on nonracial grounds.

One of his models concludes that, even after taking account of 39 nonracial variables, defendants charged with killing white victims were 4.3 times as likely to receive a death sentence as defendants charged with killing blacks. According to this model, black defendants were 1.1 times as likely to receive a death sentence as other defendants. Thus, the Baldus study indicates that black defendants, such as McCleskey, who kill white victims have the greatest likelihood of receiving the death penalty. . . .

DISCRIMINATORY INTENT AND STATISTICS

McCleskey's first claim is that the Georgia capital punishment statute violates the Equal Protection Clause of the Fourteenth Amendment. He argues that race has infected the administration of Georgia's statute. . . . McCleskey's claim of discrimination extends to every actor in the Georgia capital sentencing process, from the prosecutor who sought the death penalty and the jury that imposed the sentence, to the State itself that enacted the capital punishment statute and allows it to remain in effect despite its allegedly discriminatory application. [This] claim must fail.

[To] prevail under the Equal Protection Clause, McCleskey must prove that the decisionmakers in his case acted with discriminatory purpose. He offers no evidence specific to his own case that would support an inference that racial considerations played a part in his sentence. Instead, he . . . argues that the Baldus study compels an inference that his sentence rests on purposeful discrimination. McCleskey's claim that these statistics are sufficient proof of discrimination, without regard to the facts of a particular case, would extend to all capital cases in Georgia, at least where the victim was white and the defendant is black.

The Court has accepted statistics as proof of intent to discriminate in certain limited contexts. First, this Court has accepted statistical disparities as proof of an equal protection violation in the selection of the jury venire in a particular district. Although statistical proof normally must present a "stark" pattern to be accepted as the sole proof of discriminatory intent under the Constitution, because of the nature of the jury-selection task, we have permitted a finding of constitutional violation even when the statistical pattern does not approach such extremes. Second, this Court has accepted statistics in the form of multiple-regression analysis to prove statutory violations under Title VII of the Civil Rights Act of 1964.

But the nature of the capital sentencing decision, and the relationship of the statistics to that decision, are fundamentally different from the corresponding elements in the venire-selection or Title VII cases. Most importantly, each particular decision to impose the death penalty is made by a petit jury selected from a properly constituted venire. Each jury is unique in its composition, and the Constitution requires that its decision rest on consideration of innumerable factors that vary according to the characteristics of the individual defendant and the facts of the particular capital offense. Thus, the application of an inference drawn from the general statistics to a specific decision in a trial and sentencing simply is not comparable to the application of an inference drawn from general statistics to a specific venire-selection or Title VII case. In those cases, the statistics relate to fewer entities, and fewer variables are relevant to the challenged decisions.

Another important difference between the cases in which we have accepted statistics as proof of discriminatory intent and this case is that, in the venire-selection and Title VII contexts, the decisionmaker has an opportunity to explain the statistical disparity. Here, the State has no practical opportunity to rebut the Baldus study. Controlling considerations of public policy dictate that jurors cannot be called to testify to the motives and influences that led to their verdict. Similarly, the policy considerations behind a prosecutor's traditionally wide discretion suggest the impropriety of our requiring prosecutors to defend their decisions to seek death penalties, often years after they were made. Moreover, absent far stronger proof, it is unnecessary to seek such a rebuttal, because a legitimate and unchallenged explanation for the decision is apparent from the record: McCleskey committed an act for which the United States Constitution and Georgia laws permit imposition of the death penalty.

Finally, McCleskey's statistical proffer must be viewed in the context of his challenge. McCleskey challenges decisions at the heart of the State's criminal justice system. "[One] of society's most basic tasks is that of protecting the lives of its citizens and one of the most basic ways in which it achieves the task is through criminal laws against murder." Gregg v. Georgia, 428 U.S. 153, 226 (1976) (White, J., concurring). Implementation of these laws necessarily requires discretionary judgments. Because discretion is essential to the criminal justice process, we would demand exceptionally clear proof before we would infer that the discretion has been abused. . . . Accordingly, we hold that the Baldus study is clearly insufficient to support an inference that any of the decisionmakers in McCleskey's case acted with discriminatory purpose. . . .

ARBITRARY AND CAPRICIOUS

[McCleskey also] contends that the Georgia capital punishment system is arbitrary and capricious in application, and therefore his sentence is excessive [and contrary to the Eighth Amendment], because racial considerations may influence capital sentencing decisions in Georgia. . . .

To evaluate McCleskey's challenge, we must examine exactly what the Baldus study may show. Even Professor Baldus does not contend that his statistics prove that race enters into any capital sentencing decisions or that race was a factor in McCleskey's particular case. Statistics at most may show only a likelihood that a particular factor entered into some decisions. There is, of course, some risk of racial prejudice influencing a jury's decision in a criminal case. There are similar risks that other kinds of prejudice will influence other criminal trials. The question is at what point that risk becomes constitutionally unacceptable. McCleskey asks us to accept the likelihood allegedly shown by the Baldus study as the constitutional measure of an unacceptable risk of racial prejudice influencing capital sentencing decisions. This we decline to do.

Because of the risk that the factor of race may enter the criminal justice process, we have engaged in "unceasing efforts" to eradicate racial prejudice from our criminal justice system. Our efforts have been guided by our recognition that "the inestimable privilege of trial by jury . . . is a vital principle, underlying the whole administration of criminal justice," Ex parte Milligan, 4 Wall. 2, 123 (1866). . . .

Individual jurors bring to their deliberations qualities of human nature and varieties of human experience, the range of which is unknown and perhaps unknowable. The capital sentencing decision requires the individual jurors to focus their collective judgment on the unique characteristics of a particular criminal defendant. It is not surprising that such collective judgments often are difficult to explain. But the inherent lack of predictability of jury decisions does not justify their condemnation. On the contrary, it is the jury's function to make the difficult and uniquely human judgments that defy codification and that build discretion, equity, and flexibility into a legal system.

McCleskey's argument that the Constitution condemns the discretion allowed decisionmakers in the Georgia capital sentencing system is antithetical to the fundamental role of discretion in our criminal justice system. Discretion in the criminal justice system offers substantial benefits to the criminal defendant. Not only can a jury decline to impose the death sentence, it can decline to convict or choose to convict of a lesser offense. Whereas decisions against a defendant's interest may be reversed by the trial judge or on appeal, these discretionary exercises of leniency are final and unreviewable. Similarly, the capacity of prosecutorial discretion to provide individualized justice is firmly entrenched in American law. As we have noted, a prosecutor can decline to charge, offer a plea bargain, or decline to seek a death sentence in any particular case. Of course, the power to be lenient also is the power to discriminate, but a capital punishment system that did not allow for discretionary acts of leniency would be totally alien to our notions of criminal justice. . . .

At most, the Baldus study indicates a discrepancy that appears to correlate with race. Apparent disparities in sentencing are an inevitable part of our criminal justice system. The discrepancy indicated by the Baldus study is a far cry from the major systemic defects identified in Furman v. Georgia, 408 U.S. 238 (1972), [which struck down existing capital punishment statutes because they imposed the punishment arbitrarily and capriciously. There] can be no perfect procedure for deciding in which cases governmental authority should be used to impose death. Despite these imperfections, our consistent rule has been that constitutional guarantees are met when the mode for determining guilt or punishment itself has been surrounded with safeguards to make it as fair as possible. Where the discretion that is fundamental to our criminal process is involved, we decline to assume that what is unexplained is invidious. In light of the safeguards designed to minimize racial bias in the process, the fundamental value of jury trial in our criminal justice system, and the benefits that discretion provides to criminal defendants, we hold that the Baldus study does not demonstrate a constitutionally significant risk of racial bias affecting the Georgia capital sentencing process.

Two additional concerns inform our decision in this case. First, McCleskey's claim, taken to its logical conclusion, throws into serious question the principles that underlie our entire criminal justice system. The Eighth Amendment is not limited in application to capital punishment, but applies to all penalties. Thus, if we accepted McCleskey's claim that racial bias has impermissibly tainted the capital sentencing decision, we could soon be faced with similar claims as to other types of penalty. Moreover, the claim that his sentence rests on the irrelevant factor of race easily could be extended to apply to claims based on unexplained discrepancies that correlate to membership in other minority groups, and even to gender. Similarly, since McCleskey's claim relates to the race of his victim, other claims could apply with equally logical force to statistical disparities that correlate with the race or sex of other actors in the criminal justice system, such as defense attorneys or judges. Also, there is no logical reason that such a claim need be limited to racial or sexual bias. If arbitrary and capricious punishment is the touchstone under the Eighth Amendment, such a claim could — at least in theory — be based upon any arbitrary variable, such as the defendant's facial characteristics, or the physical attractiveness of the defendant or the victim, that some statistical study indicates may be influential in jury decision-making. As these examples illustrate, there is no limiting principle to the type of challenge brought by McCleskey. The Constitution does not require that a State eliminate any demonstrable disparity that correlates with a potentially irrelevant factor in order to operate a criminal justice system that includes capital punishment. . . .

Second, McCleskey's arguments are best presented to the legislative bodies. It is not the responsibility — or indeed even the right — of this Court to determine the appropriate punishment for particular crimes. It is the legislatures, the elected representatives of the people, that are constituted to respond to the will and consequently the moral values of the people. Legislatures also are better qualified to weigh and evaluate the results of statistical studies in terms of their own local conditions and with a flexibility of approach that is not available to the courts. Capital punishment is now the law in more than two-thirds of our States. It is the ultimate duty of courts to determine on a case-by-case basis whether these laws are applied consistently with the Constitution. Despite McCleskey's wide-ranging arguments that basically challenge the validity of capital punishment in our multiracial society, the only question before us is whether in his case the law of Georgia was properly applied. [T]his was carefully and correctly done in this case. . . .

BRENNAN, J., dissenting.

At some point in this case, Warren McCleskey doubtless asked his lawyer whether a jury was likely to sentence him to die. A candid reply to this question would have been disturbing. First, counsel would have to tell McCleskey that few of the details of the crime or of McCleskey's past criminal conduct were more important than the fact that his victim was white. Furthermore, counsel would feel bound to tell McCleskey that defendants charged with killing white victims in Georgia are 4.3 times as likely to be sentenced to death as defendants charged with killing blacks. In addition, frankness would compel the disclosure that it was more likely than not that the race of McCleskey's victim would determine whether he received a death sentence: 6 of every 11 defendants convicted of killing a white person would not have received the death penalty if their victims had been black, while, among defendants with aggravating and mitigating factors comparable to McCleskey's, 20 of every 34 would not have been sentenced to die if their victims had been black. Finally, the assessment would not be complete without the information that cases involving black defendants and white victims are more likely to result in a death sentence than cases featuring any other racial combination of defendant and victim. The story could be told in a variety of ways, but McCleskey could not fail to grasp its essential narrative line: there was a significant chance that race would play a prominent role in determining if he lived or died. . . .

Georgia's legacy of a race-conscious criminal justice system, as well as this Court's own recognition of the persistent danger that racial attitudes may affect criminal proceedings, indicates that McCleskey's claim is not a fanciful product of mere statistical artifice.

For many years, Georgia operated openly and formally precisely the type of dual system the evidence shows is still effectively in place. The criminal law expressly differentiated between crimes committed by and against blacks and whites, distinctions whose lineage traced back to the time of slavery. During the colonial period, black slaves who killed whites in Georgia, regardless of whether in self-defense or in defense of another, were automatically executed. A. Higginbotham, In the Matter of Color: Race in the American Legal Process 256 (1978).

By the time of the Civil War, a dual system of crime and punishment was well established in Georgia. See Ga. Penal Code (1861). The state criminal code contained separate sections for "Slaves and Free Persons of Color," and for all other persons. The code provided, for instance, for an automatic death sentence for murder committed by blacks, but declared that anyone else convicted of murder might receive life imprisonment if the conviction were founded solely on circumstantial testimony or simply if the jury so recommended. The code established that the rape of a free white female by a black "shall be" punishable by death. However, rape by anyone else of a free white female was punishable by a prison term not less than 2 nor more than 20 years. The rape of blacks was punishable "by fine and imprisonment, at the discretion of the court." . . .

Citation of past practices does not justify the automatic condemnation of current ones. But it would be unrealistic to ignore the influence of history in assessing the plausible implications of McCleskey's evidence. . . .

The Court . . . states that its unwillingness to regard petitioner's evidence as sufficient is based in part on the fear that recognition of McCleskey's claim would open the door to widespread challenges to all aspects of criminal sentencing. Taken on its face, such a statement seems to suggest a fear of too much justice. Yet surely the majority would acknowledge that if striking evidence indicated that other minority groups, or women, or even persons with blond hair, were disproportionately sentenced to death, such a state of affairs would be repugnant to deeply rooted conceptions of fairness. The prospect that there may be more widespread abuse than McCleskey documents may be dismaying, but it does not justify complete abdication of our judicial role.

[To] reject McCleskey's powerful evidence . . . is to ignore both the qualitatively different character of the death penalty and the particular repugnance of racial discrimination, considerations which may properly be taken into account in determining whether various punishments are "cruel and unusual." Furthermore, it fails to take account of the unprecedented refinement and strength of the Baldus study. . . .

Warren McCleskey's evidence confronts us with the subtle and persistent influence of the past. His message is a disturbing one to a society that has formally repudiated racism, and a frustrating one to a Nation accustomed to regarding its destiny as the product of its own will. Nonetheless, we ignore him at our peril, for we remain imprisoned by the past as long as we deny its influence in the present. . . .

The destinies of the two races in this country are indissolubly linked together, and the way in which we choose those who will die reveals the depth of moral commitment among the living. . . .

PROBLEM 9-1.   OFFENDER'S RACE AND RECORD

You represent Gerald Lane, a black man who is accused of murder. Lane claims that the Washoe County, Nevada, district attorney's office seeks the death penalty much more frequently when the defendant in a murder case is black. "If a person is accused of murder in Washoe County," Lane asserts, "it is better to be a white felon than a black with no prior felony convictions."

In support of this charge, you evaluate the 86 murder cases prosecuted by the Washoe County district attorney's office since Nevada's death penalty law took effect. In approximately 80% of cases involving a white defendant with at least one prior felony conviction, the district attorney did not seek the death penalty. By contrast, in approximately 80% of cases involving a black defendant without prior felony convictions, the district attorney did seek the death penalty. In other words, Lane argues that the Washoe County district attorney's office seeks the death penalty for only one out of five white murderers with past felonies and seeks the death penalty for four out of five black murderers without prior felonies.

In what legal terms will you frame the claim that might bar the use of the death penalty against Lane? How would you distinguish *McCleskey*? How would you use it? Compare Lane v. State, 881 P.2d 1358 (Nev. 1994).

NOTES

1. *Compelling evidence of intent.*   What sort of statistical study might provide the circumstantial evidence necessary to convince a court that arbitrary racial discrimination plays a large enough role in a sentencing system to invalidate the outcome in a particular case? Is such a statistical study possible? If racial discrimination does influence some decision makers in some cases, how might one demonstrate that fact in a court of law? In *McCleskey* both the court of appeals and the Supreme Court concluded that a stronger statistical showing would be necessary for racial influences in sentencing to amount to a constitutional problem. What sort of evidence did the courts have in mind?

2. *Whose race, victim's or defendant's?*   Note that the Baldus study found that the race of the *defendant* had no statistically significant effect on the use of capital punishment. In Furman v. Georgia, 408 U.S. 238 (1972), the Supreme Court struck down several capital punishment statutes, declaring that the death penalty (as administered at that time) was a "cruel and unusual punishment"

in violation of the Eighth Amendment. Several of the Justices argued that capital punishment could not stand because it was imposed disproportionately against the poor and racial minorities. Would the Supreme Court have reached a different outcome in *McCleskey* if the Baldus study had pointed to racial discrimination based on the defendant's race rather than the victim's race? Can a punishment be racially discriminatory if the government imposes it equally on defendants of all races?

3. *Other venues.* Suppose that on the day after the district court issues its order, the NAACP sends a copy of the Baldus study to a member of the Georgia legislature, and that member distributes copies. As the chair of the Senate's committee on criminal justice matters, would you hold hearings? If so, what would be the topic of the hearings — the validity of the study or the most appropriate response to the study? If the Supreme Court had concluded instead that the influence of race in Georgia's capital punishment system rendered McCleskey's sentence unconstitutional, how would you advise Georgia legislators and prosecutors to respond? Would a victory for McCleskey mean abolition of the death penalty in Georgia? Would it necessitate any other changes or inquiries into Georgia's sentencing system?

4. *Statistical studies of capital punishment after* McCleskey. The "race of the victim" effect that appeared in the Baldus study in Georgia has also appeared in statistical studies of other states. See, e.g., Glenn L. Pierce & Michael L. Radelet, Race, Region, and Death Sentencing in Illinois, 1988-1997, 81 Or. L. Rev. 39 (2002); Glenn L. Pierce & Michael L. Radelet, The Impact of Legally Inappropriate Factors on Death Sentencing for California Homicides, 1990-99, 46 Santa Clara L. Rev. 1-47 (2005). These claims have received little serious attention from courts; many simply cite *McCleskey* and refuse to consider the studies as relevant evidence of racial discrimination in the use of capital punishment. See People v. Davis, 518 N.E.2d 78 (Ill. 1987). The Supreme Court of New Jersey indicated that evidence along the lines of that presented in *McCleskey* could be sufficient to establish a prima facie case of a violation of the state constitution. The court also indicated, however, that New Jersey has not yet executed enough people to form the basis for a convincing statistical study. See State v. Bey, 645 A.2d 685, 712 (N.J. 1994) ("Our abiding problem with analyzing the effect of race is that the case universe still contains too few cases to prove that the race of a defendant improperly influences death sentencing.").

5. *The Kentucky Racial Justice Act.* In 1998 Kentucky's governor signed into law "An Act relating to the fair and reliable imposition of capital sentences":

> (1) No person shall be subject to or given a sentence of death that was sought on the basis of race.
> (2) A finding that race was the basis of the decision to seek a death sentence may be established if the court finds that race was a significant factor in decisions to seek the sentence of death in the Commonwealth at the time the death sentence was sought.
> (3) Evidence relevant to establish a finding that race was the basis of the decision to seek a death sentence may include statistical evidence or other evidence, or both, that death sentences were sought significantly more frequently:
> (a) Upon persons of one race than upon persons of another race; or
> (b) As punishment for capital offenses against persons of one race than as punishment for capital offenses against persons of another race.

(4) The defendant shall state with particularity how the evidence supports a claim that racial considerations played a significant part in the decision to seek a death sentence in his/her case. The claim shall be raised by the defendant at the pre-trial conference. The court shall schedule a hearing on the claim and shall prescribe a time for the submission of evidence by both parties. If the court finds that race was the basis of the decision to seek the death sentence, the court shall order that a death sentence shall not be sought.

(5) The defendant has the burden of proving by clear and convincing evidence that race was the basis of the decision to seek the death penalty. The Commonwealth may offer evidence in rebuttal of the claims or evidence of the defendant.

Is this law an appropriate response to the Baldus study and other evidence concerning the impact of race on the application of the death penalty? Would a capital defendant in Kentucky armed with a Kentucky version of the Baldus study be able to prevail on a claim based on this act?

As a legislator in a death penalty state, would you advocate the adoption of such a law? Does this legislation go far enough to address racial disparities in the application of the death penalty? Or does it go too far by providing all capital defendants with an additional set of arguments to delay appropriate and otherwise lawful executions?

6. *The federal death penalty.*   The federal death penalty, which had been defunct for many decades before the early 1990s, has been the focus of much recent race-based debate. More than 80% of the federal death row inmates are nonwhite. The first individual executed since the reinstitution of the federal death penalty — Timothy McVeigh — was white, however. See, e.g., U.S. Department of Justice, The Federal Death Penalty System: A Statistical Survey (1988-2000), 14 Fed. Sent'g Rep. 35 (2002); U.S. Department of Justice, The Federal Death Penalty System: Supplementary Data, Analysis and Revised Protocols for Capital Case Review, 14 Fed. Sent'g Rep. 40 (2002). Nevertheless, criticism of the racial makeup on federal death row continues. How should this debate affect prosecutorial discretion? As a federal prosecutor, would you be more inclined to ask for capital punishment in the case of a white defendant since you know about the existing disparity? Federal death penalty decisions appear to be centralized in the hands of the attorney general. Will a centralized decision-making structure protect better against racial disparity across the country? See, e.g., Robin Campbell, Issues of Consistency in the Federal Death Penalty: A Roundtable Discussion on the Role of the U.S. Attorney, 14 Fed. Sent'g Rep. 52 (2002).

3.   Discretionary Decisions and Race

Racial disparities at sentencing can result from decisions, such as the selection of charges, made at various earlier stages of the criminal justice process. If prosecutors discriminate on the basis of race (or gender or other objectionable grounds), the U.S. Supreme Court has stated that it is possible, at least in theory, to overturn a prosecutor's charging decision. A defendant who makes such a claim must establish that the prosecutor (1) made different charging decisions for similarly situated suspects (a discriminatory effect) and (2) intentionally made the decision on the basis of an "arbitrary" classification (a discriminatory intent). Arbitrary classifications would include "suspect classes" under equal protection doctrine or those defendants exercising their constitutional liberties such as freedom of speech or religion. See Oyler v. Boles, 368 U.S. 448 (1962); Wayte v. United States, 470 U.S. 598 (1985).

The *Wayte* decision made it clear that a criminal defendant claiming discrimination must demonstrate that the prosecutor chose the defendant for criminal charges "because of" and not "despite" the protected conduct or status of the defendant. This basic federal framework for analyzing constitutional challenges to discriminatory charging policies has also been influential in state courts. See, e.g., State v. Muetze, 534 N.W.2d 55 (S.D. 1995) (no proof that non–Native Americans who were not charged were similarly situated).

In 1996 the U.S. Supreme Court considered the claim of Christopher Armstrong, who was indicted in 1992 for crack distribution. He responded by filing a motion for discovery or for dismissal of the indictment, alleging that he had been selected for federal prosecution because he was black. The issue in the case was not whether Armstrong was able to show selective prosecution, but what burden he had to carry to obtain discovery on a selective prosecution claim. Armstrong based his initial motion on evidence that the defendant was black in all 24 narcotics cases closed in 1991 by the U.S. Attorney's office that had prosecuted him.

The Supreme Court rejected Armstrong's claim, holding that a court hearing a claim of selective prosecution may grant discovery to the defendant only if there is "some evidence" to support each of the elements of the claim, and finding that the "study" presented by Armstrong "failed to identify individuals who were not black, could have been prosecuted for the offenses for which respondents were charged, but were not so prosecuted." The Court did not explain how Armstrong or other claimants should obtain information about the pool of nonprosecuted suspects. Armstrong v. United States, 517 U.S. 456 (1996). Very few courts have reversed convictions on selective prosecution grounds, and no U.S. Supreme Court decisions have done so on racial grounds since Yick Wo v. Hopkins, 118 U.S. 356 (1886). In United States v. Bass, 536 U.S. 862 (2002), the Supreme Court held that national charging and plea bargaining statistics on the race of offenders in federal death penalty cases were insufficient under *Armstrong*'s credible evidence requirement to trigger a discovery order.

Claims of selective prosecution are difficult to pursue successfully, not only because of the difficult proof requirements under federal law, but also because so many actors are involved, including prosecutors, police, judges, probation officers, and decision makers in a variety of other institutions, such as schools. A strong bias in investigations or arrests may be concealed by studies showing unbiased decision making at a later stage of the process. For example, if whites and blacks who are convicted of a particular offense are punished identically, but members of one race are disproportionately investigated, then the sanction will appear neutral but will in fact be highly disparate, at least to the extent that the investigatory practices do not accurately reflect underlying behavior.

Much of the racial disparity in the criminal justice system can be explained through the offender's criminal record. As detailed in Chapter 5, offenders with prior convictions are typically punished more harshly; many minority offenders have such records. Studies indicate that one of the most discriminatory elements of the criminal justice system is the juvenile system. African American boys, in particular, are more likely to come under its supervision than white youngsters who commit similar offenses. Barry C. Feld, Juvenile and Criminal Justice Systems' Responses to Juvenile Violence, 24 Crime & Just. 189, 231-232 (1998). The juvenile case becomes the stepping-stone into the adult criminal justice system.

This section highlights the difficulty of proving the source of discrimination in large, complicated systems with many participants. Discrimination may be especially hard to unearth when it is the product of ongoing, low-level behavior of a large group of criminal justice officials and, perhaps, the result of unconscious influences on decision making. This section also raises questions about the law's capacity to change group behavior.

Freddie Stephens v. State
456 S.E.2d 560 (Ga. 1995)

FLETCHER, J.

Freddie Stephens challenges the constitutionality of OCGA §16-13-30(d), which provides for life imprisonment on the second conviction of the sale or possession with intent to distribute a controlled substance. He contends that the provision as applied is irrational and racially discriminatory in violation of the United States and Georgia Constitutions. . . . The challenged statute states:

> [Any] person who violates subsection (b) of this Code section with respect to a controlled substance in Schedule I or a narcotic drug in Schedule II shall be guilty of a felony and, upon conviction thereof, shall be punished by imprisonment for not less than five years nor more than 30 years. Upon conviction of a second or subsequent offense, he shall be imprisoned for life.

Subsection (b) makes it unlawful to "manufacture, deliver, distribute, dispense, administer, sell, or possess with intent to distribute any controlled substance." For a defendant to receive a life sentence for a second conviction, the state must notify the defendant prior to trial that it intends to seek the enhanced punishment based on past convictions.

Stephens contends that the statute as applied discriminates on the basis of race. He argues that this court should infer discriminatory intent from statewide and county-wide statistical data on sentences for drug offenders. In Hall County, where Stephens was convicted, the trial court found that one hundred percent (14 of 14) of the persons serving a life sentence under OCGA §16-13-30(d) are African-American, although African-Americans make up less than ten percent of the county population and approximately fifty to sixty percent of the persons arrested in drug investigations. Relying on evidence provided by the State Board of Pardons and Paroles, the trial court also found that 98.4 percent (369 of 375) of the persons serving life sentences for drug offenses as of May 1, 1994 were African-American, although African-Americans comprise only 27 percent of the state's population. Finally, a 1994 Georgia Department of Corrections study on the persons eligible for a life sentence under subsection (d) shows that less than one percent (1 of 168) of the whites sentenced for two or more convictions for drug sales are serving a life sentence, compared to 16.6 percent (202 of 1219) of the blacks.

In an earlier challenge to death penalty sentencing in Georgia based on statistics showing that persons who murder whites are more likely to be sentenced to death than persons who murder blacks, the United States Supreme Court held that the defendant had the burden of proving the existence of purposeful discrimination and that the purposeful discrimination had a discriminatory effect on him. McCleskey v. Kemp, 481 U.S. 279 (1987). . . .

Stephens concedes that he cannot prove any discriminatory intent by the Georgia General Assembly in enacting the law or by the Hall County district attorney in choosing to seek life imprisonment in this case. . . . These concessions preclude this court from finding an equal protection violation under the United States Constitution.

We also conclude that the statistical evidence Stephens presents is insufficient evidence to support his claim of an equal protection violation under the Georgia Constitution. Stephens fails to present the critical evidence by race concerning the number of persons eligible for life sentences under OCGA §16-13-30(d) in Hall County, but against whom the district attorney has failed to seek the aggravated sentence. Because the district attorney in each judicial circuit exercises discretion in determining when to seek a sentence of life imprisonment, a defendant must present some evidence addressing whether the prosecutor handling a particular case engaged in selective prosecution to prove a state equal protection violation. . . .

Stephens's argument about inferring intent from the statistical evidence also ignores that other factors besides race may explain the sentencing disparity. Absent from the statistical analysis is a consideration of relevant factors such as the charges brought, concurrent offenses, prior offenses and sentences, representation by retained or appointed counsel, existence of a guilty plea, circuit where convicted, and the defendant's legal status on probation, in prison, or on parole. Without more adequate information about what is happening both statewide and in Hall County, we defer deciding whether statistical evidence alone can ever be sufficient to prove an allegation of discriminatory intent in sentencing under the Georgia Constitution.

The dissent argues that McCleskey v. Kemp is not the controlling precedent, instead relying on the United States Supreme Court decision on peremptory challenges in jury selections in Batson v. Kentucky, 476 U.S. 79 (1986). We must look to *McCleskey* for a proper analysis of the substantive issue before us, rather than *Batson,* because *McCleskey* dealt with the use of statistical evidence to challenge racial disparity in sentencing, as does this case.

The Supreme Court in *McCleskey* pointed out several problems in requiring a prosecutor to explain the reasons for the statistical disparity in capital sentencing decisions. Many of these same problems exist in requiring district attorneys to justify their decisions in seeking a life sentence for drug offenses based on statewide, and even county-wide, statistics of persons serving life sentences in state prisons for drug offenses.

First, "requiring a prosecutor to rebut a study that analyzes the past conduct of scores of prosecutors is quite different from requiring a prosecutor to rebut a contemporaneous challenge to his own acts. See Batson v. Kentucky, 476 U.S. 79 (1986)." *McCleskey,* 481 U.S. at 296. Second, statewide statistics are not reliable in determining the policy of a particular district attorney. Finally, the Court stated that the policy considerations behind a prosecutor's discretion argue against requiring district attorneys to defend their decisions to seek the death penalty. Since district attorneys are elected to represent the state in all criminal cases, it is important that they be able to exercise their discretion in determining who to prosecute, what charges to bring, which sentence to seek, and when to appeal without having to account for each decision in every case. . . .

Stephens also argues that the statute violates due process and equal protection by creating an irrational sentencing scheme. Seeking to deter repeated drug sales by the same person is not irrational. Therefore, we adhere to our previous decision that there is a rational basis for the sentencing scheme in OCGA §16-13-30(d) and that it does not deprive persons of due process or equal protection under the law. . . .

THOMPSON, J., concurring.

[We] are presented once again with the claim that OGCA §16-13-30(d) is being used in a discriminatory fashion. This time, we are introduced to statewide statistical information which must give us pause: From 1990 to 1994, OCGA §16-13-30(d) was used to put 202 out of 1,107 eligible African-Americans in prison for life. During that same period, the statute was used to put 1 out of 167 eligible whites in prison for life. A life eligible African-American had a 1 in 6 chance of receiving a life sentence. A life eligible white had a 1 in 167 chance of receiving a life sentence. An African-American was 2,700 percent more likely to receive a life sentence than a white. . . . These statistics are no doubt as much a surprise to those who work and practice within the judicial system as to those who do not.

Statistical information can inform, not explain. It can tell what has happened, not why. However, only a true cynic can look at these statistics and not be impressed that something is amiss. That something lies in the fact that OCGA §16-13-30(d) has been converted from a mandatory life sentence statute into a statute which imposes a life sentence only in those cases in which a district attorney, in the exercise of his or her discretion, informs a defendant that the State is seeking enhanced punishment. . . .

McCleskey v. Kemp, 481 U.S. 279 (1987), should continue to be applied in death penalty cases where there is a system of checks and balances to ensure that death sentences are not sought and imposed autocratically. Likewise *McCleskey* should be applied in other cases where the courts have discretion to determine the length of time to be served. However, *McCleskey* probably should not be applied where a district attorney has the power to decide whether a defendant is sentenced to life, or a term of years. . . .

I am persuaded that Batson v. Kentucky, 476 U.S. 79 (1986), could be used to supply a general framework in analyzing cases of this kind. . . . Nevertheless, it is my considered view that the judgment in this case must be affirmed because the defendant has failed to meet his burden even under a *Batson*-type analysis.

In order to establish a prima facie case under *Batson,* a defendant must prove systematic discrimination in his particular jurisdiction. Although the statistics presented by defendant are indicative of a statewide pattern of discrimination in the use of OCGA §16-13-30(d), the Hall County statistics are insufficient to make such a case. They simply show that all the persons in Hall County serving a life sentence under OCGA §16-13-30(d) are African-Americans. They do not show how many African-Americans were eligible to receive a life sentence under the statute; nor do they show how many whites were eligible. Moreover, they offer no information concerning the record of the district attorney in this case. Thus, upon careful review, I must conclude that this defendant, in this case and on this record, failed to prove a pattern of systematic discrimination in his jurisdiction. . . .

Statewide, approximately 15 percent of eligible offenders receive a life sentence under OCGA §16-13-30(d). The statistical evidence presented in this case serves as notice to the General Assembly of Georgia that the mandatory life sentence provision of OCGA §16-13-30(d) has been repealed de facto. With such notice, there are at least three courses of action the legislature might now choose to pursue.

One. The General Assembly could choose to leave the mandatory life sentence on the books realizing that it is being used in a small percentage of the eligible cases. Militating against this course of action is the fact that all laws passed by the legislature should be followed. Contempt for and failure to follow any law breeds contempt for and failure to follow other laws.

Two. The General Assembly could reaffirm its commitment to a mandatory life sentence by requiring district attorneys to inform all defendants of prior convictions and thus enforce OCGA §16-13-30(d) with respect to all life eligible offenders. Militating against this course of action is the fact that mandatory life sentences are not favored by the prosecuting bar or by the defense bar. That is evidenced by the fact that from 1990 to 1994 only 203 out of 1,274 life eligible defendants actually received a life sentence under OCGA §16-13-30(d). . . .

Three. The General Assembly could choose to change the mandatory life sentence penalty to one of several sentencing options which the court could impose. For example, the penalty for a second or subsequent sale could be imprisonment for not less than 5 nor more than 30 years, or life. . . .

It is my concern that these problems be resolved in whatever way the General Assembly deems best and that, thereafter, the prosecutors and the courts carry out that legislative will.

BENHAM, P.J., dissenting.

Of those persons from Hall County serving life sentences pursuant to OCGA §16-13-30(d), which mandates a life sentence for the second conviction for sale of or possession with intent to distribute certain narcotics, 100 percent are African-American, although African-Americans comprise only approximately 10 percent of Hall County's population. In our state prison system, African-Americans represent 98.4 percent of the 375 persons serving life sentences for violating OCGA §16-13-30(d). These statistics were part of the finding of the trial court in this case. In the face of such numbing and paralyzing statistics, the majority say there is no need for inquiry. It is with this determination that I take issue and from which I respectfully dissent. . . .

[In Batson v. Kentucky, 476 U.S. 79 (1986), the Supreme Court] installed a system that shifted the burden to the prosecutor to give race-neutral reasons for the peremptory challenges once the defendant established facts supporting an inference that the prosecutor's use of peremptory challenges was racially motivated. [The] court in *Batson* stated that an inference of discriminatory intent could be drawn from certain conduct or statistical data. Beyond its effect on peremptory challenges, the importance of *Batson* was that it significantly reduced the burden on one claiming discrimination, recognizing that under certain circumstances, the crucial information about an allegedly discriminatory decision could only come from the one who made the decision.

This is the course of reasoning we need to follow in analyzing the issue in this case rather than the more restrictive course taken in McCleskey v. Kemp and applied by the majority. . . .

I am not unmindful or unappreciative of the vital and taxing role district attorneys are called upon to undertake in the ongoing battle against the blight of illicit drug trafficking. Throughout this state, they shoulder an enormous burden of responsibility for advancing the fight against drugs, and to do so successfully, they must be invested with considerable discretion in making decisions about ongoing prosecutions. However, it is the very breadth of that discretion, concentrated in a single decision-maker, which makes it necessary that the one exercising the discretion be the one, when confronted with facts supporting an inference of discriminatory application, to bear the burden of establishing that the discretion was exercised without racial influence. This case is more like *Batson* than *McCleskey* because all the discretion in the sentencing scheme involved in this case resides in the district attorney, to the exclusion of the trial court, whereas in death penalty cases such as *McCleskey*, the spread of discretion among the prosecutor, the trial court, and the jurors introduces variables which call for more rigorous statistical analysis. In addition, the complexity of the death penalty procedure, with its many safeguards and the recurring necessity of specific findings at every stage from the grand jury to the sentencing jury, differentiates it from the relative simplicity of the sentencing scheme applicable to this case.

[The] U.S. Supreme Court recognized in *McCleskey* itself that statistical proof which presents a "stark pattern" may be accepted as the sole proof of discriminatory intent. In distinguishing *McCleskey* from such a case, the Supreme Court mentioned in a footnote two cases in which "a statistical pattern of discriminatory impact demonstrated a constitutional violation." . . . The statistics in those cases presented a "stark pattern," but no more stark than the pattern presented in this case. In the present case, based on evidence from law enforcement officers who testified as to arrest rates and other relevant statistics, the trial court found that 100% of the people from that county who were serving life sentences pursuant to OCGA §16-13-30(d) were African-Americans and that statewide, 98.4% of all the persons serving life sentences pursuant to OCGA §16-13-30(d) were African-Americans. . . .

I believe it is necessary that we adopt a procedure which will make it possible to address the issue openly and honestly in the trial courts. . . . I would hold, therefore, as a matter purely of state constitutional law, that equal protection of the law in the context of OCGA §16-13-30(d) requires that the prosecution be required, when a defendant has made a prima facie showing sufficient to raise an inference of unequal application of the statute, to "demonstrate that permissible racially neutral selection criteria and procedures have produced the monochromatic result." *Batson*, 476 U.S. at 94. . . .

Because appellant has made a sufficient showing of discriminatory application of OCGA §16-13-30(d) that the State should be required to give race-neutral reasons for the "monochromatic" application of that statute in Hall

County, this court should vacate the life sentences and remand this case to the trial court for a hearing. At such a hearing, should the trial court find that the prosecution could not provide race-neutral reasons for the "monochromatic result" of the application of OCGA §16-13-30(d) in Hall County, sentencing for the offenses involved would still be permissible, but not with the aggravation of punishment authorized by OCGA §16-13-30(d). On the other hand, should the trial court find that the State has provided appropriate race-neutral reasons, the life sentences would be reimposed, whereupon appellant would be entitled to a new appeal.

Just as the prosecution was reined in by *Batson*, it must also be reined in here and called upon to give an account of itself. The statistics offered in this case show an enormous potential for injustice, and those statistics are just like the tip of an iceberg, with the bulk lying below the surface, yet to be realized. . . .

PROBLEM 9-2. TOWN AND COUNTRY

Darryl Pierre Wooden, an African American man sentenced to ten years in prison for selling illegal narcotics, believes that an Alabama law is racially discriminatory and asks for your help. His sentence was the product of the following two statutes, each of which mandates a five-year term:

- §13A-12-250. In addition to any penalties . . . provided by law for any person convicted of an unlawful sale of a controlled substance, there is hereby imposed a penalty of five years' incarceration in a state corrections facility with no provision for probation if the situs of such unlawful sale was on the campus or within a three-mile radius of the campus boundaries of any public or private school . . . or other educational institution in this state.
- §13A-12-270. In addition to any penalties . . . provided by law for any person convicted of an unlawful sale of a controlled substance, there is hereby imposed a penalty of five years' incarceration in a state corrections facility with no provision for probation if the situs of such unlawful sale was within a three-mile radius of a public housing project owned by a housing authority.

Wooden's conviction and ten-year mandatory sentence resulted from his sale to an undercover police officer of one tablet of "hydromorphone." Indisputably, this $50 transaction, which occurred on the 100 block of Fourth Avenue North in Birmingham, occurred within a three-mile radius both of a school and of a housing project. Wooden claims these statutes disproportionately impose a heavier sentence on black defendants in Jefferson County than on similar defendants in other Alabama counties because the conditions described in the statute ordinarily are present in an urban setting rather than a rural setting, and the overwhelming majority of citizens living in the city of Birmingham are black.

You gather the following evidence: Birmingham Police Officer B. H. Butler reports that of 150 persons he arrested for the "unlawful sale of a controlled substance," 145 were black and were subject to the enhanced sentence provisions of §§13A-12-250 and 13A-12-270. Officer Eric Benson asserts that of approximately 100 persons he arrested for the "unlawful sale of a controlled substance" in the preceding year, 70 were black. He also states that "any sale of a controlled substance within the city limits of Birmingham would be within three miles of both a school and a housing project, and that 98% to 99% of those living in these housing projects are black."

Alabama Administrative Office of Courts official Larry Forston provides computer data gleaned from circuit court clerks' offices throughout the state. He tells you that from 1989, when the three-mile-radius provisions were adopted, through 1994, only three black defendants and one white defendant were sentenced in Jefferson County under either statute, compared with 267 black defendants and 90 white defendants sentenced elsewhere in the state.

Is Wooden right to focus on the application of the law to his county? How would you frame that claim? What other information would you try to obtain? Whose actions are suspect? Compare Ex parte Wooden, 670 So. 2d 892 (Ala. 1995).

NOTES

1. *Who discriminates against whom?* What discrimination does Freddie Stephens claim? Other than the fact that both McCleskey and Stephens asserted that race was the basis for discrimination, were these similar claims? A controversial case at all stages, *Stephens* garnered additional attention when, 13 days before issuing the above opinion, the Georgia justices issued a slip opinion with a majority written by Justice Hugh Thompson announcing the "watershed" conclusion that under the equal protection clauses of both the federal and state constitutions these statistics required a prosecutor to provide a race-neutral explanation for the decision to apply the statute to Stephens. The slip opinion was bitterly attacked by the Georgia attorney general and the 46 state district attorneys, who together filed a brief asking that it be reversed. Attorney General Michael Bowers asserted that it was the worst decision from the Georgia Supreme Court in more than 20 years and that it "sets up sentencing quotas."

2. *Competing analogies.* Did the majority in Stephens v. State think that Stephens's claim was the same as McCleskey's? Did the concurrence think so? The dissent? Were you convinced by the competing analogy to discriminatory jury selection in Batson v. Kentucky? Did you find convincing Justice Thompson's application of *Batson* in the concurring opinion? Justice Robert Benham, dissenting in *Stephens,* argued that sentencing under the Georgia drug statute was different from capital punishment because it concentrates the decision in the hands of the district attorney. Do you agree? Are there ways a police officer might influence who receives a life sentence under the statute? Does the judge have some control over this question? The defense counsel? The state attorney general? Voters in the county or in the state?

3. *The federalization of drug law enforcement.* In many criminal cases, state and federal prosecutors both have jurisdiction. Sometimes they investigate cases together and then allocate prosecutorial responsibilities; sometimes state prosecutors call in federal investigatory assistance; and sometimes federal prosecutors refer cases, especially those of a minor nature, to the state for trial.

The different penalty structures in state and federal courts, together with procedural differences, may provide an incentive for state and federal prosecutors to send cases to federal court. This is true particularly when higher penalties exist under the federal sentencing guidelines or congressional mandatory sentences. While the so-called federalization of crime has been thoroughly criticized, it provides prosecutors with substantial additional discretion. See American Bar Association, Criminal Justice Section, Task Force on the Federalization of Criminal Law, Report on the Federalization of Criminal Law (1998). Results may also be startling. Hispanics, for example, make up 15% of the inmates in state prisons but 30% of the inmates in federal prisons. This substantial difference likely reflects Hispanics' higher rate of federal drug and especially immigration convictions. In FY 2005 42% of those sentenced under the federal guidelines were Hispanic; about 42% of all drug trafficking offenders and almost 90% of all immigration offenders were Hispanic.

In a study of charging for crack cocaine offenses in Los Angeles, Richard Berk and Alex Campbell found that black defendants are more likely than white or Latino defendants to be charged in federal court with sale of crack cocaine (which translates into more severe punishments than for comparable charges in state court). While black defendants represented 58% of those arrested by the Los Angeles Sheriff's Department for sale of crack cocaine between 1990 and 1992, they made up 83% of the defendants charged with that crime in federal court. White and Latino defendants arrested for this crime were more likely to be prosecuted in state court. Richard Berk & Alex Campbell, Preliminary Data on Race and Crack Charging Practices in Los Angeles, 6 Fed. Sent'g Rep. 36 (1993). What might explain the racially disparate federal crack prosecutions reported by Berk and Campbell?

4. *Racial patterns in charging.*   Racial minorities are charged with crimes in a number disproportionate to their percentage in the population. But are minorities charged with crimes at a higher rate, once one accounts for different levels of participation in crime? Criminologists addressing this question have studied records of large numbers of cases, using statistical techniques (especially regression analysis) to compare similar cases and to sort out racial and nonracial influences over charging decisions. See, e.g., Cassia Spohn, John Gruhl & Susan Welch, The Impact of the Ethnicity and Gender of Defendants on the Decision to Reject or Dismiss Felony Charges, 25 Criminology 175 (1987) (study of 33,000 felony cases between 1977 and 1980 to determine whether racial bias influenced prosecutors' decisions to decline felony charges; declinations occurred more frequently for white suspects after controlling for age, criminal record, and seriousness of offense); Developments in the Law — Race and the Criminal Process, 101 Harv. L. Rev. 1520, 1525-1530 (1988) (summarizing other studies). If racial discrimination in charging is indeed widespread, is it unrealistic to ask a defendant to make a prediscovery showing? Or is it necessary to limit litigation to the most egregious cases of racial discrimination in prosecutorial decision making? How egregious must the disparity be?

A factor that overlaps with race is neighborhood. As indicated in Problem 9-2, some laws that increase punishment for drug sales based on the proximity to school grounds have markedly different effects between urban and rural counties. In New Jersey, this feature of the narcotics laws led the state sentencing commission to propose a complete overhaul of the statutory structure. See Report on New Jersey's Drug-Free Zone Crimes & Proposal for Reform (Dec. 2005) (available at http://sentencing.nj.gov/publications.html).

   5. *Influence of race on sentencing in the United Kingdom.*   The United States is not the only nation in which the influence of race on sentencing has ignited controversy. In a study of the English crown courts of Birmingham, Wolverhampton, Coventry, Warwick, and Stafford in 1989, Roger Hood noted that blacks were given prison sentences rather than a nonprison alternative more often than whites (56.6% of blacks sentenced, compared with 48.4% of whites). After attempting to account statistically for differences in cases based on arguably nonracial factors such as the seriousness of the offense or past criminal record, Hood concluded that race still had a minor influence on the custody decision: There was a "5 percent greater probability of a male black defendant being sentenced to custody than a white male." Race seemed to have more influence in cases of "medium seriousness": black defendants had a 13% higher probability of receiving custody in these cases. Roger Hood, Race and Sentencing: A Study in the Crown Court 198 (1992). Why is this specific racial difference of particular concern?

PROBLEM 9-3.   THE CRACK-POWDER DIFFERENTIAL

   In 1986 Congress passed the Anti-Drug Abuse Act to increase the penalties for various drug crimes. The new law imposed heavier penalties on cocaine base (crack) than on cocaine powder, a relationship later known as the "100-to-1 ratio." An offense involving mixtures weighing 5 grams or more containing cocaine base was subject to the same punishment as an offense involving mixtures weighing 500 grams or more containing cocaine powder. Congress considered crack cocaine to be more dangerous than cocaine powder because of crack's potency, its more highly addictive nature, and its greater accessibility because of its relatively low cost.

   Some of the impetus for the federal law came from the news media. Stories associated the use of crack cocaine with social maladies such as gang violence and parental neglect among user groups. Critics of the federal law, however, argued that these social problems resulted not from the drug itself but from the disadvantaged social and economic environment in places where the drug is often used.

   In practice, the increased penalties for crack meant that African American defendants received heavier penalties than whites for possession and sale of cocaine. More than 90% of all people arrested for sale or possession of crack were African American; roughly 80% of all people arrested for sale or possession of powder cocaine were white.

   By 1989 the Minnesota legislature was debating the sentencing of crack offenses. The legislators considered a bill that would make a person who possessed three or more grams of crack cocaine guilty of a third-degree offense. Under the same statute, a person who possessed ten or more grams of cocaine powder would be guilty of the same offense; someone who possessed fewer than ten grams of cocaine powder would be guilty of a fifth-degree offense. The bill became known as the "10-to-3 ratio" law.

The sponsors of the bill argued that this structure facilitated prosecution of street-level drug dealers. Law enforcement officers who testified at legislative hearings suggested that three grams of crack and ten grams of powder indicated a level at which dealing, not merely using, took place. A person convicted of selling 100 grams of crack may often be characterized as a midlevel dealer (someone who provides the drug to street-level retailers). By comparison, 100 grams of powder usually typifies a low-level retailer; 500 grams is more indicative of a midlevel dealer. But witnesses from the Department of Public Safety Office of Drug Policy contradicted these estimates for the typical amount of drugs carried by dealers, suggesting that most cocaine powder users are dealers as well.

The customary units of sales for the two drugs are also different. The typical unit of crack is a rock weighing .1 gram, which at the time sold for $20 to $25. The customary unit of powder is the 8-ball, one-eighth of an ounce or about 3.5 grams, which sold for about $350. Ten grams of powder cocaine could be easily converted into more than three grams of crack.

Sponsors of the bill echoed Congress's argument that crack is more addictive and dangerous than cocaine powder, and witnesses at the hearings supported this contention. But other witnesses pointed out that crack and powder cocaine have the same active ingredient and produce the same type of pharmacological effects. The difference in effect between the two drugs stems from the fact that cocaine powder is sniffed through the nostrils while crack cocaine is smoked. If powder cocaine is dissolved and injected, it is just as addictive as crack.

As a member of the Minnesota legislature, would you support the 10-to-3 ratio bill? What else would you like to know before you vote? Compare State v. Russell, 477 N.W.2d 886 (Minn. 1991).

NOTES

1. *Constitutional challenges to punishment differentials: majority position.* Racial disparities in the application of death penalty laws highlight several distinct forms of discrimination. A law can be discriminatory in intent, either at the point of creation or when it is applied. Some laws have racially discriminatory effects, even though the people who create and enforce the law do not intend to burden one racial group more than another and even though they apply the law with complete evenhandedness. These effects occur when the criminal sanctions apply to behavior that people of one race engage in more often than people of other races. Would it ever be unconstitutional for a legislature to criminalize conduct when one racial group is more likely to engage in it?

A number of defendants convicted of trafficking in crack cocaine have argued for a downward departure from the guideline sentence (or an invalidation of the relevant guidelines and statutes) based on an equal protection claim. Federal courts have uniformly rejected this assertion, reasoning that any racial impact of the crack cocaine statutes and guidelines was unintentional. See, e.g., United States v. Reece, 994 F.2d 277 (6th Cir. 1993) (per curiam); United States v. Thomas, 900 F.2d 37 (4th Cir. 1990). While not often addressing such claims, high state courts have also usually rejected the constitutional challenges.

2. *Legislative response.*   The Minnesota Supreme Court struck down the legislation described in Problem 9-3 based on the state's equal protection clause in State v. Russell, 477 N.W.2d 886 (Minn. 1991). The legislature responded by increasing the penalties for powder to equal the former penalties for crack. Minn. Stat. §152.021-023. Minnesota's cocaine penalties are now among the toughest in the country — stiffer in some ways than in the federal system.

The crack-powder differential has received attention in other states as well. In Connecticut, the legislature in 2005 passed a bill equalizing the punishments for crack and powder cocaine, but Governor Jodi Rell vetoed the bill. She proposed "compromise" legislation that would place Connecticut "in the forefront of this fight" to address racial disparities in sentencing, but the state's crack penalties remain unchanged.

3. *Crack and cocaine sentences in the federal sentencing guidelines.*   For many years the federal penalty structure punished cocaine powder and crack offenders equally for amounts that differ by a factor of 100 — the so-called 100-to-1 ratio. Note that this is not a ratio of penalties but of the amounts of drugs generating similar penalties. Proposals to reduce this ratio have flared into combustible debates several times over the years. In 1994 Congress ordered the U.S. Sentencing Commission to report on cocaine punishment policies in the federal system. The following year the commission issued a report attacking the 100-to-1 quantity ratio and recommending instead a 1-to-1 crack-powder quantity ratio, to be achieved by lowering the penalties for crack while punishing behavior associated with crack offenses more severely.

The commission's proposed ratio came under attack from legislators across the political spectrum. Congress passed legislation to overturn the commission's proposal on October 18, 1995, by a vote of 332 to 83, and President Clinton signed the measure. This was the first time in the history of the commission that Congress voted to override a proposed amendment to the sentencing guidelines.

In May 2002 the commission recommended to Congress that the amount required to trigger a five-year mandatory minimum sentence be increased from 5 to at least 25 grams of crack and that the amount of crack required to trigger a ten-year mandatory sentence be increased from 50 to at least 250 grams, producing a quantity ratio of at least 20 to 1. Congress never responded to the commission's 2002 recommendation.

Finally, in May 2007, the U.S. Sentencing Commission took action on its own, amending the crack cocaine guidelines to eliminate any reliance on a 100-to-1 ratio, even though mandatory minimum penalty statutes remained in place to trump the guideline sentences in some cases. After reviewing the statutory purposes of sentencing under 18 U.S.C. §3553(a), the scientific and medical literature, and its own extensive research into sentencing patterns in drug cases, the commission found that the existing crack penalties failed in several respects:

(1) The current quantity-based penalties overstate the relative harmfulness of crack cocaine compared to powder cocaine.
(2) The current quantity-based penalties sweep too broadly and apply most often to lower level offenders.

(3) The current quantity-based penalties overstate the seriousness of most
      crack cocaine offenses and fail to provide adequate proportionality.
(4) The current severity of crack cocaine penalties mostly impacts minorities.

Report to the Congress: Cocaine and Federal Sentencing Policy 8 (2007) (available at http://www.ussc.gov/r_congress/cocaine2007.pdf). The revised guidelines use different ratios at different offense levels, with higher powder-to-crack
ratios operating at higher offense levels. The commission estimated that its
modifications to the guidelines would affect 69.7% of crack cocaine offenses
and would reduce the average sentence for all crack cocaine offenses from
121 months to 106 months. The commission also urged Congress to revise
the mandatory minimum penalties for crack cocaine to "focus the penalties
more closely on serious and major traffickers" and to exclude simple possession
of crack from the reach of any mandatory penalty. Congress appeared ready in
2007 to accept the guideline changes and possibly to debate revisions to the
penalty statutes.

What explains the different political outcomes in 1995, 2002, and 2007?
Did the commission manage the 2007 process more effectively, or did an overall
change in the political atmosphere or practical experience with drug sentencing
make the difference? As for the merits of the proposal, what might explain the
use of a ratio between powder and crack that varies depending on the seriousness of the offense?

4. *Crack sentencing after* Booker.   As we saw in Chapter 3, the Supreme
Court in United States v. Booker, 543 U.S. 220 (2005), ruled that the federal
sentencing guidelines could not compel federal sentencing judges to impose
the sentences that were indicated as "presumptive" under the guidelines. On
the other hand, appellate courts were still allowed to review sentences for
"reasonableness." In light of the *Booker* decision, dozens of district court
judges refused to apply the 100-to-1 ratio embedded in the guidelines because
they concluded that this rule violated 18 U.S.C. §3553(a), which requires the
judge to impose a sentence "sufficient, but not greater than necessary, to
comply with" the statutory purposes of sentencing. See United States v.
Perry, 389 F. Supp. 2d 278 (D.R.I. 2005). Federal appellate courts uniformly
rejected this position. United States v. Eura, 440 F.3d 625 (4th Cir. 2006).
Despite the lack of a circuit split, the Supreme Court has indicated a willingness to address the issue.

5. *Race and crack.*   Are racial differentials the central issue in the crack-
powder punishment debate, or are they rather a by-product of social structure?
Do different parts of the criminal world just happen to be controlled by groups
of a particular race or ethnicity, as the analogy to the use of racketeering laws
against the Mafia suggests? Or do you find convincing the position that, in effect,
racially disproportionate effects (but not intent) justify reworking the system to
start with a 1-to-1 quantity ratio?

In an excerpt reprinted in the first part of this section, Michael Tonry
asserted that politicians pursued the war on drugs with full knowledge that
"the greater burden of punishment [would be] borne by blacks. Crime control
politicians wanted more people in prison and knew that a larger proportion of
them would be black." Is this the sort of discriminatory intent that could

form the basis for an equal protection challenge? Does this argument create a politically viable basis for revising penalties for drug offenses?

B.   NATIVE PEOPLES

The concept of race is being undermined by the growing diversity of racialized identities. The most prominent example is professional golfer Tiger Woods. Nevertheless, race remains a powerful concept in U.S. legal discourse. Equality is constitutionally guaranteed, and limits on unequal treatment are reinforced in statutes and rules. Congress required the U.S. Sentencing Commission to "assure that the guidelines and policy statements are entirely neutral as to the race, sex, national origin, creed, and socioeconomic status of offenders." 28 U.S.C. §994(d). In accordance with this mandate, the guidelines state unequivocally that race, sex, national origin, creed, religion, and socioeconomic status "are not relevant in the determination of a sentence." U.S. Sentencing Guidelines Manual §5H1.10. Should national origin never be relevant in a sentence determination?

The strong statements of equal treatment, grounded in constitutional principle, contrast sharply with the social realities of Native Americans. This contrast generates dilemmas for courts trying to balance the defendants they see with the constitutional, statutory, and guideline nondiscrimination provisions that seem to prohibit the recognition of racial and ethnic differences.

> *Native Americans in South Dakota: An Erosion*
> *of Confidence in the Justice System*
> **South Dakota Advisory Committee to the United**
> **States Civil Rights Commission, Mar. 2000**

South Dakota Demographics.   . . . The estimated white population in South Dakota is 669,007, or 90.6 percent. American Indians are by far the largest minority group, making up 8 percent (59,292) of the population. Only Alaska and New Mexico have larger percentages of American Indian residents. . . .

Native Americans in South Dakota.   Nationwide, American Indians number approximately 1.2 million, with 900,000 living on or near Indian reservations. . . . South Dakota's nine reservations vary in size from Lower Brule, with about 1,200 residents, to Pine Ridge, with more than 30,000, making it the second largest reservation in the United States.

Economic Conditions.   Despite a booming economy, nationwide half of the potential work force in Indian Country is unemployed. For American Indians in South Dakota the statistics are even worse. [More than 50 percent of the labor force was unemployed in 1997 on 8 of the 9 reservations in the state, with unemployment reaching as high as 85 percent at Yankton and 80 percent at Cheyenne River.]

Of the 10 poorest counties in the United States in 1990, 4 were on Indian reservations in South Dakota. The poorest county in the Nation is Shannon County, which includes much of Pine Ridge Reservation: 63.1 percent of county residents have incomes that fall below the poverty line. The average annual income for families living on Pine Ridge is just $3,700.

The effects of poverty are far reaching. According to the director of [the Bureau of Indian Affairs' (BIA's)] Great Plains Regional Office, on South Dakota's reservations "economic depression has manifested itself in the form of suicides, alcohol and drug abuse, juvenile gangs, and dropping out of school, to physical abuse, sexual abuse, and child abuse."

Health.   On average, men in Bangladesh can expect to live longer than Native American men in South Dakota. A study by the Harvard School of Health in conjunction with health statisticians from the Centers for Disease Control found that Native American men living in six South Dakota counties had the shortest life expectancy in the Nation. . . . Indian men in South Dakota . . . usually live only into their mid-50s. . . .

In 1993, age-adjusted death rates for the following causes were considerably higher for American Indians [than for the general population]: alcoholism, 579 percent greater; tuberculosis, 475 percent; diabetes mellitus, 231 percent; accidents, 212 percent; suicide, 70 percent; pneumonia and influenza, 61 percent; and homicide, 41 percent. Further, infant mortality in Indian Country is double the national average, and Pine Ridge Reservation has the highest infant mortality rate in the Nation.

Crime.   In an October 1997 report, the Justice Department's Criminal Division concluded "there is a public safety crisis in Indian Country." While most of the Nation has witnessed a drastic reduction in serious crime over the past 7 years, on Indian reservations crime is spiraling upwards. Between 1992 and 1996, the overall crime rate dropped about 17 percent, and homicides were down 22 percent. For the same period, however, the Bureau of Indian Affairs reported that murders on America's Indian reservations rose sharply. Some tribes, the Justice Department report says, "have murder rates that far exceed those of urban areas known for their struggles against violent crime." And other violent crimes parallel the rise in homicide.

Tribal law enforcement agencies do not have the resources to meet their growing caseloads. The Criminal Division's report concluded, "The single most glaring problem is a lack of adequate resources in Indian Country. Any solution requires a substantial infusion of new money in addition to existing funds." A chronic shortage of personnel plagues most agencies. For example, in 1996 Indian Country residents were served by less than one-half the number of officers provided to small non-Indian communities. Tribal officers are also in dire need of training. According to the BIA, no reservation in South Dakota has a fully staffed, adequately trained law enforcement program.

[A 1999 study by the Bureau of Justice Statistics found] that American Indians experience per capita rates of violence which are more than twice those of the U.S. population. From 1992 through 1996 the average annual rate of violent victimizations among Indians 12 years and older was 124 per 1,000 residents, compared with 61 for blacks, 49 for whites, and 29 for Asians.

The rate of violent crime experienced by American Indian women is nearly 50 percent higher than that reported by black males.

Annual Average Rate of Violent Victimization by Race of Victim, 1992-96
Number of victimizations per 1,000 persons age 12 or older in each racial group

	All Races	American Indian	White	Black	Asian
Violent victimizations	50	124	49	61	29
Rape/sexual assault	2	7	2	3	1
Robbery	6	12	5	13	7
Aggravated assault	11	35	10	16	6
Simple assault	31	70	32	30	15

The report also found that in 7 out of 10 violent victimizations of American Indians the assailant was someone of a different race, a substantially higher incidence of interracial violence than experienced by white or black victims. Among white victims, 69 percent of the offenders were white; similarly, black victims are most likely to be victimized by a black assailant (81 percent). For American Indian victims of rape/sexual assault, the offender is described as white in 82 percent of the cases.

Alcohol is more often a factor in crimes committed by and against American Indians than for other races. Seventy percent of Indians in local jails for violent crimes had been drinking when they committed the offense, nearly double the rate for the general population. In 55 percent of violent crimes against American Indians, the victim said the offender was under the influence of alcohol and/or drugs. The offender's use of alcohol is less likely for white and black victims (44 and 35 percent, respectively). Other important findings of the study are as follows:

- The arrest rate for alcohol-related offenses among American Indians (drunken driving, liquor law violations and public drunkenness) was more than double that for the total population during 1996. However the drug arrest rate was lower than for other races.
- Almost four in 10 American Indians held in local jails had been charged with a public order offense — most commonly driving while intoxicated.
- During 1996 the American Indian arrest rate for youth violence was about the same as that for white youths.
- On any given day an estimated one in 25 American Indians 18 years old and older is under the jurisdiction of the nation's criminal justice system. This is 2.4 times the rate for whites and 9.3 times the per capita rate for Asians but about half the rate for blacks.
- The number of American Indians per capita confined in the state and federal prisons is about 38 percent above the national average. However, the rate of confinement in local jails is estimated to be nearly 4 times the national average.

MAJOR CONCERNS AND CONCLUSIONS

1. Many Native Americans in South Dakota have little or no confidence in the criminal justice system and believe that the administration of justice at the Federal and State levels is permeated by racism. There is a strongly held perception among Native Americans that there is a dual system of justice and that race is a critical factor in determining how law enforcement and justice functions are carried out. This perception includes a belief that violent crimes involving Native Americans are dealt with differently from those involving whites. It is believed that crimes perpetrated by whites against Indians are investigated and prosecuted with less vigor than those committed by Indians against whites. . . . Information was received by the Advisory Committee suggesting disparities in many aspects of the criminal justice system, including law enforcement stops and racial profiling, arrests, prosecutions, legal representation, and sentencing. . . .

6. The Advisory Committee heard many complaints concerning Federal sentencing guidelines. It was alleged that crimes prosecuted in the Federal system require harsher sentences than similar offenses prosecuted in State courts. Because of the much broader Federal jurisdiction applicable to crimes committed by Native Americans in Indian Country, disparate sentencing — with more severe punishment for Native Americans — may result. This serves to reinforce and strengthen the perception of unequal justice for American Indians. . . .

8. Native Americans are underrepresented in the employment of all institutions involved in the administration of justice, at the Federal, State, and local levels. They are also largely excluded from elected positions and other decisionmaking positions that govern the administration of justice. . . .

13. There appear to be limited legal resources available for Native Americans in South Dakota. Victims of discrimination often find it difficult to secure legal representation. Court-appointed defense attorney systems and local public defender programs have been described as inadequate, due to inexperience, lack of funding, and potential conflicts of interest. There are also few Native Americans in the legal professions. National civil rights legal organizations are not easily accessible, and there are few such programs at the State level. . . .

While some have overcome the obstacles and achieved great success, most American Indians have been left behind. For the most part, Native Americans are very much separate and unequal members of society. Thus, it is not surprising that they are underrepresented in terms of economic status and overrepresented in the population of the State's jails, juvenile facilities, and prisons. Systemic, institutionalized, and historic discrimination disadvantage Native Americans in many ways, and therefore the problems they encounter when caught up in the criminal justice system are wholly consistent with other forms of discrimination.

Despair is not too strong a word to characterize the emotional feelings of many Native Americans who believe they live in a hostile environment. . . .

PROBLEM 9-4. HARD WORKER

Following an evening of heavy drinking, David Big Crow and his wife, Margaret, returned from a dance to their trailer home near Porcupine, South Dakota, on the Pine Ridge Indian Reservation. They were met there by Donald Twiss and several other friends who had attended the same dance and who also had been drinking. The group gathered in the kitchen and began playing a drinking game called quarter pitch.

Some time later, David left the kitchen. When he returned, he fell on Donald, who had been asleep on the floor. Donald awoke feeling a sharp pain above his eye and bleeding from his forehead. David stood next to him with a piece of firewood in his hand, making derogatory remarks about the Twiss family. The two of them fought until Donald left the room. At that point, David hit Margaret with a folding chair. She was taken to the hospital and remained unconscious until noon the next day.

Big Crow was convicted of assault with a dangerous weapon and assault resulting in serious bodily injury. Under the Guidelines, aggravated assault has a base offense level of 15. Use of a dangerous weapon and the infliction of serious bodily injury increase the offense level by 8 levels for a total of 23. U.S.S.G. §§2A2.2(b)(2)(B), 2A2.2(b)(3)(B). Big Crow had no criminal record, and this gave him a criminal history category of I. The United States Probation Officer's presentence investigation report recommended that Big Crow receive 2 points for acceptance of responsibility, and suggested that a departure from the Guideline range might be warranted because Big Crow's offense was out of character and he had been a decent citizen living in a difficult environment. An offense level of 21 carries a range of 37-46 months.

As the sentencing judge in this case, you have received letters written on Big Crow's behalf by community leaders and a Bureau of Indian Affairs official. The letter writers include a local school principal, the president of the Oglala Sioux Tribe, and the agency safety officer of the Bureau of Indian Affairs. The presentence investigation report also noted that Big Crow has a positive reputation in his community and is well liked by his employers and area law enforcement personnel.

Big Crow, who was 23 at the time of his offense, has worked steadily since the age of 17. With his wife's help, he provides more than adequately for the needs of their family, which includes two children. During the three years before this offense, Big Crow worked as a forestry aid and firefighter for the Bureau of Indian Affairs. His employer indicated that Big Crow was "a hard worker in what is not too pleasant a job." He expressed willingness to hold Big Crow's job for him until he is released from custody. The unemployment rate on the Pine Ridge Indian Reservation is 72%. Per-capita annual income on the reservation is estimated at $1,042.

In your experience, extreme intoxication appears to play a role in a large number of crimes committed in the Indian country. Will the role of alcohol in Big Crow's offense affect the sentence you impose? Is his lack of a prior criminal record a basis for imposing a sentence below the Guideline range? Does his employment history, in the context of this community, convince you to sentence outside the Guideline range?

Guideline policy statements indicate that previous employment record, family ties and responsibilities, and community ties are "not ordinarily relevant in determining whether a sentence should be outside the guidelines." U.S.S.G. §§5H1.5, 5H1.6 (policy statements). A policy statement in the Guidelines states that race, national origin, and socioeconomic status are not relevant in the determination of a sentence. U.S.S.G. §5H1.10 (policy statement). On the other hand, the legislative history of the Sentencing Reform Act notes that the "requirement of neutrality . . . is not a requirement of blindness." S. Rep. No. 225, 98th Cong., 1st Sess. 171 n.409 (1983). Cf. United States v. David Big Crow, 898 F.2d 1326 (8th Cir. 1990).

Perhaps it is the principle of equality itself that should be moderated to take account of racial, ethnic, biological, social, or historical circumstances. The Canadian Charter, for example, mandates consideration of the disadvantaged circumstances in which Native Americans find themselves at sentencing. Does this make for fairer sentences in light of the extreme economic disadvantage of aborigines? Should all those who are defined as aborigines benefit from such special consideration, or is it designed only for those on reservations? Is the differentiating characteristic race or race "plus" some other feature(s)? Consider the solution offered by the legislature and high court in Canada.

‖ *Jamie Tanis Gladue v. R.* ‖
[1999] S.C.R. 688

CORY and IACOBUCCI, JJ.

[Criminal Code §718.2(e)] provides that all available sanctions other than imprisonment that are reasonable in the circumstances should be considered for all offenders, with particular attention to the circumstances of aboriginal offenders. This appeal must consider how this provision should be interpreted and applied.

FACTUAL AND PROCEDURAL BACKGROUND

. . . The appellant and the victim Reuben Beaver started to live together in 1993, when the appellant was 17 years old. Thereafter they had a daughter, Tanita. . . . By September 1995, the appellant and Beaver were engaged to be married, and the appellant was five months pregnant with their second child. . . .

In the early evening of September 16, 1995, the appellant was celebrating her 19th birthday. She and Reuben Beaver, who was then 20, were drinking beer with some friends and family members in the townhouse complex. The appellant suspected that Beaver was having an affair with her older sister, Tara. During the course of the evening she voiced those suspicions to her friends. The appellant was obviously angry with Beaver. She said, "the next time he fools around on me, I'll kill him." . . .

The appellant and Beaver returned separately to their townhouse and they started to quarrel. During the argument, the appellant confronted him with his infidelity and he told her that she was fat and ugly and not as good as the others. . . .

Mr. Gretchin, [a neighbor,] saw the appellant run toward Beaver with a large knife in her hand and, as she approached him, she told him that he had better run. Mr. Gretchin heard Beaver shriek in pain and saw him collapse in a pool of blood. The appellant had stabbed Beaver once in the left chest, and the knife had penetrated his heart. As the appellant went by on her return to her apartment, Mr. Gretchin heard her say, "I got you, you fucking bastard." The appellant was described as jumping up and down as if she had tagged someone. Mr. Gretchin said she did not appear to realize what she had done. At the time of the stabbing, the appellant had a blood-alcohol content of between 155 and 165 milligrams of alcohol in 100 millilitres of blood.

[After] a jury had been selected, the appellant entered a plea of guilty to manslaughter. [The government had evidence] that Beaver had subjected the appellant to some physical abuse in June 1994, while the appellant was pregnant with their daughter Tanita. Beaver was convicted of assault, and was given a 15-day intermittent sentence with one year's probation. The neighbour, Mr. Gretchin, told police that the noises emanating from the appellant's and Beaver's apartment suggested a fight. . . . Bruises later observed on the appellant's arm and in the collarbone area were consistent with her having been in a physical altercation on the night of the stabbing. However, the trial judge found that the facts as presented before him did not warrant a finding that the appellant was a "battered or fearful wife."

The appellant's sentencing took place 17 months after the stabbing. Pending her trial [she] took counselling for alcohol and drug abuse at Tillicum Haus Native Friendship Centre in Nanaimo, and completed Grade 10 and was about to start Grade 11. After the stabbing, the appellant was diagnosed as suffering from a hyperthyroid condition, which was said to produce an exaggerated reaction to any emotional situation. . . .

In his submissions on sentence at trial, the appellant's counsel did not raise the fact that the appellant was an aboriginal offender but, when asked by the trial judge whether in fact the appellant was an aboriginal person, replied that she was Cree. When asked by the trial judge whether the town of McLennan, Alberta, where the appellant grew up, was an aboriginal community, defence counsel responded: "it's just a regular community." No other submissions were made at the sentencing hearing on the issue of the appellant's aboriginal heritage. Defence counsel requested a suspended sentence or a conditional sentence of imprisonment. Crown counsel argued in favour of a sentence of between three and five years' imprisonment. The appellant was sentenced to three years' imprisonment and to a ten-year weapons prohibition. . . .

The trial judge noted that both the appellant and the deceased were aboriginal, but stated that they were living in an urban area off-reserve and not "within the aboriginal community as such." He found that there were not any special circumstances arising from their aboriginal status that he should take into consideration. He stated that the offence was a very serious one, for which the appropriate sentence was three years' imprisonment with a ten-year weapons prohibition.

The appellant appealed her sentence of three years' imprisonment [on the ground that] the trial judge failed to give appropriate consideration to the appellant's circumstances as an aboriginal offender. The appellant also sought to adduce fresh evidence at her appeal regarding her efforts since the killing to maintain links with her aboriginal heritage. . . .

INTERPRETATION OF SENTENCING PROVISION

The issue in this appeal is the proper interpretation and application to be given to §718.2(e) of the Criminal Code. The provision reads as follows:

A court that imposes a sentence shall also take into consideration the following principles: . . . (e) available sanctions other than imprisonment that are reasonable in the circumstances should be considered for all offenders, with particular attention to the circumstances of aboriginal offenders. . . .

As a general principle, §718.2(e) applies to all offenders, and states that imprisonment should be the penal sanction of last resort. Prison is to be used only where no other sanction or combination of sanctions is appropriate to the offence and the offender.

The next question is the meaning to be attributed to the words "with particular attention to the circumstances of aboriginal offenders." The phrase cannot be an instruction for judges to pay "more" attention when sentencing aboriginal offenders. It would be unreasonable to assume that Parliament intended sentencing judges to prefer certain categories of offenders over others. Neither can the phrase be merely an instruction to a sentencing judge to consider the circumstances of aboriginal offenders just as she or he would consider the circumstances of any other offender. There would be no point in adding a special reference to aboriginal offenders if this was the case. Rather, the logical meaning to be derived from the special reference to the circumstances of aboriginal offenders, juxtaposed as it is against a general direction to consider "the circumstances" for all offenders, is that sentencing judges should pay particular attention to the circumstances of aboriginal offenders *because those circumstances are unique,* and different from those of non-aboriginal offenders. The fact that the reference to aboriginal offenders is contained in §718.2(e) . . . dealing with restraint in the use of imprisonment, suggests that there is something different about aboriginal offenders which may specifically make imprisonment a less appropriate or less useful sanction. . . .

Section 718 now sets out the purpose of sentencing in the following terms:

The fundamental purpose of sentencing is to contribute, along with crime prevention initiatives, to respect for the law and the maintenance of a just, peaceful and safe society by imposing just sanctions that have one or more of the following objectives:

(a) to denounce unlawful conduct;
(b) to deter the offender and other persons from committing offences;
(c) to separate offenders from society, where necessary;
(d) to assist in rehabilitating offenders;
(e) *to provide reparations for harm done to victims or to the community;* and
(f) *to promote a sense of responsibility in offenders, and acknowledgment of the harm done to victims and to the community.* [Emphasis added.]

Clearly, §718 is, in part, a restatement of the basic sentencing aims, which are listed in paras. (a) through (d). What are new, though, are paras. (e) and (f), which along with para. (d) focus upon the restorative goals of repairing the harms suffered by individual victims and by the community as a whole, promoting a sense of responsibility and an acknowledgment of the harm caused on the part of the offender, and attempting to rehabilitate or heal the offender. [As] a general matter restorative justice involves some form of restitution and reintegration into the community. The need for offenders to take responsibility for their actions is central to the sentencing process. Restorative sentencing goals do not usually correlate with the use of prison as a sanction. In our view, Parliament's choice to include (e) and (f) alongside the traditional sentencing goals must be understood as evidencing an intention to expand the parameters of the sentencing analysis for all offenders. . . .

The parties and interveners agree that the purpose of §718.2(e) is to respond to the problem of overincarceration in Canada, and to respond, in particular, to the more acute problem of the disproportionate incarceration of aboriginal peoples. They also agree that one of the roles of §718.2(e) . . . is to encourage sentencing judges to apply principles of restorative justice alongside or in the place of other, more traditional sentencing principles when making sentencing determinations. . . .

Although the United States has by far the highest rate of incarceration among industrialized democracies, at over 600 inmates per 100,000 population, Canada's rate of approximately 130 inmates per 100,000 population places it second or third highest. Moreover, the rate at which Canadian courts have been imprisoning offenders has risen sharply in recent years, although there has been a slight decline of late. This record of incarceration rates obviously cannot instil a sense of pride. . . .

If overreliance upon incarceration is a problem with the general population, it is of much greater concern in the sentencing of aboriginal Canadians. In the mid-1980s, aboriginal people were about 2 percent of the population of Canada, yet they made up 10 percent of the penitentiary population. In Manitoba and Saskatchewan, aboriginal people constituted something between 6 and 7 percent of the population, yet in Manitoba they represented 46 percent of the provincial admissions and in Saskatchewan 60 percent. The situation has not improved in recent years. By 1997, aboriginal peoples constituted closer to 3 percent of the population of Canada and amounted to 12 percent of all federal inmates. The situation continues to be particularly worrisome in Manitoba, where in 1995-96 they made up 55 percent of admissions to provincial correctional facilities, and in Saskatchewan, where they made up 72 percent of admissions. A similar, albeit less drastic situation prevails in Alberta and British Columbia. . . .

Not surprisingly, the excessive imprisonment of aboriginal people is only the tip of the iceberg insofar as the estrangement of the aboriginal peoples from the Canadian criminal justice system is concerned. Aboriginal people are over-represented in virtually all aspects of the system. As this Court recently noted in R. v. Williams, [1998] 1 S.C.R. 1128, at para. 58, there is widespread bias against aboriginal people within Canada, and "[there] is evidence that this widespread racism has translated into systemic discrimination in the criminal justice system." . . . The figures are stark and reflect what may fairly be termed a crisis in the Canadian criminal justice system. [Section 718.2(e)] may properly be seen as Parliament's direction to members of the judiciary to inquire into the causes of the problem and to endeavour to remedy it, to the extent that a remedy is possible through the sentencing process.

It is clear that sentencing innovation by itself cannot remove the causes of aboriginal offending and the greater problem of aboriginal alienation from the criminal justice system. The unbalanced ratio of imprisonment for aboriginal offenders flows from a number of sources, including poverty, substance abuse, lack of education, and the lack of employment opportunities for aboriginal people. It arises also from bias against aboriginal people and from an unfortunate institutional approach that is more inclined to refuse bail and to impose more and longer prison terms for aboriginal offenders. There are many aspects of this sad situation which cannot be addressed in these reasons. What can and must be addressed, though, is the limited role that sentencing judges will play in remedying injustice against aboriginal peoples in Canada. Sentencing judges are among those decision-makers who have the power to influence the treatment of aboriginal offenders in the justice system. They determine most directly whether an aboriginal offender will go to jail, or whether other sentencing options may be employed which will play perhaps a stronger role in restoring a sense of balance to the offender, victim, and community, and in preventing future crime.

How are sentencing judges to play their remedial role? The words of §718.2(e) instruct the sentencing judge to pay particular attention to the circumstances of aboriginal offenders, with the implication that those circumstances are significantly different from those of non-aboriginal offenders. . . . The background factors which figure prominently in the causation of crime by aboriginal offenders are by now well known. Years of dislocation and economic development have translated, for many aboriginal peoples, into low incomes, high unemployment, lack of opportunities and options, lack or irrelevance of education, substance abuse, loneliness, and community fragmentation. These and other factors contribute to a higher incidence of crime and incarceration.

[The] circumstances of aboriginal offenders differ from those of the majority because many aboriginal people are victims of systemic and direct discrimination, many suffer the legacy of dislocation, and many are substantially affected by poor social and economic conditions. Moreover, as has been emphasized repeatedly in studies and commission reports, aboriginal offenders are, as a result of these unique systemic and background factors, more adversely affected by incarceration and less likely to be "rehabilitated" thereby, because the internment milieu is often culturally inappropriate and regrettably discrimination towards them is so often rampant in penal institutions. . . .

In cases where [unique background and systemic] factors have played a significant role [in bringing the particular offender before the courts], it is incumbent upon the sentencing judge to consider these factors in evaluating whether imprisonment would actually serve to deter, or to denounce crime in a sense that would be meaningful to the community of which the offender is a member. In many instances, more restorative sentencing principles will gain primary relevance precisely because the prevention of crime as well as individual and social healing cannot occur through other means.

Closely related to the background and systemic factors which have contributed to an excessive aboriginal incarceration rate are the different conceptions of appropriate sentencing procedures and sanctions held by aboriginal people. A significant problem experienced by aboriginal people who come into contact with the criminal justice system is that the traditional sentencing ideals of deterrence, separation, and denunciation are often far removed from the understanding of sentencing held by these offenders and their community. [Most] traditional aboriginal conceptions of sentencing place a *primary* emphasis upon the ideals of restorative justice. This tradition is extremely important to the analysis under §718.2(e).

[Restorative] justice may be described as an approach to remedying crime in which it is understood that all things are interrelated and that crime disrupts the harmony which existed prior to its occurrence, or at least which it is felt should exist. The appropriateness of a particular sanction is largely determined by the needs of the victims, and the community, as well as the offender. The focus is on the human beings closely affected by the crime.

The existing overemphasis on incarceration in Canada may be partly due to the perception that a restorative approach is a more lenient approach to crime and that imprisonment constitutes the ultimate punishment. Yet in our view a sentence focussed on restorative justice is not necessarily a "lighter" punishment. . . .

In describing the effect of §718.2(e) in this way, we do not mean to suggest that, as a general practice, aboriginal offenders must always be sentenced in a manner which gives greatest weight to the principles of restorative justice, and less weight to goals such as deterrence, denunciation, and separation. It is unreasonable to assume that aboriginal peoples themselves do not believe in the importance of these latter goals, and even if they do not, that such goals must not predominate in appropriate cases. Clearly there are some serious offences and some offenders for which and for whom separation, denunciation, and deterrence are fundamentally relevant.

Yet, even where an offence is considered serious, the length of the term of imprisonment must be considered. In some circumstances the length of the sentence of an aboriginal offender may be less and in others the same as that of any other offender. Generally, the more violent and serious the offence the more likely it is as a practical reality that the terms of imprisonment for aboriginals and non-aboriginals will be close to each other or the same, even taking into account their different concepts of sentencing. . . .

How then is the consideration of §718.2(e) to proceed in the daily functioning of the courts? The manner in which the sentencing judge will carry out his or her statutory duty may vary from case to case. In all instances it will be necessary for the judge to take judicial notice of the systemic or background factors and the approach to sentencing which is relevant to aboriginal offenders. However, for each particular offence and offender it may be that some evidence will be required in order to assist the sentencing judge in arriving at a fit sentence. Where a particular offender does not wish such evidence to be adduced, the right to have particular attention paid to his or her circumstances as an aboriginal offender may be waived. Where there is no such waiver, it will be extremely helpful to the sentencing judge for counsel on both sides to adduce relevant evidence. . . .

However, even where counsel do not adduce this evidence, where for example the offender is unrepresented, it is incumbent upon the sentencing judge to attempt to acquire information regarding the circumstances of the offender as an aboriginal person. Whether the offender resides in a rural area, on a reserve or in an urban centre the sentencing judge must be made aware of alternatives to incarceration that exist whether inside or outside the aboriginal community of the particular offender. The alternatives existing in metropolitan areas must, as a matter of course, also be explored. Clearly the presence of an aboriginal offender will require special attention in pre-sentence reports. Beyond the use of the pre-sentence report, the sentencing judge may and should in appropriate circumstances and where practicable request that witnesses be called who may testify as to reasonable alternatives.

Similarly, where a sentencing judge at the trial level has not engaged in the duty imposed by §718.2(e) as fully as required, it is incumbent upon a court of appeal in considering an appeal against sentence on this basis to consider any fresh evidence which is relevant and admissible on sentencing. [Although] §718.2(e) does not impose a statutory duty upon the sentencing judge to provide reasons, it will be much easier for a reviewing court to determine whether and how attention was paid to the circumstances of the offender as an aboriginal person if at least brief reasons are given. . . .

The fact that a court is called upon to take into consideration the unique circumstances surrounding these different parties is not unfair to non-aboriginal people. Rather, the fundamental purpose of §718.2(e) is to treat aboriginal offenders fairly by taking into account their difference. . . .

The class of aboriginal people who come within the purview of the specific reference to the circumstances of aboriginal offenders in §718.2(e) must be, at least, . . . an estimated 799,010 people [who] were identified as aboriginal in [the] 1996 [census]. Of this number, 529,040 were Indians (registered or non-registered), 204,115 Metis and 40,220 Inuit.

Section 718.2(e) applies to all aboriginal offenders wherever they reside, whether on- or off-reserve, in a large city or a rural area. Indeed it has been observed that many aboriginals living in urban areas are closely attached to their culture. . . .

Based on the foregoing, the jail term for an aboriginal offender may in some circumstances be less than the term imposed on a non-aboriginal offender for the same offence. . . .

APPLICATION OF PRINCIPLES

In most cases, errors such as those in the courts below would be sufficient to justify sending the matter back for a new sentencing hearing. It is difficult for this Court to determine a fit sentence for the appellant according to the suggested guidelines set out herein on the basis of the very limited evidence before us regarding the appellant's aboriginal background. However, as both the trial judge and all members of the Court of Appeal acknowledged, the offence in question is a most serious one, properly described . . . as a "near murder." Moreover, the offence involved domestic violence and a breach of the trust inherent in a spousal relationship. That aggravating factor must be taken into account in the sentencing of the aboriginal appellant as it would be for any offender. For that offence by this offender a sentence of three years' imprisonment was not unreasonable.

More importantly, the appellant was granted day parole on August 13, 1997, after she had served six months in the Burnaby Correctional Centre for Women. She was directed to reside with her father, to take alcohol and substance abuse counselling and to comply with the requirements of the Electronic Monitoring Program. On February 25, 1998, the appellant was granted full parole with the same conditions as the ones applicable to her original release on day parole.

In this case, the results of the sentence with incarceration for six months and the subsequent controlled release were in the interests of both the appellant and society. In these circumstances, we do not consider that it would be in the interests of justice to order a new sentencing hearing in order to canvass the appellant's circumstances as an aboriginal offender. . . .

NOTES

1. *Aboriginal offenders in prison.*   The *Gladue* court recognized the disproportionate imprisonment of aboriginal offenders in Canada. In response to the problem, Parliament added Criminal Code §718.2(e). In Australia aborigines are also overrepresented in prisons. In fact, the racial disparities in Canada and Australia between aborigines and non-aborigines are worse than those between blacks and whites in the United States. What factors account for the high imprisonment rates of natives? Much of Australia's high aboriginal imprisonment rate has been blamed on mandatory sentencing laws for relatively minor property offenses. Why would mandatory sentences not lead to *greater* ethnic equality? Should the disparate impact on minority groups be a reason for abolishing such legislation?

2. *Aboriginal sentencing practices.*   In a later decision, Canada's highest court emphasized that in cases of aboriginal offenders sentencing judges must consider "the types of sentencing procedures and sanctions which may be appropriate in the circumstances for the offender because of his or her particular Aboriginal heritage or connection. In particular, given that most traditional Aboriginal approaches place a primary emphasis on the goal of restorative justice, the alternative of community-based sanctions must be explored." R. v. Wells, [2000] S.C.R. 207, para. 53. To what extent can and should U.S. courts consider the punishment practices of native courts? While some aboriginal groups have focused on restorative justice, others have used punishment practices that many today would consider torture. How should the courts accommodate considerations of traditional practice and modern human rights concerns? See Rick Sarre, Sentencing in Customary or Tribal Settings: An Australian Perspective, 13 Fed. Sent'g Rep. 74 (2000).

3. *Native Americans, blacks, and other minority offenders.*   In many countries with native populations, natives are not the only ones overrepresented in prison. Should the situation of native offenders be any more disconcerting than the situation of offenders from other racial groups? Why? To what extent can sentencing judges be expected to "fix" racial disparity at individualized sentencing hearings? Will such attempts not merely lead to other forms of injustice?

4. *Ethnicity.*   Ethnicity has become an alternative to race in describing human diversity, but the term also carries deep ambiguities. Ethnicity focuses

on the cultural distinctiveness of a group: country of origin, language, religion, food, and values all create a particular ethnic identity. Which of these characteristics are relevant and the extent to which one should be allowed to self-classify as a member of a particular ethnic group remain ambiguous. Ethnicity allows for distinctions within racial groups (blacks emigrating from the Caribbean, for example, differ from those hailing from the African continent), but it also encompasses racial differences (blacks and whites from Brazil are both considered Hispanics). Often ethnicity appears to be a substitute for national origin, but in fact the latter is usually limited to first- and possibly second-generation immigrant populations.

5. *Culture and sentencing.* Offenders from some ethnic groups may be culturally conditioned or socialized not to enter guilty pleas. Since guilty pleas often result in a sentence reduction, offenders who insist on their right to trial may receive longer sentences. In imposing a sentence, should a court consider whether the choice of trial may be characteristic of the offender's ethnic group? If not, is the offender being punished for a cultural value that differs from that of mainstream society rather than for offense-relevant conduct? Australia's Crimes Act requires courts to consider the "cultural background" of an offender, including "ethnic, environmental and cultural matters." Would the insistence on going to trial be a cultural factor?

6. *Culture and victims.* Most crime is committed *within* a given racial or ethnic group. Sentencing patterns based on the offender's culture, therefore, often parallel the victims' ethnicity and culture. Do lower sentences based on offenders' cultural background devalue the suffering of their victims or indicate that the victims deserve less state protection?

7. *Principles of equality.* U.S. law is based on principles of equality. All individuals, independent of their race, ethnicity, or national origin, should be treated the same. The federal sentencing guidelines as well as state sentencing regimes reflect this mantra. Such neutrality can lead to injustice, however, when the situations of individuals are so different that equal treatment in the criminal justice system merely magnifies the unequal treatment in other aspects of life.

As the preceding materials indicate, Native Americans who commit offenses on reservations are tried in federal court and sentenced under the federal guidelines. Historically, the guarantee of criminal trials in federal courts was designed to protect Native Americans from discriminatory state courts. Today, however, when federal sentences are perceived as harsher than those in many states, Native Americans tend to consider themselves as being treated unfairly. While the guidelines appear to have decreased racial disparity within the federal system, federal courts have refused to undertake state-federal comparisons to determine whether a sentence is too harsh.

8. *Inequality and the state.* In contrast to the current approach to race equality, an alternative sentencing system might deliberately take group differences into account. But considering group status at sentencing could undermine the concept of "one nation" and the fundamental equality of the victims of crime. It could also excuse the state's inability or unwillingness to equalize the social and economic starting points for all members of society.

PROBLEM 9-5.   ALIEN STATUS

Peter Onwuemene, a Nigerian citizen, and other Nigerians participated in a nationwide automobile insurance fraud scheme that caused losses of about $1 million to several insurance companies. A member of the group would obtain liability insurance on an old car from 10 to 15 insurance companies. Subsequently, the policy owner would report a collision with an expensive, late-model car owned by another member of the group, who would claim damage to his car.

Onwuemene was charged with four counts of mail fraud. He pled guilty to one of the counts in return for the government's agreement to recommend dismissal of the others. Onwuemene faced a sentencing range under the federal sentencing guidelines of 6 to 12 months. The presentence investigation report recommended 6 months' incarceration and a work release program. At sentencing, Onwuemene agreed to pay restitution of $3,723.

The district court sentenced him to 12 months' imprisonment, the top of the sentencing range, because the crime was serious and could have resulted in a much greater loss if the victims had failed to discover it and because Onwuemene "failed or refused" to identify the other participants in the fraud. The court added:

> The other thing that I feel that warrants imposition at the high end of the guideline range: You are not a citizen of this country. This country was good enough to allow you to come in here and to confer upon you . . . a number of the benefits of this society, form of government, and its opportunities, and you repay that kindness by committing a crime like this. We have got enough criminals in the United States without importing any.

Onwuemene appeals. A federal sentence within the applicable guidelines range is reviewable only if it is imposed in violation of the law or as a result of an incorrect application of the guidelines. How should the appellate court rule? See United States v. Onwuemene, 933 F.2d 650 (8th Cir. 1991).

NOTES

1. *Immigration status and sentencing.* Large-scale immigration into North America and Western Europe has caused an ever-increasing number of immigrants to become involved in the criminal justice system. May a court consider an offender's immigration status at sentencing? Because of the possibility (or even likelihood) of deportation, a court could impose a lesser sentence than it would on a citizen offender. Federal courts, however, have generally rejected downward departures based on a noncitizen's deportability. See, e.g., United States v. Restrepo, 999 F.2d 640 (2nd Cir. 1993); United States v. Lopez-Salas, 266 F.3d 842 (8th Cir. 2001). But see United States v. Gallo-Vasquez, 284 F.3d 780, 784 (7th Cir. 2002) (district court may depart downward when "defendant's status as a deportable alien . . . may lead to conditions of confinement, or other incidents of punishment, that are substantially more onerous than the framers of the guidelines contemplated in fixing the punishment range for the defendant's offense").

Alternatively, a court may view an immigrant's offense as more heinous because he abused his guest status, as did the trial court in Problem 9-5. When judges explicitly refer to alien status, some federal courts have held that they are violating the Constitution by sentencing an offender on the basis of factors such as race, national origin, or alienage. See United States v. Onwuemene, 933 F.2d 650 (8th Cir. 1991) (consideration of defendant's alien status violates his constitutional rights); United States v. Borrero-Isaza, 887 F.2d 1349, 1352 (9th Cir. 1989) (imposing stricter sentence on defendant because of his national origin and alienage violated right to due process). One state court tried to impose a higher sentence on a member of an ethnic community: "[S]ometimes it is necessary in sentencing to send a message to the community, and I am sending a message by this sentence to a small segment of the Albanian community that they now live in the United States and they are governed by our laws, and we are not going to tolerate whatever the customs may be in Albania, and that includes the customs of dealing with family members as well as the use of guns." The appellate court considered this justification an impermissible consideration of defendant's national origin. People v. Gjidoda, 364 N.W.2d 698 (Mich. 1985).

2. *Noncitizen offenses.* A number of immigration offenses, such as reentry of a convicted felon, can be committed only by noncitizens. Do such statutes not discriminate based on national origin? Because of increases in congressional funding and changes in law enforcement priorities and federal sentencing, between the mid-1980s and 2000 the number of noncitizens sentenced for immigration offenses — primarily unlawful entry and reentry upon deportation — more than doubled, the rate of incarceration increased eightfold, and the length of incarceration rose from an average of 4 months to 21 months. About 80% of the offenders prosecuted for reentry offenses are Mexican nationals, and more than half of all immigration offenders hail from Mexico. 2002 Yearbook of Immigration Statistics, Enforcement, Fiscal Year 2002.

3. *Immigrants and crime.* With the growth of immigration, new groups add to the existing racial and ethnic diversity in the United States. In Western Europe and North America crime and incarceration rates for members of some minority groups greatly exceed those for the majority population. The same minority groups are also socially and economically disadvantaged (but not all disadvantaged groups are also high-crime groups). While some discrimination may be present, the principal cause of the disparities appears to be differences in offending patterns rather than official bias. How should the criminal justice system react to such increasing diversity and disparity?

One approach would be to exempt certain immigrant groups from the coverage of select substantive criminal law provisions that are legally and culturally foreign to them. So far, no one has seriously considered this idea. Another notion is to consider an offender's ethnicity at the sentencing stage. For example, when a recent immigrant from a country that allows the marriage of adult men to teenage girls is convicted of statutory rape, the sentencing court may consider as a mitigating circumstance that the immigrant and his teen "wife" viewed the marriage as legitimate. Feminists, however, have objected that such exemptions generally come at the expense of women's rights, as in many societies around the world women and girls have fewer legal rights than is the case in the United States. Can a color-blind society permit courts and prosecutors to consider ethnicity when it prohibits them from basing their sentences on race or national origin? Should the court be allowed to consider the laws prevalent in the defendants' home countries and their cultural immersion in such values? How should home and host country values and laws be reconciled? Should such special treatment exist for all first-generation immigrants? For all members of an ethnic group? For all members of an ethnic group growing up in a distinctly ethnic environment?

4. *What sentencing practices and values?*   Some have argued that immigrant offenders should be punished based on the sentence that would be appropriate in their home countries. The reason given is that the sentencing regime in the United States is too lenient to deter offenders from countries where the death penalty is available for more offenses, where physical punishments such as flogging are practiced, and where longer prison terms may be imposed for select offenses.

In a number of federal cases, courts have departed from the applicable guideline range because of the offender's adoption of American values. See, e.g., United States v. Rodriguez-Montelongo, 263 F.3d 429, 432-434 (5th Cir. 2001) (cultural assimilation considered a mitigating factor). Is this an appropriate ground for departure from the guidelines?

C. CLASS

In the United States legal scholars, sociologists, political scientists, and public commentators tend to pay less attention to class differences than do those in other Western countries. Race-based analysis has replaced much of the focus on class. While racial distinctions and poverty do not go hand in hand, they do overlap.

Class is relatively difficult to define. If a person's class is determined by annual income, some members of the Rockefeller family may be categorized as poor. If it is based on educational attainment or status of employment, to what economic class do the stay-at-home spouses of executives of major corporations belong? The intellectual tradition in the United States combined with these definitional difficulties and related challenges in data collection make it difficult to find empirical studies on class.

Courts are also reluctant to identify "class." White-collar offenses are often associated with high-class defendants, while blue-collar defendants are generally viewed as lower-class. The relationship between class and type of crime is not perfect; many embezzlers are members of the middle class, for example. To the extent that courts do discuss class, they focus on high-status offenders. A prosecutor may request a higher sentence for "someone who had choices," or a defense lawyer may argue that "family" or "community" contributions and good works justify a lower sentence. Consider the relevance of class in the following case.

|| *United States v. Frank Serafini* ||
|| 233 F.3d 758 (3d Cir. 2000) ||

RENDELL, J.

In this appeal, Frank Serafini challenges his conviction and sentence for one count of perjury in violation of 18 U.S.C. §1623. Serafini, a popular state legislator in northeastern Pennsylvania, was convicted based on his false testimony before a federal grand jury; the grand jury was investigating a scheme wherein corporate political contributions were funneled through third-party conduits in violation of federal election laws. In his grand jury testimony, Serafini had denied that he was reimbursed for a contribution he had made to Senator Bob Dole's presidential campaign. [The government appeals] Serafini's sentence, contesting . . . the District Court's three-level downward departure for exceptional civic or charitable contributions pursuant to U.S.S.G. §5H1.11. [We conclude that the District Court's downward departure was] not an abuse of its discretion. . . .

Serafini was subpoenaed to testify before a grand jury that was investigating possible violations of the Federal Election Campaign Act (FECA).[5] The principal targets of the probe were Renato Mariani, president of Empire Sanitary Landfill, Inc. (Empire), and Serafini's nephew, Michael Serafini. The apparent violations were that Michael Serafini and his secretary had solicited numerous employees, business associates, and family members to make $1,000 contributions to Senator Bob Dole's presidential campaign, and that Michael reimbursed them for these contributions; the resulting transactions between Michael and these "conduits" therefore allegedly violated FECA. . . .

Serafini was called before the grand jury to answer questions about Michael's having solicited Serafini for a $1,000 contribution and allegedly having reimbursed him for that contribution. . . . The [government] sought and received an order immunizing Serafini so that the government could compel his testimony before the grand jury; the resulting subpoena ordered him to produce "[all] documents relative to political contributions you were reimbursed for." During Serafini's appearance before the grand jury, the Assistant U.S. Attorney informed him that he could be prosecuted if he provided false testimony. Although Serafini did acknowledge that Michael had solicited and obtained from him a $1,000 contribution to Dole, he denied that a $2,000 check given to him by Michael that same week was in part a reimbursement for that contribution. Instead, Serafini maintained that the $2,000 probably represented Michael's reimbursing Serafini for payments that Serafini made to a mechanic who had fixed Michael's Porsche. [Serafini repeatedly asserted that he was not reimbursed for any contributions.

The jury convicted Serafini of perjury.] After ascertaining that the base offense level for perjury before a grand jury was 12, see U.S.S.G. §2J1.3(a), the District Court applied a three-level enhancement for "substantial interference with the administration of justice," *id.* §2J1.3(b)(2). [We] conclude that

---

5. FECA prohibits corporations from making contributions in connection with any federal election. FECA also makes it unlawful for any person to make a contribution in the name of another person (referred to in this opinion as a "conduit"), or for any person to permit his or her name to be used as a conduit. FECA limits individual contributions to federal candidates to $1,000 per election per candidate.

the enhancement for "substantial interference" was permissible. . . . When combined with Serafini's criminal history category of I, this adjusted offense level resulted in a guideline range of 18 to 24 months' imprisonment. However, the District Court granted a three-level downward departure for Serafini's community and charitable activities. The government argues that the District Court's departure is an abuse of discretion. . . .

The District Court . . . correctly determined that departing on the basis of civic and charitable good works was discouraged, but not forbidden, by the Guidelines. U.S.S.G. §5H1.11 ("Military, civic, charitable, or public service; employment-related contributions; and similar prior good works are not ordinarily relevant in determining whether a sentence should be outside the applicable guideline range"). The District Court recognized that, in order to depart downward on this basis, it must find that this factor existed "to an exceptional degree or, in some way, that makes the case different from the ordinary case in which the factor is present." The District Court made a finding that Serafini's civic and charitable contributions did exist to such an exceptional degree, or in an extraordinary manner. . . .

At the sentencing hearing, the District Court was presented with several character witnesses, and more than 150 letters. The letters submitted to the Court fall into three categories: (i) the first category presents Serafini as a good person; (ii) the second category refers to his activities as a state legislator; and (iii) the third category refers to his assistance, in time and money, to individuals and local organizations.

As to the first category, these can be quickly dismissed with the observation that being a "good person," a quality indeed to be admired, does not qualify as extraordinary or exceptional civic or charitable conduct.

As to Serafini's activities as a state legislator, they are work-related and political in character. For example, a letter from the Fire Chief of Greenfield Township Volunteer Fire Company stated that he "had worked tirelessly to obtain grant monies to help the community afford the lifesaving equipment they need." . . . Conceptually, if a public servant performs civic and charitable work as part of his daily functions, these should not be considered in his sentencing because we expect such work from our public servants. [To] the extent this second group of letters does not evidence extraordinary community service under Guideline §5H1.11, but instead, reflects merely the political duties ordinarily performed by public servants, we are of the view that they cannot form the basis of a departure.

However, unlike the first and second categories of letters the Court received, the third category of letters provided an adequate basis for the District Court's conclusion that Serafini's community service warranted a downward departure. Many of the letters that fall within this last group contain substantive descriptions of Serafini's generosity with his time as well as his money. Several constituents and friends described situations in which Serafini extended himself to them in unique and meaningful ways during times of serious need. In particular, three letters are especially noteworthy.

William Drazdowski, an accountant and "a close personal friend" of the defendant, explains Serafini's role in providing a $300,000 guarantee to Dr. Edward Zaloga so that he could secure new cutting edge data from certain Tokyo physicians for the treatment of his brother's brain tumor. Dr. Zaloga testified at the sentencing hearing that he telephoned Serafini at 1:00 A.M. seeking his assistance in raising the money. Just thirty minutes later, Serafini called back and informed Dr. Zaloga "that everything was in place." . . . In reading the Zaloga letter, both Serafini's readiness to help and his reluctance to seek gratitude make a strong impression. Such behavior is hardly part of the normal duties of a local politician.

Another letter came from George E. Seig, who also testified at the sentencing hearing. He sustained a serious injury as a result of an accident while he was a college student. The physicians' prognosis was that he would never be able to carry on any form of normal social functioning. After a year of frustrating physical therapy, Seig lost all ambition to return to school. Then, he was contacted by Serafini's office who told him that Serafini had heard of the tragic incident and wanted Seig to come work for him. The record reflects that Serafini's offer of employment went far beyond just hiring a young person on his staff. Serafini took Seig under his wing, mentored him, and strongly encouraged him to attend college. He even loaned him money until Seig could repay it. The letter from Seig — now an attorney — reflects his immense gratitude and his feeling that Serafini is responsible for turning his life around.

A third letter came from a widow who approached Serafini in tears because she was about to lose her house. He wrote her a personal check for $750 to forestall foreclosure. She expressed doubt about her future ability to repay him, but Serafini insisted that she need not do so unless she could afford it.

The remaining letters, taken as a whole, depict Serafini as an exceptionally giving person. . . . For example, the letters describe Serafini's volunteer work as an usher at St. Mary's Church; at the Abington Heights School District; and at Lackawanna Trail High School. In addition, he helped to establish a fund to defray the cost of a bone marrow transplant for a man suffering from leukemia. Several letters note that Serafini was generous with his time even with people who lived outside his district. The letters also describe Serafini's financial contributions to organizations such as The Arc (a nonprofit agency serving people with mental retardation and their families); the Rotary Run Against Drugs; the Scranton Lackawanna Human Development Agency; the Little League; the Boy Scouts; St. Francis of Assisi Kitchen; the Abington Heights School District; and the leukemia sufferer's fund mentioned above. A letter from an official at the University of Scranton refers to Serafini's financial assistance to college students, and a letter from a high school social studies teacher describes Serafini's contributions to a scholarship for graduating seniors. . . .

The District Court concluded that the letters and testimony demonstrated that Serafini had distinguished himself, "not by the amount of money [he has] given, but by the amount of time that [he has] devoted." The District Court found that these efforts made Serafini's community and charitable activities "exceptional" when compared to what an average person in Serafini's circumstances would have done:

> Those weren't acts of just giving money, they were acts of giving time, of giving one's self. That distinguishes Mr. Serafini, I think, from the ordinary public servant, from the ordinary elected official, and I had ample testimony, today, that says that Mr. Serafini distinguishes himself, that these are acts not just undertaken to assure his re-election, but are taken because of the type of person he is. . . .

We realize, as did the District Court, that Serafini's largesse was in part financial, and in part, devotion of himself and his time. Since he is a wealthy

individual, we must ensure that a district court does not run afoul of the prohibition against considering socioeconomic differences in relying on financial
contributions as a basis for a departure. See U.S.S.G. §5H1.11. However, the
District Court here recognized this particular aspect of Serafini's situation, but
nonetheless found *all* his contributions, not merely monetary ones, exceptional.

It is not our role to decide in the first instance whether Serafini's civic and
charitable contributions were exceptional given Serafini's role as a public servant and his apparent wealth. Our review is far more deferential. We conclude
that the District Court had an adequate basis for its factual finding, and that the
District Court's decision was not clearly out of line with other reported cases.
See, e.g., United States v. Woods, 159 F.3d 1132, 1136 (8th Cir. 1998) (upholding defendant's downward departure for charitable activities, which included
bringing two troubled young women into her home and paying for them to
attend a private high school, as well as helping to care for an elderly friend,
where the court found no basis to overturn the district court's finding that these
efforts were exceptional). . . .

ROSENN, J., dissenting.

. . . I believe that when it came to sentencing, the voluminous letters from
the defendant's political constituents, colleagues, and other friends misled the
Court to depart downward from the Guidelines. . . .

The Sentencing Guidelines are clear that a defendant's record of charitable work and community service are a discouraged justification for a sentencing
departure. The historical note to the Civic and Charitable Amendment to the
Guidelines (§5H1.11) "expresses the Commission's intent that the factors set
forth in this part are not ordinarily relevant in determining whether a sentence
should be outside the applicable guideline range. . . ." This appears to be a
recognition that in our culture and society, every person is expected reasonably
to contribute charity to the poor and to non-profit organizations dedicated to
educational, health, and religious purposes.[1] . . .

The defendant is not only a wealthy individual, but his federal income tax
returns show substantial income from sources other than his salary as a state
official. Included are substantial royalties from the Empire Landfill. A financial
analysis of his pertinent income returns for the period 1991 through 1996
reveals the following undisputed evidence.

Year	$ Total Income	$ Charitable Deductions	Charity as % of Income
1991	724,019	13,407	1.8
1993	857,000	22,604	2.6
1994	855,000	16,620	1.9
1995	908,172	17,385	1.9
1996	1,101,276	20,310	1.8

1. According to a national survey by Independent Sector on "Giving and Volunteering in the United States," approximately 69% of all households in the United States
made voluntary contributions to charity in 1995. See Statistical Abstract of the United
States 404 (1999).

Except for 1993, in which his contributions exceeded 2%, all of his contributions are less than 2% per annum. Donating less than 2% of one's income to charity — even 2.6% — is lackluster and pedestrian by any measure; it is not exceptional. It is far below the average measure of giving in the United States by people in the defendant's socioeconomic status.[2] . . .

As noted, the majority and the District Court were persuaded by Serafini's non-financial charitable acts. But much of Serafini's civic participation was either honorary or obligatory because of his job as a Representative. Numerous letters submitted on his behalf were written by constituents or other beneficiaries of his public position. . . . Neither Drazdowski, an accountant, nor Dr. Zaloga claim that Serafini personally made the guarantee; nor does the defendant. There is no information how the guarantee was accomplished, to whom it was made, who made it, and the substance of the guarantee, or the relationship between Dr. Zaloga and the defendant. [The] entirely obscure and mysterious incident may very well have its genesis in defendant's political agenda. In any event, it hardly rises to the level of significant community service.

The Seig letter attests to Serafini's offer to employ Seig, a young friend of the family, on the defendant's legislative staff, a loan to him of an unstated sum of money, and encouragement to Seig to attend college. The third letter reports a personal check of $750 from the defendant to a widow who was about to lose her home through foreclosure. The widow expressed doubt about her ability to repay and defendant insisted she need not do so unless able.

These three "noteworthy" letters do reflect commendable action by the defendant, but neither they, nor the other letters, show community service to an exceptional or extraordinary degree. A few acts of personal kindness to individual friends do not add up to community service; they do not fulfill the purpose of the Guidelines. The District Court relied considerably on the defendant's gift "of time." I can find no evidence of the amount of time given to community service, as distinguished from some personal favors to friends and political constituents. . . .

The 1999 Statistical Abstract of the United States reveals that in the year 1995, persons in the United States with income of $100,000 or more contributed an average of 4.4 hours per week to volunteer work without monetary pay. In this case, although Serafini earned many times more than $100,000 in 1994 and 1995, we have no record that he gave any amount of time to volunteer work, whether it was for one or more weeks during the year, or for fifty-two weeks.

The cases support the foregoing analysis. Courts may not leniently interpret the requirement of extraordinary circumstances to grant a downward departure. See, e.g., United States v. Rybicki, 96 F.3d 754, 758 (4th Cir. 1996) (defendant was a highly-decorated Vietnam veteran, had saved an innocent civilian during the My Lai massacre, and had served with the Secret Service; these deeds did not warrant a departure); United States v. McHan, 920 F.2d 244, 247 (4th Cir. 1990) (defendant's work history, family ties and responsibilities, and extensive

---

2. According to the Statistical Abstract of the United States, the average American household contributed 2.2% of its income to charity in 1991. . . . In 1995, households with greater than $100,000 income contributed 3.4% of their household income to charity. . . .

contribution to the town's economic well-being could not justify downward departure). . . .

Measured by any reasonable standard, whether it be tithing to his church and community, or other charitable contributions of money or community time, Serafini's charitable and community service was far from exceptional or extraordinary. . . . I therefore conclude that it was impermissible under the Guidelines for the District Court to depart from the Sentencing Guidelines.

NOTES

1. *Higher class status and sentencing advantage.* Is membership in a privileged class a basis for increased or decreased sentencing, or should it be irrelevant? Should monetary charity ever be considered a basis for adjusting a sentence downward? If money is a poor indicator of anything other than class, are there aspects of social or community behavior not tied to class that should nonetheless be relevant to sentencing? For a different perspective on a downward departure in the case of a wealthy white-collar defendant based on charitable giving and good deeds, see United States v. Thurston, 338 F.3d 50 (1st Cir. 2003) (review of downward departure de novo).

2. *Lower class status and sentencing disadvantage.* The striking reality of the U.S. criminal justice system is the disproportionate presence of members of the lower class. Should the disproportionate presence of the poor in U.S. courts, prisons, and jails prompt changes in our sentencing systems or our social systems? In a survey of federal judges conducted in 2002, only 54-60% of them believed that there was "almost always" neutrality with regard to the offender's socioeconomic status, in contrast to 62-68% who believed the same with regard to race and almost 90% who shared that belief with regard to religion or creed.

D.   GENDER

Criminal laws used to distinguish explicitly between men and women. Some, such as rape laws, made it impossible for women to commit the crime; others relegated women automatically to victimhood. See, e.g., M. v. Superior Court of Sonoma County, 450 U.S. 464 (1981) (state statute criminalizing only the male's conduct in sexual intercourse with an underage woman did not violate the equal protection clause); People v. Liberta, 474 N.E.2d 567 (N.Y. 1984) (statute that prohibited only forcible rape of women by men violated the equal protection clause; conviction could stand as court extended coverage to rape of men by women). Because such legislation treated women differently, often in a manner appropriate to a child, feminists urged their abolition. Ultimately these arguments succeeded; the few gender-based distinctions that remain mostly revolve around the childbearing functions of women. For example, until recently Ohio mandated the imposition of nonprison sentences involving prenatal care and drug rehabilitation for pregnant drug abusers who were willing to enter treatment.

Although gender equality has become the nominal hallmark of our criminal justice system, issues of differential treatment continue to rear their head in substantive criminal law and sentencing. Most common are charges of preferential sentencing. Traditionally, women have benefited from the paternalism and chivalry of a largely male judiciary. Women often receive lesser sentences because men believe they need protection and help.

While some of this discrimination may be due to gender stereotypes, judges may implicitly recognize the reality of the lives of many female offenders. They are dominated or abused by fathers, husbands, or boyfriends who involve them in criminal activities; their offenses are designed to benefit their families; and, perhaps most significant, their incarceration sends children into foster homes.

But prosecutors and judges do not favor all women. Rather, they distinguish between "good" and "bad" women. As crime victims the former — or their male representatives — are taken seriously; as offenders the former group appear to receive substantially lower sentences than men convicted of the same offenses. The criminal justice system, however, is often not so generous to women who violate social norms — prostitutes, for example, or women who assault and kill their children or mates — by engaging in behavior that is considered "unnatural." Minority and poor women also tend to be included among those who receive harsher sentences.

Whether anecdotal evidence of differential treatment amounts to gender-based discrimination is more difficult to determine. The number of women committing crimes (especially violent crimes) is small. Possible sentencing discrimination remains hidden behind a process that makes it difficult to determine whether similar offenders receive similar sentences. Consider the following case, in which the defendant challenged a blatantly gender-based policy.

‖ *Virginia Salaiscooper v. Eighth Judicial District* ‖
34 P.3d 509 (Nev. 2001)

PER CURIAM

Petitioner Virginia Anchond Salaiscooper contends that, in prosecuting her for solicitation of prostitution, Clark County District Attorney Stewart Bell is engaging in impermissible unconstitutional selective prosecution that violates her right to equal protection under the law. More specifically, Salaiscooper contends that the district attorney intended to discriminate against females by implementing a policy that prohibited his deputies from entering into plea negotiations with female defendants charged with solicitation of prostitution, thereby foreclosing any possibility that they could attend a diversion class in order to avoid solicitation convictions. . . .

The policy at issue was summarized in a December 1999 memo from Clark County District Attorney Stewart Bell to his deputies. The memo provided:

> In light of some changes in policy at the Las Vegas Metropolitan Police Department with regard to work card licensing for exotic dancers charged with prostitution, it has been agreed . . . that (*except in cases of first time male offenders*

who opt for the diversion program) we will not negotiate the nature of cases of soliciting prostitution, nor will we agree that they may be in the future dismissed for any reason.

The policy was implemented due to the American Civil Liberties Union's (ACLU) objection to the fact that the Las Vegas Metropolitan Police Department (Metro) was revoking adult entertainment industry employees' work cards based merely on an arrest for solicitation of prostitution. The ACLU contended that revoking a work card needed to work in the entertainment industry without an underlying conviction violated due process. In response to the ACLU's objection, the district attorney implemented a no-plea-bargain policy that prohibited his deputies from entering into a plea agreement with a defendant charged with solicitation of prostitution allowing a plea to a lesser charge. The plain language of the policy prohibiting plea bargains excepted first time male defendants.

Because the justice court was concerned with the gender-specific language used in the policy, it ordered an evidentiary hearing where both sides could present evidence to support or refute a specific finding of discriminatory purpose. . . .

The State called . . . Dr. Roxanne Clark Murphy, a clinical psychologist and the Program Coordinator for the First Offender Program for Men in Las Vegas. Murphy testified that she developed the First Offender Program in collaboration with Metro and that it boasted an extremely low recidivism rate of less than one percent. Murphy explained that the diversionary program was designed for buyers of sex that are statistically almost always male. Murphy also described the requisite for entrance into the program was that a defendant must be a first-time offender charged with soliciting a prostitute.

Murphy testified that the vast majority of sellers of sex are females. Murphy also stated that it would take a minimum of a year to successfully rehabilitate a seller of sex. Murphy explained that, in order for a diversion program to be an effective deterrent, it would need to be a residential program that would protect women from their pimps, teach them job skills, and provide substance abuse and psychological counseling. Murphy further explained that more effort is required to rehabilitate and deter sex sellers than buyers because many prostitutes have been sexually abused, selling sex since the age of 13 to 14, disassociated from their actions through the use of drugs and alcohol, and/or controlled by a violent pimp or procurer. . . .

Judge Togliatti issued a lengthy order stating that the Las Vegas Justice Court had unanimously found that the policy did not discriminate on the basis of gender and that its distinction based on buyers of sex and sellers of sex was constitutionally permissible. In so finding, Judge Togliatti qualified this conclusion by stating that the judges were relying on the district attorney's representations that his policy applied to all sellers of sex regardless of gender, and consequently ordered Mr. Bell to clarify this fact in writing to his deputies within ten days.

In response to the court's order, Mr. Bell filed a clarification of policy in the justice court, affirming that he had distributed a memo clarifying that the First Offender Program for Men was available only to buyers of sex regardless of whether they were male or female. Accordingly, under the clarified policy, if a female buyer of sex was charged with solicitation of prostitution, she, like a male buyer of sex, would have the option of attending the First Offender Program, thereby avoiding a solicitation conviction. . . .

Salaiscooper argues that, in enacting the policy, the district attorney engaged in impermissible and unconstitutional selective prosecution that violated her right to equal protection under the law. Specifically, Salaiscooper argues that the policy's distinction between buyers and sellers of sex is "nothing more than a facade" concealing "conscious, intentional discrimination" against women, and thereby violates the Equal Protection Clauses of the United States and Nevada Constitutions. We conclude that Salaiscooper's argument lacks merit.

The government's decision to deny an arrestee admission into a diversion program is a decision to prosecute and [on review is treated] as a claim of selective prosecution. A defendant alleging unconstitutional selective prosecution has an onerous burden. Indeed, a district attorney is vested with immense discretion in deciding whether to prosecute a particular defendant that "necessarily involves a degree of selectivity." In exercising this discretion, the district attorney is clothed with the presumption that he acted in good faith and properly discharged his duty to enforce the laws. Although the district attorney's prosecutorial discretion is broad, it is not without limitation. The Equal Protection Clause constrains the district attorney from basing a decision to prosecute upon an unjustifiable classification, such as race, religion or gender.

The requisite analysis for a claim of unconstitutional selective prosecution is two-fold. First, the defendant has the burden to prove a prima facie case of discriminatory prosecution. To establish a prima facie case, the defendant must show that a public officer enforced a law or policy in a manner that had a discriminatory effect, and that such enforcement was motivated by a discriminatory purpose. A discriminatory effect is proven where a defendant shows that other persons similarly situated "are generally not prosecuted for the same conduct." A discriminatory purpose or "evil eye" is established where a defendant shows that a public administrator chose a particular course of action, at least in part, because of its adverse effects upon a particular group. If a defendant proves a prima facie case, the burden then shifts to the State to establish that there was a reasonable basis to justify the unequal classification. Where the classification is based on gender, the court applies an intermediate standard of scrutiny; in other words, the court must conclude the unequal classification in the policy is "reasonable, not arbitrary, and [rests] upon some ground of difference having a fair and substantial relation to the object of the legislation."

In the instant case, the justice court found that the district attorney had a valid, gender-neutral motivation for creating the policy classification — to draw a distinction between buyers and sellers of sex in order to deter acts of prostitution. More specifically, the justice court found that it was reasonable for the district attorney to prohibit sellers of sex from attending the one-day diversion program because it would have no deterrent effect. The justice court opined that the classification was therefore necessary because buyers of sex should not be precluded from participating in a successful diversion program merely because such treatment would be ineffective in rehabilitating the sellers. Finally, the justice court found that there was "nothing sinister" about the district attorney's primary goal of obtaining solicitation of prostitution convictions against sellers of sex so that he could revoke their work cards and, ultimately, stop prostitutes from working in the adult entertainment industry.

The lower court's findings with respect to the district attorney's motivation and intent underlying the policy are findings of fact to be given deference, and they should not be reversed if supported by substantial evidence. The district court correctly concluded that there is substantial evidence in support of the justice court's factual findings. In particular, Dr. Murphy testified that the diversion class would not be an effective deterrent for sex sellers because they would need a one-year rehabilitation program in light of the deeply-entrenched culture of drug abuse, psychological abuse, and violence associated with prostitution. Moreover, [there was testimony] that the district attorney needed solicitation convictions against sellers of sex so that Metro could revoke their work cards and eradicate prostitution from the strip clubs. Because the State presented evidence that the purpose of the policy's buyer/seller distinction was to deter acts of prostitution, the justice court's findings that the policy did not run afoul of the Equal Protection Clause is supported by substantial evidence.

Other jurisdictions have reached an analogous conclusion, holding that it is constitutionally permissible to treat prostitutes differently than the customers who patronize them. In People v. Superior Court of Alameda County, 562 P.2d 1315, 1320 (Cal. 1977), the Supreme Court of California, sitting en banc, held that it was permissible for law enforcement officials to target sellers of sex, because the "sexually unbiased policy of concentrating its enforcement effort on the profiteer" was not initiated by an intent to discriminate. The court reasoned that the policy was created because of the belief that focusing criminal prosecution on the sellers of sex had the most deterrent effect: "Prostitutes, the municipal court found, average five customers per night; the average customer does not patronize prostitutes five times a year. Because of an effective grapevine, arrest of one prostitute by an undercover officer will deter others, at least for a time."

Like the law enforcement officials in *Alameda*, [the] State presented evidence in support of its belief that a one-day class would not stop a prostitute from selling sex. . . . In light of our conclusion that the policy does not violate the Equal Protection Clauses of the United States and Nevada Constitutions, we conclude that extraordinary relief is not warranted in this matter. The legislature has vested the district attorney with prosecutorial discretion, and we conclude it is within the purview of the district attorney's prosecution powers to treat buyers of sex differently than sellers of sex. After all, the decision to prosecute, including the offer of a plea bargain, is a complex decision involving multiple considerations, including prior criminal history, the gravity of the offense, the need to punish, the possibility of rehabilitation, and the goal to deter future crime. Unless a defendant can prove that a district attorney's decision to prosecute arose from an impermissible desire to discriminate on the basis of race, gender or other protected class, our federal and state constitutions do not compel our intervention. Because there is no evidence of a discriminatory motive in the case before us, we deny Salaiscooper's petition.

PROBLEM 9-6.   SENTENCING AND MOTHERHOOD

Amrhu Dyce, an immigrant in her twenties, pled guilty in federal court to conspiracy to commit possession with intent to distribute crack cocaine. She had carried drugs from New York City to North Carolina, largely to increase her limited household budget. Under the federal sentencing guidelines, Dyce faced an imprisonment range of 121 to 151 months. At sentencing she argued for a substantial downward departure based on her "extraordinary" family responsibilities, claiming that her case fell outside the heartland of cases for which the U.S. Sentencing Commission had declared family responsibilities "not ordinarily relevant." At the time of the sentencing hearing, Dyce had three small children. She breastfed the youngest, a newborn (a practice the U.S. government recommends at least for the first year of a baby's life while the World Health Organization suggests two years). The other two children were one and three years old. Dyce's boyfriend, the father of her children, was not involved in her criminal activities but seemed incapable of raising one, let alone all three, of his children. Dyce's mother and sister, who live in England, were willing and able to take in only the middle child.

Because of the father's inability to bring up two children, the youngest and the eldest may have to be placed in foster care should Dyce be sentenced to prison. Should the court consider her family circumstances extraordinary so as to allow for a nonprison sentence? Should it matter whether residential treatment facilities are available that would allow Dyce to live in a restrictive environment but keep at least the infant, and possibly even the other two children, with her? May the court consider the separation of the family and the impossibility of visitation should one of the children be removed from the United States? See United States v. Amrhu Dyce, 91 F.3d 1462 (D.C. Cir. 1996).

NOTES

1. *Backfiring.* Much feminist criticism of law enforcement has centered on gender-specific offenses such as prostitution, domestic violence, and rape. Substantive law and enforcement practices have changed in all three, but the impact of the changes is often imperceptible or ambiguous.

Consider prostitution. As *Salaiscooper* indicates, much of the enforcement of gender-neutral statutes still centers on the providers of the service — largely women. What justifies this enforcement focus? Who is in the best position to ascertain the information to make this decision?

Imagine a reverse world in which legislation criminalizes only the purchasing of sexual services. What could justify the sole prosecution and sentencing of the largely male customers? Prostitution is frequently deemed particularly harmful to the female providers, many of whom were abused as children, are drug addicts, suffer from low self-esteem, and do not view themselves as having other employment options. Would such legislation, if adopted in a U.S. jurisdiction, run afoul of the equal protection clause? See Vermont v. George, 602 A.2d 953 (Vt. 1991). What effect do you expect such a change in enforcement practice to have on the supply of and demand for prostitution services? Sweden has adopted this model, but there have been few prosecutions of male customers.

2. *Criminal law defenses and sentencing.* Feminists have charged that substantive criminal law, and especially the area of criminal defenses, focuses on men. This issue has been publicized most frequently with regard to abused women who kill their batterers. The women often argue that they acted in self-defense, and they frequently introduce the battered spouse syndrome to bolster their claim. Juries usually either reject the defense outright or find liability for a lesser, included offense. Once the defense has been fully or partially rejected, the lesser culpability of the defendant can be recognized merely through the sentence. See United States v. Whitetail, 956 F.2d 857 (8th Cir. 1992) (federal sentencing guidelines allow for consideration of battered spouse syndrome through downward departures).

The same situation occurs when a female defendant raises a duress defense. The defendant's emotional, psychological, or sexual dependence on a male partner who abused the defendant may fail as a defense at the guilt phase, but still might allow the court to impose a lesser sentence. See United States v. Gaviria, 804 F. Supp. 476 (E.D.N.Y. 1992).

3. *More female offenders?* The number of women in state and federal prison rose by 757% between 1977 and 2004. Women's Prison Association, The Punitiveness Report — Hard Hit: The Growth in Imprisonment of Women, 1977-2004 (2005) (available at http://www.wpaonline.org/institute/hardhit/index.htm). During this period the number of women imprisoned increased at almost twice the male rate. Drug offenses accounted for almost half of the rise in women's incarceration, and federal prisons outpaced state facilities in the growth of female admissions. African American and, to a lesser extent, Hispanic women bore the brunt of this development.

What explains the explosion in female imprisonment? Some blame a change in enforcement strategies; some point to enforcement and sentencing practices, stemming largely from the war on drugs, that no longer discriminate in favor of women; some see a rise of women in the drug underworld, paralleling their rise in the legitimate business world; some blame the feminization of poverty. See Phyllis Goldfarb, Counting the Drug War's Female Casualties, 6 J. Gender, Race & Just. 277 (2002).

Despite the increase in female convicts, the gender differences in incarceration rates remain striking. At year-end 2001, about 1,313,000 men (1 in 112) were incarcerated in state and federal prisons, but only about 93,000 women (1 in 1,724) were incarcerated. Why are so few women imprisoned, comparatively speaking? Victimization studies indicate that men commit more offenses, especially more violent crimes. In 1996 women accounted for 16% of all felons convicted in state courts: They made up almost one-quarter of property offenders but less than one-tenth of violent criminals. However, the number of women who commit violent crimes has been rising steadily, especially among adolescents. Of female offenders about one-third are serving time for a drug offense. Even if these numbers underestimate female offending somewhat, they raise the issue of whether biological differences or socialization, or both, explain why men are more violent and more likely to engage in crime generally.

4. *Women are different.* In contrast to people of different races, men and women truly differ. Some of these differences are clearly biological; others may or may not be. To what extent should the criminal justice system consider a

woman's ability to bear children? There is an international consensus that pregnant women should not be executed, but beyond that, criminal justice systems differ on whether and to what extent biological differences should be considered.

In imposing a 20-year prison sentence on a 25-year-old woman and a 25-year-old man, should a court consider that this makes it virtually impossible for the woman to bear a child (putting aside expensive modern reproductive technologies) but not for the man to father a child? Cf. Gerber v. Hickman, 291 F.3d 617, 623 (9th Cir. 2002) ("[T]he right to procreate while in prison is fundamentally inconsistent with incarceration."); Goodwin v. Turner, 908 F.2d 1395, 1396 (8th Cir. 1990) (Bureau of Prisons' restriction on allowing inmate to ejaculate into a clean container so that his semen could be used to artificially inseminate his wife "is reasonably related to legitimate penological interest of treating all prisoners equally"). As of December 2002, the British Home Office had granted six inmates the right to father a child through artificial insemination. The prisoners most likely to benefit are those with long prison sentences, whose spouses would likely be too old to conceive a child upon their release. The policy extends also to female inmates, but none have requested artificial insemination yet.

Concerned that women will become pregnant to avoid incarcerative sentences, courts have declined to consider pregnancy, childbirth, and the presence of a young child as mitigating sentencing factors. If courts should not and cannot consider such biological differences in their sentencing, is there a societal responsibility to create institutional facilities that would allow female offenders to keep their children with them?

5. *Pregnancy and drugs.* In 19 states and the District of Columbia, pregnant women have been prosecuted for substance abuse. Some prosecutors have argued that the small amount of drugs that travels from the mother to the child either during the pregnancy or through the umbilical cord at birth constitutes drug trafficking — and a more severe form at that, since the drugs are delivered to a minor. In South Carolina, Charleston prosecutors filed child neglect charges against women who had just given birth in a state hospital. The U.S. Supreme Court struck down this policy because the hospital's practice of collecting urine samples, without the patient's consent, to obtain evidence of the patient's criminal conduct constituted an unreasonable search. It reached this result even though the state's interest in deterring pregnant women from using cocaine is high. See Ferguson v. City of Charleston, 532 U.S. 67 (2001). Particularly disturbing is the fact that the vast majority of such drug prosecutions are aimed at poor African American women, generally because they frequent public hospitals and because of the allegedly more destructive impact of crack on a fetus.

6. *Gender equality redux.* Gender equality is writ large in the legal system. Does it make sense if there is no such equality in the larger society? While many male inmates are also fathers, data on state prisoners indicate that 90% of fathers who were incarcerated had wives who cared for their children. For female offenders, less than one-quarter had husbands who cared for their children. Because of changes in foster care and adoption laws, a likely consequence of long-term imprisonment for single parents who cannot find another caregiver for their children is loss of parental rights. While differences in caregiving may not be solely biological, should a court consider them? Such consideration would also

benefit men who are not able to find stable caregiving arrangements for their minor children during imprisonment. Alternatively, should the large numbers of single parents in the criminal justice system (and society at large) counsel against consideration of single-parent status at sentencing?

Federal courts that consider family circumstance in their departure jurisprudence frequently note the defendant's financial contribution to the family. Women who do not appear to be gainfully employed, even if they are the sole caregiver for minor children, are thus at a disadvantage. Does such an approach not privilege one type of parenting over another? May it not also discriminate against minority groups in which the mother is expected to stay at home with her children?

7. *The numbers disadvantage in imprisonment.*   Because there are substantially fewer prisons for women than for men, often the conditions of incarceration differ by gender. In the federal system especially, the small number of female offenders and the location of women's prisons often necessitate incarceration far from family and friends. This is particularly difficult for women with young children and women whose families cannot afford lengthy trips, for financial or other reasons. Should courts consider such well-known facts in deciding whether to impose a prison sentence?

Female prisons also offer different conditions than all-male institutions. Many have fewer or different educational programs, and most have only limited employment options. This may further disadvantage women who entered the system with educational and vocational deficits. Nevertheless, courts have not found equal protection violations based on different prison conditions. See Klinger v. Department of Corrections, 31 F.3d 727, 731 (8th Cir. 1994) (substantial differences between men's and women's prisons did not constitute an equal protection violation because male and female prisoners "were not similarly situated for purposes of prison programs and services"). At the same time, women often enjoy better prison facilities and more privacy than men. In those cases, courts, relying on *Klinger,* have also found no constitutional violations. See Oliver v. Scott, 276 F.3d 736 (5th Cir. 2002).

8. *Female recidivism and risk-based sentencing.*   Women commit fewer violent offenses and have lower recidivism rates than men. If the risk of future offending were the focus of sentencing, most women would receive lesser sentences than most men for a similar offense. Does risk-based sentencing violate the equal protection clause? Without risk-based sentencing, doesn't equal treatment put women at a disadvantage?

9. *Women as crime victims.*   Men are disproportionately the victims of crime. While this finding may contradict public perception, it holds true for most offenses. Women make up the majority of domestic violence and rape victims, however — both destructive, usually violent offenses that are vastly underreported. Normatively, the victimization of women is considered substantially more heinous than that of men. Why?

Women are often the targets of crime because offenders consider them more vulnerable. Imagine, for example, a young man choosing a robbery victim: The 5′2″, 90-pound woman is a more attractive target than most men, possibly barring Woody Allen. Should offenders who pick vulnerable female targets be subject to sentence enhancements? Or is a new substantive criminal law provision more appropriate? Consider one proposed definition for hate crime: "a crime in which the defendant intentionally selects a victim, or in the case of a property crime, the property that is the object of the crime, because of the actual or perceived . . . gender . . . of any person."

PROBLEM 9-7.   SAUCE FOR THE GANDER

Gilberto Redondo-Lemos was charged in Arizona federal court for acting as a drug courier. He alleged that prosecutors in the U.S. Attorney's office violated his right to equal protection by offering more favorable plea bargains to female couriers.

The district court held an evidentiary hearing. At the hearing, the assistant U.S. Attorney (AUSA) handling the Redondo-Lemos prosecution said that she offered, in exchange for a guilty plea, to recommend the lowest sentence allowed by the federal sentencing guidelines and the mandatory minimum. She testified that she assessed the strength of her case, followed the factors set out in departmental memos dealing with plea bargains generally, was not motivated by defendant's gender, and knew of no office policy of plea bargaining on the basis of gender.

Another AUSA's testimony concerned a case against a couple where the evidence was actually stronger against the woman. The AUSA nonetheless agreed to let the husband plead guilty to a lesser charge in exchange for allowing the wife to go free and take care of their three children. The AUSA noted that, after 25 years of experience, he'd observed that it was "usually the Mexican men that will stand up and take responsibility," and he'd come to expect it. The AUSA noted that when couples are faced with a choice, they usually select the woman to care for the children and that allowing this choice reflects no government policy of gender discrimination. The government argued that it was the private party, not the government, who made the decision and "discriminated." The government simply practiced compassion when it allowed parents to decide which parent would be the better caregiver for children who otherwise would be effectively orphaned.

In ten additional cases that concerned the district judge, the responsible AUSAs testified that they based their plea bargaining decisions on the strength of the evidence, the legality of the stops and searches, the defendant's cooperation, the level of the defendant's involvement, and special circumstances of particular defendants. In one case, the AUSA allowed a woman who was overdue in her pregnancy to plead guilty to a misdemeanor. Because the Marshal's Service indicated it couldn't give her proper medical care, she was sentenced to time served, while her male partner, who had a record, pleaded guilty and was sentenced to 90 months in prison. The AUSA explained that she would have responded the same way had the Marshal's Service expressed concern about medical care for a male defendant.

The court considered two sets of statistics to show intentional discrimination in plea bargaining with male "mules" in the District of Arizona. Statistics from the local probation office showed that male drug offenders in the District of Arizona were sentenced to an average of 36 months compared to 32 months for females and that only 11% of all males received probation compared with 35% of females. A U.S. Sentencing Commission report showed that nationwide, 61.5% of men who committed crimes subject to mandatory minimum sentences received them, while only 50% of women did.

The district court rejected the explanations by the AUSAs as "mere general assertions that the AUSAs did not discriminate." In the case of the couple, the court found the discriminatory plea to be unjustified. Based on that case and the two sets of statistics, the district court found intentional invidious discrimination and sentenced Redondo-Lemos below the statutory minimums for the offenses of which he was convicted.

Suppose the government appeals the finding of invidious discrimination and the remedy of ordering sentences below the statutory minimum. How should the appellate court rule? See United States v. Redondo-Lemos, 27 F.3d 439 (9th Cir. 1994).

NOTES

1. *Male claims of bias.*   A striking feature of gender bias claims is that they are often raised by men rather than women. Why? Claims of gender bias face the problems of definition and proof confronted by Warren McCleskey and others making claims of bias based on race and other factors.

2. *The centrality of plea bargaining.*   Defendants who plea bargain face two obstacles in challenging bias in their prosecution and sentence. First, by plea bargaining they may have waived some right to challenge any bias in treatment and sentence; second, bias challenges to charges and pleas are almost always based on claims of systematic rather than individual bias. Are the doctrines of equality able to make the leap from individual to collective treatment, from individual bias to disparate outcome, which may or may not be based on biased judgments and rules by the decision maker whose actions are challenged?

3. *Information on sentencing disparities.*   Does the focus on legally compelling claims of bias obscure important policy issues with respect to equal treatment? How should policymakers, scholars, or judges concerned with issues of bias in sentencing or the criminal justice system address or illuminate those issues?

=10=

Alternatives to Criminal Sentences

Criminal punishments presuppose a criminal conviction, and the collateral consequences discussed in Chapter 8 occur only after a criminal conviction. But there are alternatives to criminal punishment that create many of the effects of a criminal sanction without a criminal conviction being entered. As you read about the alternative sanctions surveyed in this chapter, ask yourself whether they differ in meaningful ways from true criminal sanctions. When might the lack of a criminal conviction make it improper or difficult to impose some of these alternatives?

A. DIVERSION PROGRAMS

Diversion threatens an offender but does not use the criminal process. Its goal is to protect the offender from the sanctions and stigma arising from a criminal conviction while preserving criminal justice resources. Precharge diversion has always been an element of prosecutorial discretion. Diversion programs started with juvenile cases and expanded to include adult drug offenses in the 1960s; more formalized programs exist today in the state and federal systems.

Diversion programs can take several forms, attaching at different points in the criminal process. Pre-arrest diversion allows the police or the prosecutors to divert offenders at the earliest stage, without ever starting the criminal process. Its informality may open the process to possible abuse and prevent structured oversight of the offender's subsequent actions. But it spares the offender the stigma of an arrest record.

Pre-arraignment diversion directs individual offenders out of the system after their arrest but prior to the formal filing of charges. This process ensures prosecutorial control over the diversion process and allows for more screening to remove unsuitable offenders from the program. In this way it saves the criminal justice system the costs of prosecution without saddling the offender with a criminal record.

Diversion may occur at later stages in the process, after formal charges have been filed but before a judgment has been rendered. Pretrial diversion, for example, allows charges to be dismissed after a defendant has successfully fulfilled the conditions the prosecutor imposed. In some cases defendants may plead guilty conditionally with the understanding that the judge will vacate the plea after the offender has met all of the required conditions.

Prosecutors and judges use diversion programs especially often in drug cases. Minor, nonviolent drug users in particular benefit from programs that move them into drug treatment. Diversion can be used for defendants ranging from juveniles to corporations. A corporation might escape potentially damaging publicity in exchange for monetary payment. The juvenile might perform community service or pay a fine. Among the more imaginative diversion programs are those using offender-victim mediation.

The prosecutor typically controls access to these diversion programs (also known as "deferred prosecution" programs). But given their functional similarity to criminal sentences, should judges also have a role in selecting who gets diverted and what conditions the defendant must meet?

|| *State v. Carolyn Curry* ||
|| **988 S.W.2d 153 (Tenn. 1999)** ||

ANDERSON, C.J.

... The defendant, Carolyn C. Curry, worked as an assistant clerk for the City of McKenzie, Tennessee, from 1985 to 1995. Over a two-year period from July of 1993 to July of 1995, Curry embezzled over $27,000 from the City. She later was indicted for theft of property valued between $10,000 and $60,000.

Curry applied for pretrial diversion. According to her application, she was a divorced, 34-year-old mother of three children, ages 19, 13, and 8. Curry had graduated from college with honors in 1983, and she served in the Tennessee National Guard from 1983 to 1990, when she was honorably discharged. She was an active member of her church and numerous charitable and community organizations including the United Way, United Neighbors, Concerned Citizens, and youth softball. Numerous letters included with her application attested to her charitable and community involvement. Curry had no prior arrests or convictions. She cooperated with authorities in this case when her actions were discovered, admitting that she took money for family and living expenses and proposing a restitution program. She stated that: "I sincerely regret my actions and regret the shame that my actions have brought to bear on myself and my family."

In denying the application for pretrial diversion, the prosecutor, in a written response, gave the following reasons:

... We have carefully reviewed the application and the attached letters. ... We have considered the defendant's past history and her conduct for two years in defrauding the City of McKenzie. This was a calculated criminal scheme that took planning and thought. It manifests a criminal intent for a long period of time and not something that happened at once. We cannot believe that it would be in the best interests of the public, the defendant, and justice to overlook a criminal scheme of this proportion and grant pre-trial diversion. ...

Curry sought review of the prosecutor's decision by filing a petition for writ of certiorari in the trial court. After hearing argument of counsel, the trial court found that diversion had been denied solely based upon the circumstances of the offense, specifically, the two-year duration, and ruled [that the district attorney's office had "abused its discretion in denying pretrial diversion" and that Curry should be placed on pretrial diversion].

The pretrial diversion program, drafted and enacted by the Legislature, allows the District Attorney General to suspend a prosecution against a qualified defendant for a period of up to two years. Tenn. Code Ann. §40-15-105(a)(1)(A). A qualified defendant pursuant to the statute is one who has not previously been granted diversion and does not have a prior misdemeanor conviction for which confinement was served or a prior felony conviction within a five year period after completing the sentence or probationary period for the conviction. The offense for which diversion is sought may *not* be a class A felony, a class B felony, a sexual offense, driving under the influence, or vehicular assault. Tenn. Code Ann. §40-15-105(a)(1)(B)(i)(c).

Any grant of diversion must be conditioned on one or more of the following conditions: that the defendant not commit any criminal offense; that the defendant refrain from activities, conduct, or associations related to the charge; that the defendant receive rehabilitative treatment, counseling, and education; that the defendant make restitution to the victim; that the defendant pay court costs and the costs of the diversion; and that the defendant abide by any other terms or conditions as may be agreed upon. Tenn. Code Ann. §40-15-105(a)(2)(A)-(H). If the defendant violates a term or condition, the prosecution may terminate diversion and resume the criminal prosecution.

One who is statutorily eligible is not presumptively entitled to diversion. Instead, whether to grant pretrial diversion to a qualified defendant who is statutorily eligible is a determination that lies in the discretion of the district attorney general. The relevant considerations for the prosecutor are as follows:

When deciding whether to enter into a memorandum of understanding under the pretrial diversion statute a prosecutor should focus on the defendant's amenability to correction. Any factors which tend to accurately reflect whether a particular defendant will or will not become a repeat offender should be considered. ... Among the factors to be considered in addition to the circumstances of the offense are the defendant's criminal record, social history, the physical and mental condition of a defendant where appropriate, and the likelihood that pretrial diversion will serve the ends of justice and the best interest of both the public and the defendant.

State v. Pinkham, 955 S.W.2d 956, 959-960 (Tenn. 1997).

736 Chapter 10. Alternatives to Criminal Sentences

If the district attorney general denies pretrial diversion, the denial must be in writing and must include an enumeration of the evidence that was considered and a discussion of the factors considered and weight accorded each. This requirement entails more than an abstract statement in the record that the district attorney general has considered these factors. Instead, the factors considered must be clearly articulable and stated in the record. . . .

The prosecutor's response must be in writing. [The written statement compels] the prosecutor to think about and justify his denial in terms of the applicable standards. [The] statement of reasons [also restricts] the prosecutor to a particular rationale and insure[s] that the prosecutor would offer no new reasons at the evidentiary hearing. The prosecutor's written response must also identify any factual disputes between the evidence relied upon and the application filed by the defendant.

If the application for pretrial diversion is denied, the defendant may appeal by petitioning the trial court for a writ of certiorari. Tenn. Code Ann. §40-15-105(b)(3). The only evidence that may be considered by the trial court is the evidence that was considered by the district attorney general. The trial court may conduct a hearing only to resolve any factual disputes raised by the prosecutor or the defendant concerning the application, but not to hear additional evidence that was not considered by the prosecutor. The action of the prosecutor is presumptively correct, and it is subject to review by the trial court only for an abuse of discretion.

[In this case,] the prosecutor's primary consideration in the written denial of diversion was the circumstances of the offense, specifically, the amount of money taken and the duration of the criminal activity. The denial letter stated that diversion was not "in the best interest of the public," which, although imprecise, arguably includes deterrence. Although the prosecutor asserts that he had "carefully reviewed the application and the attached letters," the denial does not discuss the defendant's favorable social history, lack of a criminal record, and potential for rehabilitation. Moreover, assuming these essential factors were, in fact, considered, there is no explanation as to how much weight they were afforded and no rationale as to why they were outweighed by the other factors in denying diversion.

The State argues, and the dissent writes, that the seriousness of the offense itself may justify a denial of diversion. A review of the case law reveals, however, that the circumstances of the offense and the need for deterrence may alone justify a denial of diversion, *but only if all of the relevant factors have been considered as well.* See State v. Washington, 866 S.W.2d 950, 951 (Tenn. 1993) ("circumstances of the case and the need for deterrence may be considered as two of the many factors, [but] they cannot be given controlling weight unless they are of such overwhelming significance that they . . . outweigh all other factors"). The facts and circumstances of nearly all criminal offenses are by definition serious; only by analyzing all of the relevant factors, including those favorable to the defendant, can appropriate candidates for this legislative largess be identified in a manner consistent with the purpose of the pretrial diversion act.

In *Pinkham,* for instance, the defendant was charged with falsely representing himself as a lawyer, impersonating a licensed professional, and aggravated perjury. The denial of diversion emphasized the circumstances of the offense, the losses sustained by the victim, and the "systematic and continuing criminal activity," but also gave extensive consideration to the other relevant factors:

> In making this decision to reject the defendant's diversion application, I have considered that [the defendant] is a 50 year old man with no criminal record. I have considered his exemplary social history. I have considered that [the defendant] appears to be a leader in his community, as evidenced by the character and reference letters from lawyers, teachers, professors, ministers, doctors, et al. I have considered all of the parameters of [the defendant's] social, family, personal, educational and professional background. . . . Since [the defendant] is a highly educated person who holds a law degree, [the defendant] knew that his conduct was unlawful and unethical. . . .

955 S.W.2d at 959.

In contrast, the defendant in State v. Herron, 767 S.W.2d 151, 155 (Tenn. 1989), a 24-year-old woman with no prior criminal record, was charged with two counts of larceny by trick, one offense involving $5000 and the other involving $6000. The prosecutor's denial of pretrial diversion was based primarily on the circumstances of the "contrived, deliberate" offenses and the need to deter such offenses. Although the trial court denied the defendant's petition for certiorari, [this court held that] both the prosecutor and the trial court failed to consider "that defendant did not have any criminal record, her social history, her physical and mental condition, including her educational background, her employment history as well as the stability and continued support of her family."

[The] dissent strains to conclude that the evidence regarding the defendant's background was unfavorable and that her potential for rehabilitation was minimal simply by looking only to the circumstances and time span of the offense. Under such an analysis, in which the facts and circumstances are given conclusive weight against a defendant's potential for correction, rare is the defendant who would qualify for pretrial diversion. . . .

HOLDER, J., dissenting.

. . . Pretrial diversion is a legislative largess as well as extraordinary relief. Pretrial diversion relieves criminal defendants of the burden of being tried for or convicted of a crime for which they are guilty. Once defendants have completed a diversion program, they are under no legal obligation to disclose their offenses to prospective employers, and their public records are expunged. Mere eligibility for diversion should not provide a presumption for program suitability.[1] Defendants, therefore, should at all times carry the burden of establishing suitability given the extraordinary nature of diversionary relief. . . .

The pretrial diversion statute does not enumerate specific criteria that a prosecuting attorney should use when making pretrial diversion determinations. The legislature apparently recognized the extraordinary relief provided by the pretrial diversion statute and intended to provide prosecuting attorneys substantial discretion in making pretrial diversion decisions. This grant of discretion would presumptively include the broad discretion to determine not only

---

1. Pursuant to Tenn. Code Ann. §40-15-105, defendants committing extremely serious offenses such as aggravated assault, voluntary manslaughter, vehicular homicide (not involving intoxication), kidnapping, robbery, arson, and aggravated burglary may be eligible for pretrial diversion.

the relevant criteria and considerations of each case but also the weight to be afforded the relevant considerations of each diversionary decision. Courts, however, have judicially imposed general considerations to guide a prosecuting attorney's decision.

. . . In the case now before us, the prosecuting attorney set out the following reasons in support of the pretrial diversion denial: (1) the long-term and continuing nature of the offense; (2) the fact that the circumstances of the offense reveal a systematic scheme to commit crimes which "manifest a criminal intent for a long period of time" and not a crime of impulse; (3) the magnitude of the offense, noting the amount of money ($27,368.73) embezzled during a period from July 1, 1993 to July 11, 1995; (4) the deceitful nature of the criminal violations; and (5) the deterrent effect of crimes to defraud city or municipal organizations ("[w]e cannot believe that it would be in the best interests of the public, the defendant and justice to overlook a criminal scheme of this proportion and grant pre-trial diversion to the defendant").

The reasons cited by the prosecutor are well-supported by the record and have been held sufficient for denials of pretrial diversion in numerous published opinions involving similar crimes and crimes of a less serious nature. . . . In State v. Carr, 861 S.W.2d 850, 854 (Tenn. App. 1993), the defendant's crimes were very similar to the crimes in the case now before us. Pretrial diversion was denied based on the following factors:

(1) The circumstances show "a systematic scheme to defraud . . . not a crime of impulse," involving considerable planning which would have continued absent discovery.

(2) The magnitude of the offense, noting the amount of money ($23,370.85). . . .

(3) The number of individual claims and continuing nature of the offense.

(4) The particular need for deterrence because of the considerable opportunity for Medicaid fraud, which is serious and prevalent.

(5) The defendant's statements indicate little remorse and failure to accept responsibility.

The appellate court stated that . . . in a close case, the courts should defer to the prosecutor's decision. The appellate court held that substantial evidence in the record supported the denial based on the circumstances of the crime and the need for deterrence. . . .

In the case now before us, I believe that the record is replete with substantial evidence supporting the district attorney's reasons for denying pre-trial diversion. . . . I would hold that the district attorney's letter denying diversion more than adequately addressed the criteria set forth in *Pinkham,* even though the letter could have been more detailed. . . . The circumstances of the defendant's offense and the need to deter fraud as well as thefts of large sums of money are sufficiently overwhelming to justify denial of pretrial diversion in this case. . . .

I disagree with the majority's finding that the defendant has a "favorable" social history and background. I believe that someone who continually commits serious crimes involving deception, planning, and fraud over a two-year period of time has a less than favorable social history, has an extensive criminal background, and is a poor candidate for rehabilitation. Moreover, the defendant ceased her criminal activity only when she was caught, and her criminal activity would likely have continued had she not been caught.

I disagree with the majority's decision that an abuse of discretion occurred merely due to a district attorney's failure to specifically or explicitly address non-statutory criteria. . . . The majority's holding could effectively allow defendants committing serious offenses such as manslaughter, kidnapping, and vehicular homicide to avoid prosecution merely because a district attorney commits a non-prejudicial omission affecting neither a constitutional nor a statutory right.

U.S. Attorneys' Manual, Pretrial Diversion Program
U.S. Department of Justice

9-22.100 ELIGIBILITY CRITERIA

The U.S. Attorney, in his/her discretion, may divert any individual against whom a prosecutable case exists and who is not:

1. Accused of an offense which, under existing Department guidelines, should be diverted to the State for prosecution;
2. A person with two or more prior felony convictions;
3. An addict;
4. A public official or former public official accused of an offense arising out of an alleged violation of a public trust; or
5. Accused of an offense related to national security or foreign affairs.

Criminal Resource Manual, 715 USA
Form 186 — Pretrial Diversion Agreement
U.S. Department of Justice

. . . Upon accepting responsibility for your behavior and by your signature on this Agreement, it appearing, after an investigation of the offense, and your background, that the interest of the United States and your own interest and the interest of justice will be served by the following procedure; therefore

On the authority of the Attorney General of the United States, by _____, United States Attorney for the _____ District of _____, prosecution in this District for this offense shall be deferred for the period of _____ months from this date, provided you abide by the following conditions and the requirements of this Agreement set out below.

Should you violate the conditions of this Agreement, the United States Attorney may revoke or modify any conditions of this pretrial diversion program or change the period of supervision, which shall in no case exceed eighteen months. The United States Attorney may release you from supervision at any time. The United States Attorney may at any time within the period of your supervision initiate prosecution for this offense should you violate the conditions of this Agreement. In this case [he/she] will furnish you with notice specifying the conditions of the Agreement which you have violated.

After successfully completing your diversion program and fulfilling all the terms and conditions of the Agreement, no prosecution for the offense . . . will be instituted in this District, and the charges against you, if any, will be dismissed.

Neither this Agreement nor any other document filed with the United States Attorney as a result of your participation in the Pretrial Diversion Program will be used against you, except for impeachment purposes, in connection with any prosecution for the above-described offense.

GENERAL CONDITIONS OF PRETRIAL DIVERSION

1. You shall not violate any law (Federal/State/Local). You shall immediately contact your pretrial diversion supervisor if arrested and/or questioned by any law enforcement officer.
2. You shall attend school or work regularly at a lawful occupation or otherwise comply with the terms of the special program described below. If you lose your job or are unable to attend school, you shall notify your pretrial diversion supervisor at once. You shall consult him/her prior to job or school changes.
3. You shall report to your supervisor as directed and keep him/her informed of your whereabouts.
4. You shall follow the program and such special conditions as may be described below. . . .

I hereby state that the above has been read and explained to me. I understand the conditions of my pretrial diversion program and agree that I will comply with them.

[Defendant] _____
Defense Attorney _____
United States Attorney _____
Chief Pretrial Services Officer (or Chief Probation Officer) _____

PROBLEM 10-1.　IN NEED OF TREATMENT?

Melissa has abused legal and illegal narcotics for years. One day she asks her best friend, Claire, to pick up a package for her in a neighborhood with a reputation for drug trafficking. Melissa's husband no longer allows her to leave the house without their driver, so she has no other way of getting drugs. Claire feels uncomfortable about this errand, but she owes Melissa a major favor and agrees.

Claire picks up the package and is arrested shortly after leaving the drug house. A police officer arrests Claire with about three ounces of cocaine in her pocket and informs her of her *Miranda* rights. On her way to the station house, she overhears two police officers discuss the severe sentences that apply to drug crimes. Upon arrival there, the police begin to interrogate Claire. They tell her that she has the right to an attorney but that if she cooperates with them and admits her guilt, they might be able to keep her from "going to court." Her interrogator suggests that with a quick admission of guilt, the case would basically be over for her. Surely, he intimates, she would prefer that over seeing her name and picture in the newspaper and having a criminal record. When she mentions her children, he tells her that only her agreement to go through a diversion program would guarantee that she could keep her children. Claire also speaks quickly to a harried assistant district attorney. She then agrees to enroll in a drug treatment program and to complete it successfully in exchange for the prosecutor's agreement not to file charges against her. Is Claire an appropriate candidate for diversion? What purpose(s) would the prosecutor serve by diverting her case?

NOTES

1. *Purposes of diversion.* According to the U.S. Attorneys' Manual, the purposes of diversion are to prevent future criminal activity, to save prosecutorial and judicial resources for major cases, and to provide restitution to communities and victims. Section 712 of the Criminal Resource Manual for U.S. Attorneys states that a pretrial diversion program "should be tailored to the offender's needs and may include employment, counseling, education, job training, psychiatric care," and so forth. The provision also endorses restitution and community service and strongly encourages "innovative approaches." Which of the traditional purposes of the criminal law does this provision emphasize? How successfully were any of these accomplished in Claire's case (Problem 10-1)?

2. *Prevalence of diversion.* Diversion of arrestees is less common than the outright rejection of criminal charges. Prosecutors are most likely to offer diversion to suspects who face misdemeanor charges. About 7% of all felony arrestees in the largest urban counties in 2002 took part in diversion or "deferred adjudication" programs. Bureau of Justice Statistics, Felony Defendants in Large Urban Counties, 2002 at 24 (NCJ 210818, February 2006). Federal diversion programs are even smaller: just over 1,100 suspects were handled through pretrial diversion in 2004 (compared with more than 116,000 cases prosecuted and almost 32,000 cases declined). Why do diversion programs remain relatively rare? What resource limitations might restrict their availability? See Steven Belenko, The Challenges of Integrating Drug Treatment into the Criminal Justice Process, 63 Alb. L. Rev. 833 (2000).

Are the considerations that affect the decision to defer prosecution meaningfully different when the criminal defendant is a corporate entity? Under a 2003 Department of Justice memorandum (written after the collapse of Arthur Andersen following the accounting firm's indictment), the federal government's policy is to permit a corporate defendant to enter into a "deferred prosecution agreement." After the corporation is indicted, it agrees to pay a fine and restitution to victims, to cooperate with ongoing investigations of its officers, and to institute governance reforms that will be verified by some form of external monitoring. Between 18 months and two years later, the prosecutor will dismiss the indictment if the corporation has complied with all of these conditions. What might motivate a corporation to enter such an agreement? What variations would you expect to find among such agreements in different cases? See Lawrence D. Finder & Ryan D. McConnell, Devolution of Authority: The Department of Justice's Corporate Charging Policies, 51 St. Louis L.J. 1 (2006); John C. Coffee Jr., Deferred Prosecution: Has It Gone Too Far?, Nat'l L.J. (July 25, 2005).

3. *Prosecutors and judges as gatekeepers.*   Prosecutors retain complete control over precharge diversion programs but often share authority with judges over diversion programs that begin after charges are filed. State statutes dealing with postcharge diversion programs ordinarily empower the judge to approve the prosecutor's recommendations for offenders to enter the program. See Mont. Code Ann. §46-16-130(3) ("After a charge has been filed, a deferral of prosecution may be entered into only with the approval of the court"). Yet as the Tennessee court in *Curry* recognized, it is usually the prosecutor who decides which defendants or suspects enter a pretrial diversion program, and the court is loath to interfere with the prosecutor's decision. Indeed, courts in many states refuse to review the prosecutor's decision whether to offer diversion to a suspect unless the prosecutor relies on unconstitutional grounds, such as racial discrimination. See Cleveland v. State, 417 So. 2d 653 (Fla. 1982) (decision on pretrial intervention is prosecutorial, rather than judicial, in nature and is not subject to judicial review; review of arbitrary decisions allowed in other jurisdictions because statutes explicitly authorize review). Statutes in about a dozen states give prosecutors complete control over who may enter pretrial diversion programs.

Prosecutors' offices sometimes create uniform policies to govern eligibility for diversion, at least for some types of cases. Are the guidelines provided in the U.S. Attorneys' Manual sufficiently precise to limit prosecutorial discretion? Why does the manual exclude drug addicts from access to the diversion program?

In many Continental European countries, such as Germany, where prosecutors have traditionally not been assumed to have any discretion, diversion programs may indicate an increase in prosecutorial power. Is that also true for the United States, or do diversion programs tend to circumscribe prosecutorial discretion by allowing judicial supervision over the prosecutor's choices?

4. *Other gatekeepers.*   Pre-arrest diversion programs tend to shift the police function from law enforcement to social work without providing guidance as to which offenders are well suited to a diversion program. What role should experts such as probation officers play in the initial recommendation process? In the federal system, prosecutors are instructed to refer potential candidates for pretrial diversion to the chief pretrial services officer or the chief probation officer for the district. See Criminal Resources Manual 712D. What can the probation officer add that the prosecutor does not know or see?

Should the victim have any input in deciding whether an offender may enter a diversion program? The German Juvenile Justice Act permits prosecutors to dismiss cases after the juvenile offender has tried to reach a settlement with the victim.

Legislatures also create some preconditions for defendants or suspects to participate in pretrial diversion programs. See, e.g., S.C. Code §17-22-50 (no pretrial intervention for repeat domestic violence offenders); Utah Code §77-36-2.7 (court may not approve diversion for domestic violence defendants but may hold guilty plea in abeyance during treatment program). If the prosecutor and the suspect disagree about the statutory eligibility requirements, should a court be able to review the prosecutor's decision based on its independent interpretation of the statute?

5. *Who decides if the defendant has completed the program?* Suppose a defendant believes that she has fulfilled all the conditions of the diversion program but the prosecutor disagrees and files criminal charges. Will a court review the prosecutor's conclusion that the defendant failed to complete the program? Is there any reason to treat this question differently from the question of who will enter a diversion program? Among states with statutes addressing judicial review, the majority require some sort of court approval for a decision to remove an offender from a diversion program; others (fewer than ten) grant this decision exclusively to the prosecutor. See Fla. Stat. §948.08; State v. Hancich, 513 A.2d 638 (Conn. 1986) (once defendant was admitted to pretrial alcohol education program following her first arrest for driving under the influence, she could not be removed unless court independently determined that she had lost her eligibility or that she had failed to complete the program successfully). What circumstances might make a court more willing to judge the defendant's success or failure in the program?

6. *Admission of guilt and involvement of counsel.* The existence of a diversion program may be used to pressure individuals to waive their rights and admit guilt in order to gain entrance. How could a precharge diversion program be structured to avoid such problems? The federal system requires the involvement of a defense attorney. If a suspect or defendant cannot afford counsel, one is appointed. The Canadian statute governing diversion involving juveniles requires that the juvenile, before consenting to participate in a diversion program, be "advised of his or her right to be represented by counsel and [be] given a reasonable opportunity to consult with counsel." Youth Criminal Justice Act, Part 1, 10(2)(d) (2002, c. 1) (Can.). Why does the U.S. Attorneys' Manual mandate that counsel be involved rather than simply require that defendants be informed of their right to counsel?

7. *Widening the net.* The beginning of formal diversion programs can be traced back to juvenile courts in the early twentieth century. Diversion was formally extended to narcotics cases in the 1960s. Since then concerns have existed about "widening the net" of such programs. The fear is that individuals who would have previously been released without any action are now being diverted into programs while the cases of more serious offenders, who would not be eligible for diversion, are dismissed. Does diversion amount to decriminalization of certain offenses or offender groups? Or does it instead increase the level of social control over offenders, as community service and drug treatment complement the traditional prison sanctions?

8. *Female offenders and diversion.* Might diversion programs be particularly suitable for and attractive to female defendants? Many of these offenders

commit nonviolent crimes and have dependent children. Lengthy pretrial detention or incarceration forcibly separates mothers from their children, whereas diversion programs allow them to remain together. Should such family considerations help determine which offenders qualify for admission into diversion programs? If not, should offense type be the sole determining factor?

B.   DOMESTIC VIOLENCE PROTECTION ORDERS

Crime victimization surveys show a decline in nonfatal intimate-partner violence since 1993. Nevertheless, between 1998 and 2002, almost 700,000 nonfatal violent incidents occurred annually between intimate partners in the United States. These included rapes and sexual assaults, robberies, aggravated assaults, and (most commonly) simple assaults. Eighty-five percent of that violence was directed at women.

In domestic violence cases, the state may file criminal charges against the perpetrator. But other avenues are available: in all states, a family member who is the victim of domestic violence can get a so-called civil protection or restraining order. Survey data indicate that about 17% of women and 3.5% of men who are physically assaulted by an intimate obtain such an order. Over 1.1 million victims of intimate violence obtain protective or restraining orders annually. At the end of the last decade there were an estimated 2 million active restraining orders. Patricia Tjaden & Nancy Thoennes, Extent, Nature and Consequences of Intimate Partner Violence: Findings from the National Violence Against Women Survey 52-54 (National Institute of Justice 2000); U.S. Department of Justice, Office for Victims of Crime, Legal Series Bulletin No. 4, Enforcement of Protective Orders (January 2002).

Protection orders are designed to empower the victim, allowing her to act when the state is unwilling to file a criminal complaint against the batterer. In this sense, civil protection orders create an alternative to the criminal justice process. The goal of such an order is to break the cycle of violence by removing the perpetrator from the abusive relationship without immediately involving the criminal justice system. A civil protection order prohibits a named person from harassing, stalking, or threatening an intimate partner. In addition, a protection order may forbid the person from contacting the victim, require the person to vacate a joint household, or set conditions for child visitation and financial support.

Protection orders are relatively easy to obtain, allowing a victim to proceed without an attorney. Frequently, victims get help from non-attorney domestic violence advocates. A judge issues a preliminary order after an ex parte hearing, and a final protection order follows a hearing at which both sides appear and present evidence.

Protection orders, while technically the product of a civil process, lie between the civil and criminal arenas. Those who violate a protection order can be sanctioned for disobeying the court, through misdemeanor charges,contempt charges, or both. This civil process, therefore, carries a criminal sanction if its target fails to comply with the civil order. Of course, the state may file a criminal complaint if the violation of the protection order also amounts to a substantive offense, such as assault or attempted murder. Despite these sanctions, about 60% of restraining orders are violated.

PROBLEM 10-2.   RESTRAINT

John and Miriam lived in Louisville, Kentucky, and were having marital difficulties. Even though they hoped to reconcile, they agreed that it would be best if John moved out. One night John came over to pick up their son for a walk. When John asked his son to get ready, five-year-old Ben said, "Get out of my face." John then began to shout at Miriam for failing to teach Ben respect for his father. She responded, also in a raised voice, that Ben's attitude might be John's fault because he was not a good father or husband. John lost his temper and slapped Miriam. She then yelled, "I'll divorce you." John yelled back that he would "bury" her if she filed for divorce, and he stormed off.

Based on this exchange, Miriam filed for an emergency protective order requiring John to keep his distance from her and Ben. The court granted the protective order and sent notice to John immediately after granting the order.

A week later, Miriam's car broke down on the highway. She called John at work and asked him whether he could pick her up and fix the car. John arrived immediately. While he was driving Miriam home, they began to quarrel again. After they arrived at home and got out of the car, John screamed at Miriam so loudly that her neighbor came out to see what was going on. At that point, John raised his hand as if he were about to hit Miriam, but he then thought better of it and instead continued berating her. Miriam asked the neighbor to call the police. Within minutes the police arrived and arrested John for violating the protective order.

At his trial for violation of the protective order and attempted assault, John challenges the validity of the initial protective order. He argues that the court violated the Constitution when it issued the protective order without hearing from him, and he contends that the government has not established the statutory requirements to convict him of violating the restraining order and attempted assault.

As prosecuting counsel, how would you respond? Before you answer this question, consult the following Kentucky statutes describing the relevant procedures for protective orders.

|| *Kentucky Statutes §§403.720 to 403.760* ||

§403.720

As used in [this chapter], (1) "Domestic violence and abuse" means physical injury, serious physical injury, sexual abuse, assault, or the infliction of fear of imminent physical injury, serious physical injury, sexual abuse, or assault between family members or members of an unmarried couple; (2) "Family member" means a spouse, including a former spouse, a parent, a child, a stepchild, or any other person related by consanguinity or affinity within the second degree; and (3) "Member of an unmarried couple" means each member of an unmarried couple which allegedly has a child in common, any children of that couple, or a member of an unmarried couple who are living together or have formerly lived together.

§403.740

(1) If, upon review of the petition, . . . the court determines that the allegations contained therein indicate the presence of an immediate and present danger of domestic violence and abuse, the court shall issue, upon proper motion, ex parte, an emergency protective order:

(a) Restraining the adverse party from any contact or communication with the petitioner except as directed by the court;

(b) Restraining the adverse party from committing further acts of domestic violence and abuse;

(c) Restraining the adverse party from disposing of or damaging any of the property of the parties;

(d) Directing the adverse party to vacate the residence shared by the parties to the action;

(e) [Granting] temporary custody; or

(f) [Entering] other orders the court believes will be of assistance in eliminating future acts of domestic violence and abuse; or any combination thereof.

(2) [If] the court issues an emergency protective order pursuant to subsection (1) of this section, the court shall not order or refer the parties to mediation for resolution of the issues alleged in the petition [unless the victim of the alleged domestic abuse voluntarily requests it and mediation is a realistic and viable alternative to or adjunct to a protective order].

(3) An emergency protective order issued in accordance with this section shall be issued without bond being required of the petitioner.

(4) An emergency protective order issued in accordance with this section shall be effective for a period of time fixed in the order, but not to exceed fourteen days. Upon the issuance of an emergency protective order, a date for a full hearing . . . shall be fixed not later than the expiration date of the emergency protective order. An emergency protective order shall be reissued for a period not to exceed fourteen days if service has not been made on the adverse party by the fixed court date and time or as the court determines is necessary for the protection of the petitioner. . . .

§403.745

(1) If, upon review of the petition . . . , the court determines that the allegations contained therein do not indicate the presence of an immediate and present danger of domestic violence and abuse, the court shall fix a date, time, and place for a hearing and shall cause a summons to be issued for the adverse party. . . . The hearing shall be fixed not later than fourteen days following the issuance of the summons. . . .

§403.750

(1) Following the hearing provided for under §§403.740 and 403.745, the court, if it finds from a preponderance of the evidence that an act or acts of domestic violence and abuse have occurred and may again occur, may:

(a-e) [take any actions described in §403.740(1a-e)];

(f) award temporary support;

(g) direct that either or both parties receive counseling services available in the community, except that the court shall not order or refer the parties to participate in mediation for resolution of the issues alleged in the petition filed pursuant to [the provisions on domestic violence protective orders].

(2) Any order entered pursuant to this section shall be effective for a period of time, fixed by the court, not to exceed three years and may be reissued upon expiration for an additional period of up to three years. The number of times an order may be reissued shall not be limited. With respect to whether an order should be reissued, any party may present to the court testimony relating to the importance of the fact that acts of domestic violence or abuse have not occurred during the pendency of the order. . . .

§403.760

(1) Violation of the terms or conditions of an order issued under the provisions of §§403.740 or 403.750, whether an emergency protective order, or an order following hearing, after service of the order on the respondent, or notice of the order to the respondent, shall constitute contempt of court.

(2) Any peace officer having probable cause to believe a violation has occurred of an order issued under the provisions of §§403.740 or 403.750 . . . shall arrest the respondent without a warrant for violation of a protective order. . . . Following a hearing the District Court in the county in which the peace officer made the arrest for the violation may punish the violation of a protective order. . . .

(4) Nothing in this section shall preclude the Commonwealth from prosecuting and convicting the respondent of criminal offenses other than violation of a protective order.

(5) Civil proceedings and criminal proceedings for . . . violation of a protective order shall be mutually exclusive. Once either proceeding has been initiated the other shall not be undertaken regardless of the outcome of the original proceeding.

NOTES

1. *Goals of civil protection orders.* What goals are civil protection orders intended to achieve? Why can these not be accomplished with criminal actions? Civil protection orders appear to be a valuable alternative to the criminal justice process when the criminal justice system either does not act or does not act quickly enough. Such orders also serve important symbolic ends by allowing the victim to demonstrate her ability to act, her strength, and her independent

decision-making skills. They constitute a direct action by the victim against the abuser.

Despite the support of the justice system, however, restraining orders may not reduce domestic violence. See Elaine Chiu, Confronting the Agency in Battered Mothers, 74 S. Cal. L. Rev. 1223 (2001). Is a civil process insufficiently stigmatizing to keep the offender from battering again? Many abusers in domestic violence situations have criminal records that resemble those of other violent criminals. Should restraining orders be utilized only for first-time domestic violence offenders or for individuals without a criminal record?

Some have argued that restraining orders may be unsuccessful because batterers do not perceive the process as fair. Often they do not understand the difference between the civil and criminal systems and are left alone to navigate the judicial system. Should batterers be provided with more process, such as information about the system or even the right to counsel? May such services be advisable only if it is shown that they increase compliance? See Deborah Epstein, Procedural Justice: Tempering the State's Response to Domestic Violence, 43 Wm. & Mary L. Rev. 1843 (2002).

In some counties in Kentucky, domestic violence orders have earned the nickname "the poor man's [and woman's] divorce." Domestic violence orders may be used to accomplish some of the goals of divorce, but much more quickly. How could such abuses of the system be prevented without limiting access for abused persons?

2. *Ex parte civil proceedings.* Emergency protection orders are granted without a hearing and without notice being provided to the respondent. They often stay in place for about two weeks. Many states provide extensive self-help manuals for battered spouses, explaining how to obtain a restraining order. Shortly before the emergency protection order runs out, the court holds a hearing in which both sides are present. Because the grant of civil protection orders takes place in a civil proceeding, the petitioner (note the civil terminology) has to establish the occurrence of domestic violence merely by a preponderance of the evidence.

There is no right to publicly funded counsel in civil proceedings, including hearings on civil protection orders. Petitioners, however, are frequently represented by women's advocates or law school clinics in their requests for emergency protection orders. These advocates become regular players in the process, with the respondents remaining largely unrepresented until a protection order is violated. Once criminal proceedings are under way, the alleged batterer has the right to an attorney.

3. *Specialized judges.* In some states, specially designated domestic violence judges grant civil protection orders, sit on domestic violence cases, and deal with violations of civil protection orders. What reasons are there for the institution of such "one-stop shopping"? What advantages and disadvantages flow from subject matter–focused judging? See Dag MacLeod & Julia F. Weber, Judicial Council of California, Administrative Office of the Courts, Domestic Violence Courts: A Descriptive Study (May 2000); Randal B. Fritzler & Leonore M. J. Simon, The Development of a Specialized Domestic Violence Court in Vancouver, Washington: Utilizing Innovative Judicial Paradigms, 69 UMKC L. Rev. 139 (2000).

4. *Double jeopardy and domestic violence orders.* The violation of a civil protection order may lead to a panoply of actions against the batterer. Breach of the court's order could lead to a contempt citation or a criminal prosecution for the violation; an assault and battery could also lead to a separate criminal action. In United States v. Dixon, 509 U.S. 688 (1993), the Supreme Court addressed whether charges of assault and threats were nullified by the double jeopardy clause because they were filed after a misdemeanor contempt conviction based on the same conduct. The Court, in a splintered opinion, held that the misdemeanor assault prosecution was barred, but the prosecutions for assault with intent to kill and felony threats could go forward because misdemeanor contempt and each of the latter crimes required proof of an element that the other did not. See Blockburger v. United States, 284 U.S. 299 (1932) (describing traditional "same elements" test to determine which crimes qualify as the same offense and thus are barred by double jeopardy). Does this decision deter prosecutors from filing criminal assault charges after the courts have issued contempt citations? See David M. Zlotnick, Battered Women and Justice Scalia, 41 Ariz. L. Rev. 847 (1999).

5. *Weapon possession and protection orders.* The federal Violence Against Women Act, enacted in 1994, prohibits anyone under a civil protection order from possessing firearms or ammunition. See 18 U.S.C. §922(g)(8). Federal law and most state statutes, however, prohibit possession of weapons only upon a finding of abuse after an evidentiary hearing that gives the defendant an opportunity to be heard. This means that in many states an emergency protective order will not place the respondent under the coverage of the gun ban. Some commentators argue that without an immediate confiscation of weapons when the court issues the emergency order, the threat to the victim continues until the hearing. See Carrie Chew, Domestic Violence, Guns, and Minnesota Women: Responding to New Law, Correcting Old Legislative Need, and Taking Cues from Other Jurisdictions, 25 Hamline J. Pub. L. & Pol'y 115 (2003).

6. *Control of litigation.* In situations in which physical harm is inflicted or threatened, the state asserts its interest as a representative of the people, not merely of the victim of the alleged crime. This means that the decision whether to prosecute is made by a state agent rather than the victim. In many jurisdictions, mandatory prosecution in domestic violence cases (sometimes required by statute, more often by prosecutorial office policy) does not leave the victim any option. Should she refuse to testify or choose to testify falsely, the criminal justice system can sanction her. Because the victim and the offender in a domestic violence situation have a relationship — and sometimes try to preserve that relationship — the traditional adversarial criminal justice model may break down.

In what other situations may civil actions be preferable over criminal actions? Are there other types of criminal offenses in which the victim's interests may not be adequately represented by the state? In corporate embezzlement and similar types of business crimes, businesses often choose to settle with the offenders, under the threat of reporting them to the criminal justice system, without ever involving the official system. This is possible because the victimized business is in a more advantageous bargaining position than the offender — and its sole interest is recouping its financial loss rather than vindicating a greater goal.

In fraud crimes committed against the government, prosecutors often threaten to file criminal suits while also proceeding civilly. The threat of criminal litigation can lead to more advantageous civil settlements for the government. Should there be constitutional or statutory limits on the use of such dual threats?

C. ASSET FORFEITURE

While the alternatives to criminal sentences we have considered so far all emphasize restrictions on liberty, other alternative remedies depend on taking the property of a suspected wrongdoer. Asset forfeiture is among the most important of these sanctions. Technically, most asset forfeiture occurs through civil proceedings, with no necessary connection to criminal charges. In practice, asset forfeiture is tightly integrated with criminal enforcement. Asset forfeiture has become an important part of prosecution and punishment, especially for crimes with an economic motive, such as drug offenses, money laundering, and racketeering. Forfeiture is said to "take the profit out of crime."

The effectiveness of asset forfeiture lies partly in the procedural edge it gives the prosecution. Civil asset forfeiture gives the prosecution a more favorable standard of proof, extensive discovery, and summary judgment, among other advantages. Forfeiture can also take place during proceedings following on the heels of a criminal conviction, essentially as part of the criminal sentencing. Such "criminal forfeitures" are less common than civil forfeitures, however, because of the relative procedural difficulties they present to the government.

The destination of forfeited property also makes forfeiture an attractive device for law enforcement. Federal statutes and executive policies, along with most state statutes, assign forfeited property directly to the budgets of law enforcement agencies. Funds from forfeitures carried out under state law generally go to local police and sheriff's offices, after reimbursement of prosecutors for the costs of processing the forfeiture. When federal agents complete a forfeiture, the proceeds go to the participating federal agencies. Moreover, the federal government can "adopt" the forfeitures of state or local authorities. If state or local police seize property that is forfeitable under federal law, and federal prosecutors obtain the final forfeiture order in federal court, they split the proceeds.

Because the police and prosecutors who select property for forfeiture directly benefit from the forfeitures, property owners have argued that the police have an incentive to abuse the practice. Alleged abuses in spending forfeited funds often make the headlines. For instance, news reports widely noted a small-town sheriff who seized a Rolls-Royce from a drug dealer and used it as his personal car.

In this section, we examine the asset forfeiture procedures that operate in tandem with the criminal justice system. Consider the ways in which civil forfeiture proceedings differ from criminal proceedings, and determine whether those differences are justified by the different purposes of these systems or by the different consequences flowing from them.

1. Property Subject to Forfeiture

The forfeiture laws target only property with some defined connection to a crime. It is ordinarily not enough that an accused felon owns the property; the suspect must use it to commit a crime or acquire it as a result of the crime. The materials below describe the property that the law targets for forfeiture and the property it exempts from forfeiture. Consider what these categories reveal about the objectives of the forfeiture laws and their imperfect overlap with the objectives of criminal law enforcement.

In the federal system, roughly 200 criminal statutes provide for forfeiture. Many of these statutes deal with violations of customs laws or food and drug laws. Most federal forfeitures, however, are exercised under the laws against money laundering, racketeering, and illicit drugs. The same pattern holds for most state forfeiture laws: they apply primarily to violations of drug, gambling, liquor, and racketeering laws. In a few states, any felony can serve as the basis for a forfeiture. The following case discusses the necessary connection between the crime and the forfeited property under an early federal statute.

|| **United States v. Cargo of the Brig Malek Adhel** ||
|| **43 U.S. 210 (1844)** ||

STORY, J.

[The information in this case alleged that the brig *Malek Adhel* was used to commit "piratical aggression and restraint upon the high seas" against five vessels. The government pursued forfeiture proceedings against the ship and its cargo after it arrived in Maryland. The firm of Peter Harmony and Co. of New York claimed the ship and cargo as its property and attempted to prevent the forfeiture. At the hearing in district court, the vessel was condemned and the cargo acquitted. Peter Harmony and Co. brought this appeal.]

It was fully admitted in the court below, that the owners of the brig and cargo never contemplated or authorized the acts complained of; that the brig was bound on an innocent commercial voyage from New York to Guayamas, in California; and that the equipments on board were the usual equipments for such a voyage. It appears from the evidence that the brig sailed from the port of New York on the 30th of June, 1840, under the command of one Joseph Nunez, armed with a cannon and ammunition, and with pistols and daggers on board. The acts of aggression complained of, were committed at different times under false pretences, and wantonly and wilfully without provocation or justification, between the 6th of July, 1840, and the 20th of August, 1840, when the brig arrived at Bahia; where, in consequence of the information given to the American consul by the crew, the brig was seized by the United States ship *Enterprize,* then at that port, and carried to Rio Janeiro, and from thence brought to the United States. . . . Now upon this posture of the case, it has been contended [that] neither the brig nor the cargo are liable to condemnation, because the owners neither participated in nor authorized the piratical acts, but are entirely innocent thereof. . . .

The [first] question is, whether the innocence of the owners can withdraw the ship from the penalty of confiscation under the act of Congress. Here, . . . it may be remarked that the act makes no exception whatsoever, whether the aggression be with or without the co-operation of the owners. The vessel which commits the aggression is treated as the offender, as the guilty instrument or thing to which the forfeiture attaches, without any reference whatsoever to the character or conduct of the owner. The vessel or boat (says the act of Congress) from which such piratical aggression, &c., shall have been first attempted or made shall be condemned. . . . And this is done from the necessity of the case, as the only adequate means of suppressing the offence or wrong, or insuring an indemnity to the injured party. The doctrine also is familiarly applied to cases of smuggling and other misconduct under our revenue laws. . . . In short, the acts of the master and crew, in cases of this sort, bind the interest of the owner of the ship, whether he be innocent or guilty; and he impliedly submits to whatever the law denounces as a forfeiture attached to the ship by reason of their unlawful or wanton wrongs. . . .

The ship is also by the general maritime law held responsible for the torts and misconduct of the master and crew thereof, whether arising from negligence or a wilful disregard of duty; as, for example, in cases of collision and other wrongs done upon the high seas or elsewhere within the admiralty and maritime jurisdiction, upon the general policy of that law, which looks to the instrument itself, used as the means of the mischief, as the best and surest pledge for the compensation and indemnity to the injured party. The act of Congress has therefore done nothing more on this point than to affirm and enforce the general principles of the maritime law and of the law of nations.

The remaining question is, whether the cargo is involved in the same fate as the ship. In respect to the forfeiture under the act of 1819,* it is plain that the cargo stands upon a very different ground from that of the ship. Nothing is said in relation to the condemnation of the cargo in the fourth section of the act; and in the silence of any expression of the legislature, in the case of provisions confessedly penal, it ought not to be presumed that their intention exceeded their language. . . .

So far as the general maritime law applies to torts or injuries committed on the high seas and within the admiralty jurisdiction, the general rule is, not forfeiture of the offending property; but compensation to the full extent of all damages sustained or reasonably allowable, to be enforced by a proceeding therefor in rem or in personam. It is true that the law of nations goes in many cases much farther, and inflicts the penalty of confiscation for very gross and wanton violations of duty. But, then, it limits the penalty to cases of extraordinary turpitude or violence. For petty misconduct, or petty plunderage, or petty neglect of duty, it contents itself with the mitigated rule of compensation in damages. . . .

The present case seems to us fairly to fall within the general principle of exempting the cargo. The owners are confessedly innocent of all intentional or meditated wrong. They are free from any imputation of guilt, and every

---

* The act of 1819 provides as follows: "[Whenever] any vessel or boat from which any piratical aggression . . . shall have been first attempted or made, shall be captured and brought into any port of the United States, the same shall and may be adjudged and condemned to their use and that of the captors, after due process and trial in any court have admiralty jurisdiction, . . . and the same court shall thereupon order a sale and distribution thereof accordingly, and at their discretion." — EDS.

suspicion of connivance with the master in his hostile acts and wanton misconduct. [The act of Congress limits] the penalty of confiscation to the vessel alone,
[showing] that the public policy of our government in cases of this nature is not
intended to embrace the cargo. It is satisfied by attaching the penalty to the
offending vessel, as all that public justice and a just regard to private rights
require. For these reasons, we are of opinion that the decrees condemning
the vessel and restoring the cargo, rendered in both the courts below, ought
to be affirmed. . . .

NOTES

1. *Objectives of forfeiture.* Why did the government seek forfeiture of the
ship and its cargo? The statute in question called for the forfeiture proceeds to
become government property and did not mention use of the property to compensate victims of wrongdoing. Was the forfeiture done to prevent future
criminal uses of the property? Won't future pirates be able to use some other
ordinary vessel just as readily? Did Peter Harmony and Co. do anything wrong?
Does it matter in forfeiture proceedings whether the firm was responsible for the
piracy?

2. *Statutory connection to vessel and cargo.* Why did the Court in *Malek Adhel*
interpret the statute to allow forfeiture of the vessel but not the cargo? Would
the Court have enforced a statute that clearly provided for the forfeiture of the
cargo, or could the law of admiralty and the law of nations actually trump the
statute? Why do the law of admiralty and the law of nations require gross and
wanton acts before allowing forfeiture of cargo? Consider whether this is an early
indication of a need for proportionality between the crime committed and the
assets forfeited.

3. *The expanding statutory connection.* Legislatures have steadily increased
the categories of property subject to forfeiture. Take, for instance, the evolution
of one of the primary federal forfeiture statutes, 21 U.S.C. §881. The original
1970 version of the statute applied to (1) all controlled substances; (2) all raw
materials, products, and equipment used or intended to be used to manufacture
or deliver controlled substances; (3) all containers for property described in the
first two categories; (4) all conveyances (including aircraft, vehicles, and vessels)
used or intended to be used to facilitate the transportation, sale, receipt, possession, or concealment of property described in the first two categories; and (5)
all books, records, and research used in violation of controlled substances laws.
Law enforcement officers were not able to seize much property meeting these
criteria — only $30 million during the first nine years following passage of the
law. A 1978 amendment expanded forfeiture to reach (1) all money, securities,
and other "things of value furnished or intended to be furnished" in exchange
for a controlled substance; (2) all proceeds traceable to such an exchange; and
(3) all money, negotiable instruments, and securities used or intended to facilitate a violation of the drug laws. In 1984 the statute was expanded further to
allow forfeiture of all real property used or intended "to commit, or to facilitate"
a violation of drug laws. For a discussion of the "widening net" of property
subject to forfeiture under federal laws, see Jimmy Gurulé, Sandra Guerra

Thompson & Michael O'Hear, The Law of Asset Forfeiture ch. 5 (2004). Asset
forfeiture has also become an important tool in punishing and preventing financial crimes in many European nations. See Laura Donohue, Anti-Terrorist
Finance in the United Kingdom and the United States, 27 Mich. J. Int'l L.
303 (2006) (discussing forfeiture in the United Kingdom and the United
States).

4. *Forfeiture of estate.*   None of the major forfeiture statutes attempts to
subject to forfeiture *all* of the property of a person suspected, accused, or convicted of a crime. Is there anything stopping Congress and the state legislatures
from adopting a statute along these lines? In eighteenth-century English
practice, felons and traitors forfeited all their property. As William Blackstone
explained it, allowing forfeitures of an entire estate "will help to restrain a man,
not only by the sense of his duty, and dread of personal punishment, but also by
his passions and natural affections; and will interest every dependent and relation he has, to keep him from offending." 4 William Blackstone, Commentaries
on the Laws of England *375. The U.S. Constitution forbids forfeiture of estate
as a punishment for treason, although it is allowed "during the Life of the
Person attainted." U.S. Const. art. III, §3, cl. 2. The First Congress passed a
law prohibiting federal forfeiture of estate as a punishment for other felonies.
Could a state pass a statute providing for forfeiture of estate? What abuses
might have occurred under English law to create such a reaction among early
American lawmakers?

PROBLEM 10-3.   WEAPONS ON WHEELS

In 1999 New York City introduced a "Zero Tolerance Drinking and Driving
Initiative." Under this policy, police officers who arrest someone for driving
while intoxicated (registering .10 or higher on a Breathalyzer test) may seize
the automobile. The policy prevents the police from seizing a vehicle in cases
where drivers are arrested for the lesser offense of "driving while impaired"
(registering between .06 and .10 on a Breathalyzer test). The seized car is
searched and stored in a city facility. If the driver is either the owner or principal
user of the car, the city will begin a civil forfeiture proceeding to take the car
away. If the owner of the car knew that someone else would use it to commit a
crime (including driving while intoxicated), the car is also declared subject to
forfeiture. Before the city adopted this new policy, the police held the car of
someone arrested for drunken driving until some other person arrived at the
station to pick up the car. The city sometimes asked for forfeiture of the car, but
only after a criminal conviction.

The change in policy was based on an existing provision of the Administrative Code of the City of New York. Section 14-140 provides that the Police
Property Clerk may take possession of all property "suspected of having been
used as a means of committing crime." A person who uses property in furtherance of a crime "or suffers the same to be used . . . shall not be deemed to be the
lawful claimant."

The mayor explained the new policy as follows: "It isn't punishment. It's
remedial. The car is seized to protect society against this car being driven around

in the communities of New York City because it's been demonstrated that this car will be operated unsafely." The forfeiture action is "a way of preventing the use of what, in fact, is a weapon when driven while intoxicated against the public." There were 6,368 arrests of drunken drivers in New York City in 1998, and 31 fatalities attributed to driving while intoxicated.

Francisco Almote, one of the first motorists whose vehicle was seized under the new policy, had been convicted five times previously on charges that he drove while intoxicated. Police seized his 1987 Toyota when they arrested him. A second driver whose car was seized was Pavel Grinberg, who was driving with his wife in Brooklyn one night when he was pulled over for not wearing a seat belt. Police officers said that a Breathalyzer test showed a blood alcohol level of .11 percent, so the officers arrested Grinberg and seized his 1988 Acura Integra (with a book value of about $1,650). "I was at my good friend's daughter's first birthday party and I had one beer—that was it," Grinberg said.

You are an attorney in the office of the Corporation Counsel for New York City. What difficulties (if any) do you foresee in enforcing this policy? How should the city respond in cases where the defendant charged with driving while intoxicated is willing to plead guilty to the lesser charge of driving while impaired (a charge that is not a basis for seizing the car under the city's policy)? What if the defendant is willing to "settle" the forfeiture proceeding by paying one-quarter of the car's value?

|| *Richard Austin v. United States* ||
|| 509 U.S. 602 (1993) ||

BLACKMUN, J.

In this case, we are asked to decide whether the Excessive Fines Clause of the Eighth Amendment applies to forfeitures of property under 21 U.S.C. §§881(a)(4) and (a)(7). We hold that it does and therefore remand the case for consideration of the question whether the forfeiture at issue here was excessive.

On August 2, 1990, petitioner Richard Lyle Austin was indicted on four counts of violating South Dakota's drug laws. Austin ultimately pleaded guilty to one count of possessing cocaine with intent to distribute and was sentenced by the state court to seven years' imprisonment. On September 7, the United States filed an in rem action in the United States District Court for the District of South Dakota seeking forfeiture of Austin's mobile home and auto body shop under 21 U.S.C. §§881(a)(4) and (a)(7). Austin filed a claim and an answer to the complaint.

[According to affidavits supporting a government motion for summary judgment], Austin met Keith Engebretson at Austin's body shop on June 13, 1990, and agreed to sell cocaine to Engebretson. Austin left the shop, went to his mobile home, and returned to the shop with two grams of cocaine which he sold to Engebretson. State authorities executed a search warrant on the body shop and mobile home the following day. They discovered small amounts of marijuana and cocaine, a .22 caliber revolver, drug paraphernalia, and approximately $4,700 in cash. [The district court granted summary judgment to the government, and the Eighth Circuit affirmed.]

Austin contends that the Eighth Amendment's Excessive Fines Clause applies to in rem civil forfeiture proceedings. . . . The United States now argues that "any claim that the government's conduct in a civil proceeding is limited by the Eighth Amendment generally, or by the Excessive Fines Clause in particular, must fail unless the challenged governmental action, despite its label, would have been recognized as a criminal punishment at the time the Eighth Amendment was adopted." It further suggests that the Eighth Amendment cannot apply to a civil proceeding unless that proceeding is so punitive that it must be considered criminal under [our prior cases]. We disagree. . . .

The purpose of the Eighth Amendment, putting the Bail Clause to one side, was to limit the government's power to punish. The Cruel and Unusual Punishments Clause is self-evidently concerned with punishment. The Excessive Fines Clause limits the Government's power to extract payments, whether in cash or in kind, as punishment for some offense. The notion of punishment, as we commonly understand it, cuts across the division between the civil and the criminal law. It is commonly understood that civil proceedings may advance punitive and remedial goals, and, conversely, that both punitive and remedial goals may be served by criminal penalties. Thus, the question is not, as the United States would have it, whether forfeiture under §§881(a)(4) and (a)(7) is civil or criminal, but rather whether it is punishment. . . . We turn, then, to consider whether, at the time the Eighth Amendment was ratified, forfeiture was understood at least in part as punishment and whether forfeiture under §§881(a)(4) and (a)(7) should be so understood today.

Three kinds of forfeiture were established in England at the time the Eighth Amendment was ratified in the United States: deodand, forfeiture upon conviction for a felony or treason, and statutory forfeiture [for violations of the customs and revenue laws]. Each was understood, at least in part, as imposing punishment. At common law the value of an inanimate object directly or indirectly causing the accidental death of a King's subject was forfeited to the Crown as a deodand. . . . The value of the instrument was forfeited to the King, in the belief that the King would provide the money for Masses to be said for the good of the dead man's soul, or insure that the deodand was put to charitable uses. When application of the deodand to religious or eleemosynary purposes ceased, and the deodand became a source of Crown revenue, the institution was justified as a penalty for carelessness. . . .

Of England's three kinds of forfeiture, only the third took hold in the United States. [The] common law courts in the Colonies — and later in the states during the period of Confederation — were exercising jurisdiction in rem in the enforcement of English and local forfeiture statutes. The First Congress passed laws subjecting ships and cargos involved in customs offenses to forfeiture. . . .

Our cases also have recognized that statutory in rem forfeiture imposes punishment. [This] understanding of forfeiture as punishment runs through our cases rejecting the "innocence" of the owner as a common-law defense to forfeiture. In these cases, forfeiture has been justified on two theories — that the property itself is "guilty" of the offense, and that the owner may be held accountable for the wrongs of others to whom he entrusts his property. . . . In *Brig Malek Adhel*, it reasoned that "the acts of the master and crew, in cases of this sort, bind the interest of the owner of the ship, whether he be innocent or guilty; and he impliedly submits to whatever the law denounces as a forfeiture attached to the ship by reason of their unlawful or wanton wrongs." . . . Like the guilty-property fiction, this theory of vicarious liability is premised on the idea that the owner has been negligent. . . . We conclude, therefore, that forfeiture generally and statutory in rem forfeiture in particular historically have been understood, at least in part, as punishment.

We turn next to consider whether forfeitures under 21 U.S.C. §§881(a)(4) and (a)(7) are properly considered punishment today. We find nothing in these provisions or their legislative history to contradict the historical understanding of forfeiture as punishment. Unlike traditional forfeiture statutes, §§881(a)(4) and (a)(7) expressly provide an "innocent owner" defense. . . . These exemptions serve to focus the provisions on the culpability of the owner in a way that makes them look more like punishment, not less. . . .

The legislative history of §881 confirms the punitive nature of these provisions. When it added subsection (a)(7) to §881 in 1984, Congress recognized "that the traditional criminal sanctions of fine and imprisonment are inadequate to deter or punish the enormously profitable trade in dangerous drugs." It characterized the forfeiture of real property as "a powerful deterrent." . . .

The Government argues that §§881(a)(4) and (a)(7) are not punitive but, rather, should be considered remedial in two respects. First, they remove the "instruments" of the drug trade "thereby protecting the community from the threat of continued drug dealing." Second, the forfeited assets serve to compensate the Government for the expense of law enforcement activity and for its expenditure on societal problems such as urban blight, drug addiction, and other health concerns resulting from the drug trade.

In our view, neither argument withstands scrutiny. Concededly, we have recognized that the forfeiture of contraband itself may be characterized as remedial because it removes dangerous or illegal items from society. The Court, however, previously has rejected government's attempt to extend that reasoning to conveyances used to transport illegal liquor, [because there] is nothing even remotely criminal in possessing an automobile. The same, without question, is true of the properties involved here, and the Government's attempt to characterize these properties as "instruments" of the drug trade must meet the same fate.

The Government's second argument about the remedial nature of this forfeiture is no more persuasive. We previously have upheld the forfeiture of goods involved in customs violations as a reasonable form of liquidated damages. But the dramatic variations in the value of conveyances and real property forfeitable under §§881(a)(4) and (a)(7) undercut any similar argument with respect to those provisions. . . .

Fundamentally, even assuming that §§881(a)(4) and (a)(7) serve some remedial purpose, the Government's argument must fail. A civil sanction that cannot fairly be said solely to serve a remedial purpose, but rather can only be explained as also serving either retributive or deterrent purposes, is punishment, as we have come to understand the term. In light of the historical understanding of forfeiture as punishment, the clear focus of §§881(a)(4) and (a)(7) on the culpability of the owner, and the evidence that Congress understood those provisions as serving to deter and to punish, we cannot conclude that forfeiture under §§881(a)(4) and (a)(7) serves solely a remedial

purpose. We therefore conclude that forfeiture under these provisions constitutes payment to a sovereign as punishment for some offense, and, as such, is
subject to the limitations of the Eighth Amendment's Excessive Fines Clause.

Austin asks that we establish a multifactor test for determining whether a
forfeiture is constitutionally "excessive." We decline that invitation. . . . Prudence dictates that we allow the lower courts to consider that question in the
first instance. . . . The judgment of the Court of Appeals is reversed and the case
is remanded to that court for further proceedings consistent with this opinion. It
is so ordered.

SCALIA, J., concurring.
. . . However the theory may be expressed, it seems to me that this taking of
lawful property must be considered, in whole or in part, punitive. Its purpose is
not compensatory, to make someone whole for injury caused by unlawful use of
the property. Punishment is being imposed, whether one quaintly considers its
object to be the property itself, or more realistically regards its object to be the
property's owner. . . . The Court apparently believes, however, that only actual
culpability of the affected property owner can establish that a forfeiture
provision is punitive, and sets out to establish that such culpability exists in
the case of in rem forfeitures. [But we] have never held that the Constitution
requires negligence, or any other degree of culpability, to support such forfeitures. . . .

That this forfeiture works as a fine raises the excessiveness issue, on which
the Court remands. I agree that a remand is in order, but think it worth pointing
out that on remand the excessiveness analysis must be different from that applicable to monetary fines and, perhaps, to in personam forfeitures. In the case of a
monetary fine, the Eighth Amendment's origins in the English Bill of Rights,
intended to limit the abusive penalties assessed against the king's opponents,
demonstrate that the touchstone is value of the fine in relation to the offense.
[The] same is true for in personam forfeiture. . . .

Unlike monetary fines, statutory in rem forfeitures have traditionally been
fixed, not by determining the appropriate value of the penalty in relation to the
committed offense, but by determining what property has been "tainted" by
unlawful use, to which issue the value of the property is irrelevant. Scales used to
measure out unlawful drug sales, for example, are confiscable whether made of
the purest gold or the basest metal. But an in rem forfeiture goes beyond the
traditional limits that the Eighth Amendment permits if it applies to property
that cannot properly be regarded as an instrumentality of the offense — the
building, for example, in which an isolated drug sale happens to occur. Such
a confiscation would be an excessive fine. The question is not how much the
confiscated property is worth, but whether the confiscated property has a close
enough relationship to the offense. . . .

|| *Kansas Constitution Art. 15, §9* ||

A homestead to the extent of . . . one acre within the limits of an incorporated town or city, occupied as a residence by the family of the owner, together
with all improvements on the same, shall be exempted from forced sale under

any process of law, and shall not be alienated without the joint consent of husband and wife. . . .

Philadelphia Police Department Directive 102

. . . The Police Department has established the following minimal value guidelines for seizure under Drug Forfeiture Laws:

Currency	$1,000	Vehicles	$2,500
Jewelry	$5,000	Aircraft, Vessels	$5,000
Real Estate	$10,000	Other Property	$1,000

PROBLEM 10-4.   HIGH ROLLERS

The government seeks forfeiture of the $150,000 Miami residence of Emilio and Yolanda Delio because it was used in an illegal gambling operation. Emilio Delio is an 80-year-old wheelchair-bound man residing at the property with his 66-year-old wife, Yolanda. Emilio and Yolanda own the property jointly. Their adult children also reside at the house.

Mr. Delio conducted a poker game at his home, involving some of his relatives and associates, on Wednesday nights. Government agents observed poker games at the house on five occasions between September 12 and October 10. Witnesses later said that the poker games were held at the house on a regular basis. The government charged Delio and other members of the family with directing a gambling operation and obtained criminal convictions against Emilio and three other participants (including one of Emilio's sons). The statute applied only to gambling businesses (1) owned or directed by five or more persons, (2) remaining in "substantially continuous operation" for more than 30 days, (3) with a gross revenue of $2,000 in any single day. In the separate civil forfeiture proceedings, the government seeks summary judgment.

Will the government obtain forfeiture of this property? How should the "excessiveness" of this fine be measured? Compare United States v. One Single Family Residence at 18755 North Bay Road, Miami, 13 F.3d 1493 (11th Cir. 1994).

NOTES

1. *Excessive fines and forfeitures: majority position.* The *Austin* opinion left for other courts the task of deciding how to measure the excessiveness of a forfeiture under the Eighth Amendment. The lower federal courts developed a proportionality test that weighs the severity of the offense, the harshness of the sanction, and the culpability of the claimant. Then the Supreme Court returned to the question of what standard to use in measuring the excessiveness of a forfeiture in United States v. Bajakajian, 524 U.S. 321 (1998).

Bajakajian was waiting in the Los Angeles airport to board an international flight when a customs inspector approached him and told him that he was required to report all cash in excess of $10,000 in his possession or baggage. Bajakajian lied about the amount of cash he was holding; cash-sniffing dogs indicated the presence of currency in his luggage, and customs inspectors found $357,144. Bajakajian pled guilty to the currency reporting offense and elected to have a bench trial on the forfeiture. The trial judge found that the funds were not connected to any other crime and that Bajakajian was transporting the money to repay a lawful debt; he held that forfeiture of the entire amount was constitutionally excessive and reduced the forfeiture to $15,000.

The Supreme Court held that the forfeiture was a punishment for purposes of the excessive fines clause because the statute authorized an in personam forfeiture that applied only to the property of a person who willfully fails to report the cash. The Court then described the proper method for a court to use in determining whether a forfeiture is excessive:

> [There are two considerations] that we find particularly relevant. The first . . . is that judgments about the appropriate punishment for an offense belong in the first instance to the legislature. The second is that any judicial determination regarding the gravity of a particular criminal offense will be inherently imprecise. Both of these principles counsel against requiring strict proportionality between the amount of a punitive forfeiture and the gravity of a criminal offense, and we therefore adopt the standard of gross disproportionality articulated in our Cruel and Unusual Punishments Clause precedents. See Solem v. Helm, 463 U.S. 277 (1983); Rummel v. Estelle, 445 U.S. 263 (1980).
>
> In applying this standard, the district courts in the first instance, and the courts of appeals, reviewing the proportionality determination de novo, must compare the amount of the forfeiture to the gravity of the defendant's offense. If the amount of the forfeiture is grossly disproportional to the gravity of the defendant's offense, it is unconstitutional.
>
> Under this standard, the forfeiture of respondent's entire $357,144 would violate the Excessive Fines Clause. Respondent's crime was solely a reporting offense. It was permissible to transport the currency out of the country so long as he reported it. . . . Furthermore, as the District Court found, respondent's violation was unrelated to any other illegal activities. The money was the proceeds of legal activity and was to be used to repay a lawful debt. Whatever his other vices, respondent does not fit into the class of persons for whom the statute was principally designed: He is not a money launderer, a drug trafficker, or a tax evader. And under the Sentencing Guidelines, the maximum sentence that could have been imposed on respondent was six months, while the maximum fine was $5,000. . . .
>
> The harm that respondent caused was also minimal. Failure to report his currency affected only one party, the Government, and in a relatively minor way. There was no fraud on the United States, and respondent caused no loss to the public fisc. Had his crime gone undetected, the Government would have been deprived only of the information that $357,144 had left the country. . . . Comparing the gravity of respondent's crime with the $357,144 forfeiture the Government seeks, we conclude that such a forfeiture would be grossly disproportional to the gravity of his offense.

After the Supreme Court's decision in *Bajakajian*, Congress enacted 31 U.S.C. §5332, which declares bulk cash smuggling into and out of the United States a criminal offense. The provision, a part of the U.S. PATRIOT Act, mandates criminal forfeiture and allows for civil forfeiture of the entire amount of money smuggled. The only case that has addressed the issue so far found *Bajakajian* applicable, and therefore subjected the civil forfeiture to the excessive fines clause. United States of America v. $293,316 in U.S. Currency, 349 F. Supp. 2d 638 (E.D.N.Y. 2004).

The states have assumed that the excessive fines clause of the Eighth Amendment applies to them. Like the lower federal courts, many high state courts seem content for now to ask trial judges to consider a range of factors in judging the excessiveness of fines, including the value of the property, the amount of the illicit transaction, and the physical and temporal extent of involvement between the property and the crime. Commonwealth v. Fint, 940 S.W.2d 896 (Ky. 1997); State v. Hill, 635 N.E.2d 1248 (Ohio 1994).

2. *Instrumentalities versus proceeds.* Should the proceeds of crimes be subject to a proportionality test at all? What about the property offered in exchange for illicit drugs? See United States v. 15,538 Panulirus Argus Lobster Tails, 834 F. Supp. 385 (S.D. Fla. 1993) (contraband forfeited will always be proportional to crime committed). Suppose that a government agent posing as a buyer had first approached Austin in a public park and had proposed that they complete their transaction in the privacy of Austin's shop. If the government influences the choice of property that will facilitate a crime, should the property still be forfeited?

3. *"Punitive" versus "remedial" label.*   Why was Justice Blackmun so intent on demonstrating that the forfeiture in *Austin* was individual punishment? Justice Scalia and three other justices did not agree that all forfeitures involve some type of punishment. What is at stake in this argument over the label "punishment"? Will the holding in this case apply also to statutes containing no "innocent owner" defense?

4. *Forfeiture and criminal sentencing.*   Civil forfeiture sometimes takes place after the owner has been convicted and sentenced for a crime in a separate proceeding. If the offender was fined or otherwise suffered a loss of property during the criminal process, should this reduce the amount of property subject to civil forfeiture? In other words, should proportionality analysis account for related criminal sanctions? See Sandra Guerra, Reconciling Federal Asset Forfeitures and Drug Offense Sentencing, 78 Minn. L. Rev. 805 (1994) (urging Congress and courts to factor amount of forfeited property into criminal sentence).

5. *Exempt property.*   Residences seem to create the most difficult forfeiture cases for the government. Homestead property is exempt from forfeiture under some state constitutions and statutes, even if it has a clear connection to the commission of a crime and even if its forfeiture would be proportional to the crime. State courts have vigorously enforced exceptions for homestead property.

> The purpose of the homestead exemption has been described broadly as being to protect the family, and to provide for it a refuge from misfortune, without any requirement that the misfortune arise from a financial debt. [The homestead protections] create no personal qualifications touching the moral character of the resident nor do they undertake to exclude the vicious, the criminal, or the immoral from the benefits so provided.

Butterworth v. Caggiano, 605 So. 2d 56, 60 (Fla. 1992). Does the exemption of a home used to commit a crime further the objective of family security that the drafters of the homestead exemptions hoped to achieve? Cf. Unif. Controlled Substances Act §§505(c)(3), (d) (1994) (homestead exemptions). Should a homestead exemption apply to any home, regardless of size and value? Would the same logic apply to a residence purchased with assets obtained through criminal activity? The federal government is not bound by such limitations in state law, even when seeking forfeiture of property within the state. Furthermore, the federal government offers to adopt the property seized during investigations by state law enforcers. In light of the federal adoption alternative, are the homestead exemptions under state law now dead letters?

The Philadelphia Police Department directive indicates that there is some forfeitable property that police and prosecutors will not bother to obtain. Although covered by the statute, as a practical matter such property is immune from forfeiture. Why would law enforcement agencies decline to pursue a small amount of property even when it is clearly within the coverage of the forfeiture statute? Some state statutes also exempt certain property from forfeiture if the criminal activity is relatively insignificant. For instance, a South Carolina statute exempts vehicles from forfeiture if they transport less than ten grams of cocaine or one pound of marijuana. S.C. Code §44-53-520(a)(6). Some police department rules require higher levels of certainty among officers as to the forfeitability of property when the property value is small.

2. Procedures for Resolving Forfeitures

The government may begin forfeiture proceedings in several ways. It might simply file a civil complaint against either the property (in rem) or the owner (in personam). The government might also choose criminal forfeiture proceedings, which begin as part of the criminal action and with the final forfeiture hearing occurring after conviction. In criminal forfeiture cases the government must prove beyond a reasonable doubt that the defendant committed the crime (or it must obtain a guilty plea reflecting such a conclusion). Further findings are also necessary to show the relationship between the property at issue and the crime of conviction. In most states, civil forfeiture is far more common than criminal forfeiture.

Judges and juries do not often resolve civil forfeitures; instead, most forfeitures are handled administratively. After a government attorney sends notice to all interested parties, the property owners might choose not to contest the forfeiture. For forfeitures below a designated dollar amount, the government can then take possession of the property through an uncontested administrative forfeiture without any judicial proceedings at all.

Because the property owner might attempt to dispose of the disputed property before the government can take possession, the government often seizes or arrests the property at the beginning of the civil proceedings. The government may take physical possession of a movable asset such as a vehicle; it may ask a financial institution to freeze an account. For real property, the government often files a notice of lis pendens against the property; in a few cases, it takes actual possession of the property and renegotiates the rental arrangements with residents on the property. For some ongoing businesses seized, the government continues to operate the business and collect the revenue pending the final forfeiture determination.

No property may be seized or arrested for purposes of forfeiture unless the government has probable cause to believe it is subject to forfeiture. Probable cause can be demonstrated in different ways. Most often, the government arrests the property after obtaining a warrant in an ex parte hearing. An adversarial probable cause hearing takes place after the seizure. Before real property can be seized, however, the person with a claim to the property must be given notice and an opportunity to be heard. United States v. James Daniel Good Real Property, 510 U.S. 43, 44, 58, 62 (1993) ("Because real property cannot abscond, the court's jurisdiction can be preserved without prior seizure. . . . Sale of the property can be prevented by filing a notice of lis pendens. [B]ased upon the importance of the private interests at risk and the absence of countervailing Government needs, we hold that the seizure of real property . . . is not one of those extraordinary instances that justify the postponement of notice and hearing.").

Once the government has frozen the property it seeks to obtain through forfeiture, any claimant may file a bond, hire an attorney, and contest the validity of the forfeiture. If the claimant loses the judicial challenge, she forfeits the value of the bond along with the property in dispute. The stated purpose of the bond is to reimburse the government for expenses incurred in litigating a "frivolous" forfeiture action. Does the bond requirement explain why the great majority of forfeiture cases are never challenged in court? Or do most forfeitures go unchallenged because the owners have no realistic prospect of prevailing in court? One of the most important features of the Civil Asset Forfeiture Reform Act of 2000, P.L. 106-185 (codified at 18 U.S.C. §983(a)(2)(E)), was its elimination of the bond requirement for parties challenging a forfeiture in federal court. The Act does not change the procedure in state court.

Forfeiture statutes take various positions on the relevant burden of proof and standard of proof. Consider the following constitutional decision on the subject.

Department of Law Enforcement v. Real Property
588 So. 2d 957 (Fla. 1991)

BARKETT, J.

[We hold today that the Florida Contraband Forfeiture Act] is facially constitutional provided that it is applied consistent with the minimal due process requirements of the Florida Constitution as set forth in this opinion. Charles DeCarlo was arrested on drug trafficking charges on May 15, 1990, stemming from a reverse sting operation conducted by [the] Florida Department of Law Enforcement (FDLE) and the Levy County Sheriff's Department. On May 16, the state initiated forfeiture proceedings in circuit court against [a 60-acre tract of land, part of which includes an extension of an airstrip; 420 acres subdivided for mobile home sites and 300 permanent residences; and a personal residence and property, including garages and sheds].

Based solely on an affidavit executed by an FDLE special agent, the circuit court on May 16 issued warrants to seize the aforementioned properties. The state that day also filed a notice of lis pendens against those properties and petitioned for a rule to show cause why the properties should not be forfeited. . . . The claimants moved to dismiss the petitions on constitutional grounds. . . .

The basic due process guarantee of the Florida Constitution provides that "[n]o person shall be deprived of life, liberty or property without due process of law." Art. I, §9, Fla. Const. . . . Procedural due process serves as a vehicle to ensure fair treatment through the proper administration of justice where substantive rights are at issue. Procedural due process under the Florida Constitution guarantees to every citizen the right to have that course of legal procedure which has been established in our judicial system for the protection and enforcement of private rights. It contemplates that the defendant shall be given fair notice and afforded a real opportunity to be heard and defend in an orderly procedure, before judgment is rendered against him. . . .

The process provided in the Act [as amended in 1989] enables the state to seize property—whether real or personal—"which has been or is being used" to commit one of the enumerated offenses, or "in, upon or by means of which" any enumerated violation "has taken or is taking place." . . . After seizure, the state must "promptly proceed" against the property "by rule to show cause in the circuit court," and may have the property forfeited "upon producing due proof" that the property was being used in violation of the Act. If the state does not initiate proceedings within 90 days after the seizure, the claimant may maintain an action to recover the property. . . . Owners may raise a defense only after the property has been seized, and they must bear the burden in forfeiture proceedings of proving that they neither knew, nor should have known after a reasonable inquiry, that the property was being used or was likely to be used to commit an enumerated crime. Lienholders who can establish their perfected interests also may raise a defense only after seizure, and they bear the same burden as property owners plus an additional burden of proving that they did not consent to having the property used to commit a crime. At some point, the court is to issue a "final order of forfeiture" perfecting title in the seizing agency relating back to the date of seizure. Legal title to the property, or proceeds derived from the property after satisfaction of bona fide liens, are then transferred to [a specified agency or fund].

The Act raises numerous constitutional concerns that touch upon many substantive and procedural rights protected by the Florida Constitution. In construing the Act, we note that forfeitures are considered harsh exactions, and as a general rule they are not favored either in law or equity. Therefore, this Court has long followed a policy that it must strictly construe forfeiture statutes. Strict construction, however, may clash with the traditional judicial policy that all doubts as to the validity of a statute are to be resolved in favor of constitutionality where reasonably possible. . . .

The Act provides that after the property is first seized, the state must file a petition for a rule to show cause in the circuit court, and upon producing due proof that the property was used in violation of the Act, the court shall issue a final order of forfeiture vesting legal title in the appropriate agency under the Act. However, that is the sum total of direction given by the Act.

The Act does not set out any procedures for filing the petition or issuing the rule to show cause, except that a rule shall issue upon the showing of "due proof." The Act does not address any requirements for filing the petition; which procedural rules should apply to control the litigation; what standard and burden of proof is "due" for issuance of the rule; whether a trial—with or without a jury—is required to decide the merits of the action once the rule has been issued; what standard and burden of proof apply in deciding the ultimate issue, including defenses; and whether and how property is to be divided or partitioned to ensure that only the "guilty" property is forfeited. . . .

It is now well settled that the ultimate issue of forfeiture must be decided by jury trial unless claimants waive that right. That substantive right is also subsumed within article I, section 9 of the Florida Constitution. However, the issue of standard and burden of proof has not been previously addressed by this Court. The state argues that the agency seeking forfeiture need establish its case by at most a preponderance of the evidence, whereas the claimants argue that the constitution requires proof beyond a reasonable doubt, or alternatively, by clear and convincing evidence. Case law reflects no uniformity in this state as to the appropriate burden and standard of proof.

We conclude that the state has the burden of proof at trial, which should be by no less than clear and convincing evidence. The state and the decisions on which it relies fail to recognize the significance of the constitutionally protected rights at issue and the impact forfeiture has on those rights. In forfeiture proceedings the state impinges on basic constitutional rights of individuals who may never have been formally charged with any civil or criminal wrongdoing. This Court has consistently held that the constitution requires substantial burdens of proof where state action may deprive individuals of basic rights. For example, when an individual is charged with a crime, the government cannot deprive that person of life, liberty, or property unless it carries the burden of proof beyond every reasonable doubt as to each essential element. In noncriminal contexts [such as termination of parental rights, termination of an incompetent patient's life support, defamation suits brought by public figures, or establishment of land ownership through adverse possession], this Court has held that constitutionally protected individual rights may not be impinged with a showing of less than clear and convincing evidence.

Accordingly, "due proof" under the Act constitutionally means that the government may not take an individual's property in forfeiture proceedings unless it proves, by no less than clear and convincing evidence, that the property being forfeited was used in the commission of a crime. Lack of knowledge of the holder of an interest in the property that the property was being employed in criminal activity is a defense to forfeiture, which, if established by a preponderance of the evidence, defeats the forfeiture action as to that property interest. . . .

This Court is obliged and authorized to establish rules to enforce the Florida Constitution and to administer the courts of this state. Although we are concerned with the multitude of procedural deficiencies in the Act, the procedures described above are required to satisfy due process and are not inconsistent with the language and intent of the Act. We conclude that the Act can be reasonably construed as constitutional provided that it is applied consistent with the due process requirements summarized in this opinion.

Turning to the facts of this case, it is clear that the state did not comply with due process: It seized real property, including residential property, prior to giving the claimants any notice or opportunity to be heard. Accordingly, we affirm the result reached by the [lower] court in dismissing the forfeiture action. . . .

NOTES

1. *Burden of proof: majority position.*   It is most common for civil forfeiture statutes to place the burden of proof on the state to demonstrate that the property is forfeitable; the claimant then has the burden of proof to demonstrate that any exemptions or exceptions apply. The federal government and more than 30 states allocate the burden in this way. Roughly a dozen other states follow a different approach to the burden of proof: After the prosecution establishes probable cause to believe that property is forfeitable, the claimant carries the burden of persuasion and must show that the property is not forfeitable. Court challenges to the constitutionality of this burden of proof have mostly failed.

In the federal system, the Civil Asset Forfeiture Reform Act of 2000 changed the burden of proof in civil forfeiture. Before this amendment to the federal statutes, the burden of proof on the question of forfeitability shifted to a claimant after the government showed probable cause to believe that the property was forfeitable. Would you expect this statutory amendment to lead to a different outcome in many cases? Will this amendment change more outcomes than the elimination of the bond requirement (also a part of the Civil Asset Forfeiture Reform Act)?

Civil forfeiture statutes commonly include a provision creating a "presumption of forfeitability" for certain property, such as large amounts of currency found near narcotics. This presumption effectively shifts the burden of proof back to the claimant. Is this feature of the asset forfeiture laws likely to survive a court ruling that requires the government to carry the burden of proof in forfeiture proceedings?

2. *Standard of proof: majority position.*   In more than 30 states, civil forfeiture statutes require a party to establish facts by a preponderance of the evidence. For *criminal* forfeiture actions, which are resolved after a criminal conviction for the underlying crime, the government must prove the elements of the crime beyond a reasonable doubt. But after conviction, in the sentencing phase, the government usually must establish the forfeitability of the property only by a preponderance of the evidence rather than beyond a reasonable doubt. Clear and convincing evidence is the government's standard of proof in the civil forfeiture statutes of about a half-dozen states. See Minn. Stat. §609.531(6a)(a). A handful require proof beyond a reasonable doubt for some civil forfeitures. Why would a prosecutor ever use a civil forfeiture statute that requires proof beyond a reasonable doubt?

The Florida decision in the *Real Property* case was unusual in requiring a particular burden of proof and standard of proof as a matter of constitutional law. The Florida constitution forbids one of the branches of government from invading the province of another. Did the court invade the province of the legislature with its decision in *Real Property*? Or did it instead create law within its area of special expertise — procedural fairness — at the implicit invitation of the legislature? The Florida legislature later amended the statute dealing with civil forfeiture actions — without changing the "due proof" language relating to the procedure at trial.

3. *Juries.* Most state courts have concluded that their state statutes or constitutions require a jury trial for civil asset forfeiture proceedings. The relevant constitutional provision often protects the right to jury trial in any action recognized at common law at the time the state first adopted a constitution. Since civil in rem forfeitures were common law actions available during the relevant time period, jury trial is still available. See, e.g., Idaho Department of Law Enforcement v. Real Property, 885 P.2d 381 (Idaho 1994). About a dozen states, however, have reached the opposite conclusion. Federal courts have concluded that the Seventh Amendment requires jury trial for in rem forfeitures on the question of forfeitability. In practice, juries do not hear many civil asset forfeiture cases, in part because claimants rarely exercise their right to a jury trial and because the rules of civil procedure allow the government to move for summary judgment. When these motions succeed, as they often do, the court disposes of the case before it reaches a jury.

4. *Counsel fees from frozen assets.* In civil forfeiture proceedings, there is no federal constitutional right to appointed counsel. The U.S. Supreme Court in Caplin and Drysdale, Chartered v. United States, 491 U.S. 617 (1989), concluded that the right to counsel does not prevent the government from freezing assets necessary to hire criminal defense counsel so long as the assets are potentially subject to forfeiture. Most state courts agree. See State v. Nine Thousand One Hundred Ninety-Nine Dollars, 791 P.2d 213 (Utah 1990).

Constitutions are not the only source of law that determines whether forfeitable funds may be used for attorneys' fees. Some state forfeiture statutes explicitly allow a court to order the release of some frozen assets to permit a defendant to hire an attorney. New York statutes allow the release of such funds to hire an attorney for representation during civil forfeiture proceedings, criminal forfeiture proceedings, or related criminal proceedings. See N.Y. C.P.L.R. 1312(4); N.Y. Crim. Proc. Law §480.05(3) (allows payment for "bona fide fees" for legal services).

The Civil Asset Forfeiture Reform Act of 2000 expands access to attorneys for claimants of property being subject to civil asset forfeiture proceedings in federal court. The federal government now provides legal counsel for indigent claimants of property that the government is attempting to seize, along with attorneys' fees for winning claimants. Would expanded access to fees in civil proceedings be enough to convince private defense counsel to accept a forfeiture case?

PROBLEM 10-5. JOINT OWNERS

Tina and John Bennis jointly owned an 11-year-old Pontiac. Detroit police arrested John after observing him engaged in a sexual act with a prostitute in the automobile while it was parked on a Detroit city street. He was convicted of gross indecency. The state then filed a civil action to have the car declared a public nuisance (and therefore forfeited) under Michigan statutes.

Tina defended against the forfeiture of her interest in the car on the ground that she did not know her husband would use the car to violate Michigan's indecency law. The circuit court rejected this argument and declared the car a public nuisance. Even though the statute gave the judge the authority to award half of the sale proceeds to Tina (as an innocent titleholder) and the other half to the state, the judge refused to divide the proceeds. The judge noted that the couple owned another automobile and that the Pontiac was worth only $600. Is there any constitutional bar to the forfeiture of the car under these circumstances? Compare Bennis v. Michigan, 516 U.S. 442 (1996).

NOTES

1. *Innocent owners under federal statutes.* Under 18 U.S.C. §983(d)(2)(A), an innocent property owner can reclaim property that might otherwise be forfeited if the owner can show that he "did not know of the conduct giving rise to forfeiture [or] upon learning of the conduct giving rise to the forfeiture, did all that reasonably could be expected under the circumstances to terminate such use of the property." The property owner may establish his "innocence" even if he obtains the property after the previous owner commits a crime that makes the property forfeitable. The U.S. Supreme Court, in United States v. 92 Buena Vista Avenue, Rumson, New Jersey, 507 U.S. 111 (1993), decided that the unqualified language of the "innocent owner" provision (it applies to any "owner") precludes any per se bar against using the defense, even for persons who obtain the property after it becomes forfeitable. Under what circumstances can persons who were paid with illegal proceeds for providing goods or services to drug traffickers claim to be innocent owners?

2. *Innocent owners under state statutes.* While most state forfeiture statutes do provide "innocent owner" defenses, a few statutes without such a defense remain in place. The elements of the defense vary from state to state. Compare the two major model statutes, the Forfeiture Reform Act (FRA) of the President's Commission on Model State Drug Laws, and the Uniform Controlled Substances Act (UCSA) of the National Conference of Commissioners on Uniform State Laws. When it comes to an owner who acquires property interests before the property becomes forfeitable, the FRA requires that the owner either "did not and could not reasonably have known" about the likelihood of conduct making the property forfeitable or "acted reasonably to prevent the conduct." Section 8(a). The UCSA requires that the owner either "did not know the conduct would occur" or acted "in a manner the owner reasonably believed appropriate to prevent" the wrongful conduct. Sections 505(b), (c). On which drafting commission do you think prosecutors had more influence? Would Tina Bennis have been able to meet either test?

3. *Constitutions and innocent owners.* There is no federal constitutional bar to the forfeiture of an innocent owner's property when the forfeiture is allowed by state or federal statute. In Bennis v. Michigan, 516 U.S. 442 (1996), the basis for Problem 10-5, the Supreme Court decided that due process was not violated

by the forfeiture of an innocent owner's property without compensation: A "long and unbroken line of cases holds that an owner's interest in property may be forfeited by reason of the use to which the property is put even though the owner did not know that it was to be put to such use." The Court said that forfeiture of property — even an innocent owner's property — serves a deterrent purpose by preventing further illicit use of the property and by making illegal behavior unprofitable.

In an oft-cited case, State v. Richards, 301 S.W.2d 597 (Tex. 1957), the Texas Supreme Court upheld the forfeiture of a pickup truck when the owner lent it to an acquaintance who (unbeknownst to the truck's owner) was carrying two Dolophine pills in his shirt pocket. A dissenting justice declared that the "right to acquire and own property" is a "natural right" and that forfeiture interferes with this right. Many critics of forfeiture argue that the practice should remain limited because forfeiture is based on the "legal fiction" that the property reverts to the government as soon as the crime is committed. What is a legal fiction? Aren't all property rights recognized and enforced through a fiction of sorts? Is there a difference between a government declaration that a private party owns certain property and a government declaration that property used to commit a crime automatically belongs to the government? Does your answer to these questions depend on your views of the source of individual rights?

4. *Multiple owners.* Often the criminal offender's interest in the property is less valuable than the innocent owner's interest, such as when the offender borrows or leases the property. In other cases, the innocent owner and the offender are equal co-owners of the property in question. In that situation, should the property become forfeitable even if the innocent owner qualifies in every respect for the statutory defense? If so, what is the proper remedy? Forced sale of the property followed by an equal split of the proceeds? Should the innocent owner have to pay her share of the litigation costs? A number of statutes provide special protection to spouses who own forfeitable property jointly with wrongdoers. See Wash. Rev. Code §69.50.505(d) (innocent spouse with community property interest can block forfeiture). Should a formal property interest be necessary before this protection applies? See Sandra Guerra, Family Values? The Family as an Innocent Victim of Civil Drug Asset Forfeiture, 81 Cornell L. Rev. 343 (1996).

5. *The innocent tenant.* Under section 715 of New York's Real Property Actions and Proceedings Law, the owner of any real property "used or occupied in whole or in part . . . for any illegal trade, business or manufacture" may bring expedited civil proceedings to evict the tenant. If the landlord refuses to evict the tenant, the district attorney may bring a civil action against the tenant and recover litigation expenses from the landlord. See Peter Finn, The Manhattan District Attorney's Narcotics Eviction Program (National Institute of Justice, NCJ 153146, May 1995). If the statute itself contains no provision for an innocent co-tenant, what charging limitations (if any) should the district attorney employ? Should the D.A. evict any tenant (say, a grandmother) who "knew or should have known" about illegal activity of another tenant (say, a grandson)? If "reasonable efforts" to stop the illegal activity are enough to avoid eviction, how much effort is considered reasonable? Pleading with the grandson to stop the

illegal activity? Reporting it to the police? Cf. Department of Housing and Urban Development v. Rucker, 535 U.S. 125 (2002) (Anti-Drug Abuse Act required lease terms that gave local public housing authorities discretion to terminate lease when any member of household or guest engaged in drug-related activity).

6. *Bypassing the criminal process.*   One of the virtues of asset forfeiture from the perspective of law enforcement is its efficiency. It allows the government to remove dangerous or illicit goods from circulation quickly, and as a practical matter it allows for some punishment of guilty property owners without having to clear the hurdles of the criminal process. Elsewhere in this chapter we have considered other legal procedures that accomplish some of the objectives of criminal sentences without going through the criminal process. Do these procedures differ from one another in important ways? Do some present greater potential for abuse by prosecutors or other law enforcement officials?

D.   CIVIL AND ADMINISTRATIVE REMEDIES

Rather than pursuing criminal charges against wrongdoers, government enforcers sometimes go to court to obtain civil sanctions such as fines or injunctions. Or they make their claims against the wrongdoer in administrative proceedings, without involving the judicial branch at all. Under what circumstances do government enforcers tend to ask for civil or administrative remedies rather than filing criminal charges? What are the risks for potential targets who face criminal and civil proceedings simultaneously?

|| *John Hudson v. United States* ||
522 U.S. 93 (1997)

REHNQUIST, C.J.

The Government administratively imposed monetary penalties and occupational debarment on petitioners for violation of federal banking statutes, and later criminally indicted them for essentially the same conduct. We hold that the Double Jeopardy Clause of the Fifth Amendment is not a bar to the later criminal prosecution because the administrative proceedings were civil, not criminal. . . .

During the early and mid-1980's, petitioner John Hudson was the chairman and controlling shareholder of the First National Bank of Tipton and the First National Bank of Hammon. During the same period, petitioner Jack Rackley was president of Tipton and a member of the board of directors of Hammon, and petitioner Larry Baresel was a member of the board of directors of both Tipton and Hammon. An examination of Tipton and Hammon led the Office of the Comptroller of the Currency to conclude that petitioners had used their bank positions to arrange a series of loans to third parties in violation of various federal banking statutes and regulations. According to the OCC, those loans, while nominally made to third parties, were in reality made to Hudson in order to enable him to redeem bank stock that he had pledged as collateral on defaulted loans.

On February 13, 1989, OCC issued a "Notice of Assessment of Civil Money Penalty." The notice alleged that petitioners had violated 12 U.S.C. §§84(a)(1) and 375b and 12 CFR §§31.2(b) and 215.4(b) by causing the banks with which they were associated to make loans to nominee borrowers in a manner that unlawfully allowed Hudson to receive the benefit of the loans. The notice also alleged that the illegal loans resulted in losses to Tipton and Hammon of almost $900,000 and contributed to the failure of those banks. However, the notice contained no allegation of any harm to the Government as a result of petitioners' conduct. After taking into account the size of the financial resources and the good faith of petitioners, the gravity of the violations, the history of previous violations and other matters . . . OCC assessed penalties of $100,000 against Hudson and $50,000 each against Rackley and Baresel. On August 31, 1989, OCC also issued a "Notice of Intention to Prohibit Further Participation" against each petitioner. These notices, which were premised on the identical allegations that formed the basis for the previous notices, informed petitioners that OCC intended to bar them from further participation in the conduct of any insured depository institution.

In October 1989, petitioners resolved the OCC proceedings against them by each entering into a "Stipulation and Consent Order." These consent orders provided that Hudson, Baresel, and Rackley would pay assessments of $16,500, $15,000, and $12,500 respectively. In addition, each petitioner agreed not to participate in any manner in the affairs of any banking institution without the written authorization of the OCC and all other relevant regulatory agencies.

In August 1992, petitioners were indicted in the Western District of Oklahoma in a 22-count indictment on charges of conspiracy, misapplication of bank funds, and making false bank entries. The violations charged in the indictment rested on the same lending transactions that formed the basis for the prior administrative actions brought by OCC. Petitioners moved to dismiss the indictment on double jeopardy grounds [and the trial court granted the motion].

The Double Jeopardy Clause provides that no "person [shall] be subject for the same offence to be twice put in jeopardy of life or limb." We have long recognized that the Double Jeopardy Clause does not prohibit the imposition of all additional sanctions that could, in common parlance, be described as punishment. The Clause protects only against the imposition of multiple *criminal* punishments for the same offense, and then only when such occurs in successive proceedings.

Whether a particular punishment is criminal or civil is, at least initially, a matter of statutory construction. A court must first ask whether the legislature, in establishing the penalizing mechanism, indicated either expressly or impliedly a preference for one label or the other. Even in those cases where the legislature has indicated an intention to establish a civil penalty, we have inquired further whether the statutory scheme was so punitive either in purpose or effect as to transform what was clearly intended as a civil remedy into a criminal penalty.

In making this latter determination, the factors listed in Kennedy v. Mendoza-Martinez, 372 U.S. 144, 168-169 (1963), provide useful guideposts, including: (1) whether the sanction involves an affirmative disability or restraint;

(2) whether it has historically been regarded as a punishment; (3) whether it comes into play only on a finding of scienter; (4) whether its operation will promote the traditional aims of punishment—retribution and deterrence; (5) whether the behavior to which it applies is already a crime; (6) whether an alternative purpose to which it may rationally be connected is assignable for it; and (7) whether it appears excessive in relation to the alternative purpose assigned. It is important to note, however, that these factors must be considered in relation to the statute on its face, and "only the clearest proof" will suffice to override legislative intent and transform what has been denominated a civil remedy into a criminal penalty.

Our opinion in United States v. Halper, 490 U.S. 435 (1989), marked the first time we applied the Double Jeopardy Clause to a sanction without first determining that it was criminal in nature. In that case, Irwin Halper was convicted of violating the criminal false claims statute based on his submission of 65 inflated Medicare claims each of which overcharged the Government by $9. He was sentenced to two years' imprisonment and fined $5,000. The Government then brought an action against Halper under the civil False Claims Act, 31 U.S.C. §§3729-3731. The remedial provisions of the False Claims Act provided that a violation of the Act rendered one "liable to the United States Government for a civil penalty of $2,000, an amount equal to 2 times the amount of damages the Government sustains because of the act of that person, and costs of the civil action." Given Halper's 65 separate violations of the Act, he appeared to be liable for a penalty of $130,000, despite the fact he actually defrauded the Government of less than $600.

[This Court held that a penalty of this magnitude would violate the Double Jeopardy Clause in light of Halper's previous criminal conviction. As the *Halper* Court saw it, any] sanction that was so overwhelmingly disproportionate to the injury caused that it could not "fairly be said *solely* to serve the remedial purpose" of compensating the Government for its loss, was thought to be explainable only as "serving either retributive or deterrent purposes."

The analysis applied by the *Halper* Court deviated from our traditional double jeopardy doctrine in two key respects. First, the *Halper* Court bypassed the threshold question: whether the successive punishment at issue is a "criminal" punishment. Instead, it focused on whether the sanction, regardless of whether it was civil or criminal, was so grossly disproportionate to the harm caused as to constitute "punishment." In so doing, the Court elevated a single *Kennedy* factor—whether the sanction appeared excessive in relation to its non-punitive purposes—to dispositive status. But as we emphasized in *Kennedy* itself, no one factor should be considered controlling as they may often point in differing directions. The second significant departure in *Halper* was the Court's decision to assess the "character of the actual sanctions imposed," rather than, as *Kennedy* demanded, evaluating the "statute on its face" to determine whether it provided for what amounted to a criminal sanction. . . .

As subsequent cases have demonstrated, *Halper*'s test for determining whether a particular sanction is "punitive," and thus subject to the strictures of the Double Jeopardy Clause, has proved unworkable. We have since recognized that all civil penalties have some deterrent effect. See Department of Revenue of Montana v. Kurth Ranch, 511 U.S. 767, 777 n.14 (1994) [applying a *Kennedy*-like test before concluding that Montana's dangerous drug tax was "the functional equivalent of a successive criminal prosecution"]; United States v. Ursery, 518 U.S. 267, 284-285 (1996) [civil in rem forfeitures do not violate the Double Jeopardy Clause]. If a sanction must be "solely" remedial (i.e., entirely nondeterrent) to avoid implicating the Double Jeopardy Clause, then no civil penalties are beyond the scope of the Clause.

[It] should be noted that some of the ills at which *Halper* was directed are addressed by other constitutional provisions. The Due Process and Equal Protection Clauses already protect individuals from sanctions which are downright irrational. The Eighth Amendment protects against excessive civil fines, including forfeitures. The additional protection afforded by extending double jeopardy protections to proceedings heretofore thought to be civil is more than offset by the confusion created by attempting to distinguish between "punitive" and "nonpunitive" penalties.

Applying traditional double jeopardy principles to the facts of this case, it is clear that the criminal prosecution of these petitioners would not violate the Double Jeopardy Clause. It is evident that Congress intended the OCC money penalties and debarment sanctions imposed for violations of 12 U.S.C. §§84 and 375b to be civil in nature. As for the money penalties, both §§93(b)(1) and 504(a), which authorize the imposition of monetary penalties for violations of §§84 and 375b respectively, expressly provide that such penalties are "civil." While the provision authorizing debarment contains no language explicitly denominating the sanction as civil, we think it significant that the authority to issue debarment orders is conferred upon the appropriate Federal banking agencies. That such authority was conferred upon administrative agencies is prima facie evidence that Congress intended to provide for a civil sanction.

[There] is little evidence, much less the clearest proof that we require, suggesting that either OCC money penalties or debarment sanctions are so punitive in form and effect as to render them criminal despite Congress' intent to the contrary. First, neither money penalties nor debarment has historically been viewed as punishment. We have long recognized that revocation of a privilege voluntarily granted, such as a debarment, "is characteristically free of the punitive criminal element." Helvering v. Mitchell, 303 U.S. 391, 399 (1938)....

Second, the sanctions imposed do not involve an "affirmative disability or restraint," as that term is normally understood. While petitioners have been prohibited from further participating in the banking industry, this is certainly nothing approaching the "infamous" punishment of imprisonment. Third, neither sanction comes into play "only" on a finding of scienter. The provisions under which the money penalties were imposed, 12 U.S.C. §§93(b) and 504, allow for the assessment of a penalty against any person "who violates" any of the underlying banking statutes, without regard to the violator's state of mind. "Good faith" is considered by OCC in determining the amount of the penalty to be imposed, but a penalty can be imposed even in the absence of bad faith. The fact that petitioners' "good faith" was considered in determining the amount of the penalty to be imposed in this case is irrelevant, as we look only to "the statute on its face" to determine whether a penalty is criminal in nature. Similarly, while debarment may be imposed for a "willful" disregard for the safety or soundness of an insured depository institution, willfulness is not a prerequisite to debarment; it is sufficient that the disregard for the safety and soundness of the institution was "continuing." §1818(e)(1)(C)(ii).

Fourth, the conduct for which OCC sanctions are imposed may also be criminal (and in this case formed the basis for petitioners' indictments). This fact is insufficient to render the money penalties and debarment sanctions criminally punitive, particularly in the double jeopardy context. See United States v. Dixon, 509 U.S. 688 (1993) (rejecting "same-conduct" test for double jeopardy purposes).

Finally, we recognize that the imposition of both money penalties and debarment sanctions will deter others from emulating petitioners' conduct, a traditional goal of criminal punishment. But the mere presence of this purpose is insufficient to render a sanction criminal, as deterrence may serve civil as well as criminal goals. For example, the sanctions at issue here, while intended to deter future wrongdoing, also serve to promote the stability of the banking industry. To hold that the mere presence of a deterrent purpose renders such sanctions "criminal" for double jeopardy purposes would severely undermine the Government's ability to engage in effective regulation of institutions such as banks.

In sum, there simply is very little showing . . . that OCC money penalties and debarment sanctions are criminal. The Double Jeopardy Clause is therefore no obstacle to their trial on the pending indictments, and it may proceed. . . .

STEVENS, J., concurring.

. . . As is evident from the first sentence of the Court's opinion, this is an extremely easy case. It has been settled since the decision in Blockburger v. United States, 284 U.S. 299 (1932), that the Double Jeopardy Clause is not implicated simply because a criminal charge involves "essentially the same conduct" for which a defendant has previously been punished. Unless a second proceeding involves the "same offense" as the first, there is no double jeopardy. The two proceedings at issue here involved different offenses that were not even arguably the same under *Blockburger.*

Under *Blockburger*'s "same-elements" test, two provisions are not the "same offense" if each contains an element not included in the other. The penalties imposed on the petitioners in 1989 were based on violations of 12 U.S.C. §§84(a)(1) and 375b and 12 CFR §§31.2(b) and 215.4(b). Each of these provisions required proof that extensions of credit exceeding certain limits were made, but did not require proof of an intent to defraud or the making of any false entries in bank records. The 1992 indictment charged violations of 18 U.S.C. §§371, 656, and 1005 and alleged a conspiracy to willfully misapply bank funds and to make false banking entries, as well as the making of such entries; none of those charges required proof that any lending limit had been exceeded. Thus, I think it would be difficult to find a case raising a double jeopardy claim that would be any easier to decide than this one. . . .

Despite my disagreement with the Court's decision to use this case as a rather lame excuse for writing a gratuitous essay about punishment, I do agree with its reaffirmation of the central holding of *Halper,* [which held] that sanctions imposed in civil proceedings constituted "punishment" barred by the Double Jeopardy Clause. Those holdings reconfirmed the settled proposition that the Government cannot use the "civil" label to escape entirely the Double

Jeopardy Clause's command, as we have recognized for at least six decades. That proposition is extremely important because the States and the Federal Government have an enormous array of civil administrative sanctions at their disposal that are capable of being used to punish persons repeatedly for the same offense, violating the bedrock double jeopardy principle of finality. . . .

BREYER, J. concurring.

. . . I would not decide now that a court should evaluate a statute only "on its face," rather than assessing the character of the actual sanctions imposed. *Halper* involved an ordinary civil-fine statute that as normally applied would not have created any "double jeopardy" problem. It was not the statute itself, but rather the disproportionate relation between fine and conduct as the statute was applied in the individual case that led this Court, unanimously, to find that the "civil penalty" was, in those circumstances, a second "punishment" that constituted double jeopardy. . . . It seems to me quite possible that a statute that provides for a punishment that normally is civil in nature could nonetheless amount to a criminal punishment as applied in special circumstances. And I would not now hold to the contrary. . . .

NOTES

1. *Double jeopardy and civil sanctions: majority position.* If the government seeks a penalty in a civil proceeding, it can be instituted after a criminal conviction, before a criminal conviction, or indeed in the absence of any criminal conviction or criminal charges. The possibility of facing two separate proceedings raises the concern that the government will pursue a second "punishment" for a crime if it is dissatisfied with the punishment after the first set of proceedings. Nevertheless, in *Hudson* the U.S. Supreme Court decided that civil penalties usually do not constitute "punishment" for purposes of the double jeopardy clause of the Eighth Amendment. As a result, there is no double jeopardy bar to the government's bringing both criminal charges and civil forfeiture proceedings based on the same conduct or transaction. See also United States v. Ursery, 518 U.S. 267 (1996) (civil in rem forfeiture proceedings are not punishment for double jeopardy purposes).

2. *Choice of proceedings.* While the government's ability to pursue both criminal and civil sanctions (or criminal fines and civil money penalties) is now clearly accepted, this was not always the case. For an early survey of the issues, see Walter Gellhorn, Administrative Prescription and Imposition of Penalties, 1970 Wash. L.Q. 265. Defendants might worry that the government will use civil proceedings as an insurance policy against an unfavorable outcome in the criminal process. For instance, if the government fails to obtain a conviction or the court imposes a sentence unsatisfactory to the prosecutor, the government could try to obtain a more favorable outcome by pursuing civil charges. Can courts prevent this sort of manipulation by insisting that the civil proceedings commence before the verdict or sentence in the criminal case? See Mary M. Cheh, Constitutional Limits on Using Civil Remedies to Achieve Criminal Law Objectives: Understanding and Transcending the Criminal-Civil Law

Distinction, 42 Hastings L.J. 1325 (1991); Kenneth Mann, Punitive Civil Sanctions: The Middleground Between Criminal and Civil Law, 101 Yale L.J. 1795 (1992). The government also might use the relatively broad discovery devices of civil litigation to get around the barriers built into discovery for criminal proceedings.

In the corporate context, the federal government may be inclined to threaten an entity with criminal prosecution in an attempt to leverage large civil payments. This is the case when similar statutes allow for criminal and civil fines. Whether a criminal or a civil proceeding is preferable against a corporation may be debatable, especially if the wrongdoing is limited to a handful of employees rather than being indicative of widespread corruption. See Elizabeth K. Ainslie, Indicting Corporations Revisited: Lessons from the Arthur Andersen Prosecution, 43 Am. Crim. L. Rev. 107 (2006).

3. *The publicity alternative.*   Consider this alternative to criminal proceedings: After the end of apartheid in South Africa, the government established the Truth and Reconciliation Commission to create some accountability and public disclosure for many acts of public wrongdoing during the earlier era. The commission did not impose criminal sanctions, but its proceedings and findings received intense public attention. Perpetrators of apartheid crimes who did not appear before the commission could end up in front of a criminal court—and all perpetrators could still face criminal charges before an international or non-national tribunal. In what situations is intense public scrutiny and debate an acceptable alternative to criminal punishments? To what extent should a country be allowed to opt for forgiveness instead of criminal sanctions for serious offenses, such as apartheid, torture, or crimes against humanity? See Eric Blumenson, The Challenge of a Global Standard of Justice: Peace, Pluralism, and Punishment at the International Criminal Court, 44 Colum. J. Transnat'l L. 801 (2006).

4. *Drug taxes.*   A majority of states impose taxes on illegal drugs or on those who distribute them. The statutes typically require any possessor of a controlled substance to purchase "tax stamps" for each ounce of the controlled substance. Some of the drug tax statutes apply regardless of whether the owner of the controlled substance was ever arrested or convicted. In Department of Revenue of Montana v. Kurth Ranch, 511 U.S. 767 (1994), the Supreme Court held that such a drug tax might qualify as an additional "punishment" for conduct; the double jeopardy bar means that the tax cannot be used in conjunction with a criminal prosecution. The Court described the statute and its reasons as follows:

> Montana's Dangerous Drug Tax Act . . . imposes a tax "on the possession and storage of dangerous drugs," and expressly provides that the tax is to be "collected only after any state or federal fines or forfeitures have been satisfied." The tax is either 10 percent of the assessed market value of the drugs . . . or a specified amount depending on the drug ($100 per ounce for marijuana, for example, and $250 per ounce for hashish), whichever is greater. [At] the time of arrest law enforcement personnel shall complete the dangerous drug information report as required by the department and afford the taxpayer an opportunity to sign it. If the taxpayer refuses to do so, the law enforcement officer is required to file the form within 72 hours of the arrest. . . . The taxpayer has no obligation to file a return or to pay any tax unless and until he is arrested. . . .

Whereas fines, penalties, and forfeitures are readily characterized as sanctions, taxes are typically different because they are usually motivated by revenue-raising rather than punitive purposes. Yet at some point, an exaction labeled as a tax approaches punishment, and our task is to determine whether Montana's drug tax crosses that line.

We begin by noting that neither a high rate of taxation nor an obvious deterrent purpose automatically marks this tax a form of punishment. . . . A significant part of the assessment was more than eight times the drug's market value — a remarkably high tax. That the Montana legislature intended the tax to deter people from possessing marijuana is beyond question. . . .

Other unusual features . . . set the Montana statute apart from most taxes. First, this so-called tax is conditioned on the commission of a crime. [The] assessment not only hinges on the commission of a crime, it also is exacted only after the taxpayer has been arrested for the precise conduct that gives rise to the tax obligation in the first place. . . . The Montana tax is exceptional for an additional reason. Although it purports to be a species of property tax — that is, a "tax on the possession and storage of dangerous drugs" — it is levied on goods that the taxpayer neither owns nor possesses when the tax is imposed. Indeed, the State presumably destroyed the contraband goods in this case before the tax on them was assessed.

Id. at 770, 778-783. The Court concluded that the imposition of the drug tax in Montana constituted "punishment" and therefore created a double jeopardy bar that prevented the state from bringing criminal charges for possession of drugs.

State tax provisions have withstood some, but not all, challenges under various provisions of state constitutions. The state courts have split when deciding whether their statutes violated the state or federal rules against double jeopardy. The statutes surviving a double jeopardy challenge are usually different from the Montana statute in *Kurth Ranch* because they provide for collection of the tax and punishment of violators even when there is no prosecution or conviction for other narcotics violations. See Covelli v. Commissioner of Revenue Services, 668 A.2d 699 (Conn. 1995).

5. *Driver's license.* Persons who are arrested for driving while intoxicated often lose their driver's licenses in administrative hearings and are convicted of a crime in separate criminal proceedings. The defendants sometimes claim that the two proceedings amount to double jeopardy. Such arguments have failed in about 30 states and have succeeded in almost 20 (mostly in the intermediate appellate courts). Compare State v. Young, 544 N.W.2d 808 (Neb. 1996) (no double jeopardy violation) with State v. Gustafson, 668 N.E.2d 435 (Ohio 1996) (double jeopardy violation). How might you argue that the loss of a driver's license is different from civil in rem forfeiture of assets? Should the legal analysis change if the government is threatening to remove some other form of license, such as a license to practice medicine or law?

= 11 =

‖ *Sentences Reconsidered* ‖

As discussed in Chapter 2, many institutions and individuals have input into the sentences imposed on convicted offenders. We often think of this input as culminating in the decision of a sentencing judge. Many different players, however, have the opportunity to reconsider sentencing choices made by others.

Some of the legal structures through which sentences are reconsidered involve the judiciary, as detailed in the first half of this chapter; others involve executive branch officials, as discussed in the second half. Some review structures are unique to death sentences, while others apply to all sentences. In all settings, the officials may reconsider not only specific sentencing outcomes but also some of the theoretical, policy-based, and legal arguments that influenced initial sentencing decisions.

A. JUDICIAL RECONSIDERATION OF SENTENCES

Judges are commonly viewed as central figures in sentencing. Yet, as we have seen throughout the book, many other institutions and individuals — legislatures, sentencing commissions, prosecutors, and probation officers — play a role in determining what types of sentences judges are able to impose. Indeed, when a legislature enacts a mandatory sentencing provision, or when a sentencing commission establishes strict sentencing guidelines, the judiciary's role in determining initial sentences can seem more administrative than substantive.

While many structured sentencing reforms have allowed institutions other than courts to play a larger part in initial sentencing decisions, other legal developments have increased the judiciary's role in the reconsideration of initial sentencing decisions. The judicial role in sentence reconsideration, especially through appeals and collateral review, is relatively new: Review of convictions and sentences were historically part of an appeal made to the sovereign — the governor or president. But no longer is such an appeal to the sovereign an offender's only avenue for relief. There are now elaborate legal structures and rules that give offenders a way to obtain judicial review of their convictions and sentences.

1. Sentencing Judge

The sentencing choices of legislatures, sentencing commissions, and prosecutors are inevitably reexamined and reassessed by a sentencing judge when she decides what specific sentence to impose on a particular offender. As the following case highlights, modern systems with defined sentencing rules present sentencing judges with opportunities to reconsider the appropriateness and the application of general sentencing rules in individual cases.

> ## California v. Superior Court of San Diego County (Jesus Romero, Real Party in Interest)
> ### 917 P.2d 628 (Cal. 1996)

WERDEGAR, J.

Penal Code section 1385, subdivision (a), authorizes a trial court to dismiss a criminal action "in furtherance of justice" on its own motion. . . . This case raises the question whether a court may, on its own motion, strike prior felony conviction allegations in cases arising under the law known as "Three Strikes and You're Out." . . .

I. BACKGROUND

A. The Three Strikes Law

The Three Strikes law consists of two, nearly identical statutory schemes designed to increase the prison terms of repeat felons. . . . In summary, both statutes have this effect: When a defendant is convicted of a felony, and it is pleaded and proved that he has committed one or more prior felonies defined as "violent" or "serious," sentencing proceeds under the Three Strikes law. Prior felonies qualifying as "serious" or "violent" are taken into account regardless of their age. The current felony need not be "violent" or "serious." If the defendant has only one qualifying prior felony conviction, the prescribed term of imprisonment . . . is twice the term otherwise provided as punishment for the current felony conviction. If the defendant has two or more prior qualifying felonies, the prescribed sentence is an indeterminate term of life imprisonment [with a minimum term before parole eligibility of] the greater of: (a) three times the term otherwise provided for the current conviction; (b) twenty-five years; or (c) the term required [under other statutes]. In sentencing, the court may not grant probation, suspend execution or imposition of sentence, divert the defendant, or commit the defendant to any facility other than state prison.

B. Facts

On June 3, 1994, the District Attorney of San Diego County filed an information in the superior court charging defendant Jesus Romero with possession of a controlled substance, namely 0.13 grams of cocaine base. The information also alleged defendant had previously been convicted of the following felonies on the dates indicated: second degree burglary on June 25, 1980; attempted burglary of an inhabited dwelling on November 16, 1984; first degree burglary of an inhabited dwelling on September 2, 1986; and possession of a controlled substance on April 6, 1992, and June 8, 1993.

Defendant's two prior serious felonies, namely burglary and attempted burglary of inhabited dwellings, made him eligible for a life sentence under the Three Strikes law. Without the prior felony conviction allegations, defendant's sentence would fall between one and six years. . . . Defendant pled not guilty. At a subsequent hearing, the court indicated its willingness to consider striking the prior felony conviction allegations if defendant changed his plea to guilty as charged on all counts. The prosecutor objected to that procedure, arguing the court had no power to dismiss prior felony allegations in a Three Strikes case unless the prosecutor asked the court to do so. The court disagreed [and] permitted defendant to change his plea and struck the prior felony conviction allegations. [The court] imposed a sentence of six years in state prison. . . .

II. Discussion

The ultimate question before us is whether a trial court may dismiss prior felony conviction allegations in furtherance of justice on its own motion in a case brought under the Three Strikes law. In answering this question, two statutes are of central importance. The first is section 1385. It provides as follows:

> (a) The judge or magistrate may, either of his or her own motion or upon the application of the prosecuting attorney, and in the furtherance of justice, order an action to be dismissed. The reasons for the dismissal must be set forth in an order entered upon the minutes. . . .
> (b) This section does not authorize a judge to strike any prior conviction of a serious felony for purposes of enhancement of a sentence under Section 667.

[We] have construed section 1385(a) as permitting a judge to dismiss not only an entire case, but also a part thereof, including the allegation that a defendant has previously been convicted of a felony. When a court strikes prior felony conviction allegations in this way, it does not wipe out such prior convictions or prevent them from being considered in connection with later convictions. Instead, the order striking such allegations simply embodies the court's determination that, in the interest of justice, defendant should not be required to undergo a statutorily increased penalty which would follow from judicial determination of the alleged fact.

The other statute of central importance to this case is section 667, subdivision (f). A part of the Three Strikes law, the statute provides as follows:

> (f) (1) Notwithstanding any other law, subdivisions (b) to (i), inclusive, shall be applied in every case in which a defendant has a prior felony conviction as defined in subdivision (d). The prosecuting attorney shall plead and prove each prior felony conviction except as provided in paragraph (2).
>
> (2) The prosecuting attorney may move to dismiss or strike a prior felony conviction allegation in the furtherance of justice pursuant to Section 1385, or if there is insufficient evidence to prove the prior conviction. If upon the satisfaction of the court that there is insufficient evidence to prove the prior felony conviction, the court may dismiss or strike the allegation.

Defendant argues that the Three Strikes law, if interpreted to permit a court to strike a prior felony conviction allegation *only* on the prosecutor's motion, violates the doctrine of separation of powers. [In People v. Tenorio, we held] unconstitutional a statute purporting to empower a prosecutor to veto a court's decision to dismiss a prior conviction allegation. . . . One may fairly summarize the court's reasoning in this way: [Conceding] the Legislature's power to bar a court from dismissing certain charges altogether, when the Legislature does permit a charge to be dismissed the ultimate decision whether to dismiss is a judicial, rather than a prosecutorial or executive, function; to require the prosecutor's consent to the disposition of a criminal charge pending before the court unacceptably compromises judicial independence. In subsequent cases, the court relied on People v. Tenorio to hold unconstitutional other statutes purporting to give prosecutors the power to veto similar judicial decisions related to the sentencing or other disposition of criminal charges. . . .

The Attorney General suggests the Three Strikes law serves the purpose of the separation of powers doctrine by making the decision to dismiss under section 1385 a "joint" decision, in the sense that the court and the prosecutor each may veto the other's preferred disposition. [But] interference with the traditional prerogatives of the executive cannot justify interference with the independence of the judiciary. . . . That the Legislature and the electorate may eliminate the courts' power to make certain sentencing choices may be conceded. Subject to the constitutional prohibition against cruel and unusual punishment, the power to define crimes and fix penalties is vested exclusively in the legislative branch. It does not follow, however, that having given the court the power to dismiss, the Legislature may therefore condition its exercise upon the approval of the district attorney. This court has not upheld any law purporting to subject to prosecutorial approval the court's discretion to dispose of a criminal charge. Instead, we have consistently held such laws unconstitutional. . . .

We thus arrive at this question: Does the Three Strikes law contain a "clear legislative direction" that courts may not strike sentencing allegations in furtherance of justice under section 1385 without the prosecutor's approval? [It is] self-evident that the Legislature assumed a court would at least have the power to grant the prosecutor's motion to strike a prior felony allegation in the furtherance of justice. The question then becomes: Does the court also have the power to strike such an allegation on its own motion?

[Defendant] contends, the Three Strikes law confirms that the court retains its powers under section 1385: Because section 667(f)(2) permits the prosecuting attorney to "move to dismiss or strike a prior felony conviction allegation in the furtherance of justice *pursuant to Section 1385*"(italics added), a fortiori the court must have power to grant the motion *pursuant to section 1385*. . . .

[There] is a long history of dispute among the various branches of state government over the application of section 1385 to sentencing allegations [, and] the lesson of section 1385's controversial history is that references to the section in sentencing statutes are not lightly or thoughtlessly made. The drafter's express invocation of section 1385 in the Three Strikes law, together with the absence of any language purporting to bar courts from acting pursuant to it, virtually compels the conclusion no such prohibition was intended. . . .

The district attorney . . . argues that section 1385(b) independently bars a court from striking prior felony allegations in Three Strikes cases [because it] qualifies the general power to dismiss granted to courts in section 1385(a), in these words: "This section does not authorize a judge to strike any prior conviction of a serious felony for purposes of enhancement of a sentence under Section 667." The Three Strikes law, the district attorney contends, was codified as part of section 667 and articulates a sentence "enhancement" within the meaning of section 1385(b). . . . Defendant's [main response is] that section 1385(b) cannot fairly be read as referring to the Three Strikes law [because it was enacted first and because it is not an "enhancement" under the terms of section 1385(b). Legislative] intent is the governing consideration. [The] Legislature's decision to place the Three Strikes law within section 667 falls short of a "clear legislative direction" to eliminate courts' power to strike prior felony allegations sua sponte. . . .

The district attorney [further argues that the] Three Strikes initiative was motivated by the voters' desire for longer sentences and by a mistrust of judges. The proponents of the initiative argued in its favor that "soft-on-crime judges, politicians, defense lawyers and probation officers care more about violent felons than they do victims. They spend all of their time looking for loopholes to get rapists, child molesters and murderers out on probation, early parole, or off the hook altogether."

Plainly the Three Strikes initiative, as well as the legislative act embodying its terms, was intended to restrict courts' discretion in sentencing repeat offenders. . . . Both versions of the Three Strikes law expressly declare that a court, in sentencing, may not grant probation, suspend execution or imposition of sentence, divert the defendant, or commit the defendant to any facility other than state prison. But to say the intent of a law was to restrict judicial discretion begs the question of *how* judicial discretion was to be restricted. The answer to that question can be found only by examining the language of the act. In it, one finds the express restrictions on the courts' power mentioned above, but no others. . . .

For these reasons, we conclude that section 1385(a) does permit a court acting on its own motion to strike prior felony conviction allegations in cases brought under the Three Strikes law. Our holding respects the principle that legislative acts are construed, if at all possible, to be constitutional. Our holding also avoids conflict with the principle that ambiguous penal statutes are construed to favor the defendant.

To guide the lower courts in the exercise of their discretion under section 1385(a), whether acting on their own motion or on motion of the prosecuting attorney, we emphasize the following: A court's discretion to strike prior felony conviction allegations in furtherance of justice is limited . . . and is subject to review for abuse. We reviewed the applicable principles in People v. Orin, 533 P.2d 193 (Cal. 1975):

> The trial court's power to dismiss an action under section 1385 . . . is limited by the amorphous concept which requires that the dismissal be "in furtherance of justice." . . . From the case law, several general principles emerge. Paramount among them is the rule that the language of [section 1385], "in furtherance of justice," requires consideration "both of the constitutional rights of the defendant, and *the interests of society represented by the People,* in determining whether there should be a dismissal." At the very least, the reason for dismissal must be "that which would motivate a reasonable judge." . . .

From these general principles it follows that a court abuses its discretion if it dismisses a case, or strikes a sentencing allegation, solely to accommodate judicial convenience or because of court congestion. A court also abuses its discretion by dismissing a case, or a sentencing allegation, simply because a defendant pleads guilty. Nor would a court act properly if guided solely by a personal antipathy for the effect that the Three Strikes law would have on a defendant, while ignoring defendant's background, the nature of his present offenses, and other individualized considerations.

. . . Section 1385 anticipates, and facilitates, appellate review with the requirement that "[t]he reasons for the dismissal must be set forth in an order entered upon the minutes." The statement of reasons is not merely directory, and neither trial nor appellate courts have authority to disregard the requirement. It is not enough that on review the reporter's transcript may show the trial court's motivation; the *minutes* must reflect the reason so that all may know why this great power was exercised.

Having decided that section 1385(a) applies to this case, we must determine the appropriate disposition. [Here] the record does not contain all of the material a reviewing court should consider . . . because the trial court did not set forth its reasons for striking the prior felony conviction allegations in the relevant minute order, as required by section 1385(a). . . . Under these circumstances, the appropriate remedy is to vacate the judgment, to permit defendant to withdraw his plea, and otherwise to proceed in conformity with this opinion. . . .

NOTES

1. *Means for judicial sentencing reconsideration: constitutional review.* Though the decision in *Romero* is based ultimately on an interpretation of a California statute, the court's discussion reveals that judges always have an opportunity — indeed, an obligation — to reexamine sentencing decisions made by legislatures and others in light of prevailing state and federal constitutional rules. The federal Constitution's mandates of due process and separation of powers, and its prohibition of cruel and unusual punishments create procedural and substantive limits on sentencing structures and outcomes that judges can and do enforce. Many states also have additional constitutional provisions and

precedents that enable judges to reconsider the sentencing decisions of legislatures, sentencing commissions, and others.

Because constitutional provisions are usually vague and subject to interpretation, there has been a robust debate concerning how judges should review sentencing determinations in light of constitutional norms. See Ewing v. California, 538 U.S. 11 (2003) (explaining that the Supreme Court has a long-standing tradition of deferring to state legislatures in making and implementing important policy decisions regarding sentencing); Harmelin v. Michigan, 501 U.S. 957 (1991) (developing arguments for why the Supreme Court should not rigorously review state sentencing choices on constitutional grounds). Do you think the standards for constitutional review ought to differ depending on the nature and severity of the sentence at issue — that is, should constitutional review of death sentences or lengthy prison terms be more exhaustive than review of shorter terms of imprisonment or alternative sanctions?

2. *Means for judicial sentencing reconsideration: statutory authority.*   Though influenced by constitutional concerns, the decision in *Romero* makes clear that statutes give sentencing judges in California the power to strike prior felony allegations (and thereby avoid application of the three-strikes law). The decision details inappropriate grounds for striking prior felony allegations, but it does not indicate what grounds may be appropriate. What types of reasons for striking prior felony allegations would be "in the furtherance of justice"?

Though relatively few jurisdictions give sentencing judges direct means to avoid the application of mandatory sentencing statutes, nearly all jurisdictions that employ guideline sentencing systems have granted sentencing judges some express statutory authority to depart from these guidelines. In the state of Washington, a sentencing judge may depart from the presumptive guideline sentence and impose a more or less severe sentence only when the case presents "substantial and compelling reasons justifying an exceptional sentence." Wash. Rev. Code Ann. §9.94A.535. Departures from the presumptive sentences established in the guidelines are authorized when the sentencing judges find "substantial and compelling circumstances." Like the provisions at issue in *Romero,* departure statutes generally require judges to explain the basis for any departure, and an inadequate explanation can lead to reversal on appeal.

3. *Means for judicial sentencing reconsideration: circumvention.*   In any taxonomy of the ways sentences get reconsidered, one should not overlook the extralegal "authority" judges possess to circumvent the application of sentencing rules established by legislatures and sentencing commissions. A sentencing judge who is disconcerted by the application of a mandatory sentencing provision in a particular case might condone (and even encourage) a plea bargain in which the offender pleads to a lesser offense. See U.S. Sentencing Commission, Special Report to Congress: Mandatory Minimum Penalties in the Federal Criminal Justice System 56-58 (August 1991). In a series of articles based on empirical research into the operation of the federal sentencing guidelines, Professors Stephen Schulhofer and Ilene Nagel concluded that the guidelines were circumvented in up to one-third of all federal cases during the period studied. See Schulhofer & Nagel, Plea Negotiations Under the Federal Sentencing Guidelines: Guideline Circumvention and Its Dynamics in the Post-*Mistretta* Period, 91 Nw. U. L. Rev. 1284, 1305 (1997); Schulhofer & Nagel, Negotiated

Pleas Under the Federal Sentencing Guidelines: The First Fifteen Months, 27 Am. Crim. L. Rev. 232, 272-278 (1989).

4. *Judicial override in death sentencing systems.*   Most of the 38 states that authorize capital punishment rely on juries to decide whether an offender should be sentenced to die and give the trial judge authority to reconsider a jury's capital sentencing decision. In many states, a judge has the authority to override a jury's recommendation only by imposing a life sentence after the jury has recommended death. See, e.g., Ohio Rev. Code §2727.16. But four states — Alabama, Delaware, Florida, and Indiana — use "advisory" juries in their capital sentencing process, which means that the trial judge has the authority to override a jury's recommendation in either direction: The judge might impose a life sentence when the jury voted for death or might impose a death sentence even when a jury has recommended life. See Ala. Stat. §13A-5-46; Del. Code tit. 11, §4209; Fla. Stat. §921.141; Ind. Code Ann. §35-50-2-9. The constitutionality of permitting judges to impose a death sentence has been thrown into question by the Supreme Court's decision in Ring v. Arizona, 536 U.S. 584 (2002), which held that a jury must make any factual findings that allow a sentence of death under the applicable state statute. The ruling in Blakely v. Washington, 542 U.S. 296 (2004), deepened the questions about these advisory jury jurisdictions. Most courts, however, have upheld the review of jury capital decision making by trial judges after *Ring* and *Blakely* so long as juries play a central role in finding the facts on which a death sentence is based. See Stephanos Bibas, *Apprendi* in the States, 94 J. Crim. L. & Criminology 1 (2003).

How would you expect judges and juries to view aggravating and mitigating circumstances differently? William J. Bowers et al., The Decision Maker Matters: An Empirical Examination of the Way the Role of the Judge and the Jury Influence Death Penalty Decision-Making, 63 Wash. & Lee L. Rev. 931 (2006).

2.   *Direct Appeal of Sentences*

The modern history of appellate review of criminal *convictions* extends nearly a century, with a rich set of doctrines governing when and how trial error can be corrected. The important doctrine does not come from constitutional law; the Supreme Court held in McKane v. Durston, 153 U.S. 684 (1894), that there is no federal constitutional right to appeal, and most state constitutions lack express provisions guaranteeing appeals in criminal cases. Nevertheless, all American jurisdictions have long provided for appellate review of convictions, and statutes and rules of appellate procedure establish who can file an appeal and what issues the parties can raise.

The modern history of appellate review of criminal *sentences* is far more abbreviated and much less evolved. Frequent appellate review of the outcome of capital cases did not begin until the 1970s, following the Supreme Court's decision in Furman v. Georgia, 408 U.S. 238 (1972), which struck down existing capital sentencing schemes. And, as Professor Kevin Reitz notes, serious appellate review of noncapital sentencing did not begin until a decade later, when jurisdictions started adopting guideline systems and other structured sentencing reforms:

> Prior to the guideline innovations of the 1980s, little meaningful appellate review of sentencing decisions had ever occurred in the United States, in federal or state courts. Those few appellate decisions that existed did not, for the most part, focus on substantive issues of the appropriate principles for punishment decisions, or the application of those principles to particular factual scenarios. Instead, the cases dealt primarily with constitutional issues. . . . Even in those states where a power of sentence review existed, it was used sparingly. Appellate courts refrained from interference with a sentence below unless it could be characterized as clearly excessive or as a clear abuse of discretion. . . .
>
> The absence, or near absence, of appellate input into the law of criminal punishment was due in part to the embarrassment that there was no substantive law of sentencing to be applied at the trial level. [There] were effectively no legal principles against which a sentence could be tested on review. Another disablement of appellate review was the widespread rule that trial courts were not obliged to explain the reasons for their sentencing decisions on the record, [which provided] little practical way for an appeals court to discover what thought process a trial judge had followed in a given case.

Kevin R. Reitz, Sentencing Guideline Systems and Sentence Appeals: A Comparison of Federal and State Experiences, 91 Nw. U. L. Rev. 1441, 1443-1446 (1997).

As this excerpt suggests, modern sentencing reforms radically changed the dynamics surrounding appellate review of noncapital sentencing. By creating defined sentencing law through mandatory sentencing provisions and guideline sentencing rules, structured sentencing reforms established a corpus of legal rules that sentencing judges had to apply and appellate judges could review. The following statute establishes the authority and the role of appellate courts in reviewing sentences in a typical guideline state.

‖ *42 Pennsylvania Consolidated Statutes §9781* ‖

(a) *Right to appeal.* The defendant or the Commonwealth may appeal as of right the legality of the sentence.

(b) *Allowance of appeal.* The defendant or the Commonwealth may file a petition for allowance of appeal of the discretionary aspects of a sentence for a felony or a misdemeanor to the appellate court that has initial jurisdiction for such appeals. Allowance of appeal may be granted at the discretion of the appellate court where it appears that there is a substantial question that the sentence imposed is not appropriate under this chapter.

(c) *Determination on appeal.* The appellate court shall vacate the sentence and remand the case to the sentencing court with instructions if it finds:

(1) the sentencing court purported to sentence within the sentencing guidelines but applied the guidelines erroneously;

(2) the sentencing court sentenced within the sentencing guidelines but the case involves circumstances where the application of the guidelines would be clearly unreasonable; or

(3) the sentencing court sentenced outside the sentencing guidelines and the sentence is unreasonable.

In all other cases the appellate court shall affirm the sentence imposed by the sentencing court.

(d) *Review of record.* In reviewing the record the appellate court shall have regard for:

(1) The nature and circumstances of the offense and the history and characteristics of the defendant.

(2) The opportunity of the sentencing court to observe the defendant, including any presentence investigation.

(3) The findings upon which the sentence was based.

(4) The guidelines promulgated by the commission. . . .

(f) Limitation on additional appellate review. — No appeal of the discretionary aspects of the sentence shall be permitted beyond the appellate court that has initial jurisdiction for such appeals.

PROBLEM 11-1.   HOW APPEALING?

Corrine Marie Denardi was convicted on an indictment charging conspiracy to distribute cocaine. At the time of sentencing, her attorney argued for a departure from the sentencing guidelines, citing mitigating factors such as the defendant's cooperation with the government, the absence of a prior criminal record, an exemplary work history, and a lifetime of love and devotion to friends and family. Ms. Denardi's attorney stressed that the imposition of a sentence within the recommended guideline range would cause extreme hardship on Ms. Denardi's family because she was the sole caretaker of three young children, one of whom was developmentally disabled. The relevant provision of the Pennsylvania Sentencing Guidelines states that nonguideline sentences may be imposed if the trial court determines that an aggravating or mitigating factor "is present." Such factors should be "sufficiently important to warrant a sentence" above or below the standard range."

The trial court refused to depart from the guidelines, and sentenced Ms. Denardi to 24 months' imprisonment. In so doing, the judge stated:

> I find nothing here that permits me to depart from the guidelines, and I am very much guided by them. I recognize all of the favorable points that the defendant has produced, and the best that I can do with those is to apply them to my choice of where within the guidelines the sentence would fall. I have been asking and trying to get some factor that would justify a deviation, and I haven't found any.

Based on the appellate review provisions of the Pennsylvania code, reprinted above, does Ms. Denardi have the right to appeal the trial court's decision not to depart from the sentencing guidelines? Does the answer to this question depend on whether the trial court believed it lacked the legal authority to depart or instead simply made a discretionary decision not to exercise its departure authority? Cf. United States v. Denardi, 892 F.2d 269 (3d Cir. 1989); see also David Yellen, Appellate Review of Refusals to Depart, 1 Fed. Sent'g Rep. 264 (1988).

PROBLEM 11-2. WAIVING GOOD-BYE TO AN APPEAL?

In December 2001, Walter Grange's house was burglarized. During the course of the investigation, police seized from Grange's home a microwave oven, which contained 6.44 grams of crack cocaine residue coated on the inside, and a bag containing nearly $12,000 in cash. Pursuant to a plea agreement, Grange pleaded guilty to possessing crack cocaine in violation of 21 U.S.C. §844(a). The plea agreement stated that the government and the defendant agreed that the total amount of drugs possessed was just over six grams of crack cocaine. The agreement also included the following statement:

> Defendant knowingly waives the right to appeal any sentence within the guideline range applicable to the statute of conviction as determined by the Court after resolution of any objections by either party to the presentence report to be prepared in this case, and defendant specifically agrees not to appeal the determination of the Court in resolving any contested sentencing factor. In other words, Defendant waives the right to appeal the sentence imposed in this case except to the extent, if any, that the Court may depart upwards from the applicable sentencing guideline range as determined by the Court. The defendant also waives his right to challenge his sentence or the manner in which it was determined in any collateral attack.

The probation officer investigating the offense and writing the presentence report for the sentencing court concluded that the $12,000 in cash should be converted into crack cocaine when computing the base offense level under the federal sentencing guidelines. At the sentencing hearing the prosecutor, when asked about the probation officer's computation, stated:

> On the $12,000, your Honor, I have nothing to add. I think the Probation Department set out the facts. Also, I'm in a little bit of a difficult position because I signed a plea agreement agreeing to the 6.44 grams. To be honest with the Court, it doesn't take a genius to know if you have that much residue in the facility that was cooking it, there's a little bit more involved there; but on the other hand, that was the extent of our evidence at that point.

The trial judge accepted the probation office's determination and sentenced Grange to 78 months in prison.

Under the terms of the plea agreement, can Grange appeal directly or file for a writ of habeas corpus? Can he attack the validity of the plea agreement, arguing that the government failed to live up to its promise? Can Grange assert that he received ineffective assistance of counsel as a means to try to void the plea agreement? See United States v. Brown, 328 F.3d 767 (5th Cir. 2003).

PROBLEM 11-3. PRESUMPTION ON APPEAL

Mario Claiborne was arrested for attempting to sell .23 grams of cocaine base to an undercover police officer. Six months later, police approached Claiborne when he appeared to be engaged in a drug deal. He fled through the house next door, throwing down a plastic baggie containing 5.03 grams of cocaine base. Claiborne was charged in federal court with distributing cocaine base during the first incident and possessing cocaine base during the second. He pled guilty to both counts. The district court determined that Claiborne's advisory guidelines sentencing range is 37 to 46 months in prison and imposed a 15-month sentence.

At sentencing, the district court granted Claiborne "safety valve" relief from the five-year mandatory minimum sentence under 18 U.S.C. §844(a). The court also rejected the government's position that he should receive a two-level increase under U.S.S.G. §3C1.2 for reckless endangerment because he fled through a nearby residence. These rulings resulted in a guidelines sentencing range of 37 to 46 months in prison.

Under United States v. Booker, 543 U.S. 220 (2005), the federal sentencing guidelines are no longer a mandatory regime. Instead, the district court must take the advisory guidelines into account together with other sentencing factors enumerated in 18 U.S.C. §3553(a). The district court in this case sentenced Claiborne to 15 months in prison, concluding that "the 37 month low end of the range is, in my view, excessive" because of Claiborne's lack of criminal history, young age, the small quantity of drugs involved, and the court's opinion that Claiborne was not likely to commit similar crimes in the future.

The government appealed the sentence as unreasonable under 18 U.S.C. §3553(a). In the court of appeals, when the district court has correctly determined the guidelines sentencing range, the appellate panel reviews the resulting sentence for "reasonableness," a standard akin to the traditional review for abuse of discretion.

In the Eighth Circuit (the court hearing Claiborne's appeal), the appellate court gives a "presumption of reasonableness" to any sentence falling within the designated guideline range. The presumption is based on the court's belief that "the guidelines were fashioned taking the other §3553(a) factors into account and are the product of years of careful study." Thus, when a district court varies from the guidelines range based on its analysis of the §3553(a) factors, the appeals court must examine whether "the district court's decision to grant a §3553(a) variance from the appropriate guidelines range is reasonable, and whether the extent of any §3553(a) variance is reasonable." The greater the variance from the guideline sentencing range, the heavier the scrutiny that a sentence receives on appeal.

Here, the government notes that Claiborne's lack of criminal history was taken into account when the safety valve eliminated an otherwise applicable mandatory minimum sentence. The small amount of crack cocaine seized during his two offenses was taken into account in determining his guidelines range. Substantially reducing the resulting guidelines-range sentence based on drug quantity was unreasonable, in the government's view, because it is fair to suppose that Claiborne distributed additional quantities of cocaine during the six months between the two occasions that the police witnessed.

Normally, a "presumption" instructs a finder of fact about the proper inferences to draw from the proven facts, or sets a burden of proof or standard of proof for the parties to meet at trial. What does a "presumption of reasonableness" mean for an appellate court? Would the presumption operate differently if the district court had imposed a guideline sentence despite arguments by Claiborne that a variance from the guidelines was required under

section 3553(a), and Claiborne appealed the within-guideline sentence? See
United States v. Claiborne, 439 F.3d 479 (8th Cir. 2006).

NOTES

1. *Whose right to appeal?* Under U.S. law in every jurisdiction, the prosecution cannot appeal from an acquittal, while in civil law countries such an appeal is possible. In the United States, such appeals are considered a violation of double jeopardy prohibitions; civil law countries consider the trial and appeal to be part of one proceeding, and therefore a direct appeal does not constitute double jeopardy.

As revealed by the Pennsylvania appeals provision reprinted above, this American imbalance in appellate rights has generally not carried over to sentencing; in nearly all jurisdictions, prosecutors as well as defendants may appeal after a guilty verdict and the sentence. Why should the prosecution have the right to appeal from a sentence, especially since it controls charging and has unique power during plea negotiations? Should it matter whether the case is adjudicated in a guideline or a nonguideline jurisdiction?

2. *Dual functions of error correction and lawmaking.* Appellate courts are often said to have the dual functions of correcting trial errors and expounding legal rules that control future cases through the force of precedent. Is one role more important than the other when it comes to sentencing?

Many early advocates of modern sentencing reforms urged the more active role for appellate courts, hoping that appellate review would foster an "evolutionary and principled development of a common law of sentencing." Norval Morris, Towards Principled Sentencing, 37 Md. L. Rev. 267, 284 (1977); see also Marvin E. Frankel, Sentencing Guidelines: A Need for Creative Collaboration, 101 Yale L.J. 2043, 2050 (1992). But in a thorough assessment of appellate review in three guideline jurisdictions, Professor Kevin Reitz documented that in practice, reviewing courts have favored the task of error correction over substantive lawmaking. In "hundreds of appellate decisions across different guideline jurisdictions," he notes, "one seldom encounters thoughtful opinions that advance our understanding of the substantive problems of punishment. Instead, guideline appeals lean toward technical, even technocratic, analyses." Kevin R. Reitz, Sentencing Guideline Systems and Sentence Appeals: A Comparison of Federal and State Experiences, 91 Nw. U. L. Rev. 1441, 1450 (1997). Can you imagine why the reformist vision of developing a "common law of sentencing" has proven hard to achieve in practice?

3. *Standards for review in federal sentencing.* The influence and impact of appellate review will often hinge on the standard of review employed by the court. In most appellate review settings, factual findings are reviewed for clear error, legal rulings are reviewed de novo, and discretionary judgments are reviewed for an abuse of discretion. Would you describe sentencing decisions made under guideline systems as factual findings, legal rulings, or discretionary judgments?

The original version of the appellate review portion of the federal Sentencing Reform Act stated simply in 18 U.S.C. §3742(e) that circuit courts should "give due deference to the district court's application of the guidelines to the facts." This somewhat oblique instruction led the circuit courts to develop a range of approaches to reviewing certain guideline determinations, particularly decisions to depart from the guidelines. In Koon v. United States, 518 U.S. 81, 97 (1996), the U.S. Supreme Court, interpreting section 3742(e), stated that the deference to be given on appeal depends on the nature of the guideline question presented, and that a departure decision will in most cases be "due substantial deference" because "it embodies the sentencing court's traditional exercise of discretion." The Court thus concluded that circuit courts should apply an abuse of discretion standard when reviewing departures. See Douglas A. Berman, Balanced and Purposeful Departures: Fixing a Jurisprudence that Undermines the Federal Sentencing Guidelines, 76 Notre Dame L. Rev. 21 (2000); Ian Weinstein, The Discontinuous Tradition of Sentencing Discretion: *Koon*'s Failure to Recognize the Reshaping of Judicial Discretion Under the Guidelines, 79 B.U. L. Rev. 493 (1999); Barry L. Johnson, Discretion and the Rule of Law in Federal Guidelines Sentencing: Developing Departure Jurisprudence in the Wake of *Koon v. United States*, 58 Ohio St. L.J. 1697 (1998).

Data from the U.S. Sentencing Commission show that the number of downward departures granted by district courts increased steadily between 1996 and 2003. The total number of downward departures granted for reasons other than a defendant's assistance to prosecutors nearly doubled. Concerns about the number of departures ultimately led Congress in 2003, as part of a package of reforms designed to decrease the number of downward departures, to modify the language of 18 U.S.C. §3742(e) to provide that when considering "determinations [to depart from the guidelines], the court of appeals shall review de novo the district court's application of the guidelines to the facts." Through this alteration of the appellate review standard from "abuse of discretion" to "de novo," Congress apparently intended not only that circuit judges more rigorously review questionable downward departures on appeal, but also that district judges feel more restrained in granting departures in the first instance.

4. *Presumptions on appeal.*   As we saw in Chapter 3, the Supreme Court held in Booker v. United States, 543 U.S. 220 (2005), that the "presumptive" federal sentencing guidelines violated the Sixth Amendment because they authorized judges to impose higher sentences only after finding certain facts that had not been found by a jury. Nonetheless, the Court retained the guidelines on a voluntary basis, while instructing appellate courts to review the sentences imposed in the district court for "reasonableness." In the aftermath of *Booker*, federal appellate courts started to embrace two devices that the Department of Justice urged on them: (a) the "presumption" on appeal that a guideline sentence was "reasonable" and (b) the "proportionality" principle, stating that larger variances from the guidelines require stronger justifications on appeal. The Supreme Court upheld the first of these devices in Rita v. United States, 2007 WL 1772146 (June 21, 2007), reprinted in Chapter 3. Problem 11-3 addresses the second of these devices. How do you predict trial judges will behave in light of these two presumptions that now operate in the federal appellate courts?

5. *Waivers of the right to appeal.*   Prosecutors in some federal districts routinely seek waivers of defendants' appeal rights in plea agreements. In 1995 the Department of Justice issued a memorandum to all U.S. Attorneys' offices

(discussed in Chapter 6) providing guidance on the drafting and use of appeal waivers. That memo recognized that the use of appeal waivers is "helpful in reducing the burden of appellate and collateral litigation involving sentencing issues" but also cautioned that it "could result in guideline-free sentencing of defendants in guilty plea cases, and it could encourage a lawless district court to impose sentences in violation of the guidelines." In July 1996 the Judicial Conference of the United States, in a memorandum to aid district judges and probation officers in their consideration of appeal waiver provisions, noted "that waivers have been consistently upheld as legal . . . as long as the waiver is knowing and voluntary." It also suggested that courts provide all defendants with a "qualified, yet informative, advisement of the right to appeal at sentencing," followed by a specific oral colloquy about the terms of any appeal waiver provision to which a defendant has agreed.

The federal courts have endorsed the validity of appeal waivers, while adopting a few exemptions for certain sorts of claims. Some courts exempt from the waivers any claims that a sentence is based on race discrimination, United States v. Baramdyka, 95 F.3d 840, 843 (9th Cir. 1996), is the product of ineffective assistance of counsel, United States v. Attar, 38 F.3d 727, 732-733 (4th Cir. 1994), or amounts to a "miscarriage of justice," United States v. Khattak, 273 F.3d 557, 563 (3d Cir. 2001).

A 2005 empirical analysis of appeal waivers found that defendants entered such waiver agreements in almost two-thirds of the cases settled by plea agreement. The government provides some sentencing concessions more frequently to defendants who sign waivers, such as downward departures, safety valve credits, and factual stipulations. The waivers are used more frequently in some circuits than in others. Nancy J. King & Michael E. O'Neill, Appeal Waivers and the Future of Sentencing Policy, 55 Duke L.J. 209 (2005).

5. *Appeal rights under international law.* Article 14(5) of the International Covenant on Civil and Political Rights, which the United States has ratified, grants every defendant the right to have the conviction and sentence reviewed by a higher tribunal. Similar rights are granted in the American and European Human Rights Conventions. Exceptions apply to minor offenses and cases tried in front of the nations' highest tribunals. Notably, there was no appeal from the decisions of the two post–World War II tribunals in Nuremberg and Tokyo. Because of the evolution of international human rights law as a part of the due process norm, however, appeals are explicitly mentioned in the procedural rules for the ad hoc tribunals trying offenders for atrocities committed in the former Yugoslavia and in Rwanda as well as for the International Criminal Court. The ad hoc tribunals have allowed for sentence appeals, even in the case of guilty pleas.

In contrast to noncapital sentencing, in which appellate review is relatively new and still somewhat novel, death sentences have been subject to appellate scrutiny since the early 1900s. The severity and finality of the penalty not only have prompted capital defendants to appeal in greater numbers and with greater urgency, but also have led appellate courts to examine more closely the legality and appropriateness of death sentences in individual cases. As the case below highlights, when states enacted new death penalty statutes after the Supreme Court struck down existing capital sentencing schemes in Furman v. Georgia, 408 U.S. 238 (1972), appellate review became a central tool in efforts to ensure that the death penalty was administered in a more consistent and reasoned way.

Reginald Pulley v. Robert Alton Harris
465 U.S. 37 (1984)

WHITE, J.

[Robert Alton] Harris was convicted of a capital crime in a California court and was sentenced to death. Along with many other challenges to the conviction and sentence, Harris claimed on appeal that the California capital punishment statute was invalid under the United States Constitution because it failed to require the California Supreme Court to compare Harris' sentence with the sentences imposed in similar capital cases and thereby to determine whether they were proportionate. . . .

The proportionality review sought by Harris . . . and provided for in numerous state statutes[1] [inquires whether a death sentence is] unacceptable in a particular case because disproportionate to the punishment imposed on others convicted of the same crime. The issue in this case, therefore, is whether the Eighth Amendment, applicable to the States through the Fourteenth Amendment, requires a state appellate court, before it affirms a death sentence, to compare the sentence in the case before it with the penalties imposed in similar cases if requested to do so by the prisoner. Harris insists that it does and that this is the invariable rule in every case. . . . We do not agree.

Harris' submission is rooted in Furman v. Georgia, 408 U.S. 238 (1972). In *Furman*, the Court concluded that capital punishment, as then administered under statutes vesting unguided sentencing discretion in juries and trial judges, had become unconstitutionally cruel and unusual punishment. The death penalty was being imposed so discriminatorily, so wantonly and freakishly, and so infrequently that any given death sentence was cruel and unusual. In response to that decision, roughly two-thirds of the States promptly redrafted their capital sentencing statutes in an effort to limit jury discretion and avoid arbitrary and inconsistent results. All of the new statutes provide for automatic appeal of death sentences. Most, such as Georgia's, require the reviewing court, to some extent at least, to determine whether, considering both the crime and the defendant, the sentence is disproportionate to that imposed in similar cases. Not every State has adopted such a procedure. In some States, such as Florida, the appellate court performs proportionality review despite the absence of a statutory requirement; in others, such as California and Texas, it does not.

---

1. Under the much-copied Georgia scheme, for example, the Supreme Court is required in every case to determine "[whether] the sentence of death is excessive or disproportionate to the penalty imposed in similar cases, considering both the crime and the defendant." Ga. Code Ann. §17-10-35(c)(3)(1982). If the court affirms the death sentence, it is to include in its decision reference to similar cases that it has taken into consideration. The court is required to maintain records of all capital felony cases in which the death penalty was imposed since 1970.

Four years after *Furman,* this Court examined several of the new state statutes. We upheld one of each of the three sorts mentioned above. See Gregg v. Georgia, 428 U.S. 153 (1976); Proffitt v. Florida, 428 U.S. 242 (1976); Jurek v. Texas, 428 U.S. 262 (1976). Needless to say, that some schemes providing proportionality review are constitutional does not mean that such review is indispensable. . . .

Assuming that there could be a capital sentencing system so lacking in other checks on arbitrariness that it would not pass constitutional muster without comparative proportionality review, the 1977 California statute is not of that sort. Under this scheme, a person convicted of first-degree murder is sentenced to life imprisonment unless one or more "special circumstances" are found, in which case the punishment is either death or life imprisonment without parole. Special circumstances are alleged in the charging paper and tried with the issue of guilt at the initial phase of the trial [and] must be proved beyond a reasonable doubt. If the jury finds the defendant guilty of first-degree murder and finds at least one special circumstance, the trial proceeds to a second phase to determine the appropriate penalty. Additional evidence may be offered and the jury is given a list of relevant factors [and,] guided by the aggravating and mitigating circumstances referred to in this section, [determines] whether the penalty shall be death or life imprisonment without the possibility of parole. If the jury returns a verdict of death, the . . . trial judge then reviews the evidence and, in light of the statutory factors, makes an independent determination as to whether the weight of the evidence supports the jury's findings and verdicts. The judge is required to state on the record the reasons for his findings. If the trial judge denies the motion for modification, there is an automatic appeal. The statute does not require comparative proportionality review or otherwise describe the nature of the appeal. It does state that the trial judge's refusal to modify the sentence "shall be reviewed." . . . As the California Supreme Court has said, "the statutory requirements that the jury specify the special circumstances which permit imposition of the death penalty, and that the trial judge specify his reasons for denying modification of the death penalty, serve to assure thoughtful and effective appellate review, focusing upon the circumstances present in each particular case."

By requiring the jury to find at least one special circumstance beyond a reasonable doubt, the statute limits the death sentence to a small subclass of capital-eligible cases. The statutory list of relevant factors, applied to defendants within this subclass, provides jury guidance and lessens the chance of arbitrary application of the death penalty, guaranteeing that the jury's discretion will be guided and its consideration deliberate. The jury's "discretion must be suitably directed and limited so as to minimize the risk of wholly arbitrary and capricious action." *Gregg,* 428 U.S., at 189. Its decision is reviewed by the trial judge and the State Supreme Court. On its face, this system, without any requirement or practice of comparative proportionality review, cannot be successfully challenged under *Furman* and our subsequent cases. . . .

STEVENS, J., concurring in part and concurring in the judgment.
 . . . The systemic arbitrariness and capriciousness in the imposition of capital punishment under statutory schemes invalidated by Furman v. Georgia, 408 U.S. 238 (1972), resulted from two basic defects in those schemes. First, the

systems were permitting the imposition of capital punishment in broad classes of offenses for which the penalty would always constitute cruel and unusual punishment. Second, even among those types of homicides for which the death penalty could be constitutionally imposed as punishment, the schemes vested essentially unfettered discretion in juries and trial judges to impose the death sentence. Given these defects, arbitrariness and capriciousness in the imposition of the punishment were inevitable, and given the extreme nature of the punishment, constitutionally intolerable. The statutes we have approved in *Gregg, Proffitt,* and *Jurek* were designed to eliminate each of these defects. Each scheme provided an effective mechanism for categorically narrowing the class of offenses for which the death penalty could be imposed and provided special procedural safeguards including appellate review of the sentencing authority's decision to impose the death penalty.

In *Gregg,* the [plurality opinion] indicated that some form of meaningful appellate review is required, and . . . focused on the proportionality review component of the Georgia statute because it was a prominent, innovative, and noteworthy feature that had been specifically designed to combat effectively the systemic problems in capital sentencing which had invalidated the prior Georgia capital sentencing scheme. But observations that this innovation is an effective safeguard do not mean that it is the only method of ensuring that death sentences are not imposed capriciously or that it is the only acceptable form of appellate review. [I]n each of the statutory schemes approved in our prior cases, as in the scheme we review today, meaningful appellate review is an indispensable component of the Court's determination that the State's capital sentencing procedure is valid. Like the Court, however, I am not persuaded that the particular form of review prescribed by statute in Georgia — comparative proportionality review — is the only method by which an appellate court can avoid the danger that the imposition of the death sentence in a particular case, or a particular class of cases, will be so extraordinary as to violate the Eighth Amendment.

BRENNAN, J., dissenting.

[In 1976, when considering challenges to] new death penalty statutes enacted by the States of Georgia, Florida, and Texas, a majority of the Court concluded that the procedural mechanisms included in those statutes provided sufficient protection to ensure their constitutional application. Thus began a series of decisions from this Court in which, with some exceptions, it has been assumed that the death penalty is being imposed by the various States in a rational and non-discriminatory way. Upon the available evidence, however, I am convinced that the Court is simply deluding itself, and also the American public, when it insists that those defendants who have already been executed or are today condemned to death have been selected on a basis that is neither arbitrary nor capricious, under any meaningful definition of those terms. . . .

Disproportionality among sentences given different defendants can only be eliminated after sentencing disparities are identified. And the most logical way to identify such sentencing disparities is for a court of statewide jurisdiction to conduct comparisons between death sentences imposed by different judges or juries within the State. This is what the Court labels comparative proportionality review. Although clearly no panacea, such review often serves to identify the most extreme examples of disproportionality among similarly situated defendants. At least to this extent, this form of appellate review serves to eliminate some of the irrationality that currently surrounds imposition of a death sentence. If only to further this limited purpose, therefore, I believe that the Constitution's prohibition on the irrational imposition of the death penalty requires that this procedural safeguard be provided.

Indeed, despite the Court's insistence that such review is not compelled by the Federal Constitution, over 30 States now require, either by statute or judicial decision, some form of comparative proportionality review before any death sentence may be carried out. By itself, this should weigh heavily on the side of requiring such appellate review. In addition, these current practices establish beyond dispute that such review can be administered without much difficulty by a court of statewide jurisdiction in each State. Perhaps the best evidence of the value of proportionality review can be gathered by examining the actual results obtained in those States which now require such review. For example, since 1973, . . . the Georgia Supreme Court has vacated at least seven death sentences because it was convinced that they were comparatively disproportionate. . . .

What these cases clearly demonstrate, in my view, is that comparative proportionality review serves to eliminate some, if only a small part, of the irrationality that currently infects imposition of the death penalty by the various States. Before any execution is carried out, therefore, a State should be required under the Eighth and Fourteenth Amendments to conduct such appellate review.

NOTES

1. *Proportionality review of death sentences.* As suggested in Pulley v. Harris, most states with the death penalty require their appellate courts to review the proportionality of any death sentence. In a few states, notably Florida, many death sentences have been reversed on the basis of a finding of disproportionality. See Cooper v. State, 739 So. 2d 82 (Fla. 1999). Commentators have noticed, however, that the rigor and significance of proportionality review of death sentences seems to have waned after the Supreme Court held in *Pulley* that such review was not constitutionally mandated. Professor Penny White explains the trend:

> Rather than conducting a meaningful comparison between similar cases, courts all too often simply state that a particular death sentence is proportionate and cite previous decisions without analyzing their similarities and differences, or the appropriateness of the death sentence. . . .
>
> Examples of cases in which codefendants are treated disproportionately with the least culpable receiving the death sentence are not rare. Similarly, there are many cases in which almost identical defendants commit almost identical crimes, but are sentenced differently. . . . On occasion before *Pulley*, the appellate courts in most states (when their statutes mandated) would step in and correct what would otherwise have been a tragic injustice by reducing a disproportionate death sentence to life imprisonment. However, *Pulley*'s removal of what was believed to be proportionality's constitutional underpinning, coupled with the politically charged climate that surrounds most capital cases are undermining *Furman*'s mandate for nonarbitrary, nondiscriminatory death penalty schemes.

Penny J. White, Can Lightning Strike Twice? Obligations of State Courts after Pulley v. Harris, 70 U. Colo. L. Rev. 813, 816-817, 841-842 (1999). Since the decision in *Pulley*, eight states have repealed statutory provisions calling for proportionality review while three other states have established proportionality review. (Tennessee repealed and then reenacted its proportionality requirement after *Pulley*.) See Barry Latzer, The Failure of Comparative Proportionality Review of Capital Cases (with Lessons from New Jersey), 64 Alb. L. Rev. 1161, 1168 n.31 (2001).

What is it about death penalty cases that justifies proportionality review, a procedure that seems to entitle a defendant to a reduced sentence because of a failure to impose the same harsh sentence on other, similarly situated defendants? Should all sentences, or at least all serious sentences (such as sentences of 25 or more years of imprisonment), be subject to proportionality review, or is the entire concept of substantive sentencing review unsound? Compare Latzer, 64 Alb. L. Rev. 1161 (suggesting that proportionality review in death penalty cases has been largely a waste of time and money) with Evan J. Mandery, In Defense of Specific Proportionality Review, 65 Alb. L. Rev. 883 (2002) (arguing that proportionality review with the right focus could be valuable).

2. *Automatic appellate review of death sentences.* Another unique feature of appellate review in capital cases is its automatic nature. Most states with the death penalty provide for automatic review of every death sentence, and some jurisdictions provide for expedited review by the state's highest court. See, e.g., Ala. Code §12-22-150; Del. Code tit. 11, §4209(g); Neb. Const. art. 1, §23 ("In all capital cases, appeal directly to the Supreme Court shall be as a matter of right.").

Suggesting that automatic appellate review provisions are in some ways akin to trial courts' review of negotiated plea agreements, Professor Richard Bonnie has explained that such procedures are fundamentally based in society's interest "in the integrity of its institutions of criminal punishment and in the dignity of the processes through which these punishments are carried out." Richard J. Bonnie, The Dignity of the Condemned, 74 Va. L. Rev. 1363, 1369 (1988). But Professor Bonnie has also noted that these interests have been given particularly broad application in the appellate review of death sentences:

> The practice of requiring automatic appeal of death sentences . . . would not represent a significant expansion of integrity-protecting procedures if it were limited to a review of the sufficiency of the substantive predicates for the sentence under state and federal law. The actual scope of appellate review, however, appears to be seldom so restricted. The prevailing practice appears to be to review all claims of error in automatic appeals in the same manner as they would have been reviewed had the appeal been brought at the defendant's own request. . . . In death cases — and only in death cases — state appellate courts have assumed the responsibility of assuring that the death sentence is not tainted by any legal error.

Id. at 1372-1373.

PROBLEM 11-4.   VOLUNTEERING TO DIE

On October 7, 1976, Gary Mark Gilmore was convicted of murder and sentenced to death in a Utah court for killing a motel clerk and a gas station attendant. Gilmore's death sentence was imposed before any court had conclusively ruled on the constitutionality of Utah's capital sentencing procedures. Gilmore admitted to the murders throughout his trial and demanded that his attorneys not file an appeal or seek a stay of execution on his behalf, even though he was informed about possible grounds for challenging the constitutionality of Utah's death penalty statute.

The state court in Utah, relying on psychiatric reports and other evidence, held that Gilmore was competent and legally entitled to waive his rights of appeal. Gilmore's efforts to accelerate his execution troubled his family as well as prosecutors, though Gilmore seemed to enjoy the frenzy and attention he had created. Gilmore's mother petitioned the U.S. Supreme Court for "next friend" standing to claim that her son was incompetent to waive his right to state appellate review. Her petition also raised the claim that given the importance of settling the constitutional validity of Gilmore's sentence, her son should be unable as a matter of law to waive the right to state appellate review.

Should the U.S. Supreme Court examine the state court's conclusion that Gilmore was competent to waive his appeals? Do the principles underlying automatic appellate review of all death sentences also support a claim that such review cannot be waived by the defendant? Would your answer to these questions change if the procedures through which Utah sentenced Gilmore to death were clearly constitutionally flawed? See Gilmore v. Utah, 429 U.S. 1012 (1978); see also Franklin ex rel. Berry v. Francis, 144 F.3d 429 (6th Cir. 1998) (considering efforts by family members to intervene on behalf of a death row defendant with a history of mental illness who sought to waive appeal rights).

3. Collateral Review of Sentences

A conviction and appeal are not the end of the line for the criminal defendant. Even after the direct appeal is complete, the offender can still challenge the validity of the conviction and sentence in court. These postconviction review procedures take a variety of names and have somewhat different historical roots: the best-known form, mentioned in both federal and state constitutions, is the writ of habeas corpus, though some states structure postconviction processes around the writ of error coram nobis. Others have supplanted the traditional (and often quite limited) postconviction remedies with broader statutes, typically labeled postconviction review acts. These various postconviction review procedures are known as "collateral review" because they are nominally civil proceedings, distinct from the direct appeal in criminal proceedings. Convicted offenders file a petition in trial court against a state official, alleging that their convictions or sentences are illegal or unconstitutional in some way. A judge typically has the power to grant relief by overturning the conviction or sentence.

In this section, we briefly review the doctrines and dynamics surrounding collateral review of sentences. The following case involves a direct appeal, but it provides considerable background about the nature of collateral review and its relationship to direct review of convictions and sentences. In so doing, the case provides some preliminary insights into the two central questions that arise in this arena: What distinguishes collateral review procedures from direct appeals, and to what extent are such procedures necessary at all?

|| ***Commonwealth v. Robert Freeman*** ||
|| **827 A.2d 385 (Pa. 2003)** ||

CASTILLE, J.

On June 18, 1998, a jury sitting in the Court of Common Pleas of Philadelphia County convicted appellant of two counts of first-degree murder. . . . At the penalty hearing, the jury found one aggravating circumstance — that appellant had been convicted of another murder at the time of the current offense — and no mitigating circumstances; accordingly, the jury imposed a sentence of death. Trial counsel subsequently withdrew from the matter and present counsel entered the case. This direct appeal followed.

Before turning to . . . substantive issues . . . , we note this Court's recent decision in Commonwealth v. Grant, 813 A.2d 726 (Pa. 2002). *Grant* overruled the procedural rule announced in Commonwealth v. Hubbard, 372 A.2d 687 (Pa. 1977), which required new counsel to raise claims of previous counsel's ineffectiveness at the first opportunity, even if that first opportunity is on direct appeal and the claims of ineffectiveness were not raised in the trial court. The new general rule announced in *Grant* is that a defendant "should wait to raise claims of ineffective assistance of trial counsel until collateral review." . . .

Grant affects the appeal sub judice in two ways. First, it affects the case directly because appellant is represented by new counsel on appeal and appellant raises numerous claims sounding in the ineffective assistance of trial counsel which were not raised below. Second, *Grant* affects this case indirectly because there are a number of additional claims raised in this appeal which, though they do not sound in the alleged ineffective assistance of trial counsel, nevertheless were not raised below. These waived claims of trial court error are reviewable here, if at all, only under this Court's direct capital appeal relaxed waiver doctrine. For reasons explicated below, we believe that many of the same considerations powering our decision in *Grant* require a similar reevaluation of the viability of the capital case relaxed waiver doctrine. . . .

I. INEFFECTIVE ASSISTANCE OF TRIAL COUNSEL

Appellant raises eight primary claims of ineffective assistance of trial counsel involving both the guilt and penalty phases of trial. None of these claims were raised below. Consistently with *Grant*, we dismiss the claims without prejudice to appellant's right to pursue these claims, and any other available claims, via a petition for relief under the Post Conviction Relief Act (PCRA), 42 Pa. C.S. §9541 et seq.

II. RELAXED WAIVER

Appellant also raises nine claims of trial court error. Many of these claims are waived because appellant failed to raise them in the trial court. Pa. R. A. P. 302 ("Issues not raised in the lower court are waived and cannot be raised for the first time on appeal."). However, since this is a direct appeal in a capital case, consistently with this Court's long-standing precedent, we have the discretion to reach claims of trial court error which, though waived, are resolvable from the record. . . . Nevertheless, [we find in this case] many of the same difficulties that prompted this Court . . . in *Grant* [to hold] that new claims of trial counsel ineffectiveness are generally better suited for review on collateral attack. We think a similar general rule should govern consideration of claims of trial court error in capital cases that were not raised before the trial court.

Grant noted that, as reflected in Appellate Rule 302(a), appellate courts generally will not entertain claims raised for the first time on appeal. We explained that:

> [Such] a prohibition is preferred because the absence of a trial court opinion can pose a substantial impediment to meaningful and effective appellate review. Further, . . . appellate courts do not act as fact finders, since to do so would require an assessment of the credibility of the testimony and that is clearly not our function.

[Also in *Grant*,] we noted that the general preference in the overwhelming majority of jurisdictions was to defer review of counsel ineffectiveness claims until collateral review. We also noted the difficult task facing appellate counsel . . . in attempting to uncover and develop extra-record claims of counsel ineffectiveness in the truncated time frame available on direct appeal review, a task further complicated by the fact that counsel's duty in this regard is not entirely clear, at least as a constitutional matter. . . .

Some of the same difficulties . . . also arise when this Court employs relaxed waiver in capital cases to address issues of trial error not raised below. This Court often is required to decide such issues without the benefit of a trial court opinion or other indication of the trial judge's view. We observed in *Grant* that "the trial court is in the best position to review claims related to trial counsel's error in the first instance as that is the court that observed first hand counsel's allegedly deficient performance." This is no less true for claims of alleged trial court error—and particularly where discretionary decisions, such as the admission or exclusion of evidence, which often depend upon trial context, are involved. . . .

Similarly, the uncabined availability of relaxed waiver to resurrect unpreserved claims degrades the importance of the trial itself by providing an incentive not to raise contemporaneous objections so as to build in claims for appeal. [There] are multiple, salutary reasons for this Court to encourage practices by which trial judges are given the initial opportunity to timely address claims of error, thereby ensuring prompt resolution at the most important stage of a case, and forestalling the necessity for appellate review and after-the-fact relief. . . .

In light of these difficulties with the relaxed waiver doctrine, it is worth reexamining its history, purpose, and contours to see whether there is a compelling reason to retain this broad and unique exception to the basic requirement of contemporaneous objection and issue preservation. As this Court noted in Commonwealth v. Albrecht, 720 A.2d 693 (Pa. 1998), the operating principle behind the relaxed waiver doctrine, as originally formulated, was to prevent this court from being instrumental in an unconstitutional execution. The doctrine has its genesis in [a time of uncertainty about the structure of appellate review in death penalty cases] after the United States Supreme Court issued its landmark decision in Furman v. Georgia, 408 U.S. 238 (1972). [This Court] provided the following rationale for the Court's determination not to adhere strictly to its normal rules of waiver in capital appeals:

> [Because] this Court has an independent, statutory obligation to determine whether a sentence of death was the product of passion, prejudice or some other arbitrary factor, whether the sentence is excessive or disproportionate to that imposed in similar cases, and to review the record for sufficiency of the evidence to support aggravating circumstances, we will not adhere strictly to our normal rules of waiver. The primary reason for this limited relaxation of waiver rules is that, due to the final and irrevocable nature of the death penalty, the appellant will have no opportunity for post-conviction relief wherein he could raise, say, an assertion of ineffectiveness of counsel for failure to preserve an issue or some other reason that might qualify as an extraordinary circumstance for failure to raise an issue. 19 P.S. §1180-4(2). Accordingly, significant issues perceived sua sponte by this Court, or raised by the parties, will be addressed and, if possible from the record, resolved. . . .

Commonwealth v. Zettlemoyer, 454 A.2d 937, 955 n.19 (Pa. 1982).

[Since these early cases], this Court has had extensive experience with state post-conviction review in capital cases. This experience has proven with absolute certainty that [a] fear of an absence of collateral review, the primary basis for the [expanded] relaxed waiver doctrine, is erroneous. Death-sentenced prisoners in Pennsylvania have an opportunity for full post-conviction review, via the PCRA, where they can, and do, pursue waived claims through assertions of ineffective assistance of trial counsel. . . .

In addition to deriving from a faulty "primary" rationale, the [expanded] relaxed waiver rule has evolved in a way [that sets it] adrift from its unconstitutional execution moorings, [which] envisioned only a "limited" relaxation of waiver rules to address "significant issues." In practice, the rule has become such a matter of routine that it is invoked to capture a myriad of claims, no matter how comparatively minor or routine, [and has] been routinely employed to reach claims that were not merely "technically" waived, but which in fact were not raised at all in the trial court.

It is notable that, even when applying the rule, this Court in recent years has expressed its increasing unease and concern that the doctrine [is being] employed by counsel as a litigation tool. . . .

In Commonwealth v. Brown, 711 A.2d 444, 455 (Pa. 1998), we further noted that we shared the concerns advanced by the Commonwealth in that case that the doctrine " 'sabotages' the trial court's efforts to correct errors" and "encourages defense attorneys to withhold objections during trial for tactical reasons, and by that create an error upon which this Court may later grant relief."

We are also troubled by the potential equal protection implications arising from the near-indiscriminate availability of relaxed waiver to invigorate claims never pursued below. Assume a joint capital trial of two defendants, each convicted of first-degree murder, but one receives a sentence of life imprisonment while the other receives the death penalty. Upon their appeals, these appellants perceive an identical claim, which both failed to raise below. If it is a claim premised upon a new constitutional rule that came into existence after the trial, the life-sentenced appellant will not be able to pursue it at all in the Superior Court, while the capital appellant will receive review in this Court and, possibly, relief. Even if it is not a claim based upon a new rule, the capital appellant will have the much easier road of having his claim reviewed as if it were a preserved claim of trial error (even though it was not), subject to a mere showing of error and harmfulness, while the otherwise identically-situated life-sentenced appellant will be required to make the more difficult showing required under the three-part standard applicable to ineffective assistance of counsel. Commonwealth v. Howard, 645 A.2d 1300, 1307 (Pa. 1994). Since the claims subject to capital case relaxed waiver are not limited to the penalty phase, the fact of the death sentence cannot rationally justify such a preferential, substantive treatment of a claim available to otherwise identically-situated defendants.

In light of these multiple concerns, and the unquestionable availability of the PCRA as a vehicle to consider waived claims of trial court error through the guise of claims of trial counsel ineffectiveness, we are convinced that the time has come to return the relaxed waiver doctrine to its roots. . . . Having created the rule, this Court is certainly empowered to modify or eliminate the doctrine if jurisprudential concerns warrant a change from our current practice.

We hold that, as a general rule on capital direct appeals, claims that were not properly raised and preserved in the trial court are waived and unreviewable. Such claims may be pursued under the PCRA, as claims sounding in trial counsel's ineffectiveness or, if applicable, a statutory exception to the PCRA's waiver provision. This general rule, like the rule announced in Commonwealth v. Grant, reaffirms this Court's general approach to the requirements of issue preservation. Since [our early cases] an assumption has arisen that all waived claims are available for review in the first instance on direct appeal. The general rule shall now be that they are not. In adopting the new rule, we do not foreclose the possibility that a capital appellant may be able to describe why a particular waived claim is of such primary constitutional magnitude that it should be reached on appeal. Indeed, nothing we say today shall be construed as calling into question the bedrock principles . . . concerning the necessity of reaching fundamental and plainly meritorious constitutional issues irrespective, even, of the litigation preferences of the parties. . . .

In reformulating this Court's approach to claims not raised below, we have not lost sight of the undeniable fact that a death penalty appeal is different in quality and kind because of the final and irrevocable nature of the penalty. But our abrogation of relaxed waiver does not eliminate or diminish other substantial safeguards . . . which already serve to prevent this Court from being instrumental in an unconstitutional execution. These protections, not available in other criminal matters, serve a function similar to the relaxed waiver rule. First, this Court performs a self-imposed duty to review the sufficiency of the evidence underlying the first-degree murder conviction in all capital direct appeals, regardless of whether the appellant has raised the issue. The Court is also required to conduct a statutory review of the death sentence itself to determine whether it was the product of passion, prejudice or any other arbitrary factor, and to determine whether the evidence adduced at trial was sufficient to support the aggravating circumstance(s) found by the jury. . . . In addition to these special protections afforded capital appellants, the PCRA exists for them, as for other criminal defendants, as a vehicle for a full and fair, counseled proceeding through which they may challenge the stewardship of trial counsel and pursue other appropriate collateral claims.

This new general rule will be applied prospectively, beginning with those capital direct appeals in which the appellant's brief has not yet been filed in this Court, and is not due for thirty days or more after today's decision. It will then apply to all future capital appeals. . . . Prospective application of our new approach will avoid upsetting the expectations of capital appellants and their direct appeal counsel who have already briefed, or are in the process of briefing, their appeals in reliance upon the prospect that this Court, in its discretion, might reach the merits of some of their otherwise waived claims of trial error. . . .

NOTES

1. *Means and methods of collateral review.* As the *Freeman* decision highlights, in addition to providing criminal defendants opportunities for "direct review" of convictions and sentences through traditional appellate mechanisms, jurisdictions also provide defendants with opportunities for "collateral review" through various procedural systems. The most common, and most commonly discussed, method of collateral review is the writ of habeas corpus, and defendants in some cases will have access to both state and federal habeas corpus review. Indeed, particularly in state death penalty cases (where defendants have the greatest interest and opportunity to seek every possible appellate review), it is not uncommon for a conviction and sentence to be reviewed in seven distinct stages: (1) direct review by a state intermediate court, (2) direct review by the state supreme court, (3) collateral state habeas corpus review by a state trial court, (4) appellate review of the state habeas corpus decision by a state appellate court, (5) collateral federal habeas corpus review by a federal district court, (6) appellate review of the federal habeas corpus decision by a federal circuit court, and (7) final appellate review by the U.S. Supreme Court.

Though many of these layers of review are available in all criminal cases, they are disproportionately invoked in death penalty cases. In capital cases, where the stakes are high and the consequences of an unlawful execution cannot be reversed, do you think these multiple layers of review are justified, or are capital defendants given too many "bites at the apple" of appellate review?

2. *Relationship between direct and collateral review.* As the *Freeman* case reveals, appellate courts reviewing convictions and sentences are often aware of the various other opportunities for review that a defendant might invoke, and there is an unavoidable (though not often expressly discussed) tendency for reviewing courts to alter their decisions in light of these realities. *Freeman*

provides an interesting, but somewhat rare, example of a court limiting its approach to direct review because of the availability (and perceived appropriateness) of collateral review for certain claims. It is far more common to see courts that conduct collateral review limiting their examination of certain issues or claims because such matters were already decided (or preclusively waived) during a defendant's pursuit of direct review. See, e.g., 28 U.S.C. §2254(b)-(e), (i) (setting forth various limits on when a federal court can grant a writ of habeas corpus on behalf of a person in custody following a state conviction). Is it a sound practice for reviewing courts to avoid duplicated effort by coordinating when and how certain legal claims will be examined? Or is the whole point of collateral review to give defendants a chance to have decisions made on direct review double-checked?

3. *The British Criminal Cases Review Commission.* The United Kingdom has a very limited appellate review system in criminal cases, and many defendants forgo the right to appeal. In the wake of a number of high-profile miscarriages of justice in the mid-1990s, however, the British government created the Criminal Cases Review Commission to review the applications of criminal defendants who claim to be wrongfully convicted. If the commission considers it "a real possibility that the conviction, verdict, finding or sentence would not be upheld," it refers the case to the court of appeal. As of October 2000, the Commission had referred 4.3% of the cases reviewed, and the court of appeal had overturned more than three-quarters of these convictions.

Especially in light of recent evidence that many innocent persons were wrongly convicted and were able to establish their innocence only with the help of public interest organizations that donated time and money to conduct DNA testing and other forms of investigation, do you think such a commission should be created in the United States? What might be some of the benefits of using a commission, rather than a traditional court, to review the lawfulness and appropriateness of criminal convictions and sentences? Should such a commission provide an additional means of review in criminal cases, or should it operate in place of certain levels of direct or collateral review? How would you try to structure its membership and operation to protect it from undue political influence?

4. *Political debates over federal habeas corpus review.* A highly political debate about federalism arises when federal courts review and invalidate convictions obtained in state court through collateral review. Although the federal writ of habeas corpus has a constitutional foundation and a long history, debates over postconviction judicial review began to heat up following modern expansions of habeas corpus review of state court convictions in federal court. Expanded federal habeas review began in the mid-1960s after a few groundbreaking U.S. Supreme Court decisions, although there was some significant retrenchment in the methods of review in the 1980s and 1990s. See generally Jordan Steiker, Restructuring Post-conviction Review of Federal Constitutional Claims Raised by State Prisoners: Confronting the New Face of Excessive Proceduralism, 1998 U. Chi. Legal F. 315 (discussing history and controversies over federal habeas review and suggesting ways to redesign federal habeas review of state convictions in capital cases).

The impact of politics on federal habeas corpus review was reflected in Congress's passage of the Antiterrorism and Effective Death Penalty Act

(AEDPA) in 1996 after the Oklahoma City bombing of the Murrah Federal Building by Timothy McVeigh. The AEDPA dramatically altered federal habeas corpus practice in many ways, establishing restrictions on the filing of federal habeas corpus petitions, new procedures for treating unexhausted claims and for appealing the denial or dismissal of a petition, and new standards for reviewing state court rulings. See generally Bryan A. Stevenson, The Politics of Fear and Death: Successive Problems in Capital Federal Habeas Corpus Cases, 77 N.Y.U. L. Rev. 699 (2002).

A Broken System: Error Rates in Capital Cases, 1973-1995, James S. Liebman et al. (2000)

SUMMARY OF CENTRAL FINDINGS

[We] undertook a painstaking search, beginning in 1991 and accelerating in 1995, of all published state and federal judicial opinions in the U.S. conducting direct and habeas review of state capital judgments, and many of the available opinions conducting state post-conviction review of those judgments. We then (1) checked and catalogued all the cases the opinions revealed, and (2) collected hundreds of items of information about each case from the published decisions and the NAACP Legal Defense Fund's quarterly death row census, and (3) tabulated the results. Nine years in the making, our central findings thus far are [set forth below.]

- Between 1973 and 1995, approximately 5,760 death sentences were imposed in the U.S. Only 313 (5.4%; one in 19) of those resulted in an execution during the period.
- Of the 5,760 death sentences imposed in the study period, 4,578 (79%) were finally reviewed on "direct appeal" by a state high court. Of those, 1,885 (41%; over two out of five) were thrown out because of "serious error," i.e., error that the reviewing court concludes has seriously undermined the reliability of the outcome or otherwise "harmed" the defendant.
- Nearly all of the remaining death sentences were then inspected by state post-conviction courts. Our data reveal that state post-conviction review is an important source of review in states such as Florida, Georgia, Indiana, Maryland, Mississippi, North Carolina, and Tennessee. In Maryland, at least 52 percent of capital judgments reviewed on state post-conviction during the study period were overturned due to serious error; the same was true of at least 25 percent of the capital judgments that were similarly reviewed in Indiana, and at least 20 percent of those reviewed in Mississippi.
- Of the death sentences that survived state direct and post-conviction review, 599 were finally reviewed in a first habeas corpus petition during the 23-year study period. Of those 599, 237 (40%; two out of five) were overturned due to serious error. . . .
- The "overall error-rate" is . . . the proportion of fully reviewed capital judgments that were overturned at one of the three stages due to

serious error. Nationally, over the entire 1973-1995 period, the overall error-rate in our capital punishment system was 68 percent. . . .

- The most common errors are (1) egregiously incompetent defense lawyering (accounting for 37 percent of the state post-conviction reversals), and (2) prosecutorial suppression of evidence that the defendant is innocent or does not deserve the death penalty (accounting for another 16%–19%, when all forms of law enforcement misconduct are considered). . . .

- The seriousness of these errors is . . . revealed by what happens on retrial, when the errors are cured. In our state post-conviction study, an astonishing 82 percent (247 out of 301) of the capital judgments that were reversed were replaced on retrial with a sentence less than death, or no sentence at all. In the latter regard, 7 percent (22/301) of the reversals for serious error resulted in a determination on retrial that the defendant was not guilty of the capital offense.

- The result of very high rates of serious, reversible error among capital convictions and sentences, and very low rates of capital reconviction and resentencing, is the severe attrition of capital judgments. As is illustrated by the flow chart . . . , [for] every 100 death sentences imposed and reviewed during the study period, 41 were turned back at the state direct appeal phase because of serious error. Of the 59 that got through that phase to the second, state post-conviction stage, at

The Attrition of Capital Judgments

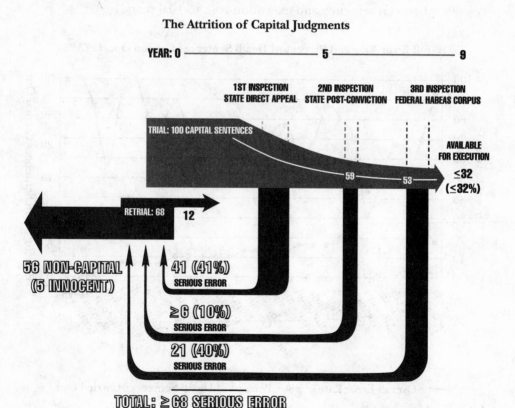

least 10 percent — meaning 6 more of the original 100 — were turned back due to serious flaws. And, of the 53 that got through that stage to the third, federal habeas checkpoint, 40 percent — an additional 21 of the original 100 — were turned back because of serious error. All told, at least 68 of the original 100 were thrown out because of serious flaws, compared to only 32 (or less) that were found to have passed muster — after an average of 9-10 years had passed. . . .

- The 68 percent rate of capital error found by the three stage inspection process is much higher than the error rate of less than 15 percent found by those same three inspections in noncapital criminal cases.

- Appointed federal judges are sometimes thought to be more likely to overturn capital sentences than state judges, who almost always are elected in capital-sentencing states. In fact, state judges are the first and most important line of defense against erroneous death sentences. They found serious error in and reversed 90 percent of the capital sentences that were overturned during the study period. . . .

- Finding all this error takes time. . . . It took an average of 7.6 years after the defendant was sentenced to die to complete federal habeas consideration in the 40 percent of habeas cases in which reversible error was found. . . . In the cases in which no error was detected at the third inspection stage and an execution occurred, the average time between sentence and execution was 9 years. Matters did not improve over time. In the last 7 study years (1989-95), the average time between sentence and execution rose to 10.6 years.

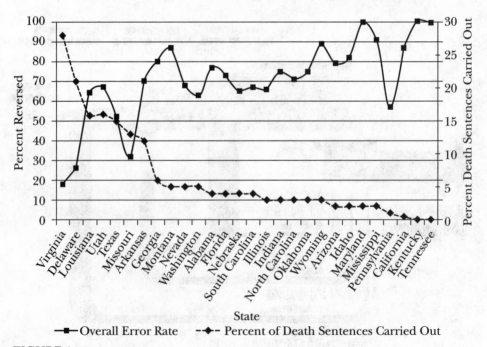

Overall Error Rate and Percent of Death Sentences Carried Out, 1973-95

FIGURE 1

• High rates of error, and the time consequently needed to filter out all that error, frustrate the goals of the death penalty system. [As Figure 1 shows], where the rate of serious reversible error in a state's capital judgments reaches 55 percent or above (as is true for the vast majority of states), the state's capital punishment system is effectively stymied — with its proportion of death sentences carried out falling below 7 percent.

The recent rise in the number of executions is not inconsistent with these findings. Instead of reflecting improvement in the quality of death sentences under review, the rising number of executions may simply reflect how many more sentences have piled up for review. If the error-induced pile-up of cases is the cause of rising executions, their rise provides no proof that a cure has been found for disturbingly high error rates. To see why, consider a factory that produces 100 toasters, only 32 of which work. The factory's problem would not be solved if the next year it made 200 toasters (or added 100 new toasters to 100 old ones previously

Persons on Death Row and Percent and Number Executed, 1974-99

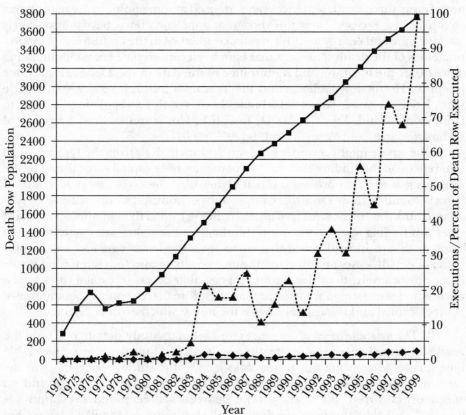

FIGURE 2

backlogged at the inspection stage), thus doubling its output of working products to 64. With, now, 136 duds to go with the 64 keepers, the increase in the latter would simply mask the persistence of crushing error rates. The decisive question, therefore, is not the number of death sentences carried out each year, but the proportion. . . .

- [As Figure 2 shows, in] contrast to the annual number of executions (the middle line in the chart), the proportion of death row inmates executed each year (the bottom line) has remained remarkably stable — and extremely low. Since post-*Furman* executions began in earnest in 1984, the nation has executed an average of about 1.3 percent of its death row inmates each year; in no year has it ever carried out more than 2.6 percent — or 1 in 39 — of those on death row. . . .

NOTES

1. *Success or failure?* Though the title of the groundbreaking report by Professor James Liebman and his colleagues speaks of "a broken system," can one rely on some of this data to claim that the system works? From 1973 to 1995, two of every three death sentences were reversed at some point in the many layers of capital case reviews. Does this show that appellate courts have appropriately invested time and energy to instill greater confidence in the lawfulness and appropriateness of the death sentences that have been carried out? For an illuminating debate over the meaning and significance of the data in the Liebman study, see Joseph L. Hoffmann, Violence and the Truth, 76 Ind. L.J. 939 (2001); Valerie West, Jeffrey Fagan & James S. Liebman, Look Who's Extrapolating: A Reply to Hoffmann, 76 Ind. L.J. 951 (2001); Joseph L. Hoffmann, A Brief Response to Liebman, Fagan, and West, 76 Ind. L.J. 957 (2001).

One way we might consider what conclusions to draw from the Liebman data is to reflect on the finding that the "68 percent rate of capital error found by the three stage inspection process is much higher than the error rate of less than 15 percent found by those same three inspections in noncapital criminal cases." Why do you think the "error rate" is so much higher in capital than in noncapital cases? Does this finding suggest that more fundamental mistakes are made in capital cases, or does it instead reveal that there are more legal regulations that apply in death penalty cases and thus many more possible bases for committing error? More provocatively, does this finding suggest that courts in capital cases review verdicts and sentences more seriously and therefore that the only major difference between capital and noncapital cases is the rate at which error is detected?

2. *The time and costs of review.* The Liebman study details not only the results of appellate review in death penalty cases, but also the considerable time it takes to conduct this review. Specifically, the study reports that "in the cases in which no error was detected at the third inspection stage and an execution occurred, the average time between sentence and execution was 9 years," and that the time needed for all the layers of appellate review has

grown longer, not shorter, over time. This timeline of appellate review is significant not only for the defendant sitting on death row and his family, but also for the family members of the victim. In addition, though not specifically calculated in the Liebman study, the economic costs of all this review of capital verdicts is considerable (some rough estimates suggest that just the appellate review stages of a fully appealed capital case may cost up to $1 million). Not to be overlooked are the lost opportunities: the time that courts, state lawyers, and defense attorneys spend on death penalty appeals that could be devoted instead to other important aspects of the criminal justice system.

In short, although it would be impossible to calculate precisely the economic and noneconomic costs of appellate review of capital cases, no one could reasonably question the conclusion that the costs are enormous in many respects. But like the data in the Liebman study, that determination does not suggest an obvious legal response. Should the enormity of the time and resources spent on appellate review in capital cases lead us to conclude that opportunities for review should be more sharply limited or that more money needs to be invested in ensuring that errors are not committed in capital cases in the first place? Or does the data suggest that we ought to abolish the death penalty altogether? See generally James Liebman, The Overproduction of Death, 100 Colum. L. Rev. 2030 (2000).

3. *Geographic and court variations in "error" data.* What conclusions can and should we draw from the fact that Professor Liebman's data reveals many variations in reversal rates based on geography and reviewing courts? This variation is most apparent in Figure 1 of the excerpt, which shows, for example, that less than 20% of all capital cases in Virginia are reversed on appeal, whereas nearly 100% of all capital cases in Tennessee are reversed on appeal. Do these numbers indicate that Tennessee is more "error-prone" in operating its capital sentencing system, or rather that the courts reviewing Tennessee death sentences detect more errors on appeal? More generally, do you need to know the reasons for reversals rather than just the cumulative numbers in order to assess what the Liebman study establishes?

4. *Appellate review and punishment purposes.* The authors of the Liebman study assert that high rates of error "and the time consequently needed to filter out all that error frustrate the goals of the death penalty system." Is that the conclusion you would draw? Does a "successful" death penalty system really depend on executing offenders efficiently and at a low cost, or should success be measured more in terms of whether defendants who deserve to die, and only those who deserve to die, are executed? More generally, can one effectively assess the success of appellate review in capital cases or of other sentencing outcomes without first reaching some conclusions about the purposes of punishment canvassed in Chapter 1?

5. *"Error" in non-death cases.* With some notable exceptions, the focus on errors in criminal convictions and sentences has been almost exclusively on death penalty cases. This is understandable because of the irreversibility of the sentence and also because many researchers have an anti–capital punishment agenda. But is a system that is error-prone in death cases likely to function

more accurately in other cases? How may the pressures vary between death and non-death cases? Would a comprehensive, Liebman-type study be advisable for non-death cases? What would you expect it to show? In countries without the death penalty, such as the United Kingdom, concern about error in criminal cases has focused almost exclusively on cases involving imprisonment.

4.   Supranational Review of Sentences

While the U.S. Supreme Court is the highest binding authority in direct appeals and collateral review in the United States, U.S. citizens and residents may bring complaints about their sentences before the Inter-American Human Rights Commission and the United Nations Human Rights Committee. Both of these institutions can issue recommendations to the U.S. government, though their decisions are not binding on any U.S. official.

In other countries, however, supranational courts may review sentences and issue decisions that can bind national governments and courts. Among such institutions are the European Court of Human Rights (ECHR) and the Judicial Committee of the Privy Council, the highest court for former Commonwealth countries that continue to accept its jurisdiction. In recent years the Judicial Committee has heard a large number of death penalty appeals. The most famous may be the one set out below.

Earl Pratt and Ivan Morgan v. The Attorney General for Jamaica
(Appeal No. 10 of 1993)

JUDGMENT OF THE LORDS OF THE JUDICIAL COMMITTEE OF THE PRIVY COUNCIL

LORD GRIFFITHS.

The appellants, Earl Pratt and Ivan Morgan, were arrested 16 years ago for a murder committed on 6th October 1977 and have been held in custody ever since. On 15th January 1979 they were convicted of murder and sentenced to death. Since that date they have been in prison in that part of Saint Catherine's prison set aside to hold prisoners under sentence of death and commonly known as death row. On three occasions the death warrant has been read to them and they have been removed to the condemned cells immediately adjacent to the gallows. . . . The statement of these bare facts is sufficient to bring home to the mind of any person of normal sensitivity and compassion the agony of mind that these men must have suffered as they have alternated between hope and despair in the 14 years that they have been in prison facing the gallows. It is unnecessary to refer to the evidence describing the restrictive conditions of imprisonment and the emotional and psychological impact of this experience, for it only reveals that which it is to be expected. These men are not alone in their suffering for there are now 23 prisoners in death row who have been awaiting execution for more than ten years and 82 prisoners who have been awaiting execution for more than five years. It is against this disturbing background that their Lordships must now determine this constitutional appeal. . . .

The death penalty in the United Kingdom has always been carried out expeditiously after sentence, within a matter of weeks or in the event of an appeal even to the House of Lords within a matter of months. Delays in terms of years are unheard of. . . . The Report of the Royal Commission on Capital Punishment 1949-53 (Cmd. 8932) gave the average delay in 1950 as six weeks if there was an appeal and three weeks if there was not. In 1947 there was great public disquiet that men convicted of a murder on the Gold Coast had been under sentence of death for two years. . . .

The murder was committed on 6th October 1977 and the appellants were sentenced to death on 15th January 1979. Their application for leave to appeal was dismissed by the Court of Appeal on 5th December 1980 who said that they would hand down their reasons later. Although notice of application for leave to appeal was given within three days of the conviction on 18th January 1979, it took almost two years to arrange a hearing by the Court of Appeal. Making every allowance for the pressure of work on the Jamaican courts this does seem a long time to arrange a hearing in a capital case which one would have expected to have been expedited.

[In the meantime, the defendants could not pursue their appeals in the Jamaican Privy Council. On 16th August 1984, Pratt] wrote to the Registrar of the Court of Appeal asking for the reasons why his application for leave to appeal was dismissed. It then transpired that no reasons had yet been prepared by the judge to whom the writing of the judgment had been assigned. The papers had apparently been put in the wrong bundle and forgotten. This was a serious oversight by the judge and by those in the office of the Court of Appeal who should have reminded him that reasons had not been provided in accordance with the practice of the Court of Appeal, which is to provide a reserved judgment or reasons within three months of a hearing. Prompted by Pratt's request reasons were quickly prepared and handed down on 24th September 1984. No immediate steps were, however, taken to petition the Judicial Committee of the Privy Council.

On 3rd October the [Inter-American Commission on Human Rights (IACHR), which Pratt had petitioned, rejected his] submission that his trial was unfair; but recommended that his sentence be commuted for humanitarian reasons. . . . On 28th January 1986 Pratt petitioned the United Nations Human Rights Committee [UNHRC] under the International Covenant on Civil and Political Rights.

On 13th March 1986 the appellants lodged notice of intention to petition for special leave to appeal to the Judicial Committee of the Privy Council. The application for special leave was heard with reasonable dispatch and special leave to appeal was refused by the Judicial Committee of the Privy Council on 17th July 1986. . . . In dismissing the application Lord Templeman expressed the concern of the Judicial Committee that three years and nine months had elapsed between the dismissal of the appeal and the delivery of the reasons. . . .

On 21st July 1986 the UNHRC requested Jamaica not to carry out the death sentence on Pratt and Morgan before it had an opportunity to consider the admissibility of the complaint. On 18th November 1986 the [Jamaican Privy Council (JPC)], apparently for the first time, considered the appellants' case.

They did not accede to the request of the UNHRC to stay the execution and the first warrant of execution was issued on 12th February 1987 for execution on 24th February.

On 23rd February the Governor-General issued a stay of execution. The reasons for the stay are not entirely clear but may have been the result of a telegram from the UNHRC urging a stay of execution and a letter from Mr. Noel Edwards Q.C., to the Governor-General informing him that the case of the appellants was due to be considered by the UNHRC on 23rd March 1987 and the IACHR on 26th March 1987. . . .

On 9th July 1987 the IACHR pursuant to further representations of Pratt and Morgan informed the Jamaican government of the following findings:

> Pratt and Morgan suffered a denial of justice during the period 1980-1984 violative of Article 5(2) of the American Convention on Human Rights. The Commission found that the fact that the Jamaican Court of Appeal issued its decision on December 5, 1980 but did not issue the reasons for that decision until four years later, September 24, 1984, was tantamount to cruel, inhuman and degrading treatment because during that four year delay the petitioners could not appeal to the Privy Council and had to suffer four years on death row awaiting execution. The Inter-American Commission on Human Rights . . . requests that the execution of Messrs. Pratt and Morgan be commuted for humanitarian reasons.

. . . On 13th October 1987 the JPC reconsidered the appellants' case. They did not accede to the request of the IACHR and on their advice the second warrant of execution was issued on 18th February 1988 for execution on 1st March.

On 29th February 1988 the second stay of execution was issued by the Governor-General. This time it appears to have been as a result of a further request from the UNHRC not to execute the men until the Committee had completed their review of the case. . . .

On 6th April 1989 the UNHRC gave their decision on the merits. They held that the failure of the Court of Appeal to deliver reasons for 45 months was a violation of Article 14 para. 3(c) and Article 14 para. 5 of the International Covenant on Civil and Political Rights and Optional Protocol which [states that everyone "shall be entitled to . . . be tried without undue delay" and "shall have the right to his conviction and sentence being reviewed by a higher tribunal according to law."].

The Committee gave the following reasons for their decision [and made the following recommendation]:

> . . . The Committee considers that the responsibility for the delay of 45 months lies with the judicial authorities of Jamaica. This responsibility is neither dependent on a request for production by the accused in a trial nor is non-fulfilment of this responsibility excused by the absence of a request from the accused. . . .
>
> In the absence of a written judgement of the Court of Appeal, the authors were not able to proceed to appeal before the Privy Council. [It] matters not that in the event the Privy Council affirmed the conviction of the authors. The Committee notes that in all cases, and especially in capital cases, accused persons are entitled to trial and appeal without undue delay, whatever the outcome of those judicial proceedings turns out to be.

[Although] capital punishment is not per se unlawful under the Covenant, it should not be imposed in circumstances where there have been violations by the State party of any of its obligations under the Covenant. The Committee is of the view that the victims of the violations of articles 14, paragraph 3(c) . . . are entitled to a remedy; the necessary prerequisite in the particular circumstances is the commutation of the sentence.

Eighteen months then passed before a decision was taken by the JPC on this recommendation of the UNHRC. Press reports of parliamentary proceedings show that in June 1990 the question of the death penalty was under review by the Cabinet but that no conclusions had yet been reached on commuting sentences.

On 17th September 1990 the JPC again reconsidered the appellants' case. They rejected the recommendations made eighteen months earlier by the UNHRC. On 18th February 1991 the warrant of execution was issued for execution on 7th March 1991, the delay in issuing the warrant of execution from 17th September 1990 to 18th February 1991 apparently being accounted for by the wish of the Governor-General to obtain the Attorney-General's advice on the legal status of decisions of human rights bodies. This is advice which it would have been appropriate to place before the members of the JPC at a much earlier date, and before they considered any recommendations of such bodies. Their Lordships have not seen the Attorney-General's advice but do not doubt that it correctly advised that, Jamaica being a signatory to the International Covenant on Civil and Political Rights and to the Optional Protocol, the views of the UNHRC should be afforded weight and respect but were not of legally binding effect; and that the like considerations applied to the IACHR.

On 28th February 1991 the appellants commenced these proceedings. . . .

The primary submission of the appellants is that to hang them after they have been held in prison under sentence of death for so many years would be inhuman punishment or other treatment and thus in breach of section 17(1) of the Constitution. Section 17 of the Constitution provides [that] "No person shall be subjected to torture or to inhuman or degrading punishment or other treatment." . . .

There is an instinctive revulsion against the prospect of hanging a man after he has been held under sentence of death for many years. What gives rise to this instinctive revulsion? The answer can only be our humanity; we regard it as an inhuman act to keep a man facing the agony of execution over a long extended period of time. But before their Lordships condemn the act of execution as "inhuman or degrading punishment or other treatment" within the meaning of section 17(1) there are a number of factors that have to be balanced in weighing the delay. If delay is due entirely to the fault of the accused such as an escape from custody or frivolous and time wasting resort to legal procedures which amount to an abuse of process the accused cannot be allowed to take advantage of that delay for to do so would be to permit the accused to use illegitimate means to escape the punishment inflicted upon him in the interest of protecting society against crime.

A much more difficult question is whether the delay occasioned by the legitimate resort of the accused to all available appellate procedures should be taken into account, or whether it is only delay that can be attributed to the shortcomings of the State that should be taken into account.

There is a powerful argument that it cannot be inhuman or degrading to allow an accused every opportunity to prolong his life by resort to appellate procedures however extended may be the eventual time between sentence and execution. This is the view that currently prevails in some States in the United States of America and has resulted in what has become known as the death row phenomenon where men are held under sentence of death for many years while their lawyers pursue a multiplicity of appellate procedures. . . . Support for this view is also to be found in previous decisions of the Privy Council. . . . There are other authorities which do not accept that delay occasioned by use of appeal procedures is to be disregarded. In Catholic Commission for Justice and Peace in Zimbabwe v. Attorney-General [Judgment No. S.C. 73/93, unreported, delivered on June 24, 1993] Gubbay C.J. said:

> It seems to me highly artificial and unrealistic to discount the mental agony and torment experienced on death row on the basis that by not making the maximum use of the judicial process available the condemned prisoner would have shortened and not lengthened his suffering. The situation could be otherwise if he had resorted to a series of untenable and vexatious proceedings which, in consequence, had the effect of delaying the ends of justice. . . .

In Soering v. United Kingdom (1989) 11 E.H.R.R. 439 the applicant, a West German national, alleged that the decision by the Secretary of State for the Home Department to extradite him to the United States of America to face trial in Virginia on a charge of capital murder would, if implemented, give rise to a breach by the United Kingdom of Article 3 of the European Convention for the Protection of Human Rights and Fundamental Freedoms (Cmd. 8969) which provides that no one should be subjected to torture or to inhuman or degrading treatment or punishment. . . . The European Court of Human Rights recognised that the death row phenomenon in Virginia where prisoners were held for a period of six to eight years before execution arose from repeated applications by the prisoner for a stay of execution but nevertheless held that such a long period of delay might go beyond the threshold set by Article 3. . . .

In their Lordships' view a State that wishes to retain capital punishment must accept the responsibility of ensuring that execution follows as swiftly as practicable after sentence, allowing a reasonable time for appeal and consideration of reprieve. It is part of the human condition that a condemned man will take every opportunity to save his life through use of the appellate procedure. If the appellate procedure enables the prisoner to prolong the appellate hearings over a period of years, the fault is to be attributed to the appellate system that permits such delay and not to the prisoner who takes advantage of it. Appellate procedures that echo down the years are not compatible with capital punishment. The death row phenomenon must not become established as a part of our jurisprudence.

The application of the appellants to appeal to the Judicial Committee of the Privy Council and their petitions to the two human rights bodies do not fall within the category of frivolous procedures disentitling them to ask the Board to look at the whole period of delay in this case. The total period of delay is shocking and now amounts to almost fourteen years. It is double the time that the European Court of Human Rights considered would be an infringement of

Article 3 of the European Convention and their Lordships can have no doubt that an execution would now be an infringement of section 17(1) of the Jamaican Constitution. . . .

Their Lordships are very conscious that many other prisoners under sentence of death are awaiting the outcome of this appeal. In an attempt to assist the Jamaican authorities who may be faced with a large number of appeals their Lordships wish to make some general observations. . . .

There may of course be circumstances which will lead the JPC to recommend a respite in the carrying out of a death sentence, such as a political moratorium on the death sentence, or a petition on behalf of the appellants to IACHR or UNHRC or a constitutional appeal to the Supreme Court. But if these respites cumulatively result in delay running into several years an execution will be likely to infringe section 17(1) and call for commutation of the death sentence to life imprisonment.

Their Lordships are very conscious that the Jamaican government faces great difficulties with a disturbing murder rate and limited financial resources at their disposal to administer the legal system. Nevertheless, if capital punishment is to be retained it must be carried out with all possible expedition. Capital appeals must be expedited and legal aid allocated to an appellant at an early stage. The aim should be to hear a capital appeal within twelve months of conviction. [It] should be possible to complete the entire domestic appeal process within approximately two years. Their Lordships do not purport to set down any rigid timetable but to indicate what appear to them to be realistic targets which, if achieved, would entail very much shorter delay than has occurred in recent cases and could not be considered to involve inhuman or degrading punishment or other treatment.

The final question concerns applications by prisoners to IACHR and UNHRC. Their Lordships wish to say nothing to discourage Jamaica from continuing its membership of these bodies and from benefiting from the wisdom of their deliberations. It is reasonable to allow some period of delay for the decisions of these bodies in individual cases but it should not be very prolonged. The UNHRC does not accept the complaint unless the author "has exhausted all available domestic remedies." . . . A complainant [can] lodge a complaint immediately after his case has been disposed of by the Judicial Committee of the Privy Council. If, however, Jamaica is able to revise its domestic procedures so that they are carried out with reasonable expedition no grounds will exist to make a complaint based upon delay. And it is to be remembered that the UNHRC does not consider its role to be that of a further appellate court.

It therefore appears to their Lordships that provided there is in future no unacceptable delay in the domestic proceedings complaints to the UNHRC from Jamaica should be infrequent and when they do occur it should be possible for the Committee to dispose of them with reasonable dispatch and at most within eighteen months.

These considerations lead their Lordships to the conclusion that in any case in which execution is to take place more than five years after sentence there will be strong grounds for believing that the delay is such as to constitute "inhuman or degrading punishment or other treatment." If, therefore, rather than waiting for all those prisoners who have been in death row under sentence of death for five years or more to commence proceedings pursuant to section 25 of the Constitution, the Governor-General now refers all such cases to the JPC who, in accordance with the guidance contained in this advice, recommend commutation to life imprisonment, substantial justice will be achieved swiftly and without provoking a flood of applications to the Supreme Court for constitutional relief pursuant to section 17(1). . . .

Their Lordships will accordingly humbly advise Her Majesty that this appeal ought to be allowed, and the sentences of the appellants be commuted to life imprisonment.

NOTES

1. *The Privy Council and its death penalty jurisprudence.*   With the expansion of the British Empire during the nineteenth century, courts in the colonies increasingly gained the right to appeal to the Privy Council and, later, its Judicial Committee. The Judicial Committee is an independent court composed of members of the high English judiciary and that of Commonwealth countries. Today it continues to hear appeals from British territories and the former English colonies that recognize it as their highest court. The modern line of death penalty jurisprudence in the Judicial Committee began with *Pratt.* In later cases, the Judicial Committee found a delay of less than five years unconstitutional. Moreover, the Judicial Committee found that not only delay but also unreasonable speed could lead to sentence commutation, since a defendant deserved reasonable notice of his execution.

As a consequence of these decisions, in the Caribbean countries scores of death sentences were commuted to life, and new appellate procedures were instituted to shorten the delay. What problems do such changes entail? For the U.S. Supreme Court's view of delay in capital cases (as well as a discussion of the value of foreign opinions on such issues), see Knight v. Florida, 528 U.S. 990 (1999) (concurrence and dissent from denial of certiorari).

2. *The Inter-American Human Rights system and the ECHR.*   The Inter-American Human Rights system consists of two organs, a commission and a court. While not all countries have accepted the court's jurisdiction, their citizens and residents have the right to petition the commission unless expressly excluded. For signatories of the American Declaration of Human Rights only, such as the United States, the commission may issue a recommendation at the end of a factual investigation; if a country signed the American Convention on Human Rights, the commission can refer a complaint to the court.

In past cases, the commission has held the United States in violation of the international prohibition of the execution of juveniles and has chastised it for the disparate application of the death penalty. The Inter-American court, while not outlawing the death penalty, has applied strict scrutiny in capital cases.

The European Human Rights system, with the European Court of Human Rights (ECHR), has only rarely had the opportunity to consider the death penalty. In a seminal decision, the court ruled that Great Britain could not extradite a German national to Virginia because of the so-called death row phenomenon — the delay between sentence imposition and execution and the conditions on death row — unless it received guarantees that the German would not be sentenced to death. Soering v. United Kingdom, 11 Eur. H.R.

Rep. 439 (Eur. Ct. H.R. 1989). This opinion has had a lasting impact on other national and supranational tribunals around the world. For details on the recent European reaction to the death penalty in the United States, see Nora V. Demleitner, The Death Penalty in the United States: Following the European Lead?, 81 Or. L. Rev. 131 (2002).

3. *The U.N. Human Rights Committee.*   The U.N. Human Rights Committee is a treaty body under the International Covenant on Civil and Political Rights and under the Convention Against Torture and Other Cruel, Inhuman or Degrading Treatment or Punishment. In that capacity it can hear a complaint once an individual has exhausted domestic remedies. In 1994 the Human Rights Committee found the use of gas chambers in select U.S. states to be a violation of the International Covenant on Civil and Political Rights. Other subcommittees and U.N. rapporteurs have focused on the question of juvenile executions. Should a governor be influenced by pronouncements of the U.N. Human Rights Committee or other U.N. institutions in individual petitions or on larger questions pertaining to the application of the death penalty?

4. *The International Court of Justice (ICJ).*   The ICJ can hear only state-to-state complaints, some of them lodged by countries on behalf of individual citizens. In 1999 Germany asked the ICJ to issue a stay of execution in the case of a German citizen sentenced to death in Arizona. It alleged that the United States had violated the Vienna Convention on Consular Rights by failing to inform him and his brother, who had already been executed, that they had the right to contact the German embassy, which would have paid for their defense attorneys. The state of Arizona proceeded to execute the German, in violation of the ICJ's stay order. The ICJ held that it had the power to issue such provisional measures and stated that in future cases in which the United States failed to live up to its treaty obligations and sentenced someone severely, a sentence commutation and monetary compensation to the German government were in order. LaGrand Case (Germany v. United States of America), 40 I.L.M. 1069 (I.C.J. 2001). The case was styled not as a death penalty case but rather as a case involving the violation of an important treaty. The Mexican government filed a similar case against the United States before the ICJ. Case Concerning Avena and other Mexican Nationals (Mex. v. U.S.), 2004 I.C.J. No. 128 (Judgment of Mar. 31). Are Germany and Mexico merely trying to protect the right to consular notification, or are they attempting to change U.S. law on the death penalty? If the latter, is such action legitimate?

B.   EXECUTIVE RECONSIDERATION OF SENTENCES

Even after trial, sentencing, appeals, and judicial postconviction challenges have ended and a convict begins to serve a sentence, the criminal justice process is not complete. A variety of mechanisms under the control of executive branch agencies determine whether, at some point before the sentence expires, an offender should be released from prison and what continuing controls are to be placed on an offender after release.

The most common mechanism for early prison release decisions and for supervising offenders after release is parole, a period of conditional supervised release following a prison term. Parole was once a fundamental component of nearly every American sentencing system, but the past quarter-century has seen dramatic reforms. The purpose, structure, and operation of parole (and parole boards) have changed in significant ways over the past several decades, and in some jurisdictions, including the federal system, parole has been technically eliminated. Nevertheless, parole remains a key aspect of most state sentencing systems, and as of year-end 2005 more than 780,000 people were on parole.

Another form of executive review takes place when a governor or president issues a pardon or commutation. The pardon power typically has a consti-tutional foundation; like the role of parole, however, the role of pardons in modern sentencing systems has evolved considerably. In recent times, an executive decision to grant a pardon or commutation has become both rare and often controversial. These two fundamental forms of executive sentence review will occupy the second part of this chapter.

1.   Parole

At the start of the twentieth century, reformers introduced parole as a cornerstone of a new approach to sentencing and corrections, and by 1950 all of the states, the federal system, and the District of Columbia relied heavily on the parole function as part of an indeterminate sentence system. In indeterminate sentencing, judges could impose both maximum and minimum sentences, choosing a range as broad as "zero to life" (though most sentences were imposed in a narrower range). Parole boards were authorized to consider offenders for release starting at a designated point within the broad sentencing ranges. Inherent in this system, and in the function of parole boards, was the belief that the primary purpose of imprisonment was to rehabilitate offenders. The prevailing belief was that experts in the social and psychological sciences would be able to determine when an individual was rehabilitated and therefore ready for release.

In the 1970s many began to doubt the ability of the criminal justice system to rehabilitate offenders. The discretion of both judges and parole boards in indeterminate sentencing systems was criticized on various grounds, and an array of reforms led to a movement in many jurisdictions toward more deter-minate sentencing, in which offenders know their release date (subject to a slight decrease for good institutional behavior, so-called good time) on the day they are sentenced. Nevertheless, the model of indeterminate sentencing that dominated American sentencing systems for most of the twentieth century can still be found in more than half of the states, and thus parole continues to be critical in many jurisdictions.

As researchers Jeremy Travis and Sarah Lawrence have explained, parole and parole boards play three critical roles:

> First, parole boards determine the actual length of a prison sentence. With indeterminate sentencing, judges sentence an offender to a prison term, specifying a minimum and a maximum length of prison stay. The parole board, an executive branch agency, then decides on a case-by-case basis whether a prisoner is ready to be released to the community.

Second, parole agencies supervise recently released individuals in the community for the remainder of their sentence. In the classic indeterminate sentencing model, a prisoner released on parole is not free. Rather, he or she is still serving a criminal sentence, in the community rather than in prison, and must abide by a number of conditions established by the parole board at the time of release. Thus, parole agencies are expected to play a critical role in overseeing the reintegration of returning prisoners.

Third, parole officers and parole boards are authorized to revoke a parolee's conditional liberty and return him or her to prison. If a parole officer (also referred to as a parole agent) determines that the parolee has failed to observe a condition of his release — for example, has committed a new crime, failed to maintain employment, or failed a drug test — the officer can recommend that parole be revoked. The parole board, or in some states a judicial officer, then decides whether to send the parolee back to prison for some or all of the remainder of the prison sentence.

Jeremy Travis & Sarah Lawrence, Beyond the Prison Gates: The State of Parole in America 2 (Urban Institute, Nov. 2002).

In the sections that follow, we first examine the composition and authority of parole commissions, the key decision makers in parole systems. We then turn to an examination of the three major functions of parole commissions: (1) determining when inmates will be released from prison, (2) supervising offenders on parole, and (3) creating rules for parole revocation. As you read these materials, it is worthwhile to review some of the doctrines and issues concerning probation covered in Chapter 8, since probation and parole both involve conditional releases into the community. They differ, however, in that probation is imposed at sentencing by a judge whereas parole is imposed by a parole board after an offender has already served a prison term.

a.   Parole Commissions and Guidelines

Early in their history parole boards had nearly unfettered discretion in making parole release decisions. One distinct feature of modern parole decision making is that boards are now typically governed by guidelines of varying detail. Usually those guidelines have been issued by the parole board itself, although they are sometimes produced under legislative direction. Some guidelines state principles to guide the parole board's release decisions; others specify particular parole terms for a given offender committing a specific offense. Some guidelines are based on an unweighted list of factors related to the underlying offense: the offender's threat to the community or to individuals, or the inmate's likelihood of reoffending. Other guidelines create a scoring system based on social science data reflecting risk factors and favor release of individuals who, based on their similarity to prior offenders, are designated as least likely to commit serious offenses in the near future.

‖ *Iowa Code §§904A.1, 904A.2* ‖

The board of parole is created to consist of five members. Each member, except the chairperson, shall be compensated on a day-to-day basis. Each member shall serve a term of four years. . . . The terms shall be staggered. The chairperson of the board shall be a full-time, salaried member of the board. A majority of the members of the board constitutes a quorum to transact business.

The membership of the board shall be of good character and judicious background, shall include a member of a minority group, may include a person ordained or designated as a regular leader of a religious community and who is knowledgeable in correctional procedures and issues, and shall meet at least two of the following three requirements:

1. Contain one member who is a disinterested layperson.
2. Contain one member who is an attorney licensed to practice law in this state and who is knowledgeable in correctional procedures and issues.
3. Contain one member who is a person holding at least a master's degree in social work or counseling and guidance and who is knowledgeable in correctional procedures and issues.

‖ *Colorado Revised Statutes §17-22.5-404(1),(2)* ‖

(1) As to any person . . . who is eligible for parole . . . , the board may consider all applications for parole, . . . and may parole any person who is sentenced or committed to a correctional facility when the board determines, by using the guidelines established by this section, that there is a strong and reasonable probability that the person will not thereafter violate the law and that his release from institutional custody is compatible with the welfare of society. The board shall first consider the risk of violence to the public in every release decision it makes.

(2)(a) In considering offenders for parole, the board shall consider, but need not be limited to, the following factors:

(I) The testimony of the victim of the crime or a relative of the victim, if the victim has died . . . ;

(II) The offender's conduct which would indicate whether he has substantially observed all of the rules and regulations of the institution or facility in which he has been confined and has faithfully performed the duties assigned to him;

(III) The offender's demonstration of good faith efforts to make restitution to the victim of his conduct for the actual damages that were sustained . . . ;

(IV) The offender's demonstration of good faith efforts to pay reasonable costs of parole supervision . . . ;

(V) The offender's demonstration of good faith efforts to devote time to a specific employment or occupation;

(VI) The offender's good faith efforts to enroll in a school, college, university, or course of vocational or technical training designed to fit the student for gainful employment;

(VII) Whether the offender has diligently attempted but has been unable to obtain employment that provides the offender sufficient income, whether the offender has an employment disability, or whether the offender's age prevents him or her from obtaining employment;

(VIII) The offender's demonstration of good faith efforts to remain within prescribed geographical boundaries and notify the court or the parole officer of any change in the offender's address or employment;

(IX) The offender's demonstration of good faith efforts to report as directed to the parole officer;

(X) The offender's demonstration of good faith efforts to participate in some type of community service work;

(XI) The offender has not harassed the victim either verbally or in writing;

(XII) The offender's demonstration of good faith efforts to provide support, including any court-ordered child support, for any minor children;

(XIII) The offender's participation in the literacy corrections programs.

(b) Nothing in this subsection . . . shall preclude the board from considering factors other than those stated in paragraph (a) . . . when considering applicants for parole.

Michael McDermott v. James McDonald
24 P.3d 200 (Mont. 2001)

Petitioner Michael McDermott (McDermott) is serving a thirty-year sentence for assault and felony bail jumping in the Crossroads Correctional Center. The Board of Pardons and Parole (Board) has denied his application for parole, based in part on his failure to participate in a sexual offender program (SOP). He petitions this Court for a writ of habeas corpus, alleging that the Board has illegally denied him parole. We deny his petition.

BACKGROUND

In May 1989, McDermott was charged by information with four counts of assault and four counts of incest against his two stepsons, then aged five and six. The information alleged that, between June 1985 and January 1986, McDermott assaulted his stepsons physically and sexually by burning their arms on the stove, knocking out their teeth, beating them on their legs, buttocks and penis with a wooden spoon and forcing them to engage in anal and oral intercourse. After being charged and released on bond, McDermott fled the jurisdiction. Eventually recaptured, he was extradited back to Montana and charged with an additional count of felony bail jumping.

McDermott pled guilty to the assault and bail jumping charges in exchange for dismissal of the four incest counts. The District Court sentenced him to five years on each assault charge and ten years on the bail jumping charge, for a total sentence of thirty years. Because of the violent nature of the assaults, because he committed them against young victims and because the court found that he represents a substantial danger to society, McDermott was designated a dangerous offender for purposes of parole.

McDermott began serving his sentence in May 1992. At that time, an initial needs assessment concluded that he suffers from "severe sexual problems" and recommended that he participate in the prison's treatment program for sexual offenders. McDermott elected not to participate in the SOP, and the Board later considered this fact during evaluations for placement in a prerelease center, for parole and for inmate classification purposes.

McDermott first applied for parole in September 1998. After notice and a hearing, the Board denied his application, citing McDermott's multiple offenses as well as their nature and severity. It noted that participation in the SOP would "enhance success on parole and further ensure that the applicant is willing and able to fulfill the obligations of a law-abiding citizen." McDermott again chose not to participate. As a result, he had four points added to his classification status for noncompliance with the Board's SOP recommendation. In September 1999, the Board again denied McDermott's parole application, citing the nature and severity of his offenses as well as his failure to comply with the Board's previous SOP recommendation.

McDermott contends that by requiring him to complete an SOP as a condition to early release on parole, the Board infringed upon his liberty interest in parole without due process of law. He petitions this Court for a writ of habeas corpus ordering his immediate release and rescinding the four points added to his classification status.

DISCUSSION

Our due process analysis requires us to determine whether McDermott has a protected liberty interest in parole, and, if so, what process he is due and whether he received that process.

A.   McDermott's Liberty Interest in Parole

As a general rule, inmates have no liberty interest in parole. Greenholtz v. Inmates of the Nebraska Penal and Correctional Complex, 442 U.S. 1, 7 (1979). We have, however, recognized an exception to this general rule for inmates who committed their offenses prior to 1989. Before that year, Montana's parole eligibility statute stated: "the board *shall* release on parole . . . any person confined in the Montana state prison . . . when in its opinion there is reasonable probability that the prisoner can be released without detriment to the prisoner or to the community." Section 46-23-201, MCA (emphasis added). The United States Supreme Court held that the mandatory language of this provision created a liberty interest in parole that is protected by the due process clause of the federal constitution. Board of Pardons v. Allen, 482 U.S. 369, 377 (1987). . . .

B.   The Process Due McDermott

There is no absolute standard for what constitutes due process. Rather, the requirements of due process are flexible, so that they may be adapted to meet the procedural protections demanded by a particular situation. Thus, the process due in any given case varies according to the factual circumstances of the case, the nature of the interests at stake, and the risk of making an erroneous decision.

It is well established that a parole release determination is not subject to all the due process protections required to convict or confine. Nor must a parole release determination provide the same due process protections as are required in a parole revocation hearing. These situations present a much greater risk of error than a parole release determination because incarceration, whether as a result of conviction or parole revocation, involves a loss of liberty. Denial of parole, on the other hand, involves the loss of the mere anticipation of freedom — freedom to which the lawfully-convicted inmate is otherwise not entitled. As a consequence, the United States Supreme Court has held that due process is satisfied when the prisoner seeking parole is, at a minimum, provided with an opportunity to be heard and a written statement explaining why he was denied parole. *Greenholtz,* 442 U.S. at 16.

C. The Board's Authority to Consider McDermott's Participation in the SOP

McDermott does not contend that he was denied an opportunity to come before the Board or that he did not receive a statement of the reasons his parole was denied. Rather, he argues that the Board does not have authority to consider his lack of participation in an SOP as a basis for denying him early release on parole. For support, he relies on two of this Court's recent decisions: State v. Ommundson, 974 P.2d 620 (Mont. 1999), in which we held that a district court could not force an offender to complete a sexual offender program that had no correlation or connection to the underlying offense, and State v. Field, 11 P.3d 1203 (Mont. 2000), in which we held that the Board had no authority to impose conditions on a probationer that were not a part of his original sentence. We conclude, however, that neither of these cases limit the Board's authority to consider McDermott's failure to participate in the recommended SOP.

In *Ommundson,* the defendant pled guilty to driving under the influence of alcohol (DUI). After a presentence investigation revealed that he had more than ten previous convictions for indecent exposure, the district court conditioned suspension of the defendant's DUI sentence on his participation in an SOP. On appeal, we struck down the SOP condition, holding that "a sentencing limitation or condition must have . . . some correlation or connection to the underlying offense for which the defendant is being sentenced." We based our decision on the requirement of MCA §46-18-202(1)(e), that a sentence be "reasonably related to the objectives of rehabilitation and protection of the victim and society." . . . Since he was not convicted of a sex offense, McDermott contends that the Board has no authority to condition his parole on his participation in an SOP. We find this argument without merit. . . .

McDermott's argument fails to recognize the fundamental difference between imposition of a sentence — as in *Ommundson* — and release on parole. A sentence, or condition included in that sentence, is a *limitation on liberty*. A condition on parole is not. The district court's authority is properly restrained when it acts to limit an individual's freedom. Once lawfully sentenced, however, a prisoner is not entitled to release prior to the completion of his full sentence. Parole, therefore, is a *grant of liberty*. A condition on parole only limits freedom to which the inmate is otherwise not entitled. As a general proposition, then, it is

826   Chapter 11.   Sentences Reconsidered

invalid to assume, as McDermott does, that the Board's authority to set conditions precedent to parole is necessarily limited by a court's sentencing authority. . . .

Under both Montana and federal precedent, parole is a privilege and not a right. Since parole is granted as a matter of grace, rather than right, the state may offer such grace under and subject to such conditions as it considers most conducive to accomplish the desired purpose. In Montana, that grace is offered only when, in the Board's opinion, three conditions have been satisfied: "there is a reasonable probability that the prisoner can be released without detriment to the prisoner or to the community," MCA §46-23-201(1); when it is in "the best interests of society"; and when the prisoner "is able and willing to fulfill the obligations of a law-abiding citizen." MCA §46-23-201(2). Rather than restricting the authority of the Board to set conditions precedent to parole, these provisions obligate the Board to ensure that no prisoner is released on parole who cannot meet these three criteria.

As a complement to its broad discretion to grant, deny, or condition parole, the Board is authorized to consider factors that may not be considered by the district court at trial and sentencing. For instance, parole authorities are not limited to consideration of formally adjudicated cases when determining the likelihood of a prisoner's success on parole. Christopher v. U.S. Board of Parole, 589 F.2d 924 (7th Cir. 1978). Moreover, they may consider evidence of offenses which were charged in dismissed counts. Robinson v. Hadden, 723 F.2d 59 (10th Cir. 1983). A parole board may even hear and consider evidence excluded at trial under the exclusionary rule. In re Martinez, 463 P.2d 734 (Cal. 1970). In Montana, the Board is specifically required to "consider all pertinent information regarding each prisoner, including the circumstances of his offense, his previous social history and criminal record, his conduct, employment and attitude in prison, and the reports of any physical and mental examinations which have been made." MCA §46-23-202.

We conclude that the Board's authority to condition parole is not limited by our holding in *Ommundson*. Furthermore, the Board's statutory authority is broad enough to permit its consideration of McDermott's dismissed incest counts, the results of his initial needs assessment showing severe sexual problems and his refusal to participate in an SOP when determining whether to grant him an early release on parole.

McDermott's second argument is based on this Court's recent holding in *Field*. In that case, we held that the Board could not impose a condition on a probationer's postrelease conduct that was not specifically authorized by his sentence. *Field* dealt with a prisoner who had served the full term of his unsuspended sentence and was released on probation. Prior to release, the Board imposed the condition that he have no unsupervised contact with minors. Violation of this condition was later used to rescind the probation and return Field to prison. On appeal, this Court applied MCA §46-18-801, which provides that no "offender may be *deprived of a civil or constitutional right* except as provided in the Montana Constitution or as specifically enumerated by the sentencing judge as a necessary condition of the sentence. . . ." We reversed recision of the suspended sentence after determining that the condition that Field have no unsupervised contact with minors was a violation of his constitutional right to freedom of association and that it was not specifically included as a condition of his sentence.

McDermott argues that the Board's authority to impose conditions on his *parole* can be no greater than its authority to impose postsentence conditions on Field. He contends that, even if the District Court had the authority to impose a condition that he participate in an SOP as part of his sentence, no such condition was included. Therefore, he asserts, as in *Field,* the Board cannot now impose it as a condition of his release. We disagree.

In applying this Court's holding in *Field,* it is important to distinguish release on *parole* and release on *probation.* Parole, as stated above, is a discretionary grant of freedom from incarceration. Probation is an original condition of sentence that, for some period of time, the offender will not be incarcerated. . . . Under *Field,* the Board has no authority to impose conditions on *probation* that were not part of the original sentence because, under the terms of the sentence, Field was entitled to be released at the time and under the conditions set by the court. But *Field* does not limit the Board's authority to place conditions on *parole.* The Board's placement of a condition on *probation* is a restriction on someone who would otherwise be free. A condition on *parole* is a limited grant of freedom to someone who would otherwise be incarcerated. We conclude that our holding in *Field* does not limit the Board's authority to impose conditions on parole and is not relevant to McDermott's case.

CONCLUSION

Under MCA §46-23-201, . . . the Board must consider "all pertinent information regarding the prisoner." McDermott, while not a convicted sex offender, had four counts of incest dismissed pursuant to a plea bargain. He has been identified as having severe sexual problems. His completion — or lack of completion — of the SOP is pertinent to his ability to be released without "detriment to the . . . community" and "to fulfill the obligations of a law-abiding citizen." Therefore, the Board was well within its authority to consider McDermott's refusal to enroll in the recommended SOP when it denied his application for an early release.

PROBLEM 11-5. BEING UNDER THE WEATHER

On October 20, 1981, Kathy Boudin was arrested in conjunction with the robbery of an armored car during which the driver, Peter Paige, had been killed. Boudin had not participated in the planning of the robbery of $1.6 million, and was unarmed at the time of her arrest. She belonged to a radical group, the Weather Underground, that was willing to use violence to support its goals. After the robbery Boudin was riding in a U-Haul truck with those who had participated in the robbery. When the U-Haul was stopped at a roadblock, Boudin immediately surrendered to the police. Shortly thereafter, as police attempted to open the back of the truck, shooting erupted, and two police officers were killed.

Boudin pled guilty under New York's felony murder statute. She was sentenced to 20 years to life in prison for her role in the robbery. No charges were filed against her in connection with the death of the officers since she had already surrendered at the time they were killed. At sentencing, Judge Ritter imposed what he characterized as a "minimal" but "just" sentence. He explained his reasons for doing so: "In my judgment there is evidence of honest contrition and remorse, and abhorrence of violence as a technique to further goals, however noble." He concluded that Boudin's role in the tragedy was a "secondary one," and stated that there was no evidence to believe she was guilty of "any form of terrorist activity." Finally, Judge Ritter stated, "I see no reason in the world why Miss Boudin should not be paroled at the expiration of the twenty years."

In prison Boudin was a model inmate. At Bedford Hills, New York's prison for women, she established a program for women inmates with HIV that served as the model for such programs nationwide. In addition, she set up programs in adult literacy and for incarcerated women with children. In that capacity she organized workshops and developed curricula. She also completed a master's degree in adult education while in prison and published widely on HIV, literacy, mother-child relationships, and higher education.

At her first parole hearing in August 2001, Boudin was denied parole; the parole board stated that "due to the violent nature and circumstances of the instant offenses," Boudin's release "would be incompatible with the welfare of society and would serve to deprecate the seriousness of the criminal behavior herein so as to undermine respect for the law." At her second parole hearing in May 2003, the board again refused to grant her parole, because of the seriousness of the crimes and the fact that three individuals died in the crime spree.

After the second parole hearing, a New York judge ordered a new hearing because the parole board had failed to consider adequately Judge Ritter's remarks at sentencing and Boudin's remarkable record while in prison. At her third hearing in the summer of 2003, the board granted Boudin parole, effective October 1, 2003.

To what extent should Judge Ritter's remarks influence the parole board's decision? Should it have mattered to the parole board that some but not all of the victims' family members opposed the grant of parole? Would the parole decision for Boudin have been different under Colorado's parole guidelines (reprinted above)? Under Montana's parole rules (discussed in the *McDermott* case above)?

NOTES

1. *Representation requirements and expertise.*   Parole board members are usually appointed by the governor for fixed terms. Traditional membership requirements include backgrounds in psychology and social work to assess the likely behavior and rehabilitation of inmates. More modern membership requirements focus on diverse representation, sometimes including specific allocation of spots to members of different political parties. The assumptions underlying the representation requirements on parole boards have changed over time. Why do statutes like the Iowa provisions now require membership of community members, religious leaders, and members of minority groups? What influence can a "disinterested layperson" have if the other members of the parole board appear to be more knowledgeable in criminal justice matters?

2. *Political insulation.* The structure and composition of parole boards can determine to what extent politics influences parole decision making. For instance, Colorado has two separate institutions to address parole issues: the parole board, which makes individual parole decisions, and the commission to review and approve parole guidelines. The commission membership includes the attorney general, the executive director of the department of public safety, the executive director of the department of corrections, the chairperson of the state board of parole, the chairperson of a community corrections board, a parole officer, a law enforcement officer, and a private citizen. Why would Colorado create a separate body to set parole policy? Should a jurisdiction seek to maximize the political insulation of parole decision makers or instead create structures that ensure political accountability in parole decisions?

3. *Right to parole.* As noted in *McDermott,* in Greenholtz v. Inmates of the Nebraska Penal and Correctional Complex, 442 U.S. 1 (1979), the Supreme Court held that state prisoners do not have a constitutional right to parole and that there is no constitutionally protected interest in receiving parole unless a state's parole statute contains mandatory language restricting the parole board's discretion. In such a case, the prisoner develops a legitimate expectation of parole that cannot be denied without due process. In *Greenholtz,* the Supreme Court held that the due process requirement was satisfied through an informal hearing in which the inmate had an opportunity to present letters and statements on his behalf.

4. *Parole procedures.* Parole hearings are typically open to the public, and the offender as well as the victim or the victim's family are allowed to make statements. The members of the parole board are furnished information about the offense committed, the offender's behavior while incarcerated, and reports from prison psychiatrists, if applicable. Although the precise contours of prisoners' due process rights in parole proceedings have not been definitively established, most jurisdictions tend to provide a hearing (with prior notice provided), a defined opportunity for the presentation of information by the inmate, notice of the criteria used to make the parole decision, and notice of the decision together with reasons for denial. See Victoria J. Palacios, Go and Sin No More: Rationality and Release Decisions by Parole Boards, 45 S.C. L. Rev. 567 (1994).

5. *Discretionary and mandatory parole releases and good time.* Parole release schemes in which parole boards have nearly unfettered discretion to determine a release date have fallen out of favor over the past few years. Parole decision making has become increasingly structured, and mandatory releases to parole supervision are much more common now than in the past. In 2005, 51% of all adults entering parole did so upon mandatory release (up from 45% in 1995). Lauren E. Glaze & Thomas E. Bonczar, Probation and Parole in the United States, 2005 (NCJ 215091, November 2006). Mandatory release occurs largely in determinate sentencing systems, in which inmates are conditionally released from prison after serving a portion of their original sentence minus any good time earned.

Inmates earn so-called good-time credit for obeying prison rules. The ceiling on good-time credits varies by jurisdiction. In the past, inmates in some systems earned a day (or more) of good time for every day served. This led to heavy criticism, as inmates were released substantially earlier than the community and the victims expected.

Many systems now cap good time at 15% of the total sentence imposed, and they have been encouraged to do so by federal funding criteria for prison construction grants. Under the federal prison-building "truth-in-sentencing" grants, states received building grants only if they kept violent offenders incarcerated for 85% of the prison time imposed. See generally Paula Ditton & Doris James Wilson, Truth in Sentencing in State Prisons (Bureau of Justice Statistics, NCJ 170032, 1999). The Minnesota system began with a good-time provision allowing credits of up to 33% of the pronounced term, but legislation later cut back on that authorization. See Minn. Stat. ch. 244. Why would a legislature decrease good-time credits inmates can earn? What advantages are there in an increase of good-time credits? Consider these questions from the perspective of a warden, a state legislator, and a member of a crime-ridden community.

6. *Elimination of parole and other changes in parole rules.*   More than a dozen states have abolished early release by a parole board for all offenders, and several others have significantly restricted parole either through formal legal limits on eligibility or through the evolving decision making by parole boards. Even in states that have retained parole, parole boards have become more hesitant to grant it. In Texas, for example, 57% of all cases considered for parole release in 1988 were approved; by 1998 that figure had dropped to 20%. See Joan Petersilia, Parole and Prisoner Reentry in the United States, 26 Crime & Just. 479 (1999).

Defendants sometimes claim that formal changes in the rules governing parole eligibility can transgress the U.S. Constitution's ex post facto clause. In Johnson v. Commissioner of Corrections, 786 A.2d 1091 (Conn. 2002), the Connecticut Supreme Court cited such constitutional concerns when interpreting a state change in release rules (the new rules made violent offenders eligible for parole release only after serving 85% rather than 50% of their sentences) to apply only prospectively. In a similar vein, but reaching a different sort of result, the Supreme Court in Garner v. Jones, 529 U.S. 244 (2000), examined whether the retroactive application of a Georgia law permitting the extension of intervals between parole considerations violated the ex post facto clause. Defining the inquiry in terms of whether Georgia's change in parole rules created "a sufficient risk of increasing the measure of punishment attached to the covered crimes," the Court sent the case back to the court of appeals to determine whether the change in Georgia's parole board rules did create a significant risk of increased punishment for inmate Jones.

7. *Supervised release under the federal sentencing guidelines.*   As part of the Sentencing Reform Act of 1984, federal law formally eliminated parole and recast post-incarceration supervision in terms of "supervised release." Federal judges must impose a term of supervised release if the offender is sentenced to at least one year in prison. The length of supervised release depends on the seriousness of the felony committed, ranging from a minimum of one year for minor felonies and the most serious misdemeanors to five years for the most serious felonies. Select offenses allow for the imposition of a life term of supervised release.

In addition, the district court may impose a specific condition of supervision so long as the condition meets four criteria: (1) it must be reasonably related to specified sentencing factors, namely the nature and circumstances of the offense and the history and characteristics of the defendant; (2) it must be reasonably related to the need to afford adequate deterrence, to protect the public from further crimes of the defendant, and to provide the defendant with necessary educational or vocational training, medical care, or other correctional treatment in the most effective manner; (3) it must involve no greater deprivation of liberty than is reasonably necessary to achieve these goals; and (4) it must be consistent with any pertinent policy statements issued by the U.S. Sentencing Commission. See 18 U.S.C. §§3583(d), 3563(d), 3553.

To what extent do parole and supervised release differ? How are they similar? Suppose a person who runs a credit repair business is convicted of conspiracy to distribute methamphetamine and has a prior conviction for passing counterfeit notes. In light of the provisions for supervised release, would it be appropriate for a court to impose on the defendant an occupational restriction demanding that he inform his clients of the conviction? See United States v. Britt, 332 F.3d 1229 (9th Cir. 2003).

8. *International tribunals.*   Under the Statute of the International Criminal Court, the court reviews a sentence after the offender has served two-thirds of the sentence imposed. At that point the sentence may be reduced and the individual may qualify for early release. The statute contemplates that early release is to be granted only to individuals who have cooperated with prosecutors, have made attempts at reparation, and appear capable of benefiting from early release. The gravity of the offense also matters. How parole is to work in practice, however, remains unresolved. It is unclear, for example, to what country the offender should be released on parole — the country of imprisonment, the home state, or possibly a third country close to the home state.

b.   Parole Conditions

Like sentencing courts, which establish conditions of probation (see Chapter 8), parole boards often establish conditions of parole. Some parole conditions are mandated by statute, but others are imposed as individualized requirements. As you review the following materials, consider what sorts of parole conditions should be mandated in all cases, and which should be applied on a case-by-case basis or never applied at all.

‖ *Alaska Statutes §33.16.150* ‖

(a) As a condition of parole, a prisoner released on special medical, discretionary, or mandatory parole

(1) shall obey all state, federal, or local laws or ordinances, and any court orders applicable to the parolee;

(2) shall make diligent efforts to maintain steady employment or meet family obligations;

(3) shall, if involved in education, counseling, training, or treatment, continue in the program unless granted permission from the parole officer assigned to the parolee to discontinue the program;

(4) shall report (A) upon release to the parole officer assigned to the parolee; (B) at other times, and in the manner, prescribed by the board or the parole officer assigned to the parolee;

(5) shall reside at a stated place and not change that residence without notifying, and receiving permission from, the parole officer assigned to the parolee;

(6) shall remain within stated geographic limits unless written permission to depart from the stated limits is granted the parolee;

(7) may not use, possess, handle, purchase, give, distribute, or administer a controlled substance . . . or a drug for which a prescription is required under state or federal law without a prescription from a licensed medical professional to the parolee;

(8) may not possess or control a firearm . . . ;

(9) may not enter into an agreement or other arrangement with a law enforcement agency or officer that will place the parolee in the position of violating a law or parole condition without the prior approval of the board;

(10) may not contact or correspond with anyone confined in a correctional facility of any type serving any term of imprisonment or a felon without the permission of the parole officer assigned to a parolee;

(11) shall agree to waive extradition from any state or territory of the United States and to not contest efforts to return the parolee to the state;

(12) shall provide a blood sample, an oral sample, or both, when requested by a health care professional acting on behalf of the state to provide the sample or samples, or an oral sample when requested by a juvenile or adult correctional, probation, or parole officer, or a peace officer, if the prisoner is being released after a conviction of an offense requiring the state to collect the sample or samples for the deoxyribonucleic acid identification system under AS 44.41.035.

(13) from a conviction for a sex offense shall submit to regular periodic polygraph examinations. . . .

(b) The board may require as a condition of special medical, discretionary, or mandatory parole, or a member of the board acting for the board under (e) of this section may require as a condition of mandatory parole, that a prisoner released on parole

(1) not possess or control a defensive weapon, a deadly weapon other than an ordinary pocket knife with a blade three inches or less in length, or ammunition for a firearm, or reside in a residence where there is a firearm capable of being concealed on one's person or a prohibited weapon . . . ;

(2) refrain from possessing or consuming alcoholic beverages;

(3) submit to reasonable searches and seizures by a parole officer, or a peace officer acting under the direction of a parole officer;

(4) submit to appropriate medical, mental health, or controlled substance or alcohol examination, treatment, or counseling;

(5) submit to periodic examinations designed to detect the use of alcohol or controlled substances;

(6) make restitution ordered by the court according to a schedule established by the board;

(7) refrain from opening, maintaining, or using a checking account or charge account;

(8) refrain from entering into a contract other than a prenuptial contract or a marriage contract;

(9) refrain from operating a motor vehicle;

(10) refrain from entering an establishment where alcoholic beverages are served, sold, or otherwise dispensed;

(11) refrain from participating in any other activity or conduct reasonably related to the parolee's offense, prior record, behavior or prior behavior, current circumstances, or perceived risk to the community, or from associating with any other person that the board determines is reasonably likely to diminish the rehabilitative goals of parole, or that may endanger the public; in the case of special medical parole, for a prisoner diagnosed with a communicable disease, comply with conditions set by the board designed to prevent the transmission of the disease. . . .

(f) In addition to other conditions of parole imposed under this section, the board may impose as a condition of special medical, discretionary, or mandatory parole for a prisoner serving a term for a crime involving domestic violence (1) any of the terms of protective orders . . . ; (2) a requirement that, at the prisoner's expense, the prisoner participate in and complete, to the satisfaction of the board, a program for the rehabilitation of perpetrators of domestic violence that meets the standards set by, and that is approved by, the department . . . ; and (3) any other condition necessary to rehabilitate the prisoner. . . .

‖ *Colorado Revised Statutes §16-11.7-105(2)* ‖

Each sex offender placed on parole by the state board of parole . . . shall be required, as a condition of such parole, to undergo treatment to the extent appropriate to such offender. . . . Any such treatment shall be at a facility or with a person certified or approved by the board and at such offender's expense, based upon such offender's ability to pay for such treatment.

PROBLEM 11-6. BANISHMENT

John Beavers was paroled from prison after serving 7 years of a 30-year sentence. As one of the special conditions of his parole, he was barred from Houston County, Alabama, where he and his family had lived prior to his incarceration. When he returned to Houston County without permission to see his two young daughters, he was arrested, and his parole was revoked. On appeal, what arguments should Beavers's counsel make to attack the revocation? Is the underlying parole condition constitutional? What purpose does the condition serve? See Beavers v. State, 666 So. 2d 868 (Ala. Crim. App. 1995).

PROBLEM 11-7. COMPUTER CONDITION

Gregory Sofsky received on his home computer via the Internet more than 1,000 images of child pornography in the form of both still and moving pictures.

He did not produce any of the images but transferred some of them to CD-ROM disks. In addition, he used the Internet to exchange images of child pornography with other (apparently like-minded) individuals. He is prosecuted for receiving child pornography, a federal offense.

The presentence report recommended that the judge impose a three-year period of supervised release. In addition to the standard conditions of supervised release, the report suggested that the court impose three special conditions: (1) the defendant must participate in mental health treatment, including a program for sexual disorders; (2) the defendant must permit a search of his premises at any time on reasonable suspicion that contraband or evidence of a violation of a condition of supervision may be found; and (3) the defendant must not view, purchase, or possess child pornography. The court followed the report's recommendations and added a fourth condition: the defendant must not "access a computer, the Internet, or bulletin board systems at any time, unless approved by the probation officer."

On appeal Sofsky challenges the conditions of his supervised release. What standard of review should the appellate court apply? How should it assess the validity of the four conditions? For different answers, see United States v. Sofsky, 287 F.3d 122 (2d Cir. 2002); United States v. Paul, 274 F.3d 155 (5th Cir. 2002); United States v. White, 244 F.3d 1199 (10th Cir. 2001); United States v. Crandon, 173 F.3d 122 (3d Cir. 1999).

NOTES

1. *Parole conditions.* Paroled inmates are released before their maximum sentence has expired, but usually they must report regularly to a parole officer and comply with a host of conditions, such as finding a job, abstaining from alcohol and illegal drugs, and not associating with convicted felons. In what settings do such apparently benign conditions become more onerous? Consider the predicament of a parolee who, having returned from prison to live with his parents, is visited one afternoon by his elder brother, a convicted felon.

At year-end 2005, about 70% of all parolees were under active parole supervision, which meant they were required to maintain regular contact with their parole officers. About 10% of parolees could not be located. Lauren E. Glaze & Thomas E. Bonczar, Probation and Parole in the United States, 2005 at 6 (NCJ 215091, November 2006).

2. *Evolving nature of parole supervision and services.* The rise of determinate sentences and the corresponding reduced reliance on parole mechanisms have significantly changed the nature of postrelease supervision. Professor Joan Petersilia has observed an evolution in parole supervision toward controlling the offender at the expense of providing social services necessary for reentry into society:

> Historically, parole agents were viewed as paternalistic figures who mixed authority with help. Officers provided direct services (e.g., counseling) and also knew the community and brokered services (e.g., job training) to needy offenders. Parole was originally designed to make the transition from prison to the community more gradual, and, during this time, parole officers were to assist the offender in addressing personal problems and searching for

employment and a place to live. Many parole agencies still do assist in these "service" activities. Increasingly, however, parole supervision has shifted away from providing services to parolees and more toward monitoring and surveillance (e.g., drug testing, monitoring curfews, and collecting restitution). . . .

There are a number of reasons for this. For one, a greater number of parole conditions are being assigned to released prisoners. In the federal system, for example, between 1987 and 1996 the proportion of offenders required to comply with at least one special supervision condition increased from 67 percent of entrants to 91 percent. . . .

It is also true that the fiscal crises experienced in most states in recent years reduced the number of treatment and job-training programs in the community at large, and given the fear and suspicion surrounding ex-convicts, these persons are usually placed at the end of the waiting lists. . . . If there is one common complaint among parole officers in the United States, it is the lack of available treatment and job programs for parolees. . . .

The main reason, however, that "services" are not delivered to most parolees is that parole supervision has been transformed ideologically from a social service to a law enforcement system.

Joan Petersilia, Parole and Prisoner Reentry in the United States, 26 Crime & Just. 479, 506-508 (1999).

c.   Parole Revocation

Should parolees be returned to prison for committing *any* infraction of the terms of parole? What procedures should be used to determine whether an offender has violated parole?

Consider the statistics described in the following study of prisoners. What accounts for the dramatic increase in reincarcerated parole violators? Should violation of a reporting condition, a geographic restriction, a work requirement, or a drug screen be cause for automatic parole revocation? If not, when is revocation called for?

> ### *Trends in Parole Supervision, 1990-2000,* *Timothy A. Hughes, Doris James Wilson,* *and Allen J. Beck*
> ### Bureau of Justice Statistics (Sept. 2001)

RE-RELEASES AN INCREASING PORTION OF STATE PAROLE ENTRIES

Among parole entries, the percentage who had been re-released rose between 1990 and 1999. Re-releases are persons leaving prison after having served time either for a violation of parole or other conditional release or for a new offense committed while under parole supervision. In 1990, 27% of entries to parole were re-releases; in 1999, 45% were re-releases. . . .

After having been returned to prison for a parole or conditional release violation, re-releases served on average 13 months in prison in 1999. From 1990 to 1999 their average time served in prison following re-admission increased by 2 months. In both years about 7 in 10 re-releases had served less than 12 months in prison. . . .

Parole Success Rates Unchanged Since 1990

Of the 410,613 discharges from State parole in 1999, 42% successfully completed their term of supervision, 43% were returned to prison or jail, and 10% absconded. In 1990, 45% of State parole discharges were successful. Between 1990 and 1999 the percent successful among State parole discharges has ranged from 42% to 49%, without any distinct trend.

States differed in their rate of success among parole discharges. States with the highest rates of success in 1999 were Massachusetts and Mississippi (at 83% each), followed by North Carolina (80%) and North Dakota (79%). Utah (18%) and California (21%) had the lowest rates of success in 1999.

When comparing State success rates for parole discharges, differences may be due to variations in parole populations, such as age at prison release, criminal history, and most serious offense. Success rates may also differ based on the intensity of supervision and the parole agency policies related to revocation of technical violators.

Success Rates Highest Among First Releases and Discretionary Parole Releases

In every year during the 1990's, first releases to State parole were more likely to have been successful than re-releases. Among State parole discharges in 1990, 56% of first releases successfully completed their supervision, compared to 15% of re-releases. Of all those exiting parole in 1999, 63% of first releases were successful, compared to 21% of re-releases.

Success rates also varied by method of release. In every year between 1990 and 1999, State prisoners released by a parole board had higher success rates than those released through mandatory parole. Among parole discharges in 1999, 54% of discretionary parolees were successful compared to 33% of those who had received mandatory parole. . . .

Among Parole Discharges, Success Rates Rose for Blacks and Hispanics; Dropped for Whites

Between 1990 and 1999 the success rates among State parole discharges increased from 33% to 39% among blacks and increased from 31% to 51% among Hispanics, but dropped from 44% to 41% among whites. The 11 percentage-point difference in success rates between white and black parole discharges in 1990 narrowed to less than 2 percentage points in 1999. . . .

For female parole discharges, the rate of success rose over 10 percentage points (from 37% in 1990 to 48% in 1999). The success rate among male parole discharges increased from 36% to 39%.

Older parole discharges had the highest rates of success in both years. Accounting for 2.1% of discharges in 1999, parolees age 55 or older had the highest rate of successful completion (55%). Among parole discharges in other age groups, success rates fluctuated between 36% and 43%. . . .

NUMBER OF PAROLE VIOLATORS RETURNED TO PRISON
CONTINUED TO RISE DURING THE 1990's

In 1999, 197,606 parole violators were returned to State prison, up from 27,177 in 1980 and 131,502 in 1990. As a percentage of all admissions to State prison, parole violators more than doubled from 17% in 1980 to 35% in 1999. Between 1990 and 1999 the number of parole violators rose 50%, while the number of new court commitments rose 7%. . . .

In 1999 parole violators accounted for more than 50% of State prison admission in California (67%), Utah (55%), Montana (53%), and Louisiana (53%). In five States — Florida (7%), Alabama (9%), Indiana (10%), Mississippi (10%) and West Virginia (10%) — parole violators comprised 10% or less of all admissions. . . .

Based on personal interviews of State inmates, an estimated 24% of prisoners in 1997 said they were on parole at the time of the offense for which they were serving time in prison (up from 22% in 1991). . . .

70% OF PAROLE VIOLATORS IN PRISON IN 1997 RETURNED
FOR A NEW OFFENSE

Among parole violators in State prison in 1997, 215,964 (85%) reported that their parole had been revoked or taken away for violating the conditions of their release. Of that number, 70% said that their parole had been revoked because of an arrest or conviction for a new offense; 22% said they had absconded or otherwise failed to report to a parole officer; 16% said they had a drug-related violation; and 18% reported other reasons such as possession of a gun, maintaining contact with known felons, or failure to maintain employment.

HALF OF PAROLE VIOLATORS INCARCERATED IN 3 STATES

The three largest State prison systems (California, Texas, and New York) held over half of all parole violators in prison in 1997. California held 22% of all parole violators in prison, Texas, 21%, and New York, 8%. Within each of these States, the percentage of prisoners who were parole violators was higher than the national level: 39% in Texas, 38% in California, and 28% in New York, compared to 24% nationally.

Among parole violators returned to prison, those held in California (60%) were the least likely to have been arrested or convicted for a new offense and the most likely to have been returned for a drug violation (23%). About 11% of parole violators in New York and Texas reported a drug violation as a reason for their return to prison. . . .

New York had the highest percentage of parole violators in prison who were black (54%), followed by Texas (50%) and California (33%). In New York, 11% of parole violators were white; in Texas, 23%; in California, 31%. The percent Hispanic among parole violators ranged from 26% to 33% in the three States.

New York had the highest percentage of parole violators convicted of a violent offense (41%), compared to 33% in Texas and 24% in California. New York also had the highest percentage of parole violators returned for a drug offense (34%), compared to 27% in California and 21% in Texas. . . .

NOTES

1. *The purposes of parole.*   Traditionally, parole was supposed to help an offender reenter society successfully. Parole officers often had a background in social work. In recent years, the function of parole and the background of parole officers have changed dramatically. Parole is increasingly viewed as a way to control offenders once they are back in the community. Parole officers more often have a criminal justice background and see themselves as enforcers of rules rather than as assistants in the reintegration project. Parole violators thus tend to be returned to prison. In some jurisdictions, however, parole may be revoked but then immediately reinstated, often with new conditions added or following a warning that continued infractions will result in imprisonment. Do such differences in the enforcement culture account for the nationally disparate numbers of parole violators who return to prison?

2. *Types of violations.*   Data on parole violations tends to distinguish technical violations from new offenses. Technical violations may include failing to meet with the parole officer, testing positive for drugs, or leaving the jurisdiction without informing the parole officer. Why should technical violations lead to reincarceration? What other sanctions are available? A recent study of juvenile parolees indicated that young parolees who test positive for drugs during their first three months on parole are more likely to commit offenses while on parole than are other parolees. How can such findings be used to prevent later parole violations?

3. *Revocation procedures.*   The rights of parolees at revocation proceedings are limited since such proceedings are not part of a criminal prosecution and the liberty of parolees is considered only conditional. In Pennsylvania Board of Probation and Parole v. Scott, 524 U.S. 357 (1998), for example, the Supreme Court held that the exclusionary rule does not apply to parole revocation hearings. In Morrissey v. Brewer, 408 U.S. 470 (1972), however, the Supreme Court set out the necessary due process protections in parole revocation hearings, including written notice of the claimed violations of parole, disclosure to the parolee of the evidence against him, opportunity to be heard in person and to present witnesses and documentary evidence, the right in general to confront and cross-examine adverse witnesses, the right to be heard by a "neutral and detached" body whose members need not be judicial officers, and a written statement by the factfinders as to the evidence relied on and reasons for revoking parole. In some states the proceeding is heard by the parole board, in others by an administrative law judge. Many states allow for appeals from an adverse decision.

4. *Reentry courts.*   Because of the large number of parole violators who return to prison and the concomitant expense, criminal justice professionals and politicians have renewed their focus on the reentry of prisoners into the community. Some federally funded projects have established reentry courts that follow the model of drug courts (discussed in Chapter 8). A judge regularly sees

a parolee and monitors her progress. Successive violations carry sanctions of increasing magnitude, and successful program participation carries small rewards. The goal is to allow for occasional violations of parole rules but to prevent future crime while assisting the offender in her reintegration.

2.   Civil Commitment

Parole provides a certain check on released offenders, largely by requiring that they report regularly to their parole officers, but it does not prevent all crime. Offenders who are considered very dangerous may be released from prison at their mandatory release date. What should society do in that situation? One possibility is an enhanced level of parole in which released offenders are monitored through electronic bracelets or are subject to unannounced visits by parole officers.

   In the highly charged cases of sexual offenders, however, state legislators may not be willing to risk another offense. Therefore, a number of states have adopted special civil commitment statutes for sexual offenders. In most such cases, civil commitment appears to equate to life imprisonment. Is civil commitment for sex offenders constitutional? What types of safeguards have to be in place?

|| *Kansas v. Leroy Hendricks* ||
521 U.S. 346 (1997)

THOMAS, J.

   In 1994, Kansas enacted the Sexually Violent Predator Act, which establishes procedures for the civil commitment of persons who, due to a "mental abnormality" or a "personality disorder," are likely to engage in "predatory acts of sexual violence." Kan. Stat. Ann. §59-29a01 et seq. The State invoked the Act for the first time to commit Leroy Hendricks, an inmate who had a long history of sexually molesting children, and who was scheduled for release from prison shortly after the Act became law. Hendricks challenged his commitment on, inter alia, "substantive" due process, double jeopardy, and ex post facto grounds. . . .

I.   BACKGROUND

A.   Sexually Violent Predator Act

   The Kansas Legislature enacted the Sexually Violent Predator Act (Act) in 1994 to grapple with the problem of managing repeat sexual offenders. [The] legislature determined that existing civil commitment procedures were inadequate to confront the risks presented by "sexually violent predators." In the Act's preamble, the legislature explained:

   [Sexually] violent predators' likelihood of engaging in repeat acts of predatory sexual violence is high. The existing involuntary commitment procedure . . . is inadequate to address the risk these sexually violent predators pose to society. The legislature further finds that the prognosis for rehabilitating sexually violent predators in a prison setting is poor, the treatment needs of this population are very long term and the treatment modalities for this population are very different than the traditional treatment modalities for people appropriate for commitment under the [general involuntary civil commitment statute].

Kan. Stat. Ann. §59-29a01.

As a result, the Legislature found it necessary to establish "a civil commitment procedure for the long-term care and treatment of the sexually violent predator." The Act defined a "sexually violent predator" as: "any person who has been convicted of or charged with a sexually violent offense and who suffers from a mental abnormality or personality disorder which makes the person likely to engage in the predatory acts of sexual violence." §59-29a02(a). A "mental abnormality" was defined, in turn, as a "congenital or acquired condition affecting the emotional or volitional capacity which predisposes the person to commit sexually violent offenses in a degree constituting such person a menace to the health and safety of others."

As originally structured, the Act's civil commitment procedures pertained to: (1) a presently confined person who, like Hendricks, "has been convicted of a sexually violent offense" and is scheduled for release; (2) a person who has been "charged with a sexually violent offense" but has been found incompetent to stand trial; (3) a person who has been found "not guilty by reason of insanity of a sexually violent offense"; and (4) a person found "not guilty" of a sexually violent offense because of a mental disease or defect.

The initial version of the Act, as applied to a currently confined person such as Hendricks, was designed to initiate a specific series of procedures. The custodial agency was required to notify the local prosecutor 60 days before the anticipated release of a person who might have met the Act's criteria. The prosecutor was then obligated, within 45 days, to decide whether to file a petition in state court seeking the person's involuntary commitment. If such a petition were filed, the court was to determine whether "probable cause" existed to support a finding that the person was a "sexually violent predator" and thus eligible for civil commitment. Upon such a determination, transfer of the individual to a secure facility for professional evaluation would occur. After that evaluation, a trial would be held to determine beyond a reasonable doubt whether the individual was a sexually violent predator. If that determination were made, the person would then be transferred to the custody of the Secretary of Social and Rehabilitation Services (Secretary) for "control, care and treatment until such time as the person's mental abnormality or personality disorder has so changed that the person is safe to be at large."

In addition to placing the burden of proof upon the State, the Act afforded the individual a number of other procedural safeguards. In the case of an indigent person, the State was required to provide, at public expense, the assistance of counsel and an examination by mental health care professionals. The individual also received the right to present and cross-examine witnesses, and the opportunity to review documentary evidence presented by the State.

Once an individual was confined, the Act required that "the involuntary detention or commitment . . . shall conform to constitutional requirements for care and treatment." Confined persons were afforded three different avenues of review: First, the committing court was obligated to conduct an annual review to determine whether continued detention was warranted. Second, the Secretary was permitted, at any time, to decide that the confined individual's condition had so changed that release was appropriate, and could then authorize the person to petition for release. Finally, even without the Secretary's permission, the confined person could at any time file a release petition. If the court found that the State could no longer satisfy its burden under the initial commitment standard, the individual would be freed from confinement.

B.   Leroy Hendricks

In 1984, Hendricks was convicted of taking "indecent liberties" with two 13-year-old boys. After serving nearly 10 years of his sentence, he was slated for release to a halfway house. Shortly before his scheduled release, however, the State filed a petition in state court seeking Hendricks' civil confinement as a sexually violent predator. . . .

Hendricks . . . requested a jury trial to determine whether he qualified as a sexually violent predator. During that trial, Hendricks' own testimony revealed a chilling history of repeated child sexual molestation and abuse, beginning in 1955. . . . He testified that despite having received professional help for his pedophilia, he continued to harbor sexual desires for children. . . .

Hendricks admitted that he had repeatedly abused children whenever he was not confined. He explained that when he "gets stressed out," he "can't control the urge" to molest children. Although Hendricks recognized that his behavior harms children, and he hoped he would not sexually molest children again, he stated that the only sure way he could keep from sexually abusing children in the future was "to die." Hendricks readily agreed with the state physician's diagnosis that he suffers from pedophilia and that he is not cured of the condition; indeed, he told the physician that "treatment is bull—." The jury unanimously found beyond a reasonable doubt that Hendricks was a sexually violent predator. The trial court subsequently determined, as a matter of state law, that pedophilia qualifies as a "mental abnormality" as defined by the Act, and thus ordered Hendricks committed to the Secretary's custody. . . .

II.   DISCUSSION

A.   Prerequisites of Civil Confinement: Dangerousness and Mental Abnormality

Kansas argues that the Act's definition of "mental abnormality" satisfies "substantive" due process requirements. We agree. Although freedom from physical restraint "has always been at the core of the liberty protected by the Due Process Clause from arbitrary governmental action," Foucha v. Louisiana, 504 U.S. 71, 80 (1992), that liberty interest is not absolute. The Court has recognized that an individual's constitutionally protected interest in avoiding physical restraint may be overridden even in the civil context.

Accordingly, States have in certain narrow circumstances provided for the forcible civil detainment of people who are unable to control their behavior and who thereby pose a danger to the public health and safety. We have consistently upheld such involuntary commitment statutes provided the confinement takes place pursuant to proper procedures and evidentiary standards. It thus cannot be said that the involuntary civil confinement of a limited subclass of dangerous persons is contrary to our understanding of ordered liberty.

The challenged Act unambiguously requires a finding of dangerousness either to one's self or to others as a prerequisite to involuntary confinement. Commitment proceedings can be initiated only when a person "has been convicted of or charged with a sexually violent offense," and "suffers from a mental abnormality or personality disorder which makes the person likely to engage in the predatory acts of sexual violence." The statute thus requires proof of more than a mere predisposition to violence; rather, it requires evidence of past sexually violent behavior and a present mental condition that creates a likelihood of such conduct in the future if the person is not incapacitated. As we have recognized, "previous instances of violent behavior are an important indicator of future violent tendencies." Heller v. Doe, 509 U.S. 312, 323 (1993). A finding of dangerousness, standing alone, is ordinarily not a sufficient ground upon which to justify indefinite involuntary commitment. We have sustained civil commitment statutes when they have coupled proof of dangerousness with the proof of some additional factor, such as a "mental illness" or "mental abnormality." These added statutory requirements serve to limit involuntary civil confinement to those who suffer from a volitional impairment rendering them dangerous beyond their control. The Kansas Act is plainly of a kind with these other civil commitment statutes: It requires a finding of future dangerousness, and then links that finding to the existence of a "mental abnormality" or "personality disorder" that makes it difficult, if not impossible, for the person to control his dangerous behavior. . . .

The mental health professionals who evaluated Hendricks diagnosed him as suffering from pedophilia, a condition the psychiatric profession itself classifies as a serious mental disorder. Hendricks even conceded that, when he becomes "stressed out," he cannot "control the urge" to molest children. This admitted lack of volitional control, coupled with a prediction of future dangerousness, adequately distinguishes Hendricks from other dangerous persons who are perhaps more properly dealt with exclusively through criminal proceedings. Hendricks' diagnosis as a pedophile, which qualifies as a "mental abnormality" under the Act, thus plainly suffices for due process purposes.

B.   Civil v. Criminal Proceedings

[Hendricks argues] that the Act establishes criminal proceedings; hence confinement under it necessarily constitutes punishment. He contends that where, as here, newly enacted "punishment" is predicated upon past conduct for which he has already been convicted and forced to serve a prison sentence, the Constitution's Double Jeopardy and Ex Post Facto Clauses are violated. We are unpersuaded by Hendricks' argument that Kansas has established criminal proceedings.

The categorization of a particular proceeding as civil or criminal is first of all a question of statutory construction. We must initially ascertain whether the legislature meant the statute to establish "civil" proceedings. If so, we ordinarily defer to the legislature's stated intent. Here, Kansas' objective to create a civil proceeding is evidenced by its placement of the Sexually Violent Predator Act within the Kansas probate code, instead of the criminal code, as well as its description of the Act as creating a "civil commitment procedure." Nothing on the face of the statute suggests that the legislature sought to create anything other than a civil commitment scheme designed to protect the public from harm.

Although we recognize that a civil label is not always dispositive, we will reject the legislature's manifest intent only where a party challenging the statute provides the clearest proof that the statutory scheme [is] so punitive either in purpose or effect as to negate [the State's] intention to deem it civil. . . .

As a threshold matter, commitment under the Act does not implicate either of the two primary objectives of criminal punishment: retribution or deterrence. The Act's purpose is not retributive because it does not affix culpability for prior criminal conduct. Instead, such conduct is used solely for evidentiary purposes, either to demonstrate that a "mental abnormality" exists or to support a finding of future dangerousness. . . . In addition, the Kansas Act does not make a criminal conviction a prerequisite for commitment—persons absolved of criminal responsibility may nonetheless be subject to confinement under the Act. An absence of the necessary criminal responsibility suggests that the State is not seeking retribution for a past misdeed. Thus, the fact that the Act may be tied to criminal activity is insufficient to render the statute punitive.

Moreover, unlike a criminal statute, no finding of scienter is required to commit an individual who is found to be a sexually violent predator; instead, the commitment determination is made based on a "mental abnormality" or "personality disorder" rather than on one's criminal intent. The existence of a scienter requirement is customarily an important element in distinguishing criminal from civil statutes. The absence of such a requirement here is evidence that confinement under the statute is not intended to be retributive.

Nor can it be said that the legislature intended the Act to function as a deterrent. Those persons committed under the Act are, by definition, suffering from a "mental abnormality" or a "personality disorder" that prevents them from exercising adequate control over their behavior. Such persons are therefore unlikely to be deterred by the threat of confinement. . . . The State has represented that an individual confined under the Act is not subject to the more restrictive conditions placed on state prisoners, but instead experiences essentially the same conditions as any involuntarily committed patient in the state mental institution. Because none of the parties argues that people institutionalized under the Kansas general civil commitment statute are subject to punitive conditions, even though they may be involuntarily confined, it is difficult to conclude that persons confined under this Act are being "punished."

Although the civil commitment scheme at issue here does involve an affirmative restraint, "the mere fact that a person is detained does not inexorably lead to the conclusion that the government has imposed punishment." United States v. Salerno, 481 U.S. 739, 746 (1987). The State may take measures to restrict the freedom of the dangerously mentally ill. This is a legitimate nonpunitive governmental objective and has been historically so regarded. . . .

Hendricks focuses on his confinement's potentially indefinite duration as evidence of the State's punitive intent. That focus, however, is misplaced. Far from any punitive objective, the confinement's duration is instead linked to the stated purposes of the commitment, namely, to hold the person until his mental abnormality no longer causes him to be a threat to others. If, at any time, the confined person is adjudged "safe to be at large," he is statutorily entitled to immediate release.

Furthermore, commitment under the Act is only *potentially* indefinite. The maximum amount of time an individual can be incapacitated pursuant to a single judicial proceeding is one year. If Kansas seeks to continue the detention beyond that year, a court must once again determine beyond a reasonable doubt that the detainee satisfies the same standards as required for the initial confinement. This requirement again demonstrates that Kansas does not intend an individual committed pursuant to the Act to remain confined any longer than he suffers from a mental abnormality rendering him unable to control his dangerousness. . . .

Finally, Hendricks argues that the Act is necessarily punitive because it fails to offer any legitimate "treatment." Without such treatment, Hendricks asserts, confinement under the Act amounts to little more than disguised punishment. Hendricks' argument assumes that treatment for his condition is available, but that the State has failed (or refused) to provide it.

[Under] the appropriate circumstances and when accompanied by proper procedures, incapacitation may be a legitimate end of the civil law. . . . While we have upheld state civil commitment statutes that aim both to incapacitate and to treat, we have never held that the Constitution prevents a State from civilly detaining those for whom no treatment is available, but who nevertheless pose a danger to others. A State could hardly be seen as furthering a "punitive" purpose by involuntarily confining persons afflicted with an untreatable, highly contagious disease. Similarly, it would be of little value to require treatment as a precondition for civil confinement of the dangerously insane when no acceptable treatment existed. To conclude otherwise would obligate a State to release certain confined individuals who were both mentally ill and dangerous simply because they could not be successfully treated for their afflictions. . . .

Although the treatment program initially offered Hendricks may have seemed somewhat meager, it must be remembered that he was the first person committed under the Act. That the State did not have all of its treatment procedures in place is thus not surprising. What is significant, however, is that Hendricks was placed under the supervision of the Kansas Department of Health and Social and Rehabilitative Services, housed in a unit segregated from the general prison population and operated not by employees of the Department of Corrections, but by other trained individuals. And, before this Court, Kansas declared "absolutely" that persons committed under the Act are now receiving in the neighborhood of 31.5 hours of treatment per week.

Where the State has "disavowed any punitive intent"; limited confinement to a small segment of particularly dangerous individuals; provided strict procedural safeguards; directed that confined persons be segregated from the general prison population and afforded the same status as others who have been civilly committed; recommended treatment if such is possible; and permitted immediate release upon a showing that the individual is no longer dangerous or mentally impaired, we cannot say that it acted with punitive intent. We therefore hold that the Act does not establish criminal proceedings and that involuntary confinement pursuant to the Act is not punitive. Our conclusion that the Act is nonpunitive thus removes an essential prerequisite for both Hendricks' double jeopardy and ex post facto claims. . . .

Because we have determined that the Kansas Act is civil in nature, initiation of its commitment proceedings does not constitute a second prosecution. Moreover, as commitment under the Act is not tantamount to "punishment," Hendricks' involuntary detention does not violate the Double Jeopardy Clause, even though that confinement may follow a prison term. . . . The Ex Post Facto Clause, which forbids the application of any new punitive measure to a crime already consummated, has been interpreted to pertain exclusively to penal statutes. . . . Because the Act does not criminalize conduct legal before its enactment, nor deprive Hendricks of any defense that was available to him at the time of his crimes, the Act does not violate the Ex Post Facto Clause. . . .

KENNEDY, J., concurring.

[I write] to caution against dangers inherent when a civil confinement law is used in conjunction with the criminal process, whether or not the law is given retroactive application. [The] power of the state to confine persons who, by reason of a mental disease or mental abnormality, constitute a real, continuing, and serious danger to society is well established. . . . The Kansas law, with its attendant protections, including yearly review and review at any time at the instance of the person confined, is within this pattern and tradition of civil confinement.

Notwithstanding its civil attributes, the practical effect of the Kansas law may be to impose confinement for life. At this stage of medical knowledge, although future treatments cannot be predicted, psychiatrists or other professionals engaged in treating pedophilia may be reluctant to find measurable success in treatment even after a long period and may be unable to predict that no serious danger will come from release of the detainee.

A common response to this may be, "A life term is exactly what the sentence should have been anyway," or, in the words of a Kansas task force member, "So be it." The point, however, is not how long Hendricks and others like him should serve a criminal sentence. With his criminal record, after all, a life term may well have been the only sentence appropriate to protect society and vindicate the wrong. The concern instead is whether it is the criminal system or the civil system which should make the decision in the first place. . . . We should bear in mind that while incapacitation is a goal common to both the criminal and civil systems of confinement, retribution and general deterrence are reserved for the criminal system alone.

On the record before us, the Kansas civil statute conforms to our precedents. If, however, civil confinement were to become a mechanism for retribution or general deterrence, or if it were shown that mental abnormality is too imprecise a category to offer a solid basis for concluding that civil detention is justified, our precedents would not suffice to validate it.

BREYER, J., dissenting.

I agree with the majority that the Kansas Act's definition of mental abnormality satisfies the "substantive" requirements of the Due Process Clause.

Kansas, however, concedes that Hendricks' condition is treatable; yet the Act did not provide Hendricks (or others like him) with any treatment until after his release date from prison and only inadequate treatment thereafter. These, and certain other, special features of the Act convince me that it was not simply an effort to commit Hendricks civilly, but rather an effort to inflict further punishment upon him. The Ex Post Facto Clause therefore prohibits the Act's application to Hendricks, who committed his crimes prior to its enactment.

[When] a State believes that treatment does exist, and then couples that admission with a legislatively required delay of such treatment until a person is at the end of his jail term (so that further incapacitation is therefore necessary), such a legislative scheme begins to look punitive. . . . I have found 17 States with laws that seek to protect the public from mentally abnormal, sexually dangerous individuals through civil commitment or other mandatory treatment programs. Ten of those statutes, unlike the Kansas statute, begin treatment of an offender soon after he has been apprehended and charged with a serious sex offense. Only seven, like Kansas, delay "civil" commitment (and treatment) until the offender has served his criminal sentence (and this figure includes the Acts of Minnesota and New Jersey, both of which generally do not delay treatment). Of these seven, however, six (unlike Kansas) require consideration of less restrictive alternatives. Only one State other than Kansas, namely Iowa, both delays civil commitment (and consequent treatment) and does not explicitly consider less restrictive alternatives. But the law of that State applies prospectively only, thereby avoiding ex post facto problems. Thus the practical experience of other States, as revealed by their statutes, confirms . . . that for Ex Post Facto Clause purposes, the purpose of the Kansas Act (as applied to previously convicted offenders) has a punitive, rather than a purely civil, purpose. . . .

To find that the confinement the Act imposes upon Hendricks is "punishment" is to find a violation of the Ex Post Facto Clause. . . . To find a violation of that Clause here, however, is not to hold that the Clause prevents Kansas, or other States, from enacting dangerous sexual offender statutes. A statute that operates prospectively, for example, does not offend the Ex Post Facto Clause. Neither does it offend the Ex Post Facto Clause for a State to sentence offenders to the fully authorized sentence, to seek consecutive, rather than concurrent, sentences, or to invoke recidivism statutes to lengthen imprisonment. Moreover, a statute that operates retroactively, like Kansas' statute, nonetheless does not offend the Clause *if the confinement that it imposes is not punishment*—if, that is to say, the legislature does not simply add a later criminal punishment to an earlier one.

The statutory provisions before us do amount to punishment primarily because, as I have said, the legislature did not tailor the statute to fit the nonpunitive civil aim of treatment, which it concedes exists in Hendricks' case. The Clause in these circumstances does not stand as an obstacle to achieving important protections for the public's safety; rather it provides an assurance that, where so significant a restriction of an individual's basic freedoms is at issue, a State cannot cut corners. Rather, the legislature must hew to the Constitution's liberty-protecting line. See The Federalist, No. 78, p. 466 (C. Rossiter ed. 1961) (A. Hamilton).

NOTES

1. *Civil commitment for sex offenders.* The Supreme Court's decision in *Hendricks* clearly labeled commitment for sex offenders a civil sanction that can follow a criminal conviction or be imposed instead of one. In Seling v. Young, 531 U.S. 250 (2001), the Court rejected the claim that Washington state's sex offender commitment statute could be found punitive as applied to a particular sex offender. It found the "as applied" determination unworkable and rejected the notion that an "as applied" challenge could lead to release on ex post facto or substantive due process grounds.

2. *Prerequisites for sex offender commitment.* In *Hendricks,* the Supreme Court held that the statutory requirement of a "mental abnormality or personality disorder" satisfied due process requirements. In Kansas v. Crane, 534 U.S. 407 (2002), the Court required the state to prove that a sex offender had *difficulty* controlling his sexual urges before he could be committed civilly. There is no constitutional requirement, however, that the individual be *unable* to control his urges before commitment. Why does the Court require the existence of a mental abnormality for civil commitment? Why does the continued dangerousness of the offender not suffice?

3. *Treatment during confinement.* While the *Hendricks* Court showed some concerns about the minimal treatment Hendricks had received, Justice Breyer appeared the most concerned about the absence of treatment during imprisonment, which in turn seemed to imply the state's lack of interest in curing Hendricks. Justice Kennedy, in his concurrence, noted that treatment, as it is currently available, may never be useful to offenders such as Hendricks, leaving them in preventive detention for the rest of their lives. For a discussion of substantive due process considerations during civil commitment, see Eric S. Janus & Wayne A. Logan, Substantive Due Process and the Involuntary Confinement of Sexually Violent Predators, 35 Conn. L. Rev. 319 (2003). Should society's inability to develop successful treatment options be sufficient reason for virtual life imprisonment of offenders after they have served their criminal justice sanctions?

4. *Alternatives to civil commitment.* Civil commitment statutes for sex offenders have generated much discussion in legal circles, but their practical impact has remained low as other risk control mechanisms have replaced or substituted for them. All states have enacted sex offender notification and registration laws (see Chapter 8), and many have lengthened criminal penalties for sex crimes. Are longer sentences for sex offenders generally desirable, based on a risk analysis? Consider that predictions of recurrent acts of sexual violence have gotten more accurate in the short term, but psychiatrists and psychologists are loath to make long-term predictions. See Eric S. Janus & Robert A. Prentky, Forensic Use of Actuarial Risk Assessment with Sex Offenders: Accuracy, Admissibility and Accountability 40 Am. Crim. L. Rev. 1443 (2003).

3. Sealed Records and Expungements

Many convicted individuals carry their criminal records with them until they die. In some states, however, administrative procedures are available to seal or expunge criminal records. Sealed records, which are common for juveniles, are inaccessible to anyone other than law enforcement agencies and courts, in case of a later conviction. Expungement of records is no longer available to every offender. Some states allow expungement of criminal records only for certain first offenses, others for offenses in which the sentence was suspended or the offender successfully completed probation. In a few jurisdictions courts expunge records; in others administrative agencies fulfill this function.

|| *Christopher John Dillingham v. INS* ||
267 F.3d 996 (9th Cir. 2001)

B. FLETCHER, J.
In this case, we consider whether an alien's right to equal protection is violated if, in the course of removal proceedings, the Immigration and Naturalization Service ("INS") refuses to recognize the effects of a British expungement[1] statute on a simple drug possession offense that would have qualified for federal first offender treatment had it occurred in the United States. . . .

I

Dillingham pled guilty in April 1984 to criminal charges in Great Britain for possessing marijuana and cocaine, paying a £50 fine. As a first-time offender convicted of a minor controlled substance offense, Dillingham's conviction was later expunged pursuant to Great Britain's Rehabilitation of Offenders Act of 1974. Under the terms of the Act, a conviction is treated as "spent" if an offender complies with his sentence and is not convicted of a subsequent offense within five years. In such cases, the statute requires that the offender be treated "for all purposes in law as a person who has not committed or been charged with or prosecuted for or convicted of or sentenced for the offense," except that any penalty resulting from the conviction that extends beyond the five-year period is unaffected, and evidence of the conviction may be introduced in a subsequent criminal proceeding.

In September 1991, seven years after his drug conviction (and two years after his rehabilitation), Dillingham married his U.S.-citizen wife. Although his conviction rendered him inadmissible to the United States under [the Immigration and Naturalization Act], he was permitted to enter the country in July

---

1. Throughout this opinion, we use the term "expungement" to refer generally to the effect of a rehabilitative statute on a prior conviction — regardless of whether, as a procedural matter, the statute allows for a deferral of the conviction itself, such that no judgment is ever entered (as under the [Federal First Offender Act]), or a judgment of conviction is entered but later removed from the books (as under various state rehabilitative statutes, as well as the British statute at issue in this case).

1992 on a six-month nonimmigrant visitor visa, pursuant to the waiver provisions of 8 U.S.C. §1182(d)(3)(A). After his authorized period of stay had expired, Dillingham applied for adjustment of status to legal permanent resident on May 13, 1993, pursuant to an immediate relative visa petition filed by his wife. The INS district director in Portland, Oregon, denied his application on September 14, 1993, on the grounds that the British Rehabilitation of Offenders Act was not a counterpart to the Federal First Offender Act ("FFOA"), and that his prior drug conviction therefore rendered him inadmissible. . . .

At his hearing before an Immigration Judge ("IJ") . . . Dillingham cited the [Board of Immigration Appeals' (BIA's) decision in In re Manrique, Interim Decision 3250 (BIA 1995)], in which the Board established a policy of treating aliens who had been convicted of simple possession and rehabilitated under any state's expungement statute equivalently to those who had been convicted and rehabilitated under the FFOA.[5]

On June 13, 1996, the IJ ruled that *Manrique* did not extend to foreign rehabilitation statutes and denied the application for adjustment of status. . . .

On appeal, the BIA (sitting en banc) . . . affirmed the IJ's decision. . . . Specifically, the Board analogized the expungement of Dillingham's prior drug offense to a foreign pardon and declined to recognize it for U.S. immigration purposes. . . .

IV . . .

A

As a general rule, the BIA does not recognize expungements of controlled substance offenses for federal immigration purposes. However, in 1970, Congress carved out a narrow exception for simple possession offenses when it enacted the Federal First Offender Act ("FFOA"). The FFOA, which applies exclusively to first-time drug offenders who are guilty only of simple possession, serves to expunge such convictions (after the successful completion of a probationary period) and was intended to lessen the harsh consequences of certain drug convictions, including their effects on deportation proceedings. Under the FFOA, no legal consequences may be imposed following expungement as a result of the defendant's former conviction. 18 U.S.C. §3607.

In Garberding v. INS, 30 F.3d 1187 (9th Cir. 1994), we rejected on equal protection grounds the BIA's policy that only expungements under exact state counterparts to the FFOA could be recognized in deportation proceedings. We held that this policy was inconsistent with the Constitution's equal protection

---

5. The BIA's decision in *Manrique* followed our holding in Garberding v. INS, 30 F.3d 1187 (9th Cir. 1994), and constituted a reversal of its former policy of not recognizing, for immigration purposes, the effects of state rehabilitation laws that were not the exact counterparts of the FFOA. Under *Manrique,* the BIA created a four-part test for determining when an expungement pursuant to a state rehabilitative statute should be recognized: (1) the alien is a first offender; (2) the alien has pled to or been found guilty of a simple possession offense; (3) the alien has not been accorded first offender treatment under any law; (4) the court has entered an order pursuant to a state rehabilitative statute either deferring or dismissing the criminal proceedings.

guarantee, because there was no rational basis for treating two persons found guilty of the identical conduct differently based on the breadth of the rehabilitation statutes in their respective states, when both persons were eligible for relief under their own state's law and both would have been had the state law been an exact counterpart of the federal Act. . . . The Constitution is concerned with the differential treatment of persons not statutes. [Absent] a rational basis (and as long as the FFOA remains extant), the INS may not discriminate against aliens convicted of simple possession offenses whose subsequent conduct would have qualified them for FFOA rehabilitation, but for the fact that they were convicted and rehabilitated under the laws of another sovereign. . . .

B

We evaluate Dillingham's constitutional challenge according to the requirements of equal protection law. In order to succeed on his challenge, the petitioner must establish that his treatment differed from that of similarly situated persons. Our prior cases dictate that persons similarly situated to petitioner for equal protection purposes are persons convicted of drug offenses based upon conduct for which they would have been eligible for relief under the FFOA, and whose convictions were ultimately expunged by the sovereign that imposed them.

For this reason, we find that the Board's categorical decision not to recognize foreign expungements for simple drug possession offenses did indeed result in differential treatment between the petitioner and persons whose federal and state expungements of identical crimes were honored by the INS. The BIA erred when it found that "the expungement of [Dillingham]'s conviction is akin to a foreign pardon and is therefore ineffective for immigration purposes." . . . By likening foreign expungements of simple drug possession offenses to foreign pardons of crimes of moral turpitude — a category of crimes for which Congress has not enacted a domestic rehabilitation statute analogous to the FFOA — the Board improperly skirted the constitutional issue of differential treatment in this case. . . .

Thus, having found differential treatment, we turn to the question of whether the Board's decision is supported by a rational basis. The government's chief contention is that its policy of not recognizing foreign expungements is justified because of the added administrative difficulty in verifying that an alien's conviction has indeed been validly expunged, and that he or she in fact complied with the requirements of the foreign expungement statute such that the alien also would have qualified for relief under the FFOA. The Supreme Court has held, however, that in cases where the petitioner's interest is substantial and the government's interest in putting forth the policy in question is unquantifiable or de minimis, such a policy cannot withstand even rational basis review. . . .

The private liberty interests involved in deportation proceedings are indisputably substantial. [Yet the BIA would] establish, by way of its decision in this case, an irrebuttable presumption against the validity of all foreign expungements — irrespective of where the offense in question occurred; how comparable to ours the system of criminal justice (including the operation of the expungement law) may be; and what degree of evidence verifying the expungement the alien may present. . . .

[Although] procedure by presumption is always cheaper and easier than individualized determination, we find that the government's interest in administrative convenience is insufficient to establish a rational basis for its categorical dismissal of foreign expungements. Indeed, we fail to see how the administrative burden of identifying and verifying foreign convictions (which the government already undertakes as a matter of course to determine whether an alien is admissible into the United States) is any different from the incremental burden of verifying foreign expungements — especially in light of the government's failure to provide any evidence in support of this claim in regard to the present case. We accordingly find the government's decision establishing an irrebuttable presumption against the validity of foreign expungements to be unacceptably overbroad, in light of an alien's substantial interest in avoiding deportation, as well as the government's minimal (or nonexistent) incremental burden in verifying that his or her conviction was expunged. Thus, we hold that the government's purported interest in administrative convenience does not constitute a legitimate basis for distinguishing aliens like Dillingham, whose illicit conduct and subsequent rehabilitation occurred on British soil (but who would otherwise have qualified for relief under the FFOA), from aliens whose convictions and expungements took place domestically under state procedures. . . .

FERNANDEZ, J., dissenting.

Dillingham argues that as a matter of constitutional law expungements in all of the countries of the world must be treated in the same manner as expungements within the United States because anything less would violate the principle of equal protection. I disagree.

While Congress could, no doubt, so decree, it is not compelled to do so by the Constitution. As in other equal protection claims, what we must ask is whether there was a rational basis for the choice made here. And in the immigration area [w]e will only overturn a classification if it is "wholly irrational."

I see nothing irrational in a determination that we will not treat aliens who obtain expungement of drug offenses in other countries in the same way that we treat those who obtain expungement of offenses in this country. Of course, under the Federal First Offender Act, 18 U.S.C. §3607, some simple drug possession convictions can be expunged. When they are, they are not used as a predicate for deportation; the Attorney General has so decided. On equal protection grounds, we have extended that to expungements under state laws.

As I see it, that is a far cry from stating that the Attorney General is equally required to treat the expungement statutes from all of the countries of the world in the same manner that he treats the FFOA and, by extension, state expungement statutes. It is no "mere fortuity" that foreign offenders are prosecuted in their own countries and not here. See Paredes-Urrestarazu v. INS, 36 F.3d 801, 812 (9th Cir. 1994). Nor do foreign expungement laws have anything to do with "uniform nationwide application of [our] immigration laws." In fact, foreign countries and their ways are not necessarily, or even particularly, the same as this country and its ways. A much more complex task is placed upon the shoulders of an administrative agency when it is told that it must not only review the varying ways and means of expungements all over the world, but also the full records of aliens who have admittedly committed foreign offenses, not to mention the difficulties that can be encountered in authenticating the accuracy of those records. . . .

That is not to say that it will be impossible to administer a system which requires ranging all over the world in that manner—we know that [people can live] with and administer just about any kind of system, no matter how difficult. But it is to say that it is perfectly rational to decline to undertake that process. . . .

In fine, equal protection does not require the progression we have here: recognition of FFOA expungements, to recognition of similar state statutes, to recognition of all state statutes and, finally, to recognition of enactments all over the world. To say that, does not enisle this country, although it does recognize that we are a separate nation. One world is a fine concept, but it is not a constitutional imperative. Not yet anyway. Thus, I respectfully dissent.

PROBLEM 11-8.   FIRE WHEN READY

In 1970 a Pennsylvania state court sentenced Philip Rice to probation for a number of felonies involving stolen auto parts. Federal law prohibits a convicted felon whose crime was "punishable by a term exceeding one year" from possessing firearms. Rice would like to get a gun dealer's license, despite this obstacle under federal law.

Another part of the federal felon-in-possession statute grants the Secretary of the Treasury the right to reinstate a former felon's firearms privileges if past good conduct indicates that his disability should be removed. Rice applied for restoration of his firearms privileges, but the Bureau of Alcohol, Tobacco and Firearms refused to consider his application because Congress had not funded that part of its operation since 1992.

Rice decided to petition a federal district court for review since the statute allows him to seek judicial review of the denial of his petition and it empowers the court to hear additional evidence to prevent a miscarriage of justice. What should the court do? See Rice v. United States Dep't of Alcohol, Tobacco and Firearms, 68 F.3d 702 (3d Cir. 1995); but see United States v. McGill, 74 F.3d 64 (5th Cir. 1996).

NOTES

1. *Expungement and sealing of records.*   While the term "expungement" carries no universally agreed-upon meaning, an expunged criminal record is generally considered to be one that is no longer available to the public. The files documenting the conviction may be physically destroyed or sealed. In the latter case they are frequently available to law enforcement personnel but not to others, such as private employers.

Once a criminal record is expunged, it has limited or no impact on the offender's future prospects. The types of conviction that can be expunged and the ramifications of expungement, however, vary widely by statute. Juvenile records, for example, are automatically expunged in almost all states once the juvenile reaches a particular age. In some states, the ex-offender does not have to reveal expunged convictions on employment applications; in other states, even expunged convictions may limit employment opportunities.

Criminal records may be expunged by administrative or judicial action. Some courts have recognized an inherent judicial power to expunge records, weighing privacy rights against the public's right of access to criminal records.

What purposes do expungement statutes serve? Some argue that ex-offenders should not continually pay for past crimes; others view expungement as a positive reward for a crime-free period. Expungement also restores the offender to the community. Without such statutes, an ever larger number of Americans would have criminal records. See Julian V. Roberts, The Role of Criminal Record in the Sentencing Process, 22 Crime & Just. 303, 356 (1997). Should expungement be available for all offenses? Should some types of crimes—such as drug offenses, sex crimes, and murder—be categorically excluded from expungement? What drawbacks, if any, do you see to expungement of criminal records? Why would Congress create but not fund a provision that would allow for the expungement of a record for a limited purpose, the ability to acquire a gun license?

2. *Prior expunged convictions at sentencing.* The availability of expungement differs dramatically between the states. As we learned in Chapter 5, an offender's criminal record influences sentencing decisions in both guideline and non-guideline states. Why should a sentencing court not be able to consider the prior conviction of an offender who benefited from a generous expungement statute? Does this scheme provide an inappropriate advantage to this offender? Or does it place at an unfair disadvantage the offender whose prior record could not have been expunged because of a less generous statutory regime?

3. *Foreign convictions and expungement.* As the *Dillingham* court indicates, foreign countries often have more generous expungement provisions than the United States. Should U.S. courts consider such expungements? Do you see practical problems to such determinations, or are you more concerned about inequities between U.S. and foreign offenders? Should a court be able to consider a foreign expunged conviction at sentencing? Are you more or less concerned about that scenario than about the impact of collateral sanctions (see Chapter 8), as in *Dillingham?*

4. Pardons, Commutations, Clemencies, and Amnesties

A form of executive review distinct from the parole system takes place when a governor or president considers a pardon or commutation. The history of the pardon power runs quite deep and has constitutional underpinnings. But the ancient origins of pardons have not insulated them from the same evolutionary developments that have occurred with the parole authority. Indeed, because pardons tend to be more visible, even though they are far less common than grants of parole, they also tend to be far more controversial. Most states give the governor unrestricted clemency power, although a substantial minority give the clemency power to special pardoning boards.

The differences among pardons, commutations, clemencies, and amnesties are slight and more a matter of semantics than of substance. *Clemency* is an umbrella term encompassing pardons, commutations, and amnesties. A *pardon* typically removes all consequences of criminal conviction and may come with strings attached. A *commutation* is a partial pardon, usually reducing a sentence but not erasing such consequences of conviction as voting bars, prohibitions from holding office, and restrictions on future gun ownership. In the United States, *amnesty* is a term often used in the context of war to connote a pardon for a war-related crime.

The number of pardons in states and the federal system has declined dramatically over the past century. Interestingly enough, in death cases more pardons were granted prior to the Supreme Court's decision in *Furman* than after it. In the early to mid-1940s governors pardoned those condemned to death in between one-fifth and one-fourth of all capital cases. In recent years presidents have granted fewer pardons and commutations. President George H. W. Bush granted 38 pardons and 1 commutation during his four-year administration. In contrast, President Ronald Reagan granted 393 pardons and 13 commutations during his eight years in office. Looking back to the 1960s, President Lyndon Johnson granted 960 pardons and 227 commutations in his five years in office. No federal pardons or commutations were granted in 1992 or 1994.

Use of pardons and commutations varies substantially among the states. Pardons are granted for a variety of reasons. They may be granted in cases of miscarriage of justice, including a violation of substantive rules, or in cases in which the accused is proven to be innocent or is deemed highly likely not to have committed the offense. In addition, individuals may be pardoned when the goals of their sentence appear to have been accomplished, such as when they appear to be fully rehabilitated. Pardons are often requested for the purpose of removing certain disabilities that go with a felony conviction, such as loss of voting rights. Occasionally a death sentence is commuted to a life sentence without the possibility of parole, but such commutations have been rare in recent years.

The use of pardons and commutations also reflects changing social perspectives on the seriousness of or justification for various kinds of crimes. Some governors, for example, have pardoned women who killed battering spouses or boyfriends after many years of abuse. At the time the women were convicted, the battered spouse syndrome was not used in their defense, and the governors believed that the women had served enough time for their offenses.

|| *U.S. Constitution Art. II, §2, Cl. 1* ||

The President shall . . . have Power to grant Reprieves and Pardons for Offences against the United States, except in Cases of Impeachment.

|| *Alabama Constitution Art. V, §124* ||

GOVERNOR; PARDONS AND COMMUTATION OF SENTENCES

The governor shall have power to remit fines and forfeitures, under such rules and regulations as may be prescribed by law; and, after conviction, to grant reprieves, paroles, commutations of sentence, and pardons, except in cases of impeachment. The attorney-general, secretary of state, and state auditor shall constitute a board of pardons, who shall meet on the call of the governor, and before whom shall be laid all recommendations or petitions, for pardon, commutation, or parole, in cases of felony; and the board shall hear them in open session, and give their opinion thereon in writing to the governor, after which or on the failure of the board to advise for more than sixty days, the governor may grant or refuse the commutation, parole, or pardon, as to him seems best for the public interest. He shall communicate to the legislature at each session every remission of fines and forfeitures, and every reprieve, commutation, parole, or pardon, with his reasons therefor, and the opinion of the board of pardons in each case required to be referred, stating the name and crime of the convict, the sentence, its date, and the date of reprieve, commutation, parole, or pardon. Pardons in cases of felony and other offenses involving moral turpitude shall not relieve from civil and political disabilities, unless approved by the board of pardons and specifically expressed in the pardon.

|| *Washington Revised Code §9.94A.728* ||

(5) The governor, upon recommendation from the clemency and pardons board, may grant an extraordinary release for reasons of serious health problems, senility, advanced age, extraordinary meritorious acts, or other extraordinary circumstances; . . .

(7) The governor may pardon any offender; . . .

|| *Ohio Adult Parole Authority v. Eugene Woodard* || 523 U.S. 272 (1998)

REHNQUIST, C.J.

The Ohio Constitution gives the Governor the power to grant clemency upon such conditions as he thinks proper. The Ohio General Assembly cannot curtail this discretionary decision-making power, but it may regulate the application and investigation process. The General Assembly has delegated in large part the conduct of clemency review to petitioner Ohio Adult Parole Authority.

In the case of an inmate under death sentence, the Authority must conduct a clemency hearing within 45 days of the scheduled date of execution. Prior to the hearing, the inmate may request an interview with one or more parole board members. Counsel is not allowed at that interview. The Authority must hold the hearing, complete its clemency review, and make a recommendation to the Governor, even if the inmate subsequently obtains a stay of execution. If additional information later becomes available, the Authority may in its discretion hold another hearing or alter its recommendation.

Respondent Eugene Woodard was sentenced to death for aggravated murder committed in the course of a carjacking. His conviction and sentence were affirmed on appeal. When respondent failed to obtain a stay of execution more than 45 days before his scheduled execution date, the Authority commenced its clemency investigation. It informed respondent that he could have a clemency interview on Sept. 9, 1994, if he wished, and that his clemency hearing would be on Sept. 16, 1994.

Respondent did not request an interview. Instead, he objected to the short notice of the interview and requested assurances that counsel could attend and participate in the interview and hearing. When the Authority failed to respond to these requests, respondent filed suit in United States District Court on September 14, alleging that Ohio's clemency process violated his Fourteenth Amendment right to due process and his Fifth Amendment right to remain silent. . . .

Respondent argues first . . . that there is a life interest in clemency broader in scope than the "original" life interest adjudicated at trial and sentencing. This continuing life interest, it is argued, requires due process protection until respondent is executed. . . .

In Connecticut Bd. of Pardons v. Dumschat, 452 U.S. 458 (1981), an inmate claimed Connecticut's clemency procedure violated due process because the Connecticut Board of Pardons failed to provide an explanation for its denial of his commutation application. The Court held that "an inmate has no constitutional or inherent right to commutation of his sentence." It noted that, unlike probation decisions, "pardon and commutation decisions have not traditionally been the business of courts; as such, they are rarely, if ever, appropriate subjects for judicial review." The Court relied on its prior decision in Greenholtz v. Inmates of Neb. Penal and Correctional Complex, 442 U.S. 1 (1979), where it rejected the claim "that a constitutional entitlement to release [on parole] exists independently of a right explicitly conferred by the State." The individual's interest in release or commutation "is indistinguishable from the initial resistance to being confined," and that interest has already been extinguished by the conviction and sentence. The Court therefore concluded that a petition for commutation, like an appeal for clemency, "is simply a unilateral hope."

Respondent's claim of a broader due process interest in Ohio's clemency proceedings is barred by *Dumschat*. The process respondent seeks would be inconsistent with the heart of executive clemency, which is to grant clemency as a matter of grace, thus allowing the executive to consider a wide range of factors not comprehended by earlier judicial proceedings and sentencing determinations. . . .

The reasoning of *Dumschat* did not depend on the fact that it was not a capital case. The distinctions accorded a life interest to which respondent and the dissent point are primarily relevant to trial. And this Court has generally rejected attempts to expand any distinctions further. . . . The Court's analysis in *Dumschat*, moreover, turned, not on the fact that it was a non-capital case, but on the nature of the benefit sought: "In terms of the Due Process Clause, a Connecticut felon's expectation that a lawfully imposed sentence will be commuted or that he will be pardoned is no more substantial than an inmate's expectation, for example, that he will not be transferred to another prison; it is simply a unilateral hope." A death row inmate's petition for clemency is also a "unilateral hope." The defendant in effect accepts the finality of the death sentence for purposes of adjudication, and appeals for clemency as a matter of grace.

Respondent also asserts that as in *Greenholtz*, Ohio has created protected interests by establishing mandatory clemency application and review procedures. . . . Ohio's clemency procedures do not violate due process. Despite the Authority's mandatory procedures, the ultimate decisionmaker, the Governor, retains broad discretion. Under any analysis, the Governor's executive discretion need not be fettered by the types of procedural protections sought by respondent. There is thus no substantive expectation of clemency. . . .

Respondent also . . . claims that under the rationale of Evitts v. Lucey, 469 U.S. 387 (1985), clemency is an integral part of Ohio's system of adjudicating the guilt or innocence of the defendant and is therefore entitled to due process protection. Clemency, he says, is an integral part of the judicial system because it has historically been available as a significant remedy, its availability impacts earlier stages of the criminal justice system, and it enhances the reliability of convictions and sentences. Respondent further suggests that *Evitts* established a due process continuum across all phases of the judicial process.

In *Evitts*, the Court held that there is a constitutional right to effective assistance of counsel on a first appeal as of right. This holding, however, was expressly based on the combination of two lines of prior decisions [indicating] that a criminal defendant has a right to effective assistance of counsel on a first appeal as of right.

The Court did not thereby purport to create a new "strand" of due process analysis. And it did not rely on the notion of a continuum of due process rights. Instead, the Court evaluated the function and significance of first appeal as of right, in light of prior cases. Related decisions similarly make clear there is no continuum requiring varying levels of process at every conceivable phase of the criminal system. Murray v. Giarratano, 492 U.S. 1, 9-10 (1989) (no right to counsel for capital inmates in state postconviction proceedings).

An examination of the function and significance of the discretionary clemency decision at issue here readily shows it is far different from the first appeal of right at issue in *Evitts*. Clemency proceedings are not part of trial—or even the adjudicatory process. They do not determine the guilt or innocence of the defendant, and are not intended primarily to enhance the reliability of the trial process. They are conducted by the Executive Branch, independent of direct appeal and collateral relief proceedings. . . . And they are usually discretionary, unlike the more structured and limited scope of judicial proceedings. While traditionally available to capital defendants as a final and alternative avenue of relief, clemency has not traditionally been the business of courts. . . .

Thus, clemency proceedings are not "an integral part of the . . . system for finally adjudicating the guilt or innocence of a defendant," *Evitts*, 469 U.S. at 393. Procedures mandated under the Due Process Clause should be consistent with the nature of the governmental power being invoked. Here, the executive's clemency authority would cease to be a matter of grace committed to the executive authority if it were constrained by the sort of procedural requirements that respondent urges. Respondent is already under a sentence of death, determined to have been lawfully imposed. If clemency is granted, he obtains a benefit; if it is denied, he is no worse off than he was before. . . .

Respondent also [argues] that the provision of a voluntary inmate interview, without the benefit of counsel or a grant of immunity for any statements made by the inmate, implicates the inmate's Fifth and Fourteenth Amendment right not to incriminate himself. . . .

The Fifth Amendment protects against compelled self-incrimination. [We] do not think that respondent's testimony at a clemency interview would be "compelled" within the meaning of the Fifth Amendment. It is difficult to see how a voluntary interview could "compel" respondent to speak. . . .

A defendant who takes the stand in his own behalf may be impeached by proof of prior convictions without violation of the Fifth Amendment privilege. A defendant whose motion for acquittal at the close of the Government's case is denied must then elect whether to stand on his motion or to put on a defense, with the accompanying risk that in doing so he will augment the Government's case against him. In each of these situations, there are undoubted pressures — generated by the strength of the Government's case against him — pushing the criminal defendant to testify. But it has never been suggested that such pressures constitute "compulsion" for Fifth Amendment purposes. . . .

Here, respondent has the same choice of providing information to the Authority — at the risk of damaging his case for clemency or for postconviction relief — or of remaining silent. But this pressure to speak in the hope of improving his chance of being granted clemency does not make the interview compelled. We therefore hold that the Ohio clemency interview, even on assumptions most favorable to respondent's claim, does not violate the Fifth Amendment privilege against compelled self-incrimination.

O'CONNOR, J., concurring in part and concurring in the judgment.

. . . When a person has been fairly convicted and sentenced, his liberty interest, in being free from such confinement, has been extinguished. But it is incorrect . . . to say that a prisoner has been deprived of all interest in his life before his execution. Thus, although it is true that pardon and commutation decisions have not traditionally been the business of courts, and that the decision whether to grant clemency is entrusted to the Governor under Ohio law, I believe that . . . some minimal procedural safeguards apply to clemency proceedings. Judicial intervention might, for example, be warranted in the face of a scheme whereby a state official flipped a coin to determine whether to grant clemency, or in a case where the State arbitrarily denied a prisoner any access to its clemency process.

In my view, however, a remand to permit the District Court to address respondent's specific allegations of due process violations is not required. [Woodard] contends that 3 days' notice of his interview and 10 days' notice of the hearing were inadequate; that he did not have a meaningful opportunity to prepare his clemency application because postconviction proceedings were pending; that his counsel was improperly excluded from the interview and permitted to participate in the hearing only at the discretion of the parole board chair; and that he was precluded from testifying or submitting documentary evidence at the hearing. I do not believe that any of these allegations amounts to a due process violation. The process respondent received, including notice of the hearing and an opportunity to participate in an interview, comports with Ohio's regulations and observes whatever limitations the Due Process Clause may impose on clemency proceedings. . . .

STEVENS, J., concurring in part and dissenting in part.

. . . The text of the Due Process Clause properly directs our attention to state action that may "deprive" a person of life, liberty, or property. When we are evaluating claims that the State has unfairly deprived someone of liberty or property, it is appropriate first to ask whether the state action adversely affected any constitutionally protected interest. [There is] no room for legitimate debate about whether a living person has a constitutionally protected interest in life. He obviously does. . . .

There are valid reasons for concluding that even if due process is required in clemency proceedings, only the most basic elements of fair procedure are required. Presumably a State might eliminate this aspect of capital sentencing entirely, and it unquestionably may allow the executive virtually unfettered discretion in determining the merits of appeals for mercy. Nevertheless, there are equally valid reasons for concluding that these proceedings are not entirely exempt from judicial review. I think, for example, that no one would contend that a governor could ignore the commands of the Equal Protection Clause and use race, religion, or political affiliation as a standard for granting or denying clemency. Our cases also support the conclusion that if a State adopts a clemency procedure as an integral part of its system for finally determining whether to deprive a person of life, that procedure must comport with the Due Process Clause. . . .

The interest in life that is at stake in this case warrants even greater protection than the interests in liberty at stake in [non-capital] cases. For "death is a different kind of punishment from any other which may be imposed in this country. . . . It is of vital importance to the defendant and to the community that any decision to impose the death sentence be, and appear to be, based on reason rather than caprice or emotion." Gardner v. Florida, 430 U.S. 349, 357-358 (1977). Those considerations apply with special force to the final stage of the decisional process that precedes an official deprivation of life. . . .

NOTES

1. *Due process in clemency procedures?* Though Woodard's claims were rejected, five justices appear to have held that at least some modicum of process is constitutionally required in clemency proceedings. What sorts of "minimum procedural safeguards" do you think are now required? What if a state denies a death row prisoner any hearing and allows its parole board members to vote individually on clemency petitions by fax or phone, without providing any reason for their votes and without even having a meeting to discuss the petition? See Faulder v. Texas Bd. of Pardons and Paroles, 178 F.3d 343, 345 (5th Cir. 1999). What if a lawyer for the state screens information before it reaches the governor so that the ultimate decision maker does not know all the mitigating facts that might justify clemency? See Alan Berlow, The Texas Clemency Memos, Atlantic Monthly (July/August 2003), at 91.

2. *The historical place for clemency.* In Herrera v. Collins, 506 U.S. 390 (1993), a defendant sentenced to death claimed that habeas corpus had to be available as a means of establishing his innocence and thus of obtaining further review of his conviction and sentence after his initial appeals had been exhausted. In the course of rejecting this claim, Chief Justice William Rehnquist discussed the role of clemency in the criminal justice system, particularly as a means to redress wrongful convictions:

Clemency is deeply rooted in our Anglo-American tradition of law, and is the historic remedy for preventing miscarriages of justice where judicial process has been exhausted.

In England, the clemency power was vested in the Crown and can be traced back to the 700's. Blackstone thought this "one of the great advantages of monarchy in general, above any other form of government; that there is a magistrate, who has it in his power to extend mercy, wherever he thinks it is deserved: holding a court of equity in his own breast, to soften the rigour of the general law, in such criminal cases as merit an exemption from punishment." 4 W. Blackstone, Commentaries *397. Clemency provided the principal avenue of relief for individuals convicted of criminal offenses — most of which were capital — because there was no right of appeal until 1907. It was the only means by which one could challenge his conviction on the ground of innocence.

Our Constitution adopts the British model and gives to the President the "Power to grant Reprieves and Pardons for Offences against the United States." Art. II, §2, cl. 1. . . . The original States were reluctant to vest the clemency power in the executive. And although this power has gravitated toward the executive over time, several States have split the clemency power between the Governor and an advisory board selected by the legislature. Today, all 36 States that authorize capital punishment have constitutional or statutory provisions for clemency.

Executive clemency has provided the "fail safe" in our criminal justice system. It is an unalterable fact that our judicial system, like the human beings who administer it, is fallible. But history is replete with examples of wrongfully convicted persons who have been pardoned in the wake of after-discovered evidence establishing their innocence. In his classic work, Professor Edwin Borchard compiled 65 cases in which it was later determined that individuals had been wrongfully convicted of crimes. Clemency provided the relief mechanism in 47 of these cases; the remaining cases ended in judgments of acquittals after new trials. Borchard, Convicting the Innocent (1932). Recent authority confirms that over the past century clemency has been exercised frequently in capital cases in which demonstrations of "actual innocence" have been made. See M. Radelet, H. Bedau, and C. Putnam, In Spite of Innocence 282-356 (1992).

In recent years, however, clemency has been granted in substantially fewer cases than was the case prior to the U.S. Supreme Court's 1972 decision declaring the form then used for administering the death penalty unconstitutional. Michael A. G. Korengold et al., And Justice for Few: The Collapse of the Capital Clemency System in the United States, 20 Hamline L. Rev. 349 (1996) (noting that in the United States from 1960 to 1970, 261 people were executed and clemency was granted to 204 death row inmates, whereas from 1985 to 1995, 281 people were executed and only 20 death row inmates were granted clemency). Among the factors accounting for this decline may be a changing political climate that encourages tougher criminal penalties and the erroneous belief that clemency is unnecessary today because death row inmates receive "super due process" in the courts.

3. *Pardon patterns.*   Although many state legislatures require the governor or pardon board to issue reports on pardons every year, there is no readily available information on the number of pardons granted in the states, the basis for particular decisions, or pardon patterns over time. Consider Professor Daniel Kobil's summary of pardons in Ohio:

At the close of his second term, former Ohio Governor Richard Celeste granted clemency to sixty-eight individuals. Many of the cases were controversial, with Celeste being alternately praised and vilified for reducing the punishments of, among others, twenty-five battered women who had killed or assaulted their purported abusers, eight condemned murderers, a famous country-western singer, and an embezzler of hundreds of thousands of dollars.

Daniel Kobil, Do the Paperwork or Die: Clemency, Ohio Style?, 52 Ohio St. L.J. 655 (1991). The country music star, for fans of such music, was Johnny Paycheck, the creator of the unforgettable song "Take This Job and Shove It." According to a newspaper article, Governor Celeste found the 7½-to-9-year sentence for the 1985 shooting of a man in a bar "unbelievably harsh." See Celeste Orders Paycheck Freed, Columbus Dispatch (January 11, 1991), at 5B, col. 1.

4. *Clemency procedures.* The chief executive traditionally holds the clemency and pardon powers, with little judicial interference. The offender has only limited due process rights, such as the right to notice of the clemency proceeding and the right to be heard at the proceeding.

Nine states require that the governor have a recommendation of clemency from a board or advisory group before granting clemency. In three states the board makes the ultimate decision, and in another three states the governor sits on this board. In the remaining states, the governor is largely responsible for the decisions herself. See generally Death Penalty Information Center, Clemency Process by State (available at www.deathpenaltyinfo.org/article.php?did=126&scid=13#process). The setup of clemency procedures influences the number of clemencies granted. They are more likely to occur when an administrative board rather than the governor holds clemency authority. Why do you suppose this is the case?

5. *The effect of a pardon.* Many, and possibly all, nations recognize some possibility of obtaining a pardon, but the effects of pardons vary. In England, for example, pardons do not exonerate the accused but merely amount to non-enforcement of the sentence. England also recognizes sentence remissions to reward prisoners who cooperate with authorities or to release those who are terminally ill. In the United States a pardon allows a person to hold himself out as innocent. However, disciplinary boards and professional licensing bodies may deny professional licenses based on the underlying criminal conduct even after the offender has received a pardon. See In re William A. Borders, Jr., 797 A.2d 716 (D.C. Ct. App. 2002).

6. *Pardons and politics.* Critics have charged that the number of pardons and the types of cases in which they are granted depend on the political situation. Governors at the end of their terms seem more inclined to take political gambles in granting pardons. Charges of influence peddling and outright corruption sometimes crop up in the pardon process. As Helen Prejean recounts, the former chair of the Louisiana Board of Pardons described some of the political maneuvering that went on:

> [The governor's chief legal counsel] told me that I knew the governor did not like to be confronted with these cases and wanted us to handle it. [This implied that the board, out of loyalty to the governor, had to follow the governor's decision, independent of their own opinion. Otherwise they would be replaced.]
>
> [Before] our Board hearings, I'd get the word from the governor's office about which deals would go down when the Board met. "The governor wants this one or that one," that's what they'd say. [T]here would be cases sometimes, where . . . some of the Board members would balk at giving the pardon, and

[I'd] have to pull them aside and tell them the governor had already committed to the pardon and their task was to put it through.

Helen Prejean, Dead Man Walking 171, 173 (1993). Here the pardon board functioned less to insulate the governor from a difficult decision-making process than to camouflage the decision already made.

Female governors seem even less inclined than their male counterparts to issue pardons and commute sentences. How do you account for this disparity?

7. *Women and clemency.*   Women receive executive clemency substantially more often than men. Even though their numbers on death row are already very small, they benefit disproportionately from gubernatorial commutations of death sentences. See Michael Heise, Mercy by the Numbers: An Empirical Analysis of Clemency and Its Structure, 89 Va. L. Rev. 239, 275-278 (2003). No longer is it the case, however, that governors can pardon women or commute their sentences merely because they are women. Frequently, pardons are granted to women who killed spouses or boyfriends who allegedly abused them and to women whose criminal activity stemmed from duress caused by a male figure in their lives. Nevertheless, governors frequently reserve such pardons and commutations for the very end of their terms in office.

8. *Clemency abroad.*   In some western European countries amnesties for entire groups of incarcerated offenders occur regularly. Often they are announced around Christmas. Why do you think such amnesties are not used in the United States?

9. *Compensation after release from wrongful conviction.*   In some cases governors have issued pardons when it became clear that an incarcerated offender was innocent of the offense but no judicial recourse remained to overturn his conviction. In such situations most European countries would allow for compensation after release from imprisonment following a wrongful conviction. The same does not hold true in all U.S. states. Moreover, even states that provide for such compensation often strictly limit it. Under New York's Unjust Conviction and Imprisonment Act, for example, the claimant must show by clear and convincing evidence that his conviction was reversed, that he did not commit any of the acts charged, and that he did not by his own conduct cause or bring about his conviction. N.Y. Ct. Cl. Act §8-b (1984). Of the 12 successful claimants in New York — out of 200 claims filed between 1984 and 2002 — the awards ranged from $40,000 to $1.9 million, the latter to compensate for almost 20 years in prison.

Pardon Us: Systematic Presidential Pardons,
Charles Shanor and Marc Miller
13 Fed. Sent'g Rep. 139 (2001)

Scholars, judges and commentators often emphasize the individualized and mercy-driven nature of the pardon power. . . . We consider whether it is constitutional and appropriate to use the pardon power in a systematic way, applied to a group of offenders selected through consistent criteria and processes, and for reasons that may reflect concerns of justice, equality, and wise policy, rather than mercy.

1. THE CONSTITUTIONALITY OF SYSTEMATIC PARDONS

One constitutional objection might be made to systematic use of the pardon power by a president to further a policy goal. If Congress passes a statute that directs differential penalties for two crimes, and the judiciary implements this law, even upholding its constitutionality in the process, does it violate the separation of powers to allow the president to undo what Congress and the courts have approved?

Of course, the president has an obligation to "take Care that the Laws be faithfully executed." Art. II, §3. However, we do not believe this obligation overrides, much less obliterates, the distinct constitutional power stating that the President "shall have Power to grant Reprieves and Pardons for Offences against the United States, except in Cases of Impeachment." Art II, §2, cl. 1.

Were the "faithful execution" duty extended so far, it would effectively remove the pardon power from the Constitution altogether. This power, explicitly given to the Executive responsible for enforcing the law rather than sharing with Congress, should be viewed as a limited exception to the general duty of the president to faithfully execute the laws. The pardon power qualifies the duty only in connection with enforcement of criminal statutes. It has no bearing on enforcement of regulatory statutes or on private civil actions established by Congress.

Moreover, even as to criminal law statutes, the pardon power operates only as a check on prosecutions or sentences; it in no way alters congressional criminalization of particular behavior. Indeed, because the pardon power is explicit in the Constitution's text, it seems less vulnerable to criticism on separation of powers grounds than the authority of the executive branch, regularly exercised, to decline to prosecute particular cases or to plea bargain for lesser offenses than those recognized by Congress as applicable to particular behaviors. . . .

At least a third of all United States presidents, including many of our greatest presidents, and from the earliest administrations, have used systematic pardons. This long history convinces us that even class-wide pardons, with the potential to dramatically limit the impact of federal criminal laws, are constitutional. . . .

1795	Washington	Pardoned participants in the Pennsylvania Whiskey Rebellion. . . .
1801	Jefferson	Pardoned all persons convicted under the Alien and Sedition Acts. . . .
1862-1864	Lincoln	Granted amnesty to Confederate sympathizers.
1865-1868	Johnson	Granted amnesty to Confederate soldiers, officials, and sympathizers. . . .
1945	Truman	Pardoned pre-war convicts who served in the U.S. armed forces during World War II subject to review by presidential board.
1961-1963	Kennedy	Pardoned offenders sentenced under mandatory minimum penalties of Narcotics Act of 1956.
1974-1975	Ford	Pardoned Vietnam-era violators of Service Act subject to review by presidential board.
1977	Carter	Pardoned Vietnam-era violators of the Selective Service Act.

While a quick review of the historical record makes it difficult to determine the extent to which these were systematic pardons, this review does suggest a history of using the pardon power, not simply as an act of individualized mercy, or as a political tool to reward supporters, but as a tool to reconcile national divisions. . . .

2.   Unpardonable and Irregular Pardons

. . . The recent focus on pardon abuse may arise in part from the fact that the federal pardon power has fallen into desuetude. There have been over 20,000 presidential pardons and commutations granted during the twentieth century, and many thousands of additional war-related amnesties falling within the pardon power. However, the vast majority of those pardons occurred before 1980, and the percentage of pardons granted to those sought has been declining steadily for the past 40 years. . . .

President	Pardons Sought	Pardons Granted	Percent Granted
Nixon	2,591	923	35.6%
Ford	1,527	404	26.5%
Carter	2,627	563	21.4%
Reagan	3,404	406	11.9%
Bush	1,466	77	5.3%
Clinton	6,622	456	6.9%

Looking back even further, around 1300 pardons and commutations were granted in Lyndon Johnson's five years in office (around 31% of requests), and around 600 pardons were granted during John Kennedy's three years (around 36% of requests). . . .

The combination of the recent controversial pardons [at the end of President Clinton's second term] and the highly sporadic use of non-controversial pardons has obscured two important dimensions of the pardon power.

First, when the numbers of pardons are insubstantial, the pardon power offers little possibility for more consistent and substantial executive assessments of sentences. The low and decreasing number of pardons is even more striking in light of [large] size of the federal prison population. . . .

The significance of the small numbers and percentages of pardons in recent years is magnified even further by the fact that, prior to the implementation of the [federal sentencing] guidelines in 1987, all sentences were subject to standardized executive review of the U.S. Parole Commission. It seems that the elimination of the Parole Commission should have led to an increase in the use of presidential pardons, since one of the two major forms of traditional executive post-conviction review and adjustment is no longer available.

Second, the irregular and seemingly random Clinton pardons obscure the possibility of presidents using the pardon power as a principled, systematic policy tool.

3. Some Modern Systematic Pardons

Presidents have sometimes issued multiple pardons on the same or different dates, and given the same reason for those pardons. Such pardons are not necessarily systematic, unless they are the product of articulated principles applied consistently to an identified group, so that all members of the group who satisfy the principles are pardoned or subject to a standard and reasonably structured process of review.

Wars. The most common form of systematic pardons in the twentieth century appear to be amnesty or clemency for those who avoided military service or even opposed the U.S. during a conflict. The most recent illustration of this type of systematic pardon was President Carter's decision to pardon Vietnam-era violators of the Selective Service Act. . . .

Drugs. An example of what may have been systematic, non-wartime, drug offense pardons appears, in brief form, in the Annual Reports of the Attorney General issued during the Kennedy administration. Those reports suggest that there was a large number of pardons or commutations reducing sentences under the Narcotic Control Act of 1956 [which included mandatory minimum sentences of five to thirty years for various drug offenses]. . . .

The 1964 report confirmed that "[as] in the years preceding, the commutations of sentence granted included some long-term narcotics offenders who, by statute, were not eligible for parole but whose sentences were considerably longer than average." The 1964 report also explicitly refers to efforts to make review of pardons and commutations more systematic:

> During the year, the Director of the Bureau of Prisons was called upon to encourage the wardens of the federal prisons to review cases in their institutions and present to the Attorney General selected cases which they considered to be worthy of clemency and whose sentences could be considered disparate. For the first time there is a policy of attempting to systematically review cases which may be deserving of commutation. As a result, a very sizeable increase in commutations has resulted.

While it is not clear whether the Narcotics Act commutations were fully systematic in the sense we suggest, they do combine a statement of principle (disparity) and a suggestion of regularized review to identify similarly situated offenders. . . .

4. Wise Use of Systematic Pardons

Even if systematic pardons are constitutional, are they a desirable tool for the president compared to other possible strategies available to the executive branch, such as advocating changes in the laws, or changing executive charging, plea, or sentencing policies?

A president might believe that a distinction made by a federal criminal law is unconstitutional. This was the basis for President Jefferson's pardons of those convicted of violating the Alien and Sedition Acts, which Jefferson believed to be unconstitutional. . . . Under the oath of office, the president not only has the power but the duty to apply the commands of the constitution in the exercise of his office.

A president also might use systematic pardons when the constitutionality of the conviction and sentence is abundantly clear. . . . Presidents Truman, Ford, and Carter all believed that a process of amnesty would help to heal the many wounds of war at home. President Kennedy did not suggest that convictions under the mandatory minimum penalties of the Narcotics Act of 1956 were unconstitutional, but he did point to the excessive and unequal sentences imposed under those laws.

As a political matter, a president might hesitate to issue a series of class-wide pardons in the face of Congressional or public criticism. When Lincoln used the pardon power in 1865, he referenced not only his constitutional authority, but also Congressional support for pardoning a large class of southerners "guilty of treason." When Congress had passed laws calling for forfeiture of property by those in rebellion against the Union, it granted the President the authority to grant pardons or amnesty "on such conditions as he may deem expedient for the public welfare." The legislation was perhaps helpful to Lincoln, but it was also unnecessary, for Lincoln could have granted the pardons without it.

Systematic pardons would likely initiate reconsideration of punishment and incarceration policies by Congress. Given the political difficulty of generating rich discussions of criminal justice policy, confident and wise chief executives may be in the best position to generate such debate. Systematic pardons thus offer the chance for a visible and public dialogue about important legal issues. On the other hand, pardons cannot and should not supplant the legislative role on a continuing basis.

NOTES

1. *Systematic clemencies.*   Perhaps one of the most noteworthy and dramatic examples of the systematic use of the clemency power occurred in January 2003, when outgoing Illinois governor George Ryan granted clemency to all of the 156 death row inmates in Illinois (as well as 11 inmates who were awaiting sentencing or resentencing) in response to the flawed process in Illinois that led to these sentences. (A portion of Governor Ryan's speech announcing his decision is reprinted in Chapter 3.) Note that these grants of clemency did not result in the release of the inmates, since many still faced sentences of life in prison. Governor Ryan also completely pardoned four wrongly convicted death row inmates.

Do you think it is appropriate for governors or presidents to use their pardon and clemency powers systematically? Are such actions an effective way to influence criminal justice or sentencing policy? Should a change in administration and in criminal justice priorities provide a sound basis for considering the systematic use of the pardon power?

2. *Unsystematic pardons.*   Perhaps equally noteworthy and even more controversial than systematic pardons or clemencies are instances in which the pardon power is used in ways that seem particularly unsystematic. Only two hours before surrendering the White House, President Bill Clinton pardoned

some persons involved in various scandals that touched the Clinton presidency, along with former Cabinet members, onetime fugitive heiress Patricia Hearst Shaw, and his own brother, Roger Clinton. The number and nature of these pardons not only surpassed the scope of last-minute pardons granted by previous presidents, but also generated widespread public outrage. Both the Senate Judiciary Committee and the House Government Reform Committee scheduled hearings to investigate particularly whether Clinton's pardon of financier Marc Rich was motivated by campaign contributions made by Rich's former wife. For an insightful discussion of these pardons and the lessons to be learned from them, see Margaret Colgate Love, Fear of Forgiving: Rule and Discretion in the Practice of Pardoning, 13 Fed. Sent'g Rep. 125 (2001). See also Harold Krent, Conditioning the President's Conditional Pardon Power, 89 Cal. L. Rev. 1665 (2001).

3. *The decline in clemency.* The drop in presidential pardons over the past few decades is startling, particularly in view of the dramatic rise in imprisonment rates during the same period (see Chapter 7). How do you explain the decrease in individual pardons? Is the current pardon process fatally flawed, as some have argued? In light of more systematic guideline sentencing, should we increasingly object to unsystematic executive clemency? Have presidents become less courageous?

PROBLEM 11-9. A CURIOUS COMMUTATION

In July 2007 President George W. Bush exercised his clemency power to commute the 30-month prison term given to former White House aide I. Lewis "Scooter" Libby before he was to start serving this sentence. The prison sentence was imposed in June 2007 after a federal court convicted Libby of perjury, obstruction of justice, and lying to investigators in the course of a special counsel's investigation of possible White House involvement in the leak of the name of a CIA operative. Here is part of the statement made by President Bush in support of his decision:

> From the very beginning of the investigation into the leaking of Valerie Plame's name, I made it clear to the White House staff and anyone serving in my administration that I expected full cooperation with the Justice Department. Dozens of White House staff and administration officials dutifully cooperated.
>
> After the investigation was under way, the Justice Department appointed United States Attorney for the Northern District of Illinois Patrick Fitzgerald as a special counsel in charge of the case. Mr. Fitzgerald is a highly qualified, professional prosecutor who carried out his responsibilities as charged.
>
> This case has generated significant commentary and debate. Critics of the investigation have argued that a special counsel should not have been appointed, nor should the investigation have been pursued after the Justice Department learned who leaked Ms. Plame's name to columnist Robert Novak. Furthermore, the critics point out that neither Mr. Libby nor anyone else has been charged with violating the Intelligence Identities Protection Act or the Espionage Act, which were the original subjects of the investigation. Finally, critics say the punishment does not fit the crime: Mr. Libby was a first-time offender with years of exceptional public service and was handed a harsh sentence based in part on allegations never presented to the jury.

Others point out that a jury of citizens weighed all the evidence and listened to all the testimony and found Mr. Libby guilty of perjury and obstructing justice. They argue, correctly, that our entire system of justice relies on people telling the truth. And if a person does not tell the truth, particularly if he serves in government and holds the public trust, he must be held accountable. They say that had Mr. Libby only told the truth, he would have never been indicted in the first place.

Both critics and defenders of this investigation have made important points. I have made my own evaluation. In preparing for the decision I am announcing today, I have carefully weighed these arguments and the circumstances surrounding this case.

Mr. Libby was sentenced to 30 months of prison, two years of probation and a $250,000 fine. In making the sentencing decision, the district court rejected the advice of the probation office, which recommended a lesser sentence and the consideration of factors that could have led to a sentence of home confinement or probation.

I respect the jury's verdict. But I have concluded that the prison sentence given to Mr. Libby is excessive. Therefore, I am commuting the portion of Mr. Libby's sentence that required him to spend 30 months in prison.

My decision to commute his prison sentence leaves in place a harsh punishment for Mr. Libby. The reputation he gained through his years of public service and professional work in the legal community is forever damaged. His wife and young children have also suffered immensely. He will remain on probation. The significant fines imposed by the judge will remain in effect. The consequences of his felony conviction on his former life as a lawyer, public servant and private citizen will be long-lasting.

The Constitution gives the president the power of clemency to be used when he deems it to be warranted. It is my judgment that a commutation of the prison term in Mr. Libby's case is an appropriate exercise of this power.

Is there something unique (and uniquely troubling) about a president's decision to use his clemency power to mitigate the sentence of an executive branch official convicted of an offense during a criminal investigation into suspect activities taking place within that president's administration? Should Congress have some means (short of initiating the process for a constitutional amendment) to oversee or regulate the use of clemency powers that may appear to be part of an effort to cover up activities of high-ranking executive branch officials?

Also, in light of all the materials in this text, are the president's stated reasons for this commutation in harmony with prevailing modern sentencing doctrines? Are they convincing?

Table of Cases

|| *Table of Statutes, Rules, and Guidelines* ||

Index